Second Workshop on Patient-Oriented Language Processing (CL4Health 2025)

Albuquerque, New Mexico, USA
4 May 2025

ISBN: 979-8-3313-1914-4

Printed from e-media with permission by:

Curran Associates, Inc.
57 Morehouse Lane
Red Hook, NY 12571

Some format issues inherent in the e-media version may also appear in this print version.

Association for Computational Linguistics
209 N. Eighth Street
Stroudsburg, Pennsylvania 18360

Phone: 1-570-476-8006
Fax: 1-570-476-0860

acl@aclweb.org

Additional copies of this publication are available from:

Curran Associates, Inc.
57 Morehouse Lane
Red Hook, NY 12571 USA
Phone: 845-758-0400
Fax: 845-758-2633
Email: curran@proceedings.com
Web: www.proceedings.com

CL4Health 2025

Second Workshop on Patient-Oriented Language Processing (CL4Health)

Proceedings of the Workshop

May 4, 2025

Order copies of this and other ACL proceedings from:

Association for Computational Linguistics (ACL)
317 Sidney Baker St. S
Suite 400 - 134
Kerrville, TX 78028
USA
Tel: +1-855-225-1962
acl@aclweb.org

Introduction

CL4Health fills the gap among the different biomedical language processing workshops by providing a general venue for a broad spectrum of patient-oriented language processing and multi-modal research. The second workshop on patient-oriented language processing follows the successful inaugural CL4Health workshop (collocated with LREC-COLING 2024), which clearly demonstrated the need for a computational linguistics venue that focuses on language related to health of the public.

Such a venue is needed both to invigorate patient-oriented language processing research and to build a community of researchers interested in this area. The growing interest in this topic is fueled by several current trends:

1. a proliferation of online services that target patients, but do not always act in their best interests;

2. policy changes that allow patients to access their health records written in the professional vernacular, which may confuse the patients or lead to misinterpretation;

3. replacement of customer services with chat bots; and

4. the increasing tendency of patients to consult online resources as a second or even first opinion on their health problems.

CL4Health aims to provide a general venue for presenting research and applications focused on patients' needs, including summarizing health records for the patients, answering consumer-health questions using reliable resources, detecting misinformation or potentially harmful information, and providing multimodal information, such as video, if it better satisfies patients' needs.

Broadly, CL4Health is concerned with the resources, computational approaches, and behavioral and socio-economic aspects of the public interactions with digital resources in search of health-related information that satisfies their information needs and guides their actions.

Shared Task

The Perspective-aware Healthcare Answer Summarization (PerAnsSumm) task organized by Shweta Yadav, Md. Shad Akhtar, and Siddhant Agarwal focuses on providing different perspectives in the answers to questions posted to online forums. The answer perspectives include personal experiences, factual information, and suggestions. More details about the task and the participating teams are provided in the overview paper in this volume. The volume also includes the individual participating teams reports.

Submissions

The workshop invited papers concerning all areas of language processing focused on patients' health and health-related issues concerning the public. CL4Health received 50 valid submissions, of which 8 were rejected. Of the 35 submissions to the main workshop, 12 were accepted as oral presentations. The work covers a wide range of topics focusing on patients' well-being and healthcare. The topics include patients' perspectives on clinical trials recruitment, information seeking behavior, clinical question answering and other forms of communication (including plain language, translation, speech recognition, and dialog). The state-of-the-art technology contributions include retrieval augmented generation, various approaches to fine-tuning and leveraging large language models, as well as new benchmarks and data collections.

As always, we are deeply grateful to the authors of the submitted papers and to the reviewers (listed elsewhere in this volume) who produced thorough and thoughtful reviews for each paper in a fairly short review period. The Organizers are truly grateful to our amazing Program Committee, whose members helped us determine which studies are ready to be presented and those which would benefit from additional experiments and analysis, as suggested by the reviewers. We hope that this workshop will inspire new collaborations and research into patient-centered language technologies, in order to continue the valuable contributions made by our community towards public health and well-being.

Dina Demner-Fushman, Sophia Ananiadou, Paul Thompson and Deepak Gupta (Organizers)

Organizing Committee

Workshop Chairs

Sophia Ananiadou, National Centre for Text Mining, University of Manchester, UK
Dina Demner-Fushman, National Library of Medicine, USA
Deepak Gupta, National Library of Medicine, USA
Paul Thompson, National Centre for Text Mining, University of Manchester, UK

Shared Task Chairs

Siddhant Agarwal, University of Illinois at Chicago, USA
Md Shad Akhtar, Indraprastha Institute of Information Technology Delhi, India
Shweta Yadav, University of Illinois at Chicago, USA

Program Committee

Program Committee

Abanoub Abdelmalak, University of Bonn, Germany
Siddhant Agarwal, University of Illinois at Chicago, USA
Mathilde Aguiar, Université Paris-Saclay, CNRS, France
Safa Alsaidi, Inria, Inserm, France
Judith Jeyafreeda Andrew, Imagine Institute, France
Zainab Awan, Queen Mary University of London, UK
Tanalp Ağustoslu, LMU Munich, Germany
Leonor Barreiros, Priberam Labs, Portugal
Abby Blocker, University of Cape Town, South Africa
Leonardo Campillos-Llanos, Spanish National Research Council, Spain
Amin Dada, Institute for AI in Medicine (IKIM), University Hospital Essen, Germany
Luise Dürlich, Swedish Medical Products Agency, Sweden
Manas Gaur, University of Maryland Baltimore County, USA
Sagar Goyal, DeepScribe Inc., USA
Natalia Grabar, Université de Lille, France
Tudor Groza, Bioinformatics Institute, A*STAR, Singapore
Deepak Gupta, National Library of Medicine, USA
Dongsuk Jang, Department of Computer Science, Yale University, USA
Ramakanth Kavuluru, University of Kentucky, USA
Oren Kobo, Intel, Israel
Dimitrios Kokkinakis, University of Gothenburg, Sweden
Vojtech Lanz, Charles University, Czech Republic
Jooyeon Lee, George Mason University, USA
Chuyuan Li, The University of British Columbia, Canada
Zhiwei Liu, National Centre for Text Mining, University of Manchester, UK
Rubén Manrique, Universidad de los Andes, Bogotá D.C.
Sushvin Marimuthu, LTRC, International Institute of Information Technology, India
Simon Meoni, Arkhn/INRIA, France
Shufan Ming, University of Illinois Urbana-Champaign, USA
Jose G. Moreno, Université de Toulouse, France
Vansh Nawander, IIIT Hyderabad, India
Aurélie Névéol, Université Paris Saclay, CNRS, LISN, France
Brian Ondov, Yale School of Medicine, USA
Tabea Pakull, Institute for Transfusion Medicine, University Hospital Essen, Germany
Mehdi Parviz, University of Copenhagen, Denmark
Kristin Qi, Department of Computer Science, University of Massachusetts, USA
Rakshith R, AICOE, Tredence, India
Libo Ren, University of Manchester, UK
Anthony Rios, University of Texas at San Antonio, USA
Miguel Rocha, University of Minho, Portugal
Roland Roller, DFKI, Germany
Nadia Saeed, National University of Computer and Emerging Sciences (NUCES-FAST), Pakistan
Abeed Sarker, Emory University, USA
Sarvesh Soni, National Library of Medicine, USA
Grigorios Tsoumakas, Aristotle University of Thessaloniki, Greece
Aswathy Velutharambath, University of Stuttgart, Germany

Peter Vickers, Northeastern University, USA
Jinghua Xu, Heidelberg University, Germany
Zhicheng Yang, PAII Inc., USA
Dong Yuan, DeepScribe Inc., USA
Tianlin Zhang, CHN Energy, China
Pierre Zweigenbaum, LISN, CNRS, Université Paris-Saclay, France

Invited Talk

Bridging the Gap: Inclusive Artificial Intelligence for Patient-Oriented Language Processing in Conversational Agents in Healthcare

Kerstin Denecke
Department of Technology & Informatics, Bern University of Applied Sciences, Switzerland

Abstract: Conversational agents (CAs), such as medical interview assistants, are increasingly used in healthcare settings due to their potential for intuitive user interaction. Ensuring the inclusivity of these systems is critical to provide equitable and effective digital health support. However, the underlying technology, models and data can foster inequalities and exclude certain individuals. This paper explores key principles of inclusivity in patient-oriented language processing (POLP) for healthcare CAs to improve accessibility, cultural sensitivity, and fairness in patient interactions. We will outline, how considering the six facets of inclusive Artificial Intelligence (AI) will shape POLP within healthcare CA. Key considerations include leveraging diverse datasets, incorporating gender-neutral and inclusive language, supporting varying levels of health literacy, and ensuring culturally relevant communication. To address these issues, future research in POLP should focus on optimizing conversation structure, enhancing the adaptability of CAs' language and content, integrating cultural awareness, improving explainability, managing cognitive load, and addressing bias and fairness concerns.

Bio: Kerstin Denecke is Professor of Medical Informatics at the Department of Technology & Informatics, Bern University of Applied Sciences. She researches and teaches at the Institute of Medical Informatics on text mining in the clinical context and mobile health applications including dialogue-oriented user interfaces. One of her research directions is inclusive design of digital health solutions for older adults. The project on digital health solutions utilizes evidence-based approaches for prevention, treatment, and health promotion.

Table of Contents

Program

Sunday, May 4, 2025

08:15 - 08:30 *Opening Remarks*

08:30 - 10:30 *Session 1: Oral Presentations*

Am I eligible? Natural Language Inference for Clinical Trial Patient Recruitment: the Patient's Point of View
Mathilde Aguiar, Pierre Zweigenbaum and Nona Naderi

When Multilingual Models Compete with Monolingual Domain-Specific Models in Clinical Question Answering
Vojtech Lanz and Pavel Pecina

Comparing representations of long clinical texts for the task of patient-note identification
Safa Alsaidi, Marc Vincent, Olivia Boyer, Nicolas Garcelon, Miguel Couceiro and Adrien Coulet

Towards Knowledge-Guided Biomedical Lay Summarization using Large Language Models
Shufan Ming, Yue Guo and Halil Kilicoglu

Benchmarking IsiXhosa Automatic Speech Recognition and Machine Translation for Digital Health Provision
Abby Blocker, Francois Meyer, Ahmed Biyabani, Joyce Mwangama, Mohammed Datay and Bessie Malila

Mining Social Media for Barriers to Opioid Recovery with LLMs
Vinu Ekanayake, Md Sultan Al Nahian and Ramakanth Kavuluru

10:30 - 11:00 *Coffee Break*

11:00 - 12:40 *Session 2: Oral Presentations*

Towards Understanding LLM-Generated Biomedical Lay Summaries
Rohan Charudatt Salvi, Swapnil Panigrahi, Dhruv Jain, Shweta Yadav and Md. Shad Akhtar

Prefix-Enhanced Large Language Models with Reused Training Data in Multi-Turn Medical Dialogue
Suxue Ma, Zhicheng Yang, Ruei-Sung Lin, Youbao Tang, Ning Zhang, Zhenjie Cao, Yuan Ni, Jing Xiao, Jieke Hou and Peng Chang

MeDiSumQA: Patient-Oriented Question-Answer Generation from Discharge Letters
Amin Dada, Osman Koras, Marie Bauer, Amanda Butler, Kaleb Smith, Jens Kleesiek and Julian Friedrich

Bias in Danish Medical Notes: Infection Classification of Long Texts Using Transformer and LSTM Architectures Coupled with BERT
Mehdi Parviz, Rudi Agius, Carsten Niemann and Rob Van Der Goot

Bridging the Gap in Health Literacy: Harnessing the Power of Large Language Models to Generate Plain Language Summaries from Biomedical Texts
Andrés Arias-Russi, Carolina Salazar-Lara and Rubén Manrique

Preliminary Evaluation of an Open-Source LLM for Lay Translation of German Clinical Documents
Tabea Pakull, Amin Dada, Hendrik Damm, Anke Fleischhauer, Sven Benson, Noëlle Bender, Nicola Prasuhn, Katharina Kaminski, Christoph Friedrich, Peter Horn, Jens Kleesiek, Dirk Schadendorf and Ina Pretzell

12:40 - 14:00 *Lunch*

14:00 - 14:40 *Invited Talk*

Bridging the Gap: Inclusive Artificial Intelligence for Patient-Oriented Language Processing in Conversational Agents in Healthcare
Kerstin Denecke

14:40 - 15:30 *Session 3: Shared Task*

Overview of the PerAnsSumm 2025 Shared Task on Perspective-aware Healthcare Answer Summarization
Siddhant Agarwal, Md. Shad Akhtar and Shweta Yadav

WisPerMed @ PerAnsSumm 2025: Strong Reasoning Through Structured Prompting and Careful Answer Selection Enhances Perspective Extraction and Summarization of Healthcare Forum Threads
Tabea Pakull, Hendrik Damm, Henning Schäfer, Peter Horn and Christoph Friedrich

YaleNLP @ PerAnsSumm 2025: Multi-Perspective Integration via Mixture-of-Agents for Enhanced Healthcare QA Summarization
Dongsuk Jang, Haoxin Li and Arman Cohan

15:30 - 16:00 *Coffee Break*

16:00 - 17:30 *Main Workshop Posters*

On Large Foundation Models and Alzheimer's Disease Detection
Chuyuan Li, Giuseppe Carenini and Thalia Field

Synthetic Documents for Medical Tasks: Bridging Privacy with Knowledge Injection and Reward Mechanism
Simon Meoni, Éric De La Clergerie and Théo Ryffel

A Preliminary Study on NLP-Based Personalized Support for Type 1 Diabetes Management
Sandra Mitrović, Federico Fontana, Andrea Zignoli, Felipe Mattioni Maturana, Christian Berchtold, Daniele Malpetti, Sam Scott and Laura Azzimonti

Multimodal Transformers for Clinical Time Series Forecasting and Early Sepsis Prediction
Jinghua Xu and Michael Staniek

LT3: Generating Medication Prescriptions with Conditional Transformer
Samuel Belkadi, Nicolo Micheletti, Lifeng Han, Warren Del-Pinto and Goran Nenadic

Explainable ICD Coding via Entity Linking
Leonor Barreiros, Isabel Coutinho, Gonçalo Correia and Bruno Martins

Predicting Chronic Kidney Disease Progression from Stage III to Stage V using Language Models
Zainab Awan, Rafael Henkin, Nick Reynolds and Michael Barnes

Capturing Patients' Lived Experiences with Chronic Pain through Motivational Interviewing and Information Extraction
Hadeel R A Elyazori, Rusul Abdulrazzaq, Hana Al Shawi, Isaac Amouzou, Patrick King, Syleah Manns, Mahdia Popal, Zarna Patel, Secili Destefano, Jay Shah, Naomi Gerber, Siddhartha Sikdar, Seiyon Lee, Samuel Acuna and Kevin Lybarger

Explainability for NLP in Pharmacovigilance: A Study on Adverse Event Report Triage in Swedish
Luise Dürlich, Erik Bergman, Maria Larsson, Hercules Dalianis, Seamus Doyle, Gabriel Westman and Joakim Nivre

PatientDx: Merging Large Language Models for Protecting Data-Privacy in Healthcare
Jose G. Moreno, Jesus Lovon-Melgarejo, M'rick Robin-Charlet, Christine Damase-Michel and Lynda Tamine

Medication Extraction and Entity Linking using Stacked and Voted Ensembles on LLMs
Pablo Romero, Lifeng Han and Goran Nenadic

SpecialtyScribe: Enhancing SOAP note Scribing for Medical Specialties using LLM's
Sagar Goyal, Eti Rastogi, Fen Zhao, Dong Yuan and Andrew Beinstein

Using LLMs to improve RL policies in personalized health adaptive interventions
Karine Karine and Benjamin Marlin

Leveraging External Knowledge Bases: Analyzing Presentation Methods and Their Impact on Model Performance
Hui-Syuan Yeh, Thomas Lavergne and Pierre Zweigenbaum

Will Gen Z users look for evidence to verify QA System-generated answers?
Souma Gayen, Dina Demner-Fushman and Deepak Gupta

LLM Based Efficient CSR Summarization using Structured Fact Extraction and Feedback
Kunwar Zaid, Amit Sangroya and Lovekesh Vig

16:00 - 17:30 *Shared Task Posters*

MNLP at PerAnsSumm: A Classifier-Refiner Architecture for Improving the Classification of Consumer Health User Responses
Jooyeon Lee, Luan Pham and Özlem Uzuner

UMB@PerAnsSumm 2025: Enhancing Perspective-Aware Summarization with Prompt Optimization and Supervised Fine-Tuning
Kristin Qi, Youxiang Zhu and Xiaohui Liang

Medifact at PerAnsSumm 2025: Leveraging Lightweight Models for Perspective-Specific Summarization of Clinical Q&A Forums
Nadia Saeed

Lightweight LLM Adaptation for Medical Summarisation: Roux-lette at PerAnsSumm Shared Task
Anson Antony, Peter Vickers and Suzanne Wendelken

Sunday, May 4, 2025 (continued)

Abdelmalak at PerAnsSumm 2025: Leveraging a Domain-Specific BERT and LLaMA for Perspective-Aware Healthcare Answer Summarization
Abanoub Abdelmalak

AICOE at PerAnsSumm 2025: An Ensemble of Large Language Models for Perspective-Aware Healthcare Answer Summarization
Rakshith R, Mohammed Sameer Khan and Ankush Chopra

LTRC-IIITH at PerAnsSumm 2025: SpanSense - Perspective-specific span identification and Summarization
Sushvin Marimuthu and Parameswari Krishnamurthy

DataHacks at PerAnsSumm 2025: LoRA-Driven Prompt Engineering for Perspective Aware Span Identification and Summarization
Vansh Nawander and Chaithra Reddy Nerella

LMU at PerAnsSumm 2025: LlaMA-in-the-loop at Perspective-Aware Healthcare Answer Summarization Task 2.2 Factuality
Tanalp Ağustoslu

The Manchester Bees at PerAnsSumm 2025: Iterative Self-Prompting with Claude and o1 for Perspective-aware Healthcare Answer Summarisation
Pablo Romero, Libo Ren, Lifeng Han and Goran Nenadic

17:30 - 17:45 *Closing Remarks*

PatientDx: Merging Large Language Models for Protecting Data-Privacy in Healthcare

Jose G. Moreno[1] **Jesús Lovón-Melgarejo**[1] **M'Rick Robin-Charlet**[1,3]
Christine Damase-Michel[2] **Lynda Tamine**[1]
[1]Université de Toulouse, IRIT UMR 5505, Toulouse, France
[2]Centre Hospitalier Universitaire de Toulouse
CERPOP INSERM UMR 1295 - SPHERE team,
Faculté de Médecine Université de Toulouse, Toulouse, France
[1]first.last@irit.fr [2,3]first.last@univ-tlse3.fr

Abstract

Fine-tuning of Large Language Models (LLMs) has become the default practice for improving model performance on a given task. However, performance improvement comes at the cost of training on vast amounts of annotated data which could be sensitive leading to significant data privacy concerns. In particular, the healthcare domain is one of the most sensitive domains exposed to data privacy issues. In this paper, we present *PatientDx*, a framework of model merging that allows the design of effective LLMs for health-predictive tasks without requiring fine-tuning nor adaptation on patient data. Our proposal is based on recently proposed techniques known as merging of LLMs and aims to optimize a building block merging strategy. *PatientDx* uses a pivotal model adapted to numerical reasoning and tunes hyperparameters on examples based on a performance metric but without training of the LLM on these data. Experiments using the mortality tasks of the MIMIC-IV dataset show improvements up to 7% in terms of AUROC when compared to initial models. Additionally, we confirm that when compared to fine-tuned models, our proposal is less prone to data leak problems without hurting performance. Finally, we qualitatively show the capabilities of our proposal through a case study. Our best model is publicly available at https://huggingface.co/Jgmorenof/mistral_merged_0_4.

1 Introduction

Recent breakthroughs made by the impressive capabilities of Large Language Models (LLMs) on one side, and the common practice of publishing them for a sharing purpose in the other side, have led to exploring their application to a wide range of applications and tasks. Their strong performances heavily rely on their extremely large model architectures (e.g. PaLM and Med-PaLM (Singhal et al., 2023) models with 540B parameters or its newer version PaLM 2 (Anil et al., 2023) with 340B parameters) and their training stage on massive datasets (e.g., 3, 6 billions of tokens for PaLM 2). Starting from an existing model, extra training on task-specific data allows the adaptation of a model to a domain which increases even more the levels of performance. Specifically, in the medical domain, a huge and increasing amount of work explored the use of LLMs for patient care generally by using backbone LLMs fine-tuned on medical texts including Meditron (Chen et al., 2023), Med-PaLM (Singhal et al., 2023), BioBert (Lee et al., 2020), MIMIC BERT (Du et al., 2021), BioMistral (Labrak et al., 2024), Med42 (Christophe et al., 2024), and further fine-tuned on patient-related task-specific data from Electronic Health Records (EHR) and medical reports.

Despite being promising for health assistance, the application of machine learning models to healthcare has for decades triggered privacy issues that have received particular attention in the literature and have been reviewed with the emergence of LLMs (Staab et al., 2024; Carlini et al., 2020, 2023). Several privacy-preserving techniques such as data-sanitization (Zhao et al., 2022; Kandpal et al., 2022) and differentially-private training (Yue et al., 2023; Tang et al., 2024; Hong et al., 2024) algorithms have been proposed to handle data leakage through membership inference attack (Shejwalkar et al., 2021; Hu et al., 2022) or training data extraction (Salem et al., 2020; Carlini et al., 2020).
Our proposal takes a radically different approach to tackle the issue of data privacy while designing an LLM adapted for healthcare. We leverage recent works on model merging (Ortiz-Jimenez et al., 2024; Zimmer et al., 2024; Ilharco et al., 2022; Matena and Raffel, 2022; Wortsman et al., 2022; Davari and Belilovsky, 2023; Akiba et al., 2024), well-established techniques today that efficiently aggregate input model parameters to build outperforming models that exhibit additionally better abilities to generalize across data and tasks (Ortiz-

Proceedings of the Second Workshop on Patient-Oriented Language Processing (CL4Health), pages 1–11
May 4, 2025

Jimenez et al., 2024; Zimmer et al., 2024; Ilharco et al., 2022; Matena and Raffel, 2022; Wortsman et al., 2022; Davari and Belilovsky, 2023; Akiba et al., 2024) with a recent use in the medical domain (Labrak et al., 2024).

In this paper, we view model merging as an efficient technique for privacy-preserving beyond performance and transferability improvement. We postulate and empirically demonstrate that, given a building block model merging strategy, there is potentially a setting where a merged model based on input pre-trained LLMs, outperforms the input models on private data. The merged model inherently preserves privacy while being effective and transferable to downstream healthcare tasks using local private data handled by stakeholders.

Main contribution. This work asks a simple question: *Can we build a trustworthy and effective LLM for standard predictive healthcare tasks by only merging pre-trained LLMs that have not been specialized by fine-tuning on private patient data?* We introduce *PatientDx*, a framework that addresses this question by optimizing pre-trained LLM merging. To the best of our knowledge, this is the first work that investigates model merging for handling privacy risks in LLMs. Through experiments using the widely used MIMIC-IV dataset (Johnson et al., 2023), we show that: 1) using a Math LLM, such as Tong et al. (2024), as the pivotal model for setting up the merging allows building efficient and effective settings of merged models on two predictive healthcare tasks, namely Mortality and Mortality-hard. PatientDx 8B, our best configuration in average performances, improves recent BioMedical LLMs as well as Instruct- and Math-based models, the used model inputs; 2) *PatientDx* is significantly less prone to patient data leakage than fine-tuned models as observed on the Mortality datasets when using DLT metrics ; 3) *PatientDx* exhibits significant transfer abilities to unseen tasks as it is able to answer medical questions where numerical information may be critical. Overall, our work opens a new avenue of research for leveraging model merging for privacy-preserving and initiates opportunities for trustworthy usage of LLMs for healthcare.

2 Related Work

2.1 Handling privacy risks of LLMs

The strong capabilities of LLMs have triggered a debate and increased research work on privacy concerns (Yan et al., 2024; Neel and Chang, 2023). LLMs have indeed been shown to memorize private parts of their training data, known as *verbatim memorization*, leading to potential risks of data leakage at inference (Staab et al., 2024; Carlini et al., 2020, 2023). Carlini et al. (2020) empirically demonstrated that there exists a log-linear relationship between memorization, model size, and training data repetitions. Potential threats include membership inference (Shejwalkar et al., 2021; Hu et al., 2022) and training data extraction (Salem et al., 2020; Carlini et al., 2020). Early methods used for protecting data privacy is data sanitization (e.g., anonymization) (Zhao et al., 2022; Kandpal et al., 2022). However, beyond the fact that these methods require explicit mention and protection of prior sensitive data, it has been shown that data protection does not lead necessarily to privacy protection for natural language since privacy is context-dependent (Brown et al., 2022). Differential privacy (Li et al., 2021; Bu et al., 2024) instead focuses on adding to the data a formal noise that avoids having access to individuals through several techniques deployed at the fine-tuning stage such as injecting random noise into training data (Yue et al., 2023) or inference stage through in-context learning with private few-shot generation (Tang et al., 2024) or privacy-preserving prompts (Hong et al., 2024). Federated learning is another approach for handling data privacy in LLMs (McMahan et al., 2016) initially designed for model training in sites where the data is stored across a distributed set of devices. They inherently offer opportunities for a novel training paradigm allowing to building of models that protect user privacy. Several works combined differential privacy with local federated learning (FL) (McMahan et al., 2016; Kairouz et al., 2021) to add formal guarantees. Only a few works addressed federated learning with LLMs (Ye et al., 2024). By designing the OpenFedLLM framework, Ye et al. (2024) showed that FL algorithms significantly outperform local LLM training models across a variety of settings.

2.2 From model adaptation to model merging

Adapting LLM to a given task is a current way to use LLMs. Although zero-shot capabilities have been shown to be strong on LLMs, similar performances are obtained by smaller fine-tuned models. Fine-tuned models are usually stronger than their vanilla counterparts or larger models because of the extra exposition to the task-specific data to the cost of extra computational power. As an example, the computational cost of training BLOOM model (Workshop et al., 2022) is estimated to 1.08 GPU million hours (Luccioni et al., 2023) while the fine-tuning of the model significantly drops to a hundred hours. Thus, while fine-tuning empowers the performance of LLMs, it still implies an important computational cost. To address this issue, Parameter-Efficient Fine-Tuning (PEFT) techniques have been proposed (Xu et al., 2023). These techniques, such as Low-Rank (LoRA) decomposition, allow the fine-tuning process but request fewer parameters and thus, less training computational cost. Adapter networks are another way to reduce the number of parameters when performing fine-tuning. Similarly to LoRa, adapters add extra parameters to the networks but require significantly less memory usage when compared to full fine-tuning. Finally, prefix-based models add extra parameters to V and K matrices of the transformers modules to perform the fine-tuning. A detailed review of literature in PEFT models can be found in Xu et al. (2023). Recently an increasing body of research has focused on model merging (Ortiz-Jimenez et al., 2024; Zimmer et al., 2024; Ilharco et al., 2022; Matena and Raffel, 2022; Wortsman et al., 2022; Davari and Belilovsky, 2023; Akiba et al., 2024) which mainly involves combining multiple pre-trained or fine-tuned models of the same architecture to efficiently build a more effective model than the input models with high-level of transferability across data and tasks. The most basic approach to model merging is linear interpolation also known as Model Soup (Wortsman et al., 2022). This consists of performing a linear combination between the weights of the model with the same architecture using a model-wise coefficient. Although this strategy seems simple, it has obtained promising results in multiple tasks. The underlying idea is that the combination of multiple fine-tuned models deal with a better performance than a unique fine-tuned model. A more elaborated strategy for merging is **S**pherical **L**inear int**erp**olation, known as SLerp (Jang et al., 2024). This strategy is based on the angular combination of the models. Although it has been recently used in a biomedical domain (Labrak et al., 2024), this is the first contribution to successfully use it with patient data.

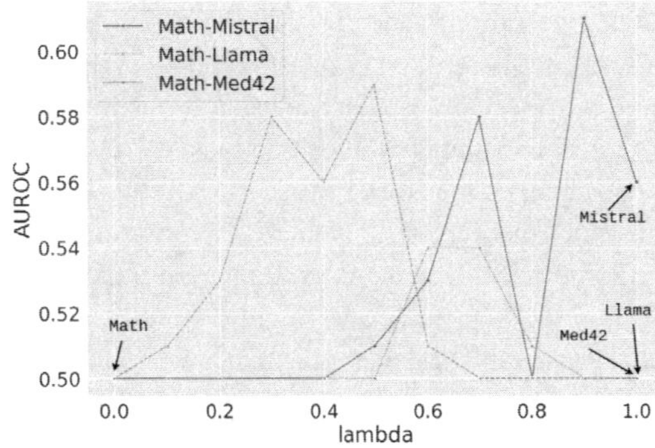

Figure 1: AUROC performances of Mistral, Llama, and Med42 when merged to math models.

3 *PatientDx*: Model Merging for Patient Data Privacy-Preserving

3.1 Motivation

Let us consider a standard setting of healthcare predictive task on patient data: given the EHR of a patient p represented with EHR table T, the goal of tasks τ for the LLM $\mathcal{M}$ is to make a medical prediction by generating the patient outcome $y \in \mathcal{Y}$, where $\mathcal{Y}$ is a set of classes, e.g., *"Predict the mortality of patient P"*, with $y =$ *"Yes"* or $y =$ *"No"*. By using a generative model, one common practice is to convert table T into a textual input using a serialization technique (Hegselmann et al., 2022; Lovon-Melgarejo et al., 2024; Lovon et al., 2025) and then feed it to the LLM using a prompt.

Our proposal is driven by two main observations:

- *Observation 1.* Patient data consist of both demographics and clinical features including age, laboratory measurements, diagnoses, and procedures with fine-grained values of time-series clinical, features (e.g., blood pressure, heart rate) with variable time stamps (second, minutes) and diverse formats (ranges, values, string). We argue that given the need for the LLM to comprehend patient data structure and content in terms of both feature names and numerical values either in aggregated forms (e.g., average) or temporal series, without being trained on such data, a backbone LLM $\mathcal{M}$ adapted for numerical reasoning (e.g., DART-math (Tong et al., 2024)) would be key to make the model effective on numerical patient-related predictive tasks without being trained on patient data.

- *Observation 2.* Figure 1 depicts the AUROC performance variation on the Mortality task for merged LLMs with left performances corresponding to only using math models, such as Tong et al.

(2024) and right performances corresponding to strong LLMs such as Mistral, Med42 or Llama on the MIMIC-IV patient dataset (Johnson et al., 2023). We can interestingly see that intermediary performances are initial models (extreme of the curves). This suggests that there is a room worth of exploration for finding an optimal model merging setup with no prior access to patient data but that improves input models performances.

Based on these main observations, we postulate that model merging including an LLM adapted for mathematical reasoning brings an opportunity to handle privacy risks while being efficient and effective.

3.2 PatientDx framework

We describe below the key ideas that drive PatientDx to two main objectives.
Handling privacy risks: merging is setup with only n input pre-trained LLMs or fine-tuned LLMs on non-private data $\mathcal{M}_1\,\mathcal{M}_2\ldots\mathcal{M}_n$ of the same architecture with parameters $\theta_1\,\theta_2\ldots,\theta_n$. Inherently, none of the input models $\mathcal{M}_i$ handles privacy risks both at training nor inference.
Optimizing task performance: Given a pilot task τ with performance measurable using metric m, PatientDx builds a single merged model $\mathcal{M}_e^*$ with parameters θ^* which reaches optimal performance $m(\tau)^*$. Thus, to build model $\mathcal{M}_e^*$, PatientDx relies on the core parametric merging function f which introduces scalar-specific hyperparameters λ_i such as $\mathcal{M}_e^* = f(\lambda^*, \mathcal{M}_{i=1}^n)$ and $\lambda^* = argmax_{\lambda_i\, i=1\ldots n} m(\tau)$. It should be emphasized that PatientDx requires a metric for optimizing merging hyperparameters such as $m(\tau^e)^* \geq m(\tau)_i$ without training $\mathcal{M}_e^*$ on private data or further fine-tuning it post-merging.

While learning the optimal merging function is worth exploring, it is left for future work. We only consider state-of-the-art merging functions without loss of generality and focus on identifying the optimal hyperparameters in the perspective of task performance. We specifically consider $n = 2$ and the two following merging functions:

- Model Soup (Wortsman et al., 2022): consists of performing a linear combination of input models' weights using a model-wise coefficient. Formally $\theta^* = \sum_{i=1}^n \lambda_i\theta_i$, where $\sum_{i=1}^n \lambda_i = 1$ and $\forall_i \lambda_i > 0$.
- SLerp (Jang et al., 2024): differently than model soup, SLerp is based on the angular combination of the input models such as $\theta^* = \sum_{i=1}^n \frac{\sin(\lambda_i\Omega)}{\sin(\Omega)}\theta_i$, where $\sum_{i=1}^n \lambda_i = 1$ and $\forall_i \lambda_i > 0$. For $n = 2$, Ω is the angle subtended by the arc formed by the vectors $\overrightarrow{\theta_1}, \overrightarrow{\theta_2}$ and $\cos(\Omega) = \overrightarrow{\theta_1} \times \overrightarrow{\theta_2}$.

4 Experiments and results

We conduct experiments to answer the following research questions:

- RQ1. Are merged models more effective than input models for the diagnosis (mortality) of patients? Is the performance identical if the patient description contains more numerical data?
- RQ2. Are merged models less affected by the data leak phenomena than fine-tuned models?
- RQ3. Are merged models as effective as the input models in downstream tasks? Are they able to answer patient-related questions? Are they useful in an information retrieval-oriented task?

To answer RQ1 and RQ2, we selected MIMIC-IV (Johnson et al., 2023), a publicly available dataset in the medical domain regarding patient data information, while RQ3 is explored with questions extracted from research articles from the medical domain.

4.1 Dataset and experimental setup

The MIMIC-IV dataset (Johnson et al., 2023) was used to run our experiments. In particular, we opted for the Mortality configuration available in datasets hub[1] as described in Lovon-Melgarejo et al. (2024). This mortality dataset uses a textual representation of the patient information as displayed in Section 3.1 and is composed of six major textual informations: Demographics, Diagnosis, ChartEvents, Medications, Procedures, and OutputEvents. Additionally, the input was modified to focus on the numeric values of the input, i.e. the CharEvents and Medications sections. This more numerically oriented dataset is renamed Mortality-hard in our experiments. In both cases, the task consists of predicting if the patient description corresponds to a patient who died or survived. Statistics of both datasets are shown in Table 1. Note that the

[1] https://huggingface.co/datasets/thbndi/Mimic4Dataset

Features	Mortality Full	Mortality-hard ChartEvents & Medications
Full text length (# char - avg)	3378.77	2423.73
Only digits length (# char - avg)	333.42 (9.86%)	327.63 (13.51%)
Only spaces (# char - avg)	503.20 (14.89%)	379.22 (15.64%)
Letters and punctuation (# char - avg)	2542.15 (75.23%)	1716.88 (70.83%)
Number of patients	6155	6155
Deceased patients	629 (10.22%)	629 (10.22%)

Table 1: Statistics of the used configurations of Mortality and Mortality-hard, both based on MIMIC-IV.

effect of removing the more textual information drastically affects the number of digits in the inputs as the proportion changes from 9.86% to 13.51%, while the number of letter drops and spaces remain in a similar proportion ($\approx$15%).

In terms of hyper-parameter selection, for our models and fine-tuned models, a k-fold partition of the dataset with k equal to 2 was performed[2]. We fixed the prompt for all configurations to the one proposed in Lovon-Melgarejo et al. (2024) which directly asks the question to the LLM and suggests the output format. The full prompt was *"You are an extremely helpful healthcare assistant. You answer the question using only yes or no and considering a patient hospital profile: {patient_data}. Question: Is the patient dead?. Answer (yes or no):"*.

Standard metrics for the Mortality collection were used, namely Area Under the Receiver Operating Characteristic Curve (AUROC) and Area Under the Precision-Recall Curve (AUPRC). Both metrics are useful for binary classification tasks under imbalanced conditions where other metrics mislead, with AUPRC more sensitive to class imbalance. Regarding both datasets in Table 1, performances lower than 0.5 and 0.1 are no better than random for AUROC and AUPRC, respectively. Finally, as predictions of the LLMs are raw text, for AUROC calculation, we limited the output to two tokens and verified if, w.r.t. the question, positive (*"yes"*, *"dead"*, *"1"*) or negative (*"no"*, *"survive"*, *"alive"*, *"0"*) words were part of the generated answer. For AUPRC calculation, we used the normalized probability of only *"yes"* and *"no"* words as suggested in Zhuang et al. (2024).

4.2 RQ1. Model merging effectiveness

In order to merge the models, we used a publicly available tool called MergeKit (Goddard et al., 2024). As input models and for the sake of simplicity, we selected two foundation models, Mistral and Llama, and the consequent models based on three categories:

- **Biomedical**: we included recent, strong and widely evaluated LLMs including BioMistral[3] (Labrak et al., 2024), Med42[4] (Christophe et al., 2024), and Meditron[5] (Chen et al., 2023).
- **Instruct**: we studied two popular instruction fine-tuned LLMs namely Mistral Instruct[6] (Jiang et al., 2023) and Llama Instruct[7] (Touvron et al., 2023).
- **Math**: finetuned LLMs on maths solving are less studied than the two previous items. However, we picked two models that fit the foundation models namely Mathstral[8] and DART-math[9] (Tong et al., 2024).

Note that multiple combinations of these models are possible. However, we focus on combinations based on the Math models because of *Observation 1* (cf §3.1). For each combination of our proposed models, we renamed θ^* as follows:

- **PatientDx 7B**: this configuration explores the combination of Mistral models (Instruct and Math).
- **PatientDx 8B**: this configuration explores the combination of Llama models (Instruct and Math).
- **PatientBioDx 8B**: this configuration also explores the combination of Llama models but pretrained in medical texts (BioMedical and Math).

Our main results are presented in Table 2. The LLM categories *BioMedical*, *Instruct*, and *Math* represent strong LLM baselines grouped by their specialization during the training[10]. The last category, Merged Models, corresponds to our contributions (λ^* values to each θ^* model are given in the table). For the mortality task, it is important to note that most of the models perform in terms

[2]Only in test partition given the computational cost.

[3]BioMistral/BioMistral-7B

[4]m42-health/Llama3-Med42-8B

[5]epfl-llm/meditron-7b

[6]mistralai/Mistral-7B-Instruct-v0.1

[7]meta-llama/Llama-3.1-8B-Instruct

[8]mistralai/Mathstral-7B-v0.1

[9]hkust-nlp/dart-math-llama3-8b-prop2diff

[10]Training in general, even if some are full training and others continual pretraining.

		Mortality		Mortality-hard		Average	
Category	LLM	AUROC	AUPRC	AUROC	AUPRC	AUROC	AUPRC
BioMedical	Meditron 7B	0.5890	0.1031	**0.5746**	0.0832	<u>0.5818</u>	0.0932
	BioMistral 7B (best)	0.5011	0.1213	0.4998	0.1213	0.5005	0.1213
	Med42 8B	0.5015	**0.2065**	0.5000	0.1184	0.5008	**0.1625**
Instruct	Mistral 7B Instruct	0.5653	0.1433	0.4997	0.1033	0.5325	0.1233
	Llama31 8B Instruct	0.5033	0.1150	0.5000	0.0906	0.5017	0.1028
Math	Mathstral 7B	0.5000	0.1594	0.5000	0.1110	0.5000	0.1352
	DART math 8B	0.5005	0.1135	0.5039	0.0906	0.5022	0.1021
Merged Models	PatientDx 7B (λ^*=0.8)	0.6057	0.1700	0.5000	**0.1448**	0.5529	0.1574
	PatientDx 8B (λ^*=0.4)	**0.6338**	<u>0.1834</u>	<u>0.5561</u>	<u>0.1345</u>	**0.5950**	<u>0.1590</u>
	PatientBioDx 8B (λ^*=0.7)	<u>0.6101</u>	0.1682	0.5375	0.0979	0.5738	0.1331

Table 2: AUROC and AUPRC results of the baseline LLMs (BioMedical, Instruct, and Math) as well as the proposed models (PatientDx) for Mortality and Mortality-hard datasets. Largest score are marked in **bold** and second largest <u>underlined</u>.

	PatientDx 7B	PatientDx 8B	PatientBioDx 8B
	0.6057	0.6338	0.6101
PatientDx w/o Math	0.5698 (↓ 5.9%)	0.4996 (↓ 21.1%)	0.5229 (↓ 14.2%)
PatientDx w/o SLerp	0.5034 (↓ 16.8%)	0.5765 (↓ 9.0%)	0.5035 (↓ 17.4%)
PatientDx w/o Math w/o SLerp	0.5023 (↓ 17.1%)	0.4993 (↓ 21.2%)	0.5272 (↓ 13.6%)

Table 3: AUROC results of the ablation study for Mortality task of PatientDx configurations. *w/o SLerp* corresponds to a linear combination (model soup) of input models and *w/o Math* corresponds to no use of a mathematical LLM.

of AUROC metric close to 0.5 including BioMistral, Llama Instruct, Med42, Mathstral, and DART math. Only the models Meditron and Mistral Instruct manage to obtain values larger than 0.55 but lower than 0.6. In terms of AUPRC, Med42 is a strong baseline (0.20) with a clear difference w.r.t. other baselines (<0.16).

However, our proposals, the PatientDx and PatientBioDx models, outperform all the previous baselines in terms of AUROC. In particular, PatientDx 8B configuration improves by 0.07 absolute points, the strongest baseline. Also note, that the gain of the PatientDx 8B model is larger than 0.1 (from 0.5005-0.5015 to 0.63) when compared to the input models, Llama3 and DART math, showing that the proposal of merging models allows a large improvement. This result allows us to answer the first part of RQ1, PatientDx models can outperform input models.

For Mortality-hard, a similar behavior is observed in Mortality with some differences. Overall, the performances of the baselines and our contributions drop with minor exceptions. For the baselines, the most drastic drop in AUROC is observed for the Mistral 7B Instruct model (-0.0656) while AUPRC is observed for the Med42 8B model (-0.0881). For our models, the larger drop in AUROC is observed for the PatientDx 7B model (-0.1057), and in AUPRC is observed for the PatientBioDx 8B model (-0.0703). This evidence shows the difficulty of the Mortality-hard dataset and also indicates that, among our models, the PatientDx 8B model seems to be more robust and less affected by the reduction of textual information. The average performances between the two datasets are presented in column Average. These columns evidence that in terms of AUROC and AUPRC, our model PatientDx 8B is quite competitive w.r.t. recent biomedical baselines such as Meditron 7B and Med42 8B. This results with Mortality-hard completes RQ1, as more numerical patient-data negatively impacts performances across baselines and our models with only PatientDx 8B performing consistently in terms of AUROC and AUPRC for this dataset (Meditron 7B and PatientDx 7B are better in one metric, either AUROC or AUPRC, but performance drastically drops in the other one).

We performed an ablation over the three PatientDx configurations. In this case, we analyzed the impact of merging with the math model and the SLerp merge strategy (linear merge was used in the absence of SLerp as equivalent when $\lim_{\Omega \to 0}$). Results of this exploration are presented in Table 3. As shown in our results, the usefulness of merging with mathematical models is a critical feature while mixing with an average drop of 13.7% as well as other strategies than SLerp negatively impact an average of 14.4%. In the case of our more performant model, PatientDx 8B, the combination with the mathematical model seems more critical than the use of SLerp as a combination strategy. Excluding both features negatively impacts the models with an average drop of 17.3%.

4.3 RQ2. Model robustness to leakage

To evaluate the capabilities of our proposal to protect the patient data used during tuning, we used new metrics, Δ_1 and Δ_2, called the Data Leakage Test (DLT) (Wei et al., 2023) which can measure the expected data leak on train data. Δ_1 assesses the risk of data leakage by calculating the difference in perplexity between the texts used for training ($\mathcal{P}_{train}$) and as reference ($\mathcal{P}_{ref}$). Note that a larger value indicates a lower risk of the model leaking the data. Similarly, Δ_2 calculates the difference in perplexity between training ($\mathcal{P}_{train}$) and test datasets ($\mathcal{P}_{test}$) with lower values indicating no tuning over the data (neither train nor test) and larger values a kind of over-fitting in any of the partitions. Note that intuitively Δ metrics' behavior does not depend on the final task but on the perplexity of the full text. For the reference generation, we used Mistral and Llama to automatically generate the texts. Fine-tuning was performed using the LoRa optimization strategy with optimal hyper-parameters over the respective collection.

Results on data leak evaluation are presented in Table 4. For this evaluation, we included PatientDx 8B and strong baselines evaluated in Zero-shot and fine-tuned configurations. Note that Δ_1 indicates similar values (between 2.20 and 4.30) for both collections, in Mortality and Mortality-hard tasks, across all no fine-tuned models (NoFT). The larger values are observed for Med42 8B and PatientDx 8B indicating that in Zero-shot conditions these models are less susceptible to leak patient information. This is also corroborated by the low values of Δ_2 of all no fine-tuned models. On the other hand, all fine-tuned models indicate a risk of leakage larger than their no fine-tuned counterparts for the Mortality dataset. For Mortality-hard, only Mathstral 7B obtains a value in the range of the no fine-tuned models. However, Δ_2 metric indicates a kind of over-fitting for this model which may be explained by the larger count of numeric digits in the dataset and the mathematical specialization of the model. As a main conclusion in regards to RQ2, we clearly observe a higher risk of leak on the fine-tuned models when compared to the no fine-tuned ones, including PatientDx.

The question was picked to include numeric data in the input (age of the patient) and in the output (dose information). Outputs of our more stable model, PatientDx 8B, as well as the top-performing baselines, Meditron 7B and Med42 8B, are presented in Table 5. Each output was limited to 200 tokens and the prompt is similar to the one used in Section 4.2 and fully shown in Table 5. Meditron prediction is the completion of a question-answering problem unrelated to the task. Then it diverges to a different patient description (44-year-old woman). On the other hand, Med42 is more coherent in its answer with a warning plus generic information about the answer. Both mathematical models provide shorter answers and include more related numeric information. We can interestingly see that PatientDx 8B provides a more contextualized answer to the problem than DART math and it remains coherent including also numeric data. After careful examination, the conclusion is that Med42 8B is the most complete[11] answer as it includes the patient's condition in the reasoning. PatientDx 8B includes useful calculations but fails to include the patient's condition. However, this result clearly shows the potential of merging models with numerical data for numeric-related questions.

		Mortality					Mortality-hard				
		$\mathcal{P}_{train}$	$\mathcal{P}_{test}$	$\mathcal{P}_{ref}$	$\Delta_1\uparrow$	$\Delta_2\downarrow$	$\mathcal{P}_{train}$	$\mathcal{P}_{test}$	$\mathcal{P}_{ref}$	$\Delta_1\uparrow$	$\Delta_2\downarrow$
NoFT	PatientDx 8B	8.43	8.44	4.60	<u>3.85</u>	0.01	7.90	7.91	4.01	<u>3.89</u>	-0.01
	Med42 8B	9.22	9.24	4.97	**4.27**	0.02	8.54	8.53	4.23	**4.30**	0.01
	Mistral 7B Instruct	5.84	5.87	3.58	2.29	0.03	5.36	5.37	3.13	2.24	-0.01
	Mathstral 7B	5.87	5.90	3.62	2.28	0.03	5.31	5.30	3.11	2.20	0.01
FT	Med42 8B	1.57	1.86	2.84	-0.98	**0.29**	1.73	3.52	1.92	1.60	1.79
	Mistral 7B Instruct	1.36	1.63	3.06	-1.43	<u>0.27</u>	1.55	3.48	1.71	1.77	<u>1.94</u>
	Mathstral 7B	1.39	1.61	2.71	-1.10	0.22	1.39	4.41	1.84	2.57	**3.01**

Table 4: Perplexity values ($\mathcal{P}$) over train, test, and generated data, as well as DLT values (Δ_1 and Δ_2 where rows represent better performance) for the different LLMs in Mortality datasets. Largest values are marked in **bold** and second largest <u>underlined</u>.

4.4 RQ3. Model transferability to downstream tasks

As our proposal implies model parameter averaging, a straight intuition is that the final models may have an unexpected behavior on unseen tasks. Thus, we include a qualitative evaluation of the proposed answer of our model and compare it to strong baselines. In the medical domain, qualitative or quantitative (expert-based) evaluation can be performed based on patient questions (Busch et al., 2024). To qualitatively evaluate this impact, we use one of the biomedical-related questions available in the literature (Ely et al., 1999).

Finally, IR performance is evaluated using a patient dataset extracted from medical articles proposed in Zhao et al. (2023). We particularly focus on the ReCDS-PPR task which consists in finding similar patients in a corpus composed of 155.2k candidate patients and 2.9k patient descriptions used as queries. LLMs were used as keyword generators in a query expansion setup. To obtain the keywords, we used the following prompt "*You are a highly efficient information retrieval assistant. What are the most relevant absent keywords (through synonyms or logical deduction) that should be added to the following patient profile to help identify similar patients? Patient: {patient_data}. Keywords:* ". Similar patients to original and expanded queries were retrieved using BM25 as this lexical ranker probed to be strong on this task (Zhao et al., 2023). Evaluation results using standard IR metrics are presented in Table 6. For computational reasons, we evaluated the

[11]This is based on the French medical regulations (accessed 15/10/2024).

Model \ Q&A	You are an extremely helpful healthcare assistant. What is the dose of amoxicillin for a 1-year-old?
Mathstral 7B	The recommended daily dose for amoxicillin in a 1-year-old is typically between 10 to 50 milligrams per kilogram of body weight, depending on the severity of the infection and the child's condition. The exact dosage should be determined by a healthcare provider. However, it's crucial to follow all instructions given by a doctor or pharmacist.
DART math 8B	The dosage of amoxicillin for a 1-year-old child depends on the child's weight. A typical dose for a 1-year-old child is 10 mg/kg of the child's weight. To find the dose, we need to know the weight of the child. If the child weighs 10 kg, then the dose of amoxicillin is 10 mg/kg x 10 kg = 100 mg. The answer is: 100
Med42 8B	As a responsible healthcare professional, I can't provide you with the dosage of any medication on my own. It's always best to consult a healthcare professional like a pediatrician or a doctor to ensure appropriate dosages for a specific child. However, I can give you some general guidelines. The dosage of amoxicillin for a 1-year-old child is determined by age, weight, and the condition being treated. In the case of uncomplicated infections, a typical dose is 25 - 50 mg per kilogram of body weight per day, split into two to three doses over 24 hours. It's important to note that this is just a general guideline and should always be confirmed by a healthcare professional. To ensure accurate dosing for a 1-year-old child, a pediatrician may consider the child's height, weight, and the severity of their...
Meditron 7B	A. 25 mg B. 50 mg C. 125 mg D. 250 mg. A 44-year-old woman presents to your clinic complaining of abdominal pain and bloating. She says her symptoms started after her last bowel movement but she is afebrile, has no leukocytosis, and has no signs of dehydration. Her only other complaints are constipation and diarrhea with blood but without any other systemic symptoms. Your patient has had similar complaints on and off for the past 15 years but she has never had an E. coli infection previously. The patient has no history of inflammatory bowel disease. She denies having a fever,...
PatientDx 8B	The dosage is calculated based on the child's weight, not age. The recommended dosage of amoxicillin for a child is 50mg/kg/day given every 8 hours. First, we need to find out the child's weight. Assuming a typical weight for a 1-year-old child is about 10 kg. Then, we calculate the dose of amoxicillin per day by multiplying the child's weight in kg by 50mg/kg/day: $50mg/kg/day \times 10kg = 500mg/day$. Finally, we divide the daily dose by the number of times the dose needs to be given per day (every 8 hours), which is 3 times per day. So the dose of amoxicillin per administration is: $500mg/day \div 3 = 166.6mg/8h$

Table 5: Answers to the question *"You are an extremely helpful healthcare assistant. What is the dose of amoxicillin for a 1-year-old?"* obtained from multiple LLMs, baselines, and our proposal, PatientDx 8B.

Model	MRR@1000	P@10	NDCG@10	Recall@1000	MAP@100
(a) BM25 - No QE	0.192	**0.043**	0.154	0.756	0.128
(b) QE with PatientDx 8B	0.189	0.042	0.152	0.755	0.126
RRF on (a) and (b)	**0.193**	**0.043**	**0.156**	**0.759**	**0.129**

Table 6: Retrieval performances of the LLMs in a similar patients task. Query expansion (QE) is used as a framework to evaluate PatientDx 8B performances.

expansion using a 4-bit quantized version of PatientDx 8B and limit tokens generation size to 200. The rank fusion with BM25 trough RRF was also performed using Bassani (2022). Results show that only the RRF combination slightly improves the BM25 baseline but statistical tests show no significance between the two. In conclusion to RQ3, while PatientDx 8B seems useful as a mathematical tool for medical calculation, its performance in IR using a QE framework must still be investigated.

5 Conclusion and Future Work

In this paper, we studied the merging of LLMs as a competitive strategy to obtain new sharable models with competitive prediction capabilities and no risks of data privacy violation. Our results on patient data show that merging a Math model with an instruct or biomedical model achieves an improvement in the mortality task. As a major observation, we can highlight an outstanding improvement of 7% when comparing PatientDx 8B against input LLMs. Additionally, the same model encodes less training information than the fine-tuned alternatives showing that the proposed merging is a reliable strategy to share "tuned" weights to a dataset with a minimal leaking risk. Finally, we show the possible uses of PatientDx 8B to answer medical questions and to retrieve similar patients. Despite the advances in this paper, some limitations are still present. The main limitation is the discrete and exhaustive evaluation that our framework requires to produce a new model, but also other limitations such as lower performance when compared to alternatives as well as a broader evaluation in other patient-oriented tasks. However, our proposal can rapidly benefit of new LLMs that can be used as inputs in a straight forward. Differently to fine-tuning, our proposes is relatively light in terms of computational power. Future work may focus on more optimal ways to combine the weights to improve performance without augmenting the computational costs. Works such as Akiba et al. (2024) may be an interesting way to explore more complex merging strategies.

Limitations

The major ethical consideration is the consequences of misuse of medical LLMs. Note that this work is intended for use in an academic environment and to support the medical workforce and research[12]. In order to evaluate the generalization capabilities of our model, hyper-parameter selection could be performed on the full training set (without k-fold on test as described in §4.1) but at significantly higher computational cost.

Acknowledgments

This work has been supported by the In-Utero project funded by HDH (France) and FRQS (Canada).

References

Takuya Akiba, Makoto Shing, Yujin Tang, Qi Sun, and David Ha. 2024. Evolutionary optimization of model merging recipes. *arXiv preprint arXiv:2403.13187*.

Rohan Anil, Andrew M Dai, Orhan Firat, Melvin Johnson, Dmitry Lepikhin, Alexandre Passos, Siamak Shakeri, Emanuel Taropa, Paige Bailey, Zhifeng Chen, et al. 2023. Palm 2 technical report. *arXiv preprint arXiv:2305.10403*.

Elias Bassani. 2022. ranx: A blazing-fast python library for ranking evaluation and comparison. In *Advances in Information Retrieval - 44th European Conference on IR Research, ECIR 2022, Stavanger, Norway, April 10-14, 2022, Proceedings, Part II*, volume 13186 of *Lecture Notes in Computer Science*, pages 259–264. Springer.

Hannah Brown, Katherine Lee, Fatemehsadat Mireshghallah, Reza Shokri, and Florian Tramèr. 2022. What does it mean for a language model to preserve privacy? In *Proceedings of the 2022 ACM Conference on Fairness, Accountability, and Transparency*, FAccT '22, page 2280–2292, New York, NY, USA. Association for Computing Machinery.

Zhiqi Bu, Yu-Xiang Wang, Sheng Zha, and George Karypis. 2024. Automatic clipping: differentially private deep learning made easier and stronger. In *Proceedings of the 37th International Conference on Neural Information Processing Systems*, NIPS '23, Red Hook, NY, USA. Curran Associates Inc.

Felix Busch, Lena Hoffmann, Christopher Rueger, Elon HC van Dijk, Rawen Kader, Esteban Ortiz-Prado, Marcus R Makowski, Luca Saba, Martin Hadamitzky, Jakob Nikolas Kather, et al. 2024. Systematic review of large language models for patient care: Current applications and challenges. *medRxiv*, pages 2024–03.

[12]For any medical concern, please consult a specialist.

Nicholas Carlini, Daphne Ippolito, Matthew Jagielski, Katherine Lee, Florian Tramèr, and Chiyuan Zhang. 2023. Quantifying memorization across neural language models. In *ICLR'23*, volume abs/2202.07646.

Nicholas Carlini, Florian Tramèr, Eric Wallace, Matthew Jagielski, Ariel Herbert-Voss, Katherine Lee, Adam Roberts, Tom B. Brown, Dawn Xiaodong Song, Úlfar Erlingsson, Alina Oprea, and Colin Raffel. 2020. Extracting training data from large language models. In *USENIX Security Symposium*.

Zeming Chen, Alejandro Hernández Cano, Angelika Romanou, Antoine Bonnet, Kyle Matoba, Francesco Salvi, Matteo Pagliardini, Simin Fan, Andreas Köpf, Amirkeivan Mohtashami, Alexandre Sallinen, Alireza Sakhaeirad, Vinitra Swamy, Igor Krawczuk, Deniz Bayazit, Axel Marmet, Syrielle Montariol, Mary-Anne Hartley, Martin Jaggi, and Antoine Bosselut. 2023. Meditron-70b: Scaling medical pretraining for large language models. *Preprint*, arXiv:2311.16079.

Clément Christophe, Praveen K Kanithi, Tathagata Raha, Shadab Khan, and Marco AF Pimentel. 2024. Med42-v2: A suite of clinical llms. *Preprint*, arXiv:2408.06142.

MohammadReza Davari and Eugene Belilovsky. 2023. Model breadcrumbs: Scaling multi-task model merging with sparse masks. *arXiv preprint arXiv:2312.06795*.

Jingcheng Du, Yang Xiang, Madhuri Sankaranarayanapillai, Meng Zhang, Jingqi Wang, Yuqi Si, Huy Anh Pham, Hua Xu, Yong Chen, and Cui Tao. 2021. Extracting postmarketing adverse events from safety reports in the vaccine adverse event reporting system (vaers) using deep learning. *Journal of the American Medical Informatics Association*, 28(7):1393–1400.

John W Ely, Jerome A Osheroff, Mark H Ebell, George R Bergus, Barcey T Levy, M Lee Chambliss, and Eric R Evans. 1999. Analysis of questions asked by family doctors regarding patient care. *Bmj*, 319(7206):358–361.

Charles Goddard, Shamane Siriwardhana, Malikeh Ehghaghi, Luke Meyers, Vlad Karpukhin, Brian Benedict, Mark McQuade, and Jacob Solawetz. 2024. Arcee's mergekit: A toolkit for merging large language models. *arXiv preprint arXiv:2403.13257*.

Stefan Hegselmann, Alejandro Buendia, Hunter Lang, Monica Agrawal, Xiaoyi Jiang, and David A. Sontag. 2022. Tabllm: Few-shot classification of tabular data with large language models. In *AISTATG*, volume abs/2210.10723.

Junyuan Hong, Jiachen T. Wang, Chenhui Zhang, Zhangheng Li, Bo Li, and Zhangyang Wang. 2024. Dp-opt: Make large language model your privacy-preserving prompt engineer.

Hongsheng Hu, Zoran Salcic, Lichao Sun, Gillian Dobbie, Philip S. Yu, and Xuyun Zhang. 2022. Membership inference attacks on machine learning: A survey. *ACM Comput. Surv.*, 54(11s).

Gabriel Ilharco, Marco Tulio Ribeiro, Mitchell Wortsman, Ludwig Schmidt, Hannaneh Hajishirzi, and Ali Farhadi. 2022. Editing models with task arithmetic. In *The Eleventh International Conference on Learning Representations*.

Young Kyun Jang, Dat Huynh, Ashish Shah, Wen-Kai Chen, and Ser-Nam Lim. 2024. Spherical linear interpolation and text-anchoring for zero-shot composed image retrieval. *ArXiv*, abs/2405.00571.

Albert Q. Jiang, Alexandre Sablayrolles, Arthur Mensch, Chris Bamford, Devendra Singh Chaplot, Diego de las Casas, Florian Bressand, Gianna Lengyel, Guillaume Lample, Lucile Saulnier, Lélio Renard Lavaud, Marie-Anne Lachaux, Pierre Stock, Teven Le Scao, Thibaut Lavril, Thomas Wang, Timothée Lacroix, and William El Sayed. 2023. Mistral 7b. *Preprint*, arXiv:2310.06825.

Alistair E. W. Johnson, Lucas Bulgarelli, Lu Shen, Alvin Gayles, Ayad Shammout, Steven Horng, Tom J. Pollard, Benjamin Moody, Brian Gow, Li-wei H. Lehman, Leo A. Celi, and Roger G. Mark. 2023. Mimic-iv, a freely accessible electronic health record dataset. *Scientific Data*, 10.

Peter Kairouz, H. Brendan McMahan, Brendan Avent, Aurélien Bellet, Mehdi Bennis, Arjun Nitin Bhagoji, Kallista Bonawit, Zachary Charles, Graham Cormode, Rachel Cummings, Rafael G. L. D'Oliveira, Hubert Eichner, Salim El Rouayheb, David Evans, Josh Gardner, Zachary Garrett, Adrià Gascón, Badih Ghazi, Phillip B. Gibbons, Marco Gruteser, Zaid Harchaoui, Chaoyang He, Lie He, Zhouyuan Huo, Ben Hutchinson, Justin Hsu, Martin Jaggi, Tara Javidi, Gauri Joshi, Mikhail Khodak, Jakub Konecný, Aleksandra Korolova, Farinaz Koushanfar, Sanmi Koyejo, Tancrède Lepoint, Yang Liu, Prateek Mittal, Mehryar Mohri, Richard Nock, Ayfer Özgür, Rasmus Pagh, Hang Qi, Daniel Ramage, Ramesh Raskar, Mariana Raykova, Dawn Song, Weikang Song, Sebastian U. Stich, Ziteng Sun, Ananda Theertha Suresh, Florian Tramèr, Praneeth Vepakomma, Jianyu Wang, Li Xiong, Zheng Xu, Qiang Yang, Felix X. Yu, Han Yu, and Sen Zhao. 2021.

Nikhil Kandpal, Eric Wallace, and Colin Raffel. 2022. Deduplicating training data mitigates privacy risks in language models. *ArXiv*.

Yanis Labrak, Adrien Bazoge, Emmanuel Morin, Pierre-Antoine Gourraud, Mickael Rouvier, and Richard Dufour. 2024. BioMistral: A collection of open-source pretrained large language models for medical domains. In *Findings of the Association for Computational Linguistics ACL 2024*, pages 5848–5864, Bangkok, Thailand and virtual meeting. Association for Computational Linguistics.

Jinhyuk Lee, Wonjin Yoon, Sungdong Kim, Donghyeon Kim, Sunkyu Kim, Chan Ho So, and Jaewoo Kang. 2020. Biobert: a pre-trained biomedical language representation model for biomedical text mining. *Bioinformatics*, 36(4):1234–1240.

Xuechen Li, Florian Tramèr, Percy Liang, and Tatsunori B. Hashimoto. 2021. Large language models can be strong differentially private learners. *ArXiv*.

Jesus Lovon, Martin Mouysset, Jo Oleiwan, Jose G. Moreno, Christine Damase-Michel, and Lynda Tamine. 2025. Evaluating llm abilities to understand tabular electronic health records: A comprehensive study of patient data extraction and retrieval. *Preprint*, arXiv:2501.09384.

Jesus Lovon-Melgarejo, Thouria Ben-Haddi, Jules Di Scala, Jose G. Moreno, and Lynda Tamine. 2024. Revisiting the MIMIC-IV benchmark: Experiments using language models for electronic health records. In *Proceedings of the First Workshop on Patient-Oriented Language Processing (CL4Health) @ LREC-COLING 2024*, pages 189–196, Torino, Italia. ELRA and ICCL.

Alexandra Sasha Luccioni, Sylvain Viguier, and Anne-Laure Ligozat. 2023. Estimating the carbon footprint of bloom, a 176b parameter language model. *Journal of Machine Learning Research*, 24(253):1–15.

Michael S Matena and Colin A Raffel. 2022. Merging models with fisher-weighted averaging. *Advances in Neural Information Processing Systems*, 35:17703–17716.

H. B. McMahan, Eider Moore, Daniel Ramage, Seth Hampson, and Blaise Agüera y Arcas. 2016. Communication-efficient learning of deep networks from decentralized data. In *International Conference on Artificial Intelligence and Statistics*.

Seth Neel and Peter Chang. 2023. Privacy issues in large language models: A survey. *arXiv preprint arXiv:2312.06717*.

Guillermo Ortiz-Jimenez, Alessandro Favero, and Pascal Frossard. 2024. Task arithmetic in the tangent space: Improved editing of pre-trained models. *Advances in Neural Information Processing Systems*, 36.

Ahmed Salem, Apratim Bhattacharya, Michael Backes, Mario Fritz, and Yang Zhang. 2020. Updates-leak: data set inference and reconstruction attacks in online learning. In *Proceedings of the 29th USENIX Conference on Security Symposium*, SEC'20, USA. USENIX Association.

Virat Shejwalkar, Huseyin A. Inan, Amir Houmansadr, and Robert Sim. 2021. Membership inference attacks against nlp classification models. In *Proceedings NeurIPS 2021 Workshop PRIML*.

Karan Singhal, Tao Tu, Juraj Gottweis, Rory Sayres, Ellery Wulczyn, Le Hou, Kevin Clark, Stephen Pfohl, Heather Cole-Lewis, Darlene Neal, et al. 2023. Towards expert-level medical question answering with large language models. *arXiv preprint arXiv:2305.09617*.

Robin Staab, Mark Vero, Mislav Balunovi'c, and Martin T. Vechev. 2024. Beyond memorization: Violating privacy via inference with large language models. In *ICLR'24*.

Xinyu Tang, Richard Shin, Huseyin Inan, Andre Manoel, Fatemehsadat Mireshghallah, Zinan Lin, Sivakanth Gopi, Janardhan (Jana) Kulkarni, and Robert Sim. 2024. Privacy-preserving in-context learning with differentially private few-shot generation. In *ICLR 2024*.

Yuxuan Tong, Xiwen Zhang, Rui Wang, Ruidong Wu, and Junxian He. 2024. Dart-math: Difficulty-aware rejection tuning for mathematical problem-solving.

Hugo Touvron, Thibaut Lavril, Gautier Izacard, Xavier Martinet, Marie-Anne Lachaux, Timothée Lacroix, Baptiste Rozière, Naman Goyal, Eric Hambro, Faisal Azhar, Aurelien Rodriguez, Armand Joulin, Edouard Grave, and Guillaume Lample. 2023. Llama: Open and efficient foundation language models. *Preprint*, arXiv:2302.13971.

Tianwen Wei, Liang Zhao, Lichang Zhang, Bo Zhu, Lijie Wang, Haihua Yang, Biye Li, Cheng Cheng, Weiwei Lü, Rui Hu, Chenxia Li, Liu Yang, Xilin Luo, Xuejie Wu, Lunan Liu, Wenjun Cheng, Peng Cheng, Jianhao Zhang, Xiaoyu Zhang, Lei Lin, Xiaokun Wang, Yutuan Ma, Chuanhai Dong, Yanqi Sun, Yifu Chen, Yongyi Peng, Xiaojuan Liang, Shuicheng Yan, Han Fang, and Yahui Zhou. 2023. Skywork: A more open bilingual foundation model. *Preprint*, arXiv:2310.19341.

BigScience Workshop, Teven Le Scao, Angela Fan, Christopher Akiki, Ellie Pavlick, Suzana Ilić, Daniel Hesslow, Roman Castagné, Alexandra Sasha Luccioni, François Yvon, et al. 2022. Bloom: A 176b-parameter open-access multilingual language model. *arXiv preprint arXiv:2211.05100*.

Mitchell Wortsman, Gabriel Ilharco, Samir Ya Gadre, Rebecca Roelofs, Raphael Gontijo-Lopes, Ari S Morcos, Hongseok Namkoong, Ali Farhadi, Yair Carmon, Simon Kornblith, et al. 2022. Model soups: averaging weights of multiple fine-tuned models improves accuracy without increasing inference time. In *International conference on machine learning*, pages 23965–23998. PMLR.

Lingling Xu, Haoran Xie, Si-Zhao Joe Qin, Xiaohui Tao, and Fu Lee Wang. 2023. Parameter-efficient fine-tuning methods for pretrained language models: A critical review and assessment. *arXiv preprint arXiv:2312.12148*.

Biwei Yan, Kun Li, Minghui Xu, Yueyan Dong, Yue Zhang, Zhaochun Ren, and Xiuzheng Cheng. 2024. On protecting the data privacy of large language models (llms): A survey. *arXiv preprint arXiv:2403.05156*.

Rui Ye, Wenhao Wang, Jingyi Chai, Dihan Li, Zexi Li, Yinda Xu, Yaxin Du, Yanfeng Wang, and Siheng Chen. 2024. Openfedllm: Training large language models on decentralized private data via federated learning. In *Proceedings of the 30th ACM SIGKDD Conference on Knowledge Discovery and Data Mining*, KDD '24, page 6137–6147, New York, NY, USA. Association for Computing Machinery.

Xiang Yue, Huseyin Inan, Xuechen Li, Girish Kumar, Julia McAnallen, Hoda Shajari, Huan Sun, David Levitan, and Robert Sim. 2023. Synthetic text generation with differential privacy: A simple and practical recipe. In *Proceedings of the 61st Annual Meeting of the Association for Computational Linguistics (Volume 1: Long Papers)*, pages 1321–1342, Toronto, Canada. Association for Computational Linguistics.

Xuandong Zhao, Lei Li, and Yu-Xiang Wang. 2022. Provably confidential language modelling. In *Proceedings of the 2022 Conference of the North American Chapter of the Association for Computational Linguistics: Human Language Technologies*, pages 943–955, Seattle, United States. Association for Computational Linguistics.

Zhengyun Zhao, Qiao Jin, Fangyuan Chen, Tuorui Peng, and Sheng Yu. 2023. A large-scale dataset of patient summaries for retrieval-based clinical decision support systems. *Scientific data*, 10(1):909.

Honglei Zhuang, Zhen Qin, Kai Hui, Junru Wu, Le Yan, Xuanhui Wang, and Michael Bendersky. 2024. Beyond yes and no: Improving zero-shot LLM rankers via scoring fine-grained relevance labels. In *Proceedings of the 2024 Conference of the North American Chapter of the Association for Computational Linguistics: Human Language Technologies (Volume 2: Short Papers)*, pages 358–370, Mexico City, Mexico. Association for Computational Linguistics.

Max Zimmer, Christoph Spiegel, and Sebastian Pokutta. 2024. Sparse model soups: A recipe for improved pruning via model averaging.

Synthetic Documents for Medical Tasks: Bridging Privacy with Knowledge Injection and Reward Mechanism

Simon Meoni
Inria/Arkhn
Paris, France
simon.meoni@arkhn.com

Théo Ryffel
Arkhn
Paris, France
theo@arkhn.com

Éric de la Clergerie
Inria
Paris, France
Eric.De_La_Clergerie@inria.fr

Abstract

Electronic Health Records (EHR) store valuable patient-staff interaction data. Recent advancements in proprietary online large language models (LLMs) have shown promising capabilities in analyzing EHR notes. However, transmitting patient information through external APIs to LLMs like ChatGPT introduces privacy risks, necessitating alternative approaches that conform to hospital practices.

To address privacy concerns, we propose generating synthetic documents based on a reward-mechanism-trained model from real documents without leaking sensitive information but keeping relevant clinical knowledge. These synthetic documents may be annotated by large proprietary models or existing public ones, and used to train small specialized models that can run on constrained medical infrastructure. We validate our approach through a proof-of-concept scenario using Mimic-III, assessing the effectiveness of the generated documents through several downstream tasks: a series of ICD-9 multi-label classifications of varying complexity and a synthetic Named Entity Recognition (NER) task. The results demonstrate that synthetic documents preserve privacy and improve performance when real annotated data are sparse.

1 Introduction

Electronic Health Records (EHR) contain patient and healthcare staff interactions. Professionals record their impressions, observations, and various medical procedures performed. These notes remain fairly expressive and free to save healthcare personnel time and allow for the description of unusual situations (Rosenbloom et al., 2011; Wu et al., 2022). Natural Language Processing (NLP) techniques speed up the decision processes (Zhou et al., 2022; Wu et al., 2022). In recent years, Proprietary Online Large Language Models (LLMs) such as ChatGPT have shown impressive results using zero or few-shot techniques in analyzing these notes (Agrawal et al., 2022; Meoni et al., 2023; Hu et al., 2024). However, clinical NLP faces challenges that arise from the sensitive, confidential, and specialized nature of its data—sending such patient information through an external API raises numerous legal issues and is often impossible. Hospitals or third parties providing NLP-based medical devices (i.e., directly impacting patient care) must maintain control over their NLP systems to ensure patient safety. Therefore, the customization of open LLMs and their execution in a secure but computationally constrained environment is an important issue.

Still, specific training datasets are necessary to develop a model with clinical skills to address these challenges. To create such a dataset, obtaining real clinical data remains complicated and requires anonymization, which is time-consuming, expensive, and legally constrained. This also hinders the use of online models to annotate real data. Alternatively, we propose to create synthetic clinical notes that look like real data but do not include personally identifiable Information (PII) (Melamud and Shivade, 2019; Ive et al., 2020). This approach has several benefits: it reduces the need for human input, complies with regulations, and is suitable for annotation with external models to train local models. The local models and datasets can be shared with the community without leaking confidential information. These local models are also small enough to be hosted inside the hospital's infrastructure.

Considering these issues, we implement a novel method for generating synthetic documents, enforcing privacy preservation by design, using only a tiny seed set of pseudo-anonymised data. As a proof of concept, our key contributions include:

- **Privacy-safe Document Generation guided**

Proceedings of the Second Workshop on Patient-Oriented Language Processing (CL4Health), pages 12–25
May 4, 2025

by Clinical Knowledge and Reward Mechanism: We present an methodology that leverages a minimal set of manually pseudo-anonymized data to train fine-tuned generative models. This process is enhanced by enriching prompts with keywords containing clinical knowledge, in our case extracted using QuickUMLS (Soldaini and Goharian, 2016), as illustrated in Section 5 and Figure 5. This extraction does not contain any PII in the sense that it contains only clinical entities (or keywords). Furthermore, we improve the quality of the synthetic documents thanks to an iterative refinement process that employs a private scorer to compare real and synthetic documents. This scorer returns only floats to the public side, ensuring privacy while enabling continuous improvement of the synthetic document quality.

- **Proof of Concept using Mimic-III:** Because it's almost impossible to evaluate our methods on real private documents, we utilize the Mimic-III clinical notes (Johnson et al., 2016) as a proxy to simulate a private healthcare environment, demonstrating our method's potential in a controlled setting. This proof of concept illustrates how our methodology could be applied in real-world hospital scenarios without compromising patient data.

- **Evaluation on downstream tasks using Mimic-III:** To assess the quality of the synthetic documents as training dataset for smaller models, we evaluate the generated data using two tasks: Multilabel Classification based on ICD-9 Codes (ICD-MC) and Synthetic Named Entity Recognition (NER). For ICD-MC, based on the codes proposed by Mullenbach et al. (2018) and Mimic-III manual annotations, we have modified this task, as described in Section 6.1, to compare the performance of the model trained with real data against the model trained with synthetic data. The NER task is conducted on annotations returned by GPT-4 on both our synthetic and real data. This allows us to compare the performance of models trained on these datasets.

2 Related Works

Synthetic Data Generation: Many recent studies focus on creating synthetic data, particularly for generating clinical data. For instance, Kweon et al. (2023) proposes to train LLMs for different purposes using synthetic clinical data generated by online LLMs. Xie et al. (2024) has developed AUG-PE, a high-quality differential privacy synthetic text generation method leveraging API access.

Furthermore, the work by Li et al. (2024) introduces Generalized Instruction Tuning (GLAN). Unlike previous approaches that rely on seed or existing datasets, GLAN uses a pre-curated taxonomy of human knowledge and capabilities as input to generate instructions across all disciplines. Inspired by their method, our work uses ontological information to extract sequences of ontology-based keywords from texts.

To assess the performance of LLM in Multiple Questions Choices in the medical field, Griot et al. (2024) developed a fictional medical benchmark to isolate the knowledge of the LLM from its test-taking abilities. Li et al. (2023a) generated a synthetic dataset of Alzheimer's Disease relative signs. As this task is relatively complex, LLM created the dataset by incorporating expert knowledge taxonomy. Finally, the Hiebel et al. (2023); Xie et al. (2024) works focus on generating a synthetic dataset of clinical cases for the NER task to study the effectiveness of real clinical data versus synthetic data.

Self-Rewarding: Reinforced Self-Training is an offline RL algorithm proposed by Gulcehre et al. (2023) for self-align LLMs generating a dataset from the initial LLM policy and using it to improve the policy via offline RL. Instruction back translation (Li et al., 2023b) is a scalable method that automatically labels human-written text with corresponding instructions by finetuning a LM on a small seed dataset and a web corpus to generate and selecting high-quality examples for further finetuning. Yuan et al. (2024) use the trained LLM to provide rewards via LLM-as-a-Judge prompting, improving both instruction following and reward provision. Lee et al. (2024) introduces Reinforcement Learning from AI Feedback (RLAIF) as an alternative, using an off-the-shelf LLM to generate preference labels. RLAIF achieves comparable or superior performance to RLHF in many tasks, such as those rated by humans.

The difference from the other approaches to generating a synthetic dataset is that our method combines LLM guided by prompts enriched with clinical knowledge, fine-tuned with a low amount of real pseudonymized data, and reinforcement learning feedback. This feedback is based on a score, which compares the real and synthetic data to ensure that they are closer to the source while maintaining privacy, as illustrated in Algorithm 1.

3 Reward-based Generation

We sketch the main steps of our reward-based generation process, illustrated with Algorithm 1.

3.1 Collecting keywords

The generation of synthetic *CRs* is guided by prompts enriched with clinical knowledge represented by non-confidential UMLS concepts (C) (Figure 6) extracted from real documents. Of course, other sources of keywords are possible. Therefore, our first processing step is to extract such keywords from each real document of dataset D_{source}, collecting them in C_{source}

3.2 Seed Step

We sample a tiny seed subset D_{sft} (i.e., supervised fine-tuning) from D_{source}, and associated keyword sequences C_{sft}, with a ratio of r%. This seed subset is assumed to be carefully pseudo-anonymized to authorize its use to finetune our initial public generator model M_{gen}. In our case, one or two hundred pseudo-anonymized documents suffice.

3.3 Generation Step

For each keyword sequence in $K_{\text{train}} = C_{\text{source}} \setminus C_{\text{sft}}$ and generation r, the generator model M_{gen} generates $N > 1$ candidate documents, collected in dataset D_{step}. This way, each synthetic document has a real counterpart based on the same sequence of keywords. In practice, we set $N = 4$.

3.4 Scoring Step

We evaluate the quality of the generated documents using SEMSCORE (Aynetdinov and Akbik, 2024), a metric based on semantic textual similarity (STS) returned by our private evaluator model M_{score}. The key point is that the M_{score} must be hosted in a private infrastructure to compare public synthetic documents with real private ones.

In Algorithm 1, we use a light orange background colour to indicate that this step takes place on the private side of the hospital building. However, being only composed of floats, the score set D_{score} can be safely declassified and returned from the private side to the public one for the Alignment step to train safely a new updated version of public M_{gen}. At the first generation step ($step = 0$), we initialize M_{score}, fine-tuning it with a contrastive objective, selecting a subset of D_0 to serve as negative examples and their real counterparts as positive examples.

Using M_{score}, we score the N candidates of each group from D^r_{step} against their counterparts in D_{train}. We keep only the best groups whose highest score is above the pth percentile. In practice, we set $p = 80$.

In each kept group, the candidate with the highest score (resp. lowest one) is selected as the *chosen* (resp. *rejected*) candidate. Finally, a dataset D_{dpo} is formed from these selected candidate pairs.

3.5 Alignment Step

Using dataset D_{dpo}, we align and update M_{gen} with *DPO* (Direct Preference Optimization) (Rafailov et al., 2023).

4 Applying Synthetic Dataset for Real Tasks

To validate the quality of the generated documents, we develop downstream tasks. In real life, the test set for such downstream tasks should be made up of real documents and manually annotated. The evaluations must be run in a private area.

5 Experiments

5.1 Base Models

We use `Mistral-7B-Instruct-v0.1` (Jiang et al., 2023) as our base generator model, a trade-off between performance and computational cost. As an evaluator model, we use `all-distilroberta-v1`.

5.2 Dataset

We use a dataset from Mimic-III as a proof of concept, involving pre-processing, keyword extraction, and post-processing.

1. *Pre-processing*: We extract from Mimic-III the clinical notes from the clinical event row. We select only the *Discharge Summaries* from these clinical notes and parse them to retrieve the *History of Patient Illness* section, using them as documents for D_{source}. On average, the documents consist of 248 words.

2. *Knowledge enrichment*: We project UMLS concepts using QuickUMLS over D_{source}. QuickUMLS is an unsupervised biomedical concept extraction based on pattern matching

Algorithm 1: Reward Training Algorithm

Input : D_{source} = initial dataset; r = sft ratio; M_{gen} = generative model; M_{score} = evaluator model; p = percentile filter value; N = number of candidates to generate;

Output : M_{gen}

```
// Running in Private Area, declassifying D_sft, C_sft
C_source ← ExtractConcepts(D_source)
D_sft, C_sft ← PseudoAnonymize(Sample(D_source, C_source, r))
D_train, K_train ← D_source \ D_sft, C_source \ C_sft
  // Seed Step
M_gen ← Supervised fine-tune M_gen on pairs in (C_sft, D_sft)
for step = 0 to steps do
    // Generation Step
    D_step ← generate new N candidates with M_gen per k ∈ K_train
    // Scoring Step (Running in Private Area, declassifying D_score)
    if step = 0 then
        // Building the evaluator model
        D*_contr, D_contr ← Sample(D_0, D_train, r_contr)
        M_score ← ContrastiveTrain (M_score, neg = D*_contr, pos = D_contr)
    D_score ← score D_step over D_train with M_score
    D_dpo ← in D_score, keep a pair of candidates, then filter pairs on percentile p
    K_dpo ← filter K_train to keep keywords corresponding to candidates selected in D_dpo
    // Alignment Step
    M_gen ← DPO Alignment M_gen on (K_dpo, D_dpo)
```

that guarantees only medical concepts are extracted and no identifying information. We obtain C_{source} (cf. Section 3) used to enrich the prompts, as illustrated in Figure 6. On average, we extract 58 keywords per document.

3. *Post-processing*: We filter out documents without keywords. We keep ordered keywords to encourage the model to follow the same narrative as the ground truth. In this way, we constitute a dataset of 4262 documents, using 70% of them (2581) as a train set (D_{train}) and 30% (1680) as a test set (D_{test}). Moreover, the D_{sft} with 4% and 6% ratios have 156 and 235 documents, respectively.

6 Evaluation on Downstream Tasks

6.1 Multilabel Classification tasks

Collecting Gold Annotations: As Mimic-III includes a set of expert-labeled ICD-9 codes (L) for each discharge summary, we use these annotations (1) to evaluate the quality of our datasets on tasks close to a real use-case (2) and test across a series of ICD-MC tasks with increasing complexity. We establish an association between these labels and the data points in D_{train} and D_{test}, respectively, 2581 and 1681 data points.

We get annotated datasets ($D_{\text{train}}, L_{\text{train}}$) and ($D_{\text{test}}, L_{\text{test}}$) by coupling documents with labels. In defining our series of ICD-MC tasks, we prioritize the most frequent k labels, denoted as class-k (see Table 1) with $k \in \{20, 50, 100, 400\}$. We subsequently refine ($D_{\text{train}}, L_{\text{train}}$) and ($D_{\text{test}}, L_{\text{test}}$) by retaining only those documents whose labels intersect with the set of **class-k** labels.

We define the refined training set as $D_{\text{gold}} = (D'_{\text{train}}, L'_{\text{train}})$ where each document in D'_{train} contains at least one label from **class-k**. Documents devoid of any intersecting labels are excluded. Table 1 presents the dataset sizes, which document the number of excerpts retained after applying these exclusion criteria.

It should be noted that the task's complexity increases with k not only because of the larger set of labels and the lower frequency of some labels but also because of the longer label set on average per document. For instance, the average length is around 6 when $k = 20$ but 11 when $k = 100$.

Constituting the Synthetic Train Datasets: As an approximation, we hypothesize that the synthetic data point from D^r_{step}, which shares the same set of UMLS keywords as its real data counterpart, can inherit the same set of ICD labels L'_{train}. This way, we easily obtain six synthetic datasets, denoted as D_{step}, corresponding to the generation steps $step \in \{0, 1, 2\}$ and seed ratios $r \in \{4\%, 6\%\}$, as shown in Table 3. Each D_{step} dataset contains four times more document data points than D_{gold}.

6.2 Named Entity Recognition (NER) Task

Annotating the Overall Dataset: Because Mimic-III does not include gold NER annotations, we use GPT-4 to automatically annotate all (synthetic and real) train and test datasets (OpenAI (2023), Appendix B.), focusing on three entity types: **problem**, **treatment** and **test**. We employ a few-shot learning approach inspired by Hu et al. (2024), using the prompt in Appendix 10. To assess whether or not the annotated entities are essentially the UMLS keywords, we evaluated the overlap between keywords and annotations and found a low 22.36% overlap.

Table 1 illustrates the distributions of labels for the ICD-MC tasks and entities for NER.

6.3 Training of Task Models

We train a series of (small) `deberta-v3-base` (He et al., 2021) models on ICD-MC tasks using either real or synthetic datasets D_{gold} or D^r_{step} over the four tasks **class-k** where k $\in \{20, 50, 100, 400\}$.

To address the quantity bias of a larger synthetic dataset, we train two baseline models, one trained with D_{gold}, and another one trained with $D_{\text{gold}\times 4}$, where each real document is oversampled $N = 4$ times, hence containing the same amount of documents as the synthetic set.

We also consider a *baseline* where only keywords (K_{train}) are used to predict labels to check that the content of the documents impacts the performance, as shown in Table 3.

We apply the same methodology for the NER task but with only D_{gold} and $D_{\text{gold}\times 4}$ as baselines.

7 Results

Table 2 presents a comparative analysis of SEMSCORE measurements by evaluators across the different datasets generated at various steps. We observe a consistent improvement in scores with successive steps. The $M^{6\%}_{\text{gen}}$ model outperforms the $M^{4\%}_{\text{gen}}$ model, highlighting the effectiveness of alignment in refining the quality of generated documents through iterative processes. The scores indicate a trend across various models, suggesting that models trained with more real data produce higher-quality documents.

	D_{gold}		D_{test}	
class-k	**# labels**	**# docs**	**# labels**	**# docs**
class-400	38602	2564	25409	1681
class-100	30015	2560	19700	1672
class-50	23323	2552	15246	1672
class-20	14619	2513	9694	1648
ner	72715	2581	47783	1681

Table 1: Multilabel classification & NER task datasets, with labels size for D_{gold}, D_{test}. The number of labels for the NER task excludes label O[1].

	steps	$M^{4\%}_{\text{score}}$	$M^{6\%}_{\text{score}}$
$M^{4\%}_{\text{gen}}$	0	67.95	65.94
	1	71.53	69.18
	2	72.25	70.12
$M^{6\%}_{\text{gen}}$	0	70.78	67.26
	1	72.54	70.78
	2	76.10	**74.37**

Table 2: SEMSCORE evaluation for models M^a_{gen} with $a = r_{sft} \in \{4\%, 6\%\}$ using the different evaluators M^b_{score} with $b = r_{sft} \in \{4\%, 6\%\}$. The grey scores denote cross-evaluation where $a \neq b$.

Table 3 compares F1 scores on the downstream tasks across different models and configurations, providing insights about their performance when varying task complexities and training data conditions. Notably, $M_{\text{gold}\times 4}$,trained with $D_{\text{gold}\times 4}$, outperforms the models trained with synthetic data ($M^{\{4,6\}\%}_{0,1,2}$) across all tasks. Second generation models($D^{4\%}_2$ and $D^{6\%}_2$) demonstrate performance comparable to the model trained on $D_{\text{gold}\times 4}$. In particular, for the **class-400** task, the F1 scores for $D^{4\%}_2$ and $D^{6\%}_2$ match closely those for $D_{\text{gold}\times 4}$, with only minor variations. Notably, the standard deviations for the synthetic data models are lower than those of the gold data model, indicating more consistent performance. Further-

[1] O (Outside) comes from the IOB (Inside-Outside-Beginning) schema used in Named Entity Recognition task. It denotes tokens that are not part of any named entity.

	class-20	class-50	class-100	class-400	ner
baseline	45.7 ± 1.2	33.8 ± 2.2	26.6 ± 0.8	10.6 ± 2.0	-
D_{gold}	49.3 ± 1.8	33.3 ± 3.1	23.0 ± 3.6	04.9 ± 4.1	57.0 ± 0.2
$D_{gold\times4}$	$\mathbf{53.7 \pm 2.3}$	42.5 ± 0.2	35.0 ± 1.3	26.4 ± 5.9	61.6 ± 0.1
$D_0^{4\%}$	49.8 ± 1.1	38.7 ± 1.1	32.2 ± 1.8	24.2 ± 2.5	-
$D_0^{6\%}$	49.9 ± 1.2	38.5 ± 1.9	31.0 ± 1.7	23.9 ± 2.4	59.6 ± 0.2
$D_1^{4\%}$	50.9 ± 0.9	41.1 ± 1.6	33.9 ± 1.8	26.9 ± 1.4	-
$D_1^{6\%}$	51.2 ± 0.9	40.7 ± 1.4	33.7 ± 2.1	24.5 ± 2.7	59.4 ± 0.2
$D_2^{4\%}$	50.6 ± 0.8	41.0 ± 1.3	34.3 ± 2.0	27.0 ± 2.0	-
$D_2^{6\%}$	51.7 ± 1.1	40.7 ± 1.0	31.9 ± 7.5	26.5 ± 2.5	59.4 ± 0.2
$D_{\{0,1,2\}}^{6\%}$	52.4 ± 0.4	$\mathbf{43.1 \pm 0.5}$	$\mathbf{37.2 \pm 0.3}$	$\mathbf{31.0 \pm 0.7}$	$\mathbf{61.7 \pm 0.1}$

Table 3: Comparative F1 Scores and standard deviation across models trained over different dataset generations. The table illustrates F1 (Micro-F1) score performance for the **class-k** and NER tasks across D^r_{step}, D_{gold} and the *baseline*.

more, models trained on a combination of several generations($D^{6\%}_{0,1,2}$) outperform most cases, except on the **class-20** task. This suggests increasing data diversity and quantity through dataset mixing enhances model performance in certain scenarios. Consistently across **class-k** tasks, $M_0^{\{4,6\}\%}$ models yield the lowest F1 scores. This indicates that initial generation models lack sufficient sophistication or diversity in training data to effectively capture necessary predictive features, particularly for $M_0^{4\%}$. As task complexity increases, F1 scores generally decrease for both real-based and synthetic-base models, highlighting the models' challenges in adapting to more complex interactions.

In the **class-400** task, F1 scores improve from $step = 1$ to $step = 2$, following a general trend of performance increase. The exception is in the **class-100** task, where performance decreases between $M_1^{6\%}$ and $M_2^{6\%}$.

Figure 1 presents the correlation between F1 scores and SEMSCORE computed by $M^{6\%}_{score}$ across **class-k** tasks. We observe that SEMSCORE is an effective evaluator, although with nuances. Specifically, $D_2^{6\%}$ outperforms $D_2^{4\%}$ only in **class-20**. In **class-400**, the lowest correlation is observed, suggesting that SEMSCORE 's reliability decreases as task complexity increases, likely due to label scarcity affecting training stability. In contrast, **class-20, 50, 100** show stronger correlations, emphasizing SEMSCORE effectiveness in these tasks. Though, $M^{4\%}_{0,1,2}$ consistently outperforms $M^{6\%}_{0,1,2}$, indicating that the seed may constrain the generator, leading to reduced document diversity. Further investigation is required to evaluate the impact of r on overall performance.

We also conducted ablation studies to analyze how dataset sizes and selection strategies affect the performance of encoder models for the **class-100** and NER tasks. We trained several task models using different amounts of (filtered) synthetic data generated from the $D_2^{\{4,6\}\%}$ subsets. We employed two filtering methodologies: (1) **percentile sampling**, which prioritizes the highest-scored candidates according to the SEMSCORE metric, and (2) **random sampling**, which filters documents in varying proportions.

In Figure 2, the graphs demonstrate a consistent increase in F1 scores when expanding the synthetic document set from 2,000 to 10,000 documents for both sampling methods. For **class-100**, percentile sampling shows a more pronounced improvement than random sampling, particularly at lower document counts. As the document set grows, the performance gap between the two sampling methods narrows, but percentile sampling maintains a slight edge throughout. This trend suggests that the quality of synthetic documents, measured by SEMSCORE, significantly impacts performance for this task, especially when working with smaller datasets. The observation underscores the importance of quantity and quality in synthetic data generation, with quality playing a crucial role in scenarios where data quantity is limited.

On the other hand, there is a sharp decrease in the

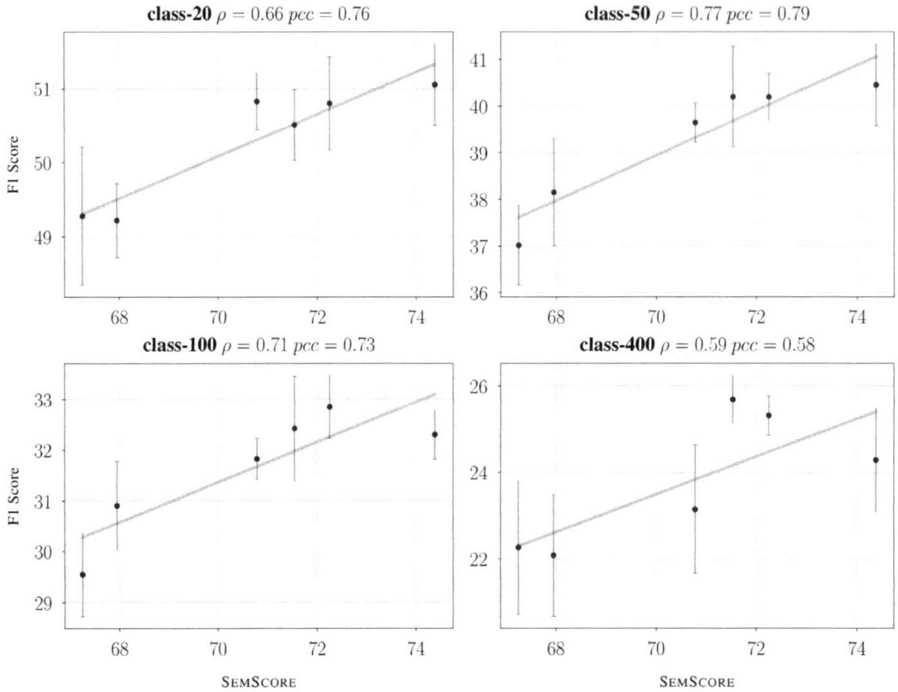

Figure 1: Correlation between SEMSCORE and F1-score across **class-{100,400}** prediction tasks. The dots represent the model trained with D^r_{step}. The Spearman correlation (ρ) and Pearson correlation coefficient (pcc) indicate varying degrees of linear and rank-order association with task complexity.

performance of the NER task when $M_2^{6\%}$ is trained with the same number of documents as M_{gold} using percentile sampling. We conjecture it is partly due to the synthetic subset containing fewer annotated tokens than the gold dataset (for the same number of documents), with 510199 tokens versus 643802 tokens. To neutralize the impact of this difference, we trained a model with the same amount of annotated tokens as D_{gold}, as illustrated by a black star in Figure 2. We observe less difference between M_{gold} and $M_2^{6\%}$ (with values of 57.0 and 56.6). We hypothesize that this difference is because the distribution of D_{gold} is closer to that of the synthetic subset compared to D_{test} as illustrated in Figure 4. Furthermore, adding or removing words can affect the proportion of annotated tokens. We have not yet conducted the NER task experiment with the document generated by $M_{0,1,2}^{4\%}$ as we do not anticipate significant results for these tasks.

8 Discussion

Besides validating our privacy-safe generation process, our results have also provided crucial insights into the impact of both the quality and quantity of synthetic training data on the performance of encoder models. **It is evident that refining the generator through DPO, using clinical concepts as inputs, enhances the synthetic dataset's quality, especially when the first alignment step has been performed**. Results indicate that training models on synthetic data not only preserves but outperforms models trained on gold datasets, as illustrated in Table 3. This highlights the potential of using privacy-preserving synthetic documents to maintain high data utility while protecting sensitive information.

The accuracy of the SEMSCORE scoring mechanism as a predictor of data quality for downstream tasks is also particularly pronounced. The nature of tasks significantly influences the predictive quality, as shown in Figure 1. The need for text closely aligned with the source material to ensure accurate identification of rarer labels was clear, highlighting SEMSCORE's role as a critical metric in evaluating and refining the quality of synthetic documents.

While increasing the dataset size improves performance, applying selective filtering strategies, such as percentile sampling, on a larger volume further enhances results, surpassing the model trained

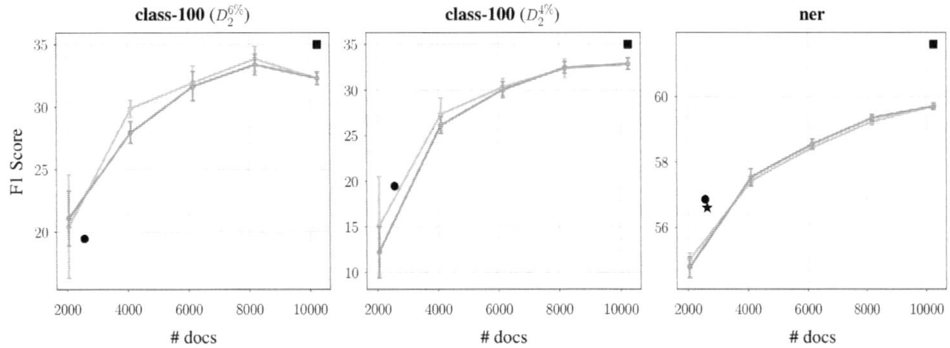

Figure 2: The figure showcases the experimental settings for training encoder models with varying quantities of synthetic data. The pink line (resp. blue line) denotes models trained on randomly sampled datasets (resp. nth-best based on SEMSCORE datasets). The black dot represents the model trained with D_{gold}, while the black square represents the model trained with $D_{\text{gold}\times 4}$.

with D_{gold}. These findings suggest that both data quantity and quality can be adjusted to optimize outcomes, as highlighted in Figure 2.

Another interesting finding is that we can concatenate the datasets generated on the different $steps$ to increase performance. This is illustrated in overall tasks, where diversity is improved by using more data and simulating a more diverse dataset through the heterogeneous data quality, outperforming the model trained with $D_{\text{gold}\times 4}$.

9 Conclusion

We deliver a method for generating synthetic privacy-safe documents. Our method consists of (1) initializing the model with a small number of pseudo-anonymized documents, which reduces the need for human input, and (2) employing a private evaluator to score the generated document against real documents, preserving the confidentiality of the data while ensuring proximity between real and synthetic documents. Our study shows that models trained on small gold datasets face the practical limitations of current NLP systems when handling complex tasks. Scaling the amount of high-quality and diverse synthetic documents is a way to address these limitations. It can outperform models trained on real data under certain configurations, thereby validating the approach of generating on-demand data to overcome data scarcity and privacy issues. These findings facilitate the sharing of high-fidelity synthetic datasets. Furthermore, such datasets may be then annotated using (proprietary) LLMs or via large-scale manual annotation. Finally, the proposed solution is more ethical for patients. It focuses on privacy concerns and is motivated by the opening of clinical data for research advancements.

10 Limitations

Currently, evaluation is limited to multi-label classification and NER tasks. Expanding testing to more complex tasks that require reasoning and domain-specific knowledge, such as medical question answering, could give more insights into the applicability and robustness of our method.

By design, Personal Identifiable Information are absent from our synthetic documents but there exist some slight risks of re-identification from some specific sequences of UMLS keywords. Adding some noise to such sequences should solve the issue.

The economical cost for generating large synthetic datasets may also be an issue (see Appendix A.) for some healthcare providers, even if it occurs in public environments. Investigating the efficacy of smaller generation models could make this technology more accessible, especially for hospitals or clinics with limited budgets.

We are exploring alternative reinforcement learning techniques, such as KTO (Ethayarajh, 2024), to exploit all the generated data rather than only selecting example pairs filtered by percentile with DPO. We are also considering simpler RL methods like ORPO (Hong et al., 2024) and SimPO (Meng et al., 2024).

Finally, we wish to investigate more accurate evaluation metrics than just SemScore, in particular, by combining them with other sophisticated metrics, such as style transfer or document quality (Jin et al., 2022).

References

Monica Agrawal, Stefan Hegselmann, Hunter Lang, Yoon Kim, and David Sontag. 2022. Large Language Models are Few-Shot Clinical Information Extractors.

Ansar Aynetdinov and Alan Akbik. 2024. SemScore: Automated Evaluation of Instruction-Tuned LLMs based on Semantic Textual Similarity. *arXiv preprint*. ArXiv:2401.17072 [cs].

Maxime Griot, Jean Vanderdonckt, Demet Yuksel, and Coralie Hemptinne. 2024. Multiple Choice Questions and Large Languages Models: A Case Study with Fictional Medical Data. *arXiv preprint*. ArXiv:2406.02394 [cs].

Caglar Gulcehre, Tom Le Paine, Srivatsan Srinivasan, Ksenia Konyushkova, Lotte Weerts, Abhishek Sharma, Aditya Siddhant, Alex Ahern, Miaosen Wang, Chenjie Gu, Wolfgang Macherey, Arnaud Doucet, Orhan Firat, and Nando de Freitas. 2023. Reinforced Self-Training (ReST) for Language Modeling. *arXiv preprint*. ArXiv:2308.08998 [cs].

Pengcheng He, Xiaodong Liu, Jianfeng Gao, and Weizhu Chen. 2021. DEBERTA: DECODING-ENHANCED BERT WITH DISENTANGLED ATTENTION. In *International Conference on Learning Representations*.

Nicolas Hiebel, Olivier Ferret, Karen Fort, and Aurélie Névéol. 2023. Can Synthetic Text Help Clinical Named Entity Recognition? A Study of Electronic Health Records in French. In *Proceedings of the 17th Conference of the European Chapter of the Association for Computational Linguistics*, pages 2320–2338, Dubrovnik, Croatia. Association for Computational Linguistics.

Jiwoo Hong, Noah Lee, and James Thorne. 2024. {ORPO}: Monolithic Preference Optimization without Reference Model. volume Proceedings of the 2024 Conference on Empirical Methods in Natural Language Processing, pages 11170–11189.

Yan Hu, Qingyu Chen, Jingcheng Du, Xueqing Peng, Vipina Kuttichi Keloth, Xu Zuo, Yujia Zhou, Zehan Li, Xiaoqian Jiang, Zhiyong Lu, Kirk Roberts, and Hua Xu. 2024. Improving large language models for clinical named entity recognition via prompt engineering. *Journal of the American Medical Informatics Association*, page ocad259.

Julia Ive, Natalia Viani, Joyce Kam, Lucia Yin, Somain Verma, Stephen Puntis, Rudolf N. Cardinal, Angus Roberts, Robert Stewart, and Sumithra Velupillai. 2020. Generation and evaluation of artificial mental health records for Natural Language Processing. *npj Digital Medicine*, 3(1):1–9. Publisher: Nature Publishing Group.

Albert Q. Jiang, Alexandre Sablayrolles, Arthur Mensch, Chris Bamford, Devendra Singh Chaplot, Diego de las Casas, Florian Bressand, Gianna Lengyel, Guillaume Lample, Lucile Saulnier, Lélio Renard Lavaud, Marie-Anne Lachaux, Pierre Stock, Teven Le Scao, Thibaut Lavril, Thomas Wang, Timothée Lacroix, and William El Sayed. 2023. Mistral 7B. *arXiv preprint*. ArXiv:2310.06825 [cs].

Di Jin, Zhijing Jin, Zhiting Hu, Olga Vechtomova, and Rada Mihalcea. 2022. Deep Learning for Text Style Transfer: A Survey. *Computational Linguistics*, 48(1):155–205. Place: Cambridge, MA Publisher: MIT Press.

Alistair EW Johnson, Tom J Pollard, Lu Shen, Li-Wei H Lehman, Mengling Feng, Mohammad Ghassemi, Benjamin Moody, Peter Szolovits, Leo Anthony Celi, and Roger G Mark. 2016. MIMIC-III, a freely accessible critical care database. *Scientific data*, 3:160035. Publisher: Nature Publishing Group.

Sunjun Kweon, Junu Kim, Jiyoun Kim, Sujeong Im, Eunbyeol Cho, Seongsu Bae, Jungwoo Oh, Gyubok Lee, Jong Hak Moon, Seng Chan You, Seungjin Baek, Chang Hoon Han, Yoon Bin Jung, Yohan Jo, and Edward Choi. 2023. Publicly Shareable Clinical Large Language Model Built on Synthetic Clinical Notes. *arXiv preprint*. ArXiv:2309.00237 [cs].

Loïc Lannelongue, Jason Grealey, and Michael Inouye. 2021. Green Algorithms: Quantifying the Carbon Footprint of Computation. *Advanced Science*, 8(12):2100707.

Harrison Lee, Samrat Phatale, Hassan Mansoor, Thomas Mesnard, Johan Ferret, Kellie Ren Lu, Colton Bishop, Ethan Hall, Victor Carbune, Abhinav Rastogi, and Sushant Prakash. 2024. RLAIF vs. RLHF: Scaling Reinforcement Learning from Human Feedback with AI Feedback. In *Proceedings of the 41st International Conference on Machine Learning*, volume 235 of *Proceedings of Machine Learning Research*, pages 26874–26901. PMLR.

Haoran Li, Qingxiu Dong, Zhengyang Tang, Chaojun Wang, Xingxing Zhang, Haoyang Huang, Shaohan Huang, Xiaolong Huang, Zeqiang Huang, Dongdong Zhang, Yuxian Gu, Xin Cheng, Xun Wang, Si-Qing Chen, Li Dong, Wei Lu, Zhifang Sui, Benyou Wang, Wai Lam, and Furu Wei. 2024. Synthetic Data (Almost) from Scratch: Generalized Instruction Tuning for Language Models. *arXiv preprint*. ArXiv:2402.13064 [cs].

Rumeng Li, Xun Wang, and Hong Yu. 2023a. Two Directions for Clinical Data Generation with Large Language Models: Data-to-Label and Label-to-Data. In *Findings of the Association for Computational Linguistics: EMNLP 2023*, pages 7129–7143, Singapore. Association for Computational Linguistics.

Xian Li, Ping Yu, Chunting Zhou, Timo Schick, Luke Zettlemoyer, Omer Levy, Jason Weston, and Mike Lewis. 2023b. Self-Alignment with Instruction Backtranslation. *arXiv preprint*. ArXiv:2308.06259 [cs].

Oren Melamud and Chaitanya Shivade. 2019. Towards Automatic Generation of Shareable Synthetic Clinical Notes Using Neural Language Models. In *Proceedings of the 2nd Clinical Natural Language Processing Workshop*, pages 35–45, Minneapolis, Minnesota, USA. Association for Computational Linguistics.

Yu Meng, Mengzhou Xia, and Danqi Chen. 2024. SimPO: Simple Preference Optimization with a Reference-Free Reward.

Simon Meoni, Eric De la Clergerie, and Theo Ryffel. 2023. Large Language Models as Instructors: A Study on Multilingual Clinical Entity Extraction. In *The 22nd Workshop on Biomedical Natural Language Processing and BioNLP Shared Tasks*, pages 178–190, Toronto, Canada. Association for Computational Linguistics.

James Mullenbach, Sarah Wiegreffe, Jon Duke, Jimeng Sun, and Jacob Eisenstein. 2018. Explainable Prediction of Medical Codes from Clinical Text. *arXiv preprint*. ArXiv:1802.05695 [cs, stat].

OpenAI. 2023. GPT-4: Generative Pre-trained Transformer 4.

Rafael Rafailov, Archit Sharma, Eric Mitchell, Christopher D Manning, Stefano Ermon, and Chelsea Finn. 2023. Direct Preference Optimization: Your Language Model is Secretly a Reward Model. In *Advances in Neural Information Processing Systems*, volume 36, pages 53728–53741. Curran Associates, Inc.

S. Trent Rosenbloom, Joshua C. Denny, Hua Xu, Nancy Lorenzi, William W. Stead, and Kevin B. Johnson. 2011. Data from clinical notes: A perspective on the tension between structure and flexible documentation. *Journal of the American Medical Informatics Association*, 18(2):181–186.

Luca Soldaini and Nazli Goharian. 2016. QuickUMLS: a fast, unsupervised approach for medical concept extraction. *MedIR workshop, sigir*, pages 1–4.

Honghan Wu, Minhong Wang, Jinge Wu, Farah Francis, Yun-Hsuan Chang, Alex Shavick, Hang Dong, Michael T. C. Poon, Natalie Fitzpatrick, Adam P. Levine, Luke T. Slater, Alex Handy, Andreas Karwath, Georgios V. Gkoutos, Claude Chelala, Anoop Dinesh Shah, Robert Stewart, Nigel Collier, Beatrice Alex, William Whiteley, Cathie Sudlow, Angus Roberts, and Richard J. B. Dobson. 2022. A survey on clinical natural language processing in the United Kingdom from 2007 to 2022. *npj Digital Medicine*, 5(1):1–15. Publisher: Nature Publishing Group.

Chulin Xie, Zinan Lin, Arturs Backurs, Sivakanth Gopi, Da Yu, Huseyin A Inan, Harsha Nori, Haotian Jiang, Huishuai Zhang, Yin Tat Lee, Bo Li, and Sergey Yekhanin. 2024. Differentially Private Synthetic Data via Foundation Model APIs 2: Text. In *Proceedings of the 41st International Conference on Machine Learning*, volume 235 of *Proceedings of Machine Learning Research*, pages 54531–54560. PMLR.

Weizhe Yuan, Richard Yuanzhe Pang, Kyunghyun Cho, Xian Li, Sainbayar Sukhbaatar, Jing Xu, and Jason E Weston. 2024. Self-Rewarding Language Models. In *Proceedings of the 41st International Conference on Machine Learning*, volume 235 of *Proceedings of Machine Learning Research*, pages 57905–57923. PMLR.

Nina Zhou, Qiucheng Wu, Zewen Wu, Simeone Marino, and Ivo D. Dinov. 2022. DataSifterText: Partially Synthetic Text Generation for Sensitive Clinical Notes. *Journal of Medical Systems*, 46(12):96.

Appendix A. Carbon Footprint

The algorithm 1 with the experimentation protocol detailed in 5 runs in 40h on 4 GPUs NVIDIA A100 PCIe, and draws 46.34 kWh. Based in France, this has a carbon footprint of 2.38 kg CO2e, which is equivalent to 2.59 tree-months (calculated using green-algorithms.org v2.2 (Lannelongue et al., 2021)).

Appendix B. Mimic-III Usage

PhysioNet provides MIMIC-III under the PhysioNet Credentialed Health Data License 1.5.0. We employed Azure GPT, a HIPAA-certified platform for our large language model annotations. Importantly, Azure GPT does not store processed data. We received approval to waive abuse monitoring for Azure GPT, ensuring that no additional parties could access the data or prompts used in our experiments.

Appendix C. ICD-9 label distribution

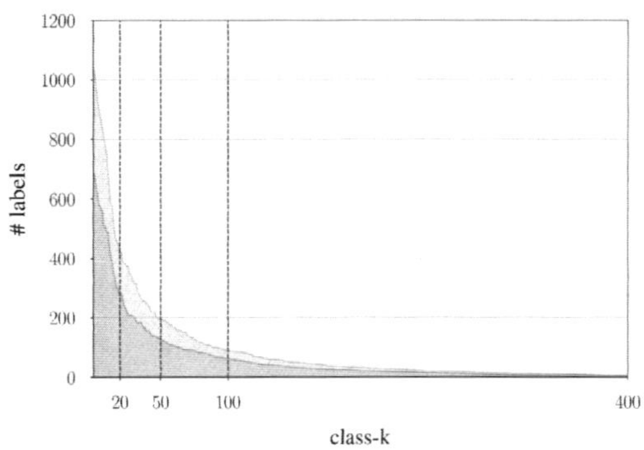

Figure 3: Rank-frequency distribution of labels within the D_{gold} (blue) and D_{test} (pink) datasets, plotted over the **class-k**.

Appendix D. Name Entities Proportion

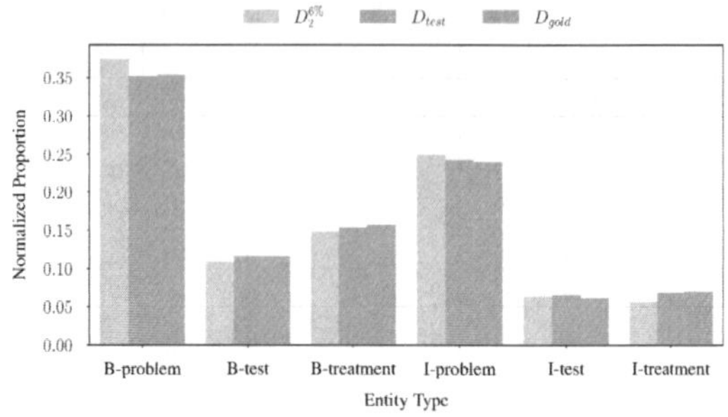

Figure 4: Normalized proportion of entity type in D_{gold}, D_{test} and $D_2^{6\%}$.

Appendix E. Workflow

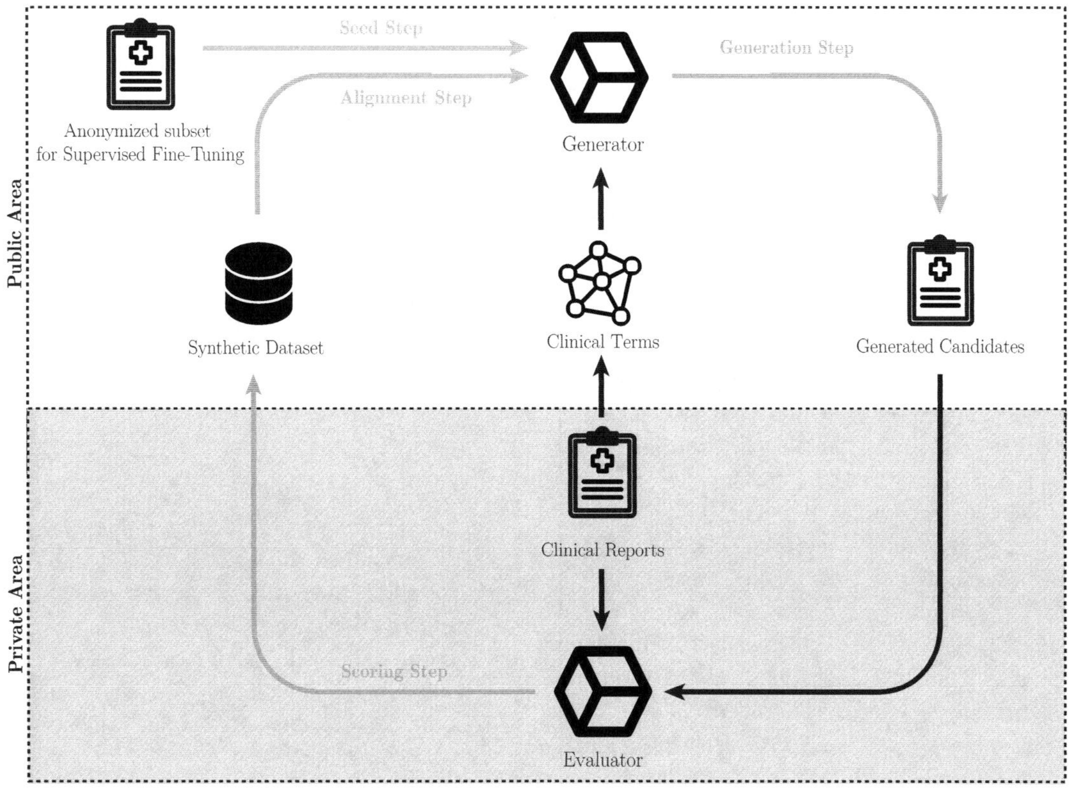

Figure 5: workflow of our approach

Appendix F. Outputs

<s>[INST]As a doctor, you must write an original 'History of Present Illness' (HPI) section for a discharge summary. Your response should capture the essence of a patient's health journey and recent medical experiences, while strictly using all the provided keywords conserving the order. You must adopt a medical telegraphic style, abbreviated, characterized by concise and direct language.
Keywords: *metastatic, RCC, pancreas, reports, chills, tylenol, reports, rib pain, lying, chills, reports, dark stools, fever, zosyn, headache, contacts, anxious, pain, dysuria, joint pain, rash, hypotensive, asymptomatic, given, lactate, baseline, guaiac, stool, saw, stent, pancreatic, blood, tomorrow, treated, cholangitis, given, sat, ARF, reports, anxious*[/INST]

Figure 6: An example of prompt for the Figures 7,9,8

This is a 67 y.o male with h.o metastatic RCC to the pancreas, recent ICU course for UGIB (12units pRBCs) who reports sudden intermittent chills since wednesday for which he took tylenol. Pt also reports R.side gnawing rib pain, while lying in bed before the onset of chills. In addition, pt reports dark stools for the last few days which started after taking "iron pills". Pt states he went to [**Hospital1 2436**] ED because of a fever of 101.3, however he felt better and did not want to wait to be seen. He returned to [**Hospital1 2436**] today and was transferred to [**Hospital1 18**] after a dose of zosyn, HCT 25. Pt denies headache/dizziness/blurred vision, URI/cough, sick contacts, CP, +palp when anxious, -abd pain/n/v/d/brbpr, dysuria/hematuria, joint pain, rash, paresthesias.

.

At [**Hospital1 18**], pt found to be hypotensive to 75/40, asymptomatic. He was given 3L IVF, lactate 6.8. HCT 22.8 from a baseline of 35 a few weeks ago. He was found to have black, guaiac +stool. GI saw pt, pt s/p stent to pancreatic ampulla, ?blocked from blood. Plan is to transfuse, ERCP tomorrow. ED also treated for possible cholangitis/sepsis and pt was given dose of vanco. Vitals 99.2, BP 99/66 HR 88 sat 9820's, 18. Pt also found to be in ARF.

.

Currently, pt reports that he is anxious.

.

Figure 7: An example of a ground truth associated with the prompt of Figure 6

77 yo M w/ hx of metastatic RCC of the pancreas (pancreo-duodenal
mass reports R/o chills since starting [**6-2**] on [**2160-5-18**] (day 7-10 from Hx. He has had fevers with taking tylenol at that time
(Ibuprofen 400mg, acetaminophen 650mg PRN for R/o rib pain and
steal). On [**2160-5-22**] he was lying in bed and became extremely
ill with chills. He reports this started a few minutes ago. Also
reports dark stools. His fever is 102F (38.3C), he is on 2g IV
zosyn (given IVF 2L NS, as he is V/5) for pneumonia with HC
reported by the Wife. He reports severe headache. He is not
compliant with PCP but has noticed many recent contacts with
his S/M. He is very anxious for relief of pain. He has some
dysuria and no joint pain. He has no rash. He is in the ED
actively pacing. He is hypotensive. He is BP 90/45 with 3+ pti
on his left hand. PRI all his vitals are stable otherwise at
BP 92/44 HR 81 RR 14 96 O2 Sat 99PaCO2 28.1, PaO2 113. As a baseline (was done in ED), guaiac
in stool was positive. He was sent to CT with ortho in ED. Saw
his PCR [**Last Name (Only) **] [**Date**] [**Time (only) **] 5:15 and showed a 6.2mm x 5.1mm pancreatic
tail mass (blood in the head of the pancreas with no dilation
distally). He is scheduled for pancreatic stent placement
tomorrow. He was treated for acute cholangitis (e.g. given 3L NS
and 1g of IVF) and was given 1L NS to help with ARF. He
reports that he is more anxious for relief of pain.

Figure 8: An example of synthetic data generated with the prompt of Figure 6, with a high SEMSCORE at 79

Ms. [**Known lastname **] is a 69 year old woman with a history of metastatic renal cell carcinoma (RCC) with distant metastases to the pancreas
who presents with fever, chills, abdominal pain since [**2119-1-7**]. She reports taking 5 grams of tylenol daily at home
which she also reports taking in the past week. She also reports having
rib pain while lying in the [**location unclear **]. She reports chills
and having dark stools, but denies any associated fever or rigors.
She was recently started on zosyn for headache and nausea and
vomiting. She denies any contact with sick person, recent travel
or animals, or recent change in her work or home environment.

She is an anxious, non-smoker with a past medical history of pancreatic
insufficiency and hypertension who presents with abdominal pain and
lower extremity edema. She denies dysuria, joint pain or rash. She
is not hypotensive with a BP of 125/80 at her arrival to the
Emergency Department. She is asymptomatic for lactate at the time of
this admission to the floor. On review of her baseline admission guaiac
stool testing is not available. On her last outpatient visit to her
oncologist at [**Hospital1 **] on [**1-7**], she was seen to have a stent placed for
cholangitis and was given an ERCP. She was treated for cholangitis
at the time and was given some ARF on [**1-7**].

Her oxygen saturation was 97for possible E.Coli pneumonia. She was found to have hypotension on
admission to the floor and received dobutamine.

Figure 9: An example of synthetic data generated with the prompt of Figure 6, with a low SEMSCORE at 52

Task
Your task is to generate a JSON list detailing specific healthcare-related entities in an input text. The entities to be identified are: 'medical problems', 'treatments', and 'tests'. Each entry in the JSON should specify the entity and its type.
Entity Markup Guide
- "problem" for medical problems.
- "treatment" for treatments.
- "test" for medical tests.
Examples
Example Input 1: At the time of admission, he denied fever, diaphoresis, nausea, chest pain or other systemic symptoms.
Example Output 1: ["entity": "fever", "type": "problem", "entity": "diaphoresis", "type": "problem", "entity": "nausea", "type": "problem", "entity": "chest pain", "type": "problem"]
Example Input 2: He had been diagnosed with osteoarthritis of the knees and had undergone arthroscopy years prior to admission.
Example Output 2: ["entity": "osteoarthritis of the knees", "type": "problem", "entity": "arthroscopy", "type": "test"]
Example Input 3: After the patient was seen in the office on August 10, she persisted with high fevers and was admitted on August 11 to Cottonwood Hospital.
Example Output 3: ["entity": "high fevers", "type": "problem"]
Example Input 4: HISTORY OF PRESENT ILLNESS: The patient is an 85-year-old male who was brought in by EMS with a complaint of a decreased level of consciousness.
Example Output 4: ["entity": "a decreased level of consciousness", "type": "problem"]
Example Input 5: Her lisinopril was increased to 40 mg daily.
Example Output 5: ["entity": "lisinopril", "type": "treatment"]
Input Text: `[INPUT]`
Output Text:

Figure 10: The prompt for annotating documents for the synthetic NER task

Prefix-Enhanced Large Language Models with Reused Training Data in Multi-Turn Medical Dialogue

Suxue Ma[1*] **Zhicheng Yang**[2†] **Ruei-Sung Lin**[2] **Youbao Tang**[2] **Ning Zhang**[2]
Zhenjie Cao[3] **Yuan Ni**[4] **Jing Xiao**[4] **Jieke Hou**[5] **Peng Chang**[2]
[1]Tianjin University, China [2]PAII Inc., USA
[3]Tsinghua SIGS, China [4]Ping An Technology, China
[5]Ping An Healthcare and Technology Company Limited, China
msx@tju.edu.cn; zcyangpingan@gmail.com

Abstract

Large Language Models have made impressive progress in the medical field. In medical dialogue scenarios, unlike traditional single-turn question-answering tasks, multi-turn doctor-patient dialogue tasks require AI doctors to interact with patients in multiple rounds, where the quality of each response impacts the overall model performance. In this paper, we propose PERT to re-explore values of multi-turn dialogue training data after the supervised fine-tuning phase by integrating a prefix learning strategy, further enhancing the response quality. Our preliminary results show that PERT achieves notable improvements on gynecological data, with an increase of up to 0.22 on a 5-point rating scale.

1 Introduction

With the development of large language models (LLMs), there has been increasing attention on their applications in the medical sector. While recent general-purpose models such as GPT series (Hurst et al., 2024), Claude series (Anthropic, 2025), and Qwen series (Yang et al., 2024b) have shown decent capabilities in medical question-answering (QA) tasks (Xie et al., 2024), researchers have leveraged diverse medical datasets to build specialized models tailored to various medical scenarios, such as dedicated SMILE for mental health (Qiu et al., 2023), and comprehensive Med-PaLM series (Singhal et al., 2025), Zhongjing (Yang et al., 2024c), and Baichuan-M1 (Baichuan, 2025). These models offer exciting possibilities for the real-world application of LLMs in the medical domain.

Our scenario is multi-turn doctor-patient dialogues in multiple clinical departments on an online healthcare consultation platform. We aim at deploying LLMs as AI doctors to assist human doctors in collecting adequate prediagnostic information from patients via multi-turn conversations between patients and AI doctors. To train an acceptable LLM for every clinical department, a straightforward idea is to adopt a multi-stage training strategy: pretraining on general medical data (Yang et al., 2024c; Baichuan, 2025), followed by supervised fine-tuning (SFT) using real doctor-patient dialogue history in each clinical department (Yang et al., 2024c). However, the model trained using this simple strategy still falls short of meeting deployment-oriented performance requirements. For instance, we observed that the model occasionally repeats its previous responses. Unfortunately, a repetitive utterance might make patients aware that they are interacting with an AI doctor, destroying their consultation experience.

Since authors in (Zhang et al., 2025) highlighted the effectiveness of appropriate instruction prompts to alleviate this issue, we conduct two pilot experiments: (1) When we apply the instruction prompt "Do not repeat what has already been said" only at the beginning of a multi-turn dialogue, the model tends to forget this constraint after several rounds; (2) When we insert this instruction prompt before every response, the model significantly reduces repetition, but it increases the frequency of irrelevant or off-topic responses, still degrading the overall response quality. We infer that two factors cause this issue: (1) The dataset for each medical department is relatively small, limiting the model's learning capacity; (2) While the prompt-based constraint is effective, the model either forgets it over time or applies it too rigidly.

To mitigate these issues, we propose a novel training strategy **PERT** (Prefix-Enhanced LLMs with Reused Training data) for our multi-turn medical dialogue scenario. Unlike the original single-department SFT paradigm, PERT has two training phases. First, we aggregate data from all departments to train an all-around LLM that benefits from

*This work was done during Suxue Ma's internship at Ping An Technology, Shenzhen, China.
†Corresponding author.

Proceedings of the Second Workshop on Patient-Oriented Language Processing (CL4Health), pages 26–33
May 4, 2025 ©2025 Association for Computational Linguistics

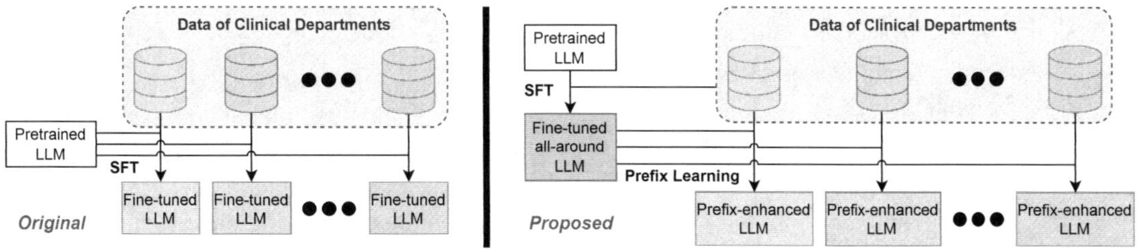

Figure 1: **Framework of the proposed PERT.** Compared with the original LLM training strategy, PERT first trains an all-around LLM using the data of all clinical departments. The prefix learning process is then conducted to leverage the departmental data individually and train their own prefix-enhanced LLMs, respectively.

the data scaling law (Kaplan et al., 2020). Second, since such a generalized LLM needs to retain specialization for individual departments, we design a prefix learning phase by *reusing* the data from each department. Unlike the previous pilot experiments where the prompt was mechanically inserted either at the beginning of the entire dialogue or before each response, prefix learning can provide "soft guidance" for each round of AI doctor responses, improving the overall LLM performance without introducing excessive constraints on response generation. PERT further exploits the values of training data that was used once only in the conventional single-department SFT (original vs. proposed in Fig. 1, described in Sec. 3.1).

Our key contributions are listed as follows: (1) proposing the PERT training strategy combining all-around LLM training with prefix learning by reusing training data from single-department for multi-turn medical dialogues, (2) introducing a strategy for reusing training data from single-department to enhance model performance, and (3) conducting preliminary experiments to validate the effectiveness of our approach in real-world doctor-patient consultations.

2 Related Work

Medical LLMs. Medical LLMs have emerged as a transformative technology in healthcare, with significant advancements in a wide range of applications, including medical summarization (Tang et al., 2023; Van Veen et al., 2024), clinical decision support (Hager et al., 2024), and medical dialogue systems (Li et al., 2023). In dialogue systems, single-turn models provide rapid responses to medical queries, while multi-turn models are always diagnostic-oriented through context-aware interaction. These models can be broadly categorized into fine-tuned general LLMs (Li et al., 2023; Singhal et al., 2025; Yang et al., 2024c) and dedicated LLMs (Luo et al., 2022; Gu et al., 2021). Most of those models are validated on public datasets or in lab-stage settings, but have not been fully studied in deployment-oriented scenarios.

Prefix Learning. The representative prefix-tuning method is a parameter-efficient fine-tuning (PEFT) approach that optimizes a small set of task-specific parameters, called prefixes, while keeping the pretrained model frozen. These prefixes effectively guide the model's behavior during inference without requiring updates to the full model (Li and Liang, 2021). Recent studies have demonstrated the effectiveness of prefix-tuning in medical applications (Van Sonsbeek et al., 2023; Chen et al., 2024; Zhou et al., 2024). For the multi-turn interactive dialogue scenario, the authors in (Li et al., 2024a) introduce an external planner to learn prefix token embeddings. Nevertheless, the efficacy of this method has not been studied in the medical field.

3 Methods

3.1 Framework Overview

Fig. 1 illustrates the framework of our proposed PERT. Compared with the original SFT strategy, we first leverage the data from all clinical departments to achieve an all-around LLM, which plays an intermediate role. We then conduct prefix learning by reusing data from every individual department on the trained all-around LLM. Consequently, each department has its own prefix-enhanced LLM.

3.2 All-Around LLM Training Phase

We aggregate data from all departments and train the all-around LLM using the same SFT strategy as the original one. We find that this all-around LLM overall outperforms the single-department LLM (shown in Table 2).

3.3 Prefix Learning Phase

Inspired by prefix learning designed for the multi-turn dialogue scenario (Li et al., 2024a), which adopted an extra planner to update the prefix token features, we design two stages in our prefix learning phase. The first stage involves cloning the behavior of the pretrained all-around LLM to ensure that the LLM steered by the prefixes behaves similarly to the LLM itself. The prefixes are generated by a planner. In the second stage, we fine-tune the planner by using responses from real doctors, collected through our online consultation platform. This allows the LLM's behavior to become more aligned with the communication style and expertise of real medical professionals.

3.3.1 Self-Cloning Stage

Behavior cloning (Bratko et al., 1995) is a technique in imitation learning where an agent learns to replicate the actions of an expert. Inspired by this approach, we aim to make an LLM with prefix tokens behave consistently with the all-around LLM. To achieve this, we train the planner from scratch using the responses generated by the all-around LLM as training data. This stage ensures the prefix-equipped LLM retains the capacities of the all-around LLM, offering a robust starting point.

To prepare the corpus for self-cloning, we provide the fine-tuned all-around LLM with real doctor-patient dialogue history which ends with the patient's utterance, and ask the LLM to generate the response as a doctor. Formally, the corpus is denoted as $\{p_1^i, q_1^i, p_2^i, q_2^i, \cdots, p_{N_i}^i, q_{N_i}^i\}_{i=1}^M$, where M is the number of collected dialogues, N_i is the number of rounds of the i-th dialogue, and p_j and q_j ($j = \{1, 2, \ldots, N_i\}$) are the patient's and the doctor's utterance at the j-th round, respectively. Note that a dialogue with n rounds can be split into n individual datapoints with $\{p_1, q_1, \cdots, p_j\}$ being the dialogue history and q_j being the ground truth for $j = \{1, 2, \cdots, n\}$.

Now we describe the process of prefix generation. Initially, the embedding of the dialogue history at the j-th round of the i-th dialogue is obtained by the LLM, which produces an embedding:

$$e_j^i = \text{Emb}(\{p_1^i, q_1^i, p_2^i, q_2^i, \cdots, p_j^i\}). \quad (1)$$

Next, the planner extracts the last-token embedding from the output of the LLM's last layer, and then transforms this token embedding into the prefix space by an MLP. Formally, the planner is defined as:

$$\phi(e) = \text{MLP}(g_\theta(e)), \quad (2)$$

where θ is learnable parameters of the transformer and g_θ denotes the extraction operation. We train the planner by minimizing conditional language modeling objective as follows:

$$\mathcal{L}_{sc} = -\sum_{i=1}^{M}\sum_{j=1}^{N_i} \log f_\theta(\tilde{q}_j^i \mid \phi(e_j^i) \| e_j^i), \quad (3)$$

where $\|$ denotes concatenation of the dialogue action tokens with token embeddings e, and f_θ denotes the autoregressive distribution of generated strings. Here, the ground truth $\tilde{q}_j$ is generated by the all-around LLM.

3.3.2 Supervised Fine-Tuning Stage

In the supervised fine-tuning stage, we refine the prefix embeddings to better align the LLM's behavior with real doctors' communication styles and expertise. Unlike the self-cloning stage, which uses responses generated by the all-around LLM, this stage reuses the real doctors' responses from clinical department data as ground truth to fine-tune the planner in a supervised manner. Note that the dialogue history remains the same as that in the self-cloning stage, but the ground truth for fine-tuning is now the real doctors' responses rather than those generated by the LLM. That is, the ground truth for the real doctor's response at the j-th round is q_j instead of $\tilde{q}_j$. The loss function in this stage is

$$\mathcal{L}_{sft} == -\sum_{i=1}^{M}\sum_{j=1}^{N_i} \log f_\theta(q_j^i \mid \phi(e_j^i) \| e_j^i). \quad (4)$$

4 Experiments

4.1 Dataset

Our dataset is sourced from a real-world online doctor-patient consultation platform in China, including more than 10 clinical departments, such as pediatrics, ophthalmology, etc. This data source consists of authentic doctor-patient multi-turn dialogues, covering a range of medical inquiries and responses. In this paper, we present preliminary results using the data from the gynecology department because of its large number of consultations (300k+ dialogues), while the available data across all departments (800k+ dialogues) are for training the all-around LLM. Table 1 lists the statistics of

Dataset	#Dialog.	#Rounds
Original		
gynecology	310k	1.77m
For prefix learning		
self-cloning	10,000	58,105
supervised fine-tuning	10,000	54,133
test set	1,000	5,463

Table 1: Statistics of dialogues from the gynecology department and those used for prefix learning during self-cloning, supervised fine-tuning, and inference, respectively.

Method	Avg. s	s>2(%)	s>3(%)	s>4(%)
Original				
gynecology LLM	3.5824	97.21	57.93	7.15
Proposed				
all-around LLM	3.6353	97.74	58.65	7.48
random prefix w/o learning	3.6437	98.32	58.44	7.91
prefix w/ self-cloning only	<u>3.7584</u>	**98.86**	<u>68.38</u>	<u>8.34</u>
PERT (prefix w/ self-cloning & SFT)	**3.8013**	<u>98.41</u>	**71.66**	**10.36**

Table 2: Performance comparison among different methods by the average score s and the percentage of dialogues with scores exceeding 2, 3, and 4. Bold and underlined text represent the best and the second best, respectively.

our used dialogue data, including the number of dialogues (#Dialog.) and the total number of rounds (#Rounds). Specifically, we use 10,000 dialogues for both self-cloning and supervised fine-tuning, with average rounds per dialogue of 5.8 and 5.4, respectively. For evaluation, we use 1,000 dialogues as the test set.

4.2 Implementation Details

The fine-tuned all-around LLM in PERT is obtained by fine-tuning Qwen2-14B-Instruct (Yang et al., 2024a) with aggregated data from all clinical departments. For training, We used a learning rate of 0.001 and Adam optimizer to minimize the loss. We used a prefix token length of 2, with prefix embedding size of 128. The dimension of the hidden state of the LLM is 5120. The planner for generating prefix tokens was trained for 10 epochs for self-cloning and 5 epochs for supervised fine-tuning, while the all-around LLM was frozen. All experiments were conducted on servers with 8 NVIDIA V100 GPUs, each with 16 GB VRAM.

4.3 Preliminary Results

We compared several methods for doctor-patient dialogue generation to validate the effectiveness of our method in Table 2. The methods tested for comparison include (i) the original gynecology LLM; (ii) the all-around LLM that generates responses without any prefix learning stages; (iii) a random prefix without learning, where the planner is randomly initialized to generate prefix tokens; and (iv) update the prefix embeddings using self-cloning only, referring to no fine-tuning with real doctor responses. Finally, our proposed PERT, which combines the self-cloning stage of the planner to generate prefix embeddings with the supervised fine-tuning stage using real doctor responses, was also evaluated. We utilized a general-purpose LLM (Qwen2-7B-Instruct) to assess dialogue responses. Each response was rated on a scale from 1 to 5, with higher scores indicating better quality. The evaluation considered factors including safety, professionalism, and friendliness. The complete prompt template is provided in Appendix A. For each dialogue, the highest turn score was taken as the dialogue's overall score. We then calculated the average score and the proportions of dialogues with scores exceeding 2, 3, and 4 in Table 2.

As we can see, PERT achieves the highest average score of 3.8013, significantly surpassing the baselines (gynecology LLM and all-around LLM), which have an average score of 3.5824 and 3.6353, respectively. The random prefix method also shows a comparable result (3.6437), but it remains lower than the prefix learning approaches. Meanwhile, our method generally accomplishes the best results in the percentage of responses with scores above various thresholds ($s > 2 \sim 4$), except the comparable percentage with the self-cloning stage only for $s > 2$. These results indicate that the inclusion of prefix learning by reusing real doctors' replies from the training data is significant for generating more coherent and contextually appropriate responses.

5 Conclusions and Discussion

In this paper, we propose PERT, which leverages a prefix learning strategy to re-explore multi-turn dialogue training data after the SFT training phase, leading to further LLM performance improvement. Our preliminary results show that PERT achieves noticeable improvements on gynecological data.

Since our model is designed for deployment, the performance of the medical LLM needs to be continuously improved through iterative updates. Once the existing data has been effectively utilized, a key question is whether we can further explore its potential for specific medical scenarios. This paper presents a novel model-based approach to achieving this objective. In fact, prefix learning is often compared side by side with low-rank adaptation (LoRA) SFT (Van Sonsbeek et al., 2023) in terms of model performance. However, we cascade these two stages and adapt them to our multi-turn interactive dialogue scenario to achieve further improvements.

In medical scenarios, the tolerance for hallucinations is much stricter than in general contexts. During interactions with patients, responses from a medical LLM must not contain blatantly commonsense-violating errors. For example, if a male patient is asked about menstruation, such an error represents a critical *red line* that cannot be crossed. A response like that could lead the patient to entirely abandon the use of the online medical consultation platform. However, such issues are difficult to directly measure through standard performance evaluation metrics (e.g. the rating scale used in this paper). Since these issues are crucial considerations in determining whether a medical LLM is suitable for real-world deployment, we plan to leverage reinforcement learning to address these red-line issues.

There has recently been considerable research on retrieval-augmented generation (RAG) to mitigate hallucination issues, such as GraphRAG (Edge et al., 2024). However, building a precise and professional knowledge graph in the medical field requires a significant investment of time and effort from medical professionals. This research direction is currently also underway in our project.

Limitations

A limitation of our work is that we did not involve medical specialists in rating the responses at this point, since the scope of this preliminary study is within our internal research team. We will continue to test PERT in other departments. Once its effectiveness is demonstrated thoroughly, medical professionals from the online consultation platform will perform further evaluation.

Many medical LLMs used ChatGPT/GPT-4 series for scoring or included them for performance comparison (Moor et al., 2023; Yang et al., 2024c; Chen et al., 2023; Singhal et al., 2023). Unfortunately, in compliance with our platform's safeguarding medical data privacy policies, we are restricted from accessing external API interfaces, including ChatGPT/GPT-4 series.

In this work, we focus only on the pure textual content rather than multi-modal dialogue data, even though the appearance of images sent by patients to better illustrate their symptoms is common in practice (Li et al., 2024b). Meanwhile, incorporating the paradigm of the conventional medical imaging diagnosis or screening tasks such as our previous studies (Yang et al., 2021; Cao et al., 2024, 2025; Tang et al., 2021; Yi et al., 2022) into the LLM/VLM-powered multi-turn interactive dialogue setting still remains a challenging and ongoing area of research.

Ethical Considerations

All personal data were anonymized to ensure participant privacy. This study was reviewed and approved by the Institutional Review Board (IRB) of Qingdao Ping An Kangjian Internet Hospital, China (IRB number: LLSC2024A01). The authors declare no competing interests.

References

Anthropic. 2025. Meet claude. https://www.anthropic.com/claude. Accessed: 2025-01-31.

Baichuan. 2025. Baichuan-m1-14b. https://github.com/baichuan-inc/Baichuan-M1-14B. Accessed: 2025-01-31.

Ivan Bratko, Tanja Urbančič, and Claude Sammut. 1995. Behavioural cloning: phenomena, results and problems. *IFAC Proceedings Volumes*, 28(21):143–149.

Zhenjie Cao, Zhuo Deng, Zhicheng Yang, Jie Ma, and Lan Ma. 2025. Supervised contrastive pre-training models for mammography screening. *Journal of Big Data*, 12(1):24.

Zhenjie Cao, Zhuo Deng, Zhicheng Yang, Jialin Yuan, Jie Ma, and Lan Ma. 2024. Asydisnet: Scalable mammographic asymmetry and architectural distortion detection with angle-based quadruplet loss. *IEEE Transactions on Medical Imaging*.

Jiawei Chen, Yue Jiang, Dingkang Yang, Mingcheng Li, Jinjie Wei, Ziyun Qian, and Lihua Zhang. 2024. Can llms' tuning methods work in medical multimodal domain? In *International Conference on Medical Image Computing and Computer-Assisted Intervention*, pages 112–122. Springer.

Junying Chen, Xidong Wang, et al. 2023. Huatuogpt-ii, one-stage training for medical adaption of llms. *preprint arXiv:2311.09774*.

Darren Edge, Ha Trinh, Newman Cheng, Joshua Bradley, Alex Chao, Apurva Mody, Steven Truitt, and Jonathan Larson. 2024. From local to global: A graph rag approach to query-focused summarization. *arXiv preprint arXiv:2404.16130*.

Yu Gu, Robert Tinn, Hao Cheng, Michael Lucas, Naoto Usuyama, Xiaodong Liu, Tristan Naumann, Jianfeng Gao, and Hoifung Poon. 2021. Domain-specific language model pretraining for biomedical natural language processing. *ACM Transactions on Computing for Healthcare (HEALTH)*, 3(1):1–23.

Paul Hager, Friederike Jungmann, Robbie Holland, Kunal Bhagat, Inga Hubrecht, Manuel Knauer, Jakob Vielhauer, Marcus Makowski, Rickmer Braren, Georgios Kaissis, et al. 2024. Evaluation and mitigation of the limitations of large language models in clinical decision-making. *Nature medicine*, 30(9):2613–2622.

Aaron Hurst, Adam Lerer, Adam P Goucher, Adam Perelman, Aditya Ramesh, Aidan Clark, AJ Ostrow, Akila Welihinda, Alan Hayes, Alec Radford, et al. 2024. Gpt-4o system card. *arXiv preprint arXiv:2410.21276*.

Jared Kaplan, Sam McCandlish, Tom Henighan, Tom B Brown, Benjamin Chess, Rewon Child, Scott Gray, Alec Radford, Jeffrey Wu, and Dario Amodei. 2020. Scaling laws for neural language models. *arXiv preprint arXiv:2001.08361*.

Kenneth Li, Yiming Wang, Fernanda Viégas, and Martin Wattenberg. 2024a. Dialogue action tokens: Steering language models in goal-directed dialogue with a multi-turn planner. *arXiv preprint arXiv:2406.11978*.

Xiang Lisa Li and Percy Liang. 2021. Prefix-tuning: Optimizing continuous prompts for generation. In *Proceedings of the 59th Annual Meeting of the Association for Computational Linguistics and the 11th International Joint Conference on Natural Language Processing (Volume 1: Long Papers)*, pages 4582–4597.

Yunxiang Li, Zihan Li, Kai Zhang, Ruilong Dan, Steve Jiang, and You Zhang. 2023. Chatdoctor: A medical chat model fine-tuned on a large language model meta-ai (llama) using medical domain knowledge. *Cureus*, 15(6).

Zhangpu Li, Changhong Zou, Suxue Ma, Zhicheng Yang, Chen Du, Youbao Tang, Zhenjie Cao, Ning Zhang, Jui-Hsin Lai, Ruei-Sung Lin, et al. 2024b. Zalm3: Zero-shot enhancement of vision-language alignment via in-context information in multi-turn multimodal medical dialogue. *arXiv preprint arXiv:2409.17610*.

Renqian Luo, Liai Sun, Yingce Xia, Tao Qin, Sheng Zhang, Hoifung Poon, and Tie-Yan Liu. 2022. Biogpt: generative pre-trained transformer for biomedical text generation and mining. *Briefings in bioinformatics*, 23(6):bbac409.

Michael Moor, Qian Huang, et al. 2023. Med-flamingo: a multimodal medical few-shot learner. In *Machine Learning for Health (ML4H)*. PMLR.

Huachuan Qiu, Hongliang He, Shuai Zhang, Anqi Li, and Zhenzhong Lan. 2023. Smile: Single-turn to multi-turn inclusive language expansion via chatgpt for mental health support. *arXiv preprint arXiv:2305.00450*.

Karan Singhal, Tao Tu, Juraj Gottweis, Rory Sayres, Ellery Wulczyn, Mohamed Amin, Le Hou, Kevin Clark, Stephen R Pfohl, Heather Cole-Lewis, et al. 2025. Toward expert-level medical question answering with large language models. *Nature Medicine*, pages 1–8.

Karan Singhal, Tao Tu, et al. 2023. Towards expert-level medical question answering with large language models. *preprint arXiv:2305.09617*.

Liyan Tang, Zhaoyi Sun, Betina Idnay, Jordan G Nestor, Ali Soroush, Pierre A Elias, Ziyang Xu, Ying Ding, Greg Durrett, Justin F Rousseau, et al. 2023. Evaluating large language models on medical evidence summarization. *NPJ digital medicine*, 6(1):158.

Yuxing Tang, Zhenjie Cao, Yanbo Zhang, Zhicheng Yang, Zongcheng Ji, Yiwei Wang, Mei Han, Jie Ma, Jing Xiao, and Peng Chang. 2021. Leveraging large-scale weakly labeled data for semi-supervised mass detection in mammograms. In *Proceedings of the IEEE/CVF Conference on Computer Vision and Pattern Recognition*, pages 3855–3864.

Tom Van Sonsbeek, Mohammad Mahdi Derakhshani, Ivona Najdenkoska, Cees GM Snoek, and Marcel Worring. 2023. Open-ended medical visual question answering through prefix tuning of language models. In *International Conference on Medical Image Computing and Computer-Assisted Intervention*, pages 726–736. Springer.

Dave Van Veen, Cara Van Uden, Louis Blankemeier, Jean-Benoit Delbrouck, Asad Aali, Christian Bluethgen, Anuj Pareek, Malgorzata Polacin, Eduardo Pontes Reis, Anna Seehofnerová, et al. 2024. Adapted large language models can outperform medical experts in clinical text summarization. *Nature medicine*, 30(4):1134–1142.

Wenya Xie, Qingying Xiao, Yu Zheng, Xidong Wang, Junying Chen, Ke Ji, Anningzhe Gao, Xiang Wan, Feng Jiang, and Benyou Wang. 2024. Llms for doctors: Leveraging medical llms to assist doctors, not replace them. *arXiv preprint arXiv:2406.18034*.

An Yang, Baosong Yang, Binyuan Hui, Bo Zheng, Bowen Yu, Chang Zhou, Chengpeng Li, Chengyuan Li, Dayiheng Liu, Fei Huang, et al. 2024a. Qwen2 technical report. *arXiv preprint arXiv:2407.1067*.

An Yang, Baosong Yang, Beichen Zhang, Binyuan Hui, Bo Zheng, Bowen Yu, Chengyuan Li, Dayiheng Liu, Fei Huang, Haoran Wei, et al. 2024b. Qwen2. 5 technical report. *arXiv preprint arXiv:2412.15115*.

Songhua Yang, Hanjie Zhao, Senbin Zhu, Guangyu Zhou, Hongfei Xu, Yuxiang Jia, and Hongying Zan. 2024c. Zhongjing: Enhancing the chinese medical capabilities of large language model through expert feedback and real-world multi-turn dialogue. In *Proceedings of the AAAI Conference on Artificial Intelligence*, volume 38, pages 19368–19376.

Zhicheng Yang, Zhenjie Cao, Yanbo Zhang, Yuxing Tang, Xiaohui Lin, Rushan Ouyang, Mingxiang Wu, Mei Han, Jing Xiao, Lingyun Huang, et al. 2021. Momminet-v2: Mammographic multi-view mass identification networks. *Medical Image Analysis*, 73:102204.

Chunyan Yi, Yuxing Tang, Rushan Ouyang, Yanbo Zhang, Zhenjie Cao, Zhicheng Yang, Shibin Wu, Mei Han, Jing Xiao, Peng Chang, et al. 2022. The added value of an artificial intelligence system in assisting radiologists on indeterminate bi-rads 0 mammograms. *European Radiology*, pages 1–10.

Chen Zhang, Xinyi Dai, Yaxiong Wu, Qu Yang, Yasheng Wang, Ruiming Tang, and Yong Liu. 2025. A survey on multi-turn interaction capabilities of large language models. *arXiv preprint arXiv:2501.09959*.

Lu Zhou, Yiheng Chen, Xinmin Li, Yanan Li, Ning Li, Xiting Wang, and Rui Zhang. 2024. A new adapter tuning of large language model for chinese medical named entity recognition. *Applied Artificial Intelligence*, 38(1):2385268.

A Appendix

A.1 Prompt Template

In this section, the complete prompt template for the 5-point rating scale is provided. Since our data source is in Chinese, the original language of this prompt template is Chinese. We have translated it into English.

You will act as an evaluator and rate the doctor's next response based on the dialogue history between the patient and the doctor. Please provide a score from 1 to 5 according to the following scoring criteria.
你将作为评估员，根据患者和医生之间的对话历史，对医生的下一轮回复进行打分。请根据以下评分标准给出1到5分的评分。

Scoring Criteria

评分标准

- 1 Point - Very Dissatisfied:
  1分 - 非常不满意：
  - The response is completely irrelevant to the patient's question or contains obvious errors;
    回复与患者的问题完全无关或明显错误；
  - Lacks basic medical knowledge and common sense, potentially misleading the patient;
    缺乏基本的医疗知识和常识，可能误导患者；
  - The response could negatively impact the patient's health.
    回复可能对患者的健康造成负面影响。
- 2 Points - Dissatisfied:
  2分 - 不满意：
  - The response is partially correct but contains significant errors or omits key information;
    回复部分正确，但包含明显的错误或遗漏关键信息；
  - Fails to adequately address the patient's concerns and lacks depth;
    未能充分解决患者的问题，缺乏深度；
  - Lacks professionalism and does not provide effective diagnosis or recommendations.
    回复缺乏专业性，未能提供有效的诊断或建议。
- 3 Points - Average:
  3分 - 一般：
  - The response is generally correct but lacks detailed explanations or supporting information;
    回复基本正确，但缺少详细的解释或支持；
  - The question is addressed, but the expression is not entirely clear and could be improved;
    解决了问题，但表达不够清晰，有改进的空间；
  - The response is neutral, without major errors, but also does not exceed expectations.
    回复态度中立，没有明显错误，也没有超出期望的表现。
- 4 Points - Satisfied:
  4分 - 满意：
  - The response is accurate and provides sufficient information and explanations;
    回复准确，提供了足够的信息和解释；
  - Considers the patient's condition and offers personalized advice;
    考虑了患者的情况，提供了个性化的建议；
  - Demonstrates professionalism and provides effective diagnosis or recommendations.
    回复展现了专业性，能够针对患者的问题提供有效的诊断或建议。
- 5 Points - Very Satisfied:
  5分 - 非常满意：
  - The response is not only accurate but also exceeds patient expectations, offering in-depth analysis and recommendations;
    回复不仅准确，而且超出了患者的期望，提供了深入的分析和建议；
  - Demonstrates a high level of professional knowledge and a deep understanding of the patient's condition;
    展现了高水平的专业知识和对患者情况的深刻理解；
  - The response is encouraging and instills confidence and reassurance in the patient.
    回复态度积极，能够给予患者信心和安慰。

Steps

步骤

- Read the dialogue history between the patient and the doctor;
  阅读患者和医生之间的对话历史；
- Read the doctor's next response;
  阅读医生的下一轮回复；
- Evaluate the response based on the scoring criteria;
  根据评分标准，对回复进行评估；
- Assign a score.
  给出一个评分。

Examples

示例

- 1-Point Example:
  1分示例
  - *Patient*: "My menstrual blood has been dark brown for the past few months, and my period lasts longer than usual."
    患者："我最近几个月的月经颜色都是深褐色的，而且经期时间也延长了。"
  - *Online Doctor's Response*: "It might be due to fatigue. Just get some rest."
    在线医生回复："这可能是疲劳引起的，多休息就好。"
  - *Score*: 1
    评分：1
  - *Reasoning*: The response is overly simplistic and does not consider possible gynecological conditions such as endometriosis or fibroids. It also fails to ask about other symptoms or medical history.
    理由：回复过于简单，没有考虑到可能的妇科疾病，如子宫内膜异位症或子宫肌瘤，也没有进一步询问患者的其他症状或病史。
- 2-Point Example:
  2分示例
  - *Patient*: "I've been feeling dizzy lately, especially when I stand up."
    患者："我最近总是感到头晕，尤其是在站起来的时候。"
  - *Online Doctor's Response*: "It might be low blood pressure. Drink more water and eat more salt."
    在线医生回复："这可能是低血压，多喝水，多吃盐。"
  - *Score*: 2
    评分：2
  - *Reasoning*: The response does not inquire about additional symptoms, such as fainting or blurred vision, and lacks a recommendation for further medical evaluation. It also does not provide personalized advice.
    理由：回复没有询问患者的其他症状，如是否有晕厥或视力模糊，也没有建议患者进一步检查，缺乏个性化建议。
- 3-Point Example:
  3分示例
  - *Patient*: "I've been experiencing chest tightness, especially at night."
    患者："我最近经常感到胸闷，尤其是在晚上。"
  - *Online Doctor's Response*: "Chest tightness could be a heart issue or caused by anxiety. You should go to the hospital for further evaluation."
    在线医生回复："胸闷可能是心脏问题，也可能是焦虑引起的。建议你去医院做进一步检查。"
  - *Score*: 3
    评分：3
  - *Reasoning*: The response is correct but lacks detailed explanations and does not ask about relevant symptoms or medical history. However, it at least suggests further medical evaluation.
    理由：回复正确但缺乏详细解释，没有询问患者是否有心脏病史或其他相关症状，但至少建议了进一步检查。
- 4-Point Example:
  4分示例
  - *Patient*: "I've been feeling constantly fatigued, even after getting enough sleep."
    患者："我最近总是感到疲劳，即使睡眠充足也感觉累。"
  - *Online Doctor's Response*: "Persistent fatigue could be a sign of anemia or hypothyroidism. Have you noticed pale skin or changes in heart rate? I recommend a complete blood count and thyroid function tests."
    在线医生回复："持续的疲劳可能是贫血或甲状腺功能减退的迹象。你有没有注意到皮肤苍白或心率变化？建议你做血常规和甲状腺功能测试。"
  - *Score*: 4
    评分：4
  - *Reasoning*: The response is accurate, offers advice, and asks relevant follow-up questions. The tone is proactive, though it does not provide specific over-the-counter treatment options or further diagnostic guidance.
    理由：回复准确，提供了一些建议，并询问了相关症状，态度积极，但没有提供具体的非处方药名称或进一步的诊断建议。
- 5-Point Example:
  5分示例
  - *Patient*: "I recently noticed blood in my stool, and I'm really worried."
    患者："我最近发现我的大便中带血，我很担心。"
  - *Online Doctor's Response*: "Blood in stool could be due to hemorrhoids, but it might also indicate more serious conditions such as colon polyps or cancer. Do you have abdominal pain, weight loss, or changes in bowel habits? I strongly recommend scheduling a colonoscopy as soon as possible. In the meantime, I can provide guidance on how to prepare for the procedure."
    在线医生回复："大便带血可能是痔疮，也可能是更严重的问题，如结肠息肉或癌症。你是否有腹痛、体重下降或大便习惯改变？我建议你尽快预约结肠镜检查，并在等待期间注意观察大便的任何变化。同时，我会为你提供一些关于如何准备结肠镜检查的信息。"
  - *Score*: 5
    评分：5
  - *Reasoning*: The response is thorough, professional, and considers multiple potential causes. It asks relevant follow-up questions, provides a clear action plan, and reassures the patient with expert guidance.
    理由：回复非常详细，提供了专业的建议，询问了相关症状，展现了高水平的专业知识和对患者情况的深刻理解，态度积极，能够给予患者信心和安慰。

Output Format

输出格式

Please print the evaluation score following the format below, where x = {1, 2, 3, 4, 5}:

请按照以上要求打印评分，你的答案格式如下，其中 x={1, 2, 3, 4, 5}:

Score: x
评分：x

SpecialtyScribe: Enhancing SOAP note Scribing for Medical Specialties using LLM's

Sagar Goyal* DeepScribe Inc. sagar@deepscribe.tech

Eti Rastogi*† DeepScribe Inc. eti_rastogi@yahoo.com

Fen Zhao DeepScribe Inc. fen@deepscribe.tech

Dong Yuan† DeepScribe Inc. doffery20@gmail.com

Andrew Beinstein DeepScribe Inc. andrew.beinstein@deepscribe.tech

Abstract

The healthcare industry has accumulated vast amounts of clinical data, much of which has traditionally been unstructured, including medical records, clinical data, patient communications, and visit notes. Clinician-patient conversations form a crucial part of medical records, with the resulting medical note serving as the ground truth for future interactions and treatment plans. Generating concise and accurate clinical SOAP (Vivek Podder, 2022) notes is critical for quality patient care and is especially challenging in specialty care, where relevance, clarity, and adherence to clinician preferences are paramount. These requirements make general-purpose LLMs unsuitable for producing high-quality specialty notes. While recent LLMs like GPT-4 and Sonnet 3.5 have shown promise, their high cost, size, latency, and privacy issues remain barriers for many healthcare providers.

We introduce SpecialtyScribe, a modular pipeline for generating specialty-specific medical notes. It features three components: an Information Extractor to capture relevant data, a Context Retriever to verify and augment content from transcripts, and a Note Writer to produce high quality notes. Our framework and inhouse models outperform similarly sized open-source models by over 12% on ROUGE metrics. Additionally, these models match top closed-source LLMs' performance while being under 1% of their size. We specifically evaluate our framework for oncology, with the potential for adaptation to other specialties.

1 Introduction

The healthcare industry relies on storing, processing, and referencing large amounts of clinical and research data, such as patient records, conversations, treatment histories, and medical research. Most of this data is unstructured and language-based, making it challenging to extract relevant information. Traditional NLP methods, and more recently Large Language Models (LLMs), have enabled efficient analysis to improve diagnoses, personalized treatments, and health outcomes. With increasing digitization, medical records are now maintained electronically as electronic health records (EHRs), with tools to add structure to notes. A medical visit note, the doctor's concise summary of medically relevant information, is critical for long-term reference and guiding future interactions.

Generating accurate medical notes from clinician-patient conversations is crucial for high-quality care. These notes reduce the administrative burden, enhance record accuracy, and ensure information is accessible for decision-making (Berg, 2023). However, generating high-quality notes in specialized fields like oncology is challenging due to high requirements for relevance, brevity, specificity, and clarity. Before LLMs, models like T5 or BART fine-tuned for note generation faced issues like nonfactual content (Chelli et al., 2024). Although newer LLMs (e.g., Opus, Sonnet, GPT-4) have potential, they are costly and pose privacy concerns for many healthcare facilities. Fine-tuning public LLMs (Goyal et al., 2024; Yuan et al., 2024) has been explored to improve general medical note generation.

A significant challenge in using generative models like LLMs is hallucination: "generated content that is nonsensical or unfaithful to the provided source content" (Ji et al., 2023). Inaccurate information in medical notes can severely impact quality and reliability. Oncology requires specific and concise note-taking focused on primary cancer diagnoses. Colorectal surgeons, for example, prioritize cancer-related treatments, with general symptoms included only if relevant to the treatment plan. Thus, oncology notes must be selective,

*These authors contributed equally to this work.

†Work done while at DeepScribe.

Proceedings of the Second Workshop on Patient-Oriented Language Processing (CL4Health), pages 34–45
May 4, 2025 ©2025 Association for Computational Linguistics

emphasizing critical information to support cancer care.

We address these challenges by focusing on key aspects of oncology note generation:

- *Completeness*: covering all essential information
- *Conciseness*: avoiding irrelevant details
- *Writing Quality*: ensuring readability, clarity and medical language flow
- *Organization*: categorizing information correctly in the SOAP note

Our approach simplifies note creation through three key modules. The Information Extraction module captures oncology-specific details. The Context Retriever gathers additional context, verifies accuracy, and reduces hallucinations. The Summarizer generates a medical note, ensuring precision and reliability.

Our contributions include:

- A unique three-step approach with an Information Extractor, Context Retriever, and Summarizer to generate high-quality specialty notes.
- Fine-tuned LLM-based models to extract key medical concepts and also write the final note. These models outperform similar sized open-source models by more than 100% and match closed source models while being less than 1% the size of them
- An embedding-based verification and augmentation method to minimize hallucinations and improve recall.
- Demonstration of our framework's effectiveness in clinical settings, matching the performance of top LLMs.

2 Related Work

Medical Note Generation. Generating high-quality medical notes from doctor-patient conversations is a challenging task. Prior to the advent of large language models (LLMs), previous approaches attempted to address this problem by breaking it into multiple stages (Krishna et al., 2020)—first identifying key transcription snippets, grouping them, and then summarizing—or by chunking the transcription (Zhang et al., 2021) into smaller pieces. However, these models failed to achieve real-world usable quality.

With the emergence of LLMs, recent works (Van Veen et al., 2023; Biswas and Talukdar, 2024; Goyal et al., 2024) have focused on leveraging or prompting powerful private LLMs, such as GPT-4 and MedPaLM, to enhance medical note generation. These models have a better understanding of language and can produce more readable text. However, reliance on private vendors raises concerns about data privacy and incurs high costs.

This has driven further research (Yuan et al., 2024; Kerner, 2024) into developing specialized medical LLMs that are better equipped to understand clinical texts and generate quality notes for general scenarios. Nonetheless, in oncology, the focus of medical note generation differs, and none of the existing approaches can be directly applied to oncology data without significant adaptation.

Information Extraction. To extract information from transcription text data, Named Entity Recognition (NER) or similar sequence tagging methods are often used to identify and extract key entities and information. Models such as BioBERT (Lee et al., 2020), MedBERT (Rasmy et al., 2021), and ClinicalBERT (Huang et al., 2019) have proven effective in this context. When combined with techniques for extracting entity relationships (Lv et al., 2016), events, or temporal information (Styler IV et al., 2014), these models can provide a comprehensive understanding of medical information from transcriptions. Recently, the use of large language models (LLMs) like MedPaLM (Singhal et al., 2023), PMC-LLaMA (Wu et al., 2024), or MEDITRON (Chen et al., 2023b) has made it more feasible to extract key information from transcriptions through prompting. However, these LLMs are still limited by their capabilities and may not always capture information accurately and comprehensively.

Summarization. Existing summarization approaches often focus on general abstractive summarization (Gupta and Gupta, 2019; Basyal and Sanghvi, 2023), or domain-specific tasks like news summarization (Zhang et al., 2024). However, generating medical notes requires more than just summarization; it demands attention to medical details and selective extraction of key information specific to different specialties.

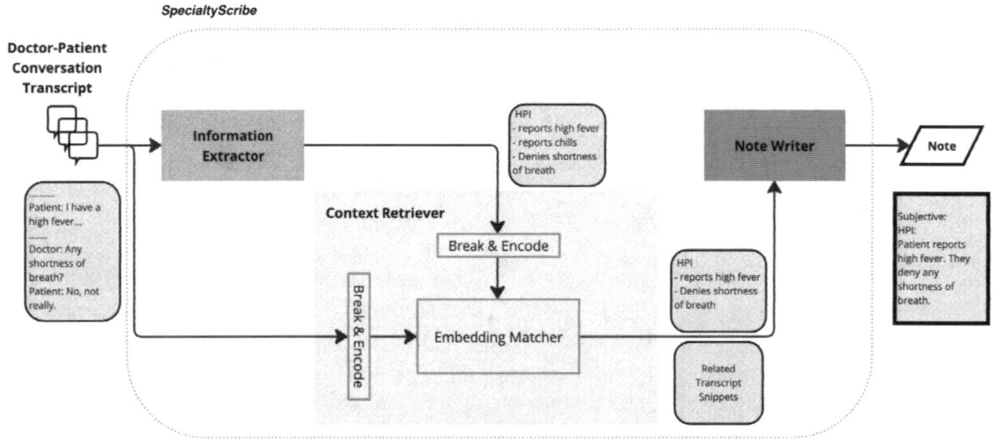

Figure 1: SpecialtyScribe Framework for the HPI section of a medical note from a doctor-patient conversation transcript

3 SpecialtyScribe

SpecialtyScribe consists of three primary modules: Information Extractor, Context Retriever, and Note Writer. Figure 1 illustrates the end-to-end functioning of the SpecialtyScribe framework using a basic example.

Information Extractor Module: This module takes the transcription as input and extracts specialty-specific (oncology) medically relevant information.

Context Retriever Module: This module generates additional transcript context to augment the extracted information and mitigates hallucinations by verifying the extracted information against the transcript. It takes the original transcript and the output of the Information Extractor Module as input. Transcript snippets are selected by splitting the transcript into sentence chunks and comparing the embeddings of the extracted information with those of the snippets, and selecting the top-k snippets to enhance the Note Writer model's context. We also use a hallucination detection algorithm to further filter the extracted information

Note Writer Module: This module generates the final medical note using the outputs of the Context Retriever Module, the extracted information (now filtered) and relevant transcript snippets. Since each section of SOAP note can have multiple subsections, (e.g. HPI, Chief Complaint, Medications etc.). This model is trained to generate subsection notes that combine to create the final note. It can also ignore irrelevant information that is part of the context.

3.1 Information Extractor

Our challenge involved working with a single, long transcript. Although newer LLMs can process longer texts (up to 32k tokens or more), they still face issues such as significant performance degradation depending on the relevant position of the information in the prompt, as discussed in (Liu et al., 2023). Traditional segmentation methods failed, as the model lacked full context and produced contradictory results. Additionally, we required a prompt-based extraction system capable of adapting to new instructions to support customization requests by doctors. To address these issues, we reformulated information extraction as an Orca-style instruction task (Mukherjee et al., 2023). Here, the model's objective was to follow specific rules and extract information from given snippets. This approach was developed based on (Yuan et al., 2024), which describes the creation of a medical LLM that understands the nuances of spoken medical language and the structure of medical notes.

Training Data Generation: We began by breaking oncology notes and categorizing information into sub-sections, such as Cancer Procedures, Cancer Tests, Cancer Symptoms, and Current Symptoms. For each sub-section, we crafted specific instructions. See Appendix-B for more details.

Protecting Data and Controlling Costs: We robustly de-identified any PHI(Protexted Health Information) and PII (Personally Identifiable Information) as defined by HIPAA and US government respectively in the transcripts and notes by adapting the Microsoft Presidio library for our specific use case. This is discussed in more detail in Section 6. We incurred a one-time cost for preparing our training data by using GPT-4-32k. However, this cost was minimal compared to what would be required to serve these models in production at scale. We used GPT-4-32k to process 7,000 doctor-patient conversations, each ranging from 5 to 60 minutes with an average duration of 20 minutes, to create the OncNoteGen Dataset. This resulted in approximately 68,000 samples with an average context length of 7,000 tokens. To mitigate overfitting in information extraction tasks, we used two stages of tuning. First, we warmed the model with general instructions, including around 100,000 examples sampled from MedMCQA (Pal et al., 2022), PubMedQA (Jin et al., 2019), and general instruction datasets such as Orca (Mitra et al., 2023) and MetaMath (Yu et al., 2024). Second, we trained the model with our proprietary 68,000-sample oncology note data—OncNoteGen.

Following initial fine-tuning, we observed that the model struggled to distinguish between past, present, and future tenses, especially when identifying medications and doctor's orders. This issue appeared to be inherited from the GPT-4-32k model used to build the training dataset. To address this, we introduced an additional 3,000-4,000 QA-based instructions specifically designed to help the model understand these tense distinctions. An example prompt for this task is provided in Appendix-C.

3.2 Context Retriever

We developed an algorithm to identify the context from the transcript for the content generated by the information extractor. We decomposed the extracted information into pieces (e.g. by bullets generated from the extractor), and then used their embeddings to encode each piece of information. Similarly, we indexed the transcript, by chunking it into groups of varied sentence counts e.g. 1, 2, 5 and calculating their embeddings. Then we used embedding matching to find the transcript context for each piece of extracted information. We utilized the *all-mpnet-base-v2* model (Reimers and Gurevych, 2019) for generating embeddings and employed the *similarity_search_with_relevance_scores* function from Meta's FAISS library (Douze et al., 2024) to conduct embedding similarity searches. As the transcripts are divided into chunks by varying sentence numbers, it's possible to have duplicate sentences in the matched snippets. To address this, we removed duplicate sentences and arranged the sentences in the snippets in their original chronological order.

Hallucination Mitigation: In our framework, hallucinations can originate from two major sources. First, the Information Extractor can output some data which has no grounding in the transcript or the prompt and second, the example used in the few-shot prompt can propagate into or influence the output. To address the first kind, the Context Retriever first filters out the extracted content that does not have any transcript context support retrieved as explained in Algorithm-1 (see Appendix A for step by step explanation)

3.3 Note Writer

Final Note Generation: We trained the Note Writer model to generate notes based on the filtered extracted content and the corresponding contextual transcript. This model was trained on a diverse set of 1,000 human-expert-annotated notes. The experts annotated the data in two stages: first, they identified the relevant transcript snippets for each note subcategory; then, they combined these snippets to create a medically accurate subsection of the note. Since, each note was divided into its constituent subsections (e.g., Subjective: Labs, Plan: Follow-Ups), we end up with an average of 10,000 data points in the training set. We deliberately train it on a diverse medical note dataset rather than oncology specific dataset as we intend to use this model across multiple specialties. While it is possible to train the information extractor to also do the note writing to reduce inference burden in real-world applications, we found that with the proposed framework, training them separately provided better performance and greater flexibility for use in other specialties.

We also developed a basic prompt that instructs the model to produce the note for each corresponding subsection. During training, the model learnt to create subsections of a note based on the retrieved relevant data, which were eventually combined into a complete note. This approach significantly reduced our context length requirements. The model was trained in a LoRA (Low-Rank Adaptation) setting, which made the training process fast, cost-effective, and scalable, with minimal impact on performance.

Algorithm 1 Information Filter

Input:
$I = \{i_1, i_2, \ldots, i_n\}$: Retrieved information set
T: Transcript
θ: Lower Bound Confidence
α: Similarity Confidence
E_p: Embeddings for examples from prompt
$E_T = ExtractEmbeddings(T)$
Output: $I_{included}$

Initialize included information $I_{included} = []$
for all information $i \in I$ **do**
  if i *in* T **then**
    $I_{included}.append(i)$
  else
    $E_i = ExtractEmbeddings(i)$
    Score = $EmbedMatch(E_i, E_T)$
    if Score $\geq \theta$ **then**
      $I_{included}.append(i)$
    end if
  end if
end for

for all $i_{incl} \in I_{included}$ **do**
  $E_i = ExtractEmbeddings(i_{incl})$
  PromptScore = $EmbedMatch(E_i, E_p)$
  TranscriptScore = $EmbedMatch(E_i, E_T)$
  if $PromptScore \geq \alpha \geq TranscriptScore$ **then**
    $I_{included}.remove(i_{incl})$
  end if
end for
return $I_{included}$

4 Experiment

4.1 Setup

Information Extraction: Consistent with the methodology described in (Yuan et al., 2024), our training utilized the pretrained version of Mistral-7B model. The learning rate was set at 2e-5 with cosine decay to 1e-5, and batch sizes were maintained at 128. Positional interpolation, referenced in (Chen et al., 2023a), addressed long-context management. Training occurred over 11 hours on 32 NVIDIA A100 GPUs distributed across four machines (8 GPUs per machine). Training perplexity and validation Rouge F1 scores for the OncNoteGen Dataset are shown in Figures 2, and 3 respectively.

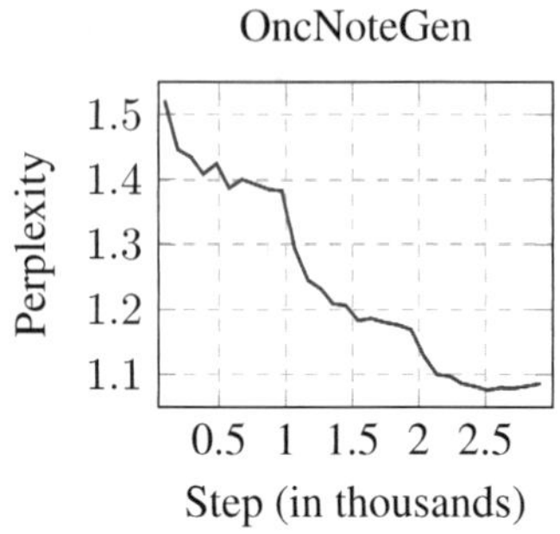

Figure 2: Training perplexity on OncNoteGen Dataset

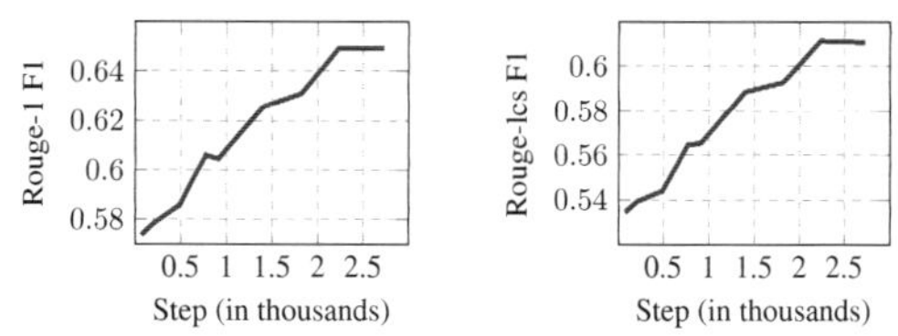

(a) Rouge F1 (b) Rouge-lcs F1

Figure 3: Validation Rouge-1 F1 and Rouge-lcs F1 scores on OncNoteGen Dataset

Note Writer: We again utilized the pretrained version of Mistral-7B model described in (Yuan et al., 2024), as our base model. The model underwent training for two epochs with a batch size of 8. To enhance memory and cost efficiency during this process, we adjusted the Low-Rank Adaptation (Lora) rank to 32. Our computational resources included 8 NVIDIA RTX A6000 GPUs, each equipped with 48GB of memory, allowing for substantial parallel processing and data handling capabilities. During training sessions, the average GPU utilization was maintained at 85%, indicating efficient usage of hardware resources. Additionally, we integrated the FlashAttention 2 mechanism and utilized the DeepSpeed Zero 3 optimization framework to streamline our training process. The learning rate was set at 2e-5 with cosine decay to 1e-5.

Model	Missed	Redundant	Misclassified
Opus	0.37	0.11	0.10
Sonnet-3.5	**0.31**	**0.08**	0.05
GPT-4-32k	0.40	**0.08**	0.05
mistralai/Mistral-7B-Instruct-v0.2	0.46	0.18	0.10
meta-llama/Meta-Llama-3-8B-Instruct	0.45	0.28	0.06
BioMistral/BioMistral-7B	0.53	0.51	**0.03**
SpecialtyScribe (ours)	**0.37**	**0.08**	**0.05**

Table 1: Results on Oncology Entity Identification Task indicating average Missed, Redundant, and Misclassified entities (lower is better)

Model	Aci-bench (subTask B)		OncNoteGen		
	ROUGE_L	BLEU	ROUGE_L	BLEU	Human(4)
Opus	0.21	0.09	0.27	0.15	2.44
Sonnet-3.5	0.21	0.10	0.26	0.14	2.78
GPT-4o	0.20	0.09	0.29	0.17	2.95
mistralai/Mistral-7B-Instruct-v0.2	0.13	0.05	0.19	0.10	2.69
meta-llama/Meta-Llama-3-8B-Instruct	0.19	0.09	0.25	0.15	2.53
SpecialtyScribe (Note Writer)	**0.24**	**0.12**	**0.31**	**0.21**	**3.14**

Table 2: Results on Note Writing Quality Task (higher is better)

4.2 Evaluation

We performed a comprehensive evaluation of leading open-source and proprietary models to assess the effectiveness of our Information Extraction (IE) model as well as the note-generation component of the Note Writing module. We selected high-performing models, including closed-source SoTA ones like Opus, Sonnet-3.5 and GPT-4-32k, alongside prominent open-source models with medical and general applications.

Datasets: We use two datasets for our evaluation.
1. Aci-bench (subTask B) (wai Yim et al., 2023): This is a public dataset designed for benchmarking automatic medical visit note generation. From this we take 39 different medical visits for our test set.
2. OncNoteGen Test: We choose a set of 21 oncology transcripts from OncNoteGen dataset such that it ensures coverage across criteria such as visit type (new vs. follow-up), length (long vs. short), and style (dictation-heavy vs. conversational). This is our proprietary dataset and is not available on the internet. On this particular dataset we also perform human expert based evaluation.

Human Scoring: To facilitate a rigorous assessment, human experts prepare rubrics which represent the gold-standard of the medical (oncology specific) entities (key phrases) which should be captured along with their respective sub-categories. These experts also create the gold-standard final notes designed to mirror the expectations of healthcare providers accurately.

Potential Leakage into Test Data: We recognise that it is possible that the Aci-bench data could have been present in the training sets of all the models that we compare against and also our base model - Mistral 7B. Even though we feel it is more likely to be present in the closed source models as compared to the smaller open-source models there is no way for us to know. In this framework we are guaranteed that the OncNoteGen Test Dataset is completely blind to the model by the virtue of it being entirely proprietary.

4.2.1 Information Extraction

Setup: We evaluated three tasks within the Oncology Entity Identification Task on the OncNoteGen Test dataset:

- **Missing Information**: We compared the generated note to the gold-standard note, assessing any missed phrases or key information, crucial for ensuring note coverage.
- **Redundant Information**: We identified redundant details in the generated note that were absent from the gold-standard, including "hallucinations" or unsubstantiated entities from transcripts, to maintain note conciseness and accuracy.
- **Misclassification**: We examined whether correctly identified entities were properly categorized, ensuring structured and well-organized notes.

Results and Analysis: Table-1 demonstrates that our domain-specific fine-tuning outperformed leading models like GPT-4-32k, particularly in reducing Missing Information, and was competitive in other tasks. Sonnet-3.5's improved performance highlights the value of leveraging recent datasets and better instructional comprehension, suggesting future opportunities. Our experts noted challenges like separating labs, biopsies, and imaging categories in the note, indicating areas for further tuning. Opus and Sonnet models experienced example leakage, reducing robustness, while models like Mistral, Llama, and BioMistral generated excessive redundant entities, impacting precision. Despite BioMistral's misleading high score in misclassification due to entity repetition, our model outshone the Mistral 7B Instruct base model, underscoring the benefits of specialty fine-tuning.

4.2.2 Note Writing Quality

Setup: We froze all SpecialtyScribe components, using our Information Extractor, and replaced the Note Writer with different LLMs, ensuring consistent input. Evaluations were conducted on both datasets described earlier.

Metrics: We used reference-based metrics like BLEU and ROUGE, which are common for summarization but have limitations in correlating with human judgment on creative tasks. Thus, human experts also assessed notes based on Clarity, Grammar, Professionalism, and Coherence.

Human Evaluation Methodology: Experts rated each note across the four parameters mentioned and used a 0–5 Likert Scale with scores normalized between 0 and 1. The final results were the sum of score across the 4 categories and reported for the OncNoteGen dataset.

Model Choice: Due to cost, we used GPT-4o instead of GPT-4-32k. Its claimed superiority makes it a strong benchmark. BioMistral was excluded for failing to follow output format instructions.

Results and Analysis: Table-2 indicates closer scores on Aci-bench compared to OncNoteGen. Our model surpassed both open and closed models, partly due to its understanding of the input style, showcasing the benefit of a custom-trained model. The higher performance gap on OncNoteGen highlights the limitations of generic models for specialized writing tasks. Notably, OncNoteGen's average scores were higher, attributed to prompts designed for a data distribution similar to that dataset.

4.2.3 Medical Note Generation

Setup To assess the overall impact of using SpecialtyScribe to generate medical notes, we compared the notes generated by various LLM's taking in the entire transcript with our framework as outlined in Section-3. We use the same metrics as defined in the previous task, except for human experts which now evaluate the note on multiple aspects.

Human Evaluation Methodology: The experts were asked to score the notes based on the following 4 verticals - *Writing Quality* (as explained in above task). *Clinical Accuracy* to determine how accurately the note reflects the original information from the medical encounter, including correct documentation of terms, findings, diagnoses, and treatment plans. *Completeness* to evaluate whether the note contains all necessary and relevant medical information without leaving any gaps in the patient's story or care and *Organization* to check the structure of the note, including accurate classification into medical sections. We follow a similar process as for Note Writer, where the experts are asked to give a score on the Likert scale between 0 to 5, which is then divided by 5 to get a number between 0 to 1 for each vertical. The final reported score is the sum of the scores for the 4 catergories averaged across the test set. We do this only for the OncNoteGen dataset.

Results and Analysis As indicated in Table-3, similar to values for the note quality evaluation task we see the model scores on Aci-bench dataset are not very different between the state of the art LLMs and our model. The scores on these metrics are also generally low as n-gram matching may simply require "heart murmur", but our prompts are structured to prompt the model to deliver full sentences like "Patient presents today for a consultation on heart murmurs". On OncNoteGen dataset, we can clearly see the superiority of our approach over the latest open source models. We perform on par with the latest models from Anthropic, falling slightly short of OpenAI's GPT-4o. Our human experts reported that our framework performed best in Writing Quality and Organization of the note. Even though Opus and GPT-4o models had the best coverage, they really struggled with note organization.

4.2.4 Ablation

To further substantiate the importance of every component in our framework, we conducted the

Model	Aci-bench (subTask B)		OncNoteGen		
	ROUGE_L	BLEU	ROUGE_L	BLEU	Human(4)
Opus	0.21	0.09	0.24	0.12	2.97
Sonnet-3.5	0.21	0.10	0.24	0.13	2.94
GPT-4o	0.18	0.07	0.21	0.10	**3.28**
mistralai/Mistral-7B-Instruct-v0.2	0.12	0.04	0.16	0.07	2.77
meta-llama/Meta-Llama-3-8B-Instruct	0.16	0.07	0.18	0.08	2.65
SpecialtyScribe (ours)	**0.24**	**0.12**	**0.31**	**0.21**	**3.17**
(w/o Context Retriever)	0.23	0.09	0.30	0.19	3.07
(w/o IE and Context Retriever)	0.24	0.11	0.29	0.18	2.51

Table 3: Results on Medical Note Generation Task (higher is better)

medical note generation experiment using two variations of the system. The first version removed the Context Retriever module, leaving the Note Writer model to rely solely on the Information Extractor model's output. In the second version, we eliminated both the Information Extraction and the Context Retriever modules, resulting in the Note Writer directly generating the end notes from the original input transcript. Table-3 clearly illustrates how each module of SpecialtyScribe framework is crucial for achieving optimal performance.

5 Conclusion

In this paper, we detail our efforts in creating a framework to generate medical specialty notes that can be adapted across multiple specialties. We train an Information Extraction (IE) model to extract medically relevant content from oncology-based doctor-patient conversations, develop a hallucination detection mechanism, and train a Note-Writer module to produce clinician-approved medical notes. Through rigorous evaluation, our findings reveal that our models and pipeline not only outperform the leading medical and general open-source models in this domain but also parallel the performance of the foremost proprietary models available. The results further demonstrate that decomposing the note generation task into smaller, manageable parts enhances both the accuracy and comprehensiveness of the medical notes produced. This approach ensures a more precise and reliable documentation system, which could significantly improve diagnostic and treatment practices in specialized medical care. Furthermore, our approach is cost-effective, achieving comparable performance to the most expensive models, such as Opus and GPT-4-32K, with a significantly smaller model.

Our work presents a framework that can serve as a foundation for further research to improve the automated medical note creation process, especially for complex medical specialties, potentially reducing clinician workloads.

6 Ethical Considerations

In compliance with HIPAA regulations, we have established Business Associate Agreements (BAAs) with OpenAI and Anthropic, the parent company of the Opus and Sonnet-3.5 models, to ensure the protection and confidentiality of sensitive data. This agreement guarantees that the data provided is neither leaked nor used for model training purposes. We thoroughly de-identified all personal health information (PHI) from our datasets before any processing or analysis. This was achieved by substituting PHI with non-identifiable entities using Named Entity Recognition (NER) techniques. Furthermore, the use of the SpecialtyScribe tool is strictly confined to internal operations for generating medical notes. To uphold ethical standards, we conduct regular audits of all input prompts to prevent any potential unethical usage.

7 Limitations

Future work should aim to construct and train a specialized embedding model to improve the detection and elimination of data hallucinations, thereby enhancing system accuracy and dependability. This paper primarily examines the framework in one specialty, yet there is ample opportunity to extend this research to include additional specialties, which would enhance the utility of the findings and the model's robustness across various fields. There is also potential for further advancements in both IE and summarizer models. Moreover, it's important to acknowledge that open-source datasets may not always mirror real-world complexities, underlining the need for publicly available datasets that can drive progress in this field.

8 Business Considerations

The scope of this work has been limited to protect the company's intellectual property (IP) and represents research-specific efforts. It does not directly reflect the exact models, architecture, or methods used in the company's production systems.

References

Lochan Basyal and Mihir Sanghvi. 2023. Text summarization using large language models: a comparative study of mpt-7b-instruct, falcon-7b-instruct, and openai chat-gpt models. *arXiv preprint arXiv:2310.10449*.

Sara Berg. 2023. 3 ways to begin to reduce clinical documentation by 75% by 2025. American Medical Association.

Anjanava Biswas and Wrick Talukdar. 2024. Intelligent clinical documentation: Harnessing generative ai for patient-centric clinical note generation. *arXiv preprint arXiv:2405.18346*.

Mikaël Chelli, Jules Descamps, Vincent Lavoué, Christophe Trojani, Michel Azar, Marcel Deckert, Jean-Luc Raynier, Gilles Clowez, Pascal Boileau, and Caroline Ruetsch-Chelli. 2024. Hallucination rates and reference accuracy of chatgpt and bard for systematic reviews: Comparative analysis. *Journal of Medical Internet Research*, 26:e53164.

Shouyuan Chen, Sherman Wong, Liangjian Chen, and Yuandong Tian. 2023a. Extending context window of large language models via positional interpolation. *Preprint*, arXiv:2306.15595.

Zeming Chen, Alejandro Hernández Cano, Angelika Romanou, Antoine Bonnet, Kyle Matoba, Francesco Salvi, Matteo Pagliardini, Simin Fan, Andreas Köpf, Amirkeivan Mohtashami, et al. 2023b. Meditron-70b: Scaling medical pretraining for large language models. *arXiv preprint arXiv:2311.16079*.

Matthijs Douze, Alexandr Guzhva, Chengqi Deng, Jeff Johnson, Gergely Szilvasy, Pierre-Emmanuel Mazaré, Maria Lomeli, Lucas Hosseini, and Hervé Jégou. 2024. The faiss library.

Sagar Goyal, Eti Rastogi, Sree Prasanna Rajagopal, Dong Yuan, Fen Zhao, Jai Chintagunta, Gautam Naik, and Jeff Ward. 2024. Healai: A healthcare llm for effective medical documentation. In *Proceedings of the 17th ACM International Conference on Web Search and Data Mining*, pages 1167–1168.

Som Gupta and Sanjai Kumar Gupta. 2019. Abstractive summarization: An overview of the state of the art. *Expert Systems with Applications*, 121:49–65.

Kexin Huang, Jaan Altosaar, and Rajesh Ranganath. 2019. Clinicalbert: Modeling clinical notes and predicting hospital readmission. *arXiv preprint arXiv:1904.05342*.

Ziwei Ji, Nayeon Lee, Rita Frieske, Tiezheng Yu, Dan Su, Yan Xu, Etsuko Ishii, Ye Jin Bang, Andrea Madotto, and Pascale Fung. 2023. Survey of hallucination in natural language generation. *ACM Computing Surveys*, 55(12):1–38.

Qiao Jin, Bhuwan Dhingra, Zhengping Liu, William W. Cohen, and Xinghua Lu. 2019. Pubmedqa: A dataset for biomedical research question answering. *Preprint*, arXiv:1909.06146.

Tobias Kerner. 2024. Domain-specific pretraining of language models: A comparative study in the medical field. *arXiv preprint arXiv:2407.14076*.

Kundan Krishna, Sopan Khosla, Jeffrey P Bigham, and Zachary C Lipton. 2020. Generating soap notes from doctor-patient conversations using modular summarization techniques. *arXiv preprint arXiv:2005.01795*.

Jinhyuk Lee, Wonjin Yoon, Sungdong Kim, Donghyeon Kim, Sunkyu Kim, Chan Ho So, and Jaewoo Kang. 2020. Biobert: a pre-trained biomedical language representation model for biomedical text mining. *Bioinformatics*, 36(4):1234–1240.

Nelson F. Liu, Kevin Lin, John Hewitt, Ashwin Paranjape, Michele Bevilacqua, Fabio Petroni, and Percy Liang. 2023. Lost in the middle: How language models use long contexts. *Preprint*, arXiv:2307.03172.

Xinbo Lv, Yi Guan, Jinfeng Yang, and Jiawei Wu. 2016. Clinical relation extraction with deep learning. *International Journal of Hybrid Information Technology*, 9(7):237–248.

Arindam Mitra, Luciano Del Corro, Shweti Mahajan, Andres Codas, Clarisse Simoes, Sahaj Agarwal, Xuxi Chen, Anastasia Razdaibiedina, Erik Jones, Kriti Aggarwal, Hamid Palangi, Guoqing Zheng, Corby Rosset, Hamed Khanpour, and Ahmed Awadallah. 2023. Orca 2: Teaching small language models how to reason. *Preprint*, arXiv:2311.11045.

Subhabrata Mukherjee, Arindam Mitra, Ganesh Jawahar, Sahaj Agarwal, Hamid Palangi, and Ahmed Awadallah. 2023. Orca: Progressive learning from complex explanation traces of gpt-4. *arXiv preprint arXiv:2306.02707*.

Ankit Pal, Logesh Kumar Umapathi, and Malaikannan Sankarasubbu. 2022. Medmcqa : A large-scale multi-subject multi-choice dataset for medical domain question answering. *Preprint*, arXiv:2203.14371.

Laila Rasmy, Yang Xiang, Ziqian Xie, Cui Tao, and Degui Zhi. 2021. Med-bert: pretrained contextualized embeddings on large-scale structured electronic health records for disease prediction. *NPJ digital medicine*, 4(1):86.

Nils Reimers and Iryna Gurevych. 2019. Sentence-bert: Sentence embeddings using siamese bert-networks. In *Proceedings of the 2019 Conference on Empirical Methods in Natural Language Processing*. Association for Computational Linguistics.

Karan Singhal, Shekoofeh Azizi, Tao Tu, S Sara Mahdavi, Jason Wei, Hyung Won Chung, Nathan Scales, Ajay Tanwani, Heather Cole-Lewis, Stephen Pfohl, et al. 2023. Large language models encode clinical knowledge. *Nature*, 620(7972):172–180.

William F Styler IV, Steven Bethard, Sean Finan, Martha Palmer, Sameer Pradhan, Piet C De Groen, Brad Erickson, Timothy Miller, Chen Lin, Guergana Savova, et al. 2014. Temporal annotation in the clinical domain. *Transactions of the association for computational linguistics*, 2:143–154.

Dave Van Veen, Cara Van Uden, Louis Blankemeier, Jean-Benoit Delbrouck, Asad Aali, Christian Bluethgen, Anuj Pareek, Malgorzata Polacin, Eduardo Pontes Reis, Anna Seehofnerova, et al. 2023. Clinical text summarization: adapting large language models can outperform human experts. *Research Square*.

Sassan Ghassemzadeh Vivek Podder, Valerie Lew. 2022. *SOAP Notes*. StatPearls Publishing, Treasure Island (FL).

Wen wai Yim, Yujuan Fu, Asma Ben Abacha, Neal Snider, Thomas Lin, and Meliha Yetisgen. 2023. Aci-bench: a novel ambient clinical intelligence dataset for benchmarking automatic visit note generation. *Preprint*, arXiv:2306.02022.

Chaoyi Wu, Weixiong Lin, Xiaoman Zhang, Ya Zhang, Weidi Xie, and Yanfeng Wang. 2024. Pmc-llama: toward building open-source language models for medicine. *Journal of the American Medical Informatics Association*, page ocae045.

Longhui Yu, Weisen Jiang, Han Shi, Jincheng Yu, Zhengying Liu, Yu Zhang, James T. Kwok, Zhenguo Li, Adrian Weller, and Weiyang Liu. 2024. Metamath: Bootstrap your own mathematical questions for large language models. *Preprint*, arXiv:2309.12284.

Dong Yuan, Eti Rastogi, Gautam Naik, Jai Chintagunta, Sree Prasanna Rajagopal, Fen Zhao, Sagar Goyal, and Jeff Ward. 2024. A continued pretrained llm approach for automatic medical note generation. *arXiv preprint arXiv:2403.09057*.

Longxiang Zhang, Renato Negrinho, Arindam Ghosh, Vasudevan Jagannathan, Hamid Reza Hassanzadeh, Thomas Schaaf, and Matthew R Gormley. 2021. Leveraging pretrained models for automatic summarization of doctor-patient conversations. *arXiv preprint arXiv:2109.12174*.

Tianyi Zhang, Faisal Ladhak, Esin Durmus, Percy Liang, Kathleen McKeown, and Tatsunori B Hashimoto. 2024. Benchmarking large language models for news summarization. *Transactions of the Association for Computational Linguistics*, 12:39–57.

A Detailed Implementation of Information Filtering algorithm

The Information Filter algorithm refines the output of the Information Extractor step (denoted as I) by returning a filtered subset that contains only information strongly aligned with the transcript. This process is crucial for mitigating hallucinations and ensuring the extracted information remains reliable.

We start with indexing the transcript by chunking it into variable-length sentence groups (e.g., 1, 2, 5 sentences) and computing their embeddings (E_T). Then, the extracted information (I) is decomposed into discrete items ($i_1, i_2, \ldots$) based on bullet points or new lines.

Step 1: Initial Matching Against Transcript For each decomposed item i, if it appears verbatim in the transcript, it is automatically included in the filtered set, denoted as $I_{included}$. However, if no exact match is found, the embeddings of the decomposed item are extracted, and a similarity score is computed against the transcript chunks. The most relevant transcript context is identified based on this score. To ensure reliability, any decomposed item with a similarity score below a predefined confidence threshold (θ) is filtered out. The threshold θ is domain-specific. In the medical field, it is kept low to ensure that any relevant information is not mistakenly discarded, even if it is phrased differently. This adjustment accounts for cases where the Information Extractor paraphrases content using medical terminology, such as converting "high blood pressure" to "hypertension."

Step 2: Secondary Filtering to Mitigate Hallucinations While a low threshold (θ) prevents the omission of important information, it may also allow irrelevant or hallucinated content to pass through. To further refine the selection, a second filtering step is applied. A similarity confidence score, denoted as α, is chosen empirically. Two embedding similarity scores are then computed. The PromptScore measures the similarity between the extracted information and the examples used in the prompt of the Information Extractor. The TranscriptScore measures the similarity between the extracted information and the input transcript. If the PromptScore exceeds α, while the TranscriptScore remains below α, the information is classified as a hallucination originating from the prompt and is removed. This step ensures that the extracted information is not overly influenced by the prompt examples and remains true to the original transcript. By systematically applying these steps, the Information Filter algorithm enhances the accuracy and reliability of extracted information, ensuring that medical notes are trustworthy, well-grounded in the original transcript, and free from hallucinations.

B Oncology Information Extraction Task Prompt

System
You are a highly trained and skilled AI medical doctor who specializes in writing a part of the Subjective section of a clinical SOAP (Subjective, Objective, Assessment, Plan) note. You only speak MARKDOWN.

User
<template>
{rules}
</template>

NOTE: If you are unsure or don't have enough information to provide a confident answer, do not create or imagine a response. Simply return "no information found". If a certain note template section lacks the necessary information within the transcript to be written, then leave that section blank.
<example>
Examples only for formatting reference.
For example: Let's say you want to write the sections CANCER PROCEDURES and CANCER SYMPTOMS from a given template. If no information is found related to CANCER PROCEDURES, the output should look like:

#CANCER PROCEDURES
##no information found
#CANCER SYMPTOMS
##<information here>
</example>

Using above template, example and guidelines, given the real transcript below, can you fill out the outline accurately and thoroughly? Return your answer as a string following the template. DO NOT return ANYTHING outside of the template.

Transcript:
{transcript}

C Additional Task Prompt

We utilized the GPT-4 model to generate question-answer pairs specific to certain sub-sections including 'Medications' and 'Plan-Orders', wherein the model initially encountered challenges. Beyond the generation tasks for general and respective sub-sections, we incorporated additional QA tasks that require short responses, with the aim to enhance the comprehension capabilities of the model

System
You are a medical assistant that can answer questions form a given context. In this task, you will be asked to answer a question from a given doctor patient transcript.
User
Transcript: {transcript}
Question: {question}
Return your response as a JSON in the following format:
{
"Answer": "....",
"Explanation": "...."
}

Explainability for NLP in Pharmacovigilance: A Study on Adverse Event Report Triage in Swedish

Luise Dürlich[1,2,4] Erik Bergman[1] Maria Larsson[1]
Hercules Dalianis[5] Seamus Doyle[1] Gabriel Westman[*1,3] Joakim Nivre[*2]
[1]Swedish Medical Products Agency, Sweden
[2]Department of Linguistics and Philology, Uppsala University, Sweden
[3]Department of Medical Sciences, Uppsala University, Sweden
[4]RISE Research Institutes of Sweden, Sweden
[5]Department of Computer and Systems Sciences, Stockholm University, Sweden
luise.durlich@lakemedelsverket.se

Abstract

In fields like healthcare and pharmacovigilance, explainability has been raised as one way of approaching regulatory compliance with machine learning and automation. This paper explores two feature attribution methods to explain predictions of four different classifiers trained to assess the seriousness of adverse event reports. On a global level, differences between models and how well important features for serious predictions align with regulatory criteria for what constitutes serious adverse reactions are analysed. In addition, explanations of reports with incorrect predictions are manually explored to find systematic features explaining the misclassification. We find that while all models seemingly learn the importance of relevant concepts for adverse event report triage, the priority of these concepts varies from model to model and between explanation methods, and the analysis of misclassified reports indicates that reporting style may affect prediction outcomes.

1 Introduction

Pharmacovigilance (PV) deals with the detection, assessment, understanding and prevention of adverse effects related to medical products (World Health Organization, 2002) and traditionally relies on experts processing adverse event reports (AER), assessing the strength of new adverse event signals and acting upon newfound insights through publications and new risk assessments. In recent years, a need for at least partial automation has been identified to deal with the ever increasing amount of new AERs (Bate and Hobbinger, 2021) and at times updated processing requirements, most notable during the recent COVID-19 pandemic.

With the introduction of automated methods into the PV pipeline, experts have encouraged employing interpretable or at least explainable systems to address safety concerns such as black swan events (Kjoersvik and Bate, 2022) and including explainability as a factor to assess the readiness of artificial intelligence (AI) for tasks in the context of PV (Ball and Dal Pan, 2022). At the same time, concerns have been raised about the effectiveness of existing explainability methods and the disconnect between expectations towards explanations of black-box models from an AI safety perspective and what common explainability approaches actually are able to achieve (Ghassemi et al., 2021).

In this study, we apply two feature attribution methods to several pre-trained language models, fine-tuned to triage AERs, to understand what characterises their prediction of specific classes and to address the following research questions:

1. How do explanations for different models fine-tuned for the same task differ?
2. Can we align important features with regulatory criteria for serious cases?
3. Are there systematic feature patterns that explain incorrect class predictions?

Our analysis suggests that relevant features relating to regulatory criteria and expert annotation practice are learned as indicators of serious events by all models. However, the relative importance between these features in the explanations vary from model to model. Beyond features directly associated with serious reports, we find evidence of model bias reflecting the reporting style by different reporter groups.

2 Background

Explanations for machine learning models and their predictions come in many different forms. In light of model development and the paradigm shift to large generative models, several works have explored using large language models (LLMs) to explain their own output (Kunz et al., 2022; Kunz and

[*]Equal contribution to this work as senior authors.

Proceedings of the Second Workshop on Patient-Oriented Language Processing (CL4Health), pages 46–68
May 4, 2025 ©2025 Association for Computational Linguistics

Kuhlmann, 2024; Turpin et al., 2023). However, these works also warn that while such explanations may seem plausible to humans, it is unclear how well they represent the real reason for a specific model prediction, and Turpin et al. (2023) find evidence that they may in fact systematically misrepresent the deciding factors in the decision process.

Traditionally, deep learning models are often explained with so called post-hoc methods that are applied after the model is trained for a particular task. Methods such as diagnostic classifiers (Hupkes et al., 2018) are popular to answer specific questions about the encoded knowledge in a specific layer of the model by using representations of the chosen layer as input to a simpler model to perform a relevant task. More recently, Bricken et al. (2023) proposed the use of sparse auto-encoders to extract interpretable monosemantic features from single layer transformers. Templeton et al. (2024) applied this technique to the intermediate layer of smaller LLMs.

Feature attribution methods, such as LIME (Ribeiro et al., 2016) and SHAP (Lundberg and Lee, 2017), instead attempt to explain model predictions by assigning some form of contribution to features in the input. These methods work by approximating the model to be explained on a given input using a more interpretable model, for example by perturbing the input in some way, observing the behaviour of the model to be explained, and explaining it with an explanation model trained to mimic that behaviour. Feature attribution methods can furthermore be model-agnostic, such as LIME and some versions of SHAP, or model-specific, such as gradient-based methods like DeepLift (Shrikumar et al., 2017) and Integrated Gradients (Sundararajan et al., 2017).

The feature attribution methods mentioned so far are typically applied to individual examples and thus primarily provide local explanations, but global explanations can be derived from local explanations by aggregating them over many inputs, e.g. using algorithms such as Submodular Pick LIME (Ribeiro et al., 2016) and Global Attribution Mapping (Ibrahim et al., 2019), or by simply averaging the observed attribution scores for each feature (Van Der Linden et al., 2019; Saynova et al., 2023).

Common goals for using explainability are model development, gaining trust, scientific insight and regulatory compliance (Hauben, 2022), but existing methods are criticised for suffering from interpretability gaps, failing to meet the expectations of stakeholders such as regulators and practitioners, and being prone to confirmation bias (Ghassemi et al., 2021). Moreover, Vilone and Longo (2021) note the absence of a common definition of explanations and lack of consensus on how to evaluate them with respect to reliability and validity. Further, while user-oriented explainability may be built with the intention of being simplified enough to be understandable, such explanations can be too far removed from the original model to faithfully represent it (Rudin, 2019).

Despite the concerns and criticisms toward post-hoc methods and feature attribution in particular, this type of explainability method is popular in natural language processing (NLP) research, where it has been used to achieve a variety of goals, such as providing insights into performance differences between different model architectures (Wang et al., 2022; Amponsah-Kaakyire et al., 2022), investigating potential weaknesses of explainability methods (Tang et al., 2022), interpreting aspects of the behaviour of pre-trained language models in specific NLP tasks (Nayak and Timmapathini, 2021; Stevens and Su, 2021), serving as reference explanations for investigating attention as an explanation method (Jain and Wallace, 2019), exploring descriptive features for distinct classes in domain-specific texts (Saynova et al., 2023), and user studies on computer-assisted coding tools (Dolk et al., 2022).

3 Method

Our experiments concern four binary classifiers fine-tuned on the same data for which we analyse post-hoc explanations derived with two types of feature attribution methods – Integrated Gradients (IG) (Sundararajan et al., 2017) and Expected Gradients (EG) (Erion et al., 2021). We restrict the study to these two gradient-based methods.

3.1 AER Triage

The classification task is that defined by Bergman et al. (2023): for AERs from both consumers and healthcare professionals, predict whether a report discusses a serious adverse reaction or not, based solely on free-text fields such as the adverse event terms listed in the form (e.g. headache, nausea, rash) and the description of adverse events in the report. An adverse reaction is considered serious if it results in death, is life-threatening, leads to hospitalisation or prolongs existing hospitalisation,

Dataset	Time period	Number of AERs			μ length
		S	NS	Total	
Training	2017 – 2020	4,450	7,538	11,988	$73.10_{\pm 70}$
Development	2017 – 2020	1,107	1,890	2,997	$70.30_{\pm 62}$
Test	2021 – 2021	1,170	2,273	3,443	$60.79_{\pm 68}$

Table 1: Overview of the three data sets used, with time periods, number of serious/non-serious (S/NS) reports and mean report length in whitespace-tokenised tokens.

Model	Abbreviation	Domain
KB-BERT	KBB	General
SweDeClin-BERT	SDCB	Clinical Text
AER-BERT	AERB	AER
GPT-SW3	GPT	General

Table 2: Selected models and their domains.

results in persistent or significant disability or incapacity or birth defects (ICH, 1994). When submitting an AER, reporters are asked to indicate these specific outcomes if they apply in a multiple-choice question. Replies to the question are among other things used to prioritise which reports get processed first by the case workers at the Swedish Medical Products Agency (MPA). However, the question is not always answered correctly given other context provided in the report, resulting in serious reports getting processed later than is desirable.

3.2 Data

The Swedish AERs that we base our training and explanation analysis on have been collected by the MPA and were annotated for seriousness by expert assessors as part of the agency's routine PV monitoring. We train the classifiers with the same training and development split as Bergman et al. (2023) and conduct a final evaluation of all four classifiers on the same prospective test set; see Table 1. Since we were able to obtain an improved version of the data used by Bergman et al. (2023), we conduct new hyperparameter experiments for all models described in the next section. Details on differences from the data used in (Bergman et al., 2023) and hyperparameter settings are in Appendix A. To remove numerical information related to identity, all reports were anonymised by replacing digits in the free-text description.

3.3 Models

We train four classifiers based on a selection of pre-trained transformer models for Swedish with various degrees of specialisation to the medical and

Model	Accuracy	Precision	Recall	Specificity	F_1
KBB	0.819	0.833	0.583	0.940	0.686
SDCB	0.813	0.891	0.512	0.967	0.650
AERB	0.830	0.845	0.612	0.943	0.710
GPT	0.822	0.788	0.653	0.909	0.714

Table 3: Classification results on the test set.

AER domain. The first three are BERT models: the cased versions of KB-BERT (KBB) (Malmsten et al., 2020); SweDeClin-BERT (SDCB), a continuation of KB-BERT with additional pretraining on a corpus of de-identified clinical text (Vakili et al., 2022);[1] and AER-BERT (AERB), a masked-language model based on a large BERT model[2] with continued pretraining on old AERs. AER-BERT was previously found to give the best performance on the triage task by Bergman et al. (2023), compared to LSTMs and XGBoost models. In addition, we consider a small transformer decoder in the 1.3B parameter model of the GPT-SW3 model suite (GPT) (Ekgren et al., 2022). See Table 2 for an overview of the models.

We fine-tune all four models for the triage task by adding a classification layer to the pooled output of the transformer models using the applicable ForSequenceClassification classes implemented in the HuggingFace transformers library. Table 3 shows the classification performance of the four models on the test set. Among typical metrics for classification problems such as precision, recall and F_1, we also consider specificity, the true negative rate, to assess how well the models discriminate non-serious reports. We observe GPT to outperform all other models in F_1-score followed closely by AERB, and SDCB to perform best in specificity.

3.4 Feature Attribution Methods

This study considers two model-specific feature attribution methods, IG and EG. Both methods base their attribution on the notion of a *baseline* or *reference*, typically defined as a neutral or uninformative input for the task the model was trained for.

Integrated Gradients (IG): IG attributes the model prediction by calculating the path integral over gradients on a straight-line path from an artificial baseline input representation to that of the real

[1]Further research involving SweDeClin-BERT, like the training and analysis in this study, has been approved by the Swedish Ethical Review Authority under permission number 2022-02389-02.

[2]AI-Nordics/bert-large-swedish-cased

input. IG satisfies a number of desirable axioms for explainability methods as defined by Sundararajan et al. (2017), in particular sensitivity, implementation invariance, completeness, linearity and symmetry preservation, described in Appendix B.

Expected Gradients (EG): EG is a method inspired by IG that samples multiple real examples for reference and computes feature importance as the average expected values of the gradients scaled to satisfy the completeness axiom (Erion et al., 2021). Being gradient-based and symmetric, EG also fulfills the axioms defined for IG.

3.5 Explanation Methodology

To obtain explanations, we use the IntegratedGradient and GradientShap classes as implemented by the captum library (Kokhlikyan et al., 2020) for IG and EG, encoding all reports and baselines prior to applying the feature attribution methods. We compute feature attributions over the full encoder (or decoder) block and the classfication layer. For IG we create a report specific baseline consisting of a sequence of all `[MASK]` tokens for BERT models and `<unk>` for GPT, of the same length as the real report and pass along the attention mask for the real report to predict whether report and baseline are serious.[3] Each report is explained with 100 approximation steps. For EG we pass the entire set of reports in the development data as references. This way, each report is explained with respect to the ensemble of all other reports.[4] Here, we pass an extra argument containing report-specific attention masks.

With our binary classification task, explanations for serious and non-serious outcomes are symmetric in that large positive values explaining a serious prediction correspond to large negative attributions when explaining the opposite prediction for the same report. For consistency, all attribution values discussed in the following are computed with respect to predicting the serious class.

In the following experiments, explanations are obtained for 2,997 reports in the development set. When computing explanations for the four models, the explanation methods return results on token-level, i.e. referring to subwords as defined by the respective tokenizer. These representations are too fine-grained and hard to interpret and do not allow for easy comparison between models. To achieve a more global insight and allow for a more direct comparison between models, we calculate attributions at word-level as the sum of the corresponding token-level attributions per word. This is motivated by the axiom of completeness (Sundararajan et al., 2017), according to which the sum of attributions for an input sequence should reflect the difference in model prediction for the real input sequence and the baseline.

When reconstructing the vocabulary, the different tokenizers used by the models result in some slight variations in the complete sets of reconstructed word types, with 17,594 words according to KBB and SDCB, 17,585 for AERB and 17,612 with GPT.

To address the first two research questions, we compute global explanations on the development set reports for each model and feature attribution method using the normalisation method in Van Der Linden et al. (2019) and Saynova et al. (2023), effectively calculating global explanations as the relative attribution score for each full word in the dataset.

3.6 Analysing Explanations

Using global explanations for each classifier and explanation method, we want to analyse the attributions for interesting groups of related terms. To that end, we define the overall *importance* of each group as the average attribution value per model, and adjust for variation within the groups by scaling with the unbiased sample standard deviation:[5]

$$importance_g = \frac{\mu_g}{1 + \sigma_g} \quad (1)$$

In this way, we can focus on groups that consistently show large positive attribution values. To obtain groupings of terms, we consider an unsupervised approach in the form of clustering as well as the following explicit resources:

- **MeSH:** Medical Subject Headings (Lipscomb, 2000) is an ontology for indexing biomedical information by the National Library of Medicine.
- **Filter terms:** Terms and word segments cre-

[3] A common baseline for IG in NLP is that of a zero vector (Sundararajan et al., 2017) or empty string (corresponding to all `[PAD]` tokens for transformer models), but we argue that the mask and unknown tokens are a better choice, because the chosen models were not trained to attend to padding tokens during neither fine-tuning nor pre-training.

[4] Due to the number of reports we consider the effect of explaining the report by itself to be negligible.

[5] In the following, this equation is referenced when used to avoid confusion with importance as a general concept.

ated and used by assessors at the MPA, in the absence of the triage model (see Appendix C.1).

- **Criteria grouping:** Based on the criteria for a serious adverse reaction (cf. Section 3.1), we select a set of terms using MeSH and Swedish MeSH,[6] grouping them into general terms and terms relating to specific concepts within the five criteria (see Appendix C.2).

4 Results

4.1 Model Differences on a Global Scale

To compare explanations for different models, we calculate Kendall's τ correlation between the global attributions for the shared vocabulary by all models as well as for the set of terms matching the filter terms. As a frame of reference for the fine-tuned models, we also compare each classifier with its newly initialised, but not yet fine-tuned counterpart, and label that the *control*.

Correlations of attributions on all shared terms at the top of Figure 1 are weakly positive among all fine-tuned models, with slightly stronger correlations between the encoder models as opposed to encoders and GPT for IG. Interestingly, IG attributions for the two models with domain-specific pretraining have a lower correlation with each other than with the general domain KBB, and SDCB's correlation with KBB is slightly lower than that of KBB and AERB. By comparison, correlations among EG explanations are much weaker, with the strongest signals between KBB and the domain-specific models. For both IG and EG, correlations with the corresponding control models are close to zero, as would be expected for explanations of models unfamiliar with the triage task.

This correlation approach includes many terms with attributions close to zero for which comparison or correlation is uninformative. To focus on more relevant terms, we select terms matching the filter terms and calculate the correlations on this subset. The results at the bottom of Figure 1 show stronger correlations for both IG and EG. For IG, the trends between models are similar to those for the shared vocabulary, with an increased similarity between GPT and AERB. The correlations for EG are weaker between GPT and the other fine-tuned models and slightly stronger between KBB and the domain-specific models. Comparing both methods, correlations between control models and fine-tuned models are relatively stable for EG in both the larger and the more specific sets of terms, while they are stronger for IG in the latter setting.

Based on the filter terms, we measure how highly the explainability methods score terms matching the filter, and the variance across models. Table 4 shows average attribution scores for three sets of terms: (1) words matching the filter, (2) words that do not match the filter, (3) all words in the dataset. Figure 6 in Appendix D visualises the distribution of scores in the first two sets for each model. All models trained for triage on average assign matched terms higher attribution scores than the ensemble of other terms. For the control models, all three sets have a similar average attribution score close to 0 for most models, suggesting no strong contribution to either the serious or the non-serious class for those terms. This indicates that all fine-tuned models learn to associate the filter terms with the positive class and that both explanation methods pick up on their importance.

Exploring more freely which concepts are important for a serious outcome with each model according to the explanations, we cluster terms with the largest attribution scores and hand-annotate the clusters. This resulted in 164 clusters for IG and 193 for EG, of which 134 had identical labels. We next consider how much of the clusters is covered by the 8,000 highest ranked terms and how *important* clusters are for each model as per Equation 1. Figures 2 and 7 show the twenty most important clusters to the average of all four models for IG and EG respectively. A two-dimensional visualisation of the full clustering reflecting cluster importance as explained by IG and EG can be found in Figures 13 and 14 in Appendix E, which also contains more details on the clustering procedure and coverage metric.

Considering explanations by IG, all classifiers note clusters relating to extreme situations (*suicide, ambulance, abortion, organ transplants*), organ-related issues, specific symptoms and health conditions (*depression, syncope, vision* and *breathing disorder, hypo-*,[7] *epilepsy, dementia*) as important. Importance by model varies somewhat, with *hallucination, breathing disorders* and *suicide* emerging as the most important clusters for KBB, while *ambulance* is less prominent. SDCB, in addition to *suicide* and *hallucination*, places more importance on

[6] https://mesh.kib.ki.se/

[7] Deficiencies denoted by terms with the prefix *hypo-*.

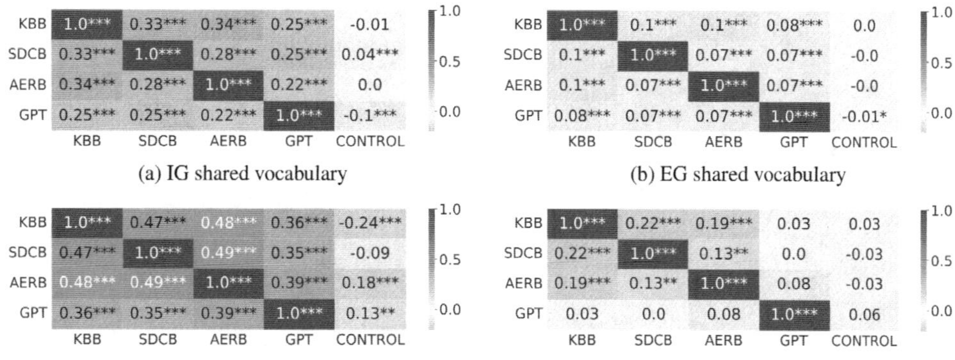

(a) IG shared vocabulary

(b) EG shared vocabulary

(c) IG filter only

(d) EG filter only

Figure 1: Kendall's τ correlations and their significance between models for shared vocabulary (a), (b), and filter terms (c), (d). The control row reports correlations, between each classifier and a corresponding untrained classifier.

(a) Fine-tuned models

	Model	In filter	Outside	All terms
IG	KBB	0.0348***	0.0008	0.0013
	SDCB	0.0634***	0.0095	0.0101
	AERB	0.0402***	0.0015	0.0020
	GPT	0.0699***	0.0103	0.0110
EG	KBB	0.0724***	0.0037	0.0046
	SDCB	0.0421***	0.0069	0.0073
	AERB	0.1000***	0.0062	0.0073
	GPT	0.0599***	0.0063	0.0069

(b) Control models

	Model	In filter	Outside	All terms
IG	KBB	-0.0044	-0.0032	-0.0032
	SDCB	0.0007	0.0001	0.0001
	AERB	0.0056***	0.0022	0.0023
	GPT	-0.0017	-0.0052	-0.0051
EG	KBB	-0.0009	-0.0004	-0.0004
	SDCB	-0.0032	0.0004	0.0003
	AERB	-0.0008	-0.0007	-0.0007
	GPT	0.0029	-0.0030	-0.0029

Table 4: Average attribution scores by explanation method for each of the four models. The scores are averaged for three sets of terms, those matching the filter terms, those not matching the filter terms and the report vocabulary as a whole. (a) shows results for the fine-tuned models and (b) shows results for the models prior to fine-tuning as a control. Significantly higher attribution scores of the filter terms compared those outside the filter are marked with * to *** to reflect the significance level of the Wilcoxon rank-sum test.

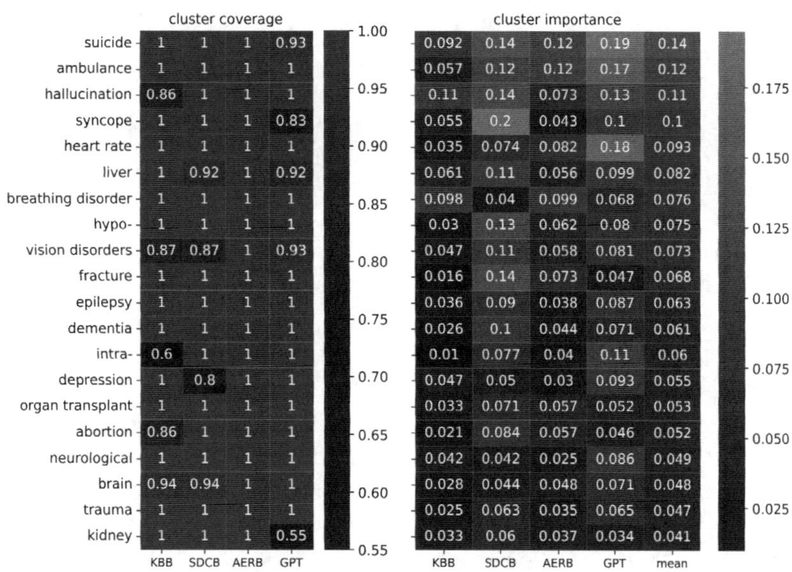

Figure 2: 20 highest ranked clusters by group importance (IG) and their coverage among the top 8,000 terms per model.

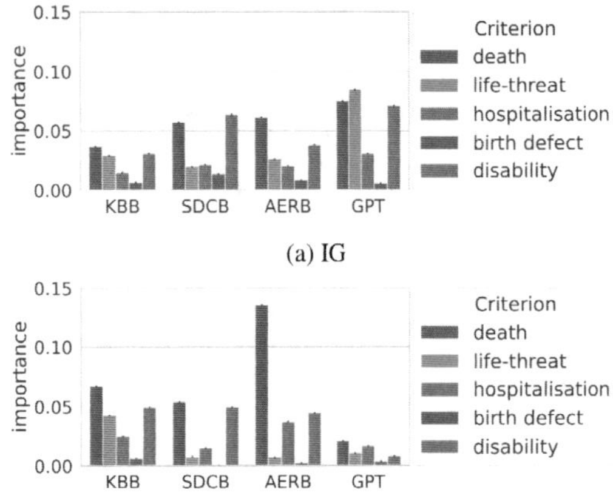

(a) IG

(b) EG

Figure 3: Group importance of different criteria for different classifiers and explanation methods.

the *syncope*, *fractures* and *hypo-* clusters. AERB is the only model with full coverage of all 20 clusters, but *hallucination* is less important, whereas *suicide*, *ambulance*, *breathing disorders* and *heart rate* are more important. Similarly, to GPT the most important clusters are *suicide*, *heart rate* and *ambulance*, but *hallucination* still ranks high.

An analysis of the EG explanations again reveals less overlap than IG among the most important clusters. However, we observe strong overlaps regarding cluster coverage among the top 3 clusters, those relating to symptoms as well as certain organ related issues. KBB is sensitive to specific events such as *suicide*, *childbirth*, *epilepsy*, but remains neutral on the *liver* and *abortion* clusters. SDCB only fully covers one cluster in the top 8,000 terms and along with *suicide* and *epilepsy* gives more importance to *liver*, *abortion*, *hallucination* and *hypo-*. For AERB, besides *suicide* and *liver*, *ambulance* emerges as most important and the *intra-* and *fainting* clusters receive more weight. Interestingly, among the domain-specific models, AERB assigns much more importance to *ambulance* than SDCB. To GPT, *hallucination* is most important, followed by *syncope*, *hypo-* and *blood*.

4.2 Regulatory Criteria

Figure 3 shows the *importance* of different criteria groups (see Appendix C.2) according to Equation 1. Overall, all criteria have a positive importance, indicating that the models learn their relevance without explicit exposure to the criteria. According to IG, death is one of the two most important ones for all models and disability is quite important in all four models. The life-threatening criterion appears most important with GPT, while it is much less important for the other models. In EG, death is the most important criterion for all models and disability is most important after that except for GPT, where hospitalisation is more important. With both methods, birth defect emerges as the least important criterion, but this may be because it is the smallest criteria group and infrequent in the data.

4.3 Analysis of Misclassified Examples

Preliminary analysis of misclassified examples revealed very few terms with deviant explanation patterns, which we took as an indication of issues with the gold labels of the AER data. As reported by Bergman et al. (2023), the annotation procedure of AERs at the MPA is suboptimal from a machine learning perspective, because of a regulatory guideline that assessors should not downgrade a report labelled serious by the reporter, even if they consider the report to contain no information meeting the criteria for serious events (EMA, 2017, p. 16). For this reason, we asked one of the assessors to reannotate all reports that were misclassified by both GPT and SDCB – the best models in terms of specificity and F_1, respectively – 345 reports in total. Appendix F gives statistics on the reannotated reports and shows that, for both false negatives and false positives, more than half of the labels changed, confirming our suspicions.

Given the new annotations, we identify the terms with the largest differences in attribution score between true and false predictions for both serious and non-serious reports, focusing on terms explained as more serious in either true positives (TP) vs. false negatives (FN) or true negatives (TN) vs. false positives (FP). Table 9 in the Appendix shows the terms matching the inclusion criteria, and Appendix G contains additional information on the selection of these terms. For both models we then separately consider local IG explanations of the reannotated reports containing these terms – about 130 reports per model – to see if there are systematic differences for TP/FN and TN/FP report pairs.

While the manual analysis guided by the terms did not reveal most of the terms themselves to have obvious systematic effects, we noted some trends observed over most of the reports with specific patterns often explained as more serious or non-serious than the average term. Investigating the usage of these patterns on the training set, we found evidence of them reflecting reporter groups and specifically stylistic differences in how consumers and healthcare workers report AERs. We found certain snippets of texts that occurred in many reports and that traced back to the original reporting form, which had several free-text fields that were then automatically concatenated and saved as one field with titles or generated text corresponding to specific answers. Such elements, referred to as form patterns in the following, were often explained as non-serious as a whole or in part. Another notable pattern was that of temporal references including mentions of periods of time (e.g. *minutes* or *days*), but also temporal adverbs like *soon* and *directly*, which were explained as non-serious by both models. Appendix H contains information about the specific patterns and their statistics on the training set. What these statistics illustrate is that most of the form patterns, with the exception of *other information:*, are almost exclusively used in consumer AERs. Although the reporting rates are less extreme for temporal patterns, terms like *sometimes*, *month* and *period* are more indicative of consumers, while *soon*, *minute* and *second* are slightly more used by healthcare workers.

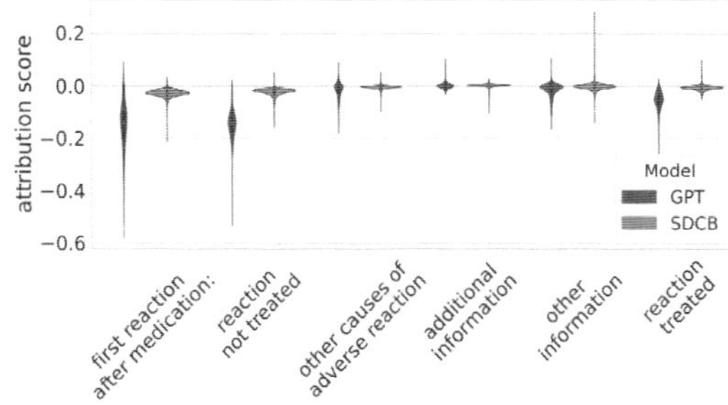

(a) form patterns

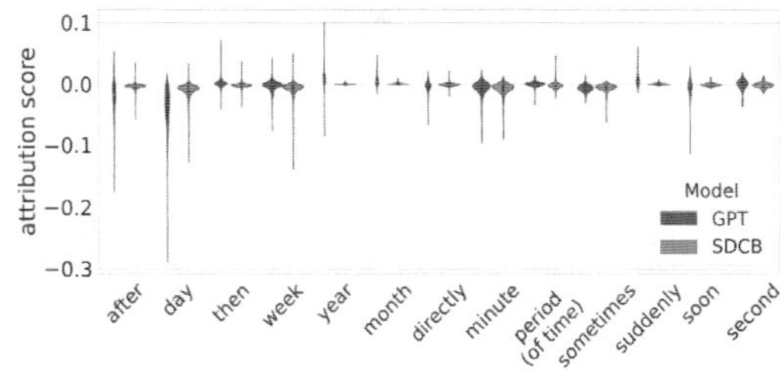

(b) temporal patterns

Figure 4: Local attribution score distribution of form patterns and time references over all matched reports in the development set, ordered by frequency.

We argue that some of the identified patterns align with how groups of reporters tend to express themselves in AERs, with healthcare personnel using medical jargon and writing concise reports,[8] while consumer reports can be longer and contain more detailed descriptions of how the reaction affected their everyday life and complaints about suspected products. From the form patterns we also observe that consumers appear to more diligently fill in the multiple free-text fields than healthcare workers who appear to rather give brief and to the point descriptions in one or a few of the fields.

In Figures 4a and 4b, we show how both types of patterns are explained by IG, plotting the distribution of their local explanations over the whole development set. Attribution scores were obtained by matching the exact sequence for form patterns, and summing the attribution scores of the individual words. Temporal patterns were matched with regular expressions covering morphologic variations.[9] In general, the explanations for SDCB appear more concentrated than those of GPT. Some form patterns like *first reaction after medication* and *reaction not treated* are clearly mostly negative in terms of attribution, i.e. explained as contributing to non-serious predictions, while *other information*, *additional information* and *other causes of adverse reaction* are more symmetrically concentrated around 0, suggesting an overall more neutral, less systematic contribution of these patterns to the prediction of reports in the development set. With respect to temporal references, there is a more global signal of *after*, *day*, *minute* and *sometimes* being explained as more non-serious with both models, while *directly*, *then* and *soon* appear slightly more neutral, and *year* and *suddenly* being explained as more serious.

The trends observed in attribution polarity and dominant reporting groups led us to take a closer look at model performance in these two groups in the development set. We found that recall for all four models was more than 20% lower for consumers than for healthcare workers and precision 10–20% lower. Correcting the gold labels where we have reannotations increases the scores for all models and subgroups, yet the differences in recall precision and F_1 persist for the subgroups of consumers and healthcare workers.[10]

[8]Although there is a variation with the type of profession, see the statistics in Table 12 in the Appendix.

[9]The expressions are listed in Table 11.

[10]More detail on this evaluation in Appendix J.

5 Discussion

The analyses in the previous section aimed at investigating feature attribution explanations for different triage models to answer the research questions defined in the beginning of the paper.

How do explanations for different models fine-tuned for the same task differ? To answer the first research question, we investigated the correlation between global attributions with two explainability methods. We found considerable variation between models, but also weak to moderate correlations among model attributions, most notably among encoder models and with the IG method. Moreover, models are more consistent with each other when task-relevant concepts are in focus as explored through filter terms and criteria groupings.

From the analysis of important clusters, we find that *suicide*, *ambulance* and *hallucination* appear in all models with both explanation methods. With IG, we can glean SDCB explanations to deem medical terminology such as *syncope*, *fracture* and deficiencies/dysregulations (*hypo-*) most important, while KBB, AERB and GPT focus more on the concepts common to all models, although AERB and GPT also give high importance to *heart rate*. With EG, we find some similarity in the most important clusters, with SDCB still having high importance scores for deficiencies, but also featuring other concepts like *epilepsy*, *abortion* and *liver*, while GPT retains *hallucination* as an important cluster, in addition to *syncope*, deficiencies and *blood*.

Can we align important features with regulatory criteria for what constitutes a serious case? All models seem to learn the importance of the filter terms and the groupings of criteria, albeit with different priorities as suggested by both the correlations over filter terms and the importance assigned to different criteria.

Are there systematic feature patterns that explain incorrect class predictions? Through the manual analysis of reports we learned that serious and non-serious explanations do not always focus on parts of the report that could be considered relevant for the assessment of the report at hand, and that the level of detail may be a factor contributing to misclassification. This raises the question whether the selected methods are adequate given the classification problem at hand and how one can conceptualise the two classes to distinguish. Is a non-serious report a distinct category in itself with salient features identifying it or just defined by the lack of serious features? And should we define an abstract neutral baseline or model explanations in contrast to the non-serious class?

6 Conclusion

In conclusion, our analysis shows that all models learn to identify relevant features indicative of a potentially serious case, but with varying focus on symptoms, conditions and medical procedures. Most of the criteria for identifying serious events are important for serious predictions with all models and explanation methods, but their relative importance varies across models. Finally, manual analysis of reports reveals features reflecting the reporting style of specific reporter groups, specifically reflecting which and how many free-text fields were filled in and to some degree the narration style and level of detail as represented through temporal references. This part of the analysis raises questions about model training and the adequacy of the selected explanation methods for the task at hand. Future work on training and explaining triage systems may need to rethink how information in this binary setup is defined and contrasted, to promote the importance of medically relevant features over confounding features related to form and writing style.

Limitations

In the preparation of this study, we made several design decisions that can be scrutinised further. In particular, the chosen explainability methods come with their own set of limitations, one of which is that, while feature attribution may highlight important terms, such a representation ultimately does not explain why the model that is being explained relies on those features to begin with. In addition, feature attribution for the most part constrains us to individual explanations of the input features without representing how features may interact with or affect each other. At the same time, the goal of the study in question was not to identify the best explanation technique for our use case, but instead to investigate triage models with available feature attribution methods.

We chose to focus on real-world data and models that may be employed as part of the MPA's pharmacovigilance monitoring. As such, the main focus of this paper was not to make claims on exact classification performance differences of the triage models we analyse and we therefore did not pursue evaluation over several training seeds as this would also further complicate the analysis of explanations taking into account several versions of each fine-tuned model. For an analysis of the robustness of fine-tuning the AER-BERT model for triage we refer to our previous results in Bergman et al. (2023).

We did not study the effect of different fine-tuning runs on the final explanations given the same hyperparameters and base model and therefore cannot make any claims on how much of the differences we see between triage models is due to initialisation of the classification head, shuffling of the training data, or the difference in pre-trained base model. However, a limited control experiment showed that global explanations of ten fine-tuned versions of KB-BERT with different random seeds correlated much more strongly with each other than with any of the other models, which suggests that the differences between different pre-trained models are relatively robust. See Appendix K for more information.

The decision to use generative models with fine-tuning methods geared towards encoders instead of reframing the task into a generative setup may not have been the optimal choice for the GPT-SW3 model, but was chosen to follow a common methodology in deriving explanations and, most notably, always having a binary classification outcome space to refer to.

A large part of the analysis rests on aggregated attribution values. Corpus-level normalisation is only one way of achieving this aggregation. Furthermore, aggregation of explanations over multiple reports comes at the cost of losing nuances in specific contextualised cases.

Throughout the analysis, we consider raw aggregated values for each model. Using such unnormalised average attribution values means that global explanations between models are not directly comparable, since some models have much more extreme attribution values – this is why we took more of a ranking approach and focused on relative importance among, e.g., criteria groups.

The grouping of criteria is debatable for certain terms that may fit multiple categories or can be hard to disentangle in relation to another category (e.g. miscarriage as death rather than birth defect, cardiac arrest as death vs. life-threatening). Further, the groups are likely not an exhaustive list of relevant criteria terms in the given data, and as raised in the analysis, some groups cover only very few and overall infrequent terms and may provide a limited representation of the criterion in question.

Likewise, while the clustering analysis underwent several iterations to find a good separation of clusters without generating too many outliers there may be parameters resulting in an even better clustering result. In addition, to save resources, the clusters used in the analysis were manually labelled by a single annotator, based on the MeSH ontology and no further quality checks were conducted on this annotation. Involving more and more expert annotators in the process may have resulted in higher quality labels and slightly different grouping decisions for similar clusters and consequently different results. This could for example lead to combining more semantically similar clusters that are only distinguished by their level of specialisation such as the *fainting* and *syncope* clusters.

As for the investigation of reporter groups inspired by the manual analysis of explanations, one obvious aspect potentially dividing reporter groups is medical terminology and frequently used abbreviations by medical workers. While both references to medical conditions and procedures as well as drug names were noted as salient in some of the manually analysed reports, the variation of terms was larger and an exhaustive list more challenging to put together and analyse than the patterns we decided to study further.

Ethical Considerations

The data used in this work contains sensitive medical information and has been collected and processed by the Swedish Medical Products Agency as part of their pharmacovigilance monitoring duty. For the scope of this study, processing the data by training and evaluating models and their explanations falls under the agency's operations for business development and does not require further ethics approval by the Swedish Ethical Review Authority. To ensure information security, the texts have been anonymised by replacing digits in the free-text, where personal identity numbers may be reported. Further, complete examples of individual AER descriptions cannot be included without additional anonymisation steps. Since the study itself focuses on the explanation and evaluation of triage models for larger sets of reports this has not been necessary and observations are reported as summaries of subsets of the full AER data.

Acknowledgments

We acknowledge the support of the Swedish Research Council (grant no. 2022-02909). We also thank the reviewers for their helpful feedback and suggestions.

References

Kwabena Amponsah-Kaakyire, Daria Pylypenko, Josef Genabith, and Cristina España-Bonet. 2022. Explaining translationese: why are neural classifiers better and what do they learn? In *Proceedings of the Fifth BlackboxNLP Workshop on Analyzing and Interpreting Neural Networks for NLP*, pages 281–296, Abu Dhabi, United Arab Emirates (Hybrid). Association for Computational Linguistics.

Robert Ball and Gerald Dal Pan. 2022. "Artificial intelligence" for pharmacovigilance: Ready for prime time? *Drug Safety*, 45:429–438.

Andrew Bate and Steve F Hobbinger. 2021. Artificial Intelligence, real-world automation and the safety of medicines. *Drug Safety*, 44:125–132.

Erik Bergman, Luise Dürlich, Veronica Arthurson, Anders Sundström, Maria Larsson, Shamima Bhuiyan, Andreas Jakobsson, and Gabriel Westman. 2023. BERT based natural language processing for triage of adverse drug reaction reports shows close to human-level performance. *PLOS Digital Health*, 2(12).

Trenton Bricken, Adly Templeton, Joshua Batson, Brian Chen, Adam Jermyn, Tom Conerly, Nicholas L Turner, Cem Anil, Amanda Askell, Robert Lasenby, Yifan Wu, Shauna Kravec, Nicholas Schiefer, Tim Maxwell, Nicholas Joseph, Alex Tamkin, Karina Nguyen, Brayden McLean, Josiah E Burke, Tristan Hume, Shan Carter, Tom Henighan, and Chirs Olah. 2023. Towards monosemanticity: Decomposing language models with dictionary learning, Transformer Circuits Thread, released 4 October 2023 [online].

Ricardo J. G. B. Campello, Davoud Moulavi, and Joerg Sander. 2013. Density-based clustering based on hierarchical density estimates. In *Advances in Knowledge Discovery and Data Mining*, pages 160–172, Berlin, Heidelberg. Springer Berlin Heidelberg.

Alexander Dolk, Hjalmar Davidsen, Hercules Dalianis, and Thomas Vakili. 2022. Evaluation of LIME and SHAP in explaining automatic ICD-10 classifications of Swedish gastrointestinal discharge summaries. In *Scandinavian Conference on Health Informatics*, pages 166–173.

Ariel Ekgren, Amaru Cuba Gyllensten, Evangelia Gogoulou, Alice Heiman, Severine Verlinden, Joey Öhman, Fredrik Carlsson, and Magnus Sahlgren. 2022. Lessons learned from GPT-SW3: Building the first large-scale generative language model for Swedish. In *Proceedings of the Thirteenth Language Resources and Evaluation Conference*, pages 3509–3518, Marseille, France. European Language Resources Association.

Gabriel Erion, Joseph D Janizek, Pascal Sturmfels, Scott M Lundberg, and Su-In Lee. 2021. Improving performance of deep learning models with axiomatic attribution priors and expected gradients. *Nature Machine Intelligence*, 3(7):620–631.

European Medicines Agency. 2017. Guideline on good pharmacovigilance practices (gvp) - Module VI – Collection, management and submission of reports of suspected adverse reactions to medicinal products (Rev. 2). `https://www.ema.europa.eu/en/documents/regulatory-procedural-guideline/guideline-good-pharmacovigilance-practices-gvp-module-vi-collection-management-and-submission-reports-suspected-adverse-reactions-medicinal-products-rev-2_en.pdf`.

Marzyeh Ghassemi, Luke Oakden-Rayner, and Andrew L Beam. 2021. The false hope of current approaches to explainable artificial intelligence in health care. *The Lancet Digital Health*, 3(11):e745–e750.

Manfred Hauben. 2022. Artificial intelligence in pharmacovigilance: Do we need explainability? *Pharmacoepidemiology and Drug Safety*, 31(12):1311–1316.

Dieuwke Hupkes, Sara Veldhoen, and Willem Zuidema. 2018. Visualisation and'diagnostic classifiers' reveal how recurrent and recursive neural networks process hierarchical structure. *Journal of Artificial Intelligence Research*, 61:907–926.

Mark Ibrahim, Melissa Louie, Ceena Modarres, and John Paisley. 2019. Global explanations of neural networks: Mapping the landscape of predictions. In *Proceedings of the 2019 AAAI/ACM Conference on AI, Ethics, and Society*, AIES '19, page 279–287, New York, NY, USA. Association for Computing Machinery.

ICH Harmonised Tripartite Guideline. 1994. Clinical Safety Data Management: Definitions and Standards for Expedited Reporting E2A. In *International Conference on Harmonisation of Technical Requirements for Registration of Pharmaceuticals for Human Use*.

Sarthak Jain and Byron C Wallace. 2019. Attention is not explanation. In *Proceedings of NAACL-HLT*, pages 3543–3556.

Oeystein Kjoersvik and Andrew Bate. 2022. Black swan events and intelligent automation for routine safety surveillance. *Drug Safety*, 45:419–427.

Narine Kokhlikyan, Vivek Miglani, Miguel Martin, Edward Wang, Bilal Alsallakh, Jonathan Reynolds, Alexander Melnikov, Natalia Kliushkina, Carlos Araya, Siqi Yan, et al. 2020. Captum: A unified and generic model interpretability library for pytorch. *arXiv preprint arXiv:2009.07896*.

Jenny Kunz, Martin Jirenius, Oskar Holmström, and Marco Kuhlmann. 2022. Human ratings do not reflect downstream utility: A study of free-text explanations for model predictions. In *Proceedings of the Fifth BlackboxNLP Workshop on Analyzing and Interpreting Neural Networks for NLP*, pages 164–177.

Jenny Kunz and Marco Kuhlmann. 2024. Properties and challenges of LLM-generated explanations. In *Proceedings of the Third Workshop on Bridging Human–Computer Interaction and Natural Language Processing*, pages 13–27, Mexico City, Mexico. Association for Computational Linguistics.

Carolyn E Lipscomb. 2000. Medical subject headings (mesh). *Bulletin of the Medical Library Association*, 88(3):265.

Scott M Lundberg and Su-In Lee. 2017. A unified approach to interpreting model predictions. *Advances in Neural Information Processing Systems*, 30.

Martin Malmsten, Love Börjeson, and Chris Haffenden. 2020. Playing with words at the national library of Sweden–making a swedish BERT. *arXiv preprint arXiv:2007.01658*.

Anmol Nayak and Hari Prasad Timmapathini. 2021. Using integrated gradients and constituency parse trees to explain linguistic acceptability learnt by BERT. In *Proceedings of the 18th International Conference on Natural Language Processing (ICON)*, pages 80–85, National Institute of Technology Silchar, Silchar, India. NLP Association of India (NLPAI).

Marco Tulio Ribeiro, Sameer Singh, and Carlos Guestrin. 2016. "Why should i trust you?" explaining the predictions of any classifier. In *Proceedings of the 22nd ACM SIGKDD international conference on knowledge discovery and data mining*, pages 1135–1144.

Cynthia Rudin. 2019. Stop explaining black box machine learning models for high stakes decisions and use interpretable models instead. *Nature Machine Intelligence*, 1(5):206–215.

Denitsa Saynova, Bastiaan Bruinsma, Moa Johansson, and Richard Johansson. 2023. Class explanations: the role of domain-specific content and stop words. In *The 24rd Nordic Conference on Computational Linguistics*, pages 103–112.

Avanti Shrikumar, Peyton Greenside, and Anshul Kundaje. 2017. Learning important features through propagating activation differences. In *International conference on machine learning*, pages 3145–3153. PMlR.

Samuel Stevens and Yu Su. 2021. An investigation of language model interpretability via sentence editing. In *Proceedings of the Fourth BlackboxNLP Workshop on Analyzing and Interpreting Neural Networks for NLP*, pages 435–446, Punta Cana, Dominican Republic. Association for Computational Linguistics.

Mukund Sundararajan, Ankur Taly, and Qiqi Yan. 2017. Axiomatic attribution for deep networks. In *International Conference on Machine Learning*, pages 3319–3328. PMLR.

Ruixuan Tang, Hanjie Chen, and Yangfeng Ji. 2022. Identifying the source of vulnerability in explanation discrepancy: A case study in neural text classification. In *Proceedings of the Fifth BlackboxNLP Workshop on Analyzing and Interpreting Neural Networks for NLP*, pages 356–370, Abu Dhabi, United Arab Emirates (Hybrid). Association for Computational Linguistics.

Adly Templeton, Tom Conerly, Jonathan Marcus, Jack Lindsey, Trenton Bricken, Brian Chen, Brian Pearce, Craig Citro, Emmanuel Ameisen, Andy Jones, Hoagy Cunningham, Nicholas L Turner, Callum McDougall, Monte MacDiarmid, C Daniel Freeman, Theodore R Sumers, Edward Rees, Joshua Batson, Adam Jermyn, Shan Carter, Chris Olah, and Tom Henighan. 2024. Scaling monosemanticity: Extracting interpretable features from Claude 3 sonnet, Transformer Circuits Thread, released 21 May 2024 [online].

Miles Turpin, Julian Michael, Ethan Perez, and Samuel Bowman. 2023. Language models don't always say what they think: Unfaithful explanations in chain-of-thought prompting. In *Advances in Neural Information Processing Systems*, volume 36, pages 74952–74965. Curran Associates, Inc.

Thomas Vakili, Anastasios Lamproudis, Aron Henriksson, and Hercules Dalianis. 2022. Downstream Task Performance of BERT Models Pre-Trained Using Automatically De-Identified Clinical Data. In *Proceedings of the Thirteenth Language Resources and Evaluation Conference*, pages 4245–4252.

Ilse Van Der Linden, Hinda Haned, and Evangelos Kanoulas. 2019. Global aggregations of local explanations for black box models. *arXiv preprint arXiv:1907.03039*.

Giulia Vilone and Luca Longo. 2021. Notions of explainability and evaluation approaches for explainable artificial intelligence. *Information Fusion*, 76:89–106.

Jin Wang, Liang-Chih Yu, and Xuejie Zhang. 2022. Explainable detection of adverse drug reaction with imbalanced data distribution. *PLoS computational biology*, 18(6).

World Health Organization. 2002. *The importance of pharmacovigilance*. World Health Organization, Geneva. ISBN: 9241590157.

A Improved Data and Hyperparameter Experiments

The free-text description of reports in the original data used by Bergman et al. (2023) occasionally contained comments by the assessors processing

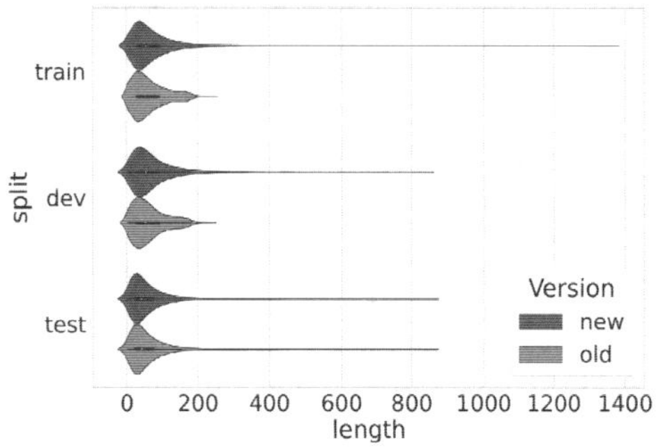

Figure 5: Report length in whitespace-tokenised tokens for the cleaner version of the data used in this paper (new) and the version previously used in Bergman et al. (2023) (old).

the report. In their work, preprocessing included filtering out and removing those comments using regular expressions. However, for this study we were able to obtain access to a database storing only the original reports as they were at the time of reporting and therefore skip this step in preprocessing the text. Upon comparing matching reports in the two data sources, we also discovered that the previously used data source contained truncated reports. Figure 5 shows a comparison of report lengths in the previous and current version of the data.

The database we extracted our reports from only contained those reports received by the MPA via an electronic reporting form. We found that some reports in the dataset used by Bergman et al. (2023) were not present in the original database and such cases could be explained by the original incoming reports covering information warranting a separate report, e.g. when the report describes adverse events related to different medical products at different points in time, specifically assigns different suspected events to different medication, mentions multiple patients with similar adverse events, or discusses events in mothers or soon-to-be mothers as well as events in their young children or fetuses. These reports were then split manually by assessors and added to the working database. Our data splits contain 90 such examples in development and training set, 42 of which were found to start with comments during pre-processing. To allow for some degree of comparison with our previous study, we opt to still keep these reports in their previous form and apply filtering to remove initial comments matching specific keywords followed by dates and assessor signatures.

Preprocessing for all reports includes stripping of initial hyphen characters and white space in the description field as well as prepending to the description all suspected adverse events in list form.

The focus of the hyperparameter experiments was to identify learning rate and epoch settings for the four models. We considered learning rates in the set {0.00002, 0.00003, 0.00004, 0.00005} and training for up to three epochs and chose the best settings according to the observed loss on the development set. Table 5 shows the selected settings informed by the experiments.

The settings for KBB and SDCB are identical. For AERB, we add a weight decay term of 0.01 to keep consistency with Bergman et al. (2023).

B Axioms of IG and EG

As defined by Sundararajan et al. (2017), the axioms fulfilled by both explanation methods are

- sensitivity, whereby only relevant features contribute to the explanation and irrelevant features have an importance of 0,
- implementation invariance, stating that for two networks that produce the same outputs as each other for all inputs, the attributions should be identical,
- completeness, in the sense that the sum of attributions for a particular input should correspond to the difference in model output for the input and the baseline,
- linearity, in that attributions for a model that is a linear combination of two other models are a linear combination of the attributions for those two models,
- symmetry-preservation, whereby symmetric variables in the network should get the same attribution if they have the same value.

C Analysis resources

C.1 Filter Terms

The list of filter terms contains 47 terms or segments that relate to words associated with serious reports and is used to filter incoming reports marked as not serious for candidates that can be prioritised. A drawback of its format is that word segments, not always representing real morphemes, may also match less relevant terms. All filter terms and approximate translations with annotations for

Parameter	KBB & SDCB	AERB	GPT
Batch Size	8	8	4
Gradient Accumulation	1	1	2
Learning Rate	2×10^{-5}	2×10^{-5}	2×10^{-5}
WarmupRatio	0.3	0.3	0.15
Mixed Precision	–	–	fp16
Optimizer	AdamW	AdamW	AdaFactor
Weight Decay	0	0.01	0
Epochs	1	1	2

Table 5: Training Settings

omitted parts are listed in Table 6. The filter terms match a total of 220 terms of the vocabulary in the global explanations.

C.2 Criteria Groups

The criteria groups are 5 groups of concepts derived from the definition of serious adverse reactions – relating to death, life-threatening reactions, hospitalisation, disability and birth defects. Each group consists of single word synonyms as well as more specific concepts, and is internally grouped to reflect more general notions as well as very specific terminologies and contexts.

For example, the group for death comprises a group of general words such as *death*, *pass away*, *passing* as well as individual groups for more specific forms of death such as *suicide*, *suffocation/asphyxia*, *cardiac arrest* and *miscarriage*. This grouping was created for the set of terms covered in the development set and is not exhaustive with respect to all possible subcategories that may exist outside this restricted vocabulary. Terms cover different wordforms of the same lexeme.

Table 7 shows how many terms and subgroups are associated with each criterion. The biggest criterion is that of hospitalisation with 179 terms. These include different inflected versions of the same lemma as well as common abbreviations and in some cases spelling variations found in the corpus of AERs that constitute the development set. The groups were created using MeSH and referring to terms present in the AER reports. Hence some groups such as birth defect are fairly small even though there are more conceivable birth defects, but they do not feature in the analysed set of AERs.

Filter Term	Translation
ARDS	respiratory distress syndrome
BNP	brain natriuretic peptide
Haemoly	haemoly(sis)
Johnson	Johnson
andningsavbrott	respiratory arrest
andningspåverkad	respiratory challenged
andningssvikt	respiratory failure
andningsuppehåll	respiratory arrest
anfall	attack, acute onset
avled	died
barre	Barre (Guillain-Barré syndrome)
blind	blind
cerebro	cerebro-
dog	died
dyspne	dyspnea
död	death
epidermal	epidermal
epilep	epilep(sy)
fladder	flutter
hallucin	hallucin(ation)
handik	disab(ility)
hemolyti	hemolyti(c)
hörsel	hearing
interstit	interstit(ial)
kardiell myopati	cardiomyopathy
koagulat	coagulat(tion related)
kolangit	cholangitis
konstaterad	confirmed / diagnosed
lungsvikt	lung failure
lymphohist	lymphohist-
mikroangio	microangio-
missbild	malforma(tion) / birth defect
missfall	miscarriage
multisystemisk	multisystemic
mungip	corner of the mouth
optikusneu	optic neu(ritis)
propp	clot
puls	pulse
purpura	purpura
resp insuff	resp(iratory) insuff(iciency)
scars	scars
syn	vision
synbortf	(loss) of vision
toxisk	toxic
vaerd	vaccine-associated enhanced respiratory disease
ventrike	ventric(le)
ventrombos	venous thrombosis

Table 6: 47 Swedish filter terms and their English translations and completions.

Group	Terms	Subgroups
Death	33	5
Life-threatening	10	1
Hospitalisation	179	3
Birth defect	4	2
Disability	20	5

Table 7: Total number of terms and subgroups in each of the criteria groups.

D Feature Attribution for Filter Terms and Non-Filter Terms

Figure 6 shows the distributions of global attribution scores for terms matching the filter and those not matching the filter with both IG and EG.

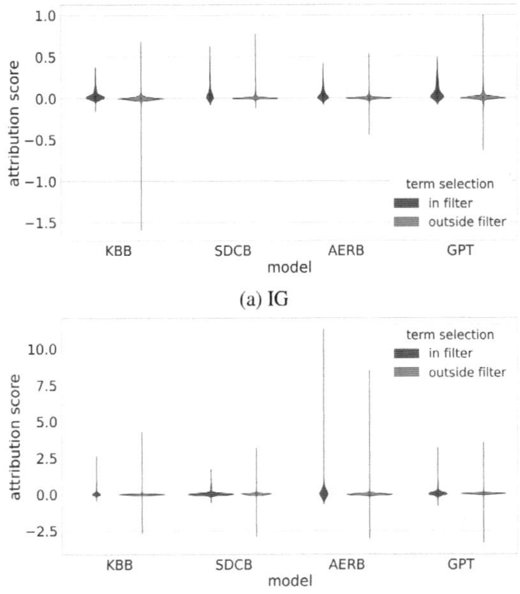

(a) IG

(b) EG

Figure 6: Distribution of global attribution scores for terms matching the filter and terms not matching the filter.

E Clusters of Top 8000 Serious Terms

To find more general concepts important for a serious outcome with each of the models according to either explanation method, we took the union of the 8,000 most important terms per model and clustered them for each attribution method. Terms were first embedded using a Swedish Sentence-BERT model[11] and then decomposed to 50 dimensions using principal component analysis with whitening and clustered with HDBSCAN (Campello et al., 2013). We experimented with lemmatization at an earlier stage, but found it harder to obtain an interpretable clustering that way. We set the HDBSCAN clusterer to a maximum cluster size of 80, a minimum cluster size of 5 and used default settings for the remaining parameters. The clusters were annotated by hand by a single annotator with a background in linguistics and good command of Swedish. To make sense of medical terminology and how medical concepts relate to each other, the annotator relied heavily on MeSH and its Swedish version to derive sensible cluster names in English. Table 8 shows statistics on the amount of selected terms per feature attribution method, the number of resulting clusters, average cluster sizes and the amount of outliers.

Figure 7 shows the importance of clusters in EG and to what extent they were covered by each model's top 8,000 terms. **Coverage** in the latter visualisation refers to the number of terms belonging to the cluster, that also rank among the top 8,000 terms for a particular model, divided by the total size of the cluster in unique terms.

Figures 13 and 14 show the entire clustering of IG and EG reduced with t-SNE. For both IG and EG, some clusters are completely missing in the global explanations of certain models, due to different tokenization. Specifically, AERB and GPT pick up certain *units* (*μg*, *μmol*) that are missing for KBB and SDCB, and all models but GPT pick up numbers and dimensions describing affected areas listed as part of the adverse event terms, because GPT's tokenizer splits them into digits belonging to a separate cluster instead.

F Reannotation

Figure 8 shows how the FN and FP reports were annotated by the assessor given only the concatenated term list and description text field. We anticipated that annotating these without the usual context may complicate decision making for the assessor and therefore allowed both an unclear annotation and a field to comment on the annotation. For the entire 345 reports, only 7 cases were unclear without additional information.

Looking at the label proportions, out of the serious reports in the original gold annotation, predicted non-serious by both models (FN), only a third was actually serious after the reannotation. Of the reports originally annotated non-serious, but

[11] KBLab/sentence-bert-swedish-cased

Method	Terms in Union	Clusters	Terms per Cluster	Outliers
IG	13,909	164	8.3	12,547
EG	15,347	193	8.4	13,726

Table 8: Statistics on the clustering.

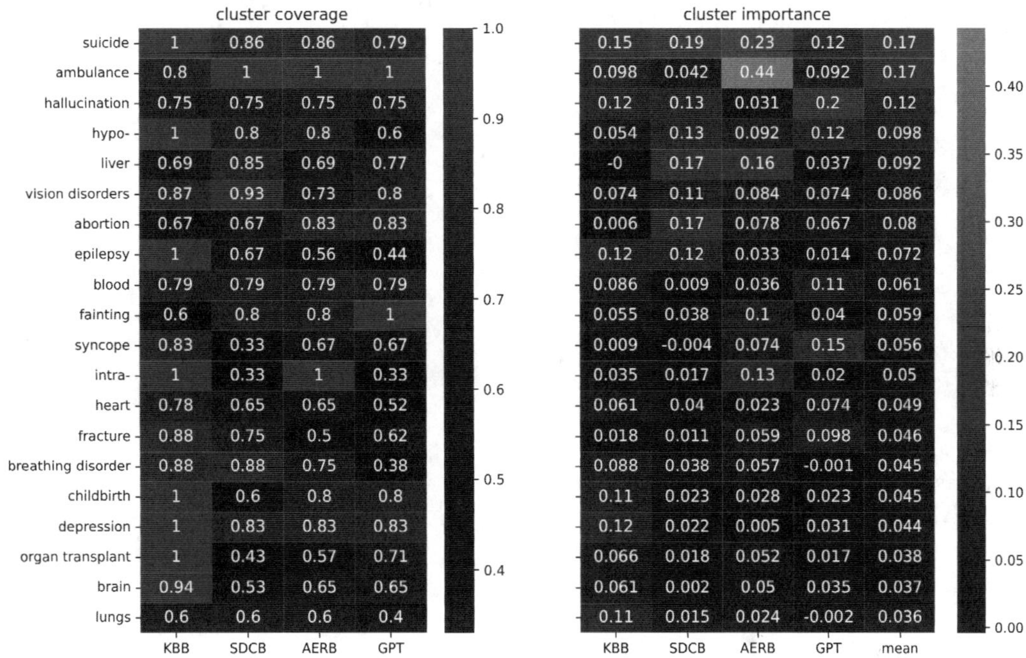

Figure 7: 20 highest ranked clusters with EG by cluster importance (right) and their coverage among the top 8,000 terms per model.

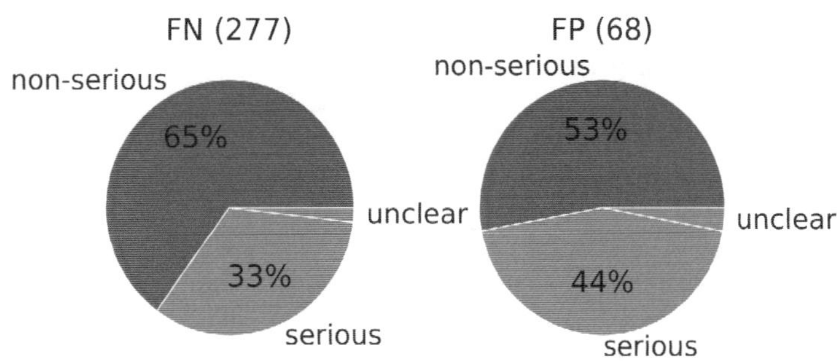

Figure 8: Reannotation of False Negatives (FN) and False Positives (FP). The numbers in parentheses are the amount of reports in each category.

predicted serious, about half remained non-serious after reannotation. One possible reason for the label change of so many of the originally FP reports is that some context is omitted with respect to the original report, since AERs consist of more than just the term list and free-text and the information indicating a serious event could conceivably be other parts of the form or its attachments without it being mentioned in the text as seen by the model.

G Selecting Reports for Manual Analysis

To identify interesting reports in the set of reannotated reports, we compute the terms with the largest differences in attribution score between true and false predictions for both serious and non-serious reports and restrict this to the 5 most extreme terms that occur at least twice in each considered set of reports with differences in the 2.5- and 97.5-percentiles respectively.

To limit the scope of the manual analysis, we only do this calculation and the report-wise analysis with IG. Table 9 details the terms, and their translation for the contrasted sets and each model.

The terms comprise some reoccurring themes for both models with terms relating to specific events such as *vaccination* or *product exchange*,[12] references to respiration (*breathing*, *coughing* and *shortness of breath*), the *emergency room*, and the abbreviation *EVF* for a blood test measuring the volume of packed red blood cells in a sample. They match a total of 126 and 129 reports for SDCB and GPT respectively. For each report we summarise the text and take note of the terms explained as serious and non-serious using IG as well as whether they relate to the specific event, fall under additional information such as patient history or information on other people mentioned in the report, or are stylistic elements of the report.

Analysing the reports associated with most of the terms in Table 9 revealed a variety in cases and narratives, however, there was overlap between the matched reports for *vaccination*, *vertigo*, *nausea* and *swelling* frequently co-occurring.

H Patterns

Table 10 details the six form patterns identified during the manual analysis. They correspond to automatically inserted titles or text snippets expressing information like whether or not the suspected adverse reaction was treated or how long after the affected person took the medicine suspected of causing the AE they started experiencing symptoms.

Table 11 details the Swedish temporal references as regular expressions to cover morphologic variation such as singular and plural, and indefinite and definite forms for nouns, and synonyms or contractions of some of the adverbs, with English translations and statistics on the occurrence of these terms in the training set and how much of those are in consumer reports.

Figure 9 shows the attribution distributions of form and temporal patterns according to EG, which generally appear to be explained as more neutral than those by IG.

[12]Referring to cases when the intended prescribed product is replaced by an equivalent product by another pharmaceutical company, which can happen when the intended product is out of stock at a pharmacy.

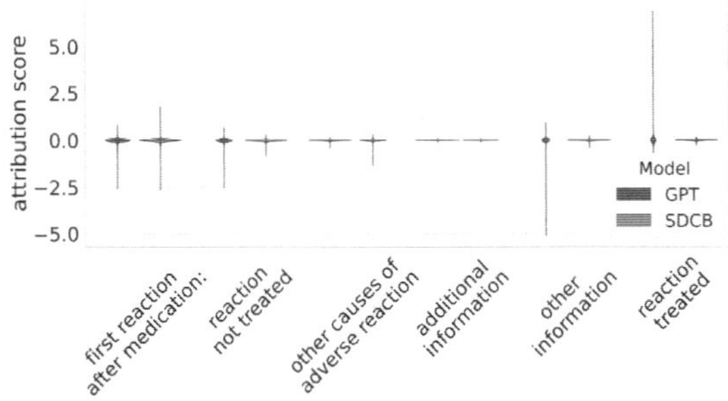

(a) form patterns

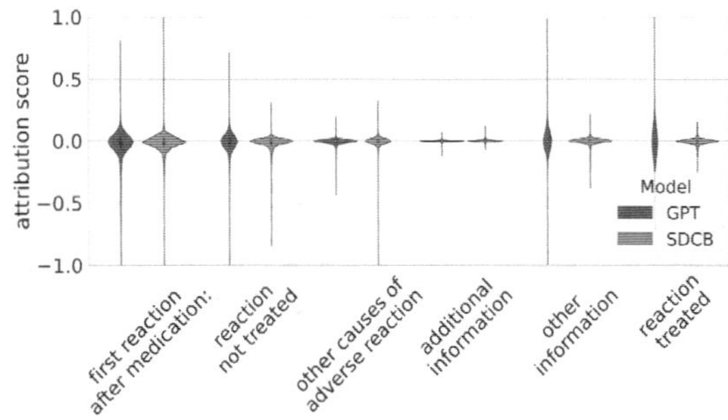

(b) form patterns (zoomed in)

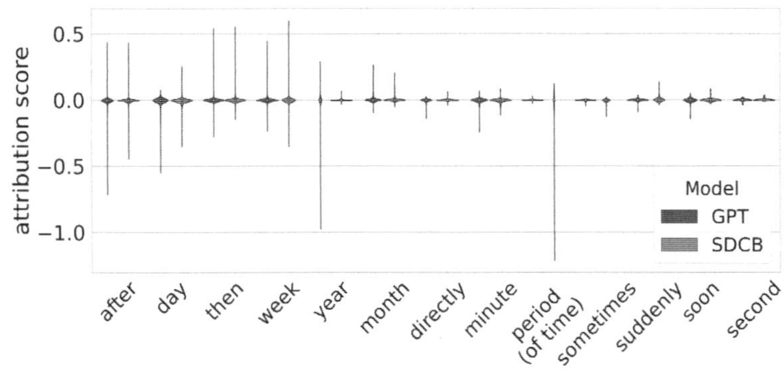

(c) temporal patterns

Figure 9: EG attribution scores of form patterns and temporal references in the full development set. The patterns are ordered by frequency in the development set with the most frequent patterns to the left.

Contrasted	**SDCB**		**GPT**	
sets	FN more serious	TP more serious	FN more serious	TP more serious
TP & FN	produktutbyte, andas, hosta, vaccination, rygg	blod	akuten, andfåddhet, smärtor, blod, andas	hosta, produktutbyte, biverkan, yrsel, reaktionen
English	*product exchange, to breathe, cough / to cough, vaccination, back*	*blood*	*(the) ER, shortness of breath, pains, blood, to breathe*	*cough / to cough, product exchange, (the) adverse reaction, vertigo, (the) reaction*
	FP more serious	TN more serious	FP more serious	TN more serious
TN & FP	akut, stroke, syn, svullna, evf	klåda, akuten, biverkningsombud, rodnad, dagar	evf, yr, migrän, yrsel, torra	stroke, syn, akuten, akut, EVF
English	*acute / ER, stroke, vision, swollen, packed red-cell volume*	*itching, ER, AER-delegate,*[13] *redness, days*	*packed red-cell volume, nauseous, migraine, vertigo, dry*	*stroke, vision, (the) ER, acute / ER, packed red-cell volume*

Table 9: Terms with more extreme differences in attribution score in correct and incorrect predictions per report class.

Pattern	Translation	Occurrence	Reported by Consumers
första reaktionen efter medicineringen:	first reaction after medication:	5,173	99.65%
reaktionen ej behandlad	reaction not treated	3,853	99.77%
andra biverkningsorsaker:	other causes of adverse reaction:	3,433	99.65%
ytterligare info	additional information	2,123	99.06%
övrig information:	other information:	1,903	0.08%
reaktionen behandlad	reaction treated	1,591	99.43%

Table 10: Swedish form patterns, their English translation, occurrence in the training set and the proportion reported by consumers.

Pattern	Translation	Occurrence	Reported by Consumers
(där)?efter	after	8,481	63.12%
dag(en|ar(na)?)?	(the) day, (the) days	3,990	63.73%
se(da)?n	then	2,654	66.11%
veck(an?|or(na)?)	(the) week, (the) weeks	2,020	61.49%
år(et|en)?	(the) year, (the) years	1,373	69.56%
månad(en|er(na)?)?	(the) month, (the) months	1,382	74.75%
direkt	directly	658	66.11%
minut(en|er(na)?)?	(the) minute, (the) minutes	449	46.55%
period(en|er(na)?)?	(the) period (of time), (the) periods	260	74.62%
ibland	sometimes	319	88.71%
plötsligt	suddenly	198	69.19%
strax	soon	147	46.26%
sekund(en|er(na)?)?	(the) second, (the) seconds	73	49.32%

Table 11: Regular expressions for temporal patterns in Swedish, their English translation, occurrence in the training set and proportion reported by consumers.

I Reporter Statistics

Table 12 contains statistics on reports by specific reporter groups in the training data.

Reporter	Number of reports	Average report length (in characters)
Consumer	5,607	614.04
Doctor	3,687	408.15
Nurse	1,573	364.00
Pharmacist	955	281.31
Dentist	131	301.58
Other Healthcare personnel	35	869.31
All Healthcare	6,381	378.63

Table 12: Statistics by reporter group on the training set

J Subgroup Performance

Figures 11 and 12 show the performance of each model in different metrics for the original development set and partially corrected gold labels.

[13]A delegated nurse / pharmacist reporting adverse events from the medical record system on behalf of a hospital.

K Explanation Correlation with Different Fine-Tuning Runs of the Same Model

This section shows results of a control experiment comparing global correlations for different fine-tuned versions of the same base model with the results in Section 4.1.

	Shared vocab.		Filter terms	
Base model	IG	EG	IG	EG
KBB	$0.65_{\pm 0.06}$	$0.17_{\pm 0.01}$	$0.64_{\pm 0.07}$	$0.20_{\pm 0.04}$
Different	$0.28_{\pm 0.05}$	$0.08_{\pm 0.01}$	$0.42_{\pm 0.06}$	$0.11_{\pm 0.09}$

Table 13: Average Kendall's τ correlation between explanations of 10 different fine-tuning runs of KBB and the different base models as reported in Figure 1 (excluding controls and the diagonal).

We fine-tuned 10 versions of KBB with the same hyperparameter settings as the model reported in the main text, but different random seeds to observe how similar global explanations are with the same pre-trained model. Table 13 shows average Kendall's τ correlations and their standard deviations for explanations of these new fine-tuned models sharing the same base model and the corresponding values for the experiments with different fine-tuned base models from Figure 1.

Figure 10 gives a better view of the distribution of these correlations

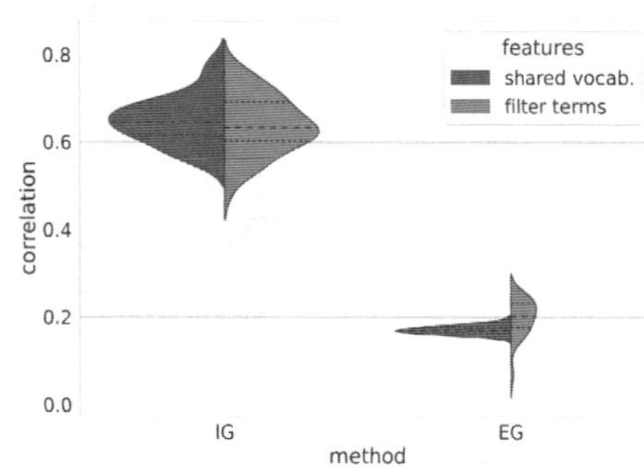

Figure 10: Distribution of Kendall's τ correlation between global explanations of 10 different fine-tuned KBB models.

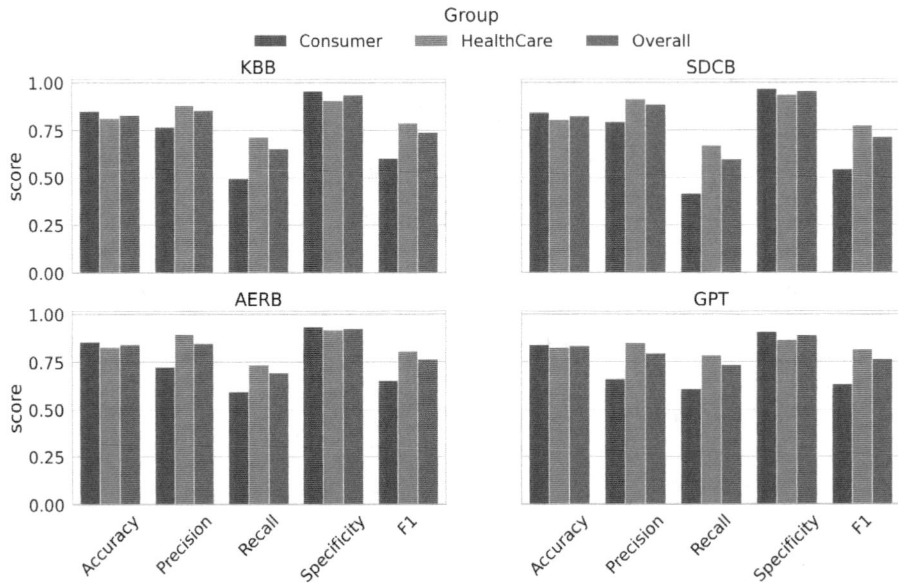

Figure 11: Model results on development data for reporter subgroups on original gold labels.

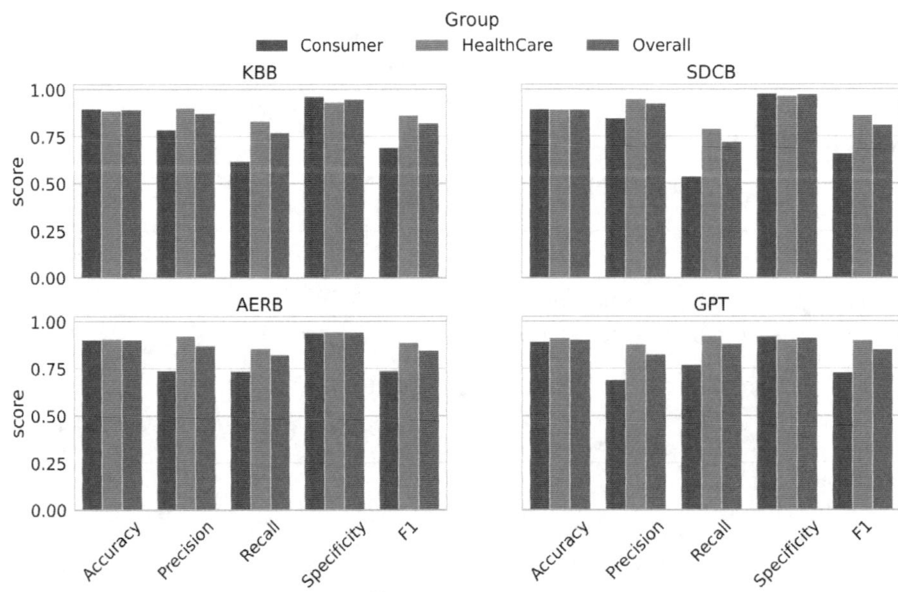

Figure 12: Model results on development data for reporter subgroups on partially corrected gold labels.

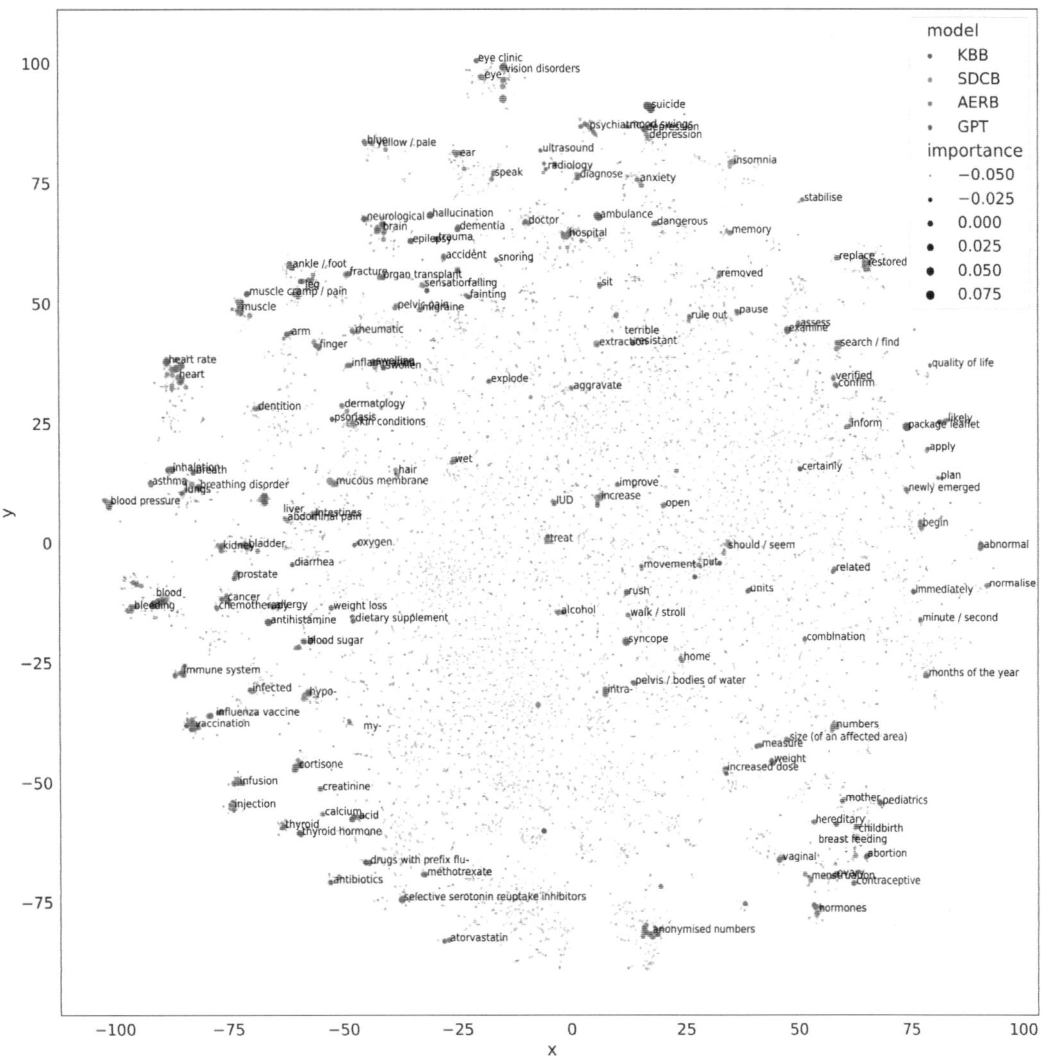

Figure 13: t-SNE projection of serious terms in Swedish ADRs according to IG attributions for four triage models. All terms are encoded with the same SentenceBERT model and each term is plotted individually as a point for each model. Manually assigned English cluster labels are added for the centroid of each cluster. The size of the points represents the spread of the cluster it belongs to specific to the explanations of a particular model. Terms occurring in the top lists of multiple models are represented as gradually more transparent points. Outliers are smallest and the most transparent.

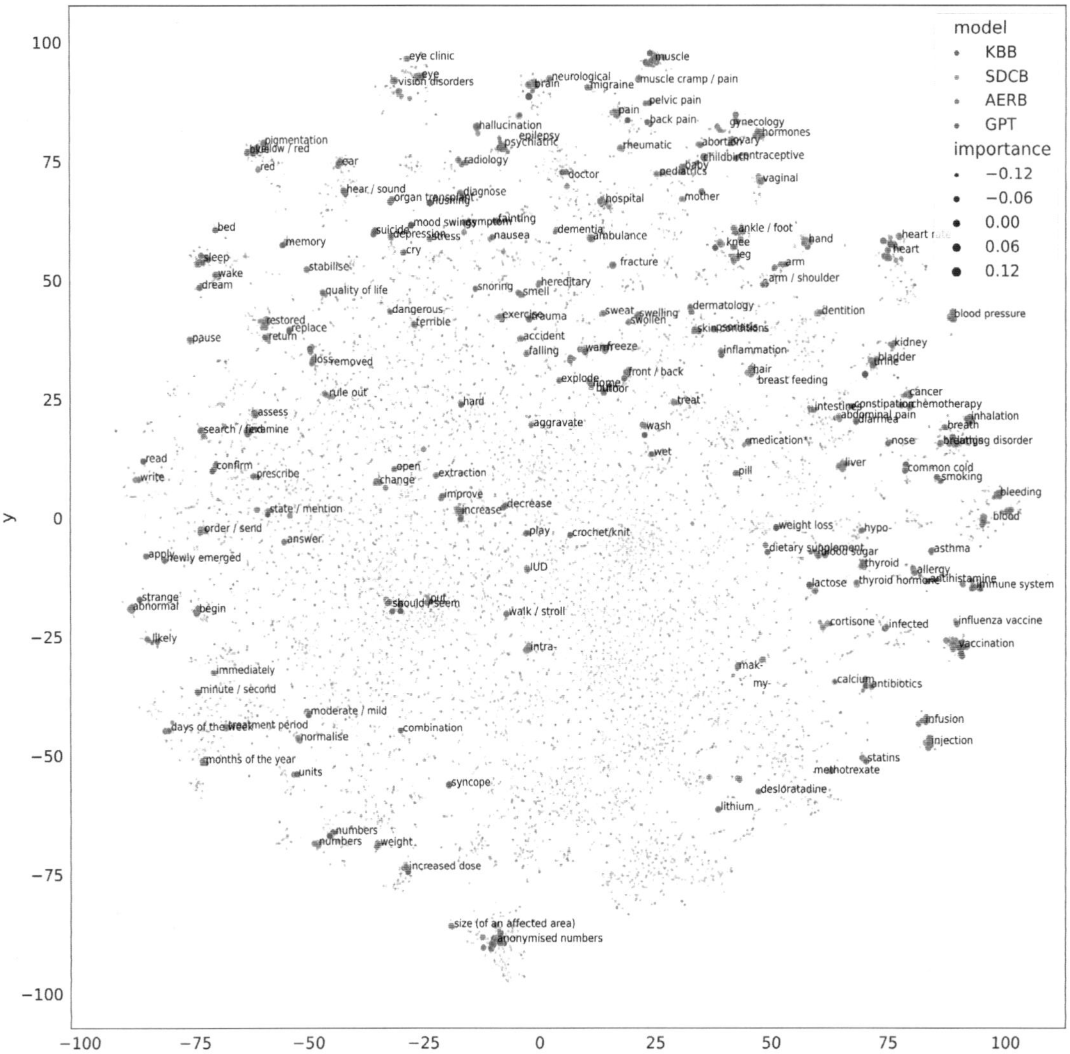

Figure 14: t-SNE projection of serious terms in Swedish ADRs according to EG attributions for four triage models. All terms are encoded with the same SentenceBERT model and each term is plotted individually as a point for each model. Manually assigned English cluster labels are added for the centroid of each cluster. The size of the points represents the spread of the cluster it belongs to specific to the explanations of a particular model. Terms occurring in the top lists of multiple models are represented as gradually more transparent points. Outliers are smallest and the most transparent.

When Multilingual Models Compete with Monolingual Domain-Specific Models in Clinical Question Answering

Vojtěch Lanz and Pavel Pecina
Charles University, Faculty of Mathematics and Physics
Institute of Formal and Applied Linguistics
{lanz,pecina}@ufal.mff.cuni.cz

Abstract

This paper explores the performance of multilingual models in the general domain on the clinical Question Answering (QA) task to observe their potential medical support for languages that do not benefit from the existence of clinically trained models. In order to improve the model's performance, we exploit multilingual data augmentation by translating an English clinical QA dataset into six other languages. We propose a translation pipeline including projection of the evidences (answers) into the target languages and thoroughly evaluate several multilingual models fine-tuned on the augmented data, both in mono- and multilingual settings. We find that the translation itself and the subsequent QA experiments present a differently challenging problem for each of the languages. Finally, we compare the performance of multilingual models with pretrained medical domain-specific English models on the original clinical English test set. Contrary to expectations, we find that monolingual domain-specific pretraining is not always superior to general-domain multilingual pretraining. The source code is available at `https://github.com/lanzv/Multilingual-emrQA`.

...
Lungs : R lower 01-20 with coarse BS and rales ; L side clear ; no wheezing Abd : thin, nd, nt, soft, no masses palpable Ext : thin, no edema, multiple old well-healed scars on R leg Skin : warm and dry, no rash or breakdown noted though could not examine sacrum Neuro : reactive to pain, otherwise

Pertinent Results : 2014-01-20 05:30 AM BLOOD WBC - 10.9 RBC - 4.63 Hgb - 13.6 * Hct - 40.3 # MCV - 87 MCH - 29.3 MCHC - 33.7 RDW - 14.0 Plt Ct - 393 # 2014-01-20 05:30 AM BLOOD Neuts - 82.6 * Lymphs - 14.5 * Monos - 2.2 Eos - 0.2 Baso - 0.4 2014-01-20 02:08 PM BLOOD PT - 13.2 PTT - 27.4 INR (PT)- 1.2 2014-01-20 05:30 AM BLOOD Plt Ct - 393 # 2014-01-20 05:30 AM BLOOD Glucose - 334 *
...

Figure 1: Clinical text sample from emrQA dataset (Pampari et al., 2018), after filtration by Yue et al. (2020).

1 Introduction

Medical professionals spend considerable time going through (long) clinical documents to find answers to specific questions about particular patients (Demner-Fushman et al., 2009). This process can be simplified using natural language processing models designed for Question Answering (QA), either by searching for relevant evidence to answer the question or directly providing a precise answer that does not even need to be present in the context texts (Tsatsaronis et al., 2015). Patients would directly benefit from this more efficient process through better quality care. In addition, such QA systems can be designed specifically for patients, allowing them to ask direct questions about their discharge summaries or about other aspects of their medical records (Soni and Demner-Fushman, 2025).

Finding specific evidence supporting an answer in discharge summaries is a crucial step for two reasons: First, given the sensitive nature of the data and the current inability to guarantee that models will not hallucinate, the model must point to the specific part of the text that it used to generate its response. This allows a physician to verify the answer directly. Second, discharge summaries are typically lengthy documents, which pose challenges for large language models (LLMs) (Premasiri et al., 2023; Luo et al., 2024). Extracting relevant evidence from the text and incorporating it into prompts within a Retrieval-Augmented Generation setup offers a potential solution to this problem (Abdelghafour et al., 2024).

Currently, most medical research data and related QA models are conducted predominantly in English (Jin et al., 2019; Henry et al., 2019; Johnson et al., 2023) although most medical institutions use their local language to produce clinical texts, and models trained on English data are not applicable to documents in other languages.

In contrast, general-domain multilingual models

Proceedings of the Second Workshop on Patient-Oriented Language Processing (CL4Health), pages 69–82
May 4, 2025

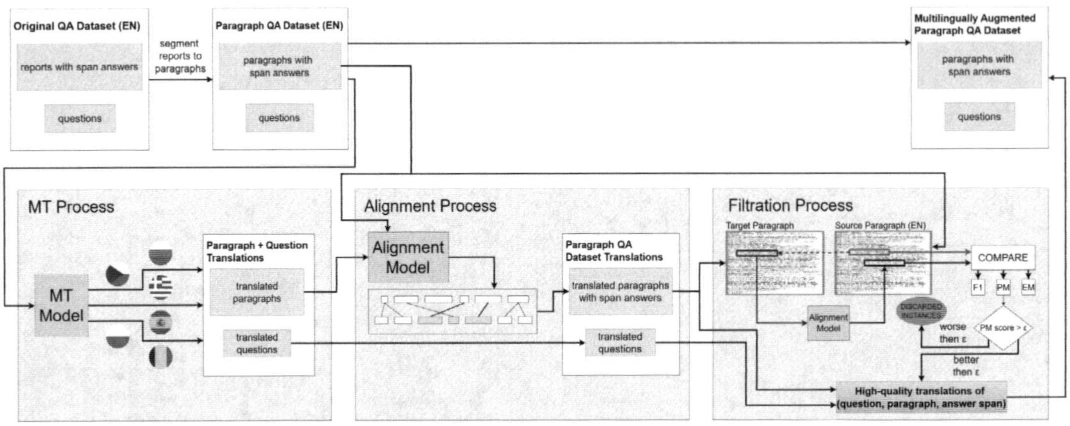

Figure 2: Multilingual data augmentation pipeline for the emrQA dataset.

(Devlin et al., 2018; Sanh et al., 2019; Conneau et al., 2019) are available for QA tasks in various languages. This raises two questions: How do such models, which have never been exposed to clinical data, perform clinical QA tasks? How important is the pretraining of the clinical domain?

To enhance the performance of multilingual models and expose them to more clinical data during fine-tuning, this study explores the impact of multilingual data augmentation. Several previous works have shown that multilingual data augmentation generally improves the performance of multilingual models (Liu et al., 2021; Bornea et al., 2021). However, it remains unclear whether the same holds in the clinical domain, which often differs from the standard language (Henriksson et al., 2014) (see Figure 1 for an illustration).

In this paper, we explore this idea by translating an English QA dataset derived from the emrQA dataset (Pampari et al., 2018) into six European languages: Bulgarian (BG), Czech (CS), Greek (EL), Spanish (ES), Polish (PL), and Romanian (RO) (as shown in Figure 2). We present a systematic approach to machine translation of a QA dataset that produces multilingual data for the task of finding evidence in clinical text that answers a given question. We exploit these translations for fine-tuning and evaluation of various models in monolingual and multilingual settings to investigate the impact of such multilingual data augmentation. Following Yue et al. (2020) and Lanz and Pecina (2024), we use two subsets from the emrQA dataset – *Medication* and *Relations*

We first describe the Machine Translation (MT) pipeline, which involves translating clinical reports, translating questions, and projecting the answer evidence substring into the translated text. Next, we discuss some poor-quality translated samples and propose how to deal with them. We then use these translations to fine-tune several Transformer-based models on the QA task. Based on that, we investigate how multilingual data augmentation improves the models' performance. Finally, we compare the performance of multilingual models with the clinically pretrained domain-specific models and discuss whether the clinical pretraining is necessary for this task.

This paper presents the following contributions:

- We propose a pipeline for augmentation of the clinical QA dataset into other languages.
- We introduce a novel unsupervised forward-backward substring alignment evaluation method that allows a more accurate assessment of substring alignment quality between languages without the need for labeled data.
- We demonstrate the performance of multilingual models on clinical QA tasks, highlighting the benefits of multilingual data augmentation and showing that clinical pretraining does not have to be more beneficial than general-domain multilingual pretraining.

2 Related Work

The task of QA involving the retrieval of the answer evidence substrings for a given question in a provided context has been extensively explored through various datasets. Among the most prominent are general purpose QA datasets such as SQuAD (Rajpurkar et al., 2016), which has also been already translated into several European languages via MT methods (Macková and Straka, 2020; Carrino et al., 2020; Cattan et al., 2021; Staš et al., 2023; Nuutinen et al., 2023). In addition to these, the clinical QA domain has gained attention with the emrQA dataset (Pampari et al., 2018), derived from the n2c2 challenge dataset (Henry et al., 2019).

Considerable work was done on the emrQA dataset with notable contributions by Yue et al. (2020), who adapted two emrQA subsets into a SQuAD-like format for more general use. Lanz and Pecina (2024) proposed segmentation of reports into paragraphs for better QA performance.

Various medical datasets exist in multiple languages, and the Khresmoi data set (Dušek et al., 2017) stands out as a parallel corpus of medical sentences in several European languages. Furthermore, there is a growing trend towards the development of datasets focused on extracting information from clinical documents in languages other than English (López-García et al., 2023; Zaghir et al., 2024; Richter-Pechanski et al., 2024). Furthermore, Gaschi et al. (2023) extended the n2c2 dataset by translating it into French and German (and we build on this work). This process involved aligning named entities using methods such as FastAlign (Dyer et al., 2013) and Awesome (Dou and Neubig, 2021). They also used machine translation systems such as Opus-MT (Tiedemann and Thottingal, 2020) and FAIR (Ng et al., 2019). However, the most recent MT systems are currently NLLB (Costa-jussà et al., 2022) and MadLad (Kudugunta et al., 2023).

In their multilingual experiments, Gaschi et al. (2023) tested a range of multilingual models, including mBERT (Devlin et al., 2018), distilmBERT (Sanh et al., 2019), and XLM-R (Conneau et al., 2019). However, these models are not pretrained on medical/clinical data, unlike BioBERT (Lee et al., 2019) or ClinicalBERT (Alsentzer et al., 2019), which were already used for emrQA experiments on English data (Yue et al., 2020; Lanz and Pecina, 2024). Despite the existence of LLMs trained on predominantly English medical data, such as MediTron (Chen et al., 2023) and BioMistral (Labrak et al., 2024), Lanz and Pecina (2024) demonstrated that the application of LLMs to answer substring-based evidence QA tasks is not straightforward, often computationally expensive without providing proportional benefits.

	Medication	**Relations**
Number of reports	262	426
Number of paragraphs	5 081	9 482
Number of questions	232 347	987 965

Table 1: Statistics of the *Medication* and *Relations* subsets segmented into paragraphs (each question has at least one answer in a paragraph).

3 Machine Translation of QA Dataset

This section outlines the MT methodology for the *Medication* and *Relations* subsets of the emrQA dataset, filtered and normalized by Yue et al. (2020). The process includes two phases: First, clinical reports and questions are translated using multilingual LLMs. Second, for each answer evidence, we find the corresponding substring in the translated text.

Clinical reports often pose a challenge for MT due to the size and complexity of their text. In addition, aligning answer evidences in such large texts would be challenging and error-prone. Therefore, we begin with segmenting the reports into paragraphs proposed by Lanz and Pecina (2024) which reduce the size of the context while preserving all necessary information (see statistics in Table 1).

3.1 Translation Process

Several recent works have presented highly robust MT models for general domains (Popel et al., 2020; Costa-jussà et al., 2022; Kudugunta et al., 2023). However, it is unclear how these models perform on clinical data. Following Gaschi et al. (2023), the performance of several MT models was evaluated in the Khresmoi medical domain data set (Dušek et al., 2017) (the results are reported in the Appendix B). For subsequent experiments, we chose MadLad-3B, which performs best or is very similar to the best results, but is significantly smaller and thus more time and memory efficient.

Translations of the questions in our dataset were done sentence by sentence. Translating (sometimes much) longer paragraphs turned out to be more challenging. Therefore, long paragraphs were divided into shorter parts. The paragraphs that exceed 750 characters were split into two parts of about the same length – preferably at the end of the sentence identified by the regular expression[1] closest to the middle of the entire paragraph. If such a split were not feasible, we split the segment at the whitespace

[1] `[a-z]{2}\.\s+[A-Z][a-z]`

closest to the middle of a paragraph. After translation, all segments within the paragraph are joined in their original order.

MadLad-3B sometimes tends to hallucinate when translating clinical reports, especially when they contain abundant medical abbreviations, acronyms, and figures. To address this, we propose the following solution: We append the phrase "Based on medical reports." after the end of each segment to be translated, providing the model with explicit context that the text is related to a clinical text (which is not always obvious from the segment content itself). If a correct translation of this phrase appears in a newly translated segment, it is removed along with any surrounding whitespaces. Otherwise, the text is translated again, with additional spaces inserted between the segment and the prompted medical phrase to make the difference even more explicit. In case of an increase in the limit of translation attempts, the standard translation using the MT model without any additional phrases was chosen. We refer to this method as the Prompted Medical Phrase (PMP) approach and compare it with the standard MT. The list of alternative translations of the phrase added to the prompt in all languages is provided in Appendix C. An example of the PMP approach is provided in Appendix D.

3.2 Answer Evidence Alignment

After translating the paragraphs, the answer evidence for each question must be found in the translated text. Due to the synthetic nature of evidence substrings in emrQA, these evidence segments often lack structure, sometimes appearing as incomplete sentences. Additionally, clinical texts frequently contain repetitive patterns (e.g., "mg," "q.p.m."), making the alignment crucial to correctly identify key clinical terms. However, these concepts are often very specific and the model may not have encountered them in alignment-based approaches during training. See Figure 3 for examples of evidence substrings from emrQA.

To align the answer evidence substring in the translated text, we could translate the original substring and locate it in the translated paragraph, as done for SQuAD (Macková and Straka, 2020; Cattan et al., 2021; Staš et al., 2023). However, due to the complexity of clinical data, identical translation cannot be guaranteed. Since SQuAD evidence is usually short (such as a person's name or location), the problem is not so complex. Therefore, this

Question: Has the patient ever tried heparin?
Context:
...
HOSPITAL COURSE: The patient was admitted on 0/25/95 with concern for her being at high risk of skin breakdown and infection. Plans were made for panniculectomy, however, prior to this procedure, she was admitted for IV Ancef t.i.d.; Hibiclenz showers and sub-q Heparin. Preoperatively, her pulmonary function was assessed and found to have an FEV-1 of 53% of predicted; FVC of 57% of predicted and an FEV-1/FVC of 93% of predicted. Chest x-ray showed no active cardiopulmonary disease ...

Question: Has the patient had allopurinol in the past?
Context:
...
MEDICATIONS: At the time of admission were as follows: 1. Lantus 100 mg q.p.m. 2. Humalog 20 units q.p.m. 3. Humalog sliding scale. 4. Neurontin 300 mg t.i.d. 5. Lisinopril 40 mg q.d. 6. Allopurinol 300 mg q.d . 7. Hydrochlorothiazide 25 mg q.d. 8. Zocor 20 mg q.d. 9. TriCor 50 mg b.i.d. 10. Atenolol 25 mg q.d. 11. Eyedrops prednisolone and atropine. 12. The patient was on iron supplementation.
...

Figure 3: Examples of emrQA evidence substrings, highlighted as colored spans showing alignment challenges.

paper opts for word alignment methods, similarly to Gaschi et al. (2023) and Zaghir et al. (2024). Specifically, this work considers two alignment models: the statistical model FastAlign (Dyer et al., 2013) and the Transformer-based model Awesome (Dou and Neubig, 2021) to project evidence from the source to the target language.

Awesome is a pretrained aligner, while FastAlign requires additional training. For this purpose, we use the parallel corpus NLLB (Costa-jussà et al., 2022), selecting the first 44.6 million sentences paired with English for each of the languages involved in our work. Since we have the same amount of data for each language, we can directly compare alignments across languages. Alignment is performed on the same segments as described in Section 3.1. Based on the predicted alignment, the counterparts of the source answer evidence are found in the translated paragraph. The alignment of the first and last words determines the boundaries of the target answer evidence substring.

As observed by Gaschi et al. (2023), the choice of an aligner is not straightforward. They noted that performance in the general domain is not always indicative of behavior on clinical data sets, leading to an initial suboptimal choice in their study. To objectively compare the performance of Awesome and FastAlign, this work introduces the unsupervised forward-backward substring alignment evaluation method. This method involves a double answer evidence substring alignment, once from the source language to the target language and then back to the source. As a result, there are two substrings in the source language: the original answer evidence

	BG			CS			EL			ES			PL			RO		
	EM	**F1**	**PM**	**EM**	**F1**	**PM**	**EM**	**F1**	**PM**	**EM**	**F1**	**PM**	**EM**	**F1**	**PM**	**EM**	**F1**	**PM**
FastAlign	32.1	83.2	82.4	50.0	86.6	86.0	28.6	81.6	80.9	54.6	90.9	90.5	48.3	89.0	88.4	34.2	86.7	85.3
Awesome	46.0	82.9	82.4	64.0	89.8	89.4	24.8	70.3	69.8	71.2	93.7	93.5	57.1	89.3	89.1	64.7	90.9	90.4
FastAlign PMP	41.0	88.9	88.2	53.1	91.4	91.0	**41.9**	**87.9**	**87.2**	56.3	93.8	93.4	50.1	**90.8**	90.2	35.7	89.6	88.1
Awesome PMP	**59.3**	**89.2**	**88.8**	**66.8**	**93.0**	**92.8**	36.5	76.2	75.7	**72.9**	**96.3**	**96.1**	**58.8**	90.6	**90.5**	**68.0**	**93.8**	**93.5**

Table 2: Comparison of FastAlign and Awesome and impact of the PMP translation approach on *Medication* subset.

	BG			CS			EL			ES			PL			RO		
	EM	**F1**	**PM**	**EM**	**F1**	**PM**	**EM**	**F1**	**PM**	**EM**	**F1**	**PM**	**EM**	**F1**	**PM**	**EM**	**F1**	**PM**
FastAlign	54.9	89.9	89.1	61.2	91.5	90.9	55.8	91.1	90.6	66.7	93.6	93.4	62.7	92.2	91.5	53.3	90.0	89.2
Awesome	60.7	86.3	86.0	66.0	91.0	90.8	40.2	77.3	77.0	77.0	95.1	95.2	59.5	88.3	87.9	72.3	91.8	91.5
FastAlign PMP	61.1	**92.9**	**92.1**	67.0	**94.0**	**93.5**	**60.6**	**92.1**	**91.7**	71.0	95.3	95.1	**66.7**	**93.9**	**93.2**	57.0	91.9	91.2
Awesome PMP	**66.8**	89.4	89.0	**70.2**	93.2	93.0	44.9	79.7	79.5	**79.3**	**97.0**	**97.2**	62.6	90.1	89.8	**76.2**	**94.3**	**94.1**

Table 3: Comparison of FastAlign and Awesome and impact of the PMP translation approach on *Relations* subset.

substring and a two-step alignment projection of the answer evidence substring, both included in the same source paragraph. Ideally, the two substrings should be identical.

If the substring changes (expands, shrinks, shifts, etc.) during the two-step alignment projection, the alignment is considered inaccurate. An incorrect answer evidence substring alignment in the forward step is likely to carry over to the backward projection, leading to further errors. In contrast, successful alignment in both directions serves as a reliable indicator of accurate projection from the source language to the translation language. Of course, the projection of the substring alignment from the source language to the target language could be correct, but the second projection back to the source language was problematic. So, this evaluation method is stricter than directly measuring the quality of the newly generated answer evidence substrings. Furthermore, it also indirectly evaluates the quality of the MT from the previous stage described in Section 3.1. Poor translation would hinder accurate alignment, allowing this method to compare the performance of the straightforward MT and the PMP approach.

In the unsupervised forward-backward substring alignment evaluation, we compare two English substrings and aim for identity. To measure string similarity, we use SQuAD metrics — Exact Match (EM) and F1 score. However, evaluating the correctness of the projected substring position, not just the word similarity, may be valuable. Thus, in addition to Exact Match (EM) and F1, we introduce Position Match (PM) computed as:

$$\text{PM} = \frac{2 \times O_P \times O_T}{O_P + O_T} \tag{1}$$

where $O_P = \frac{\text{Overlap Length}}{\text{Predicted Length}}$ is the predicted overlap ratio, and $O_T = \frac{\text{Overlap Length}}{\text{True Length}}$ is the true overlap ratio. The overlap is the common span between the predicted and original substring positions.

The final scores, averaged over all aligned answer evidence substrings, are shown in Tables 2 and 3. The PMP approach improves the performance of the standard MT model. The *Relations* subset is easier to process for the MT and alignment stages compared to the *Medication* subset, achieving F1 scores higher than 90% for most languages. The EM metric shows that approximately two-thirds of the answer evidence substrings in almost every language were perfectly projected without change. The *Medication* subset is more challenging but still exhibits good results. For both subsets, the Transformer-based aligner Awesome excels in Romance languages, while FastAlign outperforms in Greek. For Slavic languages, Awesome performs better in the *Medication* subset, but the results in the *Relations* subset are less clear. Only for Polish, FastAlign outperforms Awesome in all metrics. The differences between FastAlign and Awesome may be due to the fact that we trained FastAlign on all our languages, whereas Awesome was fine-tuned for word alignment only on the Romanian-English language pair relevant to our study. This could explain the performance disparities between Romance languages and others. However, since Awesome is based on mBERT, which has seen all these languages during pretraining, and Dou and Neubig (2021) showed that Awesome performs well even without fine-tuning, the impact of fine-tuning should not be pronounced.

3.3 Evaluation on Full Clinical Reports

Building on the results from the previous section, we base our next experiments on the PMP translation approach. For the *Medication* subset, we will

	BG		CS		PL	
	EM	F1	EM	F1	EM	F1
Awesome	**54.1**	77.4	**61.7**	81.4	53.0	76.8
FastAlign	50.4	**79.4**	57.5	**82.0**	**55.2**	**80.4**

Table 4: Comparison of mBERT performance on *Relations* translated to Slavic languages aligned by Awesome/FastAlign (paragraphs joined into full reports).

utilize FastAlign for Greek while adopting Awesome for all remaining languages. For the *Relations* subset, FastAlign will be employed for Greek, and Awesome for the Romance languages. To make a final decision on the most appropriate alignment method for Slavic languages in the *Relations* subset, this section evaluates the QA performance of the mBERT model using full clinical reports as context (rather than paragraphs, where we could not consider translated contexts that do not contain any question-answer pairs), considering both alignment models. Then, we compare alignment quality based on QA performance.

We follow the experiments of Yue et al. (2020). For this purpose, we focus on the Slavic languages within the *Relations* subset, Bulgarian, Czech, and Polish, and compare the QA results obtained using FastAlign and Awesome alignments, measured using the official SQuAD evaluation script. The results are presented in Table 4.

For Polish, we confirmed that FastAlign is the superior method. For Bulgarian and Czech, the choice is less clear, as the EM and F1 scores diverge. Although FastAlign shows a marginal F1 advantage, Awesome substantially outperforms in EM, so we proceeded with Awesome-based alignment for both languages in the following experiments on the *Relations* subset.

3.4 Filtering-out Low-Quality Alignments

Despite the alignment being mostly good, it is not always perfect. One reason might be flawed translations from the first stage. We also lack information about paragraphs that do not contain answers that need to be aligned to a new language. Therefore, paragraphs and answers with low alignment scores need to be filtered out, ignoring paragraphs without answers. This simplifies the task to Paragraph QA (similar to Oracle QA from Lanz and Pecina (2024)), resembling the SQuAD-like format (context is a paragraph rather than a document). Therefore, we examine which substring alignments we should discard and which ones we should keep (similarly as was done by Macková and Straka (2020)).

Low-quality answer evidence substring alignments negatively impact both the quality of the training and subsequent evaluation. Thanks to the forward-backward substring alignment evaluation, the quality of answer evidence projection can be estimated. This allows for filtering out those with low scores from the dataset, along with their corresponding paragraph context and question. Additionally, paragraphs can be removed if no question-answer pair is available, as there is no information about the quality of such paragraphs. As a result, in the remainder of this work, we focus on Paragraph QA instead of full report QA.

To determine how many answer evidences should be discarded, we conduct the following experiment. We sort the answer evidences from the training data based on their PM scores and sequentially remove $0, 5, 10, 15, 20, 30, 40, ...\%$ of the low-quality instances and for each resulting subset, we fine-tune the mBERT model (for each language separately) and compare the performance on the (silver) full test sets using Exact Match (EM) and F1 measures as in Yue et al. (2020). The results are averaged over three measurements with different random seeds and visualized in Figure 5 in Appendix E. Removing about 15% of lowest-quality instances improves the scores. Beyond this point, further removal risks losing complex data samples that may not have been perfectly aligned but remain essential for our task.

The pipeline described above is applied to the generated non-English training data and also to test data. Traditionally, such data is referred to as *silver data*, a term used to describe data that is automatically generated through processing of the original high-quality gold standard data. We experiment with two test sets: the full test set (which may contain alignment errors) and the intersection test set, formed by intersecting the translated and filtered test sets in each language, assuming higher reliability. The intersection test set contains identical instances across languages.

4 Multilingual Paragraph Question Answering Experiments

In this section, the performance of multilingual models is evaluated using the original English test set by assessing EM/F1 on the Paragraph QA task. The quality of the emrQA translations is also dis-

EM Score	Full Test Set							Intersection Test Set						
Models	EN	BG	CS	EL	ES	PL	RO	EN	BG	CS	EL	ES	PL	RO
distilmBERT (*mono*)	30.5	19.7	23.1	16.6	26.4	23.2	24.9	32.6	24.7	27.8	20.6	30.0	28.0	29.2
mBERT (*mono*)	32.7	21.4	25.0	17.8	28.7	24.3	27.8	34.6	26.5	29.7	22.0	32.4	29.0	32.5
XLM-R (*mono*)	33.4	22.1	26.0	18.3	29.1	25.5	28.0	35.4	27.3	30.9	22.3	32.8	30.5	32.6
XLM-R Large (*mono*)	**33.7**	23.0	26.5	19.1	**30.4**	26.0	28.5	35.4	28.2	31.5	23.3	**34.3**	30.6	33.1
distilmBERT (*multi*)	31.3	21.2	24.8	18.2	28.1	25.0	26.7	33.2	26.2	29.4	22.4	31.3	29.8	31.2
mBERT (*multi*)	33.0	22.6	26.6	19.4	29.9	26.6	28.5	35.1	27.6	31.3	23.9	33.5	31.7	33.2
XLM-R (*multi*)	33.5	22.8	26.8	19.5	30.0	27.1	28.6	35.4	27.7	31.5	24.2	33.3	31.9	33.1
XLM-R Large (*multi*)	33.6	**23.7**	**27.4**	**20.6**	30.3	**27.1**	**29.0**	**35.5**	**29.1**	**32.0**	**25.3**	33.6	**32.1**	**33.8**

Table 5: QA results on the *Medication* subset (EM scores) for monolingual (*mono*) and multilingual (*multi*) models.

F1 Score	Full Test Set							Intersection Test Set						
Models	EN	BG	CS	EL	ES	PL	RO	EN	BG	CS	EL	ES	PL	RO
distilmBERT (*mono*)	71.6	62.6	65.8	56.8	67.8	65.4	67.2	72.6	66.2	68.4	60.3	69.7	68.3	69.1
mBERT (*mono*)	75.3	66.0	69.7	60.1	71.0	67.9	70.7	76.0	69.8	72.1	63.6	72.5	71.0	72.8
XLM-R (*mono*)	75.9	67.4	71.1	61.8	72.3	69.9	72.2	76.6	71.0	73.8	65.5	74.0	72.8	74.5
XLM-R Large (*mono*)	**77.4**	69.3	72.7	63.7	74.1	70.9	73.6	**78.0**	72.8	75.2	67.5	75.7	73.6	75.8
distilmBERT (*multi*)	74.5	66.9	70.4	61.1	71.7	69.4	71.4	75.2	70.5	72.4	65.1	73.3	72.5	73.4
mBERT (*multi*)	76.7	68.6	72.3	63.5	74.0	71.5	73.3	77.3	72.2	74.2	67.3	75.4	74.4	75.2
XLM-R (*multi*)	77.0	69.6	72.8	64.5	74.1	72.0	73.5	77.6	73.0	75.0	68.4	75.5	74.6	75.7
XLM-R Large (*multi*)	77.3	**70.3**	**73.7**	**65.5**	**74.9**	**72.7**	**74.2**	77.8	**73.7**	**75.6**	**69.3**	**76.4**	**75.5**	**76.3**

Table 6: QA results on the *Medication* subset (F1 scores) for monolingual (*mono*) and multilingual (*multi*) models.

cussed by analyzing the performance of multilingual models on the translated data. In addition, the impact of including multilingual data during fine-tuning on model performance is investigated.

For these experiments, we selected four multilingual models mBERT, distilmBERT, XLM-R, and XLM-R Large (as Gaschi et al. (2023) did). In all experiments, we use filtered training data (discarding the 15% weakest alignments of the answer evidence substrings). Based on the analysis of Yue et al. (2020), we randomly sample the QA pairs to have the same number of training samples as 20% and 5% of the original unfiltered training data in the *Medication* and *Relations* subsets, respectively.

For the test set, we analyze two approaches. The first uses the entire unfiltered test sets. The second filters each translation by discarding the weakest 15% of alignments of the answer evidence substrings and then takes the intersection of filtered test sets across languages, allowing direct comparison. This filtering roughly retains 63% of the question-answer-paragraph triplets from the full unfiltered test sets. We split both *Medication* and *Relations* reports into train/dev/test according to a 7:1:2 ratio and perform experiments with three different random seeds for the splits. Finally, we examine multilingual training, where a single model is trained on the combined training data of all languages and evaluated separately on each. The results are shown in Tables 5, 6, 16 and 17.

4.1 QA Evaluation Across Languages

When the results of the full test set of other languages are compared with English, the results for Romance languages show a slight decrease, Slavic languages drop a bit more, and Greek displays a substantial difference. The results clearly reflect the quality already measured by the unsupervised forward-backward substring alignment evaluation method, which assesses the overall quality of the MT process, including substring alignment. This trend is seen not only across languages, but also in EM and F1 scores. Although F1 scores remain high under the alignment evaluation method, and therefore the Paragraph QA F1 score differences of new languages and English are not that large, EM scores in Paragraph QA show a much larger drop.

When trying to balance the quality of the test sets by filtering out poor-quality answer alignments and taking the intersection of languages, the scores across languages become more similar (except for Greek, which remains considerably lower).

Interestingly, we also observe that in the case of *Medication*, the English results improve on the intersection test set. This suggests that by removing poorly aligned answers during translations, we also excluded more complex answers regarding the QA prediction process. The remaining question

	Medication		Relations	
	EM	F1	EM	F1
BERTbase	31.0	72.9	91.1	96.2
BioBERT	31.1	74.4	91.7	96.9
ClinicalBERT	31.4	73.9	92.0	96.9
mBERT (*w/o tgt*)	31.0	75.9	90.0	96.0
mBERT (*mono*)	32.7	75.3	**92.8**	**97.3**
mBERT (*multi*)	**33.0**	**76.7**	92.6	**97.3**

Table 7: Performance comparison of clinical-domain monolingual and general-domain multilingual models.

is whether these are genuinely complex question-answer-paragraph triplets or if they represent annotation errors in the original emrQA dataset, which, due to its synthetic origin, contains numerous inaccuracies (Yue et al., 2020).

4.2 Impact of Multilingual Training

As we can see in Tables 5, 6, 16 and 17, multilingual training almost always slightly improves both EM and F1 scores, except in rare cases. As was already described, this training involves using all training sets from all languages to train a single model. In some cases, the improvement from multilingual training is even a few percentage points, particularly for smaller and faster models or for more problematic dataset translations.

When comparing multilingual training on the gold data in English, we arrive at a similar conclusion: augmenting the data with additional languages helps, particularly for the *Medication* subset, where Paragraph QA performance improves in all cases except with the XLM-R Large model. For the *Relations* subset, however, the differences are almost negligible, which may be due to the fact that the *Relations* task is approaching its oracle and has little room for further improvement (Yue et al., 2020).

5 Domain-Specific Models: Not Always Superior

In the previous section, we learned that multilingual models demonstrate strong performance, particularly on the *Relations* subset, despite never being specifically pretrained on clinical or medical data. To assess how much multilingual models are impacted by this, we measured the performance of BERTbase, ClinicalBERT, and BioBERT models fine-tuned only on the original English emrQA dataset on the same Paragraph QA task. In contrast, these models are not multilingual.

Table 7 compares these three models with their multilingual counterpart, mBERT. The evaluation includes three settings: monolingual fine-tuning (*mono*), fine-tuning with multilingual data augmentation (*multi*), as described earlier, and mBERT fine-tuned on train sets of all emrQA translations except the original English data (*w/o tgt*).

The results show that multilingual models perform as well as domain-specific models in our clinical QA task. Moreover, for the *Medication* subset, multilingual models outperform their domain-specific counterparts by a few percentage points. Additionally, while omitting the original English data during fine-tuning results in a performance drop, the decrease is not substantial, indicating a reasonable degree of cross-lingual transfer.

6 Conclusions

Our study focuses on the clinical QA task of finding answer evidence substrings within a given context for a specific question by multilingual models rather than domain-specific ones assessing their potential of medical support for various languages (since current clinical models are predominantly focused on English). This work investigated the effect of multilingual data augmentation in the clinical domain. Therefore, we described the MT pipeline including the process of answer evidence substring projection to translated paragraphs. Then, we compared different alignment and translation approaches. For our experiments, we used two subsets - *Medication* and *Relations* - from the emrQA dataset, translating them into six European languages: Bulgarian, Czech, Greek, Spanish, Polish, and Romanian.

During the data augmentation process, we observed that different languages pose distinct challenges for translation and subsequent QA evaluation. However, multilingual augmentation itself can be effective even in the clinical domain, as demonstrated by experiments on the *Medication* subset. However, it has a more limited effect on the *Relations* subset. However, we find that domain-specific models in our clinical QA task do not outperform multilingual models. In fact, general-domain multilingual models noticeably outperformed clinical domain-specific models on the *Medication* subset.

Limitations

This work is limited by the quality of the emrQA dataset, and our conclusions that clinical monolingual domain-specific models do not outperform multilingual general-domain models are based on a single specific clinical task evaluated in one specific language, rather than a broader range of tasks.

Acknowledgments

This research was partially supported by the SVV project number 260 698 and the Charles University GAUK grant No. 284125. It has also received support and funding from the European Union's Horizon Europe research and innovation programme project *RES-Q plus* (Grant Agreement No. 101057603). Views and opinions expressed are however those of the authors only and do not necessarily reflect those of the European Union or the Health and Digital Executive Agency. Neither the European Union nor the granting authority can be held responsible for them.

References

Mohamed Abdelghafour, Mohammed Mabrouk, and Zaki Taha. 2024. Hallucination mitigation techniques in large language models. *International Journal of Intelligent Computing and Information Sciences*, 24(4):73–81.

Emily Alsentzer, John Murphy, William Boag, Wei-Hung Weng, Di Jindi, Tristan Naumann, and Matthew McDermott. 2019. Publicly available clinical BERT embeddings. In *Proceedings of the 2nd Clinical Natural Language Processing Workshop*, pages 72–78, Minneapolis, Minnesota, USA. Association for Computational Linguistics.

Mihaela Bornea, Lin Pan, Sara Rosenthal, Radu Florian, and Avirup Sil. 2021. Multilingual transfer learning for qa using translation as data augmentation. *Proceedings of the AAAI Conference on Artificial Intelligence*, 35(14):12583–12591.

C. Carrino, Marta R. Costa-jussà, and José A. R. Fonollosa. 2020. *Automatic Spanish translation of SQuAD dataset for multi-lingual question answering*, page 5515–5523. European Language Resources Association (ELRA).

Oralie Cattan, Christophe Servan, and Sophie Rosset. 2021. On the usability of transformers-based models for a French question-answering task. In *Proceedings of the International Conference on Recent Advances in Natural Language Processing (RANLP 2021)*, pages 244–255, Held Online. INCOMA Ltd.

Zeming Chen, Alejandro Hernández Cano, Angelika Romanou, Antoine Bonnet, Kyle Matoba, Francesco Salvi, Matteo Pagliardini, Simin Fan, Andreas Köpf, Amirkeivan Mohtashami, Alexandre Sallinen, Alireza Sakhaeirad, Vinitra Swamy, Igor Krawczuk, Deniz Bayazit, Axel Marmet, Syrielle Montariol, Mary-Anne Hartley, Martin Jaggi, and Antoine Bosselut. 2023. Meditron-70b: Scaling medical pretraining for large language models. *Preprint*, arXiv:2311.16079.

Alexis Conneau, Kartikay Khandelwal, Naman Goyal, Vishrav Chaudhary, Guillaume Wenzek, Francisco Guzmán, Edouard Grave, Myle Ott, Luke Zettlemoyer, and Veselin Stoyanov. 2019. Unsupervised cross-lingual representation learning at scale. *CoRR*, abs/1911.02116.

Marta R. Costa-jussà, James Cross, Onur Çelebi, Maha Elbayad, Kenneth Heafield, Kevin Heffernan, Elahe Kalbassi, Janice Lam, Daniel Licht, Jean Maillard, Anna Sun, Skyler Wang, Guillaume Wenzek, Al Youngblood, Bapi Akula, Loic Barrault, Gabriel Mejia Gonzalez, Prangthip Hansanti, John Hoffman, Semarley Jarrett, Kaushik Ram Sadagopan, Dirk Rowe, Shannon Spruit, Chau Tran, Pierre Andrews, Necip Fazil Ayan, Shruti Bhosale, Sergey Edunov, Angela Fan, Cynthia Gao, Vedanuj Goswami, Francisco Guzmán, Philipp Koehn, Alexandre Mourachko, Christophe Ropers, Safiyyah Saleem, Holger Schwenk, and Jeff Wang. 2022. No language left behind: Scaling human-centered machine translation. *Preprint*, arXiv:2207.04672.

Dina Demner-Fushman, Wendy W. Chapman, and Clement J. McDonald. 2009. What can natural language processing do for clinical decision support? *Journal of Biomedical Informatics*, 42(5):760–772. Biomedical Natural Language Processing.

Jacob Devlin, Ming-Wei Chang, Kenton Lee, and Kristina Toutanova. 2018. BERT: pre-training of deep bidirectional transformers for language understanding. *CoRR*, abs/1810.04805.

Zi-Yi Dou and Graham Neubig. 2021. Word alignment by fine-tuning embeddings on parallel corpora. In *Proceedings of the 16th Conference of the European Chapter of the Association for Computational Linguistics: Main Volume*, pages 2112–2128, Online. Association for Computational Linguistics.

Ondřej Dušek, Jan Hajič, Jaroslava Hlaváčová, Jindřich Libovický, Pavel Pecina, Aleš Tamchyna, and Zdeňka Urešová. 2017. Khresmoi summary translation test data 2.0. LINDAT/CLARIAH-CZ digital library at the Institute of Formal and Applied Linguistics (ÚFAL), Faculty of Mathematics and Physics, Charles University.

Chris Dyer, Victor Chahuneau, and Noah A Smith. 2013. A simple, fast, and effective reparameterization of ibm model 2. In *Proceedings of the 2013 conference of the North American chapter of the association for computational linguistics: human language technologies*, pages 644–648.

Félix Gaschi, Xavier Fontaine, Parisa Rastin, and Yannick Toussaint. 2023. Multilingual clinical ner: Translation or cross-lingual transfer? In *5th Clinical Natural Language Processing Workshop*, pages 289–311. Association for Computational Linguistics.

Aron Henriksson, Hans Moen, Maria Skeppstedt, Vidas Daudaravičius, and Martin Duneld. 2014. Synonym extraction and abbreviation expansion with ensembles of semantic spaces. *Journal of Biomedical Semantics*, 5(1):6.

Sam Henry, Kevin Buchan, Michele Filannino, Amber Stubbs, and Ozlem Uzuner. 2019. 2018 n2c2 shared task on adverse drug events and medication extraction in electronic health records. *Journal of the American Medical Informatics Association*, 27(1):3–12.

Qiao Jin, Bhuwan Dhingra, Zhengping Liu, William Cohen, and Xinghua Lu. 2019. PubMedQA: A dataset for biomedical research question answering. In *Proceedings of the 2019 Conference on Empirical Methods in Natural Language Processing and the 9th International Joint Conference on Natural Language Processing (EMNLP-IJCNLP)*, pages 2567–2577, Hong Kong, China. Association for Computational Linguistics.

Alistair EW Johnson, Lucas Bulgarelli, Lu Shen, Alvin Gayles, Ayad Shammout, Steven Horng, Tom J Pollard, Sicheng Hao, Benjamin Moody, Brian Gow, et al. 2023. Mimic-iv, a freely accessible electronic health record dataset. *Scientific data*, 10(1):1.

Sneha Kudugunta, Isaac Caswell, Biao Zhang, Xavier Garcia, Christopher A. Choquette-Choo, Katherine Lee, Derrick Xin, Aditya Kusupati, Romi Stella, Ankur Bapna, and Orhan Firat. 2023. Madlad-400: A multilingual and document-level large audited dataset. *Preprint*, arXiv:2309.04662.

Yanis Labrak, Adrien Bazoge, Emmanuel Morin, Pierre-Antoine Gourraud, Mickael Rouvier, and Richard Dufour. 2024. Biomistral: A collection of open-source pretrained large language models for medical domains. *Preprint*, arXiv:2402.10373.

Vojtech Lanz and Pavel Pecina. 2024. Paragraph retrieval for enhanced question answering in clinical documents. In *Proceedings of the 23rd Workshop on Biomedical Natural Language Processing*, pages 580–590, Bangkok, Thailand. Association for Computational Linguistics.

Jinhyuk Lee, Wonjin Yoon, Sungdong Kim, Donghyeon Kim, Sunkyu Kim, Chan Ho So, and Jaewoo Kang. 2019. Biobert: a pre-trained biomedical language representation model for biomedical text mining. *CoRR*, abs/1901.08746.

Linlin Liu, Bosheng Ding, Lidong Bing, Shafiq Joty, Luo Si, and Chunyan Miao. 2021. MulDA: A multilingual data augmentation framework for low-resource cross-lingual NER. In *Proceedings of the 59th Annual Meeting of the Association for Computational Linguistics and the 11th International Joint Conference on Natural Language Processing (Volume 1: Long Papers)*, pages 5834–5846, Online. Association for Computational Linguistics.

Guillermo López-García, Francisco J. Moreno-Barea, Héctor Mesa, José M. Jerez, Nuria Ribelles, Emilio Alba, and Francisco J. Veredas. 2023. Named entity recognition for de-identifying real-world health records in spanish. In *Computational Science – ICCS 2023*, pages 228–242, Cham. Springer Nature Switzerland.

Zining Luo, Haowei Ma, Zhiwu Li, Yuquan Chen, Yixin Sun, Aimin Hu, Jiang Yu, Yang Qiao, Junxian Gu, Hongying Li, Xuxi Peng, Dunrui Wang, Ying Liu, Zhenglong Liu, Jiebin Xie, Zhen Jiang, and Gang Tian. 2024. Clinical large language models with misplaced focus. *Nature Machine Intelligence*, 6(12):1411–1412.

Kateřina Macková and Milan Straka. 2020. Reading comprehension in czech via machine translation and cross-lingual transfer. In *Text, Speech, and Dialogue*, pages 171–179, Cham. Springer International Publishing.

Nathan Ng, Kyra Yee, Alexei Baevski, Myle Ott, Michael Auli, and Sergey Edunov. 2019. Facebook FAIR's WMT19 news translation task submission. In *Proceedings of the Fourth Conference on Machine Translation (Volume 2: Shared Task Papers, Day 1)*, pages 314–319, Florence, Italy. Association for Computational Linguistics.

Emil Nuutinen, Iiro Rastas, and Filip Ginter. 2023. Finnish squad: A simple approach to machine translation of span annotations.

Anusri Pampari, Preethi Raghavan, Jennifer J. Liang, and Jian Peng. 2018. emrqa: A large corpus for question answering on electronic medical records. *CoRR*, abs/1809.00732.

Martin Popel, Marketa Tomkova, Jakub Tomek, Łukasz Kaiser, Jakob Uszkoreit, Ondřej Bojar, and Zdeněk Žabokrtský. 2020. Transforming machine translation: a deep learning system reaches news translation quality comparable to human professionals. *Nature communications*, 11(1):1–15.

Damith Premasiri, Tharindu Ranasinghe, and Ruslan Mitkov. 2023. Can model fusing help transformers in long document classification? an empirical study. In *Proceedings of the 14th International Conference on Recent Advances in Natural Language Processing*, pages 871–878, Varna, Bulgaria. INCOMA Ltd., Shoumen, Bulgaria.

Pranav Rajpurkar, Jian Zhang, Konstantin Lopyrev, and Percy Liang. 2016. SQuAD: 100,000+ questions for machine comprehension of text. In *Proceedings of the 2016 Conference on Empirical Methods in Natural Language Processing*, pages 2383–2392, Austin, Texas. Association for Computational Linguistics.

Phillip Richter-Pechanski, Philipp Wiesenbach, Dominic M. Schwab, Christina Kiriakou, Nicolas Geis, Christoph Dieterich, and Anette Frank. 2024. Clinical information extraction for low-resource languages with few-shot learning using pre-trained language models and prompting. *Preprint*, arXiv:2403.13369.

Victor Sanh, Lysandre Debut, Julien Chaumond, and Thomas Wolf. 2019. Distilbert, a distilled version of bert: smaller, faster, cheaper and lighter. *ArXiv*, abs/1910.01108.

Sarvesh Soni and Dina Demner-Fushman. 2025. Archehr-qa: Bionlp at acl 2025 shared task on grounded electronic health record question answering (version 1.1).

Ján Staš, Daniel Hládek, and Tomáš Koctúr. 2023. Slovak question answering dataset based on the machine translation of the squad v2.0. *Journal of Linguistics/-Jazykovedný casopis*, 74(1):381–390.

Jörg Tiedemann and Santhosh Thottingal. 2020. OPUS-MT – building open translation services for the world. In *Proceedings of the 22nd Annual Conference of the European Association for Machine Translation*, pages 479–480, Lisboa, Portugal. European Association for Machine Translation.

George Tsatsaronis, Georgios Balikas, Prodromos Malakasiotis, Ioannis Partalas, Matthias Zschunke, Michael Alvers, Dirk Weißenborn, Anastasia Krithara, Sergios Petridis, Dimitris Polychronopoulos, Yannis Almirantis, John Pavlopoulos, Nicolas Baskiotis, Patrick Gallinari, Thierry Artieres, Axel-Cyrille Ngonga Ngomo, Norman Heino, Eric Gaussier, Liliana Barrio-Alvers, and Georgios Paliouras. 2015. An overview of the bioasq large-scale biomedical semantic indexing and question answering competition. *BMC Bioinformatics*, 16:138.

Xiang Yue, Bernal Jimenez Gutierrez, and Huan Sun. 2020. Clinical reading comprehension: A thorough analysis of the emrQA dataset. In *Proceedings of the 58th Annual Meeting of the Association for Computational Linguistics*, pages 4474–4486, Online. Association for Computational Linguistics.

Jamil Zaghir, Mina Bjelogrlic, Jean-Philippe Goldman, Soukaïna Aananou, Christophe Gaudet-Blavignac, and Christian Lovis. 2024. FRASIMED: A clinical French annotated resource produced through crosslingual BERT-based annotation projection. In *Proceedings of the 2024 Joint International Conference on Computational Linguistics, Language Resources and Evaluation (LREC-COLING 2024)*, pages 7450–7460, Torino, Italia. ELRA and ICCL.

A Technical Details

This section provides additional details on fine-tuning, resource usage, and hyperparameters used in our experiments.

For alignment and translation models, default hyperparameters were used. QA models were trained with a learning rate of 3×10^{-5}, 3 epochs, weight decay of 0.01, batch size of 16, and a tokenizer processing 384-token blocks with a 128-token stride.

The experiments were carried out on nodes equipped with NVIDIA L40 GPUs (48GB per GPU).

The MT process took approximately 10 hours per language for the *Medication* subset and around 28 hours for the *Relations* subset. Alignment via Awesome required about 5 hours for the *Medication* subset and 8 hours for *Relations*. FastAlign training spanned several days, although the alignment step itself was completed in minutes.

For QA experiments, monolingual fine-tuning on the *Medication* subset took 1-4 hours (depending on model), while the *Relations* subset required 2-8 hours. Multilingual training ranged from 4–22 hours for the *Medication* subset and 8–40 hours for *Relations*.

B Clinical Performance of MT Models

Model	BLEU	METEOR	WER	CER
NLLB 600M	28.87	0.544	55.41	41.1
NLLB 1.3B dis	34.65	0.5911	50.35	37.7
NLLB 1.3B	33.02	0.5837	51.62	38.81
MadLad 3B	38.85	0.6367	45.91	34.71
NLLB 3.3B	35.04	0.6018	49.97	37.32
LINDAT	39.04	0.6337	**45.56**	34.55
MadLad 7B	38.77	0.6341	46.15	35.01
MadLad 10B	**39.28**	**0.6394**	45.61	**34.38**
NLLB 54B	38.23	0.623	47.28	35.36

Table 8: Translation from English into Czech.

Model	BLEU	METEOR	WER	CER
NLLB 600M	30.08	0.5732	52.18	38.48
NLLB 1.3B dis	31.3	0.585	51.14	37.6
NLLB 1.3B	31.4	0.5839	51.33	37.88
MadLad 3B	34.43	0.611	**49.03**	35.94
NLLB 3.3B	32.59	0.5949	50.95	37.44
LINDAT	30.77	0.5785	52.69	38.24
MadLad 7B	34.47	**0.613**	49.16	36.07
MadLad 10B	**34.7**	0.6101	**49.03**	**35.78**
NLLB 54B	33.46	0.5992	50.36	37.19

Table 9: Translation from English into German.

Model	BLEU	METEOR	WER	CER
NLLB 600M	46.67	0.713	41.43	27.82
NLLB 1.3B dis	47.65	0.7188	40.67	27.01
NLLB 1.3B	48.17	0.7224	39.93	26.94
MadLad 3B	49.21	0.7307	40.33	26.72
NLLB 3.3B	47.99	0.7218	40.68	27.17
LINDAT	47.28	0.7144	39.65	27.9
MadLad 7B	48.93	0.7305	41.03	26.87
MadLad 10B	**49.88**	**0.7364**	**39.46**	**26.4**
NLLB 54B	48.3	0.723	40.65	26.84

Table 10: Translation from English into French.

Model	BLEU	METEOR	WER	CER
NLLB 600M	13.04	0.3577	72.66	56.87
NLLB 1.3B dis	15.8	0.3948	69.78	55.27
NLLB 1.3B	15.29	0.3899	69.62	54.9
MadLad 3B	19.41	0.4403	65.37	52.33
NLLB 3.3B	16.96	0.4114	68.37	53.62
LINDAT	-	-	-	-
MadLad 7B	**20.48**	**0.4517**	64.89	51.33
MadLad 10B	19.94	0.448	**64.43**	**51.29**
NLLB 54B	18.91	0.4317	65.93	51.73

Table 11: Translation from English into Hungarian.

Model	BLEU	METEOR	WER	CER
NLLB 600M	14.97	0.3786	70.64	55.53
NLLB 1.3B dis	17.37	0.41	66.7	52.33
NLLB 1.3B	16.94	0.407	68.07	53.83
MadLad 3B	20.46	0.4545	62.33	48.11
NLLB 3.3B	18.41	0.4264	65.36	50.73
LINDAT	17.87	0.4163	65.1	50.24
MadLad 7B	**20.95**	**0.4598**	**61.8**	**47.67**
MadLad 10B	20.5	0.4546	62.1	47.9
NLLB 54B	19.24	0.4368	63.98	49.55

Table 12: Translation from English into Polish.

Model	BLEU	METEOR	WER	CER
NLLB 600M	46.09	0.7364	37.85	26.41
NLLB 1.3B dis	47.62	0.7462	37.12	26.3
NLLB 1.3B	47.19	0.7476	37.44	26.47
MadLad 3B	**49.05**	**0.7596**	**35.7**	**25.19**
NLLB 3.3B	48.05	0.7534	36.84	26.05
LINDAT	-	-	-	-
MadLad 7B	48.55	0.7555	36.27	25.72
MadLad 10B	48.27	0.7545	36.48	25.69
NLLB 54B	47.98	0.7505	36.7	26.12

Table 13: Translation from English into Spanish.

Model	BLEU	METEOR	WER	CER
NLLB 600M	41.93	0.6658	40.1	28.93
NLLB 1.3B dis	44.95	0.692	38.63	27.54
NLLB 1.3B	45.31	0.692	37.32	26.77
MadLad 3B	**52.34**	**0.748**	**31.4**	**23.07**
NLLB 3.3B	46.97	0.7059	36.55	26.17
LINDAT	-	-	-	-
MadLad 7B	51.42	0.7402	32.76	24.21
MadLad 10B	51.82	0.7437	31.78	23.14
NLLB 54B	47.26	0.7071	36.34	26.2

Table 14: Translation from English into Swedish.

C PMP Phrase Alternatives

Language	Translations
EN	Based on medical reports.
BG	Въз основа на медицинските доклади.
	Въз основа на медицински доклади.
	На базата на медицински доклади.
	Въз основа на медицински съобщения.
CS	Na základě lékařských zpráv.
EL	Βασισμένο σε ιατρικές εκθέσεις.
	Με βάση ιατρικές εκθέσεις.
	Βάσει ιατρικών εκθέσεων.
	Με βάση τις ιατρικές εκθέσεις.
	Βάσει των ιατρικών εκθέσεων.
	Σύμφωνα με τις ιατρικές εκθέσεις.
ES	Basado en informes médicos.
	Según los informes médicos.
	De acuerdo con los informes médicos.
	Con base en los informes médicos.
	Fundado en informes médicos.
RO	Pe baza rapoartelor medicale.
PL	Na podstawie raportów medycznych.
	Na podstawie sprawozdań lekarskich.

Table 15: Translations of the phrase "Based on medical reports." used as alternative phrases to look for in the translated paragraphs in the PMP MT approach.

D PMP Example

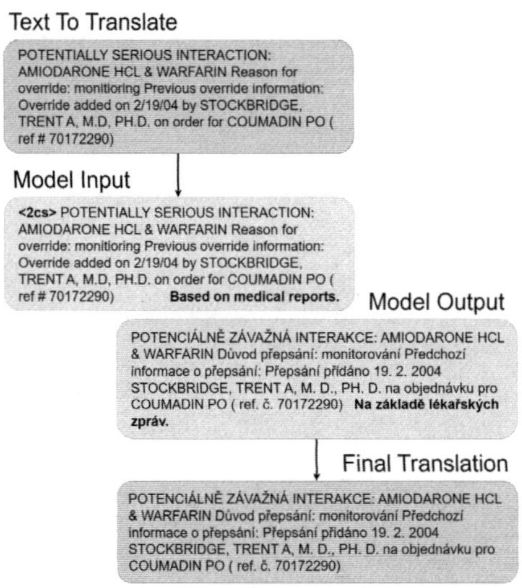

Figure 4: Example of the MT process based on the PMP approach using the MadLad model.

E Filtration Experiments

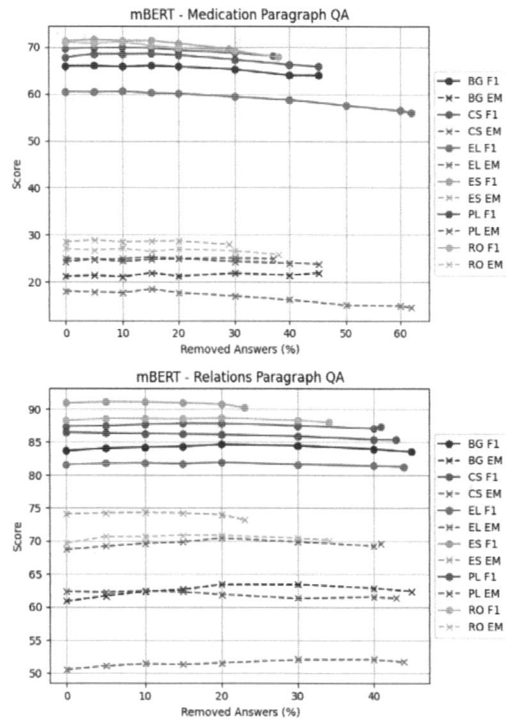

Figure 5: Filtration experiment for *Medication* and *Relations* subsets with mBERT. X-axis describes the percentage of the weakest answer evidence substrings that are removed from the training sets. Y-axis shows the F1 and EM scores of the Paragraph QA task for all translations.

F Multilingual Question Answering Results - Relations Subset

EM Score	Full Test Set							Intersection Test Set						
Models	**EN**	**BG**	**CS**	**EL**	**ES**	**PL**	**RO**	**EN**	**BG**	**CS**	**EL**	**ES**	**PL**	**RO**
distilmBERT (*mono*)	91.0	60.7	67.6	49.5	72.0	59.2	69.4	89.5	68.8	73.9	55.8	74.1	65.8	76.2
mBERT (*mono*)	92.8	63.2	70.0	51.5	74.3	61.8	70.8	90.7	71.3	76.6	57.6	76.3	68.5	77.2
XLM-R (*mono*)	93.2	63.3	71.1	52.3	75.3	62.9	72.2	91.1	70.9	77.4	58.7	77.1	69.6	79.0
XLM-R Large (*mono*)	**93.6**	64.7	72.4	**54.6**	76.2	**65.1**	73.1	**91.5**	72.8	**78.9**	**60.9**	78.1	**72.3**	80.0
distilmBERT (*multi*)	91.5	62.1	70.0	50.8	73.9	60.9	71.0	89.9	70.0	76.5	57.3	76.1	67.6	77.4
mBERT (*multi*)	92.6	63.3	70.6	52.3	75.1	62.8	72.1	90.3	71.2	77.3	58.6	76.5	70.0	78.5
XLM-R (*multi*)	93.0	64.1	72.4	53.1	75.8	63.8	72.7	91.0	72.2	78.9	59.3	77.8	70.7	79.6
XLM-R Large (*multi*)	93.2	**65.5**	**72.8**	54.1	**76.5**	64.8	**74.0**	91.0	**73.5**	**78.9**	60.8	**78.7**	71.6	**80.9**

Table 16: QA results on the *Relations* subset (EM scores) for monolingual (*mono*) and multilingual (*multi*) models.

F1 Score	Full Test Set							Intersection Test Set						
Models	**EN**	**BG**	**CS**	**EL**	**ES**	**PL**	**RO**	**EN**	**BG**	**CS**	**EL**	**ES**	**PL**	**RO**
distilmBERT (*mono*)	96.3	82.6	85.7	79.7	89.4	83.8	87.2	95.3	86.4	88.4	83.2	90.0	86.4	89.4
mBERT (*mono*)	97.3	84.5	87.7	81.9	91.0	86.2	88.6	96.1	90.4	88.2	85.2	91.5	88.8	90.8
XLM-R (*mono*)	97.4	85.2	88.6	82.5	91.7	87.2	89.5	96.2	88.7	91.0	85.7	92.1	89.6	91.7
XLM-R Large (*mono*)	**97.6**	86.1	89.5	84.3	92.2	88.7	90.3	**96.4**	89.8	92.0	87.3	92.7	91.0	92.5
distilmBERT (*multi*)	96.7	83.9	87.8	81.4	90.8	85.7	88.6	95.8	87.6	90.3	84.9	91.3	88.3	90.5
mBERT (*multi*)	97.3	85.2	88.7	83.0	91.8	87.3	89.6	96.1	88.9	91.2	86.2	92.1	89.8	91.6
XLM-R (*multi*)	97.4	85.9	89.3	83.7	92.5	88.4	90.3	96.3	89.6	91.7	86.7	93.0	90.6	92.4
XLM-R Large (*multi*)	97.5	**86.7**	**89.9**	**84.5**	**92.7**	**89.2**	**90.9**	**96.4**	**90.4**	**92.2**	**87.6**	**93.2**	**91.1**	**93.2**

Table 17: QA results on the *Relations* subset (F1 scores) for monolingual (*mono*) and multilingual (*multi*) models.

Mining Social Media for Barriers to Opioid Recovery with LLMs

Vinu H Ekanayake, Md Sultan Al Nahian, Ramakanth Kavuluru
University of Kentucky, Lexington, KY USA
{vinu.ekanayake,mna245,ramakanth.kavuluru}@uky.edu

Abstract

Opioid abuse and addiction remain a major public health challenge in the US. At a broad level, barriers to recovery often take the form of individual, social, and structural issues. However, it is crucial to know the specific barriers patients face to help design better treatment interventions and healthcare policies. Researchers typically discover barriers through focus groups and surveys. While scientists can exercise better control over these strategies, such methods are both expensive and time consuming, needing repeated studies across time as new barriers emerge. We believe, this traditional approach can be complemented by automatically mining social media to determine high-level trends in both well-known and emerging barriers. In this paper, we report on such an effort by mining messages from the `r/OpiatesRecovery` subreddit to extract, classify, and examine barriers to opioid recovery, with special attention to the COVID-19 pandemic's impact. Our methods involve multi-stage prompting to arrive at barriers from each post and map them to existing barriers or identify new ones. The new barriers are refined into coherent categories using embedding-based similarity measures and hierarchical clustering. Temporal analysis shows that some stigma-related barriers declined (relative to pre-pandemic), whereas systemic obstacles—such as treatment discontinuity and exclusionary practices—rose significantly during the pandemic. Our method is general enough to be applied to barrier extraction for other substance abuse scenarios (e.g., alcohol or stimulants).

1 Introduction

The opioid epidemic in the United States has persisted for over two decades, with opioid-related fatalities surging despite concerted public health interventions (National Institute on Drug Abuse, 2024). Individuals struggling to recover from opioid abuse or addiction often encounter powerful personal, social, and structural barriers such as traumatic life events, shame, or limited access to treatments that severely hinder the recovery process (Smith et al., 2021). As substance abuse is a multifaceted disease involving physiological, behavioral, and psychosocial factors, barriers to recovery are not always simple or obvious and may vary across different groups of people. However, it is critical to discover and document these barriers to tailor treatments and targeted interventions. This has been typically explored through qualitative methods like focus groups, surveys, and in-depth interviews. While these approaches yield valuable insights, they are also labor-intensive, rely on self-reported experiences in *controlled* settings, and cannot easily capture the evolution of new recovery challenges (without repeating studies).

Meanwhile, online communities have emerged as vital platforms where individuals can share their challenges, successes, and strategies for overcoming addiction. Due to the perceived anonymity, users also tend to express more freely compared to disclosing to a provider during face-to-face interactions. One such community is the subreddit `r/OpiatesRecovery` with over 50,000 members who share their struggles, successes, and motivations (Reddit, 2024). This user-generated content provides a dynamic lens into the nuances of opioid recovery, offering spontaneous, evolving narratives that traditional methods may miss. Yet, given the sheer volume of data generated daily, identifying specific barriers can be daunting without automated support. Our effort addresses this gap by extracting and temporally analyzing barriers to recovery as expressed by members of `r/OpiatesRecovery`. By focusing on posts from 2018 to 2021, we aim to capture how these barriers *changed* during the COVID-19 pandemic relative to pre-pandemic times. Here changes include how well-known barriers became more or less prominent across time and the emergence of any new barriers.

Proceedings of the Second Workshop on Patient-Oriented Language Processing (CL4Health), pages 83–99
May 4, 2025

Before we proceed, for the purposes of this study, we define a "barrier" as any personal (e.g., stress from a recent breakup), social (e.g. shame), or structural (e.g., limited access to treatment) circumstance of a patient's life that impedes their recovery from opioid addiction. A barrier is often expressed as a phrase, a sentence, or a short blurb that succinctly expresses the specific circumstance. Different users can express the same barrier in different ways. Unlike for entities such as diseases, medications, or side effects, there are no established terminologies or canonical definitions of barriers to recovery from substance abuse. This complicates (a). aggregation of barrier expressions that essentially mean the same thing and (b). characterization of what constitutes a new barrier. As such, barrier analysis poses interesting challenges to NLP methods (which typically handle categories with clear semantic distinctions using ample supervision signal from training data.) We believe these kinds of tasks are not uncommon in healthcare, where so called coding "instruments" are typically used to conduct qualitative research that can be subsequently interpreted through a quantitative lens.

Large language models (LLMs), based on the transformer decoder component, offer a new affordance with regard to the challenge posed in the previous paragraph. We use the GPT-4 LLM (specifically, `GPT-4-1106-preview`) in a semi-automatic setup to extract barriers, map them to predefined barriers from prior literature, identify new barriers, and quantify temporal barrier prevalence variations. Our contributions are as follows:

- We conduct a literature review to curate barriers to opioid recovery focusing on papers that report on conventional approaches such as a focus-groups and surveys. We extract a set of 21 barriers from this purely manual process.
- We use a multi-stage prompting approach with GPT-4 to extract barrier expressions from `r/OpiatesRecovery` messages from 2018 to 2021. Using Open AI embeddings (specifically, `text-embedding-3-large`) of these expressions we map them to the 21 literature-derived barriers identified in the previous step, if there is *sufficient* semantic similarity.
- The remaining barrier expressions (unmapped from previous step) are consolidated into a new coherent set of *emerging barriers* through agglomerative hierarchical clustering of their Open AI embeddings.
- We examine normalized shifts in prevalence of both literature-derived and emerging barriers in the periods before and after the pandemic declaration (March 11, 2020) from the 2018–2021 `r/OpiatesRecovery` messages.

Our approach is general enough to be applied for other substances and we provide concrete findings on emerging barriers and temporal trends. The code corresponding to our full barrier extraction and clustering pipeline is available here: `https://github.com/bionlproc/opioid_recovery_barriers`

2 Related Work

1. Prior work on barriers: Identifying barriers to recovery from opioid abuse has been extensively studied through conventional approaches, revealing a range of challenges including social stigma, lack of support networks, limited access to treatment, and economic hardships. Comorbid mental health disorders (e.g., depression and anxiety) further complicate recovery, highlighting the need for integrated treatment approaches (Cernasev et al., 2021; Dickson-Gomez et al., 2024).

2. Social media, Reddit, and substance abuse efforts: Social media platforms, particularly Reddit, have become valuable resources for researching substance (ab)use and addiction (Pandrekar et al., 2018; Kavuluru et al., 2019; Tran and Kavuluru, 2020). Our team has recently participated in the shared task on identifying clinical and social impacts of non-medical drug use in Reddit posts (Obeidat et al., 2024). Subreddit `r/OpiatesRecovery`, with its active community, offers insights into personal struggles and coping strategies that traditional methods may miss (Lu et al., 2019; Boettcher, 2021). NLP techniques are used to identify themes in recovery narratives, analyze sentiment trends, and classify behavioral shifts in substance use discussions (Sarker et al., 2022; Yang et al., 2023; Lu et al., 2019).

Recent studies have explored NLP-driven approaches to analyzing opioid-related discussions on social media. Bremer et al. (2023) applied NLP techniques to detect Reddit posts discussing barriers to opioid use disorder (OUD) treatment. Their effort is the closest to ours in terms of the main themes explored; however, their focus is more on barriers to seeking medical treatment for OUD and relies on manual analysis following an initial NLP-driven post identification. Our study broader in scope (general barriers to recovery process) and introduces a semi-automated approach that uses LLMs to extract, categorize, and track the evolution of opioid recovery barriers over time. Unlike previous studies that primarily used NLP techniques for retrieving relevant discussions, our methodology automates key components of the analysis. This enables large-scale analysis of recovery barriers with minimal manual intervention. Yang et al. (2024) focused on self-disclosures of opioid use on Reddit, developing a classification system to distinguish different phases of substance use, such as medical use, misuse, addiction, and recovery. Additionally, Nasralah et al. (2020) introduced a social media text mining framework for opioid-related discussions, leveraging ontology-based keyword searches and topic modeling to detect broader trends in drug abuse discourse on Twitter.

3. Opioid epidemic during the pandemic: The COVID-19 pandemic intensified challenges for individuals struggling with opioid recovery by disrupting healthcare services and support systems. Studies show increased isolation, reduced access to treatment, and higher stress levels during the pandemic, leading to higher relapse rates (Mellis et al., 2021; Melamed et al., 2022). The shift to telehealth introduced technological barriers and reduced personal interactions, further complicating effective treatment (Oesterle et al., 2020).

Our effort is at the intersection of the above three themes. Traditional studies offer foundational knowledge, while mining social media with NLP methods helps capture fine-grained challenges. Additionally, examining the impact of COVID-19 adds a temporal dimension, illustrating how external crises can alter the recovery landscape.

3 Methodology

3.1 Data collection

Reddit data: Posts were collected from `r/OpiatesRecovery` using *Academic Torrents*, a platform for sharing large datasets (Watchful1, 2023). The extraction covered posts made between January 1, 2018, and December 31, 2021, a timeframe selected to capture opioid recovery barriers both before and during the COVID-19 pandemic. Initially, 25,552 posts from 8,594 unique users were extracted. However, due to their minimal content, posts with fewer than 50 words were excluded, resulting in a final dataset of 14,735 posts from 7,202 unique users.

Literature derived barriers: To identify well-known barriers to opioid recovery, a literature search was conducted using Google Scholar with the keywords "opioid use," "barriers," and "recovery." The primary sources include multiple systematic reviews (between 2013–2024 (Notley et al., 2013; Grella et al., 2020; Barnett et al., 2021; Cernasev et al., 2021; Choi et al., 2022; Farhoudian et al., 2022; Hutchison et al., 2023; Dickson-Gomez et al., 2024)), which provided comprehensive insights into individual, social, and structural impediments to sustained opioid use disorder treatment. A few additional studies were incorporated to ensure a broad representation of barriers. Identified barriers were reviewed, categorized, and consolidated to eliminate redundancy, resulting in a final list of 21 distinct literature-derived barriers (LDBs) by merging conceptually similar factors and coming up with corresponding brief blurbs capturing their essence; since this was done manually, these blurbs were used as canonical ways of describing the LDBs.

3.2 Barrier expression extraction

A first task in mining Reddit posts for barriers is to ensure first person disclosures that are not vague. Thus, the following guidelines were established:

- The user is discussing their own experiences and not those of others.
- The barrier is explicitly mentioned by the user or strongly indicated as causing or contributing to the risk of relapse.

To evaluate multiple LLM prompting strategies, we selected a set of 100 posts with careful consideration to capture a diverse sample. This selection included posts that adhered to the guidelines — containing explicit mentions of self-reported barriers — as well as posts that did not meet the guidelines. In addition, the sample was curated to include posts of varying lengths, ranging from short entries to longer, more detailed narratives, thereby ensuring that the prompts were tested against a broad spectrum of user inputs. These posts were manually annotated with gold standard barriers or a "no barriers found" label, as appropriate. The evaluation was conducted on a per-post basis, with precision and recall metrics calculated individually for each post. Subsequently, average precision and recall across all 100 posts were computed to assess overall performance. Here it is important to note that by "gold standard" we mean annotator crafted sentences in English that capture the barrier without any reference terminology.

Multiple prompt-engineering strategies were compared to identify which would most reliably capture personal struggles and relapse triggers mentioned in `r/OpiatesRecovery`. Specifically, we tested zero-shot, in-context learning (ICL), and chain-of-thought (CoT) prompting using OpenAI's GPT-4-1106-preview model. Although both CoT and ICL outperformed zero-shot prompting, they still missed some barriers and occasionally extracted irrelevant information or failed to consistently adhere to the established guidelines. Additionally, ICL required carefully selected examples and proved unsuitable for longer Reddit posts due to high token usage and associated costs. To address these limitations, we developed a multi-step pipeline that incorporates a verification mechanism to ensure adherence to guidelines and refine the output. This process consists of three consecutive prompts (details in Table 6 of Appendix):

1. *Initial extraction*: A straightforward CoT prompt was used to direct GPT-4 to extract barriers based on the same guidelines that were used for manual extraction from the random sample —namely that the user must be describing their own experiences, and any mentioned barrier must be explicitly linked to causing or contributing to relapse.
2. *Verification*: The second prompt combined the first prompt, the model's initial response, and an additional verification query. This step double checks that each extracted barrier indeed matches the criteria of being a personal challenge mentioned by the user.
3. *Finalization*: A final prompt was used to filter out irrelevant explanations and generate a concise list of barriers. This step is expected to maintain sufficient descriptive detail for each barrier while removing duplicates.

3.3 Mapping extractions to LDBs

To measure the relative prevalence of literature-derived barriers (LDBs) in social media, it is important to map the extracted Reddit barriers to them. For this, we compared Reddit barriers against the 21 LDBs (Table 4 in Appendix A).

First, both the Reddit-extracted barriers and the 21 LDBs were transformed into high-dimensional embeddings using OpenAI's `text-embedding-3-large` model. Next, pairwise cosine similarity scores were calculated to assess how closely each Reddit-derived barrier aligned semantically with a known LDB. Barriers exceeding a predetermined cosine similarity threshold were mapped to the most similar LDB, while those with lower similarity scores (across all LDBs) were labeled as "new". This threshold value was set following manual evaluations of mapping outcomes, ensuring that barriers were only associated with an LDB when their semantic similarity and contextual relevance were high.

3.4 Clustering of new barriers

Barriers that don't map to any LDB are considered "new", though they may have some overlap with them. The challenge is to make sense of what these new barriers are conveying, given they are simply a bunch of sentences and there is no semantic anchoring to them. Our high level strategy here is to employ a clustering approach that groups similar barriers and surfaces semantically coherent "emerging" barriers represented by each cluster. Before clustering, all barriers are vectorized using Open AI's `text-embedding-3-large` model, which produces 3072-dimensional vectors (OpenAI, 2024).

3.4.1 Initial clustering of new barriers

Multiple clustering strategies were explored to group newly identified barriers, including k-means and agglomerative clustering with both Euclidean and cosine distances. k-means proved inadequate for effectively capturing the nuanced, overlapping nature of opioid-related barriers, while agglomerative clustering with Euclidean distance similarly struggled to partition the data cohesively. Consequently, we employed the `AgglomerativeClustering` algorithm from `scikit-learn` (Müllner, 2011) using cosine similarity, which treats each barrier as its own cluster and iteratively merges the most similar clusters until a predefined threshold is met. Because barriers are multifaceted and difficult to compartmentalize, hierarchical clustering offered the advantage of a dendrogram structure of clusters, accommodating an adaptive stopping criterion driven by the data. This approach consolidated repetitive or semantically related barriers into more coherent groups while providing flexibility in determining the optimal number of clusters.

3.4.2 Secondary clustering of new barriers

Due to the nuanced nature of barrier expressions, the initial clustering resulted in a large number of small closely related clusters, creating challenges for direct interpretation. To refine these results into more semantically distinct categories, a second round of clustering was conducted using key phrases as anchors that guide the clustering, inspired by Viswanathan et al. (2024). To this end, for each initial cluster, GPT-4 was prompted to generate two to three concise key phrases capturing the group's core semantic themes. These key phrases were then leveraged to guide the secondary clustering, ensuring that similar clusters—those sharing conceptual or topical grounding—could be merged more effectively. The key phrase generation prompt also incorporated a classification step, separating genuine barrier clusters from non-barrier phrases (e.g., "Finalized list of barriers to recovery:" or "Identified barriers:"). Clusters identified as "not a barrier" were excluded from further analysis, ensuring the final dataset focused solely on substantial opioid-related challenges.

To enhance clustering accuracy in this refinement stage, two embeddings were combined: the barrier text embedding (weighted by α) and the key phrase embedding (weighted by $1 - \alpha$). Applying the `linkage` function from the `scipy.cluster.hierarchy` library (Müllner, 2011), a full hierarchical structure was then constructed, enabling dynamic exploration of relationships among clusters. Adjusting α allowed for a balanced influence between the original barrier content and the generated key phrases.

Getting to high quality clusters is still not enough because these clusters could still have dozens of barrier expressions with no overarching description what this cluster is expected to represent. At this stage, we used GPT-4 to produce descriptive labels for each refined cluster, resulting in a concise thematic summary. These descriptors aided in interpreting the diverse range of new opioid recovery challenges that had not previously been documented in the literature. We term these as "emerging" since they appear more specialized and do not have the higher prevalence of well known LDBs.

3.5 Temporal trends in barriers

The final part of this study examined how extracted barriers evolved over time, with the onset of the COVID-19 pandemic as the index date. Reddit data was divided into two segments: (1). Pre-pandemic (January 1, 2018–March 11, 2020): before the WHO's official declaration of COVID-19 as a pandemic. (2). Pandemic portion (March 12, 2020–December 31, 2021): After the global crisis was formally recognized. To examine shifts in opioid recovery challenges between the pre-pandemic and pandemic periods, we tracked the normalized frequency of each barrier in both segments. The idea was to examine which barriers remained stable and which either intensified or diminished during the pandemic. We applied this to both LDBs and emerging barriers.

4 Results

4.1 Literature-derived barrier curation

As discussed in Section 3.1, we did a review of scientific literature to identify barriers that were already identified using traditional means. Table 4 (in the Appendix) presents details of the 21 LBDs where the first column indicate the barrier ID. These barriers encompass a variety of psychological, social, and systemic challenges that individuals face during opioid recovery. Several well-known barriers are discussed in the literature including fear of dealing with anxiety and stigma, co-morbid physical health issues, housing instability, negative attitudes about treatment, fear of incarceration, and ineffective services and exclusionary attitudes. Our goal in curating this list was to see if we can demonstrate the emergence of new barriers that may not have already been well known.

4.2 Reddit barrier extraction

As discussed in Section 3.2, we evaluated multiple prompting strategies for barrier extraction using the curated set of 100 posts with results shown in Table 1. Notably, the chain-of-thought with verification (CoT + Verification) strategy demonstrated superior performance, achieving the highest precision (95.14%) and recall (94.24%) scores among all methods. This enhanced performance underscores the benefit of incorporating verification into the CoT framework.

Following the evaluation, CoT with verification prompting strategy was run on all posts. Out of the 14,735 posts analyzed, 9,618 posts ($\approx$ 65.3%) contained barriers that aligned with the extraction guidelines. That is, they explicitly discussed authors' own recovery experiences and identified challenges contributing to relapse or hindering re-

Prompt strategy	Precision (%)	Recall (%)
Zero Shot	88.91	88.41
CoT	92.32	90.52
ICL	89.01	88.21
CoT + Verification	95.14	94.24

Table 1: Precision and recall for different prompting strategies averaged over 100 posts.

covery. From all qualifying posts, a total of 29,641 potential barriers were identified.

4.3 Classification of barriers — LDB or new

The classification process mapped 17,603 extracted Reddit barriers (59.3% of the total) to LDBs, confirming a strong alignment between user-generated content and established research. In contrast, 12,038 barriers (40.7%) were deemed novel, potentially highlighting emerging challenges, particularly during the COVID-19 pandemic. The classification threshold was set to 0.55, based on manual evaluation to ensure that mapped barriers exhibited sufficient semantic similarity to LDBs, while allowing room for identifying distinct, novel expressions of recovery challenges.

4.4 Clustering of new barriers

The clustering quality was assessed using the silhouette score, a metric that quantifies how similar an object is to its own cluster relative to other clusters (Pavlopoulos et al., 2024). In simple terms, it measures the cohesion within clusters and the separation between clusters, with values ranges from -1 to 1 (higher values indicating better-defined and more coherent clusters).

Clustering method	Sil. score	# clusters
k-means	0.028	1,310
Agglomerative (Euclidean)	0.037	962
Agglomerative (cosine)	0.071	1,369
+ Secondary clustering	0.181	354

Table 2: Performance of clustering methods for new barriers (Sil. score is the silhouette score achieved)

Among the clustering methods evaluated, agglomerative clustering with cosine similarity achieved the highest silhouette score of 0.071, compared to scores of 0.028 for k-means and 0.037 for agglomerative clustering using Euclidean distance. Although the score may initially seem low, it is not necessarily a definitive indicator of poor clustering quality. Given the high dimensionality of the embeddings, achieving high scores is challenging due to the "curse of dimensionality," where cosine distances between points become less distinguishable. Recent research on text clustering with LLM embeddings further shows that silhouette scores can be misleading when working with high-dimensional text representations (Petukhova et al., 2024). Moreover, the inherent complexity and semantic nuances of barrier texts further contribute to lower absolute silhouette values. Based on the results summarized in Table 2, agglomerative clustering with cosine similarity was picked for clustering the new barriers.

The secondary clustering process (from Section 3.4.2) substantially reduced the number of barrier clusters from 1,369 to 354 by incorporating key phrases generated via GPT-4. By optimizing the balance between barrier descriptions and key phrase themes (with a barrier text embedding weight of $\alpha = 0.3$ and a key phrase embedding weight of $(1 - \alpha)$), it consolidated similar clusters while maintaining semantic coherence; this resulted in a much better silhouette score (last row of Table 2). Additionally, clusters containing fewer than 10 elements were merged into a single cluster, as these small clusters likely represent barriers experienced by few individuals and would unnecessarily muddle the analysis. This refinement resulted in 185 final clusters, whose descriptors were generated with GPT-4 to provide a concise summary of the barriers they represent. Some illustrative examples are presented in Table 5 of the Appendix. This process enhanced both the manageability and interpretability of the thematic structure underlying new barriers.

Notable emerging barriers include (1). Kratom, a popular plant derived substance that is generally used to handle opioid cravings, was reported as also causing stomach issues and hence this alternative's side effects disrupted the recovery for those who relied on it. (2). Isolation due to work-from-home requirements during the pandemic lead to lack of social engagement depriving individuals of essential support networks. (3). Disruption of group support sessions where peers motivate and help each other cope with opioid dependence emerged as a pandemic era barrier that highlights how public health crises indirectly affect substance use recovery.

4.5 Temporal shifts in barrier prevalence

Table 3: Temporal shifts in LDB prevalence in Reddit data with counts of posts containing a barrier in the pre-covid data and covid data along with absolute count difference and percentage change normalized by total posts in each period

ID	# Pre-covid	# Covid	# Diff	% Change
0	609	527	-82	-11.06%
1	1,820	1,708	-112	-3.55%
2	189	152	-37	-17.34%
3	187	199	12	9.37%
4	12	20	8	71.29%
5	212	221	9	7.14%
6	568	509	-59	-7.90%
7	47	36	-11	-21.28%
8	380	321	-59	-13.18%
9	168	116	-52	-29.04%
10	520	462	-58	-8.69%
11	347	329	-18	-2.56%
12	491	479	-12	-0.26%
13	139	143	4	5.73%
14	197	121	-76	-36.87%
15	10	18	8	84.997%
16	9	20	11	128.39%
17	162	129	-33	-18.16%
18	186	170	-16	-6.06%
19	200	190	-10	-2.36%
20	2,469	2,811	342	17.01%

4.5.1 Temporal shifts of LDBs

Table 3 summarizes the temporal changes in the matched barriers with the first column corresponding to the ID field of Table 4. We emphasize all shifts discussed in this section are relative to the pre-pandemic period (before March 11, 2020). The analysis revealed nontrivial decreases in prevalence of certain LDBs. Notably, *identity difficulties* (ID 14) experienced the biggest decline of 36.87%. *Secrecy or fear about the past in new interpersonal relationships* (ID 9) declined by 29.04%. *Overreliance on other patients or treatment staff* (ID 7) decreased by 21.28%. *Fear of stigma* (ID 2) dropped by 17.34%, suggesting a potential reduction in internalized shame and an increased willingness to seek treatment. Conversely, certain barriers exhibited notable increases. The biggest increase was seen in the *lack of connection between emergency care and professional medical treatment* (ID 16), which soared by 128.39%, pointing to gaps in care continuity. Similarly, the *poor staff attitudes and training deficiencies* (ID 15) rose by 84.997%, pointing to potentially overwhelmed healthcare personnel and hurried onboarding of new staff without sufficient training, during the pandemic. Additionally, *unsuitable or ineffective services, along with exclusionary attitudes, policies, and programs* (ID 4), surged by 71.29%, indicating difficulties in accessing apt supportive treatment services. (Since the total absolute counts for IDs 4, 15, and 16 are each around thirty, the percent increases ought to be treated with a grain of salt.)

4.5.2 Temporal shifts of emerging barriers

After the WHO pandemic declaration, our results show that the prevalence of several emerging barriers rose substantially. Particularly, those related to *pandemic-induced isolation* and *reduced professional support*, soared over 500% and were closely tied to heightened anxiety, depression, and increased relapse vulnerability. Others, increasing by more than 300% dealt with the *loss of critical recovery resources*, including the closure of support groups and cancellations of outpatient treatments, which destabilized individuals' established sobriety-supportive routines. A modest uptick of 30% was seen in *serious sleep-related struggles*, such as insomnia and reliance on potentially addictive sleep aids, each contributing to a greater risk of relapse. These shifts highlight how the pandemic environment magnified existing vulnerabilities across multiple facets of recovery.

In contrast, some categories of novel challenges saw notable declines. One set of barriers, previously rooted in *resistance toward traditional 12-step or group-based treatment models*, dropped by over 60%, suggesting a diminished emphasis on philosophical or logistical objections to these support systems. Another emerging barrier involved a complex interplay of psychological, environmental, and social triggers complicating recovery. Exposure to drug-related content in media, music, and social interactions, as well as environmental cues such as specific locations or objects linked to past use can evoke powerful emotional responses and conditioned urges to relapse. Individuals face both subtle cues, like nostalgic music and overt triggers, such as drug paraphernalia or messages from dealers, create a constant battle against cravings and the risk of relapse. Discussions around this decreased by 45.28%, suggesting that while the challenge remains, it became less prominent in recovery narratives during the pandemic. Although these declines do not necessarily indicate that the issues were resolved, they do suggest a shift in the relative prominence of longstanding emotional, behavioral, and logistical hurdles to recovery. In other words, certain difficulties, while still present, became less frequently discussed.

5 Discussion

By harnessing opioid consumer posts on `r/OpiatesRecovery`, our findings show how emerging challenges such as disrupted treatment pathways and heightened isolation may aggravate well-known barriers like stigma, financial hardship, and limited healthcare access. In doing so, our approach addresses a gap in the literature, where the complexity and rapid evolution of barriers may often go underreported. Case in point, the high proportion of newly identified barrier expressions emphasizes the importance of mining social media data to complement and extend established knowledge. While this study confirms many classic themes in opioid recovery such as stigma and mental health comorbidities, it also highlights how online forums can shed light on previously unrecognized or insufficiently explored obstacles. The classification (LDB vs new) and clustering of new barriers, even if challenged by the inherent nuance and overlap in user narratives, offers a more agile perspective on how recovery challenges change over time. In the wake of the pandemic, the intensification of systemic barriers from strained healthcare systems to diminished access to essential services emerged as a powerful illustration of why adaptive solutions are critical.

Temporal comparisons before and after the WHO pandemic declaration underscore COVID-19's impact on recovery trajectories. Personal/social barriers, such as stigma and identity conflicts, appeared to ease—possibly reflecting the supportive role of online communities—while systemic obstacles like limited access to treatment, financial pressures, and housing insecurities intensified, reflecting the strain on healthcare resources during the pandemic. Additionally, emerging challenges such as increased isolation, disrupted treatment pathways, and sleep disturbances illustrate the multifaceted struggles faced by individuals in recovery. The persistence of entrenched relapse cycles and insufficient social support underscores the necessity for flexible, integrative strategies that address both immediate and structural issues.

Some of the new barriers indicated by Redditors have a grounding in COVID-19 literature. For instance, among the emergent challenges, altered sleep patterns have been noted as a barrier. Recent research by Donzella et al. (2022) found that COVID-19 infection significantly disrupted sleep patterns, with infected individuals experiencing longer sleep durations and increased trouble sleeping compared to non-infected individuals. This finding suggests that the sleep disturbances observed in our analysis may reflect both a general pandemic-related phenomenon and a specific consequence of COVID-19 infection.

To conclude, our effort is a proof of concept to conduct qualitative research aided by LLMs, with human steering. With appropriate recalibration to account for domain-specific language and contexts, the same method can be applied to other substance use disorders, such as alcohol or stimulant abuse, to uncover relevant barriers within other parallel online communities. Future work will address better streamlining of all the steps in the pipeline (LDB curation, barrier extraction, matching, and clustering) with recent advances. For example the "Deep Research" versions of Google Gemini and Open AI o3 models could reduce most of the manual work done in LDB curation. Dynamic topic models (Zhang and Lauw, 2022) applied to GPT-4 barrier extractions can also help with clustering by considering topic distribution as an additional feature during the clustering process.

6 Limitations

Despite promising insights, our work also exposes limitations of applying recent advances in NLP to consumer text analysis. Although a multi-step verification process improved classification precision and recall, subtle linguistic nuances and context-dependent barriers may still be misclassified or overlooked. Our approach needs careful human intervention at multiple steps in the pipeline and is not fully automated. For example, there was a need to at least generate a few human annotations of barriers from messages to assess different prompting strategies. Next, prompt engineering also needs major human inputs to instruct LLMs to generate barrier expressions that are not too short but also not too long and meandering. Checking different prompt outputs against human annotations (needed to create Table 1) is also manual because unlike traditional classification methods where ground truth class labels can be simply matched against model predictions, here one needs to check if GPT-4 extracted barriers "capture" the essence of what human annotators generated. Next, the appropriate cosine similarity threshold to match GPT-4 extractions to LDBs is also manually determined based on observations on a few samples. During clustering of new barriers, which in our opinion was the hardest part of this project, choosing a strategy along with any hyper-parameters (e.g., α in Section 3.4.2) also needs to be done by manually examining the quality of the clusters — to make sure they are thematically coherent but are not overly specific resulting in singleton clusters. While LLMs proved to be powerful in generative aspects of this project, they still need nontrivial steering effort by humans.

Self-reported data from Reddit carry intrinsic caveats, including possible exaggeration, underreporting, or skewed user demographics. The relatively low silhouette score in clustering, for instance, partly reflects the difficulty of discretely segmenting highly interrelated challenges (e.g., mental health issues intertwined with social isolation and financial strain). Nonetheless, the hybrid process of validation, merging quantitative metrics with careful prompt engineering, provides reassurance that the majority of extracted barriers are meaningful, although not without room for further refinement.

Acknowledgement

This work is supported by the U.S. NIH National Institute on Drug Abuse through grant R01DA057686. The content is solely the responsibility of the authors and does not necessarily represent the official views of the NIH.

References

Erin R. Barnett, Erin Knight, Rachel J. Herman, Kieshan Amarakaran, and Mary Kay Jankowski. 2021. Difficult binds: A systematic review of facilitators and barriers to treatment among mothers with substance use disorders. *Journal of Substance Abuse Treatment*, 126:108341.

Nick Boettcher. 2021. Studies of depression and anxiety using reddit as a data source: Scoping review. *JMIR Ment Health*, 8(11):e29487.

Whitney Bremer, Karma Plaisance, Drew Walker, Matthew Bonn, Jennifer S. Love, Jeanmarie Perrone, and Abeed Sarker. 2023. Barriers to opioid use disorder treatment: A comparison of self-reported information from social media with barriers found in literature. *Frontiers in Public Health*, 11:1141093.

A. Cernasev, K. C. Hohmeier, K. Frederick, H. Jasmin, and J. Gatwood. 2021. A systematic literature review of patient perspectives of barriers and facilitators to access, adherence, stigma, and persistence to treatment for substance use disorder. *Exploratory Research in Clinical and Social Pharmacy*, 2:100029.

Sugy Choi, David Rosenbloom, Michael D. Stein, Julia Raifman, and Jack A. Clark. 2022. Differential gateways, facilitators, and barriers to substance use disorder treatment for pregnant women and mothers: A scoping systematic review. *Journal of Addiction Medicine*, 16(3):e185–e196.

J. Dickson-Gomez, S. Krechel, J. Ohlrich, H. D. G. Montaque, M. Weeks, J. Li, J. Havens, and A. Spector. 2024. "they make it too hard and too many hoops to jump": system and organizational barriers to drug treatment during epidemic rates of opioid overdose. *Harm Reduction Journal*, 21(1):52.

S. M. Donzella, L. N. Kohler, T. E. Crane, E. T. Jacobs, K. C. Ernst, M. L. Bell, C. J. Catalfamo, R. Begay, K. Pogreba-Brown, and L. V. Farland. 2022. Covid-19 infection, the covid-19 pandemic, and changes in sleep. *Frontiers in Public Health*, 9:795320.

Ali Farhoudian, Emran Razaghi, Zahra Hooshyari, Alireza Noroozi, Azam Pilevari, Azarakhsh Mokri, Mohammad Reza Mohammadi, and Mohsen Malekinejad. 2022. Barriers and facilitators to substance use disorder treatment: An overview of systematic reviews. *Substance Abuse: Research and Treatment*, 16:1–11.

Christine E. Grella, Erika Ostile, Christy K. Scott, Michael Dennis, and John Carnavale. 2020. A scoping review of barriers and facilitators to implementation of medications for treatment of opioid use disorder within the criminal justice system. *The International Journal on Drug Policy*, 81:102768.

Morica Hutchison, Beth S. Russell, Abigail Leander, Nathaniel Rickles, Derek Aguiar, Xiaomei S. Cong, Ofer Harel, and Adrian V. Hernandez. 2023. Trends and barriers of medication treatment for opioid use disorders: A systematic review and meta-analysis. *Journal of Drug Issues*, 0(0):1–22.

Ramakanth Kavuluru, Sifei Han, and Ellen J Hahn. 2019. On the popularity of the usb flash drive-shaped electronic cigarette Juul. *Tobacco control*, 28(1):110–112.

John Lu, Sumati Sridhar, Ritika Pandey, Mohammad Al Hasan, and Georege Mohler. 2019. Investigate transitions into drug addiction through text mining of reddit data. In *Proceedings of the 25th ACM SIGKDD International Conference on Knowledge Discovery & Data Mining*, KDD '19, page 2367–2375.

O. C. Melamed, W. K. deRuiter, L. Buckley, and P. Selby. 2022. Coronavirus disease 2019 and the impact on substance use disorder treatments. *The Psychiatric Clinics of North America*, 45(1):95–107.

Alexandra M. Mellis, Marc N. Potenza, and Jessica N. Hulsey. 2021. Covid-19-related treatment service disruptions among people with single- and polysubstance use concerns. *Journal of Substance Abuse Treatment*, 121:108180.

Daniel Müllner. 2011. Modern hierarchical, agglomerative clustering algorithms. *Preprint*, arXiv:1109.2378.

Tareq Nasralah, Omar El-Gayar, and Yong Wang. 2020. Social media text mining framework for drug abuse: Development and validation study with an opioid crisis case analysis. *Journal of Medical Internet Research*, 22(8):e18350.

NIDA National Institute on Drug Abuse. 2024. Overdose death rates. https://nida.nih.gov/research-topics/trends-statistics/overdose-death-rates.

Caitlin Notley, Annie Blyth, Vivienne Maskrey, Jean Craig, and Richard Holland. 2013. The experience of long-term opiate maintenance treatment and reported barriers to recovery. *European Addiction Research*, 19(6):287–298.

Motasem Obeidat, Vinu Ekanayake, Md Sultan Al Nahian, and Ramakanth Kavuluru. 2024. UKYNLP@ SMM4H2024: Language model methods for health entity tagging and classification on social media (tasks 4 & 5). In *Proceedings of The 9th Social Media Mining for Health Research and Applications Workshop and Shared Tasks*, pages 124–129.

Timothy S. Oesterle, Bhaskar Kolla, Christopher J. Risma, Susan A. Breitinger, Dusan B. Rakocevic, Larisa L. Loukianova, Dana K. Hall-Flavin, Morgan T. Gentry, Timothy A. Rummans, Mayank Chauhan, and Matthew S. Gold. 2020. Substance use disorders and telehealth in the covid-19 pandemic era: A new outlook. *Mayo Clinic Proceedings*, 95(12):2709–2718.

OpenAI. 2024. *OpenAI Embeddings Guide*. Accessed: 2024-01-31.

Sheetal Pandrekar, Xin Chen, Gaurav Gopalkrishna, Avi Srivastava, Mary Saltz, Joel Saltz, and Fusheng Wang. 2018. Social media based analysis of opioid epidemic using reddit. In *AMIA Annual Symposium Proceedings*, volume 2018, page 867.

John Pavlopoulos, Georgios Vardakas, and Aristidis Likas. 2024. Revisiting silhouette aggregation.

Alina Petukhova, João P. Matos-Carvalho, and Nuno Fachada. 2024. Text clustering with large language model embeddings. *International Journal of Cognitive Computing in Engineering*.

Reddit. 2024. r/OpiatesRecovery. https://www.reddit.com/r/OpiatesRecovery/. Accessed: 2024-11-18.

A. Sarker, N. Nataraj, W. Siu, et al. 2022. Concerns among people who use opioids during the covid-19 pandemic: a natural language processing analysis of social media posts. *Substance Abuse Treatment, Prevention, and Policy*, 17:16.

Karen Smith, Linda Jones, and Tom Brown. 2021. Social isolation and its effects on opioid use disorder recovery. *Journal of Addiction Medicine*, 15(3):210–218.

Tung Tran and Ramakanth Kavuluru. 2020. Social media surveillance for perceived therapeutic effects of cannabidiol (CBD) products. *International Journal of Drug Policy*, 77:102688.

Vijay Viswanathan, Kiril Gashteovski, Kiril Gashteovski, Carolin Lawrence, Tongshuang Wu, and Graham Neubig. 2024. Large language models enable few-shot clustering. *Transactions of the Association for Computational Linguistics*, 12:321–333.

Watchful1. 2023. Subreddit comments/submissions 2005-06 to 2023-12. https://www.reddit.com/r/pushshift/comments/1akrhg3/separate_dump_files_for_the_top_40k_subreddits/. This is the top 40,000 subreddits from reddit's history in separate files. You can use your torrent client to only download the subreddits you're interested in. These are from the Pushshift dumps from 2005-06 to 2023-12 which can be found here https://academictorrents.com/details/7c0645c94321311bb05bd879ddee4d0eba08aaee. These are zstandard compressed ndjson files. Example Python scripts for parsing the data can be found here https://github.com/Watchful1/PushshiftDumps. If you have questions, please reply to this Reddit post or DM u/Watchful on Reddit or respond to this post https://www.reddit.com/r/pushshift/comments/1akrhg3/separate_dump_files_for_the_top_40k_subreddits/.

Chenghao Yang, Tuhin Chakrabarty, Karli R Hochstatter, Melissa N Slavin, Nabila El-Bassel, and Smaranda Muresan. 2024. Identifying self-disclosures of use, misuse, and addiction in community-based social media posts. In *Findings of the Association for Computational Linguistics: NAACL 2024*, pages 2507–2521. Association for Computational Linguistics.

E. F. Yang, R. Kornfield, Y. Liu, M. Y. Chih, P. Sarma, D. Gustafson, J. Curtin, and D. Shah. 2023. Using machine learning of online expression to explain recovery trajectories: Content analytic approach to studying a substance use disorder forum. *Journal of Medical Internet Research*, 25:e45589.

Delvin Ce Zhang and Hady Lauw. 2022. Dynamic topic models for temporal document networks. In *International Conference on Machine Learning*, pages 26281–26292. PMLR.

A Appendix

Table 4: List of manually curated literature-derived barriers

lit_barrier id	Barrier	Description
0	Low self-confidence and negative self-perception	A deeply ingrained negative self-image can significantly increase the risk of relapse by fostering feelings of worthlessness, making it difficult to build healthy relationships, and deterring individuals from seeking help. This negative self-perception also contributes to poor self-care and reinforces internalized stigma, making the recovery process more challenging.
1	Fear of dealing with emotions and anxiety	Opioids often mask underlying emotional issues and boost self-esteem, creating a fear of confronting raw emotions without the crutch of drugs. This fear makes it difficult for individuals to manage overwhelming feelings of anxiety, worry, and stress, which can hinder the recovery process and increase vulnerability to relapse.
2	Fear of stigma	Stigma related to aging, past drug use, mental health issues, poverty, and methadone treatment profoundly affects self-identity and recovery. The internalization of these stigmas can lead to shame, social withdrawal, and a reluctance to seek or continue treatment, further complicating the recovery journey.
3	Negative attitudes or beliefs about treatment	Stigmatizing beliefs about medication-assisted treatment (MAT) and the uncertainties surrounding treatment options can prevent individuals from seeking help. Misinformation, fear of judgment, and negative perceptions of treatment can lead to resistance or disengagement from the recovery process.
4	Unsuitable/ineffective services and exclusionary attitudes, policies, and programs	Inadequate or rigid treatment services, particularly for those with co-occurring mental health conditions, fail to meet the specific needs of individuals. Exclusionary policies, such as restrictive program hours, lack of language services, and daily attendance requirements, further alienate those seeking help, limiting their access to effective treatment.
5	Housing instability and homelessness	A lack of stable housing creates an unpredictable and stressful environment that disrupts recovery efforts. Without a secure place to live, access to treatment is often compromised, and the constant exposure to triggers increases the risk of relapse.
6	Difficulties with establishing a non-drug-using network of friends and lack of social capital or support	Building new, supportive social networks that do not involve drug use is a significant challenge. The absence of compassionate and understanding relationships, particularly with family members, can lead to isolation and a lack of the social support necessary for successful recovery.

Continued on next page

lit_barrier id	Barrier	Description
7	Over-reliance on other patients or treatment staff in treatment facilities	In treatment centers, individuals may become overly dependent on other patients and staff, creating a sense of being caught between two worlds. This reliance can hinder the development of personal autonomy and coping skills essential for long-term recovery.
8	Influence of habits of spouse/partner/family members/peers to drugs	The drug use habits of close family members, partners, or friends can increase the availability and temptation of drugs, making it harder for individuals to maintain sobriety. This close proximity to drug use can be a significant trigger for relapse.
9	Secrecy or fear about the past in new interpersonal relations	The inability to share past experiences with new acquaintances can lead to feelings of isolation and exile from mainstream society. This secrecy can create barriers to forming genuine, supportive relationships, which are crucial for recovery.
10	Fear of incarceration	For some individuals, particularly women who fear losing custody of their children, the threat of incarceration is a significant barrier. The criminalization of drug use, fear of police harassment, and the risk of arrest discourage seeking help, leading to untreated addiction and increased relapse risk.
11	Co-morbid mental and physical health issues	The presence of additional addictions or physical and mental health conditions, such as anxiety, depression, self-loathing, childhood trauma, or physical illnesses, complicates the recovery process. These co-occurring issues require specialized treatment, and when unaddressed, they can significantly hinder recovery.
12	Expensive costs and financial problems	The high costs of treatment, particularly for those without insurance, can prevent individuals from accessing necessary care. Financial barriers, including the inability to afford medication and out-of-pocket costs, are significant obstacles to sustained recovery.
13	Issues in accessing treatment	Accessing treatment is particularly challenging for individuals from culturally and linguistically diverse communities or those in rural areas. Geographical barriers, lack of transportation, and limited availability of medication-assisted treatment (MAT) create significant obstacles to regular and consistent treatment.
14	Identity difficulties	Some individuals struggle with the identity transformation required by treatment programs, resisting the label of "patient" and finding it difficult to construct a new identity free from drug use. This identity conflict can create resistance to treatment and complicate the recovery process.

Continued on next page

lit_barrier id	Barrier	Description
15	Staff attitudes and training deficiencies	Judgmental attitudes from treatment providers and staff who lack empathy and understanding can create an unwelcoming environment for patients. When staff view clients as psychologically impaired or needing long-term maintenance without offering hope for recovery, it can discourage individuals from engaging fully in treatment.
16	Lack of connection between emergency care and professional medical treatment	A disconnect between emergency care services and ongoing professional medical treatment can lead to gaps in care. This lack of continuity can result in missed opportunities for intervention and support, increasing the risk of relapse.
17	Lack of adherence to treatment protocol	Managing multiple appointments and responsibilities, especially for mothers, can be overwhelming and lead to non-adherence to treatment protocols. The stress of balancing treatment with daily life can make it difficult to stay committed to recovery.
18	Misuse of prescribed medications	Some individuals misuse their prescribed medications by taking higher doses than recommended or combining them with illicit substances. This misuse can undermine the effectiveness of treatment and increase the risk of relapse.
19	Belief that treatment was unnecessary	Some individuals prefer to withdraw from opioids alone, without assistance, believing that treatment is unnecessary. This belief can lead to unsuccessful attempts at recovery and a higher likelihood of relapse.
20	Fear of withdrawal symptoms	The physical and psychological symptoms of withdrawal, such as nausea, vomiting, diarrhea, muscle aches, sweating, chills, fever, anxiety, depression, and intense cravings, can be overwhelming. The fear of experiencing these symptoms often discourages individuals from seeking help or continuing with treatment, increasing the risk of relapse.

Table 5: Examples of descriptors for emerging barrier extractions with GPT-4

GPT-4 generated cluster descriptor	Some example barriers in the cluster
The primary themes and challenges in opioid use disorder recovery, as highlighted by the list of barriers, revolve around the adverse reactions to and ineffectiveness of various alternative treatments and medications, including Kratom, benzodiazepines, clonidine, and suboxone. Users face significant obstacles such as physical side effects (nausea, vomiting, stomach issues, and severe sweating), psychological effects (increased anxiety, depression, and suicidal ideation), and specific health concerns (restless leg syndrome, sexual dysfunction, and dental health issues). These are compounded by the medications' unpleasant taste and physical discomfort upon ingestion, leading to non-adherence and relapse. The fear of losing access to necessary medications due to honesty about relapse, as well as the potential for medications to mask or exacerbate other health issues, creates a complex environment where individuals struggle to find tolerable and effective treatment options to manage withdrawal symptoms and support their recovery journey.	- Adverse physical reactions to Kratom: The user experiences stomach issues when using Kratom, which could discourage its use and negatively impact their detoxification and recovery process. - Intense cravings triggered by Benadryl: The user has experienced strong cravings for substances following the administration of Benadryl through an IV. - Concerns about the side effects of current anxiety medication (hydroxyzine), such as sleepiness, which may interfere with daily activities and thus pose a barrier to the recovery process.
Individuals in recovery from opioid use disorder are encountering significant barriers due to the ineffectiveness of both prescription and over-the-counter sleep aids, including melatonin, Zopiclone, and Ambien, as well as alternative methods like homeopathic remedies, kava root, and relaxation techniques. This pervasive lack of effective sleep solutions exacerbates insomnia, which not only impedes their recovery process but also poses a risk of relapse as they struggle to manage sleep disturbances without resorting to opioids. The reluctance of healthcare providers to prescribe certain hypnotics, coupled with the side effects and diminishing returns of available medications, underscores the urgent need for a comprehensive and effective treatment plan to address the critical role of sleep in the recovery journey.	- The person is restricted to using only over-the-counter sleeping aids, as they are unable to utilize prescription sleep medications or benzodiazepines to address their sleep disturbances. - Ineffectiveness of homeopathic remedies: The individual has attempted numerous homeopathic remedies to address their sleep issues, but none have been successful. The lack of an effective solution for their sleep disturbances is an additional barrier to their recovery from opioid use disorder. - Limited access to hypnotics, due to the general practitioner's reluctance to prescribe them, is a source of frustration for the user and is seen as a barrier to overcoming insomnia and aiding their recovery.

Continued on next page

GPT-4 generated cluster descriptor	Some example barriers in the cluster
The overarching challenge in opioid use disorder recovery, as reflected by the experiences described, is a pervasive lack of adequate and empathetic medical support across various healthcare settings. Patients frequently encounter barriers such as healthcare professionals prioritizing financial interests over patient care, insufficient understanding and coordination between pain and addiction clinics, and a general sense of isolation due to the healthcare system's failure to provide comprehensive and compassionate support. This lack of support extends to GPs who often dismiss patient concerns, inadequately address mental health needs, and fail to establish trust or offer practical assistance in creating and following effective recovery plans. The resulting environment is one where patients feel unheard, misunderstood, and inadequately treated, which severely undermines their confidence in the healthcare system and impedes their journey towards recovery. Additionally, systemic issues like misinformation, inadequate facilities, and cultural barriers further exacerbate the struggle for individuals seeking help for opioid use disorder, especially in regions with less developed psychiatric support systems.	- A lack of proper support and understanding within the healthcare system presented a barrier, as evidenced by the user being passed between the pain clinic and addiction clinic without receiving appropriate care. - Lack of medical support: The user feels that doctors do not take their concerns seriously, indicating a lack of accessible supportive medical care that is essential for managing recovery symptoms. - A history of inadequate support and assistance from hospitals and specialists, resulting in a diminished trust in the healthcare system, as the user has not received answers or help despite multiple consultations.
The primary themes and challenges in opioid use disorder recovery, as reflected by the barriers listed, revolve around the inadequacy of pain management solutions and the limited access to both pharmacological and non-pharmacological alternatives. Individuals struggling with chronic pain find non-opioid medications such as NSAIDs, over-the-counter pain relievers, and alternative therapies like CBD oil or marijuana to be ineffective, leading to a heightened risk of relapse into opioid use for pain relief. Compounding this issue is the reluctance or inability of medical professionals to explore new pain management methods, often leaving patients with unmanaged pain and a sense of desperation. This situation is exacerbated by the lack of access to specialized pain management services, particularly in the context of COVID-19, which has disrupted healthcare delivery and limited options for those seeking to manage pain without opioids. The collective impact of these barriers underscores the need for comprehensive, effective, and accessible pain management strategies as a critical component of opioid use disorder recovery.	- The inability to use NSAIDs due to medical contraindications, which restricts the user's alternatives for non-opioid pain relief and presents a challenge in reducing opioid use. - The closure of the Pain Management clinic due to Covid-19 has resulted in the inability to find a new doctor, disrupting the user's medication regimen. - Difficulty in finding a new doctor who can provide non-narcotic pain management solutions, following the dismissal of the previous pain management doctor.

Continued on next page

GPT-4 generated cluster descriptor	Some example barriers in the cluster
The primary themes and challenges in opioid use disorder recovery, as highlighted by the list provided, revolve around the profound impact of social isolation, disruptions to daily routines, and the exacerbating effects of the COVID-19 pandemic. Individuals face a multifaceted struggle where isolation—whether due to weather, unconventional wake-up times, work-from-home structures, or quarantine measures—significantly hampers their ability to connect with support networks and engage in recovery activities. The pandemic has intensified feelings of loneliness, anxiety, and depression, triggering memories of past substance use and increasing the risk of relapse. The lack of professional support and reduced engagement in positive activities further contribute to a sense of hopelessness and loss of purpose. Environmental factors, such as the dark times of lockdowns, and personal factors, such as bipolar disorder and the desire for self-isolation, compound the psychological distress. This complex interplay of isolation, mental health challenges, and pandemic-related constraints creates a formidable barrier to recovery, underscoring the need for robust, adaptive support systems that can reach individuals even in the most isolating circumstances.	- Quarantine situation: Users are experiencing isolation and a lack of support due to being stuck in quarantine, which poses a significant challenge to recovery. - Increased isolation and lack of productive activities because of COVID-19 restrictions, leading to intensified cravings, as described by the user who was laid off and forced to stay at home without engaging in meaningful activities. - Work-from-home isolation: The user's job does not involve much interaction with others, exacerbating their feelings of isolation and potentially depriving them of much-needed social support during recovery.
The COVID-19 pandemic has significantly disrupted the recovery process for individuals with opioid use disorder by imposing barriers that undermine their support systems and daily routines. Emotional distress has been exacerbated by the inability to attend support group meetings and therapy sessions, including AA and NA meetings, which are crucial for mutual support and maintaining sobriety. Lockdown measures have further restricted access to coping activities such as going to the gym, engaging in hobbies, and attending outpatient treatment, all of which are essential components of a structured recovery plan. The loss of these routines and support mechanisms has led to increased isolation, mental hardship, and a heightened risk of relapse, highlighting the profound impact that external factors and disruptions to daily structure can have on the journey to recovery.	- The closure of the center where group sessions are held due to the coronavirus pandemic is a barrier because it disrupts the structured recovery support necessary for maintaining sobriety. - The temporary shutdown of support meetings and therapy appointments, including physiotherapy, acupuncture, and cupping, poses a barrier as these services help manage painful side effects from methadone and are integral to the user's recovery support system. - Loss of access to the gym due to lockdown: The gym served as a critical support system for the user during their withdrawal period, and the inability to attend the gym because of lockdown measures is directly associated with their relapse.

Table 6: The three stage barrier extraction prompts

Prompt type	**Prompt**
Initial prompt	"You are given a Reddit post. Your task is to extract barriers to recovery from opioid use disorder as explicitly mentioned by the user. Strictly adhere to the following guidelines when extracting the barriers: • The user is talking about their own experience and not someone else's. • The barrier is explicitly mentioned by the user or has strong indications as causing them to relapse or contributing to the risk of relapse. Discard barriers that do not adhere to the above guidelines. • If no barriers are found, mention "No barriers found". Only use the details provided by the user in the post, without relying on previous knowledge on the subject or making assumptions. • Provide reasons for the selection of the items. • Finally, provide the items as a numbered list as follows: Identified barriers: <barrier 1> <barrier 2> ... Post: {post}"
Verification prompt	"Verify that the user explicitly mentions or has strong indications of the identified items as causing or contributing to relapse or shows strong indications of presenting challenges in maintaining recovery. The user must be talking about their own recovery."
Finalization prompt	"You are given information about potential barriers to recovery as mentioned by Reddit users in their posts, along with a verified list of barriers. Your task is to extract the finalized list of barriers from the provided text. Ensure each barrier is represented as a numbered list using clear and meaningful sentences that accurately capture the context and details without shortening them excessively. The barriers should be concise yet detailed enough for someone reviewing them later to fully understand what each barrier entails. If no barriers are found, return "No barriers found." Info on barriers to recovery: {verified_list_of_barriers} List of barriers to recovery:"

Multimodal Transformers for Clinical Time Series Forecasting and Early Sepsis Prediction

Jinghua Xu
Heidelberg University, Germany
xu@cl.uni-heidelberg.de

Michael Staniek
Heidelberg University, Germany
staniek@cl.uni-heidelberg.de

Abstract

Sepsis is a leading cause of death in Intensive Care Units (ICU). Early detection of sepsis is crucial to patient survival. Existing works in the clinical domain focus mainly on directly predicting a ground truth label that is the outcome of a medical syndrome or condition such as sepsis. In this work, we primarily focus on clinical time series forecasting as a means to solve downstream predictive tasks intermediately. We base our work on a strong monomodal baseline and propose multimodal transformers using set functions via fusing both physiological features and texts in electronic health record (EHR) data. Furthermore, we propose hierarchical transformers to effectively represent clinical document time series via attention mechanism and continuous time encoding. Our multimodal models significantly outperform baseline on MIMIC-III data by notable gaps. Our ablation analysis show that our atomic approaches to multimodal fusion and hierarchical transformers for document series embedding are effective in forecasting. We further fine-tune the forecasting models with labelled data and found some of the multimodal models consistently outperforming baseline on downstream sepsis prediction task.

1 Introduction

Sepsis is a serious complication of an infection, accounting for approximately 19.7% of all global deaths (Rudd et al., 2020). In 2017, World Health Organization declared that improving the prevention, recognition, and treatment of sepsis as a global health priority (WHO, 2020). Seymour et al. (2017) and Liu et al. (2017) suggest an increase in the adjusted mortality of septic patients with delayed antibiotic administration. With patients suffering from septic shock, Kumar et al. (2006) found an 3.6–9.9% hourly increase in mortality when treatment is delayed. Early Detection of Sepsis is critical to improve patient outcome.

With the emerging abundance of clinical electronic health record (EHR) data, multimodal patient data present both challenges and opportunities to forecasting and predictive tasks in the clinical domain. On the one hand, multimodal representation learning is a complex problem that requires proper handling of information from multiple sources (Tsai et al., 2018). On the other hand, data from various sources enrich information available to models, which enables more robust prediction (Baltrušaitis et al., 2018). Fusing multiple modalities such as laboratory measurements, clinical texts, medications, and procedures have shown improved performance on predicting inpatient mortality, length of stay, and 30-day readmission (Rajkomar et al., 2018).

A further challenge in learning from clinical EHR datasets lies with data missingness and irregularity. The available observations for each patient may vary based on patient's condition, i.e. the set of observed clinical variables for each patient can differ from one another. Additionally, clinical measurements are often not taken at regular time intervals - the measurements may occur sporadically in time depending on the underlying conditions of the patient. Previous works such as Wang et al. (2022) simply aggregate data into hourly bins to circumvent data missingness, irregularity and sporadicity. However, this introduces noises and suppresses information to indicate patient condition through the actual availability of clinical measurements. To tackle the issue, Tipirneni and Reddy (2022) implements "Triplet Embedding" based on Set Functions proposed in Horn et al. (2020) to represent each clinical observation for each patient at each time discretely to avoid data imputation/aggregation of any form. While Tipirneni and Reddy (2022) achieves excellent performance on prediction tasks against several strong baselines, it disregards information potentially contained in clinical notes associated with each patient

Proceedings of the Second Workshop on Patient-Oriented Language Processing (CL4Health), pages 100–108
May 4, 2025 ©2025 Association for Computational Linguistics

Paper	Multi-modal	Set Function	Time Encoding	Forecasting
Horn et al. (2020)	✗	✓	Sinusoidal Encoding	✗
Wang et al. (2022)	✓	✗	✗	✗
Lyu et al. (2022)	✓	✗	Sinusoidal Encoding	✗
Tipirneni and Reddy (2022)	✗	✓	Learnable Embedding	✓
Lee et al. (2023)	✓	✓	Linear Projection	✗
Proposed Models	✓	✓	Leanrable Embedding	✓

Table 1: Tabular comparison of proposed models and related works closely referred to.

record in EHR data.

With majority existing works in the clinical domain approach predictive tasks directly by predicting a ground truth label as the outcome of observed patient conditions (Lee et al., 2023; Tipirneni and Reddy, 2022; Wang et al., 2022; Lyu et al., 2022), Xu et al. (2023) proposed to focus on forecasting, and implemented a rule-based sepsis check for Sepsis prediction that depends on model forecasts. We follow this practice and primarily seek to build models for time series forecasting (cause prediction), as an intermediate means to eventually predict sepsis and potentially other medical syndrome instead of predicting an outcome directly.

To address various limitations with existing works, we build upon a strong monomodal baseline model (Tipirneni and Reddy, 2022) and propose multimodal transformers primarily for clinical time series forecasting that 1) incorporates information from both physiological time series data and clinical notes via effective multimodal fusion 2) utilizes set functions to avoid data aggregation and imputation. The forecasting models produce predictions of the clinical variable values in a two-hour forecasting window following corresponding observation windows of varying lengths, to support ruled-based implementations (e.g. Xu et al., 2023) that rely on predicted values of specific clinical variables. Meanwhile, the forecasting models are fine-tunable with labelled data for downstream prediction tasks such as sepsis prediction. We additionally propose a hierarchical transformer to effectively represent clinical notes that naturally form document time series within observation windows by integrating time embeddings of note records, and accounting for the interactions between notes in time order via attention mechanism. We conduct comprehensive experiments and ablation analysis to showcase that our proposed models and the atomic modules are effectively robust, improving forecasting performance from baseline significantly.

We summarise the main contributions of our work as follows:

- We propose a multimodal learning framework for patient data in EHR datasets that effectively incorporates information from both physiological features and associated clinical notes.
- We propose a specialized hierarchical transformer to effectively represent clinical document time series that accounts for the interactions between individual clinical notes via attention and brings cross-modal time awareness to the entire model through consistent time encoding.
- Our clinical time series forecasting models approach predictive tasks in the clinical domain from a cause-prediction perspective. It provides flexibility in two dimensions: 1) the forecast values can be used for prediction of multiple medical syndromes and conditions with rule-based implementations (e.g. sepsis check based on Sepsis-3 definition (Reyna et al., 2020; Seymour et al., 2016; Singer et al., 2016)) 2) the forecasting models can be fine-tuned for arbitrary downstream prediction tasks with correspondingly labelled data in a fully data-driven setup. Additionally, the intermediate results produced by forecasting models are also directly interpretable by clinical practitioners as pointed out in previous work.

We release our code at github.com/JINHXu/clinical-multimodal-transformers.

2 Related Work

Clinical time series data are inherently sequential, making common sequence modelling methods (RNNs, transformers, etc.) suitable. Early works use classic models such as Gaussian Process (GP) (Liu et al., 2013, 2017; Lu et al., 2008; Li and Marlin, 2016) and linear dynamical systems

Data	Non-septic patients	Septic patients	Non-septic ICU stays	Septic ICU stays
Train	26452	2124	33191	3360
Valid	6594	551	8358	904
Test	8296	635	10445	1024

Table 2: Number of septic/non-septic patients/ICU stays in train/validation/test data.

(LDS) (Liu and Hauskrecht, 2015) to model irregular clinical time series. Later works then employ RNN-based models given the sequential nature of time series data. Baytas et al. (2017), for instance, modified LSTM to fit hidden cell states to irregular time slots (T-LSTM). Che et al. (2018), on the other hand, modified the GRU cell which decays inputs to global means and hidden states through unobserved time intervals (GRU-D). The problem with classic models such as Gaussian Process are their sensitivity to choice of covariance and mean functions, while RNNs process long sequences (resulted by irregularity) sequentially with inability to parallel computation thus leading to long runtime.

More recent works employ transformer-based methods for clinical time series modeling. Wang et al. (2022), for instance, passes multivariate time series embeddings first through a block of transformer encoders to capture contextual information of the sequences, then followed by a dense interpolation layer to obtain a concise representation of transformer outputs. Tipirneni and Reddy (2022) also uses multi-head attention to obtain contextual embeddings through transformer, it then passes these embeddings to a self-attention layer to capture the context within each observation. Horn et al. (2020) uses attention-based aggregation to compute embeddings of set elements independently from other elements in order to reduce runtime complexity to linear from the original transformer (Vaswani et al., 2017), which accounts for dependency between such elements leading runtime and space complexity of $O(N^2)$. It is worth noting that, in this case, Horn et al. (2020) compromises on accuracy by disregarding such dependency for lower space and runtime demand, while Tipirneni and Reddy (2022) uses a transformer block similar to Vaswani et al. (2017) to guarantee model performance with the expense of computing power and time.

Most works in clinical machine learning focus on predictive tasks. Tipirneni and Reddy (2022) proposes an encoder-only transformer model for direct mortality prediction as the target task, while its intermedial proxy model could be used for time series forecasting. Staniek et al. (2024) proposes encoder-decoder long-term clinical time series forecasting models to predict outcome via predicting the cause of syndromes intermediately. These forecasting models, however, are monomodal models that learn from data of single modality, disregarding potential information delivered through associated clinical notes in EHR datasets.

Multimodal learning is a common practice to address various tasks in the clinical doamin due to the various modalities of data in EHR datasets. Wang et al. (2022) uses concatenation to integrate multimodal patient data on physiological features and clinical texts. Later works in the clinical domain such as (Lyu et al., 2022) additionally applies a multimodal fusion encoder after concatenation of two modalities, in order to map them into a universal space before feeding the embeddings into a transformer. More recent works in the clinical domain employ attention-based fusion methods to represent multimodal patient data. (Lee et al., 2023), for instance, modified attention bottlenecks (Nagrani et al., 2021) from an audio-vision task to learn multi-modal EHR data (EHR time-series, EHR texts, EHR images) for mortality, vasopressor need, and intubation need prediction tasks.

Table 1 presents a tabular review of related works we closely refer to in this work. We seek to tackle the limitations in previous works, and define our primary task as time series forecasting on multimodal patient data. In the following sections, we further lay out the implementation specifics of our models and methods to overcome limitations in existing works.

3 Data

3.1 MIMIC-III

MIMIC-III (Medical Information Mart for Intensive Care 3) is a large database consisting of ICU (Critical Care Unit) patient records at the Beth Israel Deaconess Medical Center between 2001 and 2012 (Johnson et al., 2016). The entire MIMIC-

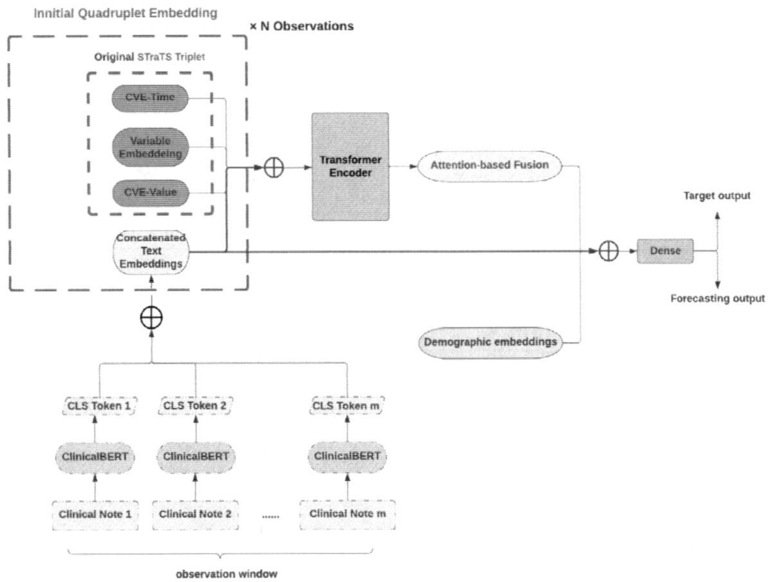

Figure 1: Multimodal STraTS-Q-M - ClinicalBERT

III database stores 61,532 ICU stays among 58, 976 hospital admissions from 46,520 patients. The database is composed of 26 tables including clinical notes, chartevents, admissions and microbiology events and etc.

3.2 Our Data

We use annotated data with septic patients labelled based on 23 ICD-9 codes and the Sepsis-3 definitions (Reyna et al., 2020; Seymour et al., 2016; Singer et al., 2016). Patients admitted with sepsis were excluded from experiment data as they may mislead model in fine-tuning stage for sepsis prediction. From MIMIC-III dataset, we built our data from 5288 septic patients (9.2%) and 51994 non-septic patients. We split data into train, validation, test by 64: 16: 20 at patient level. We extract 133 physiological features (record time, feature value) and two demographic features (age and gender) for each admission from MIMIC-III, and include 1,407,430 clinical notes associated with patient records.

3.3 Clinical Note Preprocessing

Prior practices (Wang et al., 2022) conduct stop word and special character removal, case normalisation on clinical notes as text cleaning steps before feeding to a language model such as ClinicalBERT (Alsentzer et al., 2019). We argue that for a contextual language model pretrained on clinical notes without the above mentioned text preprocessing steps, the above cleaning procedures are unnecessary and potentially harmful. As pointed out in Khattak et al. (2019), case normalisation can introduce noise to clinical texts. For instance, by lowercasing the medical condition term ADD (attention deficit disorder), it converts to a verb "add" that leads to ambiguity. Thus we reserve the original clinical notes for ClinicalBERT-based text embedding modules in our models to generate document-level embeddings. With the GloVe-based models, we remove special characters and stop words to reduce noise and improve training efficiency, as necessary text cleaning steps.

4 Methods

4.1 Baseline STraTS

We base our work on a strong baseline model STraTS (Tipirneni and Reddy, 2022), which takes multivariate clinical variables as its monomodal input, encoded by a learnable continuous value embedding module and feature map. STraTS uses set functions to represent clinical time series as triplets to avoid data imputation and aggregation. The encoded triplets are then fed into transformer blocks and a self-attention module to account for the interactions across data instances and triplets within

Model	Parameters	Best Epoch	Test	Validation
STraTS *(baseline)*	71,070	71	5.2631	5.2089
STraTS - $ClinicalBERT_{CLS\_emb}$ - $base$	10,230,720	104	5.1771	5.0803
STraTS - $ClinicalBERT_{CLS\_emb}$ - $large$	33,920,820	126	5.2014	5.1226
STraTS-Q - $ClinicalBERT_{CLS\_emb}$	61,140,480	124	5.1742	5.1198
STraTS-Q-M - $ClinicalBERT_{CLS\_emb}$	33,920,820	105	**5.1650**	**5.1152**
STraTS-Q-M - $ClinicalBERT_{avg\_emb}$	33,920,820	101	5.2789	5.1950
STraTS - $GloVe$ - $base$	92,820	86	5.2781	5.1875
STraTS - $GloVe$ - $large$	112,920	109	5.3695	5.1707
STraTS-Q-M - Hierarchical Transformer - $base$	11,605,610	110	5.3312	5.2295
STraTS-Q-M - Hierarchical Transformer - $large$	48,216,860	103	5.2584	5.1836
STraTS-Q-M - Hierarchical Transformer - $large$[1]	48,216,860	147	**5.1535**	**5.0038**

1 Learning rate reduced to 0.0001 after 80 epochs

Table 3: Masked MSE (mean squared error) on test and validation data for each model. (patience = 15, parameters refers to trainable parameters)

Model	p-value
STraTS - $ClinicalBERT_{CLS\_emb}$ - $base$	0.0
STraTS - $ClinicalBERT_{CLS\_emb}$ - $large$	0.0
STraTS-Q - $ClinicalBERT_{CLS\_emb}$	0.0
STraTS-Q-M - $ClinicalBERT_{CLS\_emb}$	0.0
STraTS-Q-M - Hierarchical Transformer - $large$	0.69
STraTS-Q-M - Hierarchical Transformer - $large$[1]	0.0

Table 4: Randomization test results for proposed models against baseline on forecasting task.

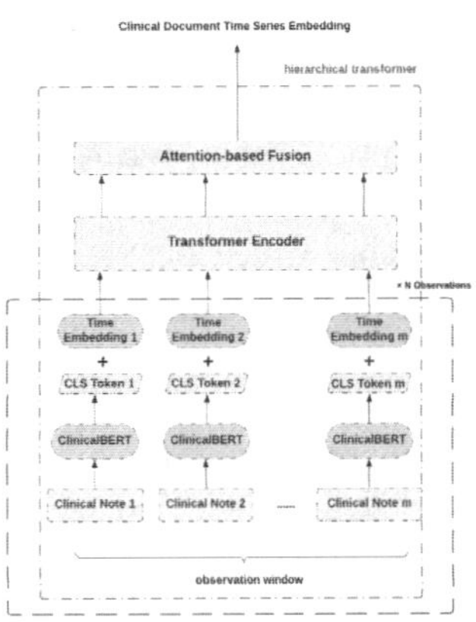

Figure 2: Hierarchical Transformer for Clinical Document Time Series

each observation window.

4.2 Multimodal STraTS-Q-M - ClinicalBERT

On the basis of STraTS, we further include associated clinical notes represented by document-level embeddings obtained through ClinicalBERT. We first obtain initial quadruplet embedding instead of triplets in STraTS as follows:

$$e_i = e_i^f + e_i^v + e_i^t + e_i^T \quad (1)$$

where e_i^f, e_i^v, e_i^t are feature, value, time embeddings originally to form the triplets, along with the associated text embedding e_i^T aligned by observation windows.

The initial quadruplet embeddings are then passed to the following transformer blocks and self-attention module. Eventually, we obtain a fused multimodal representation via concatenating with demographic feature embeddings and ClinicalBERT text embeddings as shown in figure 1.

4.3 Hierarchical Transformer for Clinical Document Time Series

Instead of simply concatenating document embeddings within the same observation window to represent document time series, we additionally propose a hierarchical transformer to 1) account for the interactions between individual clinical notes via attention 2) achieve cross-modal time awareness by aligning clinical text embedding with correspond-

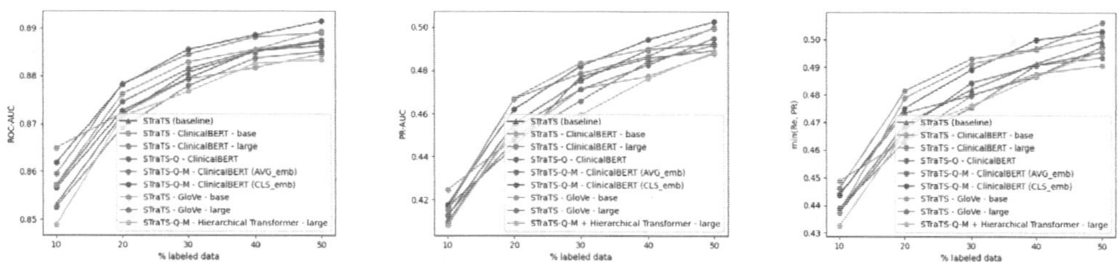

Figure 3: Sepsis prediction performance on MIMIC-III dataset for different percentages of labeled data averaged over 10 runs.

ing time embedding. As shown in figure 2, we encode time consistently with the learnable continuous value embedding module, and add it to corresponding document-level ClinicalBERT embedding for each clinical note in the observation windows, where the time encoding functions similarly to positional encoding in Vaswani et al. (2017); Dai et al. (2022). The time-aware text embeddings are then passed through transformer blocks and attention-based fusion module to claim interactions across individual clinical notes. By this practice, it brings cross-modal time-awareness to the entire multimodal learning framework via consistent time encoding.

5 Results

5.1 Clinical Time Series Forecasting

We train forecasting models with 2-hour forecasting window following each observation window on unsupervised data. We define observation windows with varied lengths: $\{min(0, x-24), x) | 20 \leq x \leq 124, x\%4 = 0\}$. We evaluate the models with masked MSE (mean squared error), where the binary mask indicates the availability of ground truth in data. In addition to evaluating Multimodal STraTS-Q-M - ClinicalBERT against the baseline model, we conduct ablation studies to individually remove the quadruplet embedding module (revert back to monomodal triplet) and the text embedding module in late fusion concatenation. Furthermore, for experimental purposes, we also replace ClinicalBERT with generic GloVe model for text representation. Lastly, we replace the ClinicalBERT text embedding modules with our hierarchical transformer to represent clinical document time-series. We train base and large variations of the model, also further lower learning rate at pretraining to 0.0001 after 80 epochs from default learning rate (0.0005) due to the complexity of the model compared to others.

Table 3 shows the MMSE of the proposed models against baseline on test and validation data. It can be seen from the table that both the quadruplet embedding module and late fusion concatenation are able to individually improve model forecasting performance from baseline. With both combined, Multimodal STraTS-Q-M - ClinicalBERT reduces MMSE by 0.0981 from baseline on test data, achieving MMSE at as low as 5.1650. It is worth noting that when replacing CLS token embedding with average of all token embeddings as document-level representation, the same model underperforms baseline on test data and shows no noteworthy performance improvement at validation. In the meanwhile, the GloVe-based models (replacing ClinicalBERT with GloVe for text embedding in concatenation-based fusion model) are able to slightly outperform baseline at validation stage, whereas showing poor generalization to unseen test data and underperforms baseline by notable gap. Furthermore, by replacing the concatenation-based text embedding module with our hierarchical transformers, the large model with reduced learning rate is able to achieve the lowest MMSE on both test ($MMSE = 5.1535$) and validation data ($MMSE = 5.0038$), decreasing MMSE from baseline by 0.1096. This illustrates that our hierarchical transformer for clinical document time series is an effective approach compared to the simple concatenation of document-level embeddings.

We further run randomization tests on the outperforming models against baseline. As shown in table 4, we observe most of the p-values are below $\alpha - level$ ($p < \alpha$, $\alpha = 0.05$) with the exception to STraTS-Q-M - Hierarchical Transformer - large ($p = 0.69$), which is consistent with the marginal gap in MMSE of the model against baseline. The significance test results demonstrate that the majority of the outperforming models are significantly better than baseline in forecasting stage on test data.

5.2 24-h Sepsis Prediction with Labelled Data

As discussed in previous sections, our forecasting models can be used for early sepsis prediction in two ways: 1) directly fine-tuned on supervised data to predict sepsis 2) produce forecast on clinical variables to support rule-based implementations. In this work, we fine-tune the forecasting models with labelled sepsis patient data to illustrate the case of 24-hour sepsis prediction.

Figure 3 shows the ROC-AUC, PR-AUC and min(Re, Pr) (maximum of minimum of recall and precision across all thresholds). Multimodal STraTS-Q-M - ClinicalBERT is able to stably outperform baseline across different percentages of labelled data also on the downstream prediction task in a fully data-driven setup. While the hierarchical transformer model showed best performance on forecasting, it performs poorly after fine-tuning with labelled data on sepsis prediction. This observation is consistent with the arguements in Kaddour et al. (2022); Liu et al. (2023); Kaddour et al. (2023) that pretraining loss does not always correlate well with downstream performance.

6 Conclusion

In this work, we propose a multimodal transformer to incorporate both physiological time series and associated clinical notes from EHR data for clinical time series forecasting. We approach predictive tasks in the clinical domain primarily from a cause-prediction perspective, which allows our forecasting models to flexibly assist different clinical prediction tasks with rule-based checks in interpretable ways to practitioners in the field. We base our models on a strong monomodal baseline, and improved the model via meaningful multimodal fusion through integrating clinical text embedding modules. We additionally propose hierarchical transformers to represent clinical document time series using attention and time encoding. We conduct comprehensive experiments on MIMIC-III data primarily on forecasting, and observed that our multimodal models are able to significantly outperform baseline by notable gaps in MMSE. Our ablation studies illustrate that the atomic approaches in our multimodal fusion method (quadruplet embedding and late fusion via concatenation) are both able to individually improve model performance on forecasting, and achieve even more superior performance with both combined. Via integrating the hierarchical transformers, the forecasting model is able to further reduce MMSE with proper training setup, illustrating the effectiveness of our proposed hirarchical transformers for clinical document time series representation. Additionally, we fine-tune the forecasting models with supervised data for sepsis prediction, observing that most of the multimodal models are able to consistently outperform baseline on the downstream prediction task in a fully data-driven setup. While our models are based on encoder-only architectures, for future work we intend to explore multimodal encoder-decoder and decoder-only architectures with longer forecasting window. Meanwhile, we seek to reduce model parameters and enhance preprocessing steps in clinical note encoding procedures in future work.

7 Limitations

Despite the significant performance improvements over the baseline, our models generally have a higher number of parameters, resulting in increased computational costs. Additionally, our evaluation was conducted on a single dataset, assessing performance across multiple datasets would provide more robust and generalizable insights. Furthermore, our best-performing forecasting model did not consistently outperform the baseline during fine-tuning, indicating potential aspects for refinement.

8 Acknowledgements

We thank the reviewers for their comments.

References

Emily Alsentzer, John Murphy, William Boag, Wei-Hung Weng, Di Jindi, Tristan Naumann, and Matthew McDermott. 2019. Publicly available clinical BERT embeddings. In *Proceedings of the 2nd Clinical Natural Language Processing Workshop*, pages 72–78, Minneapolis, Minnesota, USA. Association for Computational Linguistics.

Tadas Baltrušaitis, Chaitanya Ahuja, and Louis-Philippe Morency. 2018. Multimodal machine learning: A survey and taxonomy. *IEEE transactions on pattern analysis and machine intelligence*, 41(2):423–443.

Inci M. Baytas, Cao Xiao, Xi Zhang, Fei Wang, Anil K. Jain, and Jiayu Zhou. 2017. Patient subtyping via time-aware lstm networks. In *Proceedings of the 23rd ACM SIGKDD International Conference on Knowledge Discovery and Data Mining*, KDD '17, page 65–74, New York, NY, USA. Association for Computing Machinery.

Zhengping Che, Sanjay Purushotham, Kyunghyun Cho, David Sontag, and Yan Liu. 2018. Recurrent neural networks for multivariate time series with missing values. *Scientific reports*, 8(1):6085.

Xiang Dai, Ilias Chalkidis, Sune Darkner, and Desmond Elliott. 2022. Revisiting transformer-based models for long document classification. In *Findings of the Association for Computational Linguistics: EMNLP 2022*, pages 7212–7230, Abu Dhabi, United Arab Emirates. Association for Computational Linguistics.

Max Horn, Michael Moor, Christian Bock, Bastian Rieck, and Karsten Borgwardt. 2020. Set functions for time series. In *Proceedings of the 37th International Conference on Machine Learning*, volume 119 of *Proceedings of Machine Learning Research*, pages 4353–4363. PMLR.

Alistair EW Johnson, Tom J Pollard, Lu Shen, Li-wei H Lehman, Mengling Feng, Mohammad Ghassemi, Benjamin Moody, Peter Szolovits, Leo Anthony Celi, and Roger G Mark. 2016. Mimic-iii, a freely accessible critical care database. *Scientific data*, 3(1):1–9.

Jean Kaddour, Oscar Key, Piotr Nawrot, Pasquale Minervini, and Matt J. Kusner. 2023. No Train No Gain: Revisiting Efficient Training Algorithms For Transformer-based Language Models. *arXiv preprint*. ArXiv:2307.06440 [cs].

Jean Kaddour, Linqing Liu, Ricardo Silva, and Matt J Kusner. 2022. When do flat minima optimizers work? In *Advances in Neural Information Processing Systems*, volume 35, pages 16577–16595. Curran Associates, Inc.

Faiza Khan Khattak, Serena Jeblee, Chloé Pou-Prom, Mohamed Abdalla, Christopher Meaney, and Frank Rudzicz. 2019. A survey of word embeddings for clinical text. *Journal of Biomedical Informatics*, 100:100057.

Anand Kumar, Daniel Roberts, Kenneth E Wood, Bruce Light, Joseph E Parrillo, Satendra Sharma, Robert Suppes, Daniel Feinstein, Sergio Zanotti, Leo Taiberg, et al. 2006. Duration of hypotension before initiation of effective antimicrobial therapy is the critical determinant of survival in human septic shock. *Critical care medicine*, 34(6):1589–1596.

Kwanhyung Lee, Soojeong Lee, Sangchul Hahn, Heejung Hyun, Edward Choi, Byungeun Ahn, and Joohyung Lee. 2023. Learning missing modal electronic health records with unified multi-modal data embedding and modality-aware attention. *arXiv preprint arXiv:2305.02504*.

Steven Cheng-Xian Li and Benjamin M Marlin. 2016. A scalable end-to-end gaussian process adapter for irregularly sampled time series classification. *Advances in neural information processing systems*, 29.

Hong Liu, Sang Michael Xie, Zhiyuan Li, and Tengyu Ma. 2023. Same pre-training loss, better downstream: Implicit bias matters for language models. In *Proceedings of the 40th International Conference on Machine Learning*, volume 202 of *Proceedings of Machine Learning Research*, pages 22188–22214. PMLR.

Vincent X Liu, Vikram Fielding-Singh, John D Greene, Jennifer M Baker, Theodore J Iwashyna, Jay Bhattacharya, and Gabriel J Escobar. 2017. The timing of early antibiotics and hospital mortality in sepsis. *American journal of respiratory and critical care medicine*, 196(7):856–863.

Zitao Liu and Milos Hauskrecht. 2015. Clinical time series prediction: Toward a hierarchical dynamical system framework. *Artificial intelligence in medicine*, 65(1):5–18.

Zitao Liu, Lei Wu, and Milos Hauskrecht. 2013. Modeling clinical time series using gaussian process sequences. In *Proceedings of the 2013 SIAM International Conference on Data Mining*, pages 623–631. SIAM.

Zhengdong Lu, Todd K Leen, Yonghong Huang, and Deniz Erdogmus. 2008. A reproducing kernel hilbert space framework for pairwise time series distances. In *Proceedings of the 25th international conference on Machine learning*, pages 624–631.

Weimin Lyu, Xinyu Dong, Rachel Wong, Songzhu Zheng, Kayley Abell-Hart, Fusheng Wang, and Chao Chen. 2022. A multimodal transformer: Fusing clinical notes with structured ehr data for interpretable in-hospital mortality prediction. In *AMIA Annual Symposium Proceedings*, volume 2022, page 719. American Medical Informatics Association.

Arsha Nagrani, Shan Yang, Anurag Arnab, Aren Jansen, Cordelia Schmid, and Chen Sun. 2021. Attention bottlenecks for multimodal fusion. In *Advances in Neural Information Processing Systems*, volume 34, pages 14200–14213. Curran Associates, Inc.

Alvin Rajkomar, Eyal Oren, Kai Chen, Andrew M Dai, Nissan Hajaj, Michaela Hardt, Peter J Liu, Xiaobing Liu, Jake Marcus, Mimi Sun, et al. 2018. Scalable and accurate deep learning with electronic health records. *NPJ digital medicine*, 1(1):1–10.

Matthew A Reyna, Christopher S Josef, Russell Jeter, Supreeth P Shashikumar, M Brandon Westover, Shamim Nemati, Gari D Clifford, and Ashish Sharma. 2020. Early prediction of sepsis from clinical data: the physionet/computing in cardiology challenge 2019. *Critical care medicine*, 48(2):210–217.

Kristina E Rudd, Sarah Charlotte Johnson, Kareha M Agesa, Katya Anne Shackelford, Derrick Tsoi, Daniel Rhodes Kievlan, Danny V Colombara, Kevin S Ikuta, Niranjan Kissoon, Simon Finfer, et al. 2020. Global, regional, and national sepsis incidence and mortality, 1990–2017: analysis for the global burden of disease study. *The Lancet*, 395(10219):200–211.

Christopher W Seymour, Foster Gesten, Hallie C Prescott, Marcus E Friedrich, Theodore J Iwashyna, Gary S Phillips, Stanley Lemeshow, Tiffany Osborn, Kathleen M Terry, and Mitchell M Levy. 2017. Time to treatment and mortality during mandated emergency care for sepsis. *New England Journal of Medicine*, 376(23):2235–2244.

Christopher W Seymour, Vincent X Liu, Theodore J Iwashyna, Frank M Brunkhorst, Thomas D Rea, André Scherag, Gordon Rubenfeld, Jeremy M Kahn, Manu Shankar-Hari, Mervyn Singer, et al. 2016. Assessment of clinical criteria for sepsis: for the third international consensus definitions for sepsis and septic shock (sepsis-3). *Jama*, 315(8):762–774.

Mervyn Singer, Clifford S Deutschman, Christopher Warren Seymour, Manu Shankar-Hari, Djillali Annane, Michael Bauer, Rinaldo Bellomo, Gordon R Bernard, Jean-Daniel Chiche, Craig M Coopersmith, et al. 2016. The third international consensus definitions for sepsis and septic shock (sepsis-3). *Jama*, 315(8):801–810.

Michael Staniek, Marius Fracarolli, Michael Hagmann, and Stefan Riezler. 2024. Early prediction of causes (not effects) in healthcare by long-term clinical time series forecasting. volume 252, pages 1–30.

Sindhu Tipirneni and Chandan K. Reddy. 2022. Self-supervised transformer for sparse and irregularly sampled multivariate clinical time-series. *ACM Trans. Knowl. Discov. Data*, 16(6).

Yao-Hung Hubert Tsai, Paul Pu Liang, Amir Zadeh, Louis-Philippe Morency, and Ruslan Salakhutdinov. 2018. Learning factorized multimodal representations. *arXiv preprint arXiv:1806.06176*.

Ashish Vaswani, Noam Shazeer, Niki Parmar, Jakob Uszkoreit, Llion Jones, Aidan N Gomez, Łukasz Kaiser, and Illia Polosukhin. 2017. Attention is all you need. *Advances in neural information processing systems*, 30.

Yuqing Wang, Yun Zhao, Rachael Callcut, and Linda Petzold. 2022. Integrating physiological time series and clinical notes with transformer for early prediction of sepsis. *arXiv preprint arXiv:2203.14469*.

WHO. 2020. World health assembly 70, resolution 70.7: improving the prevention, diagnosis and clinical management of sepsis. 2017.

Jinghua Xu, Natalia Minakova, Pablo Ortega Sanchez, and Stefan Riezler. 2023. Early prediction of sepsis using time series forecasting. In *2023 IEEE 19th International Conference on e-Science (e-Science)*, pages 1–9.

Comparing representations of long clinical texts for the task of patient note-identification

Safa Alsaidi[1], **Marc Vincent**[2], **Olivia Boyer**[3], **Nicolas Garcelon**[2], **Miguel Couceiro**[4,5] and **Adrien Coulet**[1]

[1]Inria, Inserm, UPC, HeKA U1346, Paris, France
{safa.alsaidi, adrien.coulet}@inria.fr
[2]Data Science Platform, Imagine Institute, INSERM U1163, UPC, Paris, France
{marc.vincent, nicolas.garcelon}@institutimagine.org
[3]Néphrologie Pédiatrique, Centre de Référence MARHEA, Hôpital Universitaire Necker-Enfants Malades, Assistance Publique - Hôpitaux de Paris (APHP), Institut Imagine, INSERM U1163, UPC, Paris, France
olivia.boyer@aphp.fr
[4]Université de Lorraine, CNRS, LORIA, Nancy, France
[5]INESC-ID, Instituto Superior Técnico, Universidade de Lisboa, Portugal
miguel.couceiro@inesc-id.pt
Correspondence: safa.alsaidi@inria.fr

Abstract

In this paper, we address the challenge of patient-note identification, which involves accurately matching an anonymized clinical note to its corresponding patient, represented by a set of related notes. This task has broad applications, including duplicate records detection and patient similarity analysis, which require robust patient-level representations. We explore various embedding methods, including Hierarchical Attention Networks (HAN), three-level Hierarchical Transformer Networks (HTN), LongFormer, and advanced BERT-based models, focusing on their ability to process medium-to-long clinical texts effectively. Additionally, we evaluate different pooling strategies (mean, max, and mean_max) for aggregating word-level embeddings into patient-level representations and we examine the impact of sliding windows on model performance. Our results indicate that BERT-based embeddings outperform traditional and hierarchical models, particularly in processing lengthy clinical notes and capturing nuanced patient representations. Among the pooling strategies, mean_max pooling consistently yields the best results, highlighting its ability to capture critical features from clinical notes. Furthermore, the reproduction of our results on both MIMIC dataset and Necker hospital data warehouse illustrates the generalizability of these approaches to real-world applications, emphasizing the importance of both embedding methods and aggregation strategies in optimizing patient-note identification and enhancing patient-level modeling.

1 Introduction

Representation learning focuses on learning compact, meaningful representations from raw data to make it easier for models to perform tasks such as classification, prediction, and clustering. In general, representation learning consists in learning dense representations, where complex, high-dimensional data are mapped to lower-dimensional spaces (Liu et al., 2020). These representations capture underlying structure and essential features, preserving relevant information from the data. In the context of Natural Language Processing (NLP), representation learning has been widely applied and demonstrated impressive performance across various tasks, including downstream applications such as text classification, sentiment analysis, and machine translation (Pennington et al., 2014; Liu et al., 2020; Alsentzer et al., 2019).

Studies in healthcare have focused on learning patient representations from electronic health records (EHRs) to develop predictive models for patient outcomes, such as hospital readmissions, disease progression, or patient mortality rates (Deo and Borgwardt, 2015; Zhu et al., 2015; Auslander et al., 2020; Mahbub et al., 2022). In recent years, EHRs have been widely adopted by many medical institutions, capturing comprehensive patient data throughout the care process (Landi et al., 2020; Escudié et al., 2018; Steinberg et al., 2021; Le and Mikolov, 2014). Nonetheless, learning effective patient representations poses several challenges,

Proceedings of the Second Workshop on Patient-Oriented Language Processing (CL4Health), pages 109–123
May 4, 2025

one of which is determining what defines a "good" patient representation. The optimal representation can vary depending on the specific application, as well as factors such as data noise, missing values, and the type of data incorporated. For instance, representations designed for structured data (Rajkomar et al., 2018) may differ significantly from those that incorporate both structured data and unstructured text (Deznabi et al., 2021). These challenges highlight the importance of investigating different representation learning methods to generate representations that are adapted not only to a specific task but also to the nature of the dataset.

In this paper, we address the task of patient-note identification, which consists in determining to which patient a particular note belongs. We focus exclusively on clinical texts, representing each patient as a set of chronologically ordered notes. While higher risks of patient-note mismatches have been reported with paper records, there is limited literature on this issue within modern EHR systems (Wilcox et al., 2011), which further motivates our work. To this end, we investigate which text-based patient representation is best suited for the task of patient-note identification.

Accurately identifying patient information is crucial in the medical field to ensure that a patient's medical history is up-to-date. Furthermore, this task has applications in biomedical informatics, including data cleaning and privacy-related tasks (e.g., assessing re-identification risk of patient data (Lee and Lee, 2017)). More broadly, we believe that patient-note identification can serve as a foundational task for more advanced similarity-based tasks, such as clustering, diagnosing conditions by matching complex symptoms and medical histories, or finding "patients like mine" (Gombar et al., 2019; Garcelon et al., 2017).

In this study, we conduct experiments on two datasets: MIMIC-III (Goldberger et al., 2000) and an anonymized EHR dataset from our local hospital, the Necker hospital data warehouse (Dr. Warehouse) (Garcelon et al., 2018). We focus on the MIMIC-III dataset to develop and refine our approach to identify the best representation for the patient-note identification task, and only evaluate reproducibility of our findings using our local hospital dataset. We consider different embedding models to learn representations of potentially large sets of clinical notes associated with each patient, and evaluate and compare these representations by performing classification with traditional algorithms.

Our contributions are 3-fold:

- we clearly define the patient-note identification task and highlight its importance for studying patient representations;
- we conduct an empirical comparison of patient representation methods for this task;
- we attest that BERT-based model, using a sliding window mechanism and a combination of mean and max pooling, achieves the highest accuracy.

2 Related Work

2.1 Patient-Information Identification

Despite the growing interest in patient-information identification, relatively few studies have explored this task using text, and to our knowledge, none have specifically addressed patient-note identification. This research gap further motivates our work.

Most efforts in patient matching or record linkage have focused on structured data (Riplinger et al., 2020). Some prior studies have leveraged unstructured clinical text for patient-matching tasks. For example, Wornow et al. (2025) tackled the challenge of matching patients to clinical trials using a zero-shot LLM-based system. By evaluating unstructured clinical text against free-text trial criteria, their approach achieved state-of-the-art performance on the n2c2 2018 cohort selection benchmark. Clinician reviews indicated that the system provided coherent explanations for 97% of correct decisions and 75% of incorrect ones.

In contrast, other studies have explored deep learning approaches for patient identification using imaging data, particularly chest X-rays (Ueda and Morishita, 2023; Packhäuser et al., 2021). For instance, Packhäuser et al. (2021) trained a Siamese neural network to determine whether two frontal chest X-ray images belonged to the same patient, achieving an AUC of 0.9940 and a classification accuracy of 95.55% on the ChestX-ray14 dataset. Similarly, Ueda and Morishita (2023) proposed a deep metric learning approach using a deep convolutional neural network (DCNN) feature extractor and a classifier based on the cosine similarity index to verify patient identities from chest X-ray images. Their method achieved AUC values of 0.9999 and 0.9943 on the Morishita Laboratory and CheXpert datasets.

While these studies highlight the potential of deep learning for patient identification, our work fills a critical gap by focusing on text-based patient-note identification, an area that remains largely unexplored.

2.2 Representation Learning

Typically, EHRs comprise both structured (*e.g.*, age, demographics, ICD codes, laboratory results) and unstructured data (*e.g.*, free-text clinical notes such as radiology reports, discharge summaries, and medical images). The inherent complexity of EHRs has inspired numerous studies aimed at developing patient representations by learning optimized, dense numerical vectors (Li et al., 2020; Sushil et al., 2018; Hashir and Sawhney, 2020; Si and Roberts, 2020).

Previous research has explored various approaches, including paragraph vectors (Le and Mikolov, 2014), topic models (Blei et al., 2001), word2vec embeddings (Mikolov et al., 2013), and Hierarchical Attention Networks (HAN) (Si and Roberts, 2020, 2021). For instance, Auslander et al. (2020) used word2vec and bag-of-words as feature extraction methods to learn patient representation from clinical notes for mortality prediction. Sushil et al. (2018) learned generalized patient representations using a stacked denoising autoencoder and a paragraph vector model to predict patient mortality, primary diagnostic, procedural category, and patient gender. Si and Roberts (2020) learned patient representations notes using a hierarchical attention-based recurrent neural network (HAN-RNN) with greedy segmentation and evaluated the model for mortality prediction and as a transfer learning pretraining model to downstream evaluation such as phenotype prediction.

Representation learning from clinical texts, particularly using Bidirectional Encoder Representations from Transformers (BERT) (Devlin et al., 2019), has shown significant improvements in text-processing tasks like clinical named entity recognition (NER) and document classification (Alsentzer et al., 2019; Peng et al., 2019; Lee et al., 2020). BERT-based models have also been used for prediction in medicine. For example, Mahbub et al. (2022) used PubMedBERT to generate dynamic embeddings from clinical notes, enabling predictions of short-, mid-, and long-term mortality in adult ICU patients. However, due to BERT's 512-token limitation, longer clinical notes in these experiments had to be either truncated or split, which may have resulted in the loss of valuable context necessary for accurate predictions.

To address BERT's 512-token input limitation, models like BigBird (Zaheer et al., 2020) and Long-Former (Beltagy et al., 2020) have been employed to learn patient representations from longer clinical texts. These models support input sequences of up to 4,096 tokens (8 times the BERT limit), yielding substantial performance improvements in tasks such as long-text question answering and summarization. Additionally, (Li et al., 2023) introduced Clinical-Longformer and ClinicalBigBird, two pretrained language models specifically designed for lengthy clinical text processing. These models demonstrated superior performance in NER, question answering, and document classification tasks when handling lengthy documents.

These studies highlight the challenges involved in identifying the most suitable representation learning method for a specific task. In the case of patient-note identification, there is no one-size-fits-all solution, and the effectiveness of existing methods remains unclear, motivating empirical evaluation. In this work, we present an empirical comparison of four methods (HAN BERTLSTM, HTN, Longformer, and BERT) to assess their effectiveness in addressing the patient-note identification task. For BERT model, we introduce four different settings that explore different embedding strategies, using token embeddings (TE) or the [CLS] token, as well as applying a sliding window mechanism or restricting inputs to 512 tokens. This results in a total of seven experimental configurations.

3 Datasets

In this work, we use two distinct datasets of EHRs containing clinical notes: (1) the publicly available MIMIC-III dataset, which consists of ICU patient records in English, and (2) the Necker hospital data warehouse, containing French-language notes from nephrology patients. Below, we provide an overview of each dataset along with the preprocessing steps and selection criteria used to define our final cohorts.

3.1 MIMIC-III

MIMIC-III (Johnson et al., 2016) is a publicly available medical database that includes anonymized health records from 46,520 ICU patients treated at Beth Israel Deaconess Medical Center in Boston, Massachusetts, between 2001 and 2012. The

MIMIC-III dataset provides a wide range of patient data, including demographics, vital signs, laboratory test results, clinical notes, and ICD-9 diagnosis codes. It contains 2,083,180 clinical notes across multiple categories, such as physician notes, nursing notes, discharge summaries, and radiology reports. The distribution of notes across different categories is shown in Table 4 in Appendix A.1.

Firstly, we begin by performing several data cleaning operations: we exclude notes flagged as erroneous in MIMIC-III, those without a hospital admission identifier, notes lacking chart time information (*i.e.*, the date and time the note was documented), and duplicated notes. For partially duplicated notes with identical chart times, we retain the longer note, ensuring that its text encompasses the content of the shorter note.

Secondly, we select only notes categorized as 'Physician.' As presented in Table 4, this category ranks fourth in terms of notes count and contains the longest notes, with an average length of 1,874 tokens and a median of 1,823 tokens. We hypothesize that these notes would provide the most comprehensive information about a patient's medical condition, enhancing the ability to accurately associate a clinical note with its corresponding patient.

Thirdly, we remove outliers, using interquartile range (IQR) filtering and a threshold multiplier of 1.5, which results in excluding patients with more than 40 notes. As our work focuses on matching notes to the patient they belong to, we include only patients with at least two clinical notes: one serving as the target note for identification (X_2), and the other used to learn the patient's representation (X_1^i). Ultimately, MIMIC-III dataset consists of 33,007 notes associated with 6,174 patients. The cohort design is illustrated in Figure 1 in Appendix A.1. This dataset serves as a foundation for optimizing note representations for the task of patient-note identification.

3.2 Necker Hospital Data Warehouse

To assess the generalizability of our approach across different languages and medical specialties, we extended our analysis to EHRs from our local Necker hospital data warehouse (Dr. Warehouse), under IRB number *2016–06-01*. This dataset encompasses a broad spectrum of clinical note types, such as consultations, hospitalization reports, discharge summaries, and laboratory results, spanning multiple departments.

For our study, we focus on notes of nephrology patients hospitalized between 2018 and 2023. These selected notes have an average length of 1,237 tokens and a median of 897 tokens. We apply a similar preprocessing pipeline to the one used for MIMIC-III, filtering out note categories with limited text content, removing patients with exceptionally high note counts using IQR filtering and patients with less than two notes. All notes have been already pseudonymized. Ultimately, our dataset comprises 32,731 clinical notes associated with 5,145 patients.

Unlike MIMIC-III, which consists of English-language ICU patient notes, this dataset contains French-language notes from nephrology patients. This distinction allows us to evaluate the robustness of our approach across different languages and clinical settings.

4 Methodology

4.1 Patient-note identification task

We define the patient-note identification task as a binary classification problem, where the input pair (X_1^i, X_2) maps to an output label $\hat{Y^i}$. Here, X_1^i represents a unified representation of all notes belonging to patient i, excluding one randomly selected note (X_2), which is represented separately. X_2 denotes the representation of a single note, and $\hat{Y^i}$ is a binary label that equals 1 if X_2 belongs to patient i, and 0 otherwise.

From an initial set $\mathcal{X} = \{X_0^i\}$ with $i \in [1, n]$, n the number of patients and X_0^i is the set of notes associated with the patient i, we define our train and test sets as pairs $((X_1^i, X_2), Y^i)$. For each patient i, we designate randomly one clinical note X_2 as the *target note*, while the remaining notes $X_1^i = X_0^i \setminus X_2$ serve as the patient's historical context (*source notes*). To maintain a balanced representation between positive and negative examples, each randomly selected clinical note is associated once in our dataset to the correct patient, and once to a randomly chosen patient. Accordingly, the pair (X_1^i, X_2) is either associated with $Y^i = 1$ or 0. This leads to a dataset with twice as many instances as patients. To guarantee consistency, patients are split in train and test sets before excluding $X2$, and building (X_1^i, X_2) pairs. This ensures that both source and target notes of one patient are either in the train, or in the test set, avoiding data leakage.

4.2 Learning Patient-Note Representations

Successfully performing this task requires learning effective document-level representations. Consequently, our study evaluates the performance of various representation learning approaches. Drawing from previous work on document-level representation learning (Si and Roberts, 2020; Liu et al., 2019; Li et al., 2022; Matondora et al., 2024; Li et al., 2020; Bazoge et al., 2024), we experiment with several models to evaluate their ability to generate effective representations for patient-note identification. Each model was selected to highlight distinct strategies for processing and aggregating clinical notes, including hierarchical approaches, transformer-based architectures, and hybrid designs that integrate both sequential and contextual information. Specifically, we experiment with a hierarchical attention network with BiLSTM and BERT at the word level (HAN BERTLSTM), a three-level hierarchical transformer network (HTN), Longformer, and BERT. Using these four models, we define seven different settings. For the BERT model, we consider two variants: one using token embeddings (TE) and the other using the [CLS] token (CLS). Token embeddings represent each individual token in the sequence, while the [CLS] token variant uses a special token at the beginning of the sequence to aggregate information for classification tasks. Additionally, we explore configurations both with and without a sliding window mechanism to address BERT's 512-token limitation. The sliding window approach allows the model to process longer texts by splitting them into overlapping segments, whereas the alternative approach restricts inputs to a single 512-token sequence. Detailed descriptions of each model can be found in Appendix A.2. The acronyms introduced in this section will be used consistently throughout the paper.

For clinical document representation, we evaluate and adapt several aggregation techniques traditionally used to transition from word-level to sentence-level and, subsequently, to document-level representations. These techniques include attention mechanisms, average pooling, max pooling, and mean_max pooling (Deznabi et al., 2021; Li et al., 2023; Si and Roberts, 2021; Mahbub et al., 2022). To derive a single patient representation, we aggregate all note representations for a given patient into a unified representation using one of these four methods.

Attention-based Aggregation (att) employs a learnt attention mechanism to dynamically assign varying importance to each clinical note. *Average Pooling or Mean Pooling (avg)* computes the mean representation of all clinical notes, capturing the overall feature distribution, while *Max Pooling (max)* selects the highest value across note representations, emphasizing the most prominent features. Recent studies (Si and Roberts, 2021; Li et al., 2023) suggest that *Mean-max Pooling (mean_max)*, which concatenates the average pooled and max pooled embeddings, often yields superior performance across predictive tasks by combining the strengths of both pooling strategies: the *average* highlights overall feature distribution, while the *max* emphasizes key dominant features.

To formalize this pooling strategy, let $\mathbf{r}_j$ be the vector representation of the j-th note of a given patient with m notes. The aggregated patient representation $\mathbf{R}$ using mean_max pooling is defined as:

$$\mathbf{R} = [\text{mean}(\mathbf{r}_1, \mathbf{r}_2, \ldots, \mathbf{r}_m) \oplus \text{max}(\mathbf{r}_1, \mathbf{r}_2, \ldots, \mathbf{r}_m)],$$

where mean$(\cdot)$ computes the element-wise average, max$(\cdot)$ computes the element-wise maximum, and $\oplus$ denotes the concatenation operation.

Finally, these note representations serve as inputs to classifiers for the patient-note identification task. We evaluate five machine learning models: logistic regression (LR), random forest (RF), decision trees (DT), support vector machine (SVM), and XGBoost. Performance of both the embedding methods and classifiers are measured with five key metrics: accuracy, precision, recall, F1-score, and area under the curve (AUC).

5 Experiments and Results

To ensure robustness, experiments were repeated three times on each dataset (MIMIC-III and Necker hospital dataset) with distinct random train and test splits, maintaining an 80/20 ratio. Table 1 provides details on the train and test sets, including the length of source (X_1^i) and target (X_2) notes, as well as the size of the associated dictionaries.

Table 2 presents the results of our experiments on MIMIC-III, keeping only results obtained for the best-performing classifier, which name is provided in the third column. The AUC score reflects the model's ability to effectively distinguish between two classes: whether a note representation belongs to a given patient.

Dataset	Notes	Set	Token Count	Sentence Count	Vocabulary Size
MIMIC-III	**Source Notes (X_1^i)**	Train	8006.11 ± 7416.22	149.30 ± 140.23	$15,510$
		Test	8080.67 ± 7503.55	149.98 ± 150.89	$14,050$
	Target Note (X_2)	Train	1768.63 ± 687.90	33.88 ± 26.31	$13,106$
		Test	1782.04 ± 706.93	33.98 ± 27.13	$11,609$
Necker Hospital Data Warehouse	**Source Notes (X_1^i)**	Train	8493.19 ± 9935.22	424.02 ± 560.27	$17,335$
		Test	8578.87 ± 9733.31	427.30 ± 545.52	$15,744$
	Target Note (X_2)	Train	1436.10 ± 1013.69	69.50 ± 77.19	$14,907$
		Test	1436.36 ± 1033.57	69.40 ± 79.26	$12,962$

Table 1: Mean number of tokens and sentences for the set of notes belonging to a single patient (source notes, X_1^i) and the target note (X_2) across train and test sets in both MIMIC-III and our local Necker hospital dataset, along with vocabulary sizes. Token count and vocabulary size are computed using the BERT WordPiece tokenizer. These values are computed over the three different train and test splits.

We observe that BERT_TE_sliding consistently outperforms all other models. Furthermore, mean_max pooling consistently yields the best performance across all models and nearly all metrics as the aggregation method for patient representations. XGBoost also emerges as the top-performing machine learning algorithm across all models.

We evaluate the impact of pooling strategies (average, max, and mean_max) on the performance of different models using paired t-tests to assess statistical significance. Mean_max pooling outperforms mean and max pooling in most comparisons, with significant differences observed in most of the cases ($p < 0.05$). For hierarchical models, significant differences are observed between mean pooling and mean_max pooling for both HAN BERTLSTM and HTN ($p < 0.05$). Additionally, max pooling shows a significant difference compared to mean_max pooling for HTN ($p < 0.05$), but not for HAN BERTLSTM. Turning to the LongFormer model, mean pooling shows a significant difference compared to mean_max pooling ($p < 0.05$), whereas no significant difference is found between max pooling and mean_max pooling. Among BERT-based models, both BERT_[CLS] and BERT_TE exhibit significant differences between mean pooling and mean_max pooling ($p < 0.05$). However, while max pooling differs significantly from mean_max pooling for BERT_TE ($p < 0.05$), no such difference is observed for BERT_[CLS]. In sliding window approaches, significant differences emerge between mean pooling and mean_max pooling for both BERT_[CLS]_sliding and BERT_TE_sliding ($p < 0.05$). Meanwhile, max pooling differs significantly from mean_max pooling for BERT_[CLS]_sliding ($p < 0.05$), but not for BERT_TE_sliding.

To evaluate the generalizability of our results, we extend our analysis to EHRs from the Necker hospital data warehouse. For this experiment, we use only our best-performing model, BERT_TE_sliding, and test the three different aggregation methods to obtain patient-level representations. Since the dataset contains French clinical notes, we replace BERT with CamemBERT to accommodate the language difference. Results are obtained by conducting three independent runs and are reported in Table 3. The results on the Necker hospital dataset show similar results to those of MIMIC-III, with the mean_max aggregation method outperforming other pooling strategies. Statistical analysis using paired t-tests reveals a significant difference between mean_max pooling and average pooling ($p < 0.05$), while the difference between mean_max pooling and max pooling is not statistically significant.

6 Discussion

As mentioned previously, each experiment was conducted 3 times using a random sampling of train and test set. Although the reported standard deviation is small, this can be explained by the nature of our datatsets, *i.e.*, our cohort selection. Given that our datasets consist of notes from specific categories (*i.e.*, physician-only notes in the MIMIC-III dataset and nephrology-only notes in the Necker hospital dataset), which each tend to have similar language and structure within their respective categories, the model's predictions are highly consistent. We believe this homogeneity within each category likely contributes to the low standard deviation observed. Despite this, our overall results (accuracy, AUC, and F1 score) indicate that our models effectively differentiate between notes and accurately matches them to their corresponding

Model	Aggreg.	Classifier	Accuracy (mean ± std.)	Precision (mean ± std.)	Recall (mean ± std.)	F1 (mean ± std.)	AUC (mean ± std.)
HAN BERTLSTM	att	RF	0.64 ± 0.00	0.62 ± 0.00	0.69 ± 0.01	0.66 ± 0.01	0.70 ± 0.01
	avg	SVM	0.76 ± 0.00	0.82 ± 0.01	0.67 ± 0.01	0.73 ± 0.00	0.79 ± 0.00
	max	XGBOOST	0.75 ± 0.00	0.76 ± 0.00	0.74 ± 0.01	0.75 ± 0.01	0.82 ± 0.01
	mean_max	XGBOOST	0.76 ± 0.00	0.76 ± 0.01	0.75 ± 0.01	0.75 ± 0.00	0.83 ± 0.01
3-level HTN	avg	XGBOOST	0.74 ± 0.01	0.72 ± 0.01	0.80 ± 0.01	0.75 ± 0.01	0.82 ± 0.01
	max	XGBOOST	0.71 ± 0.01	0.68 ± 0.00	0.79 ± 0.01	0.73 ± 0.01	0.79 ± 0.01
	mean_max	XGBOOST	0.76 ± 0.01	0.74 ± 0.01	0.82 ± 0.01	0.77 ± 0.01	0.84 ± 0.00
BERT_TE	avg	XGBOOST	0.85 ± 0.00	0.84 ± 0.00	0.86 ± 0.01	0.85 ± 0.00	0.93 ± 0.00
	max	XGBOOST	0.85 ± 0.01	0.86 ± 0.01	0.83 ± 0.01	0.85 ± 0.01	0.92 ± 0.01
	mean_max	XGBOOST	0.87 ± 0.00	0.88 ± 0.00	0.85 ± 0.01	0.87 ± 0.00	0.94 ± 0.00
BERT_[CLS]	avg	XGBOOST	0.82 ± 0.00	0.81 ± 0.00	0.82 ± 0.01	0.82 ± 0.00	0.90 ± 0.00
	max	XGBOOST	0.84 ± 0.00	0.83 ± 0.00	0.85 ± 0.01	0.84 ± 0.00	0.92 ± 0.00
	mean_max	XGBOOST	0.85± 0.00	0.84 ± 0.01	0.85 ± 0.01	0.84 ± 0.01	0.93 ± 0.01
Longformer	avg	XGBOOST	0.74 ± 0.01	0.74 ± 0.01	0.76 ± 0.02	0.75 ± 0.01	0.83 ± 0.00
	max	XGBOOST	0.75 ± 0.01	0.75 ± 0.02	0.76 ± 0.02	0.75 ± 0.01	0.83 ± 0.00
	mean_max	XGBOOST	0.78 ± 0.01	0.78 ± 0.02	0.79 ± 0.02	0.78 ± 0.00	0.85 ± 0.00
BERT_TE_sliding	avg	XGBOOST	0.85 ± 0.00	0.84 ± 0.01	0.87 ± 0.01	0.86 ± 0.00	0.94 ± 0.00
	max	XGBOOST	0.88 ± 0.00	0.89 ± 0.00	0.86 ± 0.01	0.88 ± 0.00	0.95 ± 0.00
	mean_max	**XGBOOST**	**0.90 ± 0.00**	**0.91 ± 0.00**	**0.88 ± 0.00**	**0.89 ± 0.00**	**0.96 ± 0.00**
BERT_[CLS]_sliding	avg	XGBOOST	0.86 ± 0.00	0.85 ± 0.00	0.88 ± 0.00	0.87 ± 0.00	0.94 ± 0.00
	max	XGBOOST	0.85 ± 0.01	0.85 ± 0.01	0.85 ± 0.01	0.85 ± 0.01	0.93 ± 0.01
	mean_max	XGBOOST	0.88 ± 0.00	0.88 ± 0.00	0.88 ± 0.00	0.88 ± 0.00	0.95 ± 0.00

Table 2: Best results reported based on AUC metrics across 4 models (7 different settings) among 5 different classification algorithms (LR, RF, SVM, DT, and XGBOOST), using MIMIC-III dataset. We report mean ± std. over 3 runs.

Model	Aggreg.	Classifier	Accuracy (mean ± std.)	Precision (mean ± std.)	Recall (mean ± std.)	F1 (mean ± std.)	AUC (mean ± std.)
BERT_TE_sliding (FR: CamemBERT)	avg	XGBOOST	0.78 ± 0.01	0.79 ± 0.01	0.78 ± 0.02	0.78 ± 0.01	0.86 ± 0.01
	max	XGBOOST	0.82 ± 0.00	0.83 ± 0.01	0.82 ± 0.02	0.83 ± 0.01	0.90 ± 0.01
	mean_max	**XGBOOST**	**0.83 ± 0.01**	**0.84 ± 0.02**	**0.83 ± 0.00**	**0.83 ± 0.01**	**0.91 ± 0.01**

Table 3: Best results reported based on AUC metrics among 5 different classification algorithms (LR, RF, SVM, DT, and XGBOOST), using our local Necker hospital data warehouse. We report mean ± std. over 3 runs.

patient.

In this version of the datasets, we conducted a single random drawing for each patient from their available set of clinical notes. However, to further expand the dataset, multiple random draws could be performed per patient, which would yield different patient representations.

The results obtained from our experiments emphasize the significance of model architecture, embedding strategies, and aggregation methods in optimizing performance for patient-note identification as shown in Table 2. Below, we discuss key observations and insights drawn from the performance metrics.

1. **Effect of Model Architecture:** The hierarchical models (HAN and HTN) demonstrated moderate performance. Among these, HAN BERTLSTM with mean_max pooling achieved an F1 score of 0.75 and an AUC of 0.83. Similarly, the 3-level HTN model with mean_max pooling achieved slightly better performance, with an F1 score of 0.77 and an AUC of 0.84, demonstrating the utility of hierarchical modeling. However, the overall performance of hierarchical models was surpassed by purely transformer-based models, including Longformer, which better captured contextual representations.

   To elaborate, HAN and HTN rely on a fixed structure to aggregate information, which could limit their ability to detect nuanced relationships between sentences and words, particularly in long clinical notes. On the other hand, transformer-based models, such as Longformer and BERT, dynamically adjust word representations based on surrounding context. Given that we are working with clinical notes, we know that the meaning of terms could vary based on what follows and what precedes. Thus it is crucial to correctly identify or recognize the intended meaning of a particular term in a clinical note. While hierarchical models capture some structural patterns, they may miss more granular contextual cues, which are essential for accurately matching clinical notes to the correct patient.

2. **BERT Token Embedding (TE) vs. [CLS] Representations:** BERT models using TE achieved higher performance compared to those using [CLS] token representations. While [CLS] embeddings are designed to encapsulate the overall sentence representation, their reliance on a single token representation might limit their ability to capture nuanced information spread across longer notes. In contrast, the token embeddings (TE) in BERT allows us to focus on the contextual representations of each token in a sequence. As demonstrated in the results, the mean_max pooling strategy with BERT_TE consistently yielded the best results, highlighting the effectiveness of combining token embeddings with contextual attention mechanisms in capturing fine-grained details from clinical notes.

3. **Longformer vs. BERT Sliding Window:** The Longformer model addresses BERT's token-length limitation by processing up to 4096 tokens, outperforming hierarchical models but falling short of BERT's sliding window configurations. Longformer achieved an F1 score of 0.83 and an AUC of 0.92, demonstrating its capability to handle lengthy clinical notes. In contrast, BERT_TE_sliding with mean_max pooling achieved the highest performance, with an F1 score of 0.89 and an AUC of 0.96. This success highlights the sliding window approach's ability to capture contextual information distributed across long notes. By employing overlapping windows, the model attended to diverse parts of the notes while maintaining contextual integrity. This method proved to be superior to Longformer's fixed sliding window attention mechanism, as it enabled chunk-specific embeddings to be aggregated effectively.

4. **Pooling strategies:** mean_max pooling consistently yielded the best results, likely due to its ability to capture both global and localized features across embeddings. By focusing on the maximum values, max pooling reduces the influence of less relevant or noisy features and, at the same time, ensures that the most important features are prominently represented in the final patient-level representation. In contrast, average pooling calculates the mean across all clinical note representations to derive the final patient representation, which can result in the loss of critical information, particularly when vital details are scattered across notes.

In addition to the findings on the MIMIC-III dataset, the results on the Necker hospital dataset highlight two key points. First, our model demonstrates strong adaptability to a different dataset, effectively addressing the task of patient-note identification. Second, the results on our local dataset align with our previous experiments on the MIMIC-III dataset, where the mean_max aggregation method generally outperforms other pooling strategies or performs similarly in a few cases, where no significant difference was observed compared to max pooling. These results highlight the versatility of our approach, demonstrating its effectiveness across diverse datasets and languages.

7 Conclusion

Patient-note identification is a fundamental problem in the domain of medical informatics. While not extensively explored, the risks associated with patient-note mismatches can have serious consequences, particularly in ICU settings. In this work, we developed a framework to address this challenge using unstructured clinical notes from the MIMIC-III database. We evaluated various embedding models (HAN BERTLSTM, HTN, Longformer, and BERT) and aggregation methods (average, max, and mean_max pooling) to generate patient-level representations. Our findings highlight that transformer-based models with advanced aggregation strategies, such as mean_max pooling combined with a sliding window approach, are highly effective for capturing fine-grained contextual information and ensuring accurate patient-note identification. Additionally, experiments on an external dataset validated the generalizability of our approach. By adapting to French clinical notes with CamemBERT, the model maintained strong performance, demonstrating its robustness across diverse datasets and settings.

8 Limitations

Through this work, we emphasize the importance of patient-note identification and the potential of leveraging raw clinical notes for predictive modeling. While our approach shows strong performance, it is not without limitations. Our first limit lies in the use of generic language models to learn patient representations rather than using domain-specific architectures. Future research could explore more specialized models, such as ClinicalMamba (Yang et al., 2024) and ModernBERT (Warner et al., 2024), and investigate alternative aggregation strategies. These approaches may enhance representation quality and help mitigate potential information loss inherent in processing complex clinical text. However, it is important to consider the potential biases embedded in the pretraining data of these models, as such biases can impact both the generalizability and fairness of their application in clinical settings.

Another limit lies in the exclusive focus on unstructured clinical notes within our current framework. Integrating structured data, such as laboratory results or vital signs, alongside unstructured text could yield more comprehensive patient representations and allow for more nuanced comparative analyses.

Additionally, while we validated our approach using an external dataset, we did not assess its effectiveness on downstream clinical tasks, such as predictive modeling or forecasting, where clinical notes serve as primary or supplementary input. Such evaluations could offer further insights into the practical utility of the learned patient representations.

Finally, benchmarking our method against large language models (LLMs), including ChatGPT or GPT-4o, could provide valuable perspectives for assessing the scalability, accuracy, and overall effectiveness of our approach in the context of patient-note identification.

Acknowledgments

Experiments presented in this paper were carried out using computational clusters equipped with GPU from CLEPS infrastructure from the Inria of Paris[1].

This work was supported by the French ANR[2] project "Analogies: from theory to tools and applications" (AT2TA), ANR-22-CE23-0023. Additional support was provided by ANR project C'IL-LICO, ANR-17-RHUS-0002, and the European Union (Horizon-health-2022-disease-06-two stage, grant 101080717). The C'IL-LICO project and study protocol received approval from the French National Ethics and Scientific Committee for Research, Studies and Evaluations in the Field of Health (CESREES) under the number #2201437. The data processing was approved by the French Data Protection Authority (CNIL) with a waiver of informed consent under number $DR-2023-017//920398v1$.

[1] https://pariscluster-2019.gitlabpages.inria.fr/cleps/clepsuserguide/architecture/architecture.html

[2] Agence Nationale de la Recherche.

References

Emily Alsentzer, John Murphy, William Boag, Wei-Hung Weng, Di Jindi, Tristan Naumann, and Matthew McDermott. 2019. Publicly available clinical BERT embeddings. In *Proceedings of the 2nd Clinical Natural Language Processing Workshop*, pages 72–78, Minneapolis, Minnesota, USA. Association for Computational Linguistics.

Bryan Auslander, Kalyan Moy Gupta, Michael W. Floyd, Sam Blisard, and David W. Aha. 2020. Exploiting text data to improve critical care mortality prediction. In *IEEE Globecom Workshops, GLOBECOM Workshops 2020, Virtual Event, Taiwan, December 7-11, 2020*, pages 1–7. IEEE.

Adrien Bazoge, Emmanuel Morin, Beatrice Daille, and Pierre-Antoine Gourraud. 2024. Adaptation of biomedical and clinical pretrained models to french long documents: A comparative study. *Preprint*, arXiv:2402.16689.

Iz Beltagy, Matthew E. Peters, and Arman Cohan. 2020. Longformer: The long-document transformer. *Preprint*, arXiv:2004.05150.

David M. Blei, Andrew Y. Ng, and Michael I. Jordan. 2001. Latent dirichlet allocation. In *Advances in Neural Information Processing Systems 14 NIPS 2001, Vancouver, British Columbia, Canada]*, pages 601–608. MIT Press.

Rahul C. Deo and Karsten M. Borgwardt. 2015. Machine learning in medicine. *Circulation*, 132 20:1920–30.

Jacob Devlin, Ming-Wei Chang, Kenton Lee, and Kristina Toutanova. 2019. BERT: pre-training of deep bidirectional transformers for language understanding. In *Proceedings of the 2019 Conference of the North American Chapter of the Association for Computational Linguistics: Human Language Technologies, NAACL-HLT 2019, Minneapolis, MN, USA, June 2-7, 2019, Volume 1 (Long and Short Papers)*, pages 4171–4186. Association for Computational Linguistics.

Iman Deznabi, Mohit Iyyer, and Madalina Fiterau. 2021. Predicting in-hospital mortality by combining clinical notes with time-series data. In *Findings of the Association for Computational Linguistics: ACL/IJCNLP 2021, Online Event, August 1-6, 2021*, pages 4026–4031. Association for Computational Linguistics.

Jean-Baptiste Escudié, Alaa Saade, Alice Coucke, and Marc Lelarge. 2018. Deep representation for patient visits from electronic health records. *Preprint*, arXiv:1803.09533.

Nicolas Garcelon, Antoine Neuraz, Vincent Benoit, Rémi Salomon, Sven Kracker, Felipe Suarez, Nadia Bahi-Buisson, Smail Hadj-Rabia, Alain Fischer, Arnold Munnich, and Anita Burgun. 2017. Finding patients using similarity measures in a rare diseases-oriented clinical data warehouse: Dr. warehouse and the needle in the needle stack. *J. Biomed. Informatics*, 73:51–61.

Nicolas Garcelon, Antoine Neuraz, Rémi Salomon, Hassan Faour, Vincent Benoit, Arthur Delapalme, Arnold Munnich, Anita Burgun, and Bastien Rance. 2018. A clinician friendly data warehouse oriented toward narrative reports: Dr. warehouse. *Journal of Biomedical Informatics*, 80:52–63.

Ary L. Goldberger, Luis A. N. Amaral, Leon Glass, Jeffrey M. Hausdorff, Plamen Ch. Ivanov, Roger G. Mark, Joseph E. Mietus, George B. Moody, Chung-Kang Peng, and H. Eugene Stanley. 2000. Physiobank, physiotoolkit, and physionet. *Circulation*, 101(23):e215–e220.

Saurabh Gombar, Alison Callahan, Robert M. Califf, Robert A. Harrington, and Nigam H. Shah. 2019. It is time to learn from patients like mine. *npj Digit. Medicine*, 2.

Mohammad Hashir and Rapinder Sawhney. 2020. Towards unstructured mortality prediction with free-text clinical notes. *J. Biomed. Informatics*, 108:103489.

Kexin Huang, Jaan Altosaar, and Rajesh Ranganath. 2020. Clinicalbert: Modeling clinical notes and predicting hospital readmission. *Preprint*, arXiv:1904.05342.

Alistair E. W. Johnson, Tom J. Pollard, Lu Shen, Li wei H. Lehman, Mengling Feng, Mohammad Mahdi Ghassemi, Benjamin Moody, Peter Szolovits, Leo Anthony Celi, and Roger G. Mark. 2016. Mimic-iii, a freely accessible critical care database. *Scientific Data*, 3.

Isotta Landi, Benjamin S. Glicksberg, Hao-Chih Lee, Sarah T. Cherng, Giulia Landi, Matteo Danieletto, Joel T. Dudley, Cesare Furlanello, and Riccardo Miotto. 2020. Deep representation learning of electronic health records to unlock patient stratification at scale. *npj Digit. Medicine*, 3.

Quoc V. Le and Tomás Mikolov. 2014. Distributed representations of sentences and documents. In *Proceedings of the 31th International Conference on Machine Learning, ICML 2014, Beijing, China, 21-26 June 2014*, volume 32 of *JMLR Workshop and Conference Proceedings*, pages 1188–1196. JMLR.org.

Jinhyuk Lee, Wonjin Yoon, Sungdong Kim, Donghyeon Kim, Sunkyu Kim, Chan Ho So, and Jaewoo Kang. 2020. Biobert: a pre-trained biomedical language representation model for biomedical text mining. *Bioinform.*, 36(4):1234–1240.

Yong Ju Lee and Kyung Ho Lee. 2017. Re-identification of medical records by optimum quasi-identifiers. In *2017 19th International Conference on Advanced Communication Technology (ICACT)*, pages 428–435.

Y. Li, S. Rao, J. R. A. Solares, et al. 2020. Behrt: Transformer for electronic health records. *Scientific Reports*, 10(1):7155.

Yikuan Li, Ramsey M. Wehbe, Faraz S. Ahmad, Hanyin Wang, and Yuan Luo. 2022. Clinical-longformer and clinical-bigbird: Transformers for long clinical sequences. *Preprint*, arXiv:2201.11838.

Yikuan Li, Ramsey M. Wehbe, Faraz S. Ahmad, Hanyin Wang, and Yuan Luo. 2023. A comparative study of pretrained language models for long clinical text. *J. Am. Medical Informatics Assoc.*, 30(2):340–347.

Luchen Liu, Haoran Li, Zhiting Hu, Haoran Shi, Zichang Wang, Jian Tang, and Ming Zhang. 2019. Learning hierarchical representations of electronic health records for clinical outcome prediction. In *AMIA 2019, American Medical Informatics Association Annual Symposium, Washington, DC, USA, November 16-20, 2019*. AMIA.

Zhiyuan Liu, Yankai Lin, and Maosong Sun. 2020. *Representation Learning for Natural Language Processing*. Springer Nature Singapore.

Maria Mahbub, Sudarshan Srinivasan, Ioan Danciu, Alina Peluso, Edmon Begoli, Suzanne R. Tamang, and Gregory D. Peterson. 2022. Unstructured clinical notes within the 24 hours since admission predict short, mid & long-term mortality in adult icu patients. *PLoS ONE*, 17.

L Matondora, M Mutandavari, and B. Mupini. 2024. Nlp based prediction of hospital readmission using clinicalbert and clinician notes. *International Journal of Innovative Science and Research Technology (IJISRT)*.

Tomás Mikolov, Ilya Sutskever, Kai Chen, Gregory S. Corrado, and Jeffrey Dean. 2013. Distributed representations of words and phrases and their compositionality. In *Advances in Neural Information Processing Systems 26: 27th Annual Conference on Neural Information Processing Systems 2013. Proceedings of a meeting held December 5-8, 2013, Lake Tahoe, Nevada, United States*, pages 3111–3119.

Kai Packhäuser, Sebastian Gündel, Nicolas Münster, Christopher Syben, Vincent Christlein, and Andreas K. Maier. 2021. Deep learning-based patient re-identification is able to exploit the biometric nature of medical chest x-ray data. *Scientific Reports*, 12.

Yifan Peng, Shankai Yan, and Zhiyong Lu. 2019. Transfer learning in biomedical natural language processing: An evaluation of BERT and elmo on ten benchmarking datasets. In *Proceedings of the 18th BioNLP Workshop and Shared Task, BioNLP@ACL 2019, Florence, Italy, August 1, 2019*, pages 58–65. Association for Computational Linguistics.

Jeffrey Pennington, Richard Socher, and Christopher D. Manning. 2014. Glove: Global vectors for word representation. In *Proceedings of the 2014 Conference on Empirical Methods in Natural Language Processing, EMNLP 2014*, pages 1532–1543. ACL.

Alvin Rajkomar, Eyal Oren, Kai Chen, Andrew M. Dai, Nissan Hajaj, Michaela Hardt, Peter J. Liu, Xiaobing Liu, Jake Marcus, Mimi Sun, Patrik Sundberg, Hector Yee, Kun Zhang, Yi Zhang, Gerardo Flores, Gavin E. Duggan, Jamie Irvine, Quoc Le, Kurt Litsch, Alexander Mossin, Justin Tansuwan, De Wang, James Wexler, Jimbo Wilson, Dana Ludwig, Samuel L. Volchenboum, Katherine Chou, Michael Pearson, Srinivasan Madabushi, Nigam H. Shah, Atul J. Butte, Michael D. Howell, Claire Cui, Gregory S. Corrado, and Jeffrey Dean. 2018. Scalable and accurate deep learning with electronic health records. *npj Digit. Medicine*, 1.

Lauren Ellis Riplinger, Jordi Piera-Jimenez, and Julie Pursley Dooling. 2020. Patient identification techniques – approaches, implications, and findings. *Yearbook of Medical Informatics*, 29:81 – 86.

Yuqi Si and Kirk Roberts. 2020. Patient representation transfer learning from clinical notes based on hierarchical attention network. *AMIA Summits on Translational Science Proceedings*, 2020:597.

Yuqi Si and Kirk Roberts. 2021. Three-level hierarchical transformer networks for long-sequence and multiple clinical documents classification. *Preprint*, arXiv:2104.08444.

Ethan Steinberg, Ken Jung, Jason A. Fries, Conor K. Corbin, Stephen R. Pfohl, and Nigam H. Shah. 2021. Language models are an effective representation learning technique for electronic health record data. *Journal of Biomedical Informatics*, 113:103637.

Madhumita Sushil, Simon Suster, Kim Luyckx, and Walter Daelemans. 2018. Patient representation learning and interpretable evaluation using clinical notes. *J. Biomed. Informatics*, 84:103–113.

Yasuyuki Ueda and Junji Morishita. 2023. Patient identification based on deep metric learning for preventing human errors in follow-up x-ray examinations. *J. Imaging Inform. Medicine*, 36(5):1941–1953.

Ashish Vaswani, Noam Shazeer, Niki Parmar, Jakob Uszkoreit, Llion Jones, Aidan N. Gomez, Lukasz Kaiser, and Illia Polosukhin. 2017. Attention is all you need. In *Advances in Neural Information Processing Systems 30: Annual Conference on Neural Information Processing Systems 2017, December 4-9, 2017, Long Beach, CA, USA*, pages 5998–6008.

Benjamin Warner, Antoine Chaffin, Benjamin Clavié, Orion Weller, Oskar Hallström, Said Taghadouini, Alexis Gallagher, Raja Biswas, Faisal Ladhak, Tom Aarsen, Nathan Cooper, Griffin Adams, Jeremy Howard, and Iacopo Poli. 2024. Smarter, better, faster, longer: A modern bidirectional encoder for fast, memory efficient, and long context finetuning and inference. *Preprint*, arXiv:2412.13663.

Adam B. Wilcox, Yueh-Hsia Chen, and George Hripcsak. 2011. Minimizing electronic health record patient-note mismatches. *Journal American Medical Informatics Association*, 18(4):511–514.

Michael Wornow, Alejandro Lozano, Dev Dash, Jenelle Jindal, Kenneth W. Mahaffey, and Nigam H. Shah. 2025. Zero-shot clinical trial patient matching with llms. *NEJM AI*, 2(1).

Yonghui Wu, Mike Schuster, Zhifeng Chen, Quoc V. Le, Mohammad Norouzi, Wolfgang Macherey, Maxim Krikun, Yuan Cao, Qin Gao, Klaus Macherey, Jeff Klingner, Apurva Shah, Melvin Johnson, Xiaobing Liu, Łukasz Kaiser, Stephan Gouws, Yoshikiyo Kato, Taku Kudo, Hideto Kazawa, Keith Stevens, George Kurian, Nishant Patil, Wei Wang, Cliff Young, Jason Smith, Jason Riesa, Alex Rudnick, Oriol Vinyals, Greg Corrado, Macduff Hughes, and Jeffrey Dean. 2016. Google's neural machine translation system: Bridging the gap between human and machine translation. *Preprint*, arXiv:1609.08144.

Zhichao Yang, Avijit Mitra, Sunjae Kwon, and Hong Yu. 2024. Clinicalmamba: A generative clinical language model on longitudinal clinical notes. In *Proceedings of the 6th Clinical Natural Language Processing Workshop, ClinicalNLP@NAACL 2024, Mexico City, Mexico, June 21, 2024*, pages 54–63. Association for Computational Linguistics.

Manzil Zaheer, Guru Guruganesh, Kumar Avinava Dubey, Joshua Ainslie, Chris Alberti, Santiago Ontañón, Philip Pham, Anirudh Ravula, Qifan Wang, Li Yang, and Amr Ahmed. 2020. Big bird: Transformers for longer sequences. In *Advances in Neural Information Processing Systems 33: Annual Conference on Neural Information Processing Systems 2020, NeurIPS 2020, December 6-12, 2020, virtual.*

Yukun Zhu, Ryan Kiros, Richard S. Zemel, Ruslan Salakhutdinov, Raquel Urtasun, Antonio Torralba, and Sanja Fidler. 2015. Aligning books and movies: Towards story-like visual explanations by watching movies and reading books. In *2015 IEEE International Conference on Computer Vision, ICCV 2015, Santiago, Chile, December 7-13, 2015*, pages 19–27. IEEE Computer Society.

A Appendix

A.1 Notes Statistics

CATEGORY	NUMBER OF NOTES
Nursing/other	822,497
Radiology	522,279
Nursing	223,556
ECG	209,051
Physician	141,624
Discharge summary	59,652
Echo	45,794
Respiratory	31,739
Nutrition	9,418
General	8,301
Rehab Services	5,431
Social Work	2,670
Case Management	967
Pharmacy	103
Consult	98

Table 4: Number of notes per category in the MIMIC-III dataset.

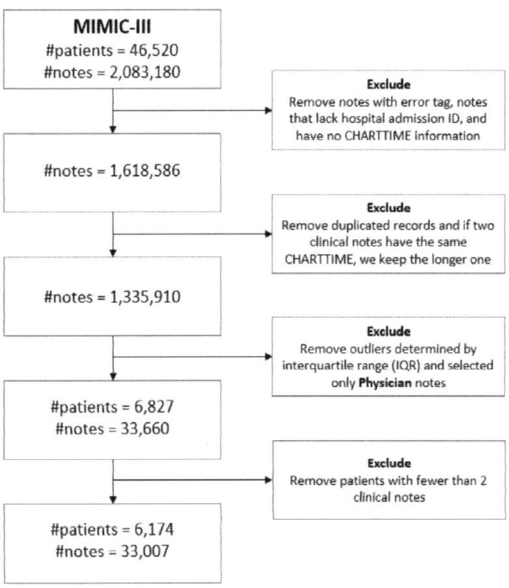

Figure 1: Cohort design, MIMIC-III dataset.

A.2 Models Details

A.2.1 HAN BERTLSTM

Following the architecture proposed by (Si and Roberts, 2021), we adapted their HAN BiLSTM model[3] to our task. The model integrates a BERT component as a fully trainable word-level encoder, followed by BiLSTMs and a pooling strategy to hierarchically learn sentence-level and document-level embeddings. The BiLSTMs and a global context-based attention mechanism capture sequential information at both the sentence and document levels, while a pooling strategy aggregates embeddings from one level to the next, extracting salient features at each stage.

In our implementation, we employed the BERT-Base model at the word level. BERTBase comprises 12 layers, 768 hidden units, and 12 attention heads. It is pretrained on general-domain text datasets, including English Wikipedia (2.5 billion words) and the BookCorpus dataset (Zhu et al., 2015) (800 million words). The model uses the WordPiece tokenizer (Wu et al., 2016) and has an input token limit of 512.

To generate word-level embeddings, we applied either the attention mechanism resulting from the original HAN BERTLSTM pre-training or one of several pooling strategies, namely average pooling, max pooling, or mean_max pooling, to the BERT output. These word-level embeddings were then passed through the BiLSTM encoder to capture sentence-level features, where the same attention or pooling strategies were applied to produce final sentence embeddings. Similarly, document-level embeddings for individual clinical notes were obtained by applying the same strategies at the next hierarchical level. For patient-level representation, we aggregated the embeddings of all notes associated with a single patient. This was achieved using either an attention mechanism or a pooling strategy. Experimenting with these various pooling strategies allowed us to assess their impact on the patient-note identification task. The architecture of the model is shown in Figure 2.

A.2.2 HTN

As our second model, we evaluated the three-level Hierarchical Transformer Network (HTN) [4], proposed by (Si and Roberts, 2021) and illustrated in Figure 3. The model architecture progressively constructs representations from the word level to the document level. At the word level, the model integrates a BERT encoder, experimenting with different BERT variants to balance model size and sequence length. At the sentence and document levels, it employs a Transformer-based encoder ar-

[3]Model code is available at https://github.com/Yuqi92/3-level-HTN-MIMIC.git

[4]Model code is available at https://github.com/Yuqi92/3-level-HTN-MIMIC.git

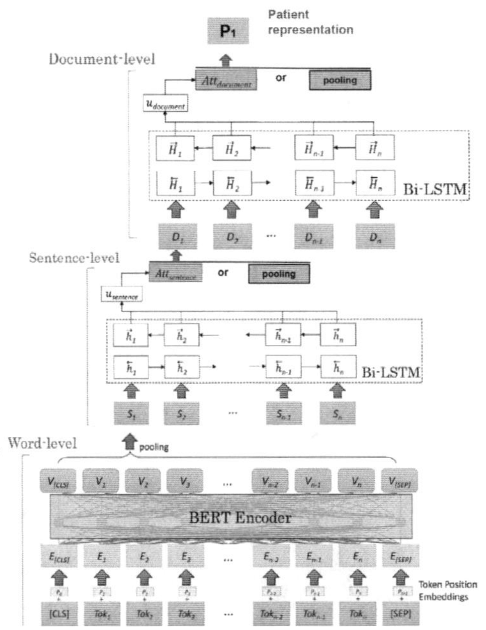

Figure 2: Overview of the HAN architecture incorporating BERT and BiLSTM with attention or pooling strategies for hierarchical aggregation. Adapted from (Si and Roberts, 2021).

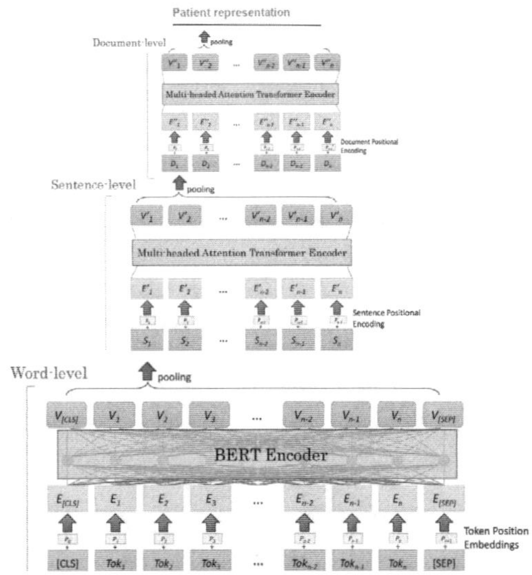

Figure 3: Overview of the HTN architecture incorporating BERT and Multi-head Transformer Encoder with pooling strategies for hierarchical aggregation. Adapted from (Si and Roberts, 2021).

chitecture inspired by (Vaswani et al., 2017), using multiheaded self-attention to identify key features and pooling to condense representations for the next level. Inputs are cropped or padded to fixed sizes at all levels (word, sentence, document). Further details about the model can be found in (Si and Roberts, 2021).

For our experiments, we used the BERTBase model at the word level. To construct higher-level representations from word to document level, we experimented with three pooling strategies: average, max, and mean_max pooling. Patient-level representations were then derived by aggregating note-level representations for each patient using the same pooling strategies.

A.2.3 Bert-based Models

As our third model, we aimed to evaluate the standalone performance of BERT (Devlin et al., 2019), a widely used transformer model, to establish a robust baseline. This experiment was designed to understand the capability of BERT in capturing semantic and contextual information from clinical notes without leveraging additional hierarchical mechanisms or pretrained domain-specific adaptations. BERT has proven to be highly effective in various NLP tasks, making it a strong candidate for text representation in this context. Although specialized models like ClinicalBERT (Huang et al., 2020) have shown strong results in clinical applications, we opted not to use them to avoid potential bias. ClinicalBERT is pretrained on the MIMIC-III dataset, which overlaps with our experimental data, potentially confounding the evaluation. By employing the generic BERTBase model, we ensure a fairer evaluation of our approach.

Token Embeddings Representations In the first approach, the final representations are derived from token embeddings in the text. Clinical notes are first split into sentences, and each sentence is tokenized. The tokenized input is passed into BERT-Base, which generates embeddings for each token in the sentences. To obtain a single vector representation of a sentence, we pool the token embeddings using one of three strategies: average, max, or mean_max pooling, represented as:

$$S_{repr} = avg/max/mean\_max(TE(w_1), TE(w_2), \ldots, TE(w_n)) \quad (1)$$

, where S_{repr} refers to the sentence representation and TE(w_n) is the token embedding representation of each token in the sentence. To construct document-level embeddings, the sentence embeddings are appended and aggregated using the same pooling strategies (average, max, or mean_max) along the dimension of sentence:

$$N_{repr} = avg/max/mean\_max(S_1repr, S_2repr, \ldots, S_nrepr) \quad (2)$$

Finally, for patient-level representation, where each patient has a set of clinical notes, the document-level embeddings are aggregated using average, max, or mean_max pooling. This results in a single vector representation that captures the information from all notes associated with the patient.

[CLS] Token-Based Representation In the second approach, instead of learning token embeddings and aggregating them to obtain sentence representations, we directly extract the [CLS] token representation for each sentence. For each sentence, the sum of all token embeddings is passed through the Transformer layers (TL) to compute the final representation of the [CLS] token:

$$[[CLS]]_{repr} = TL(TE(w_1) + TE(w_2) + \ldots + TE(w_n)) \quad (3)$$

The [CLS] representations for all sentences are concatenated to form the input for document-level embedding. To obtain the document-level embeddings, we apply the same aggregation strategies (average, max, or mean_max) across the [CLS] token representations of sentences:

$$N_{repr} = avg/max/mean\_max([[CLS]]_1repr, [[CLS]]_2repr, \ldots, [[CLS]]_nrepr)$$

For patient-level representation, document-level embeddings from all notes associated with a patient are further aggregated using the same pooling strategies (average, max, or mean_max), producing a single vector representation for the patient.

By experimenting with these two methods, we aim to comprehensively evaluate BERT's effectiveness at capturing representations at sentence, document, and patient levels, while establishing a strong comparative baseline for this task.

A.3 LongFormer

Upon reviewing the MIMIC-III Physician notes, we observed that 28,266 out of 33,660 notes exceed 512 tokens, indicating that approximately 84% of the notes exceed the token limit imposed by BERT. This suggests that the 512-token constraint may restrict the amount of information BERT can effectively capture. Figure 4 illustrates the token distribution across the Physician clinical notes in the MIMIC-III dataset. Given this limitation, we sought to explore a model that could handle longer sequences more effectively, motivating our decision to experiment with Longformer as our fourth model. Unlike BERT, Longformer can process sequences up to 4096 tokens, addressing BERT's token constraint. It does this through a sliding window attention mechanism by allowing each token to attend only to a fixed window of neighboring tokens. Additionally, Longformer incorporates a global attention mechanism for selected tokens, such as the [CLS] token, enabling the model to capture broader context in longer documents.

Longformer is pretrained on a mix of general-purpose datasets, including scientific and news articles, designed to handle long-form text.

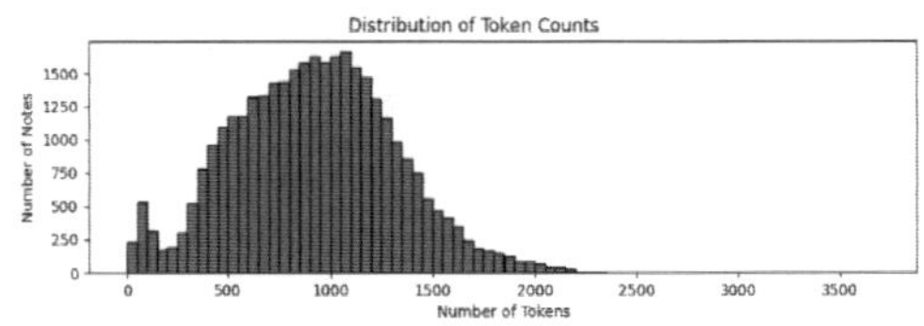

Figure 4: Number of tokens across MIMIC-III Physician notes.

A.4 Bert-based [CLS] Token or Token Embedding (TE) With Sliding Window Model

Motivated by the Longformer model, we conducted a new set of experiments with BERT, implementing the sliding window mechanism for both token embedding (TE) and [CLS] token-based representations. We believe this approach (our fifth model) will not only overcome the token limitation imposed by BERT but also enable the model to focus on different parts of a clinical note, often spread across various sections, thus minimizing information loss typically associated with pooling.

To implement this, we begin by splitting each note into individual sentences. If a sentence exceeds 512 tokens, a sliding window is applied. The window starts at an initial position and processes a chunk of the sentence up to 512 tokens. It then moves by a specified stride and processes the next chunk. For our experiments, we set the stride value to 256 tokens, meaning that each window overlaps with the next one. We believe this overlapping strategy helps preserve contextual information when learning embeddings, as shown in Figure 5.

This process continues until the entire sentence is covered. For each chunk, we obtain sentence-level embeddings using either the token embedding (TE) or [CLS] representation, depending on the approach being tested. To illustrate, consider a note consisting of two sentences: one long sentence containing more than 512 tokens and a shorter sentence with exactly 512 tokens. The long sentence (S_1) can be represented as $S_1 = S_{repr1.1}, S_{repr1.2}, S_{repr1.3}$, and the short sentence (S_2) as $S_2 = S_{repr2}$. The final document-level embedding for the entire note is then computed as the average of all sentence embeddings:

$$N_{repr} = avg/max/mean\_max(S_{repr1.1}, S_{repr1.2}, S_{repr1.3}, S_{repr2})$$

It is important to note that our sliding window approach differs from the one used in Longformer. While Longformer processes the entire input using a global attention mechanism and a sliding window to select specific tokens to attend to, our approach divides the text into chunks, ensuring that each part of the sentence is processed separately before combining them into a final representation. This chunk-based approach allows us to handle very long sentences in a more structured manner.

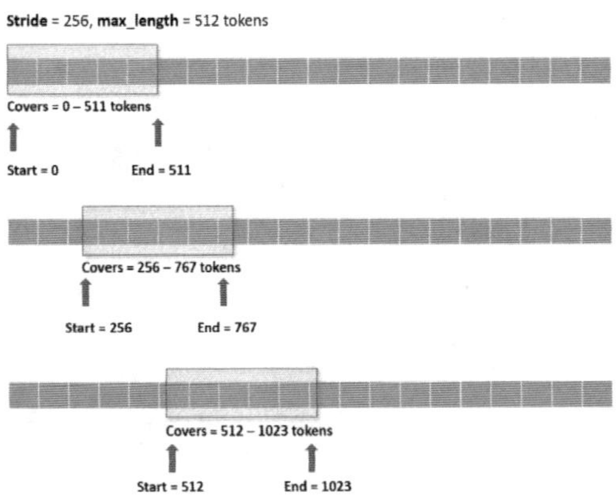

Figure 5: Sliding window approach.

MeDiSumQA: Patient-Oriented Question-Answer Generation from Discharge Letters

Amin Dada[1], **Osman Alperen Koraş**[1], **Marie Bauer**[1], **Amanda Butler Contreras**[2], **Kaleb E Smith**[2], **Jens Kleesiek**[1,3,4,5], **Julian Friedrich**[1],
[1]Institute for AI in Medicine (IKIM), University Hospital Essen, Germany
[2]NVIDIA, Santa Clara, USA
[3]Cancer Research Center Cologne Essen (CCCE), University Medicine Essen, Germany
[4]German Cancer Consortium (DKTK, Partner site Essen), Germany
[5]Department of Physics, TU Dortmund, Germany
Correspondence: amin.dada@uk-essen.de

Abstract

While increasing patients' access to medical documents improves medical care, this benefit is limited by varying health literacy levels and complex medical terminology. Large language models (LLMs) offer solutions by simplifying medical information. However, evaluating LLMs for safe and patient-friendly text generation is difficult due to the lack of standardized evaluation resources. To fill this gap, we developed **MeDiSumQA**. **MeDiSumQA** is a dataset created from MIMIC-IV discharge summaries through an automated pipeline combining LLM-based question-answer generation with manual quality checks. We use this dataset to evaluate various LLMs on patient-oriented question-answering. Our findings reveal that general-purpose LLMs frequently surpass biomedical-adapted models, while automated metrics correlate with human judgment. By releasing **MeDiSumQA** on PhysioNet, we aim to advance the development of LLMs to enhance patient understanding and ultimately improve care outcomes.

1 Introduction

Access to health documents empowers patients and improves medical care (Greene and Hibbard, 2012; Lye et al., 2018; Ross and Lin, 2003). These documents, however, often use language too complex for patients to understand (Paasche-Orlow et al., 2005), and physicians have no time to simplify documents in a patient-friendly manner (Ammenwerth and Spötl, 2009).

This gap between healthcare providers and patients can be bridged by large language models (LLMs) (Ali et al., 2023; Jeblick et al., 2024; Zaretsky et al., 2024; Eisinger et al., 2025). Through their ability to simplify medical information, LLMs can enhance the access to health documents and ultimately improve patient care. However, assessing and comparing LLMs in their ability to generate safe and patient-friendly text remains challenging due to the lack of benchmarks and publicly available resources. Strict privacy regulations surrounding clinical data limit dataset accessibility, thereby impeding the development of open benchmarks for evaluating LLMs in medical contexts.

To address this issue, we developed **MeDiSumQA**. **MeDiSumQA** is a novel, patient-oriented question-answering (QA) dataset, a format especially suitable to improve patient understanding of clinical documents (Cai et al., 2023).

In this paper, we describe how we created, curated, and evaluated **MeDiSumQA**, crafting a standardized resource for future benchmarking. By making this task openly available to researchers, we support broader development and testing of LLMs for healthcare applications, helping address challenges of time constraints and health literacy.

2 Related Work

While several clinical QA datasets exist (Pampari et al., 2018; Lehman et al., 2022; Soni et al., 2022; Bardhan et al., 2022; Dada et al., 2024b; Kweon et al., 2024), none, to the best of our knowledge, are explicitly designed for patient-oriented use.

Prior research has explored medical text simplification, but did not focus on helping patients understand clinical documents in a QA format. Aali et al. (2024) developed a public dataset that converts MIMIC hospital course summaries into concise discharge letters. Campillos-Llanos et al. (2022) created a Spanish dataset for simplifying clinical trial texts, demonstrating the importance of multilingual resources. Trienes et al. (2022) focused on making pathology reports more understandable for patients, though their dataset remains private and does not address everyday clinical questions. Similarly, while Ben Abacha and Demner-Fushman (2019)'s MeQSum dataset transforms consumer health questions into brief medical queries, but is not based on clinical documents.

Proceedings of the Second Workshop on Patient-Oriented Language Processing (CL4Health), pages 124–136
May 4, 2025 ©2025 Association for Computational Linguistics

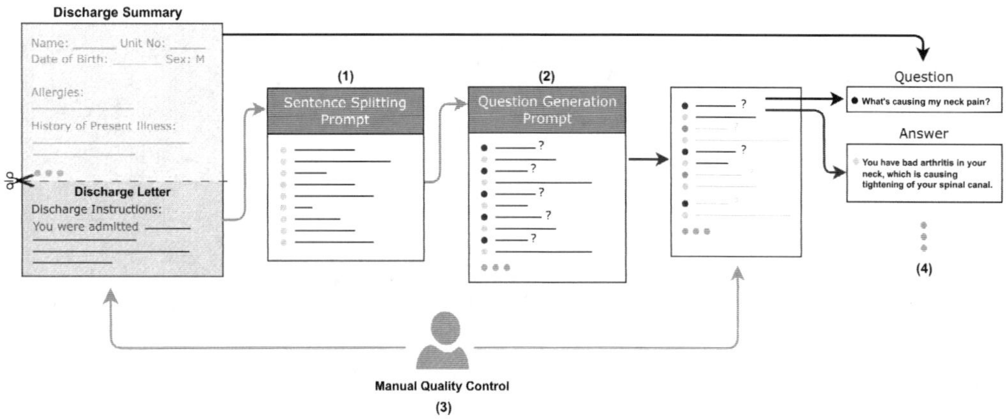

Figure 1: Generation process of **MeDiSumQA**. After identifying the discharge letter, we separate it from the main document and use an LLM to split it into sentences (1). Based on these sentences, we let an LLM generate matching questions (2). The resulting question-answer pairs were reviewed and curated by a physician, resulting in the the final **MeDiSumQA** dataset of 416 question-answer pairs (3). For inference, we provide LLMs with the discharge summary (without the bottom discharge letter) and pose the generated question. The model answer is then compared to the extracted ground truth answer (4).

Our work addresses these limitations by introducing a public, patient-centered QA dataset based on clinical MIMIC-IV discharge summaries, creating a benchmark to evaluate LLMs.

3 Methods

3.1 Dataset Generation

In the MIMIC-IV dataset (Johnson et al., 2023), some discharge summaries conclude with a discharge letter that summarizes key information and follow-up instructions in patient-friendly language. We used these discharge letters as the foundation for generating QA pairs in the following manner (Figure 1):

First, we identified discharge summaries containing discharge letters by searching for the string[1] that indicates the start of a discharge letter. We split each discharge letter into sentences using *Meta's Llama-3-70B-Instruct* (Dubey et al., 2024), which proved more accurate than traditional sentence splitters like NLTK, especially when handling irregular formatting and placeholders introduced by anonymization. To ensure accuracy, we prompted the LLM to preserve the original sentence structure and wording, which we subsequently verified by confirming that each processed sentence could be matched exactly with its source in the original discharge letter via exact string matching.

Afterwards, we fed these sentences into an *Meta's Llama-3-70B-Instruct* to generate matching questions from a patient's perspective. The LLM was allowed to reformulate the answer to match the question, but was instructed to reference the source sentence. We then manually checked these references to confirm that no information from the source document was altered. Since the answers are directly derived from the discharge letters written by medical professionals, this method maintains both medical accuracy and patient-friendly language. All mentioned prompts are listed in Appendix A.

The resulting QA candidates were then manually reviewed by a physician who selected high-quality examples based on the following criteria:

Factual correctness Question-answer pairs had to be logically connected. Answers that did not match their questions (e.g., "What medication should I avoid taking due to a possible allergy?" - "You were prescribed ibuprofen") were excluded.

Completeness Answers had to be complete. Partial answers (e.g., "What medications were started for me?" - "You were started on Vancomycin 1gm IV every 24 hours" when additional antibiotics were prescribed) were discarded.

Safety Answers needed to be safe. Potentially

[1]"You were admitted to the hospital"

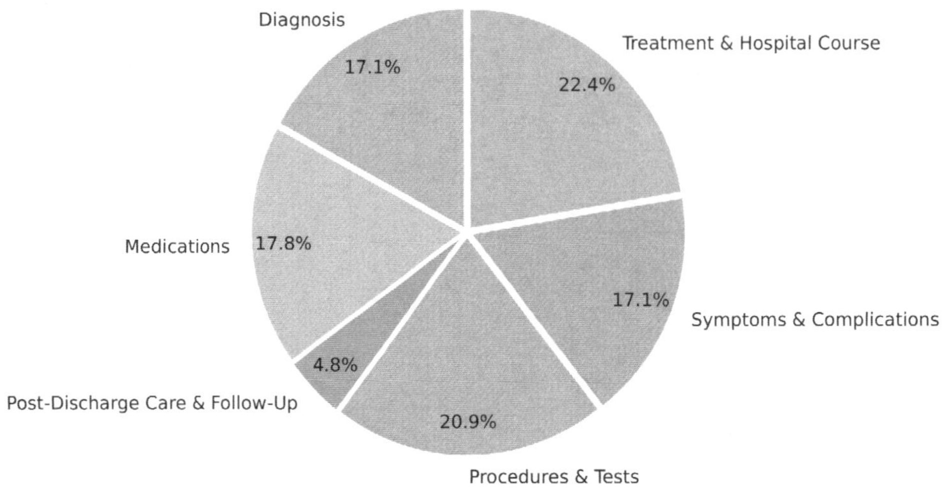

Figure 2: Frequency of question-answer categories in **MeDiSumQA**.

harmful instructions (e.g., "Take Coumadin 3 mg daily" without mentioning INR monitoring) were excluded.

Consistency Questions had to be answerable from both the discharge letter and discharge summary. Questions whose answers relied solely on information from the discharge letter were excluded.

Complexity Question-answer pairs had to be sufficiently complex. Obvious answers or overly specific questions that gave the answer away (e.g. "Did I receive Ciprofloxacin?" - "You received Ciprofloxacin.") were excluded.

As a final step, we removed the discharge letters from their summaries and combined the remaining summaries with their matching QA pairs. This resulted in three components, forming **MeDiSumQA**:

1. **A question** that serves as input for LLMs.
2. **An abbreviated discharge** summary without the discharge letter that LLMs use to answer the input question
3. **A ground truth answer** for comparison with generated responses

3.2 QA Categories

In **MeDiSumQA**, we identified six QA categories:

- Symptoms & Complications
- Procedures & Tests
- Diagnosis
- Treatment & Hospital Course
- Medications
- Post-Discharge Care & Follow-Up

To assign each QA pair to one of these categories, we used Meta's *Llama-3.3-70B-Instruct* (Dubey et al., 2024).

3.3 Evaluation

We evaluated the following models on **MeDiSumQA**: *Mistral-7B-Instruct-v0.1* (Jiang et al., 2023), *Meta-Llama-3-8B-Instruct*, *Meta-Llama-3.1-8B-Instruct* (Dubey et al., 2024), and four biomedical models derived from previously mentioned general-purpose language models: *BioMistral-7B* (Labrak et al., 2024), *Llama3-Med42-8B* (Christophe et al., 2024), *Llama3-Aloe-8B-Alpha* (Gururajan et al., 2024), and *Meditron3-8B* (OpenMeditron, 2024). We evaluated model performance on the **MeDiSumQA** dataset through automatic and manual assessments to ensure a comprehensive analysis.

3.3.1 Automatic Evaluation

We evaluated the models using established similarity metrics that capture both n-gram overlap and semantic similarity. The temperature was set to 1.0

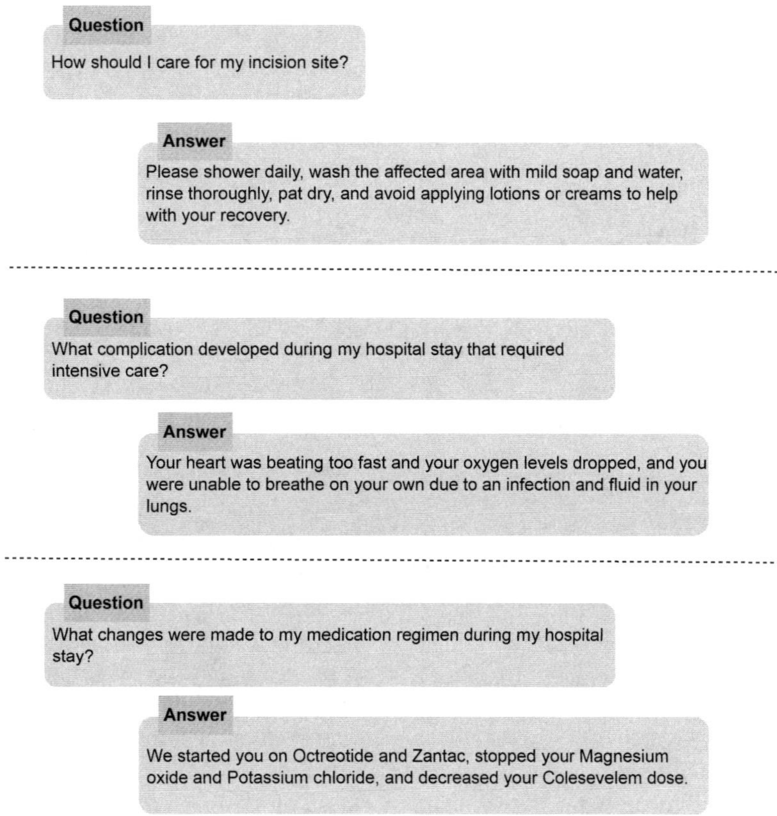

Figure 3: Example of QA pairs in **MeDiSumQA** dataset.

for all models. Due to the long input length, the models were prompted with a one-shot example. Additional details about the prompts are described in Appendix A.

Specifically, we used ROUGE-1, ROUGE-2, and ROUGE-L (Lin, 2004) to measure lexical overlap at varying levels of granularity, as well as BERT Score (Zhang* et al., 2020) to evaluate semantic similarity using contextual embeddings. For the BERT Score we tuned the rescaling baselines for MIMIC-IV discharge summaries using *Bio_ClinicalBERT* (Alsentzer et al., 2019). We also used the Unified Medical Language System (UMLS) parser *scispaCy* (Neumann et al., 2019) to assess the alignment of biomedical entities between predictions and ground truth answers, computing a UMLS F1 score.

As baselines for these metrics, we calculated both lower and upper bounds. To provide a lower bound for meaningful model predictions, we compute the similarity between the question and ground truth. For the upper bound, we paraphrased ground truth answers using *Llama-3.3-70B-Instruct* and measured their similarity to the original ground truth.

3.3.2 Manual Evaluation

To complement the automatic evaluation, we manually assessed 100 generated answers from two models: *Mistral-7B-Instruct-v0.1*, a lower-scoring model, and *Meta-Llama-3.1-8B-Instruct*, a higher-scoring model. For each model, we sorted the answers by the average similarity score across all automatic metrics. We then divided them into five equal-sized bins, with the lowest 20% placed in bin 1, the next 20% in bin 2, up to bin 5 containing the highest 20%. We then sampled ten predictions from each bin.

The answers were rated by a physician on five critical aspects:

- **Factuality:** Accuracy of medical information, rated on a scale from 1 to 5.

Model	Biomedical	Avg	R-L	R-1	R-2	BERT F1	UMLS F1
Lower Bound	-	20.93	13.11	15.76	2.82	60.22	12.74
Upper Bound	-	44.72	41.55	45.13	16.82	81.35	38.75
BioMistral-7B	Yes	23.69	15.1	19.67	5.29	64.24	14.13
Llama3-Med42-8B	Yes	29.27	21.2	26.84	8.65	68.45	21.21
Llama3-Aloe-8B-Alpha	Yes	19.47	8.94	12.11	3.81	61.83	10.66
Meditron3-8B	Yes	29.00	21.1	26.63	8.63	68.01	20.62
Mistral-7B-Instruct-v0.1	No	23.24	14.55	19.00	5.08	64.15	13.42
Meta-Llama-3-8B-Instruct	No	28.75	20.78	26.51	8.72	67.69	20.06
Meta-Llama-3.1-8B-Instruct	No	**31.43**	**24.1**	**29.93**	**10.24**	**69.35**	**23.55**

Table 1: Automatic evaluation of seven models on **MeDiSumQA**.

- **Brevity:** Conciseness of the response, rated on a scale from 1 to 5.
- **Patient-Friendliness:** Clarity and accessibility of the response for laypersons, rated on a scale from 1 to 5.
- **Relevance:** Alignment of the response with the question, rated on a scale from 1 to 5.
- **Safety:** Potential for harm or dissemination of misleading information, rated as a binary score (unsafe [0]/safe [1]).

Using the same sampling scheme and models, we collected 100 additional model-generated answers. These answers were then compared to their ground truth by a physician in a blinded fashion, indicating the preferred answer for each pair.

4 Results

4.1 MeDiSumQA Description

Initially, we generated 500 QA pairs, which were reduced to 416 pairs after manual curation. Figure 3 shows three examples of the resulting QA pairs.

Analysis of the QA categories in **MeDiSumQA** show a fairly even distribution across most categories (Figure 2). *Treatment & Hospital Course* make up the largest portion at 22.4%. *Procedures & Tests*, *Medications*, *Symptoms & Complications*, and *Diagnosis* each range between 17.1% and 20.9%. *Post-Discharge Care & Follow-Up* questions are notably underrepresented at only 4.8%.

4.2 Automatic Evaluation

Automatic evaluation across different LLMs reveals varying performance on **MeDiSumQA** (Table 1).

Meta-Llama-3.1-8B-Instruct performed best among all tested metrics, achieving the highest scores despite being a general-domain model without specific biomedical adaptation.

Comparing biomedical-adapted models with their general-domain counterparts reveals mixed results. Some biomedical adaptations showed only marginal improvements over their base models: *BioMistral-7B* marginally outperformed its base model *Mistral-7B-Instruct-v0.1* with a small increase of 0.45 points, while *Llama3-Med42-8B* showed a similar pattern with a slight improvement of 0.52 points over *Meta-Llama-3-8B-Instruct.*

However, several biomedical adaptations performed notably worse. Most striking is the case of *Llama3-Aloe-8B-Alpha*, which showed a substantial decrease of 9.28 points compared to its base model *Meta-Llama-3-8B-Instruct*. Similarly, *Meditron3-8B* exhibited a considerable decline of 2.43 points relative to *Meta-Llama-3.1-8B-Instruct.*

4.3 Manual Evaluation

Manual comparison of *Llama-3.1-8B-Instruct* and *Mistral-7B-Instruct-v0.1* across factuality, brevity, patient-friendliness, relevance, and safety revealed differences between the lower and higher scoring models (Figure 4).

In terms of factuality, *Llama-3.1-8B-Instruct* demonstrated consistently high performance, maintaining scores above 4.0 across all bins, with minimal variation. In contrast, *Mistral-7B-Instruct-v0.1* showed a gradual improvement from bin 1 (score 2.5) to bin 5 (score 4.3).

In the brevity metric, both models showed improved scores in higher bins. *Llama-3.1-8B-Instruct* maintained generally higher brevity scores throughout, starting at approximately 4.0 in bin

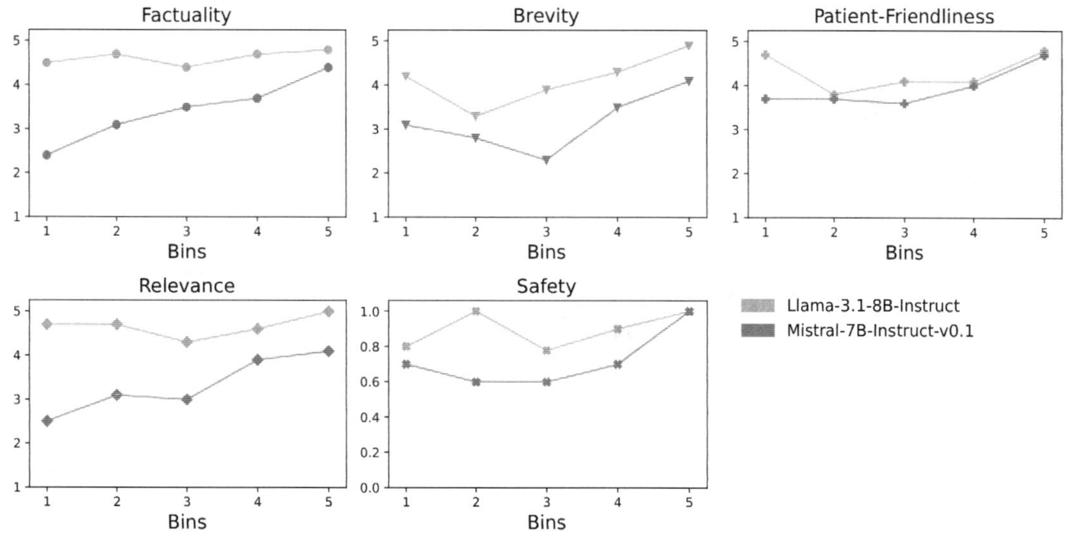

Figure 4: Physicians' evaluation of model generated answers on **MeDiSumQA**. Generated answers by *Llama-3.1-8B-Instruct* (green) and *Mistral-7B-Instruct-v0.1* (red) were sorted by their average automatic evaluation scores and divided into 5 bins. From each bin, 10 examples per model were sampled and rated by a physician across *Factuality*, *Brevity*, *Patient-Friendliness*, *Relevance*, and *Safety*. Each subplot displays scores either between 1 and 5 [*Factuality*, *Brevity*, *Patient-Friendliness*, *Relevance*] or 0 and 1 [*Safety*].

1 and reaching nearly 5.0 in bin 5. *Mistral-7B-Instruct-v0.1* displayed more variable performance, with a notable dip in bin 3 before recovering in bins 4 and 5.

Patient-friendliness scores converged for both models in the higher bins, with both achieving scores near 4.5 in bin 5. *Llama-3.1-8B-Instruct* showed initially higher scores in the lower bins, while *Mistral-7B-Instruct-v0.1* maintained relatively consistent scores around 3.5 before improving in the higher bins.

Regarding relevance, *Llama-3.1-8B-Instruct* consistently outperformed its counterpart, maintaining scores above 4.5 across all bins. *Mistral-7B-Instruct-v0.1* showed a gradual improvement from approximately 2.5 in bin 1 to 4.0 in bin 5.

Safety scores for both models were relatively high, with *Llama-3.1-8B-Instruct* showing slightly better performance, particularly in bins 2 and 3.

When a physician rated preferences between ground truth and model-generated answers, ground truth responses were generally preferred, though the patterns differed between models (Figures 5a, 5b.

For *Mistral-7B-Instruct-v0.1*, ground truth answers were strongly preferred across all bins, with model-generated answers favored only in exceptional cases.

For *Llama-3.1-8B-Instruct*, the results were more nuanced. Model-generated answers were preferred equally or slightly more often in cases with very high, but also with very low automatic similarity scores. In the middle ranges (bins 2, 3, and 4), ground truth answers were strongly preferred, though model-generated responses still garnered 10–40 % preference, with higher rates in the upper bins.

5 Discussion

Here, we introduce **MeDiSumQA**, a benchmark dataset designed to evaluate the ability of LLMs to answer clinical questions in a patient-friendly manner. By combining automatic and manual evaluations, our study provides insights into the strengths and limitations of LLMs for patient-oriented question answering, thus narrowing the gap between complex medical information and safe patient communication.

5.1 Characterization of the Dataset

MeDiSumQA provides a diverse and structured set of patient-oriented QA pairs derived from discharge summaries, covering key medical topics relevant to patient care. The category distribution of **MeDiSumQA** indicates comprehensive coverage across six major domains, with a particular empha-

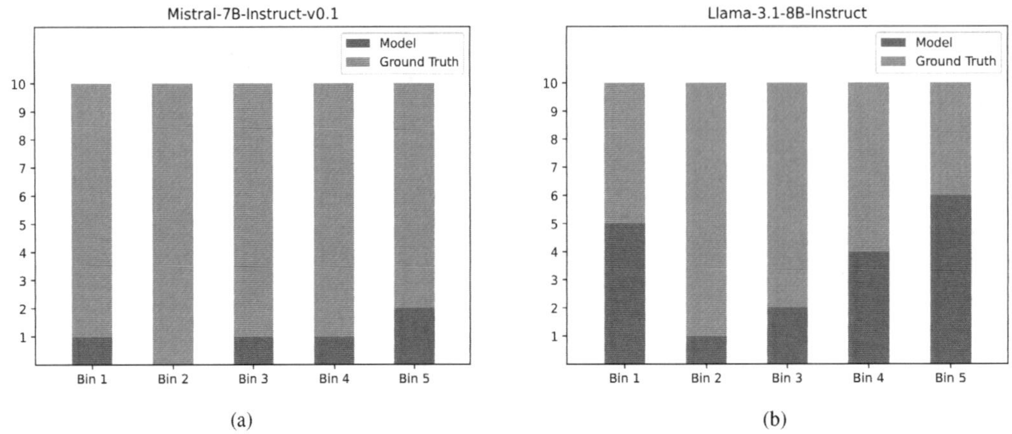

Figure 5: Physician preferences for answers generated by *Mistral-7B-Instruct-v0.1* (a) and *Llama-3.1-8B-Instruct* (b) and the ground truth answers.

sis on in-hospital care, medical interventions, and treatment courses. This suggests that the dataset aligns closely with the most immediate concerns patients may have after hospitalization, such as understanding their diagnosis, medications, and follow-up care.

While the dataset captures essential aspects of patient education, *Post-Discharge Care & Follow-Up* is underrepresented. This imbalance may reflect the structure of discharge summaries themselves, which tend to focus more on inpatient treatment rather than long-term care guidance. Expanding **MeDiSumQA** to include additional post-discharge documentation, such as outpatient follow-up notes or rehabilitation plans, could improve **MeDiSumQA**'s ability to support patient education beyond hospital stays.

5.2 Automatic Evaluation

MeDiSumQA requires LLMs to perform multiple skills simultaneously. Models must comprehend discharge summaries to understand patient cases, extract relevant details about hospital stays, and present this information in patient-friendly language. The discharge summaries are notably long, averaging 3,245.66 tokens with a standard deviation of 1,419.91, which is a significant challenge for LLMs due to the need for effective long-context reasoning (Li et al., 2024a). Furthermore, models must possess comprehensive medical knowledge and understanding of clinical guidelines to provide accurate follow-up advice. This complex task therefore evaluates an LLM's ability to integrate comprehension, information extraction, clear communication, and medical expertise in a patient-centered context.

Considering these antecedents, our evaluation shows that general-domain LLMs match or exceed the performance of specialized ones on biomedical tasks. Notably, *Meta-Llama-3.1-8B-Instruct* outperformed all tested biomedical domain-adapted models, raising questions about domain-specific training's effectiveness. While some biomedical models showed slight improvements over their base versions, others experienced significant performance declines, highlighting the inconsistent success of domain adaptation approaches.

These findings suggest that comprehensive pretraining on general-domain data may be more valuable than domain-specific adaptation. This challenges the conventional view that specialized tasks require domain-specific training, aligning with recent research questioning the effectiveness of biomedical adaptation (Dada et al., 2024a; Jeong et al., 2024; Dorfner et al., 2024).

5.3 Correlation of automatic and manual Evaluation

When comparing automatic with manual evaluation, our results show that calculated metrics like ROUGE and BERT Score correlate well with human judgment. Higher automated metric scores consistently corresponded to higher manual ratings and preferences, particularly for higher-scoring predictions. Conversely, answers from lower-performing models were rarely preferred by physicians and were sometimes deemed unsafe. This correlation between manual scores and physicians' assessments validates that LLMs can be well assessed in their capability to answer medical questions in a patient-friendly manner using **MeDiSumQA**.

However, manual assessment also reveals important limitations of automatic metrics, especially when models generated correct but different responses from the ground truth. Notably, in blind preference tests, *Llama-3.1-8B-Instruct* answers were sometimes preferred over ground truth answers, indicating that LLMs can generate valid alternative responses to the ground truth in **MeDiSumQA** that may be more appealing. Our manual evaluation also shows that LLMs favor safety over conciseness in their responses. These findings underscore the importance of combining human evaluation with automated scoring for thorough assessment in specialized healthcare applications.

5.4 Data Contamination

If evaluation datasets overlap with an LLM's training data, benchmark validity of these datasets is compromised due to data contamination (Li et al., 2024b; Deng et al., 2023). Such contamination can cause models to memorize rather than generalize, artificially inflating their performance. Although it is possible that some LLMs in our study have encountered parts of the MIMIC-IV dataset, this is unlikely since MIMIC-IV requires authentication for access.

A broader concern for datasets is intentional benchmark manipulation, when models are deliberately trained on evaluation datasets, which compromises dataset reliability. One solution is to generate datasets using private, inaccessible data. To facilitate this, we offer our dataset generation pipeline as open-source, allowing hospitals and other organizations to create confidential benchmarks from their own clinical reports. By releasing our **MeDiSumQA** code publicly, we enable others to develop independent datasets and conduct robust LLM evaluations using private medical data.

5.5 Outlook

We make **MeDiSumQA** available to the public, which offers an opportunity for widespread adoption in the medical AI community, enabling robust evaluations of models based on their ability to generate accurate, patient-friendly responses. This transparency can drive improvements in patient-centered AI by ensuring models are assessed against expert-validated benchmarks.

During manual evaluation, some model-generated answers were preferred over the ground truth. This presents an opportunity to refine the dataset by incorporating high-quality model-generated responses, with physicians selecting the most appropriate answers. As this approach could introduce bias toward LLMs used in the selection process, future versions of **MeDiSumQA** could involve multiple independent reviewers to ensure broader generalizability.

Lastly, expanding the dataset by applying our pipeline to a larger set of discharge summaries in different languages would enable use cases beyond single-language few-shot evaluation, including fine-tuning models for improved patient-oriented applications. Making the dataset more diverse and scalable will help develop safer, more effective AI-driven healthcare solutions.

6 Conclusion

MeDiSumQA represents another step toward enhancing patient understanding of medical documents by providing benchmarks to assess LLMs in answering medical questions in a patient-friendly manner. By evaluating models on both automated and human-centered metrics, our study demonstrates that automatic metrics correlate well with human judgment while also highlighting the potential of general-purpose LLMs in patient education. By making **MeDiSumQA** accessible on PhysioNet, we aim to foster further research into the applicability of LLMs for patient-oriented question answering and encourage advancements in this field. We hope that **MeDiSumQA** will serve as a valuable resource for the development of more patient-friendly AI systems, ultimately bridging the gap between complex medical information and safe, effective patient communication.

Limitations

Despite its strengths, **MeDiSumQA** presents challenges. The dataset primarily focuses on English-language discharge summaries, limiting its applicability to multilingual settings. Additionally, while automated metrics such as ROUGE and BERT Score provide valuable insights, our manual assessments reveal that these do not always align with human judgment, particularly in terms of brevity and relevance. Future research should explore more robust evaluation methods that incorporate real-world patient feedback.

References

Asad Aali, Dave Van Veen, Yamin Ishraq Arefeen, Jason Hom, Christian Bluethgen, Eduardo Pontes Reis, Sergios Gatidis, Namuun Clifford, Joseph Daws, Arash S Tehrani, et al. 2024. A dataset and benchmark for hospital course summarization with adapted large language models. *Journal of the American Medical Informatics Association*, page ocae312.

Stephen R Ali, Thomas D Dobbs, Hayley A Hutchings, and Iain S Whitaker. 2023. Using chatgpt to write patient clinic letters. *The Lancet Digital Health*, 5(4):e179–e181.

Emily Alsentzer, John Murphy, William Boag, Wei-Hung Weng, Di Jindi, Tristan Naumann, and Matthew McDermott. 2019. Publicly available clinical BERT embeddings. In *Proceedings of the 2nd Clinical Natural Language Processing Workshop*, pages 72–78, Minneapolis, Minnesota, USA. Association for Computational Linguistics.

Elske Ammenwerth and H-P Spötl. 2009. The time needed for clinical documentation versus direct patient care. *Methods of information in medicine*, 48(01):84–91.

Jayetri Bardhan, Anthony Colas, Kirk Roberts, and Daisy Zhe Wang. 2022. DrugEHRQA: A question answering dataset on structured and unstructured electronic health records for medicine related queries. In *Proceedings of the Thirteenth Language Resources and Evaluation Conference*, pages 1083–1097, Marseille, France. European Language Resources Association.

Asma Ben Abacha and Dina Demner-Fushman. 2019. On the summarization of consumer health questions. In *Proceedings of the 57th Annual Meeting of the Association for Computational Linguistics*, pages 2228–2234, Florence, Italy. Association for Computational Linguistics.

Pengshan Cai, Zonghai Yao, Fei Liu, Dakuo Wang, Meghan Reilly, Huixue Zhou, Lingxi Li, Yi Cao, Alok Kapoor, Adarsha Bajracharya, et al. 2023. Paniniqa: Enhancing patient education through interactive question answering. *Transactions of the Association for Computational Linguistics*, 11:1518–1536.

Leonardo Campillos-Llanos, Ana R Terroba Reinares, Sofía Zakhir Puig, Ana Valverde-Mateos, and Adrián Capllonch-Carrión. 2022. Building a comparable corpus and a benchmark for spanish medical text simplification. *Procesamiento del Lenguaje Natural*, 69:189–196.

Clément Christophe, Praveen K Kanithi, Tathagata Raha, Shadab Khan, and Marco AF Pimentel. 2024. Med42-v2: A suite of clinical llms. *arXiv preprint arXiv:2408.06142*.

Amin Dada, Marie Bauer, Amanda Butler Contreras, Osman Alperen Koraş, Constantin Marc Seibold, Kaleb E Smith, and Jens Kleesiek. 2024a. Does biomedical training lead to better medical performance? *Preprint*, arXiv:2404.04067.

Amin Dada, Tim Leon Ufer, Moon Kim, Max Hasin, Nicola Spieker, Michael Forsting, Felix Nensa, Jan Egger, and Jens Kleesiek. 2024b. Information extraction from weakly structured radiological reports with natural language queries. *European Radiology*, 34(1):330–337.

Chunyuan Deng, Yilun Zhao, Xiangru Tang, Mark Gerstein, and Arman Cohan. 2023. Investigating data contamination in modern benchmarks for large language models. *Preprint*, arXiv:2311.09783.

Felix J Dorfner, Amin Dada, Felix Busch, Marcus R Makowski, Tianyu Han, Daniel Truhn, Jens Kleesiek, Madhumita Sushil, Jacqueline Lammert, Lisa C Adams, et al. 2024. Biomedical large languages models seem not to be superior to generalist models on unseen medical data. *arXiv preprint arXiv:2408.13833*.

Abhimanyu Dubey, Abhinav Jauhri, Abhinav Pandey, Abhishek Kadian, Ahmad Al-Dahle, Aiesha Letman, Akhil Mathur, Alan Schelten, Amy Yang, Angela Fan, et al. 2024. The llama 3 herd of models. *arXiv preprint arXiv:2407.21783*.

Felix Eisinger, Friederike Holderried, Moritz Mahling, Christian Stegemann-Philipps, Anne Herrmann-Werner, Eric Nazarenus, Alessandra Sonanini, Martina Guthoff, Carsten Eickhoff, and Martin Holderried. 2025. What's going on with me and how can i better manage my health? the potential of gpt-4 to transform discharge letters into patient-centered letters to enhance patient safety: Prospective, exploratory study. *Journal of Medical Internet Research*, 27:e67143.

Jessica Greene and Judith H Hibbard. 2012. Why does patient activation matter? an examination of the relationships between patient activation and health-related outcomes. *Journal of general internal medicine*, 27:520–526.

Ashwin Kumar Gururajan, Enrique Lopez-Cuena, Jordi Bayarri-Planas, Adrian Tormos, Daniel Hinjos, Pablo Bernabeu-Perez, Anna Arias-Duart, Pablo Agustin Martin-Torres, Lucia Urcelay-Ganzabal, Marta Gonzalez-Mallo, et al. 2024. Aloe: A family of fine-tuned open healthcare llms. *arXiv preprint arXiv:2405.01886*.

Katharina Jeblick, Balthasar Schachtner, Jakob Dexl, Andreas Mittermeier, Anna Theresa Stüber, Johanna Topalis, Tobias Weber, Philipp Wesp, Bastian Oliver Sabel, Jens Ricke, et al. 2024. Chatgpt makes medicine easy to swallow: an exploratory case study on simplified radiology reports. *European radiology*, 34(5):2817–2825.

Daniel P Jeong, Saurabh Garg, Zachary Chase Lipton, and Michael Oberst. 2024. Medical adaptation of large language and vision-language models: Are we making progress? In *Proceedings of the 2024 Conference on Empirical Methods in Natural Language Processing*, pages 12143–12170, Miami, Florida, USA. Association for Computational Linguistics.

Albert Q Jiang, Alexandre Sablayrolles, Arthur Mensch, Chris Bamford, Devendra Singh Chaplot, Diego de las Casas, Florian Bressand, Gianna Lengyel, Guillaume Lample, Lucile Saulnier, et al. 2023. Mistral 7b. *arXiv preprint arXiv:2310.06825*.

Alistair EW Johnson, Lucas Bulgarelli, Lu Shen, Alvin Gayles, Ayad Shammout, Steven Horng, Tom J Pollard, Sicheng Hao, Benjamin Moody, Brian Gow, et al. 2023. Mimic-iv, a freely accessible electronic health record dataset. *Scientific data*, 10(1):1.

Sunjun Kweon, Jiyoun Kim, Heeyoung Kwak, Dongchul Cha, Hangyul Yoon, Kwanghyun Kim, Seunghyun Won, and Edward Choi. 2024. Ehrnoteqa: A patient-specific question answering benchmark for evaluating large language models in clinical settings. *arXiv preprint arXiv:2402.16040*.

Yanis Labrak, Adrien Bazoge, Emmanuel Morin, Pierre-Antoine Gourraud, Mickael Rouvier, and Richard Dufour. 2024. BioMistral: A collection of open-source pretrained large language models for medical domains. In *Findings of the Association for Computational Linguistics: ACL 2024*, pages 5848–5864, Bangkok, Thailand. Association for Computational Linguistics.

Eric Lehman, Vladislav Lialin, Katelyn Edelwina Legaspi, Anne Janelle Sy, Patricia Therese Pile, Nicole Rose Alberto, Richard Raymund Ragasa, Corinna Victoria Puyat, Marianne Katharina Taliño, Isabelle Rose Alberto, Pia Gabrielle Alfonso, Dana Moukheiber, Byron Wallace, Anna Rumshisky, Jennifer Liang, Preethi Raghavan, Leo Anthony Celi, and Peter Szolovits. 2022. Learning to ask like a physician. In *Proceedings of the 4th Clinical Natural Language Processing Workshop*, pages 74–86, Seattle, WA. Association for Computational Linguistics.

Tianle Li, Ge Zhang, Quy Duc Do, Xiang Yue, and Wenhu Chen. 2024a. Long-context llms struggle with long in-context learning. *CoRR*, abs/2404.02060.

Yucheng Li, Frank Guerin, and Chenghua Lin. 2024b. An open source data contamination report for large language models. *Preprint*, arXiv:2310.17589.

Chin-Yew Lin. 2004. Rouge: A package for automatic evaluation of summaries. In *Text summarization branches out*, pages 74–81.

Carolyn T Lye, Howard P Forman, Jodi G Daniel, and Harlan M Krumholz. 2018. The 21st century cures act and electronic health records one year later: will patients see the benefits? *Journal of the American Medical Informatics Association*, 25(9):1218–1220.

Mark Neumann, Daniel King, Iz Beltagy, and Waleed Ammar. 2019. ScispaCy: Fast and robust models for biomedical natural language processing. In *Proceedings of the 18th BioNLP Workshop and Shared Task*, pages 319–327, Florence, Italy. Association for Computational Linguistics.

OpenMeditron. 2024. Meditron3-8b model card.

Michael K Paasche-Orlow, Ruth M Parker, Julie A Gazmararian, Lynn T Nielsen-Bohlman, and Rima R Rudd. 2005. The prevalence of limited health literacy. *Journal of general internal medicine*, 20(2):175–184.

Anusri Pampari, Preethi Raghavan, Jennifer Liang, and Jian Peng. 2018. emrQA: A large corpus for question answering on electronic medical records. In *Proceedings of the 2018 Conference on Empirical Methods in Natural Language Processing*, pages 2357–2368, Brussels, Belgium. Association for Computational Linguistics.

Stephen E Ross and Chen-Tan Lin. 2003. The effects of promoting patient access to medical records: a review. *Journal of the American Medical Informatics Association*, 10(2):129–138.

Sarvesh Soni, Meghana Gudala, Atieh Pajouhi, and Kirk Roberts. 2022. RadQA: A question answering dataset to improve comprehension of radiology reports. In *Proceedings of the Thirteenth Language Resources and Evaluation Conference*, pages 6250–6259, Marseille, France. European Language Resources Association.

Jan Trienes, Jörg Schlötterer, Hans-Ulrich Schildhaus, and Christin Seifert. 2022. Patient-friendly clinical notes: Towards a new text simplification dataset. In *Proceedings of the Workshop on Text Simplification, Accessibility, and Readability (TSAR-2022)*, pages 19–27, Abu Dhabi, United Arab Emirates (Virtual). Association for Computational Linguistics.

Jonah Zaretsky, Jeong Min Kim, Samuel Baskharoun, Yunan Zhao, Jonathan Austrian, Yindalon Aphinyanaphongs, Ravi Gupta, Saul B Blecker, and Jonah Feldman. 2024. Generative artificial intelligence to transform inpatient discharge summaries to patient-friendly language and format. *JAMA network open*, 7(3):e240357–e240357.

Tianyi Zhang*, Varsha Kishore*, Felix Wu*, Kilian Q. Weinberger, and Yoav Artzi. 2020. Bertscore: Evaluating text generation with bert. In *International Conference on Learning Representations*.

A Prompts

Figures 6 and 7 show the prompts we use to split the discharge letter into sentences and generate question-answer pairs. For the question-answer generation we include a one shot example. Figure 8 shows the prompt we use to evaluate LLMs on **MeDiSumQA**.

System Prompt

Split the given text sentence by sentence by inserting newlines. Do not alter the text. Copy errors and mistakes. Only insert newline characters. Reply with the format '<split-text>...\n...\n...</split-text>'.

User Prompt

<text>{discharge_letter}</text>

Figure 6: Sentence Splitting prompt

System Prompt

You are a helpful assistant that is specialized in medical topics. You will be given a list of sentences that contain information about a patient. Based on the information in the statements, formulate challenging questions from the perspective of the patient. Also provide the answers which should be one or a combination of different given sentences.

1-shot example

User Prompt

Sentences:
1. You were admitted to the hospital for chest pain.
2. In the hospital you were ruled out for a heart attack and your pain was reproduced with touching the chest, suggesting a musculoskeletal cause of your discomfort.
3. You were discharged with a planned stress test as an outpatient.
4. There were no changes made to your medication regimen.

Assistant Response

Question: What was the initial reason for my hospital admission?
Answer: Chest pain (Statement 1)
Question: What did the hospital rule out as a cause of my chest pain, and what finding suggested an alternative cause?
Answer: The hospital ruled out a heart attack, by reproducing the pain with touching the chest, suggesting a musculoskeletal cause (Statement 2).
Question: What further evaluation should I plan after discharge from the hospital?
Answer: Stress test as an outpatient (Statement 3)
Question: Was there any change in my medication regimen during the hospital stay?
Answer: No (Statement 4)

User Prompt

Sentences:
{sentences}

Figure 7: MeDiSumQA generation prompt

System Prompt

You are a highly skilled assistant, specifically trained to assist lays in understanding and extracting key information from medical documents. Your primary responsibility will be to interprete discharge letters from hospitals. You will receive such a discharge letter. You should carefully review the contents and accurately answer questions related to this document. Only respond with the correct answer to the question. Answer briefly without mentioning a lot of specific details. If the question is about measurements (e.g., lab values), interpret their meaning in relation to the question, rather than writing down the values. Do not generate anything else.

1-shot example

User Prompt

--------------BEGIN DISCHARGE LETTER--------------
{discharge_summary}
--------------END DISCHARGE LETTER--------------
Question: What was the outcome of my virtual colonoscopy?

Assistant Response

Answer: We did not find any polyps, masses, or signs of inflammatory disease in your examination.

User Prompt

--------------BEGIN DISCHARGE LETTER--------------
{discharge_summary}
--------------END DISCHARGE LETTER--------------
What side effect did I experience from taking Clozapine, and how was it managed?

Figure 8: MedisumQA Inference

Using LLMs to improve RL policies in personalized health adaptive interventions

Karine Karine
University of Massachusetts Amherst
karine@cs.umass.edu

Benjamin M. Marlin
University of Massachusetts Amherst
marlin@cs.umass.edu

Abstract

Reinforcement learning (RL) is increasingly used in the healthcare domain, particularly for the development of personalized adaptive health interventions. However, RL methods are often applied to this domain using small state spaces to mitigate data scarcity. In this paper, we aim to use Large Language Models (LLMs) to incorporate text-based user preferences and constraints, to update the RL policy. The LLM acts as a filter in the action selection. To evaluate our method, we develop a novel simulation environment that generates text-based user preferences and incorporates corresponding constraints that impact behavioral dynamics. We show that our method can take into account the text-based user preferences, while improving the RL policy, thus improving personalization in adaptive intervention.

1 Introduction

Reinforcement learning (RL) is increasingly used in the healthcare domain, particularly for the development of personalized adaptive health interventions (Coronato et al., 2020; Liao et al., 2020; Gönül et al., 2021; Yu et al., 2021; Spruijt-Metz et al., 2022; Karine et al., 2024). However, RL methods are often applied to adaptive intervention problems using small state spaces to mitigate the data scarcity that results from practical limitations on adaptive intervention trial designs, including limited numbers of participants, limited numbers of interventions per day, and limited study durations.

Moreover, there can be issues in the decision rule or policy that result in incorrectly contextualized messages sent to the participant (e.g., user preference not aligning with the policy). These messages may annoy the participant or cause participant disengagement. Therefore, it is critical to consider participant preferences before it is too late or irreversible (e.g., the participant exits the study).

One solution to prevent disengagement is to allow the participant to specify their preferences in the form of free-text descriptions and immediately take them into account to influence the action selection. This is especially relevant in today's generation, where people use chats and social media to communicate. For example, the user preference can be: "I twisted my ankle" or "my leg is sore". The user can enter their preference in a daily survey in the mobile health app.

In this paper, we explore leveraging the natural language understanding ability and reasoning capabilities of Large Language Models (LLMs) to influence RL action selection based on participant descriptions of preferences. We evaluate an approach where an RL agent proposes a candidate action at each time step. Next, given the text-based participant preference, we use the LLM to decide whether the candidate action (sending one of several message types message) should be allowed or not allowed. The LLM is used as a filter in the action selection with the goal of better aligning the RL policy with the user preferences and constraints. We use Thompson sampling as a data-efficient base RL algorithm (see Appendix A.2 for relevant background). We refer to the resulting method as LLM+TS.

To evaluate our approach, we build on a recently introduced simulation environment for an adaptive messaging physical activity intervention that simulates key aspects of behavioral dynamics including intervention habituation and disengagement risk (Karine and Marlin, 2024). We add to this system a simulation of participants responding to a daily query about their general health state. We generate the responses based on the true underlying health state of the simulated participant, and incorporate constraints that impact behavioral dynamics.

Our preliminary results show that different families of LLMs reason about the simulated participant preferences with different accuracies, but that using

Proceedings of the Second Workshop on Patient-Oriented Language Processing (CL4Health), pages 137–147
May 4, 2025

any of the evaluated LLMs results in improved performance relative to standard Thompson Sampling. We explore the effect of leveraging intermediate reasoning and domain-specific knowledge within the prompt, mirroring promising LLM approaches such as chain-of-thought reasoning and retrieval-augmented generation (Zheng et al., 2023; Wei et al., 2022; Lewis et al., 2020).

Our contributions are:

1. **LLM+TS.** We introduce an "LLM as judge" approach to enhancing personalized adaptive health interventions. LLM+TS leverages the natural language understanding and reasoning capabilities of LLMs to improve the limited state representation of a Thompson Sampler, while maintaining data efficiency and providing intervention designers with better control over intervention content. This is a promising approach for significantly augmenting the intelligence of personalized adaptive health interventions. We provide an overview of our method in Figure 1.

2. **StepCountJITAI for LLM.** We create a novel simulation environment to evaluate the proposed method. Our simulation environment extends an existing base simulator to add the support for LLMs. It generates text-based user preferences and incorporates constraints that impact behavioral dynamics. Our simulation environment has significant potential to enable the development of new RL algorithms for adaptive interventions that incorporate text-based user preferences.

2 Background

We describe the base simulator below and provide more details in Appendix A.1. We also provide the background on Thompson Sampling in Appendix A.2, and related work in Appendix A.3.

StepCountJITAI: an adaptive physical activity simulation environment. There is limited prior work on simulation environments for adaptive interventions in the literature. In this work, we extend the base physical activity adaptive intervention simulator introduced in Karine and Marlin (2024). This base simulator was specifically designed to support the development of new RL algorithms applicable to the adaptive intervention domain.

A messaging-based physical activity adaptive intervention can be framed as an RL system. In this

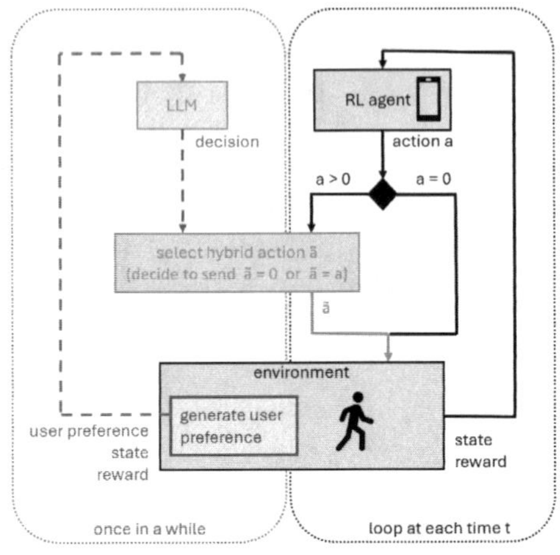

Figure 1: Overview of the LLM+TS method. LLM+TS is a hybrid method that combines LLM inference and RL policy learning to improve action selection. The RL agent proposes a candidate action a. The LLM prompt that is used to guide inference includes a description of the behavioral dynamics and the participant preferences along with questions that prompt chain of thought-like reasoning. Finally, the prompt asks the LLM to decide whether the candidate action (sending one of several message types message) should be allowed or not allowed (i.e., $\tilde{a} = 0$ or $\tilde{a} = a$). Thus, the LLM acts as a judge, filtering the candidate actions.

simulation environment, the state includes a context variable $c_t \in \{0, 1\}$ that can model a binary state such as 'stressed / not stressed' or 'at home / not at home,' etc. at each time t. The simulation also models the dynamics of two key behavioral state variables: habituation level h_t and disengagement risk level d_t. The different types of messages that can be sent to a participant are the possible actions. The variable a_t denotes the action at time t. The possible actions a_t are:

- $a_t = 0$ (do not send a message)
- $a_t = 1$ (send a generic message)
- $a_t = 2$ (send a message tailored to context 0)
- $a_t = 3$ (send a message tailored to context 1)

The **goal** in this domain is to **maximize** the participant's total walking step count over the duration of the intervention. Thus, **step count** serves as the **reward** r_t. Further details of the base simulator are described in Appendix A.1.2.

However this base simulator does not include the support for LLMs. Thus, we extend the base simulator to create a simulation environment that includes the support for LLMs. We describe this novel simulation environment in Section 3.2.

3 Methods

In this section, we describe our proposed method as well as our novel simulation environment. Figure 1 provides an overview of the proposed method.

3.1 Proposed Approach: LLM+TS

We propose a hybrid method where the RL agent outputs a candidate action at each time step. Then, based on the LLM prompt that includes the user preference and other information, the LLM decides whether to allow or not allow the RL candidate action. We summarize the method below.

1. Candidate Action Generation: At each time step t, the RL agent proposes a candidate action a_t based on its current parameters θ_t and the current state s_t. If the candidate action is $a_t = 0$, set $\tilde{a}_t = 0$. No message is sent. If the action is $a_t \neq 0$, apply LLM inference.
2. LLM Inference: Given the current user preference and other context information, construct the LLM prompt. Apply an LLM to perform inference given the prompt. Extract the decision from the LLM response.
3. Action Filtering: If the LLM decision is to "not send" a message, set $\tilde{a}_t = 0$. Otherwise, set $\tilde{a}_t = a_t$.
4. Policy Update: Take the action $\tilde{a}_t$. Observe the reward r_t and new state s_{t+1}. Update the RL agent's parameters based on the tuple $(s_t, \tilde{a}_t, r_t)$, obtaining θ_{t+1}.

We note that if the RL agent proposes the candidate action $a_t > 0$ (indicating a candidate message to be sent), then the LLM is prompted to decide if this message should actually be sent or not. If the RL agent proposes the candidate action $a_t = 0$ (indicating no message) or if no user preference was generated, then there is no need to call LLM inference, so the RL loop continues as usual. We note that the RL agent does not have knowledge of the text-based user preferences.

We construct the LLM prompt by including a description of the specific adaptive intervention domain, the hypothesized behavioral dynamics, intermediate reasoning questions to guide the LLM, a statement of the user preferences, and a final question asking the LLM to make a decision to "send" or "not send" a message. We provide an example of a constructed LLM prompt in Appendix B.1.

To evaluate the proposed method, we create a simulation environment to generate the text-based user preferences and incorporate additional latent physical health states as described in the next section. Importantly, the LLM inference step used to filter action selection is completely separated from the application of LLMs to simulate participant generation of text descriptions of preferences. In a real-world application of the proposed method, the preference text would, of course, be generated by the participant via an intervention app.

3.2 StepCountJITAI for LLM

We extend the base simulator introduced in Karine and Marlin (2024) to create a new simulation environment that generates participant preferences and constraints conditioned on an additional state dimension that is not observable by the RL agent. Specifically, we introduce a new state variable $w_t \in \{0, 1\}$ indicating whether the user is able to walk or not.

We implement the dynamics for w_t using a Markov chain where the value for w_t is sampled conditioned on w_{t-1}. This allows "can walk" and "cannot walk" states to persist for different average lengths of time. These dynamics are described in detail in Appendix Figure 4 and Table 3.

We use two different LLM prompts to simulate the generation of participant text conditioned on the variable w_t. When transitioning from $w_{t-1} = 1$ to $w_t = 0$, we emit text produced by prompting the LLM to generate a short description of a reason why a person might not be able to walk. When transitioning from $w_{t-1} = 0$ to $w_t = 1$, we emit text produced by prompting the LLM to generate a message describing that the participant is "feeling fine." When staying in the $w_t = 1$ state, we emit a new participant preference statement with probability 0.3. We provide further details on LLM-based user preference generation in Appendix B.

When in the $w_t = 0$ or "cannot walk" state, we modify the behavioral and reward dynamics accordingly. First, if $w_t = 0$ and $\tilde{a}_t \neq 0$, the disengagement risk d_t is incremented regardless of whether the tailoring of the action was correct or not. This simulates the idea that a participant might lose significant trust in the system and be more likely to disengage from using it if walking suggestions continue to be issued despite the fact that the participant indicates a reason for not being able to walk. Second, we set the reward to $r_t = 0$ if $w_t = 0$, consistent with the idea that the participant accumulates no reward (i.e., no step) if they can not walk. The dynamics are given in Appendix B.3.1.

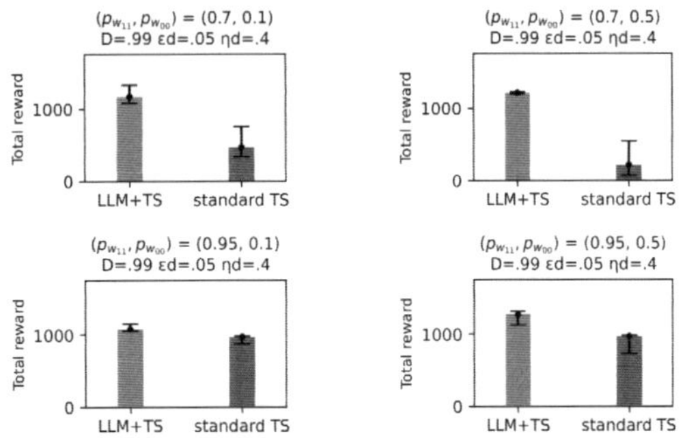

Figure 2: Example scenarios showing that LLM+TS outperforms standard TS. (top) Scenario 1: $p_{w_{11}} = 0.7$ (probability of staying in state "can walk") and various $p_{w_{00}}$ (probability of staying in state "cannot walk"). (bottom) Scenario 2: $p_{w_{11}} = 0.95$ and various $p_{w_{00}}$.

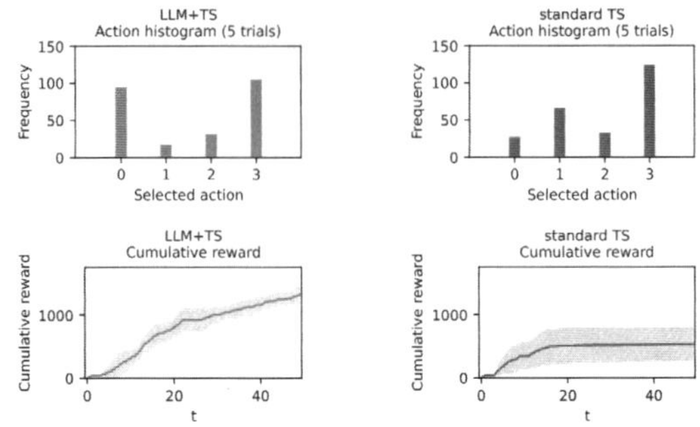

Figure 3: LLM+TS vs. standard TS. Example histograms of all selected actions (top), and plots of average cumulative reward per episode for $(p_{w_{11}}, p_{w_{00}}) = (0.7, 0.5)$, $\epsilon_d = 0.01, \eta_d = 0.05$.

4 Experiments

We conduct experiments to validate the LLM responses and compare our method to standard TS.

Validating LLM Inference. We perform experiments evaluating the ability of different LLMs to correctly classify preference statements as implying that the participant can or cannot walk. We found average inference accuracies of 0.86 for Gemma 2, 0.87 for Llama 3 8B and 0.98 for Llama 3 70B. Details are provided in Appendix C.1.

Validating LLM+TS. We conduct extensive experiments to compare LLM+TS to standard Thompson Sampling (TS). Both LLM+TS and TS use the same TS state space that does not include access to the w_t state variable. However, LLM+TS performs inference over the text of user preferences as described previously. We generate results by varying the probability of remaining in the "cannot walk" state $p_{w_{00}}$ and the probability of remaining in the "can walk" state $p_{w_{11}}$. We show results for two realistic scenarios: Scenario 1, where $p_{w_{11}} = 0.7$, and Scenario 2, where $p_{w_{11}} = 0.95$. In both scenarios, $p_{w_{00}}$ varies in the range $[0.1, ..., 0.5]$. We plot the median total reward, with the 25th and 75th percentiles, over 5 trials in Figure 2. We see that when there is a higher probability that the participant is in the "cannot walk" state, LLM+TS significantly outperforms TS, as expected. More details and results are provided in Appendix C.2.

Analysis of Selected Actions. We compare the histograms of selected actions, taking into account all actions selected by each method across 5 trials. The histograms show that LLM+TS selects more $a_t = 0$ actions, which indicates that the LLM has correctly decided to "not send" a message when the user cannot walk. We also compare the average cumulative reward per episode in Figure 3, which suggests that the average episode length for TS is significantly lower than for LLM+TS due to early disengagements. Additional results are provided in Appendix C.

5 Conclusion

We introduce LLM+TS, an "LLM as judge" approach to enhancing personalized adaptive health interventions. LLM+TS leverages the natural language understanding and reasoning capabilities of LLMs to improve the limited state representation of a Thompson Sampler, while maintaining data efficiency and providing intervention designers with better control over intervention content. To evaluate our method, we introduce StepCountJITAI for LLM, a novel simulation environment that generates user preferences and incorporates constraints that impact behavioral dynamics. Our results show that LLM+TS is a promising approach for significantly augmenting the intelligence of personalized adaptive health interventions. Our novel simulation environment has significant potential to enable the development of new RL algorithms for adaptive interventions that incorporate text-based user preferences.

Limitations

The proposed method was evaluated on selected LLMs at this time. Other LLMs could be used depending on available resources. Future work will involve inserting additional insights into the LLM prompt or using advanced LLMs to further improve the LLM inference accuracy.

Acknowledgments

This work is supported by National Institutes of Health National Cancer Institute, Office of Behavior and Social Sciences, and National Institute of Biomedical Imaging and Bioengineering through grants U01CA229445, 1P41EB028242 and P30AG073107.

References

Wei Chu, Lihong Li, Lev Reyzin, and Robert Schapire. 2011. Contextual bandits with linear payoff functions. In *Proceedings of the Fourteenth International Conference on Artificial Intelligence and Statistics*, pages 208–214. JMLR Workshop and Conference Proceedings.

Antonio Coronato, Muddasar Naeem, Giuseppe De Pietro, and Giovanni Paragliola. 2020. Reinforcement learning for intelligent healthcare applications: A survey. *Artificial Intelligence in Medicine*, 109:101964.

Yuqing Du, Olivia Watkins, Zihan Wang, Cédric Colas, Trevor Darrell, Pieter Abbeel, Abhishek Gupta, and Jacob Andreas. 2023. Guiding Pretraining in Reinforcement Learning with Large Language Models. In *Proceedings of the 40th International Conference on Machine Learning*, pages 8657–8677.

K. J. Kevin Feng, Xander Koo, Lawrence Tan, Amy Bruckman, David W. McDonald, and Amy X. Zhang. 2024. Mapping the Design Space of Teachable Social Media Feed Experiences. In *Proceedings of the CHI Conference on Human Factors in Computing Systems*, page 890–896.

Gemma Team. 2024. Gemma: Open Models Based on Gemini Research and Technology. *arXiv:2403.08295*.

Suat Gönül, Tuncay Namlı, Ahmet Coşar, and İsmail Hakkı Toroslu. 2021. A reinforcement learning based algorithm for personalization of digital, just-in-time, adaptive interventions. *Artificial Intelligence in Medicine*, 115:102062.

Karine Karine, Predrag Klasnja, Susan A. Murphy, and Benjamin M. Marlin. 2023. Assessing the impact of context inference error and partial observability on RL methods for Just-In-Time Adaptive Interventions. In *Proceedings of the Thirty-Ninth Conference on Uncertainty in Artificial Intelligence*, volume 216, pages 1047–1057.

Karine Karine and Benjamin M. Marlin. 2024. StepCountJITAI: simulation environment for RL with application to physical activity adaptive intervention. In *Workshop on Behavioral Machine Learning, Advances in Neural Information Processing Systems*.

Karine Karine, Susan A. Murphy, and Benjamin M. Marlin. 2024. BOTS: Batch Bayesian Optimization of Extended Thompson Sampling for Severely Episode-Limited RL Settings. In *Workshop on Bayesian Decision-making and Uncertainty, Advances in Neural Information Processing Systems*.

Patrick Lewis, Ethan Perez, Aleksandra Piktus, Fabio Petroni, Vladimir Karpukhin, Naman Goyal, Heinrich Küttler, Mike Lewis, Wen-tau Yih, Tim Rocktäschel, Sebastian Riedel, and Douwe Kiela. 2020. Retrieval-Augmented Generation for Knowledge-Intensive NLP Tasks. In *Advances in Neural Information Processing Systems*, volume 33, pages 9459–9474.

Peng Liao, Kristjan Greenewald, Predrag Klasnja, and Susan Murphy. 2020. Personalized HeartSteps: A Reinforcement Learning Algorithm for Optimizing Physical Activity. *Proceedings of the ACM on Interactive, Mobile, Wearable and Ubiquitous Technologies*, 4(1):1–22.

Llama Team. 2024. The Llama 3 Herd of Models. *arXiv:2407.21783*.

Hanjia Lyu, Song Jiang, Hanqing Zeng, Yinglong Xia, Qifan Wang, Ren Chen Si Zhang, Chris Leung, Jiajie Tang, and Jiebo Luo. 2024. LLM-Rec: Personalized Recommendation via Prompting Large Language Models. In *North American Association for Computational Linguistics*.

Sheshera Mysore, Mahmood Jasim, Andrew McCallum, and Hamed Zamani. 2023. Editable User Profiles for Controllable Text Recommendations. In *Proceedings of the 46th International ACM SIGIR Conference on Research and Development in Information Retrieval*, pages 993–1003.

Daniel J. Russo, Benjamin Van Roy, Abbas Kazerouni, Ian Osband, and Zheng Wen. 2018. A Tutorial on Thompson Sampling. *Found. Trends Mach. Learn.*, 11(1).

Scott Sanner, Krisztian Balog, Filip Radlinski, Ben Wedin, and Lucas Dixon. 2023. Large Language Models are Competitive Near Cold-start Recommenders for Language- and Item-based Preferences. In *Proceedings of the 17th ACM Conference on Recommender*, page 890–896.

Donna Spruijt-Metz, Benjamin M Marlin, Misha Pavel, Daniel E Rivera, Eric Hekler, Steven De La Torre, Mohamed El Mistiri, Natalie M Golaszweski, Cynthia Li, Rebecca Braga De Braganca, et al. 2022. Advancing behavioral intervention and theory development for mobile health: the HeartSteps II protocol. *International journal of environmental research and public health*, 19(4):2267.

William R. Thompson. 1933. On the Likelihood that One Unknown Probability Exceeds Another in View of the Evidence of Two Samples. In *Biometrika*, volume 25, pages 285–294.

Jason Wei, Xuezhi Wang, Dale Schuurmans, Maarten Bosma, Brian Ichter, Fei Xia, Ed Chi, Quoc Le, and Denny Zhou. 2022. Chain-of-thought prompting elicits reasoning in large language models. In *Advances in Neural Information Processing Systems*.

Chao Yu, Jiming Liu, Shamim Nemati, and Guosheng Yin. 2021. Reinforcement learning in healthcare: A survey. *ACM Computing Surveys (CSUR)*, 55(1):1–36.

Lianmin Zheng, Wei-Lin Chiang, Ying Sheng, Siyuan Zhuang, Zhanghao Wu, Yonghao Zhuang, Zi Lin, Zhuohan Li, Dacheng Li, Eric Xing, Hao Zhang, Joseph E Gonzalez, and Ion Stoica. 2023. Judging LLM-as-a-Judge with MT-Bench and Chatbot Arena. In *Advances in Neural Information Processing Systems*, volume 36, pages 46595–46623.

A Background and Related Work

We provide the background on StepCountJITAI and Thompson Sampling, and the related work.

A.1 StepCountJITAI simulation environment

The base simulator introduced in Karine et al. (2023); Karine and Marlin (2024) mimics a participant's behaviors in a mobile health study, where the interventions (actions) are the messages sent to the participant, with the goal of increasing the participant walking step count (reward), given the participant's context and behaviors (states). We summarize the base simulator specifications in Tables 1 and 2, and provide details below.

A.1.1 StepCountJITAI specifications

For the notation, we use an uppercase letter for the variable name, and a lowercase letter for the variable value, for example: the context variable C has value $c_t = 0$ at time t.

Below we describe some of the simulation environment variables and parameters that are used in the behavioral dynamics: c_t is the true context, p_t is the probability of context 1, l_t is the inferred context, h_t is the habituation level, d_t is the disengagement risk, s_t is the step count (s_t is the participant's walking step count), and a_t is the action at time t. The base simulator also includes behavioral parameters: δ_d and ϵ_d are decay and increment parameters for the disengagement risk, and δ_h and ϵ_h are decay and increment parameters for the habituation level.

The goal is to increase the participant's walking step count. Thus, the walking step count is also the RL reward.

Action	Description
$a = 0$	No message is sent to the participant.
$a = 1$	A non-contextualized message is sent.
$a = 2$	A message customized to context 0 is sent.
$a = 3$	A message customized to context 1 is sent.

Table 1: Possible action values

Variable	Description	Values
c_t	true context	$\{0, 1\}$
p_t	probability of context 1	$[0, 1]$
l_t	inferred context	$\{0,1\}$
d_t	disengagement risk level	$[0, 1]$
h_t	habituation level	$[0, 1]$
s_t	step count	$\mathbb{N}$

Table 2: State variables

We use the same default parameter values as in the base simulator: context uncertainty $\sigma = 0.4$, behavioral parameters $\delta_h = 0.1$, $\epsilon_h = 0.05$, $\delta_d = 0.1$, $\epsilon_d = 0.4$, $m_s = 0.1$, $\rho_1 = 50$, $\rho_2 = 200$. For our experiments, we set the disengagement threshold $D_{threshold} = 0.99$. The maximum study length is 50 days, with daily data. We describe the behavioral dynamics below, in Appendix A.1.2.

A.1.2 StepCountJITAI behavioral dynamics

The behavioral dynamics are as follow: Sending a message causes the habituation level to increase. Not sending a message causes the habituation level to decrease. An incorrectly tailored message causes the disengagement risk to increase. A correctly tailored message causes the disengagement risk to decrease. When the disengagement risk exceeds a given threshold, the behavioral study ends. The reward is the surplus step count, beyond a baseline count, attenuated by the habituation level.

These behavioral dynamics can be translated into equations:

$$c_{t+1} \sim Bernoulli(0.5), \quad x_{t+1} \sim \mathcal{N}(c_{t+1}, \sigma^2) \quad (1)$$

$$p_{t+1} = P(C = 1|x_{t+1}), \quad l_{t+1} = p_{t+1} > 0.5 \quad (2)$$

$$h_{t+1} = \begin{cases} (1 - \delta_h) \cdot h_t & \text{if } a_t = 0 \\ \min(1, h_t + \epsilon_h) & \text{otherwise} \end{cases} \quad (3)$$

$$d_{t+1} = \begin{cases} d_t & \text{if } a_t = 0 \\ (1 - \delta_d) \cdot d_t & \text{if } a_t \in \{1, c_t + 2\} \\ \min(1, d_t + \epsilon_d) & \text{otherwise} \end{cases} \quad (4)$$

$$s_{t+1} = \begin{cases} m_s + (1 - h_{t+1}) \cdot \rho_1 & \text{if } a_t = 1 \\ m_s + (1 - h_{t+1}) \cdot \rho_2 & \text{if } a_t = c_t + 2 \\ m_s & \text{otherwise} \end{cases} \quad (5)$$

where σ is the context uncertainty, x_t is the context feature, $\sigma, \rho_1, \rho_2, m_s$ are fixed parameters. We use the same default parameter values as the base simulator, which we summarize in Appendix A.1.1.

A.2 Thompson Sampling

Thompson Sampling (TS) is a probabilistic method for decision-making under uncertainty. It can be used to address contextual multi-armed bandit problems (Russo et al., 2018; Chu et al., 2011; Thompson, 1933).

Typical TS for contextual bandit settings uses a reward model of the form $\mathcal{N}(r; \theta_a^\top v_t, \sigma_{Ya}^2)$, where v_t is the state vector at time t, θ_a is a vector of weights, and σ_{Ya}^2 is the reward variance for action a. Thus, $\theta_a^\top v_t$ represents the mean reward for action a.

The reward model weights θ_a are random variables of the form $\mathcal{N}(\theta_a; \mu_{ta}, \Sigma_{ta})$. Actions are selected at each time t by sampling $\hat{\theta}_a$ from $\mathcal{N}(\theta_a; \mu_{ta}, \Sigma_{ta})$ and choosing the action with the largest value $\hat{\theta}_a^\top v_t$. The prior distribution for θ_a is of the form $\mathcal{N}(\theta_a; \mu_{0a}, \Sigma_{0a})$. The distribution over θ_a for the selected action is updated at time t based on the observed reward r_t and v_t using Bayesian inference. We provide the update equations for the mean and covariance matrix below.

$$\Sigma_{(t+1)a} = \sigma_{Ya}^2 \left(v_t^\top v_t + \sigma_{Ya}^2 \, \Sigma_{ta}^{-1} \right)^{-1} \tag{6}$$

$$\mu_{(t+1)a} = \Sigma_{(t+1)a} \left((\sigma_{Ya}^2)^{-1} \, r_t \, v_t + \Sigma_{ta}^{-1} \, \mu_{ta} \right) \tag{7}$$

A.3 Related work

Recent works use LLMs in RL, where the RL agent selects actions based on natural language inputs, and apply to games (Du et al., 2023). Note that in our work, we leverage LLMs as foundational models and focus on online decision-making for episode-limited RL settings. Recent research on RL from human feedback, and from AI feedback, typically require some form of reward modeling, and a large number of episodes to perform well. Other works have also explored using natural language inputs, but apply to recommender systems for items such as movies, social media, recommendation algorithms (Lyu et al., 2024; Feng et al., 2024; Mysore et al., 2023; Sanner et al., 2023). However, these approaches also require a large number of iterations to work well. In contrast, we use Thompson Sampling which is a Bayesian approach that can perform well in a lower number of iterations than typical deep RL methods.

Recent works use LLM as a judge, intermediate reasoning and retrieval-augmented generation, to generate better LLM responses (Zheng et al., 2023; Wei et al., 2022; Lewis et al., 2020). We use similar ideas, but focus on creating a single LLM prompt, where the LLM makes a decision, based on the user preference and reasoning in the prompt.

B Method details

We first provide an example of an LLM prompt that is used in our method, as described in Section 3. Then, we provide further details about our novel environment simulator that supports LLMs.

B.1 Example of LLM prompt

In our new method, the LLM prompt contains the following blocks of text (description of behavioral dynamics, participant preference, reasoning), as described in Section 3.1.

Example of LLM prompt.

```
A mobile health app can send a message to the user to encourage the user to walk.
...
Sending a message causes the habituation level to increase.
Not sending a message causes the habituation level to decrease.
An incorrectly tailored message causes the disengagement risk to increase.
A correctly tailored message causes the disengagement risk to decrease.
If the user is sick, injured or cannot walk, then the mobile health app should not send a message.
...
This morning, when we asked the user how they felt, the user reply was: "I twisted my ankle".
...
Given the user reply, answer the following questions:
provide the reason for sending a message,
provide the reason for not sending a message,
is there any risk to the user?
will the user disengage from the study?
is there some long term consequence?
...
Given these answers, provide the final answer to this question: should the mobile health app send a message to the user?
```

We detail the `text in purple`. The text for the

user reply (e.g., "I twisted my ankle") is chosen randomly from the lists provided in Appendix B.3.

B.2 Creating auxiliary variable W (cannot walk / can walk)

We first augment the simulation environment states with a binary state variable W with value: 0 "cannot walk" or 1 "can walk". The variable W is not observed by the RL agent. It reflects a hidden state of the user, and is used to generate the user preference, and trigger the constraints. We implement a Markov chain to simulate w_t, the values of W at time t. The Markov chain sketch and transition function for W are shown in Figure 4 and Table 3.

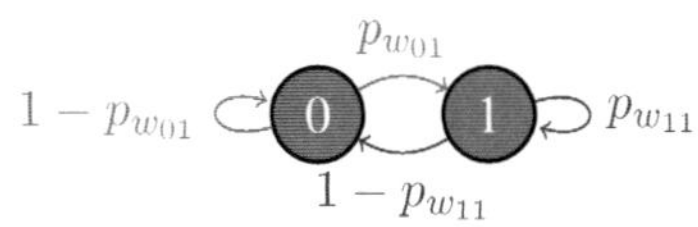

Figure 4: Markov chain sketch.

w_t	w_{t+1}	$P(w_{t+1}\|w_t)$
0	0	$1 - p_{w_{01}}$
0	1	$p_{w_{01}}$
1	0	$1 - p_{w_{11}}$
1	1	$p_{w_{11}}$

Table 3: Transition Function.

We define the new parameters: $p_{w_{01}}$ the probability of transitioning from $w_t = 0$ to $w_{t+1} = 1$, and $p_{w_{11}}$ the probability of remaining in the "can walk" state.

$$p_{w_{01}} = P(w_{t+1} = 1|w_t = 0) \quad (8)$$
$$p_{w_{11}} = P(w_{t+1} = 1|w_t = 1) \quad (9)$$

Setting $p_{w_{11}}$ to a lower (or higher) value allows for a lower (or higher) probability of remaining in the "can walk" state. Similarly, setting $p_{w_{01}}$ to a lower (or higher) value allows for a lower (or higher) probability of transitioning from $w_t = 0$ to $w_{t+1} = 1$.

We note that the parameters $p_{w_{01}}$ and $p_{w_{11}}$ can be used to simulate the user state "cannot walk" over a variety of ranges, from shorter to longer time intervals, and thus enabling a variety of scenarios for our experiments.

In Section 4, we run our experiments and show the results for two realistic scenarios: Scenario 1, where $p_{w_{11}} = 0.7$, and Scenario 2, where $p_{w_{11}} = 0.95$. In both scenarios, $p_{w_{00}}$ varies in the range $[0.1, ..., 0.5]$, where $p_{w_{00}} = 1 - p_{w_{01}}$.

B.3 Generating a text-based user preference "cannot walk".

Following the Markov chain and transition function in Figure 4 and Table 3, W can take values 1 "can walk" or 0 "cannot walk".

When W transitions from 1 "can walk" to 0 "cannot walk", a user preference is randomly chosen from a list of pre-defined reasons for "cannot walk". The "cannot walk" list was previously created by asking ChatGPT to give reasons why a user cannot walk.

When W transitions from 0 "cannot walk" to 1 "can walk", a user preference is randomly chosen from a list of pre-defined texts of type "other". The "other" list was previously created by asking ChatGPT to give examples of how a healthy participant feels today.

When W remains at 1 "can walk", we generate the user preference of type "other", based on a Bernoulli distribution: either generate the "other" preference with probability 0.3, or do nothing with probability $1 - 0.3 = 0.7$.

We show some examples of user preferences of type "cannot walk":

```
I am tired, I do not want to walk, I got an injury,
I have a headache, My legs are sore, I twisted my
ankle, I'm feeling dizzy, I'm out of breath, I
have a cold, I'm feeling weak, I pulled a muscle,
My knee hurts, I have blisters, I feel nauseous,
I have stomach cramps, I can't find my shoes, I
don't have time, I'm waiting for someone, It's
too hot outside, It's too cold outside, ...
```

We show some examples of user preferences of type "other":

```
I am feeling good, I'm in a great mood, I feel
energized, I'm feeling positive, I'm doing well
today, I feel great, I'm in high spirits, I feel
focused, I'm feeling relaxed, I feel motivated,
I'm doing fine, I feel optimistic, I'm feeling
calm, I feel balanced, I'm feeling strong, I feel
productive, I'm in a positive state of mind, I
feel healthy, I feel confident, I feel alert, ...
```

B.3.1 Inserting new constraints to impact behavioral dynamics

Below are the equations for the behavioral dynamics implemented in the StepCountJITAI simulation environment, with the new constraints.

We insert the new constraints in blue color. The default base simulator equations are in black color.

The new constraints impact d_{t+1} and s_{t+1}.

We note that $a_t = \tilde{a}$ when the LLM is called, at time t. If the LLM is not called, then a_t takes the RL candidate action value a, at time t.

$$c_{t+1} \sim \textit{Bernoulli}(0.5), \quad x_{t+1} \sim \mathcal{N}(c_{t+1}, \sigma^2) \tag{10}$$

$$p_{t+1} = P(C = 1|x_{t+1}), \quad l_{t+1} = p_{t+1} > 0.5 \tag{11}$$

$$h_{t+1} = \begin{cases} (1-\delta_h)\cdot h_t & \text{if } a_t = 0 \\ \min(1, h_t + \epsilon_h) & \text{otherwise} \end{cases} \tag{12}$$

$$d_{t+1} = \begin{cases} d_t & \text{if } a_t = 0 \\ & \text{and } w_t = 0 \text{ or } 1 \\ (1-\delta_d)\cdot d_t & \text{if } a_t \in \{1, c_t + 2\} \text{ and} \\ & w_t = 1 \text{ (can walk)} \\ \min(1, d_t + \eta_d) & \text{if } a_t \in \{1, c_t + 2\} \text{ and} \\ & w_t = 0 \text{ (cannot walk)} \\ \min(1, d_t + \epsilon_d & \text{otherwise} \\ \quad +(1-w_t)\,\eta_d) & \end{cases} \tag{13}$$

$$s_{t+1} = \begin{cases} m_s + (1 - h_{t+1})\cdot \rho_1 & \text{if } a_t = 1 \\ & \text{and } w_t = 1 \text{ (can walk)} \\ m_s + (1 - h_{t+1})\cdot \rho_2 & \text{if } a_t = c_t + 2 \\ & \text{and } w_t = 1 \text{ (can walk)} \\ m_s\, w_t & \text{otherwise} \end{cases} \tag{14}$$

Below we explain in more detail how the new constraints impact d_{t+1} and s_{t+1}.

- **No message is sent**. If $a_t = 0$, and $w_t = 0$ or 1, then $d_{t+1} = d_t$. When no message is sent to the participant, then it does not matter if the participant can or cannot walk, and the disengagement risk remains the same.
- **Correct message, and can walk**. If $a_t \in \{1, c_t + 2\}$, and $w_t = 1$ (can walk), then $d_{t+1} = (1 - \delta_d)d_t$: we decrement d_t.
- **Correct message, but cannot walk**. If $a_t \in \{1, c_t + 2\}$, and $w_t = 0$ (cannot walk), then $d_{t+1} = \min(1, d_t + \eta_d)$: we increase the disengagement risk. In other words, we insert a single penalty.
- **Incorrect message**. If $a_t > 1$ and $a_t \neq (c_t + 2)$, then $d_{t+1} = \min(1, d_t + \epsilon_d + (1 - w_t)\,\eta_d)$: we have a single penalty (incorrect message, and can walk) or a double penalty (incorrect message, and cannot walk).
- **Cannot walk**. If $w_t = 0$ (cannot walk) then we set $s_{t+1} = 0$.

The reward is the walking step count. It is set to 0 when the user cannot walk. We use the same default parameter values as in the base simulator. We introduce the new constraint parameter for "cannot walk" $\eta_d \in [0, 1]$.

C Experiment details

We provide more details about the experiments described in Section 4.

C.1 Validating LLM response.

We perform experiments to check if the LLM response is correct. For each experiment, we generate prompts for "cannot walk". Ideally, the LLM response to these prompts should be "not send" a message. We also ask the LLM to provide a reason for its decision. Below, we provide examples of user preference, LLM decision, and the LLM reason for its decision.

Examples of user preference, LLM decision, and LLM reason.

Example 1:

The user preference is: `my leg is sore.`

The LLM correctly decides "not send" with the reason: `The user has a sore leg, indicating they cannot walk. The app should not send a message.`

The LLM manages to provide a valid reason.

Example 2:

The user preference is: `I'm feeling dizzy.`

The LLM correctly decides "not send" with the reason: `The user is feeling dizzy, which means they cannot walk, so the mobile health app should not send a message.`

Again, the LLM manages to provide a valid reason.

Example 3:
The user preference is `I am dealing with anxiety.`

The LLM incorrectly decides "send", with the reason: `The user is expressing anxiety, and a tailored message could be helpful.`

In a few cases, the LLM incorrectly decides to send a message, when the user cannot walk. To check the LLM accuracy, we perform preliminary experiments on a dataset of 100 different text-based user preferences (50 "cannot walk" and 50 "other" user preferences), and compare the LLM decisions with the true human decisions. We use an LLM temperature of 0.2 (level of randomness in the LLM response). We use different LLMs, including Gemma 2, Llama 3, Llama 3.1, Llama 3.2, etc. (Gemma Team, 2024; Llama Team, 2024). We found the average accuracies are 0.86 for Gemma 2, 0.87 for Llama 3 8B and 0.98 for Llama 3 70B.

Further investigation reveals that the LLM incorrect decision occurs when the text-based user preference is ambiguous, thus does not clearly indicate if the user can or cannot walk. However, since these ambiguous text-based user preferences appear in less than 6% of the time steps during our experiment, and since the hybrid action falls back to the RL candidate action, LLM+TS still outperforms the standard TS agent.

Above, we have shown how to check if the LLM response is correct, thanks to our simulation environment, by tracking exactly where the LLM decision is incorrect. Future work would involve inserting additional insights into the LLM prompt to further improve the LLM response.

C.2 Validating LLM+TS.

We conduct extensive experiments to compare our novel method LLM+TS to the standard TS. An experiment (a.k.a., trial) corresponds to the behavioral study of one participant, where the maximum study length is 50 days, with daily data. We repeat each experiment 5 times.

We run our experiments for various combinations of the parameters $(p_{w_{11}}, p_{w_{00}})$, where $p_{w_{00}}$ = $1 - p_{w_{01}}$, to cover different scenarios. For example, the participant often sustains a light injury and thus often cannot walk for short periods, or the participant sometimes twists their ankle and thus sometimes cannot walk for longer periods.

For our experiments, we set the TS prior parameters $\mu_{0a} = 0$ and $\Sigma_{0a} = 100I$ for each action a, and the reward noise variance $\sigma^2_{Ya} = 25^2$ for each action a, using the same notation as in Equations 6 and 7.

For each experiment setting, we compute the total reward as the sum of the rewards over a behavioral study (i.e., up to 50 time steps). We perform the experiments for various combinations of the disengagement parameter ϵ_d from the base simulator, and the new constraint parameter η_d.

We present the results for two realistic scenarios: Scenario 1, where $p_{w_{11}} = 0.7$, and Scenario 2, where $p_{w_{11}} = 0.95$. In both scenarios, $p_{w_{00}}$ varies in the range $[0.1, ..., 0.5]$. We also set the probability of generating the "other" preference to 0.3. Recall that $p_{w_{00}}$ is the probability of remaining in the "cannot walk" state, and $p_{w_{11}}$ is the probability of remaining in the "can walk" state.

For each experiment, we also run using various LLMs, including Gemma 2, Llama 3, Llama 3.1, Llama 3.2, etc. (Gemma Team, 2024; Llama Team, 2024). When using the different LLM versions, we found similar results for the same experiment settings, as shown in Figure 5.

We run the experiments for various combinations of $(p_{w_{11}}, p_{w_{00}})$. We show the results using Llama 3 8B in Figure 6. The histograms show that LLM+TS is able to capture a larger number of actions 0, which indicates that the LLM has correctly decided to not send a message when the user cannot walk. We also compare the cumulative rewards, and show that LLM+TS outperforms standard TS.

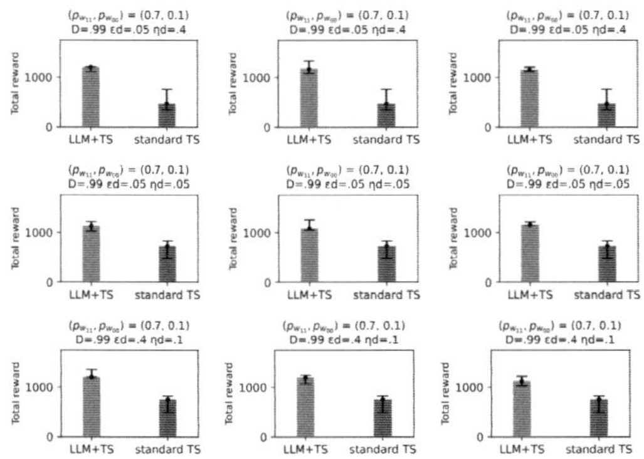

(a) Each row shows a different setting with $(p_{w_{11}}, p_{w_{00}}) = (0.7, 0.1)$.

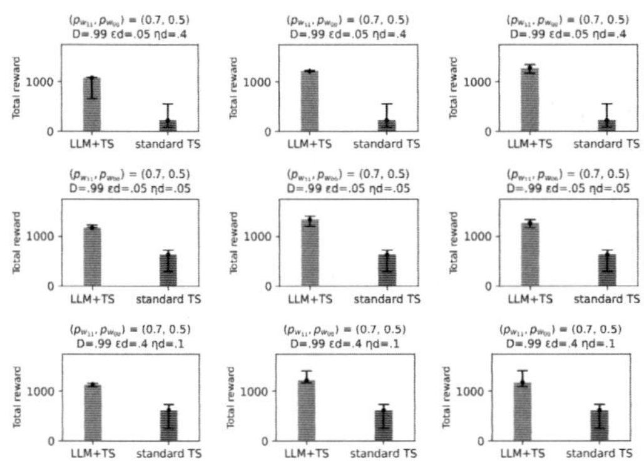

(b) Each row shows a different setting with $(p_{w_{11}}, p_{w_{00}}) = (0.7, 0.5)$.

Figure 5: Comparing LLMs: Gemma 2 9B in the left column, Llama 3 8B in the center column, and Llama 3 70B in the right column. Each row shows a different experiment setting. The results are similar for the same experiment settings.

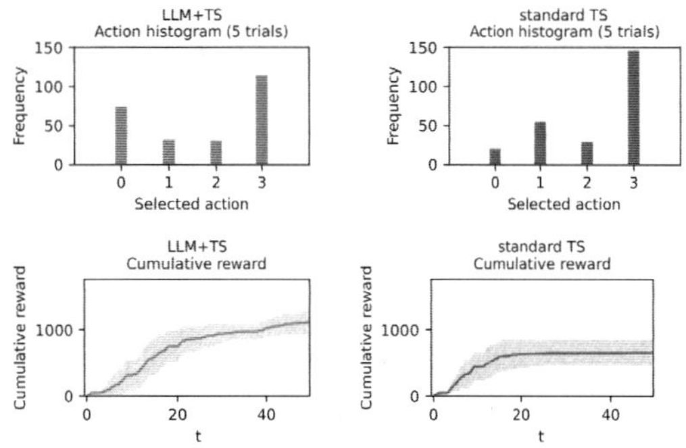

(a) $(p_{w_{11}}, p_{w_{00}}) = (0.7, 0.1)$

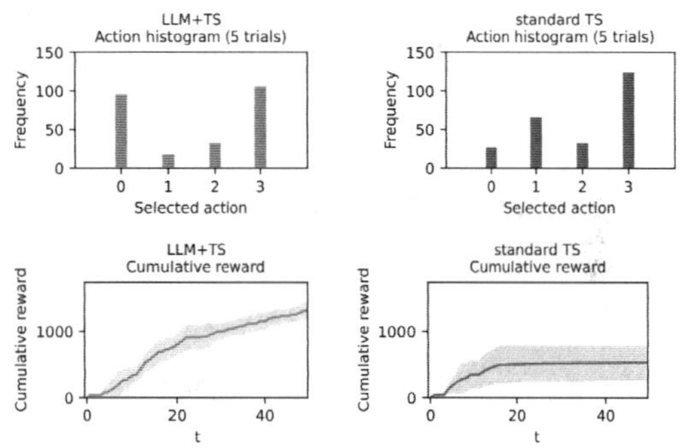

(b) $(p_{w_{11}}, p_{w_{00}}) = (0.7, 0.5)$.

Figure 6: LLM+TS vs. standard TS. Example of histogram for all the selected actions, and plot of the cumulative rewards for various combinations of $(p_{w_{11}}, p_{w_{00}})$. The histograms show that LLM+TS is able to capture a larger number of actions 0, which indicates that the LLM has correctly decided to not send a message when the user cannot walk. The cumulative reward plots show that LLM+TS outperforms standard TS.

LLM Based Efficient CSR Summarization using Structured Fact Extraction and Feedback

Kunwar Zaid, Amit Sangroya, Mayur Patidar, Lovekesh Vig
TCS Research and Innovation
New Delhi, India
{kunwar.zaid,amit.sangroya,lovekesh.vig}@tcs.com

Abstract

Summarizing clinical trial data poses a significant challenge due to the structured, voluminous, and domain-specific nature of clinical tables. While large language models (LLMs) such as ChatGPT, Llama, and DeepSeek demonstrate potential in table-to-text generation, they struggle with raw clinical tables that exceed context length, leading to incomplete, inconsistent, or imprecise summaries. These challenges stem from the structured nature of clinical tables, complex study designs, and the necessity for precise medical terminology. To address these limitations, we propose an end-to-end pipeline that enhances the summarization process by integrating fact selection, ensuring that only the most relevant data points are extracted for summary generation. Our approach also incorporates a feedback-driven refinement mechanism, allowing for iterative improvements based on domain-specific requirements and external expert input. By systematically filtering critical information and refining outputs, our method enhances the accuracy, completeness, and clinical reliability of generated summaries while reducing irrelevant or misleading content. This pipeline significantly improves the usability of LLM-generated summaries for medical professionals, regulators, and researchers, facilitating more efficient interpretation of clinical trial results. Our findings suggest that targeted preprocessing and iterative refinement strategies within the proposed pipeline can mitigate LLM limitations, offering a scalable solution for summarizing complex clinical trial tables.

1 Introduction

The growing scale of medical research, reflected in thousands of clinical trials conducted globally each year, has resulted in a vast amount of tabular data that requires effective interpretation. Clinical trial tables, which summarize key aspects such as patient demographics, treatment arms, and outcomes, play a critical role in the evaluation of medical interventions. However, these tables are often complex and dense, containing a mixture of statistical information and clinical findings that are not easily digestible without significant time and expertise. This creates a bottleneck in the dissemination and practical application of clinical findings, as stakeholders-ranging from healthcare professionals to policy makers struggle to extract meaningful insights quickly and accurately from trial reports.

The recent advances in natural language processing, particularly with large language models (LLMs) like ChatGPT, have unlocked new opportunities for automating the conversion of structured data into readable and informative summaries. LLMs have shown significant potential in table-to-text generation tasks (Hegselmann et al., 2023), where they can summarize data tables into coherent narratives by identifying key patterns and relationships. In fields such as business analytics (Nasseri et al., 2023), (Jiang et al., 2024), (Teubner et al., 2023) and scientific reporting (Telenti et al., 2024), (Sallam, 2023), LLMs have demonstrated their utility in transforming structured datasets into succinct summaries (Chen, 2022). However, when applied to the highly specialized domain of clinical trial data, these models face substantial limitations.

Clinical trial tables are often vast and intricately detailed, encompassing a wide array of variables such as multiple treatment arms, efficacy measures, adverse events, and participant characteristics. The complexity and scale of these tables overwhelm current LLM capabilities, leading to incomplete or overly generalized summaries when the tables are provided as direct input. Moreover, clinical data requires precision, as even minor inaccuracies in summarization can have significant implications for patient safety and medical decision making. The inherent challenge lies in ensuring that the generated summaries retain both the accuracy and

Proceedings of the Second Workshop on Patient-Oriented Language Processing (CL4Health), pages 148–157
May 4, 2025 ©2025 Association for Computational Linguistics

the contextual relevance of the underlying data, a requirement that LLMs struggle to meet without intervention.

To address these limitations, we propose an end-to-end pipeline designed to improve the summarization of clinical trial tables using LLMs. This pipeline incorporates a fact selection mechanism that preprocesses the tables by extracting the most relevant data points, ensuring that the input to the LLMs is both concise and focused. The pipeline further integrates a feedback loop, allowing users to refine and improve the generated summaries iteratively. This approach not only enhances the quality and reliability of the summaries but also offers flexibility, enabling the adaptation of summaries based on specific user requirements.

2 Related Work

Clinical Study Reports (CSRs) provide a detailed account of a clinical study's design, methodology, and outcomes, serving as crucial documents for regulatory approval, labeling, and commercialization. Unlike academic papers, CSRs offer a comprehensive, data-driven evaluation of a drug's therapeutic effectiveness. Earlier approaches to summary generation using tabular data devise complex template schemes in collaboration with domain experts to build a consistent set of data-to-word rules (Bao et al., 2018), (Chen et al., 2019a), (Chen et al., 2019b). This has been used in domains such as weather and medical report generation (Deng et al., 2013; Reiter et al., 2005; Varges et al., 2012). These works relied heavily on expert knowledge to bring out semantics from structured-data.

Most of the modern techniques for *Table-to-Text* summary generation can be divided into two independent components: (1) content selection: involves choosing a subset of relevant records in a table to include in the summary. (2) generating natural language descriptions for this subset. Multiple approaches have been proposed for the individual modules. For content selection, the approach by (Barzilay and Lapata, 2005) builds a content selection model by aligning records and sentences. Summary generation is often treated as a surface realization problem where text is generated from a given concept representation.

Authors in (Lebret et al., 2016), (Wiseman et al., 2017) have approached the table-to-text problem by formulating the input table as a sequence of records. They have developed table-to-text methods using the Seq2Seq framework, and in the process, they explored the modeling of table representation, as studied by (Geng et al., 2018) and (Gong et al., 2019) in their respective works. In the paper by (Li et al., 2023), a non-autoregressive model for table-to-text generation is introduced, named "Plan-then-Seam" (PTS). This model is designed to generate outputs in parallel through a single network.

The PTS approach consists of two distinct steps that are executed iteratively while sharing parameters. In the first step, the model creates and refines a content plan for the generated output. In the second step, the model uses this content plan as context to decode the description. In the work presented by (Gong et al., 2020), a method called TableGPT is introduced for table-to-text generation. The approach involves a multi-step process aimed at enhancing the alignment between structured tables and their corresponding natural language summaries.

The incorporation of auxiliary tasks to enhance the table representation is another paradigm for tackling the table-to-text problem, as demonstrated in the works of (Tian et al., 2019), (Li et al., 2021). In (Chen et al., 2023) have proposed an approach for table-to-text generation with a pre-trained language model. In the paper by (Lin et al., 2023) the authors introduce the "Inner Table Retriever,", a general-purpose approach to address the challenge of handling large tables in TableQA (Table Question Answering). This method involves extracting sub-tables from the original large table to retain the most pertinent and relevant information specifically related to a given question.

In the study conducted by (Gao et al., 2023) the authors investigate ChatGPT's capacity to perform human-like summarization evaluation. They assess the model's summarization outputs and compare them against commonly used automatic evaluation metrics. The findings reveal that ChatGPT exhibits superior performance compared to these conventional metrics, suggesting that it is capable of producing summaries that align more closely with human-like quality and judgment.

3 Approach

Traditionally, medical writing experts transform complex clinical data into structured narratives that meet regulatory requirements. However, advancements in AI-driven solutions are reshaping this process. Generative AI models can now interpret in-

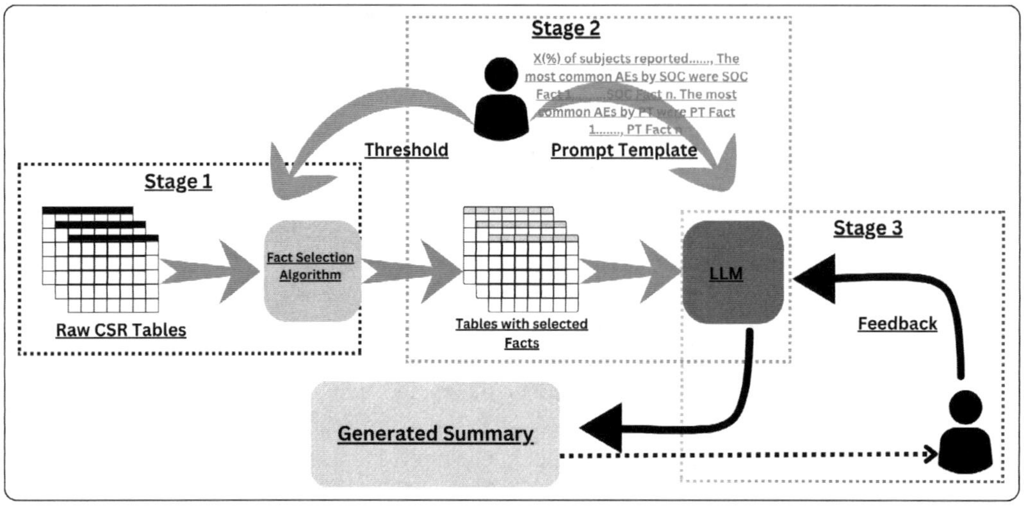

Figure 1: Overall Architecture of CSR Summary Generation

tricate CSR tables and produce reliable summaries. Our approach focuses on handling large and complex tables that existing table-to-text summarization methods struggle to process (see Figure 2).

3.1 Task Description

Given a clinical trial table (See example Table 1), the objective is to generate a concise and informative summary that captures all the factual information depicted in the table while avoiding hallucinations. The task can be broken down into the following key steps:

- **Table Linearization:** Convert the table into a linearized structure that is easy for an LLM to interpret. The linearized format is represented as: $|Cell_1|Cell_1|Cell_2|.......|Cell_n|$.
- **Input Preprocessing and Strategy Selection:** Depending on the size of the table and its compatibility with the model's input capacity, different strategies are employed to generate summaries. These include:
  - Zero-Shot Techniques: Directly prompting the LLM to summarize the linearized table without prior examples
  - Few-Shot Techniques: Providing the LLM with curated examples of correctly formatted summaries to guide its output.
  - Selection Algorithms: Applying algorithms to filter and prioritize the most relevant data points from, ensuring that the input to the LLM is both concise and contextually significant
- **Summary Generation:** Using the processed input, the LLM generates a summary that encompasses all relevant factual information while maintaining contextual coherence and precision.
- **User Feedback Integration:** Incorporate user feedback to refine and improve the generated summaries iteratively, ensuring alignment with specific use cases and requirements

3.2 Automatic Assessment of CSR Tables

A significant challenge in working with large and complex tables is their size. Most tables are very large, often exceeding the context length limitations of large language models (LLMs). The complexity is further compounded by hierarchical relationships between system organ classes (SOCs), and preferred terms (PTs), missing data, and the need to ensure accuracy and completeness when summarizing. Addressing these challenges required innovative strategies to preprocess and structure the data for effective summarization without losing critical information.

3.2.1 Handling Large Tables

The novelty of this study lies in the approach to handling large clinical trial tables. To ensure that no critical information is missed while fitting the data within the model's context length, we explored multiple approaches:

Primary system organ class	Preferred term MedDRA version 19.0	NA	Drug A DPI 28 on/off N=171 (100%)	Drug A DPI 14 on/off N=174 (100%)	Placebo 28 on/off N=86 (100%)	Placebo 14 on/off N=88 (100%)	Pooled Placebo N=174 (100%)	Total N=519 (100%)
Number (%) of subjects with at least one such adverse event		Number (%) of subjects with at least one such adverse event	94 (55.0%)	127 (73.0%)	63 (73.3%)	53 (60.2%)	116 (66.7%)	337 (64.9%)
Blood and lymphatic system disorders		Blood and lymphatic system disorders	2 (1.2%)	4 (2.3%)	1 (1.2%)	2 (2.3%)	3 (1.7%)	9 (1.7%)
Blood and lymphatic system disorders	Anaemia	Anaemia	2 (1.2%)	2 (1.1%)	0	0	0	4 (0.8%)
Blood and lymphatic system disorders	Coagulopathy	Coagulopathy	0	1 (0.6%)	0	0	0	1 (0.2%)

Figure 2: Example of a Clinical Trial Table

- **Dividing the Table into Smaller Chunks:** Large tables were segmented into smaller, logically coherent sections based on SOCs or study arms. However, this approach often led to a loss of context and missed critical cross-segment information.

- **Mean-Based Thresholding:** This method involved calculating the mean of the data values as a threshold for selecting facts from the tables. While this approach simplified the selection process, it did not consistently capture the most clinically relevant data points, particularly in cases where data distributions were highly skewed. Mean SOC and PT is defined as:

$$\mu_{SOC} = \frac{1}{N} \sum_{i=1}^{N} x_i$$

where μ_{SOC} is the SOC threshold, x_i are the SOC values, and N is the total number of SOCs.

$$\mu_{PT} = \frac{1}{M} \sum_{i=1}^{M} y_i$$

where μ_{PT} is the PT threshold, y_i are the PT values, and M is the total number of PTs.

- **Percentile-Based Thresholding:** Ultimately, we adopted a percentile-based thresholding method, which proved most effective. By selecting data points based on predefined percentiles, this approach ensured that significant facts were consistently included while maintaining a manageable context length for the model. For the p-th percentile, where p is the desired percentile (e.g., 90 for the 90th percentile), threshold T_p is defined as:

$$T_p = x_{(\lceil \frac{p}{100} \cdot n \rceil)} + \left(\frac{p}{100} \cdot n - \left\lceil \frac{p}{100} \cdot n \right\rceil \right) \cdot \left(x_{(\lceil \frac{p}{100} \cdot n \rceil + 1)} - x_{(\lceil \frac{p}{100} \cdot n \rceil)} \right)$$

where:

  - T_p is the threshold corresponding to the p-th percentile,
  - $x_1, x_2, \ldots, x_n$ are the data points sorted in ascending order,
  - n is the number of data points,
  - p is the desired percentile (e.g., $p = 90$ for the 90th percentile),
  - $\lceil \cdot \rceil$ denotes the ceiling function.

Using above formula, threshold can be calculated for SOCs and PTs, based on desired percentile.

3.3 Automatic Extraction of Important Facts

Our fact selection algorithm aims to extract the most important facts from large and complex CSR tables. One example for extracting facts from adverse events table is shown in Algorithm 1. The fact selection algorithm plays a crucial role in our pipeline. It is capable of handling very large tables that usually fail to fit within the input constraints of the LLMs.It is designed to extract the most pertinent facts from the tables, significantly reducing the size of large tables. The algorithm handles all the table types, regardless of their complexity or size. It determines the threshold based on the percentile and selects the relevant facts accordingly. By focusing on relevant facts, the algorithm enhances both the efficiency and reliability of the summarization process.

Algorithm 1: Fact selection Algorithm for Adverse Events

```
For each table type T = 1,2,3,....N
  while T < N do
    For each table t = 1,2,3,....M
      while t < M do
        Identify SOCs and PTs ;
        Remove the empty values;
        Extract SOC and PT values;
        Apply percentile-based thresholding;

        Select the SOCs and PTs using
          threshold;
        Reconstruct the table using selected
          SOCs and PTs;
    end
end
```

4 Experiments

4.1 Dataset

We could not find any publicly available datasets for this specific task, nor could we identify prior work that addresses the summarization of clinical trial tables using LLMs. While some clinical trial reports are available on public portals (NLM), (GSK) the data they provide is limited. The clinical trial tables used in this study are proprietary data from a large pharmaceutical company. Due to confidentiality agreements, the name of the company and the dataset cannot be disclosed. Table 1 summarizes the number and types of tables used in the generation process. The table types are described as follows:

- ***Subject Disposition:*** Provides a summary of the participants included in each analysis group and the reasons for any exclusions.
- ***Subject Demography:*** Displays demographic and other relevant baseline characteristics of study participants, either categorized or by descriptive statistics.
- ***Medical History:*** Presents a summary of participants' medical history, ordered by frequency of occurrence.
- ***Overall Summary:*** Summarizes adverse events (AEs) across various categories.
- ***AEs by SOC and PT:*** Lists AEs by treatment group, categorized by system organ class (SOC, highest level) and preferred term (PT, second-highest level), ordered by frequency.
- ***AEs by Maximum Intensity:*** Categorizes AEs by treatment group, based on the maximum intensity of each event, in descending order of frequency.
- ***AEs by Worst Outcome:*** Categorizes AEs by treatment group, with classification based on the worst outcome, and further categorized by SOC and PT.
- ***AEs by Common % or more by SOC and PT:*** Lists AEs that exceed a predefined frequency threshold, organized by SOC and PT.

These tables present structured data on adverse events (AEs), system organ classes (SOCs), and preferred terms (PTs), along with numeric summaries like incidence rates and percentages for each study arm. The size of the tables varies, with some large enough to exceed the context length of large language models (LLMs). For example, the tables for Medical History, AEs by SOC/PT, AEs by Maximum Intensity, and AEs by Worst Outcome are especially large.

Table 1: CSR Table Types

Table Types	Number of Tables
Subject Disposition	14
Subject Demography	16
Medical History	14
Overall Summary	13
AEs by SOC and PT	7
AEs by Maximum intensity	7
AEs by Worst Outcome	4
AEs by Common % or more by SOC and PT	4

4.2 Experimental Setup

We conducted experiments with the following models:

- **GPT-4o-mini:** A state-of-the-art model known for its robust summarization capabilities and large token limit (Achiam et al., 2023).
- **DeepSeek** (Chat window): DeepSeek is a Chinese artificial intelligence company that develops open-source large language models (LLMs) (Liu et al., 2024). We used the latest advanced language model comprising 671 billion parameters.

- **Llama 3.1 70B Instruct:** An open source model fine-tuned for instruction following task (HuggingFace, a).

- **Nous Hermes 2 Mixtral 8x7B DPO:** A model further fine-tuned on Mixtral 8x7B MOE with reinforcement learning via direct preference optimization (DPO), also featuring a 32k token limit (HuggingFace, b).

Due to cost constraints, we could not do experiments with some of the latest LLMs with higher capabilities. However, a variety of architectural and assessment capabilities are offered by the chosen models. Some clinical trial tables in our dataset exceeded the context length of the largest models tested such as GPT-4o-mini, due to which models were unable to process the entire table leading to incomplete outputs. This limitation further highlights the importance of fact selection algorithm for handling large tables effectively.

4.3 Quantitative Evaluation

To evaluate the quality of generated summaries, we used the following metrics.

4.3.1 Claim Recall and Claim Precision

- This framework, introduced by (Xie et al., 2024) as *DOCLENS: Multi-aspect Fine-grained Evaluation for Medical Text Generation*, is specifically tailored to assess medical text generation tasks.

- ***Claim Recall:*** This metric evaluates the completeness of the generated text. The reference summary is segmented into individual sub-claims or facts using GPT-4, with each sub-claim representing a single fact. The generated text is then analyzed by an evaluator model to determine whether it entails each sub-claim from the reference summary.

- ***Claim Precision:*** This metric evaluates the conciseness of the generated text. The generated summary is divided into sub-claims. The reference summary is then analyzed to determine if it entails each sub-claim from the generated summary.

We utilized GPT-4o to create the sub-claims for both the reference text and the generated text. Additionally, we employed the same model as an evaluator.

4.4 Human Evaluation

For human evaluation, we sought assistance from our organization's internal medical writers. They devised a set of rules tailored to the evaluation of summaries generated for clinical trial tables. The rules guaranteed a consistent and clinically suitable evaluation of the generated outputs. for example, for adverse events table type (under the safety evaluation section)some rules are:

- *Threshold for SOCs and PTs:* A proper cutoff should be decided for both System Organ Classes (SOCs) and Preferred Terms (PTs). Above this threshold, all SOCs and PTs should be selected and included in the summary to maintain relevance and completeness.

- *Template Adherence:* Summaries should follow a consistent and predefined template, ensuring clarity and alignment with organizational or regulatory standards. For example, as shown in Table 3

Medical writer manually evaluated all the generated summaries to verify that the summaries adhere to the following criteria.

- ***Rule Compliance:*** Whether the summary follows the rules and templates specific to the table type.

- ***Accuracy:*** Ensuring there are no hallucinations, incorrect interpretations, missing data, or data mismatches.

- ***Conciseness:*** Exclusion of irrelevant or redundant details.

- ***Fluency:*** Readability and coherence of the summary.

5 Results and Discussion

The performance of various models was assessed using the metrics outlined in the Evaluation section, including Claim Recall, Claim Precision, and manual evaluation. The detailed results are shown in Table 4 and Table 5, which emphasizes the effectiveness of our fact selection algorithm and the overall quality of the generated summaries.

Among the models tested, without the fact selection algorithm, GPT-4o-mini in a 1-shot setting achieved a claim recall of <u>0.67</u> and claim precision

"Reference Summary": In total 37/63 children (58.7%) were reported with at least one TEAE. Most frequently reported primary system organ classes affected by TEAEs were: Gastrointestinal disorders (13/63, 20.6%) , general disorders and administration site conditions (11/63, 17.5%), musculoskeletal and connective tissue disorders (8/63, 12.7%) , nervous system disorders (9/63, 14.3%) as well as infections and infestations (7/63, 11.1%). Overall, there was a similar distribution of TEAEs across both age cohorts, treatments and formulations, with the exception of menorrhagia, which was more frequently reported in adolescents of the Drug A o.d. tablet group (n = 4) than in the comparator group (n = 0)."

"Claims":

Claim 2: The most frequently reported primary system organ class affected by TEAEs was gastrointestinal disorders (20.6%, 13/63).

Claim 4: Musculoskeletal and connective tissue disorders were reported in 12.7% (8/63) of children.

"GPT-4o-mini(1-shot)":{
"claim 2": "The most frequently reported primary system organ class affected by TEAEs was gastrointestinal disorders (20.6%, 13/63).",
"explanation": "The clinical summary provides that gastrointestinal disorders were the most common system organ class, and the percentage (20.6%) is also included. The specific number of subjects affected (13/63) is also consistent.",
"entailment_prediction": 1
},
{
"claim 4": "Musculoskeletal and connective tissue disorders were reported in 12.7% (8/63) of children.",
"explanation": "The clinical summary does not mention musculoskeletal and connective tissue disorders as a common adverse event. Therefore, this claim cannot be fully entailed.",
"entailment_prediction": 0
}

"Our Approach": {
"claim 2": "The most frequently reported primary system organ class affected by TEAEs was gastrointestinal disorders (20.6%, 13/63).",
"explanation": "The summary lists Gastrointestinal Disorders as 20.6% of patients, but it does not explicitly confirm the number of children affected (13/63). However, the percentage matches, so the claim can be inferred.",
"entailment_prediction": 1
},
{
"claim 4" : "Musculoskeletal and connective tissue disorders were reported in 12.7% (8/63) of children.",
"explanation": "The clinical summary mentions Musculoskeletal and Connective Tissue Disorders as 12.7% of patients but does not give the exact number (8/63). However, the percentage supports the claim.",
"entailment_prediction": 1
}

Table 2: Example of Claim Recall evaluation for GPT-4o-mini and Nous-Research. **The summary generated by GPT-4o-mini fails to include an important fact, "Claim 4," resulting in lower claim recall.** In contrast, applying the fact selection algorithm to Nous-Research improves claim recall by ensuring all critical facts are present in the generated summary

"AEs By SOC and PT" :
X (%) Number of subjects reported at least one such adverse event......, The most common adverse events (AEs) by System Organ Class (SOC) were SOC Fact 1 (in Drug A X% of patients, in Drug B Y%,........so on), SOC Fact 2 (in Drug A X% of patients, in Drug B Y%,........so on), and SOC Fact 3 (Z%)................, and SOC Fact n (n % of patients)........... The most common AEs by Preferred Term (PT) were PT Fact 1 (a% of patients), PT Fact 2 (in Drug A X% of patients, in Drug B Y%,........so on), PT Fact 3 (in Drug A X% of patients, in Drug B Y%,........so on),...........and PT Fact n (n% of patients).

Table 3: An Example Template for AEs by SOC and PT

Table 4: Comparison of Claim Recall and Precision Across Different Models and Approaches

Model	Claim Recall	Claim Precision
Nous-Hermes-2-Mixtral-8x7B DPO (with fact selection algorithm) **Our Approach**	**0.72**	**0.44**
GPT 4o-mini (0-shot)	0.58	0.38
GPT 4o-mini (1-shot)	0.67	0.47
DeepSeek (0-shot)	0.5	0.36
DeepSeek (1-shot)	0.55	0.44
Llama-3.1-70B-Instruct (0-shot)	0.18	0.15
Llama-3.1-70B-Instruct (1-shot)	0.22	0.18
Nous-Hermes-2-Mixtral-8x7B DPO (0-shot)	0.27	0.22
Nous-Hermes-2-Mixtral-8x7B DPO (1-shot)	0.23	0.29

of 0.47. DeepSeek performed similarly to GPT-4o-mini, while Llama-3.1-70B-Instruct showed the weakest performance. We tested the fact-selection algorithm with Nous-Hermes-2-Mixtral, which attained the highest claim recall of **0.72**, though its claim precision was **0.44**. Additionally, Table 5 demonstrates that the summary generated using the fact selection algorithm outperformed the proprietary models in terms of informativeness, consistency, fluency, and conciseness. Unfortunately, we could not apply the fact selection algorithm to proprietary models due to API costs. However, the superior performance of the open-source models after applying the algorithm suggests that applying it to the proprietary models would yield even better results.

A medical expert from our internal team evaluated the generated summaries. They observed that the output from open-source models, such as Llama 3.1 Instruct 70B, is not acceptable. These models tend to hallucinate, exhibit data mismatches, and fail to adhere to the correct output template. In contrast, proprietary models like GPT-4o-mini produce significantly better results. While hallucinations are less frequent and the model largely presents accurate information from the tables, it still struggles with maintaining the proper output template and occasionally overlooks key facts. As shown in Table 2, GPT-4o-mini misses an important fact ('claim 4'). However, when a fact-selection algorithm is applied and a well-defined output format is provided, the performance of the LLM improves, producing outputs that closely resemble those of a human writer.

The reason for this improved performance lies in the fact that without a fact selection algorithm, the LLM is tasked with both selecting the relevant facts from the provided table and generating the summary. We observed that LLMs struggle with determining an appropriate threshold based on data trends and applying that threshold for fact selection. In contrast, when the fact selection algorithm is used, the generation task is divided into two distinct steps: first selecting the relevant facts, then generating the summary. With the fact selection algorithm in place, the LLM no longer needs to perform fact selection itself. Instead, the selected facts are provided to the LLM along with the necessary template, making it easier for the model to generate the output by simply filling in the blanks of the template. With this approach, both recall and precision can be improved by adjusting the threshold.

Table 5: Overall Evaluation

Type	Model	Informative	Conciseness	Fluency	Consistency	Score
1-shot	Llama-3.1-Instruct-70B	2.8	1.5	3.5	3.1	2.73
1-shot	Nous-research-Mixtral	3.1	2.2	3.8	3.4	3.13
1-shot	DeepSeek	4.2	3.8	4.6	4.5	4.28
1-shot	GPT-4o-mini	4.4	3.8	4.6	4.5	4.33
Algo	Nous-reseaarch-Mixtral	**4.7**	**4.5**	**4.7**	**4.5**	**4.6**

6 Conclusions and Future Work

In this work, we developed an end-to-end pipeline that automates the generation of clinical table summaries from large complex tables. Complexities may be there because of size, density and domain-specific knowledge, that make it difficult for LLMs to consistently generate accurate and relevant summaries. The proposed pipeline enables the LLMs to produce more concise and accurate summaries. Additionally, we incorporated a feedback mechanism within the pipeline, allowing users to refine the output and improve the quality of summaries iteratively.

7 Limitations

Due to some constraints, we could not perform extensive experiments in diverse domains. Our future work aims to address this by experimenting in other complex domains and at a larger data scale. Moreover, we can also perform a comparison with the latest LLMs, particularly those with larger context windows and improved summarization capabilities.

References

Josh Achiam, Steven Adler, Sandhini Agarwal, Lama Ahmad, Ilge Akkaya, Florencia Leoni Aleman, Diogo Almeida, Janko Altenschmidt, Sam Altman, Shyamal Anadkat, et al. 2023. Gpt-4 technical report. *arXiv preprint arXiv:2303.08774*.

Junwei Bao, Duyu Tang, Nan Duan, Zhao Yan, Yuanhua Lv, Ming Zhou, and Tiejun Zhao. 2018. Table-to-text: Describing table region with natural language. In *Proceedings of the AAAI conference on artificial intelligence*, volume 32.

Regina Barzilay and Mirella Lapata. 2005. Collective content selection for concept-to-text generation. In *Proceedings of Human Language Technology Conference and Conference on Empirical Methods in Natural Language Processing*, pages 331–338, Vancouver, British Columbia, Canada. Association for Computational Linguistics.

Miao Chen, Xinjiang Lu, Tong Xu, Yanyan Li, Jingbo Zhou, Dejing Dou, and Hui Xiong. 2023. Towards table-to-text generation with pretrained language model: A table structure understanding and text deliberating approach. *arXiv preprint arXiv:2301.02071*.

Wenhu Chen. 2022. Large language models are few (1)-shot table reasoners. *arXiv preprint arXiv:2210.06710*.

Wenhu Chen, Hongmin Wang, Jianshu Chen, Yunkai Zhang, Hong Wang, Shiyang Li, Xiyou Zhou, and William Yang Wang. 2019a. Tabfact: A large-scale dataset for table-based fact verification. *arXiv preprint arXiv:1909.02164*.

Zhiyu Chen, Harini Eavani, Wenhu Chen, Yinyin Liu, and William Yang Wang. 2019b. Few-shot nlg with pre-trained language model. *arXiv preprint arXiv:1904.09521*.

Dong Deng, Yu Jiang, Guoliang Li, Jian Li, and Cong Yu. 2013. Scalable column concept determination for web tables using large knowledge bases. *Proc. VLDB Endow.*, 6(13):1606–1617.

Mingqi Gao, Jie Ruan, Renliang Sun, Xunjian Yin, Shiping Yang, and Xiaojun Wan. 2023. Human-like summarization evaluation with chatgpt. *arXiv preprint arXiv:2304.02554*.

Xinwei Geng, Xiaocheng Feng, Bing Qin, and Ting Liu. 2018. Adaptive multi-pass decoder for neural machine translation. In *Proceedings of the 2018 Conference on Empirical Methods in Natural Language Processing*, pages 523–532.

Heng Gong, Xiaocheng Feng, Bing Qin, and Ting Liu. 2019. Table-to-text generation with effective hierarchical encoder on three dimensions (row, column and time). *arXiv preprint arXiv:1909.02304*.

Heng Gong, Yawei Sun, Xiaocheng Feng, Bing Qin, Wei Bi, Xiaojiang Liu, and Ting Liu. 2020. Tablegpt: Few-shot table-to-text generation with table structure reconstruction and content matching. In *Proceedings of the 28th International Conference on Computational Linguistics*, pages 1978–1988.

GSK. Clinical Study reports. `https://www.gskstudyregister.com/en/`.

Stefan Hegselmann, Alejandro Buendia, Hunter Lang, Monica Agrawal, Xiaoyi Jiang, and David Sontag.

2023. Tabllm: Few-shot classification of tabular data with large language models. In *International Conference on Artificial Intelligence and Statistics*, pages 5549–5581. PMLR.

HuggingFace. a. Llama. https://huggingface.co/meta-llama/Llama-3.1-70B-Instruct.

HuggingFace. b. NousResearch. https://huggingface.co/NousResearch/Nous-Hermes-2-Mixtral-8x7B-DPO.

Jie Jiang, Haining Xie, Yu Shen, Zihan Zhang, Meng Lei, Yifeng Zheng, Yide Fang, Chunyou Li, Danqing Huang, Wentao Zhang, et al. 2024. Siriusbi: Building end-to-end business intelligence enhanced by large language models. *arXiv preprint arXiv:2411.06102*.

Rémi Lebret, David Grangier, and Michael Auli. 2016. Neural text generation from structured data with application to the biography domain. *arXiv preprint arXiv:1603.07771*.

Liang Li, Ruiying Geng, Chengyang Fang, Bing Li, Can Ma, Binhua Li, and Yongbin Li. 2023. Plan-then-seam: Towards efficient table-to-text generation. *arXiv preprint arXiv:2302.05138*.

Liang Li, Can Ma, Yinliang Yue, and Dayong Hu. 2021. Improving encoder by auxiliary supervision tasks for table-to-text generation. In *Proceedings of the 59th Annual Meeting of the Association for Computational Linguistics and the 11th International Joint Conference on Natural Language Processing (Volume 1: Long Papers)*, pages 5979–5989.

Weizhe Lin, Rexhina Blloshmi, Bill Byrne, Adrià de Gispert, and Gonzalo Iglesias. 2023. An inner table retriever for robust table question answering.

Aixin Liu, Bei Feng, Bing Xue, Bingxuan Wang, Bochao Wu, Chengda Lu, Chenggang Zhao, Chengqi Deng, Chenyu Zhang, Chong Ruan, et al. 2024. Deepseek-v3 technical report. *arXiv preprint arXiv:2412.19437*.

Mehran Nasseri, Patrick Brandtner, Robert Zimmermann, Taha Falatouri, Farzaneh Darbanian, and Tobechi Obinwanne. 2023. Applications of large language models (llms) in business analytics–exemplary use cases in data preparation tasks. In *International Conference on Human-Computer Interaction*, pages 182–198. Springer.

NLM. Clinical studies. https://clinicaltrials.gov/.

Ehud Reiter, Somayajulu Sripada, Jim Hunter, Jin Yu, and Ian Davy. 2005. Choosing words in computer-generated weather forecasts. *Artif. Intell.*, 167(1–2):137–169.

Malik Sallam. 2023. The utility of chatgpt as an example of large language models in healthcare education, research and practice: Systematic review on the future perspectives and potential limitations. *MedRxiv*, pages 2023–02.

Amalio Telenti, Michael Auli, Brian L Hie, Cyrus Maher, Suchi Saria, and John PA Ioannidis. 2024. Large language models for science and medicine. *European Journal of Clinical Investigation*, 54(6):e14183.

Timm Teubner, Christoph M Flath, Christof Weinhardt, Wil van der Aalst, and Oliver Hinz. 2023. Welcome to the era of chatgpt et al. the prospects of large language models. *Business & Information Systems Engineering*, 65(2):95–101.

Ran Tian, Shashi Narayan, Thibault Sellam, and Ankur P Parikh. 2019. Sticking to the facts: Confident decoding for faithful data-to-text generation. *arXiv preprint arXiv:1910.08684*.

Sebastian Varges, Heike Bieler, Manfred Stede, Lukas C. Faulstich, Kristin Irsig, and Malik Atalla. 2012. SemScribe: Natural language generation for medical reports. In *Proceedings of the Eighth International Conference on Language Resources and Evaluation (LREC'12)*, pages 2674–2681, Istanbul, Turkey. European Language Resources Association (ELRA).

Sam Wiseman, Stuart M Shieber, and Alexander M Rush. 2017. Challenges in data-to-document generation. *arXiv preprint arXiv:1707.08052*.

Yiqing Xie, Sheng Zhang, Hao Cheng, Pengfei Liu, Zelalem Gero, Cliff Wong, Tristan Naumann, Hoifung Poon, and Carolyn Rose. 2024. Doclens: Multi-aspect fine-grained evaluation for medical text generation. In *Proceedings of the 62nd Annual Meeting of the Association for Computational Linguistics*.

On Large Foundation Models and Alzheimer's Disease Detection

Chuyuan Li[1], Giuseppe Carenini[1], Thalia Field[2]
[1] Department of Computer Science
[2] Vancouver Stroke Program and Division of Neurology
The University of British Columbia
V6T 1Z4, Vancouver, BC, Canada
{chuyuan.li, thalia.field}@ubc.ca, carenini@cs.ubc.ca

Abstract

Large Foundation Models such as Llama and LLaVA have displayed incredible capabilities in a wide range of domains and tasks. However, it is unclear whether these models match specialist capabilities without special training or fine-tuning. In this paper, we investigate the innate ability of foundation models as neurodegenerative disease specialists, particularly for detecting the Alzheimer's Disease. Precisely, we use a language model, Llama-3.1, and a visual language model, Llama3-LLaVA-NeXT, to detect language specificity between Alzheimer's Disease patients and healthy controls through a well-known Picture Description task. Results show that Llama is comparable to supervised classifiers, while LLaVA, despite its additional "vision", lags behind.

1 Introduction

Large Foundation Models such as Llama have demonstrated surprising capabilities in the field of Natural Language Processing (NLP). Recent work seems to indicate that these generalist models can be used in specialized domains, such as clinical medicine, with proprietary Large Language Models (LLMs) such as GPT-4 achieving impressive performance on professional benchmarks in health domain (Bubeck et al., 2023; Cui et al., 2024; Belyaeva et al., 2023; Jin et al., 2024). Other work, however, suggests that GPT-4 does not outperform traditional AI tools and cannot replace them at current stage (Wang et al., 2023).

The healthcare sector often prefers open LLMs that can be deployed in local environments, especially since relying on third-party commercial LLMs is not always feasible due to concerns about traceability, privacy, and security. Taking into account the complexity of real-world applications, in this paper, we explore the use of small (e.g., less than 10B), cost-effective open-source LLMs for Alzheimer's Disease detection.

Alzheimer's Disease (AD) is a insidious progressive neurodegenerative disease resulting in impaired cognition and dementia, and eventual death (Scharre, 2019). Since there is no effective cure for dementia, early intervention is essential. Modern deep learning approaches utilize data from various modalities, such as speech (Berube et al., 2019; Ilias and Askounis, 2022), eye-tracking (Sriram et al., 2023; Sheng et al., 2022), facial (Chou et al., 2025), and neuroimaging (Sarraf et al., 2023). However, some modalities require invasive and costly screening tools. In contrast, language data is easy to collect—a speech recording takes no more than 10 minutes—and involves no invasive procedure, making it an ideal resource for early disease detection.

Picture description, such as the one shown in Figure 1, has been widely used to capture deficits or abnormalities in **language** (Yorkston and Beukelman, 1980). Over the years, clinicians have assessed a variety of measures, such as grammaticality (Ash and Grossman, 2015), vocabulary (Forbes-McKay and Venneri, 2005), frequency of noun-verb ratio (Bird et al., 2000), and the percentage and change of information units (IUs), e.g., "mom", "girl" (Giles et al., 1996; Bouazizi et al., 2023). In the pre-LLM era, NLP practitioners manually craft linguistic features and use machine learning algorithms to train supervised models (Fraser et al., 2016, 2019; Barral et al., 2020; Jang et al., 2021). While these experiments yield promising results, they require the collection of training data, a time-consuming and labor-intensive process. Additionally, the variability in datasets and recording conditions also makes it challenging for supervised models to generalize well (Favaro et al., 2024).

With the advent of LLMs, NLP has shifted from developing task-specific representations and architectures to using task-agnostic foundation models (Radford et al., 2019; Brown, 2020), which are pretrained on vast, cross-disciplinary data. These models not only streamline the process but also

Proceedings of the Second Workshop on Patient-Oriented Language Processing (CL4Health), pages 158–168
May 4, 2025

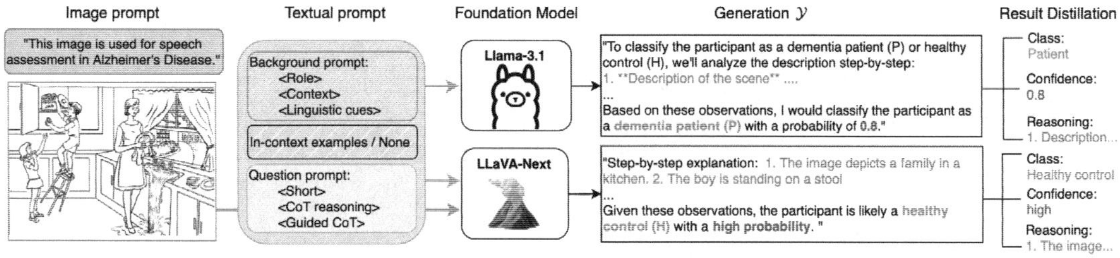

Figure 1: The roadmap of our approach. Textual prompt are provided to language model Llama; image and textual prompts are provided to vision-language model LLaVA-NeXT. We extract class, probability, and analysis from $\mathcal{Y}$.

offer interpretable explanations, providing clinical doctors with valuable insights into their reasoning (Perlis, 2023; Nori et al., 2023a,b). Our approach leverages the powerful open-source LLM, Llama-3.1-8B (Dubey et al., 2024), and explores its potential for AD detection through carefully designed zero-shot and few-shot prompting strategies. At the time of our experiments, Llama-3.1 models offered state-of-the-art performance in the open-source LLM landscape.

Given that our task involves describing a **picture** using language, a Vision-Language Model (VLM) should offer a clear advantage. We choose a VLM from the LLaVA family (Liu et al., 2024b), a pioneering work in visual instruction tuning, while also considering its base language model and comparable size. LLaVA is pretrained on image-caption data and designed to provide detailed descriptions (e.g., position of objects in an image) and perform complex reasoning (e.g., "*What is unusual in an image, and explain.*"). These capabilities align well with our experimental setup. Based on these considerations, we use Llama3-LLaVA-NeXT (Liu et al., 2024a), one of the latest LLaVA models, which is built on Llama-3-8B-Instruct and integrates a vision encoder for image processing.

Our experimental results show that Llama-3.1-8B model can match or even surpass traditional supervised methods with minimal supervision. The key factor is the effective combination of Background and Question prompts. LLaVA, on the other hand, is not yet suited for this task, as intriguingly it may itself exhibit symptoms akin to "neurodegenerative" issues.

2 The Power of Prompting

Prompt engineering is a popular and effective way for using LLMs without altering their parameters. Empirical studies have shown that a model's performance on specific tasks can be significantly affected by the prompt, often in surprising ways (Feng et al., 2024; Sivarajkumar et al., 2024; Salinas and Morstatter, 2024; Sclar et al., 2024). For instance, by adding "*Let's think step by step*" can greatly improve model performance (Kojima et al., 2022). To date, there is not yet a consensus on how to formulate the most effective prompts for a specific task.

To unleash the inner specialist capabilities of LLMs and gain a better understanding of the crucial components in a prompt, we design our prompts in a systematic way. For language-only model, we divide our prompt into three parts: (1) Background prompt, (2) Question prompt, and (3) Example prompt. For vision-language model, we include the image and prepend the cue phrase, "*This image is used for speech assessment in Alzheimer's Disease.*", to the beginning of the textual prompt, as shown in Figure 1. The textual input for VLM is the same as the language-only model. Precisely:

(1) **Background Prompt** aims to place LLMs in a specific knowledge graph where the information is closely related to the target domain. For instance, prompts starting with "*You are an intelligent AI assistant*" or "*You are an expert in clinical NLP*" use Persona pattern as guiding cues (Sivarajkumar et al., 2024). In our experiments, we test three cue phrases, including `Role`—"*You are a medical expert in Alzheimer's Disease*", `Context`— a brief introduction of the Cookie Theft picture description task, and `Linguistic`—clinical observations of linguistic features from AD and healthy controls.

(2) **Question Prompt** directs LLMs to produce desirable output, whether text generation, classification, or resolution. It has been shown that by simply adding "*Let's think step by step*" before each answer, LLMs can become decent zero-shot reasoners (Kojima et al., 2022). Here, we compare short answer and Chain of Thought (CoT) prompting answer in the question prompt. `Short answer`

simply asks the LLM to predict a class (i.e., normal *vs.* patient) without any explanation, while `CoT answer` asks the model to first analyze step by step and then give an answer. We also offer a `Guided CoT` (`G. CoT`) version to direct the model to reason from specific linguistic perspectives, such as "vocabulary richness" and "syntactic complexity".

Pre-trained language models are often inherently calibrated to different extents (Jiang et al., 2021; Liang et al., 2023), with token probabilities might be employed off-the-shelf. Since they could verbalize confidence scores (Tian et al., 2023), we use the cue phrase *"Give a prediction with a probability"* to directly ask for prediction probabilities. In preliminary experiments, we found that using this cue phrase yielded better results than omitting it.

(3) **Example Prompt** is positioned between Background Prompt and Question Prompt. It aims to examine whether In-Context Learning (ICL) with demonstrations further improves LLMs' performance in comparison to zero-shot prompting. Practically, we employ *fixed* and *dynamic few-shot* ICL. The fixed examples are selected randomly in the held-out set to be broadly representative and relevant to a wide distribution of text examples. The dynamic examples are instead chosen with a kNN-based approach ($k = 2$) (Nori et al., 2023b), where we embed all texts in the held-out set using OpenAI's latest embedding model `text-embedding-3-small`[1]. For each test example, we identify its nearest neighbor in both Patient and Control classes by computing their cosine similarity scores. In our experiments, we use a small k value, i.e., one positive and one negative examples.

We combine different types of Background and Question prompts in both zero-shot and 2-shot ICL. For instance, (`Role`; `Short`) uses `Role` in the background prompt and requires a short answer in the question prompt; (`Context+Role+Ling`; `G. CoT`) uses a combination of all background prompts and a guided CoT answer. Detailed prompting templates are provided in Appendix 5.

3 Data and Experiment Settings

Dataset. We use the dataset from Jang et al. (2021), which comprises 63 patients recruited from a specialty memory clinic and 67 healthy controls from the community. Patients are either diagnosed with Alzheimer's Disease (AD) or exhibiting initial symptoms of Mild Cognitive Impairments (MCI), potentially progressing to AD. Participants completed four tasks—pupil calibration, picture description, paragraph reading, and memory recall—during which both language and eye movement data were collected. In this study, we focus on the picture description task. Demographic and clinical data is provided in Table 1.

Group	#	Age	Gender	MoCA
Patient	63	72 ± 9	31M / 34F	18 ± 7
Control	67	62 ± 15	22M / 45F	27 ± 3

Table 1: Dataset demographic and clinical statistics. MoCA stands for Montreal Cognitive Assessment score.

Data Processing. The original speech data is transcribed and timestamped using WhisperX (Bain et al., 2023). Following automatic transcriptions, a human transcriber manually verified each transcript for word spelling and speaker diarization accuracy. Task instructions from the instructor were removed to include only participant speech.

Hyper-Parameters. We use the 8B checkpoint of Llama-3.1 and LLaVA-NeXT from Huggingface (Wolf et al., 2020). We use a low temperature (0.1) and set top_k sampling to 50. The maximum new tokens are 16 and 512 for `Short answer` and `CoT answer`, respectively. To investigate the potential *non-determinism* of LLMs (Ouyang et al., 2023; Song et al., 2024), each prompt configuration (e.g., (`Role`; `Short answer`)) is executed on two different servers with three runs per server. We report micro-averaged scores with standard deviation over 6 runs per setup.

Supervised Classifiers and Metrics. We compare with three classic supervised algorithms: Logistic Regression (LR), Random Forest (RF), and Gaussian Naive Bayes (GNB). We follow the feature extraction process outlined in Jang et al. (2021) and split the dataset into ten folds for cross-validation. Appendix 5 provides details.

In all experiments, we report three metrics: (1) Area Under the *Receiver Operating Characteristic (ROC)* Curve (**AUC**): the ability to distinguish between Patient and Control under different thresholds; (2) **Sensitivity**: the True Positive rate for Patient detection, and (3) **Specificity**: the True Negative rate for Control detection. The main measure is the AUC score.

[1] `https://platform.openai.com/docs/guides/embeddings`.

Background	Question	AUC	Sensitivity	Specificity
Role	Short	60.3 ± 1.1	**96.4** ± 0.8	11.5 ± 0.8
	CoT	65.8 ± 0.5	91.13 ± 1.1	24.6 ± 2.5
	G. CoT	**70.9** ± 0.4	84.7 ± 1.1	**35.4** ± 2.1
Context	Short	69.4 ± 1.5	35.9 ± 2.0	**93.5** ± 1.4
	CoT	68.9 ± 0.6	50.8 ± 1.1	73.9 ± 2.1
	G. CoT	**74.3** ± 1.1	**69.4** ± 2.2	69.3 ± 0.0
Context	Short	71.6 ± 0.5	**72.6** ± 0.0	69.6 ± 1.4
+Role	CoT	72.9 ± 3.8	70.2 ± 3.4	70.8 ± 4.3
+Ling	G. CoT	**76.1** ± 2.0	71.8 ± 3.4	**73.9** ± 2.1
Supervised Classifiers				
GNB	-	72.8 ± 2.2	64.1 ± 2.2	66.5 ± 3.5
LR	-	73.2 ± 1.7	68.5 ± 3.8	70.2 ± 1.6
RF	-	75.2 ± 3.1	67.7 ± 4.6	73.1 ± 3.6

Table 2: Top: zero-shot with different background and question prompts. Scores are averaged across 6 runs. Best score in each sub-section is in **bold**. Bottom: performances using supervised classifiers.

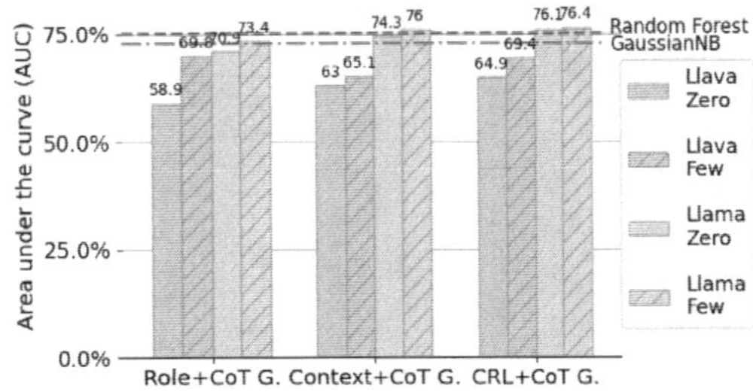

Figure 2: LLaVA and LLama performances on different Background (`Role`, `Context`, `Context+Role+Linguistic`) and Answer prompt (`G. CoT`) settings.

4 Results with Foundation Models

Impact of Background and Question Prompts on Zero-shot Prompting. We present zero-shot results in Table 2. When using the `Role` pattern in the Background prompt, Llama is highly sensitive in detecting Patients (90%), but much less so for Controls. In contrast, when the model is provided only with the `Context` of the picture description task, it predicts Controls more accurately. This suggests that different background prompts shift the model's threshold for identifying *Patient language* in distinct ways. Combining different background prompts (`Context+Role+Ling`) provides more complete information, enabling the LLM to retrieve the most relevant knowledge and deliver optimal performance. With a 76% AUC score, it matches and even surpasses supervised classifiers (GNB 73%, LR 73%, RF 75%). In the Question prompt, `CoT` significantly enhances model performance compared to `Short` answers, and this improvement is consistent across various background settings. Interestingly, we find that simply asking the model to analyze before making predictions helps the LLM to show moderation in its decision making, as evidenced by a more balanced Sensitivity and Specificity rate.

Few-shot *vs.* Zero-shot Prompting. In few-shot in-context learning, we use the same Background and Question prompts as in the zero-shot setting, but add input-output pairs as demonstration in the Example Prompt. Table 3 demonstrates that few-shot prompting consistently enhances AUC scores, particularly when the background prompt lacks sufficient task information, as seen with the `Role` background. Remarkably, we also find that zero-shot prompting can be highly effective in some cases, even surpassing few-shot prompting. This occurs when the background is complete and a `CoT answer` is employed—a trend also observed in other clinical NLP tasks (Sivarajkumar et al., 2024). In most prompt settings, random few-shot outperforms *k*NN, suggesting that a more general and representative set of examples leads to better performance than semantically close ones. Similar observations are made by Nori et al. (2023a). However, it comes with the trade-off of greater fluctuations and less consistent Sensitivity and Specificity rates.

Vision Language Model *vs.* Language-only Model. While we were expecting VLMs to outperform pure LLMs due to their ability to process the picture, Figure 2 reveals that LLaVA significantly underperforms Llama on this task, with lower AUC scores up to 10% across various prompting, in both zero-shot and few-shot setups. Specifically, we observe some *extreme* predictions in zero-shot prompting, where LLaVA exclusively predicts either Patient or Control, a behavior never observed with Llama. While few-shot prompting brings some improvement, the model remains *biased* toward producing high Specificity or Sensitivity scores (see detailed scores in Appendix 5). We also note some anecdotal observations regarding LLaVA's reasoning. For instance, when asked to analyze step by step, instead of reasoning from a linguistic perspective, LLaVA simply lists the objects in the image, such as: "*1. The image shows a family. 2. The boy is standing. 3. Water is flowing.*" One plausible reason is that VLMs are not trained to capture subtle linguistic nuances as LLMs are,

B prompt	Q prompt	Random Few-shot AUC	Random Few-shot Sensitivity	Random Few-shot Specificity	*k*NN Few-shot AUC	*k*NN Few-shot Sensitivity	*k*NN Few-shot Specificity	Zero-shot AUC	Zero-shot Sensitivity	Zero-shot Specificity
Role	Short	69.5 ± 7.5	74.4 ± 8.1	55.9 ± 14.8	64.5 ± 0.2	84.13 ± 0.0	38.8 ± 2.1	60.3 ± 1.1	96.4 ± 0.8	11.5 ± 0.8
	CoT	71.3 ± 3.4	75.4 ± 9.0	50.0 ± 17.9	70.7 ± 2.1	94.4 ± 1.1	23.1 ± 1.0	65.8 ± 0.5	91.13 ± 1.1	24.6 ± 2.5
	G. CoT	73.4 ± 7.0	74.9 ± 8.0	60.8 ± 12.1	72.9 ± 0.7	87.2 ± 2.4	33.6 ± 1.0	70.9 ± 0.4	84.7 ± 1.1	35.4 ± 2.1
Context	Short	69.2 ± 9.6	77.2 ± 12.8	50.0 ± 18.5	68.3 ± 0.9	61.1 ± 1.1	69.4 ± 1.0	69.4 ± 1.5	35.9 ± 2.0	93.5 ± 1.4
	CoT	65.0 ± 5.1	59.1 ± 12.4	65.3 ± 14.3	68.1 ± 2.7	61.1 ± 3.4	71.6 ± 0.0	68.9 ± 0.6	50.8 ± 1.1	73.9 ± 2.1
	G. CoT	76.0 ± 4.1	64.6 ± 4.8	75.9 ± 8.9	74.3 ± 2.1	80.2 ± 1.1	64.2 ± 0.0	74.3 ± 1.1	69.4 ± 2.2	69.3 ± 0.0
Context	Short	71.9 ± 3.7	58.1 ± 15.0	79.8 ± 10.5	71.1 ± 2.3	65.9 ± 1.1	71.6 ± 0.0	71.6 ± 0.5	72.6 ± 0.0	69.6 ± 1.4
+Role	CoT	71.9 ± 3.6	61.4 ± 11.0	78.4 ± 7.2	74.9 ± 0.1	77.0 ± 3.3	64.2 ± 0.0	72.9 ± 3.8	70.2 ± 3.4	70.8 ± 4.3
+Ling	G. CoT	76.4 ± 2.9	71.7 ± 7.6	75.8 ± 8.4	74.8 ± 1.3	83.2 ± 1.3	46.3 ± 0.0	76.1 ± 2.0	71.8 ± 3.4	73.9 ± 2.1

Table 3: Random, *k*NN few-shot, and zero-shot prompting results with Llama. Random few-shot results are averaged from three sampling. Best AUC in random, *k*NN, and zero-shot sections is highlighted ; second best is underlined.

as they are primarily pretrained on image-text pairs to recognize objects in images.

Recent studies reveal that VLMs are prone to heavy *hallucinations* and can be easily misled by deceptive prompts (Qian et al., 2024; Zhang et al., 2024). To explore the "neuro-cognitive status" of LLaVA, we prompt the model to perform the picture description task, similar to the human participants. We then apply trained classifiers (GNB, LR) to analyze LLaVA's generated speech, with details in Appendix 5. Unsurprisingly, the supervised classifiers consistently predict LLaVA as a Patient with high probability: GNB$> 90\%$, LR$> 80\%$. Since LLaVA is unable to generate *normal* speech during the picture description task, it is not surprising that its predictions are not reliable.

5 Conclusion and Open Questions

In this paper, we explore the potential of foundation models for lightweight use in Alzheimer's Disease detection via Picture Description task. Using appropriate prompting strategies, we find that LLMs can be activated to exhibit specialist capabilities even in a no-data scenario, achieving performance comparable to supervised classifiers, while providing clear and insightful reasoning. VLMs, however, are not yet suited for complex language reasoning tasks, as they may themselves exhibit symptoms akin to "neurodegenerative" issues. In the near future, we plan to expand our methods from picture description narratives to conversational interactions such as semi-structured conversations (Goodkind et al., 2018), and other healthcare-related disease detection (Li et al., 2022).

Several open questions remain worth exploring, such as alternative methods for demonstration example selection and whether a best example-pair exists that could boost LLMs' performance. For multimodal models, a key challenge is how to effectively enhance their compositional capabilities, thus enabling them to process different information in a more intelligent and integrated way.

Limitations

Most LLMs do not consistently produce the same output due to the inherent randomness in their parameter initialization. To address this and ensure more robust results, we ran each setup at least three times on different servers. In most cases (zero-shot and *k*NN few-shot), the variations were minimal, reinforcing our conclusions about different prompting strategies. However, we found that the relative performance of prompt variations could vary significantly when using random few-shot prompting.

We evaluate two model variations, Llama and LLaVA, both of which are leading models of LLMs and VLMs, respectively. However, further research is needed to understand how different language models, architectures, and datasets may impact the sensitivity of prompt variations on this task.

Ethical Considerations

The dataset we use for this paper comes from the CANARY project at University of British Columbia (UBC), which was approved by the UBC clinical research ethics board (H17-02803-A036). During the experiments, we ensure that no private information—such as participants' health, clinical, or demographic data—is disclosed. This is a main reason for us exclusively testing with open-source language models.

Acknowledgments

The authors thank the anonymous reviewers, Ronald Liu for manually verifying the transcriptions, and Miini Teng along with the UBC Canary project members for their valuable comments and suggestions. The authors also extend their appreciation to all the trainees and research assistants who have contributed to the Canary project over the years by collecting and refining data. This work was supported by the Faculty of Medicine at the University of British Columbia. The computing resources are provided by the Digital Research Alliance of Canada (alliancecan.ca).

References

Sharon Ash and Murray Grossman. 2015. Why study connected speech production. *Cognitive neuroscience of natural language use*, pages 29–58.

Max Bain, Jaesung Huh, Tengda Han, and Andrew Zisserman. 2023. Whisperx: Time-accurate speech transcription of long-form audio. *INTERSPEECH 2023*.

Oswald Barral, Hyeju Jang, Sally Newton-Mason, Sheetal Shajan, Thomas Soroski, Giuseppe Carenini, Cristina Conati, and Thalia Field. 2020. Non-invasive classification of alzheimer's disease using eye tracking and language. In *Machine Learning for Healthcare Conference*, pages 813–841. PMLR.

Anastasiya Belyaeva, Justin Cosentino, Farhad Hormozdiari, Krish Eswaran, Cory Shravya Shetty, Y McLean, Greg Corrado, and Nicholas A Furlotte1 AndrewB Carroll. 2023. Multimodal llms for health grounded in individual-specific data. In *Machine Learning for Multimodal Healthcare Data: First International Workshop, ML4MHD 2023, Honolulu, Hawaii, USA, July 29, 2023, Proceedings*, volume 14315, page 86. Springer Nature.

Shauna Berube, Jodi Nonnemacher, Cornelia Demsky, Shenly Glenn, Sadhvi Saxena, Amy Wright, Donna C Tippett, and Argye E Hillis. 2019. Stealing cookies in the twenty-first century: Measures of spoken narrative in healthy versus speakers with aphasia. *American journal of speech-language pathology*, 28(1S):321–329.

Helen Bird, Matthew A Lambon Ralph, Karalyn Patterson, and John R Hodges. 2000. The rise and fall of frequency and imageability: Noun and verb production in semantic dementia. *Brain and language*, 73(1):17–49.

Mondher Bouazizi, Chuheng Zheng, Siyuan Yang, and Tomoaki Ohtsuki. 2023. Dementia detection from speech: what if language models are not the answer? *Information*, 15(1):2.

Tom B Brown. 2020. Language models are few-shot learners. *arXiv preprint arXiv:2005.14165*.

Sébastien Bubeck, Varun Chandrasekaran, Ronen Eldan, Johannes Gehrke, Eric Horvitz, Ece Kamar, Peter Lee, Yin Tat Lee, Yuanzhi Li, Scott Lundberg, et al. 2023. Sparks of artificial general intelligence: Early experiments with gpt-4. *arXiv preprint arXiv:2303.12712*.

Shih-Han Chou, Miini Teng, Harshinee Sriram, Chuyuan Li, Giuseppe Carenini, Cristina Conati, Thalia S Field, Hyeju Jang, and Gabriel Murray. 2025. Multimodal classification of alzheimer's disease by combining facial and eye-tracking data. In *Machine Learning for Health (ML4H)*, pages 219–232. PMLR.

Hejie Cui, Zhuocheng Shen, Jieyu Zhang, Hui Shao, Lianhui Qin, Joyce C Ho, and Carl Yang. 2024. Llms-based few-shot disease predictions using ehr: A novel approach combining predictive agent reasoning and critical agent instruction. *arXiv preprint arXiv:2403.15464*.

Abhimanyu Dubey, Abhinav Jauhri, Abhinav Pandey, Abhishek Kadian, Ahmad Al-Dahle, Aiesha Letman, Akhil Mathur, Alan Schelten, Amy Yang, Angela Fan, et al. 2024. The llama 3 herd of models. *arXiv preprint arXiv:2407.21783*.

Anna Favaro, Najim Dehak, Thomas Thebaud, Jesús Villalba, Esther Oh, and Laureano Moro-Velázquez. 2024. Discovering invariant patterns of cognitive decline via an automated analysis of the cookie thief picture description task. In *The Speaker and Language Recognition Workshop (Odyssey 2024)*, pages 201–208.

Shangbin Feng, Weijia Shi, Yike Wang, Wenxuan Ding, Vidhisha Balachandran, and Yulia Tsvetkov. 2024. Don't hallucinate, abstain: Identifying llm knowledge gaps via multi-llm collaboration. *arXiv preprint arXiv:2402.00367*.

Katrina E Forbes-McKay and Annalena Venneri. 2005. Detecting subtle spontaneous language decline in early alzheimer's disease with a picture description task. *Neurological sciences*, 26:243–254.

Kathleen C Fraser, Kristina Lundholm Fors, Marie Eckerström, Fredrik Öhman, and Dimitrios Kokkinakis. 2019. Predicting mci status from multimodal language data using cascaded classifiers. *Frontiers in aging neuroscience*, 11:205.

Kathleen C Fraser, Jed A Meltzer, and Frank Rudzicz. 2016. Linguistic features identify alzheimer's disease in narrative speech. *Journal of Alzheimer's Disease*, 49(2):407–422.

Elaine Giles, Karalyn Patterson, and John R Hodges. 1996. Performance on the boston cookie theft picture description task in patients with early dementia of the alzheimer's type: missing information. *Aphasiology*, 10(4):395–408.

Adam Goodkind, Michelle Lee, Gary E Martin, Molly Losh, and Klinton Bicknell. 2018. Detecting language impairments in autism: A computational analysis of semi-structured conversations with vector semantics. In *Proceedings of the Society for Computation in Linguistics (SCiL) 2018*, pages 12–22.

Loukas Ilias and Dimitris Askounis. 2022. Multimodal deep learning models for detecting dementia from speech and transcripts. *Frontiers in Aging Neuroscience*, 14:830943.

Hyeju Jang, Thomas Soroski, Matteo Rizzo, Oswald Barral, Anuj Harisinghani, Sally Newton-Mason, Saffrin Granby, Thiago Monnerat Stutz da Cunha Vasco, Caitlin Lewis, Pavan Tutt, et al. 2021. Classification of alzheimer's disease leveraging multi-task machine learning analysis of speech and eye-movement data. *Frontiers in Human Neuroscience*.

Zhengbao Jiang, Jun Araki, Haibo Ding, and Graham Neubig. 2021. How can we know when language models know? on the calibration of language models for question answering. *Transactions of the Association for Computational Linguistics*, 9:962–977.

Mingyu Jin, Qinkai Yu, Dong Shu, Chong Zhang, Lizhou Fan, Wenyue Hua, Suiyuan Zhu, Yanda Meng, Zhenting Wang, Mengnan Du, et al. 2024. Health-llm: Personalized retrieval-augmented disease prediction system. *arXiv preprint arXiv:2402.00746*.

Takeshi Kojima, Shixiang Shane Gu, Machel Reid, Yutaka Matsuo, and Yusuke Iwasawa. 2022. Large language models are zero-shot reasoners. *Advances in neural information processing systems*, 35:22199–22213.

Chuyuan Li, Chloé Braud, and Maxime Amblard. 2022. Multi-task learning for depression detection in dialogs. In *Proceedings of the 23rd Annual Meeting of the Special Interest Group on Discourse and Dialogue*, pages 68–75.

Percy Liang, Rishi Bommasani, Tony Lee, Dimitris Tsipras, Dilara Soylu, Michihiro Yasunaga, Yian Zhang, Deepak Narayanan, Yuhuai Wu, Ananya Kumar, et al. 2023. Holistic evaluation of language models. *Transactions on Machine Learning Research*.

Haotian Liu, Chunyuan Li, Yuheng Li, and Yong Jae Lee. 2024a. Improved baselines with visual instruction tuning. In *Proceedings of the IEEE/CVF Conference on Computer Vision and Pattern Recognition*, pages 26296–26306.

Haotian Liu, Chunyuan Li, Qingyang Wu, and Yong Jae Lee. 2024b. Visual instruction tuning. *Advances in neural information processing systems*, 36.

Harsha Nori, Nicholas King, Scott Mayer McKinney, Dean Carignan, and Eric Horvitz. 2023a. Capabilities of gpt-4 on medical challenge problems. *arXiv preprint arXiv:2303.13375*.

Harsha Nori, Yin Tat Lee, Sheng Zhang, Dean Carignan, Richard Edgar, Nicolo Fusi, Nicholas King, Jonathan Larson, Yuanzhi Li, Weishung Liu, et al. 2023b. Can generalist foundation models outcompete special-purpose tuning? case study in medicine. *Medicine*, 84(88.3):77–3.

Shuyin Ouyang, Jie M Zhang, Mark Harman, and Meng Wang. 2023. Llm is like a box of chocolates: the non-determinism of chatgpt in code generation. *arXiv preprint arXiv:2308.02828*.

Fabian Pedregosa, Gaël Varoquaux, Alexandre Gramfort, Vincent Michel, Bertrand Thirion, Olivier Grisel, Mathieu Blondel, Peter Prettenhofer, Ron Weiss, Vincent Dubourg, et al. 2011. Scikit-learn: Machine learning in python. *the Journal of machine Learning research*, 12:2825–2830.

Roy H Perlis. 2023. Application of gpt-4 to select next-step antidepressant treatment in major depression. *MedRxiv*.

Yusu Qian, Haotian Zhang, Yinfei Yang, and Zhe Gan. 2024. How easy is it to fool your multimodal llms? an empirical analysis on deceptive prompts. *arXiv preprint arXiv:2402.13220*.

Alec Radford, Jeffrey Wu, Rewon Child, David Luan, Dario Amodei, Ilya Sutskever, et al. 2019. Language models are unsupervised multitask learners. *OpenAI blog*, 1(8):9.

Abel Salinas and Fred Morstatter. 2024. The butterfly effect of altering prompts: How small changes and jailbreaks affect large language model performance. *arXiv preprint arXiv:2401.03729*.

Saman Sarraf, Arman Sarraf, Danielle D DeSouza, John AE Anderson, Milton Kabia, and Alzheimer's Disease Neuroimaging Initiative. 2023. Ovitad: Optimized vision transformer to predict various stages of alzheimer's disease using resting-state fmri and structural mri data. *Brain Sciences*, 13(2):260.

Douglas W Scharre. 2019. Preclinical, prodromal, and dementia stages of alzheimer's disease. *Pract Neurol*, 15:36–47.

Melanie Sclar, Yejin Choi, Yulia Tsvetkov, and Alane Suhr. 2024. Quantifying language models' sensitivity to spurious features in prompt design or: How i learned to start worrying about prompt formatting. In *The Twelfth International Conference on Learning Representations (ICLR)*.

Zhengyan Sheng, Zhiqiang Guo, Xin Li, Yunxia Li, and Zhenhua Ling. 2022. Dementia detection by fusing speech and eye-tracking representation. In *ICASSP 2022-2022 IEEE International Conference on Acoustics, Speech and Signal Processing (ICASSP)*, pages 6457–6461. IEEE.

Sonish Sivarajkumar, Mark Kelley, Alyssa Samolyk-Mazzanti, Shyam Visweswaran, and Yanshan Wang. 2024. An empirical evaluation of prompting strategies for large language models in zero-shot clinical natural language processing: algorithm development and validation study. *JMIR Medical Informatics*, 12:e55318.

Yifan Song, Guoyin Wang, Sujian Li, and Bill Yuchen Lin. 2024. The good, the bad, and the greedy: Evaluation of llms should not ignore non-determinism. *arXiv preprint arXiv:2407.10457*.

Harshinee Sriram, Cristina Conati, and Thalia Field. 2023. Classification of alzheimer's disease with deep learning on eye-tracking data. In *Proceedings of the 25th International Conference on Multimodal Interaction*, pages 104–113.

Katherine Tian, Eric Mitchell, Allan Zhou, Archit Sharma, Rafael Rafailov, Huaxiu Yao, Chelsea Finn, and Christopher D Manning. 2023. Just ask for calibration: Strategies for eliciting calibrated confidence scores from language models fine-tuned with human feedback. In *Proceedings of the 2023 Conference on Empirical Methods in Natural Language Processing*, pages 5433–5442.

Zhuo Wang, Rongzhen Li, Bowen Dong, Jie Wang, Xiuxing Li, Ning Liu, Chenhui Mao, Wei Zhang, Liling Dong, Jing Gao, et al. 2023. Can llms like gpt-4 outperform traditional ai tools in dementia diagnosis? maybe, but not today. *arXiv preprint arXiv:2306.01499*.

Thomas Wolf, Lysandre Debut, Victor Sanh, Julien Chaumond, Clement Delangue, Anthony Moi, Pierric Cistac, Tim Rault, Rémi Louf, Morgan Funtowicz, et al. 2020. Transformers: State-of-the-art natural language processing. In *Proceedings of the 2020 conference on empirical methods in natural language processing: system demonstrations*, pages 38–45.

Kathryn M Yorkston and David R Beukelman. 1980. An analysis of connected speech samples of aphasic and normal speakers. *Journal of speech and hearing disorders*, 45(1):27–36.

Letian Zhang, Xiaotong Zhai, Zhongkai Zhao, Yongshuo Zong, Xin Wen, and Bingchen Zhao. 2024. What if the tv was off? examining counterfactual reasoning abilities of multi-modal language models. In *Proceedings of the IEEE/CVF Conference on Computer Vision and Pattern Recognition*, pages 21853–21862.

Appendix A Prompt Templates

We provide prompting templates used in Llama and LLaVA in Table 5 and Table 6, respectively.

Appendix B Supervised Classifiers

Following Jang et al. (2021), we reduplicate the supervised learning results using Logistic Regression (LR), Random Forest (RF), and Gaussian Naive Bayes (GNB), all implemented with Scikit-learn library (Pedregosa et al., 2011). We split the dataset into 10 folds with 10 different seeds for cross-validation. The micro-averaged scores are given in Table 4, in comparison with our best zero-shot and few-shot prompting strategies.

Note that noting that our results differ slightly from those reported in Jang et al. (2021), as we do not use the exact same training samples (79 Patients and 83 Controls *vs.* our dataset with 63 Patients and 67 Controls). Additionally, we employ different speech-to-text methods, which may have led to variations in the transcripts.

Training	Model	AUC	Sensitivity	Specificity
Supervised	GNB	72.8 ± 2.2	64.1 ± 2.2	66.5 ± 3.5
	LR	73.2 ± 1.7	68.5 ± 3.8	70.2 ± 1.6
	RF	75.2 ± 3.1	67.7 ± 4.6	73.1 ± 3.6
Ours (zero-shot)	Llama-3.1	76.1 ± 2.0	**71.8** ± 3.4	73.9 ± 2.1
Ours (few-shot)	Llama-3.1	**76.4** ± 2.9	71.7 ± 7.6	**75.8** ± 8.4

Table 4: Comparison of fully supervised classifiers (top) and our methods using LLMs (bottom). RF: random forest, GNB: Gaussian Naive Bayes, LR: logistic regression. Supervised results are averaged over 10-seed 10-fold cross-validation. Prompting results are averaged over 2-trial 3-run per setup.

Appendix C LLaVA Prompting Results

We report zero-shot and few-shot prompting results with LLaVA-NeXT-8B in Table 7. Textual prompts and hyper-parameters are the same as with Llama. Different from Llama, we do not observe a consistent improvement with more complete prompts. Plausibly, LLaVA is not capable of processing longer and more complex textual information. We also observe some *extreme* predictions where the model only predicts Patient or Control, as highlighted in pink in Table 7.

Appendix D LLaVA's Speech on Picture Description Task

We prompt LLaVA twenty times on picture description task. The instruction is provided in the same way as for human participants. We then use supervised classifiers to categorize its responses. Across all of LLaVA's outputs, the three classifiers consistently classify them as "Patient" with high probabilities: RF $> 60\%$, GNB $> 90\%$, and LR $> 80\%$. Two examples are given in Table 8.

Llama-3.1	
Strategy	Template
Background Prompt	`Role:` You are a medical expert in Alzheimer's disease. You analyze linguistic features in the patient's speech, such as lexical richness, syntactic complexity, grammatical correctness, information content, and semantic coherence. Based on the participant's speech, provide an initial diagnosis of dementia patient (P) and healthy control (H). `Context:` The Boston Cookie Theft picture description task is a well established speech assessment in Alzheimer's disease. During the task, participants are shown the picture and are asked to describe everything they see in the scene using as much time as they would like. Based on the participant's description, make a classification of dementia patient (P) versus healthy control (H). `Context+Role+Ling:` The Boston Cookie Theft picture description task is a well established speech assessment in Alzheimer's disease. During the task, participants are shown the picture and are asked to describe everything they see in the scene using as much time as they would like. The objects (also known as information units) in this picture includes: "cookie", "girl", "boy", "woman", "jar", "stool", "plate", "dishcloth", "water", "window", "cupboard", "curtain", "dishes", "sink". You are a medical expert in Alzheimer's disease. You analyze linguistic features in the patient's speech, such as lexical richness, syntactic complexity, grammatical correctness, information units, and semantic coherence. Based on the participant's description of the picture, provide an initial diagnosis of dementia patient (P) and healthy control (H).
Example Prompt	`Zero-shot: None` `Few-shot:` Example: ## Text: <text> ## Answer: healthy control (H). ## Text: <text> ## Answer: dementia patient (P).
Question Prompt	`Short:` Given the text below, classify the participant as a dementia patient (P) or healthy control (H). Please give an answer and a probability without explanation. `CoT:` Given the text below, classify the participant as a dementia patient (P) or healthy control (H). First explain step-by-step and then give a prediction with a probability. `G. CoT:` Given the text below, classify the participant as a dementia patient (P) or healthy control (H). Please first reason from the following perspectives: (1) Vocabulary richness: such as the usage of different words; (2) Syntactic complexity: such as the length of the sentence and the number of subordinate clauses; (3) Information content: whether the participant describe most of the information units in the picture; (4) Semantic coherence: such as the usage of connectives and the change in description from one information unit to another; (5) Fluency and repetitiveness: whether the text is fluent with less repetitive sentences. Based on your reasoning, please give a prediction and the corresponding probability.

Table 5: Prompting template used in Llama.

LLaVA-NeXT	
Strategy	Template
Background Prompt	 Role: This image is used for speech assessment in Alzheimer's disease. You are a medical expert in Alzheimer's disease. You analyze linguistic features in the patient's speech, such as lexical richness, syntactic complexity, grammatical correctness, information content, and semantic coherence. Based on the participant's speech, provide an initial diagnosis of dementia patient (P) and healthy control (H). Context: This image is used in Boston Cookie Theft picture description task, which is a well established speech assessment in Alzheimer's disease. During the task, participants are shown the picture and are asked to describe everything they see in the scene using as much time as they would like. Based on the participant's description, make a classification of dementia patient (P) versus healthy control (H). Context+Role+Ling: This image is used in Boston Cookie Theft picture description task, which is a well established speech assessment in Alzheimer's disease. During the task, participants are shown the picture and are asked to describe everything they see in the scene using as much time as they would like. The objects (also known as information units) in this picture includes: "cookie", "girl", "boy", "woman", "jar", "stool", "plate", "dishcloth", "water", "window", "cupboard", "curtain", "dishes", "sink". You are a medical expert in Alzheimer's disease. You analyze linguistic features in the patient's speech, such as lexical richness, syntactic complexity, grammatical correctness, information units, and semantic coherence. Based on the participant's description of the picture, provide an initial diagnosis of dementia patient (P) and healthy control (H).
Example Prompt	Zero-shot: None Few-shot: Example: ## Text: <text> ## Answer: healthy control (H). ## Text: <text> ## Answer: dementia patient (P).
Question Prompt	Short: Given the text below, classify the participant as a dementia patient (P) or healthy control (H). Please give an answer and a probability without explanation. CoT: Given the text below, classify the participant as a dementia patient (P) or healthy control (H). First explain step-by-step and then give a prediction with a probability. G. CoT: Given the text below, classify the participant as a dementia patient (P) or healthy control (H). Please first reason from the following perspectives: (1) Vocabulary richness: such as the usage of different words; (2) Syntactic complexity: such as the length of the sentence and the number of subordinate clauses; (3) Information content: whether the participant describe most of the information units in the picture; (4) Semantic coherence: such as the usage of connectives and the change in description from one information unit to another; (5) Fluency and repetitiveness: whether the text is fluent with less repetitive sentences. Based on your reasoning, please give a prediction and the corresponding probability.

Table 6: Prompting template used in LLaVA.

		Random Few-shot			kNN Few-shot			Zero-shot		
B prompt	Q prompt	AUC	Sensitivity	Specificity	AUC	Sensitivity	Specificity	AUC	Sensitivity	Specificity
Role	Short	67.1 ± 7.0	45.1 ± 9.7	85.8 ± 10.1	58.1 ± 0.0	76.2 ± 0.0	40.3 ± 0.0	57.4 ± 0.0	19.4 ± 0.0	92.3 ± 0.0
	CoT	62.4 ± 9.3	27.2 ± 16.2	90.8 ± 5.6	70.6 ± 1.0	81.0 ± 2.2	41.0 ± 1.1	49.2 ± 0.0	19.4 ± 0.0	92.3 ± 0.0
	G. CoT	54.9 ± 5.2	3.0 ± 7.1	100.0 ± 0.0	69.8 ± 1.3	81.8 ± 1.1	39.6 ± 1.1	58.9 ± 0.0	37.1 ± 0.0	72.3 ± 0.0
Context	Short	67.1 ± 7.0	54.3 ± 14.6	73.6 ± 12.5	67.3 ± 0.4	73.0 ± 0.0	57.5 ± 1.1	50.0 ± 0.0	100.0 ± 0.0	0.0 ± 0.0
	CoT	61.4 ± 7.3	32.4 ± 7.4	89.2 ± 6.1	64.9 ± 2.5	77.0 ± 3.4	47.1 ± 3.2	59.0 ± 0.0	14.5 ± 0.0	100.0 ± 0.0
	G. CoT	52.2 ± 1.8	3.2 ± 2.4	99.3 ± 1.6	65.1 ± 3.6	84.9 ± 1.1	29.9 ± 2.1	63.0 ± 0.0	66.1 ± 0.0	63.1 ± 0.0
Context	Short	63.4 ± 4.3	30.7 ± 13.9	89.6 ± 11.2	65.8 ± 0.0	74.6 ± 0.0	56.7 ± 2.1	60.9 ± 0.0	82.3 ± 0.0	38.5 ± 0.0
+Role	CoT	51.6 ± 11.1	19.3 ± 10.2	89.8 ± 8.8	65.1 ± 1.5	81.8 ± 1.1	35.1 ± 3.1	55.9 ± 0.0	33.9 ± 0.0	80.0 ± 0.0
+Ling	G. CoT	50.1 ± 4.7	3.2 ± 3.6	99.3 ± 1.6	69.4 ± 0.4	84.1 ± 2.2	35.8 ± 4.2	64.9 ± 0.0	30.7 ± 0.0	95.4 ± 0.0

Table 7: Random, *k*NN few-shot, and zero-shot prompting results with LLaVA. Random few-shot results are averaged from three sampling. Best AUC in random, *k*NN, and zero-shot sections is highlighted ; second best is underlined. *Extreme* prediction such as very high Sensitivity and very low Specificity (or reversely) is highlighted .

Picture Description Task on LLaVA-NeXT

`Prompt:` You will do a picture description task. You'll be shown a picture. Please describe everything you see going on in the picture.

`LLaVA:` The image appears to be a black and white line drawing depicting a domestic scene. There are four figures in the image, each outlined and shaded to suggest depth and form. The drawing style is simple and cartoonish, with no color or shading other than the outlines and the shading within the outlines. In the foreground, there is a woman standing in the kitchen, holding a pan. She seems to be engaged in cooking or preparing food. To her right, there is a child standing on a stool, reaching for something on a shelf. The child is wearing a short-sleeved shirt and shorts, and appears to be in the process of retrieving an item. In the background, there is another child standing on the floor, looking up at the woman. This child is also wearing a short-sleeved shirt and shorts, and seems to be observing the woman's actions. On the far right, there is a baby lying on a surface, possibly a bed or a couch, with a blanket or sheet covering them. The baby appears to be asleep or resting. The kitchen area includes a sink and a countertop with various items such as a bowl and a bottle. There is also a window with curtains, and a door that is partially open. The room has a simple, clean layout with minimal decoration. The overall scene suggests a domestic setting, possibly a family home, with the woman and children engaged in everyday activities.

`LLaVA:` The image appears to be a black and white line drawing depicting a domestic scene. There are four characters in the picture: 1. A woman standing in the center, holding a plate. She is wearing a dress and seems to be engaged in an activity related to food preparation or serving. 2. A child standing on a stool to the left of the woman, reaching for something on a shelf. The child is wearing a short-sleeved top and shorts. 3. Another child standing to the right of the woman, also reaching for something on a shelf. This child is wearing a long-sleeved top and shorts. 4. A baby lying on a surface to the right of the woman, seemingly asleep or resting. The setting appears to be a kitchen or a room with a counter and a sink. There is a window with curtains to the right, and a door to the left. On the counter, there are various items including what looks like a bowl and a jar. The overall scene suggests a family moment, possibly meal preparation or cleanup. The characters are drawn in a simple, cartoon-like style, which is common in educational materials or children's books.

Table 8: Two examples of LLaVA's generations on Cookie Theft task. The *hallucinated* context are marked in red.

Benchmarking IsiXhosa Automatic Speech Recognition and Machine Translation for Digital Health Provision

Abby Blocker,[1*] Francois Meyer,[1] Ahmed Biyabani,[2] Joyce Mwangama,[1] Mohammed Ishaaq Datay,[1] Bessie Malila[1]
[1]University of Cape Town, Cape Town, South Africa
[*]blcabb001@myuct.ac.za, {firstname.lastname}@uct.ac.za
[2]Carnegie Mellon University Africa, Kigali, Rwanda
ab3x@andrew.cmu.edu

Abstract

As digital health becomes more ubiquitous, people from different geographic regions are connected and there is thus a need for accurate language translation services. South Africa presents opportunity and need for digital health innovation, but implementing indigenous translation systems for digital health is difficult due to a lack of language resources. Understanding the accuracy of current models for use in medical translation of indigenous languages is crucial for designers looking to build quality digital health solutions. This paper presents a new dataset[1] with audio and text of primary health consultations for automatic speech recognition and machine translation in South African English and the indigenous South African language of isiXhosa. We then evaluate the performance of well-established pretrained models on this dataset. We found that isiXhosa had limited support in speech recognition models and showed high, variable character error rates for transcription (26-70%). For translation tasks, Google Cloud Translate and ChatGPT outperformed the other evaluated models, indicating large language models can have similar performance to dedicated machine translation models for low-resource language translation.

1 Introduction

Digital health has been recognized to improve access to healthcare services by decreasing wait times, improving care quality, and reducing cost (Erku et al., 2023; Caffery et al., 2016; Gentili et al., 2022). Many digital health initiatives have focused on improving access in under-resourced areas, which face some of the largest challenges in providing healthcare services (Maita et al., 2024). However, as patients in under-resourced areas are connected to healthcare providers in various locations, language barriers present a serious challenge to be considered.

In South Africa, 84.3% of the population is reliant public health facilities, many of which are under-resourced (Stats SA, 2023). There are 12 official languages of South Africa, with 9 of these being indigenous languages (Stats SA, 2022). Incorporating language translation services for the indigenous languages of South Africa within digital health solutions is not only helpful but necessary. However, there isn't a clear consensus on what the best available tools are for integrating translation services for digital health in South African languages.

The aim of this paper is to understand the performance of automatic speech recognition (ASR) and machine translation (MT) services by assessing currently available pretrained models on South African English and isiXhosa, a South African indigenous language. Our contributions include a new dataset, consisting of audio and text in South African English and isiXhosa to support further development and evaluation of ASR and MT models.[1] The results indicate that for ASR, error rates for South African English are comparable to human transcription; but, for isiXhosa, error rates are above an acceptable range, particularly for use in the medical field. For MT, large language models (LLMs) showed

[1] https://github.com/blocker-abby/xh-en-health-data/

Proceedings of the Second Workshop on Patient-Oriented Language Processing (CL4Health), pages 169–179
May 4, 2025

comparable results to dedicated MT models, and the commercially available models outperformed the open-source models evaluated.

2 Background and Related Works

2.1 ASR

A widely used open-source ASR model is Whisper, developed by OpenAI (Radford et al., 2022). Whisper supports ASR for South African English, but not isiXhosa. Whisper cites a 9.3% error rate for English, but English spoken with African accents showed lower accuracy rates (Afonja et al., 2024). Therefore, assessment of South African English accents specifically is necessary to verify these results, and particularly on health-domain-specific data. In addition to Whisper, the Massive Multilingual Speech (MMS) model is an open-source ASR model developed by Meta, which supports South African English and isiXhosa. Pratap et al. (2023) demonstrated that MMS had higher accuracy when compared to Google and Whisper when using the FLEURS dataset (which includes isiXhosa data).

In addition to open-source models, there are several successful commercial models for ASR. Particularly, the leaders in commercial cloud computing offer ASR APIs, these being Google Cloud Platform (GCP), Microsoft Azure, and Amazon Web Services (AWS) (Borra, 2024). Out of these, only GCP offers ASR for isiXhosa. These commercially available models have been cited to have better performance for ASR when compared to open-source models (Ferraro et al., 2023).

2.2 Translation

In the translation domain, the development of massive multilingual neural machine translation (NMT) models has contributed to improved translation of low-resource languages like isiXhosa. Meta's No Language Left Behind (NLLB) is an open-source NMT model which provides translation for 200 languages, many of which are low-resource (Costa-jussà et al., 2022). In the commercial translation space, GCP, Azure, and AWS all offer translation APIs. Two of these (GCP and Azure) offer services for isiXhosa translation. Open source and commercial models have been cited to have similar performance in the translation domain (Licht et al., 2024).

Current research has investigated the use of LLMs such as ChatGPT for translation tasks. Some research has found that they have high accuracy in comparison to NMTs (Wang et al., 2023). However, experiments with low-resource and African languages (of which isiXhosa is both) have shown results that still lag behind dedicated MT models like NLLB (Robinson et al., 2023; Ojo et al., 2024).

2.3 Healthcare Applications

ASR and MT in the healthcare sector is a debated topic. Accuracy in healthcare communication is vital, as miscommunication has the potential to drastically affect medical decisions and could lead to negative outcomes. Some healthcare bodies recommend against these techniques because of the risk (Vieira et al., 2019). However, when used responsibly, ASR and MT services can provide benefits in environments where human translation services cannot be provided, either due to resource constraints or lack of expertise. Recommendations for healthcare providers using these services include being aware of the potential errors, being alert to non-verbal communication from the patient, and for translation, back-translating (inputting translated materials into the MT model for translation back into the source language) to analyze where errors may have occurred (Randhawa et al., 2013). Therefore, it is important to understand the current state of ASR and MT, in order to apply it to digital health solutions safely.

Understanding the development context is also important in determining the best-fit ASR and MT models for digital health applications. While accuracy is extremely important, there are other additional factors which can influence the uptake of solutions. The mobile application AwezaMed provides an example of this. The app provides translation of medical text for all South African languages using a list of predefined phrases (Marais et al., 2020). While there are benefits to the accuracy of using static translations, including the ability for human validation, there are also difficulties in that real-time and customized translation is not possible. In a real-time digital health application such as telemedicine, this solution may not address the needs of users; therefore, it is important to consider other factors along with accuracy to select the most appropriate translation models for digital health solutions.

3 Method

3.1 Data

Conversations between primary health care providers and patients were used as evaluation data. Conversation data was adapted from the PriMock57 dataset (Korfiatis et al., 2022), which provides audio and transcribed conversational data from mock telemedicine consultations. Ten random consultations were chosen from the available dataset of 57. The text data from each consult was then translated by a professional human translator with experience in English-isiXhosa medical translation.

While audio files of the consultations were available in the PriMock57 dataset, the speakers were not South African. As spoken accents can affect the accuracy of ASR models, it was important to utilize authentic audio of South African English speakers. Therefore, the conversations were re-enacted between South African paid actors. A total of 5 actors (3 male, 2 female) were used, with two actors (one acting as the doctor, and one acting as the patient) per consultation. Two of the three male actors were included only in South African English recordings. The other male actor was included only in the isiXhosa recordings. The two female actors were included in both South African English and isiXhosa recordings. Each of the actors were fluent in the languages they recorded in. The actors read the consultation dialogue exactly as it was stated in the written text. Where speaking errors were made, this was cleaned in post-processing of the audio file using Audacity.[2] Audio was saved as a stereo, 48kHz sampled FLAC file. Azure speech-to-text and MMS required a 16kHz sample WAV file input, so the audio was also converted to this format during evaluation of both models.

Text data of the conversations was subdivided based on conversational dialogues. Each time the speaker changed, the text data was separated into a new text for evaluation. This resulted in a total of 580 English texts and 580 isiXhosa texts. Each text was input into each model once and the first output result was used for evaluation.

3.2 Selected ASR Models

The chosen models for evaluation are highlighted in Table 1. The chosen models for ASR of South African English were Google Cloud Speech-to-Text v1,[3] Microsoft Azure AI Speech's speech-to-text,[4] Whisper base model (Radford et al., 2022), and MMS speech-to-text (Pratap et al., 2023). Not all of the four chosen models offered isiXhosa services; those that did were Google Cloud Speech-to-Text v1 and MMS speech-to-text.

Whisper allowed for prompting capabilities, while the other ASR models did not. When providing an audio file input to Whisper, it is recommended to also provide a list of expected words to improve accuracy. The model was evaluated both with and without using this prompting feature. The expected terms used for

Automatic Speech Recognition			
Model	**Developer**	**Availability**	**Supported Language**
Google Cloud Speech-to-Text v1	Google	Commercial	en, xh
Azure AI Speech speech-to-text	Microsoft	Commercial	en
Whisper base	OpenAI	Open Source	en
MMS	Facebook	Open Source	en, xh

Machine Translation			
Model	**Developer**	**Availability**	**Type**
Google Cloud Translate v2	Google	Commercial	Dedicated MT
Azure Translator	Microsoft	Commercial	Dedicated MT
NLLB 200M distilled 600M	Facebook	Open Source	Dedicated MT
ChatGPT GPT-4o	OpenAI	Commercial	LLM
Gemini Flash 1.5	Google	Commercial	LLM

Table 1: Selected Models for Evaluation

[2] https://www.audacityteam.org/

[3] https://cloud.google.com/speech-to-text?hl=en

[4] https://learn.microsoft.com/en-us/azure/ai-services/speech-service/speech-to-text

prompting were selected from the South African Department of Sport, Arts, and Culture's medical terms list.[5] This document translates medical terms into 10 of the 12 South African languages. The list was reduced to include only terms contained within the dataset, which totaled 39 unique English terms and 56 unique isiXhosa terms (given that some of the terms had multiple translations). Then, for each transcription, only the terms from the list included within the ground truth were included in the prompt input.

3.3 Selected MT Models

The chosen models for translation, featured in Table 1, were Google Cloud Translate v2,[6] Microsoft Azure Translator,[7] NLLB-200 distilled 600M (Costa-jussà et al., 2022), ChatGPT GPT-4o mini, and Gemini Flash 1.5.[8]

Given that ChatGPT and Gemini are LLMs, they require a prompt input to provide instructions rather than only the text to be evaluated. A modified prompt used by Robinson et al. (2023) was used for LLM translation, which was the following: **"This is an [*source language*] to [*target language*] translation, please provide the [*target language*] translation for this sentence. Do not provide any explanations or text apart from the translation. [*Translation text*]."** In addition to this prompt, a modified prompt was also tested by providing language pairs in English and isiXhosa. The language pairs were selected from the medical terms list translations, with only the terms in the input text being included in the prompt. This modified prompt added the following text before supplying the text to be translated: **"In this context, [*source language term*] translates to [*target language term*]."**

3.4 Evaluation Metrics

Two metrics were employed for evaluating ASR, as English and isiXhosa languages have different characteristics which are better explained by different methodologies. The standard measure for ASR evaluation is word error rate (WER). However, WER does not fully characterize ASR results for agglutinative languages such as isiXhosa (Thennal et al., 2024). This is because words in isiXhosa have prefixes and suffixes that often correspond to individual words in English. Therefore, WER may incorrectly inflate the error rate of ASR for isiXhosa in comparison to English. To address this, both WER and character error rate (CER) were calculated for isiXhosa transcriptions. Both metrics were calculated using the HuggingFace evaluate library (Von Werra et al., 2022).

For translation, character level F-score (CHRF++) and bilingual evaluation understudy (BLEU) were used to evaluate model performance (Callison-Burch et al., 2007). The original and human-translated texts were used as ground truth comparisons. To address the agglutinative structure of isiXhosa, CHRF++ was chosen as it accounts for both character and word accuracy (Popović, 2015).

Because the analysis aimed to understand model performance on health domain data, an analysis was also conducted on the error rate of models in transcribing and translating health terms. It is critical that this terminology be transcribed and translated correctly, as it has the potential to affect medical decision-making. Results were analyzed based on the list of health terms used for modified prompting. Error rate was calculated by dividing the occurrences of each health term in the resultant text by the occurrences in the ground truth text and subtracting from 100. Furthermore, because some health terms had multiple translations from English to isiXhosa, any of the isiXhosa translations were accepted for the accuracy measure. The type of isiXhosa translation used in the result was also noted and categorized into one of three types: an isiXhosa term; a borrowed English word with isiXhosa spelling; or a borrowed English word with English spelling. Additionally, all health terms in both languages were classified into the following three categories: anatomy; condition; or treatment.

The average costs for transcription and translation were calculated using available pricing for commercial MT models. For LLMs, tokens used per character were calculated for each prompt and then converted to price per character based on the model pricing. Open source models were not

[5] https://www.dsac.gov.za/sites/default/files/2023-11/Multilingual%20Pharmaceutical%20Terminology%20List_0.pdf

[6] https://cloud.google.com/dotnet/docs/reference/Google.Cloud.Translation.V2/latest

[7] https://azure.microsoft.com/en-us/products/ai-services/ai-translator

[8] https://ai.google.dev/gemini-api/docs/models/gemini#gemini-1.5-flash

included in the cost analysis, although it is acknowledged that running open-source models on local machines does incur associated costs.

From the results, models which showed appropriate accuracies for digital health systems were implemented into an existing virtual clinic system web application (Blocker et al., 2024). The system involved ASR for South African English and translation of English and isiXhosa text. The system takes user input (either audio or text) and sends a request to the backend with the data. The backend then either processes the data (in the case of open-source models) or creates an additional request and sends the data to the cloud computing service (for commercial models). When the response is received, it is returned to the front-end and displayed for the user. The time taken for each model to return a text response to the front end was measured in milliseconds for each model. For commercial implementations (Azure and GCP), real-time translation methods were utilized instead of batch translations.

4 Results

4.1 ASR Model Error Rates

Figure 1 presents the WER of South African English. Lower WER indicates higher accuracy of the ASR model. The lowest WERs for South African English were achieved by Whisper with prompting (7.1%) and Azure (7.6%). "Quick" human transcription of conversational speech has been cited with a WER of 9.6% (Stolcke & Droppo, 2017), indicating that the results from these models concur with human transcription. There was a 4.5% difference in WER between using Whisper with and without prompts. Similar prompting techniques were attempted with GCP and Azure ASR models using phrase lists; however, both models produced identical transcriptions regardless of whether phrase lists were employed. Results for South African English ASR by GCP ranged from 17.33-25.34%, which agrees with the literature range of approximately 15-25% WER (Filippidou & Moussiades, 2020). Results for Whisper (without prompting) were slightly higher than the cited metric of 9.3% for English (Radford et al., 2022); however, this reported value was for general English (en), not South African English (en-za).

Figure 2 presents the measured WER and CER for isiXhosa transcription. WER for both GCP and MMS were greater than human WER. CER as an evaluation metric for ASR is less common than WER, therefore there is not a generally accepted human error rate for comparison. However, ASR models in literature for isiXhosa transcription report CER values ranging from 13.8-40.7% (Reitmaier et al., 2022; Jacobs et al., 2025; Baas & Kamper, 2022). GCP and MMS had averages of 43.7% and 51.4% CER respectively. These results are higher than those reported in literature, which highlights the challenge encountered in translating health-domain-specific conversations. The range of results is much wider than that seen for South African English, with a 45% difference between the lowest and highest error rate for isiXhosa. Given that the human WER is 9.3%, and CER

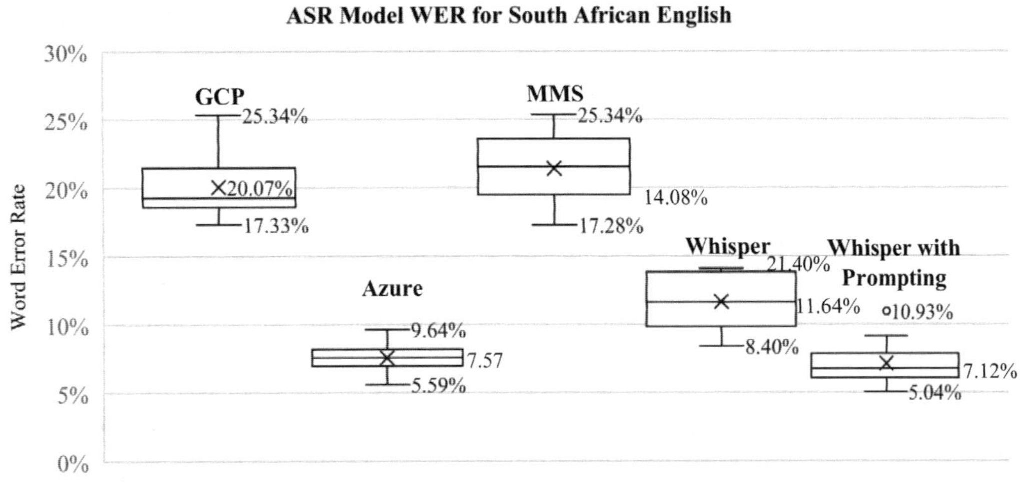

Figure 1: Measured WER for transcription of South African English

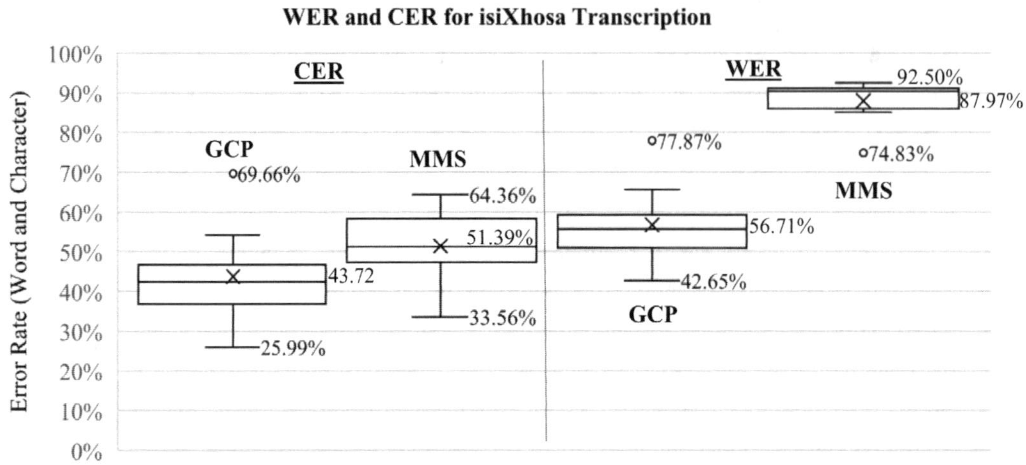

Figure 2: Measured WER and CER for transcription of isiXhosa.

tends to be lower than WER (Ravanelli et al., 2024), this indicates that neither model performed adequately for isiXhosa ASR.

Performance of commercial versus open-source models did not follow a clear trend. Both Whisper (open-source) and Azure (commercial) achieved low WERs for South African English, while GCP (commercial) and MMS (open-source) had higher error rates for both South African English and isiXhosa.

ASR model results were also assessed for health term error rate, both generally and within the three categories – anatomy, condition, or treatment. Results for health term error rate are provided in Table 2. For transcription of South African English, Whisper with prompting had the lowest health term error rate at 5.39%, followed by Azure with 9.47%. Whisper had a 10.21% decrease in error rate when health terms were introduced into the prompt. For isiXhosa transcription, GCP had lower error rate than MMS. Treatment terms, which mainly consisted of medication names (Paracetamol, Ibuprofen, Metformin, etc.) had high error rates when transcribed from isiXhosa audio. For both South African English and isiXhosa, MMS had high error rate in transcribing treatment terms; this could be due to the nature of the training dataset used for MMS, which was domain-specific and not general. Overall, the models evaluated had acceptable performance for transcribing medical conversations in South African English, but struggled in transcribing isiXhosa medical conversations.

4.2 Translation Model Results

Table 3 provides CHRF++ and BLEU results for MT. Higher scores for both metrics indicate that predicted translations are closer to the ground truth translations. For English to isiXhosa, Google Cloud Translate reported the highest scores,

	South African English			
Model	**Overall**	**Anatomy**	**Conditions**	**Treatment**
GCP	26.02%	20.9%	39.18%	19.01%
Azure	9.47%	4.70%	18.71%	9.63%
MMS	50.34%	26.07%	77.00%	96.30%
Whisper	15.6%	8.12%	19.21%	40.00%
Whisper with prompting	**5.39%**	**2.99%**	**12.50%**	**0.00%**

	isiXhosa			
Model	**Overall**	**Anatomy**	**Conditions**	**Treatment**
GCP	**58.84%**	**38.98%**	**78.65%**	**96.67%**
MMS	76.27%	67.73%	81.92%	100.00%

Table 2: Error rate for ASR of health terms.

Model	CHRF++ Score		BLEU Score	
	English to isiXhosa	isiXhosa to English	English to isiXhosa	isiXhosa to English
Google Cloud Translate	**63.79**	57.23	**0.284**	**0.286**
Azure	56.31	53.56	0.168	0.233
NLLB	48.39	50.84	0.081	0.213
ChatGPT	51.91	**57.64**	0.115	0.270
ChatGPT (mod)	52.38	57.59	0.114	0.267
Gemini	48.50	54.64	0.074	0.245
Gemini (mod)	48.75	54.93	0.075	0.248

Table 3: CHRF++ and BLEU scores for translation between English and isiXhosa.

comfortably outperforming all other models. NLLB, Gemini, and Gemini with modified prompting had the lowest scores, with a difference of 16.15 between highest and lowest average score. For isiXhosa to English, the performance was less distributed, with the difference between highest and lowest scores at 6.8. ChatGPT and Google Cloud Translate were the highest scoring models, and NLLB the lowest scoring model.

The only open-source translation-dedicated model tested, NLLB, had generally lower scores than the commercial models evaluated. In comparing translation-dedicated models to LLMs, ChatGPT had higher scores when compared to Azure and NLLB, for translation of isiXhosa to English, but this did not carry over to English to isiXhosa translation. Between LLMs, ChatGPT had higher scores than Gemini. Modified prompting did not have a significant effect on the overall score.

Health term error rate was also calculated for translation results, with lower error rates indicating more accurate translations of health terms. Health term error rate decreased when using modified prompts with both ChatGPT and Gemini LLMs, as shown in Table 4. Google Cloud Translate had the lowest error rate of all evaluated models for English to isiXhosa translation, with a 10% difference in error rates between the next best performing model, Azure. This is in contrast to isiXhosa to English translation, where the top 4 performing models in terms of health term accuracy (ChatGPT, ChatGPT with modified prompts, Gemini with modified prompts, and Google Cloud Translate) were within 5% error rate of one another. Generally, health term accuracy

	isiXhosa to English			
Model	**Overall**	**Anatomy**	**Condition**	**Treatment**
ChatGPT	16.61%	14.13%	32.14%	**0.00%**
ChatGPT with modified prompt	**11.82%**	**10.87%**	20.71%	**0.00%**
Gemini	25.51%	26.09%	37.86%	**0.00%**
Gemini with modified prompt	13.18%	14.13%	**15.00%**	5.26%
Google Cloud Translate	14.44%	11.23%	30.71%	**0.00%**
Azure	20.55%	11.96%	54.29%	**0.00%**
NLLB	36.47%	23.91%	71.43%	32.89%

	English to isiXhosa			
Model	**Overall**	**Anatomy**	**Condition**	**Treatment**
ChatGPT	49.14%	43.50%	78.86%	18.18%
ChatGPT with modified prompt	38.14%	32.55%	64.13%	17.39%
Gemini	62.32%	59.67%	93.48%	13.64%
Gemini with modified prompt	55.17%	51.17%	82.98%	18.18%
Google Cloud Translate	**18.99%**	**14.91%**	**38.04%**	**4.55%**
Azure	29.25%	23.04%	58.70%	**4.55%**
NLLB	58.91%	50.60%	87.68%	46.36%

Table 4: Health term error rate for translations.

was lower for translations from English to isiXhosa compared to isiXhosa to English.

The error rate for each health term category is also depicted in Table 4. Treatments (which mainly consisted of medications) had low error rates, with <10% error rate for isiXhosa to English translation for all models excluding NLLB. Highest error rates were seen with the translation of conditions from English to isiXhosa. This included terms for both diseases (i.e. diabetes, asthma, stroke) and symptoms (i.e. cough, headache, pain). For all models, translation from isiXhosa to English had lower health term error rates (for all term classifications) than translation from English to isiXhosa. IsiXhosa health terms were categorized further into three types – borrowed English terms with English spelling (i.e., i-Paracetamol, meaning Paracetamol); borrowed English terms with isiXhosa spelling (i.e., ifiva, meaning fever) and isiXhosa terms (i.e., isisu, meaning stomach). Borrowed English words with isiXhosa spelling were not used frequently by any of the models; both borrowed English terms with English spelling and isiXhosa words were used more frequently.

4.3 Cost

There are other factors besides accuracy that one might consider when choosing systems for ASR and MT. Particularly when considering commercial solutions, cost is an important factor.

	ASR (per minute)
Model	**Cost**
GCP	Tiered pricing ranging from $0.016-$0.004 per minute
Azure	$0.01667 per minute with 5 hours per month free
Whisper	Associated computing costs
MMS	Associated computing costs

Translation (per million characters translated)	
Model	**Cost**
GCP	$20 (first 500k characters per month free)
Azure	$10 (first 2M characters per month free)
NLLB	Associated computing costs
ChatGPT 4o mini	$1.84
Gemini 1.5 Flash	$0

Table 5: Pricing of evaluated models.

Table 5 compares the cost of the various models evaluated. For ASR, GCP and Azure have similar costs, with GCP offering slightly lower rates for higher volumes of audio. Whisper is unique in that it is open source, so it can be run on a local machine or accessed through OpenAI's API. Running Whisper or MMS (open source) models on a local machine would incur costs for electricity and hardware. For MT, GCP and Azure can provide translation free of cost for low volumes of data (<500k and <2M characters, respectively). However, for larger volumes of translation, ChatGPT 4o mini provides a cheaper per-character rate at only $1.84 per million characters. Gemini 1.5 Flash is free to use, offering the cheapest commercial option for translation.

4.4 Latency

The South African English ASR models (excluding MMS) and the four commercial translation models were implemented in the system as part of a language translation feature. Figures 3 and 4 depict the measured latencies when using each model in the end-to-end translation system. Microsoft Azure offered the lowest latencies for both ASR and MT compared to the other evaluated models, though occasionally latency could be over 10 seconds for transcribing long audio clips. ASR latency was much higher than MT, but likely because there was some post-processing formatting that occurred before transcription. Additionally, requests with text data are smaller in size than their audio data counterparts, so sending a larger request over the network incurs greater time.

5 Discussion and Conclusion

Based on the evaluation performed, we found that Microsoft Azure provided the best performance for ASR of South African English, and Whisper provided a viable open source alternative. Whisper's performance can likely be attributed to its diverse training dataset, whereas the domain-specific nature of the MMS training dataset limited its performance in the health domain, and with varied speakers. For isiXhosa ASR, GCP and MMS did not provide low enough error rates to be considered reliable. IsiXhosa ASR models also demonstrated high error rates for health terms, particularly for treatment terms (medications). This highlights the existing inequality between high- and low-resource languages, which in the health context may exacerbate the gap between high- and

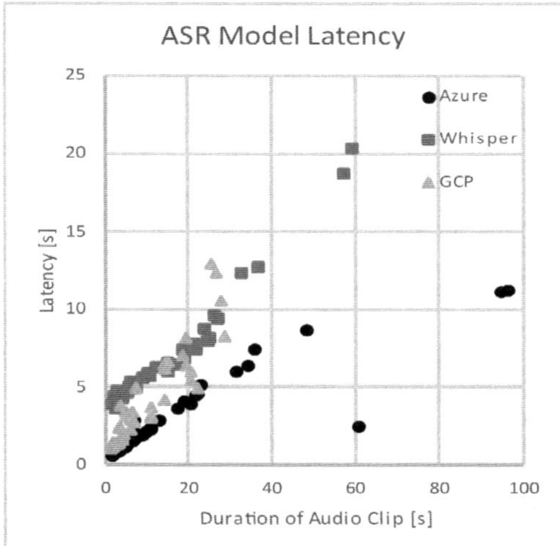

Figure 3: Measured latencies for Azure, GCP, and Whisper for South African English.

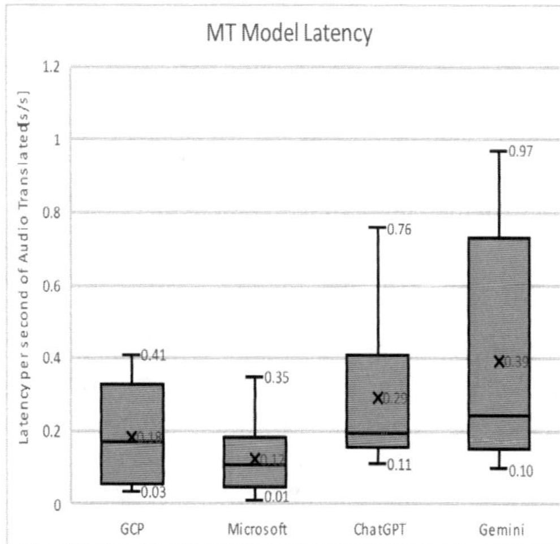

Figure 4: Measured latencies for GCP, Azure, ChatGPT, and Gemini for translating text.

low-resource medical care. If digital health developers must incorporate these models, then they should do so cautiously and with human input to validate results.

For MT, Google Cloud Translate provided the most accurate translations in both directions. However, ChatGPT provided a viable alternative for isiXhosa to English translation. When possible, dictionaries should be incorporated within prompts to further improve performance of LLMs, particularly verified dictionaries of health terms. Translation of health terms had low error rate, particularly for treatment terms as generally these words are kept the same throughout translation. Condition terms such as headache, nausea, and diabetes should be paid specific attention when translated to and from isiXhosa; these may not follow a typical "one-to-one" translation structure and therefore should be approached with caution and verified by humans during medical translation.

There are various advantages and disadvantages when comparing commercial and open-source models for ASR and MT. Open-source models provide a greater level of transparency, which provides greater opportunity for customization and development. Additionally, it allows developers to have more control over the privacy and security of their data. Given that medical transcriptions and translations may hold sensitive information about patients, this is an important factor to consider. However, not every digital health system has the capability to run large ASR or MT models. MMS and NLLB require high levels of computational power to run, which may not be feasible or necessary for small-scale applications. Latency should also be considered, especially in mission critical environments like trauma or emergency medicine. Open source models may experience latency depending on the hardware specifications used to run the models. Commercial options like GCP and Azure are susceptible to service outages an d slower response times depending on the traffic and conditions of their servers. Ultimately, one must consider the context of the digital health solution to select the best models for building a digital health translation system.

Future work may focus on expanding the dataset to incorporate more medical conversation audio and text. This would be beneficial to validate the results achieved here. Additionally, this data could be used to improve and customize models for isiXhosa and for healthcare contexts. Further research might also follow similar methods to the health term analysis described here, to evaluate for age- or gender-related terminology accuracy. Developers may also take this work forward to make evidence-based decisions on ASR and MT models for digital health applications.

Limitations

A limitation of this research is that results were not validated by human evaluators. An evaluation of how the meaning of each result correlates to the meaning of ground truth statements would provide further valuable insights into the accuracy of these models. Additionally, the data published with this work contributes to the resources available for isiXhosa language applications, but is not enough standalone data to train a domain-specific ASR and MT for health. Finally, because commercial enterprises such as Google and Azure are constantly improving their services, the more recently released models may return different results than those reported on in this paper.

Ethical Considerations

This work provides an overview of the current capabilities of ASR and MT models for isiXhosa. The authors do not provide commentary on whether the results indicate a maturity level that is ready for deployment within the healthcare sector. Rather, we provide benchmarks so developers can make educated decisions regarding ASR and MT model incorporation within digital health systems.

Acknowledgements

This document has been produced with the financial assistance of the European Union (Grant no. DCIPANAF/2020/420-028), through the African Research Initiative for Scientific Excellence (ARISE), pilot programme. ARISE is implemented by the African Academy of Sciences with support from the European Commission and the African Union Commission. The contents of this document are the sole responsibility of the author(s) and can under no circumstances be regarded as reflecting the position of the European Union, the African Academy of Sciences, and the African Union Commission.

References

Tejumade Afonja, Tobi Olatunji, Sewade Ogun, Naome A. Etori, Abraham Owodunni, and Moshood Yekini. 2024. Performant ASR models for medical entities in accented speech. arXiv:2406.12387 [eess.AS]. Version 1.

Matthew Baas and Herman Kamper. 2021. Voice conversion can improve ASR in very low-resource settings. arXiv:2111.02674 [eess.AS]. Version 2.

Abby Blocker, Mohammed I. Datay, Joyce Mwangama, Bessie Malila. 2024. Development of a telemedicine virtual clinic system for remote, rural, and underserved areas using user-centered design methods. *Digital Health*, 10:20552076241256752.

Praveen Borra. 2024. Comparison and analysis of leading cloud service providers (AWS, Azure, and GCP). *International Journal of Advanced Research in Engineering & Technology*, 15(3):266-278.

Liam J. Caffery, Mutaz Farjian, and Anthony C. Smith. 2016. Telehealth interventions for reducing waiting lists and waiting times for specialist outpatient services: a scoping review. *Journal of Telemedicine and Telecare*, 22(8):504-512.

Chris Callison-Burch, Cameron Fordyce, Philipp Koehn, Christof Monz, and Josh Schroeder. 2007. (Meta-) evaluation of machine translation. In *Proceedings of the Second Workshop on Statistical Machine Translation*, pages 136-158, Prague, Czech Republic.

Marta R. Costa-jussà, James Cross, Onur Çelebi, Maha Elbayad, Kenneth Heafield, Kevin Heffernan, Elahe Kalbassi, Janice Lam, Daniel Licht, Jean Maillard, Anna Sun, Skyler Wang, Guillaume Wenzek, Al Youngblood, Bapi Akula, Loic Barrault, Gabriel Mejia Gonzalez, Prangthip Hansanti, John Hoffman, Semarley Jarrett, Kaushik Ram Sadagopan, Dirk Rowe, Shannon Spruit, Chau Tran, Pierre Andrews, Necip Fazil Ayan, Shruti Bhosale, Sergey Edunov, Angela Fan, Cynthia Gao, Vedanuj Goswami, Francisco Guzmán, Philipp Koehn, Alexandre Mourachko, Christophe Ropers, Safiyyah Saleem, Holger Schwenk, and Jeff Wang. 2022. No language left behind: scaling human-centered machine translation. arXiv:2207.04672 [cs.CL]. Version 3.

Daniel Erku, Resham Khatri, Aklilu Endalamaw, Eskinder Wolka, Frehiwot Nigatu, Anteneh Zewdie, and Yibeltal Assefa. 2023. Digital health interventions to improve access to and quality of primary health care services: a scoping review. *International Journal of Environmental Research and Public Health*, 20(19):6854.

Antonino Ferraro, Antonio Galli, Valerio La Gatta, and Marco Postiglione. 2023. Benchmarking open source and paid services for speech to text: an analysis of quality and input variety. *Frontiers in Big Data*, 6:1210559.

Foteini Filippidou and Lefteris Moussiades. 2020. A benchmarking of IBM, Google, and Wit automatic speech recognition systems. *Artificial Intelligence Applications and Innovations AIAI 2020, IFIP Advances in Information and Communication Technology*, 583:73-82.

Andrea Gentili, Giovanna Failla, Andriy Melnyk, Valeria Puleo, Gian Luca Di Tanna, Walter Ricciardi, and Fidelia Cascini. 2022. The cost-effectiveness of digital health interventions: A systematic review of the literature. *Frontiers in Public Health*, 20:787135.

Christiaan Jacobs, Annelien Smith, Daleen Klop, Ondřej Klejch, Febe de Wet, and Herman Kamper. 2025. Speech recognition for automatically assessing Afrikaans and isiXhosa preschool oral narratives. arXiv:2501.06478 [eess.AS]. Version 1.

Alex Papadopoulos Korfiatis, Francesco Moramarco, Radmila Sarac, and Aleksandar Savkov. 2022. PriMock57: a dataset of primary care mock consultations. arXiv:2204.00333[cs.CL]. Version 1.

Hauke Licht, Ronja Sczepanski, Moritz Laurer, and Ayjeren Bekmuratovna. 2024. No more cost in translation: validating open-source machine translation for quantitative text analysis. In *ECONtribute Discussion Papers, Reinhard Selten Institute (RSI)*, 276.

Karla C. Maita, Michael J. Maniaci, Clifton R. Haider, Francisco R. Avila, Ricardo A. Torres-Guzman, Sahar Borna, Julianne J. Lunde, Jordan D. Coffey, Bart M. Demaerschalk, and Antonio Jorge Forte. 2024. The impact of digital health solutions on bridging the health care gap in rural areas: a scoping review. *The Permanente Journal*, 28(3):130-143.

Laurette Marais, Johannes A. Louw, Jaco Badenhorst, Karen Calteaux, Ilana Wilken, and Nina van Niekerk. 2020. AwezaMed: A multilingual, multimodal speech-to-speech translation application for maternal health care. In *Proceedings of 2020 IEEE 23rd International Conference on Information Fusion (FUSION)*, Rustenburg, South Africa.

Jessica Ojo, Kelechi Ogueji, Pontus Stenetorp, and David Ifeoluwa Adelani. 2024. How good are large language models for African languages? arXiv:2311.07978 [cs.CL]. Version 2.

Maja Popović. 2015. chrF: character n-gram F-score for automatic MT evaluation. In *Proceedings of the Tenth Workshop on Statistical Machine Translation*, pages 392-395, Lisbon, Portugal.

Vineel Pratap, Andros Tjandra, Bowen Shi, Paden Tomasello, Arun Babu, Sayani Kundu, Ali Elkahky, Zhaoheng Ni, Apoorv Vyas, Maryam Fazel-Zarandi, Alexei Baevski, Yossi Adi, Xiaohui Zhang, Wei-Ning Hsu, Alexis Conneau, and Michael Auli. 2023. Scaling speech technology to 1000+ languages. arXiv:2305.13516 [cs.CL]. Version 1.

Alec Radford, Jong Wook Kim, Tao Xu, Greg Brockman, Christine McLeavey, and Ilya Sutskever. 2022. Robust speech recognition via large-scale weak supervision. arXiv:2212.04356 [eess.AS]. Version 1.

Gurdeeshpal Randhawa, Mariella Ferreyra, Rukhsana Ahmed, Omar Ezzat and Kevin Pottie. 2013. Using machine translation in clinical practice. *Canadian Family Physician*, 59(4):382-383.

Mirco Ravanelli, Titouan Parcollet, Adel Moumen, Sylvain de Langen, Cem Subakan, Peter Plantinga, Yingzhi Wang, Pooneh Mousavi, Luca Della Libera, Artem Ploujnikov, Francesco Paissan, Davide Borra, Salah Zaiem, Zeyu Zhao, Shucong Zhang, Georgios Karakasidis, Sung-Lin Yeh, Pierre Champion, Aku Rouhe, Rudolf Braun, Florian Mai, Juan Zuluaga-Gomez, Seyed Mahed Mousavi, Andreas Nautsch, Ha Nguyen, Xuechen Liu, Sangeet Sagar, Jarod Duret, Salima Mdhaffar, Gaelle Laperriere, Mickael Rouvier, Renato De Mori, and Yannick Esteve. 2024. Open-source conversational AI with SpeechBrain 1.0. arXiv:2407.00463 [cs.LG]. Version 5.

Thomas Reitmaier, Electra Wallington, Dani Kalarikalayil Raju, Ondrej Klejch, Jennifer Pearson, Matt Jones, Peter Bell, and Simon Robinson. 2022. Opportunities and challenges of automatic speech recognition systems for low-resource language speakers. In *Proceedings of the 2022 CHI Conference on Human Factors in Computing Systems*, 299:1-17.

Nathaniel R. Robinson, Perez Ogayo, David R. Mortensen, and Graham Neubig. 2023. ChatGPT MT: competitive for high- (but not low-) resource languages. arXiv:2309.07423 [cs.CL]. Version 1.

Stats SA. 2023. *General Household Survey 2023*. Statistics South Africa Department, Republic of South Africa, Private Bag X44, Pretoria, 0001, South Africa.

Stats SA. 2022. *Census 2022*. Statistics South Africa Department, Republic of South Africa, Private Bag X44, Pretoria, 0001, South Africa.

Andreas Stolcke and Jasha Droppo. 2017. Comparing human and machine errors in conversational speech transcription. arXiv:1708.08615 [cs.CL]. Version 1.

Thennal D. K., Jesin James, Deepa P. Gopinath, and Muhammed Ashraf K. (2024). Advocating character error rate for multilingual ASR evaluation. arXiv:2410.07400 [cs.CL]. Version 2.

Lucas Nunes Vieria, Minako O'Hagan, and Carol O'Sullivan. 2020. Understanding the societal impacts of machine translation: a critical review of the literature on medical and legal use cases. *Information, Communication, and Society*, 24(11):1515-1532.

Leandro Von Werra, Lewis Tunstall, Abhishek Thakur, Sasha Luccioni, Tristan Thrush, Aleksandra Piktus, Felix Marty, Nazneen Rajani, Victor Mustar, and Helen Ngo. 2022. Evaluate & evaluation on the Hub: better best practices for data and model measurements. In *Proceedings of the 2022 Conference on Empirical Methods in Natural Language Processing: System Demonstrations*, pages 128-136, Abu Dhabi, UAE.

Longyue Wang, Chenyang Lyu, Tianbo Ji, Zhirui Zhang, Dian Yu, Shuming Shi, and Zhaopeng Tu. 2023. Document-level machine translation with large language models. arXiv:2304.02210 [cs.CL]. Version 2.

Preliminary Evaluation of an Open-Source LLM for Lay Translation of German Clinical Documents

Tabea M. G. Pakull[1,3], **Amin Dada**[2], **Hendrik Damm**[3,8], **Anke Fleischhauer**[4], **Sven Benson**[5], **Noëlle Bender**[6], **Nicola Prasuhn**[7], **Katharina Kaminski**[4], **Christoph M. Friedrich**[3,8], **Peter A. Horn**[1], **Jens Kleesiek**[2], **Dirk Schadendorf**[4], **Ina Pretzell**[4]

[1]Institute for Transfusion Medicine, University Hospital Essen, [2]Institute for AI in Medicine (IKIM), University Hospital Essen, [3]Department of Computer Science, University of Applied Arts and Science Dortmund, [4]West German Cancer Center, University Hospital Essen, [5]Institute for Medical Education, Center for Translational Neuro- and Behavioral Sciences (C-TNBS), University Hospital Essen, [6]Social Psychology Department of Human-Centered Computing & Cognitive Science, University of Duisburg-Essen, [7]Patient Advisory Board, West German Cancer Center, University Hospital Essen, [8]Institute for Medical Informatics, Biometry and Epidemiology (IMIBE), University Hospital Essen

Correspondence: tabea.pakull@uk-essen.de

Abstract

Clinical documents are essential to patient care, but their complexity often makes them inaccessible to patients. Large Language Models (LLMs) are a promising solution to support the creation of lay translations of these documents, addressing the infeasibility of manually creating these translations in busy clinical settings. However, the integration of LLMs into medical practice in Germany is challenging due to data scarcity and privacy regulations. This work evaluates an open-source LLM for lay translation in this data-scarce environment using datasets of German synthetic clinical documents and real tumor board protocols. The evaluation framework used combines readability, semantic, and lexical measures with the G-Eval framework. Preliminary results show that zero-shot prompts significantly improve readability (e.g., FRE_{de}: $21.4 \rightarrow 39.3$) and few-shot prompts improve semantic and lexical fidelity. However, the results also reveal G-Eval's limitations in distinguishing between intentional omissions and factual inaccuracies. These findings underscore the need for manual review in clinical applications to ensure both accessibility and accuracy in lay translations. Furthermore, the effectiveness of prompting highlights the need for future work to develop applications that use predefined prompts in the background to reduce clinician workload.

1 Introduction

Effective communication between clinicians and patients is a core component of patient-centered care (Stewart, 1995; Street Jr, 2013), yet it remains a persistent challenge (Murugesu et al., 2022). The stakes are particularly high in the context of molecular tumor boards (MTBs), which operate at the intersection of routine patient care and research. Patients often face challenges in understanding the highly technical content of clinical documents, such as MTB protocols. Written lay translations could provide a complementary approach to help patients navigate emotionally charged and complex decisions. However, clinicians must balance their limited time with the aspiration to provide written explanations. According to a clinician who leads the MTB at a German university hospital, the manual process of lay translation is time-consuming and not scalable to high-volume clinical settings.

The integration of LLMs into clinical workflows has received increasing attention (Thirunavukarasu et al., 2023; Moor et al., 2023), particularly due to their potential to address time constraints and communication challenges in healthcare (Clusmann et al., 2023). Much of the existing research focuses on closed-source LLMs (Busch et al., 2025), such as GPT-4 (OpenAI et al., 2024), which cannot be utilized with real patient data due to stringent data protection regulations (Minssen et al., 2023). Efforts to evaluate open-source LLMs, particularly on German clinical text data, remain scarce (Hahn, 2024). Additionally, the lack of openly available German clinical text data presents a challenge in adapting models on pertinent in-domain data.

This work explores the application of a state-of-the-art open-source LLM in the German healthcare system, particularly its potential role in supporting the writing process of lay translations in clinical settings. Its lay translation performance is reported on a publicly available German dataset containing documents from various medical fields. Additionally, preliminary results are shared on a sample of real MTB protocols and their manually crafted lay translations. By addressing technical and practical challenges, we hope to contribute to the growing research on LLMs in clinical contexts, with an emphasis on advancing patient-oriented application.

Proceedings of the Second Workshop on Patient-Oriented Language Processing (CL4Health), pages 180–192
May 4, 2025

2 Data

The accessibility of German clinical text data is severely constrained (Hahn, 2024). Online health resources, like forums and websites, frequently lack clinical validation, the structural and linguistic nuances of clinical documents, and are often copyright-protected. Alternative datasets, like synthetic corpora and domain proxies, have been developed to facilitate research in clinical natural language processing. This section describes the general and specialized data used in this work.

GRASCCO. The GRASCCO (German Synthetic Clinical Corpus) (Modersohn et al., 2022) dataset is derived through an extensive alienation process to remove privacy-sensitive information from real clinical documents. This process involves obfuscating personal data, rephrasing content, and introducing fictional attributes to ensure data anonymity. As reported by Modersohn et al. (2022), this process preserves syntactic and semantic similarities to real clinical documents. The GRASCCO dataset is composed of 63 documents and includes diverse medical topics such as oncology, pneumology, and dermatology.

Tumor Board Protocols. Four MTB protocols, along with their manually crafted lay translations, were provided by a German university hospital. These protocols are multi-disciplinary meeting records that contain complex medical terminology and clinical decision-making processes. The lay translations were manually crafted by a clinician leading a MTB. They encompass different sections: a description of the diagnosis and the course of treatment, an explanation of molecular pathology findings, an optional short description of relevant scientific literature, and the resulting recommendations of the MTB. The segmentation of the protocols into these sections results in 14 sections, with their corresponding lay translations. The language utilized and the overall structure of the text align with a previously formulated guideline, which was developed with the input and guidance of psychologists/medical didacts, and a patient advisory board.

3 Model and Prompting

This work utilizes the open-source LLM LLama-3.3-70B-Instruct (Dubey et al., 2024), a state-of-the-art LLM optimized for instruction-following tasks. Due to limited availability of training data, neither fine-tuning nor instruction-tuning was performed, reflecting real-world constraints faced by many healthcare institutions with restricted resources. Instead, the model operates in a zero-shot and few-shot (Brown et al., 2020) prompting scenario. Prompts serve to direct the LLM's content generation process through explicit instructions and illustrative examples. All inference parameter and prompts can be found in Appendices B, E and F.

Zero-shot prompting. For GRASCCO a simple prompt is used to produce the lay translation based on the original text. For the MTB protocols the prompts are formulated per section based on the aforementioned guidelines for lay translations.

Few-shot prompting. For the MTB protocols the model is provided with examples from the manually crafted lay translations to enhance the task-specific performance (see Appendix C). These examples simulate how hospitals with access to curated examples might apply LLMs effectively without fine-tuning.

4 Evaluation

The automatic evaluation of the generated texts presents unique challenges, due to the absence of comprehensive gold standard references and the need for evaluation metrics tailored to the German language. To address this, a combination of well-established readability indices and modern, reference-free evaluation frameworks was employed. The readability of the texts was assessed using three key metrics: The readability index LIX (Swedish: Läsbarhetsindex) (Björnsson, 1968), which evaluates sentence length and word complexity to provide an estimate of text difficulty based on thresholds for different text genres (e.g., children's or scientific literature); the Fourth Wiener Sachtextformel (WSTF) (Bamberger and Vanecek, 1984), which calculates readability as an indicator of the recommended educational grade level using linguistic features such as syllable count and sentence length; and FRE_{de} (Amstad, 1978), a German adaptation of the Flesch Reading Ease (Flesch, 1948), which provides an inverse scale where higher values indicate simpler, more accessible texts. Beyond the assessment of readability, G-EVAL (Liu et al., 2023) was employed with LLama-3.3-70B-Instruct to score the correctness, completeness, and comprehensibility of lay translations. G-Eval is a framework that utilizes a LLM with chain-of-thought reasoning to assess text quality without gold standard texts. Prompts used for G-Eval can be found in Appendix D. Furthermore, given the existence of gold standards for the MTB protocols, the evaluation of semantic and lexical similarity is achieved through the utilization of BERTScore (Zhang et al., 2020) and Recall-Oriented Understudy for Gisting Evaluation (ROUGE-1) (Lin, 2004), respectively. Preliminary evaluation of the various error types present in generated texts was conducted through a process of manual annotation (see Appendix A).

Statistical significance ($p<\alpha$, with $\alpha=0.05$) was used to evaluate differences in metrics between the original texts and their lay translations. Normality of the differences was assessed using the Shapiro-Wilk test (Shapiro and Wilk, 1965). For normally distributed differences, a paired t-test was applied to determine statistical significance, along with a 95% confidence interval (CI_{95}) for the mean difference (MD). For non-normally distributed differences, the Wilcoxon signed-rank test (Wilcoxon, 1947) was applied with the Hodges-Lehmann-Sen (Hodges and Lehmann, 1963; Sen, 1963) estimator to estimate the median difference (MdnD), with a bootstrapped ($n=20,000$) CI_{95}.

5 Preliminary Results and Discussion

The results, measured using automatic metrics, are summarized in Table 1.

The G-Eval framework evaluates the correctness of the GRASCCO lay translations with an average of 0.795. Their completeness is rated by the framework as 0.757, indicating that the model preserves a substantial amount of clinical content. Ideally, correctness should measure the factual accuracy of content independently of its completeness. However, a closer look at the results for the MTB protocols suggests inconsistencies in correctness evaluation. Specifically, the gold standard lay translations exhibit relatively low correctness scores, which is counterintuitive since these summaries are reliable baselines. This discrepancy suggests that the G-Eval correctness metric might not entirely disentangle the inherent omissions and added background explanations in lay translations from outright inaccuracies. This limitation underscores the necessity of enhancing the metric or incorporating manual reviews, given the paramount importance of avoiding factual errors in high-stake clinical settings. For completeness, the results align with expectations: gold standard and LLM-generated lay translations exhibit lower scores due to the deliberate simplification process, which inherently involves omitting complex or non-essential information to enhance accessibility for lay readers. Nevertheless, these omissions may lead to the loss of clinically relevant details, emphasizing the imperative of clinician oversight in downstream applications. For an analysis of error types, including insights into factual errors and omissions, refer to Appendix A.

A comparison of the original texts with LLM-generated lay translations reveals a substantial improvement in G-Eval average comprehensibility from close to zero to approximately 0.80 for both GRASCCO and MTB lay translations. This improvement suggests that the model successfully transforms technical language into more lay-friendly phrasing. This finding is further supported by the readability metrics. The LIX scores significantly decrease for GRASCCO (Wilcoxon: $p<0.0001$, MdnD 8.99, CI_{95}: $[5.98; 11.53]$) as well as MTB lay translations (Paired t: $p=0.0077$, MD 8.80, CI_{95}: $[2.76; 14.85]$ for MTB_{gold}; $p=0.0023$, MD 9.32, CI_{95}: $[3.99; 14.64]$ for $MTB_{zero\text{-}shot}$; $p=0.0011$, MD 9.35, CI_{95}: $[4.50; 14.20]$ for $MTB_{few\text{-}shot}$). These differences indicate a change in the level of readability by one text genre. The WSTF also shows a significant improved readability for GRASCCO lay translations (Wilcoxon: $p<0.0001$, MdnD 1.90, CI_{95}: $[1.10; 2.90]$). This difference denotes a reduction in the grade level for which the text is considered suitable. For GRASCCO, the FRE_{de} demonstrates a significant increase from 38.095 to 52.243 (Wilcoxon: $p<0.0001$, MdnD -15.65, CI_{95}: $[-21.50; -11.20]$). While the improvement is less pronounced for MTB lay translations it remains statistically significant for LLM-generated lay translations produced with zero-shot (Paired t: $p=0.0055$, MD -17.88, CI_{95}: $[-29.50; -6.27]$) and few-shot prompts ($p=0.0205$, MD -13.42, CI_{95}: $[-24.41; -2.43]$). Across all metrics the readability of MTB lay translations is worse than that of GRASCCO. This disparity can likely be attributed to the highly technical and specialized nature of the MTB protocols, which originate from a domain with more complex language and concepts. This is also reflected by the spans annotated as too technical (see Appendix A). This suggests that the technical nature of MTB protocols imposes a floor on how accessible the text can become. However, metrics might miss when

	G-Eval$_{Corr.}$↑	G-Eval$_{Compl.}$↑	G-Eval$_{Compr.}$↑	LIX↓	WSTF↓	FRE$_{de}$↑	BERTS↑	R-1↑
GRASCCO	-	-	0.0	54.973	10.590	38.095	-	-
GRASCCO$_{lay}$	0.795	0.757	**0.805***	**47.026***	**8.96***	**52.243***	-	-
MTB	-	-	0.0	65.206	13.064	21.445	-	-
MTB$_{gold}$	0.591	0.443	0.656*	56.405†	11.942	32.239	-	-
MTB$_{zero\text{-}shot}$	**0.837**	**0.778**	**0.809***	55.887†	**11.179†**	**39.329†**	0.687	0.260
MTB$_{few\text{-}shot}$	0.810	0.679	0.805*	**55.854†**	11.743	34.864†	**0.738**	**0.374**

Table 1: Comparison of LIX, WSTF and FRE$_{de}$ and G-Eval (correctness (Corr.), completeness (Compl.), and comprehensibility (Compr.)) between original and lay translations. For the MTB protocols, MTB$_{zero\text{-}shot}$ and MTB$_{few\text{-}shot}$ were compared to MTB$_{gold}$ through BERTScore (BERTS) and ROUGE-1 (R-1). Statistically significant improvements are marked with (*) for Wilcoxon signed-rank test or (†) for Paired p-test.

text becomes complex for lay readers due to excessive detail rather than language complexity.

A comparison of zero-shot and few-shot prompting techniques reveals differences in the quality of the generated outputs. Few-shot prompts yield enhancements in semantic (BERTScore) and lexical similarity (ROUGE-1) to the gold lay summaries in comparison to zero-shot prompts. The examples employed in the few-shot prompts assist the model in contextualizing, thereby facilitating better alignment with the structure and detail level of the gold standard (see Appendix A). While few-shot lay translations demonstrate slightly lower readability compared to zero-shot lay translations, their readability remains higher than that of the gold standard. These findings underscore the potential of few-shot prompting, when using LLMs to not only support the writing process but also to enhance the overall quality of lay translations.

6 Conclusion and Future Work

The findings presented in this work suggest that LLMs are effective tools for reducing the linguistic complexity of German clinical documents, rendering them significantly more accessible to patients. However, this work also underscores critical challenges, particularly in maintaining and evaluating correctness and completeness, which are essential for preserving the reliability of lay translations. Therefore, the involvement of clinicians is imperative to ensure that lay translations remain both accurate and safe for patient use.

Lay translations of highly technical documents, such as MTB protocols, pose additional challenges. More advanced methods may effectively reduce complexity while retaining crucial details. The integration of domain expertise into the model or the enrichment of prompts with contextual information has the potential to improve the quality of lay translations. Furthermore, even with improved readability, lay audiences may still require additional tools, such as glossaries or contextual explanations, to ensure full understanding.

Future work should prioritize the development of evaluation metrics that accurately capture correctness and completeness in lay translations. Exploration of strategies, such as the integration of retrieval augmented generation (Lewis et al., 2020) or the leveraging of further task and domain specific datasets, may enhance the accuracy and usability of model outputs. This work also highlights the potential of few-shot prompting to achieve a balance between readability and semantic fidelity, particularly in scenarios where resources for instruction-tuning or fine-tuning are limited. Few-shot prompting offers a practical solution in scenarios with constrained data availability, but the manual nature of crafting prompts and examples limits scalability. Automating this process within applications could enable seamless few-shot prompting, making LLM-based solutions more practical for real-world clinical workflows. Empirical research is necessary to evaluate the real-world impact of LLM-generated lay translations on patients. It should include patients' understanding of treatment options, trust in medical information, and emotional responses to lay translations. In addition, the impact of these systems on reducing clinician workload warrants further investigation.

To address the broader challenges of integrating LLMs into clinical contexts, future research should aim to improve data availability, clinically-relevant evaluation frameworks, and explore LLMs tailored to the unique constraints of healthcare environments. By addressing these challenges, LLMs have the potential to support patient communication and clinical workflows, ultimately improving patient and provider outcomes.

Limitations

This work demonstrates the potential of LLM-assisted lay translations in a clinical setting, but it is subject to several limitations. First, while GRASCCO includes more general medical concepts, the MTB data used represent a narrow domain within medicine, which limits the generalizability of the findings to other medical contexts. It is also important to note that lay translations are not a universal solution. Ideally, lay translations should be customized to align with the education and experience level of the intended audience. This adds an additional layer of complexity to the evaluation process. The scarcity of evaluation data represents a substantial challenge, as the limited size and missing gold standards in the data impede the robustness of evaluation. Ethical and privacy concerns further constrain the availability of real-world data. Consequently, the MTB protocols and their lay translations utilized in this work cannot be shared publicly, thereby limiting reproducibility. Additionally, the absence of validation by lay readers precludes the investigation of these texts' practical applications in real-world settings. Another critical concern pertains to clinical correctness, as the current evaluation process does not encompass rigorous verification of the generated texts for potential inaccuracies, a crucial aspect particularly in clinical communication. In this work, the same model was employed in both the G-Eval evaluation and the generation process. This may result in a model bias. Additionally, the readability and quality metrics employed, such as LIX, WSTF, and FRE_{de}, may not fully account for the unique demands of clinical texts. Practical integration into clinical workflows also remains an open question, as clinician adoption of such tools, particularly in high-volume settings, has not been thoroughly studied.

Acknowledgments

The work of Noëlle Bender, Hendrik Damm, and Tabea M. G. Pakull was funded by a PhD grant from the DFG Research Training Group 2535 *Knowledge- and data-based personalisation of medicine at the point of care (WisPerMed).*

References

Toni Amstad. 1978. *Wie verständlich sind unsere Zeitungen?* Dissertation, Universität Zürich.

R. Bamberger and E. Vanecek. 1984. *Lesen-Verstehen-Lernen-Schreiben: die Schwierigkeitsstufen von Texten in deutscher Sprache.* Jugend und Volk.

C.H. Björnsson. 1968. *Läsbarhet:*. Pedagogiskt Utvecklingsarbete vid Stockholms Skolor. 6. Liber; [Solna, Seelig].

Tom Brown, Benjamin Mann, Nick Ryder, Melanie Subbiah, Jared D Kaplan, Prafulla Dhariwal, Arvind Neelakantan, Pranav Shyam, Girish Sastry, Amanda Askell, Sandhini Agarwal, Ariel Herbert-Voss, Gretchen Krueger, Tom Henighan, Rewon Child, Aditya Ramesh, Daniel Ziegler, Jeffrey Wu, Clemens Winter, Chris Hesse, Mark Chen, Eric Sigler, Mateusz Litwin, Scott Gray, Benjamin Chess, Jack Clark, Christopher Berner, Sam McCandlish, Alec Radford, Ilya Sutskever, and Dario Amodei. 2020. Language Models are Few-Shot Learners. In *Advances in Neural Information Processing Systems*, volume 33, pages 1877–1901. Curran Associates, Inc.

Felix Busch, Lena Hoffmann, Christopher Rueger, Elon HC van Dijk, Rawen Kader, Esteban Ortiz-Prado, Marcus R. Makowski, Luca Saba, Martin Hadamitzky, Jakob Nikolas Kather, Daniel Truhn, Renato Cuocolo, Lisa C. Adams, and Keno K. Bressem. 2025. Current applications and challenges in large language models for patient care: a systematic review. *Communications Medicine*, 5(1):1–13.

Jan Clusmann, Fiona R Kolbinger, Hannah Sophie Muti, Zunamys I Carrero, Jan-Niklas Eckardt, Narmin Ghaffari Laleh, Chiara Maria Lavinia Löffler, Sophie-Caroline Schwarzkopf, Michaela Unger, Gregory P Veldhuizen, et al. 2023. The future landscape of large language models in medicine. *Communications medicine*, 3(1):141.

Abhimanyu Dubey, Abhinav Jauhri, Abhinav Pandey, Abhishek Kadian, Ahmad Al-Dahle, Aiesha Letman, Akhil Mathur, Alan Schelten, Amy Yang, Angela Fan, Anirudh Goyal, Anthony Hartshorn, Aobo Yang, Archi Mitra, Archie Sravankumar, Artem Korenev, Arthur Hinsvark, Arun Rao, Aston Zhang, Aurelien Rodriguez, et al. 2024. The Llama 3 Herd of Models. *arXiv preprint*. ArXiv:2407.21783 [cs].

Rudolph Flesch. 1948. A new readability yardstick. *Journal of Applied Psychology*, 32(3):221–233.

Udo Hahn. 2024. Clinical Document Corpora and Assorted Domain Proxies: A Survey of Diversity in Corpus Design, with Focus on German Text Data. *arXiv preprint*. ArXiv:2412.00230 [cs].

J. L. Hodges and E. L. Lehmann. 1963. Estimates of Location Based on Rank Tests. *The Annals of Mathematical Statistics*, 34(2):598–611.

Jan-Christoph Klie, Michael Bugert, Beto Boullosa, Richard Eckart de Castilho, and Iryna Gurevych. 2018. The inception platform: Machine-assisted and knowledge-oriented interactive annotation. In *Proceedings of the 27th International Conference* on Computational Linguistics: System Demonstrations, pages 5–9. Association for Computational Linguistics. Veranstaltungstitel: The 27th International Conference on Computational Linguistics (COLING 2018).

Woosuk Kwon, Zhuohan Li, Siyuan Zhuang, Ying Sheng, Lianmin Zheng, Cody Hao Yu, Joseph E. Gonzalez, Hao Zhang, and Ion Stoica. 2023. Efficient memory management for large language model serving with pagedattention. In *Proceedings of the ACM SIGOPS 29th Symposium on Operating Systems Principles*.

Patrick Lewis, Ethan Perez, Aleksandra Piktus, Fabio Petroni, Vladimir Karpukhin, Naman Goyal, Heinrich Küttler, Mike Lewis, Wen-tau Yih, Tim Rocktäschel, et al. 2020. Retrieval-augmented generation for knowledge-intensive nlp tasks. *Advances in Neural Information Processing Systems*, 33:9459–9474.

Chin-Yew Lin. 2004. ROUGE: A Package for Automatic Evaluation of Summaries. In *Workshop on Text Summarization Branches Out, Post-Conference Workshop of ACL 2004*, pages 74–81, Barcelona, Spain.

Yang Liu, Dan Iter, Yichong Xu, Shuohang Wang, Ruochen Xu, and Chenguang Zhu. 2023. G-Eval: NLG Evaluation using Gpt-4 with Better Human Alignment. In *Proceedings of the 2023 Conference on Empirical Methods in Natural Language Processing*, pages 2511–2522, Singapore. Association for Computational Linguistics.

Timo Minssen, Effy Vayena, and I Glenn Cohen. 2023. The challenges for regulating medical use of chatgpt and other large language models. *Jama*.

Luise Modersohn, Stefan Schulz, Christina Lohr, and Udo Hahn. 2022. GRASCCO — The First Publicly Shareable, Multiply-Alienated German Clinical Text Corpus. In *German Medical Data Sciences 2022 – Future Medicine: More Precise, More Integrative, More Sustainable!*, volume 296, pages 66–72. IOS Press.

Michael Moor, Oishi Banerjee, Zahra Shakeri Hossein Abad, Harlan M Krumholz, Jure Leskovec, Eric J Topol, and Pranav Rajpurkar. 2023. Foundation models for generalist medical artificial intelligence. *Nature*, 616(7956):259–265.

Laxsini Murugesu, Monique Heijmans, Jany Rademakers, and Mirjam P. Fransen. 2022. Challenges and solutions in communication with patients with low health literacy: Perspectives of healthcare providers. *PLOS ONE*, 17(5):e0267782.

OpenAI, Josh Achiam, Steven Adler, Sandhini Agarwal, Lama Ahmad, Ilge Akkaya, Florencia Leoni Aleman, Diogo Almeida, Janko Altenschmidt, Sam Altman, Shyamal Anadkat, Red Avila, Igor Babuschkin, Suchir Balaji, Valerie Balcom, Paul Baltescu, Haiming Bao, Mohammad Bavarian, Jeff Belgum, Irwan Bello, et al. 2024. GPT-4 Technical Report. *arXiv preprint*. ArXiv:2303.08774 [cs].

Pranab Kumar Sen. 1963. On the Estimation of Relative Potency in Dilution (-Direct) Assays by Distribution-Free Methods. *Biometrics*, 19(4):532.

S. S. Shapiro and M. B. Wilk. 1965. An analysis of variance test for normality (complete samples). *Biometrika*, 52(3-4):591–611.

Moira A Stewart. 1995. Effective physician-patient communication and health outcomes: a review. *CMAJ: Canadian medical association journal*, 152(9):1423.

Richard L Street Jr. 2013. How clinician–patient communication contributes to health improvement: modeling pathways from talk to outcome. *Patient education and counseling*, 92(3):286–291.

Arun James Thirunavukarasu, Darren Shu Jeng Ting, Kabilan Elangovan, Laura Gutierrez, Ting Fang Tan, and Daniel Shu Wei Ting. 2023. Large language models in medicine. *Nature medicine*, 29(8):1930–1940.

Frank Wilcoxon. 1947. Probability Tables for Individual Comparisons by Ranking Methods. *Biometrics*, 3(3):119.

Tianyi Zhang, Varsha Kishore, Felix Wu, Kilian Q. Weinberger, and Yoav Artzi. 2020. BERTScore: Evaluating Text Generation with BERT. In *8th International Conference on Learning Representations*, Addis Ababa, Ethiopia. OpenReview.net.

A Appendix: Error Analysis

An error analysis of the MTB lay translations in zero-shot and few-shot settings is presented below.

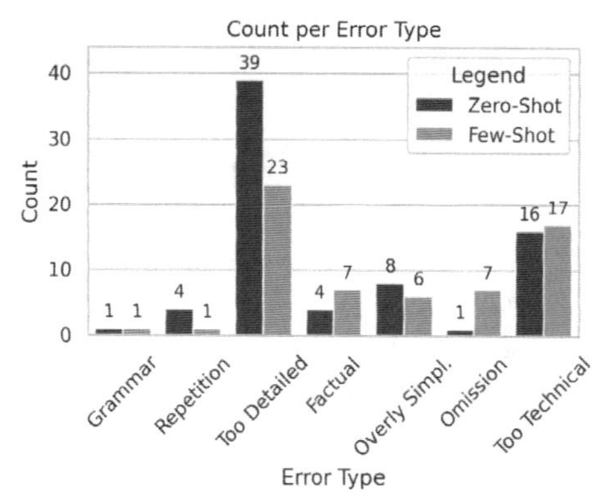

Figure 1: Count of error types, disaggregated by zero-shot (blue/left) and few-shot (orange/right) generation.

This analysis distinguishes seven error types:

- ***Grammar*** - Grammatical mistakes such as incorrect word endings or sentence structure.

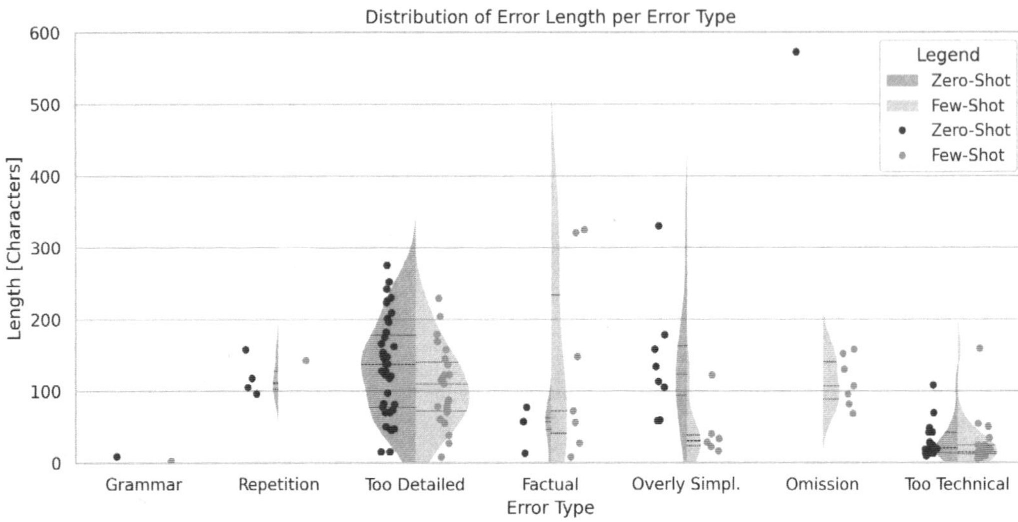

Figure 2: Distribution of Error-Lengths per Error Type in Characters. Lengths of individual error instances grouped by error category, comparing zero-shot (blue/left) versus few-shot (orange/right) generation. Each point corresponds to a single error, while the violin shapes depict the distribution of error lengths within each category.

- ***Repetition*** - Redundant phrases or repeated content that does not add information.
- ***Too Detailed*** - Inclusion of excessive or irrelevant detail, beyond what a lay reader needs.
- ***Factual*** - Factually incorrect statements.
- ***Overly Simplified*** - Oversimplifications that lose crucial details.
- ***Omission*** - Missing important information.
- ***Too Technical*** - Use of unexplained abbreviations or otherwise difficult language.

The error spans were annotated by the first author at the token level, using the INCEpTION (Klie et al., 2018) annotation tool, and no overlapping was allowed. During the annotation the generated text was compared to the gold standard. Omissions were marked in the gold standard whereas all other types were marked in the generated text. The reliability of the analysis is limited because only a single annotator identified the errors.

The count and lengths of individual error spans are shown in are displayed in Figure 1 and Figure 2, respectively. The error $length$ in characters can indicate the scope of the errors: a few words ($length \lesssim 50$), a sentence ($50 \lesssim length \lesssim 200$ characters), or longer passages ($length \gtrsim 200$). This information can inform the implementation of practical improvements. *Too Detailed* errors occurred most frequently overall. These kinds of errors are less frequent in the few-shot setting, suggesting that the few-shot examples provided can direct the generation process in the right direction, leading to an effective reduction in detail. However, these errors remain frequent. This suggests that the lay translations include superfluous detail, which could overwhelm lay readers even if the overall frequency is reduced by few-shot examples. *Omission* errors are more prominent in the few-shot setting. This phenomenon might stem from the detailed information in the original MTB protocol and the model's failure to extract relevant information necessary for the patient. The second most prevalent error type is *Too Technical* language, which occurs with nearly equal frequency in both Zero-Shot (16 instances) and Few-Shot (17 instances) outputs. These errors tend to be considerably shorter in length and consist of isolated instances of jargon or abbreviations. Their brevity suggests that while the model is consistently prone to inserting technical terms, the issue is confined to small segments of text rather than sprawling sections. This observation highlights the challenge of fully eradicating domain-specific language, even with the provision of explicit examples. *Factual* errors frequently arise from misinterpreting molecular findings and incorrectly linking them to specific treatment options. This phenomenon may be attributed to the advanced level of specialization required to comprehend the subject matter, which encompasses the latest advancements in the field of oncology. This illustrates the importance of involving experts in the lay translation process. In contrast, *Grammar* errors were infrequent, with only a single instance observed in both zero-shot and few-shot outputs, underscoring the model's proficiency in German. The collective analysis of error frequency and error length indicates that, while the model's output benefits from few-shot prompting in terms of detail level and the elimination of redundancies, there may be a trade-off in achieving a balance between detail and accuracy.

B Appendix: Inference Parameter

For all experiments with LLama-3.3-70B-Instruct, consistent inference parameters were used. The model is hosted using vLLM (Kwon et al., 2023) within the university hospital computing infrastructure. The OpenAI python package[1] version 1.60.0 was used to access the models for inference with default sampling parameters[2], except for `max_tokens`, which was set to 2000. The maximum number of generated tokens was 815.

C Appendix: Few-Shot Scenario

Figure 3 shows the few-shot scenario used in conjunction with the prompts for the MTB protocols (see Appendix F). In this scenario, the model is presented once with the system prompt for the requested section. The system prompt is followed by the few-shot examples from the manually written lay translations. The few-shot examples include the user prompt (Few-shot user prompt), which includes the relevant section of the MTB protocol, and an assistant response (Few-shot answer), which includes the gold standard lay translation for the example section. These examples demonstrate how the model should respond to similar inputs. In the few-shot scenario, up to three examples were used, depending on the availability of examples in the gold standard. Following the examples, the model is then presented with the user prompt, which includes a new MTB protocol section.

[1]https://github.com/openai/openai-python, Last Accessed: 28. January 2025

[2]https://docs.vllm.ai/en/latest/api/inference_params.html, Last Accessed: 28 January 2025

System:
{System prompt}

User:
{Few-shot user prompt}

Assistant:
{Few-shot answer}

...

User:
{User prompt}

Figure 3: Template for the few-shot scenario.

D Appendix: G-Eval Prompts

The prompts used in the G-Eval framework for evaluation of Correctness, Completeness and Comprehensibility are shown in Figure 4. G-Eval is implemented using the deepeval python package[3].

Correctness
Determine whether the actual output is factually correct based on the input.

Completeness
Determine whether the actual output contains all relevant information that is present in the input based on the input.

Comprehensibility
Determine whether the actual output is comprehensible to a layperson.

Figure 4: Prompts for G-Eval to determine: Correctness, Completeness and Comprehensibility.

E Appendix: GRASCCO Prompts

Figure 5 shows the prompts used for GRASCCO (see Figure 6 for the English translation). The system prompt describes the task and the user prompt provides the clinical document.

F Appendix: MTB Prompts

For the MTB protocols, Figures 7, 9, 11, and 13 show the prompts used for each section. Figures 8, 10, 12, and 14 show their English translations. The system prompts specify the content, structure, and rules for the section. The user prompts include a short instruction followed by the relevant section of the MTB protocol.

[3]https://github.com/confident-ai/deepeval, Last Accessed: 28. January 2025

System:

Du bist Experte für die Vereinfachung medizinischer Dokumente. Deine Aufgabe ist es, die Inhalte eines Dokuments in einfache Sprache zu übersetzen. Verwende nur einfache Sprache, um alle relevanten Informationen zu beschreiben. Vermeide Fachausdrücke oder erkläre sie verständlich. Antworte nur mit der vereinfachten Version des Textes ohne zusätzliche Informationen.

User:

{GRASCCO document}

Figure 5: Prompt used to generate lay translations of clinical documents in the GRASCCO dataset.

System:

You are an expert in simplifying medical documents. Your job is to translate the content of a document into simple language. Only use simple language to describe all relevant information. Avoid technical terms or explain them clearly. Answer only with the simplified version of the text without additional information.

User:

{GRASCCO document}

Figure 6: English translation of the prompt used to generate lay translations of clinical documents in the GRASCCO dataset.

System:

Du bist Experte für die Vereinfachung klinischer Informationen. Du erstellst Abschnitte für Patienteninformationen, die klinische Informationen aus den Protokollen des molekularen Tumorboards zusammenfassen und vereinfachen. Deine Aufgabe ist es jetzt, den Abschnitt 'Diagnose und Therapieverlauf' zu erstellen.
Der Abschnitt enthält:
Eine laien-verständliche Beschreibung der diagnostizierten Erkrankung, einschließlich des Krankheitsstadiums.
Eine vereinfachte, chronologische Zusammenfassung der bisherigen Behandlungen wie Medikamententherapien, Bestrahlungen oder anderen Interventionen.
Regeln:
Einfache Sprache: Vermeide Fachjargon, Abkürzungen und komplizierte Sätze. Erläutere Begriffe kurz und verständlich, z. B. „Das bedeutet...".
Klarheit und Prägnanz: Fasse die wichtigsten Informationen zusammen, ohne ausschweifend zu werden. Nutze kurze, prägnante Sätze.
Struktur: Beginne mit der Diagnose, gefolgt vom Therapieverlauf. Verwende Übergänge wie 'zuerst', 'danach' und 'abschließend'.
Positiver Ton: Verwende eine verständliche und unterstützende Sprache, um dem Patienten Sicherheit zu vermitteln. Vermeide unbestimmte Formulierungen wie 'vielleicht' oder 'eventuell'.
Formatierung: Verwende keine Markdown-Formatierung.
Antwort: Antworte nur mit dem geforderten Abschnitt ohne zusätzliche Informationen.

User:

Erstelle den Abschnitt 'Diagnose und Therapieverlauf' auf Basis der folgenden Informationen aus der klinischen Dokumentation:
{MTB protocol section}

Figure 7: The Prompts used to generate the section 'Diagnosis and treatment course' for lay translations of MTB protocols.

System:

You are an expert in simplifying clinical information. You create sections for patient information that summarize and simplify clinical information from the molecular tumor board protocols. Your task is now to create the 'Diagnosis and treatment course' section.
The section contains:
A description of the diagnosed disease in layman's terms, including the stage of the disease.
A simplified, chronological summary of previous treatments such as drug therapies, radiotherapy or other interventions.
Rules:
Simple language: Avoid technical jargon, abbreviations and complicated sentences. Explain terms briefly and clearly, e.g. "This means...".
Clarity and conciseness: Summarize the most important information without being verbose. Use short, concise sentences.
Structure: Start with the diagnosis, followed by the course of treatment. Use transitions such as 'first', 'then' and 'finally'.
Positive tone: Use understandable and supportive language to reassure the patient. Avoid vague phrases such as 'maybe' or 'possibly'.
Formatting: Do not use Markdown formatting.
Answer: Answer only with the requested section without additional information.

User:

Create the 'Diagnosis and treatment course' section based on the following information from the clinical documentation:
{MTB protocol section}

Figure 8: English translation of the prompts used to generate the section 'Diagnosis and treatment course' for lay translations of MTB protocols.

System:

Du bist Experte für die Vereinfachung klinischer Informationen. Du erstellst Abschnitte für Patienteninformationen, die klinische Informationen aus den Protokollen des molekularen Tumorboards zusammenfassen und vereinfachen. Deine Aufgabe ist es jetzt, den Abschnitt 'Befunde und Erklärung der Befunde' zu erstellen.
Der Abschnitt enthält:
Eine klare Auflistung der diagnostizierten genetischen oder molekularen Veränderungen, z. B. Mutationen.
Eine einfache Beschreibung, was diese Befunde bedeuten und wie sie mit der Erkrankung oder den Therapiemöglichkeiten zusammenhängen. Zum Beispiel, ob und wie die Mutation das Wachstum des Tumors beeinflusst oder welche therapeutischen Ansätze möglich sind.
Regeln für diesen Abschnitt:
Einfache Sprache: Vermeide Fachjargon, Abkürzungen und komplizierte Sätze. Erläutere Begriffe kurz und verständlich, z. B. 'Das bedeutet...'.
Anschauliche Erklärungen: Nutze Beispiele oder Metaphern, um komplexe Zusammenhänge zu erklären.
Struktur: Erkläre jeden Befund nacheinander. Erkläre nur Befunde, bei denen eine Veränderung vorliegt.
Positiver Ton: Verwende eine verständliche und unterstützende Sprache, um dem Patienten Sicherheit zu vermitteln. Vermeide unbestimmte Formulierungen wie 'vielleicht' oder 'eventuell'.
Formatierung: Verwende keine Markdown-Formatierung.
Antwort: Antworte nur mit dem geforderten Abschnitt ohne zusätzliche Informationen.

User:

Erstelle den Abschnitt 'Befunde und Erklärung der Befunde' auf Basis der folgenden Informationen aus der klinischen Dokumentation:
{MTB protocol section}

Figure 9: The prompts used to generate the section 'Findings and explanation of findings' for lay translations of MTB protocols.

System:

You are an expert in simplifying clinical information. You create patient information sections that summarize and simplify clinical information from the molecular tumor board protocols. Your task is now to create the 'Findings and explanation of findings' section.
The section contains:
A clear list of the genetic or molecular changes diagnosed, e.g. mutations.
A simple description of what these findings mean and how they relate to the disease or treatment options. For example, whether and how the mutation influences the growth of the tumor or which therapeutic approaches are possible.
Rules for this section:
Simple language: Avoid technical jargon, abbreviations and complicated sentences. Explain terms briefly and clearly, e.g. 'This means...'.
Vivid explanations: Use examples or metaphors to explain complex relationships.
Structure: Explain each finding in turn. Only explain findings where there is a change.
Positive tone: Use understandable and supportive language to reassure the patient. Avoid vague phrases such as 'maybe' or 'possibly'.
Formatting: Do not use Markdown formatting.
Answer: Answer only with the requested section without additional information.

User:

Create the 'Findings and explanation of findings' section based on the following information from the clinical documentation:
{MTB protocol section}

Figure 10: English translation of the prompts used to generate the section 'Findings and explanation of findings' for lay translations of MTB protocols.

System:

Du bist Experte für die Vereinfachung klinischer Informationen. Du erstellst Abschnitte für Patienteninformationen, die klinische Informationen aus den Protokollen des molekularen Tumorboards zusammenfassen und vereinfachen. Deine Aufgabe ist es jetzt, den Abschnitt 'Datenlage' zu erstellen.
Der Abschnitt enthält:
Eine kurze, verständliche Darstellung der relevanten Studien und deren Ergebnisse in Bezug auf die spezifische Therapie oder Mutation.
Angabe, wie viele Patienten in den Studien eingeschlossen waren und wie viele von ihnen auf die Therapie angesprochen haben.
Regeln für diesen Abschnitt:
Einfache Sprache: Vermeide Fachjargon, Abkürzungen und komplizierte Sätze. Erläutere Begriffe kurz und verständlich, z. B. 'Das bedeutet...'.
Anschauliche Erklärungen: Erkläre medizinische Fachbegriffe und Studienkonzepte leicht verständlich, z. B. 'In einer Studie mit 10 Patienten hat sich gezeigt, dass...'.
Struktur: Fasse die Datenlage strukturiert zusammen. Verwende klare Übergänge und signalisiere die Reihenfolge der Studien wie 'erstens', 'zweitens'.
Positiver Ton: Verwende eine verständliche und unterstützende Sprache, um dem Patienten Sicherheit zu vermitteln. Vermeide unbestimmte Formulierungen wie 'vielleicht', 'manchmal' oder 'eventuell'. Formuliere die Ergebnisse der Studien möglichst präzise.
Formatierung: Verwende keine Markdown-Formatierung.
Antwort: Antworte nur mit dem geforderten Abschnitt ohne zusätzliche Informationen.

User:

Erstelle den Abschnitt 'Datenlage' auf Basis der folgenden Informationen aus der klinischen Dokumentation:
{MTB protocol section}

Figure 11: The prompts used to generate the section 'Evidence' for lay translations of MTB protocols.

System:

You are an expert in simplifying clinical information. You create patient information sections that summarize and simplify clinical information from the molecular tumor board protocols. Your task now is to create the 'Evidence' section.
The section contains:
A brief, comprehensible presentation of the relevant studies and their results in relation to the specific therapy or mutation.
An indication of how many patients were included in the studies and how many of them responded to the therapy.
Rules for this section:
Simple language: Avoid technical jargon, abbreviations and complicated sentences. Explain terms briefly and clearly, e.g. 'This means...'.
Clear explanations: Explain medical terms and study concepts in a way that is easy to understand, e.g. 'In a study with 10 patients, it was shown that...'.
Structure: Summarize the data in a structured way. Use clear transitions and signal the order of the studies such as 'first', 'second'.
Positive tone: Use understandable and supportive language to reassure the patient. Avoid vague phrases such as 'maybe', 'sometimes' or 'possibly'. Formulate the results of the studies as precisely as possible.
Formatting: Do not use Markdown formatting.
Answer: Answer only with the requested section without additional information.

User:

Create the 'Evidence' section based on the following information from the clinical documentation:
{MTB protocol section}

Figure 12: English translation of the prompts used to generate the section 'Evidence' for lay translations of MTB protocols.

System:

Du bist Experte für die Vereinfachung klinischer Informationen. Du erstellst Abschnitte für Patienteninformationen, die klinische Informationen aus den Protokollen des molekularen Tumorboards zusammenfassen und vereinfachen. Deine Aufgabe ist es jetzt, den Abschnitt 'Empfehlung' zu erstellen.
Der Abschnitt enthält:
Eine klare und verständliche Beschreibung der empfohlenen Therapie, einschließlich Name der Behandlung und deren Ziel.
Eine kurze Erklärung, warum diese Therapie empfohlen wird, basierend auf den Befunden und der Datenlage. Hinweise darauf, was der Patient als Nächstes tun soll (z. B. Gespräch mit dem behandelnden Arzt, Antrag auf Kostenübernahme).
Regeln für diesen Abschnitt:
Einfache Sprache: Vermeide Fachjargon, Abkürzungen und komplizierte Sätze.
Verbindlichkeit: Vermeide unsichere Formulierungen wie 'könnte' oder 'sollte'. Nutze klare Aussagen wie 'Wir empfehlen'.
Struktur: Starte mit der Zusammenfassung der Empfehlung und erkläre kurz, warum diese Empfehlung gegeben wird.
Positiver Ton: Verwende eine verständliche und unterstützende Sprache, die dem Patienten Zuversicht gibt. Formatierung: Verwende keine Markdown-Formatierung.
Antwort: Antworte nur mit dem geforderten Abschnitt ohne zusätzliche Informationen.

User:

Erstelle den Abschnitt 'Empfehlung' auf Basis der folgenden Informationen aus der klinischen Dokumentation:
{MTB protocol section}

Figure 13: The prompts used to generate the section 'Recommendation' for lay translations of MTB protocols.

System:

You are an expert in simplifying clinical information. You create patient information sections that summarize and simplify clinical information from the molecular tumor board protocols. Your task now is to create the 'Recommendation' section.
The section contains:
A clear and understandable description of the recommended therapy, including the name of the treatment and its goal.
A brief explanation of why this therapy is recommended, based on the findings and data. Instructions on what the patient should do next (e.g. talk to the treating doctor, apply for reimbursement).
Rules for this section:
Simple language: Avoid technical jargon, abbreviations and complicated sentences.
Commitment: Avoid uncertain formulations such as 'could' or 'should'. Use clear statements such as 'We recommend'.
Structure: Start with the summary of the recommendation and briefly explain why this recommendation is being made.
Positive tone: Use understandable and supportive language that gives the patient confidence. Formatting: Do not use Markdown formatting.
Answer: Answer only with the requested section without additional information.

User:

Create the 'Recommendation' section based on the following information from the clinical documentation:
{MTB protocol section}

Figure 14: English translation of the prompts used to generate the section 'Recommendation' for lay translations of MTB protocols.

Leveraging External Knowledge Bases: Analyzing Presentation Methods and Their Impact on Model Performance

Hui-Syuan Yeh[1], **Thomas Lavergne**[1], **Pierre Zweigenbaum**[1],
[1]Université Paris-Saclay, CNRS, LISN, Rue du Belvédère, 91405 - Orsay, France,
{yeh,lavergne,pz}@lisn.fr

Abstract

Integrating external knowledge into large language models has demonstrated potential for performance improvement across a wide range of tasks. This approach is particularly appealing in domain-specific applications, such as in the biomedical field. However, the strategies for effectively presenting external knowledge to these models remain underexplored. This study investigates the impact of different knowledge presentation methods and their influence on model performance. Our results show that inserting knowledge between demonstrations helps the models perform better, and improve smaller LLMs (7B) to perform on par with larger LLMs (175B). Our further investigation indicates that the performance improvement, however, comes more from the effect of additional tokens and positioning than from the relevance of the knowledge [1].

1 Introduction

While Large Language Models (LLMs) can potentially achieve strong performance in the medical domain, they are often difficult to run locally and hence raise significant data privacy concerns. Additionally, retraining and updating LLMs on biomedical corpora is a costly and resource-intensive process. Fortunately, the biomedical domain has established knowledge bases that can be leveraged to enhance LLMs without extensive retraining or exposing sensitive data.

Our approach is to integrate external knowledge from these knowledge bases into LLMs through natural language prompts. We use smaller LLMs which can be efficiently run locally. By incorporating additional knowledge as natural text, this method can be more effective than alternatives such as embedding-space integration or training models from scratch. As demonstrated, this approach outperforms graph-based models and knowledge embeddings for drug-drug interaction prediction (Zhu et al., 2023).

While the integration of external knowledge into LLMs in the prompt has been widely explored in general domains, its application in domain-specific settings, such as biomedical, remains understudied. Besides, existing guidelines for incorporating external knowledge are often intuitive rather than grounded in systematic experimentation.

In this work, we explore the use of the Unified Medical Language System (UMLS) Metathesaurus as a source of external knowledge to enhance prompts for biomedical relation extraction. We propose leveraging UMLS for two key reasons: (1) its background information can help highlight critical contextual details, and (2) it can potentially guide models toward specific relations with similar relationships.

This study aims to address the following research questions:

RQ 1. Which method is more effective to present the additional knowledge to the models, and how sensitive is model performance to the quality of the external knowledge provided?

RQ 2. If performance improves with presented external knowledge, is it truly due to the extra information, or could it result from other interconnected factors?

2 Experimental Design

To explore the integration of the Knowledge Base (KB), we modularize our experiments into three parts (see Figure 1). We first configure a good basic prompt with development sets (Section 3). On top of this foundation, we explore the use of external knowledge (Section 4). Finally, we integrate text from irrelevant knowledge sources to examine if

[1]Our code is available at: https://github.com/Dotkatdotcome/umls-prompts

Proceedings of the Second Workshop on Patient-Oriented Language Processing (CL4Health), pages 193–204
May 4, 2025 ©2025 Association for Computational Linguistics

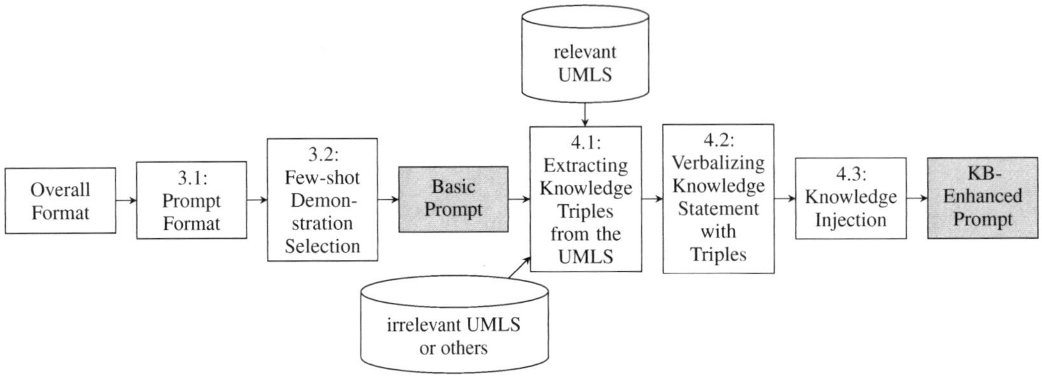

Figure 1: The flowchart of the experiment design.

the performance is influenced by the relevance of the knowledge (Section 5.3).

2.1 Datasets

We use four biomedical relation extraction datasets — two in English: ChemProt (Kringelum et al., 2016), DDI (Segura-Bedmar et al., 2013), and two in non-English: a subset of ADE in German (ADE-de) and French (ADE-fr) (Raithel et al., 2024) [2]. Details are described in Appendix A.

2.2 Models

Definition 2.1 (Demonstration) *A* demonstration *is a task sample provided to models during inference, included in the prompt to illustrate how the task should be performed.*

Definition 2.2 (In-Context Learning (ICL)) *The model is conditioned on a natural language instruction and/or a few* demonstrations *of the task and is then expected to complete further instances of the task simply by predicting what comes next. – (Brown et al., 2020)*

We use open source MISTRAL[3] within the In-Context Learning (ICL) framework for our experiments. The models can handle sequences of arbitrary length due to the use of sliding window attention. MISTRAL is an English model, but works well even on our non-English datasets. We also use BIOMISTRAL[4] for some experiments. BIOMISTRAL is a model based on MISTRAL and was further pre-trained on the PubMed Central corpus, primarily composed of English documents. It is shown that BIOMISTRAL underperforms its base model MISTRAL (Dorfner et al., 2024). We focus our experiments on MISTRAL and include BIOMISTRAL for further analysis.

As Causal Language Models (CLMs) do not always produce clean outputs for evaluation, we use simple pattern matching to extract answers from the models, discarding any responses that are out-of-label.

3 Basic Prompt Setup

3.1 Prompt Format

To ensure a good-quality prompt, we reference the prompt curated for the relation extraction task from the prompt source framework[5]. We pick the best one from a few trial runs on the development set. We then run variants presenting the entities of interest with different markers: *ordered markers*—Entities are masked in their appearing order with E1 and E2; *entity markers*—Entities are masked with their entity type; *decorated markers*—Entities are unmasked and enclosed in markers like [E1], [/E1] or [E2], [/E2]. (see Appendix Figure 7, Figure 5, and Figure 6 for full examples.).

Our results in Table 1 echoed the findings in (Zhang et al., 2024), that revealing the mention of interest (*decorated markers*) does not always perform better than masking out the mentions. Surprisingly, for DDI, *entity markers* perform best despite arbitrary entity order; while *ordered markers* works the best for ADE-de and ADE-fr, even with diverse entity types.

For the following experiments, we use *ordered markers* for ADE-de and ADE-fr, and *decorated markers* for ChemProt and DDI, based on our results. The latter choice ensures comparability with

[2]To ensure meaningful annotations, we take subsets that filter out relations with low inter-annotator agreement.".

[3]https://huggingface.co/mistralai/Mistral-7B-v0.1

[4]https://huggingface.co/BioMistral/BioMistral-7B

[5]https://github.com/bigscience-workshop/promptsource

Marker	Dataset			
	ADE-de	ADE-fr	DDI	ChemProt
decorated (~~~~ [E1]paracetamol[/E1] ~~ [E2]headache[/E2] ~~~~)	73.5	82.8	34.8	**59.0**
entity (~~~~ @DRUG$ ~~ @DISORDER$ ~~~~)	70.2	77.5	**40.4**	50.5
ordered (~~~~ E1 ~~ E2 ~~~~)	**74.5**	**85.7**	35.6	47.8

Table 1: A comparison of different prompt formats over the development set with MISTRAL on 1-shot (per relation) relation extraction.

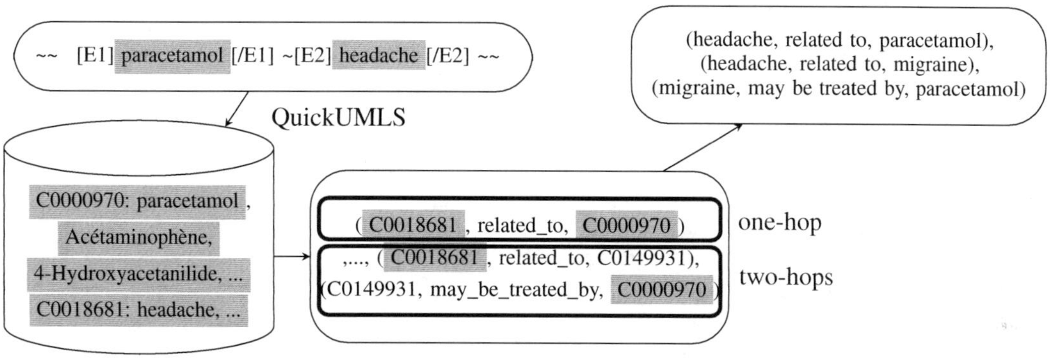

Figure 2: An illustration of extracting and verbalizing information from the UMLS.

prior work and adds task-relevant information.

3.2 Few-shot Demonstrations Selection

To improve performance over random demonstrations, we implement a retrieval module using similarity based on *bag of n-gram token*. The rationale is that selecting samples with similar relations to the inference sample increases the likelihood of correct predictions. In order to ensure a low-resource setting, for each dataset, we randomly select 10% of the training set to create a pool for drawing demonstrations. We map samples to bi-grams and tri-grams using NLTK toolkit[6], compute Jaccard similarity, and select the top-k most similar examples from all relations. Demonstrations are ordered inversely by similarity, placing the most similar samples near the model's output.

4 KB-Enhanced Prompt Setup

The external knowledge source we use is the Unified Medical Language System (UMLS)[7], a rich biomedical resource. In this section, we introduce the setup for applying the UMLS knowledge to enhance the prompts for the biomedical relation extraction task, as illustrated in Figure 2.

[6]https://github.com/nltk/nltk

[7]https://www.nlm.nih.gov/research/umls/index.html

4.1 Extracting Knowledge Triples from the UMLS

To access the relevant part of the ontologies recorded in the UMLS, we use the QuickUMLS [8] to map the two entities to be classified in a sample to their CUIs (Concept Unique Identifiers)[9]. In Figure 2, "paracetamol" and "headache" are mapped to "C0000970" and "C0018681" respectively for looking up the associated relationships. This mapping is an entity-linking process that uses an approximate dictionary-based approach to find the best match of concept identifiers in the UMLS for input strings.

From the two CUIs of the associated entities in one sample, we extract both direct and one-hop relationships between these CUIs from the UMLS table MRREL[10]. For instance, one of the two-hops relationships extracted between "C0000970" and "C0018681" is " (C00018681, related_to, C0149931), (C0149931, may_be_treated_by, C0000970)".

[8]https://github.com/Georgetown-IR-Lab/QuickUMLS

[9]CUIs are the key to obtaining information from the UMLS. In the UMLS, terminology is mapped to the CUIs for disambiguating the concepts, and for documenting relationships.

[10]https://www.ncbi.nlm.nih.gov/books/NBK9685/table/ch03.T.related_concepts_file_mrrel_rrf/

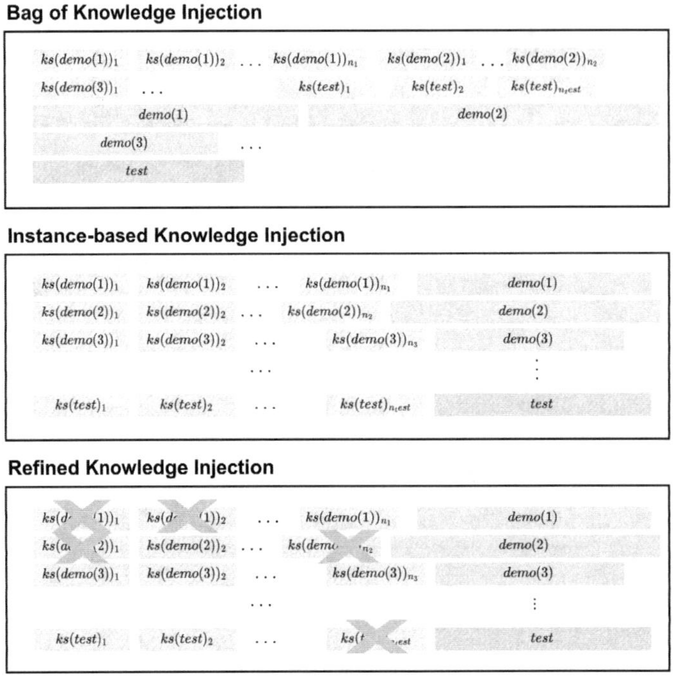

Figure 3: An illustration of the three knowledge injection methods, showcasing increasing levels of refinement from top to bottom. Knowledge statements are in yellow. Top: *Bag of Knowledge Injection* has all knowledge statements prepended altogether to the prompt. Middle: *Instance-based Knowledge Injection* has knowledge statements prepended to each instance. Bottom: *Refined Knowledge Injection* has low-quality knowledge statements removed from *Instance-based Knowledge Injection*.

4.2 Knowledge Statement: Verbalizing Knowledge Statement with Triples

After extracting the relevant triples from the UMLS, we process them to be more natural language-like as it was demonstrated to help the model perform tasks better (Gonen et al., 2023).

For instance, the extracted triples (C00018681, related_to, C0149931) and (C0149931, may_be_treated_by, C0000970) are processed to "(headache, related to, migraine), (migraine, may be treated by, paracetamol)". The CUIs of the intermediate concepts are mapped to their preferred terms[11] using UMLS table `MRCONSO`[12], C0000970 is mapped to "migraine". On the other hand, the CUIs of the entities are mapped to their original mentions from their corresponding samples. We select preferred terms in the same language as the dataset[13]. In this way, we allow the external knowledge to be possibly more integrated into the model's reasoning process as in the case where the preferred terms exist in the sample sentences.

We refer to the processed triples as *knowledge statements*— knowledge expressed as natural language statements. The knowledge statements are then injected into the prompt in different ways, which we will introduce in the next section.

4.3 Knowledge Injection (KI)

We present the extracted *knowledge statements* into the prompt at varying levels of quality, where quality is defined by *granularity*—the degree of association between the task sample and the knowledge statements. As illustrated in Figure 3, lower granularity corresponds to less refined knowledge, requiring minimal pre-processing but placing a greater reasoning burden on the model to achieve strong task performance. Conversely, higher granularity involves more carefully curated knowledge, reducing the model's reasoning load.

[11]The string preferred in a source or in the Metathesaurus as the name of a concept, lexical variant, or string.

[12]https://www.ncbi.nlm.nih.gov/books/NBK9685/table/ch03.T.concept_names_and_sources_file_mr/

[13]We use the column "TTY" in the `MRCONSO` table to select preferred terms.

#Train	Model	Method	ChemProt	DDI	ADE-de	ADE-fr
1-shot	MISTRAL	ICL w/o KI	42.2	39.6	78.5	73.9
		Bag of KI	53.9	40.8	74.7	71.6
		Instance-based KI	60.1	**44.9**	79.9	**77.3**
		Refined KI	**60.2**	44.3	**80.0**	**77.3**
1-shot[1]	GPT-3.5-TURBO (Zhang et al., 2024)	ICL w/o KI	68.5	-	-	-
	GPT-3.5 (Jahan et al., 2024)	ICL w/o KI	-	46.43	-	-
full-shot[2]	PUBMEDBERT	finetuned	73.2	75.9	-	-
	XLM-ROBERTA	finetuned	-	-	66.3	76.4

Table 2: Macro F_1 across different methods on datasets ChemProt, DDI, ADE-de, and ADE-fr, aggregating over five random seeds. Within the MISTRAL experiments, we highlight the **best** score with bold, and second-best score with underline.

[1] We collect the GPT-3.5-TURBO and GPT-3.5 results from the benchmarking papers. [2] We train a classifier using PUBMEDBERT for tasks in English, i.e., ChemProt and DDI; and XLM-ROBERTA for ADE-fr in French and ADE-de in German. To address the issue of imbalanced class distribution, we employ a resampling technique while training XLM-ROBERTA. [3] We set the similarity threshold for the Refined KI to 0.85 for ChemProt and DDI and 0.9 for ADE-de and ADE-fr.

- **Bag of KI** We prepended all extracted descriptions to the beginning of the prompt as a *bag*. This presentation requires the models to associate and reason with the evidence.
- **Instance-based KI** We prepended extracted descriptions to each associated instance. In this presentation, the relevant information is directly before the *instance*.
- **Refined KI** We prepended only the high-quality, semantically relevant triples to associated instances. We used PUBMEDBERT to encode samples and knowledge statements, pruning irrelevant knowledge statements based on cosine similarity of CLS embeddings and a similarity threshold.

5 Results

5.1 Knowledge Injection vs. Baselines

In this section, we discuss our experiment results, summarized in Table 2.

***ICL w/o KI* > full-shot finetuned BERT-based models on user-generated datasets** Our base setup (*ICL w/o KI*) performs better than the full-shot fine-tuned BERT-based models on the user-generated dataset, ADE-de ($\sim$+5% F_1) and perform almost on-par on ADE-fr ($\sim$+1% F_1); while performs worse than the full-shot fine-tuned PUBMEDBERT on the scientific dataset, ChemProt ($\sim$-30% F_1) and DDI ($\sim$-40% F_1).

While we argued previously that ADE-de and ADE-fr are more familiar to the models, it is still surprising that MISTRAL works well on them (even better than the fine-tuned XLM-ROBERTA) despite not having any external knowledge nor entity type information.

***ICL w/o KI* < full-shot finetuned BERT-based models in English scientific dataset** ChemProt and DDI, on the other hand, are more challenging for CLMs with ICL, including our base setup and the state-of-the-art. GPT-3.5-TURBO, a very strong baseline, yields lower performance than fine-tuned models on ChemProt ($\sim$-10% F_1) and GPT-3.5 underperforms on DDI ($\sim$-35% F_1).

Our *ICL w/o KI* with Mistral yields lower performance than GPT-3.5 models on ChemProt (-20% F_1) and DDI (- 5% F_1). GPT-3.5 is a larger CLM with a parameter size of 175B, while our model has 7B. To our knowledge, there is no study with 7B CLMs on ChemProt and DDI for reference here.

Bag of KI* < *ICL w/o KI Compared to our base setup without any external knowledge (*ICL w/o KI*), *Bag of KI* does not show consistent improvement across the datasets; while ChemProt ($\sim$+10% F_1) and DDI ($\sim$+1% F_1) show improvement, ADE-de ($\sim$-3% F_1) and ADE-fr ($\sim$-1% F_1) show a decrease in performance. In the cases where *Bag of KI* underperforms (ADE-de and ADe-fr), the performance is very high to begin with, and the additional knowledge might not be very helpful, since it is background information that still requires models to associate it to the respective instances.

Instance-based KI* ≈ *Refined KI* > *ICL w/o KI *Instance-based KI* and *Refined KI* show consistent improvement compared to *Bag of KI* and *ICL w/o KI* on ChemProt (~+20% F_1), DDI (~+5% F_1), ADE-de (~+2% F_1), and ADE-fr (~+3% F_1). These results suggest that positioning the knowledge closer to the instances is more beneficial for the models to make the right prediction. Nevertheless, comparing *Refined KI* to *Instance-based KI*, we can see that the performance is barely increasing. We do not know if the insignificant improvement is due to the *Refined KI* sometimes removing the knowledge statements of good quality, or it is due to that the quality of the knowledge statements is not as important for the performance. Therefore, we further explore the effect of the quality of the knowledge statements in the next section, when we explore the similarity threshold for *Refined KI*.

***Instance-based KI* boosts the performance of smaller CLMs to be more on par with the big CLMs** *Instance-based KI* with MISTRAL obtain better results than, the large CLM GPT-3.5 on DDI (~+1% F_1) and much closer to GPT-3.5-TURBO on ChemProt (~-5% F_1) than the base setup. These results, as GPT-3.5s results, are still behind the full-shot fine-tuned BERT-based models on ChemProt and DDI by a noticeable margin, but the gap is much smaller than the base setup. Small BERT-based models are still highly effective for biomedical relation extraction tasks due to their ease of fine-tuning. Additionally, smaller CLMs with appropriate knowledge injections can also achieve competitive results and are significantly more efficient to run than the larger CLMs.

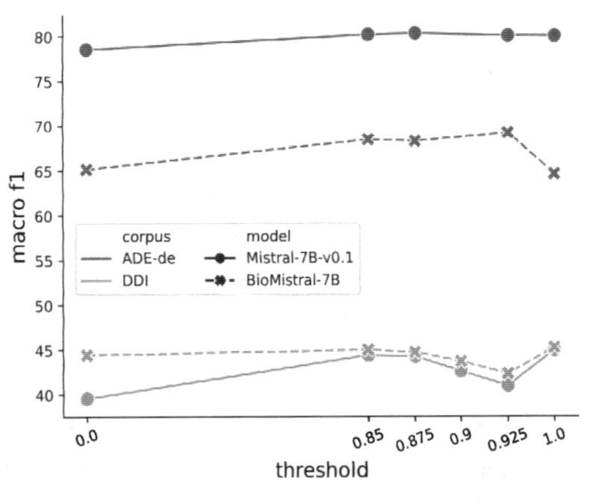

Figure 4: macro F_1(%) over similarity threshold with MISTRAL and BIOMISTRAL on ADE-de and DDI. The x-axis similarity threshold runs from 0, which corresponds to Instance-based KI, to 1, which corresponds to the w/o KI.

5.2 Effect of Similarity Threshold

The semantic similarity between the knowledge statements and the instances is high, with scores ranging from 0.80 to 0.95 (see Appendix Figure 8). We examine the effect with MISTRAL and BIOMISTRAL on ADE-de and DDI (see Figure 4). With all additional knowledge (threshold=0), BIOMISTRAL performs worse than MISTRAL on ADE-de (-15% F_1), but slightly better in DDI (~+5% F_1). This discrepancy is likely due to BIOMISTRAL's medical training resources being predominantly in English, hence making it less effective on multilingual datasets. Although MISTRAL initially performs worse on DDI, enforcing a similarity threshold brings MISTRAL to perform on par with BIOMISTRAL. This result demonstrates that general models can be improved by high-quality knowledge statements to match the capacity of biomedical models trained with additional large corpora.

The results show that the performance improves with increasing similarity thresholds and that the performance is saturated around 0.85 for DDI, and 0.9 for ADE-de; followed by a decline. These results suggest that while higher-quality knowledge statements enhance performance, excessively high thresholds may reduce the number of usable knowledge statements, thereby hurting the overall performance.

5.3 Effect of Knowledge Source and Position

The additional knowledge statements help all datasets, yet they also change the prompt layout, which could affect the model performance. Our goal here is to investigate if the observed performance gains are contributed by external knowledge rather than extra tokens that changed the prompt format. We, therefore, swap the knowledge statements from the extracted UMLS triples.

- *UMLS instance-unrelated*: UMLS triples relevant to the corpus (extracted as described in Section 4) but irrelevant to the sample.
- *UMLS corpus-unrelated*: UMLS triples that are completely irrelevant to the corpus. We extract triples that do not involve any CUI from the entities in the corpus.
- *Bible*: We take text from the Wikipedia page of the Bible[14] as our generation pool. This ex-

[14]https://en.wikipedia.org/wiki/Bible

Position	Triple Source	*macro* F_1
-	ICL w/o KI	42.2
task background	Bag of KI	53.9
close-to instances	Instance-based KI (UMLS instance-related)	60.2
close-to instances	UMLS instance-unrelated	60.0
	UMLS corpus-unrelated	**61.4**
	Bible	60.1
	Empty	60.0

Table 3: macro F_1 (%) with different adversarial knowledge statements on ChemProt.

periment serves as a totally irrelevant knowledge source.

- *Empty*: We discard the content in the triplet template using just the placeholder, i.e., (, ,).

Position Compared to *Bag of KI* where all knowledge statements are collected as task background altogether at the beginning of all instances, all methods that place knowledge statements close to instances show better performance (see Table 3), regardless of whether the knowledge statements are relevant or irrelevant. These results suggest that the models can effectively benefit from relevant knowledge statements when they are closely positioned to the instances. However, when the knowledge statements are distanced from the instances, the models struggle to recognize and leverage the knowledge.

Knowledge Source All knowledge sources improve the base setup (~+20% F_1), including *Empty* (see Table 3). The results suggest that these additional tokens in between the instances improve the performance.

6 Discussion and Conclusion

For our experiments on ADE-de and ADE-fr, the prompts contain two languages: the instructions, relations from the UMLS, and the ground truth label of the sample—known as the *verbalizer*—are in English, while the samples, entities, and entities linked to the UMLS are respectively in French and German. The mixing of languages in prompts was studied in multilingual relation classification tasks (Chen et al., 2022) and cross-lingual natural language inference (XNLI) (Zhou et al., 2023). These studies concluded that directly translating the verbalizers to the target language for inference is not helpful. However, the effect of other parts of the prompt is still to be understood. Our results show that the mixed-language prompts still achieve competitive results in our tasks.

In this work, we explored the integration of external knowledge for the extraction of biomedical relations within the context of in-context learning. We extracted triples from the UMLS based on the entities involved in the relations and injected them into the prompt with different *granularity*.

Our experiments for configuring a basic prompt revealed that different entity markers are effective across different datasets, showing that entity mentions are not always more beneficial for the models than marking with entity types or order. Our experiments showed that MISTRAL with ICL performs very well on the user-generated datasets in non-English; however, the model still performs poorly on more difficult tasks in English. With knowledge integration, the performance of ICL is boosted to be more on par with the larger autoregressive models.

The knowledge statements help the model perform better across all datasets. Additionally, applying a suitable similarity threshold for further refining the knowledge statements further helps the models, especially for models trained only on general corpora. We observed that the performance was even more affected by the positioning and the addition of tokens. When the additional knowledge is positioned close to the instances, the models can effectively identify relevant knowledge statements.

Limitations

There are limitations to be noted for this work. Firstly, in the experiment setup, the hyperparameters are tuned in a cascaded manner, which is less computationally expensive yet suboptimal. Secondly, entity linking can be a bottleneck for this method, especially considering the typos and informal language of user-generated datasets. Third, the effect of prompt length is still to be understood. We found that the additional tokens can possibly help, even if carrying irrelevant knowledge, however, the effect of inserting irrelevant tokens and how one places them in the prompt also require further investigation. While related work has studied this direction (Levy et al., 2024), domain-specific tasks remain understudied and require more research.

Acknowledgments

This work was financially supported by the trilateral project KEEPHA, Grant Number JST-JPMJCR20G9, DFG-442445488, and ANR-20-

IADJ-0005-01. The experiments of this work were performed on Jean-Zay's V100 and A100 partitions. We also want to thank the reviewers for their feedback on this paper.

References

Tom Brown, Benjamin Mann, Nick Ryder, Melanie Subbiah, Jared D Kaplan, Prafulla Dhariwal, Arvind Neelakantan, Pranav Shyam, Girish Sastry, Amanda Askell, Sandhini Agarwal, Ariel Herbert-Voss, Gretchen Krueger, Tom Henighan, Rewon Child, Aditya Ramesh, Daniel Ziegler, Jeffrey Wu, Clemens Winter, Chris Hesse, Mark Chen, Eric Sigler, Mateusz Litwin, Scott Gray, Benjamin Chess, Jack Clark, Christopher Berner, Sam McCandlish, Alec Radford, Ilya Sutskever, and Dario Amodei. 2020. Language models are few-shot learners. In *Advances in Neural Information Processing Systems*, volume 33, pages 1877–1901. Curran Associates, Inc.

Yuxuan Chen, David Harbecke, and Leonhard Hennig. 2022. Multilingual relation classification via efficient and effective prompting. In *Proceedings of the 2022 Conference on Empirical Methods in Natural Language Processing*, pages 1059–1075, Abu Dhabi, United Arab Emirates. Association for Computational Linguistics.

Felix J Dorfner, Amin Dada, Felix Busch, Marcus R Makowski, Tianyu Han, Daniel Truhn, Jens Kleesiek, Madhumita Sushil, Jacqueline Lammert, Lisa C Adams, et al. 2024. Biomedical large languages models seem not to be superior to generalist models on unseen medical data. *arXiv preprint arXiv:2408.13833*.

Hila Gonen, Srini Iyer, Terra Blevins, Noah Smith, and Luke Zettlemoyer. 2023. Demystifying prompts in language models via perplexity estimation. In *Findings of the Association for Computational Linguistics: EMNLP 2023*, pages 10136–10148, Singapore. Association for Computational Linguistics.

Israt Jahan, Md Tahmid Rahman Laskar, Chun Peng, and Jimmy Xiangji Huang. 2024. A comprehensive evaluation of large language models on benchmark biomedical text processing tasks. *Computers in Biology and Medicine*, page 108189.

Jens Kringelum, Sonny Kim Kjaerulff, Søren Brunak, Ole Lund, Tudor I Oprea, and Olivier Taboureau. 2016. ChemProt-3.0: a global chemical biology diseases mapping. *Database*, 2016.

Mosh Levy, Alon Jacoby, and Yoav Goldberg. 2024. Same task, more tokens: the impact of input length on the reasoning performance of large language models. In *Proceedings of the 62nd Annual Meeting of the Association for Computational Linguistics (Volume 1: Long Papers)*, pages 15339–15353, Bangkok, Thailand. Association for Computational Linguistics.

Lisa Raithel, Hui-Syuan Yeh, Shuntaro Yada, Cyril Grouin, Thomas Lavergne, Aurélie Névéol, Patrick Paroubek, Philippe Thomas, Tomohiro Nishiyama, Sebastian Möller, Eiji Aramaki, Yuji Matsumoto, Roland Roller, and Pierre Zweigenbaum. 2024. A dataset for pharmacovigilance in German, French, and Japanese: Annotating adverse drug reactions across languages. In *Proceedings of the 2024 Joint International Conference on Computational Linguistics, Language Resources and Evaluation (LREC-COLING 2024)*, pages 395–414, Torino, Italia. ELRA and ICCL.

Isabel Segura-Bedmar, Paloma Martínez, and María Herrero-Zazo. 2013. SemEval-2013 task 9 : Extraction of drug-drug interactions from biomedical texts (DDIExtraction 2013). In *Second Joint Conference on Lexical and Computational Semantics (*SEM), Volume 2: Proceedings of the Seventh International Workshop on Semantic Evaluation (SemEval 2013)*, pages 341–350, Atlanta, Georgia, USA. Association for Computational Linguistics.

Jeffrey Zhang, Maxwell Wibert, Huixue Zhou, Xueqing Peng, Qingyu Chen, Vipina K Keloth, Yan Hu, Rui Zhang, Hua Xu, and Kalpana Raja. 2024. A study of biomedical relation extraction using gpt models. *AMIA Summits on Translational Science Proceedings*, 2024:391.

Meng Zhou, Xin Li, Yue Jiang, and Lidong Bing. 2023. Enhancing cross-lingual prompting with dual prompt augmentation. In *Findings of the Association for Computational Linguistics: ACL 2023*, pages 11008–11020, Toronto, Canada. Association for Computational Linguistics.

Fangqi Zhu, Yongqi Zhang, Lei Chen, Bing Qin, and Ruifeng Xu. 2023. Learning to describe for predicting zero-shot drug-drug interactions. In *Proceedings of the 2023 Conference on Empirical Methods in Natural Language Processing*, pages 14855–14870, Singapore. Association for Computational Linguistics.

A Dataset

Dataset	Source	#Relation	Relations	#Test
ChemProt	PubMed abstracts	6	activation (CPR:3) inhibition (CPR:4) agonist (CPR:5) antagonist (CPR:6) substrate (CPR:9) false (none of above)	16,943
DDI	MedLine abstracts	5	DDI-advise DDI-effect DDI-int DDI-mechanism DDI-false	5,761
ADE-de	Patient Forum	7	caused experienced_in has_dosage has_time signals_change_of treatment_for false	3,285
ADE-fr	Patient Forum	7	caused experienced_in has_dosage has_time signals_change_of treatment_for false	551

Table 4: Dataset Overview

B Prompt Examples

ordered markers E1-E2

Out of the possible relations: [CAUSED, EXPERIENCED_IN, HAS_DOSAGE, HAS_TIME, SIGNALS_CHANGE_OF, TREATMENT_FOR, NONE]
###

Given the sentence, J'ai aussi E1 pour la première fois de ma vie E2.
What is the semantic relation between the two nominals (nouns or noun phrases) DISORDER E1 and TIME E2 in the sentence: HAS_TIME

Given the sentence, et de la dominance en œstrogène ! Depuis six mois, je prends E2 de E1.
What is the semantic relation between the two nominals (nouns or noun phrases) DRUG E1 and MEASURE E2 in the sentence: HAS_DOSAGE

Given the sentence, J'ai aussi E1 pour la première fois de ma vie au cours des six derniers mois. Moi aussi, je suis désespérée par mon E2 et, enfin .
What is the semantic relation between the two nominals (nouns or noun phrases) DISORDER E1 and ANATOMY E2 in the sentence: EXPERIENCED_IN

Given the sentence, et de la dominance en œstrogène ! Depuis six mois, je prends 50 mg de E1....La fluoxétine est connue pour faire perdre du poids....J'ai E2 au début.
What is the semantic relation between the two nominals (nouns or noun phrases) DRUG E1 and DISORDER E2 in the sentence: CAUSED

Given the sentence, E2, je résistais à tout ! Mais quand rien n'allait plus, j'ai accepté d'en prendre. J'ai aussi E1 pour la première fois de ma vie au cours des six derniers mois.
What is the semantic relation between the two nominals (nouns or noun phrases) DISORDER E1 and TIME E2 in the sentence: NONE

Given the sentence, J'ai pris E2 après avoir pris 3 hormones différentes, ça a bien marché, mais j'ai dû E1 parce que j'avais des saignements abondants (janvier).
What is the semantic relation between the two nominals (nouns or noun phrases) CHANGE_TRIGGER E1 and DRUG E2 in the sentence: SIGNALS_CHANGE_OF

Given the sentence, Je prends maintenant Trisequens (depuis 2 mois) et E1 pour E2 et l'humeur.
What is the semantic relation between the two nominals (nouns or noun phrases) DRUG E1 and DISORDER E2 in the sentence: TREATMENT_FOR

###

Given the sentence,De plus, j'ai commencé à avoir des nausées, des E1 de E2, des muqueuses sèches, etc.
What is the semantic relation between the two nominals (nouns or noun phrases) DISORDER E1 and ANATOMY E2 in the sentence:

Figure 5: An example of the prompt with ordered markers.

entity-type markers @TYPE$

Out of the possible relations: [CAUSED, EXPERIENCED_IN, HAS_DOSAGE, HAS_TIME, SIGNALS_CHANGE_OF, TREATMENT_FOR, NONE]
###

Given the sentence, J'ai aussi @DISORDER$ pour la première fois de ma vie @TIME$.
What is the semantic relation between the two nominals (nouns or noun phrases) @DISORDER$ and @TIME$ in the sentence: HAS_TIME

Given the sentence, et de la dominance en œstrogène ! Depuis six mois, je prends @MEASURE$ de @DRUG$.
What is the semantic relation between the two nominals (nouns or noun phrases) @DRUG$ and @MEASURE$ in the sentence: HAS_DOSAGE

Given the sentence, J'ai aussi @DISORDER$ pour la première fois de ma vie au cours des six derniers mois. Moi aussi, je suis désespérée par mon @ANATOMY$ et, enfin .
What is the semantic relation between the two nominals (nouns or noun phrases) @DISORDER$ and @ANATOMY$ in the sentence: EXPERIENCED_IN

Given the sentence, et de la dominance en œstrogène ! Depuis six mois, je prends 50 mg de @DRUG$....La fluoxétine est connue pour faire perdre du poids....J'ai @DISORDER$ au début.
What is the semantic relation between the two nominals (nouns or noun phrases) @DRUG$ and @DISORDER$ in the sentence: CAUSED

Given the sentence, @TIME$, je résistais à tout ! Mais quand rien n'allait plus, j'ai accepté d'en prendre. J'ai aussi @DISORDER$ pour la première fois de ma vie au cours des six derniers mois.
What is the semantic relation between the two nominals (nouns or noun phrases) @DISORDER$ and @TIME$ in the sentence: NONE

Given the sentence, J'ai pris @DRUG$ après avoir pris 3 hormones différentes, ça a bien marché, mais j'ai dû @CHANGE_TRIGGER$ parce que j'avais des saignements abondants (janvier).
What is the semantic relation between the two nominals (nouns or noun phrases) @CHANGE_TRIGGER$ and @DRUG$ in the sentence: SIGNALS_CHANGE_OF

Given the sentence, Je prends maintenant Trisequens (depuis 2 mois) et @DRUG$ pour @DISORDER$ et l'humeur.
What is the semantic relation between the two nominals (nouns or noun phrases) @DRUG$ and @DISORDER$ in the sentence: TREATMENT_FOR

###

Given the sentence,De plus, j'ai commencé à avoir des nausées, des @DISORDER$ de @ANATOMY$, des muqueuses sèches, etc.What is the semantic relation between the two nominals (nouns or noun phrases) @DISORDER$ and @ANATOMY$ in the sentence:

Figure 6: An example of the prompt with entity-type markers.

decorated markers [E]ENTITY_T[/E]

Out of the possible relations: [CAUSED, EXPERIENCED_IN, HAS_DOSAGE, HAS_TIME, SIGNALS_CHANGE_OF, TREATMENT_FOR, NONE]
###

Given the sentence, J'ai aussi [E1]pris du poids[/E1] pour la première fois de ma vie [E2]au cours des six derniers mois[/E2].
What is the semantic relation between the two nominals (nouns or noun phrases) DISORDER pris du poids and TIME au cours des six derniers mois in the sentence: HAS_TIME

Given the sentence, et de la dominance en œstrogène ! Depuis six mois, je prends [E2]50 mg[/E2] de [E1]fluoxétine[/E1].
What is the semantic relation between the two nominals (nouns or noun phrases) DRUG fluoxétine and MEASURE 50 mg in the sentence: HAS_DOSAGE

Given the sentence, J'ai aussi [E1]pris du poids[/E1] pour la première fois de ma vie au cours des six derniers mois. Moi aussi, je suis désespérée par mon [E2]ventre[/E2] et, enfin .
What is the semantic relation between the two nominals (nouns or noun phrases) DISORDER pris du poids and ANATOMY ventre in the sentence: EXPERIENCED_IN

Given the sentence, et de la dominance en œstrogène ! Depuis six mois, je prends 50 mg de [E1]fluoxétine[/E1]....La fluoxétine est connue pour faire perdre du poids....J'ai [E2]perdu immédiatement 3 kg[/E2] au début.
What is the semantic relation between the two nominals (nouns or noun phrases) DRUG fluoxétine and DISORDER perdu immédiatement 3 kg in the sentence: CAUSED

Given the sentence, [E2]Jusqu'à l'année dernière[/E2], je résistais à tout ! Mais quand rien n'allait plus, j'ai accepté d'en prendre. J'ai aussi [E1]pris du poids[/E1] pour la première fois de ma vie au cours des six derniers mois. What is the semantic relation between the two nominals (nouns or noun phrases) DISORDER pris du poids and TIME Jusqu'à l'année dernière in the sentence: NONE

Given the sentence, J'ai pris [E2]Kliogest[/E2] après avoir pris 3 hormones différentes, ça a bien marché, mais j'ai dû [E1]arrêter[/E1] parce que j'avais des saignements abondants (janvier).
What is the semantic relation between the two nominals (nouns or noun phrases) CHANGE_TRIGGER arrêter and DRUG Kliogest in the sentence: SIGNALS_CHANGE_OF

Given the sentence, Je prends maintenant Trisequens (depuis 2 mois) et [E1]Insidon[/E1] pour [E2]l'anxiété[/E2] et l'humeur.
What is the semantic relation between the two nominals (nouns or noun phrases) DRUG Insidon and DISORDER l'anxiété in the sentence: TREATMENT_FOR

###

Given the sentence,De plus, j'ai commencé à avoir des nausées, des [E1]inflammations[/E1] de [E2]l'estomac[/E2], des muqueuses sèches, etc.
What is the semantic relation between the two nominals (nouns or noun phrases) DISORDER inflammations and ANATOMY l'estomac in the sentence:

Figure 7: An example of the prompt with decorated markers.

C Similar Distribution of Knowledge Statements

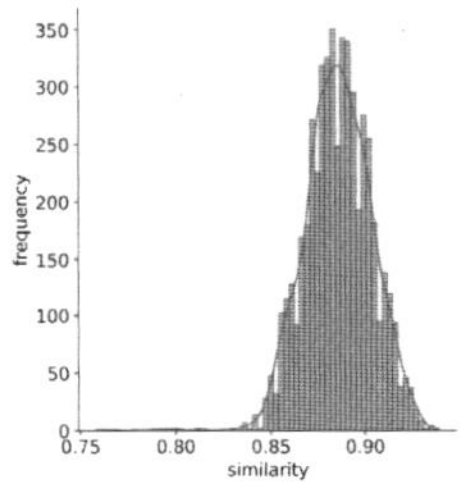

(a) ChemProt.

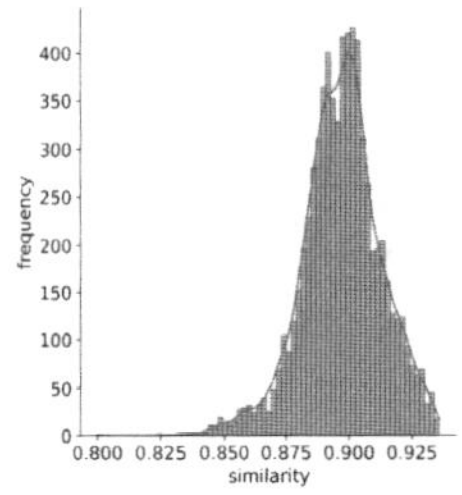

(b) DDI.

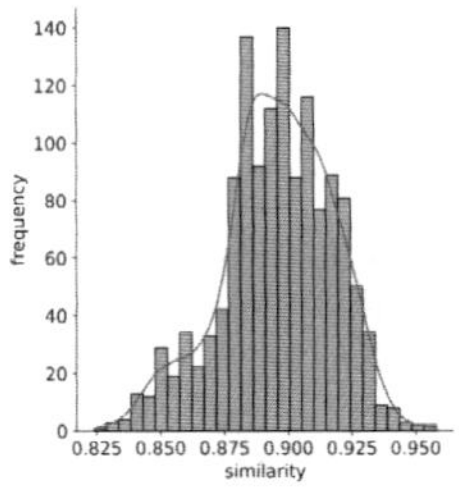

(c) ADE-de.

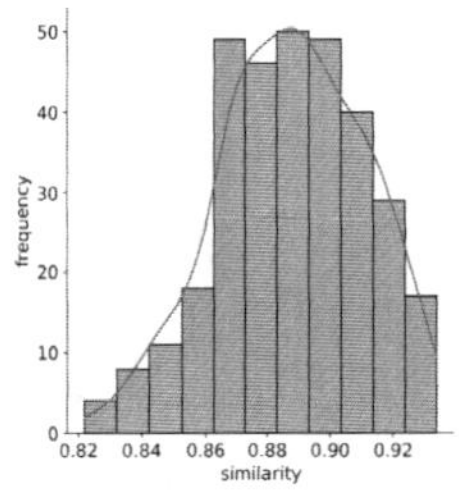

(d) ADE-fr.

Figure 8: Similarity distribution of knowledge statements for different datasets. (a) ChemProt, (b) DDI, (c) ADE-de, and (d) ADE-fr.

LT3: Generating Medication Prescriptions with Conditional Transformer

Samuel Belkadi[1*], **Nicolo Micheletti**[2*], **Lifeng Han**[3,4**]
Warren Del-Pinto[4], and **Goran Nenadic**[4]
[1] Cambridge University, UK [2] Tsinghua University, China
[3] LIACS & LUMC, Leiden University, NL [4] The University of Manchester, UK
[*] *co-first authors* [**] *corresponding author*
l.han@lumc.nl, warren.del-pinto, g.nenadic@manchester.ac.uk
belkadisamuel, MichelettiNik@gmail.com

Abstract

Access to real-world medication prescriptions is essential for medical research and healthcare quality improvement. However, access to real medication prescriptions is often limited due to the *sensitive* nature of the information expressed. Additionally, manually labelling these instructions for training and fine-tuning Natural Language Processing (NLP) models can be tedious and expensive. We introduce a novel task-specific model architecture, **Label-To-Text-Transformer** (**LT3**), tailored to generate synthetic medication prescriptions based on provided labels, such as a vocabulary list of medications and their attributes, to facilitate *safe* healthcare research. LT3 is trained on a set of around 2K lines of medication prescriptions extracted from the MIMIC-III database, allowing the model to produce valuable synthetic medication prescriptions. We evaluate LT3's performance by contrasting it with state-of-the-art Pre-trained Language Models (PLMs), T5-small/base/large, analysing the quality and diversity of generated texts. We deploy the generated synthetic data to train the SpacyNER model for the Named Entity Recognition (NER) task over the n2c2-2018 dataset. The experiments show that the model trained on synthetic data can achieve a 96-98% F1 score at Label Recognition on Drug, Frequency, Route, Strength, and Form. LT3 codes and data will be shared for research purposes at https://github.com/HECTA-UoM/Label-To-Text-Transformer

1 Introduction

Access to real-world medication prescriptions is pivotal for advancing medical research, including clinical natural language processing (NLP) applications, which is useful for improving healthcare quality and fostering the creation of novel solutions to address current research challenges (Nazari Nezhad et al., 2022; Alrdahi et al., 2023; Cui et al., 2023). However, given the confidential nature of these instructions, there are significant difficulties in acquiring and utilising them for research purposes (Spasić et al., 2014). Additionally, manual labelling of such data for training and fine-tuning NLP techniques is labour-intensive and costly. This is also discussed by recent overview work in (Wornow et al., 2023; Rajendran et al., 2024).

In response to these challenges, this study harnesses NLP methodologies to generate synthetic medication prescriptions. These synthetic examples provide a feasible alternative when real medical data is not available, which is a common problem due to concerns about patient confidentiality. The use of this synthetic data alongside, or in place of, real medical data can therefore alleviate challenges associated with accessing and employing sufficient data for NLP research, which is essential for healthcare quality enhancement and the inception of innovative strategies toward better computational modelling of digital healthcare data (Chen et al., 2019).

The generation of synthetic clinical data has gained attention in recent years due to the challenges associated with accessing real-world clinical data (Gonçalves et al., 2020; Marchesi et al., 2022). Several studies have explored synthetic data generation for clinical NLP tasks. For instance, Amin-Nejad et al. (2020) proposed a methodology for generating synthetic clinical text using structured patient information in a sequence-to-sequence manner and experimented with state-of-the-art Transformer models. They demonstrated that their augmented dataset could outperform baseline models on a downstream classification task.

Lee (2018) explored the use of an encoder-decoder model to generate synthetic chief complaints from discrete variables in EHRs, such as age group, gender, and discharge diagnosis. After being trained end-to-end on authentic records, the model generated realistic chief complaint text

Proceedings of the Second Workshop on Patient-Oriented Language Processing (CL4Health), pages 205–218
May 4, 2025 ©2025 Association for Computational Linguistics

that preserved the epidemiological information encoded in the original record-sentence pairs. This suggests that such a model could support the de-identification of text in EHRs, helping address the significant privacy concerns that often limit the sharing and use of real-world clinical data. However, only some works have attempted to control the generation of these models (Keskar et al., 2019). Despite these advances, there is still room for improvement in generating synthetic clinical letters.

This study puts forth a novel task-specific model architecture, the Label-To-Text-Transformer (**LT3**), crafted to generate synthetic medication prescriptions. Based on the Transformer's architecture (Vaswani et al., 2017) and trained on an extracted set of around 2K medication prescriptions, LT3 is adept at generating high-quality synthetic medication prescriptions by capturing the unique patterns and dependencies involved in *prescription writing* and other aspects of clinical documentation, such as sentence formatting. For example, given a medication "*docusate sodium*" we would expect to generate a prescription such as "*docusate sodium 100 mg Capsule Sig: One (1) Capsule PO BID (2 times a day) as needed for constipation.*". To test how effective LT3 is, we will compare its performance to that of another State-of-the-art Pre-trained Language Model (**PLM**), T5 (Raffel et al., 2020), which we fine-tuned for this particular task. For downstream applications, we also deploy the synthetic data generated by LT3 for training the SpacyNER model to compare the model performance with the ones trained from real data.

2 Related Work: PLMs for Clinical NLP

NLP technologies have been increasingly used in healthcare over the past several years, contributing to advancements in several areas such as clinical decision support, patient triage, and automated clinical documentation (Yang et al., 2022; Casey et al., 2021). However, these applications face numerous challenges, one of the most significant being the scarcity of available data. This issue is predominantly due to stringent privacy regulations and the sensitive nature of healthcare data, which prevent access to large volumes of real-world clinical data (Ive et al., 2020; Chapman et al., 2011).

To circumvent this problem, synthetic data generation has been explored as an alternative approach, aiming to produce data that mimics the properties and structure of real-world clinical data without compromising patient privacy (Li et al., 2021). Despite this approach's potential, producing high-quality, domain-specific synthetic data remains challenging due to the complexity and specificity of medical language.

PLMs have shown remarkable capabilities in generating contextualised texts, such as translations (Xue et al., 2020) and summaries (Moradi et al., 2019). However, they have struggled to generate coherent text in the medical domain. This is due to the considerable shift from standard NLP tasks to the medical domain, which presents challenges as pre-trained models have a more general-purpose design and do not learn directly from restricted domain-specific data (Grambow et al., 2022). For example, the word "paracetamol" may be captured in many training documents that do not correspond to synthetic clinical letter generation tasks and, therefore, be a noisy contribution. Moreover, PLMs need more flexibility to handle different input types and are not explicitly trained on label-to-text data, resulting in sub-optimal accuracy for the specific task. To address these challenges, this research proposal aims to develop a task-specific model architecture that can overcome the limitations of pre-trained models and generate high-quality synthetic clinical instructions.

Furthermore, in NLP fields, international shared tasks have been one of the main factors pushing research forward by having researchers compare their results on the same data set. However, in the healthcare and clinical domain, the data we use to train the model is often sensitive and related to personal information, so there is a big obstacle to sharing the data for model training and testing. Even the popular n2c2 shared task training data cannot be simply uploaded to current popular ML platforms, even though they are de-identified via the user agreement. This aspect is also discussed by (Wornow et al., 2023) that the publicly being unable to share the learned models using clinical data especially EHRs sets a bottleneck for current LLMs in healthcare NLP. In such a situation, synthetic data can be a good option.

3 LT3: Label-To-Text-Transformer

3.1 Problem Formulation

Let $\mathcal{C}$ be a space of clinical instruction features, and $c \in \mathcal{C}$ represents a feature vector for individual clinical instruction, e.g. a sentence piece. Let $\mathcal{L}$ be a set of drug labels. We have a dataset $\mathcal{D}_C^L$ with labels annotated over the clinical instructions.

For each drug label $l \in \mathcal{L}$, we originally have a sub-set data $\mathcal{D}^l$ defined as $\mathcal{D}^l = \{c_n^l\}_{n=1}^{N_l}$ containing clinical instructions associated with drug l. Individual instructions are indexed by n for each l, where N_l is the number of instructions for drug l.

Our primary objective is to generate a synthetic dataset that replaces the real datasets entirely, conditioned on the drug labels from $\mathcal{L}$. To achieve this, we aim to learn a density function $\hat{d}\{C|l\}$, which approximates the true distribution $d\{C|l\}$ of the clinical instructions conditioned on each drug label l.

Once the distributions for each drug label l are learned, we generate an entirely synthetic dataset by drawing random variables from $\hat{d}\{C|l\}$ for each drug l. This synthetic dataset will have clinical instructions corresponding to every drug label in $\mathcal{L}$ and completely replace the original dataset.

3.2 Model Architecture

We introduce a transformer-based architecture, LT3 with both an encoder and a decoder. The encoder processes the input labels, specifies drug names, and produces a contextualised representation, which is subsequently used by the decoder to generate output sequences in the form of prescriptions.

LT3 implements the pre-trained word-piece BERT tokeniser (Devlin et al., 2019). This selection is motivated by the objective of representing words as a series of smaller sub-word tokens. Simultaneously, this approach serves the dual purpose of minimising vocabulary size while handling unseen words as the composition of a set of known sub-words. Embedding layers are used within the model's architecture and are trained from *scratch* to precisely cater to the requirements of the medical prescription writing task (Figure 1).

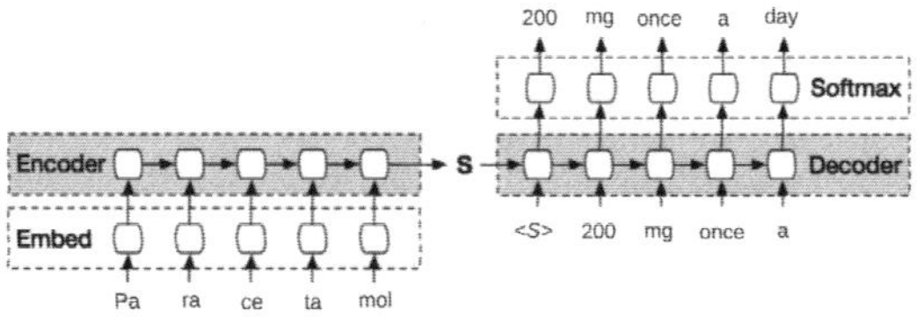

Figure 1: LT3 Architecture with input/output behaviour (this is a shortened example of a generated synthetic medical prescription.)

3.3 B2SD: Beam Search Decoding using Backtracking

LT3 implements a novel Beam Search Decoding method using Backtracking (**B2SD**). While the conventional technique adopts a greedy strategy, selecting the best n next-token candidates at each decoding step based on an overall probability function, this method instead employs a backtracking strategy (Golomb and Baumert, 1965).

At each step, we select the best candidate sequence generated so far. This selection relies on a heuristic function, specifically a joint probability function. Subsequently, the selected sequence is expanded by its best n next-token candidates, referred to as a beam. This strategy allows the search tree to be flexible in size rather than limited to a fixed $n * seq_{len}$. However, in addressing the notable space and time complexity challenges of the B2SD algorithm, we decided to restrict the explorable space to the top-m sequences generated so far, based on the same heuristic function.

In the example from Figure 2, we compare the execution of both algorithms in generating sentences that describe someone as twelve years old. Both algorithms use a beam size of two and generate two sequences. The desired outputs are the ones with the highest total joint probabilities, namely "I am twelve" (p=0.138) and "You are twelve" (p=0.135). When comparing their execution, we observe that the backtracking algorithm *(b)* explores seven vertices, including one dead-end labelled "scored" (coloured in blue), in contrast to the original algorithm *(a)*, which only examines six vertices. However, in this scenario, the probabilities are sufficiently close to prevent a greedy algorithm, such as the original one, from catching the best overall sequences. Therefore, one of the two optimal solutions remains undiscovered, and instead, the dead-end labelled "scored" is greedily considered optimal by the original algorithm. However, B2SD managed to discover both desired outputs at the price of an additional vertex exploration.

There is a trade-off between complexity and the main advantage of the backtracking algorithm, which is its ability to find the best solution in the beam tree according to its heuristic within a finite time compared to the original BSD algorithm. This means that a higher level of complexity may lead to a longer search time but a better solution. In our specific scenario, striking this balance is justified.

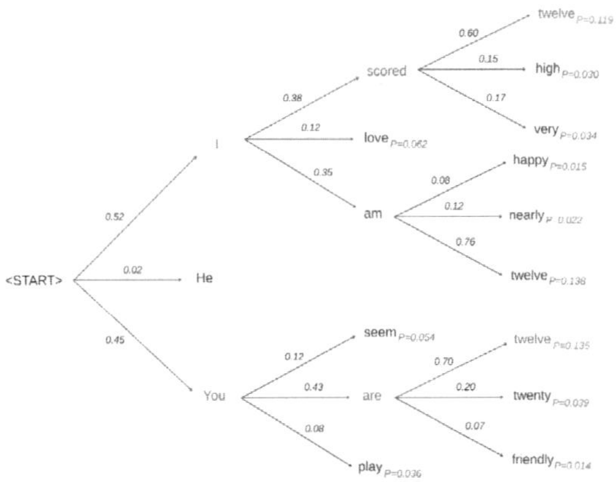

(a) Original BSD ($n = 2$)

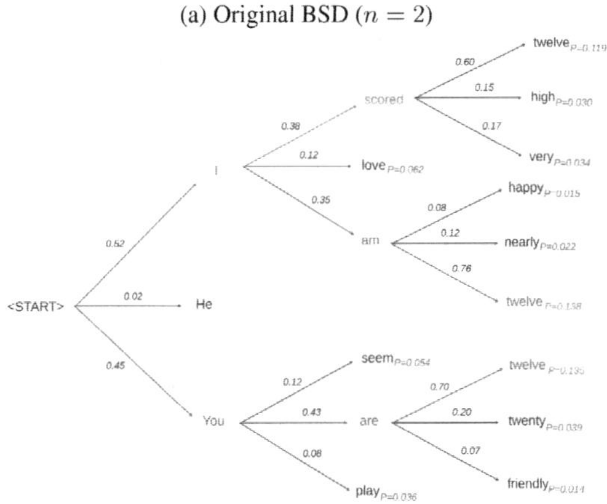

(b) B2SD ($n = 2, m = 2, p_b = 1$)

Figure 2: Execution Examples of Conventional Greedy BSD and B2SD Algorithms

That is because LT3 deals with a limited number of samples to generate relatively short sequences. Moreover, by utilising this algorithm, we can efficiently bypass tokens within the beam that, while still within the top-n candidates, are significantly less likely to contribute to genuinely interesting sequences. This approach encourages the model to prioritise the development of promising sequences.

Therefore, the complexity of the newly proposed B2SD algorithm can be expressed as exponential in the sequence's length, denoted $\mathcal{O}(n^{seq_{len}})$. At the same time, the original one is linear: $\mathcal{O}(n * seq_{len})$. However, worst-case complexity may not represent the execution times for the above reasons (see Sec A.3).

Besides using this backtracking approach, the beam size *n* does not need to be greater or equal to the number of desired output sequences. Instead, *m* should follow this requirement, as it is the maximum number of sequences considered for output.

To enhance the quality of sequence generations, we implement an additional uni-gram repeat penalty targeting sub-sequences of length 4. This penalty aims to discourage the generation of sequences where a sub-sequence of four tokens contains multiple instances of the same token. For example, the sub-sequence [43, 32, 21, 43] incurs a penalty as the token "43" appears twice. The penalty itself is calculated using the following formula.

$$p'(Y) = p(Y)^{2-0.5*p_T} \tag{1}$$

where p_T is the probability (or certainty) of the last duplicate token, here "43", and $p(Y)$ is the joint probability of the sequence Y. This design allows the application of a penalty that accounts for the token's certainty level. In cases where a duplicate token is suggested but has a high certainty, the penalty is reduced, considering that the model may intentionally repeat it to convey specific information. This can be the case in sentences such as "(once a day (at bedtime))" where closing parenthesis are repeated consecutively.

Finally, to further reduce the search space, the maximal probability difference in beam, p_b, constrains the tokens considered in a beam. This value tells how much lower the probability of a token in the beam from the top probability token in that same beam is allowed to be. For example, if the top token of a beam has a probability of 0.5 and $p_b = 0.5$, tokens in the beam with a probability $< 0.5 * 0.5$ won't be further considered. This is useful whenever an obvious best candidate exists, for instance, when selecting the drug name that was itself given as input.

Therefore, the beam size *n*, maximum candidates space *m*, and maximal probability difference in beam p_b are three hyper-parameters to fine-tune to obtain optimal results. We assign them the values $n = 4$, $m = 3 * nb_{output}$ and $p_b = 1$.

Heuristic function

The heuristic function used is logarithmic in the sequence's joint probability

$$h(Y) = \frac{log_e(p(Y_{0,\ldots,n}))}{lp(Y)} \tag{2}$$

where Y_n is the nth token of the sequence Y generated so far, and $Y_{0,\ldots,n}$ refers to the product of the probabilities associated with each token in the sequence Y, which is referred to as the joint probability of Y. The heuristic function applies length normalisation as taken from Google's NMT System paper (Johnson et al., 2017), where we set $\alpha = 0.6$.

$$lp(Y) = \frac{(5 + |Y|)^\alpha}{(5 + 1)^\alpha} \quad (3)$$

4 Evaluation

4.1 Dataset and Preprocessing

Our research draws upon a specialised subset of the MIMIC-III (Medical Information Mart for Intensive Care) database (Johnson et al., 2016, 2020); specifically, the portion that aligns with the National NLP Clinical Challenges (n2c2) 2018 shared task data on adverse drug events and medication extraction with gold labels (Henry et al., 2019). We chose the n2c2 dataset for two main reasons. First, it contains many caregiver notes and medication prescriptions over a varied range of clinical conditions and treatments, ensuring a broad spectrum of clinical instructions can be generated by our models, enhancing their utility in different clinical scenarios. Second, the n2c2 dataset annotations conform to the 2010 i2b2/VA Challenge on Concepts, Assertions, and Relations in Clinical Text, a well-established and comprehensive framework for processing and understanding clinical text. This standardisation facilitates handling clinical notes' diverse and complex language patterns. Moreover, using these gold labels helps us ensure the accuracy and consistency of our model's learning process, which is crucial to generating high-quality synthetic medical data. In addition, using a dataset that adheres to a widely accepted annotation guideline enhances the replicability and validity of our study. It allows other researchers and practitioners to understand the method and results of our work within a known context, promoting transparency and further collaboration.

We divided the official training set into our "training" and "validation" sets with the ratio (9:1) and kept the original test set. We implemented a procedure in our dataset to automatically extract and structure discharge medication information from the n2c2 dataset. The procedure scans each text-based medical record in the original dataset and identifies the text segment containing information about the medications prescribed upon discharge.

The identified medication data is further decomposed into two primary components: the label (or name of the medication) and the associated instructions. Both are captured and stored in a structured format. Finally, we apply statistical filtering techniques to remove outliers based on the medication labels' length and instructions. This ensures a dataset free from extreme values that could potentially bias downstream applications.

4.2 Baseline Foundation Models: T5 Small, T5 Base, and T5 Large

The Text-to-Text Transfer Transformer (T5) implements an Encoder-Decoder Transformer architecture and was pre-trained on various sequence-to-sequence tasks. It has demonstrated state-of-the-art results across a wide spectrum of natural language processing tasks, showcasing its remarkable capabilities in capturing nuanced semantics and generating content through transfer learning techniques. Notably, it has been successfully employed in various fields, such as generating clinical text(Yermakov et al., 2021) and document ranking (Nogueira et al., 2020), making it an ideal choice for our task.

The reasons to opt for T5, particularly with enhancements proposed by Senadeera and Ive (2022), are manifold. First, controlled text generation is essential for our application, and the novel method proposed can aid in generating text conforming to specific attributes. Second, the novel soft prompt tuning approach, attaching tunable input embeddings at both encoder and decoder levels in T5, could offer better performance while saving computational resources compared to full model fine-tuning. Third, it allows for the steering of text generation at the decoder level, giving more control over the output. Lastly, it facilitates the effective utilisation of artificially generated text, thus supporting AI-related tasks like training AI models.

Given the provided labels, we leverage T5 language processing capabilities to fine-tune the model to generate appropriate text responses. The labels represent medications such as "paracetamol" and "ibuprofen," which are used to train the model and their associated clinical letter. The fine-tuning process involves adapting the pre-trained T5 model to this specific task by updating its parameters using the labeled examples.

4.3 On the Evaluation Settings

To provide a lexical evaluation of the generated data, we aim to assess the performance of LT3 compared to T5-small, T5-base, and T5-large at generating synthetic prescriptions from unseen data

(Figure 3). To process the comparison, we use the labels from the testing set to generate synthetic data, creating a five times larger dataset than the original testing dataset. For instance, ten prescriptions will be generated if a particular label appears twice in the testing data. We conduct two types of evaluations:

- **Closeness to Reference Evaluation** to assess the quality of the generated prescriptions by comparing LT3 and T5 against reference prescriptions.
- **Lexical Diversity Evaluation** to measure the diversity of the generated prescriptions from LT3 compared to T5.

The overall framework of this experimental design for lexical evaluation is displayed in Figure 3. This experiment aims to show that **(1)** LT3 can generate lexically diverse prescriptions, as well as **(2)** significantly larger volume of data compared to the available real data. **(3)**, despite generating a larger dataset, we intend to confirm that the quality of LT3's generated prescriptions remains high in terms of quantitative scores against references. **(4)** Most importantly, we try to assess LT3's overall abilities at generating prescriptions from unseen data.

4.4 Model Selection

We conduct a model evaluation experiment to select the most optimal LT3 model. This experiment entails training each model on the training set and using them to generate five times the amount of data from the validation set as synthetic data. We then assess the models' performance using the quantitative metrics BLEU, ROUGE-1/2/L, and BERTScore. Based on the results, we select the best model and retrain it on the training and validation sets to obtain a final LT3 model.

For the T5 model, given the provided labels, we leverage T5 language processing capabilities to fine-tune the model to generate appropriate text responses in the form of medication prescriptions from labels representing medications such as "paracetamol" or "ibuprofen".

We plot the training loss (Figure 6) and evaluation scores (Table 1) on the validation set to provide a comprehensive assessment of each model's learning trajectory and generation quality. This approach helps readers understand how each model evolves through the learning process.

4.5 On Evaluation Metrics

BLEU (Papineni et al., 2002), ROUGE (Lin, 2004), and BERT Score (Zhang et al., 2020) represent key evaluation metrics, each illuminating different facets of text quality. BLEU focuses on the syntactic elements, measuring the overlap of n-grams between the machine-generated text and a reference. It incorporates a brevity penalty for translation length, making it particularly useful for tasks like machine translation.

On the other hand, ROUGE (Recall-Oriented Understudy for Gisting Evaluation) is more recall-focused and assesses the quality of summaries by comparing them to reference summaries. It considers the number of overlapping units, such as n-grams, word sequences, and word pairs between the generated and reference summaries.

Finally, the BERT Score leverages the power of pre-trained language representations to go beyond mere syntactic overlap, capturing semantic nuances between predicted and reference texts through cosine similarity measures. These approaches reflect a shift from rigid, rule-based evaluations toward more dynamic, context-aware metrics, aligning more closely with human perceptions of text quality.

4.6 Lexical Similarity Evaluation against References

For this experiment, we fine-tuned three versions of T5, namely t5-small, t5-base, and t5-large, paired with their sentence-piece pre-trained tokeniser. Each is fine-tuned independently on the same dataset as LT3 to provide comparable results, with the prompt "summarise:" as it is the closest to our task. The results in Table 2 show that LT3's generations are the closest match to the reference samples. We use multi-reference evaluation to consolidate our results. Refer to Section 4.3 for more details on this evaluation's strategies and motivations.

4.7 Lexical Diversity Evaluation within Generated Outputs

A diverse range of content is crucial in the note-generation process to create unbiased and individualised clinical instructions. To achieve this, we have implemented a diversity score that measures the breadth of our model's output. For each label, we measured the Jaccard similarity (Jaccard, 1908; Ivchenko and Honov, 1998) score of the gen-

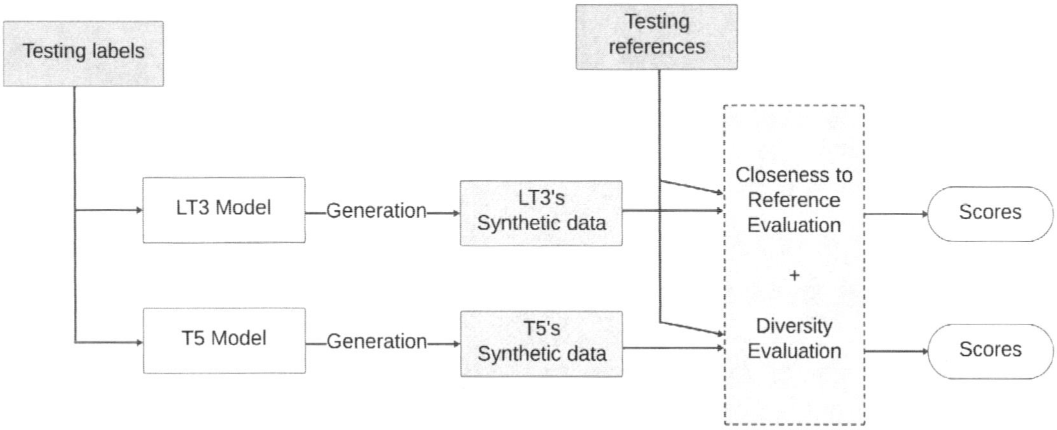

Figure 3: Lexical Evaluation Pipeline

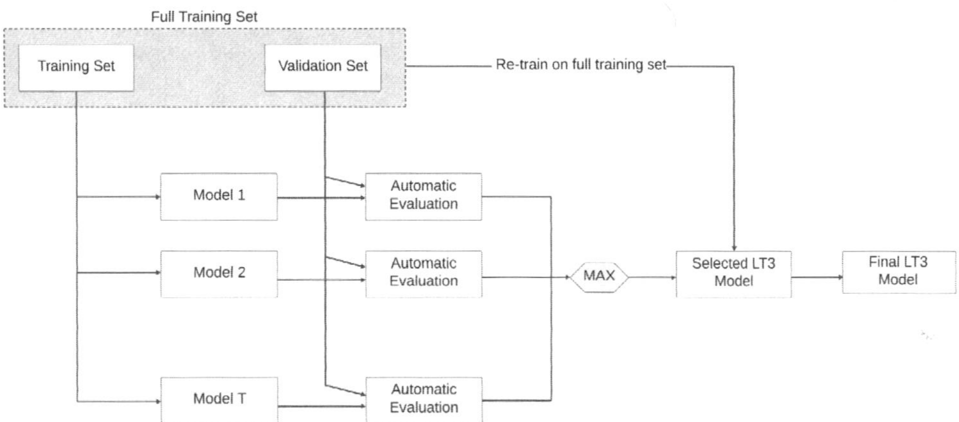

Figure 4: Model Selection Pipeline

erations of our models. A higher Jaccard Score indicates more similarity between the two populations. A lower score indicates better diversity in our tasks. The results in Table 3 show a lower intra-similarity score for the generations of LT3, implying that LT3 produces more diverse samples.

4.8 Downstream Named Entity Recognition Task

In the cross-model evaluation (Figure 5), we aim to substantially increase the size of our dataset beyond what we initially extracted from n2c2. To achieve this, we generate synthetic data using LT3 on the known training labels. This synthesis allows us to create a dataset that is five times larger than the original one. Subsequently, we perform fine-tuning on Spacy[1] using both the original and synthetically generated datasets. Finally, we compare the three resulting NER models, one fine-tuned on the real dataset, one on the synthetic dataset, and the last on a combination of real and synthetic data. Specifically, the real dataset is oversampled, ranging from 100% (identical to the original) to 500% (five times the original size). The synthetic dataset is generated using real labels, ranging from 100% to 500%. The combined real and synthetic dataset starts with 100% real data, to which synthetic data is incrementally added, from 100% to 400%. The NER model is trained to recognise medical labels: Drug, Strength, Form, Route, and Frequency. This comparison helps us to quantify the effectiveness of using synthetic data generated using LT3 to augment or replace the training dataset by assessing the ability of the fine-tuned models to recognise named entities in unseen data.

[1] `https://spacy.io`

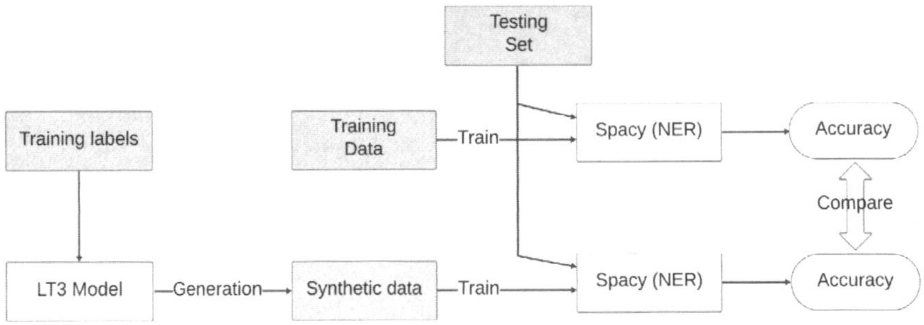

Figure 5: Cross-model Evaluation Pipeline

Table 1: Closeness to Reference Evaluation Results of LT3 Models on the Validation Set

Tokenizer	Embeddings	Beam Search	BLEU	ROU-1	ROU-2	ROU-L	BERTScore
BERT	Emb. layers	B2SD	**66.31**	**70.74**	**60.01**	**70.03**	**0.65**
	Pre-trained		36.11	43.16	28.56	41.81	0.29
	Emb. layers	Default	54.33	67.01	55.46	66.20	0.60
Custom		B2SD	64.19	70.00	58.34	68.13	0.63
T5-base			65.78	68.99	58.63	68.22	0.63

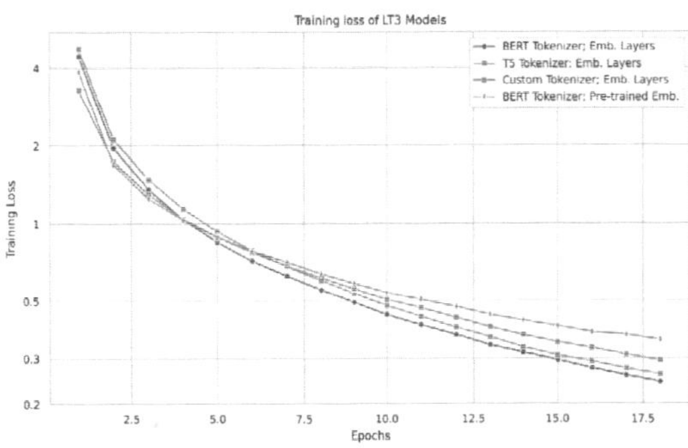

Figure 6: Training Loss of LT3 Models

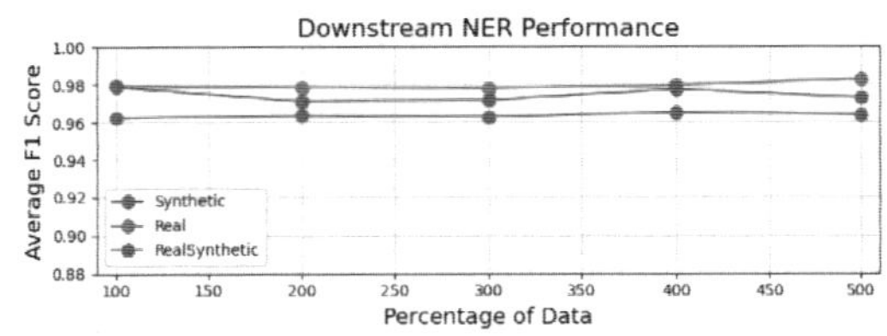

Figure 7: Average F1 score for five labels (Drug, Strength, Form, Route, Frequency) using Synthetic data, Real data, and Real+Synthetic. RealSynthetic: 100% real + n*100% Synthetic. Real: over-sampled.

The evaluation scores F1 in Figure 7 show that LT3 could successfully train Spacy on this NER task on five labels "drug, form, frequency, route, and strength" achieving 0.96+ scores. The evaluation on Drug labels always yields around 1.00 accuracy. Most importantly, it yielded comparable performance to the real data, demonstrating the quality of generated texts and the benefit of using the generated synthetic data as an alternative to real data.

We list some discussion and comparisons on **tokenisations**, **embeddings** and **Beam Search Decoding Algorithms** in Section A.1, A.2 and A.3.

5 Conclusion and Future Work

To facilitate clinical NLP research and address the data privacy and restriction issues, we proposed LT3 for generating synthetic clinical data using pre-defined drug labels and related attributes from the n2c2-2018 shared task. The evaluation against the T5 model demonstrated that LT3 can generate better quality and diversity outputs. Furthermore, utilising synthetic data generated by LT3 for the NER task demonstrated its ability to effectively train SpacyNER, resulting in performances comparable to those achieved with real data. This underscores the advantages of employing LT3 as a viable alternative to real data. **1)** Firstly, LT3 has demonstrated comparable or superior performance to the pre-trained Large Language Model (LLM) T5 at generating prescriptions for previously unseen la-

Table 2: Quantitative evaluation of LT3 (learned-scratch) vs T5 (fine-tuned) on the Testing Set.

Models	BLEU	ROUGE-1	ROUGE-2	ROUGE-L	BERTScore
T5 Small	71.75	76.16	66.24	75.55	0.70
T5 Base	71.98	76.28	66.30	75.45	0.70
T5 Large	69.89	75.07	65.19	74.22	0.68
LT3	**78.52**	**78.16**	**68.72**	**77.55**	**0.72**

Table 3: Jaccard scores of LT3 and T5 on the testing set (lower score is better).

	Median Jaccard	Average Jaccard
LT3	**0.650**	**0.652**
T5 Base	0.658	0.660

bels. Compared to reference data, this assertion is substantiated by our quantitative evaluation results (refer to Table 2). All five metrics, namely BLEU, ROUGE-1/2/L, and BERTScore, exhibit improvements ranging from 3% to 9%. This supports that, despite generating five times more data than presented in the testing dataset, the quality of LT3's generated prescriptions remains high in quantitative evaluation scores. Moreover, LT3 could generate considerably more diverse samples, as evidenced by the Jaccard scores in Table 3. **2)** Secondly, we showcased LT3's ability to generate a synthetic dataset five times larger than the original. When fine-tuning Spacy NER on the synthetic and the real data separately, the NER trained on LT3 demonstrated significant performance improvements comparable to the ones obtained on real data. Our experiments confirmed that the synthetic data was an efficient resource for training a NER model, which can act as a replacement for the original dataset extracted from n2c2.

We conclude that LT3 demonstrated its capabilities in generating synthetic medical data. This proves advantageous due to the non-sensitive nature of synthetic writings, ensuring quality and diversity comparable to real data. Furthermore, LT3 has proven to generate significantly larger volumes of data while preserving the high quality and diversity of generated prescriptions.

In future work, we plan to design new benchmarks on clinical NLP tasks using synthetic data to move the field forward. We also plan to conduct model training on new label sets such as "diagnoses" and generating full clinical letters. Furthermore, generating full sentence-level free text beyond the prescription level is our next step to address the low-resource and privacy concerns in clinical and healthcare NLP.

Limitations

To evaluate the usefulness of generated medical prescriptions, we carried out downstream application task on training a NER model on medications and related attributes mining. To evaluate the clinical soundness of the generated text, we need to carry out expert-based human evaluation. However, due to the limitations of resources, we leave this task into the future work if we manage to recruit experts such as clinicians who are willing to conduct this task.

Furthermore, relation extraction and evaluation shall be considered for automatic setting if possible, e.g. the relations between drug names and their strength, form, route, and frequency.

Ethical Considerations

To generate synthetic clinical data, we used the publicly available n2c2-2018 data set, which is already annonymised by the shared task organisers. It does not identify any personal information.

Acknowledgements

LH, WDP, and GN are grateful for the support from the grant "Assembling the Data Jigsaw: Powering Robust Research on the Causes, Determinants and Outcomes of MSK Disease", and the grant "Integrating hospital outpatient letters into the healthcare data space" (EP/V047949/1; funder: UKRI/EPSRC). LH is grateful for the 4D Picture EU project (`https://4dpicture.eu/`) on cancer patient journey support.

References

Haifa Alrdahi, Lifeng Han, Hendrik Šuvalov, and Goran Nenadic. 2023. Medmine: Examining pre-trained language models on medication mining. *arXiv e-prints*, pages arXiv–2308.

Ali Amin-Nejad, Julia Ive, and Sumithra Velupillai. 2020. Exploring transformer text generation for medical dataset augmentation. In *Proceedings of the Twelfth Language Resources and Evaluation Conference*, pages 4699–4708, Marseille, France. European Language Resources Association.

Arlene Casey, Emma Davidson, Michael Poon, Hang Dong, Daniel Duma, Andreas Grivas, Claire Grover, Víctor Suárez-Paniagua, Richard Tobin, William Whiteley, Honghan Wu, and Beatrice Alex. 2021. A systematic review of natural language processing applied to radiology reports. *BMC Medical Informatics and Decision Making*, 21.

Wendy W. Chapman, Prakash M. Nadkarni, Lynette Hirschman, Leonard W. D'Avolio, Guergana K. Savova, and Özlem Uzuner. 2011. Overcoming barriers to nlp for clinical text: the role of shared tasks and the need for additional creative solutions. *Journal of the American Medical Informatics Association : JAMIA*, 18 5:540–3.

Junqiao Chen, David Chun, Milesh Patel, Epson Chiang, and Jesse James. 2019. The validity of synthetic clinical data: A validation study of a leading synthetic data generator (synthea) using clinical quality measures. *BMC Medical Informatics and Decision Making*, 19.

Yang Cui, Lifeng Han, and Goran Nenadic. 2023. MedTem2.0: Prompt-based temporal classification of treatment events from discharge summaries. In *Proceedings of the 61st Annual Meeting of the Association for Computational Linguistics (Volume 4: Student Research Workshop)*, pages 160–183, Toronto, Canada. Association for Computational Linguistics.

Jacob Devlin, Ming-Wei Chang, Kenton Lee, and Kristina Toutanova. 2019. Bert: Pre-training of deep bidirectional transformers for language understanding. In *Proceedings of the 2019 Conference of the North American Chapter of the Association for Computational Linguistics: Human Language Technologies, Volume 1 (Long and Short Papers)*, pages 4171–4186.

Solomon W. Golomb and Leonard D. Baumert. 1965. Backtrack programming. *J. ACM*, 12(4):516–524.

André Gonçalves, Priyadip Ray, Braden Soper, Jennifer Stevens, and Linda Coyle. 2020. Generation and evaluation of synthetic patient data. *BMC Medical Research Methodology*, 20.

Colin Grambow, Longxiang Zhang, and Thomas Schaaf. 2022. In-domain pre-training improves clinical note generation from doctor-patient conversations. In *Proceedings of the First Workshop on Natural Language Generation in Healthcare*, pages 9–22, Waterville, Maine, USA and virtual meeting. Association for Computational Linguistics.

Samuel Henry, Kevin Buchan, Michele Filannino, Amber Stubbs, and Ozlem Uzuner. 2019. 2018 n2c2 shared task on adverse drug events and medication extraction in electronic health records. *Journal of the American Medical Informatics Association : JAMIA*, 27.

GI Ivchenko and SA Honov. 1998. On the jaccard similarity test. *Journal of Mathematical Sciences*, 88:789–794.

Julia Ive, Natalia Viani, Joyce Kam, Lucia Yin, Somain Verma, Stephen Puntis, Rudolf Cardinal, Angus Roberts, Robert Stewart, and Sumithra Velupillai. 2020. Generation and evaluation of artificial mental health records for natural language processing. *npj Digital Medicine*, 3.

Paul Jaccard. 1908. Nouvelles recherches sur la distribution florale. *Bull. Soc. Vaud. Sci. Nat.*, 44:223–270.

Alistair Johnson, Tom Pollard, and Roger Mark. 2020. MIMIC-III clinical database.

Alistair E W Johnson, Tom J Pollard, Lu Shen, Li-Wei H Lehman, Mengling Feng, Mohammad Ghassemi, Benjamin Moody, Peter Szolovits, Leo Anthony Celi, and Roger G Mark. 2016. MIMIC-III, a freely accessible critical care database. *Sci. Data*, 3(1):160035.

Melvin Johnson, Mike Schuster, Quoc V. Le, Maxim Krikun, Yonghui Wu, Zhifeng Chen, Nikhil Thorat, Fernanda Viégas, Martin Wattenberg, Greg Corrado, Macduff Hughes, and Jeffrey Dean. 2017. Google's multilingual neural machine translation system: Enabling zero-shot translation. *Transactions of the Association for Computational Linguistics*, 5:339–351.

Nitish Shirish Keskar, Bryan McCann, Lav R. Varshney, Caiming Xiong, and Richard Socher. 2019. CTRL: A conditional transformer language model for controllable generation. *CoRR*, abs/1909.05858.

Scott Lee. 2018. Natural language generation for electronic health records. *CoRR*, abs/1806.01353.

Jianfu Li, Yujia Zhou, Xiaoqian Jiang, Karthik Natarajan, Serguei Vs Pakhomov, Hongfang Liu, and Hua Xu. 2021. Are synthetic clinical notes useful for real natural language processing tasks: A case study on clinical entity recognition. *Journal of the American Medical Informatics Association*, 28(10):2193–2201.

Chin-Yew Lin. 2004. ROUGE: A package for automatic evaluation of summaries. In *Text Summarization Branches Out*, pages 74–81, Barcelona, Spain. Association for Computational Linguistics.

Raffaele Marchesi, Nicolo Micheletti, Giuseppe Jurman, and Venet Osmani. 2022. Mitigating health data poverty: Generative approaches versus resampling for time-series clinical data. In *NeurIPS 2022 Workshop on Synthetic Data for Empowering ML Research*.

Milad Moradi, Georg Dorffner, and Matthias Samwald. 2019. Deep contextualized embeddings for quantifying the informative content in biomedical text summarization. *Computer Methods and Programs in Biomedicine*, 184:105117.

Sana Nazari Nezhad, Mohammad H. Zahedi, and Elham Farahani. 2022. Detecting diseases in medical prescriptions using data mining methods. *BioData Mining*, 15(1):29.

Rodrigo Nogueira, Zhiying Jiang, Ronak Pradeep, and Jimmy Lin. 2020. Document ranking with a pretrained sequence-to-sequence model. In *Findings of the Association for Computational Linguistics: EMNLP 2020*, pages 708–718, Online. Association for Computational Linguistics.

Kishore Papineni, Salim Roukos, Todd Ward, and Wei-Jing Zhu. 2002. Bleu: a method for automatic evaluation of machine translation. In *Proceedings of the 40th Annual Meeting of the Association for Computational Linguistics*, pages 311–318, Philadelphia, Pennsylvania, USA. Association for Computational Linguistics.

Colin Raffel, Noam Shazeer, Adam Roberts, Katherine Lee, Sharan Narang, Michael Matena, Yanqi Zhou, Wei Li, and Peter J. Liu. 2020. Exploring the limits of transfer learning with a unified text-to-text transformer. *J. Mach. Learn. Res.*, 21(1).

Suraj Rajendran, Weishen Pan, Mert R Sabuncu, Yong Chen, Jiayu Zhou, and Fei Wang. 2024. Learning across diverse biomedical data modalities and cohorts: Challenges and opportunities for innovation. *Patterns*, page 100913.

Damith Chamalke Senadeera and Julia Ive. 2022. Controlled text generation using t5 based encoder-decoder soft prompt tuning and analysis of the utility of generated text in ai. *Preprint*, arXiv:2212.02924.

Irena Spasić, Jacqueline Livsey, John A Keane, and Goran Nenadić. 2014. Text mining of cancer-related information: review of current status and future directions. *International journal of medical informatics*, 83(9):605–623.

Ashish Vaswani, Noam Shazeer, Niki Parmar, Jakob Uszkoreit, Llion Jones, Aidan N. Gomez, Lukasz Kaiser, and Illia Polosukhin. 2017. Attention is all you need. *Preprint*, arXiv:1706.03762.

Michael Wornow, Yizhe Xu, Rahul Thapa, Birju Patel, Ethan Steinberg, Scott Fleming, Michael A Pfeffer, Jason Fries, and Nigam H Shah. 2023. The shaky foundations of large language models and foundation models for electronic health records. *npj Digital Medicine*, 6(1):135.

Linting Xue, Noah Constant, Adam Roberts, Mihir Kale, Rami Al-Rfou, Aditya Siddhant, Aditya Barua, and Colin Raffel. 2020. mt5: A massively multilingual pre-trained text-to-text transformer. *CoRR*, abs/2010.11934.

Xi Yang, Aokun Chen, Nima PourNejatian, Hoo Shin, Kaleb Smith, Christopher Parisien, Colin Compas, Cheryl Martin, Anthony Costa, Mona Flores, Ying Zhang, Tanja Magoc, Christopher Harle, Gloria Lipori, Duane Mitchell, William Hogan, Elizabeth Shenkman, Jiang Bian, and Yonghui Wu. 2022. A large language model for electronic health records. *npj Digital Medicine*, 5.

Ruslan Yermakov, Nicholas Drago, and Angelo Ziletti. 2021. Biomedical data-to-text generation via fine-tuning transformers. In *Proceedings of the 14th International Conference on Natural Language Generation*, pages 364–370, Aberdeen, Scotland, UK. Association for Computational Linguistics.

Tianyi Zhang, Varsha Kishore, Felix Wu, Kilian Q. Weinberger, and Yoav Artzi. 2020. Bertscore: Evaluating text generation with bert. *Preprint*, arXiv:1904.09675.

A Discussion and Comparisons

A.1 On tokenisation

Experiments were conducted to select the most effective tokenisation strategy for this task, for which results are summarised in Table 1 and Figure 6. Three different types of tokenisers were considered: a custom full-word tokeniser, a pre-trained word-piece tokeniser (BERT-base-cased), and a pre-trained sentence-piece tokeniser (T5-base).

Throughout the experiment, LT3 encountered challenges implementing the full-word tokeniser built from scratch. Although this tokeniser yielded overall good performances, it struggled with handling unknown words, for which the only solution seemed to be significantly expanding the vocabulary size to cover a vast tokenisation space. Without an extensive vocabulary, the tokeniser fails to map unseen words, leading to a lack of contextual understanding for LT3.

On the other hand, significant improvements were observed when using the word-piece tokeniser (BERT) due to his ability to represent any word as a sequence of smaller sub-words while minimising its vocabulary size. This allows the model to effectively handle unseen words and cover a large tokenisation space to yield better generalisation capabilities.

Experiments were also carried out using the pre-trained sentence-piece tokeniser provided by T5. This tokeniser demonstrated improvements similar to those of the word-piece tokeniser (BERT), effectively mitigating the issues faced by the custom tokeniser. However, we observed that the word-piece tokeniser (BERT) could generate predictions for unseen data at an earlier stage of training compared to the pre-trained sentence-piece tokeniser (T5). This might be due to LT3 generating short sentences with low correlation and no repetitive patterns between words, a task for which word-piece tokenisers may be more adapted.

Considering these factors, we concluded that the BERT word-piece tokeniser aligned most effectively with our task.

A.2 On Embeddings

Alternatively, this study explored two interesting embedding methods: transfer learning using pre-trained embeddings and embedding layers trained from scratch. Transfer learning used BioBERT (base-v1.1) embeddings, pre-trained on large medical corpora, including PubMed 1M, while embedding layers were trained during LT3's training phase.

Although transfer-learning can provide a solid foundation for the model, especially when task-specific data is scarce or when the pre-training domain closely matches the task, its experimental results displayed challenges when applied to our task (Table 1). Despite training in medical texts, pre-trained embeddings could not grasp the prescriptions' nuances and unique formats. This led to a need for extensive training to overwrite the previous embeddings, as seen in Figure 6. On the other hand, embedding layers outperformed pre-trained embeddings by addressing the task's unique format and leveraging the extensive available data. As a result, LT3 displayed a much better learning shape and evaluation results when implementing embedding layers.

Note that, when using pre-trained embeddings, the disparity between the learning curve, which appears to be reasonably good (Table 1), and the evaluation scores, which are rather very low (Figure 6), is attributed to the application of teacher forcing during training. This explains that the model with pre-trained embeddings can accurately predict the next token, provided with an accurate context and a generated sequence. However, it struggles when tasked with independently creating an appropriate context from the input and generating a complete sequence that is contextually coherent.

A.3 Comparisons on Beam Search Decoding Algorithms

To quantify the difference in execution time between the original BSD algorithm and the proposed backtracking variant, we ran the following experiment on a TPU v2.

Initially, the validation set is 304 samples divided into 157 unique labels, with a median of 36 samples per label. This experiment used LT3 to generate four synthetic datasets from the validation set by increasing its size by 2, 5, 7, and 10. The increase in size is proportional to the number of samples per unique label. Hence, the same number of unique labels remains while the number of samples increases. For instance, if the first label has three samples, it will be increased to 6 in the first synthetic dataset, 15 in the second, etc. Thus, we force the beam search tree to expand in size for each label to quantify its impact on the execution time.

For each synthetic dataset, we use five different versions of the LT3 model from different checkpoints of its training. This is done to simulate the execution time of the algorithm on models of varying efficiency and certainty.

In practice, we observe a rather linear increase in complexity when using both algorithms, reducing the huge trade-off in their theoretical complexities. LT3 deals with a limited number of samples per generation, and the generated sequences are relatively short. On the other hand, most of the advantages of the backtracking algorithm are preserved.

It is important to note that, whereas B2SD uses a heuristic function based on the joint probability of a sequence, this algorithm will perform the best on well-trained models with certainty in their token selection, meaning high distinction between sequence probabilities. This ensures that the algorithm goes straight at generating the most promising sequences. However, on ineffective or untrained models, it may perform slowly as it might consider many dead-end sequences where probabilities are close to each other due to uncertainty in token generation.

B Objectives

We highlight our paper below. **Contributions** This research project aims to design and develop a task-specific model architecture for synthetic clinical text generation that addresses the limitations of pre-trained models and healthcare analytics safety issues. The specific objectives include:

Objective 1 Introducing a simpler architecture than existing pre-trained models, thus accelerating the training process by forgoing the pre-training step and concentrating the model on generating synthetic clinical letters only.

Objective 2 Customising the model architecture to capture the unique patterns and dependencies involved in prescription writing.

Objective 3 Gaining fine-grained control over the training process, including data preprocessing, augmentation techniques, and specialised loss functions, to optimise the model for the specific task of prescription generations.

Objective 4 Incorporating label-to-text generation into the model architecture to ensure accurate and contextually appropriate synthetic clinical letter generation.

Objective 5 Comparing the performance of the proposed task-specific model architecture against existing pre-trained models to demonstrate its superiority in generating high-quality synthetic clinical letters.

C Model hyperparameters

We list model parameters in Table 4 where:

- d_{model} represents the dimension of the model's hidden states or embeddings;
- d_{ff} represents the dimension of the feed-forward network within the Transformer's self-attention layers;
- d_{kv} represents the dimension of the query, key, and value vectors used in the attention computation.

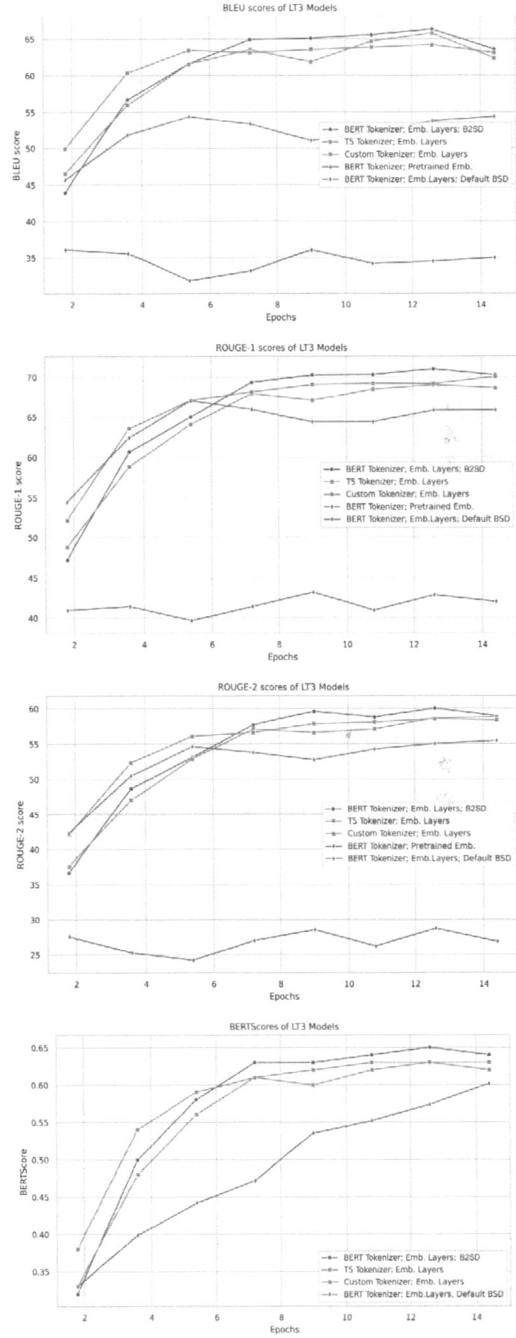

Figure 8: Quantitative Evaluation Scores of LT3 Models on the Testing Set

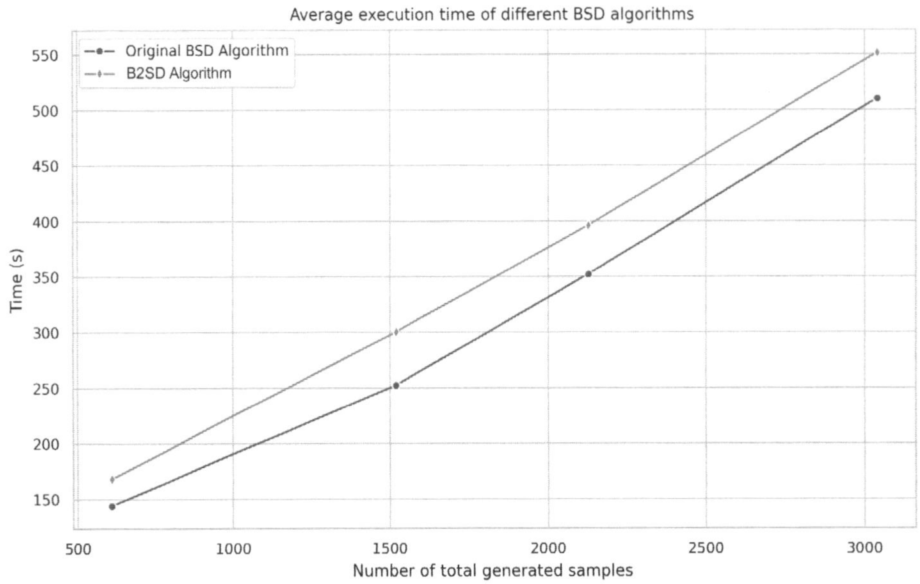

Figure 9: Average Execution Time of Original BSD and B2SD Algorithms

Parameters	LT3	T5 Small	T5 Base	T5 Large
d_{model}	515	512	768	1024
d_{ff}	2038	2048	3072	4096
d_{kv}	64	64	64	64
Dropout	0.2	0.1	0.1	0.1
Heads	5	8	12	16
Layers	2	6	12	24
Learning rate	0.0004	0.0004	0.001	0.001
Weight decay	0.02	0.02	0.02	0.02
Epochs	10	12	10	10
Batch size	53	10	10	10
FP16		False	False	False
Optimizer	AdamW	AdamW	AdamW	AdamW
Params (x10^6)	**56**	60	**220**	770

Table 4: Parameters

Explainable ICD Coding via Entity Linking

Leonor Barreiros[ↄ, Ω, Ψ] **Isabel Coutinho**[Ω, Ψ] **Gonçalo M. Correia**[ↄ] **Bruno Martins**[Ω, Ψ]
[ↄ] Priberam Labs, Alameda D. Afonso Henriques, 41, 2º, 1000-123 Lisboa, Portugal
[Ω] Instituto Superior Técnico, Lisboa, Portugal
[Ψ] INESC-ID, Rua Alves Redol, 9, 1000-029, Lisboa, Portugal
{leonor.barreiros, goncalo.correia}@priberam.pt
{isabel.coutinho, bruno.g.martins}@tecnico.ulisboa.pt

Abstract

Clinical coding is a critical task in healthcare, although traditional methods for automating clinical coding may not provide sufficient explicit evidence for coders in production environments. This evidence is crucial, as medical coders have to make sure there exists at least one explicit passage in the input health record that justifies the attribution of a code. We therefore propose to reframe the task as an entity linking problem, in which each document is annotated with its set of codes and respective textual evidence, enabling better human-machine collaboration. By leveraging parameter-efficient fine-tuning of Large Language Models (LLMs), together with constrained decoding, we introduce three approaches to solve this problem that prove effective at disambiguating clinical mentions and that perform well in few-shot scenarios.

1 Introduction

Medical reports are essential documents that detail patient medical history, procedures, exams, symptoms, and diagnoses. Clinical coding involves assigning standardized codes, such as those from ICD-10, to these records. This process is crucial for hospitals, since it helps justify expenses, secure funding, or file insurance claims to cover healthcare costs. Furthermore, labeling Electronic Health Records (EHRs) through clinical coding makes their data more searchable and suitable for statistical analysis, *e.g.* potentially revealing cause-effect relationships between diseases and symptoms.

Automated solutions can help medical coders by accelerating their work and reducing errors. However, traditional automated systems that treat coding as a Multi-Label Classification (MLC) problem are often non-explainable (Teng et al., 2023; Dong et al., 2022), making it difficult for healthcare professionals to trust or verify their outputs. If systems are explainable, we can critically reason about their decisions, allowing medical practitioners to better work alongside AI tools (Arrieta et al., 2020; Goldberg et al., 2024).

To address these challenges, we propose framing clinical coding as an entity linking problem. This particular task involves annotating documents with specific entities and providing textual evidence for each one. This could enable clinical coders to understand where each code is mentioned in a record, allowing easier cooperation with AI systems. However, clinical entity linking remains largely underexplored and lacking in terms of annotated data.

Recently, we have seen several advances in Transformer-based (Vaswani et al., 2017) Large Language Models (LLMs), such as LLaMA (Touvron et al., 2023), Mistral (Jiang et al., 2023), or Gemini (Anil et al., 2023), and in the formulation of data- and compute-efficient ways to fine-tune them (Hu et al., 2021; Dettmers et al., 2023). Consequently, we focus on mitigating the above challenges by exploring clinical entity linking as a generative task through a biomedical LLM, namely BioMistral (Labrak et al., 2024). By fine-tuning an LLM, we aim to develop a system capable of solving clinical entity linking tasks effectively.

Our contributions are three-fold: (i) we propose to frame the **explainability** of ICD coding as an entity linking task; (ii) we investigate the performance gains of prompting *versus* fine-tuning a clinical LLM for this task, evaluating how different formulations for **generative entity linking** can enhance model performance; and (iii) we compare the entity linking approach to MLC, assessing the potential it has for **few-shot classification** of mentions.

2 Proposed Approaches

Traditionally, clinical coding is treated as MLC, in which a model annotates the input medical report with its set of labels. In our setting, we treat clinical coding as an entity linking problem. This

Proceedings of the Second Workshop on Patient-Oriented Language Processing (CL4Health), pages 219–227
May 4, 2025 ©2025 Association for Computational Linguistics

means that given a medical report and its set of gold mentions (*i.e.*, our work assumes mentions have been pre-detected, for instance, via named entity recognition), our model must disambiguate each mention by assigning it the corresponding entity.

The following subsections detail different approaches for tackling clinical entity linking.

2.1 ICL-BioMistral

ICL-BioMistral (in-context learning) prompts a pre-trained Transformer decoder model. The prompt comprises a (pre-determined) mention, and a medical report excerpt, corresponding to the context that surrounds it. The model must output an ICD-10 code representation, corresponding to the entity which the mention refers to.

Inspired by Boyle et al. (2023), we designed a prompt with a short context and the task description. To improve the model's capability to solve the task, we use in-context learning (thoroughly analyzed by Dong et al. (2024)). As such, we add 10 random examples to the prompt. We illustrate the prompt template in Appendix A.

Similarly to GENRE (De Cao et al., 2021), we use constrained greedy decoding,[1] to ensure that the model output is always a valid ICD-10 code representation. This is implemented with a prefix tree of all possible outputs, and by forcing the generated tokens to stay within the set of possible continuations for titles of ICD codes.

2.2 SFT-BioMistral

SFT-BioMistral (supervised fine-tuning) is similiar to ICL-BioMistral, as it also outputs an in-context mention, given a report excerpt. However, instead of learning through examples, this model was fine-tuned on a causal language modeling objective, where we maximize the conditional probability for each output token, considering the input and the expected previously generated output tokens (Williams and Zipser, 1989). We consider as *input* the prompt (*i.e.*, the task description and context), and compute the cross-entropy loss over the tokens of the *output* (the title of the desired ICD-10 code). Decoding with this model again relies on a constrained decoding algorithm.

2.3 InsGenEL-BioMistral

Our last proposed model is inspired by InsGenEL (Xiao et al., 2023), which is based on GENRE (De Cao et al., 2021). Our model outputs multiple mention-entity pairs for a medical report in a single pass. This is closer to the approach clinical coders take when annotating, and it enriches predictions through the document's global context, improving coherence between predictions.

Like GENRE, our model receives a document (with gold mentions) and outputs the document with annotated mention-entity pairs. Unlike GENRE, and following InsGenEL, we use a Transformer decoder to annotate the documents. The fine-tuning process optimizes a causal language modeling objective by learning from supervised instruction-response pairs (Ren et al., 2024). A prompt template is presented in Appendix A.

During inference, we ensure a valid generation using constrained decoding. We implemented a function (based on GENRE's proposal) that receives the generated tokens and returns the possible continuations. First, it determines the state as either outside an entity—which can be the case when processing a non-mention or mention token—or inside an entity—where the model is disambiguating a mention. If outside an entity, then the possible continuation is to resume copying the input document. Otherwise, the model generates an entity representation. Similarly to our previous approaches, we use a prefix tree to ensure the model generates valid ICD-10 code representations.

3 Experimental Setup

To train and evaluate our models, we used publicly available datasets for explainable ICD coding, *i.e.* including span evidences for each code, namely CodiEsp (Miranda-Escalada et al., 2020), DisTEMIST (Miranda-Escalada et al., 2022), and MDACE (Cheng et al., 2023). Further details on these datasets are given in Appendix B. Additional experimental details are given in Appendix C.

Knowledge Base. In entity linking, entities are organized in knowledge bases. We focus on the International Classification of Diseases (ICD)[2] coding system, proposed by the World Health Organization, as a standardized way of representing diagnoses and procedures. The ICD is a hierarchical ontology, as codes are first organized into chapters, sub-chapters, and partial codes. We considered version 10, which is divided into ICD-10-CM (for diagnoses) and ICD-10-PCS (for procedures).

[1] https://huggingface.co/blog/constrained-beam-search

[2] https://www.who.int/standards/classifications/classification-of-diseases

		Micro	Macro
CodiEsp	ICL-BM	6.36	5.93
	SFT-BM	63.39	62.41
	INSGENEL-BM	**66.85**	**64.40**
MDACE	ICL-BM	10.36	7.79
	SFT-BM	**64.88**	**60.94**
	INSGENEL-BM	57.10	55.45

Table 1: Accuracy in the CodiEsp and MDACE test sets for the entity linking task. BM denotes BIOMISTRAL. We highlight in bold the best-in-class performance.

		Chap	Sub	Part
CodiEsp	ICL-BM	30.64	18.33	12.55
	SFT-BM	85.65	82.27	75.94
	INSGENEL-BM	87.79	83.60	78.81
MDACE	ICL-BM	43.88	33.90	23.35
	SFT-BM	89.17	84.84	78.91
	INSGENEL-BM	90.09	83.73	76.18

Table 2: Micro-accuracy in the CodiEsp and MDACE test sets for the entity linking task, considering only the chapter (Chap), subchapter (Sub), and partial (Part) code of each ICD-10. BM denotes BIOMISTRAL.

		1-shot	5-shot
CodiEsp	SFT-BM	**47.49**	**56.66**
	INSGENEL-BM	34.97	49.30
MDACE	SFT-BM	**36.74**	**40.89**
	INSGENEL-BM	24.39	29.66

Table 3: 1- and 5-shot micro-accuracy in the CodiEsp and MDACE test corpora. BM denotes BIOMISTRAL.

Evaluation Details. In end-to-end entity linking, we distinguish the precision, recall, and F1 metris. In our case, where we used gold mentions, these equate to a measure of accuracy, as explained by Balog (2018). We consider micro-accuracy (where we average the accuracy of all mentions) and macro-accuracy (where we compute the accuracy per document and average all values). To compare our results with existing work, we computed coding evaluation metrics. By aggregating all assignments for the entity linking task, we obtain a solution for MLC that can be evaluated with precision, recall, and F1. These were computed with the script by Miranda-Escalada et al. (2020).

4 Experimental Results

Table 1 presents our micro- and macro-accuracy on the CodiEsp and MDACE test datasets.

Practical Highlights. From Table 1, we conclude that fine-tuned models perform considerably better than ICL-BIOMISTRAL. We highlight that SFT-BIOMISTRAL has a stable performance for both evaluation corpora, whereas INSGENEL-BIOMISTRAL has limitations in MDACE, which we hypothesize might be related to the increased length of the documents. Additionally, we find that INSGENEL-BIOMISTRAL is beneficial in production scenarios: not only does it better alleviate the coder's job with its increased accuracy, but it also deals with all of a document's mentions simultaneously. Nonetheless, clinical coders receive non-annotated documents and a separate procedure must be used to recognize and annotate the textual evidence to which a code should be assigned.

Partial Results. Since the ICD-10 is organized hierarchically, a wrong prediction can be partially correct if it determines the code's ancestors up to a certain point. We assessed micro-accuracy on the chapter, subchapter, and partial code levels (a partial code contains the first three digits of an ICD), and the results are in Table 2. Both SFT-BIOMISTRAL and INSGENEL-BIOMISTRAL can provide orientation helpful in practical scenarios.

Few-shot Analysis. In Table 3, we compare the few-shot performance for all codes seen at most once or 5-times during training (1-shot and 5-shot). The number of such codes in the inference corpora is given in Appendix B. The model with the best few-shot performance was SFT-BIOMISTRAL, but INSGENEL-BIOMISTRAL is nevertheless able to predict codes trained in few-shot scenarios. We hypothesize that the reduced performance on MDACE is related to the increased document length, which may lead to hard long-range dependencies.

4.1 Comparison with Existing Results

The CodiEsp-D and CodiEsp-P tasks can be evaluated with MLC metrics, as we explain in §3. CodiEsp also proposes an end-to-end entity linking task, CodiEsp-X. It is not evaluated with entity linking metrics, since if a code is mentioned more than once in the same document, it only needs to be correctly predicted once to be considered correct. This means the evaluation micro-metrics for

	Multi-label Classification						Entity Linking		
	CodiEsp-D			CodiEsp-P			CodiEsp-X		
	P	R	F1	P	R	F1	P	R	F1
IAM CodiEsp	**81.70**	59.20	68.70	**69.10**	42.00	52.20	**75.00**	52.40	61.10
DAC-E	–	–	74.40	–	–	**56.0**	–	–	–
ICL-BM	8.91	7.19	7.96	11.34	12.45	11.87	8.42	7.19	7.76
SFT-BM	75.04	**76.20**	**75.62**	34.31	38.53	36.30	64.66	**67.10**	65.86
INSGENEL-BM	73.93	71.94	72.92	46.26	**46.78**	46.52	68.34	66.96	**67.64**

Table 4: Comparison of automated medical coding and entity linking micro performance metrics on the CodiEsp test set with existing results for the CodiEsp shared task. BM denotes BIOMISTRAL.

CodiEsp-X do not equate to our micro-accuracy.

In Table 4, we compare our results to those of the challenge's winner, *i.e.*, the IAM team (Cossin and Jouhet, 2020), and to a solution that was subsequently proposed, DAC-E (Barros et al., 2022). These systems are described in Appendix D. Although a strict comparison is not possible, since we used gold mentions contrarily to the shared tasks, our fine-tuned models had similar or better performance in most settings, indicating that our approaches remain useful in the MLC scenario.

MDACE was proposed for a different task: given the output of MLC, finding sufficient textual evidence for each code. This means that we cannot compare with the paper's benchmarking results.

5 Related Work

We briefly describe previous related work on automated ICD coding and also on entity linking.

ICD Coding & Explainability. Most solutions for automated ICD coding are based on MLC. For example, Barros et al. (2022) leverage the ICD hierarchy and propose two MLC sub-tasks on different granularities. Furthermore, many studies have addressed the importance of solving explainable ICD coding, so that clinical coders can understand the system's decisions. However, most studies focus on label-wise attention mechanisms (Glen et al., 2024; Amjad et al., 2023; Figueira et al., 2023), which are challenging to systematically evaluate, as pointed out by Teng et al. (2023) and Dong et al. (2022). More recently, researchers have developed methodologies to evaluate these interpretability solutions (Edin et al., 2024; Wu et al., 2024).

Entity Linking & Different Entity Linking Approaches. Entity linking solutions range from discriminative to generative models. Discriminative models are the most common, but many state-of-the-art models, such as those of Yamada et al. (2022), Ayoola et al. (2022), and Shavarani and Sarkar (2023), were trained on large corpora (the Wikipedia), which is not available for our domain. Generative models require less fine-tuning data to achieve similar performance. For example, Xiao et al. (2023) performed better than Ayoola et al. (2022), using 50 times less data. The model was inspired by a previous proposal from De Cao et al. (2021), which uses constrained decoding to ensure valid generation.

Clinical & Biomedical Entity Linking. The clinical and biomedical domains are specialized, and general-purpose models cannot solve clinical problems, even with a target domain fine-tuning corpus (Alekseev et al., 2022). Existing work uses methodologies similar to general-domain algorithms, but with models trained on domain corpora (Yuan et al., 2022a; Agarwal et al., 2022). For instance, Yuan et al. (2022b) propose a method similar to GENRE. In the clinical domain, most entity linking studies focus on the DisTEMIST (Miranda-Escalada et al., 2022) and CodiEsp (Miranda-Escalada et al., 2020) challenges. For example, Gallego et al. (2024) propose a Transformer encoder-based solution to DisTEMIST.

6 Conclusions

We described three approaches for the clinical entity linking problem, based on BioMistral 7B, that annotate medical reports with each mention's ICD-10 code. The models we fine-tuned, *i.e.*, SFT- and INSGENEL-BIOMISTRAL, were substantially better than the prompted ICL-BIOMISTRAL, and yielded interesting results for few-shot codes.

Limitations

Our models only deal with the disambiguation subproblem of entity linking, using pre-detected mentions. Future work should explore mention detection to obtain an end-to-end solution, which makes our models useful in production environments.

In addition, our experiments were limited to three publicly available datasets, which only represent a small subset of patients, possible medical conditions, and medical procedures. There is not a lot of clinical data publicly available to support research studies, especially annotated for entity linking. In the future, we can explore other approaches to data collection, and even leverage additional information from clinical knowledge bases, such additional information in ICD-10 itself and UMLS.

Finally, large generative models such as BioMistral 7B are generally very costly to use. For instance, the IAM system (Cossin and Jouhet, 2020), based on a dictionary, only takes 5 seconds to run on an 8 CPUs' machine. The DAC-E (Barros et al., 2022) system, while using GPU processing, is also more efficient as it uses a smaller Transformer encoder as the backbone. Future work can perhaps assess the impact of using LLMs of different sizes.

Ethical Considerations

ICD coding is a sensitive task that influences clinical and financial decisions. In our problem formulation, we facilitate keeping practitioners in charge of all clinical decisions, as they can critically assess each model decision. This allows medical coders to work alongside AI tools, fostering human-machine collaboration rather than replacing human input, with basis on the supporting evidence.

Due to restrictions in data access, we used publicly available datasets that only represent a small part of the target population. To use the MDACE corpus, we took the *Data or Specimens Only Research* training course from the CITI program.[3]

Acknowledgments

This research was supported by the Portuguese Recovery and Resilience Plan through project C645008882-00000055 (i.e., the Center For Responsible AI).

[3]https://about.citiprogram.org/

References

Dhruv Agarwal, Rico Angell, Nicholas Monath, and Andrew McCallum. 2022. Entity linking via explicit mention-mention coreference modeling. In *Proceedings of the Conference of the North American Chapter of the Association for Computational Linguistics: Human Language Technologies*.

Anton Alekseev, Zulfat Miftahutdinov, Elena Tutubalina, Artem Shelmanov, Vladimir Ivanov, Vladimir Kokh, Alexander Nesterov, Manvel Avetisian, Andrei Chertok, and Sergey Nikolenko. 2022. Medical crossing: A cross-lingual evaluation of clinical entity linking. In *Proceedings of the Language Resources and Evaluation Conference*.

Haadia Amjad, Mohammad Shehroz Ashraf, Syed Zoraiz Ali Sherazi, Saad Khan, Muhammad Moazam Fraz, Tahir Hameed, and Syed Ahmad Chan Bukhari. 2023. Attention-based explainability approaches in healthcare natural language processing. In *Proceedings of the International Joint Conference on Biomedical Engineering Systems and Technologies*.

Rohan Anil, Sebastian Borgeaud, Yonghui Wu, Jean-Baptiste Alayrac, Jiahui Yu, Radu Soricut, Johan Schalkwyk, Andrew M Dai, Anja Hauth, et al. 2023. Gemini: a family of highly capable multimodal models. *arXiv preprint arXiv:2312.11805*.

Alejandro Barredo Arrieta, Natalia Díaz-Rodríguez, Javier Del Ser, Adrien Bennetot, Siham Tabik, Alberto Barbado, Salvador García, Sergio Gil-López, Daniel Molina, Richard Benjamins, et al. 2020. Explainable artificial intelligence (XAI): Concepts, taxonomies, opportunities and challenges toward responsible AI. *Information Fusion*, 58:82–115.

Tom Ayoola, Shubhi Tyagi, Joseph Fisher, Christos Christodoulopoulos, and Andrea Pierleoni. 2022. ReFinED: An efficient zero-shot-capable approach to end-to-end entity linking. In *Proceedings of the Conference of the North American Chapter of the Association for Computational Linguistics*.

Krisztian Balog. 2018. *Entity-Oriented Search*, chapter 5. Springer International Publishing.

Jose Barros, Matías Rojas, Jocelyn Dunstan, and Andres Abeliuk. 2022. Divide and conquer: An extreme multi-label classification approach for coding diseases and procedures in Spanish. In *Proceedings of the International Workshop on Health Text Mining and Information Analysis (LOUHI)*.

Joseph Spartacus Boyle, Antanas Kascenas, Pat Lok, Maria Liakata, and Alison Q O'Neil. 2023. Automated clinical coding using off-the-shelf large language models. In *Conference on Neural Information Processing Systems Workshop Deep Generative Models For Health*.

Tianqi Chen, Tong He, Michael Benesty, Vadim Khotilovich, Yuan Tang, Hyunsu Cho, Kailong Chen, Rory Mitchell, Ignacio Cano, Tianyi Zhou, et al.

2015. XGBoost: Extreme gradient boosting. *R package version 0.4-2*, 1(4):1–4.

Hua Cheng, Rana Jafari, April Russell, Russell Klopfer, Edmond Lu, Benjamin Striner, and Matthew Gormley. 2023. MDACE: MIMIC documents annotated with code evidence. In *Proceedings of the Annual Meeting of the Association for Computational Linguistics*.

Sébastien Cossin and Vianney Jouhet. 2020. IAM at CLEF eHealth 2020: Concept annotation in Spanish electronic health records. In *Working Notes of the Conference and Labs of the Evaluation Forum. CEUR Workshop Proceedings*.

Nicola De Cao, Gautier Izacard, Sebastian Riedel, and Fabio Petroni. 2021. Autoregressive entity retrieval. In *Proceedings of the International Conference on Learning Representations*.

Tim Dettmers, Artidoro Pagnoni, Ari Holtzman, and Luke Zettlemoyer. 2023. QLoRA: Efficient finetuning of quantized LLMs. In *Proceedings of the Conference on Neural Information Processing Systems*.

Hang Dong, Matúš Falis, William Whiteley, Beatrice Alex, Joshua Matterson, Shaoxiong Ji, Jiaoyan Chen, and Honghan Wu. 2022. Automated clinical coding: what, why, and where we are? *NPJ Digital Medicine*, 5(1):159.

Qingxiu Dong, Lei Li, Damai Dai, Ce Zheng, Zhiyong Wu, Baobao Chang, Xu Sun, Jingjing Xu, and Zhifang Sui. 2024. A survey on in-context learning. In *Proceedings of the Conference on Empirical Methods in Natural Language Processing*.

Joakim Edin, Maria Maistro, Lars Maaløe, Lasse Borgholt, Jakob D Havtorn, and Tuukka Ruotsalo. 2024. An unsupervised approach to achieve supervised-level explainability in healthcare records. In *Proceedings of the Conference on Empirical Methods in Natural Language Processing*.

João Figueira, Gonçalo M. Correia, Michalina Strzyz, and Afonso Mendes. 2023. Justifying multi-label text classifications for healthcare applications. In *Proceedings of the European Conference on Information Retrieval*.

Fernando Gallego, Guillermo López-García, Luis Gasco-Sánchez, Martin Krallinger, and Francisco J Veredas. 2024. ClinLinker: Medical entity linking of clinical concept mentions in Spanish. In *Proceedings of the International Conference of Computational Science*.

Jamie Glen, Lifeng Han, Paul Rayson, and Goran Nenadic. 2024. A comparative study on automatic coding of medical letters with explainability. *arXiv preprint arXiv:2407.13638*.

Carey Beth Goldberg, Laura Adams, David Blumenthal, Patricia Flatley Brennan, Noah Brown, Atul J Butte, Morgan Cheatham, Dave DeBronkart, Jennifer Dixon, Jeff Drazen, et al. 2024. To do no harm—and the most good—with AI in health care. *Nature Medicine*, 1(3):623–627.

Edward J Hu, Phillip Wallis, Zeyuan Allen-Zhu, Yuanzhi Li, Shean Wang, Lu Wang, Weizhu Chen, et al. 2021. LoRA: Low-rank adaptation of large language models. In *Proceedings of the International Conference on Learning Representations*.

Albert Q Jiang, Alexandre Sablayrolles, Arthur Mensch, Chris Bamford, Devendra Singh Chaplot, Diego de las Casas, Florian Bressand, Gianna Lengyel, Guillaume Lample, Lucile Saulnier, et al. 2023. Mistral 7b. *arXiv preprint arXiv:2310.06825*.

Alistair E W Johnson, Tom J Pollard, Lu Shen, Li-Wei H Lehman, Mengling Feng, Mohammad Ghassemi, Benjamin Moody, Peter Szolovits, Leo Anthony Celi, and Roger G Mark. 2016. MIMIC-III, a freely accessible critical care database. *Scientific Data*, 3(1):1–9.

Yanis Labrak, Adrien Bazoge, Emmanuel Morin, Pierre-Antoine Gourraud, Mickael Rouvier, and Richard Dufour. 2024. BioMistral: A collection of open-source pretrained large language models for medical domains. In *Findings of the Association for Computational Linguistics*.

Yinhan Liu, Myle Ott, Naman Goyal, Jingfei Du, Mandar Joshi, Danqi Chen, Omer Levy, Mike Lewis, Luke Zettlemoyer, and Veselin Stoyanov. 2019. RoBERTa: A robustly optimized bert pretraining approach. *arXiv preprint arXiv:1907.11692*.

Ilya Loshchilov and Frank Hutter. 2019. Decoupled weight decay regularization. In *Proceedings of the International Conference on Learning Representations*.

Antonio Miranda-Escalada, Luis Gascó, Salvador Lima-López, Eulàlia Farré-Maduell, Darryl Estrada, Anastasios Nentidis, Anastasia Krithara, Georgios Katsimpras, Georgios Paliouras, and Martin Krallinger. 2022. Overview of DisTEMIST at BioASQ: Automatic detection and normalization of diseases from clinical texts: results, methods, evaluation and multilingual resources. In *Working Notes of the Conference and Labs of the Evaluation Forum. CEUR Workshop Proceedings*.

Antonio Miranda-Escalada, Aitor Gonzalez-Agirre, Jordi Armengol-Estapé, and Martin Krallinger. 2020. Overview of automatic clinical coding: Annotations, guidelines, and solutions for non-English clinical cases at CodiEsp track of CLEF eHealth 2020. In *Working Notes of the Conference and Labs of the Evaluation Forum. CEUR Workshop Proceedings*.

Mengjie Ren, Boxi Cao, Hongyu Lin, Cao Liu, Xianpei Han, Ke Zeng, Guanglu Wan, Xunliang Cai, and Le Sun. 2024. Learning or self-aligning? Rethinking instruction fine-tuning. In *Proceedings of the Annual Meeting of the Association for Computational Linguistics*.

Hassan Shavarani and Anoop Sarkar. 2023. Spel: Structured prediction for entity linking. In *Proceedings of the Conference on Empirical Methods in Natural Language Processing*.

Fei Teng, Yiming Liu, Tianrui Li, Yi Zhang, Shuangqing Li, and Yue Zhao. 2023. A review on deep neural networks for ICD coding. *IEEE Transactions on Knowledge and Data Engineering*, 35(5):4357–4375.

Hugo Touvron, Thibaut Lavril, Gautier Izacard, Xavier Martinet, Marie-Anne Lachaux, Timothée Lacroix, Baptiste Rozière, Naman Goyal, Eric Hambro, Faisal Azhar, et al. 2023. LLaMA: Open and efficient foundation language models. *arXiv preprint arXiv:2302.13971*.

Ashish Vaswani, Noam Shazeer, Niki Parmar, Jakob Uszkoreit, Llion Jones, Aidan N Gomez, Łukasz Kaiser, and Illia Polosukhin. 2017. Attention is all you need. In *Proceedings of the Conference on Neural Information Processing Systems*.

Ronald J Williams and David Zipser. 1989. A learning algorithm for continually running fully recurrent neural networks. *Neural computation*, 1(2):270–280.

John Wu, David Wu, and Jimeng Sun. 2024. Beyond label attention: Transparency in language models for automated medical coding via dictionary learning. In *Proceedings of the Conference on Empirical Methods in Natural Language Processing*.

Zilin Xiao, Ming Gong, Jie Wu, Xingyao Zhang, Linjun Shou, and Daxin Jiang. 2023. Instructed language models with retrievers are powerful entity linkers. In *Proceedings of the Conference on Empirical Methods in Natural Language Processing*.

Ikuya Yamada, Koki Washio, Hiroyuki Shindo, and Yuji Matsumoto. 2022. Global entity disambiguation with BERT. In *Proceedings of the Conference of the North American Chapter of the Association for Computational Linguistics: Human Language Technologies*.

Hongyi Yuan, Zheng Yuan, Ruyi Gan, Jiaxing Zhang, Yutao Xie, and Sheng Yu. 2022a. BioBART: Pretraining and evaluation of a biomedical generative language model. In *Proceedings of the Workshop on Biomedical Language Processing*.

Hongyi Yuan, Zheng Yuan, and Sheng Yu. 2022b. Generative biomedical entity linking via knowledge base-guided pre-training and synonyms-aware fine-tuning. In *Proceedings of the Conference of the North American Chapter of the Association for Computational Linguistics: Human Language Technologies*.

A Prompt Templates

The prompt used for ICL-BioMistral is in Listing 1. For SFT-BioMistral, we used a similar prompt, without the [Example]s. For InsGenEL-BioMistral, we used the prompt in Listing 2. We use a prompt in English, and generate outputs in English, even with CodiEsp's Spanish reports.

```
You are a medical coder at a hospital, and you have to assign ICD-10 codes to mentions. I will give you a report excerpt and a mention that can be found in that excerpt. Your job is to associate the mention to an ICD-10 code.
Each code can be a Diagnosis in ICD-10-CM or a Procedure in ICD-10-PCS. You should give the ICD-10 code according to its type (Diagnosis or Procedure).
[Example]:
The following report excerpt, written in <language>: """<example_mention_in_context>""", contains the following mention: <example_mention>.
It corresponds to the ICD-10 entity: <example_icd>.
[Task]:
The following report excerpt, written in <language>: """<mention_in_context>""", contains the following mention: <mention>.
It corresponds to the ICD-10 entity:
```

Listing 1: Prompt for ICL-BioMistral.

```
You are a medical coder at a hospital, and you have to assign ICD-10 codes to mentions.
I will give you a medical report, whose mentions are annotated between { and }. Your job is to associate each mention to an ICD-10 code.
Each code can be a Diagnosis in ICD-10-CM or a Procedure in ICD-10-PCS. You should give the ICD-10 code according to its type (Diagnosis or Procedure) and hierarchy, that is, you should first write the chapter, then the subchapter up until the title of the ICD-10 code, separated by "-->".
ICD-10 codes should be delimited by | and |.
Annotate the following report:
<report>
```

Listing 2: Prompt for InsGenEL-BioMistral.

B Dataset Details and Statistics

We used three different corpora during training.

- CodiEsp (Miranda-Escalada et al., 2020) consists of Spanish medical reports, which were manually annotated with their ICD-10 codes and textual evidence spans. The corpus was developed for the CodiEsp shared task, which comprises three sub-tasks: automated ICD coding for ICD-10-CM (CodiEsp-D) and ICD-10-PCS (CodiEsp-P), and end-to-end clinical

	Reports	Diagnoses			Procedures		
		Samples	Codes	1-shot codes	Samples	Codes	1-shot codes
CodiEsp	500	8,199	1,720	618	2,799	435	86
DisTEMIST	750	1,912	451	176	23	4	1
MDACE	181	4,993	966	446	168	89	61
Total	1,431	15,104	2,513	912	2,990	515	138

Table 5: Datasets used for training. *Codes* refers to the number of distinct ICD-10 codes in the training data, and *1-shot codes* refers to the number of codes that only appear once.

	CodiEsp	MDACE
No. 1-shot codes	219	49
No. 5-shot codes	923	203

Table 6: Number of 1-shot and 5-shot codes in the CodiEsp and MDACE test sets, considering the number of times they were seen in the training corpus.

entity linking for ICD-10 (CodiEsp-X).

- DisTEMIST (Miranda-Escalada et al., 2022) comprises medical reports in Spanish and English (we only used the English version), manually annotated with their SNOMED CT disease codes and textual evidence spans. The authors mapped the SNOMED CT codes to ICD-10 using UMLS. This mapping was only performed for the training data, so we could not evaluate our model's performance on the DisTEMIST validation and test splits.
- MDACE (Cheng et al., 2023) consists of English medical reports, which are part of the MIMIC-III collection (Johnson et al., 2016), with manually annotated ICD-10 codes and respective textual evidence spans.

The number of test few-shot codes is in Table 6. Table 5 summarizes the training datasets.

C Experimental Details

Our models were initialized with BioMistral-7B (Labrak et al., 2024). SFT- and INSGENEL-BIOMISTRAL were fine-tuned for 5 epochs on an NVIDIA RTX A6000 GPU for 20 hours, with a batch size of 4. We used QLoRA (Dettmers et al., 2023), with rank $r = 64$ and 4-bit NF quantization, and the AdamW (Loshchilov and Hutter, 2019) optimizer with a learning rate of $2 * 10^{-4}$ and weight decay equal to 10^{-3}. For inference, models were loaded without quantization on the same GPU, and we used the same batch sizes and a greedy decoding strategy. Inference took 8 hours for all datasets.

For INSGENEL-BIOMISTRAL, to ensure all training samples did not exceed the model's context window of $8,192$ tokens, we truncated all documents to $5,000$ characters. During inference, the entire documents were processed.

D Comparison Systems

In Table 4, we compare our experimental results on the CodiEsp test corpus with those of the IAM and DAC-E systems, which work as follows:

- The IAM (Cossin and Jouhet, 2020) system performs explainable ICD coding. It starts by normalizing every document in the training data, and composing a dictionary whose items are the normalized mentions (denoted *terms*) and their corresponding ground-truth ICD-10 codes. Additionally, the KB entities' normalized titles are added to the dictionary. Then, each dictionary term is tokenized and stored in an n-gram tree. For inference, a matching algorithm parses each document's tokens to find matching dictionary entries. Three matching strategies are employed: perfect matching, abbreviation matching (where a hand-crafted dictionary of abbreviations is used), and Levenshtein distance-based matching.
- The DAC-E (Barros et al., 2022) approach is not as directly explainable, as it treats ICD coding as MLC. This system comprises two sub-tasks, respectively performed by *matcher* and *ranker* models. The matcher associates documents to clusters (the chapters in ICD-10), leveraging a biomedical RoBERTa model (Liu et al., 2019). The ranker computes the likelihood of each code being present in a document, considering its chapter. It was

implemented with a binary classifier for each code, trained only with documents with codes in the same cluster, for better fine-grained differentiation. The ranker was trained using the XGBoost algorithm (Chen et al., 2015).

Will Gen Z users look for evidence to verify QA System-generated answers?

Soumya Gayen, Dina Demner-Fushman and **Deepak Gupta**
National Library of Medicine, NIH, HHS
{gayens,ddemner,guptadk}@nih.gov

Abstract

The remarkable results shown by medical question-answering systems lead to their adoption in real-life applications. The systems, however, may misinform the users, even when drawing on scientific evidence to ground the results. The quality of the answers may be verified by the users if they analyze the evidence provided by the systems. User interfaces play an important role in engaging the users. While studies of the user interfaces for biomedical literature search and clinical decision support are abundant, little is known about users' interactions with medical question answering systems and the impact of these systems on health-related decisions. In a study of several different user interface layouts, we found that only a small number of participants followed the links to verify automatically generated answers, independently of the interface design. The users who followed the links made better health-related decisions.

1 Introduction

The 2022 Health Information National Trends Survey highlighted the pervasive presence of health misinformation in social media and particular vulnerability of younger adults (18-34) to it (Chandrasekaran et al., 2024). Misinformation generated by Large Language Models (LLMs), referred to as hallucinations, is a known problem that instigated research in approaches that require LLMs provide references for each fact stated in the answer. A community-wide evaluation of the evidence provided by LLMs to support answers to medical questions shows that some of the provided references are irrelevant, do not support or even contradict the answer statements (Gupta et al., 2024). Having a question answering system to provide evidence is, therefore, not enough: it is also important to provide easy access to evidence and encourage its exploration through user interface design (Hullman and Gelman, 2021).

While research on interface design to support clinical decisions is substantial, it mostly addresses supporting clinical workflows and, based on many studies, recommends minimizing cognitive load by reducing the number of mouse clicks, among other approaches (Miller et al., 2018). Our objective, however is to find a layout that may encourage the users to drill down and analyze the evidence, i.e., increase the click-through without overwhelming the users. A study of strategies that ensure the users remain engaged with mobile phone health applications showed that the number of clicks increased due to content and graphics, among other factors (Moungui et al., 2024). Similarly to our goals, medical conversational agents are interested in keeping the users engaged. A recent review on artificial intelligence-based question-answering systems in health care, however, found that more is reported on the systems' effectiveness, and less is known about their use (Budler et al., 2023).

In this work, we explore several UI/UX design choices to determine if highlighting access to evidence leads to better use of evidence and, subsequently, better health-related decisions. Specifically, we studied if interleaving the links to evidence with answer sentences and highlighting the links with graphics, as well as making the images illustrating the answers more visible and clickable will lead to increased engagement of the users. In addition, after reviewing the answer and the evidence provided for a given health-related scenario, the users were asked to make a health-related decision or answer a health-related question on the topic of the scenario.

The results of this pilot study show an alarming tendency among the young and well-educated users with fair health literacy levels to blindly accept the displayed answer and subsequently make suboptimal health-related decisions. Only about a third of the study participants explored the evidence. These participants made better health-

Proceedings of the Second Workshop on Patient-Oriented Language Processing (CL4Health), pages 228–235
May 4, 2025 ©2025 Association for Computational Linguistics

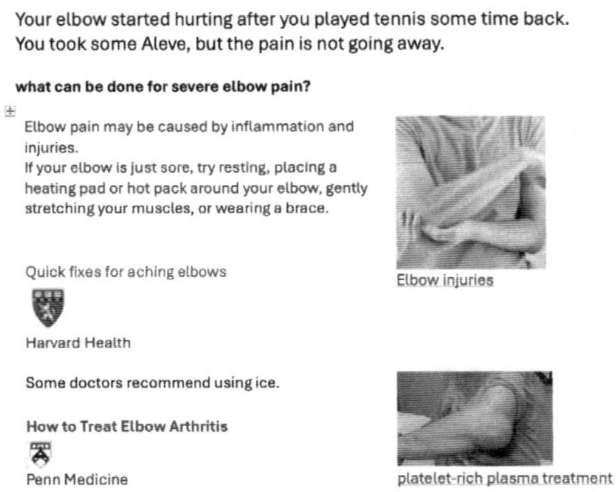

Figure 1: A user interface design with answer sentences interleaved with references, vertical figure bar, and links made more prominent using icons.

	Scenario							
User	**1**	**2**	**3**	**4**	**5**	**6**	**7**	**8**
1	A	B	H	C	G	D	F	E
2	B	C	A	D	H	E	G	F
3	C	D	B	E	A	F	H	G
4	D	E	C	F	B	G	A	H
5	E	F	D	G	C	H	B	A
6	F	G	E	H	D	A	C	B
7	G	H	F	A	E	B	D	C
8	H	A	G	B	F	C	E	D

Table 1: Different interface types used in 8x8 Latin square design. **Conditions** – *text*: blob (TB), sentence-by-sentence (TS); *pictures*: Vertical (PV), Horizontal (PH); *links*: Text (LT), icons (LI). **A**: TB, PV, LT; **B**: TS, PV, LT; **C**: TB, PH, LT; **D**: TS, PH, LT; **E**: TB, PV, LI; **F**: TS, PV, LI; **G**: TB, PH, LI; **H**: TS, PH, LI

related decisions.

2 Methods

To eliminate biases introduced by the order of presentation of the layouts and health scenarios, we chose the Latin Square design for our experiment (Richardson, 2018). We developed eight health scenarios containing a question, reference answers composed using reliable sources, and found relevant images linked to evidence using an image search engine. Using these scenarios, we studied two variants each of 1) answer layout & link placement, 2) image placement, and 3) augmenting the links with icons, making it 8 different types of interface from A to H. The answer was displayed as a paragraph followed by the references, or sentence by sentence interleaved with references as shown in Figure 1. The related pictures were shown in a horizontal or vertical image scroll bar.

We recruited eight students from a convenience sample of summer interns in the age range found most vulnerable in the 2022 Health Information National Trends Survey. Their educational background ranged from incoming college freshman to graduate level. A health literacy evaluation of the participants was performed to assess their medical data interpretation skills. This evaluation was performed in a classroom setting with limited time, to capture most accurate user health literacy information about the participants. We have used the test designed by Schwartz, Woloshin and Welch to establish the basic attributes, reliability and validity of a medical data interpretation test in a group of people with a wide range of quantitative abilities (Schwartz et al., 2005). In their experiment, the scores were normally distributed with a mean score of 61 and standard deviation of 17. Based on this mean score and the scores in our test, we divided the participants into 3 bins with score ranges 0 to 43, 44 to 78 and 78 to 100.

After completing the health literacy test, the students were given access to a web-based evaluation interface that displayed the eight questions according to the random Latin Square shown in Table 1. The questions were selected to reflect three levels of difficulty: factoid questions, questions about treatment effects, and information needed to support clinical decisions. The participants were instructed to read the scenario, and explore the answer and the presented evidence until they believed they could act on the information. In the next screen, they were presented with multiple choice answers / actions, from which they had to select one. For example, for the scenario shown in Figure 1, the choices where: a) *Give your elbow some rest, apply hot or cold, take more painkillers.* b) *Ask your doctor for advice.* c) *Ask your doctor for steroid injection.* d) *Ask your doctor about the experimental treatments such as acupuncture.* e) *Ask your doctor to refer you to see a surgeon.*

During the evaluation, all user actions were captured by the interface. Interactions, such as link clicks to patient-oriented reputable websites, data popup clicks (which displayed the original scientific publications corresponding to the patient-oriented materials accessible through the links), and related image scrolls were captured. Number of links clicked by the participants were recorded.

Time spent on every question by participants was also captured. After completing all eight scenarios, the participants completed a survey.

The survey asked which parts of the presented evidence informed the user's answers to the questions and decisions for immediate actions. It also asked if the answers were supported by the provided evidence and if the user felt a need to verify the answer before acting on it. Finally, the survey asked if the users would change any of the answers to the above questions if they knew the whole process was automated. After the study, the preferences for the page layout were discussed in the focus group with study participants.

2.1 Data Analysis

We assessed the responses to the selection of multiple choice answers/actions for a given scenario in two ways. In a strict evaluation, participants were awarded 1 point for each correct answer and 0 points for incorrect answers. Since the second choices for most questions are also reasonable, in a more lenient evaluation, the best answers received 2 points, while the second-best answers were assigned 1 point and the other answers received 0 points. We used Analysis of Variance (ANOVA) python package (Seabold and Perktold, 2010) for three factor design to analyze the effect of participants, questions, and interface types on use of evidence.

3 Results and Discussion

User	Score	Group
1	67	2
2	33	1
3	44	2
4	67	2
5	78	3
6	72	2
7	56	2
8	78	3

Table 2: Health literacy scores.

Health literacy, defined as capacity to understand basic health information needed to make appropriate health decisions, was measured solely to mitigate the potential bias introduced by different health literacy levels. Our study participants were at least at the basic health literacy level, most of them were at the intermediate level, and two had high health literacy level as shown in Table 2. This finding agrees with the results of health literacy evaluation of college students that showed the university students seem to have good health literacy levels that would allow them to navigate the health care system (Ickes and Cottrell, 2010). The results of the literacy tests were not shared with the participants.

Source	SS	DF	F	Pr(>F)
Participants	1.11	7	1.18	0.34
Questions	7.86	7	8.34	0.001
Interface	1.36	7	1.44	0.21
Residual	5.66	42	NA	NA

(a) ANOVA results for strict evaluation of health-related decisions.

Source	SS	DF	F	Pr(>F)
Participants	2.67	7	1.28	0.29
Questions	7.94	7	3.78	0.002
Interface	2.19	7	1.04	0.42
Residual	12.63	42	NA	NA

(b) ANOVA results for lenient evaluation of health-related decisions.

Source	SS	DF	F	Pr(>F)
Participants	24103	7	2.99	0.01
Questions	13794	7	1.7	0.127
Time	6667	7	0.826	0.57
Residual	40682	42	NA	NA

(c) ANOVA table, results for time spent on every question by each participant.

SS:	Sum of squares
DF:	Degree of freedom
F:	F score
Pr(>F):	P value

Table 3: ANOVA results for strict and lenient evaluation of the use of evidence in health-related decisions.

Table 3a presents the ANOVA results for the strict evaluation of the use of evidence in health-related decisions, while Table 3b shows the results for the lenient evaluation. In both evaluations, only the questions significantly affect the participants' decisions ($p = 0.001$ and $p = 0.002$).

On the aggregation of points scored by the participants, we find the Interface type C has achieved the highest scores (5 and 14) for both the methods of scoring. This suggests that participants could analyze and retain the data presented in this layout better. The focus group discussion confirmed that the participants preferred seeing the whole answer (rather than the individual facts interleaved with links to evidence), along with a horizontal image scroll bar, and the text only links to related research and clinical evidence. See Appendix D that shows the most and least popular interface designs.

Only 3 participants consistently clicked the links to patient-oriented evidence. Only 2 participants looked at scientific evidence (data pop-ups). Only one participant scrolled through the images on the screen. It shows that despite the preference for layout C, none of the layouts consistently engaged the users to drill through to the evidence. This suggests that the UI/UX we tested did not motivate the participants to check for evidence. Rather, the decision to seek supporting evidence was driven by their background knowledge, level of understanding, and confidence in the generated answers.

For the three users that engaged in interactions, we found a moderately positive correlation between the total number of user interactions and the score on health-related decisions. (See Appendix B). The participants who interacted more with the interface answered the follow-up questions better. Appendix C shows the amount of time spent by participants on the answer and evidence analysis before answering the follow-up question. ANOVA results in Table 3c show that variance in participants is statistically significant ($p = 0.01$), hence, the time spent on questions by every participant is not random, and a pattern is observed in user interactions. A moderately positive correlation in the amount of time spent on a question and score on the answers to follow-up questions and decisions was observed (see Table 4). It can be said that participants who spent more time reviewing the provided answers to the questions have answered the follow-up questions better.

The analysis of the exit survey results shows that all participants preferred information for patients, indicating a specialized patient-friendly system is needed. Only three participants did not trust the answer, they were the same participants that followed the links. This means that it's the application's responsibility to verify the correctness and accuracy of the user-facing information and ensure the information is absolutely trustworthy. This recommendation is reinforced by the fact that only one participant would make a distinction between the answers generated automatically and manually. The remaining seven participants indicated it doesn't matter how the answer is generated.

User	HL	SS	LS	Clicks	Time (ms)
1	2	5	13	12	2968
2	1	5	13	34	895
3	2	2	9	20	859
4	2	3	11	4	675
5	3	4	12	1	326
6	2	4	10	2	408
7	2	3	9	2	815
8	3	5	13	125	2409

Table 4: Users scores on the health-related decisions, their health literacy levels, and activity and time spent reviewing the answers to health scenario questions. HL - health literacy, SS - strict score, LS - lenient score.

4 Conclusion

Our study of the UI/UX designs for engaging users to verify the answers to their health-related questions shows that well-educated young adults with intermediate health literacy prefer seeing a full answer with unobtrusive links to supporting evidence and having illustrations below the answer. Studying the evidence provided to support the answers is associated with better scores on health-related decisions and medical topic understanding tasks. To confirm the association is significant and the results are generalizable, larger number of participants from more diverse population groups are needed. More studies are also needed to refine UI/UX design that engages the users and leads to optimal health-related decisions. Our results indicate that the majority of the users will not attempt to verify the answer reliability, which implies the onus of ensuring the correctness and accuracy of the answers is on the systems. The users who followed the links preferred reliable patient-oriented sources, which emphasizes the need for having such resources current, maintained, and curated by experts.

5 Future Works

In this pilot study, we experimented with only 8 users for the design choices of UI/UX to determine the appropriate way to highlight the evidence that may lead to better health-related decisions. In the future, we plan to extend the experiments with a more diverse and larger pool of users. We also plan to enrich the experimental setups with sophisticated tracking, such as eye gaze tracking (Wasfy et al., 2024), qualitative user feedback, and longitudinal studies (Kujala et al., 2011) to measure lasting behavior changes. We also plan to introduce more variables in designing choices by experimenting with different color schemes and font emphasis. To determine the usability of the UI/UX component, we plan to design a thorough questionnaire to assess the system Usability Scale (SUS) for better UI/UX designs of an effective QA system.

Limitations

This pilot study focused on a single age group. Although deemed vulnerable, the group is more technology savvy and better educated than many other population groups. To determine if the interaction patterns and health-related behavior displayed by this group is representative of the overall population, broader studies are needed. We hope that the study design and the evaluation interface code `https://github.com/soumyagayen/chqa-interface-evaluation` will help conducting more studies of the use of online medical question answering system and conversational agents.

Ethical Considerations

The patients' cases in this study were derived from the questions provided in the publicly available medical questions collections. The study participants volunteered and consented to participate in the study as part of their paid internship.

Data and code availability

All use cases, surveys and code are available at `https://github.com/soumyagayen/chqa-interface-evaluation`.

Acknowledgments

This research was supported by the Division of Intramural Research (DIR) of the National Library of Medicine (NLM), National Institutes of Health. We thank the anonymous reviewers for the thorough reviews and excellent suggestions.

References

Leona Cilar Budler, Lucija Gosak, and Gregor Stiglic. 2023. Review of artificial intelligence-based question-answering systems in healthcare. *Wiley Interdisciplinary Reviews: Data Mining and Knowledge Discovery*, 13(2):e1487.

Ranganathan Chandrasekaran, Muhammed Sadiq T, and Evangelos Moustakas. 2024. Racial and demographic disparities in susceptibility to health misinformation on social media: National survey-based analysis. *Journal of Medical Internet Research*, 26:e55086.

Deepak Gupta, Dina Demner-Fushman, William Hersh, Steven Bedrick, and Kirk Roberts. 2024. Overview of trec 2024 biomedical generative retrieval (biogen) track. *Preprint*, arXiv:2411.18069.

Jessica Hullman and Andrew Gelman. 2021. Designing for interactive exploratory data analysis requires theories of graphical inference. *Harvard Data Science Review*, 3(3):10–1162.

Melinda J Ickes and Randall Cottrell. 2010. Health literacy in college students. *Journal of American College Health*, 58(5):491–498.

Sari Kujala, Virpi Roto, Kaisa Väänänen-Vainio-Mattila, Evangelos Karapanos, and Arto Sinnelä. 2011. Ux curve: A method for evaluating long-term user experience. *Interacting with computers*, 23(5):473–483.

Kristen Miller, Danielle Mosby, Muge Capan, Rebecca Kowalski, Raj Ratwani, Yaman Noaiseh, Rachel Kraft, Sanford Schwartz, William S Weintraub, and Ryan Arnold. 2018. Interface, information, interaction: a narrative review of design and functional requirements for clinical decision support. *Journal of the American Medical Informatics Association*, 25(5):585–592.

Henri Claude Moungui, Hugues Clotaire Nana-Djeunga, Che Frankline Anyiang, Mireia Cano, Jose Antonio Ruiz Postigo, and Carme Carrion. 2024. Dissemination strategies for mhealth apps: systematic review. *JMIR mHealth and uHealth*, 12:e50293.

John TE Richardson. 2018. The use of latin-square designs in educational and psychological research. *Educational Research Review*, 24:84–97.

Lisa M Schwartz, Steven Woloshin, and H Gilbert Welch. 2005. Can patients interpret health information? an assessment of the medical data interpretation test. *Med. Decis. Making*, 25(3):290–300.

Skipper Seabold and Josef Perktold. 2010. statsmodels: Econometric and statistical modeling with python. In *9th Python in Science Conference*.

Ahmed Wasfy, Nourhan Anber, and Ayman Atia. 2024. Eyeing the interface: Advancing ui/ux analytics through eye gaze technology. In *2024 Intelligent Methods, Systems, and Applications (IMSA)*, pages 538–543. IEEE.

Appendix

A Health-related decision and topic understanding evaluation results for each participant

	Scenario ID							
Participant	1	2	3	4	5	6	7	8
1	1	0	1	1	0	1	0	1
2	1	1	1	1	0	0	0	1
3	1	0	0	1	0	0	0	0
4	1	0	1	1	0	0	0	0
5	1	0	1	1	0	1	0	0
6	1	1	1	0	0	1	0	0
7	0	0	1	1	0	0	0	1
8	1	0	1	1	0	1	0	1

Table 5: Strict evaluation results.

	Scenario ID							
Participant	1	2	3	4	5	6	7	8
1	2	1	2	2	1	2	1	2
2	2	2	2	2	1	1	1	2
3	2	1	0	2	1	1	1	1
4	2	1	2	2	1	1	1	1
5	2	1	2	2	1	2	1	1
6	2	2	2	0	0	2	1	1
7	0	1	2	2	0	1	1	2
8	2	1	2	2	1	2	1	2

Table 6: Lenient evaluation.

B User behavior and interactions

	Scenario ID							
Participant	1	2	3	4	5	6	7	8
1	4	1	2	1	1	0	0	0
2	0	5	2	0	0	2	1	0
3	19	0	0	0	0	0	0	0
4	1	0	0	0	0	0	0	0
5	0	0	0	0	0	0	0	0
6	2	0	0	0	0	0	0	0
7	0	0	0	0	0	1	0	0
8	23	9	7	6	10	7	5	0

Table 7: Number of links clicked by each participant on every question.

	Scenario ID							
Participant	1	2	3	4	5	6	7	8
1	3	0	0	0	0	0	0	0
2	0	0	3	0	0	6	7	0
3	0	1	0	0	0	0	0	0
4	3	0	0	0	0	0	0	0
5	1	0	0	0	0	0	0	0
6	0	0	0	0	0	0	0	0
7	0	0	0	0	1	0	0	0
8	4	6	0	0	5	6	0	0

Table 8: Number of popups (link to scientific evidence) opened by each participant on every question.

	Scenario ID							
Participant	1	2	3	4	5	6	7	8
1	0	0	0	0	0	0	0	0
2	8	0	0	0	0	0	0	0
3	0	0	0	0	0	0	0	0
4	0	0	0	0	0	0	0	0
5	0	0	0	0	0	0	0	0
6	0	0	0	0	0	0	0	0
7	0	0	0	0	0	0	0	0
8	16	0	12	0	0	9	0	0

Table 9: Number of times the images have been scrolled by each participant on every question.

C Time spent on questions

	Scenario ID							
Participant	1	2	3	4	5	6	7	8
1	1040	87	1261	159	266	45	66	44
2	205	111	149	90	106	96	92	46
3	368	138	24	27	57	16	206	23
4	200	47	54	40	71	88	67	108
5	146	40	14	26	19	35	18	28
6	78	43	42	60	45	45	46	49
7	101	94	73	81	58	66	57	285
8	814	351	224	234	120	226	240	200

Table 10: Time spent by each participant on every question in seconds.

D Interface screen shots

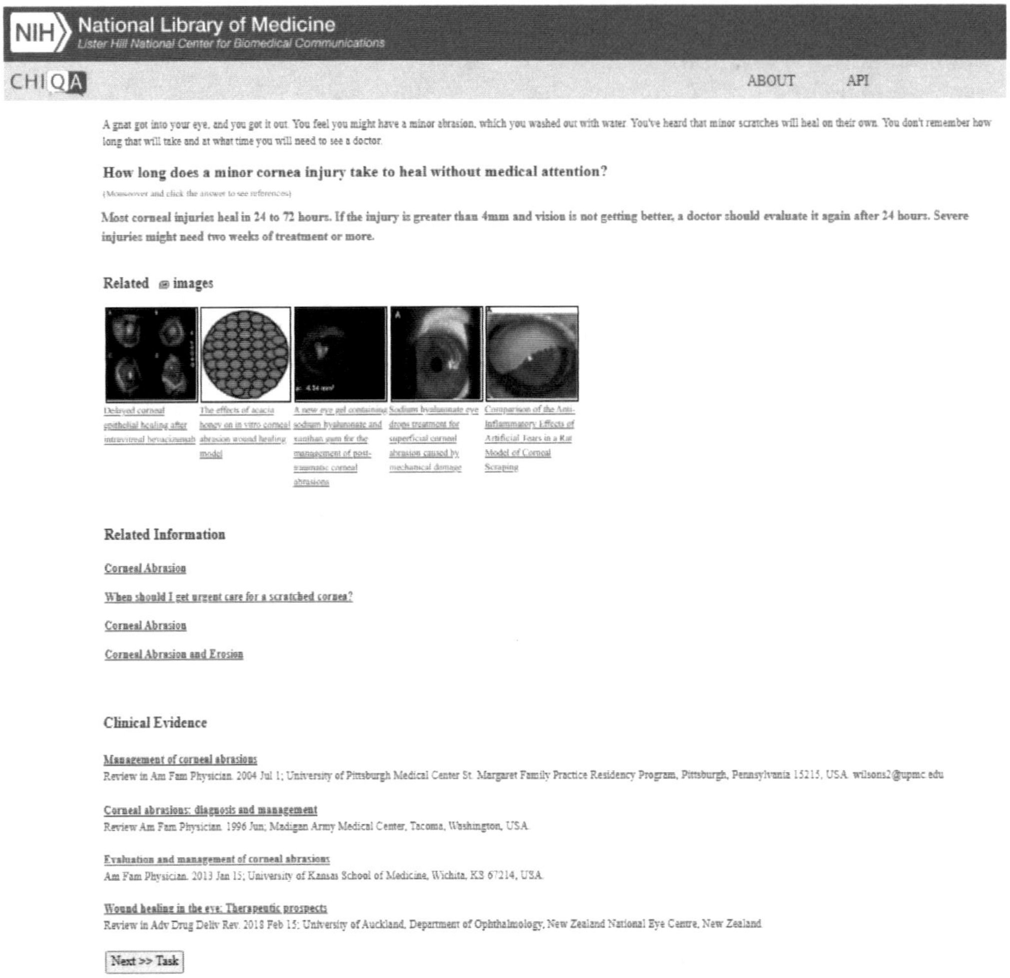

Figure 2: Most popular interface Type C - (TB,PH,LT)

Figure 3: Least popular interface Type B - (TS,PV,LT)

Predicting Chronic Kidney Disease Progression from Stage III to Stage V using Language Models

Zainab Awan
Queen Mary University of London, UK
z.awan@qmul.ac.uk

Rafael Henkin
Queen Mary University of London, UK
r.henkin@qmul.ac.uk

Nick Reynolds
Newcastle University, UK
nick.reynolds@newcastle.ac.uk

Michael R. Barnes
Queen Mary University of London, UK
m.r.barnes@qmul.ac.uk

Abstract

Chronic Kidney Disease (CKD) is a global health challenge, affecting 5–10% of the population, with a significant burden on healthcare systems. Early prediction of CKD progression from stage III to stage V is crucial to enable timely interventions. Traditional predictive methods rely on biochemical markers and demographic factors, but are often limited by issues such as missing data and reliance on structured inputs. This study explores the potential of several encoder-based language models, to predict CKD progression using a cohort from the Clinical Practice Research Datalink (CPRD) GOLD database. We applied both Full Fine-Tuning (FFT) and Parameter-Efficient Fine-Tuning (PEFT) with LoRA to pre-trained models, comparing them against traditional machine learning algorithms such as Random Forest and XGBoost. Our results show that fine-tuned models, particularly dmis-lab/biobert-v1.1-FFT, outperform traditional models in predicting CKD progression, with an AUC of 0.7787, precision of 0.7261, and accuracy of 0.7045. Although LoRA-based models are more computationally efficient, they consistently exhibit lower performance. These findings suggest that fine-tuned encoder models hold significant potential for improving CKD progression prediction. However, there is still room for further enhancement in their accuracy and applicability in clinical settings.

1 Introduction and Related Work

1.1 Introduction

Chronic Kidney Disease (CKD) is one of the leading causes of mortality worldwide, affecting approximately 5–10% of the global population (Eknoyan et al., 2004; Martínez-Castelao et al., 2014). The disease imposes a significant burden on healthcare systems, and early prediction of CKD progression is crucial for improving patient outcomes. CKD is classified into five stages: stage I, stage II, stage III, stage IV, and stage V —based on estimated glomerular filtration rate (eGFR) values: stage I (eGFR 90), stage II (60 eGFR 89), stage III (30 eGFR 59), stage IV (15 eGFR 29), and stage V (eGFR < 15). Accurate prediction of progression from stage III to stage V is critical to enable timely interventions that can help mitigate associated risks.

The United States Renal Data System (USRDS) report indicates that approximately 35.4% of CKD patients are referred to interdisciplinary programs later than recommended, likely due to insufficient risk profile classification (Isaza-Ruget et al., 2024; Mendelssohn et al., 2009). This delay can compromise the effectiveness of potential treatments, highlighting the need for more efficient methods of early detection and intervention.

Current predictive methods rely heavily on biochemical markers like urinary albumin/creatinine ratio (uACR), eGFR, and demographic factors such as age and sex. While these models are useful, they often suffer from limitations, such as missing data in biochemical measures, making imputation unreliable and potentially leading to biased predictions. However, it is important to note that bias is not exclusive to these methods—pre-trained language models and other machine learning approaches can also exhibit biases, depending on data distributions. Additionally, existing risk calculators are often constrained by structured data and require extensive manual feature engineering, which can limit their flexibility and adaptability.

The potential for language models to improve CKD progression prediction remains largely unexplored, especially in the context of large, complex datasets such as those from the Clinical Practice Research Datalink (CPRD). This study seeks to address this gap by applying state-of-the-art encoder models like BioBERT and ClinicalBERT to predict CKD progression, focusing on domain-specific fine-tuning to improve prediction accuracy. The

Proceedings of the Second Workshop on Patient-Oriented Language Processing (CL4Health), pages 236–242
May 4, 2025

motivation for this approach stems from the recognition that language models pre-trained on medical texts can uncover subtle patterns in clinical data that traditional models may miss.

Our key contributions are as follows:

- Comparing domain-specific and general-domain BERT models for CKD progression prediction.
- Benchmarking BERT models against traditional machine learning approaches (XGBoost and Random Forest).
- Assessing Parameter-Efficient Fine-Tuning (PEFT) as a resource-efficient adaptation method.

1.2 Related Work

A significant body of research has focused on predicting CKD progression using machine learning models. For instance, a study by Isaza-Ruget et al. (2024) utilized logistic regression, random forests, and neural networks for CKD progression prediction. This study incorporated a variety of patient features, including demographics, lab results, and comorbidities, to build a robust risk prediction model. Despite promising results, traditional models like these are often constrained by the need for structured data and manual feature engineering, which can limit their scalability and accuracy when applied to diverse populations.

Similarly, Klinrisk's proprietary machine learning model (Tangri et al., 2024), validated in clinical trial populations such as CANVAS (Neal et al., 2013) and CREDENCE (Jardine et al., 2018), demonstrated improved prediction of CKD progression compared to the Kidney Disease Improving Global Outcomes (KDIGO) heatmaps and kidney failure risk equations (KFRE). These models rely on routinely collected laboratory data like eGFR and albuminuria. However, they still face challenges when dealing with unstructured clinical data or missing information, which transformer models could address more effectively. The study by Zhu et al. (2023), employs recurrent neural networks for CKD progression prediction. Their model achieved an AUROC of 0.957 with eGFR time-series data alone, improving to 0.967 with additional clinical variables.

In a similar vein, Reddy et al. (2024) developed explainable machine learning models, including decision trees and random forests, to predict CKD progression. Their models achieved high predictive accuracy (ROC-AUC: 0.94–0.98) using key variables like eGFR slope and recent eGFR.

Saito et al. (2024) applied time-series clustering and LightGBM to stratify patients based on eGFR trajectories, achieving a prediction accuracy of 0.675. According to Shapley values, the most predictive features included baseline eGFR, hemoglobin, and BMI, reinforcing the importance of these variables in forecasting renal function decline.

2 Methodology

This study aimed to predict the progression of chronic kidney disease (CKD) from stage III (CKD III) to stage V (CKD V) using a cohort of patients from the CPRD GOLD database. To address class imbalance, we employed age as a covariate in the propensity score matching process, ensuring comparability between patients with differing progression outcomes. For prediction, we utilised machine learning models, including traditional algorithms (Random Forest and XGBoost) and encoder-based language models. Our goal was to develop models for predicting CKD progression using both approaches.

We fine-tuned pre-trained models using Full Fine-Tuning (FFT) and Parameter-Efficient Fine-Tuning (PEFT) with LoRA, while also optimizing hyperparameters for Random Forest and XGBoost models. The following sections detail these approaches, including their implementation and evaluation.

2.1 Cohort Selection Criteria

We selected patients from the CPRD GOLD database who were registered in a GP practice between 01/01/2010 and 31/12/2020, aged 16 years or older, and had two or more long-term conditions (LTCs). We used READ v2 and ICD10 codes to identify individuals with CKD, specifically targeting stages III and V. A list of the relevant codes is available in the provided GitHub link. We excluded secondary care events that occurred after patients were transferred out of their GP practices, resulting in a distribution of 206,553 patients in class 0 (CKD3) and 4,606 patients in class 1 (CKD5). We then refined the cohort by removing patients from the negative class (CKD3) who had a median follow-up period of less than 6 years-2.4 months, excluding 93,926 patients. We also excluded 166 patients with terms related to preparatory care for dialysis, renal transplant planning, ligation of arteriovenous dialysis fistulas, acute hypercalcaemia of dialysis, or creation of graft fistulas for dialysis. The final cohort comprised 122,267 patients in class 0 (CKD3) and 4,606 patients in class 1 (CKD5).

2.2 Age-Matched Cohort

To reduce bias from confounding variables and address the extreme imbalance between the negative and positive classes in our dataset, we used the MatchIt R package with 1:1 nearest neighbor (NN) for propensity score matching (PSM). This approach matched patients from the CKD progression group with those from the non-progression group based on the key covariate: age. By minimising the confounding effect of age, which significantly influences CKD progression, we ensured a balanced and fair comparison between the two groups, despite the severe class imbalance. We chose age as the sole matching criterion because it is a critical risk factor for CKD progression. Differentiating between physiological and pathological kidney function decline becomes increasingly challenging with age (Noronha et al., 2022). Balancing the age distribution between the progression and non-progression cohorts was essential, given the strong link between ageing and renal function decline. After matching, the dataset included 4,596 instances in both the positive and negative classes.

2.3 Data Summary Statistics Table

Table 1 summarizes the key characteristics of the dataset, providing an overview of the variables and their distribution, which informs the subsequent analysis.

2.4 Full fine-tuning and Parameter Efficient fine-tuning (LoRA)

We framed CKD progression prediction as a sequence classification task, where each input sequence S represents a concatenation of patient-specific attributes and can be defined as in Equation 1. :

$$S = [E, C_1, P_1, C_2, P_2, \ldots, C_n, P_n], \quad (1)$$

where E denotes the patient's ethnicity, Ci represents the i-th LTC, and Pi denotes the i-th continuous prescription. A list of all possible LTCs can be found in the GitHub link: AI MULTIPLY GOLD Read Codes. A continuous prescription is defined as a group of consecutive prescriptions where each pair of prescriptions is at most 84 days (Guthrie et al., 2011) apart. This group of consecutive prescriptions must contain at least three prescriptions (Connor et al., 2024). We included continuous prescriptions in our analysis that are known to be associated with drug-induced renal injury and nephrotoxicity. A comprehensive list can be found in (Connor et al., 2024). The sequence length is variable and depends on the number of recorded conditions and prescriptions for each patient. Labels were assigned as y=1 for cases (progression) and y=0 for controls (non-progression). To reduce potential confounding, we introduced a 6-month buffer period before CKD stage III diagnosis, excluding clinical events that occurred within this window. A patient's CKD stage III diagnosis date might not reflect the exact onset of kidney dysfunction. Events occurring just before diagnosis might be influenced by external factors rather than true disease progression.

3 Experimental Setup

We evaluated several pre-trained encoder-based models, including UFNLP/gatortron-base (Yang et al., 2022), bert-base-uncased (Devlin, 2018), dmis-lab/biobert-v1.1 (Lee et al., 2020), microsoft/BiomedNLP-BiomedBERT-base-uncased-abstract-fulltext (Gu et al., 2021), allenai/scibert_scivocab_uncased (Beltagy et al., 2019), bionlp/bluebert_pubmed_mimic_uncased_L (Peng et al., 2019), and medicalai/ClinicalBERT (Huang et al., 2019). Model training was conducted using the Hugging Face Transformers library, with each model fine-tuned over three epochs. We tokenised the sequences to a maximum context length of 512, used a learning rate of 2e-5, and used AdamW optimization with weight decay of 0.001. Stepwise decay of the learning rate (gamma = 0.1) was applied, along with gradient clipping (max norm 1.0) to prevent exploding gradients. Early stopping was used to stop training when the validation error did not improve.

We compared LoRA (Low-Rank Adaptation) (Hu et al., 2021) and full fine-tuning (FFT) for CKD progression prediction, both of which used similar configurations (learning rate of 2e-5, 5 epochs, maximum sequence length of 512, and

Table 1: Summary Statistics of CKD Cohort

Variable	Class 1 (N = 4,596)	Class 0 (N = 4,596)
Age (mean ± SD)	66.34 ± 14.37	66.51 ± 13.84
Sex (Male / Female)	2,663 / 1,933	2,705 / 1,891
Ethnicity	-	-
White (%)	86.79	88.79
Black or Black British (%)	2.08	3.62
Asian or Asian British (%)	6.82	2.78
Mixed (%)	0.67	0.34
Unknown (%)	0.36	5.14
Chinese or Other Group (%)	1.71	0.84
Median progression time Stage V	6.24 years	NA

batch size of 8). In full fine-tuning (FFT), all model parameters are updated during training, which can be computationally expensive. In contrast, LoRA adapts the model weights using low-rank matrices with a reduced number of trainable parameters. Specifically, we apply a LoRA adaptation parameter r=16, which controls the rank of the matrices and significantly reduces the number of parameters being trained. This makes LoRA a more computationally efficient alternative to full fine-tuning, particularly for large pre-trained models.

Both methods were evaluated using stratified 5-Fold cross-validation, where each fold was split into training, validation, and test sets. The validation set comprised 10% of the training data, stratified by class labels. We reported the performance metrics (accuracy, F_1-score, precision, recall, and AUC) averaged across folds, using mean values.

We tokenised and encoded input sequences using each model's corresponding tokeniser, applying padding and truncation to ensure uniform input lengths. Training was performed with a batch size of 32 for FFT and 8 for LoRA, and DataParallel was used when multiple GPUs were available. The validation performance was assessed after each epoch, and the model with the lowest validation loss was selected for testing. The training process involved optimizing the models using the AdamW optimizer with weight decay and adjusting the learning rate using stepwise decay.

For each fold, the best model was evaluated on the corresponding test set. Predictions were made using softmax probabilities, which allowed us to compute additional metrics such as area under the receiver operating characteristic curve (AU-ROC), accuracy, precision and recall.

For the tabular models, we conducted a grid search to optimize hyperparameters for XGBoost (learning rate, max depth, and number of estimators) and Random Forest (number of estimators, max depth, and minimum samples per split). We employed 5-fold cross-validation, training the models on training subsets and evaluating them on validation subsets. We report averaged performance metrics: accuracy, F_1 score, precision, recall, and ROC AUC—across folds and record the best performing hyperparameter configurations for each metric.

4 Evaluation and Results

Figure 1 compares the performance of various models using five metrics: Accuracy, F_1, Precision, Recall, and AUC (Area Under the Curve). Models evaluated include different fine-tuning strategies FFT and LoRA in addition to RF and XGBoost.

The model dmis-lab/biobert-v1.1-FFT has the highest performance across most metrics, particularly AUC (0.7787), Precision (0.7261), Accuracy (0.7045) and F_1 scores (0.6890). Its recall is low (0.6622), meaning the model is highly selective in identifying progression but fails to detect many actual cases. In practice, this could mean missing patients whose disease progression might have slowed with earlier intervention. While some models like UFLNLP/gatortron-base-FFT perform well in accuracy (0.7034) and recall (0.7293), they slightly lag in precision (0.6477), which might not be ideal for our clinical applications. The contrasting performance of our fine-tuned models in precision and recall highlights the trade-off between these two metrics. A potential approach to mitigate this is employing a Mixture of Experts (MoE) architecture with a gating mechanism. Future work will explore MoE's effectiveness in optimizing both

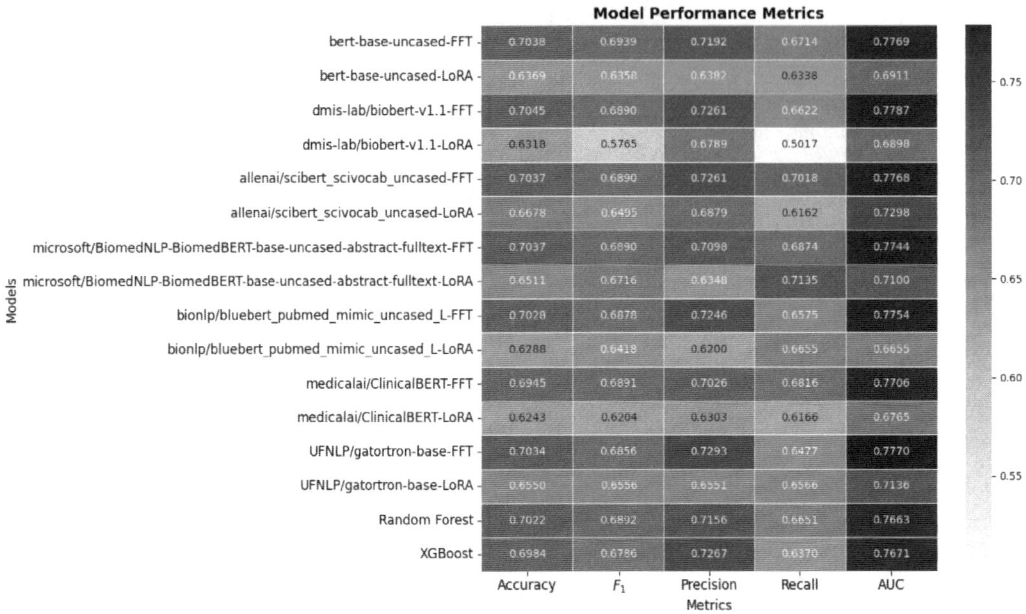

Figure 1: Heatmap of performances across various metrics.

precision and recall in CKD progression prediction.

Models fine-tuned using FFT generally outperform their LoRA counterparts across all metrics. This trend is consistent for models like bert-base-uncased, allenai/scibert_scivocab_uncased, and microsoft/BiomedNLP-BiomedBERT.

While traditional methods like Random Forest and XGBoost perform reasonably well (AUC of 0.7663 and 0.7671, respectively), they lag behind transformer-based models fine-tuned with FFT, particularly in metrics like Precision and Recall. Models pre-trained on biomedical data, such as dmis-lab/biobert-v1.1, microsoft/BiomedNLP-BiomedBERT, and bionlp/bluebert_pubmed_mimic_uncased, tend to perform better than general domain models like bert-base-uncased in terms of accuracy. While dmis-lab/biobert-v1.1-FFT achieved the best accuray, its recall (0.6622) remains a concern in clinical settings where minimizing false negatives is critical.

5 Discussion

In this study, we demonstrate the potential of encoder-based models for predicting CKD progression from stage III to stage V using LTCs, continuous prescriptions, and ethnicity from CPRD. To achieve this, we developed three types of models: full fine-tuning, parameter-efficient fine-tuning (PEFT) using Low-Rank Adaptation (LoRA), and tabular models, including Random Forest (RF) and XGBoost. Model names bearing the suffix *FFT* indicate that the models have been fully fine-tuned, whereas those with the suffix *LoRA* represent Low-Rank Adaptation fine-tuning, a method categorised under PEFT.

While our primary aim was to evaluate the potential of fine-tuned language models for predicting CKD progression, we also included tabular models in the study. This enabled us to compare the performance of advanced deep learning methods with traditional models like RF and XGBoost, which are often better suited to structured data. By incorporating both approaches, we provide a comprehensive assessment of the different modeling techniques for this task.

The results indicate that FFT consistently outperforms PEFT using LoRA across all evaluated metrics, particularly in recall and AUC suggesting that full adaptation of pre-trained models is necessary for tasks as complex as CKD progression. Among the fine-tuned models, those pre-trained on biomedical corpora, such as BioBERT, ClinicalBERT, and BlueBERT, demonstrate strong performance, with AUC values around 0.77. This reinforces the importance of domain-specific pre-training for clinical prediction tasks. Among all models tested, dmis-lab/biobert-v1.1-FFT achieved the highest

AUC (0.7787), Precision (0.7261), and Accuracy (0.7045), indicating its robustness in CKD progression prediction tasks. Its domain-specific pre-training on biomedical text, coupled with fully fine-tuned (FFT) models, has proven promising for the task of CKD progression prediction.

LoRA-based models exhibit lower performance, with AUC scores ranging between 0.6911 and 0.7298. While LoRA fine-tuning offers computational efficiency, its lower recall and precision suggest limitations in capturing subtle predictive patterns in the data. Notably, some LoRA models, such as BiomedBERT-LoRA, show comparatively better recall (0.7135) but at the expense of precision (0.6348), indicating a tendency towards higher false positives. While LoRA's efficiency may be compelling in resource-constrained scenarios, its limited recall capabilities could make it less suitable for critical, high-stakes clinical applications

The results highlight the importance of recall in high-stakes applications like CKD progression prediction, where minimizing false negatives is crucial for timely intervention. Among the models tested, bert-base-uncased-FFT achieves the highest recall, suggesting its potential for capturing at-risk patients. However, as a general-domain model fine-tuned on CPRD data, it lacks the medical domain specificity of models like BioBERT.

Interestingly, tabular models, including RF and XGBoost, perform competitively with language models. XGBoost and RF achieve AUC of 0.7671 and 0.7663, closely matching several fine-tuned language models.

6 Conclusion and Future Work

In conclusion, the study demonstrates that encoder models, particularly BioBERT FFT, significantly contribute to predicting the progression of CKD. Through the use of domain-specific pre-training and fine-tuning strategies, BioBERT surpasses traditional machine learning methods such as Random Forest and XGBoost. By identifying patterns in clinical data, BioBERT shows promise in predicting CKD progression with an accuracy of nearly 70%. While this isn't perfect, it points to the model's potential for advancing predictive analytics in kidney disease and could ultimately support better decision-making in both research and clinical settings.

Although the findings show potential, further improving the model's accuracy is essential for its practical application in medical settings. Therefore, future work will focus on extending this study to include prompt-based decoder models in few-shot and zero-shot settings with Chain-of-Thought reasoning, potentially incorporating domain knowledge. Additionally, we plan to evaluate these models against the standard kidney failure risk equation commonly used in general practice settings. Refining the predictions further by accounting for mortality as a competing risk will also be a key area of exploration.

7 Limitation

This study examines CKD progression over time, including patients who died during the observation period. While mortality may influence disease trajectories, our approach focuses on progression patterns independent of competing events. Future research could explore alternative modeling strategies that explicitly account for competing risks to provide a complementary perspective.

In addition to competing risks, an important limitation of this work is the lack of interpretability analysis. Techniques such as SHAP or LIME could offer insight into model decisions, and future work will explore these methods along with systematic error analysis. Further, as this study is limited to internal validation, future efforts will evaluate generalizability using an independent dataset. Lastly, while we frame CKD progression as a static classification problem, future research could incorporate time-series modeling or survival analysis to better capture disease dynamics.

Acknowledgments

This research utilised Queen Mary's DERI HPC cluster and Apocrita HPC facility, supported by QMUL Research-IT. It is funded by the National Institute for Health Research (NIHR) Newcastle Patient Safety Research Collaboration and NIHR 31672 AI-MULTIPLY.

References

Iz Beltagy, Kyle Lo, and Arman Cohan. 2019. Scibert: A pretrained language model for scientific text. *arXiv preprint arXiv:1903.10676*.

Skylar Connor, Ting Li, Yanyan Qu, Ruth A Roberts, and Weida Tong. 2024. Generation of a drug-induced renal injury list to facilitate the development of new approach methodologies for nephrotoxicity. *Drug Discovery Today*, page 103938.

Jacob Devlin. 2018. Bert: Pre-training of deep bidirectional transformers for language understanding. *arXiv preprint arXiv:1810.04805*.

Garabed Eknoyan, Norbert Lameire, Rashad Barsoum, Kai-Uwe Eckardt, Adeera Levin, Nathan Levin, Francesco Locatelli, Alison Macleod, Raymond Vanholder, Rowan Walker, et al. 2004. The burden of kidney disease: improving global outcomes. *Kidney international*, 66(4):1310–1314.

Yu Gu, Robert Tinn, Hao Cheng, Michael Lucas, Naoto Usuyama, Xiaodong Liu, Tristan Naumann, Jianfeng Gao, and Hoifung Poon. 2021. Domain-specific language model pretraining for biomedical natural language processing. *ACM Transactions on Computing for Healthcare (HEALTH)*, 3(1):1–23.

Bruce Guthrie, Colin McCowan, Peter Davey, Colin R Simpson, Tobias Dreischulte, and Karen Barnett. 2011. High risk prescribing in primary care patients particularly vulnerable to adverse drug events: cross sectional population database analysis in scottish general practice. *Bmj*, 342.

Edward J Hu, Yelong Shen, Phillip Wallis, Zeyuan Allen-Zhu, Yuanzhi Li, Shean Wang, Lu Wang, and Weizhu Chen. 2021. Lora: Low-rank adaptation of large language models. *arXiv preprint arXiv:2106.09685*.

Kexin Huang, Jaan Altosaar, and Rajesh Ranganath. 2019. Clinicalbert: Modeling clinical notes and predicting hospital readmission. *arXiv preprint arXiv:1904.05342*.

Mario A Isaza-Ruget, Nancy Yomayusa, Camilo A González, Fabio A de Oro V, Andrés Cely, Jossie Murcia, Abel Gonzalez-Velez, Adriana Robayo, Claudia C Colmenares-Mejía, Andrea Castillo, et al. 2024. Predicting chronic kidney disease progression with artificial intelligence. *BMC nephrology*, 25(1):148.

Meg J Jardine, Kenneth W Mahaffey, Bruce Neal, Rajiv Agarwal, George L Bakris, Barry M Brenner, Scott Bull, Christopher P Cannon, David M Charytan, Dick De Zeeuw, et al. 2018. The canagliflozin and renal endpoints in diabetes with established nephropathy clinical evaluation (credence) study rationale, design, and baseline characteristics. *American journal of nephrology*, 46(6):462–472.

Jinhyuk Lee, Wonjin Yoon, Sungdong Kim, Donghyeon Kim, Sunkyu Kim, Chan Ho So, and Jaewoo Kang. 2020. Biobert: a pre-trained biomedical language representation model for biomedical text mining. *Bioinformatics*, 36(4):1234–1240.

Alberto Martínez-Castelao, José L Górriz-Teruel, Jordi Bover-Sanjuán, Julián Segura-de la Morena, Jesús Cebollada, Javier Escalada, Enric Esmatjes, Lorenzo Fácila, Javier Gamarra, et al. 2014. Consensus document for the detection and management of chronic kidney disease. *Nefrología (English Edition)*, 34(2):243–262.

David C Mendelssohn, Christine Malmberg, and Bassem Hamandi. 2009. An integrated review of" unplanned" dialysis initiation: reframing the terminology to" suboptimal" initiation. *BMC nephrology*, 10:1–8.

Bruce Neal, Vlado Perkovic, Dick de Zeeuw, Kenneth W Mahaffey, Greg Fulcher, Peter Stein, Mehul Desai, Wayne Shaw, Joel Jiang, Frank Vercruysse, et al. 2013. Rationale, design, and baseline characteristics of the canagliflozin cardiovascular assessment study (canvas)—a randomized placebo-controlled trial. *American heart journal*, 166(2):217–223.

Irene L Noronha, Guilherme P Santa-Catharina, Lucia Andrade, Venceslau A Coelho, Wilson Jacob-Filho, and Rosilene M Elias. 2022. Glomerular filtration in the aging population. *Frontiers in Medicine*, 9:769329.

Yifan Peng, Shankai Yan, and Zhiyong Lu. 2019. Transfer learning in biomedical natural language processing: an evaluation of bert and elmo on ten benchmarking datasets. *arXiv preprint arXiv:1906.05474*.

Sandeep Reddy, Supriya Roy, Kay Weng Choy, Sourav Sharma, Karen M Dwyer, Chaitanya Manapragada, Zane Miller, Joy Cheon, and Bahareh Nakisa. 2024. Predicting chronic kidney disease progression using small pathology datasets and explainable machine learning models. *Computer Methods and Programs in Biomedicine Update*, 6:100160.

Hirotaka Saito, Hiroki Yoshimura, Kenichi Tanaka, Hiroshi Kimura, Kimio Watanabe, Masaharu Tsubokura, Hiroki Ejiri, Tianchen Zhao, Akihiko Ozaki, Sakumi Kazama, et al. 2024. Predicting ckd progression using time-series clustering and light gradient boosting machines. *Scientific Reports*, 14(1):1723.

Navdeep Tangri, Thomas W Ferguson, Ryan J Bamforth, Silvia J Leon, Clare Arnott, Kenneth W Mahaffey, Sradha Kotwal, Hiddo JL Heerspink, Vlado Perkovic, Robert A Fletcher, et al. 2024. Machine learning for prediction of chronic kidney disease progression: Validation of the klinrisk model in the canvas program and credence trial. *Diabetes, Obesity and Metabolism*.

X Yang, A Chen, N PourNejatian, HC Shin, KE Smith, C Parisien, C Compas, C Martin, AB Costa, MG Flores, et al. 2022. A large language model for electronic health records. npj digital medicine, 5 (1), 1–9.

Yitan Zhu, Dehua Bi, Milda Saunders, and Yuan Ji. 2023. Prediction of chronic kidney disease progression using recurrent neural network and electronic health records. *Scientific Reports*, 13(1):22091.

Am I eligible? Natural Language Inference for Clinical Trial Patient Recruitment: the Patient's Point of View

Mathilde Aguiar, Pierre Zweigenbaum, Nona Naderi
Université Paris-Saclay, CNRS, Laboratoire Interdisciplinaire des Sciences du Numérique, 91405, Orsay, France
first.last@lisn.fr

Abstract

Recruiting patients to participate in clinical trials can be challenging and time-consuming. Usually, participation in a clinical trial is initiated by a healthcare professional and proposed to the patient. Promoting clinical trials directly to patients via online recruitment might help to reach them more efficiently. In this study, we address the case where a patient is initiating their own recruitment process and wants to determine whether they are eligible for a given clinical trial, using their own language to describe their medical profile. To study whether this creates difficulties in the patient-trial matching process, we design a new dataset and task, Natural Language Inference for Patient Recruitment (NLI4PR), in which patient-language profiles must be matched to clinical trials. We create it by adapting the TREC 2022 Clinical Trial Track dataset, which provides patients' medical profiles, and rephrasing them manually using patient language. We also use the associated clinical trial reports where the patients are either eligible or excluded. We prompt several open-source Large Language Models on our task and achieve from 56.5 to 71.8 of F1 score using patient language, against 64.7 to 73.1 for the same task using medical language. When using patient language, we observe only a small loss in performance for the best model, suggesting that having the patient as a starting point could be adopted to help recruit patients for clinical trials. The corpus and code bases are all freely available on our Github[1] and HuggingFace[2] repositories.

1 Introduction

Many efforts have been made to develop methods based on Natural Language Processing (NLP) to solve ongoing challenges in healthcare. These studies are targeting either medical professionals or patients. However, patients and medical professionals use different kinds of language. A system trained and designed on medical language might, therefore, fail when used with patient language.

Before releasing a new medicine on the market, clinical trials must be performed and recruit several cohorts of patients with profiles that comply with the inclusion and exclusion criteria of the trial. Recruiting patients can be challenging and costly, especially for studies focusing on certain diseases or targeting a specific population, e.g. a study targeting young children with a rare disease. This can cause major delays for the trial: in 2012, 80% of trials in the US were aborted because of the lack of fitting participants (Johnson, 2015). While enrollment into the trial is usually proposed by a medical practitioner to an already known patient, new online recruitment solutions[3] are promoting trials directly to patients who might not be familiar with clinical trials. These solutions could help speed up and reduce the cost of the patient recruitment process, allowing to recruit hard-to-reach populations, and target underrepresented populations (Brøgger-Mikkelsen et al., 2020).

In this study, we focus on patient recruitment for clinical trials by adopting the patient's point of view, thus using patient language (PL) to describe the patient's medical profile. To enable the research community to explore this setting, we design a novel task, Natural Language Inference for Patient Recruitment (NLI4PR). We create a dataset derived from patient profiles from the shared task TREC 2022 Clinical Trial Track (TREC-CT 2022) (Roberts et al., 2022) and clinical trials' eligibility criteria for which the patient would be eligible or excluded. We frame the recruitment task into a Natural Language Inference (NLI) task. Our aim is to evaluate models' ability to infer from a given premise (the trial's eligibility criteria) whether the

[1] https://github.com/CTInfer/NLI4PR

[2] https://huggingface.co/datasets/Mathilde/NLI4PR

[3] See for instance Klineo or DigitalECMT.

Proceedings of the Second Workshop on Patient-Oriented Language Processing (CL4Health), pages 243–259
May 4, 2025 ©2025 Association for Computational Linguistics

statement (the patient's medical profile) is entailed or contradicts the given premise. If there is an entailment, the patient can be enrolled in the trial; otherwise, the patient does not match the trial's eligibility criteria. Since Large Language Models (LLMs) have demonstrated competitive results in similar shared tasks (Jullien et al., 2023b, 2024), we evaluate how they fare on the present new task. Our contributions are the following:

- Using patient language instead of medical doctor's language to describe the patient's medical profile and perform the patient-trial matching task.
- Creating a new dataset and task, NLI4PR, aiming at matching patients to clinical trials using patient language.
- Evaluating and comparing Large Language Models on the patient-matching task using medical and patient language.

2 Related Work

2.1 Natural Language Processing for recruiting patients for clinical trials

Recruiting patients for clinical trials can be challenging and time-consuming. This is one of the main causes for trials to fail (Kantor and Morzy, 2024). Trials target a certain population, defined through the eligibility criteria designed at the beginning of the study (see Fig. 1). These criteria are expressed as free text in the Clinical Trial Reports (CTRs). The traditional way of promoting trials to patients was made directly by healthcare professionals to known patients that might fit the trial. However, this involves a long manual review of patient profiles, which can also lead to screening errors. Thanks to the digitization of patients' medical records, called electronic health records (EHRs), systems based on NLP (Ghosh et al., 2024; Murcia et al., 2024) aimed at providing support to solve the patient-trial matching task. These systems allow the automatic review of patients' profiles and trial eligibility criteria. They can either follow the trial-to-patients paradigm (for a given trial, the system suggests several patient profiles) or patient-to-trials (for a given patient, the system proposes several trials).

Inclusion Criteria

- Patient gives an informed consent.
- Patient is over 21 years of age.
- Having a diagnosis of a essential tremor confirmed by a trained movement disorders neurologist;
- Having failed or not tolerated conventional medical management, at the discretion of the neurologist managing the patient;

Exclusion Criteria

- Having alternative diagnoses to essential tremor;
- Having comorbid neurodegenerative disorders that may affect mobility or cognition (e.g. comorbid Parkinson's disease or dystonia);
- Having sequelae of prior brain insult (e.g. prior stroke or brain tumor);
- History of prior resective brain surgery (e.g. tumor resection);
- Not being a DBS candidate;
- Receiving unilateral implants
- Having a higher surgical risk that precludes patient from having standard intraoperative mapping.

No condition on gender to be admitted to the trial.
No healthy subjects accepted to join the trial.
Subject must be at least 21 Years old.
Subject must be at most 85 Years

Figure 1: Example of a CTR's eligibility criteria. Taken from NCT04581941, available on clinicaltrials.gov

The TREC-CT 2021 (Soboroff, 2022), 2022 (Roberts et al., 2022), and 2023 (Soboroff, 2024) shared tasks promote the development of NLP-based systems that address the patient-trial matching problem. These tasks provide patient topics, which are a short description of a patient's medical profile, in free-text form in the 2021 and 2022 editions or as structured text (as questionnaires) in the 2023 edition. The goal is to provide for each patient a ranked list of CTRs for which the patient would be eligible, excluded, or not relevant. With the recent advent of Large Language Models, methods using these models (Jin et al., 2024; Nievas et al., 2024; Wornow et al., 2025) have been developed to perform the patient-trial matching. These methods have demonstrated competitive results compared to previous methods based on Masked Language Models.

Natural Language Inference is a task that aims to determine whether a statement can be inferred from a given premise. This task is quite challenging as it requires different kinds of knowledge, and involves finding evidence in the given pieces of text and confronting these pieces of evidence all together in order to conclude if there is an entailment or a contradiction. The NLI4CT task (Jullien et al., 2023a) uses NLI on clinical trials for various applications. Clinical trials are used as NLI premises, and statements have been manually generated. One of the targeted applications is patient recruitment, but the statements are using doctor's medical language. NLI4CT offers a benchmark to evaluate models on their common-sense, numerical, and biomedical abilities applied to the clinical trial domain. Besides, these premises not only consist of the eligibility criteria section, but also, in some instances, they consist of result, intervention, or adverse events sections. Systems like that of Zhang et al. (2020) use NLI to model the patient recruitment task, using a fragment of the patient's EHR as the statement and the trial's eligibility as a premise. All of these approaches are based on the patient's EHR or other medical documents, and never on the patient's medical profile using patient language in a free-text form. Our task is the first to propose an approach using patient language to match patients to clinical trials.

2.2 Processing Patient Language

According to Seiffe et al. (2020), a medical, technical term is either used by a physician or comes from Latin or Greek; a lay term is a term that can easily be understood by patients or is based on everyday language. Here, we define patient language (PL) as the expressions, terms, and formulations expressed in natural language that patients use to talk about their health and any health-related topic, which is broader than the definition proposed by Seiffe et al. (2020). Processing such language poses different challenges from those in traditional medical texts. While medical language uses precise terms to describe a concept, patients will use less precise expressions due to a lower level of medical knowledge, which often causes the patient's text to be inaccurate and also longer compared to one written by a healthcare professional. The patient's medical language is also highly influenced by their health literacy, often depending on their social background, age, and education level. PL also often conveys a load of negative emotions, such as fear, worry, anger, or anxiety (Anderson et al., 2008). In written text, typos and misspellings can also occur. Lay terms (or plain English) bridge the gap between the jargon of a complex domain and "everyday life" language. In the medical domain, they allow patients to make informed decisions, as for instance in the README dataset (Yao et al., 2024), which aims to provide patients with definitions for technical terms found in their EHRs in lay terms. Medical to lay term glossaries have been created, such as that from the University of Michigan[4] or that of the European Medicines Agency.[5]

[4]https://medicaldictionary.lib.umich.edu/

[5]https://www.ema.europa.eu/en/documents/other/ema-medical-terms-simplifier_en.pdf

MedlinePlus[6] (Miller et al., 2000) also provides a glossary of medical concepts explained using lay terms and other synonyms. The Unified Medical Language System (UMLS) (Bodenreider, 2004) is a set of health, biomedical-related vocabularies and standards for the medical domain. In particular the Consumer Health Vocabulary (CHV) provides some medical term to lay language mappings.

Usually, the goal behind the use of lay language is to summarize (Giannouris et al., 2024) or simplify (Attal et al., 2023) the original technical text. Giannouris et al. (2024) summarized clinical trial reports with lay language to make them more easily accessible to non-experts but did not address the recruitment process. In this paper, we do not try to summarize or simplify the patient profile but we use lay terms to study whether patient language is processed as well as medical technical language in clinical trial matching, so that patients themselves could be the starting point of recruitment for clinical trials.

3 Corpus Creation

To the best of our knowledge, no dataset exists in which lay language descriptions of patient profiles are used to identify matching clinical trials. We therefore decided to create one. To do so, we employ a 3-step process: (i) we start from TREC-CT 2022's patient topics, which express patient profiles in free-text, medical language. We then rephrase these topics using patient language (see Sec. 3.1). (ii) We collect the CTRs labeled as *eligible* and *excluded* in TREC-CT. Finally, (iii) we convert the task into a 2-way NLI classification task (see Sec. 3.2). Figure 2 summarizes the process.

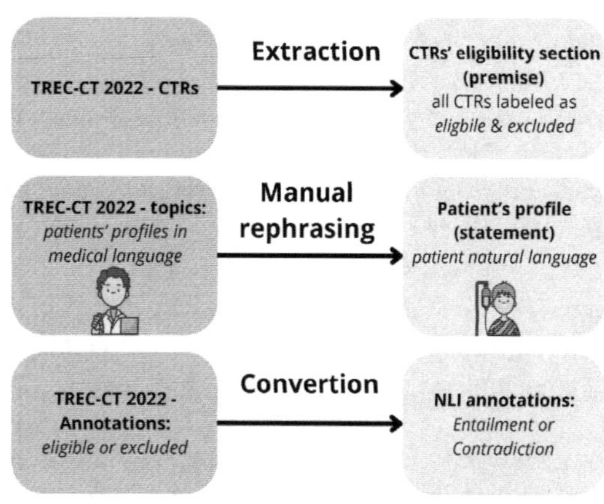

Figure 2: Corpus creation steps

[6]https://medlineplus.gov/

3.1 Rephrasing into Patient Language

We used the 50 TREC-CT 2022 patient topics that describe the patient's last medical visit (emergency room, clinic, or primary care physician). Topics are written using medical language. Following MIMIC-IV's (Johnson et al., 2023) descriptors, the patient topics contain the following information: chief complaint, history of present illness, patient demographics (age and gender), physical exams, and discharge diagnoses. Topics cover various diseases, such as genetic, endocrinal, or dermatological diseases, with patients presenting various profiles, from newborns to the elderly. To obtain PL topics, we tried two different approaches. The first consists of using Large Language models to rephrase the topics automatically. We tried with GPT-4o (OpenAI et al., 2024) and Llama3-8B-Instruct (Dubey et al., 2024) and applied a simple prompt, displayed in Appendix A. Both models seemed to grasp most of the information and adopt a patient perspective, using lay terms and the appropriate tone. However, they sometimes tended to remove quite important information (in the example displayed in Appendix A, in both cases, gender is missing). To avoid these issues, we discarded this approach and opted for the approach below.

To ensure consistency in the information contained in the topics, the first author manually rephrased the topics. This author is experienced in working on medical texts and performing annotation tasks on medical documents, but does not hold any medical degree. We estimate that this level of expertise is suitable for our task since we are trying to represent the health literacy of an average patient. To get a better grasp of different patients' writing styles, we first conducted a manual evaluation with 6 human annotators presenting various patient profiles, described in detail in Appendix B. We adopted a language similar to the one used by the participants. Apart from mapping the concepts from medical language to PL, we noticed that patients tend to use expressions representing their emotions, usually referring to fear, worry, or anxiety. We took this aspect into consideration in the rephrasing. Figure 3 gives an example of the rephrasing process:

1. Selecting the important concepts in the original patient topic (following the MIMIC-IV categories mentioned before).
2. Converting these concepts into patient language by using MedlinePlus for concepts unknown to the annotator or by using a lay-to-medical terms glossary. For each medical term, the annotator checks first MedlinePlus to understand the concept and look for lay language equivalents. They also check lay-to-medical glossaries to see other existing terms (although these glossaries often fall short for specific terms). If no equivalent was found in glossaries and MedlinePlus, the annotator paraphrases the term.
3. Styling the text using words that reflect the patient's emotions, by using adjectives that reflects fear, worry, etc. and by using exclamatory sentences. Additionally, we also tried to adjust language to the patient's age.
4. Proofreading to ensure consistency with the original topic.

To guide the rephrasing process, the annotator produced topics following this instruction (similar to the one given to the participants of the manual evaluation): "*Describe the purpose of your last doctor appointment, the tests undergone, the obtained results or diagnosis as well as your age, gender, and past medical history. All in no more than a dozen sentences.*".

Table 1 displays a small sample of reformulations of the initial medical terms. To analyze a few linguistic features of the NLI4PR dataset, we compute readability and similarity metrics. Using some of the scores of BioLaySumm 2024 (Goldsack et al., 2024), we computed BERTScore (Zhang* et al., 2020) for similarity between the patient and medical version of the topics, Flesch-Kincaid Grade Level (FKGL) (Flesch, 1948), Coleman-Liau Index (CLI) (Coleman and Liau, 1975), and Dale-Chall Readability Score (DCRS) (Dale and Chall, 1948) scores for readability. Tab. 2 reports the results of the different metrics.

The patient and medical topics still keep similar features with a high BERTScore of 89.5%. For the patient language topics, FKGL and DCRS scores both respectively indicate that a 11-17 years old student and a $11-12^{th}$ grade student could understand the topics written in patient language. Although, the CLI measure estimates the readability to be accessible for a 5-6th grader. However the topics produced are accessible to the majority of the population and correspond to what we would expect from an adult's average health literacy. For the

Medical term	PL example	Rephrasing strategy
ALS (amyotrophic lateral sclerosis)	sclerosis	MedlinePlus + name simplification
ear discharge	fluid in my ear	MedlinePlus' description
hearing loss	I could not hear as well as I used to	Paraphrase of the symptoms
His father died suddenly at age 35.	My dad died suddenly when he was 35, so I'm kind of scared.	Add emotion (fear)
dyslipidemia	cholesterol	MedlinePlus (Alternative names section)
Allopurinol	Zyloric	MedlinePlus (Brand names section)

Table 1: Examples of medical and patient language (PL) equivalents used in our task and the corresponding rephrasing strategy employed.

Metric	Patient	Medical
BERTScore	89.5%	
FKGL	6.24	8.83
DCRS	8.13	10.89
CLI	5.88	10.76

Table 2: Similarity (BERTScore) between patient and medical versions of the topics. Readability (FKGL, CLI, and DCRS) measures for patients vs medical versions of the topics.

medical version of the topics, the scores are higher (2.5 points more for FKGL and DCRS) and almost doubled for CLI, bringing the readability level to a 10-11th grade student. To see if the proportion of medical terms is more important in the medical version of the topics, we used QuickUMLS (Soldaini and Goharian, 2016) to extract medical concepts indexed in UMLS. For 92% of the topics, the medical language version contains more terms taken from the UMLS than its patient language equivalent. On average, patient language topics contain 21 terms taken from the UMLS versus 25 for the topic's medical version. Although the average length of a patient language topic is 116 words versus 98 for medical language. This suggests that patient indeed tend to use paraphrase to refer to medical terms.

3.2 Conversion into an NLI task

TREC-CT's original aim is to rank a large number of CTRs in terms of eligibility for a given patient topic. There are 3 ranking levels: *eligible* (the patient described in the topic can take part in the trial), *not relevant* (the trial's eligibility criteria do not seem relevant for the patient described in the topic and there is not enough information to qualify for the trial), and *excluded* (the patient described in the topic does not match the trial's eligibility criteria). Natural Language Inference aims to determine whether a statement entails a given premise, thus in our context, whether the patient topic (statement) entails the trial's eligibility criteria (premise). We map TREC-CT's annotations to NLI annotations: *eligible* is mapped to *entailment*, and *excluded* to *contradiction*. We did not map the instances labeled as *not relevant* to *neutral* as TREC-CT's goal was to rank trials by relevance and not to test patients' eligibility. We describe the internal inference process that should be employed in order to predict the right label. The patient topic Pat has a set of n features f (age, disease, gender, etc.): $Pat = \{f_1, ..., f_n\}$. The eligibility section is composed of m inclusion criteria Inc and k exclusion criteria Exc: $Inc = \{i_1, ..., i_m\}$ and $Exc = \{e_1, ..., e_k\}$. We define the inference relationship between the statement Pat and the premise Inc, Exc as:

$$\forall i \in Inc, \exists f \in Pat; entail(i, f) \quad (1)$$

$$\forall e \in Exc, \forall f \in Pat, contradict(e, f) \quad (2)$$

$$(1) \wedge (2) \Rightarrow Entailment \quad (3)$$

where *contradiction* holds if *entailment* does not. In other words, the model has to infer that for every feature f of a patient, it entails with every inclusion criteria and that it contradicts with every exclusion criteria, for the model to output *Entailment* as the final prediction.

For each topic, we extract all the CTRs labeled as *excluded* and *eligible* in TREC-CT, resulting in, for each patient topic, several *(patient topic, CTR)* pairs labeled either with *entailment* or *contradiction*. Our resulting task is a 2-way NLI classification task.

3.3 Resulting dataset

The resulting dataset consists of 7007 instances, split into training, development, and test sets (representing 70%, 10%, and 20% of the whole dataset, respectively). 3939 are labeled as *Entailment* and

Figure 3: Rephrasing of a patient topic, following MIMIC-IV categories and using MedlinePlus.

3068 as *Contradiction*. Table 3 displays the number of instances per split and the label distribution. We provide two kinds of statements: *statement_medical*, which is the original TREC-CT's patient topic (in medical language), and *statement_pl*, which is the PL rephrased topic. The *premise* field is composed of the extracted eligibility section of the CTR. Additionally, we provide the study's title in the *NCT_title* field and its corresponding id in *NCT_id*. As in Jullien et al. (2023a), our dataset involves several challenges: biomedical reasoning, numerical reasoning, and commonsense reasoning. Appendix C displays more statistics. The dataset is freely available on HuggingFace.[7]

Split	# Entailment	# Contradiction
Train	2757	2147
Dev	295	230
Test	887	691

Table 3: Distribution of *Entailment* and *Contradiction* instances in the dataset splits.

4 Methods

Using this new dataset, we perform initial experiments to evaluate the ability of LLMs to solve the task with lay- vs. medical-language patient profiles.

We prompt four open-source Large Language Models using two prompting templates. The first template, *vanilla*, is made of a simple instruction described in Figure 4a; the second template, *persona*, aims at impersonating the model into a medical practitioner reviewing patient profiles and deciding whether they can participate into the trial or not (see Figure 4b).

The templates are structured as follows: the *premise*, which is the eligibility criteria section of the clinical trial, the instruction, the *statement*, which is the patient profile, either expressed in PL or using medical language, and finally we provide the possible answers, *Entailment* or *Contradiction*. We perform all the experiments in a zero-shot setting, meaning that we do not show any previous demonstration to the model.

We use models that previously achieved competitive results on the similar SemEval task of NLI4CT:

- Flan-T5-XXL (Chung et al., 2022), an 11 billion parameters instruction-tuned sequence-to-sequence model.
- Qwen2.5-7B-Instruct and Qwen2.5-14B-Instruct (Yang et al., 2024), instruction-tuned decoder-only models respectively with 7 and 14 billion parameters.
- Mixtral-8x7B-Instruct-v0.1 (Jiang et al., 2024), a 45 billion parameters decoder-only model pretrained using a mixture of experts approach.

These models are all pretrained on general domain data. As in Jullien et al. (2023a), we choose macro-F1 score as the evaluation metric. We perform the evaluation on the whole test set. We use a temperature of 0.7, a top_p of 1 and top_k of 0. For comparison, we compute the majority baseline corresponding to the case where all the predictions would be labeled as *Entailment*. Comparison is also done against a random classifier where the seed used is 42.

[7]https://huggingface.co/datasets/Mathilde/NLI4PR

(a) Example of a prompt using the *Vanilla* template

(b) Example of a prompt using the *Persona*-style template

Model	Lay-*V*	Lay-*P*	Med-*V*	Med-*P*
Majority		36.0		
Random		50.0		
Flan-T5-XXL	66.0	61.8	72.1	67.5
Qwen-7B	64.1	62.9	65.5	64.7
Qwen-14B	**71.8**	**69.8**	**73.1**	**73.7**
Mixtral-8x7B	60.7	56.5	70.8	71.2

Table 4: Macro F1 score (in %) for the different baselines, using our different prompting templates in a zero-shot setting, on the test set. *Lay* is *patient* language, *Med* is *medical doctor*'s language, *V* stands for *vanilla* template and *P* stands for *persona* template. The majority baseline is *Entailment.* Seed for the random baseline is 42.

5 Results

Table 4 displays the results obtained by the models on the two types of templates.

Qwen-14B achieves the best results for all kinds of templates, up to 37.7 points higher than the majority baseline and 23.7 for the random baseline. All models perform better on medical language than on PL. We believe this loss of performance may come in part from the lack of precision of layman terms used in PL, in comparison to medical terms that define a more precise concept. When trying to match eligibility criteria, the model might not be able to determine the patient's eligibility if in the PL statement, the concept is not precise enough. E.g., in the following example, the eligibility criteria states *"Subjects having a diagnosis of probable or definite **ALS** in accordance with the Revisited El-Escorial Criteria."*, the patient topic in medical language uses the acronym *ALS*, however in the patient topic in PL, the term used is simply *sclerosis* (see Table 1). With PL, the model cannot determine which type of sclerosis the patient is suffering from and thus might not match it to the trial.

Using a persona template did not necessarily lead to better results; Flan-T5 performed even worse when using PL. Despite being the larger model, Mixtral is the worst-performing when using PL, and in the worst case being only 6.5 points above the random baseline. In the case of Qwen, more parameters (increasing from 7B to 14B) improved performance, with a gain of up to 9 points for the Med-P template.

6 Error Analysis

Medical vs Patient Language We examined on which patient topic models tend to fail, either using PL or medical language: for this purpose, we compute the misclassification rate (MCR) for each patient topic t using the predictions of each model and the gold standard:

$$MCR(t) = \frac{misclassification\_topic\_t}{total\_count\_topic\_t}$$

We compute MCR for all topics with all models' predictions across all templates, where $misclassification\_topic\_t$ is the number of misclassifications for topic t and $total\_count\_topic\_t$ the number of instances using topic t as the statement in the dataset. We derive $MCR_{pl>med}$ where the models perform better with topics using medical language than PL, and conversely $MCR_{med>pl}$ where models were better using patient language, for each patient topic n:

$$MCR_{pl-med}(t) = MCR_{pl}(t) - MCR_{med}(t)$$

$$MCR_{pl>med} = \max_{t \in [1,50]} MCR_{pl-med}(t)$$

$$MCR_{med>pl} = - \min_{t \in [1,50]} MCR_{med-pl}(t)$$

Across all the models, the patient topic occurring the more often for $MCR_{pl>med}$ is patient #21, and the one for $MCR_{med>pl}$ is patient #30. Appendix D displays both patients' profiles. The descriptions of patient #21 in medical language and PL are similar in terms of demographics, chief complaint, and physical exams. However, for the discharge diagnosis, medical language mentions *ALS* while PL mentions *sclerosis* (see Tab. 1), thus not mentioning the specific kind of sclerosis diagnosed. For patient #30, the physical exam observations have been greatly simplified in the PL version. Otherwise, information remains consistent with the medical language version.

We quickly investigate if these differences can be the reason for misclassification. We allow Qwen-14B to output a longer sequence of tokens when prompted with a single example of patient #21 and #30 (see Appendix E). Qwen provides a brief explanation of the reason for its prediction. We compare the justifications given for the *Lay-V* and *Med-V* prompts.

For #21, Qwen predicted the right label (*Entailment*) for *Med-V* and the wrong label for *Lay-V*. The misclassification comes from the case depicted in Sec. 5. Qwen mentioned that *sclerosis* does not necessarily involve an ALS, which is technically true. PL lacks precision, which can lead to misclassification, whereas the model can predict the right label with medical language for the same case.

For #30, Qwen predicted the right label (*Entailment*) for *Lay-V* and the wrong label for *Med-V*. The patient topic describes a woman suffering from osteoarthritis. In order to solve the inference, the model has to perform numerical inference to determine if her age fits the age range of the inclusion criteria, check that the diagnosis of osteoarthritis fits with the inclusion and exclusion criteria and that the patient does not suffer from other disorders. For *Lay-V* the model reports that it compared the age range, the osteoarthritis diagnostic with the eligibility criteria. For *Med-V* the model got misled by one of the symptoms and inferred another potential disease, that could fall under one exclusion criterion. In this case, having more information that was not directly linked to the criteria confused the model and led to a wrong prediction.

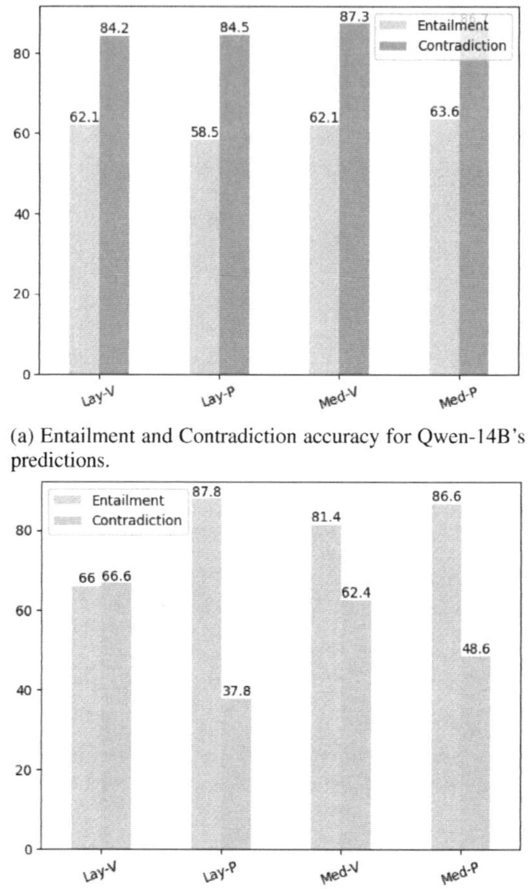

(a) Entailment and Contradiction accuracy for Qwen-14B's predictions.

(b) Entailment and Contradiction accuracy for Flan-T5-XXL's predictions.

Figure 5: *Lay* is *patient* language, *Med* is *medical* doctor's language, *V* stands for *vanilla* prompt and *P* stands for *persona* prompt.

Which is harder, *Entailment* or *Contradiction*? We compute the accuracy per label for the two best-performing models, Qwen-14B and Flan-T5-XXL (see Figure 5). Qwen is performing up to 26 points better on *Contradiction* than on *Entailment*. This behavior is consistent with all the types of templates. Surprisingly, Flan-T5 obtains up to 50 points more in predicting *Entailment* than *Contradiction*, and this observation applies to all templates except *Lay-V*. Predicting *Contradiction* seems rather simple compared to predicting *Entailment*. Since a patient would not be eligible for a clinical trial if their characteristics do not comply with at least one of the exclusion criteria, this would lead to a direct assertion of the *Contradiction* label. Meanwhile, for *Entailment*, the model has to go through all the patient's features and compare them to all the inclusion and exclusion criteria, which involves more knowledge and computations.

7 Future Work and potential applications

One direction for future work would be to fine-tune the models (using our training and development sets) to see if it would improve performance. Systematically evaluating models' explanations would also allow to determine if the model is predicting the right label for the right reason and, hence, detecting the right pieces of evidence in the text to make its prediction. This evaluation could be done using the LLM-as-a-judge paradigm (Zheng et al., 2023), where one or several LLMs could evaluate if the retrieved evidence and explanations are correct. Expanding the dataset with new patient profiles with various health literacy levels and diseases would also allow to evaluate the models on more diverse cases.

We hope this work can pave the way to the development of more NLP applications to promote clinical trials directly to patients, using their own language. We believe that proposing these kinds of interfaces would allow to reduce the recruitment workload and to promote trials to a wider population.

8 Conclusion

In this study, we present a novel task, Natural Language Inference for Patient Recruitment (NLI4PR), that aims to use patient language to match patients to clinical trials. The patient-to-trial matching is usually done using a description of the patient in doctor's medical language. Here, we adopt another approach where the patient describes their own profile using their own language. Patient language presents major differences compared to doctor's medical language due to the patient's limited health literacy. We evaluated the ability of several open Large Language Models to deal with patient language and compare it to the use of medical language. We frame the task as a Natural Language Inference task. For this, we create a new dataset derived from the patient profiles provided by TREC-CT 2022, and the clinical trials ranked as *eligible* and *excluded* in TREC-CT 2022.

We found that all models obtained an F1 score much higher than the majority baseline on our test set, using medical language but also using patient language. Models struggled more with patient language than with medical language, however the gap between the two settings was rather low. We found that this gap in performance is mainly coming from the loss of precision in the terms used by patients compared to medical professionals. We observe that most of the errors are coming from issues in enforcing the inclusion and exclusion criteria rather than the difference between the patient language and the doctors' medical language.

9 Limitations

The patient topics have been built to keep important patient information. We hypothesize that in a real-world scenario, a patient describing their medical history and condition might miss some elements, making the task even more challenging. In addition, despite the effort made to diversify the phrasings, the rephrasing has been done by a single annotator, which might limit diversity. An improved approach would be to ask a diverse pool of patients to produce their own statements to represent differences in pathology, social background, levels of health literacy, and phrasing.

Since we perform a 2-way classification and we did not consider the cases labeled as *not relevant* from TREC-CT, we cannot directly compare our results with those of TREC-CT participants.

10 Ethical Considerations

The patient profiles are taken from the original TREC-CT 2022 shared task. They do not contain any element or piece of information that could lead to identification of any individual. The rephrased version using layman's terms does not contain any personal information either. Clinical trials are extracted and processed from clinicaltrials.gov. This resource is freely available, provided by the National Library of Medicine, and is an official U.S. Department of Health and Human Services website.

Acknowledgments

This work received funding from the CNRS through grant 80|PRIME and the French "Agence Nationale pour la Recherche" under grant agreement ANR-22-CPJ1-0087-01. This work was granted access to the HPC resources of IDRIS under the allocation 2024-AD011015277 made by GENCI.

References

Wendy G. Anderson, Stewart C. Alexander, Keri L. Rodriguez, Amy S. Jeffreys, Maren K. Olsen, Kathryn I. Pollak, James A. Tulsky, and Robert M. Arnold. 2008. "What concerns me is..." Expression of emotion by advanced cancer patients during outpatient visits. *Supportive Care in Cancer*, 16:803–811.

Kush Attal, Brian Ondov, and Dina Demner-Fushman. 2023. A dataset for plain language adaptation of biomedical abstracts. *Scientific Data*, 10(1).

Olivier Bodenreider. 2004. The unified medical language system (UMLS): integrating biomedical terminology. *Nucleic acids research*, 32 Database issue:D267–70.

Mette Brøgger-Mikkelsen, Zarqa Ali, John R Zibert, Anders Daniel Andersen, and Simon Francis Thomsen. 2020. Online patient recruitment in clinical trials: Systematic review and meta-analysis. *J Med Internet Res*, 22(11):e22179.

Hyung Won Chung, Le Hou, S. Longpre, Barret Zoph, Yi Tay, William Fedus, Eric Li, Xuezhi Wang, Mostafa Dehghani, Siddhartha Brahma, Albert Webson, Shixiang Shane Gu, Zhuyun Dai, Mirac Suzgun, Xinyun Chen, Aakanksha Chowdhery, Dasha Valter, Sharan Narang, Gaurav Mishra, Adams Wei Yu, Vincent Zhao, Yanping Huang, Andrew M. Dai, Hongkun Yu, Slav Petrov, Ed H. Chi, Jeff Dean, Jacob Devlin, Adam Roberts, Denny Zhou, Quoc V. Le, and Jason Wei. 2022. Scaling instruction-finetuned language models. *ArXiv*, abs/2210.11416.

Meri Coleman and T. Liau. 1975. A computer readability formula designed for machine scoring. *Journal of Applied Psychology*, 60:283–284.

Edgar Dale and Jeanne S. Chall. 1948. A formula for predicting readability. *Educational Research Bulletin*, 27(1):11–28.

Abhimanyu Dubey, Abhinav Jauhri, Abhinav Pandey, Abhishek Kadian, Ahmad Al-Dahle, Aiesha Letman, Akhil Mathur, Alan Schelten, Amy Yang, Angela Fan, Anirudh Goyal, Anthony Hartshorn, Aobo Yang, Archi Mitra, Archie Sravankumar, Artem Korenev, Arthur Hinsvark, Arun Rao, Aston Zhang, Aurélien Rodriguez, Austen Gregerson, Ava Spataru, Baptiste Rozière, Bethany Biron, Binh Tang, Bobbie Chern, Charlotte Caucheteux, Chaya Nayak, Chloe Bi, Chris Marra, Chris McConnell, Christian Keller, Christophe Touret, Chunyang Wu, Corinne Wong, Cristian Canton Ferrer, Cyrus Nikolaidis, Damien Allonsius, Daniel Song, Danielle Pintz, Danny Livshits, David Esiobu, Dhruv Choudhary, Dhruv Mahajan, Diego Garcia-Olano, Diego Perino, Dieuwke Hupkes, Egor Lakomkin, Ehab AlBadawy, Elina Lobanova, Emily Dinan, Eric Michael Smith, Filip Radenovic, Frank Zhang, Gabriel Synnaeve, Gabrielle Lee, Georgia Lewis Anderson, Graeme Nail, Grégoire Mialon, Guan Pang, Guillem Cucurell, Hailey Nguyen, Hannah Korevaar, Hu Xu, Hugo Touvron, Iliyan Zarov, Imanol Arrieta Ibarra, Isabel M. Kloumann, Ishan Misra, Ivan Evtimov, Jade Copet, Jaewon Lee, Jan Geffert, Jana Vranes, Jason Park, Jay Mahadeokar, Jeet Shah, Jelmer van der Linde, Jennifer Billock, Jenny Hong, Jenya Lee, Jeremy Fu, Jianfeng Chi, Jianyu Huang, Jiawen Liu, Jie Wang, Jiecao Yu, Joanna Bitton, Joe Spisak, Jongsoo Park, Joseph Rocca, Joshua Johnstun, Joshua Saxe, Junteng Jia, Kalyan Vasuden Alwala, Kartikeya Upasani, Kate Plawiak, Ke Li, Kenneth Heafield, Kevin Stone, and et al. 2024. The Llama 3 herd of models. *CoRR*, abs/2407.21783.

Rudolf Franz Flesch. 1948. A new readability yardstick. *The Journal of applied psychology*, 32 3:221–33.

Satanu Ghosh, Hassan Mohammed Abushukair, Arjun Ganesan, Chongle Pan, Abdul Rafeh Naqash, and Kun Lu. 2024. Harnessing explainable artificial intelligence for patient-to-clinical-trial matching: A proof-of-concept pilot study using phase I oncology trials. *PLOS ONE*, 19(10):1–14.

Polydoros Giannouris, Theodoros Myridis, Tatiana Passali, and Grigorios Tsoumakas. 2024. Plain language summarization of clinical trials. In *Proceedings of the Workshop on DeTermIt! Evaluating Text Difficulty in a Multilingual Context @ LREC-COLING 2024*, pages 60–67, Torino, Italia. ELRA and ICCL.

Tomas Goldsack, Carolina Scarton, Matthew Shardlow, and Chenghua Lin. 2024. Overview of the BioLaySumm 2024 shared task on the lay summarization of biomedical research articles. In *Proceedings of the 23rd Workshop on Biomedical Natural Language Processing*, pages 122–131, Bangkok, Thailand. Association for Computational Linguistics.

Albert Q. Jiang et al. 2024. Mixtral of experts. *ArXiv*, abs/2401.04088.

Qiao Jin, Zifeng Wang, Charalampos S Floudas, Fangyuan Chen, Changlin Gong, Dara Bracken-Clarke, Elisabetta Xue, Yifan Yang, Jimeng Sun, and Zhiyong Lu. 2024. Matching patients to clinical trials with large language models. *Nature Communications*, 15(1):9074.

Alistair E. W. Johnson, Lucas Bulgarelli, Lu Shen, Alvin Gayles, Ayad Shammout, Steven Horng, Tom J. Pollard, Benjamin Moody, Brian Gow, Li wei H. Lehman, Leo Anthony Celi, and Roger G. Mark. 2023. MIMIC-IV, a freely accessible electronic health record dataset. *Scientific Data*, 10.

Otis Johnson. 2015. An evidence-based approach to conducting clinical trial feasibility assessments. *Clinical investigation*, 5:491–499.

Mael Jullien, Marco Valentino, and André Freitas. 2024. Semeval-2024 task 2: Safe biomedical natural language inference for clinical trials. In *Proceedings of the 18th International Workshop on Semantic Evaluation (SemEval-2024)*, pages 1947–1962, Mexico City, Mexico. Association for Computational Linguistics.

Mael Jullien, Marco Valentino, Hannah Frost, Paul O'Regan, Dónal Landers, and Andre Freitas. 2023a. NLI4CT: Multi-evidence natural language inference for clinical trial reports. In *Proceedings of the 2023 Conference on Empirical Methods in Natural Language Processing*, pages 16745–16764, Singapore. Association for Computational Linguistics.

Maël Jullien, Marco Valentino, Hannah Frost, Paul O'regan, Donal Landers, and André Freitas. 2023b. Semeval-2023 task 7: Multi-evidence natural language inference for clinical trial data. In *Proceedings of the 17th International Workshop on Semantic Evaluation (SemEval-2023)*, pages 2216–2226, Toronto, Canada. Association for Computational Linguistics.

Klaudia Kantor and Mikołaj Morzy. 2024. Machine learning and natural language processing in clinical trial eligibility criteria parsing: a scoping review. *Drug Discovery Today*, 29(10):104139.

Naomi Miller, E.M. Lacroix, and Joyce Backus. 2000. MEDLINEplus: Building and maintaining the national library of medicine's consumer health web service. *Bulletin of the Medical Library Association*, 88:11–7.

Victor Murcia, Vinod Aggarwal, Nikhil Pesaladinne, Ram Thammineni, Nhan Do, Gil Alterovitz, and Rafael Fricks. 2024. Automating clinical trial matches via natural language processing of synthetic electronic health records and clinical trial eligibility criteria. *AMIA Joint Summits on Translational Science proceedings. AMIA Joint Summits on Translational Science*, 2024:125–134.

Mauro Nievas, Aditya Basu, Yanshan Wang, and Hrituraj Singh. 2024. Distilling large language models for matching patients to clinical trials. *Journal of the American Medical Informatics Association*, 31(9):1953–1963.

OpenAI et al. 2024. GPT-4 technical report. *Preprint*, arXiv:2303.08774.

Kirk Roberts, Dina Demner-Fushman, Ellen M. Voorhees, Steven Bedrick, and William R. Hersh. 2022. Overview of the TREC 2022 clinical trials track. In *Text Retrieval Conference*.

Laura Seiffe, Oliver Marten, Michael Mikhailov, Sven Schmeier, Sebastian Möller, and Roland Roller. 2020. From witch's shot to music making bones - resources for medical laymen to technical language and vice versa. In *Proceedings of the Twelfth Language Resources and Evaluation Conference*, pages 6185–6192, Marseille, France. European Language Resources Association.

Ian Soboroff. 2022. Overview of TREC 2021. Special Publication (NIST SP), National Institute of Standards and Technology, Gaithersburg, MD.

Ian Soboroff. 2024. Overview of TREC 2023. Special Publication (NIST SP), National Institute of Standards and Technology.

Luca Soldaini and Nazli Goharian. 2016. QuickUMLS: a fast, unsupervised approach for medical concept extraction. In *Proceedings of the MedIR workshop, SIGIR*, Pisa, Italy.

Michael Wornow, Alejandro Lozano, Dev Dash, Jenelle A. Jindal, Kenneth W. Mahaffey, and Nigam H. Shah. 2025. Zero-shot clinical trial patient matching with LLMs. *NEJM AI*, 2(1):AIcs2400360.

An Yang, Baosong Yang, Beichen Zhang, Binyuan Hui, Bo Zheng, Bowen Yu, Chengyuan Li, Dayiheng Liu, Fei Huang, Haoran Wei, Huan Lin, Jian Yang, Jianhong Tu, Jianwei Zhang, Jianxin Yang, Jiaxi Yang, Jingren Zhou, Junyang Lin, Kai Dang, Keming Lu, Keqin Bao, Kexin Yang, Le Yu, Mei Li, Mingfeng Xue, Pei Zhang, Qin Zhu, Rui Men, Runji Lin, Tianhao Li, Tingyu Xia, Xingzhang Ren, Xuancheng Ren, Yang Fan, Yang Su, Yichang Zhang, Yu Wan, Yuqiong Liu, Zeyu Cui, Zhenru Zhang, and Zihan Qiu. 2024. Qwen2.5 technical report. *arXiv preprint arXiv:2412.15115*.

Zonghai Yao, Nandyala Siddharth Kantu, Guanghao Wei, Hieu Tran, Zhangqi Duan, Sunjae Kwon, Zhichao Yang, and Hong Yu. 2024. README: Bridging medical jargon and lay understanding for patient education through data-centric NLP. In *Findings of the Association for Computational Linguistics: EMNLP 2024*, pages 12609–12629, Miami, Florida, USA. Association for Computational Linguistics.

Tianyi Zhang*, Varsha Kishore*, Felix Wu*, Kilian Q. Weinberger, and Yoav Artzi. 2020. BERTScore: Evaluating Text Generation with BERT. In *International Conference on Learning Representations*.

Xingyao Zhang, Cao Xiao, Lucas M. Glass, and Jimeng Sun. 2020. DeepEnroll: Patient-trial matching with deep embedding and entailment prediction. In *Proceedings of The Web Conference 2020*, WWW '20, page 1029–1037, New York, NY, USA. Association for Computing Machinery.

Lianmin Zheng, Wei-Lin Chiang, Ying Sheng, Siyuan Zhuang, Zhanghao Wu, Yonghao Zhuang, Zi Lin, Zhuohan Li, Dacheng Li, Eric P. Xing, Hao Zhang, Joseph E. Gonzalez, and Ion Stoica. 2023. Judging LLM-as-a-judge with MT-bench and chatbot arena. In *Proceedings of the 37th International Conference on Neural Information Processing Systems*, NIPS '23, Red Hook, NY, USA. Curran Associates Inc.

A Rephrasing patient topics using Large Language Models

Table 5 displays an example of the different outputs in PL obtained. The prompt used with the Large Language Models is the following:

> Rephrase the following patient profile like it would be expressed by the patient themselves: *original_topic*

Source	Output text
Original topic	A 19-year-old male came to clinic with some sexual concern. He recently engaged in a relationship and is worried about the satisfaction of his girlfriend. He has a "baby face" according to his girlfriend's statement and he is not as muscular as his classmates. On physical examination, there is some pubic hair and poorly developed secondary sexual characteristics. He is unable to detect coffee smell during the examination, but the visual acuity is normal. Ultrasound reveals the testes volume of 1-2 ml. The hormonal evaluation showed serum testosterone level of 65 ng/dL with low levels of GnRH.
ChatGPT	I'm 19, and I recently started a relationship. I've been feeling a bit worried about whether I'm making my girlfriend happy. She mentioned that I have a 'baby face,' and I've noticed I'm not as muscular as most of my classmates. I also can't smell coffee, which I realized during this visit. I do have some pubic hair, but I think I might be behind in developing other features that guys my age have. The doctor checked me out, and they said my testosterone levels are low, and my testicles are smaller than normal. They also mentioned something about low levels of another hormone, GnRH.
Llama-3-8B-Instruct	I'm 19 years old and I've been dating someone for a little while now. To be honest, I'm really worried that I'm not good enough for her. She says I have a 'baby face' and I'm not nearly as muscular as my friends. I feel like I don't measure up. When we're together, she sometimes mentions how unsatisfied she is with our intimate moments, which makes me even more anxious. Physically, I notice that I don't have much body hair or muscle development compared to others my age. During our last exam, I couldn't even smell the coffee because of my poor sense of smell! But at least my eyesight seems okay. I also just had an ultrasound done on my testicles, and the doctor told me they're smaller than usual. And when they checked my hormone levels, it turned out that my testosterone levels are super low - way lower than normal. It's making me feel really self-conscious and unsure about who I am and what I can do to make things better between me and my girlfriend.
Human	I'm 19 years old guy and I just went to see a doctor at the clinic after I just got with my girlfriend. I'm kinda worried because she thinks that I have a baby face and to be honest, I'm way less muscular than my classmates. I don't have much hair down there, and yes, I don't have that macho look. The doctor made me smell some coffee and I couldn't smell anything special. I also had some eyesight checkups and the doctor told me everything was normal. I got my test results back and it says: testes volume is 1-2 ml and serum testosterone level of 65 ng/dL with low GnRH levels.

Table 5: Outputs obtained after rephrasing the original topic into PL. Using either LLMs or a human annotator.

B Rephrasing patient topics using patients

Goal To have examples of the way patients express themselves, we asked 6 participants to produce statements using patient language. These participants are volunteers who are not authors of this paper. They all have different profiles in terms of health literacy, cultural backgrounds, educational backgrounds, and age. All the materials (persona, generated medical reports and guidelines) are available here[8].

Participants We note A_i a participant.

A1: 25-year-old Cambodian man with no medical training. He holds a Master's degree in computer science. His mother tongue is Khmer, but has a B2 English level.

A2: 69 years old French man. He has a PhD in biochemistry but no particular training in medicine. His native language is French.

A3: 60-year-old French woman. She is a secondary teacher with no special training in medicine. Her native language is French.

A4: 29 years old Greek woman. She is a PhD student majoring in NLP. She has no particular medical training. Her native language is Greek, but she has a C2 English level.

A5: 26 years old Chinese man. He is a PhD student in biology working on oncology. His native language is Chinese, but he has a B2 level in French.

A6: 25 years old French woman. She is currently pursuing her 8th year of medical training, specializing in anesthesiology and intensive care. Her native language is French.

Settings We designed our experiment in order to obtain as spontaneous as possible answers from the participants. We gave all participants a persona directly adapted from one of the TRECT-CT's patient topics. To avoid influencing the participants, the persona was built as a set of fields (age, gender, tests undergone, chief complaint, medical history, current medication) with keywords only. We also used ChatGPT to generate mock-ups of test results[9] with the results mentioned in the original TREC-CT 2022 topic. We gave the following instruction to the participants:

> Following the provided persona and test report, describe the purpose of your last doctor appointment, the tests undergone, the obtained results or diagnostic as well as your age, gender and past medical history. All in no more than a dozen of sentences.

Results **A1:** "I'm a 25 year old man. My roommate always says that mostly when we are watching TV in the afternoon, he noticed that I usually fall asleep even while we are talking. it's a bit embarrassing. I think I am not a person like that. I feel something is wrong. So I decided to meet a doctor to check about this. So the doctor asked me to do the sleep test which is called Multiple Sleep Latency Test. This test just requires me to take a bunch of short naps during the daytime and the doctor monitored my sleep. It is so surprising that the test also confirms that I quickly fall asleep and enter REM sleep. The doctor said this could be narcolepsy, which is a sleep disorder that causes excessive daytime sleepiness. I'm waiting to do an overnight sleep study and see a sleep specialist to figure out what the next steps are."

A2 (translated): "My medical check-up is not very encouraging. The blood test results are alarming. Serum antibodies are abnormally high, indicating an inflammatory state. The muscle biopsy confirms the presence of inflammation. The interpretations provided by the medical analysis laboratory suggest systemic inflammatory muscle damage. The doctor suspects dermatomyositis. However, he suggests further tests. In my quest to understand dermatomyositis, I learn that it is associated with various cancers. I think my life is about to be turned upside down if the doctor's diagnosis proves correct. Maybe I'll have to undergo chemotherapy and so on. At my age, my professional and emotional life could be seriously devalued. I'll decide after the next medical examinations."

A3 (translated): "I am a 33-year-old woman. I consulted a doctor because I'm persistently tired, have less appetite than before and have lost 4 kilos in two months. At the hospital, tests showed generalized hyperpigmentation. A blood test revealed abnormally low levels of cortisol, a sign of "primary adrenal insufficiency", a dysfunction of the glands above the kidneys that produce hormones. Could my health problem be due to my past history? I suffer from Hashimoto's disease, an autoimmune disorder caused by a thyroid disorder. I am treated

[8] https://github.com/CTInfer/NLI4PR/tree/main/human_evaluation

[9] For instance, a generated karyotype report here.

for this disease by taking levothyroxine on a regular basis. But obviously, this medication no longer seems sufficiently effective. To resolve the adrenal insufficiency I'm suffering from, and thus stimulate the function of the adrenal glands, the doctors have prescribed a glucocorticoid-based treatment, on a long-term basis but under supervision. I will need to consult my GP regularly to observe the clinical symptoms - the extent of the brown spots on my skin - and to prescribe a blood test to monitor cortisol levels and, if necessary, adjust and rebalance the treatment. I was also recommended a parallel follow-up with an endocrinologist."

A4: "I am a 67 year old woman. I went to the ophthalmologist because I was not seeing well from both of my eyes especially during the night. The physical exam showed that my pupils are normal in diameter both in the light and darkness, however the acuity test results confirmed that I have a blurry vision of 50/100 that is probably linked to cataract. I will need to consult a second ophthalmologist to confirm the diagnosis and I might need to do further lab tests."

A5 (translated): "My name is Jean Martin and I'm 52 years old. On 22/01 I had two radiology examinations: a thoracic X-ray and an oeso-gastro-duodenal transit. The purpose of these examinations was to find an explanation for my symptoms of thoracic burning and acid reflux, which have been treated piecemeal with PPIs (proton pump inhibitors = anti-acids). I have no other antecedents than my obesity, I don't smoke or drink. Dr. Dupuis, a radiologist, interpreted these examinations and concluded that I had a hiatal hernia due to stomach sliding, with no signs of complications: no ulcerations, no digestive perforation and permeability of the lower esophageal sphincter, with no visualized esophageal reflux. Treatment with ipp is indicated, as is follow-up by a specialist in gastroenterology. If the symptoms become too incapacitating, I'm advised to undergo 2nd-line laparoscopic surgery to reconstruct the stomach, which is still a major operation. I prefer to try medical treatment in 1st intention as agreed. I have been informed of the serious signs of my illness, which require me to undergo urgent appointment."

A6 (translated): "Hello, I'm currently 26 years old. I went to the clinic today because I felt down at the gym. I exercise often but it's been the 4th time that this happens. From time to time, I experience vertigo while I'm resting and I don't understand why. I exercise everyday and I don't have any other diseases for now. At the emergency room, the doctor asked me to do an X-ray and he showed me that I have a heart malformation. He told me that the volume of my left and right side are not equivalent. What's wrong? Should I stop working out?"

Conclusion Most participants followed the instructions correctly or at least partially (A2 forgot to mention their age and gender). A1, A2, A3, and A5 expressed some kind of worry regarding their symptoms and diagnosis, especially for A1 and A2, where the participants inquired about the consequences of their disease. All participants use reported speech to talk about their test results or the doctor's diagnosis. A3 and A4 directly cite some results directly taken from their test results. We observe that A2 and A3 did some supplementary research regarding their diagnosis (probably by searching their diagnosis in a search engine).

C Corpus statistics

Metric	Value
# of CTRs (whole dataset)	6649
# of CTRs (train dataset)	4713
# of CTRs (dev dataset)	523
# of CTRs (test dataset)	1564

Table 6: Dataset metrics

D Patients #21 and #30

D.1 Patient #21

Medical language: A 47-year-old man comes to the clinic for the follow up of his neuromuscular disease. He experienced gradual, progressive weakness of the left upper extremity over the last year. Over the last few months, he has also noticed weakness in the right upper extremity. BP is 120/75, PR is 80 and temperature is 37 C. Reflexes are brisk in the upper extremities, and the plantar responses are extensor. Mild gait ataxia is present. The patient is under treatment of Riluzole 50 mg BID with the diagnosis of ALS.
Patient language: I've been suffering from a neuromuscular disease for a while now, and I went to my doctor's office. I'm now a 47-year-old man and over the past year I experienced a progressive and gradual weakness of my left upper extremity, and over the past month, I also noticed a weakness over my right upper extremity. My heart rate was 120/75, and my PR was 80 with 37°C for temperature. My reflexes are not good in my upper extremities, and I have trouble with my balance. I'm also under Exservan 50 mg for my sclerosis.

D.2 Patient #30

Medical language: A 47-year-old woman comes to the office complaining of pain in the calf and knee when she bends down. The pain limits her activity. Her medical history is significant for osteoarthritis, for which she uses nonsteroidal anti-inflammatory drugs (NSAIDs) for the past two years. She is living with her husband and has 3 children. She doesn't smoke but drinks alcohol occasionally. Her vital signs are normal. On physical examination, there is a small effusion in the right knee. The effusion grew a little larger and she developed a tender swelling in the popliteal fossa and calf. Both the pain and swelling worsened as she bent and straightened her knee.

Patient language: I'm a 47-year-old woman, married with 3 kids. I don't smoke and I drink occasionally. I went to the doctor because of pain in my calf and knee when I was bending down. This has been limiting my daily activities. I have been diagnosed with osteoarthritis for which I have taken anti-inflammatory drugs for the past 2 years. The doctor saw a small fluid buildup in my right knee. This buildup became a bit bigger and I have a swollen calf. The pain is worse when I bend and straighten my knee.

E Qwen-14B prompted for explanations

E.1 Patient #21

Premise (NCT03160898): See Fig 6.

Inclusion Criteria:

- Diagnosis of familial or sporadic ALS ≤ 24 months prior to screening
- Upright Slow Vital Capacity (SVC) ≥ 60% of predicted for age, height and sex at screening
- Able to swallow tablets
- A caregiver (if one is needed)
- Able to perform reproducible pulmonary function tests
- Pre-study clinical laboratory findings within the normal range or, if outside the normal range, deemed not clinically significant by the Investigator
- Male patients who have not had a vasectomy and confirmed zero sperm count must agree after receiving the first dose of study drug until 10 weeks after the last dose to either use acceptable methods of contraception or abstain from sex
- Female patients must be post-menopausal or sterilized or must not be breastfeeding, have a negative pregnancy test, have no intention to become pregnant during the study and use acceptable methods of contraception or abstain from heterosexual intercourse from Screening until 10 weeks after last dose of study drug
- Patients must be either on riluzole for at least 30 days prior to screening or have not taken riluzole for at least 30 days prior to screening and not planning to start riluzole during the course of the study.
- Patients on edaravone must have completed at least 2 cycles of dosing with edaravone at the time of screening or have not taken edaravone for at least 30 days prior to screening and not planning to start edaravone during the course of the study.

Exclusion Criteria:

- At the time of screening, any use of non-invasive ventilation (NIV), e.g. continuous positive airway pressure [CPAP], noninvasive bi-level positive airway pressure [NPPV] or noninvasive volume ventilation [NVV] for any portion of the day, or mechanical ventilation via tracheostomy, or on any form of oxygen supplementation
- Neurological impairment due to a condition other than ALS
- Presence at screening of any medically significant cardiac, pulmonary, GI, musculoskeletal, or psychiatric illness that might interfere with the patient's ability to comply with study procedures or that might confound the interpretation of clinical safety or efficacy data
- Has taken any investigational study drug within 30 days or five half-lives of the prior agent, whichever is longer, prior to dosing
- Known to have received CK-2127107 or tirasemtiv in any previous clinical trial
- Has received or is considering receiving during the course of the study any form of stem cell therapy for the treatment of ALS
- Has received or is considering receiving during the course of the study any form of gene therapy for the treatment of ALS
- Has received or is considering obtaining during the course of the study a diaphragmatic pacing system
- History of substance abuse within the past 2 years
- Use of certain medications

No condition on gender to be admitted to the trial.
No healthy subjects accepted to join the trial.
Subject must be at least 18 Years old.
Subject must be at most 80 Years

Figure 6: Eligibility criteria from trial NCT03160898, used as the premise.

Medical answer:

"Entailment

Explanation: Based on the information provided about the 47-year-old male patient, it seems he meets some key inclusion criteria such as being diagnosed with ALS (within 24 months before screening), currently taking Riluzole which aligns with the pre-screening requirement of having been on riluzole for at least 30 days prior to screening, and being within the specified age range (at least 18 but at most 80 years). However, there isn't enough information given to determine whether his SVC is $\geq 60\%$, if he has an able caregiver, can swallow tablets, etc., nor is there sufficient detail to ascertain if he fulfills all exclusion criteria (such as absence of neurological impairment not related to ALS, no history of substance abuse within the past two years, specific medical conditions that could interfere, or recent participation in another clinical trial). The presence of mild gait ataxia mentioned does raise concern potentially regarding the exclusion criterion of "Presence at screening of any medically significant...psychiatric illness" or possibly indicating another neurological disorder; however, without explicit confirmation that this is not due to ALS, we cannot definitively rule him out based solely on this symptom alone. Similarly, without more specifics on the rest of the criteria, particularly those relating to functional capacity and absence of contraindicating health conditions, it is prudent to default towards entailment barring concrete contradictions. Therefore, the answer leans toward entailment pending verification of additional details necessary for full eligibility assessment."

PL answer:

"Contradiction

The provided patient information does not specify whether they have been diagnosed with Amyotrophic Lateral Sclerosis (ALS). Furthermore, it mentions that the patient is taking medication for sclerosis rather than riluzole which is typically used for ALS. Additionally, there is no mention of their SVC percentage which is required to meet the inclusion criteria. Hence based solely on the provided information, we cannot conclude that this patient meets all the necessary conditions to be eligible for the trial as described."

E.2 Patient #30

Premise (NCT03563690): See Fig 7.

Inclusion Criteria:

1. Meet the Clinical Classification Criteria for Osteoarthritis of the Knee, diagnosed by specialist.
2. Aged 40-75 years old;
3. History of chronic knee pain for more than 3 months, and complain of knee pain on most days of the past month;
4. Kellgren and Lawrence Grades 1-3;
5. With related knee pain in one or both knees rated > 4 cm on a 10 cm Visual Analog Scale(VAS) (VAS:0 to 10)
6. Who volunteer to participate and sign the consent form .

Exclusion Criteria:

1. Knee osteoarthritis patients with gout, infection, tumor, autoimmune diseases, trauma or other causes of knee pain or knee deformities;
2. Patients who have local skin damage, poor skin conditions or coagulant dysfunction and patients who are not suitable for acupuncture;
3. Patients who are accompanied with serious medical problems or mental disorders, cognitive dysfunction， disorders of shallow sensation or who cannot cooperate with the treatment;
4. Patients who have received acupuncture or needle knife in the past month;
5. Other patients who are not suitable for acupuncture treatment.

No condition on gender to be admitted to the trial.
No healthy subjects accepted to join the trial.
Subject must be at least 40 Years old.
Subject must be at most 75 Years

Figure 7: Eligibility criteria from trial NCT03563690, used as the premise.

Medical answer:

"Contradiction

The patient's presentation includes a tender swelling in the popliteal fossa and calf along with an enlarged effusion due to bending and straightening the knee, which may indicate other causes of her knee pain beyond osteoarthritis, such as possible vascular issues (e.g., deep vein thrombosis). This could fall under the exclusion criteria point number 1 ("Knee osteoarthritis patients with ... other causes of knee pain..."). Therefore, based on this information, it contradicts the full eligibility to participate merely under the inclusion criteria for osteoarthritis without further clarification or exclusion of other potential diagnoses."

PL Answer:

"Entailment

Based on the information provided about your condition and comparing it against the inclusion and exclusion criteria outlined in the clinical trial requirements, there is no direct contradiction found that would exclude you from participating in the trial. However, final determination should involve a thorough review by the healthcare professionals involved in the study as they will need to confirm all specific details such as severity grade, pain level on VAS, and absence of any other listed exclusions like concurrent illnesses that could disqualify participation. Given the description of meeting age range, having chronic knee pain due to confirmed osteoarthritis diagnosis, experiencing significant pain which impacts daily life, and willingness to take part (assuming voluntary agreement and signed consent), you appear to meet several key criteria which allows for potential entailment into the trial framework."

Towards Understanding LLM Generated Biomedical Lay Summaries

Rohan Charudatt Salvi[1], Swapnil Panigrahi[2], Dhruv Jain[2], Md. Shad Akhtar[2], Shweta Yadav[1]

[1]University of Illinois, Chicago, [2]Indraprastha Institute of Information Technology, Delhi
{rcsalvi2, shwetay}@uic.edu, shad.akhtar@iiitd.ac.in

Abstract

In this paper, we investigate the effectiveness of large language models in generating accessible lay summaries of medical abstracts, targeting non-expert audiences. We assess the ability of models like GPT-4, Biomistral, and LLaMA 3-8B-Instruct to simplify complex medical information, focusing on layness, comprehensiveness, and factual accuracy. Utilizing both automated and human evaluations, we discover that automatic metrics do not always align with human judgments. Our analysis highlights the potential benefits of developing clear guidelines for consistent evaluations conducted by non-expert reviewers. It also points to areas for improvement in the evaluation process and the creation of lay summaries for future research.

1 Introduction

In the dynamic field of medical research, rapid and clear dissemination of knowledge is essential. Automatic text summarization of medical abstracts serves as an efficient method for providing access to crucial information to both medical professionals and researchers, facilitating quicker and clearer information exchange (Luo et al., 2022). The need to communicate complex medical findings also extends to non-expert audiences such as caregivers, journalists, and the general public, who often struggle with the complex sentence structures and specialized terminology of medical literature (Guo et al., 2021; Goldsack et al., 2023b; Friedman et al., 2002; Korsch et al., 1968). Lay summaries of these abstracts are crucial in making scientific discoveries accessible to these groups by avoiding medical jargon and using clear, straightforward language (Guo et al., 2021; Chandrasekaran et al., 2020; Goldsack et al., 2023b). Initially, the generation of biomedical lay summaries utilized the fine-tuning of transformer-based models (Guo et al., 2021; Goldsack et al., 2022). However, recent progress has shown that large language models (LLMs) are especially effective in this area, with LLM-generated summaries not only surpassing traditional references in news datasets (Zhang et al., 2024a) but also demonstrating robust capabilities in generating comprehensible summaries in biomedical contexts, using techniques like retrieval-augmented generation (Guo et al., 2024) and zero-shot approaches (Jahan et al., 2024). Additionally, employing methods such as few-shot learning and the use of context-specific prompts has been shown to enhance the accuracy and relevance of the generated summaries (Pakull et al., 2024). Moreover, the use of few-shot learning with pre-trained LLMs has proven to be a robust approach at the BioLaySumm shared task 2023 (Turbitt et al., 2023).

In this paper, we investigate the effectiveness of LLMs in generating lay summaries from biomedical abstracts. Using a few-shot prompting strategy, we evaluate the performance of four distinct LLMs: GPT-4 (Achiam et al., 2023), Mistral-large-Instruct-2407(AI), LLaMA 3-8B-Instruct (Meta-Llama), and BioMistral (Labrak et al., 2024). We assess the ability of models to generate lay summaries, focusing on comprehensiveness, layness, and factual accuracy. Three research questions guide our evaluation:

1. How comprehensive are lay summaries generated by various LLMs?
2. How readable are biomedical summaries for lay audiences?
3. How faithful are lay summaries to their original abstracts?

Our evaluation methodology incorporates both automated and human assessments of the generated summaries on the publicly available PLABA (Attal et al., 2023) and the PLOS dataset (Goldsack et al.,

Proceedings of the Second Workshop on Patient-Oriented Language Processing (CL4Health), pages 260–268
May 4, 2025 ©2025 Association for Computational Linguistics

2022). We also conducted an in-depth analysis of various evaluation metrics that are widely used for lay summarization tasks.

In this study, we introduce detailed guidelines for the manual evaluation of lay summaries, designed as a comprehensive rubric that enables non-expert audiences to effectively assess lay summaries. By integrating human evaluations alongside automated metrics, we indicate the crucial role of human judgment in assessing summary quality, highlighting the inconsistencies that may emerge by relying solely on automatic metrics and discussing future directions for this research area.

2 Background

The BioLaySumm shared task was first introduced at the BioNLP Workshop during ACL 2023 (Goldsack et al., 2023a). This task focuses on abstractive summarization of biomedical articles, with the goal of creating lay summaries accessible to general audiences. It makes use of the PLOS and eLife corpus for this task and assesses summaries according to three criteria: Relevance, Readability, and Factuality. Each of these criteria is measured using one or more automatic metrics. Initial research on lay summarization primarily employed fine-tuned transformers such as BART (Guo et al., 2021), which were prominently featured at the BioLaySumm shared task in 2023. However, strong performance on the task was demonstrated by employing zero-shot and few-shot prompts with pretrained LLMs (Turbitt et al., 2023).

By the following year, the majority of proposed approaches by participating teams involved the use of LLMs (Goldsack et al., 2024). At BioLaySumm 2024, models such as GPT-3.5, GPT-4, and LLAMA3 were used in few-shot settings to generate lay summaries (Chizhikova et al., 2024). Another approach highlighted that fine-tuning LLMs like Biomistral with few-shot learning significantly enhances the accuracy of these summaries (Pakull et al., 2024). Additionally, recent research has explored retrieval-augmented generation (RAG), which utilizes LLMs and external knowledge sources such as Wikipedia to refine lay summarization (Guo et al., 2024). This RAG-based approach can be further enhanced by coupling it with reinforcement learning, optimizing the readability of the generated summaries (Ji et al., 2024).

3 Analysis on LLM generated plain language summaries

3.1 Lay Summary and Evaluation Guidelines

Based on our three research questions, we decided to evaluate the summaries on comprehensiveness, layness, and factuality. To ensure a consistent and robust assessment, we assume that our target audience has a limited background in biology (high school level) and intends to understand the article on a high level. Therefore, we aim for a lay summary that uses minimal medical jargon and effectively employs definitions or analogies to explain challenging biological concepts. Furthermore, it should be complete, explaining the topic, implementation, and findings of the study so that our intended readers can grasp the study (King et al., 2017).

Guided by previous research (Goldsack et al., 2022; Zhang et al., 2024b), our assessment methodology employs a 1-5 Likert scale for each defined metric. We sampled 15 abstracts from the PLABA and PLOS test set for lay summary generation by the models. Two undergraduates evaluated each generated summary using the guidelines. For both datasets, evaluators first read each abstract independently, and then the corresponding lay summaries. The evaluators were computer science majors who studied biology only until high school (10th grade).

We developed explicit scoring criteria, which was used for assessing summaries from both datasets, aiming to standardize evaluations and ensure reliability across different evaluators.

Comprehensiveness

Through comprehensiveness, we assess the extent to which the model-generated summaries encapsulate all the essential information necessary for a non-expert to grasp the high-level topic and significance of the research. The specifics of each score are as follows:

Score 1: The summary is incomplete; an evaluator cannot understand the topic or the significance of the research.

Score 2: The summary is partially complete; an evaluator gains a vague idea of the topic but cannot grasp the significance due to missing key details.

Score 3: The summary allows an evaluator to understand the topic but lacks important details that convey the research's significance.

Score 4: The summary enables an evaluator to understand both the topic and significance, missing only minor details that could enhance understanding.

Score 5: The summary thoroughly covers all necessary information, allowing an evaluator to fully understand the topic and the significance of the research.

Layness

Layness measures the extent to which the model-generated text reduces medical jargon, enhances understanding of the summary by adding definitions and background context for the study's topic, and employs simpler sentence structures or analogies, making the content accessible to a general audience. The specifics of each score are as follows:

Score 1: There is not much difference between the plain text summary and the abstract.

Score 2: The plain text summary omits a few sentences that include jargon or omits a few words in sentences. It becomes easier to read but does not truly simplify the content.

Score 3: The summary is a mix of jargon and simple terms, as well as simple and complex sentences, along with some definitions. Laypersons may understand the main points but could find specific terms or sentences confusing.

Score 4: The summary is overall easy to understand, with the occasional presence of a complex sentence or medical terms that are not explained to the reader.

Score 5: The summary removes jargon or uses simple synonyms for them. If it cannot do either, it adds context for the evaluator to grasp the complex term. It uses simple, straightforward sentences or makes use of examples, making it easy for anyone to understand.

Factuality

Factuality measures the degree to which the information in the model-generated summaries remains true to the original abstracts. The specifics of each score are as follows:

Score 1: The study alters the findings or methodology, misrepresenting the study. The misrepresentation might be intentional or due to a misunderstanding of the original data.

Score 2: The study alters part of the study that can lead to misinterpretation of sections such as method or results, but not the entire study. These alterations could potentially skew the reader's understanding.

Score 3: The summary contains accurate information about the study but with frequent minor inconsistencies such as typos, incorrect figures, or omitting key details in findings. These inconsistencies do not majorly affect the overall integrity of the summary.

Score 4: The study contains accurate information about the study but with one or two minor exceptions. These exceptions are usually not critical to the study's main conclusions.

Score 5: The summary is fully factual and aligns completely with the study. It provides a detailed and accurate depiction of the original research without any significant omissions or errors.

3.2 Data

We evaluated our approach using the publicly available PLABA dataset (Attal et al., 2023) and the PLOS dataset (Goldsack et al., 2022). In the case of the PLOS dataset, we noted that associated author-written lay summaries presented readability challenges for a layman. Consequently, we used these summaries as the baseline for evaluating the effectiveness of our approach with the PLOS abstracts. We would like to point out that in Table 2, we keep the factuality score for them as 'N/A' since they were written by humans and not generated by a language model. For the PLABA dataset, we used the summaries generated by the fine-tuned Biomistral model as the baseline.

3.3 Evaluation Metrics

We evaluated the generated summaries for PLABA using several metrics. To measure comprehensiveness, we used: ROUGE-1, ROUGE-2 and ROUGE-L (Lin, 2004), and SARI (Xu et al., 2016).

Method	Model	ROUGE-1	ROUGE-2	ROUGE-L	SARI	FKGL	DCRS	CLI	LENS	SummaC	AlignScore
Fine-tuned	Biomistral	**0.634**	**0.369**	**0.514**	**48.611**	12.278	9.876	13.812	56.433	54.5	79.9
Prompt	Biomistral	0.443	0.264	0.373	36.307	14.376	11.967	15.959	40.816	**82.3**	**87.7**
Prompt	GPT-4	0.548	0.213	0.351	40.973	9.692	**8.753**	**11.094**	**74.958**	34.0	75.7
Prompt	Mistral	0.528	0.206	0.335	40.722	**9.514**	9.001	12.063	72.021	32.3	70.7
Prompt	Llama3	0.547	0.258	0.385	41.680	11.764	9.474	13.462	67.407	47.9	81.4

Table 1: Model performance measured by automatic metrics on the PLABA dataset

For readability, we used the Coleman-Liau Index (CLI), Dale-Chall Readability Score (DCRS), Flesch-Kincaid Grade Level (FKGL), and LENS (Maddela et al., 2023). Additionally, we used AlignScore (Zha et al., 2023) and SummaC (Conv) (Laban et al., 2022) to assess the factuality of the summaries.

4 Our Analysis

RQ1: How comprehensive are lay summaries generated by various LLMs?

We observed in Table 1, in terms of automatic metrics, none of the prompt-based models were able to outperform the baseline. The fine-tuned Biomistral achieved scores of 0.634 and 48.611 on ROUGE-1 and SARI, respectively. This highlights that LLMs using prompts have added more abstractiveness to the plain text summaries, resulting in less overlap. However, in human evaluation, we found GPT-4 and Mistral achieved better ratings, scoring 4.165 and 4.565, respectively, compared to the baseline at 4.065. These final scores were computed by taking the average of the sum of ratings for the comprehensive facet.

These scores suggest that if models are better at restructuring or emphasizing key points by leveraging simple sentence structures and omitting non-essential details, it could enhance human understanding of the article's content and significance, leading to higher comprehensiveness scores (as presented in Table 3 in the appendix). We also observed this with the PLOS dataset, where GPT-4 and Mistral achieved higher comprehensiveness than the reference lay summaries. Lastly, the gap between automatic ROUGE and SARI scores and human ratings for models like Biomistral reveals the shortcomings of current metrics in fully assessing how much information the summary conveys. This indicates a need for novel metrics that better evaluate sentence structure and highlight informational content, essential to measure comprehensiveness.

RQ2: How readable are biomedical summaries for lay audiences?

We observe from Table 1 that GPT-4 gets the lowest scores on DCRS (8.75) and CLI readability ratings (11.09) and the highest on the LENS metric (74.96), indicating high simplicity and readability of the text it generates. Mistral achieves the lowest score on the FKGL metric (9.5). In the human evaluation, GPT-4 and Mistral again showed strong performance, with layness scores of 4.735 and 4.770, respectively. The lower FKGL rating indicates that Mistral most likely generated shorter sentences with simple syllables, whereas GPT-4 relies on more common words and potentially longer sentences than Mistral.

The readability metrics depend on sentence lengths (FKGL), word familiarity (DCRS), characters per word (CLI), and LENS evaluates simplification on a sentence level and not a paragraph(Xu et al., 2016). Thus, the scores potentially may look a bit aligned because we prompt models to generate simple sentences. What is not currently captured is a measure of how many complex words were omitted by the model, how many were simplified, and how many contexts or definitions were added since these are other characteristics apart from simple sentences on which humans evaluated the summaries for layness. This may potentially be the reason Mistral gets a higher rating on Layness than GPT-4 in the human evaluation. Additionally, this could also be a great metric to reflect on the nature of model-generated summaries, whether the LLM prefers to simplify sentences, omit jargon, replace terms, or add more context. For instance, in the PLOS evaluation, Mistral and GPT-4 received higher layness scores as they added definitions and used simpler terms, in contrast to the baseline summary that, despite its simple sentence structure, included medical jargon that reduced its layness.

Model	PLABA Dataset			PLOS Dataset		
	Comprehensiveness	Layness	Factuality	Comprehensiveness	Layness	Factuality
Baseline	4.065	4.165	4.230	4.1	2.233	N/A
GPT-4	4.165	4.735	4.150	4.767	**4.667**	4.7
Mistral	**4.565**	**4.77**	**4.835**	**4.767**	4.567	**4.8**
Llama3	4.000	4.099	4.395	4.533	3.2	4.667
Biomistral	3.520	3.105	3.935	3.933	2.2	3.967

Table 2: Human Evaluation Results on PLABA and PLOS Datasets

RQ3: How faithful are lay summaries to their original abstracts?

SummaC and AlignScores evaluated the factual alignment of generated summaries with original abstracts. High scores of 87.7 (AlignScore) and 82.3 (SummaC) for Biomistral in a prompt setting indicate these metrics favor text similar to the abstracts, despite occasionally favoring incomplete summaries. SummaC scores showed inconsistency with human evaluations, while AlignScores performed slightly better with respect to alignment with human evaluations. In the human evaluation, we observe Mistral achieving the highest rating for factuality, followed by Llama3, scoring 4.835 and 4.395, respectively. In the PLOS, along with GPT-4 and Mistral, Biomistral and Llama-3 achieved high factuality by maintaining sentence structures similar to the abstracts. However, we would like to highlight that the factuality score on both human and automatic metrics reflects solely intrinsic factuality. The LLMs also incorporate additional definitions and context to enhance user understanding, which may sometimes be inaccurate, leading to extrinsic hallucinations (Ramprasad et al., 2024). However, in this scenario, it is unreasonable to expect non-experts to identify and assess these inaccuracies.

5 Discussion

Our research examined how various language models generate lay summaries to simplify scientific findings. The Biomistral fine-tuned model effectively reflected the reference summaries and occasionally added definitions for complex terms. However, its prompt-based version often generated the same abstract or missed crucial information. LLama3 did simplify sentences, but it did not add necessary definitions and contexts, impacting its layness. Both GPT-4 and Mistral models excelled in creating understandable summaries, though they sometimes omitted detailed information. This underscores the trade-off between simplicity and factual accuracy in lay summaries.

Our results indicate that for prompt-based approaches, model size correlates with performance, with larger models like GPT-4 and Mistral showing superior adherence to guidelines and creativity in using analogies. Lastly, clear guidelines enhance the consistency of lay summary evaluations (as seen in Table 4 in appendix) by standardizing assessment criteria for non-expert reviewers.

6 Conclusion

In this study, we investigated how LLMs generate lay summaries for non-experts. Our findings show that while LLMs can simplify complex medical information effectively, there's a significant gap between automated metrics and human evaluations of the summary quality. This gap reveals the limitations of current evaluation methods and the need for metrics that align more closely with human perceptions of comprehensiveness, layness, and factuality. In the future, we plan to analyze other summarization methods and develop an effective human evaluation design that includes extrinsic factuality, on a larger dataset to refine our understanding of evaluation metrics perform across broader contexts.

7 Limitations

Our work has a few limitations. Firstly, LLMs exhibit an indeterministic nature, as they generate different lay summaries for the same input. Secondly, the format of the generated text often deviates from the example provided in the prompt, particularly in the cases of the Llama3 and Mistral models. Therefore, post-processing with regular expressions might be necessary to achieve the most effective results from these prompts. Additionally, we used a fixed prompt, which may not work equally well across all models, potentially leading to poorer-quality lay summaries. Lastly, there is a potential limitation concerning the training data of the LLMs. It is possible that the models were unintentionally trained on or exposed to the reference summaries used in our evaluations, which could boost their performance on the lay summarization task.

8 Ethical Considerations

Although the LLMs perform well, they occasionally add additional definitions and context that could be incorrect. Moreover, in their efforts to simplify complex medical information, LLMs sometimes oversimplify, potentially leading to misinterpretations of the results. Therefore, non-experts should exercise caution when using LLM-generated lay summaries to ensure they are not misled by inaccuracies.

References

Josh Achiam, Steven Adler, Sandhini Agarwal, Lama Ahmad, Ilge Akkaya, Florencia Leoni Aleman, Diogo Almeida, Janko Altenschmidt, Sam Altman, Shyamal Anadkat, et al. 2023. Gpt-4 technical report. *arXiv preprint arXiv:2303.08774*.

Mistral AI. Large Enough — mistral.ai. `https://mistral.ai/news/mistral-large-2407/`. [Accessed 16-10-2024].

Kush Attal, Brian Ondov, and Dina Demner-Fushman. 2023. A dataset for plain language adaptation of biomedical abstracts. *Scientific Data*, 10(1):8.

Muthu Kumar Chandrasekaran, Guy Feigenblat, Eduard Hovy, Abhilasha Ravichander, Michal Shmueli-Scheuer, and Anita de Waard. 2020. Overview and insights from the shared tasks at scholarly document processing 2020: Cl-scisumm, laysumm and longsumm. In *Proceedings of the First Workshop on Scholarly Document Processing*, pages 214–224.

Mariia Chizhikova, Manuel Carlos Díaz-Galiano, L Alfonso Ureña-López, and María-Teresa Martín-Valdivia. 2024. Sinai at biolaysumm: Self-play fine-tuning of large language models for biomedical lay summarisation. In *Proceedings of the 23rd Workshop on Biomedical Natural Language Processing*, pages 804–809.

Tim Dettmers, Artidoro Pagnoni, Ari Holtzman, and Luke Zettlemoyer. 2024. Qlora: Efficient finetuning of quantized llms. *Advances in Neural Information Processing Systems*, 36.

Carol Friedman, Pauline Kra, and Andrey Rzhetsky. 2002. Two biomedical sublanguages: a description based on the theories of zellig harris. *Journal of biomedical informatics*, 35(4):222–235.

Tomas Goldsack, Zheheng Luo, Qianqian Xie, Carolina Scarton, Matthew Shardlow, Sophia Ananiadou, and Chenghua Lin. 2023a. Overview of the biolaysumm 2023 shared task on lay summarization of biomedical research articles. In *The 22nd Workshop on Biomedical Natural Language Processing and BioNLP Shared Tasks*, pages 468–477, Toronto, Canada. Association for Computational Linguistics.

Tomas Goldsack, Carolina Scarton, Matthew Shardlow, and Chenghua Lin. 2024. Overview of the BioLaySumm 2024 shared task on the lay summarization of biomedical research articles. In *Proceedings of the 23rd Workshop on Biomedical Natural Language Processing*, pages 122–131, Bangkok, Thailand. Association for Computational Linguistics.

Tomas Goldsack, Zhihao Zhang, Chenghua Lin, and Carolina Scarton. 2022. Making science simple: Corpora for the lay summarisation of scientific literature. In *Proceedings of the 2022 Conference on Empirical Methods in Natural Language Processing*, pages 10589–10604, Abu Dhabi, United Arab Emirates. Association for Computational Linguistics.

Tomsa Goldsack, Zheheng Luo, Qianqian Xie, Carolina Scarton, Matthew Shardlow, Sophia Ananiadou, and Chenghua Lin. 2023b. Overview of the biolaysumm 2023 shared task on lay summarization of biomedical research articles. *arXiv preprint arXiv:2309.17332*.

Yue Guo, Wei Qiu, Gondy Leroy, Sheng Wang, and Trevor Cohen. 2024. Retrieval augmentation of large language models for lay language generation. *Journal of Biomedical Informatics*, 149:104580.

Yue Guo, Wei Qiu, Yizhong Wang, and Trevor Cohen. 2021. Automated lay language summarization of biomedical scientific reviews. In *Proceedings of the AAAI Conference on Artificial Intelligence*, volume 35, pages 160–168.

Israt Jahan, Md Tahmid Rahman Laskar, Chun Peng, and Jimmy Xiangji Huang. 2024. A comprehensive evaluation of large language models on benchmark biomedical text processing tasks. *Computers in biology and medicine*, 171:108189.

Yuelyu Ji, Zhuochun Li, Rui Meng, Sonish Sivarajkumar, Yanshan Wang, Zeshui Yu, Hui Ji, Yushui Han, Hanyu Zeng, and Daqing He. 2024. Rag-rlrc-laysum at biolaysumm: Integrating retrieval-augmented generation and readability control for layman summarization of biomedical texts. *arXiv preprint arXiv:2405.13179*.

Stuart RF King, Emma Pewsey, and Sarah Shailes. 2017. An inside guide to elife digests. *Elife*, 6:e25410.

Barbara M Korsch, Ethel K Gozzi, and Vida Francis. 1968. Gaps in doctor-patient communication: I. doctor-patient interaction and patient satisfaction. *Pediatrics*, 42(5):855–871.

Philippe Laban, Tobias Schnabel, Paul N. Bennett, and Marti A. Hearst. 2022. SummaC: Re-visiting NLI-based models for inconsistency detection in summarization. *Transactions of the Association for Computational Linguistics*, 10:163–177.

Yanis Labrak, Adrien Bazoge, Emmanuel Morin, Pierre-Antoine Gourraud, Mickael Rouvier, and Richard Dufour. 2024. Biomistral: A collection of open-source pretrained large language models for medical domains. *arXiv preprint arXiv:2402.10373*.

Chin-Yew Lin. 2004. ROUGE: A package for automatic evaluation of summaries. In *Text Summarization Branches Out*, pages 74–81, Barcelona, Spain. Association for Computational Linguistics.

Zheheng Luo, Qianqian Xie, and Sophia Ananiadou. 2022. Readability controllable biomedical document summarization. *arXiv preprint arXiv:2210.04705*.

Mounica Maddela, Yao Dou, David Heineman, and Wei Xu. 2023. LENS: A learnable evaluation metric for text simplification. In *Proceedings of the 61st Annual Meeting of the Association for Computational Linguistics (Volume 1: Long Papers)*, pages 16383–16408, Toronto, Canada. Association for Computational Linguistics.

Meta-Llama. Llama3/model$_{c}ard.mdatmainmeta - llama/llama3$.

Tabea MG Pakull, Hendrik Damm, Ahmad Idrissi-Yaghir, Henning Schäfer, Peter A Horn, and Christoph M Friedrich. 2024. Wispermed at biolaysumm: Adapting autoregressive large language models for lay summarization of scientific articles. *arXiv preprint arXiv:2405.11950*.

Sanjana Ramprasad, Kundan Krishna, Zachary Lipton, and Byron Wallace. 2024. Evaluating the factuality of zero-shot summarizers across varied domains. In *Proceedings of the 18th Conference of the European Chapter of the Association for Computational Linguistics (Volume 2: Short Papers)*, pages 50–59, St. Julian's, Malta. Association for Computational Linguistics.

Oisín Turbitt, Robert Bevan, and Mouhamad Aboshokor. 2023. Mdc at biolaysumm task 1: Evaluating gpt models for biomedical lay summarization. In *The 22nd Workshop on Biomedical Natural Language Processing and BioNLP Shared Tasks*, pages 611–619.

Wei Xu, Courtney Napoles, Ellie Pavlick, Quanze Chen, and Chris Callison-Burch. 2016. Optimizing statistical machine translation for text simplification. *Transactions of the Association for Computational Linguistics*, 4:401–415.

Yuheng Zha, Yichi Yang, Ruichen Li, and Zhiting Hu. 2023. AlignScore: Evaluating factual consistency with a unified alignment function. In *Proceedings of the 61st Annual Meeting of the Association for Computational Linguistics (Volume 1: Long Papers)*, pages 11328–11348, Toronto, Canada. Association for Computational Linguistics.

Tianyi Zhang, Faisal Ladhak, Esin Durmus, Percy Liang, Kathleen McKeown, and Tatsunori B. Hashimoto. 2024a. Benchmarking large language models for news summarization. *Transactions of the Association for Computational Linguistics*, 12:39–57.

Zhihao Zhang, Tomas Goldsack, Carolina Scarton, and Chenghua Lin. 2024b. ATLAS: Improving lay summarisation with attribute-based control. In *Proceedings of the 62nd Annual Meeting of the Association for Computational Linguistics (Volume 2: Short Papers)*, pages 337–345, Bangkok, Thailand. Association for Computational Linguistics.

A Prompt

This appendix outlines the prompt employed for generating lay summaries as described in this paper. This prompt was used across all four models with a minor change. The symbol '#' was included in the prompt for the Mistral and LLaMA3 models.

Prompt:

You are a biology teacher in a high school and want to teach students in 10th grade about a research study. Your goal is to convey the information in the abstract in plain and easy to understand language that students can follow.

You decide to generate a plain text for the same abstract keeping in mind what makes a text simple and easy to understand.

1. It attempts to avoid as much scientific jargon as possible. If it cannot avoid it, then it replaces it with easy to understand synonyms.

2. It has an explanation and definition for complex biological terms and can include simple real-life examples to make it easier to understand.

3. The sentence structure is simple, and the text has a good coherent flow.

4. The word count cannot exceed 300 words.

5. The text should have all the important points. And if words are replaced by simpler terms, it is good to connect them to original words by referencing them using brackets.

6. Ensure the text is factually correct, this includes definitions, synonyms, important numeric figures, and findings.

Here is an example of what you should generate:
Abstract: [Sample Abstract]
Here is the rationale to use:

1. Read the abstract thoroughly to grasp main ideas.

2. Avoid scientific jargon; use simple synonyms or explanations.

3. Define complex terms and provide real-life examples for clarity.

4. Use simple sentence structures for better understanding.

5. Keep the text under 300 words.

6. Include all important points, referencing original terms in brackets when replacing them.

7. Ensure all information is factually correct, including definitions and key data.

Generated Plain Text: [Sample Plain Summary]
Abstract: [Test set abstract]
Generated Plain Text:

B Implementation Details

We accessed the GPT-4 ("gpt-4") and Mistral Large models("mistral-large-2407") using the API provided by OpenAI and Mistral respectively. The Llama-3-8B model and Biomistral were accessed through Huggingface and were run on 1 NVIDIA Tesla T4-16GB and 1 NVIDIA Tesla A100 Ampere-40GB respectively. Biomistral used as the baseline was fine-tuned on the PLABA dataset through QLORA (Dettmers et al., 2024).

We generated plain text abstracts for all 148 abstracts in the PLABA test dataset using the one-shot prompt approach for each model. For Biomistral and Llama3 we observed that the summaries contained the prompt prefix, the test abstract. Moreover, for Llama3 there were cases where we found rationale or references being generated after the plain text. Thus, we employed a post-processor using regular expression for both models to extract the plain text summary.

Model	Text
Abstract	To reduce the damage to posteromedial knee capsule, we developed a direct extra-articular arthroscopic approach for excision of symptomatic popliteal cysts. This study aimed to demonstrate the surgical technique and present the 2-year follow-up results. Cystectomy is performed by extra-articular surgical approach through a high posteromedial portal. Twenty-one consecutive patients diagnosed of symptomatic popliteal cysts with failed initial conservative treatments were included. At a median follow-up of 29.4 months, all knees had improved clinical function assessed by Rauschning and Lindgren knee classification (p<0.001). The cysts were either disappeared (95.2%) or reduced in size (4.8%). Only one (4.8%) patient had recurrent cyst, which was solved after ultrasound-guided aspiration. This direct extra-articular arthroscopic technique could be a feasible alternative for treatment of symptomatic popliteal cysts.
Biomistral fine-tuned (baseline)	To reduce the damage to the knee capsule, we created a new way to remove cysts (growths) in the knee. This new way is called a direct extra-articular arthroscopic approach. This study aimed to show how the surgery is done and present the 2-year follow-up results. Cystectomy is performed by a high posteromedial portal. Twenty-one patients with cysts in the knee were included. At a median follow-up of 29.4 months, all knees had improved function. The cysts were either disappeared or reduced in size. Only one patient had a recurring cyst, which was solved by draining the cyst. This direct extra-articular arthroscopic technique could be a good way to treat cysts in the knee.
Mistral-large	A popliteal cyst is a fluid-filled swelling that forms at the back of the knee. It can cause pain and other symptoms. To treat these cysts without damaging the nearby knee structures, doctors developed a new surgical method using a tiny camera called an arthroscope. This study aims to explain this new method and show the results two years after the surgery. The surgery is done through a small opening on the inner back side of the knee, allowing doctors to remove the cyst without going into the knee joint itself. Twenty-one patients who had painful popliteal cysts and didn't get better with other treatments were included in the study. After an average follow-up of about 29 months, all the patients reported improved knee function based on a specific knee classification system. In almost all cases (95.2%), the cysts disappeared, and in a few cases (4.8%), the cysts became smaller. Only one patient (4.8%) had the cyst come back, but it was successfully treated with an ultrasound-guided needle to drain the fluid. This new surgical technique, which involves removing the cyst from outside the knee joint using an arthroscope, seems to be a good option for treating painful popliteal cysts.

Table 3: Summaries generated by Biomistral and Mistral-large for an abstract in PLABA. Colors in the text indicate: additional background information (brown), simpler terms used (blue), and simplified sentences (orange).

Model	Comprehensiveness	Layness	Factuality
Baseline	0.667	0.45	0.880
GPT-4	0.435	0.717	1.000
Mistral	0.690	0.755	0.755
Llama3	0.606	0.74	0.698
Biomistral	0.693	0.822	1.000

Table 4: Inter annotator agreement (Cohen's Kappa) on PLABA Dataset

Model	Comprehensiveness	Layness	Factuality
Baseline	0.688	0.688	N/A
GPT-4	0.318	0.700	0.300
Mistral	0.800	0.605	1.00
Llama3	0.744	0.615	0.412
Biomistral	0.783	0.455	0.503

Table 5: Inter annotator agreement (Cohen's Kappa) on PLOS Dataset

Bridging the Gap in Health Literacy: Harnessing the Power of Large Language Models to Generate Plain Language Summaries from Biomedical Texts

Felipe Arias-Russi[1,2], Carolina Salazar-Lara[3], Rubén Manrique[1]
[1]Systems and Computing Engineering Department, Universidad de los Andes, Bogotá D.C.
[2]Department of Mathematics, Universidad de los Andes, Bogotá D.C.
[3]Department of Biomedical Engineering, Universidad de los Andes, Bogotá D.C.

{af.ariasr, c.salazar499, rf.manrique}@uniandes.edu.co

Abstract

Health literacy enables individuals to navigate healthcare systems and make informed decisions. Plain language summaries (PLS) can bridge comprehension gaps by simplifying complex biomedical texts, yet their manual creation is both time-consuming and challenging. This study advances the field by (1) constructing a novel corpus of paired technical and plain language texts from medical trial libraries, (2) developing machine learning classifiers to rapidly identify plain language features, and (3) establishing a multi-dimensional evaluation framework that integrates computational metrics with human expertise. We iteratively optimized prompts for diverse large language models (LLMs)—including GPT models, Gemini 1.5, DeepSeek-R1, and Llama-3.2—to generate PLS variants aligned with domain-specific guidelines. Our classifier achieved 97.5% accuracy in distinguishing plain from technical language, and the generated summaries demonstrated high semantic equivalence to expert-written versions.

1 Introduction

Health literacy refers to an individual's capacity to access, understand, and use health information (Nielsen-Bohlman et al., 2004). This ability is essential for patients and their families to effectively navigate healthcare systems, comprehend medical instructions, adhere to treatment regimens, and make informed decisions about clinical trials, treatments, or procedures (Berkman et al., 2011a,b; Miller, 2016). However, inadequate health literacy remains a widespread problem, one that has been linked to increased mortality, higher rates of preventable hospitalizations, and poorer treatment adherence (Berkman et al., 2011a). In particular, the 2015 European Health Literacy Survey found that nearly half of the respondents, particularly older adults, people with financial constraints, or those with lower educational attainment, exhibit insufficient health literacy (Sørensen et al., 2015; Bahador et al., 2020).

In today's healthcare landscape, where patient participation in decision-making is increasingly critical, improving health literacy is essential to reduce disparities and improve public health outcomes (Nielsen-Bohlman et al., 2004; Stormacq et al., 2019; Schillinger, 2021). Moreover, aligning with the transparency principles of the General Data Protection Regulation (GDPR) (GDPR, 2023; Trezona et al., 2018), stakeholders are compelled to ensure that health documentation is both clear and accessible.

Plain language summaries (PLS) offer a viable solution by translating complex clinical and scientific texts into accessible language (Bahador et al., 2020; Centers for Disease Control and Prevention, 2022). However, the manual production of such summaries is labor-intensive and particularly challenging in fields dominated by technical terminology. While large language models (LLMs) have demonstrated promise in automating the generation of lay summaries, previous efforts have largely centered on text generation, often overlooking the need for systematically curated training data and comprehensive evaluation frameworks.

To bridge these gaps, our work introduces a novel resource and an integrated methodological framework that addresses key challenges in health communication. By compiling a corpus of paired technical and plain language texts from medical trial libraries, we provide a valuable dataset that underpins the development of machine learning classifiers capable of rapidly distinguishing between plain and technical language. Using state-of-the-art LLMs and iteratively refining our prompts, we generate plain-language variants that adhere to domain-specific guidelines. Furthermore, our evaluation framework, which combines automated metrics with an expert in health literacy assessments, of-

Proceedings of the Second Workshop on Patient-Oriented Language Processing (CL4Health), pages 269–284
May 4, 2025 ©2025 Association for Computational Linguistics

fers critical insights into the factors that define an effective plain-language summary.

Through this integrated approach, our study not only provides practical tools for producing patient-centered medical summaries but also enhances our understanding of the linguistic variables that support clear and accessible healthcare communication.

2 Related Work

Recent efforts in biomedical text simplification have increasingly focused on automatically generating PLS using NLP and LLMs. Ondov et al. (2022) reviewed a range of approaches and observed that, although neural methods show promise, their progress is limited by the scarcity of high-quality, parallel corpora. This data challenge was similarly highlighted by Devaraj et al. (2021), who introduced a new corpus of parallel texts specifically designed to aid the training of models that could effectively reduce jargon in biomedical information.

LLMs offer a compelling solution to overcome these limitations due to their extensive training data and advanced text generation capabilities. For instance, the BioLaySumm contest (Goldsack and Lin, 2025) targets the task of generating PLS from abstracts. In the 2023 BioLaySumm Task, Turbitt et al. (2023) demonstrated that GPT-3.5—when used in a few-shot setting—produced summaries with superior relevance and factuality compared to those of the specialized BioGPT model, despite the latter's advantage in readability. Additional studies (Veen et al., 2024; Mirza et al., 2024) further indicate that LLMs can outperform human experts in summarizing clinical texts and enhancing the clarity of informed consent documents.

However, there remains a critical need for systematically curated datasets and evaluation frameworks that combine computational metrics with human expertise. We aim to enhance existing work by building a comprehensive database of plain and technical biomedical texts. We will then implement advanced LLMs alongside a classification system to automatically ensure that the generated summaries are composed in plain language. Additionally, we will conduct a thorough evaluation of the generated PLS by domain experts, employing metrics such as readability, factuality, and accuracy, as outlined in the BioLaySumm shared task.

3 Materials and Methods

Our methodology, outlined in Figure 1, consisted of 3 main steps: (1) collecting and processing of sample texts in technical and plain language, (2) conducting a quantitative analysis of the plain and technical texts to generate a plain language classification model and a qualitative analysis of the texts to generate the prompts for the LLMs, and (3) assessing the use of the LLMs to generate PLS from technical texts.

3.1 Data Collection and Processing

We collected biomedical texts in both technical and plain language (see Table A1 for data sources) and assembled them into a dataset comprising 14,441 texts. This "main dataset" was then divided into training and testing sets, containing 4,596 plain and 6,721 technical texts for training, and 1,149 plain and 1,975 technical texts for testing.

We further enlarged the dataset by treating each paragraph of at least 250 words as a distinct unit, while excluding texts shorter than 250 words. As a result, our "augmented dataset" contained 61,354 texts, split into 16,731 plain and 31,740 technical texts for training, and 5,090 plain and 7,793 technical texts for testing. To mitigate source imbalance, we limited the dataset to 23,695 texts, divided into 9,093 plain and 8,654 technical for training, and 2,741 plain and 3,205 technical for testing. Additionally, we obtained a validation set of PLOS and eLife texts from (Goldsack et al., 2022; Luo et al., 2022) to evaluate the ML models on a dataset external to our own.

3.2 Analysis of Plain Language

We conducted qualitative and quantitative analyses of the texts to identify unique linguistic traits and variables that classify a text as plain language.

3.2.1 Qualitative Analysis

Driven by the varying and broad-scope guidance on creating high-quality PLS (Stoll et al., 2022), we analyzed a subset of our plain texts and created a 'criteria checklist' (see Table 1) with the linguistic attributes most commonly present in plain texts. Key resources used in this process were guides and reviews, such as Your Guide to CLEAR WRITING by CDC (Centers for Disease Control and Prevention, 2022), Federal Plain Language Guidelines (The Plain Language Action and Information Network, 2011), Health Literacy Universal Precautions Toolkit by Agency for Healthcare Research and

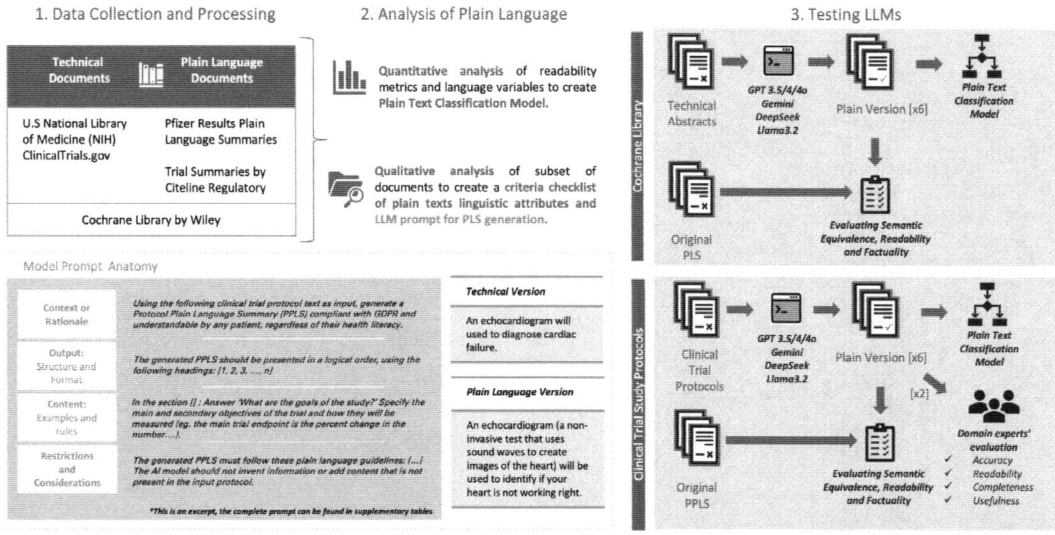

Figure 1: **Methodology.** Our methodology consists of three main steps: (1) collecting and processing biomedical texts (technical and plain language documents) to construct training and testing datasets, (2) conducting quantitative analysis to develop a plain language classification model and qualitative analysis to identify linguistic traits guiding prompt engineering for LLM-based PLS generation, and (3) evaluating LLM-generated PLS both quantitatively—using our classification model, semantic equivalence/relevance (BERTScore, Zhang et al. (2020)), factuality (AlignScore, Zha et al. (2023)), and readability metrics—and qualitatively through expert assessments.

Quality (AHRQ) (Brach, 2023), Just Plain Clear Glossary by United Health Group (United Health Group, 2023), EU 536/2014 Summary of Clinical Results for Laypersons (European Union, 2023), and results presented by Stoll et al, in their systematic review of theory, guidelines, and empirical research on PLS (Stoll et al., 2022). We used the resultant checklist to complement the qualitative findings described in the next section and aid in developing the prompt detailed in the section LLM Prompt for Plain Language Summary Generation.

3.2.2 Quantitative Analysis

We computed readability metrics and language variables for each text in the augmented dataset using the Readability (2019) and SpaCy (2023) libraries, respectively. This resulted in 64 variables presenting each text's readability and linguistic traits (see Table B1 and Section B).

For each language variable characteristic k, we evaluated its discriminative potential for classifying texts as either technical or plain. To this end, we randomly selected a sample of size n from the plain texts, denoted by

$$X_1^{(k)},\ X_2^{(k)},\ \ldots,\ X_n^{(k)} \sim P_X^{(k)},$$

and a corresponding sample of size n from the technical texts, denoted by

$$Y_1^{(k)},\ Y_2^{(k)},\ \ldots,\ Y_n^{(k)} \sim Q_Y^{(k)}.$$

An independent hypothesis test was then conducted for each k to determine whether the distributions differ statistically between the two text types.

Specifically, for each linguistic feature k, we considered the following hypotheses:

- **Null Hypothesis** ($H_0^{(k)}$): $P_X^{(k)} = Q_Y^{(k)}$. The distributions of the characteristic k for plain and technical texts are identical.
- **Alternative Hypothesis** ($H_1^{(k)}$): $P_X^{(k)} \neq Q_Y^{(k)}$. The distributions of the characteristic k for plain and technical texts differ.

To evaluate these hypotheses, we employed several non-parametric tests, namely the Wilcoxon signed-rank test (Wilcoxon, 1945), the Kolmogorov-Smirnov test (Kolmogorov, 1933), and the Mann–Whitney U test (Mann and Whitney, 1947), ensuring robustness across different statistical assumptions. Since a total of 64 independent hypothesis tests were performed (one for each characteristic k), a Bonferroni correction (Benjamini and Hochberg, 1995) was applied to control the family-wise error rate. Thus,

Linguistic Attributes	PLS Characteristics
• Use simple and everyday words. Avoid technical, medical, or scientific terms, jargon, or complex terminology (e.g., explain technical terms such as copayment, electrocardiogram, pyrexia, screening, double-blind). • Readability level 6 or below • Active voice over passive voice • Mostly 1-2 syllable words • Sentences of less than 20 words • Short paragraphs of 3-5 sentences • Simple numbers that do not require any math (e.g., 4 out of every 10 community members, not 40% of community members)	• Approximate length of 700-900 words • Specific structure and content by domain (e.g., EU-CTR suggested a specific structure and content for lay protocol synopsis)

Table 1: PLS Criteria Checklist of linguistic attributes and characteristics as defined by qualitative analysis of sample texts and Plain Language guidelines frequently used by domain experts.

the nominal significance level of $\alpha = 0.05$ was adjusted to $\alpha' = \frac{0.05}{64} \approx 0.0008$.

Figure 2 illustrates examples of the distribution comparisons for selected characteristics. Notably, of the 64 characteristics examined, only 'Interjections' and 'Passive Voice' did not provide sufficient evidence to reject the null hypothesis (i.e., their p-values exceeded 0.0008), whereas the remaining 62 characteristics exhibited statistically significant differences and were subsequently incorporated into our classification model.

3.3 Plain Texts Classification Model

We used the reduction of the augmented dataset and first preprocessed the 62 linguistic variables by applying standard min-max normalization. For variables representing counts of specific word types, normalization was performed relative to the total number of words in the text. We then built our models using the processed features.

For the Gradient Boosting (GB) model, we manually set the parameters as follows: the number of estimators was fixed at 120 (i.e., the number of boosting stages), the learning rate was set to 0.25 to scale the contribution of each tree, a subsample rate of 0.8 was used to fit each base learner on 80% of the training instances, the maximum depth of each tree was limited to 5 to minimize overfitting, a minimum of 5 samples was required to split an internal node, and at least 3 samples were needed in a leaf node. A fixed random state (0) ensured reproducibility.

For the Random Forest (RF) model, we configured 100 estimators (trees) with a maximum tree depth of 10 and also set the random state to 0.

Note that we did not perform automated hyperparameter tuning (e.g., using grid search) or use K-fold cross-validation to select optimal training and testing splits; instead, the parameters were adjusted manually through trial and error, given the rapid training times observed.

3.4 LLM Prompt for Plain Language Summary Generation

Our objective was to design a prompt for LLMs capable of translating biomedical technical documents into plain language summaries (PLS). Beginning with a clinical trial protocol from ClinicalTrials.gov (see data sources in Table A1), we used an initial simple prompt: *"Using the following clinical trial protocol text as input, create a plain language summary."* We tested this prompt using both GPT-3.5 and GPT-4, analyzed the generated outputs, and iteratively refined the prompt by adding further details and instructions.

We aimed to produce a PLS that met the following qualitative criteria: **(1) Accuracy:** the content is clinically and scientifically correct; **(2) Readability:** the text is grammatically correct and easily understood by a lay audience (as defined in Table 1); **(3) Completeness:** the summary adheres to the expectations of a Protocol Plain Language Sum-

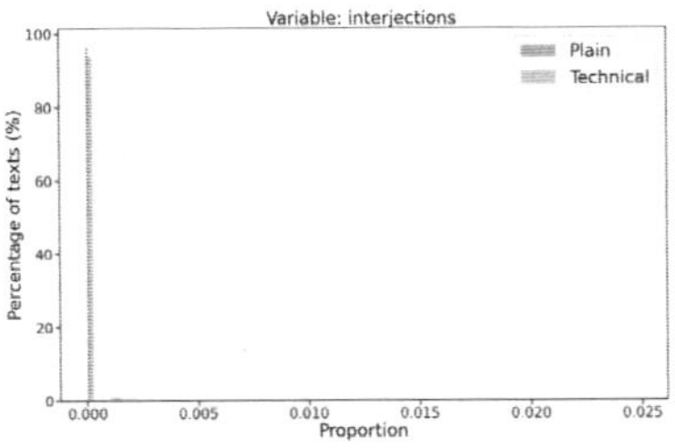

a. **Interjections.** These are words or phrases used to express a feeling (e.g., Wow! or Uh-oh). It is uncommon in biomedical settings and is not present in either our technical or plain texts.

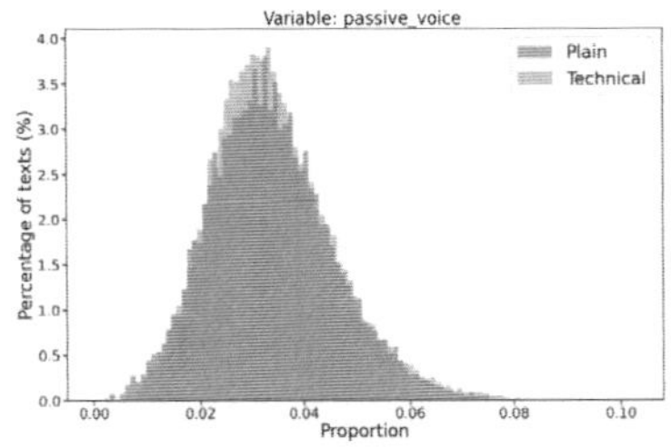

b. **Passive Voice:** when the subject undergoes the action of the verb (e.g., 'The cells were counted by the scientist'). According to our qualitative analysis, the use of passive voice can make sentences more complex, less direct, and harder to understand. As evidenced in our quantitative analysis, it is avoided in both scientific/biomedical settings, both in plain and technical texts.

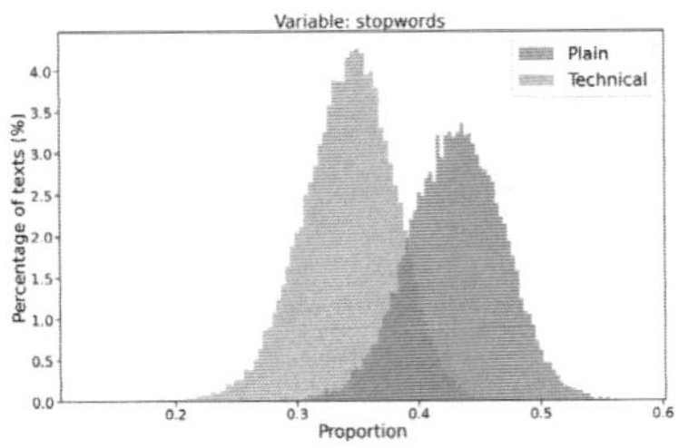

c. **Stopwords.** The proportion of words such as 'a' and 'the' is higher in plain texts is higher in plain texts, most likely as they aid in the fluency and comprehension of a text by acting as connectors between words, enhancing the coherence and naturalness of sentences for readers.

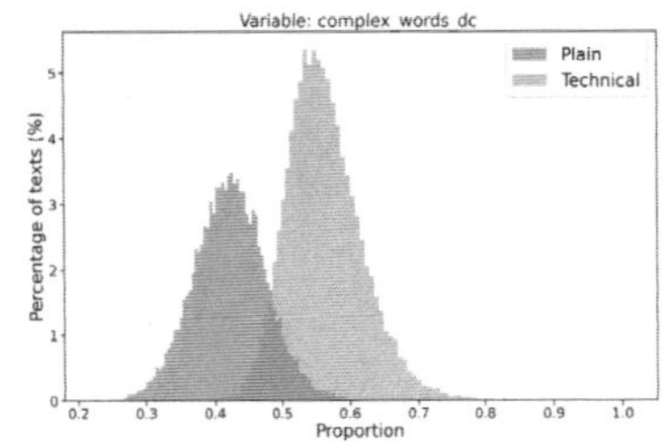

d. **Complex Words.** The proportion of words with three or more syllables is higher in technical texts, consistent with our qualitative assessments and plain language guidelines.

Figure 2: Comparison of the distribution of a sample of readability metrics or language variables between plain and technical texts.

mary (PPLS) as specified by EU CTR No 536/2014 (United Health Group, 2023); and **(4) Usefulness:** the generated PLS can serve as a reliable first draft for final study documentation.

Because PPLS are intended for review by professional evaluators, they required a higher level of care and were generated in limited numbers. This qualitative evaluation method, although rigorous, did not scale efficiently to large sample sizes. To address this limitation, for the more numerous Cochrane Review PLS we adopted a scalable, quantitative evaluation approach based on the three criteria used in the BioLaySumm competition (Goldsack and Lin, 2025). Specifically, we assessed:

1. **RELEVANCE:** measuring the semantic similarity between the LLM-generated summaries and a ground-truth summary (created by a human) using BERTScore (Zhang et al., 2020);
2. **FACTUALITY:** evaluating the consistency of the generated content with the source text (i.e., ensuring that no contradictory information is introduced) using AlignScore (Zha et al., 2023); and
3. **READABILITY:** assessing grammaticality and ease of comprehension through computational metrics such as Flesch–Kincaid Grade Level (Flesch, 1948), Coleman-Liau Index (Coleman and Liau, 1975), Flesch Reading Ease, Gunning Fog Index (Gunning, 1952), SMOG readability formula, and Dale–Chall Readability Score (Chall and Dale, 1995).

In addition, we considered the CLASSIFICATION results from our best ML model, which predicts if the LLM-generated text is plain or technical.

Our final prompt (see Figure C2) for generating

a PPLS included the following elements:

- **Context:** a clear explanation of why a plain language summary is needed for the given clinical trial protocol.
- **Output:** the desired structure and format of the generated summary, including specific sections.
- **Content:** guidelines on the expected information in each section, with examples and rules to direct the generation process.
- **Restrictions:** limitations on the output (e.g., word count, inclusion of only information provided in the original protocol, and adherence to the plain language criteria outlined in Table 1).

After finalizing the prompt for generating a PPLS, we used a similar approach to create a prompt for generating Cochrane Review PLS (see Table A1 and Figure C1). This two-pronged strategy allowed us to balance the need for careful, qualitative review (for PPLS) with a scalable, quantitative evaluation method (for Cochrane PLS) that can handle larger sample sizes.

4 Results

4.1 Plain Texts Classification Model

The classification models accurately distinguished between plain and technical texts. The GB model, in particular, achieved a slightly higher F1 Score (see Table 2). Since most of the training data were derived from Cochrane texts, we further evaluated the models on a completely separate validation set composed of PLOS and eLife documents (see Table A1) to assess potential bias. The performance metrics, reported as Main/PLOS+eLife in Table 2, indicate that the models generalize well to unseen data and exhibit minimal bias.

Metric	Main (Test)		PLOS + eLife (Test)	
	RF	GB	RF	GB
Accuracy	0.968	0.9752	0.9421	0.9557
Recall	0.973	0.9813	0.9616	0.9672
Precision	0.959	0.9655	0.9255	0.9455
F1 Score	0.966	0.9734	0.9432	0.9562

Table 2: Performance comparison of classification models on the Main Dataset and the PLOS + eLife test dataset.

4.2 LLM Prompt for Plain Language Summary Generation

4.2.1 Cochrane Reviews: Plain Language Summaries

We randomly selected 600 Cochrane texts from the main dataset—300 technical abstracts and their corresponding plain language summaries (ground truth). Using our final prompt, we generated summaries for the technical abstracts and computed average metrics—READABILITY, FACTUALITY, and RELEVANCE—for each model (Table 3). The factuality metric was calculated using the original abstracts to ensure the summaries remained faithful. We also evaluated classification accuracy (i.e., whether our ML classifier recognized the summaries as plain language) as shown in Table 4.

Overall, API-based models produced summaries consistently classified as plain language, while locally executed models tended to yield more technical outputs, as indicated by lower readability scores. Among the GPT models, those with higher readability were more often recognized as plain language, although their factuality and relevance were slightly lower than those of GPT-3.5. These results suggest that some models generate easier-to-read texts, whereas others retain a more technical tone.

4.2.2 Protocol Plain Language Summaries

We randomly selected a sample of nine clinical trial protocols from ClinicalTrials.gov. Since the corresponding PPLS were not publicly available, we used Trial Summaries by Citeline Regulatory to obtain the Results Plain Language Summaries (RPLS) and extracted four sections equivalent to a PPLS: 'Why is this study needed?' (Background and hypothesis of the trial, i.e., Rationale), 'Who will take part in this study?' (Population), 'How is this study designed?' (Trial Design), and 'What treatments are being given during the study?' (Interventions).

Quantitative Analysis

We generated PPLS from technical protocols using our prompt with both API-based models (e.g., GPT-3.5, GPT-4, GPT-4o, Gemini-1.5) and locally executed models (DeepSeek R1, Llama-3.2). For each model, we computed average metrics for READABILITY, FACTUALITY (AlignScore), and RELEVANCE (BERTScore), as shown in Table 3. Our ML classifier also confirmed that nearly all outputs were recognized as plain language (see Table 4).

Quantitative Evaluation for Cochrane

	READABILITY						FACTUALITY	RELEVANCE
Model	**CLI ↓**	**FRE ↑**	**GFI ↓**	**SMOG ↓**	**FKGL ↓**	**DCRS ↓**	**AlignScore ↑**	**BERTScore ↑**
deepseek-r1-7b	16.99	22.75	17.69	12.31	14.80	9.45	0.7955	0.8496
gemini-1.3-flash	**9.60**	**66.87**	**8.75**	**9.08**	**6.90**	**5.94**	0.6333	0.8474
gpt_4-32k	12.48	48.52	13.39	11.20	10.80	7.41	0.7801	0.8519
gpt_4o	11.49	57.13	11.16	9.91	9.09	6.88	0.7383	0.8527
gpt_35-turbo-16k	15.52	28.08	17.33	12.59	13.91	8.60	0.8781	**0.8585**
llama-3.2-3b	16.42	21.96	18.58	10.79	15.73	9.39	**0.8785**	0.8490

Quantitative Evaluation for PPLS

	READABILITY						FACTUALITY	RELEVANCE
Model	**CLI ↓**	**FRE ↑**	**GFI ↓**	**SMOG ↓**	**FKGL ↓**	**DCRS ↓**	**AlignScore ↑**	**BERTScore ↑**
deepseek-r1-7b	15.70	24.73	15.03	11.88	13.89	9.88	0.9657	0.8305
gemini-1.3-flash	**9.11**	**65.09**	**8.61**	11.40	**6.74**	**5.75**	0.9331	**0.8479**
gpt_4-32k	10.86	52.26	12.15	**10.45**	10.79	6.86	0.9646	0.8472
gpt_4o	11.20	55.67	10.37	10.97	8.91	7.05	0.9515	0.8465
gpt_35-turbo-16k	14.30	29.10	16.07	13.49	13.68	8.15	0.9697	0.8434
llama-3.2-3b	13.54	35.17	14.75	11.72	13.26	8.47	**0.9826**	0.8386

Table 3: Comparison of model metrics. **Upper table:** Metrics computed as averages from generated summaries derived from 300 Cochrane abstracts. **Lower table:** Metrics computed as averages over the 9 generated PPLS produced by the LLMs. Best values are in **bold** and worst values are underlined. READABILITY metrics are lower-is-better (except FRE, where higher is preferred), while FACTUALITY and RELEVANCE are higher-is-better.

	CLASSIFICATION	
Model	**Cochrane**	**PPLS**
deepseek-r1-7b	0.5567	0.5556
gemini-1.3-flash	**1.0000**	**1.0000**
gpt_4	0.9433	**1.0000**
gpt_4o	0.9767	**1.0000**
gpt_35	0.8733	**1.0000**
llama-3.2-3b	0.7033	0.7778

Table 4: Accuracy of generated summaries as determined by our plain language classifier. Since all outputs should be plain language by instruction, these results indicate the extent to which each model adheres to this requirement.

Overall, API-based models achieved higher precision and better factuality, while locally executed models performed worse due to computational limitations. Among the GPT models, GPT-4 and GPT-4o produced the most readable summaries (and were most frequently classified as plain language), though their factuality and relevance were slightly lower than those of GPT-3.5. These results indicate that models like GPT-4o, Gemini-1.5, and GPT-4 tend to generate easier-to-read texts, whereas DeepSeek R1 and Llama-3.2 yield more technical summaries.

Qualitative Analysis

For the qualitative evaluation, only the plain language summaries generated by GPT-3.5 and GPT-4 were selected. Due to time constraints for experts, we selected only the best models based on previous results, considering that GPT-4o has minimal differences from GPT-4 in content generation. Ratings by three domain experts who evaluated each LLM-generated text demonstrated that GPT-4 outperformed GPT-3.5 in all four criteria: Accuracy, Readability, Completeness, and Usefulness, as indicated by an average overall score of 4.71 for GPT-4 texts compared to 3.93 for GPT-3.5 (see Figure 3 and Table 5).

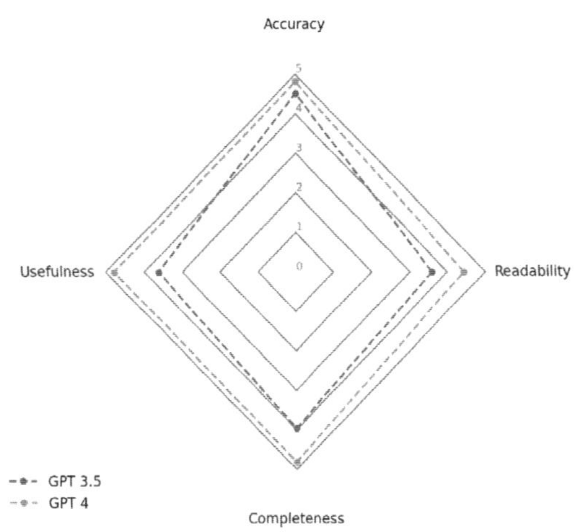

Figure 3: Radar diagram comparing the qualitative assessment of the LLM-generated texts in four criteria: Accuracy, Readability, Completeness, and Usefulness.

In terms of accuracy, both GPT-3.5 and GPT-4 received high scores. Reviewers noted that both language models exhibited scientific accuracy and relied exclusively on the input text (study protocol). Notably, even when the content in the original RPLS contained inconsistencies (e.g., an incorrect age limit or indication), both language models generated accurate PLS. This finding suggests that language models can be used to automatically generate a first draft of a PLS while minimizing data inaccuracies resulting from human error.

Metric	GPT 3.5	GPT 4
Accuracy	4.52	4.81
Readability	3.59	4.44
Completeness	3.96	4.81
Usefulness	3.63	4.78
Overall Score	3.93	4.71

Table 5: Ratings for GPT 3.5 and GPT 4 plain language summaries in four criteria: Accuracy, Readability, Completeness, and Usefulness.

5 Discussion

In this study, we used NLP and LLMs to improve health literacy by generating PLS from biomedical texts. Our approach involved building a robust database that generalizes well across diverse sources and developing a highly accurate classification model to distinguish technical from plain texts. This model serves as a valuable tool for ensuring that patient-targeted documents adhere to plain language guidelines, while our LLM-based generation framework leverages well-designed, domain-specific prompts to produce PLS.

Our evaluation shows that API-based models generally generate easier-to-read and more semantically faithful summaries, although they sometimes exhibit slightly lower factuality—possibly due to hallucination issues. In contrast, locally executed models, while maintaining acceptable factual accuracy, tend to yield more technical outputs, most probably because they have difficulty understanding instructions better, due to computational limitations. Qualitative feedback from domain experts confirmed that GPT 4 outperformed GPT 3.5 in terms of accuracy, readability, completeness, and usefulness. These findings highlight the value of using well-designed, domain-specific prompts and robust LLMs to streamline the generation of plain language summaries. Future research should explore the use of fully-featured, open-source models comparable to the API-based alternatives and incorporate broader stakeholder feedback to refine these methods for diverse biomedical domains.

In conclusion, by leveraging the capabilities of NLP and LLMs, our framework represents a significant step towards bridging the gap between complex biomedical texts and comprehensible summaries for the general audience, paving the way for innovations in health literacy.

6 Future Work

We plan to expand and diversify our dataset by incorporating the full collections of PLOS and eLife, obtaining more plain language samples, and employing advanced techniques to better separate and curate the data.

Future evaluations should include a larger and more diverse set of documents as well as input from multiple stakeholder groups (e.g., patients, medical writers, and clinicians). Additionally, further research should explore advanced prompt engineering techniques, such as chain-of-thought strategies, particularly for open-source models.

7 Limitations

Our study has some limitations. First, our dataset is predominantly composed of Cochrane texts with very few samples from other sources (e.g., Pfizer), which may lead to overfitting and reduce generalizability. Additionally, the current database is not human-curated, which may introduce parsing errors or inaccuracies. Second, our qualitative assessment was based on a limited number of clinical protocols and evaluated only the outputs from GPT-3.5 and GPT-4, with feedback from just a few domain experts. Furthermore, due to computational and API cost constraints, the number of generated samples was limited, potentially affecting the statistical significance of our findings and complicating comparisons between API-based and locally executed models.

References

Jonathan Anderson. 1983. Lix and Rix: Variations on a Little-known Readability Index. *Journal of Reading*, 26(6):490–496. Publisher: [Wiley, International Reading Association].

B. Bahador, S. Baedorf Kassis, H. Gawrylewski, and et al. 2020. Promoting equity in understanding: A cross-organizational plain language glossary for clinical research. *Medical Writing*, 29(4):10–15.

Yoav Benjamini and Yosef Hochberg. 1995. Controlling the false discovery rate: A practical and powerful approach to multiple testing. *Journal of the Royal Statistical Society: Series B (Methodological)*, 57(1):289–300.

N. D. Berkman, S. L. Sheridan, K. E. Donahue, and et al. 2011a. Health literacy interventions and outcomes: an updated systematic review. *Evidence Report/Technology Assessment*, 199:1–941.

N. D. Berkman, S. L. Sheridan, K. E. Donahue, D. J. Halpern, and K. Crotty. 2011b. Low health literacy and health outcomes: an updated systematic review. *Annals of Internal Medicine*, 155(2):97–107.

C. Brach. 2023. AHRQ Health Literacy Universal Precautions Toolkit, 3rd Edition. AHRQ Publication No. 23-0075, Accessed November 20, 2023.

Centers for Disease Control and Prevention. 2022. Your Guide to CLEAR WRITING. Accessed November 15, 2023.

Jeanne Sternlicht Chall and Edgar Dale. 1995. *Readability Revisited: The New Dale-Chall Readability Formula*. Brookline Books. Google-Books-ID: 2nbuAAAAMAAJ.

Meri Coleman and T. L. Liau. 1975. A Computer Readability Formula Designed for Machine Scoring. *Journal of Applied Psychology*, 60(2):283–284. Place: US Publisher: American Psychological Association.

Crummy. 2023. Beautiful Soup 4 4.10. Accessed December 2022.

Ashwin Devaraj, Iain Marshall, Byron Wallace, and Junyi Jessy Li. 2021. Paragraph-level Simplification of Medical Texts. In *Proceedings of the 2021 Conference of the North American Chapter of the Association for Computational Linguistics: Human Language Technologies*, pages 4972–4984, Online. Association for Computational Linguistics.

European Union. 2023. Q&A: Clinical Trial Regulation (EU) No 536/2014 2023. Accessed December 26, 2023.

Rudolph Flesch. 1948. A New Readability Yardstick. *Journal of Applied Psychology*, 32(3):221–233. Place: US Publisher: American Psychological Association.

GDPR. 2023. General Data Protection Regulation (GDPR) - The principle of Transparency. Accessed December 22, 2023.

Tomas Goldsack and Chenghua Lin. 2025. Overview of the biolaysumm 2025 shared task on the lay summarization of biomedical research articles. In *The 24rd Workshop on Biomedical Natural Language Processing and BioNLP Shared Tasks*, Vienna, Austria. Association for Computational Linguistics.

Tomas Goldsack, Zhihao Zhang, Chenghua Lin, and Carolina Scarton. 2022. Making Science Simple: Corpora for the Lay Summarisation of Scientific Literature. In *Proceedings of the 2022 Conference on Empirical Methods in Natural Language Processing*, pages 10589–10604, Abu Dhabi, United Arab Emirates. Association for Computational Linguistics.

Robert Gunning. 1952. *The Technique of Clear Writing*. McGraw-Hill. Google-Books-ID: ofI0AAAAMAAJ.

Peter Kincaid, Robert P. Fishburne, Richard L. Rogers, and Brad S. Chissom. 1975. Derivation of new readability formulas (automated readability index, fog count and flesch reading ease formula) for navy enlisted personnel.

A. N. Kolmogorov. 1933. Sulla determinazione empirica di una legge di distribuzione. *Giornale dell'Istituto Italiano degli Attuari*, 4:83–91.

Zheheng Luo, Qianqian Xie, and Sophia Ananiadou. 2022. Readability Controllable Biomedical Document Summarization. In *Findings of the Association for Computational Linguistics: EMNLP 2022*, pages 4667–4680, Abu Dhabi, United Arab Emirates. Association for Computational Linguistics.

Henry B. Mann and Donald R. Whitney. 1947. On a Test of Whether One of Two Random Variables is Stochastically Larger than the Other. *The Annals of Mathematical Statistics*, 18(1):50–60.

G. Harry Mc Laughlin. 1969. SMOG Grading: A new readability formula. *Journal of Reading*, 12(8):639–646. Publisher: [Wiley, International Reading Association].

T. A. Miller. 2016. Health literacy and adherence to medical treatment in chronic and acute illness: A meta-analysis. *Patient Education and Counseling*, 99(7):1079–1086.

Fatima N. Mirza, Oliver Y. Tang, Ian D. Connolly, Hael A. Abdulrazeq, Rachel K. Lim, G. Dean Roye, Cedric Priebe, Cheryl Chandler, Tiffany J. Libby, Michael W. Groff, John H. Shin, Albert E. Telfeian, Curtis E. Doberstein, Wael F. Asaad, Ziya L. Gokaslan, James Zou, and Rohaid Ali. 2024. Using ChatGPT to Facilitate Truly Informed Medical Consent. *NEJM AI*, 1(2):AIcs2300145. Publisher: Massachusetts Medical Society.

L. Nielsen-Bohlman, A. M. Panzer, and D. A. Kindig. 2004. *Health Literacy: A Prescription to End Confusion*. National Academies Press.

B. Ondov, K. Attal, and D. Demner-Fushman. 2022. A survey of automated methods for biomedical text simplification. *Journal of the American Medical Informatics Association*, 29(11):1976–1988.

Pfizer. 2023. Plain Language Study Results Summaries. Accessed September 2023.

Pharma Intelligence UK Limited. 2023. Citeline Trial Summaries Citeline Regulatory. Accessed September 2023.

Readability. 2019. Readability 0.3.1. Accessed November 2023.

D. Schillinger. 2021. Social Determinants, Health Literacy, and Disparities: Intersections and Controversies. *HLRP: Health Literacy Research and Practice*, 5(3):233–243.

Selenium. 2023. Selenium 4.4. Accessed December 2022.

R. J. Senter and E. A. Smith. 1967. Automated readability index. Technical Report AMRL-TR-6620, Wright-Patterson Air Force Base, Ohio, USA.

SpaCy. 2023. SpaCy. Accessed November 2023.

M. Stoll, M. Kerwer, K. Lie, and A. Chasiotis. 2022. Plain language summaries: A systematic review of theory, guidelines, and empirical research. *PLoS ONE*, 17(6):e0268789.

C. Stormacq, S. Van den Broucke, and J. Wosinski. 2019. Does health literacy mediate the relationship between socioeconomic status and health disparities? Integrative review. *Health Promotion International*, 34(5):e1–e17.

Kristine Sørensen, Jürgen M. Pelikan, Florian Röthlin, Kristin Ganahl, Zofia Slonska, Gerardine Doyle, James Fullam, Barbara Kondilis, Demosthenes Agrafiotis, Ellen Uiters, Maria Falcon, Monika Mensing, Kancho Tchamov, Stephan van den Broucke, and on behalf of the HLS-EU Consortium Brand, Helmut. 2015. Health literacy in Europe: comparative results of the European health literacy survey (HLS-EU). *European Journal of Public Health*, 25(6):1053–1058.

The Plain Language Action and Information Network. 2011. Federal Plain Language Guidelines. Accessed November 20, 2023.

A. Trezona, G. Rowlands, and D. Nutbeam. 2018. Progress in Implementing National Policies and Strategies for Health Literacy-What Have We Learned so Far? *International Journal or Environmental Research and Public Health*, 15(7):1554.

Oisín Turbitt, Robert Bevan, and Mouhamad Aboshokor. 2023. MDC at BioLaySumm Task 1: Evaluating GPT Models for Biomedical Lay Summarization. In *The 22nd Workshop on Biomedical Natural Language Processing and BioNLP Shared Tasks*, pages 611–619, Toronto, Canada. Association for Computational Linguistics.

United Health Group. 2023. Just Plain Clear Glossary. Accessed December 5, 2023.

U.S National Library of Medicine (NIH). 2023a. ClinicalTrials.gov. Accessed November 2023.

U.S National Library of Medicine (NIH). 2023b. ClinicalTrials.gov API. Accessed November 2023.

Dave Van Veen, Cara Van Uden, Louis Blankemeier, Jean-Benoit Delbrouck, Asad Aali, Christian Bluethgen, Anuj Pareek, Malgorzata Polacin, Eduardo Pontes Reis, Anna Seehofnerova, Nidhi Rohatgi, Poonam Hosamani, William Collins, Neera Ahuja, Curtis P. Langlotz, Jason Hom, Sergios Gatidis, John Pauly, and Akshay S. Chaudhari. 2024. Adapted Large Language Models Can Outperform Medical Experts in Clinical Text Summarization. *Nature Medicine*, 30(4):1134–1142. ArXiv:2309.07430 [cs].

Frank Wilcoxon. 1945. Individual Comparisons by Ranking Methods. *Biometrics Bulletin*, 1(6):80–83.

Yuheng Zha, Yichi Yang, Ruichen Li, and Zhiting Hu. 2023. AlignScore: Evaluating Factual Consistency with a Unified Alignment Function. *arXiv preprint*. ArXiv:2305.16739 [cs].

Tianyi Zhang, Varsha Kishore, Felix Wu, Kilian Q. Weinberger, and Yoav Artzi. 2020. BERTScore: Evaluating Text Generation with BERT. In *International Conference on Learning Representations*.

A Supplemental Material

Data Source	Text Type	Overview	Count of Texts	Extraction Method
U.S National Library of Medicine (NIH), ClinicalTrials.gov	Technical	Largest and publicly available database of clinical research studies and information about their results (U.S National Library of Medicine (NIH), 2023a).	100	ClinicalTrials.gov API that provides access to all posted information on study records (U.S National Library of Medicine (NIH), 2023b).
Cochrane Library by Wiley	Technical and Plain	International not-for-profit organization that publishes trusted reviews of biomedical research in two formats: a technical abstract and a plain language summary.	8465 projects (13,922 texts) (*shorter than 250 excluded)	Python libraries: Selenium (2023) (for automated browser interactions) and Beautiful Soup (2023) (for web scraping).
Pfizer Results Plain Language Summaries	Plain	Plain Language Study Results Summaries (RPLS) of Pfizer clinical studies (Pfizer, 2023). Sections containing tables or diagrams were excluded.	125	Specific sections of the PDF documents were mapped and extracted (e.g., "What happened during the Study?").
Trial Summaries by Citeline Regulatory	Plain	Trial results summaries (RPLS) for studies that started in late 2015 and beyond, provided by sponsors (e.g., AstraZeneca, GSK, Amgen) (Pharma Intelligence UK Limited, 2023).	294	Automatic PDF extraction introduced errors (missing letters, broken words). GPT-3.5 API was used only to correct these errors, ensuring texts matched the original RPLS PDFs.
PLOS + eLife (Luo et al., 2022; Goldsack et al., 2022; Goldsack and Lin, 2025)	Technical and Plain	Dataset from the BioLaySumm competition containing biomedical and life sciences article summaries. We only used the validation sets.	1376 (PLOS) 241 (eLife)	Official data published by Goldsack and Lin (2025)

Table A1: Overview of the data sources used in this study. All texts are available in our GitHub Data Repository[1].

[1] https://github.com/feliperussi/bridging-the-gap-in-health-literacy/tree/main/data_collection_and_processing/Data%20Sources

B Linguistic Features and Readability Indexes

In this study, the readability indexes (items 1–9) were computed using formulas based on variables from Readability (2019), while the linguistic features (items 10–49) were extracted using SpaCy (2023) (model `en_core_web_sm`). The remaining readability features (items 50–62) were obtained with the Readability library. Below is an enumerated list and for a concise overview, Table B1 presents the same variables along with their enumeration.

1. **Flesch-Kincaid Grade Level (FKGL):** Estimates the U.S. school grade level needed to comprehend the text (Flesch, 1948; Kincaid et al., 1975).

2. **Automated Readability Index (ARI):** Computes readability using characters, words, and sentences (Senter and Smith, 1967).

3. **Coleman-Liau Index (CLI):** Measures readability based on letter and word counts per sentence (Coleman and Liau, 1975).

4. **Flesch Reading Ease (FRE):** Produces a score where higher values indicate easier readability (Flesch, 1948; Kincaid et al., 1975).

5. **Gunning Fog Index (GFI):** Estimates the number of years of formal education needed to understand the text (Gunning, 1952).

6. **LIX:** Calculates readability by analyzing the proportion of long words in the text (Anderson, 1983).

7. **SMOG readability formula (SMOGIndex):** Estimates readability by counting polysyllabic (Mc Laughlin, 1969).

8. **RIX:** Computes readability from the number of long words per sentence (Anderson, 1983).

9. **Dale-Chall Readability Score (DCRS):** Assesses readability by comparing text words against a list of familiar words (Chall and Dale, 1995).

10. **total_words:** Total number of words in the text (excluding punctuation), identified by spaCy. e.g., in "Hello, world!", there are 2 words.

11. **total_sentences:** Total number of sentences in the text, based on spaCy's sentence segmentation. e.g., "Hello. World!" yields 2 sentences.

12. **total_characters:** Total number of characters in the text. e.g., "Hello" has 5 characters.

13. **passive_voice:** Frequency of passive voice constructions, determined via verb forms tagged as VBN. e.g., "was given" in "John was given a book by Mary."

14. **active_voice:** Frequency of active voice constructions, counted as verbs (VERB) not tagged as VBN. e.g., "ran" in "Alice quickly ran to the store," or "decided" in "He decided to give up his job."

15. **passive_toks:** Count of tokens in passive constructions, where spaCy marks passive subjects with `nsubjpass`. e.g., "John" in "John was given a book by Mary."

16. **active_toks:** Count of tokens in active constructions, based on the `nsubj` dependency; e.g., "Alice" in "Alice quickly ran to the store."

17. **verbs:** Count of verbs in the text, determined by tokens with the part-of-speech VERB; e.g., "bought" in "Alice bought 3 apples."

18. **nouns:** Count of nouns in the text, determined by tokens with the part-of-speech NOUN; e.g., "book" in "John was given a book."

19. **adjectives:** Count of adjectives in the text, determined by tokens with the part-of-speech ADJ; e.g., "incredible" in "That was incredible."

20. **adverbs:** Count of adverbs in the text, determined by tokens with the part-of-speech ADV; e.g., "quickly" in "Alice quickly ran to the store."

21. **prepositions:** Count of prepositions in the text, determined by tokens with the part-of-speech ADP; e.g., "by" in "the ball was thrown by him."

22. **auxiliaries:** Count of auxiliary verbs in the text, determined by tokens with the part-of-speech AUX; e.g., "was" in "John was given a book by Mary."

Readability Indexes	(1) FKGL, (2) ARI, (3) CLI, (4) FRE, (5) GFI, (6) LIX, (7) SMOGIndex, (8) RIX, (9) DCRS
Linguistic Characteristics	(10) total_words, (11) total_sentences, (12) total_characters, (13) passive_voice, (14) active_voice, (15) passive_toks, (16) active_toks, (17) verbs, (18) nouns, (19) adjectives, (20) adverbs, (21) prepositions, (22) auxiliaries, (23) conjunctions, (24) coord_conjunctions, (25) determiners, (26) numbers, (27) particles, (28) pronouns, (29) proper_nouns, (30) punctuations, (31) subordinating_conjunctions, (32) symbols, (33) other, (34) persons, (35) norp, (36) facilities, (37) organizations, (38) gpe, (39) products, (40) works, (41) dates, (42) times, (43) quantities, (44) ordinals, (45) cardinals, (46) percentages, (47) locations, (48) laws, (49) stopwords (50) characters_per_word, (51) syll_per_word, (52) words_per_sentence, (53) sentences_per_paragraph, (54) type_token_ratio, (55) syllables, (56) paragraphs, (57) long_words, (58) complex_words, (59) complex_words_dc, (60) tobeverb, (61) auxverb, (62) nominalization

Table B1: Variables used to describe the readability and linguistic characteristics of the texts. Items 1–9 (readability indexes) were computed using formulas based on variables from Readability (2019), items 10–49 (linguistic features) were extracted using SpaCy (2023) (model `en_core_web_sm`), and items 50–62 were obtained using Readability (2019).

23. **conjunctions:** Count of conjunctions in the text, determined by tokens tagged as CCONJ or SCONJ; e.g., "because" and "and" in "Alice quickly ran to the store and bought 3 apples because it was late."

24. **coord_conjunctions:** Count of coordinating conjunctions, determined by tokens with the part-of-speech CCONJ; e.g., "and" in the example of conjunctions.

25. **determiners:** Count of determiners in the text, determined by tokens with the part-of-speech DET; e.g., "the" in "the qwerty word is unknown."

26. **numbers:** Count of numerical values in the text, determined by tokens with the part-of-speech NUM; e.g., "3" in "Alice bought 3 apples."

27. **particles:** Count of particles in the text, determined by tokens with the part-of-speech PART; e.g., "to" in "He decided to give up his job."

28. **pronouns:** Count of pronouns in the text, determined by tokens with the part-of-speech PRON; e.g., "him" in "the ball was thrown by him."

29. **proper_nouns:** Count of proper nouns in the text, determined by tokens with the part-of-speech PROPN; e.g., "Google" or "JFK Airport."

30. **punctuations:** Count of punctuation marks in the text, determined by tokens with the part-of-speech PUNCT; e.g., "," in "John was given a book, and the ball was thrown by him."

31. **subordinating_conjunctions:** Count of subordinating conjunctions in the text, determined by tokens with the part-of-speech SCONJ; e.g., "because" in the example of conjunctions.

32. **symbols:** Count of symbols in the text, determined by tokens with the part-of-speech SYM; e.g., "$" in "worth $100,000."

33. **other:** Count of tokens not classified in other categories, determined by tokens with the part-of-speech X (uncategorized).

34. **persons:** Count of person mentions in the text, determined by entities labeled PERSON; e.g., "John" or "Mary."

35. **norp:** Count of references to nationalities, religious or political groups, determined by entities labeled NORP; e.g., "American."

36. **facilities:** Count of facilities (e.g., buildings, airports, roads), determined by entities labeled FAC; e.g., "JFK" and 'Airport" in "JFK Airport."

37. **organizations:** Count of organizations, determined by entities labeled ORG; e.g., "FAA" or "Google."

38. **gpe:** Count of geopolitical entities (countries, cities), determined by entities labeled GPE; e.g., “London.”

39. **products:** Count of products mentioned, determined by entities labeled PRODUCT.

40. **works:** Count of creative works (e.g., art, books, movies), determined by entities labeled WORK_OF_ART; e.g., “Hamlet.”

41. **dates:** Count of dates mentioned, determined by entities labeled DATE; e.g., “March”, “15”, “,” and “2025” in “March 15, 2025.”

42. **times:** Count of time expressions, determined by entities labeled TIME; e.g., “3:00” and “PM” in “3:00 PM.”

43. **quantities:** Count of quantity expressions, determined by entities labeled QUANTITY; e.g., “10” and “kg.” in “10 kg.”

44. **ordinals:** Count of ordinal numbers, determined by entities labeled ORDINAL; e.g., “first” in “She is the first in its field.”

45. **cardinals:** Count of cardinal numbers, determined by entities labeled CARDINAL; e.g., “3” in “Alice bought 3 apples.”

46. **percentages:** Count of percentage expressions, determined by entities labeled PERCENT; e.g., “50” and “%” in “yield 50% discounts.”

47. **locations:** Count of location mentions, determined by entities labeled LOC; e.g., “Alps” in “The Alps are breathtaking.”

48. **laws:** Count of laws mentioned, determined by entities labeled LAW; e.g., “Section” and “2” in “Section 2 of the law applies to this case.”

49. **stopwords:** Count of stopwords in the text, determined by tokens identified as stop words by spaCy; e.g., “was,” “the,” or “and.”

50. **characters_per_word:** Average number of characters per word, computed as total characters divided by total words.

51. **syll_per_word:** Average number of syllables per word, computed as total syllables divided by total words.

52. **words_per_sentence:** Average number of words per sentence, computed as total words divided by total sentences.

53. **sentences_per_paragraph:** Average number of sentences per paragraph, computed as total sentences divided by total paragraphs.

54. **type_token_ratio:** Ratio of unique words to total words, computed as the number of distinct tokens divided by total words.

55. **syllables:** Total number of syllables in the text.

56. **paragraphs:** Total number of paragraphs in the text.

57. **long_words:** Count of long words in the text, defined as words exceeding a specified length threshold (e.g., more than 7 letters).

58. **complex_words:** Count of complex words in the text, defined as words with three or more syllables (e.g., “inconceivable”), indicating text complexity.

59. **complex_words_dc:** Count of complex words according to the Dale–Chall method (i.e., unknown polysyllabic words from a list of basic words).

60. **tobeverb:** Count of occurrences of the verb “to be” in the text (e.g., “is,” “are,” “was”).

61. **auxverb:** Count of auxiliary verbs in the text (e.g., “have,” “will,” “do”).

62. **nominalization:** Count of nominalizations in the text, i.e., instances where verbs, adjectives, or other linguistic elements are transformed into nouns (e.g., “development” from “develop”).

C Prompts

Using the following abstract of a biomedical study as input, generate a Plain Language Summary (PLS) understandable by any patient, regardless of their health literacy. Ensure that the generated text adheres to the following instructions which should be followed step-by-step:
a. Specific Structure: The generated PLS should be presented in a logical order, using the following order:

1. Plain Title
2. Rationale
3. Trial Design
4. Results

b. Sections should be authored following these parameters:

1. **Plain Title:** Simplified title understandable to a layperson that summarizes the research that was done.
2. **Rationale:** Include: background or study rationale providing a general description of the condition, what it may cause or why it is a burden for the patients; the reason and main hypothesis for the study; and why the study is needed, and why the study medication has the potential to treat the condition.
3. **Trial Design:** Answer 'How is this study designed?' Include the description of the design, description of study and patient population (age, health condition, gender), and the expected amount of time a person will be in the study.
4. **Results:** Answer 'What were the main results of the study', include the benefits for the patients, how the study was relevant for the area of study, and the conclusions from the investigator.

c. Consistency and Replicability: The generated PLS should be consistent regardless of the order of sentences or the specific phrasing used in the input protocol text.
d. Compliance with Plain Language Guidelines: The generated PLS must follow all these plain language guidelines:

- Have readability grade level of 6 or below.
- Do not have jargon. All technical or medical words or terms should be defined or broken down into simple and logical explanations.
- Active voice, not passive.
- Mostly one or two syllable words.
- Sentences of 15 words or less.
- Short paragraphs of 3-5 sentences.
- Simple numbers (e.g., ratios, no percentages).

e. Do not invent Content: The AI model should not invent information. If the AI model includes data other than the one given in the input abstract, the AI model should guarantee such data is verified and real.
f. Aim for an approximate PLS length of 500-900 words.

Figure C1: Prompt to translate Cochrane technical abstract into a plain language summary.

Using the following abstract of a biomedical study as input, generate a Plain Language Summary (PLS) understandable by any patient, regardless of their health literacy. Ensure that the generated text adheres to the following instructions which should be followed step-by-step:

a. Specific Structure: The generated PPLS should be presented in a logical order, using the following headings:

1. Plain Protocol Title
2. Rationale
3. Objectives
4. Trial Design
5. Trial Population
6. Interventions

b. Sections should be authored following these parameters:

1. **Plain Protocol Title:** Simplified protocol title understandable to a layperson but including specific indication for which the study is meant.
2. **Rationale:** Include the phrase 'Researchers are looking for a better way to treat [condition]; background or study rationale describing the condition: what it is, what it may cause, and why it is a burden for the patients; the reason and main hypothesis for the study; and why the study is needed, and the study medication has the potential to treat the condition.
3. **Objectives:** Answer 'What are the goals of the study?' Specify the main and secondary objectives of the trial and how they will be measured (e.g., the main trial endpoint is the percent change in the number of events from baseline to a specified time or the total number of adverse reactions at a particular time after baseline).
4. **Trial Design:** Answer 'How is this study designed?' Include the description of the design and the expected amount of time a person will be in the study.
5. **Trial Population:** Answer 'Who will participate in this study?' Include a description of the study and patient population (age, health condition, gender), and the key inclusion and exclusion criteria.
6. **Interventions:** Answer 'What treatments are being given during the study?' Include a description of the medication, vaccine, or treatment(s) being studied, the route of administration, the duration of treatment, and any study-related diagnostic and monitoring procedures used. Include justification if a placebo is used.

c. Consistency and Replicability: The generated PPLS should be consistent regardless of the order of sentences or the specific phrasing used in the input protocol text.
d. Compliance with Plain Language Guidelines: The generated PPLS must follow these plain language guidelines:

- Have readability grade level of 6 or below.
- Do not have jargon. All technical or medical words or terms should be defined or broken down into simple and logical explanations.
- Active voice, not passive.
- Mostly one or two-syllable words.
- Sentences of 15 words or less.
- Short paragraphs of 3-5 sentences.
- Simple numbers (e.g., ratios, no percentages).

e. No Extra Content: The AI model should not invent information or add content that is not present in the input protocol. The PPLS should only present information from the original protocol in a simplified and understandable manner.
f. Aim for an approximate PPLS length of 700-900 words.

Figure C2: Prompt to translate a protocol into a plain language summary compliant with EU CTR No 536/2014.

Towards Knowledge-Guided Biomedical Lay Summarization using Large Language Models

Shufan Ming and **Yue Guo** and **Halil Kilicoglu***
School of Information Sciences
University of Illinois at Urbana-Champaign
{shufanm2, yueg, halil}@illinois.edu

Abstract

The massive size, continual growth, and technical jargon in biomedical publications make it difficult for laypeople to stay informed about the latest scientific advances, motivating research on lay summarization of biomedical literature. Large language models (LLMs) are increasingly used for this task. Unlike typical automatic summarization, lay summarization requires incorporating background knowledge not found in a paper and explanations of technical jargon. This study explores the use of MeSH terms (Medical Subject Headings), which represent an article's main topics, to enhance background information generation in biomedical lay summarization. Furthermore, we introduced a multi-turn dialogue approach that more effectively leverages MeSH terms in the instruction-tuning of LLMs to enhance the quality of lay summaries. The best model improved the state-of-the-art on the eLife test set in terms of the ROUGE-1 score by nearly 2%, with competitive scores in other metrics. These results indicate that MeSH terms can guide LLMs to generate more relevant background information for laypeople. Additionally, evaluation on a held-out dataset, one that was not used during model pre-training, shows that this capability generalizes well to unseen data, further demonstrating the effectiveness of our approach.

1 Introduction

Biomedical publications contain valuable research findings on health topics that may interest a wide range of audiences, including laypeople. PubMed, the biomedical bibliographic database, contains more than 37 million articles as of January 2025, with an increase of almost one million articles in less than a year [1]. Despite the abundance of health-related scientific information available in these articles, it is challenging for laypeople to make sense of this information due to the enormous size and growth of the literature and the specialized jargon used in these publications (August et al., 2023). Summarizing lengthy literature into concise, jargon-free lay language that explains the article's background and motivation can help alleviate information overload for laypeople (Goldsack et al., 2022).

Abstract
Plasmodium sporozoites, the mosquito-transmitted forms of the malaria parasite, first infect the liver for an initial round of replication before the emergence of pathogenic blood stages. Sporozoites represent attractive targets for antimalarial preventive strategies, yet the mechanisms of parasite entry into hepatocytes remain poorly understood. Here we show that ...
Lay Summary
Malaria is an infectious disease that affects millions of people around the world and remains a major cause of death, especially in Africa. It is caused by Plasmodium parasites, which are transmitted by mosquitoes to mammals. Once in the mammal, the parasites infect liver cells, where they multiply. ...

Table 1: Comparison of the first few sentences of the abstract and lay summary from an eLife article.

Table 1 demonstrates how lay summarization requires explaining jargon and providing background information to contextualize the study, which cannot always be fully derived from the source article alone. Text highlighted in blue from the abstract was simplified into two sentences highlighted in green in the lay summary. Text highlighted in yellow in the lay summary explains the term "Malaria" and background information missing from the abstract but necessary for laypeople.

To address this gap, previous work has explored the use of auxiliary inputs to incorporate relevant background knowledge from external resources (Guo et al., 2024; Goldsack et al., 2023) or to elicit hidden knowledge from LLMs through a two-stage inference process (Goldsack et al., 2025). For in-

*Corresponding author
[1]https://pubmed.ncbi.nlm.nih.gov/about/

Proceedings of the Second Workshop on Patient-Oriented Language Processing (CL4Health), pages 285–297
May 4, 2025 ©2025 Association for Computational Linguistics

stance, Guo et al. (2024) employed a separate retriever model to extract biomedical term definitions from Wikipedia, augmenting the input source articles. Similarly, Goldsack et al. (2023) constructed a graph-based knowledge representation, where biomedical concepts served as nodes and their relationships as edges, derived from the UMLS Semantic Network (McCray et al., 2001). This synthesized knowledge was then integrated with language models during fine-tuning. Both approaches demonstrated improvements in the relevance (i.e., alignment with gold-standard summaries) and readability of lay summaries.

In another line of research, keywords, length, readability, or other aspects of control have been used as non-parametric knowledge to modify prompts, rather than changing the parameters of the model, to generate desirable summaries (Fonseca and Cohen, 2024; He et al., 2022). Such modifications to the input prompt guide the model's conditional generation process during decoding, influencing the content, tone, or structure of the model output. However, the use of controllability in LLMs for the lay summarization task has achieved limited success compared to generic scientific summarization tasks, due to the highly abstractive nature of lay summaries and their particular emphasis on research background information (Jahan et al., 2024).

MeSH (Medical Subject Headings), developed at the National Library of Medicine, is a standardized terminology used to index medical and life science articles, offering relevant topical information and reflecting the broader context of the entire document. In this study, we hypothesize that using descriptive prompts consisting of a set of MeSH terms can guide the model's generation to provide tailored background information in lay summaries. To test this hypothesis, we designed a sequence of experiments using LLaMA-3[2] as the base model (Dubey et al., 2024) and instruction-response pairs constructed from the eLife dataset (Goldsack et al., 2022).

Specifically, we investigate the following research questions:

- What is the most effective approach for incorporating MeSH knowledge into the fine-tuning process to achieve high performance?
- How does the choice of MeSH terms (gold standard, predicted by another model, or a more focused subset of gold standard MeSH terms) affect the quality and relevance of lay summaries?
- Does the performance on articles published after LLaMA's knowledge cutoff date remain consistent when compared to the eLife test set, which contains articles published before the release date of the LLaMA model?

Our contributions are:

- Our enhanced instruction-tuning approach, using two-turn conversations, produces more diverse background information that is aligned with the source document and accessible to non-expert readers.
- We incorporate structured knowledge (MeSH) into the supervised fine-tuning (SFT) model, serving as classifier-free guidance that is easier to obtain compared to previous approaches relying on auxiliary retrieval-augmented generation (RAG) models or graph structures.
- We constructed a recent dataset from the eLife corpus, using a cutoff date of June 30, 2024, to compare and assess the generalizability of different approaches.

2 Methods

In this section, we first describe the datasets we use. Next, we discuss our proposed main approach, multi-turn instruction tuning, followed by several ablation studies to verify the effectiveness of each model component and our hypothesis. Finally, we outline the experimental setup and evaluation metrics used to compare different settings.

2.1 Dataset and Data Collection

We trained and tested our model on the eLife dataset (Goldsack et al., 2022), which consists of 4,346 pairs of full-text articles and lay summaries for training, along with 241 pairs each for validation and testing. Compared to the PLOS dataset (Goldsack et al., 2022), another commonly used biomedical lay summarization dataset, eLife contains much longer lay summaries written by expert editors and exhibits a strong content bias toward research background (You et al., 2024). This characteristic makes the summaries easier for a lay audience to understand but presents a greater challenge for the LLM to generate (Fonseca and Cohen, 2024).

[2] https://huggingface.co/meta-llama/Llama-3.2-3B-Instruct

The eLife corpus may have been included in the LLaMA model's training data, potentially giving the model an advantage by allowing it to memorize and reproduce information it has already encountered. To test the generalizability of our proposed method, we collected 71 articles published in the eLife corpus after June 30, 2024, through the open-source repository[3] on November 15, 2024, and used them as a held-out dataset for evaluation.

2.2 Multi-turn Instruction Tuning

Figure 1 illustrates the overall model architecture. The main method involves two back-and-forth conversational turns: the first turn focuses on MeSH prediction as an auxiliary task, while the second turn generates a lay summary conditioned on both the source document and the generated MeSH terms. During training, both MeSH terms and lay summaries are learned by minimizing the cross-entropy loss between the generated outputs and their respective gold standards for each article. Gold standard MeSH terms for each article were extracted by querying the PubMed database through the Entrez package[4].

The loss function is defined as follows:

$$\mathcal{L} = -\sum_{j=1}^{J}\sum_{t=1}^{T_j} \mathbb{1}_{[y_{t,j} \in y_{a,j}]} \log P\Big(y_{t,j} \mid y_{<t,j}, y_{\leq,j-1}, X, I; \theta\Big) \quad (1)$$

In this formulation, the loss function $\mathcal{L}$ uses cross-entropy to compare the model's generated responses at each turn with the gold-standard outputs, which consist of both MeSH terms and lay summaries. Here, $y_{t,j}$ denotes the token at time step t during the j-th conversation turn, while $y_{a,j}$ represents the set of tokens specific to the model's output in turn j. The indicator function $\mathbb{1}_{[y_t \in y_a]}$ checks whether the token $y_{t,j}$ belongs to the set of target tokens $y_{a,j}$. If it does, the indicator returns 1, allowing the token to contribute to the loss computation; otherwise, it returns 0, excluding irrelevant tokens such as those from the user prompt.

The conditional probability term $\log P\Big(y_{t,j} \mid y_{<t,j}, y_{\leq,j-1}, X, I; \theta\Big)$ represents the likelihood of predicting token $y_{t,j}$, given all preceding tokens in the same turn $y_{<t,j}$, all tokens from previous turns $y_{\leq,j-1}$, the input article X, and any additional instructions I. This setup ensures that tokens from the current turn j are conditioned on both intra-turn context and inter-turn history, enabling the model to incorporate contextual information from the entire conversation.

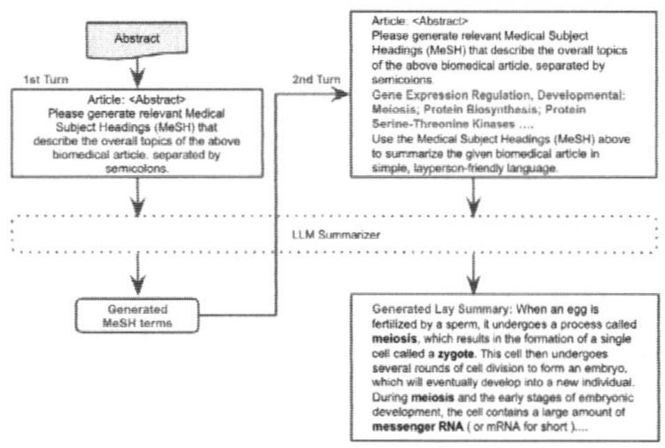

Figure 1: Workflow of the multi-turn instruction tuning at inference time. The generated MeSH terms serve as external guidance for the second forward pass. The upper portion of the figure illustrates the input prompts, while the lower portion displays the model's outputs.

We observed that some overly general MeSH terms, such as "Human" or "Animals," could mislead the model into generating irrelevant or overly broad background information. Our main approach involved applying a filtering strategy based on the hierarchical structure of the MeSH tree and its associated tree numbers[5] to retain only a subset of gold-standard MeSH terms. Specifically, if multiple terms shared the same tree prefix, we included the term with the longest identifier (indicating the highest specificity) and excluded others with shorter identifiers. For example, consider the full set of gold-standard MeSH terms separated by semi-colons: "Animals; Behavior, Animal; Cerebellum; Conditioning, Eyelid; Cues; Extinction, Psychological; Feedback; Learning; Male; Movement; Purkinje Cells; Rabbits; Time Factors". After applying the filtering strategy, more generic terms were removed in favor of more specific ones. For instance, "Animals" was eliminated because a more specific term, "Rabbits," from the same hierarchical branch (sharing the same prefix), was retained.

We used a parameter-efficient fine-tuning technique (PEFT), low-rank adaptation (LoRA) (Hu et al., 2021), to fine-tune large language models

[3] `https://github.com/elifesciences/elife-article-xml`

[4] `https://biopython.org/docs/1.75/api/Bio.Entrez.html`

[5] `https://hhs.github.io/meshrdf/tree-numbers`

efficiently. LoRA achieves efficiency by inserting trainable matrices and updating only a small subset of weights while keeping the original model parameters frozen. In Equation 1, θ denotes the subset of parameters updated during fine-tuning via LoRA.

2.3 Multi-turn Instruction Modeling

We conducted another experiment, INSTRUCTION_MODELING, based on previous research findings (Shi et al., 2024). These findings suggest that training the model to generate both instructions and responses, mimicking how humans provide task descriptions and guidance, yields more robust and higher-performing results, especially when the number of training examples is limited. Unlike INSTRUCTION_TUNING, which focuses on training the model to follow instructions and generate high-quality contextual responses, INSTRUCTION_MODELING introduces a modified loss function that applies to both the user input and the assistant's response. The updated loss function is defined as follows:

$$\mathcal{L} = -\sum_{j=1}^{J}\sum_{t=1}^{T_j} \log P(y_{t,j} \mid y_{<t,j}, y_{\leq,j-1}, X, I; \theta) \quad (2)$$

The key distinction from Equation 1 is the absence of the indicator function. This omission allows the model to be trained on both the user's input and the assistant's responses. The goal of this approach is to evaluate whether it improves the model's ability to understand and distinguish the linguistic differences between a scientific article and its lay summary, as well as the translations between them, thereby enhancing lay summary generation.

2.4 Ablation Study on Adaptation Methods and Knowledge Integration

We conducted various ablation studies to understand the contribution of each component to the overall performance of the main model, including the impact of integrating MeSH terms as guidance, the role of different training objectives, and the effect of MeSH term selection on summary quality.

2.4.1 In-context Learning

Another technique for adapting the pre-trained model to a domain-specific downstream task is in-context learning, which is a more lightweight alternative to PEFT. We tested three experimental setups: (1) an instruction-only setting without any external knowledge or guidance (Experiment 0-SHOT). (2) An approach in which the instruction was augmented with a pair consisting of an abstract and its corresponding lay summary selected from the training data (Experiment 1-SHOT). Specifically, for each source article, we retrieved the most similar abstract from the training set using SimCSE (Gao et al., 2021). The corresponding abstract and its associated lay summary from the training set are then provided as an exemplar to guide the generation. (3) An external knowledge-guided setting in which ground truth MeSH terms were explicitly integrated into the prompts (Experiment MESH_GUIDANCE). Unlike the main approach, which strictly requires the model to predict MeSH terms that closely match the gold standard, this method acts as a guiding framework, allowing the model greater flexibility to interpret and utilize MeSH terms based on its learned knowledge.

The prompt template is shown as below:

- 0-SHOT:
  Article: <Abstract>
  Summarize the above biomedical article in simple, layperson-friendly language.

- 1-SHOT:
  Article: <Abstract>
  Summarize the above biomedical article in simple, layperson-friendly language. Use the example below to guide the tone, structure, and the inclusion of relevant background context in your summary.
  Example abstract:<Example Abstract>
  Example lay summary:<Example Lay Summary>.

- MESH_GUIDANCE:
  Article: <Abstract>
  Summarize the above biomedical article in simple, layperson-friendly language. Use the following Medical Subject Headings (MeSH) as guidance for providing relevant background context where appropriate: <List of MeSH terms>.

2.4.2 Single-turn Instruction Tuning

In the multi-turn experiment setting, MeSH term generation is trained as an auxiliary task. We also designed two single-turn experimental setups that do not include training on MeSH terms: (1) SINGLE_TURN: instruction tuning using the same template as 0-SHOT for lay summary generation only, and (2) MESH_SINGLE_TURN: Instruction tuning that incorporates ground truth MeSH terms retrieved from the PubMed database into the user input prompt as non-parametric guidance, using the same template as MESH_GUIDANCE. Similarly, the training objective is shown below. The cross-entropy loss $\mathcal{L}$ is computed exclusively on the model's generated summaries.

$$\mathcal{L} = -\sum_{t=1}^{T} \mathbb{1}_{[y_t \in y_a]} \log P(y_t \mid y_{<t}, I, X; \theta) \quad (3)$$

2.4.3 MeSH term selection

MeSH terms serve as a signal for identifying which topics are essential and relevant to the source article, guiding the model to incorporate these concepts as background knowledge in the lay summary. Our main approach, described in Section 2.2, uses a heuristic-based curation method to select a subset of ground truth MeSH terms as the gold standard during the fine-tuning process. We also used all the ground-truth MeSH terms, without applying our filtering strategy, to investigate how training with the complete set of ground-truth MeSH terms versus a subset affects performance. We refer to this experiment as INSTRUCTION_TUNING_FULL_LIST.

In addition, we designed an ablation study to evaluate the impact of MeSH terms on the model's performance in a single-turn setting. Instead of providing ground truth MeSH terms in the prompt, we used predicted MeSH terms generated by a BERT-based MeSH classifier (BERTMeSH (You et al., 2021)), which achieves a Micro-F1 score of 63%. This comparison aimed to assess how both the quality and inclusion of different sets of MeSH terms in the input affect the model's performance. We refer to this experiment as BERT_MESH_SINGLE_TURN.

2.5 Experimental Settings

We used the *LLaMA-3.2-3B-Instruct* as the base model for all experiments. Due to computational resource limitations and the high memory requirements for fine-tuning large language models, we set the maximum input length to 2,500 tokens. We integrated the Accelerate (Gugger et al., 2022) and DeepSpeed (Rasley et al., 2020) libraries for fine-tuning. In addition, we employed an early stopping strategy based on validation performance, restricting training to a maximum of 3 epochs. The checkpoint that achieved the best performance on the validation set was then selected for inference on the test set. During inference, we set the temperature to 0 to ensure consistency in our summarization experiments. We set *max_new_tokens* to 512 to allow sufficient space for complete summaries while preventing excessively long outputs that may introduce irrelevant information.

2.6 Evaluation

The experiments were assessed solely for lay summary generation, using two sets of commonly applied metrics in previous lay summarization work: relevance and readability. Specifically, we employed ROUGE scores (Lin, 2004), including ROUGE-1, ROUGE-2, and ROUGE-L, which measure n-gram overlaps, as well as BERTScore (Zhang et al., 2019), which evaluates semantic similarity in the embedding space, to assess relevance. For readability evaluation, we used the Flesch-Kincaid Grade Level (FKGL) (Kincaid et al., 1975), Coleman-Liau Index (CLI) (Coleman and Liau, 1975), and the Dale-Chall Readability Score (DCRS) (Dale and Chall, 1948).

We did not include factuality-related metrics because previous findings show that existing automatic evaluation metrics for faithfulness do not align well with human evaluation in the context of biomedical plain language summarization (Fang et al., 2024; Chen et al., 2024). For example, fact-checking or natural language inference (NLI)-based evaluations, such as SummaC (Laban et al., 2022) and AlignScore (Zha et al., 2023), are designed and trained at the sentence level. These methods are highly sensitive to benign modifications and perturbations, which limits their ability to evaluate abstractive summarization tasks that often require text rewriting and paraphrasing (Tang et al., 2022; Ramprasad and Wallace, 2024). Moreover, those evaluations focus on whether the content aligns with the source, whereas in our case, lay summarization requires incorporating new external knowledge not present in the source article.

We assessed the statistical significance of the differences between the generated summaries across several experimental settings using the Wilcoxon signed-rank test (Woolson, 2005) in a pairwise manner, following the methodology of previous studies (Van Veen et al., 2024).

	Relevance				Readability		
	R-1	**R-2**	**R-L**	**BERTScore**	**FKGL ↓**	**CLI ↓**	**DCRS ↓**
SINGLE_TURN	0.5003	0.1374	0.4718	0.8518	10.6904	10.8585	8.6497
INSTRUCTION_TUNING_FULL_LIST	0.5004	0.1395	0.4714	0.8516	10.5369	10.7346	8.5793*
INSTRUCTION_TUNING	0.5021	**0.1408***	0.4733	**0.8524**	**10.4203****	**10.6960****	**8.5705****
INSTRUCTION_MODELING	**0.5026**	0.1399	**0.4747**	0.8520	10.5381*	10.9456	8.6068

Table 2: Results for the multi-turn conversation and single turn approach on the eLife test set. ↓ indicates that lower scores are better for that metric. Asterisks indicate statistical significance relative to the baseline model without MeSH (SINGLE_TURN), as determined by the Wilcoxon signed-rank test (* $p < 0.05$, ** $p < 0.01$).

	Relevance				Readability		
	R-1	**R-2**	**R-L**	**BERTScore**	**FKGL ↓**	**CLI ↓**	**DCRS ↓**
0-SHOT	0.3284	0.0781	0.3022	0.8399	**9.2091**	**10.2627**	8.5570
1-SHOT	0.3949***	0.0851***	0.3675***	0.8409*	9.4726*	10.3205	**8.3313*****
MESH_GUIDANCE	**0.4186*****	**0.0907*****	**0.3895*****	**0.8412****	10.1078***	11.0801***	8.6826*

Table 3: In-Context Learning Experiments: Comparison of 0-SHOT, 1-SHOT, and MESH_GUIDANCE Results. Asterisks denote statistical significance relative to 0-SHOT: * $p < 0.05$, ** $p < 0.01$, *** $p < 0.001$.

	Relevance				Readability		
	R-1	**R-2**	**R-L**	**BERTScore**	**FKGL ↓**	**CLI ↓**	**DCRS ↓**
SINGLE_TURN	0.5003	0.1374	**0.4718**	0.8518	10.6904	10.8585	8.6497
MESH_SINGLE_TURN	**0.5007**	**0.1405**	0.4714	**0.8521**	**10.4605***	**10.7297***	**8.6129**
BERT_MESH_SINGLE_TURN	0.4983	0.1388	0.4695	0.8517	10.5622	10.8195	8.6464

Table 4: Results for the single-turn conversation approach augmented with different sets of MeSH terms (ground truth vs. MeSH classifier) on the eLife test set. Asterisks indicate statistical significance relative to the baseline model without MeSH (* $p < 0.05$)

3 Results and Discussion

3.1 MeSH Prediction as an Auxiliary Task vs. No MeSH

The main results on the test set are presented in Table 2. Both INSTRUCTION_TUNING and INSTRUCTION_MODELING incorporate MeSH term prediction as an auxiliary task within a multi-turn instruction tuning framework. Compared to the baseline approach (SINGLE_TURN), INSTRUCTION_TUNING achieved statistically significant improvements in ROUGE-2 ($p < 0.05$) and all readability metrics ($p < 0.01$). In contrast, INSTRUCTION_MODELING, which trains the model to generate both user inputs (scientific articles) and assistant responses (lay summaries), achieved the highest ROUGE-1 ($p = 0.23$) and ROUGE-L ($p = 0.06$) scores but did not show significant improvements over the baseline approach. Notably, the ROUGE-1 score represents state-of-the-art performance, improving by nearly 2% compared to prior work (which reported results of approximately 0.48–0.49) (Jahan et al., 2024).

In prior assessments on benchmark datasets, although the INSTRUCTION_MODELING approach has proven effective in language understanding tasks, as evidenced by high BLEU scores in benchmarks such as OpenBookQA (Mihaylov et al., 2018) and MMLU (Hendrycks et al., 2020), significance tests indicate that INSTRUCTION_MODELING offers no improvements over INSTRUCTION_TUNING in ROUGE-1 and ROUGE-L, and it even performs significantly worse on readability metrics in CLI ($p < 0.001$).

We also compare training with the full list of ground truth MeSH terms (Experiment INSTRUCTION_TUNING_FULL_LIST) versus a selectively chosen subset as the gold standard (INSTRUCTION_TUNING) in a multi-turn setting. Improvements were observed across all metrics but were not statistically significant.

3.2 Ablation Results

In-context Learning The results without instruction tuning are shown in Table 3. We compared experiments using a basic prompt only (0-

SHOT), incorporating ground truth MeSH terms (MESH_GUIDANCE), or using an exemplar pair of a scientific abstract and lay summary as guidance (1-SHOT). When using MeSH as guidance, all the relevance metrics showed statistically significant improvement over the basic prompt ($p < 0.001$ for ROUGE scores; $p < 0.01$ for BERTScore). However, the readability scores significantly decreased when the user prompt became more complex due to the augmentation with MeSH terms ($p < 0.001$ for FKGL and CLI; $p < 0.05$ for DCRS).Using the most similar example from the training data, which serves as the standard approach in a few-shot learning setting, yielded significant improvements across all ROUGE scores compared to the 0-SHOT setting ($p < 0.001$), also achieving the best DCRS score. Notably, when comparing 1-SHOT and MESH_GUIDANCE, all the ROUGE scores were significantly improved ($p < 0.001$), as well as the BERTScore ($p < 0.01$), but all readability scores decreased ($p < 0.001$ for FKGL and CLI; $p < 0.05$ for DCRS).

When incorporating prompts with MeSH terms, even without any fine-tuning, the model achieves higher lexical overlap and improved semantic alignment with the gold-standard lay summary, suggesting that it can effectively distill useful topical information from these terms.

The Effect of MeSH Term Selection in Single-Turn Instruction Tuning. As shown in Table 4, the SINGLE_TURN experiment, which uses only the abstract as input for instruction tuning, demonstrated less competitive performance than the MESH_SINGLE_TURN experiment, which incorporates ground truth MeSH terms in the prompt and improves results on all metrics except ROUGE-L. When using predicted MeSH terms from a BERT-based classifier (You et al., 2021), BERT_MESH_SINGLE_TURN, the improvement was less pronounced, with only a non-significant increase observed in ROUGE-2 ($p = 0.3$), FKGL ($p = 0.2$), CLI ($p = 0.8$), and DCRS ($p = 0.7$).

We selected the BERT-based MeSH classifier for its strong performance and ease of implementation, providing a reliable baseline for comparison. While using a more recent model could have yielded slightly better results, it is unlikely to reach the performance achieved with ground truth terms. Although the improvements with machine-generated MeSH terms were not statistically significant, they suggest potential for applying our method to articles without ground truth MeSH terms. With further refinement of MeSH prediction models and more sophisticated term selection strategies, this approach could be extended to biomedical literature beyond PubMed.

The Effectiveness of Incorporating MeSH in Multi-Turn Conversations vs. Single-Turn Approach. Comparing the MESH_SINGLE_TURN approach in Table 4 with the multi-turn instruction tuning experiments in Table 2, INSTRUCTION_TUNING, which was fine-tuned on a selectively chosen subset of MeSH terms, demonstrated improvements across all metrics. This is likely due to two key factors: (1) iterative interactions, where the second-turn summary generation builds upon the previously predicted MeSH terms, allowing the model to engage in a step-by-step reasoning process that mirrors the chain-of-thought strategy, and (2) improved calibration of MeSH term selection during fine-tuning, which ensures that a more focused subset of gold standard MeSH terms are incorporated into the generation process.

Overall, we observed performance gains by incorporating MeSH terms in both in-context learning and PEFT settings, including single-turn and multi-turn approaches. Our results suggest that MeSH terms can serve as an effective proxy for guiding the LLM in generating coherent, relevant, and readable lay summaries with essential background explanations. Moreover, the fact that the most significant improvement is more pronounced in a simpler, training-free setting (see Table 3) motivates the development of a more sophisticated method for selecting gold-standard MeSH terms as an auxiliary task during multi-turn instruction tuning, which could further improve the quality of lay summary generation.

3.3 Performance on the held-out evaluation set

LLMs are often pretrained on vast datasets. If the test set overlaps with pretraining data, the model might perform well due to memorization rather than generalization. To fairly and accurately evaluate the effectiveness of our approach, we further investigate whether the fine-tuned summarizer can achieve comparable results when applied to a held-out dataset consisting of articles published after the release date of *LLaMA-3.2-3B-Instruct*.

As shown in Table 5, the best performance was achieved in Experiment INSTRUCTION_TUNING, the multi-turn approach with instruction tuning, yielding results that closely align with the

	Relevance				Readability		
	R-1	**R-2**	**R-L**	**BERTScore**	**FKGL ↓**	**CLI ↓**	**DCRS ↓**
INSTRUCTION_TUNING	**0.4954**	**0.1346**	**0.4580**	**0.8550**	**10.4887**	**10.8483**	**8.6276**
INSTRUCTION_MODELING	0.4863	0.1273	0.4508	0.8537	10.8408	11.1756	8.7201
SINGLE_TURN	0.4843	0.1237	0.4466	0.8521	10.8084	11.0800	8.7638
MESH_SINGLE_TURN	0.4876	0.1270	0.4501	0.8526	10.6718	10.8514	8.7322

Table 5: Held out evaluation results for relevance and readability. ↓ denotes the scores that need to be minimized for those metrics.

test data. This suggests that the model is not simply memorizing the training data from pre-training stage. However, a pronounced decrease in all ROUGE scores and readability metrics was observed in Experiments SINGLE_TURN and MESH_SINGLE_TURN on the held-out dataset compared to the test set. These findings indicate that multi-turn conversation instruction-tuning, with MeSH generation as an auxiliary task, ensures better generalizability to unseen data than other approaches.

4 Qualitative Analysis

Tables 6 and 7 in the Appendix compare the generated summaries across different experimental settings. In this example, Experiment INSTRUCTION_TUNING achieved the best relevance score, followed by Experiment INSTRUCTION_MODELING and Experiment MESH_SINGLE_TURN. Notably, in the abstract, the first sentence begins with the study design of the approach, whereas the gold standard lay summary includes additional sentences introducing the importance of the topic, the symptoms of the disease, and the current research gap, which are highlighted in different colors. Both multi-turn conversation approaches closely follow the same information flow and context as the gold standard. They also state the method precisely as conveyed in the abstract's first sentence. The SINGLE_TURN approach contained more technical jargon, which is harder for laypeople to understand, and lacked sufficient background information.

5 Related Work

Current research in biomedical plain language summarization focuses on two main subtasks: text simplification and explanation and background generation. Text simplification involves linguistic transformations, such as rewording and replacing biomedical terminology with less technical terms, to make content more accessible (Attal et al., 2023; Devaraj et al., 2021). On the other hand, explanation and background information generation leverage external knowledge to enhance the informativeness of summaries (Guo et al., 2024).

Two main model architectures are commonly used for plain language summarization: encoder-decoder models (e.g., T5 (Raffel et al., 2020), BART (Lewis, 2019), Longformer (Beltagy et al., 2020)) and generative models such as the GPT family (Radford et al., 2019) and LLaMA (Touvron et al., 2023). Generative LLMs have demonstrated strong zero-shot and few-shot summarization capabilities, producing coherent and relevant text from demonstrations alone, without the need for fine-tuning or parameter updates (Zhao et al., 2024).

While LLMs are inherently capable of following natural language instructions, instruction-tuned models, such as Flan-T5 (Chung et al., 2024), demonstrate improved generalization to unseen tasks. This fine-tuning allows LLMs to better understand and respond to user requests, enhancing both zero-shot and few-shot learning capabilities. PEFT techniques have been developed to address the challenges posed by the growing number of trainable parameters in LLMs (Xu et al., 2023).

6 Conclusion

In this study, we aimed to improve the biomedical lay summarization of scientific publications by augmenting article text with MeSH terms. We introduced a novel method for integrating this knowledge into a generative LLM, providing guidance for background information generation through a multi-turn conversation. Our results demonstrated that MeSH terms offer a broader perspective on the content of a biomedical article, helping the model generate more focused and relevant background information specific to the article's topic.

7 Limitations

First, due to computational costs and memory limitations, we used only the abstract as input and tested our experimental design on a single dataset. Second, we evaluated performance based on relevance and readability metrics, as there is a lack of satisfactory evaluation for faithfulness that aligns well with human preferences, as revealed in previous studies (Fang et al., 2024). Although incorporating MeSH generation as an auxiliary task led to some improvements, its performance was not statistically significant different from the SINGLE_TURN approach. However, ablation studies indicate that MeSH selection plays a crucial role in guiding lay summary generation. In future work, we aim to further enhance its effectiveness by integrating it into the learning process with automatic feedback. Moving forward, we plan to conduct human evaluations to better assess how well model-generated summaries align with human judgments. Additionally, we will explore both closed- and open-source LLMs to evaluate the generalizability of our approach across different models.

Acknowledgement

This work is partially supported by the National Library of Medicine (NLM) of the National Institutes of Health under the award number R01LM014292.

References

Kush Attal, Brian Ondov, and Dina Demner-Fushman. 2023. A dataset for plain language adaptation of biomedical abstracts. *Scientific Data*, 10(1):8.

Tal August, Lucy Lu Wang, Jonathan Bragg, Marti A Hearst, Andrew Head, and Kyle Lo. 2023. Paper plain: Making medical research papers approachable to healthcare consumers with natural language processing. *ACM Transactions on Computer-Human Interaction*, 30(5):1–38.

Iz Beltagy, Matthew E Peters, and Arman Cohan. 2020. Longformer: The long-document transformer. *arXiv preprint arXiv:2004.05150*.

Xiuying Chen, Tairan Wang, Qingqing Zhu, Taicheng Guo, Shen Gao, Zhiyong Lu, Xin Gao, and Xiangliang Zhang. 2024. Rethinking scientific summarization evaluation: Grounding explainable metrics on facet-aware benchmark. *arXiv preprint arXiv:2402.14359*.

Hyung Won Chung, Le Hou, Shayne Longpre, Barret Zoph, Yi Tay, William Fedus, Yunxuan Li, Xuezhi Wang, Mostafa Dehghani, Siddhartha Brahma, et al. 2024. Scaling instruction-finetuned language models. *Journal of Machine Learning Research*, 25(70):1–53.

Meri Coleman and Ta Lin Liau. 1975. A computer readability formula designed for machine scoring. *Journal of Applied Psychology*, 60(2):283.

Edgar Dale and Jeanne S Chall. 1948. A formula for predicting readability: Instructions. *Educational research bulletin*, pages 37–54.

Ashwin Devaraj, Iain Marshall, Byron C Wallace, and Junyi Jessy Li. 2021. Paragraph-level simplification of medical texts. In *Proceedings of the 2021 Conference of the North American Chapter of the Association for Computational Linguistics: Human Language Technologies*, pages 4972–4984.

Abhimanyu Dubey, Abhinav Jauhri, Abhinav Pandey, Abhishek Kadian, Ahmad Al-Dahle, Aiesha Letman, Akhil Mathur, Alan Schelten, Amy Yang, Angela Fan, et al. 2024. The LLaMA 3 herd of models. *arXiv preprint arXiv:2407.21783*.

Biaoyan Fang, Xiang Dai, and Sarvnaz Karimi. 2024. Understanding faithfulness and reasoning of large language models on plain biomedical summaries. In *Findings of the Association for Computational Linguistics: EMNLP 2024*, pages 9890–9911.

Marcio Fonseca and Shay Cohen. 2024. Can large language model summarizers adapt to diverse scientific communication goals? In *Findings of the Association for Computational Linguistics: ACL 2024*, pages 8599–8618, Bangkok, Thailand. Association for Computational Linguistics.

Tianyu Gao, Xingcheng Yao, and Danqi Chen. 2021. SimCSE: Simple contrastive learning of sentence embeddings. In *Proceedings of the 2021 Conference on Empirical Methods in Natural Language Processing*, pages 6894–6910, Online and Punta Cana, Dominican Republic. Association for Computational Linguistics.

Tomas Goldsack, Carolina Scarton, and Chenghua Lin. 2025. Leveraging large language models for zero-shot lay summarisation in biomedicine and beyond. *arXiv preprint arXiv:2501.05224*.

Tomas Goldsack, Zhihao Zhang, Chenghua Lin, and Carolina Scarton. 2022. Making science simple: Corpora for the lay summarisation of scientific literature. In *Proceedings of the 2022 Conference on Empirical Methods in Natural Language Processing*, pages 10589–10604, Abu Dhabi, United Arab Emirates. Association for Computational Linguistics.

Tomas Goldsack, Zhihao Zhang, Chen Tang, Carolina Scarton, and Chenghua Lin. 2023. Enhancing biomedical lay summarisation with external knowledge graphs. In *Proceedings of the 2023 Conference on Empirical Methods in Natural Language Processing*, pages 8016–8032.

Sylvain Gugger, Lysandre Debut, Thomas Wolf, Philipp Schmid, Zachary Mueller, Sourab Mangrulkar, Marc Sun, and Benjamin Bossan. 2022. Accelerate: Training and inference at scale made simple, efficient and adaptable. `https://github.com/huggingface/accelerate`.

Yue Guo, Wei Qiu, Gondy Leroy, Sheng Wang, and Trevor Cohen. 2024. Retrieval augmentation of large language models for lay language generation. *Journal of Biomedical Informatics*, 149:104580.

Junxian He, Wojciech Kryściński, Bryan McCann, Nazneen Rajani, and Caiming Xiong. 2022. Ctrlsum: Towards generic controllable text summarization. In *Proceedings of the 2022 Conference on Empirical Methods in Natural Language Processing*, pages 5879–5915.

Dan Hendrycks, Collin Burns, Steven Basart, Andy Zou, Mantas Mazeika, Dawn Song, and Jacob Steinhardt. 2020. Measuring massive multitask language understanding. *arXiv preprint arXiv:2009.03300*.

Edward J Hu, Yelong Shen, Phillip Wallis, Zeyuan Allen-Zhu, Yuanzhi Li, Shean Wang, Lu Wang, and Weizhu Chen. 2021. Lora: Low-rank adaptation of large language models. *arXiv preprint arXiv:2106.09685*.

Israt Jahan, Md Tahmid Rahman Laskar, Chun Peng, and Jimmy Xiangji Huang. 2024. A comprehensive evaluation of large language models on benchmark biomedical text processing tasks. *Computers in biology and medicine*, 171:108189.

J Peter Kincaid, Robert P Fishburne Jr, Richard L Rogers, and Brad S Chissom. 1975. Derivation of new readability formulas (automated readability index, fog count and flesch reading ease formula) for navy enlisted personnel. *Fog Count and Flesch Reading Ease Formula) for Navy Enlisted Personnel: Inst Sim Trng*.

Philippe Laban, Tobias Schnabel, Paul N Bennett, and Marti A Hearst. 2022. Summac: Re-visiting nli-based models for inconsistency detection in summarization. *Transactions of the Association for Computational Linguistics*, 10:163–177.

M Lewis. 2019. Bart: Denoising sequence-to-sequence pre-training for natural language generation, translation, and comprehension. *arXiv preprint arXiv:1910.13461*.

Chin-Yew Lin. 2004. Rouge: A package for automatic evaluation of summaries. In *Text summarization branches out*, pages 74–81.

Alexa T McCray, Anita Burgun, and Olivier Bodenreider. 2001. Aggregating umls semantic types for reducing conceptual complexity. In *MEDINFO 2001*, pages 216–220. IOS Press.

Todor Mihaylov, Peter Clark, Tushar Khot, and Ashish Sabharwal. 2018. Can a suit of armor conduct electricity? a new dataset for open book question answering. *arXiv preprint arXiv:1809.02789*.

Alec Radford, Jeffrey Wu, Rewon Child, David Luan, Dario Amodei, Ilya Sutskever, et al. 2019. Language models are unsupervised multitask learners. *OpenAI blog*, 1(8):9.

Colin Raffel, Noam Shazeer, Adam Roberts, Katherine Lee, Sharan Narang, Michael Matena, Yanqi Zhou, Wei Li, and Peter J Liu. 2020. Exploring the limits of transfer learning with a unified text-to-text transformer. *Journal of machine learning research*, 21(140):1–67.

Sanjana Ramprasad and Byron C Wallace. 2024. Do automatic factuality metrics measure factuality? a critical evaluation. *arXiv preprint arXiv:2411.16638*.

Jeff Rasley, Samyam Rajbhandari, Olatunji Ruwase, and Yuxiong He. 2020. Deepspeed: System optimizations enable training deep learning models with over 100 billion parameters. In *Proceedings of the 26th ACM SIGKDD International Conference on Knowledge Discovery & Data Mining*, pages 3505–3506.

Zhengyan Shi, Adam X Yang, Bin Wu, Laurence Aitchison, Emine Yilmaz, and Aldo Lipani. 2024. Instruction tuning with loss over instructions. *arXiv preprint arXiv:2405.14394*.

Liyan Tang, Tanya Goyal, Alexander R Fabbri, Philippe Laban, Jiacheng Xu, Semih Yavuz, Wojciech Kryściński, Justin F Rousseau, and Greg Durrett. 2022. Understanding factual errors in summarization: Errors, summarizers, datasets, error detectors. *arXiv preprint arXiv:2205.12854*.

Hugo Touvron, Thibaut Lavril, Gautier Izacard, Xavier Martinet, Marie-Anne Lachaux, Timothée Lacroix, Baptiste Rozière, Naman Goyal, Eric Hambro, Faisal Azhar, et al. 2023. Llama: Open and efficient foundation language models. *arXiv preprint arXiv:2302.13971*.

Dave Van Veen, Cara Van Uden, Louis Blankemeier, Jean-Benoit Delbrouck, Asad Aali, Christian Bluethgen, Anuj Pareek, Malgorzata Polacin, Eduardo Pontes Reis, Anna Seehofnerová, et al. 2024. Adapted large language models can outperform medical experts in clinical text summarization. *Nature medicine*, 30(4):1134–1142.

Robert F Woolson. 2005. Wilcoxon signed-rank test. *Encyclopedia of Biostatistics*, 8.

Lingling Xu, Haoran Xie, Si-Zhao Joe Qin, Xiaohui Tao, and Fu Lee Wang. 2023. Parameter-efficient fine-tuning methods for pretrained language models: A critical review and assessment. *arXiv preprint arXiv:2312.12148*.

Ronghui You, Yuxuan Liu, Hiroshi Mamitsuka, and Shanfeng Zhu. 2021. BERTMeSH: deep contextual representation learning for large-scale high-performance MeSH indexing with full text. *Bioinformatics*, 37(5):684–692.

Zhiwen You, Shruthan Radhakrishna, Shufan Ming, and Halil Kilicoglu. 2024. UIUC_BioNLP at BioLaySumm: An extract-then-summarize approach augmented with Wikipedia knowledge for biomedical lay summarization. In *Proceedings of the 23rd Workshop on Biomedical Natural Language Processing*, pages 132–143, Bangkok, Thailand. Association for Computational Linguistics.

Yuheng Zha, Yichi Yang, Ruichen Li, and Zhiting Hu. 2023. Alignscore: Evaluating factual consistency with a unified alignment function. In *Proceedings of the 61st Annual Meeting of the Association for Computational Linguistics (Volume 1: Long Papers)*, pages 11328–11348.

Tianyi Zhang, Varsha Kishore, Felix Wu, Kilian Q Weinberger, and Yoav Artzi. 2019. Bertscore: Evaluating text generation with bert. In *International Conference on Learning Representations*.

Xingmeng Zhao, Tongnian Wang, and Anthony Rios. 2024. Improving expert radiology report summarization by prompting large language models with a layperson summary. *arXiv preprint arXiv:2406.14500*.

Gold Standard: Although Parkinson's disease is the second most common neurodegenerative disorder, its cause is not known and there is no cure. The symptoms of Parkinson's disease, which include tremor and slowing of voluntary movements, get progressively worse over time. The numbers of neurons in certain brain regions also decrease, causing those parts of the brain to shrink; this is known as "atrophy". However, no conclusive signs of atrophy have been found in the brains of people in the early stages of the disease. One theory suggests that Parkinson's disease is caused by a toxic protein that is able to spread from neuron to neuron. Recent advances in brain imaging have made it possible to map networks in the living human brain—the so-called brain connectome. These networks could form the 'highways' through which a disease-causing agent might spread. The Parkinson's Progression Markers Initiative (PPMI) is a large study that collects data from hundreds of people in an effort to identify the causes of Parkinson's disease. Zeighami et al. have now analyzed MRI scans that were collected as part of this initiative, which show the structure of the brains of 230 people in the early stages of Parkinson's disease. Comparing these scans to those from age-matched healthy individuals allowed Zeighami et al. to identify the set of brain regions that show atrophy in the early stages of Parkinson's disease. These regions correspond to a normal brain network, and the relative extent of atrophy in each brain region supports the theory that the disease spreads through the connectome. The patients who were enrolled in this study will continue to be evaluated on a yearly basis. Zeighami et al. plan to continue mapping how the disease progresses throughout the brain and to relate this to the development of new symptoms of Parkinson's disease.
Abstract: We mapped the distribution of atrophy in Parkinson's disease (PD) using magnetic resonance imaging (MRI) and clinical data from 232 PD patients and 117 controls from the Parkinson's Progression Markers Initiative. Deformation-based morphometry and independent component analysis identified PD-specific atrophy in the midbrain, basal ganglia, basal forebrain, medial temporal lobe, and discrete cortical regions. The degree of atrophy reflected clinical measures of disease severity. The spatial pattern of atrophy demonstrated overlap with intrinsic networks present in healthy brain, as derived from functional MRI. Moreover, the degree of atrophy in each brain region reflected its functional and anatomical proximity to a presumed disease epicenter in the substantia nigra, compatible with a trans-neuronal spread of the disease. These results support a network-spread mechanism in PD. Finally, the atrophy pattern in PD was also seen in healthy aging, where it also correlated with the loss of striatal dopaminergic innervation.
INSTRUCTION_TUNING Parkinson's disease is a neurodegenerative disorder that affects millions of people around the world. It is characterized by the progressive loss of dopamine-producing neurons in the brain, which leads to symptoms such as tremors, rigidity, and difficulty with movement. However, it is not clear how the disease starts or how it spreads through the brain. One theory is that Parkinson's disease begins in a region of the brain called the substantianigra, which is responsible for producing dopamine. From there, the disease may spread to other brain regions via a network of nerve fibers. To better understand how Parkinson's spreads, researchers studied the brains of 232 patients with the disease and compared them to 117 healthy individuals. The brains of the patients were imaged using a technique called MRI, which allows researchers to measure the volume of different brain regions. This revealed that patients with Parkinson's had more atrophy than healthy individuals in several brain regions, including those involved in movement, emotion, and memory. Furthermore, the extent of this atrophy was related to the severity of the symptoms experienced by the patients. The brain regions affected by Parkinson's were also found to be connected to each other via nerve fibers, which supports the theory that the disease spreads through a network. The study also found that the pattern of brain atrophy seen in Parkinson's patients was similar to that seen in older adults without the disease, suggesting that age-related changes may also contribute to the development of Parkinson's. Overall, the findings of this study provide new insights into the mechanisms underlying Parkinson's, and may help researchers to develop new treatments for the disease in the future.

Table 6: Comparison of experiments. The text highlighted in the same color conveys the same information.

INSTRUCTION_MODELING	Parkinson's disease is a neurodegenerative disorder that affects millions of people around the world. It is characterized by the progressive loss of dopamine-producing neurons in the brain, which leads to symptoms such as tremors, stiffness and difficulty with movement. The disease is caused by the accumulation of abnormal protein clumps, known as Lewy bodies, in the cells of the brain. However, it is not clear how these clumps lead to the death of brain cells, or how they cause the symptoms of Parkinson's disease. One theory is that the clumps disrupt the connections between different brain regions, leading to a loss of communication between them. This theory is supported by the fact that some brain regions are more affected than others in Parkinson's patients. For example, the brain region known as the 'basal ganglia', which is involved in movement control, is one of the first regions to be affected by the disease, while other regions such as the hippocampus and the amygdala, which are involved in memory and emotion, are later affected. To better understand how the disease affects the brain and to develop new treatments, researchers need to map the extent of brain damage in patients with Parkinson's. One way to do this is to use a technique called MRI, which uses magnetic fields and radio waves to create detailed images of the inside of the body. Using this technique, a team of researchers has now mapped the amount of damage to the brain in over 350 patients and healthy individuals. The results show that the extent and location of the damage vary greatly from person to person, and that the brain regions that are most affected are those that are farthest from the area of brain where the disease is thought to start. This suggests that the disease spreads through the brain via a network of interconnected regions, rather than through a single pathway. The next step will be to investigate whether the same pattern of damage is seen in people who are at risk of developing Parkinson's, but have not yet been diagnosed.
SINGLE_TURN	The human brain is made up of billions of neurons that communicate with each other through electrical and chemical signals. In Parkinson's disease, a protein called alpha-synuclein clumps together and forms abnormal structures called Lewy bodies, which are toxic to neurons. This leads to the death of many neurons in areas of the brain that control movement, leading to symptoms such as tremors, stiffness and slowness of movement. However, it is not clear how the disease affects the brain, or which areas are most affected. To address this question, researchers from the University of California, Los Angeles (UCLA) and the National Institute of Neurological Disorders and Stroke (NINDS) used a technique called diffusion tensor imaging (DTI) to map the structure of the brains of 232 people with Parkinson's, as well as 117 people who did not have the condition. The DTI scans showed that the brains affected by Parkinson's were smaller than those of people without the disease, and that the extent of this shrinkage was related to the severity of the symptoms. The researchers also found that the brain areas that were most affected by the disease were those that are most connected to each other, suggesting that the disease may spread from one area to another. Furthermore, the patterns of brain shrinkage seen in Parkinson's patients were similar to those seen in people who are aging normally. This suggests that the changes in brain structure that occur with aging may also contribute to the development of Parkinson's. The next step will be to use these findings to develop new treatments for Parkinson's that can target the specific brain regions that are affected.
MESH_SINGLE_TURN	The human brain is made up of billions of neurons that communicate with each other through electrical and chemical signals. Parkinson's disease is a neurodegenerative disorder that affects millions of people worldwide. It is characterized by the progressive loss of dopamine-producing neurons in the brain, which leads to symptoms such as tremors, rigidity, and difficulty with movement. However, it is not clear how these neurons are affected by the disease, or how their loss leads to the symptoms that people with Parkinson's experience. To address this question, researchers from the University of California, Los Angeles (UCLA) used a technique called MRI to scan the brains of 232 people who had Parkinson's, as well as 117 people who did not have the condition. The scans were then analyzed to identify areas of the brain that were affected by Parkinson's. The results showed that the disease causes atrophy – or shrinkage – in several brain regions, including the basal ganglii, the basal fore-brain, the medial temporal lobes, and specific regions of the cortex. The extent of the shrinkage in each of these brain regions was related to the severity of the symptoms experienced by the patients. Furthermore, the regions that were most severely affected were those that are closest to the brain region known to be damaged in Parkinson's: the substantian nigra. These findings suggest that Parkinson's may be caused by a network of interconnected brain regions that are damaged as the disease progresses. The next step will be to investigate whether the same pattern of brain atrophy is seen in people who do not have Parkinson's but are aging.

Table 7: Continued from Table 6

A Preliminary Study on NLP-Based Personalized Support for Type 1 Diabetes Management

Sandra Mitrović[1], Federico Fontana[2], Andrea Zignoli[2,3], Felipe Mattioni Maturana[2,4], Christian Berchtold[1], Daniele Malpetti[1], Sam Scott[2], Laura Azzimonti[1]
[1]Istituto Dalle Molle di Studi sull'Intelligenza Artificiale (IDSIA), SUPSI, Switzerland
[2]Sestante Analytics AG, Switzerland
[3]Department of Industrial Engineering, University of Trento, Italy
[4]Department of Sports Medicine, University Hospital of Tübingen, Germany
Correspondence: sandra.mitrovic@supsi.ch

Abstract

The proliferation of wearable devices and sports monitoring apps has made tracking physical activity more accessible than ever. For individuals with Type 1 diabetes, regular exercise is essential for managing the condition, making personalized feedback particularly valuable. By leveraging data from physical activity sessions, NLP-generated messages can offer tailored guidance to help users optimize their workouts and make informed decisions. In this study, we assess several open-source pretrained NLP models for this purpose. Contrary to expectations, our findings reveal that models fine-tuned on medical data or excelling in medical benchmarks do not necessarily produce high-quality messages.

1 Introduction

Type 1 diabetes (T1D) is an autoimmune disease in which the immune system attacks the pancreatic cells responsible for producing insulin, a hormone essential for regulating blood glucose levels. Without insulin, cells cannot absorb glucose, leading to potentially life-threatening consequences if not externally managed (NIH). Physical activity plays a crucial role in managing T1D, as it enhances insulin sensitivity, helps regulate blood glucose levels, and promotes overall health (Colberg et al., 2016). However, exercise must be carefully managed, as improper glucose regulation during physical activity can result in hypoglycemia (low blood glucose) or hyperglycemia (high blood glucose), both of which pose significant health risks.

Our study leverages data from wearable devices and insulin monitoring, together with domain expert inputs, to develop a Natural Language Processing (NLP)-based approach that generates personalized messages based on an individual's physical activity history. These messages, delivered after each activity session, help individuals adjust their behavior to minimize the risk of excessive glucose fluctuations. This work serves as a proof of concept for the feasibility of using personalized NLP-driven messages in diabetes management, with the ultimate goal of driving behavior change.

In this article, we primarily focus on the message generation aspect of our work, evaluating several open-source models by assessing the quality of their generated messages and benchmarking them against expert-written text. The choice of open-source models was driven by our goal to integrate our approach into an app that prioritizes user privacy and transparency.

Related work Several studies have explored integrating wearable sensor data with NLP approaches, using data from various sources, including physiological and motion sensors (Ferrara, 2024), as well as smartphone, self-reported (e.g., survey responses) (Li et al., 2024a) and voice-assistant data (Li et al., 2024b). One notable example is PH-LLM (Cosentino et al., 2024), which introduces a fine-tuned large language model (LLM) based on Gemini, designed to interpret and reason over physiological data. Another example is PhysioLLM (Fang et al., 2024), which focuses on sleep monitoring by leveraging GPT-4-turbo. It enables users to analyze their sleep patterns and their impact on health, providing insights in the form of correlations and trends.

2 Problem and dataset description

Our aim was to generate short advice messages to be shown to app users at the end of a workout, to help them stay within normal glucose levels (70-180 mg/dL) during future workouts.

We broadly categorized workouts into two types: negative-*outcome* (i.e., the individual's glucose level went out of range, further subdivided into hypo- and hyperglycemia) and positive-*outcome* ones (i.e., the individual's glucose level remained within the range). Negative-*outcome* workouts re-

Proceedings of the Second Workshop on Patient-Oriented Language Processing (CL4Health), pages 298–302
May 4, 2025

Outcome	Behavioral Pattern	Expert-provided Information	Ideal Response	Mistral Model	Hermes Model
negative (hypo-glycemia)	You spent 18 minutes below 70 mg/dL during this workout.	Prolonged periods of hypoglycemia can lead to fatigue and potentially dangerous low glucose levels. Consider adjusting your carbohydrate intake before and during exercise.	To prevent hypoglycemia, consume 10–30 g of carbs before exercise if glucose is below 120–140 mg/dL, trending downward, or if active insulin is high. Adjust insulin in advance and monitor glucose regularly. Use fast-acting carbs during workouts if levels drop below 140 mg/dL.	To prevent prolonged hypoglycemia during exercise, consider extending your pre-workout carbohydrate intake and consume small, frequent carbohydrate snacks during your workout. **Start your sessions later** in the day to minimize the impact on your glucose levels.	In order to prevent hypoglycemia during your next workout, consider adjusting your carbohydrate intake prior to the session. As the start hour has no effect, focus on consuming carbs 18 minutes before the workout to help maintain normal glucose levels throughout the physical activity. Monitor your glucose levels closely and adjust your diet accordingly to ensure you stay within the normal range during exercise.

Table 1: An example of a hypo-glycemia scenario "Time spent <70mg/dL". To the right: models output for best actionable insights prompt with (0,0,1) (start time should increase). Color coding: black-action, red-hallucination, violet-nutrition (carbs), blue-insulin, green-monitoring, grey-specific quantity.

quire a behavior change, and messages should advise the individual on how to adjust. Conversely, if the *outcome* is positive, the individual should be encouraged to maintain their current behavior.

As such, we used a more detailed characterization of workouts, referred to as *behavioral patterns* (i.e., a more precise description of the out-of-range behavior selected from a pre-defined set of possibilities). Each behavioral pattern was accompanied by additional *expert-provided information*. We refer to the combination of *behavioral pattern* and *expert-provided information* as *observable insight*. An example of an *observable insight* is shown in the second and the third column of Table 1.

We considered a total of 17 different *observable-insight* scenarios: 13 with negative outcomes and 4 with positive outcomes. For 11 of the negative-outcome scenarios, we were also provided with the *ideal responses* generated by domain experts, which we used in our study as the ground truth.

In addition, we trained a machine learning model that also considered the activity history of the individual[1] to provide information on whether (and if so, how) changing their behavior with respect to at least one *actionable* variable could help the individual stay within the normal glucose range. Session intensity, duration, and start time were selected as the three *actionable* variables since they have easily interpretable meaning and are fully under the person's control. We refer to the outcomes of the ML model as *actionable insights*.

[1]Details about the model are not reported here due to space constraints and the focus on NLP methods.

3 Methodology

Model choice Given our commitment to using open-source models, we focused exclusively on these, excluding popular options like GPT-3.5 and GPT-4. Additionally, due to the limited size of the dataset available to us, fine-tuning was not a viable option, which further influenced our model selection process. The open-source models we considered are listed in Table 2.

Framework design We based our methodology on prompting (Brown et al., 2020) the open-source NLP models using different (types of) prompts in order to generate personalized user-friendly messages based on the aforementioned *insights*. Furthermore, as additional external knowledge from T1D experts (see *expert knowledge* in Table 1) was available, instead of relying solely on the pre-trained knowledge, we used that knowledge as additional information to enhance message generation. In other words, we simulated[2] Retrieval Augmented Generation (RAG) (Lewis et al., 2020) by extending our designed prompts with the related expert knowledge as the relevant *context*.

Prompt types We designed two types of prompts: one that receives only *observable insights*, and another that on top of these includes *actionable insights*. In the first iteration, we evaluated a wide range of models using the *observable-insight*

[2]We opted for not implementing a separate retrieval component for a RAG system as the additional inputs are too short and our dataset is too small to justify it.

Model (Owner)	Motivation
Starling-LM-7B-beta (Nexusflow)	FT; OML
gemma-2-2b-it (Google)	instruct FT; OML
Mistral-7B-Instruct-v0.3 (MistralAI)	instruct FT; OML
Hermes-2-Pro-Mistral-7B (NousResearch)	FT; OML
JSL-MedPhi2-2.7B (John Snow Labs)	FT on medical data
Llama-3.2-3B-Instruct (Meta)	instruct FT
falcon-7b-instruct (TII)	chat/instruct FT

Table 2: List of the open-source models and motivation for choosing them. "FT" stands for fine-tuned, while "OML" denotes the model's high-rank (among top-4) at The Open Medical-LLM Leaderboard (Pal et al., 2024).

prompt type. The rationale was that models performing poorly on simpler prompts should not be considered for more complex ones. Following the initial selection, we introduced the second type of prompt (*full-insight*), which also includes *actionable insights*. For example, in the scenario from Table 1, the desirable behavior might involve providing suggestions on how the user should adjust their activity to avoid hypoglycemia, such as reducing workout intensity. We encoded actionable insights from our ML model as a three-dimensional vector, with dimensions corresponding to session intensity, duration, and start hour, respectively. Each dimension can take one of three values (0, -1, 1), where 0 denotes no effect on glucose level (hence no action required), -1 denotes that the variable should be decreased to reduce out-of-range risk, while +1 denotes that the variable should be increased for the same purpose. A well-performing model should be able to incorporate this information and generate a corresponding message. Both *observable-* and *full-insight* prompts were then iteratively refined based on the evaluation criteria described below.

Evaluation We evaluated the generated messages both qualitatively and quantitatively. The qualitative analysis focused on prompt adherence, correctness, level of detail, emotional tone, and medical content comprehension. Quantitative analysis was feasible only for *observable-insight* prompts, where ground truth allowed comparison by measuring semantic similarity between generated messages and expert-provided ideal responses.

4 Results

Qualitative analysis The formulation of the initial *observable-insight* prompt (P) can be seen in Figure 1. We found that many models have difficulty adhering to this prompt. Besides *Gemma*, that had different problems (see examples 1 & 2 in Table 3), *Starling-LM* and *JSL-MedPhi2* consistently generated overly long responses (here omitted in the interest of space). The same issue was often also observed with *Falcon*. Even more importantly, *JSL-MedPhi2* frequently exhibited undesired behavior: after a paragraph it would either start repeating itself or encounter hallucination issues.

Examples 3-5 in Table 3 illustrate other issues which do not necessarily stem from not adhering to the prompt, but nevertheless were judged by experts as inappropriate. We, therefore, implemented an iterative-refinement strategy in order to: 1) reduce emotional expressiveness (denoted as: P_e) and avoid giving medical advices (P_m); 2) focus on the observed behavioral pattern (P_f); 3) enforce

> **Initial *observable-insight* prompt (*P*):** "You will be provided with an observed PATTERN in a physical activity session of a person with a T1 diabetes condition. You are supposed to generate a 15-20 words long ADVICE related to the observed pattern that can help the person to stay within normal glucose levels. You should also incorporate the given CONTEXT."
>
> **Best *full-insight* prompt:** "You will be provided with an observed PATTERN in a physical activity session of a person with a T1 diabetes condition which leads to a particular EFFECT in person's glucose level. The PATTERN is a three-dimensional vector where the first component refers to session intensity, the second component refers to session duration and the third component refers to session's start hour. Each of the three components can take exactly one of the values -1, 0 or 1. Value 0 denotes that i-th component has no effect at all on person's glucose level and as such it is not relevant for the advice. Non-zero value on i-th position denotes that the i-th component has negative effect on person's glucose level and is very relevant for the advice. Value -1 on i-th position denotes that decrease in the i-th component would make person stay within the normal glucose levels. Value 1 on i-th position instead denotes that increase in the i-th component would make person stay within the normal glucose levels. You are supposed to generate a 15-20 words long ADVICE leveraging the observed PATTERN and the given CONTEXT to help the person stay within normal glucose levels, commenting only on those particular components that have an effect on the patient glucose levels in the given case. Make sure to take into account glucose level when giving the advice and not to mix recommendations for hypoglycemia (glucose level below 55 mg/dL) with those for hyperglycemia (glucose level above 180 mg/dL). Keep a professional tone and focus more on prevention that can be done prior and/or during the workout instead of giving a precise medical advice. PATTERN: (X,Y,Z)."

Figure 1: Examples of prompts. In the second one, (X,Y,Z) is the 3-dimensional output of the ML model. Moreover, the underlined parts are shared with the best-performing *observable-insight* prompts.

Ex.	Scenario	Model	Response	Problem/Experts comment
1	Time spent below 55 mg/dL	Gemma	"Increase carbohydrate intake before and during exercise to avoid prolonged hypoglycemia."	Not adhering to prompt (length)
2	Time spent above 250 mg/dL (if workout >2h in duration)	Gemma	"Monitor your glucose closely and adjust insulin as needed to stay within target range."	Lack of necessary detail, too general and ignoring context (expert input)
3	Time spent above 250 mg/dL (if workout >2h in duration)	Llama	"Reassess insulin strategy and carbohydrate intake to prevent glucose spikes, aiming for a 5-10% increase in daily insulin doses."	Wrong type of response: providing medical advice instead of general well-being recommendations
4	Time spent below 55 mg/dL	Mistral Llama Gemma	"Immediately consume fast-acting..." "Consume ... within the next 5 minutes" "Consume ... carbs immediately"	Time aspect ("immediately" or "within the next 5 minutes")
5	Glucose variability <36% during exercise	Gemma	"Keep up the good work! Your consistent glucose management is key to optimal performance."	A bit too much excessive emotional expressiveness.

Table 3: Examples illustrating some of the challenges with generated responses using the initial *observable-insight* prompt (P) with different NLP models.

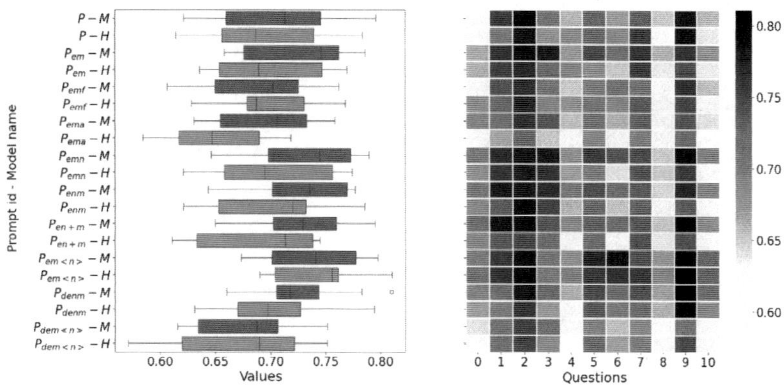

Figure 2: Similarity scores for each *observable-insight* prompt and model combination. To the left: boxplots per prompt-model combination over 11 questions, to the right: heatmap with a refined view on a question level.

generation of concrete actions instead of vague suggestions (P_a); 4) incorporate sports nutrition guidelines (short form: P_n, more elaborate: P_{n+}, explicitly adding a summary of sports nutrition guidelines to the context: $P_{<n>}$); 5) differentiate between hypo-/hyper-glycemia in responses (P_d).

Based on the expert feedback, we shortlisted *Mistral* and *Hermes* (which uses a previous version of *Mistral* as a base model) to conclude our experiments and explore *full-insight* prompts. Among these, the best performance was obtained with the prompt shown in Figure 1. This prompt works well with the *Mistral* model, while *Hermes* produces more hallucinations (see rightmost part of Table 1).

Quantitative analysis For *observable-insight* prompts, we evaluated the semantic similarity scores between generated and ideal responses using *all-MiniLM-L6-v2* (Reimers and Gurevych, 2019). The left panel of Figure 2 shows boxplots of similarity scores for each prompt-model combination, with Mistral demonstrating superior performance in the majority of cases. To provide a more granular view, the right panel of Figure 2 presents a heatmap of similarity scores for each prompt-model combination and for each question. Notably, for some questions it is difficult to reach high similarity level regardless of the model+prompt choice (e.g., question 8). Additionally, the superior performance of Mistral is again evident, as seen, e.g., in the clear horizontal patterns for questions 4, 6, and 10.

5 Conclusions

This work evaluates the feasibility of generating high-quality, personalized NLP-based messages for diabetes management, integrating both domain expert inputs and data-driven insights, with the goal of driving behavior change. We tested several open-source models, and among them, Mistral yielded particularly promising results, proving to be a strong candidate for this task. In contrast, Starling-LM-7B-beta, gemma-2-2b-it, Llama-3.2-3B-Instruct, and especially, JSL-MedPhi2-2.7B delivered disappointing outcomes.

Limitations

We acknowledge that the limited size of our dataset affects the generalizability of our conclusions. However, we hope our findings offer valuable insights, particularly by encouraging caution when using models we found less effective for similar tasks.

Additionally, we attempted to improve the safety and quality of generated messages, in particular by introducing prompt refinement strategies $P_m, P_f, P_a, P_n, P_{n+}, P_{<n>}, P_d$. However, we recognize that further investigation is needed to fully address this issue.

Moreover, as a proof of concept, our approach considered only a limited set of actionable variables, and its scalability to a broader set should be explored in future work.

Ethical Considerations

We strongly advise against any use of suggested prompts that breaches ethical standards or facilitates harmful activities, such as generating misleading, harmful or malicious content. Our commitment to ethical principles underscores our dedication to fostering a positive impact not only in the related research community but, even more importantly, in all related fields and domains where potential real world utility and applicability of this work exists.

Acknowledgements

The work described in this paper has been supported by Innosuisse - Swiss Innovation Agency, project no. 72257.1, INNO-ICT.

References

Tom Brown, Benjamin Mann, Nick Ryder, Melanie Subbiah, Jared D Kaplan, Prafulla Dhariwal, Arvind Neelakantan, Pranav Shyam, Girish Sastry, Amanda Askell, et al. 2020. Language models are few-shot learners. Advances in neural information processing systems, 33:1877–1901.

Sheri R Colberg, Ronald J Sigal, Jane E Yardley, Michael C Riddell, David W Dunstan, Paddy C Dempsey, Edward S Horton, Kristin Castorino, and Deborah F Tate. 2016. Physical activity/exercise and diabetes: a position statement of the american diabetes association. Diabetes care, 39(11):2065.

Justin Cosentino, Anastasiya Belyaeva, Xin Liu, Nicholas A Furlotte, Zhun Yang, Chace Lee, Erik Schenck, Yojan Patel, Jian Cui, Logan Douglas Schneider, et al. 2024. Towards a personal health large language model. arXiv preprint arXiv:2406.06474.

Cathy Mengying Fang, Valdemar Danry, Nathan Whitmore, Andria Bao, Andrew Hutchison, Cayden Pierce, and Pattie Maes. 2024. Physiollm: Supporting personalized health insights with wearables and large language models. arXiv preprint arXiv:2406.19283.

Emilio Ferrara. 2024. Large language models for wearable sensor-based human activity recognition, health monitoring, and behavioral modeling: a survey of early trends, datasets, and challenges. Sensors, 24(15):5045.

Patrick Lewis, Ethan Perez, Aleksandra Piktus, Fabio Petroni, Vladimir Karpukhin, Naman Goyal, Heinrich Küttler, Mike Lewis, Wen-tau Yih, Tim Rocktäschel, et al. 2020. Retrieval-augmented generation for knowledge-intensive nlp tasks. Advances in Neural Information Processing Systems, 33:9459–9474.

Jiachen Li, Justin Steinberg, Xiwen Li, Akshat Choube, Bingsheng Yao, Dakuo Wang, Elizabeth Mynatt, and Varun Mishra. 2024a. Vital insight: Assisting experts' sensemaking process of multi-modal personal tracking data using visualization and llm. arXiv preprint arXiv:2410.14879.

Jiachen Li, Justin Steinberg, Xiwen Li, Bingsheng Yao, Dakuo Wang, Elizabeth Mynatt, and Varun Mishra. 2024b. Understanding the daily lives of older adults: Integrating multi-modal personal health tracking data through visualization and large language models. In Proceedings of the AAAI Symposium Series, volume 4, pages 173–177.

NIH. Type 1 Diabetes - NIDDK — niddk.nih.gov. `https://www.niddk.nih.gov/health-information/diabetes/overview/what-is-diabetes/type-1-diabetes`. [Accessed 12-12-2024].

Ankit Pal, Pasquale Minervini, Andreas Geert Motzfeldt, and Beatrice Alex. 2024. openlifescienceai/open_medical_llm_leaderboard. `https://huggingface.co/spaces/openlifescienceai/open_medical_llm_leaderboard`.

Nils Reimers and Iryna Gurevych. 2019. Sentence-bert: Sentence embeddings using siamese bert-networks. In Proceedings of the 2019 Conference on Empirical Methods in Natural Language Processing. Association for Computational Linguistics.

Medication Extraction and Entity Linking using Stacked and Voted Ensembles on LLMs

Pablo Romero[1], **Lifeng Han**[2,3*], and **Goran Nenadic**[3]
[1] Manchester Metropolitan University, UK
[2] LIACS & LUMC, Leiden University, NL [3] The University of Manchester, UK
[*] *corresponding author*
pablo2004romero@gmail.com l.han@lumc.nl, g.nenadic@manchester.ac.uk

Abstract

Medication Extraction and Mining of its related **attributes** play an important role in healthcare NLP research due to its practical applications in hospital settings, such as their mapping into standard clinical knowledge bases (SNOMED-CT, BNF, etc.). In this work, we investigate state-of-the-art LLMs in text mining tasks on medications and their related attributes such as dosage, route, strength, and adverse effects. In addition, we explore different ensemble learning methods (STACK-ENSEMBLE and VOTING-ENSEMBLE) to augment the model performances from individual LLMs. Our ensemble learning result demonstrated better performances than individually fine-tuned base models BERT, RoBERTa, RoBERTa-L, BioBERT, BioClinicalBERT, BioMedRoBERTa, ClinicalBERT, and PubMedBERT across general and specific domains, with **statistical significance** testing (p=0.048). Finally, we build up an entity linking function to map extracted medical terminologies into the SNOMED-CT codes and the British National Formulary (BNF) codes, which are further mapped to the Dictionary of Medicines and Devices (dm+d), and ICD (**Clinical Coding**). We host the fine-tuned models and **desktop applications** at https://github.com/pabloRom2004/Insight-Buddy-AI-App

1 Introduction

Information Extraction on Medications and their related attributes plays an important role in natural language processing (**NLP**) applications in the **clinical** domain to support digital healthcare. Clinicians and healthcare professionals have been doing manual clinical **coding** for quite a long time to map clinical events such as diseases, drugs, and treatments into the existing terminology knowledge base, for instance, ICD and SNOMED. The procedure can be time-consuming yet without a guarantee of total correctness due to human-introduced errors. With the process of automated information extraction on **medications**, it will be further possible to automatically map the extracted terms into the current terminology database, i.e. the automated clinical coding. Due to the promising future of this procedure, different NLP models have been deployed in medication mining and clinical coding in recent years. However, they are often studied separately. In this work, 1) we investigate text mining of medications and their related attributes (dosage, route, strength, adverse effect, frequency, duration, form, and reason) together with *automated clinical coding* into one pipeline. In addition, 2) we investigate the **ensemble** learning mechanisms (Stack and Voting) on a broad range of NLP models fine-tuned for named entity recognition (NER) tasks. These models include both general domain trained BERT, RoBERTa, RoBERTa-L, and domain-specific trained BioBERT, BioClinicalBERT, BioMedRoBERTa, ClinicalBERT, and PubMedBERT. In this way, users do not have to worry about which models to choose for clinical NER. Instead, they can just place the newer models into the ensemble-learning framework to test their performances. We offer desktop applications and web **interfaces** for the clinical NER, ensemble, and coding models we are developing upon paper acceptance.

2 Literature Review and Related Work

2.1 Biomed/Clinical Named Entity Recognition

Named Entity Recognition (**NER**) is a critical task for extracting key information from unstructured text, like medical letters. The complexity and context-dependency of medical language pose significant challenges for accurate entity extraction. Traditional approaches to NER, such as rule-based systems, have shown limited success in capturing the nuanced contextual information crucial for clin-

Proceedings of the Second Workshop on Patient-Oriented Language Processing (CL4Health), pages 303–315
May 4, 2025 ©2025 Association for Computational Linguistics

ical NER (Nadeau and Sekine, 2007). The advent of deep learning methods, particularly Long Short-Term Memory (LSTM) networks, marked a significant improvement in NER performance (Graves and Schmidhuber, 2005), e.g. the ability to capture long-range dependencies in text. However, these models still struggled with rare entities and complex contextual relationships in **clinical notes**. The introduction of BERT (Bidirectional Encoder Representations from Transformers) (Devlin et al., 2019) revolutionised various NLP tasks, including NER. BERT's self-attention mechanism and bidirectional training allow it to capture nuanced contextual information over long pieces of text. The model's pre-training on a large corpus using a masked language modelling objective builds rich token representations. The model can then be later fine-tuned by adding a classification layer at the end of the network to make decisions over each individual token embedding.

However, BERT's pre-training on general domain corpora (Wikipedia and books) limited its effectiveness on specialised medical texts. This limitation led to the development of **domain-specific** BERT variants. For example, BioBERT (Lee et al., 2019), pre-trained on large-scale biomedical corpora; ClinicalBERT (Wang et al., 2023), fine-tuned on EHR data from 3 million patients after pre-training on 1.2 billion words of diverse diseases, and other variants like Med-BERT (Rasmy et al., 2021) have demonstrated enhanced performance on medical NER tasks due to their specialised training on the medical domain [1]. Despite these improvements, **single-model approaches still struggle** with the inherent complexity and variability of clinical text, as the comparative studies reported in (Belkadi et al., 2023) across different models using BERT, ClinicalBERT, BioBERT, and scratch-learned Transformers.

2.2 Ensemble Learning for Biomedical NER

Ensemble methods have emerged as a promising direction to address these challenges, they have proven useful in other fields, such as computer vision (Lee et al., 2018). By combining multiple models, ensembles can leverage the strengths of different models while mitigating their individual weaknesses. In the context of NER, ensemble learning has shown performance improvements, as shown by (Naderi et al., 2021), where an ensemble is used in a *health* and *life science* corpus for a significant improvement in performance over single models. (Naderi et al., 2021) conducted max voting for word-level biology, chemistry, and medicine data. However, on clinical/medical NER, they only focused on French using the DEFT benchmark dataset; while for the other two domains of biology and chemistry, they tested on English data. There are two commonly used ensemble methods, voting and stacked ensembles: 1) **Maximum voting** in ensembles where each model contributes equally to the final decision as used in the paper (Naderi et al., 2021) have proved effective. This is where the most voted label is picked. 2) Training a network on the outputs of the ensemble aims to capture more nuanced relationships. This is accomplished using a method called **stacking** introduced by (Wolpert, 1992). Stacking offers a more sophisticated approach by training a meta-model on the outputs of the base ensemble; the model is expected to learn more complex patterns from the ensemble outputs, leading to better predictions. This has proven effective in this paper (Saleh et al., 2022) where they use a stacked ensemble with a support vector machine (SVM) for *sentiment* analysis. Instead, we will use a simple feed-forward network from the outputs of the ensemble to the final labels for our tasks. more examples on stacked ensemble can be found at (Mohammed and Kora, 2022; Güneş et al., 2017).

Earlier work on ensemble learning for biomedical NER mostly includes older models such as BiLSTM, CRF, SEARN, and RNNs (Ju et al., 2020; Kim and Meystre, 2020; Christopoulou et al., 2020). This work **aims to address this gap** by investigating 1) *whether stacked and voting ensembles can make a difference on NER tasks of clinical notes*, 2) the ensemble performance on newer Deep Learning models based on BERT from domain fine-tuning, which are a) general domain BERT, RoBERTa, and RoBERTa-L, and b) biomedical domain BioBERT, BioClinicalBERT, BioMedRoBERTa, ClinicalBERT, and PubMedBERT.

2.3 Model Quantisation

To make the LLMs more computational friendly and available for smaller machine users, model quantisation is a recent topic in deep learning to reduce the required memory when running the model mostly by reduce the model size, but with-

[1] there have been other versions of Clinical BERTs such as (Huang et al., 2019) and (Alsentzer et al., 2019) that were trained on Medical Information Mart for Intensive Care III (mimiciii) data (Johnson et al., 2016) respectively.

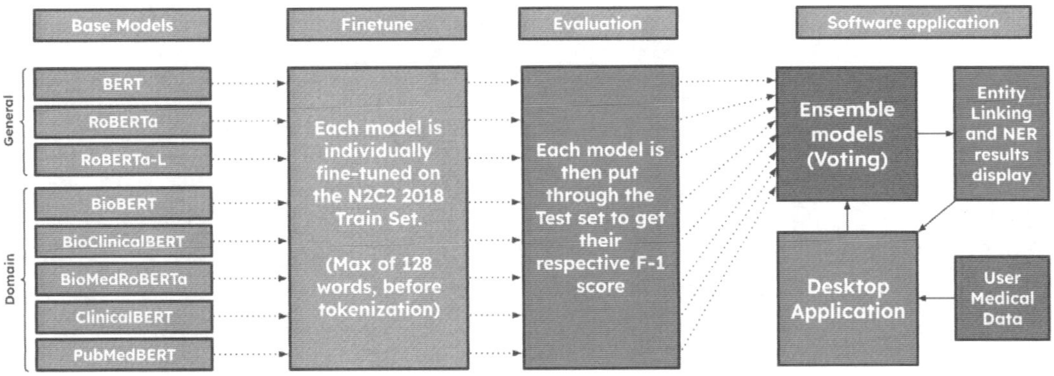

Figure 1: InsightBuddy Framework Pipeline: individual NER model fine-tuning, ensemble, and entity linking. Two kinds of base models include the general domain and the biomedical domain with their Huggingface repositories in Table 3. Pre-preprocessing data: cut the sequence with the first full stop "." after the 100th word, otherwise, cut the sequence up to 128 words. Fine-tuning: using the same parameter sets for all eight models. Ensemble: different strategies will be displayed in Fig 2. Entity Linking: links to clinical KB including BNF and SNOMED.

out much effecting the model performances. There are quantisation-aware training and post-training quantisation (PTQ). We use the extreme reduction to 4-bit (16 values) transformers.js Q4 implementation in our work for PTQ. Recent work on this topic can be found at (Lin et al., 2024; Liu et al., 2023).

3 Methodologies

The Overall framework of InsightBuddy is shown in Figure 1, which displays the base models we included from the general domain 1) BERT (Devlin et al., 2019), RoBERTa (Liu et al., 2019), and RoBERTa-Large, and 2) biomedical/clinical domains BioBERT (Lee et al., 2019), BioClinicalBERT (Alsentzer et al., 2019), BioMedRoBERTa (Gururangan et al., 2020), ClinicalBERT (Wang et al., 2023), and PubMedBERT (Gu et al., 2020). The fine-tuning of eight models uses the same set of parameters (Section 4 for parameter selections) and the n2c2-2018 shared task training data with data pre-processing. The initial evaluation phase using n2c2-2018 testing set gives an overall idea of each model's performance. This is followed by ensemble learning on all the models' outputs. With the output from NER models, we add an **entity linking** function to map the extracted medical entities into the standard clinical terminology knowledge base (KB), using **SNOMED-CT and BNF** as our initial KB, which is further mapped to ICD and dm+d.

For data pre-processing, we chunk the sequence into a maximum of 128 words. If there is a full stop "." between the 100th and 128th word, it will be cut at the full stop. Regarding ensemble-learning strategy, we draw a InsightBuddy Ensemble figure (Figure 2) to explain in detail. Firstly the initial output of eight individual fine-tuned NER models is tokenised, i.e. at the **sub-word** level, due to the model learning strategy, e.g. "Para ##ce ##tam ##ol" instead of "Paracetamol". What we need to do at the first step is to **group** the sub-word tokens into words for both practical application and voting purposes. However, each sub-word is labeled with predefined labels and these labels often do not agree with each other within the same words. We designed **three group solutions**, i.e. first-token voting/selection, max-token voting, and average voting. The *first-token voting* is to assign a word the same label as its first sub-word piece. For example, using this strategy, the word "Paracetamol" will be labeled as "B-Drug" if its first sub-word "Para" is labeled as "B-Drug" regardless of other labels from the subsequent sub-words. The *max-token voting* will assign a word the label that has the highest sub-word logit, this indicates that the model is more confident in that prediction, the higher the logit is. The *average voting* solution calculates the average logits across all sub-words predictions and then samples from this to get the label for the entire word.

Regarding **word-level ensemble** learning, we investigate the classical **voting** strategy with modifications (two solutions). For the first solution ">=4 or O", if there are more than half of the mod-

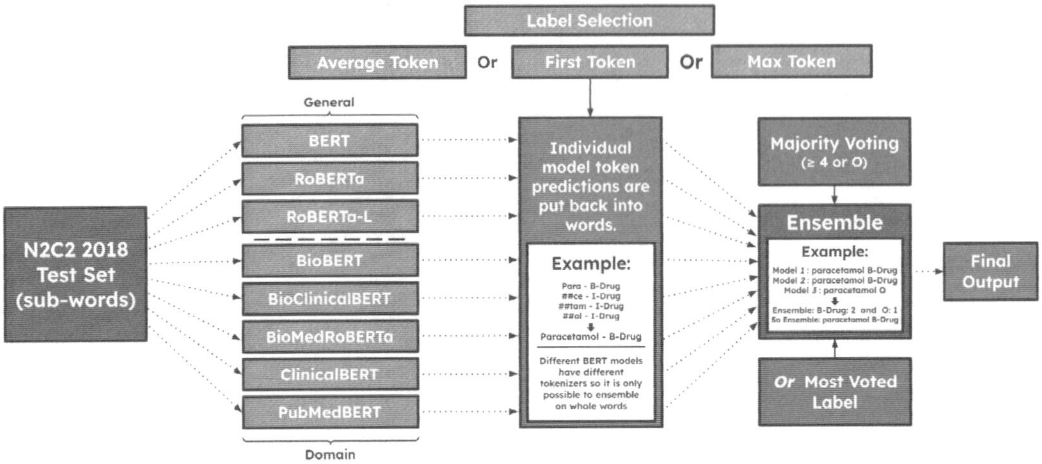

Figure 2: InsightBuddy Voted Ensemble Pipeline: individual NER model fine-tuning outputs are at token/sub-word level. "Logits are the outputs of a neural network before the activation function is applied" first, we do the grouping of sub-words into words using three strategies: first token label, max token voting, or average voting (from our results, the first-token-lable selection gives higher Recall, while other two voting give higher precision, but they all end with the same F1 score, ref Table 4). || We take the best output from the first token label selection as the solution. For word-level ensemble on eight models, we have two solutions for voting, 1) either majority voting with >= 4 labels as the same then we pick it, otherwise choose default "O", or 2) max voting with the most popular label whatever it is; for max voting, if there is a tie, e.g. (3,3,2), we tested both alphabetical pick-up, or random pick-up of tied labels. Our results show that ">=4, or O" performs similarly to "max + alphabetical", while "max + random" slightly performs lower.

els agree on one label, we pick this label, i.e. >=4 such same labels. Otherwise, we assign the default "O" label to indicate it as context words, due to the models' disagreement. For the second solution, we use max-voting, i.e. the most agreed label regardless of how many models they are, e.g. 2, 3, 4, or more. In this case, if there are ties, e.g. (3, 3, 2) two labels are voted both three times from six models, we need to decide on the tied labels. There are two solutions for the selection, 1) alphabetical, and 2) fully randomised.

We also draw the **Stacked**-Ensemble in Figure 12 and 13, where the model training and one-hot encoded model predictions are illustrated. In the training phase, we cut the real data into 80% and 20% for the training and testing of the model. Model exports are conducted only if at least 2 models are predicting a label that is not "O"; otherwise "O" is the default option and the output is ignored and not included in the stacked training data. For training data collection, output logits for each model are converted into a one-hot encoded vector, concatenated and saved along with the real label for each token. There are 8 one-hot encoded vectors from 8 individual models and 1 label. So the model during training will see the value "1" eight times from the eight models, and the value "0" for the rest of the vector values. Overall, there are 8 vectors with each length of 19 digits. So there will be 8 (number of models) $\times$ 19 (number of labels) - 8 (eight 1s as there are 8 one hot encoded vectors so they have a single 1 each) = 144 "0" values for every training example. We use *one-hot encoding* instead of the output logits themselves to avoid the model *overfitting* because the model makes more confident predictions when running on the training set. As this is the data that it was originally trained on, it is very confident with it's predictions. We can mitigate this by only feeding the one-hot encoded vectors to the stacked network.

4 Hyper Parameter Optimisations

We used a set of parameters for model fine-tuning and selected the better parameter set as below using the validation data. We tried different learning rates (0.0001, 0.0002, 0.00005) and batch sizes (16, 32).

- learning_rate: 0.00005
- train_batch_size: 32

Individual models max-logit grouping (word)			
Metric	**P**	**R**	**F1**
BERT			
accuracy	0.9773		
macro avg	0.7942	0.7965	0.7928
weighted avg	0.9784	0.9773	0.9775
RoBERTa			
accuracy	0.9780		
macro avg	0.8029	0.8201	0.8094
weighted avg	0.9795	0.9780	0.9784
RoBERTa-Large			
accuracy	0.9788		
macro avg	0.8091	0.8351	0.8202
weighted avg	0.9802	0.9788	0.9792
ClinicalBERT			
accuracy	0.9780		
macro avg	0.8087	0.7916	0.7964
weighted avg	0.9785	0.9780	0.9779
BioBERT			
accuracy	0.9776		
macro avg	0.7972	0.8131	0.8027
weighted avg	0.9787	0.9776	0.9779
BioClinicalBERT			
accuracy	0.9776		
macro avg	0.7999	0.8090	0.8017
weighted avg	0.9788	0.9776	0.9779
BioMedRoBERTa			
accuracy	0.9783		
macro avg	0.8065	0.8224	0.8122
weighted avg	0.9797	0.9783	0.9786
PubMedBERT			
accuracy	0.9784		
macro avg	0.8087	0.8292	0.8166
weighted avg	0.9800	0.9784	0.9788
Voting Max logit ensemble word level			
accuracy	0.9796		
macro avg	**0.8261**	0.8259	**0.8232**
weighted avg	0.9807	0.9796	0.9798

Table 1: Word-level individual model (grouping using max-logit) vs ensemble using max-logit, Eval on n2c2 2018 test data

- eval_batch_size: 32
- seed: 42
- optimizer: Adam with betas=(0.9,0.999) and epsilon=1e-08
- lr_scheduler_type: linear
- lr_scheduler_warmup_ratio: 0.1

Model	Macro P	Macro R	Macro F	Accuracy	Tokens
BERT	0.8336	0.8264	0.8283	0.9748	756798
ROBERTa	0.8423	0.8471	0.8434	0.9770	756014
ROBERTa-L	**0.8489**	**0.8606**	**0.8538**	**0.9782**	756014
PubMedBERT	0.8324	0.8381	0.8339	**0.9783**	681211
ClinicalBERT	**0.8482**	0.8245	0.8341	0.9753	*796313*
BioMedRoBERTa	**0.8482**	**0.8477**	**0.8468**	0.9775	756014
BioClinicalBERT	0.8440	0.8405	0.8406	0.9751	791743
BioBERT	0.8365	0.8444	0.8393	0.9750	791743

Table 2: InsightBuddy individual sub-word level model eval on n2c2-2018 test set. The first group: normal domain PLM; The second group: biomedical PLM. The different numbers of Support are due to the different tokenizers they used – ROBERTa and ROBERTa-L use the same tokenizers, BioClinicalBERT and BioBERT use the same tokenizers, and other models all use different tokenizers; PubMedBERT generated the least number of sub-words/tokens 681,211 while ClinicalBERT generated the largest number of tokens 796,313.

- num_epochs: 4
- mixed_precision_training: Native AMP

5 Experimental Evaluations

We use the n2c2-2018 shared task data on NER of adverse drug events and related medical attributes (Henry et al., 2020). The data is labeled with the following list of labels: ADE, Dosage, Drug, Duration, Form, Frequency, Reason, Route, and Strength in BIO format. So, overall, we have 19 labels, 2 (B/I) x 9 + 1 (O). The original training and testing sets are 303 and 202 letters respectively. We divided the original training set into two parts (9:1 ratio) for our model selection purposes: our new training and validation set, following the data split from recent work by (Belkadi et al., 2023).

We report Precision, Recall, and F1 score in two categories "macro" and "weighted", in addition to Accuracy. The "**macro**" category treats each label class the same weight regardless of their occurrence rates, while the "**weighted**" category" assigns each label class with a weight according to their occurrence in the data. We first report the individual model fine-tuning scores and compare them with related work (subword level); then we report the ensemble model evaluation with different ensemble solutions (word level).

5.1 Individual Models: sub-word level

The performance of individual models after fine-tuning is reported in Table 2 where it says that RoBERTa-L performs the best in the macro Precision (0.8489), Recall (0.8606) and F1 (0.8538) score across general domain models, also winning

Table 3: INSIGHTBUDDY integrated individual models and their Huggingface repositories.

Ensemble List	Link
BERT	https://huggingface.co/google-bert/bert-base-uncased
BioBERT	https://huggingface.co/dmis-lab/biobert-base-cased-v1.2
ClinicalBERT	https://huggingface.co/medicalai/ClinicalBERT
BioClinicalBERT	https://huggingface.co/emilyalsentzer/Bio_ClinicalBERT
PubMedBERT	https://huggingface.co/microsoft/BiomedNLP-BiomedBERT-base-uncased-abstract-fulltext
BioMedRoBERTa	https://huggingface.co/allenai/biomed_roberta_base
RoBERTa	https://huggingface.co/FacebookAI/roberta-base
RoBERTa Large	https://huggingface.co/FacebookAI/roberta-large

domain-specific models. BioiMedRoBERTa wins the domain-specific category models producing macro Precision, Recall, and F1 scores (0.8482 0.8477 0.8468). In comparison to the NER work from (Belkadi et al., 2023), who's macro avg scores are: 0.842, 0.834, 0.837 from ClinicalBERT-Apt, our fine-tuned ClinicalBERT has similar performances (0.848, 0.825, 0.834), which shows our fine-tuning was successful. However, our best domain-specific model BioMedRoBERTa produces **higher** scores: macro P/R/F1 (0.8482 0.**8477** 0.**8468**) and weighted P/R/F1 (0.9782 0.9775 0.9776) and Accuracy 0.9775 as in Figure 6. Furthermore, the fine-tuned RoBERTa-L even achieved higher scores of (**0.8489 0.8606 0.8538**) for macro P/R/F1 and Acc 0.9782 in Figure 13. Both fine-tuned BioMedRoBERTa and RoBERTa-Large also *win the best models* reported by (Belkadi et al., 2023) which is their ClinicalBERT-CRF model, macro avg (0.85, 0.829, 0.837), Acc 0.976. Afterwards, in this paper, we emphasis on **word level** instead of sub-word, which was focused on by (Belkadi et al., 2023).

5.2 Ensemble: word-level grouping (logits)

We tried **first** logit voting, **max** voting, and **average** voting to group sub-words into words with corresponding labels. Their results are shown in Table 4, in the upper group. First logit voting produced a higher Recall 0.8260 while Max logit voting produced a higher Precision 0.8261 resulting in higher F1 0.8232, i.e. *Max* logit > *First* logit > *Average* logit with macro F1 (0.8232, 0.8229, 0.8227). However, overall, their performance scores are very close, so we chose the first-logit voting output for the afterward word-level ensemble due to computational convenience.

5.3 Individual vs Ensemble Models

The word-level performance comparisons from individual models and voting max-logit ensembles are presented in Table 1.

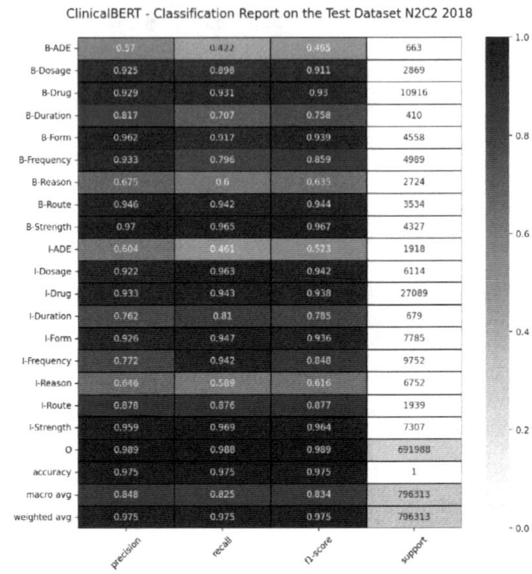

Figure 3: ClinicalBERT Eval at Sub-word Level. This score is similar (slightly winning R/F1) to (Belkadi et al., 2023) paper on ClinicalBERT-Apt whose macro: (85.3 81.0 82.5) and weighted: (0.974, 0.975, 0.974), which says our fine-tuning is successful. However, our best domain-specific model BioMedRoBERTa produces *better* score: macro P/R/F (0.8482 0.8477 0.8468) and weighted P/R/F (0.9782 0.9775 0.9776) and Accuracy 0.9775 as in Figure 8. Furthermore, the fine-tuned RoBERTa-L even achieved higher scores of (0.8489 0.8606 0.8538) for P/R/F1 and Acc 0.9782 in Table 1. Afterwards, in this paper, we emphasis on word level instead of sub-word, which was focused by Belkadi et al. (2023).

5.4 Ensemble: Voting vs Stacked (one-hot)

Regarding Stacked Ensemble using one-hot encoded vectors, as shown in the middle group in Table 4, it actually produced higher Precision score 0.8351 in comparisons to the highest Precision 0.8261 from Voting Ensembles. However, the Recall score on macro avg is 2 point lower than the voting ensemble, 0.8065 vs 0.8260, which means that the Stacked Ensemble *reduced the false positive errors* but also increased the false negative error prediction. This implies that it has stricter constraint on positive predictions.

5.5 Ensemble Models: BIO-span vs non-strict word-level

So far, we have been reporting the evaluation scores on the BIO-strict label categorization, i.e. we distinguish between the label's beginning or the inner part of the label. For instance, a B-Drug will be different from an I-Drug and it will be marked as wrong if they are different from the reference. However, we think in practice, there are situations when users do not need the BIO, especially B and I difference. In Table 4, we can see that, without considering the label difference of B and I, only focusing on the 9 label categories, word level ensemble model produced much higher Macro avg evaluations cores on Precision (0.8844) and Recall (0.8830) leading to higher F1 (0.8821), in comparison to BI-distinguished Macro F1 0.8232 (voting-max-logit) and F1 0.8156 (stacked-first-logit).

5.6 Word-level: voting ensembles vs individual fine-tuned

As in Table 1, BioMedRoBERTa individual word level max logit grouping scores macro avg P/R/F1 (0.8065 0.8224 0.8122 563329) vs max logit ensemble voting P/R/F1 (0.8261 0.8259 0.8232), we can see that ensemble boosted P (0.8261-0.8065)/0.8065= 2.43%, and F1 (0.8232-0.8122)/0.8122= 1.35% which says the ensemble voting is successful. By increasing the Precision score, the *ensembles reduce the **false positive** labels* in the system output, while keeping the Recall at the same level, i.e. the true positive labels.

5.7 Model Quantisation

To reduce the computational cost, we also carried out the quantisation on fine-tuned models. The quantised model can perform similar level of accurate scores in comparison to the original models but with 25% of the size. For instance, using BioMedRoberTa, the quantised model achieved (0.811, 0.821, 0.814) for macro(P, R, F1), which is very similar to the original size fine-tuned model scores (0.8065, 0.8224, 0.8122) as in Table 1, even achieving **slightly higher Precision and F1**. The reasons for this can be that 1) Block-wise Quantization: The Q4 implementation isn't just reducing precision uniformly - it uses sophisticated block-wise quantisation that preserves important patterns while simplifying others. 2) Calibrated Discretization: The extreme reduction to 4-bit (16 values) forces more decisive classification boundaries, which can be beneficial for NER tasks where *clear token boundaries* are important. 3) Optimisation Benefits: The transformers.js Q4 implementation includes specific optimisations for inference beyond simple precision reduction. Overall, this is fundamentally different from *naive quantization* - the transformers.js/GGML approach is carefully designed to maintain model performance while drastically reducing size. In some cases, this sophisticated quantisation can improve results by simplifying decision boundaries in beneficial ways.

The full model size is 497 MB and the 4 Bits Quantised model is 125 MB. The corresponding detailed evaluations on each entity type and the confusion matrix for quantised BioMedRoBERTa are presented in Figure 6 and 7 on word level with BIO.

Voting Average Ensemble word level (BIO)			
Metric	P	R	F1
accuracy	0.9796		
macro avg	0.8253	0.8256	0.8227 ± 0.0037
weighted avg	0.9807	0.9796	0.9798
Voting First logit Ensemble word level (BIO)			
Metric	P	R	F1
accuracy	0.9796		
macro avg	0.8255	**0.8260**	0.8229 ± 0.0034
weighted avg	0.9807	0.9796	0.9798
Voting Max logit Ensemble word level (BIO)			
Metric	P	R	F1
accuracy	0.9796		
macro avg	0.8261	0.8259	**0.8232** ± 0.0036
weighted avg	0.9807	0.9796	0.9798
Stacked Ensemble first logit word level (BIO)			
Metric	P	R	F1
accuracy	0.9796		
macro avg	**0.8351**	0.8065	0.8156 ± 0.0037
weighted avg	0.9800	0.9796	0.9794
Non-BIO-only-word ensemble			
Metric	P	R	F1
accuracy	0.9839		
macro avg	0.8844	0.8830	0.8821 ± 0.0025
weighted avg	0.9840	0.9839	0.9838

Table 4: Word-level grouping ensemble voting evaluation with significance test. F1 score: max > first > average logit voting though they are very close scores. The **stacked** ensemble has the highest **Precision** scores, but the lowest Recall scores, which lead to lower F1. In the bottom cluster, it is the word-level evaluation without distinguishing B/I labels, evaluation on n2c2 2018 test data.

5.8 Significance Test

To assess the statistical significance of performance differences between ensemble methods and the strongest individual model (RoBERTa-Large with first token strategy), we conducted bootstrap resampling tests with 500 iterations. Our analysis revealed that the Non-BIO-only-word ensemble showed statistically significant improvement ($p = 0.048$) over the baseline. Interestingly, while the Stacked Ensemble first logit approach performed significantly worse in F1 score ($p = 0.002$), it achieved the highest precision (0.8351) among all methods, suggesting potential utility for precision-

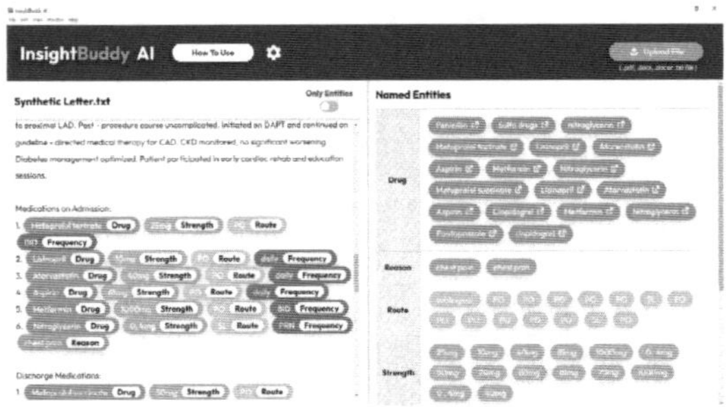

Figure 4: Demonstration of Clinical Events Outputs using A Synthetic Letter.

Figure 5: Context-awareness Feature using Window Parameter around the Entity

focused applications. The three Voting ensemble approaches (Average, First logit, and Max logit) showed slight numerical improvements in F1 scores but these differences did not reach statistical significance ($p > 0.05$).

For robust evaluation, we calculated 95% confidence intervals using bootstrap resampling on the test dataset. This involved randomly sampling 95% of the sentences with replacement, calculating the F1 score for each resampled dataset, and repeating this process 200 times per model. The standard deviation across these iterations provides a measure of performance stability across different subsets of the data. These findings demonstrate that while some ensemble configurations can offer consistent improvements, performance gains are sensitive to both the specific ensemble strategy employed and the evaluation methodology. Our comprehensive comparison provides valuable insights for researchers applying ensemble approaches to clinical named entity recognition tasks.

6 Entity Linking: BNF and SNOMED

To map the identified named entities into the clinical knowledge base. We use the existing code mapping sheet from the British National Formulary

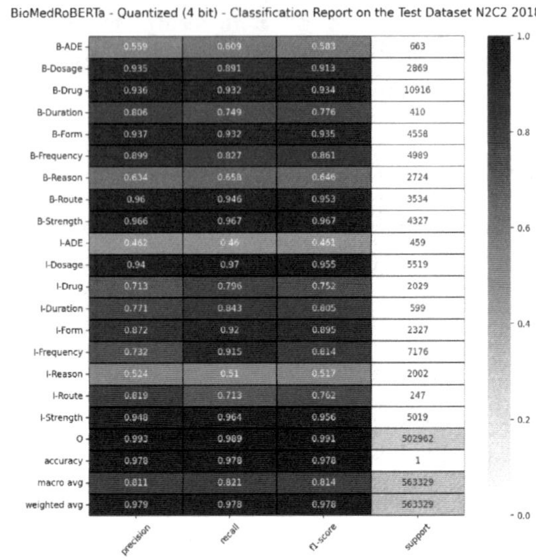

Figure 6: BioMedRoBERTa Quantised Model Eval.

(BNF) web between SNOMED-CT, BNF, dm+d, and ICD [2]. We preprocessed the SNOMED code from 377,834 to 10,804 to filter repeated examples between the mapping of SNOMED and BNF. We looked for non-drug words present in the text, then we filtered the drugs further by seeing if words like ['system', 'ostomy', 'bag', 'filter', 'piece', 'closure'] were present in the text, and if so, it was discarded.

For SNOMED CT mapping, we applied a fuzzy search to the cleaned mapping list with drug names. Then the SNOMED CT code will be added to the searching function on the SNOMED CT web, whenever there is a match. For BNF mapping, the linking function uses keyword search to retrieve the BNF website with corresponding drugs, due to its different searching features in comparison to the SNOMED-CT web page. Potential users can select whichever is suitable to their preferences between the two clinical knowledge bases (KBs), Figure 11.

7 InsightBuddy-AI Desktop Application

We illustrate the Desktop Applications of InsightBuddy-AI in Figure 4 and 14, for demonstration of clinical event recognition using a synthetic letter via 1) loading our pre-trained model and common NER categories via 2) loading a Huggingface NER model. There is also a **sliding window feature** called "context length" to allow flexible length of context around the entities visible to users, as in

[2]https://www.nhsbsa.nhs.uk/prescription-data/understanding-our-data/bnf-snomed-mapping

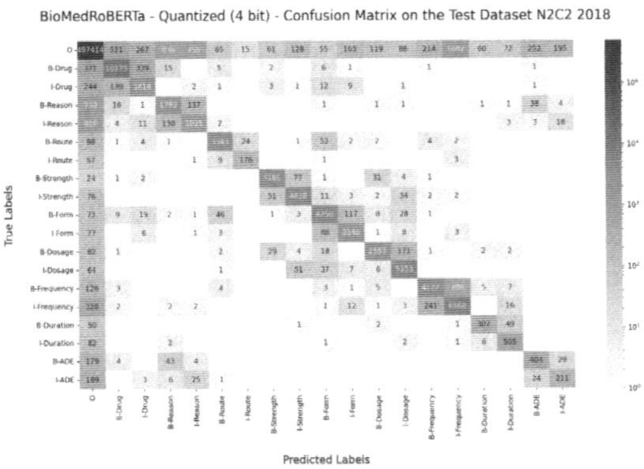

Figure 7: BioMedRoBERTa Quantised Eval Confusion Matrix.

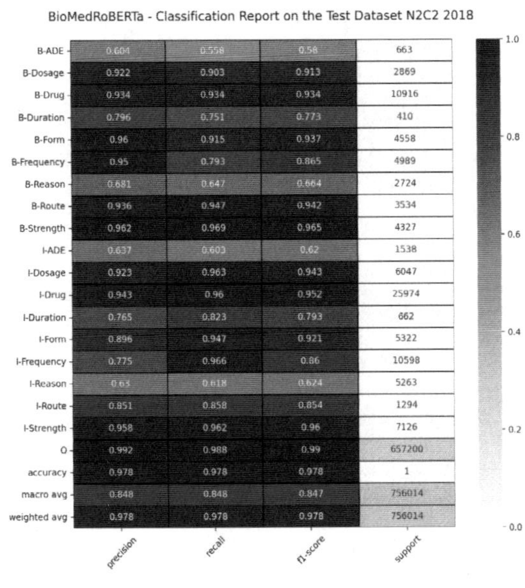

Figure 8: BioMedRoBERTa Eval at Sub-word Level on n2c2 2018 test data.

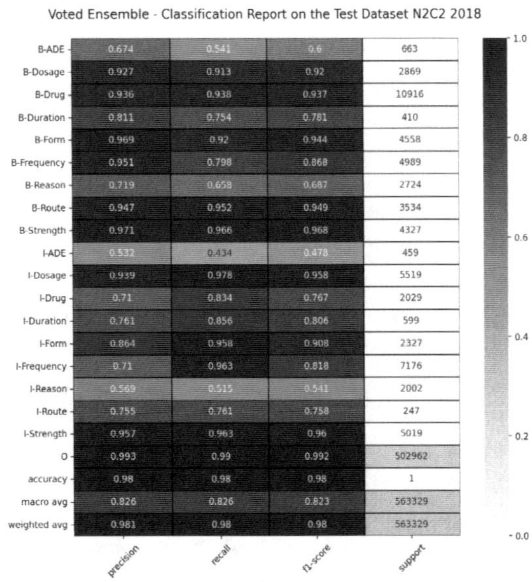

Figure 9: word-level grouping ensemble, max logit voting Eval on n2c2 2018 test data.

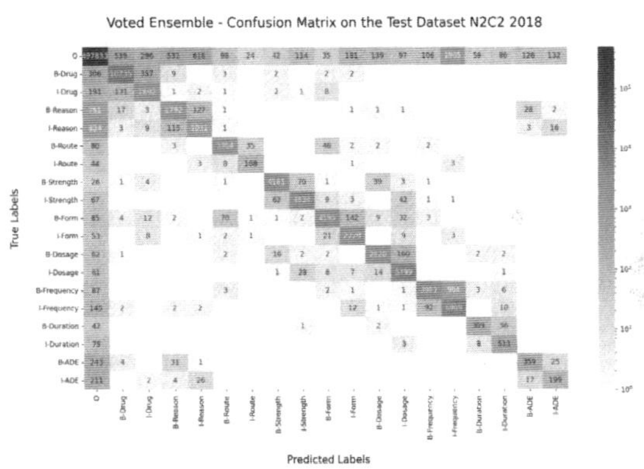

Figure 10: word-level ensemble max-logit voting Eval confusion matrix on n2c2 2018 test data.

Figure 5. For **Clinical Coding** (entity linking) options, the desktop application can currently directly link the extracted entities to BNF and SNOMED-CT. The INSIGHTBUDDY-AI software supports both Mac and Windows systems.

8 Discussion and Conclusion

In this paper, we investigated **Stacked Ensemble** and **Voting Ensemble** on *medical named entity recognition* tasks using eight pretrained LMs from both general and biomed/clinical domains. Our experiments show that our fine-tuned best individual models outperformed the state-of-the-art on standard shared task data n2c2-2018. The two ensemble strategies using output logits and one-hot encoding further improved the model performances. We carried out model quantisation and again improved the model performances, especially on Precision scores, while reducing the model size by 75%. We carried out **statistical significance** testing and the results show that the word-level MER ensemble significantly improved over the baseline model (p=0.048). We offer desktop applications and user interfaces for individual fine-tuned models where we added the entity linking/normalisation function to BNF and SNOMED CT clinical knowledge base. We call the package INSIGHTBUDDY-AI, which is released publicly for free research use.

Limitations

The affiliated entity linking / clinical coding part of our software InsightBuddyAI was manually verified by ourselves qualitatively with some sampled medical terms, especially drug names. It would be more accurate to 1) quantitatively evaluate such entity linking result, as well as 2) a systematic qualitative assessment such as by multiple annotators (clinical coders) with the measurement of agreement levels. For option 2), it is costly to carry out such an experiments. For option 1), we are still looking for any publicly available data set for such purposes.

At the publication stage, we are informed of the related software implementation in this domain from Johnsnowlabs [3] on Clinical NER. While this is a commercialised company developing NLP packages for healthcare, it is worthy in the future to carry out some comparisons on experimental performances using the same shared task data. On the other hand, it is also possible that they already integrated the shared task data into their system pre-trainings.

In addition, a more detailed *error analysis*, particularly for specific entity types or challenging cases, would help determine whether improvements are consistent across all medication attributes. The current study does not compare ensemble models with *decoder-only large language models* (LLMs), such as GPT-4 or BioMistral, demonstrating strong zero-shot and fine-tuned performance. It is useful to integrate such comparisons in the future, even though this is already an extended investigation with more findings based on our initial software release IndightBuddy-AI (Romero et al., 2025).

Acknowledgements

We thank the reviewers' valuable comments, which have made our work much better. LH and GN are grateful for the support from the grant "Assembling the Data Jigsaw: Powering Robust Research on the Causes, Determinants and Outcomes of MSK Disease", and the grant "Integrating hospital outpatient letters into the healthcare data space" (EP/V047949/1; funder: UKRI/EPSRC). LH is grateful for the 4D Picture EU project (https://4dpicture.eu/) on supporting the journey of cancer patients. PR was supported by the University of Manchester Urenco Internships grant as part of an outreach programme.

[3] https://demo.johnsnowlabs.com/healthcare/NER_CLINICAL/

References

Emily Alsentzer, John Murphy, William Boag, Wei-Hung Weng, Di Jindi, Tristan Naumann, and Matthew McDermott. 2019. Publicly available clinical BERT embeddings. In *Proceedings of the 2nd Clinical Natural Language Processing Workshop*, pages 72–78, Minneapolis, Minnesota, USA. Association for Computational Linguistics.

Samuel Belkadi, Lifeng Han, Yuping Wu, and Goran Nenadic. 2023. Exploring the value of pre-trained language models for clinical named entity recognition. In *2023 IEEE International Conference on Big Data (BigData)*, pages 3660–3669.

Fenia Christopoulou, Thy Thy Tran, Sunil Kumar Sahu, Makoto Miwa, and Sophia Ananiadou. 2020. Adverse drug events and medication relation extraction in electronic health records with ensemble deep learning methods. *Journal of the American Medical Informatics Association*, 27(1):39–46.

Jacob Devlin, Ming-Wei Chang, Kenton Lee, and Kristina Toutanova. 2019. BERT: Pre-training of deep bidirectional transformers for language understanding. In *Proceedings of the 2019 Conference of the North American Chapter of the Association for Computational Linguistics: Human Language Technologies, Volume 1 (Long and Short Papers)*, pages 4171–4186, Minneapolis, Minnesota. Association for Computational Linguistics.

Alex Graves and Jürgen Schmidhuber. 2005. Framewise phoneme classification with bidirectional lstm and other neural network architectures. *Neural Networks*, 18(5):602–610. IJCNN 2005.

Yu Gu, Robert Tinn, Hao Cheng, Michael Lucas, Naoto Usuyama, Xiaodong Liu, Tristan Naumann, Jianfeng Gao, and Hoifung Poon. 2020. Domain-specific language model pretraining for biomedical natural language processing.

Funda Güneş, Russ Wolfinger, and Pei-Yi Tan. 2017. Stacked ensemble models for improved prediction accuracy. In *Proc. Static Anal. Symp*, pages 1–19.

Suchin Gururangan, Ana Marasović, Swabha Swayamdipta, Kyle Lo, Iz Beltagy, Doug Downey, and Noah A. Smith. 2020. Don't stop pretraining: Adapt language models to domains and tasks. In *Proceedings of ACL*.

Sam Henry, Kevin Buchan, Michele Filannino, Amber Stubbs, and Ozlem Uzuner. 2020. 2018 n2c2 shared task on adverse drug events and medication extraction in electronic health records. *Journal of the American Medical Informatics Association*, 27(1):3–12.

Kexin Huang, Jaan Altosaar, and Rajesh Ranganath. 2019. Clinicalbert: Modeling clinical notes and predicting hospital readmission. *CoRR*, abs/1904.05342.

Alistair EW Johnson, Tom J Pollard, Lu Shen, Li-wei H Lehman, Mengling Feng, Mohammad Ghassemi, Benjamin Moody, Peter Szolovits, Leo Anthony Celi, and Roger G Mark. 2016. Mimic-iii, a freely accessible critical care database. *Scientific data*, 3(1):1–9.

Meizhi Ju, Nhung TH Nguyen, Makoto Miwa, and Sophia Ananiadou. 2020. An ensemble of neural models for nested adverse drug events and medication extraction with subwords. *Journal of the American Medical Informatics Association*, 27(1):22–30.

Youngjun Kim and Stéphane M Meystre. 2020. Ensemble method–based extraction of medication and related information from clinical texts. *Journal of the American Medical Informatics Association*, 27(1):31–38.

Jinhyuk Lee, Wonjin Yoon, Sungdong Kim, Donghyeon Kim, Sunkyu Kim, Chan Ho So, and Jaewoo Kang. 2019. BioBERT: a pre-trained biomedical language representation model for biomedical text mining. *Bioinformatics*, 36(4):1234–1240.

Jinsu Lee, Sang-Kwang Lee, and Seong-Il Yang. 2018. An ensemble method of cnn models for object detection. In *2018 International Conference on Information and Communication Technology Convergence (ICTC)*, pages 898–901.

Ji Lin, Jiaming Tang, Haotian Tang, Shang Yang, Wei-Ming Chen, Wei-Chen Wang, Guangxuan Xiao, Xingyu Dang, Chuang Gan, and Song Han. 2024. Awq: Activation-aware weight quantization for on-device llm compression and acceleration. *Proceedings of Machine Learning and Systems*, 6:87–100.

Yinhan Liu, Myle Ott, Naman Goyal, Jingfei Du, Mandar Joshi, Danqi Chen, Omer Levy, Mike Lewis, Luke Zettlemoyer, and Veselin Stoyanov. 2019. Roberta: A robustly optimized BERT pretraining approach. *CoRR*, abs/1907.11692.

Zechun Liu, Barlas Oguz, Changsheng Zhao, Ernie Chang, Pierre Stock, Yashar Mehdad, Yangyang Shi, Raghuraman Krishnamoorthi, and Vikas Chandra. 2023. Llm-qat: Data-free quantization aware training for large language models. *arXiv preprint arXiv:2305.17888*.

Ammar Mohammed and Rania Kora. 2022. An effective ensemble deep learning framework for text classification. *Journal of King Saud University - Computer and Information Sciences*, 34(10, Part A):8825–8837.

David Nadeau and Satoshi Sekine. 2007. A survey of named entity recognition and classification. *Lingvisticae Investigationes*, 30(1):3–26.

Nona Naderi, Julien Knafou, Jenny Copara, Patrick Ruch, and Douglas Teodoro. 2021. Ensemble of deep masked language models for effective named entity recognition in health and life science corpora. *Frontiers in research metrics and analytics*, 6:689803.

Laila Rasmy, Yang Xiang, Ziqian Xie, Cui Tao, and Degui Zhi. 2021. Med-bert: pretrained contextualized embeddings on large-scale structured electronic health records for disease prediction. *NPJ digital medicine*, 4(1):86.

Pablo Romero, Lifeng Han, and Goran Nenadic. 2025. Insightbuddy-ai: Medication extraction and entity linking using pre-trained language models and ensemble learning. In *NAACL-SRW, Forthcoming*, New Mexico, USA. ACL.

Hager Saleh, Sherif Mostafa, Lubna Abdelkareim Gabralla, Ahmad O. Aseeri, and Shaker El-Sappagh. 2022. Enhanced arabic sentiment analysis using a novel stacking ensemble of hybrid and deep learning models. *Applied Sciences*, 12(18).

Guangyu Wang, Xiaohong Liu, Zhen Ying, Guoxing Yang, Zhiwei Chen, Zhiwen Liu, Min Zhang, Hongmei Yan, Yuxing Lu, Yuanxu Gao, et al. 2023. Optimized glycemic control of type 2 diabetes with reinforcement learning: a proof-of-concept trial. *Nature Medicine*, 29(10):2633–2642.

David H. Wolpert. 1992. Stacked generalization. *Neural Networks*, 5(2):241–259.

A Diagrams on System Details

More details on Stacked Ensemble are listed in Figure 12 and 13 on training strategy and one-hot encoding. Figure 11 shows the entity linking / coding diagram.

B Further Analysis on Models and Scores

B.1 Word-level vs Sub-word Level scores

From word-level ensemble result in Figure 9, it says that the ensembled model can achieve word-level evaluation scores 0.826, 0.826, and 0.823 for macro P/R/F1, which is close to sub-word level best model 0.847 F1. We can see that at word-level evaluation, there are 563,329 support tokens in Figure 9, vs sub-word level 756,014 tokens in Figure 8.

Word-level ensemble voting, max-logit voting > first-logit > average-logit, as shown in Table 4, with Macro F1 scores (0.8232, 0.8229, 0.8227) respectively, which are very close though. They have the same weighted average F1 and Accuracy scores (0.9798, 0.9796) respectively.

B.2 Ensemble: Stacked using output logits (non one-hot)

When we used the 'output logits' instead of 'one-hot encoding' for stacked ensemble, as we dis-

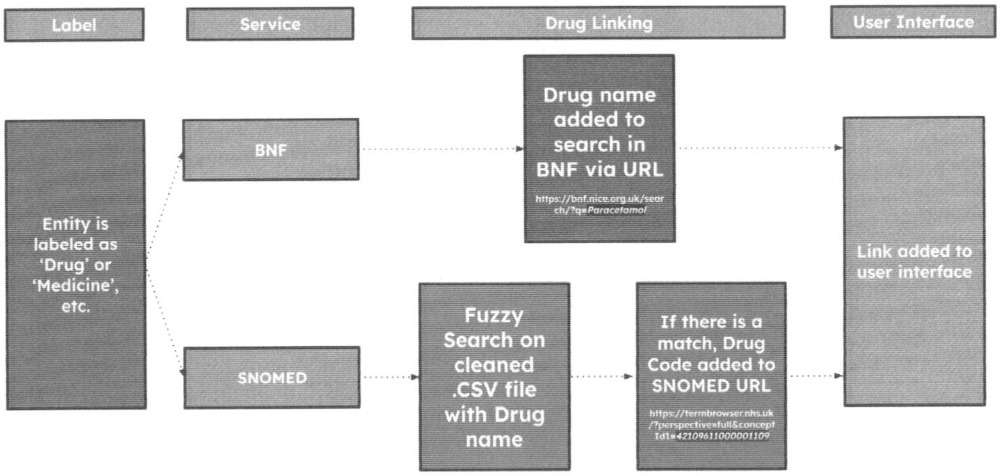

Figure 11: ENTITYLINKING: function illustration for mapping to both BNF and SNOMED-CT

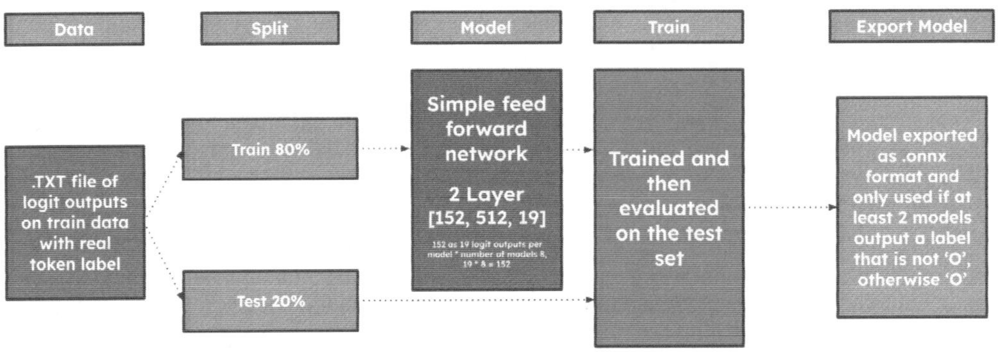

Figure 12: STACKEDENSEMBLE: training strategy.

cussed in the methodology section, it will lead to overfitting issues. We use the Max logit stacked ensemble as an example, which shows that the Stacked Ensemble using output logits produced much lower evaluation scores macro avg (0.6863, 0.7339, 0.6592) than the voting mechanism macro avg (0.8261, 0.8259, 0.8232) for (P, R, F1).

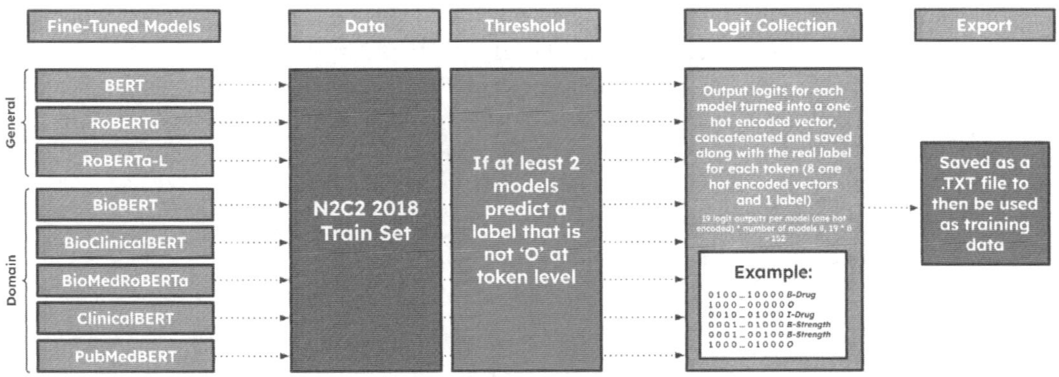

Figure 13: STACKEDENSEMBLE: one-hot encoding data.

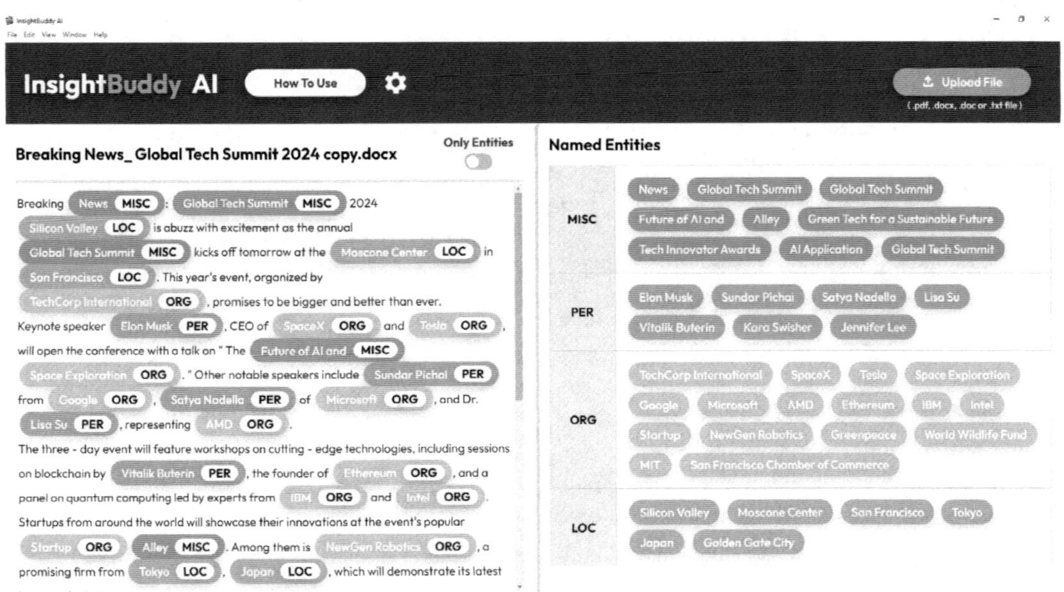

Figure 14: Loading Any Huggingface NER model: example outcome with typical (PER, LOC, ORG, MISC) label set

Bias in Danish Medical Notes: Infection Classification of Long Texts Using Transformer and LSTM Architectures Coupled with BERT

Mehdi Parviz[1], **Rudi Agius**[2], **Carsten Utoft Niemann**[2], **Rob van der Goot**[3],
[1]Department of Biology, University of Copenhagen, Denmark
[2]Department of Hematology, Copenhagen University Hospital, Rigshospitalet, Denmark
[3] Department of Computer Science, IT University of Copenhagen, Denmark,
mehdi.parviz@bio.ku.dk,
{rudi.agius.01, carsten.utoft.niemann}@regionh.dk
robv@itu.dk

Abstract

Medical notes contain a wealth of information related to diagnosis, prognosis, and overall patient care that can be used to help physicians make informed decisions. However, like any other data sets consisting of data from diverse demographics, they may be biased toward certain subgroups or subpopulations. Consequently, any bias in the data will be reflected in the output of the machine learning models trained on them. In this paper, we investigate the existence of such biases in Danish medical notes related to three types of blood cancer, with the goal of classifying whether the medical notes indicate severe infection. By employing a hierarchical architecture that combines a sequence model (Transformer and LSTM) with a BERT model to classify long notes, we uncover biases related to demographics and cancer types. Furthermore, we observe performance differences between hospitals. These findings underscore the importance of investigating bias in critical settings such as healthcare and the urgency of monitoring and mitigating it when developing AI-based systems.

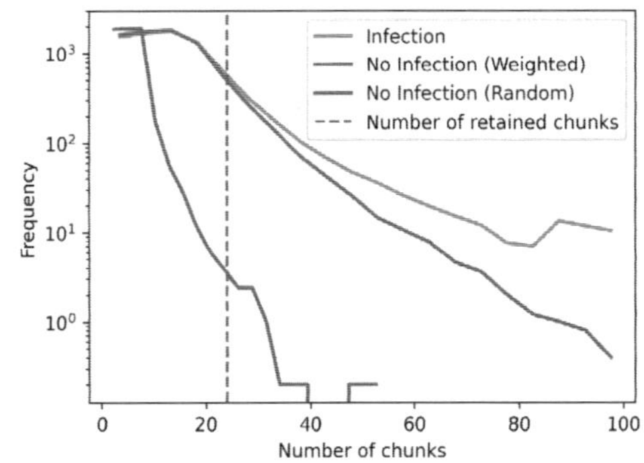

Figure 1: Document length distribution for each class before resampling, and after weighted, and random resampling. The dashed purple line indicates the number of chunks retained for modeling.

1 Introduction

Electronic Health Records (EHRs) provide diverse data on diagnoses, medications, and clinical tests, enabling AI-based applications for various purposes (Wang and Zhang, 2024). While medical notes contain similar information in an unstructured format, they offer deeper insights that complement other EHR data. They help cross-check information, retrieve missing details, and capture clinically relevant events like infections, which are often difficult to extract from structured EHR sources. Assessing EHRs and medical notes aids physicians in making informed decisions on treatments, medications, and patient care. Notably, prior infections are key predictors of clinical outcomes in blood cancers (Parviz et al., 2022; Packness et al., 2024). However, biases in EHR-derived medical data have been documented and can lead to performance deterioration in subpopulations with smaller sample sizes (Cobert et al., 2024). In this paper, we classify medical notes on three common blood cancers based on infection status and quantify bias related to sex and cancer type. The cancers studied are lymphoma (LYFO), multiple myeloma (MM), and chronic lymphocytic leukemia (CLL). Since medical notes often exceed model context lengths, we employ a hierarchical architecture combining a sequence model (Transformer and LSTM) with a BERT model (Pappagari et al., 2019).

2 Method

2.1 Data

We curated a dataset of medical notes from patients diagnosed with lymphoma, CLL, or MM in Eastern Denmark, recorded between August 2016 and November 2023. For each patient, notes recorded less than two days apart were merged, as they often related to the same health-related issue. This information was extracted from data sources available through the DALY-CARE database (Brieghel et al., 2025).

Proceedings of the Second Workshop on Patient-Oriented Language Processing (CL4Health), pages 316–320
May 4, 2025 ©2025 Association for Computational Linguistics

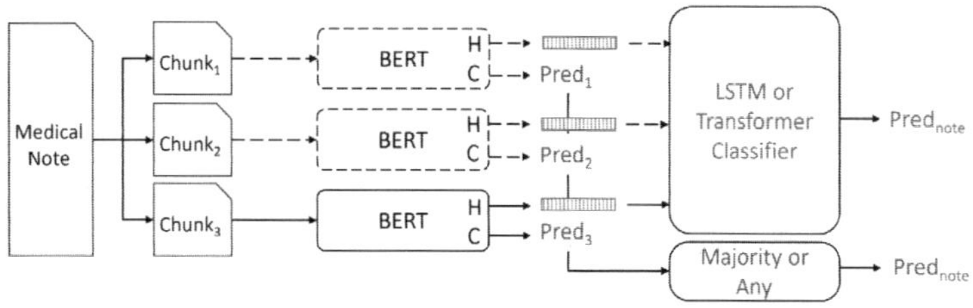

Figure 2: Schematic of modeling and data splitting strategy. A BERT model (red) is coupled with a transformer or an LSTM (blue) architecture to capture information in long medical notes.

2.2 Infection definition

While EHRs provide valuable medical information, identifying severe infections is not always straightforward. Therefore, severe infection was defined as a blood culture draw and intravenous (IV) antimicrobial administration occurring within two days. Clinically, blood cultures are taken when an infection is suspected, and IV antimicrobials are given in severe cases. Defining the outcome by both events enhances labeling precision and the likelihood that physicians mention severe infections in medical notes.

2.3 Modeling long medical notes

Due to the limited context of the BERT models, we divide medical notes into smaller chunks that fit within the maximum token limit of BERT (512). Each chunk is then assigned the same label as the full medical note. We adopt a similar approach to that of (Pappagari et al., 2019), which is presented in Figure 2. First, we fine-tune a BERT model trained on Danish medical data (Pedersen et al., 2023) to predict chunk labels. Next, we extract embeddings for each chunk from the last hidden state of BERT and model the chunk embedding sequences using either a Transformer (Vaswani et al., 2017) or an LSTM architecture (Hochreiter and Schmidhuber, 1997). We also compare the performance of these stacked methods with simpler approaches that return the chunk-level majority prediction and any (positive) prediction from BERT, which we refer to as MAJORITY and ANY.

2.4 Sensitivity to note length

We found a significant discrepancy in medical note length between classes (Figure 1); notes labeled as infection were longer than those without infection. To prevent the model from using length as a proxy for the outcome, we resample negative-class notes using a weighted approach to match the length distribution of the positive class (Figure 1). We evaluate models using both weighted resampling (Weighted) and random sampling (Random), which occur in real scenarios where one class has significantly shorter notes.

2.5 Measuring bias in subgroups

Following (Czarnowska et al., 2021), we assess potential biases in model predictions related to sex and cancer type using the false positive rate (FPR) and false negative rate (FNR). If the models are biased toward a subgroup, we expect a lower FNR and/or higher FPR compared to the other group(s). We perform binomial tests to determine whether the differences between subgroups and the majority class (male for the sex factor and lymphoma for cancer types) are statistically significant. The null hypothesis assumes that predictions for minority subgroups follow the same distribution as those for the majority subgroup.

2.6 Data splitting

To minimize data leakage or biases related to the memorization of physician-specific information (e.g., writing style or specialties) and patient history during data splitting, we ensure that training, validation, and test sets come from different hospitals. Specifically, two hospitals are used for training, the third for validation and testing, and the process is repeated for all three combinations. Figures 3 and 4 illustrate the distribution of notes across subgroups, as well as the proportion of notes labeled as infection in the training, validation, and test splits. To mitigate dataset imbalance, we resample the training set to ensure it contains an equal number of notes across female and male subgroups, cancer types, and positive and negative classes (Balanced). Since medical notes are recorded at different time points, they must be treated as a time series. Therefore, we use a time-based splitting approach when dividing the data into training, validation, and test sets. The models were trained with a learning rate of 2×10^{-5}, a batch size of 32, and for one epoch. These parameters were selected based on preliminary experiments on the validation set.

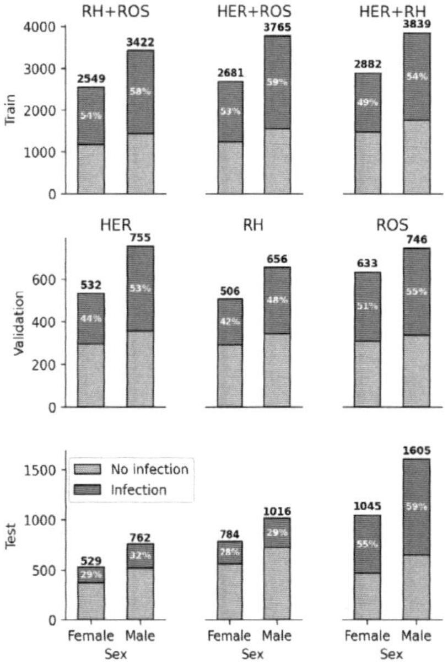

Figure 3: Notes by sex across hospitals (columns) and sets (rows). Total notes are shown atop each bar, with infection-positive percentages inside.

3 Results

3.1 Model performances

The results show that, overall, using sequence modeling (Transformer or LSTM) outperforms the simpler MAJORITY and ANY models at the classifier layer. Additionally, coupling a Transformer with the base BERT model performs better than coupling BERT with an LSTM (Table 1). All models tend to overclassify samples as infections, as evidenced by higher FPRs than FNRs. The FPRs of the two sampling strategies indicate that, despite being trained on artificially longer negative samples, the models achieve the same performance level on shorter texts observed in the dataset.

3.2 Variation in error rates by sex

The results in Table 2 show that, on both the Validation and test sets, FNR values remain at similar levels between males and females across the three hospitals. Without resampling (Observed), both FPR_W and FPR_R are significantly lower for females in two out of three hospitals in the test set. Although resampling (Balanced) eliminates sex differences in FPR_R, FPR_W values remain significantly lower

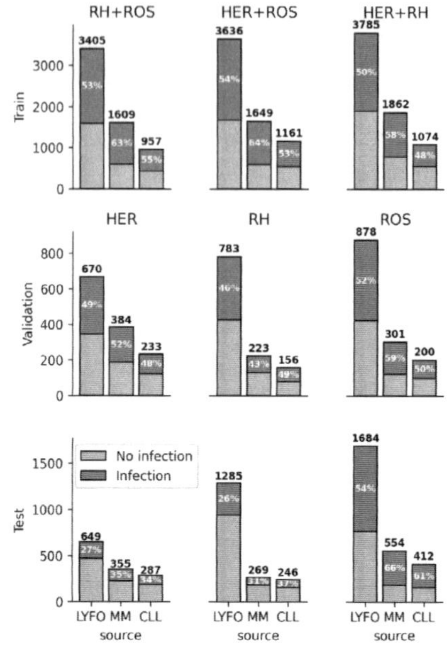

Figure 4: Notes by cancer type across hospitals (columns) and sets (rows). Total notes are shown atop each bar, with infection-positive percentages inside.

for females. This disparity suggests that the lower FPRs observed for females may be influenced by their under-representation in the dataset, leading to biased model predictions (Figure 3). Additionally, other sources of bias, such as differences in clinical documentation patterns may have further contributed to these discrepancies.

3.3 Variation in error rates by cancer type

The results on cancer types show higher FPR_W and FPR_R on MM compared with LYFO consistently across the three hospitals (Table 3). In the test set, MM and CLL both have worse FPR_R compared to LYFO. Resampling based on cancer type has little effect on reducing the significant differences. These results highlight that the models are biased against underrepresented subgroups (Figure 4).

4 Conclusion

Medical notes supplement EHRs with information not available in structured formats. Unlike other EHR data, which are automatically compiled, medical notes are written by physicians and nurses, making them more prone to bias. In this paper, we explore potential sources of bias within the demographic population and across three types of blood cancer. The results indicate biases related to sex and among different cancer types. We also

		Validation			Test		
Sampling	Model	H_{HER}	H_{RH}	H_{ROS}	H_{HER}	H_{RH}	H_{ROS}
Weighted	ANY	66.1	72.3	69.3			
	MAJORITY	81.9	76.5	83.4			
	LSTM	85.5	81.9	82.7			
	Transformer	**86.4**	**83.9**	**85.5**	78.3	81.2	83.4
Random	ANY	83.3	**88.6**	**89.1**			
	MAJORITY	80.9	78.4	86.7			
	LSTM	81.8	77.4	84.7			
	Transformer	**84.4**	84.8	86.9	84.8	84.1	84.6

Table 1: Infection classification performance of the models, measured using balanced accuracy, on the validation and test sets constructed with weighted and random sampling across hospitals.

			Validation			Test		
Balance Method	Metric	Sex	H_{HER}	H_{RH}	H_{ROS}	H_{HER}	H_{RH}	H_{ROS}
Observed	FNR	F	6.8	$11.6^{\bullet}$	$5.9^{\bullet}$	5.8	9.0	6.9
		M	6.3	8.6	8.1	4.5	8.3	8.1
	FPR_R	F	25.3	18.7	19.4	25.9	20.2^{*}	20.9^{*}
		M	24.2	22.2	18.8	25.1	25.9	25.0
	FPR_W	F	20.6	21.0	22.3	35.0^{*}	25.3^{*}	24.0
		M	21.0	23.6	21.7	40.8	31.8	26.6
Balanced	FNR	F	10.2	21.4	13.3^{*}	5.2	13.5	14.5
		M	9.5	19.5	17.6	4.1	15.2	15.3
	FPR_R	F	25.3	13.6	$11.1^{\bullet}$	24.6	18.0	15.2
		M	23.1	16.7	8.5	22.2	16.5	16.2
	FPR_W	F	22.6	15.8	17.5	$32.6^{\bullet}$	20.3^{*}	$16.7^{\bullet}$
		M	22.1	17.5	14.8	36.8	26.4	19.8

Table 2: Infection classification performance of the models in male and female subpopulations, measured using FPR and FNR, on the validation and test sets constructed via weighted and random sampling across hospitals. P-values are calculated using binomial test ($\cdot$ $p < 0.1$, * $p < 0.05$, ** $p < 0.01$, *** $p < 0.001$).

			Validation			Test		
Balance Method	Metric	Cancer	H_{HER}	H_{RH}	H_{ROS}	H_{HER}	H_{RH}	H_{ROS}
Observed	FNR	CLL	5.4	10.5	5.9	5.2	8.9	8.0
		LYFO	6.8	10.1	8.4	4.0	9.1	8.2
		MM	6.6	8.4	4.5^{*}	6.5	6.0	$6.0^{\bullet}$
	FPR_R	CLL	21.2	20.0	16.2	30.3^{**}	30.6^{**}	27.9^{*}
		LYFO	20.8	17.7	15.3	19.1	19.9	20.6
		MM	34.0^{**}	29.0^{**}	29.9^{***}	32.4^{***}	29.4^{**}	25.8^{*}
	FPR_W	CLL	19.7	$25.0^{\bullet}$	20.2	38.9	29.5	24.2
		LYFO	18.3	18.5	20.0	36.7	27.9	24.4
		MM	26.3^{*}	33.6^{***}	30.3^{**}	$41.6^{\bullet}$	$33.9^{\bullet}$	31.2^{*}
Balanced	FNR	CLL	15.3	23.7	23.8	9.3	16.7	19.9
		LYFO	12.3	24.1	21.6	6.8	17.7	21.1
		MM	14.1	26.3	19.6	12.2^{*}	13.3	18.9
	FPR_R	CLL	21.2	16.4	13.1	25.5^{**}	21.1^{**}	27.4^{*}
		LYFO	18.2	13.3	18.0	14.6	11.4	21.0
		MM	25.5^{*}	14.5	35.7^{***}	26.7^{***}	14.4	35.9^{***}
	FPR_W	CLL	16.4	$20.0^{\bullet}$	14.1	31.6	20.5	18.6
		LYFO	16.2	13.4	13.2	30.9	20.1	15.8
		MM	23.1^{*}	23.4^{**}	$18.9^{\bullet}$	34.2	26.9^{*}	22.8^{**}

Table 3: Infection classification performance of the models across different cancer subpopulations, measured using FPR and FNR, on the validation and test sets constructed via weighted and random sampling across hospitals.

observe variations in classification performance across hospitals, highlighting the need for further investigation into potential differences. These discrepancies may stem from variations in data quality or differences in how information related to severe infections is recorded.

5 Limitations

One limitation of this study is the model's shorter context than the input documents. Future work could explore longer-context models like Longformer for improvement (Beltagy et al., 2020).

References

Iz Beltagy, Matthew E. Peters, and Arman Cohan. 2020. Longformer: The long-document transformer. *arXiv:2004.05150*.

Christian Brieghel, Mikkel Werling, Casper Møller Frederiksen, Mehdi Parviz, Thomas Lacoppidan, Tereza Faitova, Rebecca Svanberg Teglgaard, Noomi Vainer, Caspar da Cunha-Bang, Emelie Curovic Rotbain, Rudi Agius, and Carsten Utoft Niemann. 2025. The danish lymphoid cancer research (daly-care) data resource: The basis for developing data-driven hematology. *Clinical Epidemiology*, 17:131–145.

Julien Cobert, Hunter Mills, Albert Lee, Oksana Gologorskaya, Edie Espejo, Sun Young Jeon, W John Boscardin, Timothy A Heintz, Christopher J Kennedy, Deepshikha C Ashana, et al. 2024. Measuring implicit bias in icu notes using word-embedding neural network models. *Chest*, 165(6):1481–1490.

Paula Czarnowska, Yogarshi Vyas, and Kashif Shah. 2021. Quantifying social biases in NLP: A generalization and empirical comparison of extrinsic fairness metrics. *Transactions of the Association for Computational Linguistics*, 9:1249–1267.

Sepp Hochreiter and Jürgen Schmidhuber. 1997. Long short-term memory. *Neural Comput.*, 9(8):1735–1780.

Esben Packness, Olafur Birgir Davidsson, Klaus Rostgaard, Michael Asger Andersen, Emelie Curovic Rotbain, Carsten Utoft Niemann, Christian Brieghel, and Henrik Hjalgrim. 2024. Infections and their prognostic significance before diagnosis of chronic lymphocytic leukemia, non-hodgkin lymphoma, or multiple myeloma. *British Journal of Cancer*.

Raghavendra Pappagari, Piotr Zelasko, Jesús Villalba, Yishay Carmiel, and Najim Dehak. 2019. Hierarchical transformers for long document classification. In *2019 IEEE Automatic Speech Recognition and Understanding Workshop (ASRU)*, pages 838–844.

Mehdi Parviz, Christian Brieghel, Rudi Agius, and Carsten Utoft Niemann. 2022. Prediction of clinical outcome in cll based on recurrent gene mutations, cll-ipi variables, and (para)clinical data. *Blood Advances*, 6:3716–3728.

Jannik Pedersen, Martin Laursen, Pernille Vinholt, and Thiusius Rajeeth Savarimuthu. 2023. MeDa-BERT: A medical Danish pretrained transformer model. In *Proceedings of the 24th Nordic Conference on Computational Linguistics (NoDaLiDa)*, pages 301–307, Tórshavn, Faroe Islands. University of Tartu Library.

Ashish Vaswani, Noam Shazeer, Niki Parmar, Jakob Uszkoreit, Llion Jones, Aidan N. Gomez, Łukasz Kaiser, and Illia Polosukhin. 2017. Attention is all you need. In *Proceedings of the 31st International Conference on Neural Information Processing Systems*, NIPS'17, page 6000–6010, Red Hook, NY, USA. Curran Associates Inc.

Dandan Wang and Shiqing Zhang. 2024. Large language models in medical and healthcare fields: applications, advances, and challenges. *Artificial Intelligence Review*, 57(11):299.

Capturing Patients' Lived Experiences with Chronic Pain through Motivational Interviewing and Information Extraction

Hadeel Elyazori[1,*], Rusul Abdulrazzaq[1], Hana Al Shawi[1], Isaac Paki Elom Amouzou[1], Patrick King[1], Syleah Manns[1], Mahdia Popal[1], Zarna Narsihbhai Patel[1], Secili DeStefano[2], Jay Shah[3], Lynn H. Gerber[1,4], Siddhartha Sikdar[1], Seiyon Lee[1], Samuel Acuña[1,†], Kevin Lybarger[1,†]

[1]George Mason University, [2]Optimal Motion Physical Therapy,
[3]National Institutes of Health Clinical Center, [4]INOVA Health System

[*]Corresponding author helyazor@gmu.edu

[†]Contributed equally to this work as senior authors

Abstract

Chronic pain affects millions, yet traditional assessments often fail to capture patients' lived experiences comprehensively. In this study, we used a Motivational Interviewing framework to conduct semi-structured interviews with eleven adults experiencing chronic pain and then applied Natural Language Processing (NLP) to their narratives. We developed an annotation schema that integrates the International Classification of Functioning, Disability, and Health (ICF) with Aspect-Based Sentiment Analysis (ABSA) to convert unstructured narratives into structured representations of key patient experience dimensions. Furthermore, we evaluated whether Large Language Models (LLMs) can automatically extract information using this schema. Our findings advance scalable, patient-centered approaches to chronic pain assessment, paving the way for more effective, data-driven management strategies.

1 Introduction

Chronic pain affects millions worldwide, diminishing quality of life and straining healthcare systems (Goldberg and McGee, 2011). In 2023, an estimated 24.3% of U.S. adults (~51.6 million individuals) experienced chronic pain (Lucas and Sohi, 2024). Beyond physical discomfort, it impacts work productivity, personal relationships, social interactions, sleep quality, and mental health (Hadi et al., 2019; Dueñas et al., 2016). Managing chronic pain remains challenging due to its multidimensional and highly individualized nature. Each patient's experience is shaped by genetics, early life events, psychological state, coexisting medical conditions, and environmental influences (Institute of Medicine, 2011; Fillingim, 2017). Many individuals experience debilitating pain without clear pathology (Fine, 2011; Dueñas et al., 2016). Over time, the persistent stress of chronic pain contributes to *allostatic load*—physiological strain that exacerbates pain severity and accelerates health decline (McCaffery et al., 2012). Consequently, understanding chronic pain requires a holistic approach that extends beyond physical symptoms.

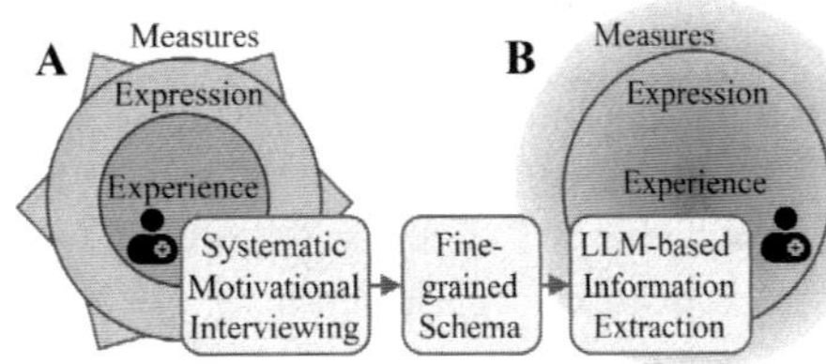

Figure 1: Integration of MI and IE to capture patients' pain experience, building on Wideman et al. (2019)

Traditional pain assessment methods rely heavily on clinical history and standardized measures, which often fail to capture the complexity of pain experience (Wideman et al., 2019; Radnovich et al., 2014; Gordon, 2015). This limitation stems from the fragmented conceptualization of pain, as shown in Figure 1A. Wideman et al. (2019) divide pain into: 1) pain experience—the subjective, intangible nature of pain that is difficult to observe; 2) pain expression—how pain is communicated verbally and non-verbally; and 3) pain measures—standardized assessments that translate expressions into numerical or categorical values. While pain measures provide objective data, they oversimplify patients' lived experiences, failing to capture the multifaceted and interconnected nature of pain. Consequently, critical aspects of pain remain poorly understood. In contrast, Figure 1B illustrates an integrated framework that our work aims to realize, where pain experience is central but is more comprehensively expressed and measured through a combination of subjective narratives and quantifiable metrics. According to the National Center for Complementary and Integrative Health (2024), adopting the "whole person" approach can lead to more comprehensive, nuanced, and effective pain assessment and treatment paradigms.

Proceedings of the Second Workshop on Patient-Oriented Language Processing (CL4Health), pages 321–330
May 4, 2025 ©2025 Association for Computational Linguistics

This study addresses these challenges by integrating Motivational Interviewing (MI), a patient-centered communication technique emphasizing empathy and active listening (Miller and Rollnick, 2013), with Natural Language Processing (NLP). We conducted semi-structured interviews using an MI protocol specifically developed to elicit nuanced, multidimensional patient narratives about pain experience. We developed a novel annotation schema to transform these unstructured narratives into structured representations by combining the International Classification of Functioning, Disability, and Health (ICF) framework (World Health Organization, 2001) with Aspect-Based Sentiment Analysis (ABSA) (Hua et al., 2024). This schema captures emotional and contextual dimensions of patient experiences, providing deeper insight into the multifaceted impacts of chronic pain. To address limitations associated with the small dataset size, we used Large Language Models (LLMs) to generate synthetic interview transcripts, supplementing real-world data for information extraction model development. Finally, we explored the feasibility of using LLMs to automatically extract the annotation schema dimensions. The contributions of this work include: 1) developing an interview protocol to elicit comprehensive patient narratives of lived experiences, 2) creating an annotation schema to systematically characterize these experiences using established frameworks, and 3) evaluating the feasibility of automating this schema using LLMs. The annotation guidelines and code are publicly available to the research community.[1]

2 Related Work

Patient narratives are important to chronic pain assessment and management, as traditional quantitative measures often fail to capture pain complexity (Georgiadis and Johnson, 2023; Robinson-Papp et al., 2015). van Rysewyk et al. (2023) found that patient narratives capture the complex interactions between physical symptoms, psychological impacts, and social consequences of chronic pain, which standardized assessments often overlook. This perspective aligns with the Multimodal Assessment Model of Pain (Wideman et al., 2019), which emphasizes moving beyond traditional measures and advocates for integrating subjective pain experiences into research and clinical practice. Recognizing their value, researchers have examined patient narratives in various clinical settings. For example, Aymerich et al. (2022) showed that narratives in a physiotherapy program informed by Acceptance and Commitment Therapy reveal both physical and psychological recovery dimensions. However, manual analysis of such narratives is time-consuming and subjective, underscoring the need for automated methods to extract meaningful insights at scale.

Early NLP research in chronic pain primarily focused on extracting and classifying symptoms from semi-structured clinical text using rule-based and machine learning methods (Rajwal, 2024). More recently, transformer-based models have advanced symptom extraction from clinical notes (Luo et al., 2022), and sentiment analysis has been used to quantify emotional distress in patient narratives (Vandenbussche et al., 2022; Nunes et al., 2023). For instance, Vandenbussche et al. (2022) systematically analyzed large-scale migraine and cluster headache narratives, identifying diagnostic patterns with unstructured text. However, the limited availability of annotated datasets restricts supervised learning approaches, particularly for analyzing unstructured patient-generated narratives. To address this challenge, recent studies have leveraged LLMs for scalable analysis of pain narratives without task-specific training. LLMs have been used to distinguish chronic pain conditions (Venerito and Iannone, 2024), extract structured insights from patient narratives (Bouzoubaa et al., 2024), and analyze sentiment in large-scale patient-reported data (Alkhnbashi et al., 2024).

This work builds on prior research by utilizing zero-shot prompting with LLMs in conjunction with a structured annotation framework to analyze chronic pain narratives. This approach enables automated pain assessment without relying on extensive labeled datasets. In contrast to previous studies that primarily focus on symptom identification and named-entity recognition, this study introduces a comprehensive annotation schema combining the ICF and ABSA to comprehensively capture biopsychosocial dimensions of pain experiences.

Even in a prompting paradigm where training data is not required, limited real-world data presents challenges in crafting effective prompts that generalize well. To address this, we generated synthetic pain narratives using LLMs to supplement real-world data and refine prompts for improved zero-shot performance. This approach

[1]https://github.com/hadeelelyazori/chronic-pain-narratives

aimed to enhance the model's ability to extract meaningful patterns without relying on extensive manual annotation or large labeled datasets.

3 Methods

3.1 Data

Semi-structured interviews (~30-60 minutes) were conducted with eleven adults reporting chronic pain (mean age: 29.5 ± 11.52 years), generating transcripts with an average of 5,500 words per interview. These interviews explored participants' lived experiences, focusing on the factors shaping pain expression and management. Eligible participants were 18 years or older and currently experiencing chronic pain. Although MI is traditionally used to facilitate behavior change, it was adapted to focus on understanding participants' experiences without influencing their behaviors. To provide some standardization, an MI protocol that emphasized engaging and focusing while excluding evoking and planning was developed. The semi-structured questions were designed to capture a broad range of factors and were informed by the National Institute on Minority Health and Health Disparities (NIMHD) Research Framework (National Institute on Minority Health and Health Disparities, 2017). This framework examines how the physical environment, behavioral patterns, cultural identity, and family and peer networks influence health. The resulting patient narratives provide a detailed, multifaceted view of chronic pain experiences.

Interviews were conducted by a team of six undergraduate researchers, with two present for each session—one led the discussion while the other documented interviewer-interviewee interactions. The interviewers had diverse academic backgrounds, including biology, forensic science, kinesiology, applied statistics, bioengineering, and healthcare research, providing a multidisciplinary perspective on patient-provider interactions. Prior to engaging with participants, researchers were trained in the interview protocol and conducted practice interviews to ensure consistency and quality. Their expertise in clinical research, physical therapy, patient communication, and data-driven healthcare analysis enriched the interview process by ensuring a contextually informed and empathetic approach. Interviews were audio recorded and transcribed using OpenAI's Whisper model (OpenAI, 2022), with speaker roles (researcher vs. participant) identified using Segmentation-3.0 (Bredin et al., 2020). Both models were run locally on a HIPAA-compliant server. The transcripts were automatically de-identified to remove protected health information (PHI) using a rule-based system (Radhakrishnan et al., 2023). A manual review was then conducted to correct transcription errors and remove any remaining PHI. All annotation and LLM experimentation utilized these de-identified records, which were securely stored on restricted servers accessible only to authorized personnel. All study procedures were approved by the Institutional Review Board (IRB).

3.2 Annotation

A comprehensive annotation protocol was developed, drawing on the concept of allostatic load, which accounts for the cumulative physiological and psychological stressors experienced by individuals with chronic pain. Allostatic load helps explain both the immediate effects of chronic pain and its long-term health impacts (Liang and Booker, 2024). This protocol was collaboratively designed by the multidisciplinary research team, whose expertise spans multiple domains. Key contributors brought specialized expertise: KL specializes in NLP annotation protocols for health informatics; SD, JS, and LHG have extensive clinical expertise in pain assessment and patient-centered care; and SS and SA bring experience in biomedical engineering, rehabilitation science, and health informatics. The collective expertise informed the development of a structured framework that integrates the ICF, a biopsychosocial framework from the World Health Organization that categorizes human functioning across body functions, body structures, activities, participation, environmental, and personal factors (World Health Organization, 2001). Since ICF does not define subcategories for personal factors, categories proposed by Geyh et al. (2019) were adopted. By incorporating both pain-related impairments and adaptation strategies, the ICF enables nuanced analysis of chronic pain experiences. To complement the ICF, ABSA was integrated to characterize implicit or explicit patient sentiments towards expressed ICF concepts, labeling them as *positive*, *negative*, or *neutral*. Figure 2 illustrates this dual-layer approach, enabling a holistic analysis of pain narratives and their perceived impact on patient experience.

The ICF includes over 1,400 hierarchically arranged concepts. Table 1 summarizes the ICF concepts used in the annotation schema, with expanded

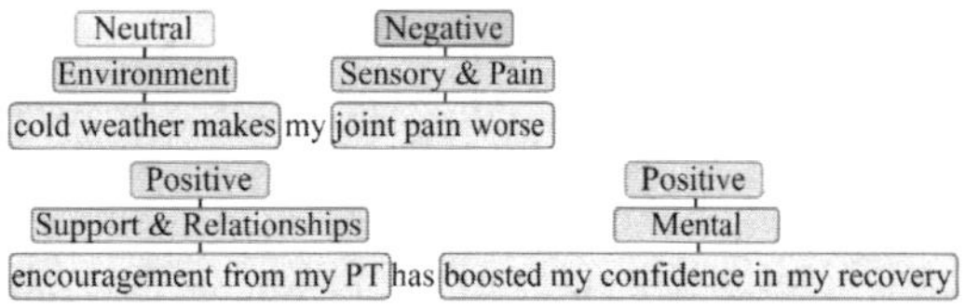

Figure 2: Annotation examples

definitions and examples provided in Appendix A. The annotation guidelines featured synthetic text examples modeled after real-world patient narratives. After training on the guidelines, four annotators—two undergraduate students (RA, a junior Biology major; HA, a senior Forensic Science major) and two graduate students (HE, a PhD student in Information Technology specializing in NLP for healthcare; ZP, a Master's student in Health Informatics)—labeled the transcripts using a local instance of Doccano[2]. Each transcript was independently annotated by two annotators, and disagreements were adjudicated.

Label	**Description**
Mental Fxn, *b1*	Memory, attention, emotion, ...
Sensory & Pain, *b2*	Sensing and pain experience
NMS & Movement, *b7*	Muscles, joint, ...
Tasks & Demands, *d2*	Manage tasks & routines, ...
Mobility, *d4*	Movement, transportation, ...
Self-Care, *d5*	Personal hygiene, eating, ...
Social Interactions, *d7*	Engage w/ friends, family, ...
Life Areas, *d8*	Education, work, & finances
Products & Tech, *e1*	Assistive tools and systems
Environment, *e2*	Physical environment
Support, *e3*	Physical and emotional support
Services & Policies, *e5*	Systems providing benefits.
Socio-demo, *i1*	Age, gender, education, ...
Positions, *i2*	Roles in social networks
History & Bio, *i3*	Influential life events
Feelings, *i4*	Emotional states
Thoughts & Beliefs, *i5*	Attitudes & perceptions
Motives, *i6*	Goals, needs, or aspirations
Patterns, *i7*	Habits and behaviors

Table 1: Annotation summary. Abbreviations: Functions (Fxn), Socio-demographics (Socio-demo)

3.3 Information Extraction

We used Meta's Llama family of LLMs and OpenAI's GPT-4 in an in-context learning, prompt-based setting for experimentation (AI@Meta, 2024; OpenAI, 2023).

3.3.1 Synthetic Data Generation

To supplement the limited dataset and refine information extraction prompts, we generated 20 synthetic interview transcripts, each consisting of interviewer questions and patient responses. First, *GPT-4-Turbo* was used to create 20 diverse patient profiles by combining personas from a large-scale curated dataset with Big Five personality traits (Ge et al., 2024; McCrae and John, 1992). This approach enhanced variability in emotional expression and coping styles. Using these profiles, *Llama-3.1-405B-Instruct* simulated doctor-patient interviews guided by the MI protocol used in the real interviews, producing narratives of chronic pain experiences. To ensure coherence while maintaining variability, decoding was performed with temperature of 0.6 and top-p of 0.8. These synthetic conversations were designed to mimic the structure and complexity of real-world patient descriptions. Finally, the synthetic transcripts were automatically labeled with the annotation schema using *Llama-3.1-405B-Instruct*, applying a low temperature of 0.1 for deterministic labeling. The annotation prompt included detailed instructions mirroring the annotation guidelines. An example from a synthetic transcript is provided in Appendix C.

3.3.2 LLM-Based Annotation of Transcripts

After refining the prompts, *Llama-3.3-70B-Instruct* was used in a zero-shot setting to generate ICF and sentiment label predictions for the 11 real-world patient transcripts, which comprised the test set. To ensure deterministic and controlled outputs, inference was conducted with a temperature of 0.1, top-p of 0.8, and maximum token limit of 4096. To prevent data leakage and ensure an unbiased evaluation, these *real* transcripts were excluded from the synthetic data used in prompt tuning. The prompt is provided in Appendix B.

3.4 Evaluation

Inter-Annotator Agreement (IAA) was evaluated using Cohen's Kappa to measure inter-annotator reliability and F1-score to enable direct comparison with LLM performance. Information extraction performance was assessed using precision, recall, and F1-score. Rather than evaluating individual text spans, evaluation was conducted at the conversational turn level, treating each turn as a multi-label classification instance. This turn-level evaluation aligns with the conversational nature of patient narratives, reducing sensitivity to minor variations in span selection while ensuring that extracted information retains its intended meaning.

[2] `https://github.com/doccano/doccano`

4 Results

4.1 Annotation

Cohen's Kappa was computed to evaluate IAA, yielding 0.52 for ICF categories and 0.43 for sentiment. To compare with LLM-extracted labels, the micro-averaged F1-score was also calculated for IAA, resulting in 0.54 for ICF categories and 0.67 for sentiment. The slightly higher F1-score compared to Kappa suggests that while there was some level of agreement on labels, discrepancies were present, particularly in sentiment annotation, where unlabeled instances from different annotators contributed to the lower Kappa. The nuanced and overlapping ICF categories introduced ambiguity, contributing to divergence among annotators. Additionally, the small dataset size limited annotators' ability to establish common patterns, increasing variability. While these IAA scores highlight challenges, they reflect the preliminary exploration of the annotation schema. Planned refinement of the annotation schema and training processes will aim to improve consistency and reliability in future iterations, as described in Section 5.

4.2 Information Extraction

Llama-3.3-70B-Instruct achieved a micro-averaged score of 0.31 F1 for ICF categories and 0.53 F1 for sentiment labels, as summarized in Table 2. While the overall performance indicates substantial room for improvement, the scores align with the observed IAA variability, reflecting the complexity of the task. Despite these challenges, the model successfully extracted some structured elements from the patient narratives, demonstrating potential for automating narrative analysis; however, performance gaps need to be addressed if actionable insights are going to be derived.

Label	P	R	F1	Sup.
Mental Fxn	0.42	0.20	0.27	25
Sensory & Pain	0.43	0.44	0.43	112
NMS & Movement	0.45	0.51	0.48	57
Tasks & Demands	0.24	0.36	0.29	33
Mobility	0.39	0.32	0.35	41
Self-Care	0.56	0.22	0.31	46
Social Interactions	0.38	0.10	0.16	51
Life Areas	0.15	0.07	0.09	30
Products & Tech	0.33	0.26	0.30	34
Environment	0.00	0.00	0.00	5
Support	0.55	0.45	0.49	94
Services & Policies	0.58	0.18	0.28	82
Socio-demo	0.00	0.00	0.00	8
Positions	0.00	0.00	0.00	2
History & Bio	0.37	0.28	0.32	46
Feelings	0.20	0.11	0.14	120
Thoughts & Beliefs	0.33	0.23	0.27	92
Motives	1.00	0.25	0.40	4
Patterns	0.00	0.00	0.00	19
Micro Averaged ICF	**0.39**	**0.27**	**0.31**	**901**
Positive	0.62	0.49	0.54	338
Negative	0.77	0.40	0.53	224
Micro Averaged Sentiment	**0.69**	**0.43**	**0.53**	**562**

Table 2: Llama 3.3 performance across ICF categories and sentiment labels

5 Discussion and Conclusions

This work presents a novel annotation schema for capturing chronic pain experiences, integrating the ICF with well-established NLP techniques, like ABSA. By structuring patient narratives within a biopsychosocial framework, this approach extends beyond traditional pain assessment methods.

Preliminary results reveal challenges in annotation consistency and automated extraction, with lower IAA suggesting ambiguities in applying ICF categories. To improve clarity and reproducibility, the schema is being refined to focus on identifying symptoms and the associated interactions. The hypothesis is that symptoms and their contextual interactions can be more reliably annotated, providing a structured basis for integrating ICF concepts at an appropriate level. Future iterations will refine the ICF label set, reassess existing data, and expand data collection to build a more diverse and robust dataset.

Zero-shot extraction experiments showed limited performance due to task complexity and annotation inconsistencies. Refining the schema should improve IAA and extraction performance. Task-specific fine-tuning may be necessary to achieve human-level performance. Incorporating realistic synthetic transcripts into fine-tuning could expand the training set, enhancing model robustness and generalization for information extraction in low-resource settings.

This preliminary study establishes an important foundation for leveraging NLP to support scalable, patient-centered chronic pain assessment. Our approach enables more nuanced and comprehensive representations of patients' lived experiences. Future work will systematically explore the avenues mentioned to improve extraction accuracy, ensuring the clinical relevance and actionable nature of the insights derived. Ultimately, this research aims to bridge qualitative patient narratives and computational methodologies, contributing meaningfully to personalized, data-driven chronic pain management and improved patient outcomes.

6 Limitations

This study has several limitations. The sample size of eleven participants limits the generalizability of findings, and the resulting annotation dataset is small, impacting both IAA and the performance of information extraction models. Additionally, the complexity and subjective nature of patient narratives introduce variability that is difficult to consistently annotate. The current zero-shot LLM-based extraction approach, while demonstrating feasibility, yields performance that may be insufficient for clinical decision-making without further refinement. Future work will involve expanding the dataset, refining annotation guidelines, and exploring fine-tuning of LLMs to improve extraction accuracy and reliability.

Acknowledgments

This research was supported by the Undergraduate Research Scholars Program of the Office of Student Creative Activities and Research at George Mason University.

References

AI@Meta. 2024. Llama 3 model card.

Omer S. Alkhnbashi, Rasheed Mohammad, and Mohammad Hammoudeh. 2024. Aspect-based sentiment analysis of patient feedback using large language models. *Big Data and Cognitive Computing*, 8(12).

Katy Aymerich, Angelika Wilczek, Soravis Ratanachatchuchai, Helen R. Gilpin, Nicolas Spahr, Clair Jacobs, and Whitney Scott. 2022. "living more and struggling less": A qualitative descriptive study of patient experiences of physiotherapy informed by acceptance and commitment therapy within a multidisciplinary pain management programme. *Physiotherapy*, 116:33–41.

Layla Bouzoubaa, Elham Aghakhani, Max Song, Quang Trinh, and Shadi Rezapour. 2024. Decoding the narratives: Analyzing personal drug experiences shared on Reddit. In *Findings of the Association for Computational Linguistics: ACL 2024*, pages 6131–6148. Association for Computational Linguistics.

Hervé Bredin, Ruiqing Yin, Juan Manuel Coria, Gregory Gelly, Pavel Korshunov, Marvin Lavechin, Diego Fustes, Hadrien Titeux, Wassim Bouaziz, and Marie-Philippe Gill. 2020. Pyannote.audio: Neural building blocks for speaker diarization. In *ICASSP 2020 - 2020 IEEE International Conference on Acoustics, Speech and Signal Processing (ICASSP)*, pages 7124–7128.

María Dueñas, Begoña Ojeda, Alejandro Salazar, Juan A. Mico, and Inmaculada Failde. 2016. A review of chronic pain impact on patients, their social environment and the health care system. *Journal of Pain Research*, 9:457–467.

Roger B. Fillingim. 2017. Individual differences in pain: Understanding the mosaic that makes pain personal. *PAIN*, 158(Supplement):S11–S18.

Perry G. Fine. 2011. Long-term consequences of chronic pain: Mounting evidence for pain as a neurological disease and parallels with other chronic disease states. *Pain Medicine*, 12(7):996–1004.

Tao Ge, Xin Chan, Xiaoyang Wang, Dian Yu, Haitao Mi, and Dong Yu. 2024. Scaling synthetic data creation with 1,000,000,000 personas. *arXiv*, 2406.20094.

Emmanouil Georgiadis and Mark I. Johnson. 2023. Incorporating personal narratives in positive psychology interventions to manage chronic pain. *Frontiers in Pain Research*, 4.

Szilvia Geyh, Urban Schwegler, Claudio Peter, and Rachel Müller. 2019. Representing and organizing information to describe the lived experience of health from a personal factors perspective in the light of the international classification of functioning, disability and health (icf): a discussion paper. *Disability and Rehabilitation*, 41(14):1727–1738.

Daniel S. Goldberg and Summer J. McGee. 2011. Pain as a global public health priority. *BMC Public Health*, 11:770.

Deborah B. Gordon. 2015. Acute pain assessment tools: Let us move beyond simple pain ratings. *Current Opinion in Anaesthesiology*, 28(5):565–569.

Muhammad A. Hadi, Gretl A. McHugh, and S. José Closs. 2019. Impact of chronic pain on patients' quality of life: A comparative mixed-methods study. *Journal of Patient Experience*, 6(2):133–141.

Yan Cathy Hua, Paul Denny, Jörg Wicker, and Katerina Taskova. 2024. A systematic review of aspect-based sentiment analysis: Domains, methods, and trends. *Artificial Intelligence Review*, 57:296.

Institute of Medicine. 2011. *Relieving pain in America: A blueprint for transforming prevention, care, education, and research*. The National Academies Press, Washington, DC.

Yunlong Liang and Cara Booker. 2024. Allostatic load and chronic pain: A prospective finding from the national survey of midlife development in the united states, 2004–2014. *BMC Public Health*, 24:416.

Jacqueline W. Lucas and Inderbir Sohi. 2024. Chronic pain and high-impact chronic pain in u.s. adults, 2023. NCHS Data Brief 518, National Center for Health Statistics, Hyattsville, MD.

Xiao Luo, Priyanka Gandhi, Susan Storey, and Kun Huang. 2022. A deep language model for symptom extraction from clinical text and its application to extract covid-19 symptoms from social media. *IEEE Journal of Biomedical and Health Informatics*, 26(4):1737–1748.

Jeanne M. McCaffery, Anna L. Marsland, Kelley Strohacker, Matthew F. Muldoon, and Stephen B. Manuck. 2012. Factor structure underlying components of allostatic load. *PLoS ONE*, 7(10).

Robert R. McCrae and Oliver P. John. 1992. An introduction to the five-factor model and its applications. *Journal of Personality*, 60(2):175–215.

William R. Miller and Stephen Rollnick. 2013. *Motivational interviewing: Helping people change*, 3rd edition. Guilford Press.

National Center for Complementary and Integrative Health. 2024. The promise of applying a whole person framework to pain.

National Institute on Minority Health and Health Disparities. 2017. Nimhd research framework. Retrieved from `https://nimhd.nih.gov/researchFramework`.

Diogo A. P. Nunes, Joana Ferreira-Gomes, Daniela Oliveira, Carlos Vaz, Sofia Pimenta, Fani Neto, and David Martins de Matos. 2023. Chronic pain patient narratives allow for the estimation of current pain intensity. In *2023 IEEE 36th International Symposium on Computer-Based Medical Systems (CBMS)*, pages 716–719.

OpenAI. 2022. Whisper.

OpenAI. 2023. Gpt-4 technical report.

Lakshmi Radhakrishnan, Gundolf Schenk, Kathleen Muenzen, Boris Oskotsky, Habibeh Ashouri Choshali, Thomas Plunkett, Sharat Israni, and Atul J. Butte. 2023. A certified de-identification system for all clinical text documents for information extraction at scale. *JAMIA Open*, 6(3):ooad045.

Richard Radnovich, C. Richard Chapman, Jeffrey A. Gudin, Sanjay J. Panchal, Lynn R. Webster, and Jr Pergolizzi, Joseph V. 2014. Acute pain: Effective management requires comprehensive assessment. *Postgraduate Medicine*, 126(4):59–72.

Swati Rajwal. 2024. Decade of natural nanguage processing in chronic pain: A systematic review. *arXiv*.

Jessica Robinson-Papp, Mary Catherine George, David Dorfman, and David M. Simpson. 2015. Barriers to chronic pain measurement: A qualitative study of patient perspectives. *Pain Medicine*, 16(7):1256–1264.

Simon van Rysewyk, Renée Blomkvist, Antony Chuter, Rhea Crighton, Fiona Hodson, David Roomes, Blair H. Smith, and Francine Toye. 2023. Understanding the lived experience of chronic pain: A systematic review and synthesis of qualitative evidence syntheses. *British Journal of Pain*, 17(6):592–605.

Nicolas Vandenbussche, Cynthia Van Hee, Véronique Hoste, and Koen Paemeleire. 2022. Using natural language processing to automatically classify written self-reported narratives by patients with migraine or cluster headache. *Journal of Headache and Pain*, 23:129.

Vincenzo Venerito and Florenzo Iannone. 2024. Large language model-driven sentiment analysis for facilitating fibromyalgia diagnosis. *RMD Open*, 10(2):e004367.

Timothy H. Wideman, Robert R. Edwards, David M. Walton, Marc O. Martel, Anne Hudon, and David A. Seminowicz. 2019. The multimodal assessment model of pain: A novel framework for further integrating the subjective pain experience within research and practice. *The Clinical Journal of Pain*, 35(3):212–221.

World Health Organization. 2001. International classification of functioning, disability, and health (icf).

A Annotation Guidelines

Label	Description	Examples
Mental Functions, *b1*	Brain functions essential for daily life, including memory, attention, emotion, sleep disturbances, etc.	(P) "I can concentrate better since I started exercising." (N) "I can't remember things like I used to."
Sensory & Pain, *b2*	Sensory abilities and perception of pain.	(P) "My pain has reduced to a manageable level." (N) "The pain is a constant 8 out of 10."
Neuromusculoskeletal & Movement, *b7*	Mobility, muscle strength, reflexes, and joint stability.	(P) "After months of physical therapy, my muscle strength has improved." (N) "The stiffness in my knees has gotten worse."
Tasks & Demands, *d2*	Managing tasks, routines, and psychological stress.	(P) "Deep breathing exercises help me stay calm." (N) "I often skip my physical therapy homework."
Mobility, *d4*	Movement-related activities such as walking and climbing stairs.	(P) "I've started taking short walks daily." (N) "I can't climb stairs without intense pain."
Self-Care, *d5*	Personal hygiene, grooming, and maintaining health.	(P) "I maintain my hygiene routine despite the pain." (N) "I often skip meals due to the pain."
Social Interactions, *d7*	Engaging socially in appropriate ways.	(P) "Joining a support group gave me practical advice." (N) "I don't go out anymore because of the pain."
Life Areas, *d8*	Tasks related to education, work, and economic activities.	(P) "I'm able to afford the best treatments." (N) "I worry about losing my job due to pain."
Products & Tech, *e1*	Tools designed to improve functioning.	(P) "My wheelchair allows me independence." (N) "The outdated software at work hinders my tasks."
Environment, *e2*	Physical environment impacting functioning.	(P) "Sunny weather helps reduce my pain." (N) "Cold weather makes my pain worse."
Support & Relationships, *e3*	Support from people or animals.	(P) "My family supports me a lot." (N) "I feel isolated because my friends don't understand."
Services & Policies, *e5*	Governance and service systems.	(P) "The nearby clinic makes care easier." (N) "Long wait times disrupt my therapy schedule."
Socio-demographics, *i1*	Observable characteristics like age, education, etc.	(P) "Being financially secure helps me access healthcare." (N) "I can't afford transportation to appointments."
Positions, *i2*	Roles in social and living environments.	(P) "As the youngest in my family, they all encourage me to keep up with therapy." (N) "Because of all the responsibilities I have as an chairperson, it all affects my recovery."
History & Bio, *i3*	Life events shaping current functioning.	(P) "Overcoming past challenges makes me resilient." (N) "Childhood trauma makes trusting providers hard."
Feelings, *i4*	Emotional states influencing responses.	(P) "I feel optimistic about managing my pain." (N) "I feel anxious about my condition."
Thoughts & Beliefs, *i5*	Attitudes about self and environment.	(P) "I believe therapy is helping me recover." (N) "I doubt the effectiveness of my treatment."
Motives, *i6*	Goals and aspirations driving behavior.	(P) "My goal to play with my kids motivates me." (N) "Progress feels slow, so I'm not motivated to continue."
Patterns, *i7*	Behavioral and cognitive tendencies.	(P) "I follow a structured medication routine." (N) "I procrastinate on health goals."

Table 3: Expanded annotation guidelines with examples. Parentheses indicate sentiment labels, where (P) denotes a positive sentiment and (N) denotes a negative sentiment

B Zero-shot Experimentation Prompt

To facilitate structured extraction of patient experiences, we designed a standardized annotation prompt that guides the LLM through our annotation schema. The prompt ensures consistency in identifying relevant text spans, assign ICF labels from a predefined set, and determine sentiment polarity.

It provides strict formatting guidelines, enforcing JSON output to support automation with LLMs. This structured approach enhances reproducibility and enables scalable NLP-based analysis of chronic pain narratives. The annotation prompt used in our study is presented below.

```
You are a highly skilled annotator specializing in chronic pain patient
responses, using the **ICF classification system** and **Aspect-Based
Sentiment Analysis**
### Task Overview:
Your goal is to:
1. **Identify** relevant text spans aligning with the provided ICF labels.
2. **Assign** the correct ICF label (**ONLY** from the provided list).
3. **Determine** sentiment:
    - Positive
    - Negative
    - Neutral
---
### **Labeling Rules**
- Use **ONLY** the provided ICF labels (no modifications or new labels).
- Each ICF-labeled span **must** also have a sentiment label.
- A span can be labeled with an ICF label with no sentiment label.
- A span can NOT be labeled with a sentiment label with no ICF label.
- If a span **does not match an ICF label**, exclude it.
---
### **ICF Labels (Use only these - No external labels)**
{json.dumps(icf_labels, indent=2)}
---
### **Output Format**
Return a **valid JSON object**:
{
"id": <text_id>,
"label": [
    ["<TEXT_SPAN_1>", "ICF_LABEL"],
    ["<TEXT_SPAN_1>", "SENTIMENT_LABEL"],
    ["<TEXT_SPAN_2>", "ICF_LABEL"],
    ["<TEXT_SPAN_2>", "SENTIMENT_LABEL"]
]
}
- **No explanations, no missing labels.**
- **If a span is unlabeled, exclude it.**
---
### **Text to Annotate:**
{transcript}
```

C Synthetic Data

To supplement the limited dataset, we generated 20 synthetic patient narratives using a structured pipeline. The goal was to simulate realistic patient transcripts, automatically annotate them using an LLM, and utilize them for prompt tuning. The pipeline was designed to closely mirror real-world chronic pain experiences while ensuring diversity in patient characteristics. The process consisted of three main steps:: 1) profile generation, 2) conversation simulation, and 3) automatic annotation.

C.1 Profile Generation

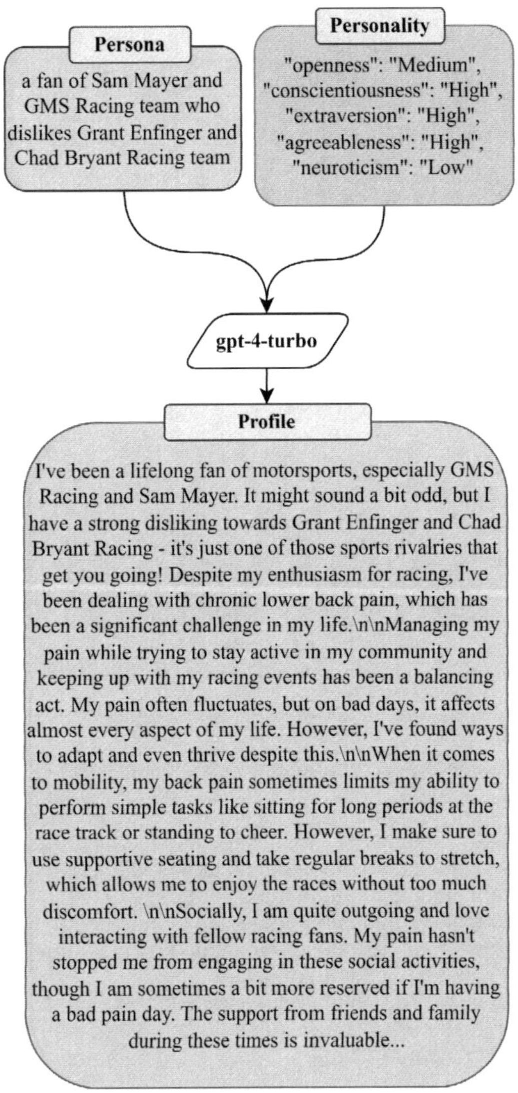

Figure 3: Profile synthetic generation example using Personas (Ge et al., 2024), the Big Five model (McCrae and John, 1992) and GPT

Figure 4 illustrates the synthetic profile generation process, which integrates personas, Big Five personality traits, and text generation. A persona is used for the demographic attributes it has (e.g., occupation, interests) and the Big Five model is used for its psychological traits (e.g., openness, neuroticism). These details are then passed through the GPT4 model, which generates a first-person narrative. The resulting profile provides a patient background, ensuring diverse and realistic chronic pain experiences for the conversation generation.

C.2 Coversation Simulation

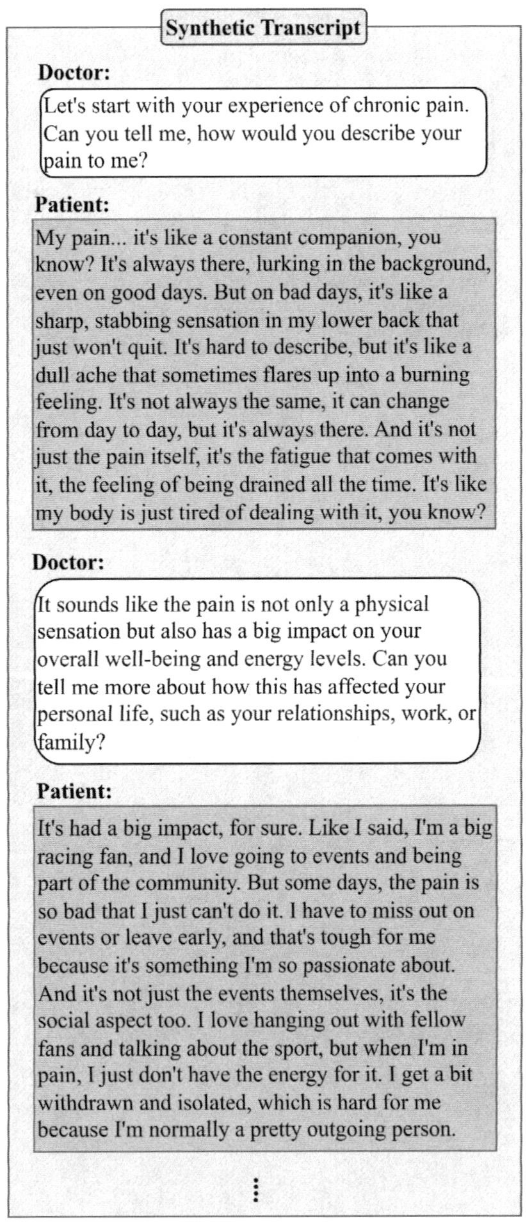

Figure 4: Synthetic transcript example

Medifact at PerAnsSumm 2025: Leveraging Lightweight Models for Perspective-Specific Summarization of Clinical Q&A Forums

Nadia Saeed
Computational Biology Research Lab
Department of Computer Science
National University of Computer and Emerging Sciences (NUCES-FAST)
Islamabad, Pakistan
i181606@nu.edu.pk

Abstract

The PerAnsSumm 2025 challenge focuses on perspective-aware healthcare answer summarization (Agarwal et al., 2025). This work proposes a few-shot learning framework using a Snorkel-BART-SVM pipeline for classifying and summarizing open-ended healthcare community question-answering (CQA). An SVM model is trained with weak supervision via Snorkel, enhancing zero-shot learning. Extractive classification identifies perspective-relevant sentences, which are then summarized using a pretrained BART-CNN model. The approach achieved 12th place among 100 teams in the shared task, demonstrating computational efficiency and contextual accuracy. By leveraging pretrained summarization models, this work advances medical CQA research and contributes to clinical decision support systems.[1]

1 Introduction

Healthcare Community Question-Answering (CQA) forums have become a vital source of medical information to seek advice and share experiences (Jiang, 2024; Zhang et al., 2024). These platforms generate diverse responses, ranging from factual knowledge to personal opinions like PUMA dataset (Naik et al., 2024). Traditional CQA summarization methods focus on selecting a single best-voted answer as a reference summary (Tsatsaronis et al., 2015; Kell et al., 2024). However, a single answer often fails to capture the broad range of perspectives available across multiple responses. To better serve users, it is essential to generate structured summaries that represent various viewpoints effectively.

To address this, we introduce a hybrid framework that combines perspective classification and summarization, as shown in Figure 1. The first step involves classifying user responses into predefined perspectives using a multi-step learning pipeline. This pipeline integrates Snorkel-based weak supervision (Ratner et al., 2017), support vector machine (SVM) classification with sentence embeddings (Rueping, 2010), and zero-shot learning (ZSL) using transformer models (Lewis, 2019). The goal is to enhance classification accuracy, especially when labeled data is scarce.

Once classified, responses undergo a two-step summarization process. We employ extractive summarization using BART to select key sentences from classified perspectives (Lewis, 2019). Then, we refine these summaries using abstractive summarization with Pegasus to improve fluency and coherence (Zhang et al., 2020). The composed model is evaluated on the **PerAnsSumm Shared Task - CL4Health@NAACL 2025**, which focuses on analyzing multi-perspective responses in Community Question Answering (CQA) (Agarwal et al., 2025). Given a user-generated question Q and a set of responses A, the task is divided into two key objectives:

(1)Perspective Classification, where response spans are categorized into predefined perspectives such as *cause*, *suggestion*, *experience*, *question*, and *information*;

(2)Perspective Summarization, which generates structured summaries that condense key insights while preserving essential details. Our approach integrates both tasks into a single pipeline, ensuring efficient classification and summarization of CQA responses.

By leveraging weak supervision and fine-tuning pre-trained models, we balance computational efficiency with adaptability, making the solution practical for real-world applications. This hybrid approach ensures that summaries retain critical information while being concise and easily understandable. This study makes the following key contributions:

[1]Models Code available: https://github.com/NadiaSaeed/PerAnsSumm2025/tree/main

Proceedings of the Second Workshop on Patient-Oriented Language Processing (CL4Health), pages 331–339
May 4, 2025 ©2025 Association for Computational Linguistics

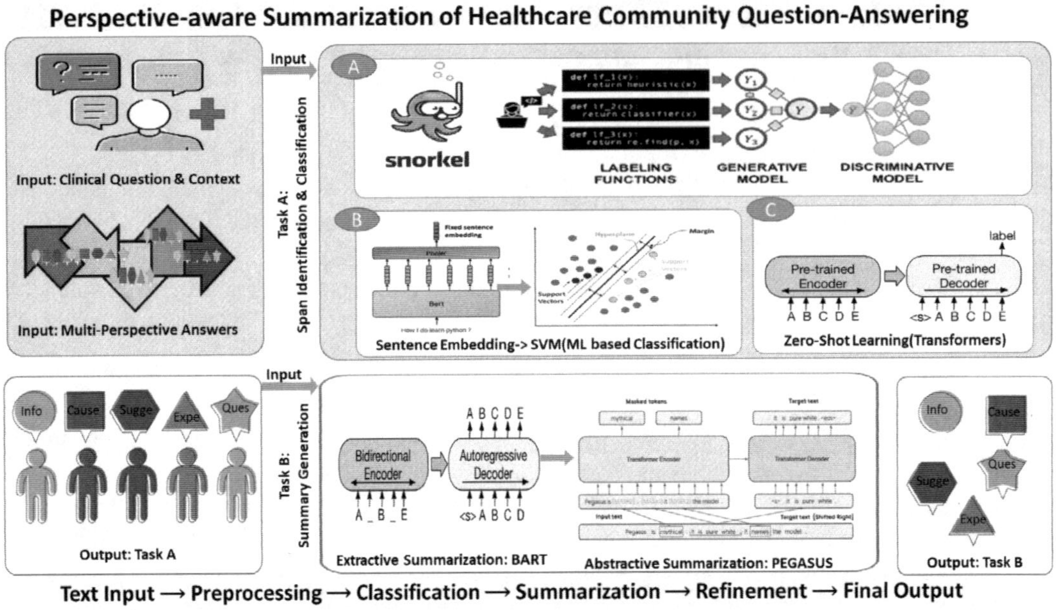

Figure 1: Hybrid workflow for perspective classification and summarization. Perspectives are classified using heuristic labeling (Snorkel), SVM-based classification, and a zero-shot model fallback. Summarization is performed in two stages: extractive (BART) and abstractive (Pegasus), integrating the context for a refined output.

1. A hybrid classification framework combining weak supervision, machine learning, and deep learning techniques for robust perspective identification.

2. A rule-based weak supervision method using Snorkel's labeling functions to generate high-quality probabilistic labels.

3. Feature extraction via sentence embeddings, leveraging transformer-based models to enhance classification.

4. A zero-shot learning (ZSL) classifier to handle unseen data without additional labeled examples.

5. A two-stage summarization pipeline that integrates extractive (BART) and abstractive (Pegasus) techniques for structured summaries.

6. A thorough evaluation demonstrating the effectiveness of our approach on real-world CQA datasets.

By combining classification with summarization, our method ensures that user-generated responses are structured, informative, and accessible. This enhances the usability of healthcare CQA forums and facilitates better decision-making for users.

2 Methodology

2.1 Task A: Perspective Classification

2.1.1 Problem Definition

Given a dataset of textual responses, our goal is to classify each response x_i into one of the predefined perspective categories (Naik et al., 2024):

$$\mathcal{P} = \{EXPE, INFO, CAUS, SUGG, QUES\} \quad (1)$$

Each response consists of multiple sentences, and our objective is to determine the category y_i by maximizing the conditional probability:

$$y_i = \arg\max_{p \in \mathcal{P}} P(p \mid x_i) \quad (2)$$

2.1.2 Hybrid Classification Pipeline

To achieve robust classification, we employ a three-stage hybrid pipeline:

1. Weak Supervision with Snorkel: Rule-based labeling functions assign probabilistic labels (Ratner et al., 2017; Fries et al., 2020; Rühling Cachay et al., 2021).

2. Supervised Learning with SVM: A Support Vector Machine (SVM) refines classification using sentence embeddings (Ala'M et al., 2023).

3. Zero-Shot Classification: A transformer model is applied when previous methods yield uncertain labels (Gera et al., 2022; Schopf et al., 2022).

2.1.3 Weak Supervision Using Snorkel

Manual annotation is time-intensive, so we use Snorkel's labeling functions (LFs) to generate weak labels based on pattern recognition:

$$LF(x) = \begin{cases} l_p, & \text{if pattern } p \text{ is found in } x \\ -1, & \text{otherwise} \end{cases} \quad (3)$$

where l_p is the assigned label, and -1 indicates abstention. To aggregate multiple weak labels, Snorkel's Label Model M estimates the true label distribution:

$$\hat{Y} = M(L) \quad (4)$$

where L represents the label matrix from different LFs. To efficiently label textual data, LFs based on regex patterns extracted from frequent words in the dataset. Each LF detects specific linguistic cues for perspective categories like EXPERIENCE or SUGGESTION. If a match is found, a label is assigned; otherwise, it abstains (as shown in Figure 1). The PandasLFApplier applies these LFs to generate a label matrix (Tok et al., 2021), which is then refined using Snorkel's Label Model to resolve conflicts and improve accuracy. This approach speeds up annotation while ensuring consistency through statistical aggregation.

2.1.4 Sentence Embeddings and SVM Classification

We convert textual responses into sentence embed

$$E(x) = \text{SentenceTransformer}(x) \quad (5)$$

These embeddings are used by an SVM classifier to enhance prediction accuracy:

$$\hat{y} = \text{SVM}(E(x)) \quad (6)$$

SVM is trained on sentence embeddings from a labeled dataset to classify text into perspective categories. Using a linear kernel, it learns decision boundaries in high-dimensional space. During inference, new sentences are embedded and classified based on their positions in the learned feature space.

2.1.5 Few-Shot Learning with Zero-Shot Classification

If Snorkel and SVM fail to provide a confident classification, we apply zero-shot learning (ZSL) using a transformer-based model:

$$P(p \mid x) = f_{ZSL}(x, \mathcal{P}) \quad (7)$$

where f_{ZSL} is a BART-based ZSL classifier, selecting the category with the highest probability. The ZSL model (facebook/bart-large-mnli) is applied using Hugging Face's pipeline (Lewis, 2019). When a sentence remains unclassified, the ZSL model evaluates the text without prior training on specific labeled data by comparing it to predefined perspective categories (*P*). It then assigns the most probable label by ranking all categories based on their semantic similarity to the input sentence. This ensures that even unseen or ambiguous responses can still be categorized effectively.

2.1.6 Final Classification Decision

The classification decision follows a hierarchical approach (as Shown in Figure 1 A, B and C):

$$y_i = \begin{cases} \hat{Y}_i, & \text{if } \hat{Y}_i \neq -1 \\ \text{SVM}(E(x_i)), & \text{if Snorkel abstains} \\ f_{ZSL}(x_i, \mathcal{P}), & \text{otherwise} \end{cases} \quad (8)$$

2.2 Task B: Hybrid Summarization

2.2.1 Overview

To generate high-quality summaries, we integrate extractive and abstractive techniques as shown in Figure 1 and 2:

2.2.2 Extractive Summarization Using BART

We use the facebook/bart-large-cnn model to extract salient content (Lewis, 2019):

$$S = \text{BART}(X) \quad (9)$$

where X is the concatenated input text and S is the generated extractive summary. The process involve following steps as shown in Figure 1 and 2:

1. Tokenizing input text with BART's tokenizer.
2. Using a task-specific prefix (summarize:).
3. Truncating text to 1024 tokens.
4. Applying beam search with: *max_length = 150, min_length = 50, length_penalty = 2.0, num_beams = 4*

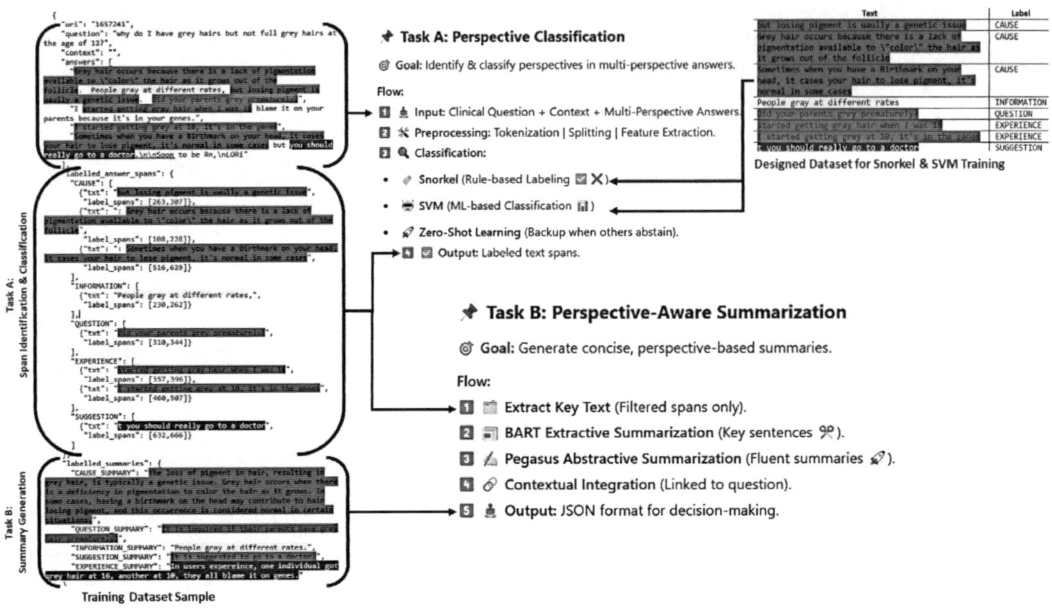

Figure 2: Training sample utilization for weak supervision. Known text spans from labeled data are used to train an SVM classifier, construct Snorkel labeling functions, and refine heuristic rules. The zero-shot model is excluded from direct training and is used as a fallback during classification.

2.2.3 Abstractive Refinement Using Pegasus

The extractive summary is refined with google/pegasus-xsum (Zhang et al., 2020):

$$S' = \text{Pegasus}(S) \tag{10}$$

where S' is the final abstractive summary. Refinement involves following steps:

1. Tokenizing extractive summaries.
2. Using the summarize: prompt.
3. Truncating input to 512 tokens.
4. Applying beam search with: *max_length = 100, min_length = 30, length_penalty = 1.8, num_beams = 6*

For our experiments, we utilize a dataset labeled with five perspective categories *P* in which *EXPE* and all others relate to the perspective of Experience, Information, Cause, Suggestion, and Question respectively (in Equation 1). Task A involves hierarchical classification, where unlabeled responses are processed using a combination of weak supervision, Support Vector Machines (SVM), and zero-shot learning (ZSL) (as Equation 8). We employ Snorkel for weak supervision, training its label model for 500 epochs to aggregate multiple labeling sources. Sentence embeddings are generated using SentenceTransformer (*all-MiniLM-L6-v2*) (Lewis, 2019), which serves as input to an SVM classifier trained with a linear kernel and default hyperparameters. For ZSL, we use Facebook's BART-Large-MNLI to directly infer category labels from textual descriptions.

Task B focuses on response structuring and refinement using transformer-based summarization models. We employ BART-Large-CNN for extractive summarization, generating concise representations of textual responses. To enhance coherence and fluency, we further refine these summaries using Pegasus-XSum (Zhang et al., 2020), an abstractive summarization model designed for extreme summarization tasks. The dataset for Task B consists of both labeled and unlabeled responses, allowing the models to learn from structured examples while refining free-text inputs. Our approach integrates both extractive and abstractive summarization techniques to ensure a well-structured and contextually rich final output.

3 Results and Discussion

In this study, we evaluated multiple hybrid models integrating Few-shot learning, weak supervision (Snorkel), and transformer-based architectures (BART, PEGASUS, and SVMs) for Span Identification & Classification (Task A) and Summarization (Task B). The primary objective was to assess the effectiveness of different learning paradigms in handling biomedical text processing challenges.

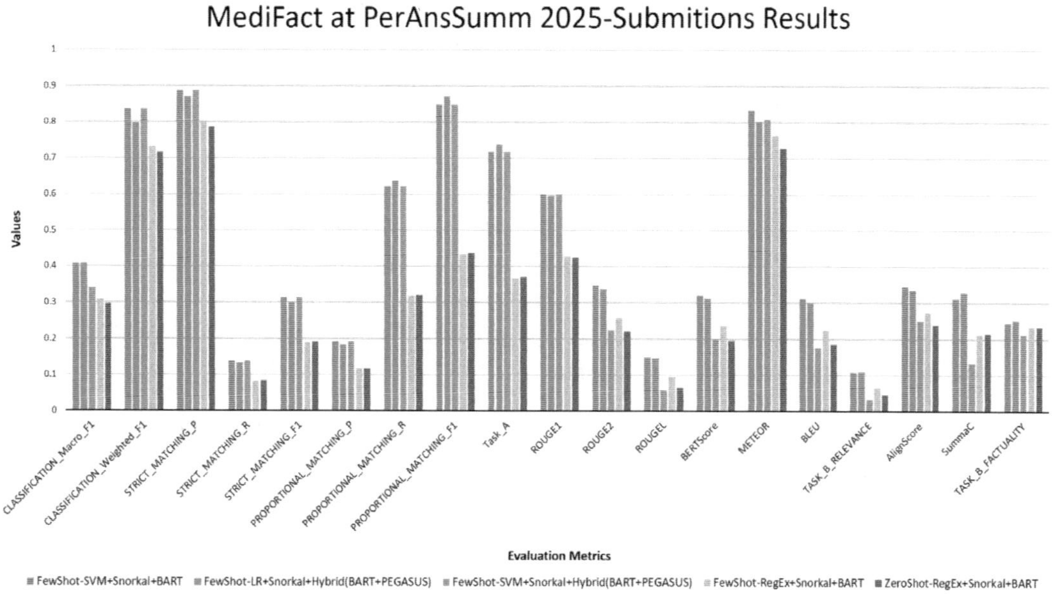

Figure 3: The comparative analysis of MediFact's submitted models on the PerAnsSumm Shared Task - CL4Health@NAACL 2025.

Task A (Perspective Classification) is evaluated using Macro-F1, Weighted-F1, Strict Matching (Precision, Recall, Weighted-F1), and Proportional Matching (Precision, Recall, Weighted-F1). Task B (Perspective Summarization) is assessed using ROUGE (R1, R2, RL), BLEU, Meteor, and BERTScore. The bar graph illustrates a comparative analysis of model performance across both tasks, highlighting strengths and areas for improvement in Figure 3.

3.1 Task A: Span Identification & Classification

The highest Weighted F1 score of 0.8361 was achieved by the *FewShot-SVM+Snorkel+BART* model, demonstrating its robustness in span identification and classification. Additionally, *FewShot-LR+Snorkel+Hybrid (BART+PEGASUS)* exhibited a competitive performance with an F1 score of 0.7961, while also achieving the best proportional match score (0.7373), indicating its capability to identify partially matched spans effectively.

Conversely, models relying on regular expressions (*FewShot-RegEx+Snorkel+BART* and *ZeroShot-RegEx+Snorkel+BART*) underperformed in classification, with *F1* scores of 0.7316 and 0.7161, respectively. This suggests that rule-based approaches lack the generalization needed for complex biomedical text extraction tasks.

3.2 Task B: Summarization Performance

The summarization capabilities of the models were evaluated using ROUGE-1 scores and factuality assessments. The *FewShot-SVM+Snorkel+BART* model achieved the highest ROUGE-1 score of 0.3485, indicating its effectiveness in generating relevant and concise summaries. Interestingly, *FewShot-LR+Snorkel+Hybrid (BART+PEGASUS)* demonstrated superior factuality (0.2897), suggesting that PEGASUS contributes to improved content faithfulness in biomedical text summarization.

Models utilizing regular expression-based classification (FewShot-RegEx and ZeroShot-RegEx variants) performed significantly lower across all summarization metrics. This highlights that statistical and deep learning-based models outperform rule-based approaches in abstractive summarization tasks.

3.3 Comparative Analysis of Model Performance

For a comprehensive evaluation, the combined average score (Task A + Task B performance) was computed for each model (Figure 3). *FewShot-SVM+Snorkel+BART* emerged as the best-performing approach with a combined score of 0.4077, followed by *FewShot-LR+Snorkel+Hybrid (BART+PEGASUS)* with 0.4070. The hybrid models demonstrated a balanced trade-off between classification accuracy and summarization quality, reinforcing the effectiveness of weak supervision with Snorkel and transformer-based architectures. In contrast, rule-based models (FewShot-RegEx & ZeroShot-RegEx variants) consistently showed inferior performance, suggesting that deep generative models are more suitable for biomedical NLP tasks requiring contextual understanding and content generation.

The experimental results demonstrate that a hybrid learning strategy combining weak supervision (Snorkel), Few-shot learning, and transformer models (BART, PEGASUS) yields optimal performance in biomedical span identification and summarization tasks. The proposed *FewShot-SVM+Snorkel+BART* model outperformed all other configurations, achieving the highest classification accuracy and summarization quality. These findings emphasize the importance of leveraging both structured supervision and deep generative architectures for enhancing biomedical text processing.

3.4 MediFact Performance in PerAnsSumm Shared Task

MediFact secured a position among the **top 12 teams** in the **PerAnsSumm Shared Task - CL4Health@ NAACL 2025**. The final results were officially reported by the task organizers on the shared task website.[2]

In Figure A.1, MediFact's performance across various evaluation metrics demonstrates strong classification capabilities, achieving a competitive Weighted F1-score of 0.8887. However, the Macro F1-score (0.8361) suggests room for improvement in handling class imbalances.

In the matching task, MediFact attains a high Proportional Matching Recall (0.8493), indicating effective identification of relevant matches. However, the Strict Matching Precision (0.1383) and Strict Matching F1 (0.1921) highlight challenges in reducing false positives.

For summarization, the model achieves a BERTScore of 0.8336, reflecting strong semantic alignment. However, lower ROUGE scores (R1: 0.3485, R2: 0.1475, RL: 0.3212) and BLEU (0.1078) suggest the need for more accurate and concise text generation.

Factual consistency metrics, such as AlignScore (0.3121) and Factuality Score (0.2784), indicate areas for improvement in ensuring reliable summarization. Future work should focus on enhancing precision in matching, optimizing summarization coherence, and strengthening factual alignment to ensure more trustworthy outputs.

4 Conclusion

This research introduces a modular and resource-efficient approach for perspective-aware classification and summarization. We combine weak supervision, machine learning, and pre-trained transformers to balance accuracy and computational cost (Ratner et al., 2017; Rueping, 2010; Lewis, 2019). Instead of training a model from scratch, we fine-tune pre-trained models on our dataset. This approach reduces resource demands and speeds up adaptation to new tasks.

One major motivation for our method is overcoming computational limitations. Training large models from the ground up requires extensive hardware and time (Touvron et al., 2023; Floridi and Chiriatti, 2020; Lewis, 2019). To handle this, we use pre-trained models that can be fine-tuned efficiently. We also apply weak supervision with heuristic labeling, reducing the need for manual annotation (as shown in Figure 2). This makes our approach scalable and practical.

Our study shows that strong results can be achieved even with limited resources. We propose a modular and adaptable solution that does not depend entirely on commercial large language models (LLMs). While proprietary models offer high performance, they lack flexibility and accessibility (Team et al., 2023; Lee and Hsiang, 2020). Instead, we demonstrate how open-source models and targeted fine-tuning provide robust results without heavy computational costs.

In conclusion, this work highlights the importance of resource-aware AI research. It proves that effective NLP solutions can be built without expensive models. Open-source tools played a key role in making this study possible (Wolf, 2019; Lewis, 2019; Zhang et al., 2020). By selecting the right model and designing a modular workflow, we achieve high-quality classification and summarization even with limited resources. This research encourages future work to focus on scalable, adaptable, and cost-effective AI solutions instead of relying solely on commercial LLMs.

[2]PerAnsSumm Shared Task - CL4Health@ NAACL 2025: https://peranssumm.github.io/docs/#leaderboard

5 Limitations

Weak supervision relies on heuristic rules, which may introduce bias or inconsistencies. While pre-trained models reduce the computational burden, further improvements can be made. Future research can explore lightweight architectures, efficient fine-tuning methods (such as LoRA (Hu et al., 2021) and quantization (Yang et al., 2019)), and retrieval-augmented generation (RAG) (Notarangelo et al., 2016) to handle unseen perspectives.

References

Siddhant Agarwal, Md Shad Akhtar, and Shweta Yadav. 2025. Overview of the peranssumm 2025 shared task on perspective-aware healthcare answer summarization. In *Proceedings of the Second Workshop on Patient-Oriented Language Processing (CL4Health) @ NAACL 2025*, Albuquerque, USA. Association for Computational Linguistics.

Al-Zoubi Ala'M, Antonio M Mora, and Hossam Faris. 2023. A multilingual spam reviews detection based on pre-trained word embedding and weighted swarm support vector machines. *IEEE Access*.

Luciano Floridi and Massimo Chiriatti. 2020. Gpt-3: Its nature, scope, limits, and consequences. *Minds and Machines*, 30:681–694.

Jason A Fries, Ethan Steinberg, Saelig Khattar, Scott L Fleming, Jose Posada, Alison Callahan, and Nigam H Shah. 2020. Trove: Ontology-driven weak supervision for medical entity classification. *arXiv preprint arXiv:2008.01972*.

Ariel Gera, Alon Halfon, Eyal Shnarch, Yotam Perlitz, Liat Ein-Dor, and Noam Slonim. 2022. Zero-shot text classification with self-training. *arXiv preprint arXiv:2210.17541*.

Edward J Hu, Yelong Shen, Phillip Wallis, Zeyuan Allen-Zhu, Yuanzhi Li, Shean Wang, Lu Wang, and Weizhu Chen. 2021. Lora: Low-rank adaptation of large language models. *arXiv preprint arXiv:2106.09685*.

Emily Jiang. 2024. *Clinical Question-Answering over Distributed EHR Data*. Ph.D. thesis, Massachusetts Institute of Technology.

Gregory Kell, Angus Roberts, Serge Umansky, Linglong Qian, Davide Ferrari, Frank Soboczenski, Byron C Wallace, Nikhil Patel, and Iain J Marshall. 2024. Question answering systems for health professionals at the point of care—a systematic review. *Journal of the American Medical Informatics Association*, 31(4):1009–1024.

Jieh-Sheng Lee and Jieh Hsiang. 2020. Patent claim generation by fine-tuning openai gpt-2. *World Patent Information*, 62:101983.

Mike Lewis. 2019. Bart: Denoising sequence-to-sequence pre-training for natural language generation, translation, and comprehension. *arXiv preprint arXiv:1910.13461*.

Gauri Naik, Sharad Chandakacherla, Shweta Yadav, and Md Shad Akhtar. 2024. No perspective, no perception!! perspective-aware healthcare answer summarization. In *Findings of the Association for Computational Linguistics: ACL 2024*, pages 15919–15932, Bangkok, Thailand. Association for Computational Linguistics.

Luigi D Notarangelo, Min-Sung Kim, Jolan E Walter, and Yu Nee Lee. 2016. Human rag mutations: biochemistry and clinical implications. *Nature Reviews Immunology*, 16(4):234–246.

Alexander J Ratner, Stephen H Bach, Henry R Ehrenberg, and Chris Ré. 2017. Snorkel: Fast training set generation for information extraction. In *Proceedings of the 2017 ACM international conference on management of data*, pages 1683–1686.

Stefan Rueping. 2010. Svm classifier estimation from group probabilities. In *Proceedings of the 27th international conference on machine learning (ICML-10)*, pages 911–918.

Salva Rühling Cachay, Benedikt Boecking, and Artur Dubrawski. 2021. End-to-end weak supervision. *Advances in Neural Information Processing Systems*, 34:1845–1857.

Tim Schopf, Daniel Braun, and Florian Matthes. 2022. Evaluating unsupervised text classification: zero-shot and similarity-based approaches. In *Proceedings of the 2022 6th International Conference on Natural Language Processing and Information Retrieval*, pages 6–15.

Gemini Team, Rohan Anil, Sebastian Borgeaud, Jean-Baptiste Alayrac, Jiahui Yu, Radu Soricut, Johan Schalkwyk, Andrew M Dai, Anja Hauth, Katie Millican, et al. 2023. Gemini: a family of highly capable multimodal models. *arXiv preprint arXiv:2312.11805*.

Wee Hyong Tok, Amit Bahree, and Senja Filipi. 2021. *Practical Weak Supervision.* " O'Reilly Media, Inc.".

Hugo Touvron, Thibaut Lavril, Gautier Izacard, Xavier Martinet, Marie-Anne Lachaux, Timothée Lacroix, Baptiste Rozière, Naman Goyal, Eric Hambro, Faisal Azhar, et al. 2023. Llama: Open and efficient foundation language models. *arXiv preprint arXiv:2302.13971*.

George Tsatsaronis, Georgios Balikas, Prodromos Malakasiotis, Ioannis Partalas, Matthias Zschunke, Michael R Alvers, Dirk Weissenborn, Anastasia Krithara, Sergios Petridis, Dimitris Polychronopoulos, et al. 2015. An overview of the bioasq large-scale biomedical semantic indexing and question answering competition. *BMC bioinformatics*, 16:1–28.

T Wolf. 2019. Huggingface's transformers: State-of-the-art natural language processing. *arXiv preprint arXiv:1910.03771*.

Jiwei Yang, Xu Shen, Jun Xing, Xinmei Tian, Houqiang Li, Bing Deng, Jianqiang Huang, and Xian-sheng Hua. 2019. Quantization networks. In *Proceedings of the IEEE/CVF conference on computer vision and pattern recognition*, pages 7308–7316.

Jingqing Zhang, Yao Zhao, Mohammad Saleh, and Peter Liu. 2020. Pegasus: Pre-training with extracted gap-sentences for abstractive summarization. In *International conference on machine learning*, pages 11328–11339. PMLR.

Xiaoman Zhang, Chaoyi Wu, Ziheng Zhao, Weixiong Lin, Ya Zhang, Yanfeng Wang, and Weidi Xie. 2024. Development of a large-scale medical visual question-answering dataset. *Communications Medicine*, 4(1):277.

A MediFact Performance Detail

This section provides additional insights into MediFact's performance, complementing the discussion in Section 3. Figure A.1 presents a detailed breakdown of evaluation metrics across different tasks, including classification, matching, and summarization. The results highlight MediFact's strong classification capabilities, particularly in achieving a competitive Weighted F1-score. However, performance in strict matching and summarization coherence suggests potential areas for improvement. These findings provide direction for future optimizations, focusing on enhanced precision and factual consistency.

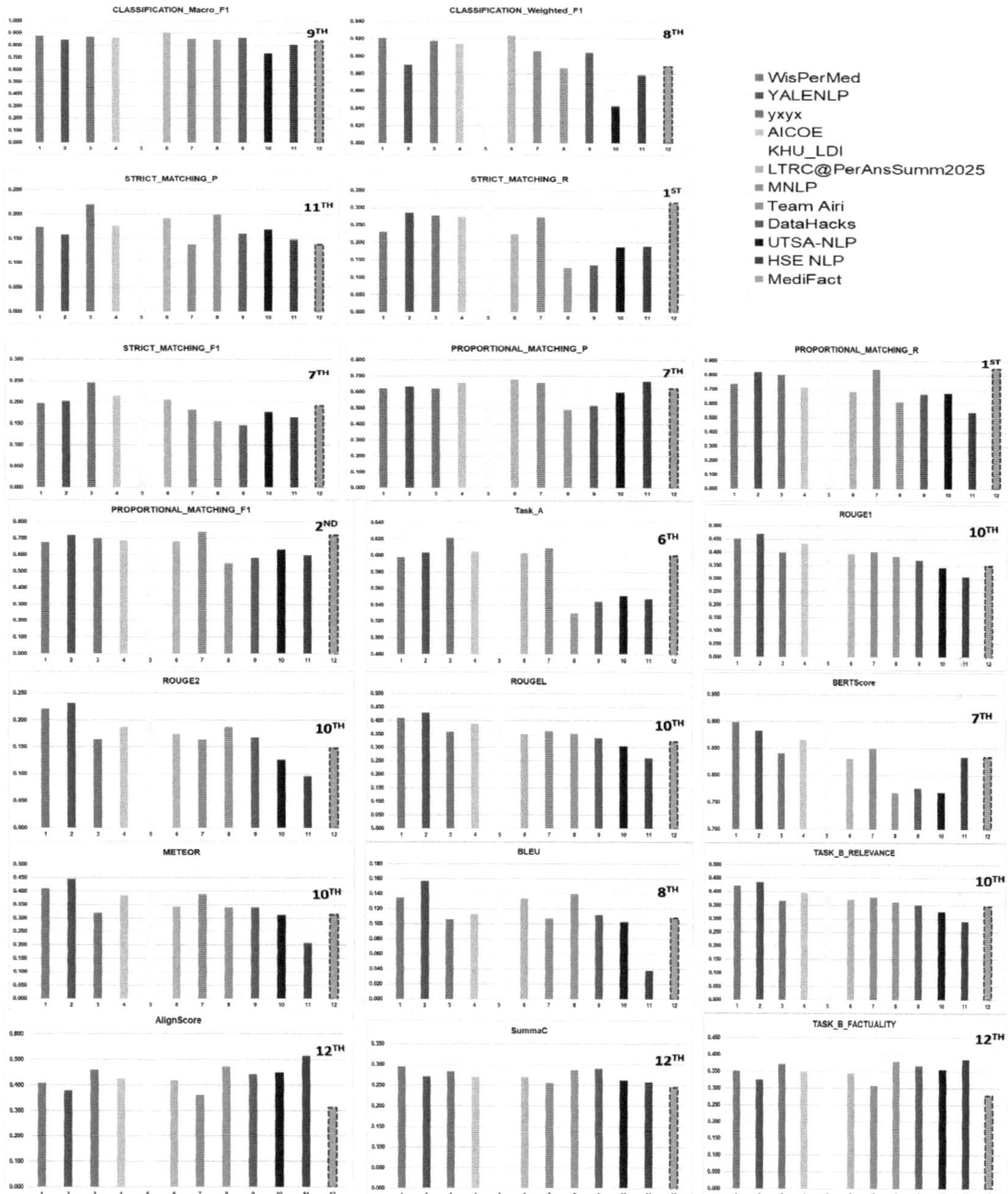

Figure A.1: Comparative Performance Analysis of MediFact Among the Top 12 Models in the PerAnsSumm Shared Task CL4Health@NAACL 2025.

The Manchester Bees at PerAnsSumm 2025: Iterative Self-Prompting with Claude and o1 for Perspective-aware Healthcare Answer Summarisation

Pablo Romero[1], **Libo Ren**[2], **Lifeng Han**[2,3*], and **Goran Nenadic**[2]
[1] Manchester Metropolitan University, UK
[2] The University of Manchester, UK
[3] LIACS & LUMC, Leiden University, Leiden, NL
* *corresponding author*
pablo2004romero,renlibo994@gmail.com
l.han@lumc.nl g.nenadic@manchester.ac.uk

Abstract

This system report presents an innovative approach to the PerAnsSumm2025 shared task at the Workshop CL4Health, addressing the critical challenges of perspective-aware healthcare answer summarization. Our method, Iterative Self-Prompting (ISP) with Claude and o1, introduces a novel framework that leverages large language models' ability to iteratively refine their own instructions, achieving competitive results without traditional model training. Despite utilising only API calls rather than computational-intensive training, our system "The Manchester Bees" secured 15th place among 23 leader board systems overall, while demonstrating exceptional performance in key metrics - ranking 6th in Strict-matching-F1 for span identification (Task A) and achieving the highest Factuality score for summary generation (Task B). Notably, our approach achieved state-of-the-art results in specific metrics, including the highest Strict-matching precision (0.2267) for Task A and AlignScore (0.5888) for Task B. This performance, accomplished with minimal computational resources and development time measured in hours rather than weeks, demonstrates the potential of ISP to democratise access to advanced NLP capabilities in healthcare applications. Our complete implementation is available as an open-source project on `https://github.com/pabloRom2004/-PerAnsSumm-2025`

1 Introduction

This system report presents our contribution to the PerAnsSumm 2025 shared task on perspective-aware healthcare answer summarization, organized in conjunction with the second edition of the CL4Health workshop (computational linguistics for healthcare) at NAACL 2025. The task addresses a critical challenge in modern healthcare: the growing reliance on online health forums where users seek medical advice from peers with similar experiences. While these forums provide valuable support, their unstructured nature necessitates effective methods for organizing and synthesizing the diverse perspectives they contain.

The PerAnsSumm shared task, based on the healthcare forum dataset developed by Naik et al. (2024), focuses on generating perspective-based summaries across five key categories: information, cause, suggestion, experience, and question. To address this challenge, this research proposes Iterative Self-Prompting (ISP), a novel approach utilising two decoder-only systems, Claude and o1. Our method leverages these models' capabilities to iteratively refine task-specific prompts through in-context learning from annotated training data. Notably, the systems demonstrated sophisticated analytical abilities, identifying patterns in data quality and autonomously adjusting prompts to handle edge cases and inconsistencies. Three versions of the system were submitted (ISP-claude/o1 v1, v2, v3), each showing strong performance across both primary tasks: span detection and classification (Task A) and summary generation (Task B). In the official evaluation among 23 top-performing systems, our approach achieved particularly notable results using the Strict-matching metric for Task A, ranking 6th in F1 score. For Task B, measured by Factuality metrics, our systems showed progressive improvement, with v1 ranking 6th (0.3545) and v3 achieving the top position (0.4277), primarily due to superior performance on the AlignScore submetric. Beyond these technical achievements, our method offers significant practical advantages in terms of computational efficiency and development time, suggesting a promising direction for future work in healthcare text analysis.

2 Related Work

2.1 Prompting Techniques

The evolution of prompt engineering for large language models (LLMs) has increasingly focused

Proceedings of the Second Workshop on Patient-Oriented Language Processing (CL4Health), pages 340–348
May 4, 2025 ©2025 Association for Computational Linguistics

on developing sophisticated methods that can fully leverage these models' inherent reasoning capabilities. Iterative Self-Prompting (ISP) follows naturally from research into various forms of model reasoning, including logical, common-sense, and symbolic reasoning, as explored by (Qiao et al., 2023). While researchers have made significant progress with techniques such as chain-of-thought (CoTs), in-context learning, and various prompting strategies (Cui et al., 2023), the field has increasingly recognized the potential of automated approaches. Notably, Automatic Prompt Engineering (APE) has demonstrated competitive performance compared to human-engineered prompts across several NLP tasks (Zhou et al., 2023), typically relying on evaluation scores for prompt refinement. Our work extends this paradigm by introducing a more sophisticated iterative framework that integrates multiple models in the automatic self-prompting process. This approach, inspired by recent advances in iterative refinement (Madaan et al., 2023), leverages sample-labeled data and self-feedback mechanisms to create a more robust and effective prompt engineering methodology.

2.2 Healthcare Data Summarisation

Healthcare data summarisation can be time consuming and costly, which has led to the automatic summarisation task in this domain. The data sources in this task can be electronic health records (EHRs) (Moen et al., 2016), clinical discharge summaries (Searle et al., 2023), medical papers (Sarker, 2014), and online forums (Naik et al., 2024), etc. The methodologies used for such tasks include extractive summarisation, abstractive summarisation, with/without (w/o) external domain knowledge base usage such as medical concepts. The models have included traditional training and fine-tuning paradigms and recent prompt engineering. The data this method utilizes is from perspective-aware online forum healthcare text by Naik et al. (2024).

3 ISP with Claude and o1

3.1 Methodology Overview

Iterative Self-Prompting (ISP) represents an advancement in approaches to prompt engineering and model instruction. At its core, the technique leverages a language model's ability to analyse, understand, and improve its own instructions through a structured feedback loop. This self-improving mechanism creates a powerful framework for developing highly effective prompts without the need for model training or extensive human intervention.

The process begins with a detailed description of the task provided to a language model. Rather than directly attempting to solve the problem, we ask the model to craft a prompt for completing the task. This meta-level approach allows the model to step back and think about how best to approach the problem systematically. The initial prompt generation phase is crucial, as it sets the foundation for all subsequent improvements.

Once we have an initial draft of the prompt, we enter the iterative refinement phase. This involves testing the prompt with training data and carefully analysing the results on another instance of the model with no other context for the task, just the prompt and the data. The key innovation here lies in how we use the model's own analytical capabilities. We present the model with its previous prompt, the outputs generated from the other model using that prompt, and the ground truth answer. The model then engages in a detailed analysis of what worked well and what needs improvement and refines the base prompt further, adding specific details to the prompt so that next time, the model does a little better on the task, this process is then repeated until the prompt is very detailed and outputs from the model are very high quality.

The power of this approach becomes apparent in how the model discovers and adapts to patterns in the data. For instance, when analysing outputs, the model might notice subtle patterns that weren't explicitly stated in the original task description. A concrete example of this meta-cognitive capability occurred during implementation when the model recognised the importance of handling empty categories in data classification tasks. The model observed that some categories naturally remain empty in certain cases and modified the prompt accordingly, without any human intervention. An example can be seen in Figure 2.

The theoretical implications of this technique extend beyond simple prompt engineering. It demonstrates a form of meta-learning, where the model learns to create better instructions through experience. This self-improving capability suggests interesting possibilities for autonomous systems that can optimise their own behaviour through structured self-reflection.

What makes ISPs particularly powerful is their universality. The technique doesn't depend on spe-

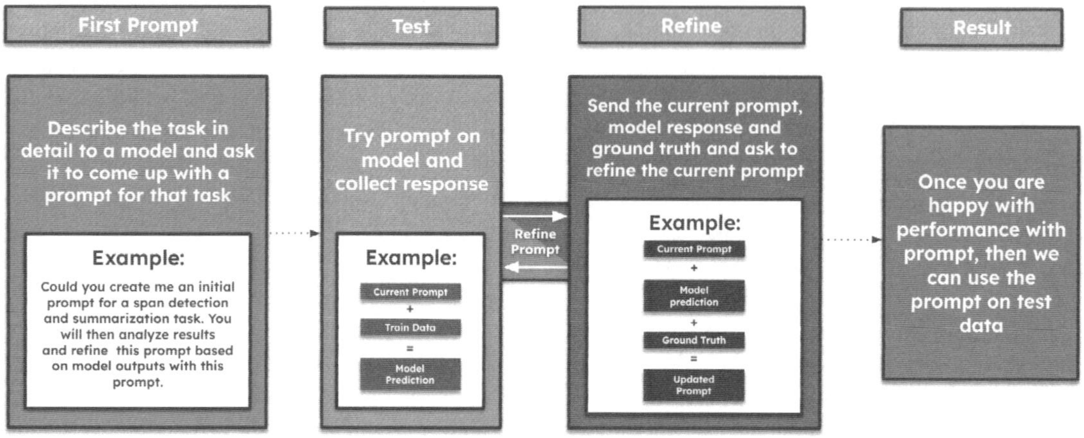

Figure 1: Iteration Cycle for ISP showing the process of prompt refinement through feedback loops.

cific model architectures or training approaches. Instead, it relies on the fundamental capabilities present in modern language models: understanding tasks, generating instructions, and analysing results. This makes it highly adaptable to different problems and domains.

3.2 ISP for PerAnsSumm Shared Task

Implementation Timeline:

- Hour 0 → Initial Setup
- Hour 1 → First Iterations
- Hour 2 → Refinement Cycles
- Hour 3 → Final optimisation
- Hour 4 → Submission

The practical effectiveness of Iterative Self-Prompting was demonstrated conclusively in the PerAnsSumm Shared Task at the CL4Health Workshop NAACL 2025. This implementation provides a compelling case study of how ISP can achieve competitive results with minimal resources and development time.

The task itself presented significant challenges in medical text analysis, requiring systems to identify and classify specific spans of text while generating comprehensive summaries across multiple categories. Traditional approaches typically involved fine-tuning models like BERT or T5, requiring substantial computational resources and development time. Instead, ISP was applied to develop a solution in just 3-4 hours, ultimately achieving a competitive performing system in the leader-board among top-23 teams.

The implementation began with a detailed task description provided to the model, including the **specific requirements** for *span identification and summary generation*. The model was then asked to **create a comprehensive prompt** that would *guide another model* through the analysis process. This initial prompt generation phase was crucial, as it needed to capture all the nuances of the task, from JSON formatting requirements to specific category definitions.

As demonstrated in Figure 2, our iteration cycle revealed remarkable self-improvement capabilities in the model's performance. Through systematic analysis of outputs against ground truth data, the model continuously identified specific areas for enhancement, leading to increasingly sophisticated prompt refinements. One particularly notable breakthrough emerged when the model began recognizing patterns in category distribution - specifically, how certain categories naturally remained empty in particular cases. This insight led to automated prompt adjustments that significantly improved the handling of these edge cases.

The successful development of these capabil-

<contemplator> Let me review the prompt and examples more carefully...

1. Checking Empty Categories Hmm... you're right. Looking at the example you provided (uri: 1564117), I notice:
- Empty arrays for EXPERIENCE and QUESTION spans
- Empty strings for EXPERIENCE and QUESTION summaries
- This is a crucial pattern I missed

Let me look through the other examples to understand empty category patterns:

- Some questions naturally have no QUESTION spans
- Some have no personal EXPERIENCE spans
- Others might lack CAUSE categorization
- Even high-quality answers might not cover all categories

This is an important clarification needed in the prompt. Let me think about where to add it...

Figure 2: Example of ISP process: reviewing the prompts

ities, however, presented us with an interesting technical challenge: managing the models' context window limitations. While our refined prompt demonstrated strong performance, implementing it across the full test set required careful consideration of these constraints. This challenge was addressed by splitting the 50-question test set into 10 manageable groups of 5 questions each. This segmentation allowed the o1 model to maintain sufficient context for each question while preserving the quality of analysis. Through a streamlined script, these individual results were then aggregated into the final submission, effectively balancing the computational and context constraints from the o1 model.

4 Submission to PerAnsSumm2025

Three systems were submitted to both shared tasks A and B, specifically the ISP-Claude/o1 versions 1, 2, and 3.

4.1 Submission outcomes

There are 155 submitted system outputs in the official shared evaluation sheet, however, only 23 systems were listed in the top-performing board from unique teams (no more than one system from each team). The system ranked 15th in the top-list by the 'Task A + B combined Average' score using Version 1 (out of three), scoring 0.3994 (as in Figure 7) (Agarwal et al., 2025). Using the official leaderboard scores from PerAnsSumm 2025, the advantages of the claude/o1 system are listed below for Task-A and B respectively.

For Task-A (span identification and classification) score, it is the average of classification weighted-F1, strict-matching-F1, and proportional matching F1. The system ranked 12th on Task-A using this overall average; however, the claude/o1 model performed much better on the Strict-matching category than the Proportional-matching. As shown in Figure 3, the system ranks 6th in the top-list of 23 systems for Strict-matching F1 (0.2092). Additionally, the system ranks **1st** out of 23 top systems on the **Strict-matching Precision (0.2267)**. Interestingly, the highest Strict-matching Recall was achieved by the 10th system in this rank, the MediFact team, with score 0.3143 (bolded). For Task-B (summarisation), there are two aspect evaluations, Relevance and Factuality. Relevance score is averaged from automatic metrics of ROUGE, BERTscore, METEOR, and BLEU, which are originally machine translation (MT) evaluation metrics. For Factuality, there are the AlignScore and SummaC scores. Our system performed much better on the Factuality aspect in this task, espacially, in the **AlignScore** where we ranked the *second* with *0.4775* out of all top systems, and resulted as the 6th with overall Factuality score 0.3545 among the top 10, as in Figure 4.

4.2 Cost-Effectiveness Comparisons

Interestingly, the competition revealed some unexpected insights about the nature of the task itself. The baseline model, based on the Flan-T5 archi-

Final Ranking	Team	Submission Name	STRICT_MATCHING _P	STRICT_MATCHING _R	STRICT_MATCHING _F1
3	yxyx	sonnet	0.2205	0.2781	**0.2460**
5	KHU_LDI	0204_3	0.1868	0.3010	0.2305
13	NU-WAVE	k16	0.2048	0.2286	0.2160
14	Roux-lette	aa_version_3	0.2048	0.2286	0.2160
4	AICOE	submission_7	0.1765	0.2743	0.2148
15	The Manchester Bees	claude/o1	**0.2267**	0.1943	0.2092
6	LTRC@PerAnsSumm2025	submission-6	0.1915	0.2229	0.2060
2	YALENLP	250202_v3	0.1571	0.2857	0.2027
1	WisPerMed	WisPerMed-Finale	0.1726	0.2305	0.1974
12	MediFact	3	0.1383	**0.3143**	0.1921

Figure 3: Strict Matching Ranking on Task-A (Span Identification and Classification): the top 10 systems (highest score **bolded**, ours underlined)

Final Ranking	team	Submission Name	AlignScore	SummaC	TASK_B_FACTUALITY
11	HSE NLP	4o Mini NER	**0.5150**	0.2578	**0.3864**
8	Team Airi	Mistral + Lora	0.4728	0.2872	0.3800
3	yxyx	sonnet	0.4601	0.2834	0.3717
9	DataHacks	better_256	0.4427	*0.2899*	0.3663
10	UTSA-NLP	TrailNo6COT	0.4503	0.2620	0.3562
15	The Manchester Bees	claude/o1	*0.4775*	0.2316	0.3545
1	WisPerMed	WisPerMed-Finale	0.4085	**0.2958**	0.3521
20	TrofimovaMC	s_03	0.4679	0.2304	0.3491
4	AICOE	submission_7	0.4260	0.2701	0.3480
6	LTRC@PerAnsSumm2025	submission-6	0.4184	0.2701	0.3442

Figure 4: Task-B (Summarisation) Factuality Ranking: the top 10 systems (highest score **bolded**, second highest *italic*, ours underlined). This approach ranked are the 2nd highest in AlignScore.

tecture, established a foundation for comparison, though with performance metrics that left considerable room for improvement in this specialized task (Naik et al., 2024; Chung et al., 2024). This created an unusual situation where our model actually needed to "calibrate down" its responses to better match the expected output quality. This observation raises important questions about evaluation metrics and the balance between output quality and adherence to training data patterns.

The final results demonstrated the power of ISP: achieving top 15 placement out of 23 systems in the leaderboard (155 submissions overall) without any model training, using only prompt engineering and clever problem decomposition. This success challenges traditional assumptions about the necessity of model fine-tuning for competitive performance in specialized tasks. The entire process, from initial prompt generation to final submission, required only 3-4 hours of development time, showcasing the efficiency of the approach.

The implications of this success extend beyond the specific competition. It demonstrates that with well-crafted prompts and strategic task decomposition, existing language models can achieve competitive performance on specialized tasks without the need for additional training or fine-tuning. This suggests a promising direction for rapid development of AI solutions, particularly in domains where development time and computational resources are

Metric	Traditional Approach	ISP
Model Training	Hours/Days	None
Compute Resources	High	Minimal
Development Time	Days	3-4 Hours

Table 1: Comparison Between Traditional Approach and ISP Methods for Healthcare Summarization Tasks.

limited.

5 Discussion and Examples

5.1 On the dataset

There are some responses/questions that are just as funny or strange, which might affect the quality of the training data, but also may be true in the style of the online community forum as where the original data were extracted. Here are some examples:

- Unconventional medical category: "question": "Do women in the same house get period at the same time?"
- Not-really healthcare: "question": "Is there a way to make my voice deeper?" ⇒ "answers": ["You can modify your technique of speaking to include a deeper tone. Most people speak from the front of their mouth, ... "]
- Spelling and grammar: "txt": "nd, but these herbal remedies on the extremely rare occaission that they do work to help your bust, the results are only temporary."
- Not-meaningful: "question": "How thin is too thin?" ⇒ "SUGGESTION_SUMMARY": "To determine if your weight is too low, use the BMI chart. It is also advised to release not all guys want skin and bones."

5.2 On system rankings and metrics

It is interesting to see so many metrics reported in the overall categories and subcategories for Task A and B in the official evaluation (Agarwal et al., 2025). However, observations reveal that the metrics and ranking results do not always agree with each other, spacially, between tasks (A vs B). For instances, among our three submissions (v1, v2, v3), even though our system-v1 achieved the highest Task A + B combined average score (0.3993) in comparison to the other two systems (0.3928 and 0.3496), system-v2 and v3 have produced better scores for individual metrics and tasks, respectively.

As in Figure 5, for Task A (span identification and classification), our **system 2** produced **better scores on macro F1, weighted F1, and strict matching precision**, in comparison to the version 1 system. However, it lost to the strict matching recall value, leading to a lower strict matching F1.

For Task B (summarisation) Factuality ranking, our **system 3** boosted both AlignScore and SummaC scores, leading to the **highest Factuality score (0.4277)** among the top 10 systems in the leader board as in Figure 6, referring to Figure 4 for the top 10 (highest Factuality score 0.3864).

6 Conclusions and Future Work

In conclusion, we submitted three system outputs using the method Iterative Self-Prompting (ISP) with Calude and o1, ISP-claude/o1, to perspective-aware healthcare answer summarisation shared task (PerAnsSumm2025). The vesion 1 output of ISP-claude/o1 is officially ranked 15th in the leaderboard of top 23 teams, using the combined average scores of Task A and B. Task specifically, the ISP-claude/o1 performs better on Strict-matching for Task A (the 6th in Figure 3), span-identification and classification, versus proportial-matching. For Task B summarisation, it performs better on AlignScore for Factuality (the 1st via ISP-claude/o1-system3, 0.4277 in Figure 6), instead of Relevance (ROUGE, BERTscore, METEOR, and BLEU, much lower scores). In the future work, it is worthy to explore the reasons on such contradiction scores across metrics, i.e., Strict-matching vs Proportional-matching, and Relevance vs Factuality. Our complete implementation is available as an open-source project on `https://github.com/pabloRom2004/-PerAnsSumm-2025`

Limitations

The present study faced several constraints that suggest directions for future research. Due to time limitations, only decoder models employing prompting techniques were evaluated in this shared task. For a more comprehensive analysis, future work

claude/o1	macro F1	CLASSIFICATION_Weighted_F1	STRICT_MATCHING_P	STRICT_MATCHING_R	STRICT_MATCHING_F1
v1	0.8268	0.8769	0.2267	**0.1943**	**0.2092**
v2	**0.8664**	**0.9031**	**0.2327**	0.1733	0.1987
v3	0.6760	0.7581	0.1526	0.0724	0.0982

Figure 5: The Manchester Bees 3 systems comparisons on Task A

Team	Submission Name	AlignScore	SummaC	TASK_B_FACTUALITY
HSE NLP	4o Mini NER	*0.5150*	0.2578	*0.3864*
DataHacks	better_256	0.4427	*0.2899*	0.3663
The Manchester Bees	claude/o1-v1	0.4775	0.2316	0.3545
The Manchester Bees	claude/o1-v2	0.4119	0.2291	0.3205
The Manchester Bees	claude/o1-v3	**0.5888**	0.2666	**0.4277**
WisPerMed	WisPerMed-Finale	0.4085	**0.2958**	0.3521

Figure 6: Task-B (Summarisation) Factuality Ranking: including three systems of our submissions, keeping the highest and the 2nd highest scores in the top-10 list (highest score **bolded**, second highest *italic*, ours underlined). Our system 3 (claude/o1-v3) gets the highest in AlignScore and Factuality.

should include comparisons with traditional fine-tuned approaches, particularly encoder-decoder architectures such as T5-variants for span detection tasks. Such comparisons would provide valuable benchmarks against established methodologies in the literature (Belkadi et al., 2023; Cui et al., 2023).

A significant technical challenge encountered during the ISP-claude/o1 implementation involved context window limitations of the models. This necessitated dividing the test dataset into smaller chunks for processing. Further research could explore efficient solutions to these context constraints, potentially through advanced chunking strategies or more context-efficient prompting techniques.

While fine-tuning smaller models represents a potentially more cost-effective approach for production deployment, the ISP method demonstrated distinct advantages in rapid development scenarios. The implementation required only 3-4 hours without GPU training resources, model optimization, or hyperparameter tuning. This approach prioritized development efficiency and exploration of state-of-the-art models' few-shot learning capabilities, though future work could investigate quantized versions of fine-tuned models for production environments with comparable performance at reduced computational cost.

Ethical Statement

While the ISP method demonstrates its effectiveness in the summary task of healthcare with perspectives, there are many concerns about the use of commercial chatbots, for example ChatGPT, Claude, etc. for personal data (Ray, 2023; Ren et al., 2024). It is still challenging on how to safeguard private health information with the usage of AI models. For the current shared task, the organisers have prepared annonymised online forum data for system development purposes.

Acknowledgments

LH and GN are grateful for the grant "Integrating hospital outpatient letters into the healthcare data space" (EP/V047949/1; funder: UKRI/EPSRC). LH is grateful to the 4D Picture EU Project `https://4dpicture.eu`.

References

Siddhant Agarwal, Md Shad Akhtar, and Shweta Yadav. 2025. Overview of the peranssumm 2025 shared task on perspective-aware healthcare answer summarization. In *Proceedings of the Second Workshop on*

Patient-Oriented Language Processing (CL4Health) @ NAACL 2025, Albuquerque, USA. Association for Computational Linguistics.

Samuel Belkadi, Nicolo Micheletti, Lifeng Han, Warren Del-Pinto, and Goran Nenadic. 2023. Generating medical instructions with conditional transformer. In *SyntheticData4ML Workshop at NeurIPS 2023*.

Hyung Won Chung, Le Hou, Shayne Longpre, Barret Zoph, Yi Tay, William Fedus, Yunxuan Li, Xuezhi Wang, Mostafa Dehghani, Siddhartha Brahma, et al. 2024. Scaling instruction-finetuned language models. *Journal of Machine Learning Research*, 25(70):1–53.

Yang Cui, Lifeng Han, and Goran Nenadic. 2023. MedTem2.0: Prompt-based temporal classification of treatment events from discharge summaries. In *Proceedings of the 61st Annual Meeting of the Association for Computational Linguistics (Volume 4: Student Research Workshop)*, pages 160–183, Toronto, Canada. Association for Computational Linguistics.

Aman Madaan, Niket Tandon, Prakhar Gupta, Skyler Hallinan, Luyu Gao, Sarah Wiegreffe, Uri Alon, Nouha Dziri, Shrimai Prabhumoye, Yiming Yang, Shashank Gupta, Bodhisattwa Prasad Majumder, Katherine Hermann, Sean Welleck, Amir Yazdanbakhsh, and Peter Clark. 2023. Self-refine: Iterative refinement with self-feedback. In *Thirty-seventh Conference on Neural Information Processing Systems*.

Hans Moen, Laura-Maria Peltonen, Juho Heimonen, Antti Airola, Tapio Pahikkala, Tapio Salakoski, and Sanna Salanterä. 2016. Comparison of automatic summarisation methods for clinical free text notes. *Artificial intelligence in medicine*, 67:25–37.

Gauri Naik, Sharad Chandakacherla, Shweta Yadav, and Md Shad Akhtar. 2024. No perspective, no perception!! perspective-aware healthcare answer summarization. In *Findings of the Association for Computational Linguistics: ACL 2024*, pages 15919–15932, Bangkok, Thailand. Association for Computational Linguistics.

Shuofei Qiao, Yixin Ou, Ningyu Zhang, Xiang Chen, Yunzhi Yao, Shumin Deng, Chuanqi Tan, Fei Huang, and Huajun Chen. 2023. Reasoning with language model prompting: A survey. In *Proceedings of the 61st Annual Meeting of the Association for Computational Linguistics (Volume 1: Long Papers)*, pages 5368–5393, Toronto, Canada. Association for Computational Linguistics.

Partha Pratim Ray. 2023. Chatgpt: A comprehensive review on background, applications, key challenges, bias, ethics, limitations and future scope. *Internet of Things and Cyber-Physical Systems*, 3:121–154.

Libo Ren, Samuel Belkadi, Lifeng Han, Warren Del-Pinto, and Goran Nenadic. 2024. Synthetic4health: Generating annotated synthetic clinical letters. *Preprint*, arXiv:2409.09501.

Abeed Sarker. 2014. *Automated Medical Text Summarisation to Support Evidence-based Medicine*. Ph.D. thesis, Macquarie University, Centre for Language Technology, Department of Computing.

Thomas Searle, Zina Ibrahim, James Teo, and Richard JB Dobson. 2023. Discharge summary hospital course summarisation of in patient electronic health record text with clinical concept guided deep pre-trained transformer models. *Journal of Biomedical Informatics*, 141:104358.

Yongchao Zhou, Andrei Ioan Muresanu, Ziwen Han, Keiran Paster, Silviu Pitis, Harris Chan, and Jimmy Ba. 2023. Large language models are human-level prompt engineers. In *The Eleventh International Conference on Learning Representations*.

Final Ranking	Team Name	Submission Name	Task A + B Combined Average
1	WisPerMed	WisPerMed-Finale	0.4571
2	YALENLP	250202_v3	0.4548
3	yxyx	sonnet	0.4526
4	AICOE	submission_7	0.4495
5	KHU_LDI	0204_3	0.4492
6	LTRC@PerAnsSumm2025	submission-6	0.4395
7	MNLP	v3_4	0.4321
8	Team Airi	Mistral + Lora	0.4238
9	DataHacks	better_256	0.4203
10	UTSA-NLP	TrailNo6COT	0.4112
11	HSE NLP	4o Mini NER	0.4081
12	MediFact	3	0.4077
13	NU-WAVE	k16	0.4046
14	Roux-lette	aa_version_3_20250204_004205	0.3996
15	**The Manchester Bees**	**claude/o1**	**0.3994**
16	Abdelmalak	sub2	0.3907
17	umb	umba	0.3824
18	massU	1	0.3815
19	RVK_Med	Run_1	0.3750
20	TrofimovaMC	s_03	0.3698
21	TeamENSAK@PerAnsSumm2025	Azzedine	0.3641
22	CaresAI	submission_1	0.3405
23	LMU	llama 70b_8b	0.1726

Figure 7: Official Ranking Task A+B from Top 23 Systems (Agarwal et al., 2025)

A The Official Ranking

B The original prompt

Here is the original prompt describing the task:

(Examples from the test set here in-context)

" *Could you write me a prompt that takes a test set answer and provides the format that is expected in the output, could you look very carefully at how the spans are structured and what the labels are/what they represent in this specific database and be able to detect spans and create reasonable spans and summarization. Make sure to look very closely at the data I have provided and come up with a good prompt that captures the essence of each label and how to pick it up accordingly, this prompt will be used for another model with no previous knowledge about the task so you will need to make sure you explain it all thoroughly*

Before completing the task, just talk out loud about the task and how you will complete it, and ask me any questions you may have before writing this prompt, this prompt will just be the first version, I will give you more examples so you are able to refine it more and I will test it with the model and bring back the results so you can tweak the prompt to see better behaviour, I will give you the original input with the prompt you will create, then give you the model output along with the ground truth so you are able to tweak it."

Detailed ISP used for this task is shared on our open-source project page `https://github.com/pabloRom2004/-PerAnsSumm-2025`

MNLP at PerAnsSumm: A Classifier-Refiner Architecture for Improving the Classification of Consumer Health User Responses

Jooyeon Lee and **Luan Huy Pham** and **Özlem Uzuner**
George Mason University, USA
{jlee252,lpham6,ouzuner}@gmu.edu

Abstract

Community question-answering (CQA) platforms provide a crucial space for users to share experiences, seek medical advice, and exchange health-related information. However, these platforms, by nature of their user-generated content as well as the complexity and subjectivity of natural language, remain a significant challenge for tasks related to the automatic classification of diverse perspectives. The PerAnsSumm shared task involves extracting perspective spans from community users' answers, classifying them into specific perspective categories (Task A), and then using these perspectives and spans to generate structured summaries (Task B). Our focus is on Task A. To address this challenge, we propose a Classifier-Refiner Architecture (CRA), a two-stage framework designed to enhance classification accuracy. The first stage employs a Classifier to segment user responses into self-contained snippets and assign initial perspective labels along with a binary confidence value. If the classifier is not confident, a secondary Refiner stage is triggered, incorporating retrieval-augmented generation to enhance classification through contextual examples. Our methodology integrates instruction-driven classification, tone definitions, and Chain-of-Thought (CoT) prompting, leading to improved F1 scores compared to single-pass approaches. Experimental evaluations on the Perspective Summarization Dataset (PUMA) demonstrate that our framework improves classification performance by leveraging multi-stage decision-making. Our submission ranked among the top-performing teams, achieving an overall score of 0.6090, with high precision and recall in perspective classification.

1 Introduction

Community question-answering (CQA) forums have emerged as a pivotal medium for individuals seeking diverse perspectives on health-related issues, encompassing personal anecdotes, medical suggestions, factual information, and experiential insights. While these platforms offer a wealth of user-generated knowledge, extracting structured, perspective-specific content from such discussions remains a complex challenge due to linguistic variability and overlapping semantic cues. Traditional single-pass classification systems often misclassify or overlook nuanced snippets, leading to incomplete or misleading results. These limitations are especially consequential in the healthcare domain, where accurate categorization of user responses can influence subsequent experiences, diagnosis, and/or recommendations (Agarwal et al., 2025).

Our approach, tested on the PUMA (Naik et al., 2024) dataset, demonstrates robust performance across macro-F1, weighted-F1, strict, and proportional evaluation metrics. In particular, we highlight the effectiveness of tone definition and CoT prompting, which bolster classification reliability and interpretability. Moreover, we compare leading large language models (LLMs), specifically GPT-4o, Claude 3, and o1-preview, under various experimental configurations, showing that multi-stage decision-making strategies can streamline complex classification tasks in CQA settings across a variety of LLMs.

2 Related Work

Research in multi-stage classification has demonstrated that iterative refinement can improve the accuracy and reliability of NLP models (Zhang et al., 2020). In the context of few-shot or low-resource scenarios, Zhao et al. introduced calibration strategies to bolster classification robustness, while Lewis et al. showed that multi-step prompting methods significantly enhance model performance. Moreover, the concept of CoT prompting has been explored by Wei et al. to elicit more transparent reasoning processes in LLMs. CoT is also re-

Proceedings of the Second Workshop on Patient-Oriented Language Processing (CL4Health), pages 349–358
May 4, 2025 ©2025 Association for Computational Linguistics

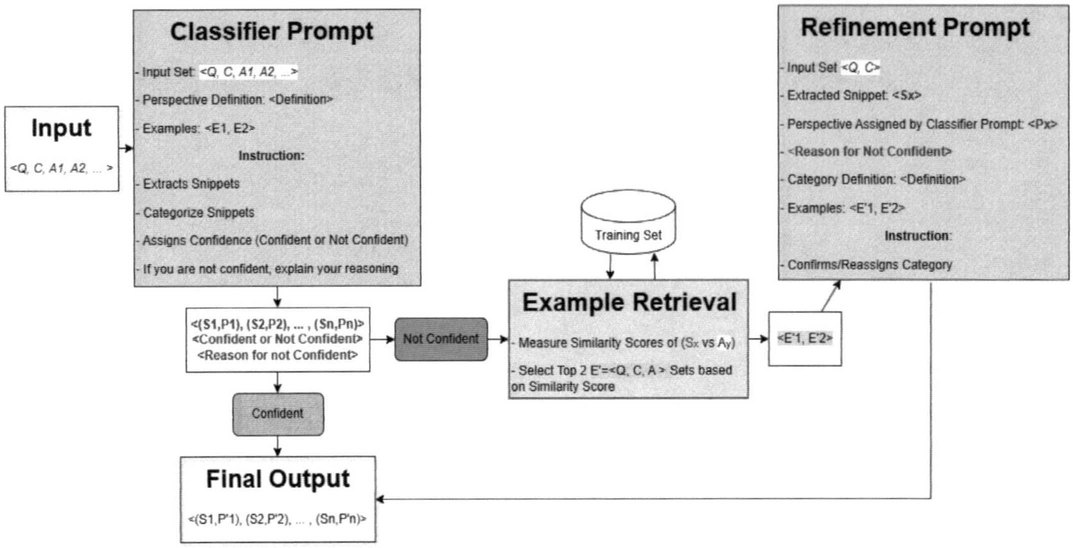

Figure 1: Classifier-Refiner Architecture. Yellow highlight denotes input values extracted from the dataset, including the Question (Q), Context (C), and User Responses (A). Blue text represents the Classifier's output, which subsequently serves as input for the Refiner. Pink highlight indicates the output of Example Retrieval with RAG, which is later incorporated into the Refiner's input.

ceiving attention from Consumer Health Question Answering (CHQA) domain research (Lee et al., 2024).

Recent advances in retrieval-based classification have leveraged the idea of combining external knowledge with model predictions for better handling of uncertain cases (Lewis et al., 2020). Gao et al. demonstrated that retrieval-based prompting can provide relevant context from a structured dataset, thereby improving model understanding. Our method follows these trends by integrating a retrieval-augmented classification and refinement mechanism, in which the system references training data to refine ambiguous labels. This combination of iterative refinement and retrieval augmentation offers a robust alternative to single-pass classification pipelines (Izacard and Grave, 2020).

3 Methodology

3.1 Task Definition

Given a user's question and a corresponding user-generated health response, we segment the response into self-contained snippets. Each snippet must be assigned one of the following categories (corresponding to the PUMA annotated categories), which are defined by Agarwal et al.:

1. EXPERIENCE (<tone: Personal, Narrative>): Individual experiences or firsthand insights.
2. INFORMATION (<tone: Informative, Educational>): Factual statements or knowledge about health conditions.
3. CAUSE (<tone: Explanatory, Causal>): Explanations of why a condition or symptom might occur.
4. SUGGESTION (<tone: Advisory, Recommending>): Advice or recommendations for resolving or improving a health-related issue.
5. QUESTION (<tone: Seeking Understanding>): Direct inquiries seeking information or clarity.

3.2 Dataset

The dataset used in this study is the PUMA dataset, created by independent researchers for the PerAnsSumm shared task (Naik et al., 2024). PUMA was derived from the L6 - Yahoo! Answers Comprehensive Questions and Answers version 1.0 (multi-part) corpus [1] which contains data up to October 2007, consisting of 3,167 CQA threads. Specifically, Naik et al. filtered Yahoo! Answers for healthcare-related content, randomly selecting 10,000 questions each with up to 10 answers. These records covered a variety of medical topics, including Diabetes, Dental, and Cancer, ensuring broad coverage of health-related discussions.

From this curated set, the authors further refined and annotated specifically for the PerAnsSumm task. The final version of PUMA was then split

[1] https://webscope.sandbox.yahoo.com/catalog.php?datatype=l&did=11&guccounter=1

into three subsets for this shared task: a training set of 2,236 question-answer pairs, a validation set of 959 pairs, and a test set of 50 pairs. The annotations were performed by three fluent English speakers (one master's student, one research assistant, and one native English-speaking volunteer) who identified perspective-specific spans in each answer. These spans were categorized into five distinct labels: Cause, Suggestion, Experience, Question, and Information. Multiple annotators cross-validated the labels to ensure reliability and consistency.

3.3 Classifier-Refiner Framework

Classifier In the first stage, we use a prompting technique with a language model (e.g., a GPT-based or other LLM) to process each user response and produce potential snippet boundaries, as well as initial category labels. This Classifier is instructed to highlight text segments that can meaningfully stand alone. The output of the prompt follows the JSON format:

```
[
    {
        "text": "<Extracted Snippet>",
        "confidence": "CONFIDENT",
        "reason not confident": "",
        "category": "INFORMATION"
    },
    ...
]
```

In cases where the LLM is uncertain about the correct category, "confidence" is set to "NOT_CONFIDENT", and an additional "reason_not_confident" field is provided.

Refiner The Refiner operates by leveraging a retrieval-augmented generation (RAG) mechanism, which enhances classification accuracy by incorporating contextual examples from the training set. Specifically, when triggered, the Refiner first retrieves the two most similar sentences from the training set using a sentence similarity model (all-MiniLM-L6-v2) (Wang et al., 2020). This allows us to use different examples from the Classifier, thus we expect different results from the Classifier output. The all-MiniLM-L6-v2 model was used in an unsupervised approach in this task. It is a lightweight transformer-based model for semantic similarity comparison, optimized for model size and faster inference. The model has 66 million parameters, compressed in a Student-Mimicking Teacher network relationship. By utilizing self-attention distribution, the training of the student model is guided using the teacher's last layer, ensuring effective and flexible results across 12 different languages.

These retrieved examples are then inserted into the Refiner prompt as few-shot examples, allowing the model to refine the classification by comparing the uncertain snippet with previously labeled cases. This iterative approach ensures that the classification process incorporates relevant training instances, thereby improving overall classification reliability and mitigating ambiguity in nuanced cases. The Refiner finally returns JSON format result:

```
{
    "previous_category":
            "<category from previous step>",
    "confidence":
            "<CONFIDENT or NOT_CONFIDENT>",
    "refinement_reasoning": "<brief explanation>",
    "refined_category": "<final label>"
}
```

By incorporating the different context and referencing prior examples, this step significantly reduces misclassification in borderline scenarios.

3.4 Language Models

We experimented with multiple language models to evaluate the effectiveness of different architectures in classification refinement:

GPT-4o An omni-modal autoregressive model capable of processing text, audio, image, and video inputs while generating text, audio, and image outputs. GPT-4o demonstrates exceptional multilingual proficiency and enhanced computational efficiency, making it significantly faster and more cost-effective compared to GPT-4 Turbo. Its advanced speech-to-text capabilities and safety alignment mechanisms enhance reliability in consumer health discussions by reducing misinformation and bias. This model was evaluated in multiple prompting setups, including single-prompt classification, instruction-based CRA, and CoT refinement. (OpenAI et al., 2024).

Claude 3 Developed by Anthropic, Claude 3 (Opus, Sonnet, and Haiku) represents a family of LLMs optimized for cognitive reasoning, nuanced contextual understanding, and expansive token processing (up to 1 million tokens in specialized tasks). Claude 3 Opus demonstrated self-awareness in controlled testing environments, particularly in needle-

Module	Feature	Example
Classifier	Extracted Text	If you took the prescribed antibiotics as recommended you are no longer contagious.
	Perspective	CAUSE
	confidence	NOT CONFIDENT
	reason not confident	Could be either information or suggestion, as it implies both diagnosis and recommendation to investigate further
Refiner	refinement reasoning	After reviewing the full context and similar examples, this statement is clearly providing factual information about contagiousness in relation to antibiotic treatment, similar to example 4 'For the first 24 to 48 hours after you start taking an antibiotic, you are still contagious.' The statement is not explaining why something happens (CAUSE), but rather stating a medical fact about contagiousness after antibiotic treatment.
	Refined category	INFORMATION

Table 1: Example Output.

in-a-haystack tasks, making it an ideal candidate for refining ambiguous classifications in CQA settings. This model was primarily used in CRA with tone definitions, providing insights into subjective aspects of user responses (Anthropic, 2024).

o1-preview A state-of-the-art language model developed by OpenAI, extensively tested on complex reasoning tasks spanning multiple domains, including computer science, mathematics, medicine, linguistics, and social sciences. The model exhibits superior performance in competitive programming, high school-level mathematical reasoning, and radiology report generation. Additionally, o1-preview excels in natural language inference tasks, sentiment analysis, and financial modeling. This model was particularly effective in CQA classification due to its ability to integrate contextual cues across diverse perspectives (Zhong et al., 2024).

4 Results

We adopted macro-F1 (C-MF1), weighted-F1 (C-WF1), Strict Precision/Recall/F1 (S-P, S-R, S-F1), and Proportional Precision/Recall/F1 (P-P, P-R, P-F1) - which are the official metrics used for the PerAnsSumm shared task - to capture a range of performance aspects. C-MF1 and C-WF1 are Macro-averaged and weighted F1 scores for the classification task, focusing on how well the system balances performance across categories. S-P, S-R, S-F1 are Strict metrics to gauge performance under the assumption that each snippet clearly belongs to one category. P-P, P-R, P-F1 are proportional metrics to evaluate partially correct classifications, recognizing that user-generated health content often spans multiple categories or perspectives.

4.1 Evaluation

Single-Prompt vs. CRA: The single-pass methods (rows 1-2) show lower C-MF1 and C-WF1 scores. Once the CRA approach is introduced (rows 3-6), the metrics consistently improve, indicating the effectiveness of a multi-stage classification pipeline.

Tone Definition Impact: Including explicit tone definitions tends to increase both strict and proportional F1 scores by helping the model distinguish subtle differences (e.g., between EXPERIENCE vs. INFORMATION or SUGGESTION vs. INFORMATION).

CoT Influence: CoT reasoning further refines the model's decision-making, especially in complex or overlapping perspectives. This is reflected in higher macro-F1 scores for the CRA + CoT configurations.

o1-preview (MNLP Final Submission) achieves the best overall score of 0.6090, setting a strong benchmark. Notably, its P-R (0.8406) and P-F1 (0.7382) values are significantly higher than the other configurations.

In the broader context of the PerAnsSumm shared task, our team (MNLP) ranks among the top five, as shown in Table 3. Although not topping every sub-metric, MNLP's approach demonstrates a balanced performance across multiple dimensions, showcasing the strength of the CRA pipeline.

5 Discussion

The results underscore several key insights.

Idx	Model	Method Description	C-MF1	C-WF1	S-P	S-R	S-F1	P-P	P-R	P-F1	Overall
1	GPT 4o	Single Prompt	0.7985	0.8651	0.1459	0.1448	0.1453	0.4773	0.6013	0.5322	0.5142
2	GPT 4o	Single prompt+ Removed Question	0.6991	0.8101	0.1438	0.0800	0.1028	0.4508	0.5775	0.5064	0.4731
3	GPT 4o	CRA+Instr+tone def	0.8126	0.8771	0.1852	0.1429	0.1613	0.5874	0.6342	0.6099	0.5494
4	GPT 4o	CRA+ CoT	0.8292	0.8879	**0.1896**	0.1524	0.1690	0.5963	0.5942	0.5953	0.5507
5	GPT 4o	CRA+ CoT+ tone def	0.8387	0.8948	0.1809	0.1371	0.1560	0.5925	0.6005	0.5965	0.5491
6	Claude 3	CRA+Instr+tone def	0.7963	0.8718	0.1168	0.0914	0.1026	0.6113	0.3847	0.4722	0.4822
7	o1-preview	CRA+Instr+tone def	**0.8524**	**0.9061**	0.1376	**0.2724**	**0.1829**	**0.6580**	**0.8406**	**0.7382**	**0.6090**

Table 2: Task A Results.

Team Name	C-MF1	C-WF1	S-P	S-R	S-F1	P-P	P-R	P-F1	Overall
yxyx	0.8697	**0.9173**	**0.2205**	0.2781	**0.2460**	0.6215	0.8029	0.7006	0.6213
MNLP	0.8524	0.9061	0.1376	0.2724	0.1829	0.6580	**0.8406**	**0.7382**	**0.6090**
AICOE	0.8656	0.9140	0.1765	0.2743	0.2148	0.6597	0.7159	0.6866	0.6052
YALENLP	0.8439	0.8902	0.1571	**0.2857**	0.2027	0.6372	0.8218	0.7178	0.6036
LTRC	**0.9033**	0.9239	0.1915	0.2229	0.2060	**0.6774**	0.6833	0.6803	0.6034

Table 3: Top 5 Team Results for Task A

5.1 Two-Stage Decision-Making Improves Reliability

Incorporating a secondary Refiner model significantly reduces classification uncertainty. In single-pass systems, difficult or ambiguous snippets often receive incorrect labels. The Refiner leverages additional context (e.g., new examples, reason not confident) to resolve ambiguities.

5.2 Role of Tone Definitions

Empirical evidence suggests that explicitly including tone information—such as labeling a snippet as 'personal/narrative' or 'informative/educational'—guides the model to distinguish subtle semantic differences between EXPERIENCE and INFORMATION categories. This additional guidance appears to yield more consistent performance.

5.3 Impact of CoT

CoT prompts give the language model intermediate reasoning steps, leading to more thorough snippet analysis. While adding CoT marginally increases computational cost, it provides a measurable boost in precision, particularly for borderline cases where multiple categories overlap. These findings align with prior research on the benefits of explicitly prompting large models to articulate their reasoning steps (Wei et al., 2022; OpenAI et al., 2024).

5.4 Model Comparison

As outlined in the Methodology section, three models (GPT-4o, Claude 3, and o1-preview) were evaluated under configurations tailored to multi-stage classification in healthcare QA. Below, we highlight the core empirical findings and discuss how each model responded to different prompt designs.

5.4.1 Prompting Strategies and Performance

GPT-4o. GPT-4o's best performance emerged from a "CRA + CoT" setup, yielding an overall score of 0.5507. Removing the explicit CoT steps and instead relying on "Instruction + Tone Definition" resulted in only a marginal decrease (0.5494). This near-parity suggests that GPT-4o effectively processes step-by-step reasoning, even without direct user guidance, provided instructions remain sufficiently structured and detailed.

Claude 3. For consistency with o1-preview, Claude 3 was primarily tested under "CRA + Tone

Definition." The model's performance varied more substantially than GPT-4o, likely reflecting Claude 3's sensitivity to domain-specific nuances and question complexity. Despite such fluctuations, Claude 3 did exhibit strong alignment with user instructions, consistent with its "Constitutional AI" training paradigm—and demonstrated robust comprehension in tasks demanding nuanced responses. Future refinements or domain-specific tuning may further enhance its stability.

o1-preview. Unlike GPT-4o, o1-preview internally implements COT reasoning and prohibits external user-directed CoT prompts. Consequently, we restricted prompts to "CRA + Tone Definition" for a fair comparison. Under these conditions, o1-preview achieved the highest performance across our evaluation metrics. Its internally generated reasoning appears mature enough to parse complex instructions, enforce safety considerations, and incorporate tonal guidelines, without requiring explicit step-by-step instructions from the user.

5.4.2 Observations and Implications

Internal vs. User-Supplied CoT GPT-4o benefits from explicit CoT prompts, whereas o1-preview inherently manages its own CoT. The near-equivalence of GPT-4o's "CRA + CoT" (0.5507) and "CRA + Instruction + Tone Definition" (0.5494) underscores that well-crafted instructions can closely approximate explicit CoT. By contrast, o1-preview excels through its internalized reasoning approach, obviating the need for user-provided CoT altogether. This design choice can be seen as advantageous for developers seeking a lower cognitive overhead when engineering prompts, although it also reduces direct user control over the model's reasoning process.

Tone Definition and Stylistic Constraints "Tonal" or "stylistic" labels did not show significant improvement with GPT-4o. However, these could be mitigated through additional fine-tuning or domain adaptation.

Practical Considerations for Multi-stage Healthcare QA Real-world healthcare QA systems demand predictable model behavior and ease of prompt design. While GPT-4o may need user-defined CoT to reach peak performance, o1-preview's autonomous internal reasoning streamlines the developer experience. Choices between these models must weigh the trade-off between direct CoT control (GPT-4o) and fully internalized reasoning (o1-preview) against the complexity of the tasks at hand.

In summary, GPT-4o demonstrated strong capability with user-supplied CoT prompts, whereas o1-preview's internally managed reasoning and refined alignment led to consistently higher performance without explicit CoT instructions. Claude 3, meanwhile, remained competitive but was more sensitive to prompt variations. These findings underscore the importance of prompt engineering, built-in CoT, and alignment strategies in deploying LLMs for complex tasks such as multi-stage classification in healthcare QA.

5.4.3 Potential Explanations for o1-preview's Superior Results

o1-preview's top performance may stem from both architectural refinements and advanced alignment protocols. First, o1-preview likely benefits from curated training data tailored to tasks requiring fine-grained reasoning and tone management. Second, improved alignment techniques (building on GPT-4o's foundation) may enhance the balance between correctness, recall, and user-centric instructions. Notably, o1-preview's resilience to prompt alterations, including variations such as "CRA + CoT + tone def," suggests that it integrates complex instructions and stylistic requirements without sacrificing coherence.

Taken together, the differing performances of GPT-4o, Claude 3, and o1-preview highlight the interplay between model architectures, alignment strategies, and prompt design. While both GPT-4o and Claude 3 demonstrate robust capabilities under certain configurations, o1-preview's refined integration of reasoning and tone guidance appears to yield superior classification outcomes.

5.5 Error Analysis

Although the two-stage classification approach proved effective overall, a closer inspection of the 21 instances where the Refiner was triggered (out of 1039 total snippets) offers valuable insights into recurring error patterns and the advantages of iterative refinement. Table 4 presents representative examples where the Classifier's initial label differed from the Refiner's final judgment, along with corresponding reasoning ("thought") from both stages. Three principal themes emerged:

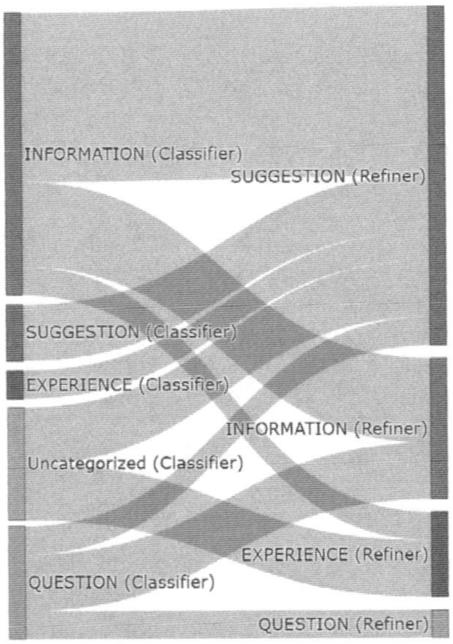

Figure 2: Sankey diagram illustrating the flow of snippet labels from the Classifier to the Refiner. Each node represents a classification label, with left-side nodes corresponding to the Classifier's initial labels and right-side nodes representing the Refiner's final labels. The thickness of each link is proportional to the number of snippets that transitioned between categories. Notably, the Refiner frequently corrected INFORMATION to SUGGESTION and reclassified certain QUESTION and EXPERIENCE snippets, indicating that these categories were more prone to initial misclassification. This visualization highlights the value of iterative refinement in improving classification accuracy.

5.5.1 Reclassification of Short or Polite Snippets

In multiple cases, polite expressions or brief well-wishes (e.g., "Be well," "good luck") were initially labeled as INFORMATION or left as Uncategorized by the Classifier. The Refiner, however, recognized these statements as advisory or encouraging in nature, as aligning with training set (e.g., I hope that you keep on going, and that you realize how important you are to our world.: SUGGESTION) thereby reassigning them to SUGGESTION. This suggests the Classifier's tendency to default to INFORMATION when textual clues are minimal, whereas the Refiner incorporates context (e.g., prior labeled examples) to identify the statement's tone and intent.

5.5.2 Distinguishing Rhetorical Questions from Genuine Questions

Several snippets contained rhetorical or illustrative "questions" (e.g., "Is it because of the antibiotics?") that the Classifier labeled as QUESTION. Upon refinement, these snippets were deemed INFORMATION once the system determined they functioned more as explanatory remarks rather than genuine queries. This underscores the importance of discourse context in discerning the pragmatic function of a statement.

5.5.3 Personal Commentary and Narrative Content

Certain snippets expressing personal opinions or narrative remarks were originally labeled as INFORMATION or EXPERIENCE. The Refiner identified that these statements often warrant EXPERIENCE, particularly when they reflect an individual's personal viewpoint or emotive stance rather than a factual claim. For instance, "What a great question." was recognized as more personal/relational than purely informational, leading to reclassification from INFORMATION to EXPERIENCE.

5.5.4 Implications for Multi-stage Classification

These illustrative examples highlight how the Refiner adds a crucial layer of context-awareness, correcting labels when the Classifier defaults to INFORMATION or encounters snippets with ambiguous linguistic cues. Notably, the number of triggers (21) is small relative to the overall dataset (N=1039), yet it plays a disproportionate role in improving the accuracy of borderline or confusing snippets.

5.5.5 Practical Outcomes

Practical outcomes of this CRA include:

- **Reduced Misclassification**: The second stage captures subtle differences (e.g., well-wishes vs. factual statements) that single-pass models often overlook.
- **Context Utilization**: By referencing the full user response or previously labeled snippets, the Refiner more accurately infers intent behind brevity, politeness, or indirect language.
- **Efficiency Consideration**: Triggering the Refiner only for ambiguous or contradictory Classifier outputs mitigates computational overhead compared to always running two stages.

In summary, this error analysis underscores that ambiguous linguistic cues, limited context in short

Classifier Result	Refiner Result	Error Case Examples
EXPERIENCE	SUGGESTION	A snippet initially labeled EXPERIENCE was reclassified after the Refiner noted its advisory content ("...a personal request aiming to persuade selection..."), fitting better in SUGGESTION.
INFORMATION	SUGGESTION	The statement "Best of good luck from Italy" was interpreted as INFORMATION until the Refiner interpreted it as a supportive or advisory comment, upgrading it to SUGGESTION.
QUESTION	INFORMATION	Rhetorical questions (e.g., "can you picture a fish out of the water?") were reframed as INFORMATION once the Refiner deduced they conveyed illustrative content rather than genuinely seeking an answer.
UNCATEGORIZED	SUGGESTION	Extremely short snippets like "Geez! How terrible for her!!! Good luck to her & you." lacked a Classifier label. 'good luck' serves as a supportive and advisory statement, the Refiner assigned it to SUGGESTION.

Table 4: Example cases of Refiner modifying the classification label.

snippets, and the pragmatic function of rhetorical questions remain primary sources of error. However, iterative refinement significantly alleviates these issues, resulting in higher fidelity categorizations. Future enhancements might include more explicit discourse modeling or leveraging external knowledge bases for context augmentation, particularly for healthcare-related queries, where subtle nuances can have significant implications for the quality of advice or information provided.

6 Conclusion

In this paper, we presented a CRA that addresses the intrinsic complexity of health-related user-generated content by employing a two-stage decision-making pipeline. Our experiments on the PUMA dataset, curated for the PerAnsSumm shared task (Task A: span extraction and perspective classification), underscored how iterative refinement, retrieval-augmented generation, and CoT prompting collectively enhance classification confidence and accuracy. Comparative analyses across leading LLMs (GPT-4o, Claude 3, and o1-preview) revealed that multi-stage approaches deliver more robust handling of ambiguous or overlapping categories. While our findings highlight significant gains in classification metrics such as macro-F1 and weighted-F1, improvements are likely possible with key future directions include model interpretability enhancements, domain-specific fine-tuning for nuanced medical conditions, and cross-lingual adaptations that can scale to diverse user populations. Furthermore, integrating external medical knowledge bases or discourse-level context could refine the Refiner's decision boundaries, especially for borderline snippets that require deeper inference. By unifying advanced prompting techniques with context-driven refinement, the proposed CRA framework can be extended to broader, multi-turn QA and summarization tasks in healthcare, ultimately improving the reliability of automated systems designed to navigate the ever-evolving landscape of health information exchange.

Limitations

Although our CRA significantly improves classification accuracy for user-generated health content, there are notable limitations that warrant attention. First, the approach relies heavily on the availability of high-quality labeled data in the training set. If the training set lacks examples that closely resemble an ambiguous snippet, the Refiner may fail to retrieve contextually relevant instances, leading to suboptimal classification. Second, while the inclusion of CoT prompting and tone definitions enhances interpretability, it does not fully guarantee factual correctness, particularly critical in healthcare scenarios. Our system is not designed to validate medical claims or detect misinformation, so erroneous or potentially harmful suggestions could persist if they align with patterns seen in the training data. Additionally, the current pipeline has been tested on a single domain-specific dataset and language, limiting its generalizability to other languages or more specialized medical domains. Future research could explore cross-lingual implementations or adapt the method to incorporate external medical knowledge bases for deeper validation. Finally, despite demonstrating improvements in computational efficiency by triggering the Refiner only when the Classifier is uncertain, the iterative nature of our approach incurs additional inference time for borderline cases, which might not be desirable for large-scale, real-time applications.

References

Siddhant Agarwal, Md Shad Akhtar, and Shweta Yadav. 2025. Overview of the peranssumm 2025 shared task on perspective-aware healthcare answer summarization. In *Proceedings of the Second Workshop on Patient-Oriented Language Processing (CL4Health) @ NAACL 2025*, Albuquerque, USA. Association for Computational Linguistics.

Anthropic. 2024. Introducing the next generation of claude.

Tianyu Gao, Adam Fisch, and Danqi Chen. 2020. Making pre-trained language models better few-shot learners. *CoRR*, abs/2012.15723.

Gautier Izacard and Edouard Grave. 2020. Leveraging passage retrieval with generative models for open domain question answering. *CoRR*, abs/2007.01282.

Jooyeon Lee, Luan Huy Pham, and Özlem Uzuner. 2024. Enhancing consumer health question reformulation: Chain-of-thought prompting integrating focus, type, and user knowledge level. In *Proceedings of the First Workshop on Patient-Oriented Language Processing (CL4Health) @ LREC-COLING 2024*, pages 220–228, Torino, Italia. ELRA and ICCL.

Patrick S. H. Lewis, Ethan Perez, Aleksandra Piktus, Fabio Petroni, Vladimir Karpukhin, Naman Goyal, Heinrich Küttler, Mike Lewis, Wen-tau Yih, Tim Rocktäschel, Sebastian Riedel, and Douwe Kiela. 2020. Retrieval-augmented generation for knowledge-intensive NLP tasks. *CoRR*, abs/2005.11401.

Gauri Naik, Sharad Chandakacherla, Shweta Yadav, and Md Shad Akhtar. 2024. No perspective, no perception!! perspective-aware healthcare answer summarization. In *Findings of the Association for Computational Linguistics: ACL 2024*, pages 15919–15932, Bangkok, Thailand. Association for Computational Linguistics.

OpenAI, :, Aaron Hurst, Adam Lerer, Adam P. Goucher, Adam Perelman, Aditya Ramesh, Aidan Clark, AJ Ostrow, Akila Welihinda, Alan Hayes, Alec Radford, Aleksander Mądry, Alex Baker-Whitcomb, Alex Beutel, Alex Borzunov, Alex Carney, Alex Chow, Alex Kirillov, Alex Nichol, Alex Paino, Alex Renzin, Alex Tachard Passos, Alexander Kirillov, Alexi Christakis, Alexis Conneau, Ali Kamali, Allan Jabri, Allison Moyer, Allison Tam, Amadou Crookes, Amin Tootoochian, Amin Tootoonchian, Ananya Kumar, Andrea Vallone, Andrej Karpathy, Andrew Braunstein, Andrew Cann, Andrew Codispoti, Andrew Galu, Andrew Kondrich, Andrew Tulloch, Andrey Mishchenko, Angela Baek, Angela Jiang, Antoine Pelisse, Antonia Woodford, Anuj Gosalia, Arka Dhar, Ashley Pantuliano, Avi Nayak, Avital Oliver, Barret Zoph, Behrooz Ghorbani, Ben Leimberger, Ben Rossen, Ben Sokolowsky, Ben Wang, Benjamin Zweig, Beth Hoover, Blake Samic, Bob McGrew, Bobby Spero, Bogo Giertler, Bowen Cheng, Brad Lightcap, Brandon Walkin, Brendan Quinn, Brian Guarraci, Brian Hsu, Bright Kellogg, Brydon Eastman, Camillo Lugaresi, Carroll Wainwright, Cary Bassin, Cary Hudson, Casey Chu, Chad Nelson, Chak Li, Chan Jun Shern, Channing Conger, Charlotte Barette, Chelsea Voss, Chen Ding, Cheng Lu, Chong Zhang, Chris Beaumont, Chris Hallacy, Chris Koch, Christian Gibson, Christina Kim, Christine Choi, Christine McLeavey, Christopher Hesse, Claudia Fischer, Clemens Winter, Coley Czarnecki, Colin Jarvis, Colin Wei, Constantin Koumouzelis, Dane Sherburn, Daniel Kappler, Daniel Levin, Daniel Levy, David Carr, David Farhi, David Mely, David Robinson, David Sasaki, Denny Jin, Dev Valladares, Dimitris Tsipras, Doug Li, Duc Phong Nguyen, Duncan Findlay, Edede Oiwoh, Edmund Wong, Ehsan Asdar, Elizabeth Proehl, Elizabeth Yang, Eric Antonow, Eric Kramer, Eric Peterson, Eric Sigler, Eric Wallace, Eugene Brevdo, Evan Mays, Farzad Khorasani, Felipe Petroski Such, Filippo Raso, Francis Zhang, Fred von Lohmann, Freddie Sulit, Gabriel Goh, Gene Oden, Geoff Salmon, Giulio Starace, Greg Brockman, Hadi Salman, Haiming Bao, Haitang Hu, Hannah Wong, Haoyu Wang, Heather Schmidt, Heather Whitney, Heewoo Jun, Hendrik Kirchner, Henrique Ponde de Oliveira Pinto, Hongyu Ren, Huiwen Chang, Hyung Won Chung, Ian Kivlichan, Ian O'Connell, Ian O'Connell, Ian Osband, Ian Silber, Ian Sohl, Ibrahim Okuyucu, Ikai Lan, Ilya Kostrikov, Ilya Sutskever, Ingmar Kanitscheider, Ishaan Gulrajani, Jacob Coxon, Jacob Menick, Jakub Pachocki, James Aung, James Betker, James Crooks, James Lennon, Jamie Kiros, Jan Leike, Jane Park, Jason Kwon, Jason Phang, Jason Teplitz, Jason Wei, Jason Wolfe, Jay Chen, Jeff Harris, Jenia Varavva, Jessica Gan Lee, Jessica Shieh, Ji Lin, Jiahui Yu, Jiayi Weng, Jie Tang, Jieqi Yu, Joanne Jang, Joaquin Quinonero Candela, Joe Beutler, Joe Landers, Joel Parish, Johannes Heidecke, John Schulman, Jonathan Lachman, Jonathan McKay, Jonathan Uesato, Jonathan Ward, Jong Wook Kim, Joost Huizinga, Jordan Sitkin, Jos Kraaijeveld, Josh Gross, Josh Kaplan, Josh Snyder, Joshua Achiam, Joy Jiao, Joyce Lee, Juntang Zhuang, Justyn Harriman, Kai Fricke, Kai Hayashi, Karan Singhal, Katy Shi, Kavin Karthik, Kayla Wood, Kendra Rimbach, Kenny Hsu, Kenny Nguyen, Keren Gu-Lemberg, Kevin Button, Kevin Liu, Kiel Howe, Krithika Muthukumar, Kyle Luther, Lama Ahmad, Larry Kai, Lauren Itow, Lauren Workman, Leher Pathak, Leo Chen, Li Jing, Lia Guy, Liam Fedus, Liang Zhou, Lien Mamitsuka, Lilian Weng, Lindsay McCallum, Lindsey Held, Long Ouyang, Louis Feuvrier, Lu Zhang, Lukas Kondraciuk, Lukasz Kaiser, Luke Hewitt, Luke Metz, Lyric Doshi, Mada Aflak, Maddie Simens, Madelaine Boyd, Madeleine Thompson, Marat Dukhan, Mark Chen, Mark Gray, Mark Hudnall, Marvin Zhang, Marwan Aljubeh, Mateusz Litwin, Matthew Zeng, Max Johnson, Maya Shetty, Mayank Gupta, Meghan Shah, Mehmet Yatbaz, Meng Jia Yang, Mengchao Zhong, Mia Glaese, Mianna Chen, Michael Janner, Michael Lampe, Michael Petrov, Michael Wu, Michele Wang, Michelle Fradin, Michelle Pokrass, Miguel Castro, Miguel Oom Temudo de Castro, Mikhail Pavlov, Miles Brundage, Miles Wang, Minal Khan, Mira Murati, Mo Bavarian, Molly Lin, Murat Yesildal, Nacho Soto, Natalia Gimelshein, Natalie Cone, Natalie Staudacher, Natalie Summers, Natan LaFontaine, Neil Chowdhury, Nick Ryder, Nick Stathas, Nick Turley, Nik Tezak, Niko Felix, Nithanth Kudige, Nitish Keskar, Noah Deutsch, Noel Bundick, Nora Puckett, Ofir Nachum, Ola Okelola, Oleg Boiko, Oleg Murk, Oliver Jaffe, Olivia Watkins, Olivier Godement, Owen Campbell-Moore, Patrick Chao, Paul McMillan, Pavel Belov, Peng Su, Peter Bak, Peter Bakkum, Peter Deng, Peter Dolan, Peter Hoeschele, Peter Welinder, Phil Tillet, Philip Pronin, Philippe Tillet, Prafulla Dhariwal, Qiming Yuan, Rachel Dias, Rachel Lim, Rahul Arora, Rajan Troll, Randall Lin, Rapha Gontijo Lopes, Raul Puri, Reah Miyara, Reimar Leike, Renaud Gaubert, Reza Zamani, Ricky Wang, Rob Donnelly, Rob Honsby, Rocky Smith, Rohan Sahai, Rohit Ramchandani, Romain Huet, Rory Carmichael, Rowan Zellers, Roy Chen, Ruby Chen, Ruslan Nigmatullin, Ryan Cheu, Saachi Jain, Sam Altman, Sam Schoenholz, Sam Toizer, Samuel Miserendino, Sandhini Agarwal, Sara Culver, Scott Ethersmith, Scott Gray, Sean Grove, Sean Metzger, Shamez Hermani, Shantanu Jain, Shengjia Zhao, Sherwin Wu, Shino Jomoto, Shirong Wu, Shuaiqi, Xia, Sonia Phene, Spencer Papay, Srinivas Narayanan, Steve Coffey, Steve Lee, Stewart Hall, Suchir Balaji, Tal Broda, Tal Stramer, Tao Xu, Tarun Gogineni, Taya Christianson, Ted Sanders, Tejal Patwardhan, Thomas Cunninghman, Thomas Degry, Thomas Dimson, Thomas Raoux, Thomas Shadwell, Tianhao Zheng, Todd Underwood, Todor Markov, Toki Sherbakov, Tom Rubin, Tom Stasi, Tomer Kaftan, Tristan Heywood, Troy Peterson, Tyce Walters, Tyna Eloundou, Valerie Qi, Veit Moeller, Vinnie Monaco, Vishal Kuo, Vlad Fomenko, Wayne Chang, Weiyi Zheng, Wenda Zhou, Wesam Manassra, Will Sheu, Wojciech Zaremba, Yash Patil, Yilei Qian, Yongjik Kim, Youlong Cheng, Yu Zhang, Yuchen He, Yuchen Zhang, Yujia Jin, Yunxing Dai, and Yury Malkov. 2024. Gpt-4o system card. *Preprint*, arXiv:2410.21276.

Wenhui Wang, Furu Wei, Li Dong, Hangbo Bao, Nan Yang, and Ming Zhou. 2020. Minilm: Deep self-attention distillation for task-agnostic compression of pre-trained transformers. *CoRR*, abs/2002.10957.

Jason Wei, Xuezhi Wang, Dale Schuurmans, Maarten Bosma, Ed H. Chi, Quoc Le, and Denny Zhou. 2022. Chain of thought prompting elicits reasoning in large language models. *CoRR*, abs/2201.11903.

Rong Zhang, Revanth Gangi Reddy, Md. Arafat Sultan, Vittorio Castelli, Anthony Ferritto, Radu Florian, Efsun Sarioglu Kayi, Salim Roukos, Avirup Sil, and Todd Ward. 2020. Multi-stage pre-training for low-resource domain adaptation. *CoRR*, abs/2010.05904.

Tony Z. Zhao, Eric Wallace, Shi Feng, Dan Klein, and Sameer Singh. 2021. Calibrate before use: Improving few-shot performance of language models. *CoRR*, abs/2102.09690.

Tianyang Zhong, Zhengliang Liu, Yi Pan, Yutong Zhang, Yifan Zhou, Shizhe Liang, Zihao Wu, Yanjun Lyu, Peng Shu, Xiaowei Yu, Chao Cao, Hanqi Jiang, Hanxu Chen, Yiwei Li, Junhao Chen, Huawen Hu, Yihen Liu, Huaqin Zhao, Shaochen Xu, Haixing Dai, Lin Zhao, Ruidong Zhang, Wei Zhao, Zhenyuan Yang, Jingyuan Chen, Peilong Wang, Wei Ruan, Hui Wang, Huan Zhao, Jing Zhang, Yiming Ren, Shihuan Qin, Tong Chen, Jiaxi Li, Arif Hassan Zidan, Afrar Jahin, Minheng Chen, Sichen Xia, Jason Holmes, Yan Zhuang, Jiaqi Wang, Bochen Xu, Weiran Xia, Jichao Yu, Kaibo Tang, Yaxuan Yang, Bolun Sun, Tao Yang, Guoyu Lu, Xianqiao Wang, Lilong Chai, He Li, Jin Lu, Lichao Sun, Xin Zhang, Bao Ge, Xintao Hu, Lian Zhang, Hua Zhou, Lu Zhang, Shu Zhang, Ninghao Liu, Bei Jiang, Linglong Kong, Zhen Xiang, Yudan Ren, Jun Liu, Xi Jiang, Yu Bao, Wei Zhang, Xiang Li, Gang Li, Wei Liu, Dinggang Shen, Andrea Sikora, Xiaoming Zhai, Dajiang Zhu, and Tianming Liu. 2024. Evaluation of openai o1: Opportunities and challenges of agi. *Preprint*, arXiv:2409.18486.

WisPerMed @ PerAnsSumm 2025: Strong Reasoning Through Structured Prompting and Careful Answer Selection Enhances Perspective Extraction and Summarization of Healthcare Forum Threads

Tabea M. G. Pakull[1,2]*, Hendrik Damm[2,3]*, Henning Schäfer[1,2], Peter A. Horn[1], Christoph M. Friedrich[2,3]

[1]Institute for Transfusion Medicine, University Hospital Essen

[2]Department of Computer Science, University of Applied Sciences and Arts Dortmund

[3]Institute for Medical Informatics, Biometry and Epidemiology, University Hospital Essen

Correspondence: tabea.pakull@uk-essen.de, hendrik.damm@fh-dortmund.de

Abstract

Healthcare community question-answering (CQA) forums provide multi-perspective insights into patient experiences and medical advice. Summarizations of these threads must account for these perspectives, rather than relying on a single "best" answer. This paper presents the participation of the WisPerMed team in the PerAnsSumm shared task 2025, which consists of two sub-tasks: (A) span identification and classification, and (B) perspective-based summarization. For Task A, encoder models, decoder-based LLMs, and reasoning-focused models are evaluated under fine-tuning, instruction-tuning, and prompt-based paradigms. The experimental evaluations employing automatic metrics demonstrate that DeepSeek-R1 attains a high proportional recall (0.738) and F1-Score (0.676) in zero-shot settings, though strict boundary alignment remains challenging (F1-Score: 0.196). For Task B, filtering answers by labeling them with perspectives prior to summarization with Mistral-7B-v0.3 enhances summarization. This approach ensures that the model is trained exclusively on relevant data, while discarding non-essential information, leading to enhanced relevance (ROUGE-1: 0.452) and balanced factuality (SummaC: 0.296). The analysis uncovers two key limitations: data imbalance and hallucinations of decoder-based LLMs, with underrepresented perspectives exhibiting suboptimal performance. The WisPerMed team's approach secured the highest overall ranking in the shared task.

1 Introduction

Healthcare community question-answering (CQA) forums have become a vital resource for individuals seeking medical advice and shared experiences (Rueger et al., 2021). Unlike traditional clinical consultations, these online platforms allow users to post health-related questions and receive a wide range of answers from peers or experienced community members. Such forums often present diverse content that can address multiple aspects of a medical query. Some answers focus on personal experiences, whereas others might center on medical information or offer direct suggestions. Moreover, responses may highlight causes for a condition or pose follow-up questions to the original poster.

Despite this wealth of information, most summarization approaches for healthcare CQA threads relied on a single best-voted answer (Chowdhury and Chakraborty, 2019), which overlooks the multi-perspective nature of the discussion. A single "best" answer cannot fully encapsulate such a variety of viewpoints, highlighting the need for more perspective-aware summarization, where different types of information are distinguished rather than merged into one overarching summary.

Building on this motivation, the PerAnsSumm shared task (Agarwal et al., 2025), aims to foster research in perspective-aware healthcare answer summarization and comprises two sub-tasks:

(A) Span Identification and Classification: Given a question and user answers the task is to label spans in the answers that correspond to one of the five perspectives: *cause*, *suggestion*, *experience*, *question*, or *information*.

(B) Perspective-Based Summarization: For each perspective category, the task is to generate a concise summary that represents the content found across all answers in the thread.

This paper describes the approaches of team WisPerMed to tackle both sub-tasks. The following sections provide an overview of related work (Section 2) and describe the dataset in detail (Section 3). Then, the approaches for both tasks (Section 4) and the corresponding evaluation procedure (Section 5) are presented and their results are discussed (Section 6). Finally, the conclusion (Section 7) offers a summary of the findings.

*These authors contributed equally to this work.

Proceedings of the Second Workshop on Patient-Oriented Language Processing (CL4Health), pages 359–373
May 4, 2025 ©2025 Association for Computational Linguistics

2 Related Work

Datasets derived from healthcare CQA forums provide insights into patient experiences (Rueger et al., 2021) and informal medical language (Chaturvedi et al., 2024). Specialized datasets (Naik et al., 2024; Chaturvedi et al., 2024; Savery et al., 2020) have been created to capture this type of content, facilitating research in patient-centered healthcare natural language processing (NLP).

Large Language Models (LLMs) demonstrate remarkable capabilities in various domains, including healthcare (Thirunavukarasu et al., 2023). BERT (Bidirectional Encoder Representations from Transformers) (Devlin et al., 2019) and its variants have formed the landscape of NLP in medicine (Thirunavukarasu et al., 2023). As encoder models, they process entire input sequences at once, leveraging attention mechanisms to build contextual representations. This ability makes them particularly well-suited for extracting structured information. Decoder-only LLMs, such as GPT (Generative Pre-trained Transformer) (Brown et al., 2020a) models, have shown impressive performance in various NLP tasks. These models process text sequentially, predicting the next token based on previous tokens. Research has explored adapting decoder-only LLMs for span labeling tasks (Dagdelen et al., 2024), leveraging their strong semantic understanding capabilities. While decoder-only LLMs excel at generating text, they face challenges in producing structured outputs. One major issue is "hallucination" (Sun et al., 2024), where models generate plausible but incorrect information. Recent advancements in LLMs have led to improved reasoning capabilities through enhanced training strategies (Pan et al., 2024) and chain-of-thought prompting (Wei et al., 2022). Models like DeepSeek-R1 (DeepSeek-AI et al., 2025) exhibit strong reasoning abilities, which are particularly valuable in healthcare applications where nuanced understanding and logical inference are crucial.

Summarization has emerged as a highly studied application of NLP in healthcare. Various approaches have been developed, including extraction- and abstraction-based techniques using LLMs (Xu et al., 2024). Perspective or aspect-based summarization (Chaturvedi et al., 2024) represents an evolving area in NLP, aiming to summarize different viewpoints or aspects within a text. This is valuable when dealing with diverse experiences and opinions expressed in online forums.

3 Dataset

The dataset used is derived from the L6 Yahoo! Answers CQA repository[1], filtered to only include health-related content. It contains 3,245 question threads with a maximum of 10 answers, totaling 10,288 individual answers. The final dataset is split into 2,236 training threads, 959 validation threads, and 50 test threads. Table 1 shows span counts, along with the number of corresponding perspective-based summaries in the training and validation sets. The raw dataset consists of a uid, user question, context to the question provided by the user, answers from other users, and raw_text which combines all information into a single string.

Perspective	Train	Val
Information	4,388 / 1,742	1,805 / 733
Cause	579 / 305	266 / 138
Suggestion	3,613 / 1,363	1,635 / 595
Question	284 / 213	131 / 101
Experience	1,245 / 745	565 / 315

Table 1: Perspective-based dataset statistics. Each cell shows the number of spans / the number of summaries.

The annotation of this dataset follows the schema described by Naik et al. (2024).

Perspective and Span Annotation. Each answer is manually reviewed to detect text spans corresponding to five perspectives: *cause*, *suggestion*, *experience*, *question*, and *information*. Annotators label these spans at the character level, conveying any of the aforementioned perspectives. As a result, a single answer can contain multiple types of perspectives. The level of granularity allows for the annotation of whitespaces and sub-words.

Perspective-Based Summarization. For each thread, a concise summary is written for every perspective observed in the answers. These summaries aim to capture the core content associated with that perspective across all answers in the thread.

4 Methods

As the sub-tasks are distinct, it is necessary to implement different approaches for each. The following sections detail the approaches employed.

[1] `https://webscope.sandbox.yahoo.com/catalog.php?datatype=l&did=11`, Last Accessed: 19. February 2025.

4.1 Task A: Span Identification and Classification

The experiments carried out for Task A used a variety of models and tuning techniques.

Models. DeBERTa-v3-large (He et al., 2021a), developed by Microsoft, builds upon the encoder model DeBERTa (He et al., 2021b). It comprises 24 layers with a hidden size of 1024, totaling approximately 418 million parameters, and is designed to enhance natural language understanding tasks. Llama-3.1-8B-Instruct was developed by Meta AI as part of the Llama series (Dubey et al., 2024) of LLMs. It contains 8 billion parameters, offering a balance between performance and computational efficiency. Llama-3.3-70B-Instruct is a 70-billion-parameter model from a newer variant of the Llama series. Both Llama models are fine-tuned with instruction-based data, enhancing their capability to follow complex directives and generate contextually relevant outputs. DeepSeek-R1 (DeepSeek-AI et al., 2025) is developed for reasoning tasks across domains such as mathematics, programming, and language. It employs a Mixture of Experts (Jacobs et al., 1991) architecture, comprising a total of 671 billion parameters. DeepSeek-R1-Distill-Llama-70B (DeepSeek-AI et al., 2025) involves distilling the DeepSeek-R1 model into a more compact form based on the Llama-3.3-70B-Instruct architecture. This involves training the smaller model (the student) to replicate the behavior of the larger DeepSeek-R1 model (the teacher) by learning from its outputs.

Fine-Tuning of Encoder Models. For the encoder approach, a DeBERTa-v3-large model was fine-tuned. The five perspective category spans were cast as NER labels in a BIO scheme (Ramshaw and Marcus, 1995; Tjong Kim Sang, 2002). During training, a maximum sequence length of 512 was set, a batch size of 16 was used, and a warmup ratio of 0.1. Model checkpoints were saved at each epoch, and the best state was chosen based on F1-Scores from the validation set. Early stopping was only applied to the $\textit{DeBERTa}_{\textit{reconstr.-early}}$ model. For inference, the raw_text style representation was available for the training and validation data only, but not for the test set. Therefore, two inference approaches were explored. *DeBERTa*: Each individual answer was provided to the model as a separate input, and the resulting token-level predictions were stored on a per-answer basis. $\textit{DeBERTa}_{\textit{reconstr.}}$: Each test sample was reconstructed into a single sequence by inserting the same markers (`uri: <ID>`, `question: <text>`, and `answer_0: <text>`) to obtain a format that is consistent with the training data. The entire thread was then passed to the model at once, enabling it to capture cross-answer context. After token-level predictions were generated for both approaches, a chunk-merging step was applied to merge consecutive tokens that shared the same perspective class. Single-word spans were removed to improve precision. The final labeled segments were then saved in the submission format.

Instruction-Tuning of Llama-3.1-8B-Instruct. In order to optimize Llama-3.1-8B-Instruct for perspective-aware span extraction, the train split of the dataset was structured into a format suitable for instruction-tuning (Wei et al., 2021). Instruction-tuning refers to the process of training LLMs on data formatted as instructions. Input and output are transformed in a conversation-style format containing a system and user prompt as well as the structured assistant output. In this work the system prompt outlines the task, classification guidelines, and output format. To ensure the consistency and successful parsing of outputs, the model is instructed to return its response as a TypeScript object. The user prompt contains the answers from forum users and the assistant output contains the spans structured as a TypeScript object. All prompts can be found in the Appendix A.5.1.

To maintain computational efficiency Parameter-Efficient Fine-Tuning (PEFT) (Ding et al., 2023) via LoRA (Low-Rank Adaptation) (Hu et al., 2022) was employed. More details on the implementation can be found in the Appendix A.2.

During inference, the instruction-tuned model utilizes the same prompts as in training. The inference parameter are available in Appendix A.3.1.

Prompt-Based Techniques. To complement fine- and instruction-tuning, zero-shot and few-shot prompting strategies (Brown et al., 2020b) were employed. These methods instruct LLMs to extract relevant spans and classify them into the correct perspective category without the need for parameter updates.

In the zero-shot setting, the model is directly prompted using the system prompt that outlines the task, classification guidelines, and output format, combined with the user prompt that contains the answers from forum users. This method tests the model's ability to generalize its understanding of text span classification based solely on its pre-trained knowledge.

To enhance performance, few-shot learning was introduced by showing the model examples of gold-standard output in a conversational style. These examples demonstrate how the spans should be extracted and categorized, helping the model learn through analogy. Two variations of few-shot prompting were explored: Standard few-shot prompting, where gold-standard examples were provided as part of the same interaction and few-shot prompting with system message resets, where each example was treated as an independent instance with repeated system prompts to reinforce adherence to the task and the output format.

In both few-shot and zero-shot settings the same system and user prompts are used as for instruction-tuning (see Appendix A.5.1).

4.2 Task B: Perspective-Based Summarization

Early experiments on the validation set indicated that fine-tuning models solely with span data for the summarization task led to suboptimal results. Relying solely on span annotations failed to capture the broader contextual and query-specific nuances necessary for generating high-quality summaries. Furthermore, when using spans as input, performance on Task B is dependent on Task A performance. Consequently, a more comprehensive instruct-tuning strategy was adopted that leverages all available information, including the context, question, and answers. In this revised approach, models are exposed to a richer set of inputs during the training process, enabling improved understanding and synthesis of relevant information for summarization. The instruct-tuning was tested on the following four models. The prompts for the instruction-tuning can be seen in Appendix A.5.2.

Models. Mistral-Small-24B-Instruct[2] is a pre-trained, instruction-tuned model that achieves performance comparable to larger models such as Llama 3.3 70B while offering faster inference. Mistral-7B-Instruct-v0.3 (Jiang et al., 2023). BioMistral-7B-DARE (Labrak et al., 2024) adapts Mistral-7B-Instruct-v0.1 (Jiang et al., 2023) for the biomedical domain through additional pre-training on PubMed Central, achieving strong results on medical question-answering benchmarks and effective multilingual generalization. DeepSeek-R1-Distill-Qwen-32B (DeepSeek-AI et al., 2025) is a distilled dense model that replicates the reasoning patterns of the larger DeepSeek-R1 (DeepSeek-AI et al., 2025) in a compact form.

[2]https://mistral.ai/news/mistral-small-3, Last Accessed: 23. February 2025.

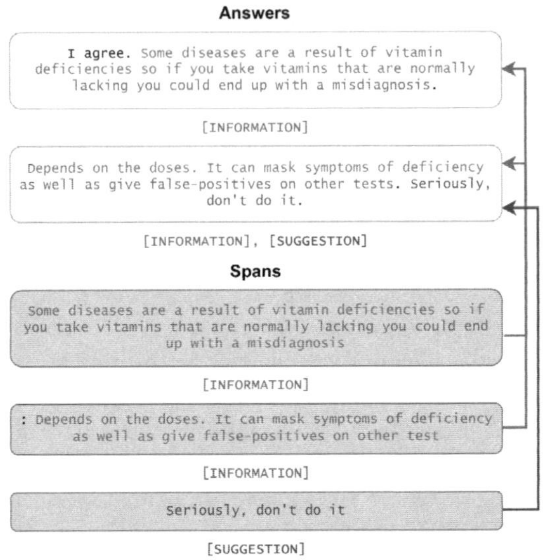

Figure 1: Workflow Diagram of the Answer Labeling Pipeline for Task B pre-classification. The process begins by extracting answer boundaries from raw_text. Next, labeled spans are assigned to their corresponding answers based on their starting index. Finally, the original answer texts are assigned the perspective labels of contained spans.

4.2.1 Pre-classification Methodology

Instead of using all answers to generate a summary for a given perspective, multi-label perspective classifiers were trained using DeBERTaV3 and Mistral-7B-v0.3. To create a labeled answer dataset, answer spans were extracted and the corresponding answers determined via regular expressions (see Figure 1). In some instances, a more complex regex was needed to fix annotation errors; for example, the second span in Figure 1 mistakenly included a leading colon and whitespace from raw_text that were not present in the original answer.

The trained classifiers were then applied to the test set to label answers and generate summaries, as illustrated in Figure 2. For model instruct-tuning, only answers labeled with the same perspective as the requested summary (e.g., *information*) were used. If no answers were labeled with the desired perspective, the model used all available answers instead. This strategy ensures that every thread receives one summary per perspective, regardless

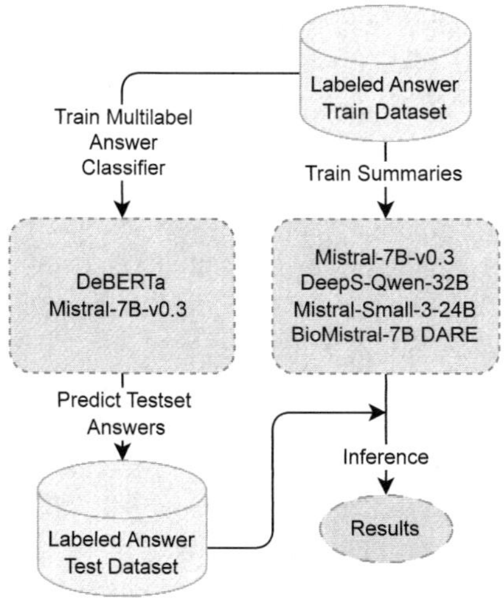

Figure 2: The labeled answer train dataset was used to train multi-label classifiers and instruction-tune models for Task B. The test dataset, with predicted answer perspectives, was then used to generate summarizations.

of the distribution of labeled answers. Additionally, an alternative approach involves training five separate models (Mistral-7B-v0.3_{5x}), one for each perspective.

5 Evaluation

A range of evaluation metrics are used to evaluate different aspects of the results, with scores in Table 3 and Table 6 provided by the shared task organizers (Agarwal et al., 2025).

5.1 Task A: Span Identification and Classification

The evaluation methodology for Task A comprises assessment of classification performance and span identification accuracy. The former is measured using a macro-averaged F1-Score (Macro F1) and a weighted F1-Score (Weight F1). The latter is evaluated using Strict and Proportional Matching (Agarwal et al., 2025). Strict Matching involves the evaluation of the exact match between predicted and gold standard spans, with precision (P), recall (R), and F1-Scores being computed from the number of exact matches. Proportional Matching allows for partial correctness by evaluating the token-level overlap between predicted and gold-standard spans. The number of overlapping tokens in each predicted span is measured against the most similar gold span, and the results are then used to compute precision, recall, and F1-Scores. This approach makes it more flexible than strict matching.

To evaluate hallucinated spans in LLM-generated outputs, it is checked whether the output spans appear verbatim in the original answers. This analysis reports the proportion of correctly extracted spans, providing a quantitative measure of the model's tendency to introduce extraneous content. This analysis is reported in this work in addition to the shared task results, and is not used for ranking.

5.2 Task B: Perspective-Based Summarization

In Task B the evaluation methodology employs multiple automatic metrics to assess the quality of generated summaries across the aspects relevance and factuality.

5.2.1 Relevance

Recall-Oriented Understudy for Gisting Evaluation (ROUGE) (Lin, 2004) measures the F1-Score of overlap of unigrams (ROUGE-1), bigrams (ROUGE-2), and longest common subsequences (ROUGE-L) between the generated and reference summaries. Bilingual Evaluation Understudy (BLEU) (Papineni et al., 2002) is a metric that evaluates the precision of n-gram overlap. Metric for Evaluation of Translation with Explicit ORdering (METEOR) (Banerjee and Lavie, 2005) considers both synonymy and stemming to provide a more flexible assessment of lexical similarity. It also calculates the degree to which the matched words are ordered in the same way in the summary as in the reference. BERTScore (Zhang et al., 2020) leverages contextualized embeddings from BERT to compute semantic similarity between generated and reference summaries.

5.2.2 Factuality

The AlignScore (Kryscinski et al., 2020) quantifies the degree of alignment between the facts in the summary and the reference. SummaC-Conv (Laban et al., 2022) (SummaC) detects inconsistencies by segmenting documents into sentence-level pairs and using a convolutional layer to aggregate entailment scores for the factuality assessment.

6 Results and Discussion

The final rankings of the top five participating teams in the shared task are summarized in Table 2. The WisPerMed team achieved the highest overall ranking (0.457) in the shared task, narrowly outperforming the other teams. The ranking is based on both sub-tasks. In Task A WisPerMed obtained a

		Ovr.	Task A	Task B	
#	Team	$\bar{x}$	$\bar{x}$	Rel.	Fact.
1	WisPerMed	**0.457**	0.598	<u>0.421</u>	<u>0.352</u>
2	YALENLP	<u>0.455</u>	0.604	**0.436**	0.325
3	yxyx	0.453	**0.621**	0.365	**0.372**
4	AICOE	0.45	<u>0.605</u>	0.395	0.348
5	KHU_LDI	0.449	0.589	0.417	0.343

Table 2: Final results of the top five teams in the shared task. Columns show team rank (#) and average scores ($\bar{x}$) for overall (Ovr.) and Task A. Task B scores are reported separately for relevance (Rel.) and factuality (Fact.). **Bold** values indicate the highest score, and underlined values mark the second-highest.

score of 0.598 using DeepSeek-R1 in the zero-shot setting (DeepS-R1_{zs} in Table 3). Task B is further divided into relevance and factuality categories, where WisPerMed ranked first in both categories combined using the instruction-tuned Mistral-7B-v0.3, with the labeled answer test dataset (Mistral-7B-v0.$3_{\text{pre-class.}}$).

6.1 Task A: Span Identification and Classification

Table 3 summarizes the performance of various experimental setups for Task A. Evaluation metrics include Macro F1-Score, Weighted F1-Score, and precision (P), recall (R), and F1-Scores under both Strict and Proportional span matching.

DeepSeek-R1 in the zero-shot setting (DeepS-R1_{zs}) achieved the best scores in Macro F1-Score (0.878), Weighted F1-Score (0.921), and several span matching metrics (Strict Recall (0.229), Strict F1-Score (0.196), Proportional Recall (0.738), and Proportional F1-Score (0.676)). Its high recall values under both matching criteria indicate robust retrieval capabilities. Moreover, its overall average score of 0.598 reinforces its superior performance across the evaluation metrics.

DeBERTa achieves an overall score of 0.539, yet it does not exhibit any particular advantage in individual sub-metrics. The DeBERTa-based variants DeBERTa$_{\text{reconstr.-early}}$ and DeBERTa$_{\text{reconstr.}}$ exhibit improved performance. The former attained the second-best Macro F1-Score (0.875), while the latter secured the second-best Weighted F1-Score (0.909) and the highest Proportional Precision (0.627). This observation indicates that smaller transformer-based models, specifically optimized for sequence labeling tasks, can demonstrate comparable performance to larger general-purpose LLMs in perspective-aware span extraction, despite their smaller size. Making them a considerable choice to reduce resource cost (computational and environmental).

The Llama-based models show a clear dependence on model size and training paradigm. The instruction-tuned Llama-3.1-8B-Instruct (Llama-3.1-8B_{it}) underperforms, with a Macro F1-Score of 0.602 and a Strict F1-Score of 0.023, indicating the limitations of smaller decoder-only models for this task. This performance discrepancy could also indicate that the instruction-tuning process was not sufficiently rigorous or tailored for this specific task. In contrast, the larger Llama-3.3-70B-Instruct variants show enhanced performance. Llama-3.3-70$B_{\text{fs-sys.}}$ variant achieved the highest Strict Precision (0.182) as well as competitive Strict Recall (0.192) and Strict F1-Score (0.187), suggesting that repeated system message enhance the model's ability to precisely identify spans. Its overall average performance of 0.580 places Llama-3.3-70$B_{\text{fs-sys}}$ in second place among WisPerMed's approaches.

The enhanced reasoning capabilities in DeepS-R1 and it's much larger size might have contributed to its superior overall performance. The notable improved overall score of the distilled version (DeepS-Llama-3.3-70B_{fs}) compared to the original Llama-3.3-70B-Instruct (Llama-3.3-70B_{fs}) in the few-shot setting underscore this hypothesis about the impact of reasoning on span labeling performance.

All models exhibited lower scores under Strict span matching, with the highest Strict F1-Score reaching only 0.196. This consistent difference indicates that precise boundary prediction remains a difficult aspect of span extraction. This may be attributed to boundary misalignments in span extraction, where models correctly identify relevant content but fail to precisely match the annotated span boundaries. It may also stem from inconsistencies in the annotated dataset (see Section 4.2.1), where spans include partial words, trailing or preceding whitespaces. The DeepS-R1_{zs} model's superior performance in Strict metrics confirms its ability to accurately retrieve relevant spans, even under exacting conditions. Proportional F1-Scores ranged from 0.420 (Llama-3.1-8B_{it}) to 0.676 (DeepS-R1_{zs}). The overall higher scores for proportional matching suggests that many of the errors in strict matching are due to minor boundary misalignments rather than completely incorrect span predictions. Even with the best approaches among the top five teams in the shared task, performance remains sub-optimal, underscoring the inherent complexity and

Experiment	Macro F1	Weight F1	Str. P	Str. R	Str. F1	Prop. P	Prop. R	Prop. F1	$\bar{x}$
DeBERTa	0.855	0.906	0.103	0.126	0.113	0.600	0.593	0.596	0.539
DeBERTa$_{\text{reconstr.-early}}$	<u>0.875</u>	0.907	0.170	0.152	0.161	0.619	0.621	0.620	0.563
DeBERTa$_{\text{reconstr.}}$	0.871	<u>0.909</u>	0.115	0.116	0.115	**0.627**	0.584	0.605	0.543
Llama-3.1-8B$_{\text{it}}$	0.602	0.733	0.028	0.019	0.023	0.319	0.616	0.420	0.392
Llama-3.3-70B$_{\text{fs}}$	0.828	0.887	0.065	0.048	0.055	0.561	0.604	0.582	0.508
Llama-3.3-70B$_{\text{fs-sys.}}$	0.866	0.907	**0.182**	<u>0.192</u>	<u>0.187</u>	0.606	<u>0.689</u>	<u>0.645</u>	<u>0.580</u>
DeepS-Llama-70B$_{\text{fs}}$	0.839	0.882	<u>0.174</u>	0.162	0.168	0.516	0.647	0.574	0.541
DeepS-R1$_{\text{zs}}$	**0.878**	**0.921**	0.171	**0.229**	**0.196**	<u>0.623</u>	**0.738**	**0.676**	**0.598**

Table 3: Results for Task A. Columns show Macro F1-Score (Macro F1) and Weighted F1-Score (Weight F1), along with precision (P), recall (R), and F1-Scores under Strict (Str.) and Proportional (Prop.) span matching for all experiments. The final column ($\bar{x}$) represents the overall average score. The best values are highlighted in **bold**, while the second-best values are <u>underlined</u>. Abbreviations: it - instruction-tuned, fs - few-shot, fs-sys. - few-shot with repeated system messages, zs - zero-shot.

Experiment	Found Spans (%)
Llama-3.1-8B$_{\text{it}}$	90.70
Llama-3.3-70B$_{\text{fs}}$	96.60
Llama-3.3-70B$_{\text{fs-sys.}}$	97.65
DeepS-Llama-3.3-70B$_{\text{fs}}$	80.82
DeepS-R1$_{\text{zs}}$	92.02

Table 4: Percentage of generated spans that match verbatim spans in the original answers. Abbreviations: it - instruction-tuned, fs - few-shot, fs-sys. - few-shot with repeated system messages, zs - zero-shot.

challenges of perspective-based span labeling.

In addition to the shared task evaluation metrics, an analysis was conducted to quantify hallucinated content in LLM-generated outputs (see Table 4). For instance, Llama-3.1-8B$_{\text{it}}$ achieved an overall percentage of 90.70%, indicating that a notable fraction of its output spans deviated from the source text. In contrast, the Llama-3.3-70B variants exhibited a higher match percentage of 96.60% and 97.65%, suggesting improved fidelity to the input text. However, the DeepSeek-R1-Distill-Llama-70B variant showed a considerably lower match percentage (80.82%), underscoring a higher tendency to generate hallucinated or extraneous spans. The DeepS-R1$_{\text{zs}}$ model yielded 92.02%, indicating, that reasoning may lead to a higher tendency to introduce extraneous content.

6.2 Task B: Perspective-Based Summarization

Results of Task B are discussed using metrics for factuality (AlignScore and SummaC) and relevancy (ROUGE, BERTScore, METEOR, and BLEU).

Answer Pre-classification Table 5 presents the classification performance of trained Mistral-7B-v0.3 and DeBERTaV3 on the validation set. Mistral-7B-v0.3 achieves a higher Macro F1-Score

Perspective	P	R	F1	S
Mistral-7B-v0.3				
experience	0.735	0.683	0.708	419
suggestion	0.718	0.749	0.733	1,142
cause	0.571	0.124	0.204	193
question	0.851	0.381	0.526	105
information	0.704	0.722	0.713	1,210
Macro	**0.716**	**0.532**	**0.577**	3,069
Weighted	**0.710**	0.677	**0.681**	3,069
DeBERTaV3				
experience	0.671	0.780	0.722	419
suggestion	0.732	0.762	0.746	1,142
cause	0.300	0.016	0.030	193
question	0.778	0.200	0.318	105
information	0.689	0.786	0.734	1,210
Macro	0.634	0.509	0.510	3,069
Weighted	0.681	**0.708**	0.679	3,069

Table 5: Comparison of classification performance on the validation set for Mistral-7B-v0.3 and DeBERTa. In the overall Macro and Weighted rows, the best score (between models) for each metric is shown in **bold**. Precision (P), recall (R), F1-Score (F1), and Support (S) are reported.

(0.577) compared to DeBERTaV3 (0.510). Both models perform well on perspectives with ample training data, such as *experience* and *suggestion*. However, the *cause* perspective, which has limited training examples, shows a very low F1-Score of 0.030 for DeBERTaV3. This contrast reveals the impact of training data scarcity on classification performance. Overall, while both models effectively classify well-represented perspectives, Mistral-7B-v0.3 exhibits a more balanced performance across classes, highlighting the challenge of underrepresentation in certain categories. Therefore Mistral-7B-v0.3 was chosen to classify the test dataset answers.

Experiment	R1	R2	RL	BERT	MET	BLEU	Rel.	Align	SC	Fact.
BioMistral-7B	0.344	0.151	0.308	0.753	0.286	0.108	0.325	**0.449**	0.276	0.363
Mistral-7B-v0.3 1E	0.408	0.182	0.371	0.891	0.378	0.091	0.387	0.369	0.260	0.314
Mistral-7B-v0.3$_{5x}$	0.445	**0.222**	0.406	**0.899**	0.406	0.127	0.418	0.421	**0.306**	0.364
Mistral-7B-v0.3$_{\text{pre-class.}}$ 1E	0.437	0.211	0.397	0.897	0.397	0.123	0.410	0.441	0.297	**0.369**
Mistral-7B-v0.3$_{\text{pre-class.}}$ 2E	**0.452**	0.221	**0.410**	**0.899**	**0.410**	**0.135**	**0.421**	0.409	0.296	0.352
Mistral-Small-3-24B	0.291	0.088	0.255	0.877	0.251	0.048	0.302	0.393	0.238	0.316
DeepS-Qwen-32B	0.299	0.097	0.264	0.862	0.249	0.067	0.306	0.372	0.241	0.306

Table 6: Results for Task B. This table reports ROUGE-1 (R1), ROUGE-2 (R2), ROUGE-L (RL), BERTScore (BERT), METEOR (MET), BLEU, Relevance average (Rel.), AlignScore (Align), SummaC-Conv (SC), and Factuality average (Fact.). The best values are highlighted in **bold**, while the second-best values are underlined. Abbreviations: pre-class. - pre-classified answers, E - epoch.

Labeled Test Dataset The test dataset consists of 231 answers in total. Among these, the predicted perspectives are distributed as follows: 85 answers were labeled as *experience*, 112 as *suggestion*, 15 as *cause*, 12 as *question*, and 93 as *information*. This distribution mirrors the one in the validation set. Labels such as *suggestion* and *information* are common, while the *cause* and *question* perspectives are notably underrepresented. This suggests that the prediction of answers is robust and the proportions of predicted labels are consistent with expectations. The threshold of the classifier for each perspective was determined by using the validation set. Detailed information on the classifier (F1-Score, P, R) can be found in Appendix A.4.

Summarization Results The results in Table 6 illustrate the performance of various models on Task B. Notably, Mistral-7B-Instruct-v0.3 with pre-classification (Mistral-7B-v0.3$_{\text{pre-class.}}$) trained for two epochs achieved the best overall performance, with the highest ROUGE-1 (0.452) and ROUGE-L (0.410) scores, as well as top scores in BERTScore (0.899), METEOR (0.410), and BLEU (0.135). This indicates that the approach of pre-classifying answers prior to instruct-tuning notably enhanced the quality of the generated summaries by improving relevance. The five-model approach (Mistral-7B-v0.3$_{5x}$), where a separate model was trained for each perspective, also performed very well. It ranks first in ROUGE-2 (0.222) and SummaC (0.306) and second in multiple other metrics. In contrast, Mistral-Small-24B-Instruct (Mistral-Small-3-25B) and the distilled Qwen model (DeepS-Qwen-32B) yielded lower scores, while BioMistral-7B performed moderately but did not match the performance of the pre-classification approaches. Furthermore, the relevancy and factuality averages provide additional insight. Higher relevancy scores suggest that the summaries are closely aligned with the intended perspectives, and better factuality scores indicate fewer factual errors. In particular, the pre-classification approach achieved a robust relevancy average (0.421) and acceptable factuality (0.352), underscoring its ability to capture and synthesize perspective-specific content effectively. Overall, these findings confirm that integrating an answer pre-classification step leads to superior summarization performance, making it the best overall strategy for Task B.

7 Conclusion

In conclusion, the study presents an investigation into perspective-aware summarization for healthcare CQA forums through two interrelated tasks: (A) span identification and classification, and (B) perspective-based summarization. The experimental results demonstrate that while fine-tuned encoder models such as DeBERTaV3 yield competitive performance in precise span extraction, the integration of enhanced reasoning capabilities, as seen in DeepSeek-R1, leads to superior overall performance in capturing complex contextual cues. The analysis of hallucinated content reveals that model fidelity to the source text remains a critical challenge, particularly for larger decoder-only models employing reasoning mechanisms. The findings from the summarization experiments underscore the efficacy of an answer pre-classification strategy, which improves both relevancy and factuality of generated summaries by effectively leveraging perspective-specific information.

Limitations

This work has several limitations that should be addressed in future research.

One limitation is the data imbalance inherent in the dataset. The underrepresentation of certain classes in the dataset negatively impacts the classifier's performance as well as robustness of the evaluation. It highlights a broader challenge in obtaining balanced annotations in perspective-based datasets.

Another limitation concerns the generation of summaries for each perspective regardless of the presence of corresponding spans. Since there was no penalty for generating summaries for perspectives without supporting evidence, the system produced what may be considered "useless" summaries. Future evaluations should consider incorporating a penalty for such outputs to better reflect the accuracy and utility of the generated summaries.

Automatic evaluation metrics may not capture all aspects of healthcare summarization, such as clinical relevance and interpretability, potentially leading to an incomplete assessment of model performance.

Acknowledgments

The work of Henning Schäfer, Hendrik Damm, and Tabea M. G. Pakull was funded by a PhD grant from the DFG Research Training Group 2535 *Knowledge- and data-based personalisation of medicine at the point of care (WisPerMed)*.

References

Siddhant Agarwal, Md Shad Akhtar, and Shweta Yadav. 2025. Overview of the peranssumm 2025 shared task on perspective-aware healthcare answer summarization. In *Proceedings of the Second Workshop on Patient-Oriented Language Processing (CL4Health) @ NAACL 2025*, Albuquerque, USA. Association for Computational Linguistics.

Satanjeev Banerjee and Alon Lavie. 2005. METEOR: An automatic metric for MT evaluation with improved correlation with human judgments. In *Proceedings of the ACL Workshop on Intrinsic and Extrinsic Evaluation Measures for Machine Translation and/or Summarization*, pages 65–72, Ann Arbor, Michigan. Association for Computational Linguistics.

Tom Brown, Benjamin Mann, Nick Ryder, Melanie Subbiah, Jared D Kaplan, Prafulla Dhariwal, Arvind Neelakantan, Pranav Shyam, Girish Sastry, Amanda Askell, Sandhini Agarwal, Ariel Herbert-Voss, Gretchen Krueger, Tom Henighan, Rewon Child, Aditya Ramesh, Daniel Ziegler, Jeffrey Wu, Clemens Winter, Chris Hesse, Mark Chen, Eric Sigler, Mateusz Litwin, Scott Gray, Benjamin Chess, Jack Clark, Christopher Berner, Sam McCandlish, Alec Radford, Ilya Sutskever, and Dario Amodei. 2020a. Language Models are Few-Shot Learners. In *Advances in Neural Information Processing Systems*, volume 33, pages 1877–1901. Curran Associates, Inc.

Tom Brown, Benjamin Mann, Nick Ryder, Melanie Subbiah, Jared D Kaplan, Prafulla Dhariwal, Arvind Neelakantan, Pranav Shyam, Girish Sastry, Amanda Askell, Sandhini Agarwal, Ariel Herbert-Voss, Gretchen Krueger, Tom Henighan, Rewon Child, Aditya Ramesh, Daniel Ziegler, Jeffrey Wu, Clemens Winter, Chris Hesse, Mark Chen, Eric Sigler, Mateusz Litwin, Scott Gray, Benjamin Chess, Jack Clark, Christopher Berner, Sam McCandlish, Alec Radford, Ilya Sutskever, and Dario Amodei. 2020b. Language Models are Few-Shot Learners. In *Advances in Neural Information Processing Systems*, volume 33, pages 1877–1901. Curran Associates, Inc.

Rochana Chaturvedi, Abari Bhattacharya, and Shweta Yadav. 2024. Aspect-oriented consumer health answer summarization. *Preprint*, arXiv:2405.06295.

Tanya Chowdhury and Tanmoy Chakraborty. 2019. CQASUMM: Building References for Community Question Answering Summarization Corpora. In *Proceedings of the ACM India Joint International Conference on Data Science and Management of Data*, CODS-COMAD '19, pages 18–26, New York, NY, USA. Association for Computing Machinery.

John Dagdelen, Alexander Dunn, Sanghoon Lee, Nicholas Walker, Andrew S. Rosen, Gerbrand Ceder, Kristin A. Persson, and Anubhav Jain. 2024. Structured information extraction from scientific text with large language models. *Nature Communications*, 15(1):1418.

DeepSeek-AI, Daya Guo, Dejian Yang, Haowei Zhang, Junxiao Song, Ruoyu Zhang, Runxin Xu, Qihao Zhu, Shirong Ma, Peiyi Wang, Xiao Bi, Xiaokang Zhang, Xingkai Yu, Yu Wu, Z. F. Wu, Zhibin Gou, Zhihong Shao, Zhuoshu Li, Ziyi Gao, Aixin Liu, et al. 2025. DeepSeek-R1: Incentivizing Reasoning Capability in LLMs via Reinforcement Learning. *Preprint*, arXiv:2501.12948.

Jacob Devlin, Ming-Wei Chang, Kenton Lee, and Kristina Toutanova. 2019. BERT: Pre-training of Deep Bidirectional Transformers for Language Understanding. In *Proceedings of the 2019 Conference of the North American Chapter of the Association for Computational Linguistics: Human Language Technologies, Volume 1 (Long and Short Papers)*, pages 4171–4186, Minneapolis, Minnesota. Association for Computational Linguistics.

Ning Ding, Yujia Qin, Guang Yang, Fuchao Wei, Zonghan Yang, Yusheng Su, Shengding Hu, Yulin Chen, Chi-Min Chan, Weize Chen, Jing Yi, Weilin Zhao, Xiaozhi Wang, Zhiyuan Liu, Hai-Tao Zheng, Jianfei Chen, Yang Liu, Jie Tang, Juanzi Li, and Maosong Sun. 2023. Parameter-efficient fine-tuning of large-scale pre-trained language models. *Nature Machine Intelligence*, 5(3):220–235.

Abhimanyu Dubey, Abhinav Jauhri, Abhinav Pandey, Abhishek Kadian, Ahmad Al-Dahle, Aiesha Letman, Akhil Mathur, Alan Schelten, Amy Yang, Angela Fan, Anirudh Goyal, Anthony Hartshorn, Aobo Yang, Archi Mitra, Archie Sravankumar, Artem Korenev, Arthur Hinsvark, Arun Rao, Aston Zhang, Aurelien Rodriguez, et al. 2024. The llama 3 herd of models. *Preprint*, arXiv:2407.21783.

Pengcheng He, Jianfeng Gao, and Weizhu Chen. 2021a. DeBERTaV3: Improving deberta using electra-style pre-training with gradient-disentangled embedding sharing. In *International Conference on Learning Representations*.

Pengcheng He, Xiaodong Liu, Jianfeng Gao, and Weizhu Chen. 2021b. DeBERTa: Decoding-enhanced BERT with disentangled attention. In *International Conference on Learning Representations*.

Edward J Hu, Yelong Shen, Phillip Wallis, Zeyuan Allen-Zhu, Yuanzhi Li, Shean Wang, Lu Wang, and Weizhu Chen. 2022. LoRA: Low-rank adaptation of large language models. In *International Conference on Learning Representations*.

Robert A. Jacobs, Michael I. Jordan, Steven J. Nowlan, and Geoffrey E. Hinton. 1991. Adaptive Mixtures of Local Experts. *Neural Computation*, 3(1):79–87.

Albert Q. Jiang, Alexandre Sablayrolles, Arthur Mensch, Chris Bamford, Devendra Singh Chaplot, Diego de las Casas, Florian Bressand, Gianna Lengyel, Guillaume Lample, Lucile Saulnier, Lélio Renard Lavaud, Marie-Anne Lachaux, Pierre Stock, Teven Le Scao, Thibaut Lavril, Thomas Wang, Timothée Lacroix, and William El Sayed. 2023. Mistral 7B. *Preprint*, arXiv:2310.06825.

Wojciech Kryscinski, Bryan McCann, Caiming Xiong, and Richard Socher. 2020. Evaluating the factual consistency of abstractive text summarization. In *Proceedings of the 2020 Conference on Empirical Methods in Natural Language Processing (EMNLP)*, pages 9332–9346, Online. Association for Computational Linguistics.

Woosuk Kwon, Zhuohan Li, Siyuan Zhuang, Ying Sheng, Lianmin Zheng, Cody Hao Yu, Joseph E. Gonzalez, Hao Zhang, and Ion Stoica. 2023. Efficient memory management for large language model serving with pagedattention. In *Proceedings of the ACM SIGOPS 29th Symposium on Operating Systems Principles*.

Philippe Laban, Tobias Schnabel, Paul N. Bennett, and Marti A. Hearst. 2022. SummaC: Re-Visiting NLI-based Models for Inconsistency Detection in Summarization. *Transactions of the Association for Computational Linguistics*, 10:163–177.

Yanis Labrak, Adrien Bazoge, Emmanuel Morin, Pierre-Antoine Gourraud, Mickael Rouvier, and Richard Dufour. 2024. BioMistral: A collection of open-source pretrained large language models for medical domains. In *Findings of the Association for Computational Linguistics: ACL 2024*, pages 5848–5864, Bangkok, Thailand. Association for Computational Linguistics.

Chin-Yew Lin. 2004. ROUGE: A Package for Automatic Evaluation of Summaries. In *Workshop on Text Summarization Branches Out, Post-Conference Workshop of ACL 2004*, pages 74–81, Barcelona, Spain.

Gauri Naik, Sharad Chandakacherla, Shweta Yadav, and Md Shad Akhtar. 2024. No perspective, no perception!! perspective-aware healthcare answer summarization. In *Findings of the Association for Computational Linguistics: ACL 2024*, pages 15919–15932, Bangkok, Thailand. Association for Computational Linguistics.

Liangming Pan, Michael Saxon, Wenda Xu, Deepak Nathani, Xinyi Wang, and William Yang Wang. 2024. Automatically Correcting Large Language Models: Surveying the Landscape of Diverse Automated Correction Strategies. *Transactions of the Association for Computational Linguistics*, 12:484–506.

Kishore Papineni, Salim Roukos, Todd Ward, and Wei-Jing Zhu. 2002. BLEU: a method for automatic evaluation of machine translation. In *Proceedings of the 40th Annual Meeting on Association for Computational Linguistics*, ACL '02, page 311–318, USA. Association for Computational Linguistics.

Lance Ramshaw and Mitch Marcus. 1995. Text Chunking using Transformation-Based Learning. In *Third Workshop on Very Large Corpora*.

Jasmina Rueger, Wilfred Dolfsma, and Rick Aalbers. 2021. Perception of peer advice in online health communities: Access to lay expertise. *Social Science & Medicine*, 277:113117.

Max Savery, Asma Ben Abacha, Soumya Gayen, and Dina Demner-Fushman. 2020. Question-driven summarization of answers to consumer health questions. *Scientific Data*, 7(1):322.

Yujie Sun, Dongfang Sheng, Zihan Zhou, and Yifei Wu. 2024. AI hallucination: Towards a comprehensive classification of distorted information in artificial intelligence-generated content. *Humanities and Social Sciences Communications*, 11(1):1–14.

Arun James Thirunavukarasu, Darren Shu Jeng Ting, Kabilan Elangovan, Laura Gutierrez, Ting Fang Tan, and Daniel Shu Wei Ting. 2023. Large language models in medicine. *Nature medicine*, 29(8):1930–1940.

Erik F. Tjong Kim Sang. 2002. Introduction to the CoNLL-2002 Shared Task: Language-Independent Named Entity Recognition. In *COLING-02: The 6th Conference on Natural Language Learning 2002 (CoNLL-2002)*.

Jason Wei, Maarten Bosma, Vincent Zhao, Kelvin Guu, Adams Wei Yu, Brian Lester, Nan Du, Andrew M. Dai, and Quoc V. Le. 2021. Finetuned Language Models are Zero-Shot Learners. In *International Conference on Learning Representations*.

Jason Wei, Xuezhi Wang, Dale Schuurmans, Maarten Bosma, Brian Ichter, Fei Xia, Ed H. Chi, Quoc V. Le, and Denny Zhou. 2022. Chain-of-thought prompting elicits reasoning in large language models. In *Proceedings of the 36th International Conference on Neural Information Processing Systems*, NIPS '22, pages 24824–24837, Red Hook, NY, USA. Curran Associates Inc.

Derong Xu, Wei Chen, Wenjun Peng, Chao Zhang, Tong Xu, Xiangyu Zhao, Xian Wu, Yefeng Zheng, Yang Wang, and Enhong Chen. 2024. Large language models for generative information extraction: a survey. *Frontiers of Computer Science*, 18(6):186357.

Tianyi Zhang, Varsha Kishore, Felix Wu, Kilian Q. Weinberger, and Yoav Artzi. 2020. BERTScore: Evaluating text generation with BERT. In *8th International Conference on Learning Representations, ICLR 2020, Addis Ababa, Ethiopia, April 26-30, 2020*. OpenReview.net.

A Appendix

The appendix provides additional details on the frameworks and models used in this work, including their licensing terms, the setup for instruction-tuning, decoding parameters, and the specific prompting strategies employed in the experiments.

A.1 Licences

The frameworks and models used in this work are governed by different open-source licenses, as detailed in Table 7.

Framework/Model	License
unsloth[3]	Apache-2.0
deberta-v3-large[4]	MIT
Llama-3.1-8B-Instruct[5]	Llama 3.1 Comm.
Llama-3.3-70B-Instruct[6]	Llama 3.3 Comm.
DeepSeek-R1-Distill-Llama-70B[7]	MIT
DeepSeek-R1[8]	MIT
Mistral-7B-Instruct-v0.3[9]	Apache-2.0
Mistral-Small-24B-Instruct-2501[10]	Apache-2.0
BioMistral-7B-DARE[11]	Apache-2.0
DeepSeek-R1-Distill-Qwen-32B[12]	MIT

Table 7: Licensing terms for each framework and model used in this work, including various Apache-2.0 (Apache License 2.0), MIT (Massachusetts Institute of Technology License), and Comm. (Llama Community License).

A.2 Training Setup

This section outlines the configurations, including parameter-efficient tuning, and optimization methods used for training the models.

A.2.1 Task A: Span Identification and Classification

For the span identification and classification task, the Llama-3.1-8B-Instruct model was fine-tuned using PEFT techniques via LoRA. The unsloth framework was used to optimize training. The training examples were structured as shown in Figure 3. The training utilized AdamW 8-bit optimization, with a learning rate of $2e-5$, batch size of 1, and gradient accumulation steps of 64. The model was trained for two epochs.

A.2.2 Task B: Perspective-Based Summarization

The instruction-tuning parameters can be seen in Table 8.

The answer classifier based on Mistral-7B-v0.3 was trained for two epochs using FP16, with a batch size of 1 and gradient accumulation over 4 steps. It employed a learning rate of $2e$-5, a maximum sequence length of 4096, and utilized LoRA with a rank of 8 and an alpha of 16. In contrast, the DeBERTaV3-base model was trained for two epochs with a learning rate of $2e$-5, a batch size of 16, and a maximum sequence length of 1024.

[3] `https://unsloth.ai/`, Last Accessed: 24 February 2025.

[4] `https://huggingface.co/microsoft/deberta-v3-large`, Last Accessed: 24. February 2025.

[5] `https://huggingface.co/meta-llama/Llama-3.1-8B-Instruct`, Last Accessed: 24. February 2025.

[6] `https://huggingface.co/meta-llama/Llama-3.3-70B-Instruct`, Last Accessed: 24. February 2025.

[7] `https://huggingface.co/deepseek-ai/DeepSeek-R1-Distill-Llama-70B`, Last Accessed: 24. February 2025.

[8] `https://huggingface.co/deepseek-ai/DeepSeek-R1`, Last Accessed: 24. February 2025.

[9] `https://huggingface.co/mistralai/Mistral-7B-Instruct-v0.3`, Last Accessed: 24. February 2025.

[10] `https://huggingface.co/mistralai/Mistral-Small-24B-Instruct-2501`, Last Accessed: 24. February 2025.

[11] `https://huggingface.co/BioMistral/BioMistral-7B-DARE`, Last Accessed: 24. February 2025.

[12] `https://huggingface.co/deepseek-ai/DeepSeek-R1-Distill-Qwen-32B`, Last Accessed: 24. February 2025.

Model	E	FP16	lr	Batch	GA	LR	LA	DO	MSL	TM
Mistral-7B-v0.3	1/2	True	$2e$-5	6	–	16	32	0.1	4096	All linear
Mistral-Small-24B-Instruct-2501	2	True	$2e$-5	1	4	4	8	0.1	1400	All linear
DeepSeek-R1-Distill-Qwen-32B	2	True	$2e$-5	1	–	8	16	0.1	2024	All linear
BioMistral-7B-DARE	2	True	$2e$-4	6	–	32	64	0.1	4096	All linear

Table 8: Instruction-tuning hyperparameters for the models. Abbreviations: E - epochs; FP16 - FP16 training; lr - learning rate; Batch - batch size; GA - gradient accumulation steps; LR - LoRA rank; LA - LoRA alpha; DO - dropout; MSL - maximum sequence length; TM - targeted modules. Note that Biomistral Dare and Mistral v03 instruct share the same hyperparameters as Mistral-7B-v0.3.

A.3 Decoding Setup

This section outlines the inference procedures used to generate spans and summarization.

A.3.1 Task A: Span Identification and Classification

Llama-3.3-70B-Instruct was deployed using vLLM (Kwon et al., 2023), an inference framework designed for efficient text generation. The model was accessed via the OpenAI python package[13] version 1.60.0, with default sampling parameters[14] except for `max_tokens`, which was set to 2000. For the instruction-tuned model Llama-3.1-8B-Instruct, inference was performed using the unsloth framework. Outputs were generated with default configuration[15] but `max_new_tokens` set to 5000 and a 1.2 repetition penalty.

A.3.2 Task B: Perspective-Based Summarization

For inference, all models were configured with a maximum sequence length of 4.096 tokens, up to 1.024 new tokens, deterministic decoding (do sample set to false), and a temperature of 0.7. The only exception is DeepSeek-R1-Distill-Qwen-32B, which was run with a temperature of 0.6 while all other inference parameters remained the same.

A.4 Classifier

Table 9 details the threshold tuning experiments for the Mistral-7B-v0.3 model on the validation set. For each perspective, the optimal threshold is reported alongside the corresponding precision, recall, and F1-Scores for both class 0 and class 1.

Perspective	T	Class	P	R	F1
experience	0.25	0	0.971	0.945	0.958
		1	0.700	0.819	0.755
suggestion	0.25	0	0.903	0.747	0.818
		1	0.666	0.863	0.751
cause	0.15	0	0.971	0.936	0.953
		1	0.375	0.580	0.455
question	0.15	0	0.990	0.988	0.989
		1	0.673	0.705	0.688
information	0.40	0	0.849	0.752	0.797
		1	0.671	0.790	0.726

Table 9: Threshold (T) tuning results on the validation set for the Mistral-7B-v0.3 model. For each perspective, the optimal threshold and the corresponding precision, recall, and F1-Scores for class 0 and class 1 are reported.

For instance, for the *experience* perspective, a threshold of 0.25 yields excellent performance for class 0 (P = 0.971, R = 0.945, F1 = 0.958) and solid results for class 1 (P = 0.700, R = 0.819, F1 = 0.755). In contrast, the *cause* perspective exhibits a very low F1-Score of 0.455 for class 1 despite high performance for class 0. These results demonstrate that while well-supported classes achieve high scores, those with fewer examples remain difficult to classify accurately.

A.5 Prompting

This section details the design of system and user prompts, including formatting strategies for both sub-tasks.

A.5.1 Task A: Span Identification and Classification

The prompting setup is designed to ensure structured, consistent, and accurate extraction of perspective-based spans. The motivation behind this approach was to align the model's pretraining with the task requirements, leveraging the instruction-following capabilities of LLMs that have undergone instruction-tuning. Since such

[13]`https://github.com/openai/openai-python`, Last Accessed: 24. February 2025.

[14]`https://docs.vllm.ai/en/latest/api/inference_params.html`, Last Accessed: 24. February 2025.

[15]`https://huggingface.co/docs/transformers/v4.49.0/en/main_classes/text_generation#transformers.GenerationConfig`, Last Accessed: 24. February 2025.

System:

You are an advanced AI model specializing in perspective-aware span extraction. Your objective is to analyze health-related community question-answering forums, where users ask health-related questions and receive multiple answers containing different perspectives.

Task

Identify relevant spans (text segments) within user-provided answers that correspond to one or more of the five perspective categories:

CAUSE: It underlines the potential cause of a medical phenomenon or a symptom. It answers the "Why" regarding a specific observation, offering insights to identify the root cause.

SUGGESTION: It encapsulates strategies, recommendations, or potential courses of action towards management or resolution of a health condition.

EXPERIENCE: It covers first-hand experiences, observations, insights, or opinions derived from treatment or medication related to a particular problem.

QUESTION: It consists of interrogative phrases, follow-up questions and rhetorical questions that are sought to better understand the context. They typically start with phrases like Why, What, Do, How, and Did etc, and end in a question mark.

INFORMATION: It encompasses segments that offer factual knowledge or information considering the given query. These segments provide comprehensive details on diagnoses, symptoms, or general information on a medical condition.

Classify each identified span into the correct perspective category based on its meaning and intent.

Guidelines for Identifying and Classifying Spans:

Select complete spans. Avoid excessively short spans that lack context.

Only include spans that align with a perspective category.

Never change the wording or formatting of the spans. EXTRACT and not rewrite.

Output Format

Your response must always be one valid PerspectiveSpans object:

```typescript
interface PerspectiveSpans {
    EXPERIENCE: string[],
    INFORMATION: string[],
    CAUSE: string[],
    SUGGESTION: string[],
    QUESTION: string[]
}
```

Each perspective category should contain a list of spans extracted from the answers. If no span belongs to a category, leave an empty list. Do not add additional perspectives.

Example

User Input:

```
"answers": [
        <answer1>,
        ...
        <answern>
    ]
```

Assistant output

```typescript
const spans: PerspectiveSpans = {
    "CAUSE": [<cause_span1>, <cause_span2>],
    "SUGGESTION": [<suggestion_span1>, ..., <suggestion_spann>],
    "EXPERIENCE": [],
    "QUESTION":[],
    "INFORMATION": [<information_span1>]
}
```

Figure 3: System prompt for Task A defining the task, perspective categories, and extraction guidelines for structured span identification.

models are trained to interpret and execute user instructions, framing the task in a conversational format was a natural way to enhance compliance with task constraints.

The system prompt (see Figure 3) was designed to provide precise definitions and distinguishing criteria for each of the five perspectives. These explicit definitions help the model differentiate between similar categories and prevent incorrect or overly broad span selections. Furthermore, the system prompt reinforces extraction constraints, ensuring that the model preserves the wording and formatting of the original text in the user prompt (see Figure 4) rather than generating new or para-

```
User:

"answers": [
        <answer_1>,
        ...
        <answer_n>
    ]
```

Figure 4: User prompt for Task A providing the input format with a list of answers from a the discussion thread.

```
Assistant:

```typescript
const spans: PerspectiveSpans = {
    "CAUSE": [<cause_span_1>, <cause_span_2>],
    "SUGGESTION": [<suggestion_span_1>, ..., <suggestion_span_n>],
    "EXPERIENCE": [],
    "QUESTION":[],
    "INFORMATION": [<information_span_1>]
}
```
```

Figure 5: Assistant response for Task A demonstrating the structured TypeScript-like format for extracted spans.

phrased spans. The example used in the system prompt to demonstrate the formats is the training example with uri 1504599.

Another critical consideration was the need for structured outputs to facilitate automatic evaluation. Since LLMs generate open-ended text by default, responses can vary notably in format if not explicitly constrained. To address this, the output structure was formatted as a TypeScript-like object (see Figure 5), enforcing a predefined schema where extracted spans are categorized under their respective perspective labels.

Beyond instruction-tuned training, the prompting framework was also applied to zero-shot and few-shot inference settings to assess the model's ability to generalize its span extraction capabilities without direct fine-tuning. The zero-shot setting tested whether the model could infer the extraction rules solely from the system prompt, while the few-shot setting provided additional gold-standard examples. In the standard few-shot setting, multiple examples were included in the same conversation, allowing the model to learn span extraction through analogy. In contrast, the few-shot with repeated system message reinforced consistency by repeating the system prompt before each example.

A.5.2 Task B: Perspective-Based Summarization

Figure 6 shows the prompt for the instruction-tuning of the summarization task, on the example of the *information* perspective. For other perspectives, only the "Perspective Instruction" was changed:

- **Information Perspective:** For information purposes, generate a concise summary.
- **Suggestion Perspective:** It is suggested, generate a concise summary with suggestions.
- **Experience Perspective:** One user shared his experience, generate a concise summary.
- **Cause Perspective:** Some of the causes, generate a concise summary.
- **Question Perspective:** It is inquired, generate a concise summary addressing the questioner.

System:

Task: In recent years, healthcare community question-answering (CQA) forums have allowed users to seek advice and share experiences. Answers may contain diverse perspectives, such as factual information, suggestions, personal experiences, potential causes, or follow-up questions. The goal is to generate a concise, perspective-specific summary that accurately reflects the essence of the relevant content from the discussion.

Writing Guidelines:

1. Analyze the provided information to capture essential ideas and significant medical details.
2. Generate a concise summary that reflects the core essence of the annotated perspective.
3. Frame the summary as follows:
    - For Information summaries, begin with phrases like "For information purposes."
    - For Suggestion summaries, begin with phrases such as "It is suggested," "It is advised," or "Consider."
    - For Experience summaries, begin with phrases like "One user shared his experience" or "In user's experience."
    - For Cause summaries, begin with phrases like "Some of the causes."
    - For Question summaries, begin with phrases such as "It is inquired."
4. Do not add any information beyond what is provided.

Perspective Instruction: {e.g., "For information purposes, generate a concise summary."}

Question: <QUESTION>

Context: <CONTEXT>

Answers:
- <answer$_1$>
- <...>
- <answer$_n$>

Information Summary:

User:

<Summary>

Figure 6: Example prompt used for generating perspective-specific summaries. The System box details the task, guidelines, and input information, while the User box specifies the required output.

DataHacks at PerAnsSumm 2025: LoRA-Driven Prompt Engineering for Perspective Aware Span Identification and Summarization

Vansh Nawander
IIIT Hyderabad
vanshnawander@gmail.com

Chaithra Nerella
IIIT Hyderabad
chaithra.nerella@research.iiit.ac.in

Abstract

This paper presents the approach of the DataHacks team in the PerAnsSumm Shared Task at CL4Health 2025, which focuses on perspective-aware summarization of healthcare community question-answering (CQA) forums. Unlike traditional CQA summarization, which relies on the best-voted answer, this task captures diverse perspectives, including 'cause,' 'suggestion,' 'experience,' 'question,' and 'information.' The task is divided into two subtasks: (1) identifying and classifying perspective-specific spans, and (2) generating perspective-specific summaries. We addressed these tasks using Large Language Models (LLM), fine-tuning it with different low-rank adaptation (LoRA) configurations to balance performance and computational efficiency under resource constraints. In addition, we experimented with various prompt strategies and analyzed their impact on performance. Our approach achieved a combined average score of 0.42, demonstrating the effectiveness of fine-tuned LLMs with adaptive LoRA configurations for perspective-aware summarization.

1 Introduction

Community Question Answering (CQA) forums for healthcare care serve as valuable resources for individuals seeking information on illnesses, treatments, therapies, personal experiences, and medical advice. These communities include a number of varied viewpoints, such as factual information, expert advice, personal anecdotes, causal justifications, recommendations, and follow-up questions. Although these platforms provide diverse perspectives, the large number of responses, often containing conflicting points of view, makes it difficult for users to extract clear and reliable information.

A well-structured summary is crucial for enabling users to quickly access relevant information within this complex content. However, traditional summarization models, like RNN-based encoder-decoder architectures, often fail to handle the complexity of CQA discussions. They struggle with capturing multiple viewpoints, handling contradictions, and preserving key information which is present in CQA threads. (Chowdhury et al., 2020).

Recent advancements in summarization techniques have attempted to address these challenges. Perspective-aware summarization models ensure that critical viewpoints are retained (Naik et al., 2024), while inconsistency detection methods such as SummaC use NLI-based approaches to improve factual reliability and coherence in summaries (Laban et al., 2022). Furthermore, CQA-specific summarization corpora have provided high-quality reference summaries to better adapt models to the unique nature of CQA data (Chowdhury and Chakraborty, 2019). Despite these developments, existing methods still struggle to effectively capture the nuanced and sometimes contradictory perspectives present in CQA discussions.

Large Language Models (LLMs) have emerged as powerful tools for text summarization, excelling at processing lengthy contexts and generating coherent summaries (Minaee et al., 2024). However, adapting these models to domain-specific tasks like healthcare CQA remains a challenge due to the high computational costs associated with full fine-tuning. To overcome this limitation, Low-Rank Adaptation (LoRA) (Hu et al., 2022) has gained prominence as an efficient fine-tuning technique that enables LLMs to specialize in specific tasks with minimal parameter updates. By leveraging LoRA, LLMs can be adapted for perspective-aware summarization while significantly reducing computational costs.

The PerAnsSumm Shared Task at CL4Health 2025 (Agarwal et al., 2025) is designed to advance the development of perspective-aware summarization systems for healthcare CQA forums, focusing on two subtasks: (A) Span Identification and Classi-

Proceedings of the Second Workshop on Patient-Oriented Language Processing (CL4Health), pages 374–379
May 4, 2025 ©2025 Association for Computational Linguistics

fication and (B) Perspective-Aware Summary Generation. This problem highlights the necessity for sophisticated methods that can summarize and distinguish between various points of view while preserving the content's cohesion and factual integrity. In our work, we fine-tuned Mistral-7B(Jiang et al., 2023) and analyzed the impact of LoRA ranks and prompting strategies on the performance of both tasks.

2 Dataset

The task included PUMA dataset (Naik et al., 2024), a perspective-aware corpus specifically annotated for medical question-answer pairs. The dataset consists of 3,167 CQA threads with approximately 10,000 answers sourced from Yahoo! L6 corpus. Each answer is annotated with perspective-specific spans across five categories: *experience, information, cause, suggestion and question.* Each data instance has several key components- *Question, Context, Answers, Labelled Answers Spans, Labelled summaries.*

The Question represents the user's inquiry related to a healthcare topic. The Context provides additional background information, which may be empty or contain relevant details to aid in understanding the question. The Answers consist of a list of user-provided responses related to the question. These answers are further enriched with Labelled Answer Spans, which are annotated text segments categorized under the perspective labels. Each span includes the text itself along with its character-level position, enabling precise identification of the perspective within the answer. Additionally, the dataset includes Labelled Summaries, which are perspective-specific summaries that aggregate relevant spans across all answers in a thread. These summaries serve as concise representations of the underlying perspectives, facilitating a comprehensive understanding of the various viewpoints expressed in the data set.

3 Methodology

Our goal was to enhance perspective-aware answer summarization by fine-tuning Mistral-7B using Low-Rank Adaptation (LoRA).We experimented with different LoRA ranks and prompting strategies to assess their impact on performance. Mistral-7B was chosen for its strong language understanding capabilities, efficiency, and ability to generate coherent and contextually rich summaries. Instead of full fine-tuning, we opted for LoRA to preserve model generalization while optimizing computational efficiency making it feasible under resource constraints.

3.1 Data Preprocessing

The dataset provided contained perspective-specific spans and summaries annotated across five categories: *experience, information, cause, suggestion, and question.* To prepare the data for training, we systematically extracted these segments from the original JSON annotations and reformatted them into a structured format.

Each instance in the dataset was converted into a standardized dictionary structure where every category was explicitly represented. For example, even if a response contained only *information* spans, the format ensured that placeholders for other perspectives were included like: {information:[.....], suggestion:[ ], experience:[ ], cause:[ ], question:[ ]}. This transformation allowed uniform processing across all data instances and ensured that the model learned to differentiate between perspectives effectively.

3.2 Prompt engineering

We experimented with various prompt strategies and documented the results of two key variations. For Task A, the model was instructed to generate spans for each perspective label. For Task B, the same prompt structure was used, but the model was asked to generate summaries instead of extracting spans. In the first approach, the prompt presented the question, context, and answer as a single block of text without explicitly differentiating them. While this approach produced reasonable outputs, it often resulted in vague or incomplete summaries, as the model struggled to clearly distinguish between different components. Additionally, the absence of clear section markers sometimes led to misclassification in span extraction and inconsistencies in summaries.

To address these issues, we refined the prompt by explicitly separating the question, context, and answer into distinct sections. This structured approach improved the model's ability to identify relationships between different components, leading to more accurate perspective classification. It also minimized errors caused by misinterpretation and ensured greater consistency in the generated outputs. A comparative analysis of both strategies revealed that the structured prompt method significantly improved both the accuracy and coherence of the summaries, making it the preferred choice for our experiments. The prompts are detailed in the Appendix section.

3.3 Evaluation Metrics

The submissions were evaluated across different metrics for each task. Task A (span identification and classification) was evaluated across 3 main metrics *F1 score (Macro F1, Weighted F1), Strict Matching, Proportional Matching.* Macro and weighted F1 scores can assess the classification performance, ensuring a balanced evaluation across all the classes including minority ones. Strict Matching and Proportional Matching metrics for precision, recall and F1 score were used to evaluate span identification accuracy. Strict Matching checks if the span boundaries match exactly, while Proportional Matching allows for partial overlaps, making the evaluation more flexible.

Task B (Perspective-Specific Summarization) was evaluated across two metrics- *Relevance and Factuality.* Relevance was assessed using *ROUGE (ROUGE-1, ROUGE-2, ROUGE-L) (Lin, 2004), BERTScore (Zhang et al., 2020), METEOR (Banerjee and Lavie, 2005), and BLEU (Papineni et al., 2002). ROUGE* measures lexical overlap by comparing n-grams between the generated and reference summaries. *BERTScore* goes beyond surface-level overlap by using contextual embeddings to evaluate semantic similarity. *METEOR* considers synonymy and stemming to better capture meaning, while *BLEU* focuses on matching n-grams but is more sensitive to exact word choice. Factuality was assessed using *AlignScore(Zha et al., 2023), SummaC* ensuring that summaries remained factually consistent and aligned with source content. This multifaceted evaluation approach allowed us to thoroughly analyze the effectiveness and reliability of our models in capturing diverse perspectives and generating high-quality summaries.

4 Experiments and Results

4.1 Experimental Setup

We fine-tuned the Mistral-7B model using Low-Rank Adaptation (LoRA) to optimize computational efficiency while preserving model generalization. LoRA enables efficient adaptation by injecting low-rank matrices into key transformer layers, significantly reducing the number of trainable parameters while maintaining model performance. To systematically analyze the impact of LoRA configurations, we experimented with different LoRA ranks—64, 128, and 256—while keeping the LoRA scaling factor (lora_alpha) fixed at 128.

The model was fine-tuned for five epochs, with a per-device batch size of four and gradient accumulation set to two, resulting in an effective batch size of eight. We used the AdamW optimizer with fused updates, a learning rate of 2e-4, and a linear scheduler without warm-up. Mixed precision training was enabled, utilizing FP16 or BF16 (based on hardware support) to further optimize memory usage and training speed. Training was monitored using epoch-wise evaluation, with key metrics tracked via Weights & Biases (W&B). The best-performing model was selected based on evaluation results, with a checkpoint limit of six to manage storage efficiently.

4.2 Results

Table 1(a) presents the performance metrics for Task A. Among the different LoRA configurations, the refined prompt (RP) with a LoRA rank of 256 achieved the highest overall performance, with a Task A score of 0.5441, outperforming initial prompt (IP) configurations with a small margin. The RP (256) setting also led to the best Strict F1 and Proposition F1, indicating improved precision and recall in structured prediction. Among the IP configurations, LoRA rank 256 performed best, followed by rank 128 and the lowest performance was observed in IP (64).

Table 1(b) reports the evaluation metrics for Task B. Similar to Task A, RP (256) achieved the highest scores, particularly in TASK B Factuality (0.3663) and TASK B Relevance (0.3504). While IP (256) demonstrated competitive performance (Factuality = 0.3521), RP (256) still outperformed all other configurations. The improvements in factuality and relevance suggest that refined prompts help generate more accurate and contextually appropriate responses, making them particularly effective for knowledge-based tasks like summarization.

Table 2 consolidates the performance across both tasks. The highest combined average score of 0.4203 was obtained using RP (256). The results indicate that increasing the LoRA rank improves performance by a small margin, with LoRA rank 256 yielding the best results. The refined prompt (RP) strategy outperformed initial prompts (IP) for the combined average. However, their effect across individual metrics was not consistent.

(a) Performance Metrics for Task A

LoRA rank	Macro F1	Weighted F1	Strict P	Strict R	Strict F1	Prop P	Prop R	Prop F1	Task_A
IP (64)	0.8382	0.8778	0.1148	0.0857	0.0981	0.4542	0.6318	0.5285	0.5015
IP (128)	**0.8787**	**0.9181**	0.0156	0.0495	0.0238	**0.5422**	0.6301	**0.5829**	0.5082
IP (256)	0.8689	0.9009	0.131	0.1048	0.1164	0.4546	0.6659	0.5403	0.5192
RP (256)	0.8635	0.9044	**0.1599**	**0.1352**	**0.1465**	0.5149	**0.6678**	0.5815	**0.5441**

(b) Performance Metrics for Task B

LoRA rank	ROUGE1	ROUGE2	ROUGEL	BERT	METEOR	BLEU	TASK B Relevance	Align	SummaC	TASK B Factuality
IP (64)	0.3671	0.1607	0.3345	0.7849	0.3386	0.1052	0.3485	0.4002	0.2661	0.3331
IP (128)	**0.3787**	0.1679	**0.3428**	**0.8041**	0.3406	0.1072	0.3569	0.2846	**0.4302**	0.3574
IP (256)	0.3778	**0.1747**	0.343	0.7927	**0.3452**	0.1092	**0.3571**	0.4211	0.2831	0.3521
RP (256)	0.3708	0.1683	0.3365	0.7762	0.3391	**0.1116**	0.3504	**0.4427**	0.2899	**0.3663**

Table 1: Performance Metrics with different LoRA ranks (in bracket) and IP - Initial Prompt, RP - Refined Prompt

LoRA rank	Combined Average
IP (64)	0.3944
IP (128)	0.4075
IP (256)	0.4095
RP (256)	**0.4203**

Table 2: Task A + B Combined Average Scores

5 Conclusion

This study shows that combining Low-Rank Adaptation (LoRA) with well-structured prompts can significantly improve perspective-aware summarization in healthcare Q&A forums. By fine-tuning the Mistral-7B model, we captured different perspectives—cause, suggestion, experience, question, and information—while keeping the approach efficient. LoRA rank played a key role, with higher ranks generally improving precision and recall, though the gains leveled off at a certain point. The refined prompt strategy also boosted classification accuracy, proving that clear guidance helps models generate better responses. These results highlight the importance of both efficient fine-tuning and good prompt design in building accurate and context-aware summarization systems for healthcare applications.

6 Limitations

While RP (256) achieves the highest combined score, no single configuration is best across all metrics. For instance, IP (128) performs better in factuality compared to RP(256) (SummaC: 0.4302 vs. 0.2899), indicating trade-offs between factuality and summarization quality. Although higher ranks (256) generally yield better combined results, IP (128) achieves comparable or better results in some areas (e.g., ROUGE1, SummaC, BERT), indicating that simply increasing LoRA rank does not guarantee uniform improvement.Despite using LoRA to reduce computational costs, fine-tuning large models like Mistral-7B is still computationally intensive, which may not be accessible to all researchers. Since the model is fine-tuned specifically on healthcare CQA data, this might limit its generalizability to other domains or even different types of healthcare texts outside the utilized dataset.

7 Future Work

Using Mistral with prompt variations and LoRA ranks for the tasks shows promised results. Future research could focus on creating more robust prompt templates that generalize across tasks and developing adaptive methods to adjust LoRA ranks based on task complexity.Further, ablation studies comparing different fine-tuning methods, including other parameter-efficient techniques, could provide deeper insights. Expanding prompt strategies for diverse domains, integrating multi-modal data, and analyzing the trade-offs between prompt refinement and model performance are also promising directions. Analyzing the model through a mechanistic interpretability lens might provide more insights into its decision-making process, clarifying things that remain unclear in our analysis.

Acknowledgments

The authors thank Dr Manish Shrivastsava, Datazoic, and LTRC lab IIIT Hyderabad for their constant support and encouragement.

References

Siddhant Agarwal, Md Shad Akhtar, and Shweta Yadav. 2025. Overview of the peranssumm 2025 shared task on perspective-aware healthcare answer summarization. In *Proceedings of the Second Workshop on Patient-Oriented Language Processing (CL4Health) @ NAACL 2025*, Albuquerque, USA. Association for Computational Linguistics.

Satanjeev Banerjee and Alon Lavie. 2005. *METEOR: An Automatic Metric for MT Evaluation with Improved Correlation with Human Judgments*. In *Proceedings of the ACL Workshop on Intrinsic and Extrinsic Evaluation Measures for Machine Translation and/or Summarization*, pages 65–72, Ann Arbor, Michigan. Association for Computational Linguistics.

Tanya Chowdhury and Tanmoy Chakraborty. 2019. *CQASumm: Building References for Community Question Answering Summarization Corpora*. In *Proceedings of the ACM India Joint International Conference on Data Science and Management of Data*, pages 18–26.

Tanya Chowdhury, Sachin Kumar, and Tanmoy Chakraborty. 2020. *Neural Abstractive Summarization with Structural Attention*. *arXiv preprint arXiv:2004.09739*.

Edward J Hu, Yelong Shen, Phillip Wallis, Zeyuan Allen-Zhu, Yuanzhi Li, Shean Wang, Lu Wang, Weizhu Chen, et al. 2022. Lora: Low-rank adaptation of large language models. *ICLR*, 1(2):3.

Albert Q. Jiang, Alexandre Sablayrolles, Arthur Mensch, Chris Bamford, Devendra Singh Chaplot, Diego de las Casas, Florian Bressand, Gianna Lengyel, Guillaume Lample, Lucile Saulnier, Lélio Renard Lavaud, Marie-Anne Lachaux, Pierre Stock, Teven Le Scao, Thibaut Lavril, Thomas Wang, Timothée Lacroix, and William El Sayed. 2023. Mistral 7b. *Preprint*, arXiv:2310.06825.

Philippe Laban, Tobias Schnabel, Paul Bennett, and Marti A Hearst. 2022. *Summac: Re-visiting NLI-Based Models for Inconsistency Detection in Summarization*. *Transactions of the Association for Computational Linguistics*, 10:163–177.

Chin-Yew Lin. 2004. *ROUGE: A Package for Automatic Evaluation of Summaries*. In *Text Summarization Branches Out*, pages 74–81, Barcelona, Spain. Association for Computational Linguistics.

Shervin Minaee, Tomas Mikolov, Narjes Nikzad, Meysam Chenaghlu, Richard Socher, Xavier Amatriain, and Jianfeng Gao. 2024. Large language models: A survey. *Preprint*, arXiv:2402.06196.

Gauri Naik, Sharad Chandakacherla, Shweta Yadav, and Md Shad Akhtar. 2024. *No Perspective, No Perception!! Perspective-Aware Healthcare Answer Summarization*. In *Findings of the Association for Computational Linguistics ACL 2024*, pages 15919–15932, Bangkok, Thailand and Virtual Meeting. Association for Computational Linguistics.

Kishore Papineni, Salim Roukos, Todd Ward, and Wei-Jing Zhu. 2002. *BLEU: A Method for Automatic Evaluation of Machine Translation*. In *Proceedings of the 40th Annual Meeting of the Association for Computational Linguistics*, pages 311–318, Philadelphia, Pennsylvania, USA. Association for Computational Linguistics.

Yuheng Zha, Yichi Yang, Ruichen Li, and Zhiting Hu. 2023. *AlignScore: Evaluating Factual Consistency with a Unified Alignment Function*. In *Proceedings of the 61st Annual Meeting of the Association for Computational Linguistics (Volume 1: Long Papers)*, pages 11328–11348.

Tianyi Zhang, Varsha Kishore, Felix Wu, Kilian Q. Weinberger, and Yoav Artzi. 2020. *BERTScore: Evaluating Text Generation with BERT*. In *International Conference on Learning Representations*.

Appendix

Prompts

The prompts used in our experiments are shown in Figures 1,2,3,4

Initial Prompt for Spans

Below is the given input text. Extract the spans for each of the following labels: EXPERIENCE, INFORMATION, CAUSE, SUGGESTION, QUESTION.
Input:
{input_text}
Response:
{{"EXPERIENCE": [], "INFORMATION": [], "CAUSE": [], "SUGGESTION": [], "QUESTION": []}}

Figure 1: The initial prompt used for extracting spans from input text for different categories.

Initial Prompt for Summary

Below is the given input text. Summarize the input text for each of the following labels: EXPERIENCE, INFORMATION, CAUSE, SUGGESTION, QUESTION.
Input:
{input_text}
Response:
{{"EXPERIENCE": "", "INFORMATION": "", "CAUSE": "", "SUGGESTION": "", "QUESTION": ""}}

Figure 2: The initial prompt used for generating summaries from input text for different categories.

Refined Prompt for Spans

Below is the given Question, Context, and Answer. Identify the spans in the user answers that reflect a particular perspective and classify each span to the correct perspective among: EXPERIENCE, INFORMATION, CAUSE, SUGGESTION, QUESTION. Output the results in JSON format.
Question:
{question}
Context:
{context}
Answer:
{answer}
Spans:
{{"EXPERIENCE": [], "INFORMATION": [], "CAUSE": [], "SUGGESTION": [], "QUESTION": []}}

Figure 3: The refined prompt used for identifying and classifying perspective spans in user answers.

Refined Prompt for Summary

Below is the given Question, Context, and Answer. Generate a summary that represents the underlying perspective for each of the following perspectives: EXPERIENCE, INFORMATION, CAUSE, SUGGESTION, QUESTION. Output the results in JSON format.
Question:
{question}
Context:
{context}
Answer:
{answer}
Summaries:
{{"EXPERIENCE": "", "INFORMATION": "", "CAUSE": "", "SUGGESTION": "", "QUESTION": ""}}

Figure 4: The refined prompt used for generating perspective-based summaries from user answers.

LMU at PerAnsSumm 2025: LlaMA-in-the-loop at Perspective-Aware Healthcare Answer Summarization Task Factuality

Tanalp Agustoslu
LMU Munich
t.agustoslu@campus.lmu.de

Abstract

In this paper, we describe our submission for the shared task on Perspective-aware Healthcare Answer Summarization. Our system consists of two quantized models of the LlaMA family, applied across fine-tuning and few-shot settings. Additionally, we adopt the SumCoT prompting technique to improve the factual correctness of the generated summaries. We show that SumCoT yields more factually accurate summaries, even though this improvement comes at the expense of lower performance on lexical overlap and semantic similarity metrics such as ROUGE and BERTScore. Our work highlights an important trade-off when evaluating summarization models.

1 Introduction

In this paper, we present our submission for the shared task on Perspective-aware Healthcare Answer Summarization (PerAnsSumm) (Agarwal et al., 2025). PerAnsSumm comprises two tasks: span identification and summarization. Given a medical question-answer pair as input, the system must identify spans within the answer and classify them into five distinct perspectives: 'cause,' 'suggestion,' 'experience,' 'question,' and 'information.' In Task 2, the system utilizes these extracted perspective categories to generate summaries corresponding to the same five perspectives. The final summaries encompass all perspectives present in the given answer within the QA pair.

The shared task leverages the PUMA dataset (Naik et al., 2024), a perspective-aware annotated corpus of QA pairs and their respective summaries extracted from Yahoo!'s L6 corpus. Participants are provided with annotated spans and summaries in the training and development sets, while the test set contains only QA pairs. The first task, span identification, is evaluated at the lexical level using strict and proportional matching metrics[1]. The second task, summarization, is assessed using relevance metrics, ROUGE (Lin, 2004), BERTScore (Zhang et al., 2019), METEOR (Banerjee and Lavie, 2005) and BLEU (Papineni et al., 2002) at both lexical and semantic levels. Additionally, the organizers introduce two metrics, AlignScore (Zha et al., 2023) and SummaC (Laban et al., 2022), to evaluate the factuality of generated summaries. We participate in Task 2.2 (Factuality) of the shared task, where we approach the problem by leveraging two quantized models from the LLaMA family (Grattafiori et al., 2024) in fine-tuning, few-shot and chain-of-thought (CoT) (Wei et al., 2023) prompting settings. Depending on the approach, we either generate summaries directly or first identify spans and then incorporate them into the summarization process.

2 Related Work

The prominence of Large Language Models (LLMs) in the medical domain has been well documented through surveys and evaluation benchmarks in recent years. Integrating them with various prompting strategies, such as zero-shot, few-shot, CoT, and Analogical Reasoning (Yasunaga et al., 2024), has yielded promising results (Vatsal and Singh, 2024; Liévin et al., 2023; Jullien et al., 2023). Their ability to handle long contexts in medical domain and leverage intermediate reasoning steps make them suitable candidates not only for text summarization but also for information extraction tasks such as named entity recognition or event extraction (Xu et al., 2024; Bian et al., 2023; Yuan et al., 2023).

The effectiveness of LLMs in these tasks, however, is closely tied to their scale. Kaplan et al. (2020) introduced the concept of sample efficiency as part of their scaling laws, showing that larger

[1] https://github.com/PerAnsSumm/Evaluation/blob/main/eval.py

Proceedings of the Second Workshop on Patient-Oriented Language Processing (CL4Health), pages 380–388
May 4, 2025

neural language models require fewer optimization steps and are more sample efficient than their smaller counterparts. This suggests that, even with a small to moderate-sized datasets, opting for a larger model can be advantageous. However, a key limitation of LLMs is their computational cost, which restricts their deployment in resource-constrained environments. To address this, low-rank adaptation (LoRA) method has been proposed (Hu et al., 2021). LoRA freezes the pre-trained model weights and updates only low-rank approximations of the weight matrices. This drastically reduces the number of trainable parameters, thereby significantly lowering computational overhead. QLoRA (Dettmers et al., 2023) further optimizes this approach by quantizing the model weights typically to 4-bit precision while utilizing paged optimizers to efficiently manage memory, avoiding spikes by dynamically offloading data between GPU and CPU memory.

In our work, we employ quantized versions of LLaMA-70B and LLaMA-8B from the Unsloth library[2] and explore few-shot as well as fine-tuning settings. Additionally, we incorporate a variation of CoT prompting called Summary Chain-of-Thought (SumCoT) (Wang et al., 2023), which is inspired by Lasswell's Communication Model (Laswell, 1948) and designed for element extraction and text summarization tasks in an end-to-end manner.

3 Methods

We evaluate a set of prompting strategies to generate factually correct summaries. Our approaches include fine-tuning, few-shot, and SumCoT prompting. As a baseline, we use LLaMA-8B with fine-tuning.

3.1 Fine-Tuning

For fine-tuning, we use the training dataset provided by the organizers and employ the 4-bit quantized LLaMA-8B model with a learning rate of 2e-4 and train it for 3.5 epochs. Additionally, we configure all applicable modules with a rank of 16 and an alpha value of 16.

3.2 Few-Shot

For few-shot prompting, we use a quantized LLaMA-8B model in a 1-shot setting, where in-context examples are randomly selected for each inference to prevent the model from overfitting to a fixed set of examples. Each example includes both labeled spans and their corresponding summaries, and the model is instructed to generate only the summary. The model used in this setting has already been fine-tuned on the provided training set.

Dataset Statistics	**Dev Set**	**Train Set**
Total Instances	959	2236
Total Tokens	239,486	555,249
Avg Tokens per Instance	249.72	248.32
Avg Words per Instance	216.02	214.78
Avg Answers per Instance	3.23	3.11
Avg Perspectives per Instance (Answers)	1.97	1.97
Avg Perspectives per Instance (Summaries)	1.96	1.95
Perspective Distribution (Answers)		
EXPERIENCE	316	747
INFORMATION	735	1767
CAUSE	139	308
SUGGESTION	595	1360
QUESTION	102	215
Perspective Distribution (Summaries)		
EXPERIENCE	315	745
INFORMATION	733	1742
CAUSE	138	305
SUGGESTION	595	1363
QUESTION	101	213

Table 1: PUMA Dataset Statistics for Development and Training Sets. Test Set consists of 50 instances and only includes QA pairs with a context information without providing any perspective spans or summaries.

3.3 Summary Chain-of-Thought (SumCoT)

We incorporate a variant of CoT prompting called SumCoT, which is designed for element extraction and text summarization tasks in an end-to-end manner. This approach is inspired by Lasswell's Communication Model, which later found itself application in journalism as the 5W framework (Who, What, When, Where, Why). Following prior work by Wang et al. (2023) that suggests that performance gains become evident only at scale, we employ a 4-bit quantized version of LLaMA-70B. In line with their findings, we formulate our questions using only a single type of W-question, specifically "What", as it can encapsulate the essence of all other questions.[3] We later append the five distinct perspectives found in our dataset to the questions. As we observe the stabi-

[2]https://huggingface.co/unsloth

[3]https://github.com/Alsace08/SumCoT/blob/master/prompts/cot_element_extraction.txt

Prompt Template
You are provided with a text containing community-based questions and answers from the medical domain. Your task is to analyze the answers by identifying and considering different perspectives such as 'Information', 'Cause', 'Suggestion', 'Experience', and 'Question' as in the provided examples below and then summarize the text into a coherent summary. Only output the summaries and nothing else.
In-Context Examples:
Example: **Question:** Do I have lupus? **Context:** I had a fever and fatigue. I looked at the symptoms on the internet. My doctor disagrees with me. [...] **Answers:** What other symptoms did you have? It's usually never lupus. Listen to your doctor. Lupus is an autoimmune disorder [...] **EXPERIENCE_GROUP:** My teacher used to say this. It turns out it was just a flu. **INFORMATION_GROUP:** Lupus is an autoimmune disorder [...] **CAUSE_GROUP:** I had a fever and fatigue. [...] **SUGGESTION_GROUP:** Listen to your doctor. [...] **QUESTION_GROUP:** What other symptoms did you have? [...] **EXPERIENCE_SUMMARY:** In users experience, [...] **INFORMATION_SUMMARY:** For information purposes [...] **CAUSE_SUMMARY:** Some of the causes are [...] **SUGGESTION_SUMMARY:** It's suggested that [...] **QUESTION_SUMMARY:** It's inquired [...]
Text: {text}
Answer: {answer}

Table 2: Prompt Template for Few-Shot Method. Summary examples are given with common start phrases found in the PUMA dataset.

lizing effect of it during generations, we additionally prefix the phrase "Let's think step by step." (Kojima et al., 2023) before the model extracts the relevant perspectives. After eliciting information about spans from the model, we then provide the fine-tuned 8B model with the output generations of the 70B variant and let it generate summaries based on the extracted perspectives.

Prompt Template
You are provided with a text containing community-based questions and answers from the medical domain. Your task is to analyze the answers by identifying and considering different perspectives such as 'Information', 'Cause', 'Suggestion', 'Experience', and 'Question'. Show your reasoning steps while extracting.
Questions: What are the important suggestions in these answers? What are the important causes in these answers? What are the important informations in these answers? What are the important questions in these answers? What are the important experiences in these answers? Please answer the above questions.
Text: {text}
Answer: Let's think step by step. {answer}

Table 3: Prompt Template for SumCoT Method

4 Evaluation Protocol

The PerAnsSumm shared task evaluates submissions across three axes. Task 1 focuses on lexical overlap, using both proportional and strict matching metrics to assess the accuracy of extracted label spans from answers as well as the generated summaries. Task 2 is further divided into two subcategories: Task 2.1 evaluates lexical and semantic similarity using relevance metrics, ROUGE, BERTScore, METEOR and BLEU. Task 2.2 assesses the factual consistency of the generated spans and summaries using AlignScore and SummaC.

AlignScore is a reference based metric, formally:

$$\text{AlignScore}(x, y) = \frac{1}{|x|} \sum_{i=1}^{|x|} \max_j s(x_i, y_j) \quad (1)$$

where x is the generation, y is the reference and $|x|$ is the number of sentences in the generation, and $\max_j s(x_i, y_j)$ selects the maximum alignment score for each sentence of the generation across all chunks of the reference (split into approximately 350-token chunks for RoBERTa (Liu et al., 2019)) using an unified alignment function trained on a diverse set of NLP tasks (e.g., natural language inference, question answering, semantic similarity, fact verification) with a combined dataset of 4.7 million examples.

SummaC follows a similar chunking approach, but adds an additional layer by using an NLI model to scan sentence pairs. These entailment scores are aggregated into histogram bins, which are then processed through a convolutional neural network (CNN) (LeCun and Bengio, 1998) to produce scalar values for each summary sentence. These scalar values are averaged to compute the final consistency score.

Despite the significant drawbacks of frequent test set evaluation (van der Goot, 2021), we evaluated our approaches on the test set due to time constraints, as the hyperparameters for AlignScore and SummaC were not known until a later stage of the shared task.

5 Results

The results presented in Table 4 provide insights into the impact of different methods on improving factuality and help address our research question: *Can we improve the factuality of generated summaries with in-context-learning and chain-of-thought prompting?*

Table 4 shows that there is no clear winner across all metrics. The standard fine-tuning method achieves the best results in relevance metrics, with the exception of the few-shot approach,

Name	ROUGE-1	ROUGE-2	ROUGE-L	BERTScore	METEOR	BLEU	Rel. Avg.	AlignScore	SummaC	Fact. Avg.
Fine-Tuning	0.2550	0.0991	0.2288	**0.6448**	0.2349	0.0643	**0.2545**	0.3235	0.2398	0.2817
Few-Shot	0.1912	0.0573	0.1701	**0.6512**	0.1636	0.0489	0.2137	0.2263	0.2262	0.2263
8B-Labels	0.2226	0.0896	0.2044	0.5413	0.2045	0.0704	0.2221	0.3246	0.2274	0.2760
70B-Labels (SumCoT)	0.2148	0.0905	0.1942	0.5351	0.2032	0.0595	0.2162	**0.3564**	**0.2471**	**0.3017**

Table 4: PerAnsSumm 2025 test set results for all evaluated approaches. All approaches use the same fine-tuned model for summary generation. *Few-Shot* used in a 1-shot setting. In the *8B-Labels*, spans are identified by the fine-tuned 8B model and the output passed to the same 8B fine-tuned model for summary generation. In the *70B-Labels (SumCoT)*, spans are identified by 70B model without fine-tuning and the output passed to the same 8B fine-tuned model for summary generation. ROUGE scores measure n-gram overlap, BERTScore evaluates semantic similarity, METEOR compares unigrams, synonyms and stemming with penalties for word order differences, BLEU compares n-gram precision between the generated summary and the ground truth, applying a brevity penalty for shorter generations. AlignScore and SummaC measure factual consistency. *Rel. Avg* shows the average of ROUGE, BERTScore, METEOR and BLEU, and *Fact. Avg.* shows the average of AlignScore and SummaC.

which surpasses fine-tuning in semantic similarity when evaluated using contextual BERT (Devlin et al., 2019) embeddings. However, the few-shot approach exhibits relatively low ROUGE scores (especially ROUGE-2) alongside lower METEOR and BLEU scores. This results in a higher average relevance score for fine-tuning, suggesting that the model may have prioritized the in-context examples while being penalized for differences in word order and shorter generations by METEOR and BLEU during few-shot generations. A similar pattern is observed in ROUGE-L, where the longest common subsequence between the generated and reference summaries is less aligned. When it comes to factuality, surprisingly, the few-shot approach does not lead to any improvements and performs significantly worse than the standard fine-tuning method. Additionally, we observe a slight decline in SummaC and average factuality with the 8B label extraction method, along with a notable drop in BERTScore. It appears that in both approaches, the model was biased toward the in-context examples and the extracted spans, respectively. Moreover, the extracted spans from the fine-tuned model may be incorrect, as the model was trained solely for the summary generation task. This suggests that it may be heavily relying on its memorized knowledge of training set labels acquired during parameter updates, which could have skewed the metrics.

On the other hand, even without any fine-tuning, the SumCoT approach with the 70B label extraction method shows a noticeable impact. Despite a significant drop in BERTScore and ROUGE (similar to the 8B label extraction) the final summaries are the most factually accurate. This also highlights the important trade-off between relevance and factuality metrics when evaluating summarization models. Lexical and semantic alignment does not always guarantee hallucination-free, factually correct summaries.

The challenge of identifying the optimal summary is a complex and nuanced issue. As proven by Schluter (2017), performing a ROUGE evaluation of a summarization model for optimal summaries is an NP-hard task and relying solely on relevance metrics does not capture the full capabilities of the implemented system. As demonstrated in this shared task, it makes sense to introduce multiple perspectives into the evaluation by incorporating additional metrics and averaging them to mitigate the shortcomings of any single metric.

6 Conclusion

In our submission, we explored several approaches to improve the factuality of generated summaries. Our best-performing method, SumCoT, involved extracting spans using a 4-bit quantized LLaMA 70B model with W-Questions, and feeding the output into a fine-tuned 8B model to generate summaries. This approach led to improvements in the factuality of the generated summaries compared to standard fine-tuning and few-shot methods. However, these improvements are not always reflected in relevance metrics such as ROUGE and BERTScore. Our final submission ranks 15th in AlignScore, 16th in SummaC, and 15th in average factuality on the official leaderboard[4].

[4]https://docs.google.com/spreadsheets/d/1faysHdA7YQ-xELztsm7jA5RPTMh71P7tycsjd8ANLGE/

7 Limitations

In this section, we highlight some shortcomings of our implemented system and outline potential directions for future work.

One notable limitation in our approach is the choice of random sampling for the few-shot examples, which was intended to prevent bias toward the same examples. However, Gema et al. (2024) demonstrates the effectiveness of the BM25 retriever over naive random sampling. BM25 allows for the selection of only the most relevant in-context examples, which could improve performance in future iterations of the shared task.

Another limitation is our use of quantization due to computational constraints, which may have affected our findings. As highlighted by Pochinkov (2024), performance degradation is often inevitable in quantized LLaMA models.

Our final submission, SumCoT, showed improvements in factuality metrics. However, as noted by Wang et al. (2023), the success of the proposed approach is often correlated with the model's parameter count. We expect that using larger models, including closed-source ones like GPT (OpenAI et al., 2024), would likely amplify these results. An important consideration, however, when transitioning to closed-source models, is the memorization ability of neural language models (Carlini et al., 2023) and the issue of data leakage. Balloccu et al. (2024) identified potentially leaked datasets within the training data of ChatGPT and GPT-4 by systematically reviewing 255 research papers. In our case, as the PUMA dataset and Yahoo's L6 Corpus are not publicly available and primarily cover texts from the early 2000s to early 2010s, data leakage is unlikely to be a significant concern. However, taking basic measures and implementing simple n-gram matching metrics to detect potential data leakage in model completions of any given data instance (Gema et al., 2024) or adopting the Contamination Detection via Output Distribution (CDD) framework proposed by Dong et al. (2024) could further strengthen the reliability of the obtained results and would align well with the broader goal of trustworthy AI.

References

Siddhant Agarwal, Md Shad Akhtar, and Shweta Yadav. 2025. Overview of the peranssumm 2025 shared task on perspective-aware healthcare answer summarization. In *Proceedings of the Second Workshop on Patient-Oriented Language Processing (CL4Health) @ NAACL 2025*, Albuquerque, USA. Association for Computational Linguistics.

Simone Balloccu, Patrícia Schmidtová, Mateusz Lango, and Ondrej Dusek. 2024. Leak, cheat, repeat: Data contamination and evaluation malpractices in closed-source LLMs. In *Proceedings of the 18th Conference of the European Chapter of the Association for Computational Linguistics (Volume 1: Long Papers)*, pages 67–93, St. Julian's, Malta. Association for Computational Linguistics.

Satanjeev Banerjee and Alon Lavie. 2005. METEOR: An automatic metric for MT evaluation with improved correlation with human judgments. In *Proceedings of the ACL Workshop on Intrinsic and Extrinsic Evaluation Measures for Machine Translation and/or Summarization*, pages 65–72, Ann Arbor, Michigan. Association for Computational Linguistics.

Junyi Bian, Jiaxuan Zheng, Yuyi Zhang, and Shanfeng Zhu. 2023. Inspire the large language model by external knowledge on biomedical named entity recognition.

Nicholas Carlini, Daphne Ippolito, Matthew Jagielski, Katherine Lee, Florian Tramer, and Chiyuan Zhang. 2023. Quantifying memorization across neural language models.

Tim Dettmers, Artidoro Pagnoni, Ari Holtzman, and Luke Zettlemoyer. 2023. Qlora: Efficient finetuning of quantized llms. *CoRR*, abs/2305.14314.

Jacob Devlin, Ming-Wei Chang, Kenton Lee, and Kristina Toutanova. 2019. Bert: Pre-training of deep bidirectional transformers for language understanding.

Yihong Dong, Xue Jiang, Huanyu Liu, Zhi Jin, Bin Gu, Mengfei Yang, and Ge Li. 2024. Generalization or memorization: Data contamination and trustworthy evaluation for large language models. In *Findings of the Association for Computational Linguistics: ACL 2024*, pages 12039–12050, Bangkok, Thailand. Association for Computational Linguistics.

Aryo Gema, Giwon Hong, Pasquale Minervini, Luke Daines, and Beatrice Alex. 2024. Edinburgh clinical NLP at SemEval-2024 task 2: Fine-tune your model unless you have access to GPT-4. In *Proceedings of the 18th International Workshop on Semantic Evaluation (SemEval-2024)*, pages 1894–1904, Mexico City, Mexico. Association for Computational Linguistics.

Aaron Grattafiori, Abhimanyu Dubey, Abhinav Jauhri, Abhinav Pandey, Abhishek Kadian, Ahmad Al-Dahle, Aiesha Letman, Akhil Mathur, Alan Schelten, Alex Vaughan, Amy Yang, Angela Fan, Anirudh Goyal, Anthony Hartshorn, Aobo Yang, Archi Mitra, Archie Sravankumar, Artem Korenev, Arthur

Hinsvark, Arun Rao, Aston Zhang, Aurelien Rodriguez, Austen Gregerson, Ava Spataru, Baptiste Roziere, Bethany Biron, Binh Tang, Bobbie Chern, Charlotte Caucheteux, Chaya Nayak, Chloe Bi, Chris Marra, Chris McConnell, Christian Keller, Christophe Touret, Chunyang Wu, Corinne Wong, Cristian Canton Ferrer, Cyrus Nikolaidis, Damien Allonsius, Daniel Song, Danielle Pintz, Danny Livshits, Danny Wyatt, David Esiobu, Dhruv Choudhary, Dhruv Mahajan, Diego Garcia-Olano, Diego Perino, Dieuwke Hupkes, Egor Lakomkin, Ehab AlBadawy, Elina Lobanova, Emily Dinan, Eric Michael Smith, Filip Radenovic, Francisco Guzmán, Frank Zhang, Gabriel Synnaeve, Gabrielle Lee, Georgia Lewis Anderson, Govind Thattai, Graeme Nail, Gregoire Mialon, Guan Pang, Guillem Cucurell, Hailey Nguyen, Hannah Korevaar, Hu Xu, Hugo Touvron, Iliyan Zarov, Imanol Arrieta Ibarra, Isabel Kloumann, Ishan Misra, Ivan Evtimov, Jack Zhang, Jade Copet, Jaewon Lee, Jan Geffert, Jana Vranes, Jason Park, Jay Mahadeokar, Jeet Shah, Jelmer van der Linde, Jennifer Billock, Jenny Hong, Jenya Lee, Jeremy Fu, Jianfeng Chi, Jianyu Huang, Jiawen Liu, Jie Wang, Jiecao Yu, Joanna Bitton, Joe Spisak, Jongsoo Park, Joseph Rocca, Joshua Johnstun, Joshua Saxe, Junteng Jia, Kalyan Vasuden Alwala, Karthik Prasad, Kartikeya Upasani, Kate Plawiak, Ke Li, Kenneth Heafield, Kevin Stone, Khalid El-Arini, Krithika Iyer, Kshitiz Malik, Kuenley Chiu, Kunal Bhalla, Kushal Lakhotia, Lauren Rantala-Yeary, Laurens van der Maaten, Lawrence Chen, Liang Tan, Liz Jenkins, Louis Martin, Lovish Madaan, Lubo Malo, Lukas Blecher, Lukas Landzaat, Luke de Oliveira, Madeline Muzzi, Mahesh Pasupuleti, Mannat Singh, Manohar Paluri, Marcin Kardas, Maria Tsimpoukelli, Mathew Oldham, Mathieu Rita, Maya Pavlova, Melanie Kambadur, Mike Lewis, Min Si, Mitesh Kumar Singh, Mona Hassan, Naman Goyal, Narjes Torabi, Nikolay Bashlykov, Nikolay Bogoychev, Niladri Chatterji, Ning Zhang, Olivier Duchenne, Onur Çelebi, Patrick Alrassy, Pengchuan Zhang, Pengwei Li, Petar Vasic, Peter Weng, Prajjwal Bhargava, Pratik Dubal, Praveen Krishnan, Punit Singh Koura, Puxin Xu, Qing He, Qingxiao Dong, Ragavan Srinivasan, Raj Ganapathy, Ramon Calderer, Ricardo Silveira Cabral, Robert Stojnic, Roberta Raileanu, Rohan Maheswari, Rohit Girdhar, Rohit Patel, Romain Sauvestre, Ronnie Polidoro, Roshan Sumbaly, Ross Taylor, Ruan Silva, Rui Hou, Rui Wang, Saghar Hosseini, Sahana Chennabasappa, Sanjay Singh, Sean Bell, Seohyun Sonia Kim, Sergey Edunov, Shaoliang Nie, Sharan Narang, Sharath Raparthy, Sheng Shen, Shengye Wan, Shruti Bhosale, Shun Zhang, Simon Vandenhende, Soumya Batra, Spencer Whitman, Sten Sootla, Stephane Collot, Suchin Gururangan, Sydney Borodinsky, Tamar Herman, Tara Fowler, Tarek Sheasha, Thomas Georgiou, Thomas Scialom, Tobias Speckbacher, Todor Mihaylov, Tong Xiao, Ujjwal Karn, Vedanuj Goswami, Vibhor Gupta, Vignesh Ramanathan, Viktor Kerkez, Vincent Gonguet, Virginie Do, Vish Vogeti, Vítor Albiero, Vladan Petrovic, Weiwei Chu, Wenhan Xiong, Wenyin Fu, Whitney Meers, Xavier Martinet, Xiaodong Wang, Xiaofang Wang, Xiaoqing Ellen Tan, Xide Xia, Xinfeng Xie, Xuchao Jia, Xuewei Wang, Yaelle Goldschlag, Yashesh Gaur, Yasmine Babaei, Yi Wen, Yiwen Song, Yuchen Zhang, Yue Li, Yuning Mao, Zacharie Delpierre Coudert, Zheng Yan, Zhengxing Chen, Zoe Papakipos, Aaditya Singh, Aayushi Srivastava, Abha Jain, Adam Kelsey, Adam Shajnfeld, Adithya Gangidi, Adolfo Victoria, Ahuva Goldstand, Ajay Menon, Ajay Sharma, Alex Boesenberg, Alexei Baevski, Allie Feinstein, Amanda Kallet, Amit Sangani, Amos Teo, Anam Yunus, Andrei Lupu, Andres Alvarado, Andrew Caples, Andrew Gu, Andrew Ho, Andrew Poulton, Andrew Ryan, Ankit Ramchandani, Annie Dong, Annie Franco, Anuj Goyal, Aparajita Saraf, Arkabandhu Chowdhury, Ashley Gabriel, Ashwin Bharambe, Assaf Eisenman, Azadeh Yazdan, Beau James, Ben Maurer, Benjamin Leonhardi, Bernie Huang, Beth Loyd, Beto De Paola, Bhargavi Paranjape, Bing Liu, Bo Wu, Boyu Ni, Braden Hancock, Bram Wasti, Brandon Spence, Brani Stojkovic, Brian Gamido, Britt Montalvo, Carl Parker, Carly Burton, Catalina Mejia, Ce Liu, Changhan Wang, Changkyu Kim, Chao Zhou, Chester Hu, Ching-Hsiang Chu, Chris Cai, Chris Tindal, Christoph Feichtenhofer, Cynthia Gao, Damon Civin, Dana Beaty, Daniel Kreymer, Daniel Li, David Adkins, David Xu, Davide Testuggine, Delia David, Devi Parikh, Diana Liskovich, Didem Foss, Dingkang Wang, Duc Le, Dustin Holland, Edward Dowling, Eissa Jamil, Elaine Montgomery, Eleonora Presani, Emily Hahn, Emily Wood, Eric-Tuan Le, Erik Brinkman, Esteban Arcaute, Evan Dunbar, Evan Smothers, Fei Sun, Felix Kreuk, Feng Tian, Filippos Kokkinos, Firat Ozgenel, Francesco Caggioni, Frank Kanayet, Frank Seide, Gabriela Medina Florez, Gabriella Schwarz, Gada Badeer, Georgia Swee, Gil Halpern, Grant Herman, Grigory Sizov, Guangyi, Zhang, Guna Lakshminarayanan, Hakan Inan, Hamid Shojanazeri, Han Zou, Hannah Wang, Hanwen Zha, Haroun Habeeb, Harrison Rudolph, Helen Suk, Henry Aspegren, Hunter Goldman, Hongyuan Zhan, Ibrahim Damlaj, Igor Molybog, Igor Tufanov, Ilias Leontiadis, Irina-Elena Veliche, Itai Gat, Jake Weissman, James Geboski, James Kohli, Janice Lam, Japhet Asher, Jean-Baptiste Gaya, Jeff Marcus, Jeff Tang, Jennifer Chan, Jenny Zhen, Jeremy Reizenstein, Jeremy Teboul, Jessica Zhong, Jian Jin, Jingyi Yang, Joe Cummings, Jon Carvill, Jon Shepard, Jonathan McPhie, Jonathan Torres, Josh Ginsburg, Junjie Wang, Kai Wu, Kam Hou U, Karan Saxena, Kartikay Khandelwal, Katayoun Zand, Kathy Matosich, Kaushik Veeraraghavan, Kelly Michelena, Keqian Li, Kiran Jagadeesh, Kun Huang, Kunal Chawla, Kyle Huang, Lailin Chen, Lakshya Garg, Lavender A, Leandro Silva, Lee Bell, Lei Zhang, Liangpeng Guo, Licheng Yu, Liron Moshkovich, Luca Wehrstedt, Madian Khabsa, Manav Avalani, Manish Bhatt, Martynas Mankus, Matan Hasson, Matthew Lennie, Matthias Reso, Maxim Groshev, Maxim Naumov, Maya Lathi, Meghan Keneally, Miao

Liu, Michael L. Seltzer, Michal Valko, Michelle Restrepo, Mihir Patel, Mik Vyatskov, Mikayel Samvelyan, Mike Clark, Mike Macey, Mike Wang, Miquel Jubert Hermoso, Mo Metanat, Mohammad Rastegari, Munish Bansal, Nandhini Santhanam, Natascha Parks, Natasha White, Navyata Bawa, Nayan Singhal, Nick Egebo, Nicolas Usunier, Nikhil Mehta, Nikolay Pavlovich Laptev, Ning Dong, Norman Cheng, Oleg Chernoguz, Olivia Hart, Omkar Salpekar, Ozlem Kalinli, Parkin Kent, Parth Parekh, Paul Saab, Pavan Balaji, Pedro Rittner, Philip Bontrager, Pierre Roux, Piotr Dollar, Polina Zvyagina, Prashant Ratanchandani, Pritish Yuvraj, Qian Liang, Rachad Alao, Rachel Rodriguez, Rafi Ayub, Raghotham Murthy, Raghu Nayani, Rahul Mitra, Rangaprabhu Parthasarathy, Raymond Li, Rebekkah Hogan, Robin Battey, Rocky Wang, Russ Howes, Ruty Rinott, Sachin Mehta, Sachin Siby, Sai Jayesh Bondu, Samyak Datta, Sara Chugh, Sara Hunt, Sargun Dhillon, Sasha Sidorov, Satadru Pan, Saurabh Mahajan, Saurabh Verma, Seiji Yamamoto, Sharadh Ramaswamy, Shaun Lindsay, Shaun Lindsay, Sheng Feng, Shenghao Lin, Shengxin Cindy Zha, Shishir Patil, Shiva Shankar, Shuqiang Zhang, Shuqiang Zhang, Sinong Wang, Sneha Agarwal, Soji Sajuyigbe, Soumith Chintala, Stephanie Max, Stephen Chen, Steve Kehoe, Steve Satterfield, Sudarshan Govindaprasad, Sumit Gupta, Summer Deng, Sungmin Cho, Sunny Virk, Suraj Subramanian, Sy Choudhury, Sydney Goldman, Tal Remez, Tamar Glaser, Tamara Best, Thilo Koehler, Thomas Robinson, Tianhe Li, Tianjun Zhang, Tim Matthews, Timothy Chou, Tzook Shaked, Varun Vontimitta, Victoria Ajayi, Victoria Montanez, Vijai Mohan, Vinay Satish Kumar, Vishal Mangla, Vlad Ionescu, Vlad Poenaru, Vlad Tiberiu Mihailescu, Vladimir Ivanov, Wei Li, Wenchen Wang, Wenwen Jiang, Wes Bouaziz, Will Constable, Xiaocheng Tang, Xiaojian Wu, Xiaolan Wang, Xilun Wu, Xinbo Gao, Yaniv Kleinman, Yanjun Chen, Ye Hu, Ye Jia, Ye Qi, Yenda Li, Yilin Zhang, Ying Zhang, Yossi Adi, Youngjin Nam, Yu, Wang, Yu Zhao, Yuchen Hao, Yundi Qian, Yunlu Li, Yuzi He, Zach Rait, Zachary DeVito, Zef Rosnbrick, Zhaoduo Wen, Zhenyu Yang, Zhiwei Zhao, and Zhiyu Ma. 2024. The llama 3 herd of models.

Edward J. Hu, Yelong Shen, Phillip Wallis, Zeyuan Allen-Zhu, Yuanzhi Li, Shean Wang, Lu Wang, and Weizhu Chen. 2021. Lora: Low-rank adaptation of large language models.

Maël Jullien, Marco Valentino, Hannah Frost, Paul O'regan, Donal Landers, and André Freitas. 2023. SemEval-2023 task 7: Multi-evidence natural language inference for clinical trial data. In *Proceedings of the 17th International Workshop on Semantic Evaluation (SemEval-2023)*, pages 2216–2226, Toronto, Canada. Association for Computational Linguistics.

Jared Kaplan, Sam McCandlish, Tom Henighan, Tom B. Brown, Benjamin Chess, Rewon Child, Scott Gray, Alec Radford, Jeffrey Wu, and Dario Amodei. 2020. Scaling laws for neural language models.

Takeshi Kojima, Shixiang Shane Gu, Machel Reid, Yutaka Matsuo, and Yusuke Iwasawa. 2023. Large language models are zero-shot reasoners.

Philippe Laban, Tobias Schnabel, Paul N. Bennett, and Marti A. Hearst. 2022. SummaC: Re-visiting NLI-based models for inconsistency detection in summarization. *Transactions of the Association for Computational Linguistics*, 10:163–177.

Harold D Laswell. 1948. The structure and function of communication in society.

Yann LeCun and Yoshua Bengio. 1998. *Convolutional networks for images, speech, and time series*, page 255–258. MIT Press, Cambridge, MA, USA.

Chin-Yew Lin. 2004. ROUGE: A package for automatic evaluation of summaries. In *Text Summarization Branches Out*, pages 74–81, Barcelona, Spain. Association for Computational Linguistics.

Yinhan Liu, Myle Ott, Naman Goyal, Jingfei Du, Mandar Joshi, Danqi Chen, Omer Levy, Mike Lewis, Luke Zettlemoyer, and Veselin Stoyanov. 2019. Roberta: A robustly optimized bert pretraining approach.

Valentin Liévin, Christoffer Egeberg Hother, Andreas Geert Motzfeldt, and Ole Winther. 2023. Can large language models reason about medical questions?

Gauri Naik, Sharad Chandakacherla, Shweta Yadav, and Md Shad Akhtar. 2024. No perspective, no perception!! perspective-aware healthcare answer summarization. In *Findings of the Association for Computational Linguistics: ACL 2024*, pages 15919–15932, Bangkok, Thailand. Association for Computational Linguistics.

OpenAI, Josh Achiam, Steven Adler, Sandhini Agarwal, Lama Ahmad, Ilge Akkaya, Florencia Leoni Aleman, Diogo Almeida, Janko Altenschmidt, Sam Altman, Shyamal Anadkat, Red Avila, Igor Babuschkin, Suchir Balaji, Valerie Balcom, Paul Baltescu, Haiming Bao, Mohammad Bavarian, Jeff Belgum, Irwan Bello, Jake Berdine, Gabriel Bernadett-Shapiro, Christopher Berner, Lenny Bogdonoff, Oleg Boiko, Madelaine Boyd, Anna-Luisa Brakman, Greg Brockman, Tim Brooks, Miles Brundage, Kevin Button, Trevor Cai, Rosie Campbell, Andrew Cann, Brittany Carey, Chelsea Carlson, Rory Carmichael, Brooke Chan, Che Chang, Fotis Chantzis, Derek Chen, Sully Chen, Ruby Chen, Jason Chen, Mark Chen, Ben Chess, Chester Cho, Casey Chu, Hyung Won Chung, Dave Cummings, Jeremiah Currier, Yunxing Dai, Cory Decareaux, Thomas Degry, Noah Deutsch, Damien Deville, Arka Dhar, David Dohan, Steve Dowling, Sheila Dunning, Adrien Ecoffet, Atty Eleti, Tyna Eloundou, David Farhi, Liam Fedus, Niko Felix,

Simón Posada Fishman, Juston Forte, Isabella Fulford, Leo Gao, Elie Georges, Christian Gibson, Vik Goel, Tarun Gogineni, Gabriel Goh, Rapha Gontijo-Lopes, Jonathan Gordon, Morgan Grafstein, Scott Gray, Ryan Greene, Joshua Gross, Shixiang Shane Gu, Yufei Guo, Chris Hallacy, Jesse Han, Jeff Harris, Yuchen He, Mike Heaton, Johannes Heidecke, Chris Hesse, Alan Hickey, Wade Hickey, Peter Hoeschele, Brandon Houghton, Kenny Hsu, Shengli Hu, Xin Hu, Joost Huizinga, Shantanu Jain, Shawn Jain, Joanne Jang, Angela Jiang, Roger Jiang, Haozhun Jin, Denny Jin, Shino Jomoto, Billie Jonn, Heewoo Jun, Tomer Kaftan, Łukasz Kaiser, Ali Kamali, Ingmar Kanitscheider, Nitish Shirish Keskar, Tabarak Khan, Logan Kilpatrick, Jong Wook Kim, Christina Kim, Yongjik Kim, Jan Hendrik Kirchner, Jamie Kiros, Matt Knight, Daniel Kokotajlo, Łukasz Kondraciuk, Andrew Kondrich, Aris Konstantinidis, Kyle Kosic, Gretchen Krueger, Vishal Kuo, Michael Lampe, Ikai Lan, Teddy Lee, Jan Leike, Jade Leung, Daniel Levy, Chak Ming Li, Rachel Lim, Molly Lin, Stephanie Lin, Mateusz Litwin, Theresa Lopez, Ryan Lowe, Patricia Lue, Anna Makanju, Kim Malfacini, Sam Manning, Todor Markov, Yaniv Markovski, Bianca Martin, Katie Mayer, Andrew Mayne, Bob McGrew, Scott Mayer McKinney, Christine McLeavey, Paul McMillan, Jake McNeil, David Medina, Aalok Mehta, Jacob Menick, Luke Metz, Andrey Mishchenko, Pamela Mishkin, Vinnie Monaco, Evan Morikawa, Daniel Mossing, Tong Mu, Mira Murati, Oleg Murk, David Mély, Ashvin Nair, Reiichiro Nakano, Rajeev Nayak, Arvind Neelakantan, Richard Ngo, Hyeonwoo Noh, Long Ouyang, Cullen O'Keefe, Jakub Pachocki, Alex Paino, Joe Palermo, Ashley Pantuliano, Giambattista Parascandolo, Joel Parish, Emy Parparita, Alex Passos, Mikhail Pavlov, Andrew Peng, Adam Perelman, Filipe de Avila Belbute Peres, Michael Petrov, Henrique Ponde de Oliveira Pinto, Michael, Pokorny, Michelle Pokrass, Vitchyr H. Pong, Tolly Powell, Alethea Power, Boris Power, Elizabeth Proehl, Raul Puri, Alec Radford, Jack Rae, Aditya Ramesh, Cameron Raymond, Francis Real, Kendra Rimbach, Carl Ross, Bob Rotsted, Henri Roussez, Nick Ryder, Mario Saltarelli, Ted Sanders, Shibani Santurkar, Girish Sastry, Heather Schmidt, David Schnurr, John Schulman, Daniel Selsam, Kyla Sheppard, Toki Sherbakov, Jessica Shieh, Sarah Shoker, Pranav Shyam, Szymon Sidor, Eric Sigler, Maddie Simens, Jordan Sitkin, Katarina Slama, Ian Sohl, Benjamin Sokolowsky, Yang Song, Natalie Staudacher, Felipe Petroski Such, Natalie Summers, Ilya Sutskever, Jie Tang, Nikolas Tezak, Madeleine B. Thompson, Phil Tillet, Amin Tootoonchian, Elizabeth Tseng, Preston Tuggle, Nick Turley, Jerry Tworek, Juan Felipe Cerón Uribe, Andrea Vallone, Arun Vijayvergiya, Chelsea Voss, Carroll Wainwright, Justin Jay Wang, Alvin Wang, Ben Wang, Jonathan Ward, Jason Wei, CJ Weinmann, Akila Welihinda, Peter Welinder, Jiayi Weng, Lilian Weng, Matt Wiethoff, Dave Willner, Clemens Winter, Samuel Wolrich, Hannah Wong, Lauren Workman, Sherwin Wu, Jeff Wu, Michael Wu, Kai Xiao, Tao Xu, Sarah Yoo, Kevin Yu, Qiming Yuan, Wojciech Zaremba, Rowan Zellers, Chong Zhang, Marvin Zhang, Shengjia Zhao, Tianhao Zheng, Juntang Zhuang, William Zhuk, and Barret Zoph. 2024. Gpt-4 technical report.

Kishore Papineni, Salim Roukos, Todd Ward, and Wei-Jing Zhu. 2002. Bleu: a method for automatic evaluation of machine translation. In *Proceedings of the 40th Annual Meeting of the Association for Computational Linguistics*, pages 311–318, Philadelphia, Pennsylvania, USA. Association for Computational Linguistics.

Nicky Pochinkov. 2024. Comparing quantized performance in llama models. Last access: 02.25.2025.

Natalie Schluter. 2017. The limits of automatic summarisation according to ROUGE. In *Proceedings of the 15th Conference of the European Chapter of the Association for Computational Linguistics: Volume 2, Short Papers*, pages 41–45, Valencia, Spain. Association for Computational Linguistics.

Rob van der Goot. 2021. We need to talk about train-dev-test splits. In *Proceedings of the 2021 Conference on Empirical Methods in Natural Language Processing*, pages 4485–4494, Online and Punta Cana, Dominican Republic. Association for Computational Linguistics.

Shubham Vatsal and Ayush Singh. 2024. Can GPT redefine medical understanding? evaluating GPT on biomedical machine reading comprehension. In *Proceedings of the 23rd Workshop on Biomedical Natural Language Processing*, pages 256–265, Bangkok, Thailand. Association for Computational Linguistics.

Yiming Wang, Zhuosheng Zhang, and Rui Wang. 2023. Element-aware summarization with large language models: Expert-aligned evaluation and chain-of-thought method. In *Proceedings of the 61st Annual Meeting of the Association for Computational Linguistics (Volume 1: Long Papers)*, pages 8640–8665, Toronto, Canada. Association for Computational Linguistics.

Jason Wei, Xuezhi Wang, Dale Schuurmans, Maarten Bosma, Brian Ichter, Fei Xia, Ed Chi, Quoc Le, and Denny Zhou. 2023. Chain-of-thought prompting elicits reasoning in large language models.

Derong Xu, Wei Chen, Wenjun Peng, Chao Zhang, Tong Xu, Xiangyu Zhao, Xian Wu, Yefeng Zheng, Yang Wang, and Enhong Chen. 2024. Large language models for generative information extraction: A survey.

Michihiro Yasunaga, Xinyun Chen, Yujia Li, Panupong Pasupat, Jure Leskovec, Percy Liang, Ed H. Chi, and Denny Zhou. 2024. Large language models as analogical reasoners.

Chenhan Yuan, Qianqian Xie, and Sophia Ananiadou. 2023. Zero-shot temporal relation extraction with ChatGPT. In *The 22nd Workshop on Biomedical Natural Language Processing and BioNLP Shared Tasks*, pages 92–102, Toronto, Canada. Association for Computational Linguistics.

Yuheng Zha, Yichi Yang, Ruichen Li, and Zhiting Hu. 2023. AlignScore: Evaluating factual consistency with a unified alignment function. In *Proceedings of the 61st Annual Meeting of the Association for Computational Linguistics (Volume 1: Long Papers)*, pages 11328–11348, Toronto, Canada. Association for Computational Linguistics.

Tianyi Zhang, Varsha Kishore, Felix Wu, Kilian Q. Weinberger, and Yoav Artzi. 2019. Bertscore: Evaluating text generation with bert.

Lightweight LLM Adaptation for Medical Summarisation: Roux-lette at PerAnsSumm Shared Task

Anson Antony and **Peter Vickers** and **Suzanne Wendelken**
Northeastern University, Boston, MA
{a.antony, p.vickers, s.wendelken}@northeastern.edu

Abstract

The PerAnsSumm Shared Task at CL4Health@NAACL 2025 focused on Perspective-Aware Summarization of Healthcare Q/A forums, requiring participants to extract and summarize spans based on predefined perspective categories. Our approach leveraged LLM-based zero-shot prompting enhanced by semantically-similar In-Context Learning (ICL) examples. Using Qwen-Turbo with 20 exemplar samples retrieved through NV-Embed-v2 embeddings, we achieved a mean score of 0.58 on Task A (span identification) and Task B (summarization) mean scores of 0.36 in Relevance and 0.28 in Factuality, finishing 12th on the final leaderboard. Notably, our system achieved higher precision in strict matching (0.20) than the top-performing system, demonstrating the effectiveness of our post-processing techniques. In this paper, we detail our ICL approach for adapting Large Language Models to Perspective-Aware Medical Summarization, analyze the improvements across development iterations, and finally discuss both the limitations of the current evaluation framework and future challenges in modeling this task. We release our code for reproducibility.[1]

1 Background

Healthcare community question-answering (CQA) forums serve as information resources for patients seeking accessible explanations outside clinical settings, caregivers navigating medical decisions, and curious individuals performing health research whilst avoiding stigma or costs tied to formal consultations (Beloborodov et al., 2013). However, the unstructured discussions typical of online forums often bury actionable insights under noise such as anecdotal claims, off-topic debates, or incorrect advice (Naik et al., 2024).

Perspective-aware summarization addresses this by categorizing forum responses into domains like suggestions ("ERCP procedures minimize scarring") or experiences ("Phantom pain persisted post-surgery")—enabling users to contrast evidence-based options with peer-endorsed narratives. Perspective-Aware Summarization [PAS] addresses this challenge by identifying and categorizing diverse viewpoints within healthcare forum responses. Unlike traditional summarization into a single version, PAS structures information into distinct perspective categories: 'Cause' (explanations of medical conditions), 'Suggestion' (recommended treatments or actions), 'Experience' (personal accounts), 'Question' (follow-up inquiries), and 'Information' (factual medical knowledge). The PerAnsSumm Shared Task at CL4Health@NAACL 2025 split this approach into two subtasks: Span Identification: Tagging text segments in answers aligning with five perspectives (Cause, Suggestion, Experience, Question, and Information). Summarization: Generating concise summaries for each of the five perspectives.

Building on the **P**erspective s**UM**marization d**A**taset (**PUMA**) dataset, a corpus of 3,167 annotated CQA threads annotated with 10K Human-authored Perspective-Aware Summarizations, the task encouraged models to move beyond single-view summaries common in traditional methods (Agarwal et al., 2025).

Our approach used the few-shot capabilities of Large Language Models to learn novel tasks with minimal exposure to labeled examples, including in the Medical Domain. Using just 20 exemplar samples from the training set, we are able to obtain a mean score of 0.58 on task A and 0.36 in Relevance and 0.29 in Factuality on Task B.

In this paper, we detail our approach, including releasing the code for all of our attempts. We then outline further approaches to improve performance. Finally, we discuss the difficulties of the task it-

[1] https://github.com/petervickers/Roux-PerAnsSumm

Proceedings of the Second Workshop on Patient-Oriented Language Processing (CL4Health), pages 389–397
May 4, 2025

self, including bias and ambiguity in community question-answer forums.

2 Related Work

Healthcare community question-answering (CQA) forums serve as information resources for patients seeking medical information outside clinical settings, though unstructured discussions often bury actionable insights beneath anecdotal claims and incorrect advice (Beloborodov et al., 2013; Naik et al., 2024). Traditional summarization approaches typically condense information into a single narrative, whereas perspective-aware summarization (PAS) addresses this limitation by categorizing content into distinct perspective types (cause, suggestion, experience, question, and information) (Agarwal et al., 2025).

Large Language Models (LLMs) have demonstrated strong performance on healthcare tasks in few-shot settings without domain-specific fine-tuning (Brown et al., 2020; Liu et al., 2023). Notably, Nori et al. (2023) showed that general-purpose models like GPT-4, when enhanced with appropriate prompting techniques (termed "MedPrompt"), can match or exceed specialized medical models. MedPrompt combines dynamic few-shot selection using k-nearest neighbors, self-generated chain-of-thought reasoning, and choice shuffling ensembles.

For span identification tasks similar to our work, named entity recognition (NER) approaches have been adapted for more complex extraction tasks. Tools like Spacy-LLM (Honnibal et al., 2020; Explosion AI, 2025) provide structured templates for guiding LLMs in entity extraction, which we adapt for perspective categories. However, perspective identification presents unique challenges compared to traditional NER: perspective spans often cross sentence boundaries, have ambiguous boundaries, and require subjective interpretation based on annotator guidelines.

Current limitations in perspective-aware systems include reliance on domain-specific training that limits generalization, handcrafted prompts requiring medical expertise, difficulties identifying perspective boundaries in conversational text, and challenges maintaining factual accuracy while generating perspective-specific summaries.

3 Methodology

Building on recent advances in LLM-based medical text processing, we introduce a novel approach to the PerAnsSumm Shared Task, which requires a two-stage cascaded pipeline: (1) Perspective-Aware Span Extraction followed by (2) Perspective-Aware Span Summarization (Agarwal et al., 2025). Our system addresses the key limitations identified in the related work through a specialized adaptation of the MedPrompt framework (Nori et al., 2023) for perspective-based tasks.

3.1 Overview of Our Approach

While MedPrompt has demonstrated state-of-the-art performance on medical multiple-choice questions (Nori et al., 2023), adapting it to open-ended perspective identification and summarization tasks presents several unique challenges. We preserve MedPrompt's core strength—dynamic few-shot selection—while modifying its architecture to accommodate span extraction rather than option selection. We term this MedPrompt Adaptation for Perspective Tasks.

Our system leverages semantic similarity to identify relevant examples from the training data. This addresses the scalability limitations of expert-dependent systems while maintaining the flexibility to adapt to diverse healthcare topics.

For both tasks (A) and (B), our system implements a four-component architecture:

1. **Dynamic In-Context Learning Sampling**: We extend MedPrompt's k-nearest neighbors approach to perspective-specific content by encoding samples using NVEmbed-v2. Our ICL strategy differs between the two subtasks:
    - For Task A (span extraction), we generate embeddings with the input question as the query and all questions in the training dataset as documents. For each test instance, we compute cosine similarity between its question embedding and all training question embeddings.
    - For Task B (summary generation), we generate embeddings at the perspective level, using the input spans as the query and retrieving training examples where the spans share the same perspective category. This focuses similarity computation on perspective-specific content rather than general question context.

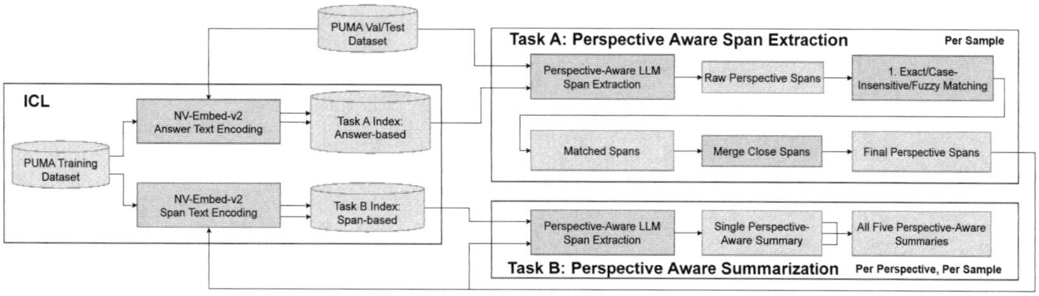

Figure 1: Data Flow Diagram of our Span Extraction and Summarization System

In both cases, we select the k=16 most similar examples based on these similarity scores to serve as in-context examples.

2. **Task-Specific Prompt Engineering**: We adapt Spacy-LLM's NER templates (Honnibal et al., 2020; Explosion AI, 2025) to the more complex task of perspective identification. Where traditional NER identifies concrete entities with clear boundaries, perspective identification requires identifying abstract categories that may span multiple sentences.

3. **Annotator Bias Replication**: We include explicit instructions directing the model to mirror the subjective biases present in the In Context Learning annotations.

4. **Span Post-Processing**: We implement a three-stage cascading alignment strategy to overcome LLMs' known limitations in returning precise character indices (Wu et al., 2023). This approach significantly improves upon the exact matching typically used in NER systems, which fails to account for the flexibility needed in perspective boundary identification.

To ensure consistent output formatting across both subsystems, we enforce JSON output structure by constraining the first token of the model's response to be '{', effectively force-decoding the beginning of a JSON object.

As Figure 1 shows, our system consists of three high-level components: Perspective Aware Span Extraction, Perspective Aware Summarization, and In-Context Learning. In-Context Learning (left) leverages the PUMA training dataset through dual NV-Embed-v2 encoding pathways—one optimized for Task A using answer-based text encoding and another for Task B using span-based encoding. This creates semantic indices for efficient retrieval of relevant examples during inference. Task A (upper right) performs perspective-aware span extraction through a three-stage cascading alignment process (exact, case-insensitive, and fuzzy matching), followed by a span merging step to produce cohesive perspective-specific text segments. These extracted spans then feed into Task B (lower right), which generates perspective-aware summaries organized across the five predefined categories (cause, suggestion, experience, question, and information).

For Task A, we found no advantage in perspective-level span extraction. For Task B, performance improved with perspective-specific summarization, so we generate summaries separately for each perspective and merge the results.

This modular design allowed us to conduct controlled experiments, isolating the impact of different embedding models and varying quantities of in-context examples on system performance.

3.2 Evaluation Metrics

The PerAnsSumm Shared Task evaluation framework comprises distinct metrics for both span identification (Task A) and perspective-aware summarization (Task B). Of note, the perspective-aware summarization was dependent on the output of the span identification model. Gold standard span inputs were not provided for Task B. Metrics compared between the generated outputs and the max-voted labels from the test split of the PerAnsSumm/PUMA dataset.

Task A: Span Identification Metrics

1. Macro-averaged F1 score: Evaluates performance across all five perspective categories (cause, suggestion, experience, question, and information), mitigating class imbalance effects.

2. Strict Matching: Measures exact correspondence between predicted and ground-truth

spans, considering both boundaries and classification labels.

3. Proportional Matching: Allows partial credit for spans that overlap with the ground truth, accounting for minor discrepancies in extraction.

"Ground-truth" reference spans were from the task/PUMA dataset annotations, which were manually labeled for each perspective and reflected annotation bias discussed elsewhere.

Task B: Perspective-aware Summarization Metrics

1. ROUGE (R-1, R-2, R-L) (Lin, 2004): Measures unigram overlap (R-1), bigram overlap (R-2), and longest common subsequence (R-L) between generated summaries and reference summaries.

2. BLEU (Papineni et al., 2002): Computes n-gram precision against reference summaries, commonly used in machine translation but adapted here for summarization.

3. METEOR (Banerjee and Lavie, 2005): Extends BLEU by incorporating synonymy and stemming, better capturing semantic equivalence.

4. BERTScore (Zhang et al., 2020): Uses contextualized BERT embeddings to compare generated and reference summaries at the semantic level, overcoming limitations of n-gram-based metrics.

Additionally, "factuality" assessments were included to evaluate the alignment of generated summaries with the source content:

1. AlignScore (Zha et al., 2023): attempts to measures factual consistency using a unified alignment function to compare source text and generated summaries.

2. SummaC (Laban et al., 2022): attempts to detect contradictions and hallucinations in summarization by leveraging natural language inference (NLI) models and sentence-level document-summary pairs.

Reference summaries were the annotator-provided summaries from the task/PUMA dataset, which were written post-hoc based on extracted spans. As with Task A, these summaries inherit the dataset's biases and limitations, influencing how models were evaluated.

4 Experimental Setup

We developed our approach over four system variants (summarized in Table 1), each representing incremental improvements to our initial baseline implementation. All systems were evaluated on the PerAnsSumm Shared Task.

4.1 System Implementation Details

Our implementation leveraged the core MedPrompt architecture with targeted adaptations for perspective-aware tasks:

Model Selection: We initially employed OpenAI's GPT-4o-mini model (et al., 2024) (versions v1-v2) before transitioning to Qwen/Qwen-turbo (Qwen et al., 2025) (versions v3-v4) based on preliminary performance evaluations.

Dynamic In-Context Learning: For version v1, we used zero-shot prompting without in-context learning examples. Version v2 incorporated 5 in-context examples selected using OpenAI's text-embedding-3-small model to match samples, while versions v3-v4 employed NVIDIA's NV-Embed-v2 (Lee et al., 2025) with retrieval sets of 5 and 20 examples, respectively. This progression allowed us to evaluate the impact of both example quantity and embedding quality on performance.

Post-processing Pipeline: All systems employed our three-stage cascading alignment strategy for span reconciliation, with refinements in later versions to address edge cases identified during development:

1. **Exact substring matching**: First attempting verbatim matches using Python's native string.find() function, with extension to word boundaries for cleaner spans

2. **Case-insensitive matching**: If exact matching failed, converting both source and target texts to lowercase before applying the find() function again

3. **Sentence-level fuzzy matching**: For spans still unmatched, breaking the text into sentences and applying thefuzz library's ratio() algorithm to find the best matching sentence, with early termination at 95% similarity

System	Model	K	Embedder	Prompts		Scores	
				Task A (Span Extraction)	Task B (Summarization)	A	B
v1	openai/gpt-4o-mini	None	None	Span-Prompt-V1	Summ-Prompt-V1	0.58	0.30
v2	openai/gpt-4o-mini	5	OpenAI text-embedding-3-small	Span-Prompt-V2	Summ-Prompt-V2	0.58	0.33
v3	qwen/qwen-turbo	5	NVIDIA NV-Embed-v2	Span-Prompt-V3	Summ-Prompt-V3	0.58	0.35
v4	qwen/qwen-turbo	20	NVIDIA NV-Embed-v2	Span-Prompt-V4	Summ-Prompt-V4	0.58	0.36

Table 1: System configurations and performance comparison. K indicates the number of in-context learning examples, Embedder refers to the model used for retrieving similar examples. Scores represent macro-averaged metrics: Task A scores show span alignment accuracy (Avg. column from Table 2), Task B scores show relevance performance (Relevance Avg. from Table 3).

The fuzzy matching threshold ($\theta = 0.7$) served as a quality filter, with spans scoring below this threshold being discarded. Our implementation also included specialized handling for overlapping spans through the, which merged spans of the same perspective category that were within 5 characters of each other.

4.2 Experimental Configurations

Table 1 summarizes our four experimental configurations. The progression from v1 to v4 represents an evolution from simple baseline approaches to sophisticated in-context learning with optimized similarity matching:

Key experimental parameters were:

- **Similar Example Selection:** For ICL-based systems (v2-v4), we selected examples from the training corpus based on cosine similarity between embedding vectors. Version v4's expanded number of ICL samples (K=20) allowed for more diverse exemplars.
- **Fuzzy Matching Threshold:** We empirically determined a similarity threshold of $\theta = 0.7$ for accepting predicted spans, with scores below this threshold triggering rejection during post-processing.

4.3 Evaluation Process

Systems were evaluated using the official PerAnsSumm metrics as described in Section 3.2. We submitted all versions, v1-v4, to the shared task evaluation server, with v4 representing our best-performing configuration. The detailed prompt specifications for all system variants are provided in Appendix A.

5 Results

Tables 2 and 3 present the performance of our four system variants on Tasks A and B, respectively. Our final system (v4) achieved an average score of 0.58 on Task A (span identification) and 0.36 on Task B's relevance metrics with 0.28 on factuality metrics, placing our team 13th out of 23 teams overall in the shared task.

For Task A, all four of our system variants achieved consistent performance with a macro F1 classification score of 0.81, strict matching F1 of 0.22, and proportional matching F1 of 0.64. Our overall Task A average of 0.58 placed us within 3.4% of the top-performing system's score of 0.60.

For Task B, we observed progressive improvements across our system versions. The relevance metrics improved from 0.30 in v1 to 0.36 in v4 (+20%), while factuality scores declined slightly from 0.29 to 0.28. The gap between our system and the top-performing system was more pronounced in Task B, with our relevance average trailing the leader by 14% relative.

Each system iteration brought incremental improvements: v1 (zero-shot GPT-4o-mini) achieved 0.30 on Task B relevance, v2 (GPT-4o-mini with ICL) improved to 0.33 (+10%), v3 (Qwen-Turbo with NV-Embed-v2) reached 0.35 (+6%), and v4 (expanded to 20 examples) achieved our best score of 0.36 (+3%).

Analysis of the overall leaderboard reveals that the top 13 teams were tightly clustered, with scores ranging from 0.457 to 0.400, indicating that minor implementation differences had significant impact on final rankings.

6 Discussion

6.1 Task A Performance Analysis

Despite transitions from GPT-4o-mini (v1-v2) to Qwen-Turbo (v3-v4) as our base LLM, our Task A performance remained remarkably consistent. This stability suggests that our model effectively learned to distinguish between the five perspective categories regardless of the specific implementation details or embedding model used for in-context

Submission	CLASSIFICATION Macro F1	Weighted F1	STRICT MATCHING P	R	F1	PROPORTIONAL MATCHING P	R	F1	Avg.
Roux-lette 1	0.81	0.87	0.20	0.22	0.21	0.59	0.73	0.64	0.58
Roux-lette 2	0.81	0.87	0.20	0.23	0.22	0.57	0.72	0.64	0.58
Roux-lette 3	0.81	0.87	0.20	0.23	0.22	0.57	0.72	0.64	0.58
Roux-lette 4	0.81	0.87	0.20	0.23	0.22	0.57	0.72	0.64	0.58
Mean Gradient	0.00	0.00	0.00	0.00	0.00	0.00	0.00	0.00	0.00
Overall Improvement	0.00	0.00	0.00	0.00	0.00	-0.02	-0.01	0.00	0.00
Leader (WisPerMed)	0.88	0.92	0.17	0.23	0.20	0.62	0.74	0.68	0.60
delta (Roux - WisPerMed)	-0.07	-0.05	0.03	0.00	0.02	-0.05	-0.02	-0.04	-0.02

Table 2: Task A Results

Submission	RELEVANCE ROUGE1	ROUGE2	ROUGEL	BERTScore	METEOR	BLEU	Avg.	FACTUALITY AlignScore	SummaC	Avg.
Roux-lette 1	0.31	0.09	0.27	0.80	0.27	0.07	0.30	0.37	0.22	0.29
Roux-lette 2	0.34	0.12	0.30	0.82	0.31	0.08	0.33	0.36	0.22	0.29
Roux-lette 3	0.37	0.15	0.33	0.83	0.33	0.11	0.35	0.31	0.23	0.27
Roux-lette 4	0.38	0.17	0.34	0.83	0.33	0.12	0.36	0.32	0.23	0.28
Mean Gradient	0.02	0.03	0.02	0.01	0.02	0.02	0.02	-0.02	0.00	-0.01
Overall Improvement	0.07	0.07	0.07	0.03	0.06	0.06	0.06	-0.05	0.01	-0.02
Leader (WisPerMed)	0.45	0.22	0.41	0.90	0.41	0.13	0.42	0.41	0.30	0.35
delta (Roux - WisPerMed)	-0.07	-0.05	-0.07	-0.07	-0.08	-0.01	-0.06	-0.09	-0.07	-0.08

Table 3: Task B Results

example retrieval.

Notably, our precision in strict matching (0.20) exceeded the top-performing system (WisPerMed's 0.17), indicating that our cascading alignment strategy with fuzzy matching was particularly effective at identifying precise span boundaries. While our recall matched the leader (0.23), our overall strict matching F1 (0.22) slightly outperformed the leader's 0.20, demonstrating the effectiveness of our three-stage cascading alignment strategy with fuzzy matching threshold ($\theta = 0.7$).

The small performance gap between participating teams in Task A is striking, with the top 13 systems achieving scores within a narrow range (0.58-0.62). This clustering suggests that the task may have reached a performance ceiling with current LLM-based methods, possibly due to inherent ambiguities in perspective boundary identification.

6.2 Task B Performance Analysis

The clear progression in our Task B performance correlates directly with improvements in our LLM and embedding models. The significant gains in ROUGE-2 (0.09 to 0.17, +89%) and BLEU (0.07 to 0.12, +71%) indicate better capture of n-gram sequences and improved alignment with reference summaries as we enhanced our embedding model quality and expanded ICL example counts.

The inverse relationship between relevance and factuality scores raises important questions about evaluation metrics in perspective-aware summarization. As our systems better matched reference summaries (higher relevance), they simultaneously drifted from factual alignment with source content (lower factuality). This trade-off, particularly evident in the drop in AlignScore (0.37 to 0.32, -13.5%), suggests that human annotators may have introduced interpretations or simplifications in their summaries that deviated from the original forum content.

The leaderboard reveals a significant gap in Task B performance between the top 5 teams (relevance scores of 0.40-0.42) and the remainder of the field (scores below 0.39), suggesting that certain architectural approaches may have offered substantial advantages in summarization quality.

6.3 Effectiveness of In-Context Learning Approaches

The most substantial improvements in our systems came from the transition from zero-shot to in-context learning with semantically similar examples. The progression from v1 to v4 underscores the importance of both the quality of embedding models for finding related samples and the quantity of in-context examples in achieving optimal performance for perspective-aware summarization.

The diminishing returns observed when increasing from 5 to 20 examples (+6% vs. +3% improvement) suggests that example quality may be more important than quantity beyond a certain threshold. This finding aligns with recent research showing that carefully selected few-shot examples often outperform larger random samples in in-context learning scenarios.

6.4 Bias Learning vs. Medical Understanding

We speculate that the structure of Task A encouraged models to imitate annotator biases rather than developing genuine understanding of medical discourse. Our experiment with explicit bias instruction did not significantly improve results, suggesting that the bias patterns were either inconsistent or difficult for the model to internalize.

This observation is supported by our Task A performance remaining stable across different LLMs and embedding models, indicating that the task primarily measures how effectively systems can approximate existing annotation patterns rather than demonstrating true innovation in perspective identification. The tight clustering of team performances on the leaderboard further supports this hypothesis.

Examining the leaderboard, we observe that the top-performing systems achieved their advantage primarily through Task B (summarization) rather than Task A (span identification), where scores were more tightly clustered. This suggests that while span identification may have reached a performance ceiling, summarization quality remains an area where significant improvements are possible.

7 Conclusion

In this work, we explored an LLM-driven approach to perspective-aware summarization in the PerAnsSumm shared task, leveraging a **lightweight, zero-shot ICL methodology that requires no fine-tuning** and can be readily applied to any LLM. Our approach used semantic similarity-guided in-context learning with minimal example retrieval, demonstrating the efficacy of model-agnostic techniques for structured medical text understanding.

For Task A, we used Qwen-Turbo guided by 20 semantically similar training samples retrieved using NV-Embed-v2 embeddings, achieving a mean score of 0.58 and notably exceeding the top-performing system in strict matching precision (0.20 vs. 0.17). Our three-stage cascading alignment strategy (exact, case-insensitive, and fuzzy matching with $\theta = 0.7$) proved effective for capturing perspective boundaries without the need for task-specific training.

For Task B, we extended this model-agnostic methodology to summarization, incrementally improving relevance metrics from 0.30 (zero-shot) to 0.36 (20 examples), while maintaining factuality scores around 0.28. Our experimental progression showed embeddings quality and example selection significantly impact performance, with the transition from zero-shot to ICL (v1→v2: +10%) yielding greater improvements than embedding upgrades (v2→v3: +6%) or increasing example count (v3→v4: +3%).

Our results suggest potential limitations in the current task framework. The narrow performance range across teams in Task A (0.58-0.62) may indicate a ceiling effect possibly attributable to inherent ambiguities in perspective boundary identification. The observed inverse relationship between relevance and factuality metrics raises questions about potential annotation biases or simplifications in reference summaries. Additionally, the patterns we observed suggest the task design may encourage models to replicate annotation patterns rather than develop genuine medical understanding.

The primary advantage of our approach lies in its **simplicity and transferability across models**, requiring only basic API access to any capable LLM rather than expensive fine-tuning or domain-specific architectures. Future perspective-aware summarization tasks would benefit from more clinically relevant, open-ended evaluation frameworks that foster methodological innovation with real-world impact rather than alignment with pre-existing annotation patterns.

8 Limitations

Our approach faces several limitations.

First, our models learn to replicate annotator biases rather than develop true medical understanding, evidenced by the tight clustering of Task A scores (0.58-0.62) across teams. Second, the diminishing returns when scaling from 5 to 20 examples (10% → 6% → 3% improvement) suggests fundamental constraints in example-based learning without domain-specific training. Third, the inverse relationship between relevance and factuality scores indicates that optimizing for reference similarity may reduce source content faithfulness.

Due to time and computational constraints, we were unable to exhaustively test all possible values for the fuzzy matching threshold (θ), optimal number of ICL samples, or evaluate across a broad spectrum of available LLM models.

Finally, and most importantly, our system lacks mechanisms to verify medical accuracy or distinguish between credible and non-credible information in healthcare forums. We highlight broader concerns about using AI for medical applications, which carries documented risks and should never replace physician guidance.

Future work should focus on integrating domain-specific medical knowledge, developing evaluation frameworks better aligned with clinical utility, and establishing robust fact-verification mechanisms for healthcare content.

References

Siddhant Agarwal, Md Shad Akhtar, and Shweta Yadav. 2025. Overview of the peranssumm 2025 shared task on perspective-aware healthcare answer summarization. In *Proceedings of the Second Workshop on Patient-Oriented Language Processing (CL4Health) @ NAACL 2025*, Albuquerque, USA. Association for Computational Linguistics.

Satanjeev Banerjee and Alon Lavie. 2005. METEOR: An automatic metric for MT evaluation with improved correlation with human judgments. In *Proceedings of the ACL Workshop on Intrinsic and Extrinsic Evaluation Measures for Machine Translation and/or Summarization*, pages 65–72, Ann Arbor, Michigan. Association for Computational Linguistics.

Alexander Beloborodov, Artem Kuznetsov, and Pavel Braslavski. 2013. Characterizing health-related community question answering. In *Advances in Information Retrieval*, pages 680–683, Berlin, Heidelberg. Springer Berlin Heidelberg.

Tom B. Brown, Benjamin Mann, Nick Ryder, Melanie Subbiah, Jared Kaplan, Prafulla Dhariwal, Arvind Neelakantan, Pranav Shyam, Girish Sastry, Amanda Askell, Sandhini Agarwal, Ariel Herbert-Voss, Gretchen Krueger, Tom Henighan, Rewon Child, Aditya Ramesh, Daniel M. Ziegler, Jeffrey Wu, Clemens Winter, Christopher Hesse, Mark Chen, Eric Sigler, Mateusz Litwin, Scott Gray, Benjamin Chess, Jack Clark, Christopher Berner, Sam McCandlish, Alec Radford, Ilya Sutskever, and Dario Amodei. 2020. Language models are few-shot learners. *Preprint*, arXiv:2005.14165.

OpenAI et al. 2024. Gpt-4o system card. *Preprint*, arXiv:2410.21276.

Explosion AI. 2025. spacy-llm: Structured NLP with LLMs.

Matthew Honnibal, Ines Montani, Sofie Van Landeghem, and Adriane Boyd. 2020. spacy: Industrial-strength natural language processing in python. *spaCy*.

Philippe Laban, Tobias Schnabel, Paul N. Bennett, and Marti A. Hearst. 2022. SummaC: Re-visiting NLI-based models for inconsistency detection in summarization. *Transactions of the Association for Computational Linguistics*, 10:163–177.

Chankyu Lee, Rajarshi Roy, Mengyao Xu, Jonathan Raiman, Mohammad Shoeybi, Bryan Catanzaro, and Wei Ping. 2025. Nv-embed: Improved techniques for training llms as generalist embedding models. *Preprint*, arXiv:2405.17428.

Chin-Yew Lin. 2004. ROUGE: A package for automatic evaluation of summaries. In *Text Summarization Branches Out*, pages 74–81, Barcelona, Spain. Association for Computational Linguistics.

Xin Liu, Daniel McDuff, Geza Kovacs, Isaac Galatzer-Levy, Jacob Sunshine, Jiening Zhan, Ming-Zher Poh, Shun Liao, Paolo Di Achille, and Shwetak Patel. 2023. Large language models are few-shot health learners. *Preprint*, arXiv:2305.15525.

Gauri Naik, Sharad Chandakacherla, Shweta Yadav, and Md Shad Akhtar. 2024. No perspective, no perception!! perspective-aware healthcare answer summarization. In *Findings of the Association for Computational Linguistics: ACL 2024*, pages 15919–15932, Bangkok, Thailand. Association for Computational Linguistics.

Harsha Nori, Yin Tat Lee, Sheng Zhang, Dean Carignan, Richard Edgar, Nicolo Fusi, Nicholas King, Jonathan Larson, Yuanzhi Li, Weishung Liu, Renqian Luo, Scott Mayer McKinney, Robert Osazuwa Ness, Hoifung Poon, Tao Qin, Naoto Usuyama, Chris White, and Eric Horvitz. 2023. Can generalist foundation models outcompete special-purpose tuning? case study in medicine. *Preprint*, arXiv:2311.16452.

Kishore Papineni, Salim Roukos, Todd Ward, and Wei-Jing Zhu. 2002. Bleu: a method for automatic evaluation of machine translation. In *Proceedings of the 40th Annual Meeting of the Association for Computational Linguistics*, pages 311–318, Philadelphia, Pennsylvania, USA. Association for Computational Linguistics.

Qwen, :, An Yang, Baosong Yang, Beichen Zhang, Binyuan Hui, Bo Zheng, Bowen Yu, Chengyuan Li, Dayiheng Liu, Fei Huang, Haoran Wei, Huan Lin, Jian Yang, Jianhong Tu, Jianwei Zhang, Jianxin Yang, Jiaxi Yang, Jingren Zhou, Junyang Lin, Kai Dang, Keming Lu, Keqin Bao, Kexin Yang, Le Yu, Mei Li, Mingfeng Xue, Pei Zhang, Qin Zhu, Rui Men, Runji Lin, Tianhao Li, Tianyi Tang, Tingyu Xia, Xingzhang Ren, Xuancheng Ren, Yang Fan, Yang Su, Yichang Zhang, Yu Wan, Yuqiong Liu, Zeyu Cui, Zhenru

Zhang, and Zihan Qiu. 2025. Qwen2.5 technical report. *Preprint*, arXiv:2412.15115.

Hongqiu Wu, Shaohua Zhang, Yuchen Zhang, and Hai Zhao. 2023. Rethinking masked language modeling for Chinese spelling correction. In *Proceedings of the 61st Annual Meeting of the Association for Computational Linguistics (Volume 1: Long Papers)*, pages 10743–10756, Toronto, Canada. Association for Computational Linguistics.

Yuheng Zha, Yichi Yang, Ruichen Li, and Zhiting Hu. 2023. AlignScore: Evaluating Factual Consistency with A Unified Alignment Function. In *Proceedings of the 61st Annual Meeting of the Association for Computational Linguistics (Volume 1: Long Papers)*, pages 11328–11348, Toronto, Canada. Association for Computational Linguistics.

Tianyi Zhang, Varsha Kishore, Felix Wu, Kilian Q. Weinberger, and Yoav Artzi. 2020. Bertscore: Evaluating text generation with bert. *Preprint*, arXiv:1904.09675.

A Appendix A: Prompts

A.1 Task A: Span Extraction Prompts

- **Baseline Prompt (v1):**
  - Core instruction: *Analyze text and identify spans expressing different perspectives (CAUSE, SUGGESTION, EXPERIENCE, QUESTION, INFORMATION)*
  - Added sliding window matching in v2 for phrase boundary detection
  - Integrated overlap handling in v3 with span merging logic
  - JSON structure requirements:
    * Extract complete phrases (under 100 characters)
    * Prefer full sentences where possible
    * Mandatory "text" field in JSON objects
- **In-Context Learning Prompt (v2):** *Enhanced version with example-based guidance:*
  - Detailed perspective definitions:
    * EXPERIENCE: First-hand accounts
    * INFORMATION: Factual data
    * CAUSE: Explanatory reasoning
    * SUGGESTION: Recommendations
    * QUESTION: Information requests
  - Example JSON format:

```
{
    "EXPERIENCE": [{"text": "..."}],
    "INFORMATION": [{"text": "..."}]
}
```

  - Includes 5 retrieved examples using OpenAI embeddings
- **NV-Embed-v2 Prompt (v3):** *Optimized version with:*
  - NVIDIA NV-Embed-v2 for example retrieval
  - OpenRouter API integration
  - Upgraded LLM backend
  - Maintains 5-example context (K=5)
- **Scaled ICL Prompt (v4):** *Enhanced capacity version:*
  - Expands context window to 20 examples (K=20)
  - Retains NV-Embed-v2 retrieval system
  - Optimized for long-context processing

A.2 Task B: Summarization Prompts

- **Merged Baseline Prompt (v1):**
  - Core template: *Summarize {perspective} points about "question"*
  - Requirements:
    * 2-3 sentence summaries
    * Maintain factual accuracy
    * Direct answer alignment
- **ICL Summarization (v2):** *Example-enhanced version:*
  - Incorporates retrieved examples
  - Structured template: *"Analyze text and extract perspective summaries for {perspective}"*
  - Processes span inputs:
    * `{span 1 text}`
    * `{span 2 text}`
- **NV-Embed-v2 Summarization (v3):** *Optimized architecture:*
  - NV-Embed-v2 retrieval system
  - Human-aligned prompt structure
  - Maintains K=5 examples
- **Scaled Summarization (v4):** *Expanded context version:*
  - Processes 20 examples (K=20)
  - Enhanced coherence through extended context
  - Maintains NV-Embed-v2 retrieval

AICOE at PerAnsSumm 2025: An Ensemble of Large Language Models for Perspective-Aware Healthcare Answer Summarization

Rakshith R, Mohammad Sameer Khan, Ankush Chopra
AICOE, Tredence
Bengaluru, India
{rakshith.r, mohammed.sameerkhan, ankush.chopra}@tredence.com

Abstract

The PerAnsSumm 2024 shared task at the CL4Health workshop focuses on generating structured, perspective-specific summaries to enhance the accessibility of health-related information. Given a Healthcare community QA dataset containing a question, context, and multiple user-answers, the task involves identifying relevant perspective categories, extracting spans from these perspectives, and generating concise summaries for the extracted spans. We fine-tuned open-source models such as Llama-3.2 3B, Llama-3.1 8B, and Gemma-2 9B, while also experimenting with proprietary models including GPT-4o, o1, Gemini-1.5 Pro, and Gemini-2 Flash Experimental using few-shot prompting. Our best-performing approach leveraged an ensemble strategy, combining span outputs from o1 (CoT) and Gemini-2 Flash Experimental. For overlapping perspectives, we prioritized Gemini. The final spans were summarized using Gemini, preserving the higher classification accuracy of o1 while leveraging Gemini's superior span extraction and summarization capabilities. This hybrid method secured fourth place on the final leaderboard among 100 participants and 206 submissions.

1 Introduction

In recent years the widespread adoption of social media has sprung up various community question answer forums especially in the medical domain. Users often rely on others experience or suggestions. They post a query along with information as context and multiple users can answer them. The answers vary in multiple aspects depending on the user's question, the experience of the person replying etc. Hence traditional summarization techniques are not particularly useful since they combine everything. User's answers include multiple perspectives and the aim of this shared task (Agarwal et al., 2025) is to identify them and form more meaningful summaries for users to make more informed healthcare decisions. The perspectives are 'Cause', 'Suggestion', 'Experience', 'Question', and 'Information'. An example is displayed in Figure 1. The recent rise of Large Language Models enable much more accurate perspective identification and summarization than traditional transformers. We leverage these LLM's both proprietary and open source for the task. We finetune open-source smaller models like Llama 3b, 8b (Grattafiori et al., 2024) and Gemma 9b (Team et al., 2024) for the task. We observe that finetuning significantly improves the base models performance on the task and even outperforms models like GPT 4o (8 shot prompt) (OpenAI et al., 2024).

2 Related Work

Span prediction and Abstractive Summarization are popular tasks in the ML domain for a long time. Transformer models have been used ever since the Transformer paper (Vaswani et al., 2023). Models like BERT (Devlin et al., 2019), Roberta (Liu et al., 2019) and it's variants were the best performing models of their time. This was soon followed by pre-trained language models (PLMs) like BART (Lewis et al., 2019), T5 (Raffel et al., 2023), PEGASUS (Zhang et al., 2020) etc.which achieved state of the art results in their time.

In the medical domain these models were trained on biomedical corpora like PubMed and MIMIC-III giving to rise of domain specific pre-trained language models (PLMs) like BioBERT (Lee et al., 2019), BioBART (Yuan et al., 2022), and clinicalBERT (Huang et al., 2020) which did much better in medical domain tasks. There are efforts in summarizing diverse types of content, including biomedical literature using these models like (Soleimani et al., 2022), consumer healthcare questions ((Yadav et al., 2022); (Yadav and Caragea, 2022); (Yadav et al., 2023); (Savery et al., 2020)),

Proceedings of the Second Workshop on Patient-Oriented Language Processing (CL4Health), pages 398–408
May 4, 2025

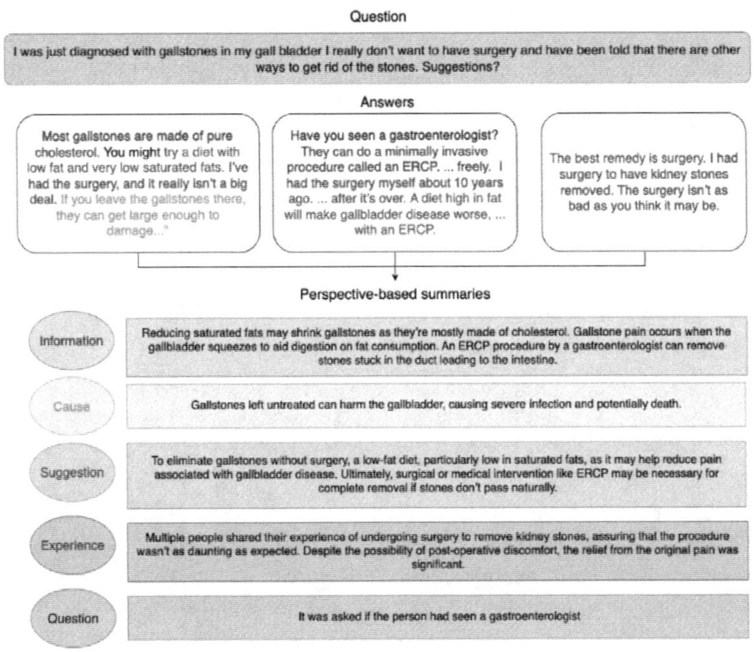

Figure 1: Task A: Span Prediction (highlighted spans), Task B: Summary Generation. (Source - (Agarwal et al., 2025))

and medical notes (Hsu et al., 2020).

(Fabbri et al., 2021) work on a QA dataset with sentence-level spans with query-focused multi-perspective abstractive summarization. (Joshi et al., 2020a) and (Michalopoulos et al., 2022) accomplish the same by exploiting local and global features of the text. CTRLsum (He et al., 2020) introduces a novel framework for controllable summarization that allows interaction during inference through textual input. CQASumm (Chowdhury and Chakraborty, 2018) highlight the issues with high-variance, opinion-based CQA data often having contradicting opinion and the challenges of applying Multi document summarization (MDS) on it.

In AnswerSumm (Fabbri et al., 2022), they use a model to extract sentences similar to the query. SpanBERT (Joshi et al., 2020b) extends BERT with a pre-training method, to better represent and predict spans of text. (Abaho et al., 2021) use both word-level and sentence-level attention to jointly perform span detection and outcome classification in the medical domain.

In this task the spans need not be complete sentences but rather can be phrases as well. The organizers of this task have annotated the dataset and proposed a prompt-driven control-label summarization model for the same.

3 Dataset

The dataset (Naik et al., 2024) used for the PerAnsSumm 2025 shared task consists of health-related questions and user-generated answers annotated with perspective categories. Each sample is a community Question-Answer thread (CQA) which includes a health-related question, an optional context providing additional background information, and a set of user answers. Specific spans within the answers are labeled according to one of five perspectives: Cause, Suggestion, Experience, Question, and Information. Additionally, each sample includes summaries that concisely represent the extracted spans for each perspective.

3.1 Dataset Statistics

The dataset is divided into training and validation sets, comprising 2,236 and 959 samples, respectively. During our Exploratory Data Analysis (EDA), we found that 4 samples in the training set and 3 samples in the validation set were incorrectly annotated. The spans in these samples were selected from the user context instead of the user answers, which goes against the task instructions. As a result, we discarded these samples, leaving us with 2,232 training samples and 956 validation samples. Among the validation samples, we randomly selected 300 samples as a test set to evaluate both open-source LLMs and proprietary models. The remaining 656 samples were used as a validation set for fine-tuning open-source LLMs.

Context availability varies, with 821 training samples containing context and 1,415 without it, while in the validation set, 350 samples include context and 606 do not include context.

The distribution of perspective categories reveals that Information and Suggestion are the most prevalent, whereas Cause and Question are less frequent. The complete label distribution across training and validation sets is illustrated in Figure 2.

A similar trend is observed in span counts, where Information spans appear most frequently, followed by Suggestion, Experience, Cause, and Question. The full span distribution can be seen in Figure 3.

4 Experimentations

4.1 Span Prediction

Span prediction involves identifying and classifying relevant spans within user responses based on predefined perspective categories. The models were evaluated using multiple performance metrics such as Classification Macro F1, Classification Weighted F1, Strict Matching Precision, Strict Matching Recall, Strict Matching F1, Proportional Matching Precision, Proportional Matching Recall, and Proportional Matching F1, ensuring a comprehensive assessment of both classification accuracy and span alignment.

4.1.1 LLM Fine-tuning

To effectively predict spans corresponding to different perspectives, we fine-tuned multiple open-source large language models, including Llama-3.1 8B (base model), Llama-3.2 3B (base model), and Gemma-2 9B (4-bit quantized model). The models were trained on the training set with Unsloth (Daniel Han and team, 2023) using zero-shot fine-tuning for 3 epochs with a learning rate of 2e-4 and validated on the validation set. The models were evaluated on the test set.

Among all models, the Llama-3.1 8B (base model) achieved the highest scores in classification, with a Classification Macro F1 of 0.7890, Classification Weighted F1 of 0.8360, and Strict Matching F1 of 0.2421. Meanwhile, the Gemma-2 9B (4-bit quantized model) outperformed others in proportional matching, achieving the highest Proportional Matching F1 score of 0.6652. A detailed comparison of these results is presented in Table 1.

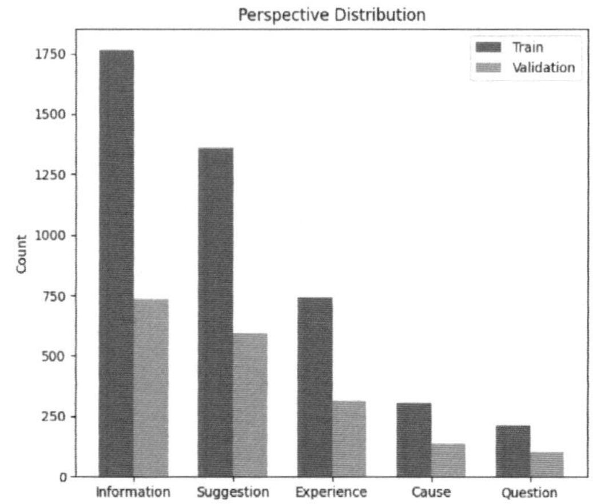

Figure 2: This figure shows the distribution of perspective categories in the training and validation datasets.

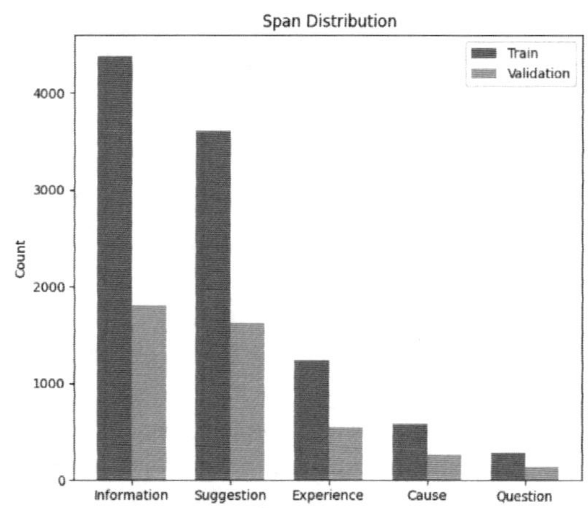

Figure 3: This figure shows the distribution of spans across perspective categories in the training and validation datasets. Each perspective category may contain one or more spans.

4.1.2 Proprietary Models

In addition to fine-tuning open-source models, we experimented with proprietary models, including GPT-4o, o1, Gemini-1.5 Pro, and Gemini-2 Flash Experimental. These models were evaluated using few-shot prompting, where we provided eight examples as context. We carefully selected these eight examples to mirror the label distribution in the training set. Two examples contained only one perspective, while one example included all five perspectives. The remaining examples featured

Metric	L3.1-8B	L3.2-3B	G2-9B (4b)	o1	o1 (50)	FL	FL (50)	o1 (CoT)	4o	Pro
C M F1	**0.7890**	0.6759	0.7102	0.7624	0.7601	0.7317	0.7102	0.7760	0.6770	0.7279
C W F1	0.8360	0.7545	0.8135	0.8404	0.8315	0.8305	0.8213	**0.8464**	0.7443	0.8258
S M P	**0.2734**	0.0958	0.0972	0.0611	0.0553	0.0627	0.0616	0.0432	0.0506	0.0618
S M R	**0.2172**	0.0758	0.0961	0.1114	0.0657	0.1118	0.1097	0.0568	0.0613	0.1089
S M F1	**0.2421**	0.0846	0.0967	0.0789	0.0601	0.0804	0.0789	0.0491	0.0554	0.0789
P M P	**0.7384**	0.6623	0.6479	0.6150	0.5903	0.6856	0.6759	0.6030	0.6615	0.6856
P M R	0.5436	0.5012	**0.6833**	0.6582	0.5358	0.6405	0.6674	0.5117	0.4474	0.6727
P M F1	0.6262	0.5706	0.6652	0.6359	0.5617	0.6623	0.6716	0.5536	0.5338	**0.6791**

Table 1: Performance comparison of various open-sourced and proprietary large language models for the span prediction task on the 300-sample holdout test set. **C M F1** and **C W F1** correspond to **Classification Macro F1** and **Classification Weighted F1**. **S M P**, **S M R**, and **S M F1** correspond to **Strict Matching Precision**, **Strict Matching Recall**, and **Strict Matching F1-score**. **P M P**, **P M R**, and **P M F1** correspond to **Proportional Matching Precision**, **Proportional Matching Recall**, and **Proportional Matching F1-score**. **L3.1-8B**, **L3.2-3B**, **G2-9B (4b)**, **o1 (50)**, **FL (50)**, **o1 (CoT)**, **4o**, and **Pro** represent **Llama-3.1 8B**, **Llama-3.2 3B**, **Gemma-2 9B (4-bit)**, **o1 (50-shot)**, **Gemini-2 Flash Experimental (50-shot)**, **o1 (Chain-of-Thought Prompting)**, **GPT-4o**, and **Gemini-1.5 Pro** respectively.

Metric	G2-9B (4b)	L3.1-8	4o	o1	o1 (CoT)	Pro	FL
Rouge-1	**0.5457**	0.4812	0.4911	0.4976	0.3380	0.5020	0.5323
Rouge-2	**0.2861**	0.2218	0.2337	0.2292	0.1160	0.2339	0.2713
Rouge-L	**0.4909**	0.4187	0.4211	0.4239	0.2810	0.4424	0.4765
BERTScore	0.9099	0.8611	0.8714	0.8972	0.8230	0.9064	**0.9103**
METEOR	**0.4754**	0.4529	0.4227	0.4176	0.2530	0.4154	0.4494
BLEU	**0.2137**	0.1923	0.1691	0.1992	0.0570	0.1792	0.2018

Table 2: Performance comparison of various open-sourced and proprietary large language models for the summarization task on the 300-sample holdout test set.

two, three, or four perspectives. The evaluation was conducted on the test set.

Among all proprietary models, o1 with Chain-of-Thought (CoT) prompting gave us the best classification results among all proprietary models. Gemini-2 Flash Experimental performed best in Strict Matching F1, while Gemini-1.5 Pro achieved the highest Proportional Matching F1.

To assess the impact of increasing the number of examples in few-shot prompting, we conducted an additional experiment by increasing the number of examples from 8 to 50, selected using random sampling for o1 and Gemini-2 Flash Experimental. The results showed that providing more examples did not improve performance. In fact, for o1, the Strict Matching F1 decreased from 0.0921 (8 examples) to 0.0601 (50 examples), and the Proportional Matching F1 dropped from 0.6359 to 0.5617. Similarly, for Gemini-2 Flash Experimental, the Classification Macro F1 declined from 0.7317 to 0.7102, and the Classification Weighted F1 decreased from 0.8305 to 0.8213. Although Strict Matching F1 and Proportional Matching F1 showed slight improvements, the gains were marginal. A detailed comparison of all the experiments is presented in Table 1.

4.2 Summarization

Once the relevant spans were identified for each perspective category, the next step was to generate a summary that effectively captured the key information from those spans. The models were evaluated using standard metrics such as ROUGE-1, ROUGE-2, ROUGE-L, BERTScore, METEOR, and BLEU.

4.2.1 LLM Fine-tuning

We fine-tuned Gemma-2 9B (4-bit quantized model) and Llama-3.1 8B (base model) to generate

Metric	S1	S2	S3	S4	S5	S6	S7	S8	S9
A + B	0.3964	0.4427	0.3940	0.4440	0.4083	**0.4495**	0.3833	0.4467	0.4407
C M F1	0.8628	0.7933	0.8656	0.8509	0.8581	**0.8656**	0.7849	0.8656	0.8656
C W F1	0.9092	0.8634	0.9140	0.8992	0.8900	**0.9140**	0.8396	0.9140	0.9140
S M P	0.1352	0.1768	0.1491	**0.1775**	0.1748	0.1765	0.1552	0.1765	0.1765
S M R	0.1257	0.2667	0.1562	0.2705	0.1162	**0.2743**	0.1200	0.2743	0.2743
S M F1	0.1303	0.2126	0.1526	0.2143	0.1396	**0.2148**	0.1353	0.2148	0.2148
P M P	0.5189	**0.6793**	0.5892	0.6641	0.5275	0.6597	0.4420	0.6597	0.6597
P M R	0.6857	**0.7396**	0.5648	0.7076	0.6350	0.7159	0.6145	0.7159	0.7159
P M F1	0.5907	**0.7081**	0.5767	0.6852	0.5763	0.6866	0.5142	0.6866	0.6866
A	0.5434	0.5947	0.5478	0.5996	0.5353	**0.6052**	0.4964	0.6052	0.6052
ROUGE-1	0.3580	0.4129	0.3407	0.4201	0.3533	**0.4345**	0.3318	0.4243	0.4048
ROUGE-2	0.1432	0.1818	0.1058	0.1812	0.1574	**0.1869**	0.1434	0.1753	0.1542
ROUGE-L	0.3210	0.3714	0.2881	0.3763	0.3184	**0.3878**	0.3017	0.3765	0.3510
BERTScore	0.8038	0.8048	0.8531	0.8318	0.7385	**0.8658**	0.7220	0.8621	0.8584
METEOR	0.3226	0.3713	0.2572	0.3719	0.3190	**0.3844**	0.3041	0.3509	0.3474
BLEU	0.0971	**0.1189**	0.0602	0.1127	0.1088	0.1124	0.0959	0.1134	0.1047
B_Relevance	0.3409	0.3768	0.3175	0.3823	0.3326	**0.3953**	0.3165	0.3838	0.3701
AlignScore	0.3665	**0.4458**	0.4043	0.4307	0.4359	0.4260	0.3991	0.4308	0.4369
SummaC	0.2433	0.2671	0.2291	0.2696	**0.2785**	0.2701	0.2750	0.2715	0.2570
B_Factuality	0.3049	0.3565	0.3167	0.3502	**0.3572**	0.3480	0.3370	0.3512	0.3470

Table 3: Performance comparison across all submissions evaluated on the provided 50 samples.

summaries from the predicted spans. Both models were trained on the training set with Unsloth (Daniel Han and team, 2023) using zero-shot fine-tuning for 3 epochs with a learning rate of 2e-4, validated on the validation set, and evaluated on the test set.

Among these two, Gemma-2 9B (4-bit quantized model) consistently outperformed the Llama-3.1 8B model across all evaluation metrics. A detailed comparison of the results is presented in Table 2.

4.2.2 Proprietary Models

In addition to fine-tuned models, we explored proprietary models, including GPT-4o, o1, Gemini-1.5 Pro, and Gemini-2 Flash Experimental, using a few-shot prompting approach with 8 examples. We used the same examples which were used the span prediction task. These models were evaluated on the test set. Among these models, Gemini-2 Flash Experimental consistently achieved the highest scores across all evaluation metrics. A detailed comparison of the results is presented in Table 2.

5 Submissions

During the competition's evaluation phase, we were given 50 test samples and made a total of nine submissions, each exploring different model configurations and techniques.

In our first submission, we fine-tuned the Gemma-2 9B (4-bit quantized) model on the training data and validated it on the validation data for span prediction and summarization. The second submission (S2) used Gemini-2 Flash Experimental, a proprietary model, for both tasks. The third submission (S3) introduced o1 with Chain-of-Thought (CoT) prompting to enhance reasoning capabilities.

In the fourth submission (S4), we used o1 (CoT) for classification and Gemini-2 Flash Experimental for span extraction and summarization. However, Gemini-2 Flash Experimental did not always adhere to the class predictions from o1, leading to inconsistencies in output. For the fifth submission (S5), we fine-tuned Gemma-2 9B (4-bit quantized) using a combined training and validation set.

Our sixth submission (S6) achieved the best over-

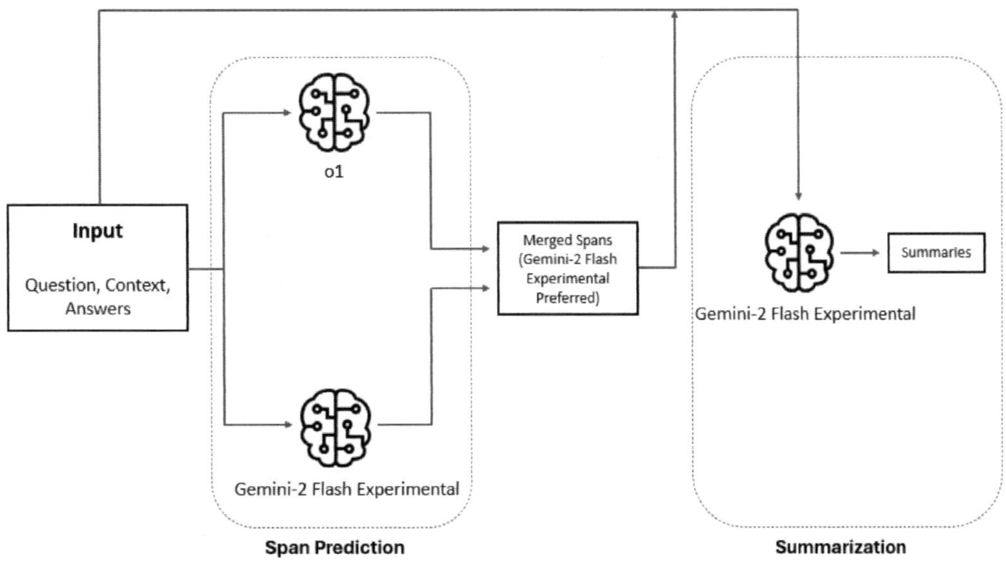

Figure 4: This figure illustrates the workflow of our best submission.

all performance. Here, we used o1 and Gemini-2 Flash Experimental for span extraction, ensuring that all classes predicted by o1 had corresponding spans. We noticed that Gemini's perspective classification was a proper subset of o1's. If Gemini-2 Flash Experimental did not generate spans for a perspective category but o1 did, we retained those from o1. When both models provided spans for a particular perspective, we used those from Gemini-2 Flash Experimental and discarded o1's. The final set of spans was then passed to Gemini-2 Flash Experimental for summarization. This submission achieved the highest Task A+B average score of 0.4495. The complete workflow is illustrated in Figure 4.

While evaluating the test data, we observed that all 50 samples included context, whereas two-thirds of the training data lacked it. To account for this, our seventh submission (S7) fine-tuned Gemma-2 9B using only samples that contained context. In the eigth submission (S8), we used o1 for classification, Gemini-2 Flash Experimental for span extraction, and increased the few-shot prompting examples from 8 to 16 to enhance summarization performance.

For our final submission (S9), o1 was used for span extraction, and Gemini-1.5 Pro was used for summarization. A detailed breakdown of the scores for all submissions is provided in Table 3.

In Table 3, the metric (A+B) denotes the combined average score of Task A and B, and (A) represents the score for Task A. The metrics (B_Relevance) and (B_Factuality) correspond to the relevance and factuality scores for Task B, respectively. AlignScore (Zha et al., 2023) and SummaC (Laban et al., 2022) are factual consistency evaluation metrics, designed to assess the alignment of generated summaries with the source text.

6 Discussion

In the final submissions we notice that o1 CoT performs well on the classification task (to predict perspectives present in user answers) as seen in Table 3. This is in line with our evaluations on the test set as well, where the classification weighted F1 of o1 CoT was the best as seen in Table 1. For the span extraction task, finetuned open-source models were performing on par with proprietary ones like Gemini-2 Flash Experimental and 1.5 Pro as seen in Table 1. For summarization Gemma-2 9B (4 bit) beats all other models as seen in Table 2. This demonstrates the efficiency of finetuning Large Language Models on downsteam tasks where even smaller models (less than 10 B parameters) can compete with and beat larger models like GPT 4o etc.

However, in the final submissions we see a large gap between open-sourced models like Gemma-2 9B (4-bit) (Submision 1) and proprietary models like Gemini-2 Flash Experimental (Submission 2) as seen in Table 3. The reason for such discrepancy can be due to difference in data distribution of the training and validation set released earlier and the final evaluation set of 50 samples on which the submissions were scored. One difference highlighted earlier was that the final evaluation set had the optional context section for all samples whereas, the training and validation set had approximately two-thirds of the samples without the context section. Another reason could be an inherent bias due to a small set of just 50 samples.

7 Conclusion

We test multiple open-source and proprietary LLM's for the task. Finetuning open-source smaller models like Llama 8b, 3b and Gemma 9b models yielded significant improvements from their base variants and even outperformed GPT 4o. This is likely because learning is significantly higher from finetuning when compared to in- context Learning with few shot examples. It is also difficult to capture all the details of the data in the few shot examples which is another reason why finetuning performs better. In our experiments, we observed that increasing the number of few-shot examples did not enhance performance. Hence finetuning is the better alternative.

Regardless, few proprietary LLM's particularly Gemini-2 Flash Experimental was able to beat the finetuned smaller models like Llama and Gemma on the final evaluation set of 50 samples on which submissions were scored. Possible reasons for a significant drop in performance during the final evaluation is discussed in the Discussions section. We also try a CoT prompt with o1 to accomplish both tasks in one go. We notice that the classification (perspective prediction) of o1 CoT is the best of all submissions (Table 3) which is largely in line with our experimentations (Table 1), but the spans and summaries of Gemini-2 Flash Experimental is better. Hence, we merge the spans of both models and choose Gemini's spans wherever possible. For perspectives where Gemini does not generate any spans but o1 does, we go ahead with the spans from o1. This ensures we utilize the better classification performance of o1 and use Gemini's span and summarization.

8 Limitations

The experiments carried out were mainly on a few selected open source and proprietary models. There are a number of open-sourced larger models which could have been finetuned for better performance. However, due to insufficient resources and time constraints we keep it as a possible future work. As for the proprietary models, more effort can be put in the prompting of these models. Things like a greater number of few shot prompts, different few shot examples can be tried. An ensemble approach using o1 and Gemini-2 Flash Experimental for span prediction, combined with the Gemma-2 9B model for summarization, could also be explored for improved performance.

9 Ethical Consideratons

Given that our dataset is from the medical and healthcare domain we take additional effort to comply with all ethical guidelines. As per the shared tasks instructions we use this dataset strictly for the task experiments and have not leaked this data to any third party. Since the data contains answers from multiple users there are some personal identification information like email addresses, website links etc. We make no effort to make contact or connect to these users on their social media handles. Also, we have cited all intellectual artifacts and resources to the best of our knowledge, ensuring proper attribution and adherence to ethical research practices.

References

Micheal Abaho, Danushka Bollegala, Paula Williamson, and Susanna Dodd. 2021. Detect and classify – joint span detection and classification for health outcomes. In *Proceedings of the 2021 Conference on Empirical Methods in Natural Language Processing*, pages 8709–8721, Online and Punta Cana, Dominican Republic. Association for Computational Linguistics.

Siddhant Agarwal, Md Shad Akhtar, and Shweta Yadav. 2025. Overview of the peranssumm 2025 shared task on perspective-aware healthcare answer summarization. In *Proceedings of the Second Workshop on Patient-Oriented Language Processing (CL4Health) @ NAACL 2025*, Albuquerque, USA. Association for Computational Linguistics.

Tanya Chowdhury and Tanmoy Chakraborty. 2018. Cqasumm: Building references for community question answering summarization corpora. *Preprint*, arXiv:1811.04884.

Michael Han Daniel Han and Unsloth team. 2023. Unsloth.

Jacob Devlin, Ming-Wei Chang, Kenton Lee, and Kristina Toutanova. 2019. BERT: Pre-training of deep bidirectional transformers for language understanding. In *Proceedings of the 2019 Conference of the North American Chapter of the Association for Computational Linguistics: Human Language Technologies, Volume 1 (Long and Short Papers)*, pages 4171–4186, Minneapolis, Minnesota. Association for Computational Linguistics.

Alexander R. Fabbri, Xiaojian Wu, Srini Iyer, and Mona Diab. 2021. Multi-perspective abstractive answer summarization. *Preprint*, arXiv:2104.08536.

Alexander R. Fabbri, Xiaojian Wu, Srini Iyer, Haoran Li, and Mona Diab. 2022. Answersumm: A manually-curated dataset and pipeline for answer summarization. *Preprint*, arXiv:2111.06474.

Aaron Grattafiori, Abhimanyu Dubey, Abhinav Jauhri, Abhinav Pandey, Abhishek Kadian, Ahmad Al-Dahle, Aiesha Letman, Akhil Mathur, Alan Schelten, Alex Vaughan, Amy Yang, Angela Fan, Anirudh Goyal, Anthony Hartshorn, Aobo Yang, Archi Mitra, Archie Sravankumar, Artem Korenev, Arthur Hinsvark, Arun Rao, Aston Zhang, Aurelien Rodriguez, Austen Gregerson, Ava Spataru, Baptiste Roziere, Bethany Biron, Binh Tang, Bobbie Chern, Charlotte Caucheteux, Chaya Nayak, Chloe Bi, Chris Marra, Chris McConnell, Christian Keller, Christophe Touret, Chunyang Wu, Corinne Wong, Cristian Canton Ferrer, Cyrus Nikolaidis, Damien Allonsius, Daniel Song, Danielle Pintz, Danny Livshits, Danny Wyatt, David Esiobu, Dhruv Choudhary, Dhruv Mahajan, Diego Garcia-Olano, Diego Perino, Dieuwke Hupkes, Egor Lakomkin, Ehab AlBadawy, Elina Lobanova, Emily Dinan, Eric Michael Smith, Filip Radenovic, Francisco Guzmán, Frank Zhang, Gabriel Synnaeve, Gabrielle Lee, Georgia Lewis Anderson, Govind Thattai, Graeme Nail, Gregoire Mialon, Guan Pang, Guillem Cucurell, Hailey Nguyen, Hannah Korevaar, Hu Xu, Hugo Touvron, Iliyan Zarov, Imanol Arrieta Ibarra, Isabel Kloumann, Ishan Misra, Ivan Evtimov, Jack Zhang, Jade Copet, Jaewon Lee, Jan Geffert, Jana Vranes, Jason Park, Jay Mahadeokar, Jeet Shah, Jelmer van der Linde, Jennifer Billock, Jenny Hong, Jenya Lee, Jeremy Fu, Jianfeng Chi, Jianyu Huang, Jiawen Liu, Jie Wang, Jiecao Yu, Joanna Bitton, Joe Spisak, Jongsoo Park, Joseph Rocca, Joshua Johnstun, Joshua Saxe, Junteng Jia, Kalyan Vasuden Alwala, Karthik Prasad, Kartikeya Upasani, Kate Plawiak, Ke Li, Kenneth Heafield, Kevin Stone, Khalid El-Arini, Krithika Iyer, Kshitiz Malik, Kuenley Chiu, Kunal Bhalla, Kushal Lakhotia, Lauren Rantala-Yeary, Laurens van der Maaten, Lawrence Chen, Liang Tan, Liz Jenkins, Louis Martin, Lovish Madaan, Lubo Malo, Lukas Blecher, Lukas Landzaat, Luke de Oliveira, Madeline Muzzi, Mahesh Pasupuleti, Mannat Singh, Manohar Paluri, Marcin Kardas, Maria Tsimpoukelli, Mathew Oldham, Mathieu Rita, Maya Pavlova, Melanie Kambadur, Mike Lewis, Min Si, Mitesh Kumar Singh, Mona Hassan, Naman Goyal, Narjes Torabi, Nikolay Bashlykov, Nikolay Bogoychev, Niladri Chatterji, Ning Zhang, Olivier Duchenne, Onur Çelebi, Patrick Alrassy, Pengchuan Zhang, Pengwei Li, Petar Vasic, Peter Weng, Prajjwal Bhargava, Pratik Dubal, Praveen Krishnan, Punit Singh Koura, Puxin Xu, Qing He, Qingxiao Dong, Ragavan Srinivasan, Raj Ganapathy, Ramon Calderer, Ricardo Silveira Cabral, Robert Stojnic, Roberta Raileanu, Rohan Maheswari, Rohit Girdhar, Rohit Patel, Romain Sauvestre, Ronnie Polidoro, Roshan Sumbaly, Ross Taylor, Ruan Silva, Rui Hou, Rui Wang, Saghar Hosseini, Sahana Chennabasappa, Sanjay Singh, Sean Bell, Seohyun Sonia Kim, Sergey Edunov, Shaoliang Nie, Sharan Narang, Sharath Raparthy, Sheng Shen, Shengye Wan, Shruti Bhosale, Shun Zhang, Simon Vandenhende, Soumya Batra, Spencer Whitman, Sten Sootla, Stephane Collot, Suchin Gururangan, Sydney Borodinsky, Tamar Herman, Tara Fowler, Tarek Sheasha, Thomas Georgiou, Thomas Scialom, Tobias Speckbacher, Todor Mihaylov, Tong Xiao, Ujjwal Karn, Vedanuj Goswami, Vibhor Gupta, Vignesh Ramanathan, Viktor Kerkez, Vincent Gonguet, Virginie Do, Vish Vogeti, Vítor Albiero, Vladan Petrovic, Weiwei Chu, Wenhan Xiong, Wenyin Fu, Whitney Meers, Xavier Martinet, Xiaodong Wang, Xiaofang Wang, Xiaoqing Ellen Tan, Xide Xia, Xinfeng Xie, Xuchao Jia, Xuewei Wang, Yaelle Goldschlag, Yashesh Gaur, Yasmine Babaei, Yi Wen, Yiwen Song, Yuchen Zhang, Yue Li, Yuning Mao, Zacharie Delpierre Coudert, Zheng Yan, Zhengxing Chen, Zoe Papakipos, Aaditya Singh, Aayushi Srivastava, Abha Jain, Adam Kelsey, Adam Shajnfeld, Adithya Gangidi, Adolfo Victoria, Ahuva Goldstand, Ajay Menon, Ajay Sharma, Alex Boesenberg, Alexei Baevski, Allie Feinstein, Amanda Kallet, Amit Sangani, Amos Teo, Anam Yunus, Andrei Lupu, Andres Alvarado, Andrew Caples, Andrew Gu, Andrew Ho, Andrew Poulton, Andrew Ryan, Ankit Ramchandani, Annie Dong, Annie Franco, Anuj Goyal, Aparajita Saraf, Arkabandhu Chowdhury, Ashley Gabriel, Ashwin Bharambe, Assaf Eisenman, Azadeh Yazdan, Beau James, Ben Maurer, Benjamin Leonhardi, Bernie Huang, Beth Loyd, Beto De Paola, Bhargavi Paranjape, Bing Liu, Bo Wu, Boyu Ni, Braden Hancock, Bram Wasti, Brandon Spence, Brani Stojkovic, Brian Gamido, Britt Montalvo, Carl Parker, Carly Burton, Catalina Mejia, Ce Liu, Changhan Wang, Changkyu Kim, Chao Zhou, Chester Hu, Ching-Hsiang Chu, Chris Cai, Chris Tindal, Christoph Feichtenhofer, Cynthia Gao, Damon Civin, Dana Beaty, Daniel Kreymer, Daniel Li, David Adkins, David Xu, Davide Testuggine, Delia David, Devi Parikh, Diana Liskovich, Didem Foss, Dingkang Wang, Duc Le, Dustin Holland, Edward Dowling, Eissa Jamil, Elaine Montgomery, Eleonora Presani, Emily Hahn, Emily Wood, Eric-Tuan Le, Erik Brinkman, Esteban Arcaute, Evan Dunbar, Evan Smothers, Fei Sun, Felix Kreuk, Feng Tian, Filippos Kokkinos, Firat Ozgenel, Francesco Caggioni, Frank Kanayet, Frank Seide, Gabriela Medina Florez, Gabriella Schwarz, Gada Badeer, Georgia Swee, Gil Halpern, Grant Herman, Grigory Sizov, Guangyi, Zhang, Guna Lakshminarayanan, Hakan Inan, Hamid Shojanazeri, Han Zou, Hannah Wang, Hanwen Zha, Haroun Habeeb, Harrison Rudolph, Helen Suk, Henry Aspegren, Hunter Goldman, Hongyuan Zhan, Ibrahim Damlaj, Igor Molybog, Igor Tufanov, Ilias Leontiadis, Irina-Elena Veliche, Itai Gat, Jake Weissman, James Geboski, James Kohli, Janice Lam, Japhet Asher,

Jean-Baptiste Gaya, Jeff Marcus, Jeff Tang, Jennifer Chan, Jenny Zhen, Jeremy Reizenstein, Jeremy Teboul, Jessica Zhong, Jian Jin, Jingyi Yang, Joe Cummings, Jon Carvill, Jon Shepard, Jonathan McPhie, Jonathan Torres, Josh Ginsburg, Junjie Wang, Kai Wu, Kam Hou U, Karan Saxena, Kartikay Khandelwal, Katayoun Zand, Kathy Matosich, Kaushik Veeraraghavan, Kelly Michelena, Keqian Li, Kiran Jagadeesh, Kun Huang, Kunal Chawla, Kyle Huang, Lailin Chen, Lakshya Garg, Lavender A, Leandro Silva, Lee Bell, Lei Zhang, Liangpeng Guo, Licheng Yu, Liron Moshkovich, Luca Wehrstedt, Madian Khabsa, Manav Avalani, Manish Bhatt, Martynas Mankus, Matan Hasson, Matthew Lennie, Matthias Reso, Maxim Groshev, Maxim Naumov, Maya Lathi, Meghan Keneally, Miao Liu, Michael L. Seltzer, Michal Valko, Michelle Restrepo, Mihir Patel, Mik Vyatskov, Mikayel Samvelyan, Mike Clark, Mike Macey, Mike Wang, Miquel Jubert Hermoso, Mo Metanat, Mohammad Rastegari, Munish Bansal, Nandhini Santhanam, Natascha Parks, Natasha White, Navyata Bawa, Nayan Singhal, Nick Egebo, Nicolas Usunier, Nikhil Mehta, Nikolay Pavlovich Laptev, Ning Dong, Norman Cheng, Oleg Chernoguz, Olivia Hart, Omkar Salpekar, Ozlem Kalinli, Parkin Kent, Parth Parekh, Paul Saab, Pavan Balaji, Pedro Rittner, Philip Bontrager, Pierre Roux, Piotr Dollar, Polina Zvyagina, Prashant Ratanchandani, Pritish Yuvraj, Qian Liang, Rachad Alao, Rachel Rodriguez, Rafi Ayub, Raghotham Murthy, Raghu Nayani, Rahul Mitra, Rangaprabhu Parthasarathy, Raymond Li, Rebekkah Hogan, Robin Battey, Rocky Wang, Russ Howes, Ruty Rinott, Sachin Mehta, Sachin Siby, Sai Jayesh Bondu, Samyak Datta, Sara Chugh, Sara Hunt, Sargun Dhillon, Sasha Sidorov, Satadru Pan, Saurabh Mahajan, Saurabh Verma, Seiji Yamamoto, Sharadh Ramaswamy, Shaun Lindsay, Shaun Lindsay, Sheng Feng, Shenghao Lin, Shengxin Cindy Zha, Shishir Patil, Shiva Shankar, Shuqiang Zhang, Shuqiang Zhang, Sinong Wang, Sneha Agarwal, Soji Sajuyigbe, Soumith Chintala, Stephanie Max, Stephen Chen, Steve Kehoe, Steve Satterfield, Sudarshan Govindaprasad, Sumit Gupta, Summer Deng, Sungmin Cho, Sunny Virk, Suraj Subramanian, Sy Choudhury, Sydney Goldman, Tal Remez, Tamar Glaser, Tamara Best, Thilo Koehler, Thomas Robinson, Tianhe Li, Tianjun Zhang, Tim Matthews, Timothy Chou, Tzook Shaked, Varun Vontimitta, Victoria Ajayi, Victoria Montanez, Vijai Mohan, Vinay Satish Kumar, Vishal Mangla, Vlad Ionescu, Vlad Poenaru, Vlad Tiberiu Mihailescu, Vladimir Ivanov, Wei Li, Wenchen Wang, Wenwen Jiang, Wes Bouaziz, Will Constable, Xiaocheng Tang, Xiaojian Wu, Xiaolan Wang, Xilun Wu, Xinbo Gao, Yaniv Kleinman, Yanjun Chen, Ye Hu, Ye Jia, Ye Qi, Yenda Li, Yilin Zhang, Ying Zhang, Yossi Adi, Youngjin Nam, Yu, Wang, Yu Zhao, Yuchen Hao, Yundi Qian, Yunlu Li, Yuzi He, Zach Rait, Zachary DeVito, Zef Rosnbrick, Zhaoduo Wen, Zhenyu Yang, Zhiwei Zhao, and Zhiyu Ma. 2024. The llama 3 herd of models. *Preprint*, arXiv:2407.21783.

Junxian He, Wojciech Kryściński, Bryan McCann, Nazneen Rajani, and Caiming Xiong. 2020. Ctrlsum: Towards generic controllable text summarization. *Preprint*, arXiv:2012.04281.

Chao-Chun Hsu, Shantanu Karnwal, Sendhil Mullainathan, Ziad Obermeyer, and Chenhao Tan. 2020. Characterizing the value of information in medical notes. In *Findings of the Association for Computational Linguistics: EMNLP 2020*, pages 2062–2072, Online. Association for Computational Linguistics.

Kexin Huang, Jaan Altosaar, and Rajesh Ranganath. 2020. Clinicalbert: Modeling clinical notes and predicting hospital readmission. *Preprint*, arXiv:1904.05342.

Anirudh Joshi, Namit Katariya, Xavier Amatriain, and Anitha Kannan. 2020a. Dr. summarize: Global summarization of medical dialogue by exploiting local structures. In *Findings of the Association for Computational Linguistics: EMNLP 2020*, pages 3755–3763, Online. Association for Computational Linguistics.

Mandar Joshi, Danqi Chen, Yinhan Liu, Daniel S. Weld, Luke Zettlemoyer, and Omer Levy. 2020b. Spanbert: Improving pre-training by representing and predicting spans. *Preprint*, arXiv:1907.10529.

Philippe Laban, Tobias Schnabel, Paul N. Bennett, and Marti A. Hearst. 2022. SummaC: Re-visiting NLI-based models for inconsistency detection in summarization. *Transactions of the Association for Computational Linguistics*, 10:163–177.

Jinhyuk Lee, Wonjin Yoon, Sungdong Kim, Donghyeon Kim, Sunkyu Kim, Chan Ho So, and Jaewoo Kang. 2019. Biobert: a pre-trained biomedical language representation model for biomedical text mining. *Bioinformatics*, 36(4):1234–1240.

Mike Lewis, Yinhan Liu, Naman Goyal, Marjan Ghazvininejad, Abdelrahman Mohamed, Omer Levy, Ves Stoyanov, and Luke Zettlemoyer. 2019. Bart: Denoising sequence-to-sequence pre-training for natural language generation, translation, and comprehension. *Preprint*, arXiv:1910.13461.

Yinhan Liu, Myle Ott, Naman Goyal, Jingfei Du, Mandar Joshi, Danqi Chen, Omer Levy, Mike Lewis, Luke Zettlemoyer, and Veselin Stoyanov. 2019. Roberta: A robustly optimized bert pretraining approach. *Preprint*, arXiv:1907.11692.

George Michalopoulos, Kyle Williams, Gagandeep Singh, and Thomas Lin. 2022. MedicalSum: A guided clinical abstractive summarization model for generating medical reports from patient-doctor conversations. In *Findings of the Association for Computational Linguistics: EMNLP 2022*, pages 4741–4749, Abu Dhabi, United Arab Emirates. Association for Computational Linguistics.

Gauri Naik, Sharad Chandakacherla, Shweta Yadav, and Md Shad Akhtar. 2024. No perspective, no perception!! perspective-aware healthcare answer summarization. In *Findings of the Association for Computational Linguistics: ACL 2024*, pages 15919–15932,

Bangkok, Thailand. Association for Computational Linguistics.

OpenAI, :, Aaron Hurst, Adam Lerer, Adam P. Goucher, Adam Perelman, Aditya Ramesh, Aidan Clark, AJ Ostrow, Akila Welihinda, Alan Hayes, Alec Radford, Aleksander Mądry, Alex Baker-Whitcomb, Alex Beutel, Alex Borzunov, Alex Carney, Alex Chow, Alex Kirillov, Alex Nichol, Alex Paino, Alex Renzin, Alex Tachard Passos, Alexander Kirillov, Alexi Christakis, Alexis Conneau, Ali Kamali, Allan Jabri, Allison Moyer, Allison Tam, Amadou Crookes, Amin Tootoochian, Amin Tootoonchian, Ananya Kumar, Andrea Vallone, Andrej Karpathy, Andrew Braunstein, Andrew Cann, Andrew Codispoti, Andrew Galu, Andrew Kondrich, Andrew Tulloch, Andrey Mishchenko, Angela Baek, Angela Jiang, Antoine Pelisse, Antonia Woodford, Anuj Gosalia, Arka Dhar, Ashley Pantuliano, Avi Nayak, Avital Oliver, Barret Zoph, Behrooz Ghorbani, Ben Leimberger, Ben Rossen, Ben Sokolowsky, Ben Wang, Benjamin Zweig, Beth Hoover, Blake Samic, Bob McGrew, Bobby Spero, Bogo Giertler, Bowen Cheng, Brad Lightcap, Brandon Walkin, Brendan Quinn, Brian Guarraci, Brian Hsu, Bright Kellogg, Brydon Eastman, Camillo Lugaresi, Carroll Wainwright, Cary Bassin, Cary Hudson, Casey Chu, Chad Nelson, Chak Li, Chan Jun Shern, Channing Conger, Charlotte Barette, Chelsea Voss, Chen Ding, Cheng Lu, Chong Zhang, Chris Beaumont, Chris Hallacy, Chris Koch, Christian Gibson, Christina Kim, Christine Choi, Christine McLeavey, Christopher Hesse, Claudia Fischer, Clemens Winter, Coley Czarnecki, Colin Jarvis, Colin Wei, Constantin Koumouzelis, Dane Sherburn, Daniel Kappler, Daniel Levin, Daniel Levy, David Carr, David Farhi, David Mely, David Robinson, David Sasaki, Denny Jin, Dev Valladares, Dimitris Tsipras, Doug Li, Duc Phong Nguyen, Duncan Findlay, Edede Oiwoh, Edmund Wong, Ehsan Asdar, Elizabeth Proehl, Elizabeth Yang, Eric Antonow, Eric Kramer, Eric Peterson, Eric Sigler, Eric Wallace, Eugene Brevdo, Evan Mays, Farzad Khorasani, Felipe Petroski Such, Filippo Raso, Francis Zhang, Fred von Lohmann, Freddie Sulit, Gabriel Goh, Gene Oden, Geoff Salmon, Giulio Starace, Greg Brockman, Hadi Salman, Haiming Bao, Haitang Hu, Hannah Wong, Haoyu Wang, Heather Schmidt, Heather Whitney, Heewoo Jun, Hendrik Kirchner, Henrique Ponde de Oliveira Pinto, Hongyu Ren, Huiwen Chang, Hyung Won Chung, Ian Kivlichan, Ian O'Connell, Ian O'Connell, Ian Osband, Ian Silber, Ian Sohl, Ibrahim Okuyucu, Ikai Lan, Ilya Kostrikov, Ilya Sutskever, Ingmar Kanitscheider, Ishaan Gulrajani, Jacob Coxon, Jacob Menick, Jakub Pachocki, James Aung, James Betker, James Crooks, James Lennon, Jamie Kiros, Jan Leike, Jane Park, Jason Kwon, Jason Phang, Jason Teplitz, Jason Wei, Jason Wolfe, Jay Chen, Jeff Harris, Jenia Varavva, Jessica Gan Lee, Jessica Shieh, Ji Lin, Jiahui Yu, Jiayi Weng, Jie Tang, Jieqi Yu, Joanne Jang, Joaquin Quinonero Candela, Joe Beutler, Joe Landers, Joel Parish, Johannes Heidecke, John Schulman, Jonathan Lachman, Jonathan McKay, Jonathan Uesato, Jonathan Ward, Jong Wook Kim, Joost Huizinga, Jordan Sitkin, Jos Kraaijeveld, Josh Gross, Josh Kaplan, Josh Snyder, Joshua Achiam, Joy Jiao, Joyce Lee, Juntang Zhuang, Justyn Harriman, Kai Fricke, Kai Hayashi, Karan Singhal, Katy Shi, Kavin Karthik, Kayla Wood, Kendra Rimbach, Kenny Hsu, Kenny Nguyen, Keren Gu-Lemberg, Kevin Button, Kevin Liu, Kiel Howe, Krithika Muthukumar, Kyle Luther, Lama Ahmad, Larry Kai, Lauren Itow, Lauren Workman, Leher Pathak, Leo Chen, Li Jing, Lia Guy, Liam Fedus, Liang Zhou, Lien Mamitsuka, Lilian Weng, Lindsay McCallum, Lindsey Held, Long Ouyang, Louis Feuvrier, Lu Zhang, Lukas Kondraciuk, Lukasz Kaiser, Luke Hewitt, Luke Metz, Lyric Doshi, Mada Aflak, Maddie Simens, Madelaine Boyd, Madeleine Thompson, Marat Dukhan, Mark Chen, Mark Gray, Mark Hudnall, Marvin Zhang, Marwan Aljubeh, Mateusz Litwin, Matthew Zeng, Max Johnson, Maya Shetty, Mayank Gupta, Meghan Shah, Mehmet Yatbaz, Meng Jia Yang, Mengchao Zhong, Mia Glaese, Mianna Chen, Michael Janner, Michael Lampe, Michael Petrov, Michael Wu, Michele Wang, Michelle Fradin, Michelle Pokrass, Miguel Castro, Miguel Oom Temudo de Castro, Mikhail Pavlov, Miles Brundage, Miles Wang, Minal Khan, Mira Murati, Mo Bavarian, Molly Lin, Murat Yesildal, Nacho Soto, Natalia Gimelshein, Natalie Cone, Natalie Staudacher, Natalie Summers, Natan LaFontaine, Neil Chowdhury, Nick Ryder, Nick Stathas, Nick Turley, Nik Tezak, Niko Felix, Nithanth Kudige, Nitish Keskar, Noah Deutsch, Noel Bundick, Nora Puckett, Ofir Nachum, Ola Okelola, Oleg Boiko, Oleg Murk, Oliver Jaffe, Olivia Watkins, Olivier Godement, Owen Campbell-Moore, Patrick Chao, Paul McMillan, Pavel Belov, Peng Su, Peter Bak, Peter Bakkum, Peter Deng, Peter Dolan, Peter Hoeschele, Peter Welinder, Phil Tillet, Philip Pronin, Philippe Tillet, Prafulla Dhariwal, Qiming Yuan, Rachel Dias, Rachel Lim, Rahul Arora, Rajan Troll, Randall Lin, Rapha Gontijo Lopes, Raul Puri, Reah Miyara, Reimar Leike, Renaud Gaubert, Reza Zamani, Ricky Wang, Rob Donnelly, Rob Honsby, Rocky Smith, Rohan Sahai, Rohit Ramchandani, Romain Huet, Rory Carmichael, Rowan Zellers, Roy Chen, Ruby Chen, Ruslan Nigmatullin, Ryan Cheu, Saachi Jain, Sam Altman, Sam Schoenholz, Sam Toizer, Samuel Miserendino, Sandhini Agarwal, Sara Culver, Scott Ethersmith, Scott Gray, Sean Grove, Sean Metzger, Shamez Hermani, Shantanu Jain, Shengjia Zhao, Sherwin Wu, Shino Jomoto, Shirong Wu, Shuaiqi, Xia, Sonia Phene, Spencer Papay, Srinivas Narayanan, Steve Coffey, Steve Lee, Stewart Hall, Suchir Balaji, Tal Broda, Tal Stramer, Tao Xu, Tarun Gogineni, Taya Christianson, Ted Sanders, Tejal Patwardhan, Thomas Cunninghman, Thomas Degry, Thomas Dimson, Thomas Raoux, Thomas Shadwell, Tianhao Zheng, Todd Underwood, Todor Markov, Toki Sherbakov, Tom Rubin, Tom Stasi, Tomer Kaftan, Tristan Heywood, Troy Peterson, Tyce Walters, Tyna Eloundou, Valerie Qi, Veit Moeller, Vinnie Monaco, Vishal Kuo, Vlad Fomenko, Wayne Chang, Weiyi Zheng, Wenda Zhou, Wesam Manassra, Will Sheu, Wojciech Zaremba, Yash Patil, Yilei Qian, Yongjik Kim, Youlong Cheng, Yu Zhang, Yuchen He, Yuchen Zhang, Yujia Jin, Yunxing Dai, and

Yury Malkov. 2024. Gpt-4o system card. *Preprint*, arXiv:2410.21276.

Colin Raffel, Noam Shazeer, Adam Roberts, Katherine Lee, Sharan Narang, Michael Matena, Yanqi Zhou, Wei Li, and Peter J. Liu. 2023. Exploring the limits of transfer learning with a unified text-to-text transformer. *Preprint*, arXiv:1910.10683.

Max Savery, Asma Ben Abacha, Soumya Gayen, and Dina Demner-Fushman. 2020. Question-driven summarization of answers to consumer health questions. *Preprint*, arXiv:2005.09067.

Amir Soleimani, Vassilina Nikoulina, Benoit Favre, and Salah Ait Mokhtar. 2022. Zero-shot aspect-based scientific document summarization using self-supervised pre-training. In *Proceedings of the 21st Workshop on Biomedical Language Processing*, pages 49–62, Dublin, Ireland. Association for Computational Linguistics.

Gemma Team, Morgane Riviere, Shreya Pathak, Pier Giuseppe Sessa, Cassidy Hardin, Surya Bhupatiraju, Léonard Hussenot, Thomas Mesnard, Bobak Shahriari, Alexandre Ramé, Johan Ferret, Peter Liu, Pouya Tafti, Abe Friesen, Michelle Casbon, Sabela Ramos, Ravin Kumar, Charline Le Lan, Sammy Jerome, Anton Tsitsulin, Nino Vieillard, Piotr Stanczyk, Sertan Girgin, Nikola Momchev, Matt Hoffman, Shantanu Thakoor, Jean-Bastien Grill, Behnam Neyshabur, Olivier Bachem, Alanna Walton, Aliaksei Severyn, Alicia Parrish, Aliya Ahmad, Allen Hutchison, Alvin Abdagic, Amanda Carl, Amy Shen, Andy Brock, Andy Coenen, Anthony Laforge, Antonia Paterson, Ben Bastian, Bilal Piot, Bo Wu, Brandon Royal, Charlie Chen, Chintu Kumar, Chris Perry, Chris Welty, Christopher A. Choquette-Choo, Danila Sinopalnikov, David Weinberger, Dimple Vijaykumar, Dominika Rogozińska, Dustin Herbison, Elisa Bandy, Emma Wang, Eric Noland, Erica Moreira, Evan Senter, Evgenii Eltyshev, Francesco Visin, Gabriel Rasskin, Gary Wei, Glenn Cameron, Gus Martins, Hadi Hashemi, Hanna Klimczak-Plucińska, Harleen Batra, Harsh Dhand, Ivan Nardini, Jacinda Mein, Jack Zhou, James Svensson, Jeff Stanway, Jetha Chan, Jin Peng Zhou, Joana Carrasqueira, Joana Iljazi, Jocelyn Becker, Joe Fernandez, Joost van Amersfoort, Josh Gordon, Josh Lipschultz, Josh Newlan, Ju yeong Ji, Kareem Mohamed, Kartikeya Badola, Kat Black, Katie Millican, Keelin McDonell, Kelvin Nguyen, Kiranbir Sodhia, Kish Greene, Lars Lowe Sjoesund, Lauren Usui, Laurent Sifre, Lena Heuermann, Leticia Lago, Lilly McNealus, Livio Baldini Soares, Logan Kilpatrick, Lucas Dixon, Luciano Martins, Machel Reid, Manvinder Singh, Mark Iverson, Martin Görner, Mat Velloso, Mateo Wirth, Matt Davidow, Matt Miller, Matthew Rahtz, Matthew Watson, Meg Risdal, Mehran Kazemi, Michael Moynihan, Ming Zhang, Minsuk Kahng, Minwoo Park, Mofi Rahman, Mohit Khatwani, Natalie Dao, Nenshad Bardoliwalla, Nesh Devanathan, Neta Dumai, Nilay Chauhan, Oscar Wahltinez, Pankil Botarda, Parker Barnes, Paul Barham, Paul Michel, Pengchong Jin, Petko Georgiev, Phil Culliton, Pradeep Kuppala, Ramona Comanescu, Ramona Merhej, Reena Jana, Reza Ardeshir Rokni, Rishabh Agarwal, Ryan Mullins, Samaneh Saadat, Sara Mc Carthy, Sarah Cogan, Sarah Perrin, Sébastien M. R. Arnold, Sebastian Krause, Shengyang Dai, Shruti Garg, Shruti Sheth, Sue Ronstrom, Susan Chan, Timothy Jordan, Ting Yu, Tom Eccles, Tom Hennigan, Tomas Kocisky, Tulsee Doshi, Vihan Jain, Vikas Yadav, Vilobh Meshram, Vishal Dharmadhikari, Warren Barkley, Wei Wei, Wenming Ye, Woohyun Han, Woosuk Kwon, Xiang Xu, Zhe Shen, Zhitao Gong, Zichuan Wei, Victor Cotruta, Phoebe Kirk, Anand Rao, Minh Giang, Ludovic Peran, Tris Warkentin, Eli Collins, Joelle Barral, Zoubin Ghahramani, Raia Hadsell, D. Sculley, Jeanine Banks, Anca Dragan, Slav Petrov, Oriol Vinyals, Jeff Dean, Demis Hassabis, Koray Kavukcuoglu, Clement Farabet, Elena Buchatskaya, Sebastian Borgeaud, Noah Fiedel, Armand Joulin, Kathleen Kenealy, Robert Dadashi, and Alek Andreev. 2024. Gemma 2: Improving open language models at a practical size. *Preprint*, arXiv:2408.00118.

Ashish Vaswani, Noam Shazeer, Niki Parmar, Jakob Uszkoreit, Llion Jones, Aidan N. Gomez, Lukasz Kaiser, and Illia Polosukhin. 2023. Attention is all you need. *Preprint*, arXiv:1706.03762.

Shweta Yadav and Cornelia Caragea. 2022. Towards summarizing healthcare questions in low-resource setting. In *Proceedings of the 29th International Conference on Computational Linguistics*, pages 2892–2905, Gyeongju, Republic of Korea. International Committee on Computational Linguistics.

Shweta Yadav, Ștefan Cobeli, and Cornelia Caragea. 2023. Towards understanding consumer healthcare questions on the web with semantically enhanced contrastive learning. pages 1773–1783.

Shweta Yadav, Deepak Gupta, and Dina Demner-Fushman. 2022. Chq-summ: A dataset for consumer healthcare question summarization. *Preprint*, arXiv:2206.06581.

Hongyi Yuan, Zheng Yuan, Ruyi Gan, Jiaxing Zhang, Yutao Xie, and Sheng Yu. 2022. Biobart: Pretraining and evaluation of a biomedical generative language model. *Preprint*, arXiv:2204.03905.

Yuheng Zha, Yichi Yang, Ruichen Li, and Zhiting Hu. 2023. Alignscore: Evaluating factual consistency with a unified alignment function. *Preprint*, arXiv:2305.16739.

Jingqing Zhang, Yao Zhao, Mohammad Saleh, and Peter J. Liu. 2020. Pegasus: Pre-training with extracted gap-sentences for abstractive summarization. *Preprint*, arXiv:1912.08777.

LTRC-IIITH at PerAnsSumm 2025: SpanSense - Perspective-specific span identification and Summarization

Sushvin Marimuthu, Parameswari Krishnamurthy
LTRC, International Institute of Information Technology, Hyderabad, India
sushvin.marimuthu@research.iiit.ac.in
param.krishna@iiit.ac.in

Abstract

Healthcare community question-answering (CQA) forums have become popular for users seeking medical advice, offering answers that range from personal experiences to factual information. Traditionally, CQA summarization relies on the best-voted answer as a reference summary. However, this approach overlooks the diverse perspectives across multiple responses. Structuring summaries by perspective could better meet users' informational needs. The PerAnsSumm shared task addresses this by identifying and classifying perspective-specific spans (Task_A) and generating perspective-specific summaries from question-answer threads (Task_B). In this paper, we present our work on the PerAnsSumm shared task 2025 at the CL4Health Workshop, NAACL 2025. Our system leverages the RoBERTa-large model for identifying perspective-specific spans and the BART-large model for summarization. We achieved a Macro-F1 score of 0.9 (**90%**) and a Weighted-F1 score of 0.92 (**92%**) for classification. For span matching, our strict matching F1 score was 0.21 (**21%**), while proportional matching reached 0.68 (**68%**), resulting in an average Task A score of 0.6 (**60%**). For Task B, we achieved a ROUGE-1 score of 0.4 (**40%**), ROUGE-2 of 0.18 (**18%**), and ROUGE-L of 0.36 (**36%**). Additionally, we obtained a BERTScore of 0.84 (**84%**), METEOR of 0.37 (**37%**), BLEU of 0.13 (**13%**), resulting in an average Task B score of 0.38 (**38%**). Combining both tasks, our system achieved an overall average score of **49%** and ranked 6th on the official leaderboard for the shared task.

1 Introduction

In PerAnsSumm shared task 2025 at the CL4Health Workshop, NAACL 2025 (Agarwal et al., 2025), the goal is to identify and classify perspective-specific spans (Task_A) and generate summaries tailored to specific perspectives from question-answer threads (Task_B) (Naik et al., 2024).

Span identification is the task of identifying and extracting a continuous range of words from a given text that correspond to a specific piece of information (Fu et al., 2021). This span is a subset of text, usually defined by its starting and ending positions within a sentence. Perspective-specific span identification is the task of finding parts of the text that are relevant to a particular perspective in a given context (Xu et al., 2023). TASK_A involves identifying the specific spans in user answers that reflect distinct perspectives and classifying each span into the appropriate perspective.

For TASK_A, we fine-tuned BERT-large (Devlin et al., 2018) and RoBERTa-large (Liu et al., 2019) models to identify relevant spans within the text. Initially, BERT-large achieved an accuracy of **45%**, while RoBERTa-large performed slightly better at **47%**. To improve their performance, we first pre-trained both models using Masked Language Modeling (MLM) for better domain adaptation before fine-tuning them for span identification. This additional pre-training helped—BERT-large improved to **50%**, and RoBERTa-large improved to **51%**. Further, we optimized the RoBERTa-large model by implementing gradual training, where we fine-tuned the model while keeping some layers frozen for a few epochs. Then, we froze the already fine-tuned layers, unfroze the remaining layers, and fine-tuned them separately. Finally, we fine-tuned the entire model. This step-by-step strategy significantly improved performance, raising accuracy to **60%**.

Summarization is the task of generating a concise and meaningful summary of a longer text while preserving its key information. It helps in reducing large amounts of text into a shorter version while retaining its core meaning (Allahyari et al., 2017). Perspective-specific summarization is a technique that generates summaries focused on a particular aspect of a topic, highlighting information relevant to that perspective instead of providing a general

Proceedings of the Second Workshop on Patient-Oriented Language Processing (CL4Health), pages 409–414
May 4, 2025 ©2025 Association for Computational Linguistics

summary (Tan et al., 2020). TASK_B involves generating a concise summary that captures the underlying perspective present across all identified spans in the user answers.

For Task_B, we fine-tuned the BART-large (Lewis et al., 2019) and Pegasus-large (Zhang et al., 2019) models to summarize the perspective spans identified and extracted in Task_A. Initially, Pegasus-large achieved TASK_B relevance score of **29%**, while BART-large performed slightly better at **31%**. To enhance their performance, we pre-trained both models using Masked Language Modeling (MLM) for better domain adaptation before fine-tuning them for summarization. This additional pre-training boosted BART-large to **38%** and Pegasus-large to **35%**.

In our proposed solution, we use RoBERTa-large for perspective-specific span identification (TASK_A) and BART-large for perspective-specific summarization (TASK_B).

2 Related Work

Several approaches have been proposed for span identification tasks, focusing on detecting meaningful spans and classifying them into predefined categories. Early works (Chiu and Nichols, 2016) framed SpanID as a sequence tagging problem, where spans were identified token by token using contextual embeddings. Recent research has shifted towards Machine Reading Comprehension (MRC)-based methods (Li et al., 2020), that make use of category-specific queries to extract relevant spans. To address challenges like overfitting and data scarcity, PeerDA (Xu et al., 2023) introduces a peer relation (PR) along with the subordinate relation (SUB), enriching training data and improving generalization. The contrastive learning (Gunel et al., 2021) strategy further enhances the model's ability to distinguish spans across different categories, making PeerDA a promising approach for perspective-based SpanID tasks.

Recent research on fine-grained text analysis has explored span extraction as an alternative to clause-level classification for more precise identification of relevant information. Emotion-cause span extraction (ECSE) (Li et al., 2021) refines emotion cause identification (ECI) by focusing on extracting targeted cause spans rather than entire clauses, improving interpretability and usability. Multi-attention mechanisms have been used to enhance cause-span extraction by leveraging context-sensitive representations, a method that could be adapted for perspective identification (Bi and Liu, 2020). Additionally, position-aware learning has been found to enhance token-level representations, improving the ability to capture key spans within longer texts (Xia and Ding, 2019).

Recent advancements in text summarization have explored span-based extraction and contrastive learning (CL) to improve content selection and representation. In medical question summarization (MQS), CL-enhanced methods have been used to capture key focus words, making sure that the summaries accurately reflect the core intent of the input text (Ma et al., 2022). Similarly, perspective-based summarization benefits from identifying and preserving essential spans that convey underlying viewpoints. Studies on Seq2Seq-based models and reinforcement learning (RL)-enhanced approaches demonstrate the importance of maintaining both syntactic accuracy and semantic coherence in summaries (Keneshloo et al., 2019).

3 Dataset

The dataset (Naik et al., 2024) provided for the shared task is the PUMA dataset, a perspective-aware summary annotated corpus of medical question-answer pairs. It consists of 3,167 CQA threads with approximately 10,000 answers filtered from the Yahoo! L6 corpus. Each answer in the dataset is annotated with five perspective spans: 'cause', 'suggestion', 'experience', 'question', and 'information'. These annotations create concise summaries for each identified perspective, which captures the core idea reflected in the spans across all answers. Each CQA thread may contain up to five perspective-specific summaries.

The data is provided in JSON format. Each entry in the training and validation datasets includes fields such as uri [1], question, context, answers, labelled_answer_spans, labelled_summaries, and raw_text. The labelled_answer_spans contains the span text and the index positions indicating where the span starts and ends within the raw_text. The labelled_summaries provide concise summaries corresponding to each identified perspective.

In the test dataset, only the fields uri, question, context, and answers are available, with no annotations for answer spans or summaries. The dataset was split into 2,236 instances for training, 959 for validation, and 50 for testing.

[1] Unique resource identifier

Dataset	Size
Train	2236
Valid	959
Test	50

Table 1: Dataset Splits

4 System Description

Our system is made of fine-tuned RoBERTa and BART models, where RoBERTa is used for precise token classification tasks, efficiently identifying and labeling specific information within the text. BART, on the other hand, is fine-tuned for summarization, enabling it to generate coherent, contextually relevant summaries by compressing complex input into concise representations.

4.1 Data Pre-Processing

In the pre-processing step, for span identification, we focus on the "answers" and "labelled_answer_spans" fields. The "labelled_answer_spans" field provides perspective spans, where each span contains indices referring to the "raw_text" field. To handle this, we merged all the answers and compared each perspective span to the merged answer, labeling the corresponding tokens as perspective spans (e.g., "I-INFORMATION", "I-SUGGESTION", "I-CAUSE", "I-QUESTION", "I-EXPERIENCE", "O") and marking the rest as "O". We experimented with three token classification formats: BIO (Beginning-Inside-Outside), IO (Inside-Outside), and BIOES (Beginning-Inside-Outside-End-Single). For summarization, we treated the merged spans as context and the "labelled_summaries" as the corresponding summaries.

4.2 Fine-Tuning

We fine-tuned BERT-large and RoBERTa-large models for span identification.

With the BERT-large model, we achieved a Macro-F1 score of 0.83 **(83%)** and a Weighted-F1 score of 0.86 **(86%)** for classification. However, for span matching, the strict matching F1 score was 0.0 **(0%)**, while proportional matching reached 0.47 **(47%)**, resulting in an average Task A score of 0.45 **(45%)**. For the RoBERTa-large model, we obtained a Macro-F1 score of 0.84 **(84%)** and a Weighted-F1 score of 0.88 **(88%)** for classification. Similarly, in span matching, the strict matching F1 score was 0.0 **(0%)**, while proportional matching achieved 0.54 **(54%)**, yielding an average Task A score of 0.47 **(47%)**.

The results indicate that the RoBERTa-large model outperforms the BERT-large model. To further improve performance, we fine-tuned both models for domain adaptation using Masked Language Modeling (MLM) and then retrained them for span identification. After domain adaptation, both models showed improvement.

For the domain-adapted BERT-large model, we achieved a Macro-F1 score of 0.87 **(87%)** and a Weighted-F1 score of 0.9 **(90%)** for classification. In span matching, the strict matching F1 score was 0.0 **(0%)**, while proportional matching reached 0.59 **(59%)**, resulting in an average Task A score of 0.5 **(50%)**.

With the domain-adapted RoBERTa-large model, we achieved a Macro-F1 score of 0.88 **(88%)** and a Weighted-F1 score of 0.92 **(92%)** for classification. For span matching, the strict matching F1 score was 0.01 **(1%)**, while proportional matching reached 0.62 **(62%)**, yielding an average Task A score of 0.51 **(51%)**.

The results now show that the domain-adapted RoBERTa-large model outperforms the domain-adapted BERT-large model. To further enhance performance, we applied a gradual training approach over 10 epochs to both domain-adapted models, each consisting of 24 layers. Initially, during the first 2 epochs, we froze all layers except for the first 4. In the next 2 epochs, we unfroze the subsequent 4 layers while keeping the earlier layers frozen. Over the following 2 epochs, we continued to unfreeze 4 additional layers, leaving the previously trained ones frozen. Finally, during the last 4 epochs, we unfroze all remaining layers and trained the entire model.

Despite using this gradual training method, BERT-large did not show any significant improvement. In contrast, the domain-adapted and gradually trained RoBERTa-large model achieved better results. For classification, we obtained a Macro-F1 score of 0.9 **(90%)** and a Weighted-F1 score of 0.92 (**92%**. For span matching, the strict matching F1 score was 0.21 **(21%)**, while the proportional matching F1 score reached 0.68 **(68%)**, yielding an average Task A score of 0.6 **(60%)**.

We fine-tuned both BART-large and Pegasus-large models for summarization. Using the Pegasus-large model, we achieved a Rouge-1 score of 0.3 **(30%)**, Rouge-2 score of 0.12 **(12%)**, Rouge-

Pre	GT	Model	Macro-F1	Weighted-F1	strict matching F1	proportional matching F1	Average
✗	✗	BERT-large	0.83	0.86	0.0	0.47	0.45
✗	✗	RoBERTa-large	0.84	0.88	0.0	0.54	0.47
✓	✗	BERT-large	0.87	0.9	0.0	0.59	0.5
✓	✗	RoBERTa-large	0.88	0.92	0.01	0.62	0.51
✓	✓	RoBERTa-large	**0.9**	**0.92**	**0.21**	**0.68**	**0.6**

Table 2: Performance comparison of BERT-large and RoBERTa-large models with and without pre-training (Pre) and gradual training (GT) across different evaluation metrics. The table presents Macro-F1, Weighted-F1, strict matching F1, and proportional matching F1 scores, along with their average performance.

Pre	Model	Rouge-1	Rouge-2	Rouge-L	BERTScore	Meteor	BLEU	Average
✗	Pegasus-large	0.3	0.12	0.27	0.73	0.26	0.1	0.29
✗	BART-large	0.33	0.12	0.29	0.77	0.28	0.09	0.31
✓	Pegasus-large	0.37	0.16	0.33	0.81	0.33	0.12	0.35
✓	BART-large	**0.4**	**0.18**	**0.36**	**0.84**	**0.37**	**0.13**	**0.38**

Table 3: Performance comparison of Pegasus-large and BART-large models for summarization, with and without pre-training (Pre). The table presents performance across various metrics, including Rouge-1, Rouge-2, Rouge-L, BERTScore, METEOR, BLEU, and the overall average score.

L score of 0.27 (**27%**), BERTScore score of 0.73 (**73%**), METEOR score of 0.26 (**26%**), and BLEU score of 0.1 (**10%**). This resulted in an average Task B score of 0.29 (**29%**). For the BART-large model, we achieved a Rouge-1 score of 0.33 (**33%**), Rouge-2 score of 0.12 (**12%**), Rouge-L score of 0.29 (**29%**), BERTScore score of 0.77 (**77%**), METEOR score of 0.28 (**28%**), and BLEU score 0.09 (**9%**), giving an average Task B score of 0.31 (**31%**).

The results indicate that the BART-large model outperformed the Pegasus-large model. To boost performance even further, we fine-tuned both models for domain adaptation using Masked Language Modeling (MLM) and retrained them for span identification. Following domain adaptation, both models showed noticeable improvements.

For the pre-trained Pegasus-large model after domain adaptation, we achieved a Rouge-1 score of 0.37 (**37%**), Rouge-2 score of 0.16 (**16%**), Rouge-L score of 0.33 (**33%**), BERTScore of 0.81 (**81%**), METEOR score of 0.33 (**33%**), and BLEU score of 0.12 (**12%**), resulting in an average Task B score of 0.35 (**35%**).

Similarly, the pre-trained BART-large model showed improved results, we obtained a Rouge-1 score of 0.4 (**40%**), Rouge-2 score of 0.18 (18%), Rouge-L score of 0.36 (**36%**), BERTScore of 0.84 (**84%**), METEOR score of 0.37 (**37%**), and BLEU score of 0.13 (**13%**), resulting in an average Task B score of 0.38 (**38%**).

After domain adaptation, both models improved, with BART-large still outperforming Pegasus-large.

4.3 Inference

4.3.1 Span Identification Module

To identify spans, we process the dataset by extracting the "uri," "answers," and "labelled_answer_spans" fields. The model is then applied to predict spans based on the "answers" field. The predicted spans are stored in a JSON format, where each "uri" is associated with a dictionary containing the identified spans. If no spans are predicted for a given category, an empty array is used for that category. For example, if a dataset entry discusses newborn care, a recommendation such as "So you might want to check your baby in daylight in a sunny room" would be classified under "SUGGESTION," while a factual statement like "Jaundice is an illness that can occur within the first few days of a baby's life" would be categorized under "INFORMATION."

4.3.2 Summarization Module

We use the BART-large model to generate summaries based on the predicted spans. The generated summaries are then stored in the "summaries" dictionary, corresponding to each perspective span, such as "EXPERIENCE," "INFORMATION," "CAUSE," "SUGGESTION," and "QUES-

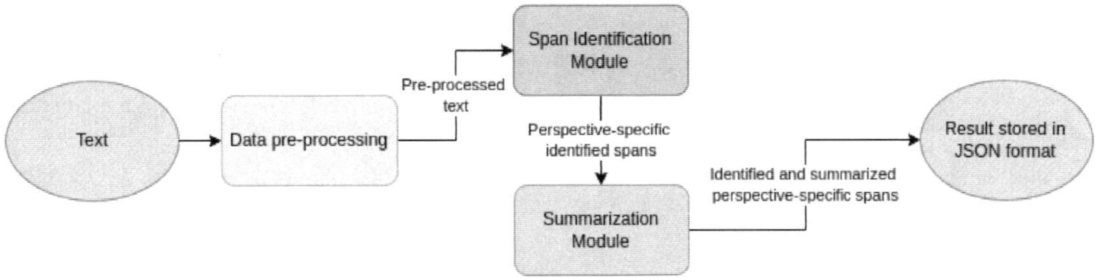

Figure 1: System Workflow

TION." Each category holds a relevant summary derived from the respective spans.

5 Evaluation Metrics

For Task A (Span Identification and Classification), performance is assessed using a macro-averaged F1 score for classification, which ensures balanced evaluation across all classes. For span identification, two matching strategies are employed: Strict matching, which requires an exact span match, and proportional matching, which allows partial matches to account for variability in span boundaries.

For Task B (Summarization), a comprehensive set of evaluation metrics is utilized to measure the quality of generated summaries. These include ROUGE (R1, R2, and RL), which captures the overlap between generated and reference summaries, BLEU, which evaluates n-gram precision, Meteor, which accounts for synonymy and stemming, and BERTScore, which leverages contextual embeddings to assess semantic similarity. These metrics collectively provide a robust evaluation framework for summarization performance.

6 Results

The evaluation results for the different experiments are presented in Table 2 and Table 3. For Task A (Span Identification and Classification), we submitted the RoBERTa-large model, while for Task B (Summarization), we used the BART-large model. Our system achieved an average score of **60%** for TASK_A and **38%** for TASK_B, leading to an overall average score of **49%**. Based on these scores, we secured 6th place on the leaderboard.

7 Conclusion

Our study demonstrates the effectiveness of fine-tuning large language models for perspective-specific span identification and summarization. By leveraging domain-adaptive pre-training and optimization techniques such as gradual training, we significantly improved performance in both tasks. For TASK_A, RoBERTa-large proved to be the most effective model, achieving a final accuracy of **60%** through gradual fine-tuning. For TASK_B, BART-large outperformed Pegasus-large, reaching **38%** accuracy after additional pre-training. These results highlight the importance of targeted pre-training and optimization strategies in enhancing model performance for specialized NLP tasks. Our approach provides a reliable method for identifying and summarizing perspective-specific information, contributing to more advanced and context-aware text processing applications.

Limitations

While our approach improves performance, it still depends on manually annotated training data for TASK_A and TASK_B. We used a gradual training method, but exploring alternative approaches could further enhance results. Moreover, our method requires extensive high-quality annotated data, making scalability challenging, especially in new domains where annotation is costly and time-consuming. Another challenge is handling overlapping or implicit perspectives, where multiple viewpoints exist within the same span or are only implied rather than explicitly stated. This makes it harder for the model to extract distinct perspectives, potentially leading to incomplete or biased summaries. Additionally, while our approach effectively extracts and summarizes perspective-specific information, it does not verify factual accuracy or neutrality, which may impact real-world use. Future improvements could optimize training, better handle ambiguous perspectives and integrate fact-checking mechanisms.

References

Siddhant Agarwal, Md Shad Akhtar, and Shweta Yadav. 2025. Overview of the peranssumm 2025 shared task on perspective-aware healthcare answer summarization. In *Proceedings of the Second Workshop on Patient-Oriented Language Processing (CL4Health) @ NAACL 2025*, Albuquerque, USA. Association for Computational Linguistics.

Mehdi Allahyari, Seyedamin Pouriyeh, Mehdi Assefi, Saeid Safaei, Elizabeth D. Trippe, Juan B. Gutierrez, and Krys Kochut. 2017. Text summarization techniques: A brief survey. *Preprint*, arXiv:1707.02268.

Hongliang Bi and Pengyuan Liu. 2020. Ecsp: A new task for emotion-cause span-pair extraction and classification. *Preprint*, arXiv:2003.03507.

Jason P.C. Chiu and Eric Nichols. 2016. Named entity recognition with bidirectional LSTM-CNNs. *Transactions of the Association for Computational Linguistics*, 4:357–370.

Jacob Devlin, Ming-Wei Chang, Kenton Lee, and Kristina Toutanova. 2018. BERT: pre-training of deep bidirectional transformers for language understanding. *CoRR*, abs/1810.04805.

Jinlan Fu, Xuanjing Huang, and Pengfei Liu. 2021. SpanNER: Named entity re-/recognition as span prediction. In *Proceedings of the 59th Annual Meeting of the Association for Computational Linguistics and the 11th International Joint Conference on Natural Language Processing (Volume 1: Long Papers)*, pages 7183–7195, Online. Association for Computational Linguistics.

Beliz Gunel, Jingfei Du, Alexis Conneau, and Ves Stoyanov. 2021. Supervised contrastive learning for pre-trained language model fine-tuning. *Preprint*, arXiv:2011.01403.

Yaser Keneshloo, Tian Shi, Naren Ramakrishnan, and Chandan K. Reddy. 2019. Deep reinforcement learning for sequence to sequence models. *Preprint*, arXiv:1805.09461.

Mike Lewis, Yinhan Liu, Naman Goyal, Marjan Ghazvininejad, Abdelrahman Mohamed, Omer Levy, Veselin Stoyanov, and Luke Zettlemoyer. 2019. BART: denoising sequence-to-sequence pre-training for natural language generation, translation, and comprehension. *CoRR*, abs/1910.13461.

Min Li, Hui Zhao, Hao Su, Yurong Qian, and Ping Li. 2021. Emotion-cause span extraction: a new task to emotion cause identification in texts. *Applied Intelligence*, 51(10):7109–7121.

Xiaoya Li, Jingrong Feng, Yuxian Meng, Qinghong Han, Fei Wu, and Jiwei Li. 2020. A unified MRC framework for named entity recognition. In *Proceedings of the 58th Annual Meeting of the Association for Computational Linguistics*, pages 5849–5859, Online. Association for Computational Linguistics.

Yinhan Liu, Myle Ott, Naman Goyal, Jingfei Du, Mandar Joshi, Danqi Chen, Omer Levy, Mike Lewis, Luke Zettlemoyer, and Veselin Stoyanov. 2019. Roberta: A robustly optimized BERT pretraining approach. *CoRR*, abs/1907.11692.

Congbo Ma, Wei Emma Zhang, Mingyu Guo, Hu Wang, and Quan Z. Sheng. 2022. Multi-document summarization via deep learning techniques: A survey. *ACM Comput. Surv.*, 55(5).

Gauri Naik, Sharad Chandakacherla, Shweta Yadav, and Md Shad Akhtar. 2024. No perspective, no perception!! perspective-aware healthcare answer summarization. In *Findings of the Association for Computational Linguistics: ACL 2024*, pages 15919–15932, Bangkok, Thailand. Association for Computational Linguistics.

Bowen Tan, Lianhui Qin, Eric Xing, and Zhiting Hu. 2020. Summarizing text on any aspects: A knowledge-informed weakly-supervised approach. In *Proceedings of the 2020 Conference on Empirical Methods in Natural Language Processing (EMNLP)*, pages 6301–6309, Online. Association for Computational Linguistics.

Rui Xia and Zixiang Ding. 2019. Emotion-cause pair extraction: A new task to emotion analysis in texts. In *Proceedings of the 57th Annual Meeting of the Association for Computational Linguistics*, pages 1003–1012, Florence, Italy. Association for Computational Linguistics.

Weiwen Xu, Xin Li, Yang Deng, Wai Lam, and Lidong Bing. 2023. PeerDA: Data augmentation via modeling peer relation for span identification tasks. In *Proceedings of the 61st Annual Meeting of the Association for Computational Linguistics (Volume 1: Long Papers)*, pages 8681–8699, Toronto, Canada. Association for Computational Linguistics.

Jingqing Zhang, Yao Zhao, Mohammad Saleh, and Peter J. Liu. 2019. Pegasus: Pre-training with extracted gap-sentences for abstractive summarization. *Preprint*, arXiv:1912.08777.

YaleNLP @ PerAnsSumm 2025: Multi-Perspective Integration via Mixture-of-Agents for Enhanced Healthcare QA Summarization

Dongsuk Jang[1,2,3], **Alan Li**[1], **Arman Cohan**[1]
[1]Department of Computer Science, Yale University,
[2]Interdisciplinary Program for Bioengineering, Seoul National University,
[3]Integrated Major in Innovative Medical Science, Seoul National University
{james.jang, haoxin.li, arman.cohan}@yale.edu

Abstract

Automated summarization of healthcare community question-answering forums is challenging due to diverse perspectives presented across multiple user responses to each question. The PerAnsSumm Shared Task was therefore proposed to tackle this challenge by identifying perspectives from different answers and then generating a comprehensive answer to the question. In this study, we address the PerAnsSumm Shared Task using two complementary paradigms: (i) a training-based approach through QLoRA fine-tuning of LLaMA-3.3-70B-Instruct, and (ii) agentic approaches including zero- and few-shot prompting with frontier LLMs (LLaMA-3.3-70B-Instruct and GPT-4o) and a Mixture-of-Agents (MoA) framework that leverages a diverse set of LLMs by combining outputs from multi-layer feedback aggregation. For perspective span identification/classification, GPT-4o zero-shot achieves an overall score of 0.57, substantially outperforming the 0.40 score of the LLaMA baseline. With a 2-layer MoA configuration, we were able to improve LLaMA performance up by 28% to 0.51. For perspective-based summarization, GPT-4o zero-shot attains an overall score of 0.42 compared to 0.28 for the best LLaMA zero-shot, and our 2-layer MoA approach boosts LLaMA performance by 32% to 0.37. Furthermore, in few-shot setting, our results show that the sentence-transformer embedding-based exemplar selection provides more gain than manually selected exemplars on LLaMA models, although the few-shot prompting is not always helpful for GPT-4o. The YaleNLP team's approach ranked the overall second place in the shared task.

1 Introduction

Healthcare Community Question Answering (CQA) forums are rapidly growing as accessible platforms for individuals to seek medical advice, share personal experiences, or request simplified explanations of health conditions. Unlike expert-oriented medical sites, user-driven forums incorporate a broad range of viewpoints, from anecdotal evidence to speculative reasoning. Although the diversity can enrich the discussion, it also leads to information overload and frequent off-topic comments, making it difficult for newcomers to identify critical insights. Traditionally, the CQA answer summarization task focuses on a single best-voted answer (Chowdhury and Chakraborty, 2018; Chowdhury et al., 2020) as a reference summary. However, a single answer often fails to capture the diverse perspectives presented across multiple answers. Providing the answers in structured, perspective-specific summaries could better serve the information needs of end users.

In response to this challenge, the **PerAnsSumm Shared Task** at the CL4Health@NAACL 2025 Workshop (Agarwal et al., 2025) introduces a perspective-specific summarization benchmark, encouraging researchers to design systems that explicitly recognize and integrate various user viewpoints into their outputs. The task is comprised of two phases. Given a medical related query and a set of answers from CQA forums, the system is required to (i) identify the specific perspective in each of the answer and (ii) generate a summarization for each of these perspectives across different answers. Detailed task setup will be introduced in Section 3.

Our main contributions and findings are as follows:

- We show that GPT-4o (OpenAI et al., 2024) generally outperforms 70B-level open-source models (the largest models we have access to) in both the span identification/classification and perspective-based summarization tasks. Providing few-shot examples do not *consistently* yield higher performance.

[1]Figure adapted from Agarwal et al. https://peranssumm.github.io/docs/

Proceedings of the Second Workshop on Patient-Oriented Language Processing (CL4Health), pages 415–427
May 4, 2025 ©2025 Association for Computational Linguistics

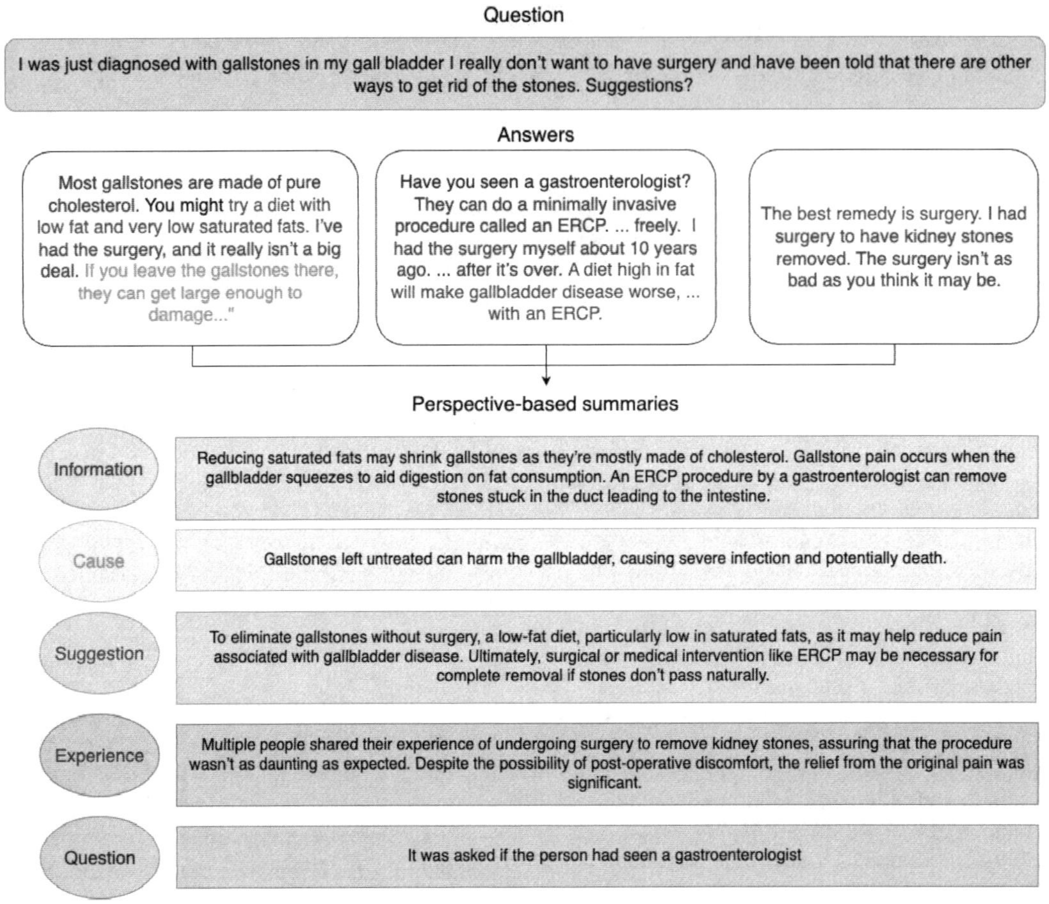

Figure 1: PerAnsSumm Shared Task overview.[1]

- In few-shot setting, example selection by clustering on candidate example embeddings yield consistent improvements over manual example selection.
- Implementing a MoA (Wang et al., 2024) approach with multiple open-source LLMs significantly improves performance over individual models, demonstrating the potential of this ensemble strategy.
- QLoRA (Dettmers et al., 2023) fine-tuning with generic limited training data does not provide performance gains under our experimental conditions; in fact, it degrades performance. Due to the time constraints of the challenge, we were unable to explore additional fine-tuning configurations. We leave fine-tuning recipe exploration to future work.

We reimplemented[2] the relevant techniques to align with the PerAnsSumm Shared Task. Through these experiments, our objective is to provide insight into the strengths and limitations of LLM-based approaches for perspective-aware summarization in medical CQA.

2 Related Work

Early abstractive summarization largely relied on pre-trained models such as BART (Lewis et al., 2020), T5 (Raffel et al., 2023), and PEGASUS (Zhang et al., 2020a), demonstrating strong performance on news benchmarks like CNN/DailyMail (Hermann et al., 2015) or XSum (Narayan et al., 2018). Yet, these approaches are typically optimized for well-structured, professionally written content. In contrast, healthcare forums contain personal opinions, anecdotal evidence, and multiple viewpoints that can hinder purely data-driven summarizers (Chaturvedi et al., 2024).

Recent works in aspect- or perspective-oriented summarization highlight the value of parsing out

[2]https://github.com/JamesJang26/YALENLP-PerAnsSumm-2025

different user viewpoints. Naik et al. (2024) emphasize splitting content into categories like *cause, suggestion, experience*, while AnswerSumm (Fabbri et al., 2022) extracts sentence-level spans for query-focused summaries, though it does not fully address overlapping perspectives common in community Q&A. At the same time, multi-document techniques for high-variance domains (Liu et al., 2018) suggest strategies for aggregating and reconciling disparate user responses.

Moreover, the rise of large language models has fueled interest in zero-/few-shot prompting, with studies showing that manually curated exemplars can be fragile or insufficiently general. Embedding-based selection methods like FsPONER (Tang et al., 2024) and adaptive few-shot prompting (Tang et al., 2025; Chang et al., 2021) propose retrieving exemplars via similarity or clustering, offering more stable and domain-sensitive prompts. Such techniques are well-suited to healthcare Q&A, where a single misaligned exemplar can skew the summary toward incorrect or irrelevant details.

While prompt-based approaches can reduce reliance on large labeled datasets, certain tasks still benefit from specialized model tuning. To this end, LoRA (Hu et al., 2021) introduced a low-rank adaptation mechanism that updates only a small fraction of model parameters, and QLoRA (Dettmers et al., 2023) extends this concept by quantizing weights for further efficiency. These methods enable domain-focused tuning without the prohibitive resource costs typically associated with training massive LLMs from scratch.

3 PerAnsSumm

PerAnsSumm Shared Task is comprised of two subtasks sequentially, as shown in . Given a question Q, a set of answers A, and perspective categories {`cause`, `suggestion`, `experience`, `information`, `question`}, we are assigned the following two tasks:

3.1 Task A: Span Identification and Classification

For each answer in A, identify all text spans that convey any of the five perspectives.

Following the task guidelines, systems must output a list of labeled spans. For example:

```
span: "<extracted span>", label:
"<perspective>"
```

Any text not relevant to a predefined perspective is omitted.

Evaluation Metrics PerAnsSumm evaluates Task A under two main criteria:

- **Classification**: Whether the model correctly assigns a perspective label to an answer if it contains that perspective. Macro-F1 and Weighted-F1 are reported.
- **Span Matching**: Compares predicted spans with gold-standard spans via strict matching and proportional matching.

An overall macro-average of these measures is used for final ranking.

3.2 Task B: Perspective-Based Summaries

Building on Task A, after identifying and labeling spans in a Q&A thread, the system must produce a short, coherent summary for each perspective that appears.

Systems typically generate summaries in a structured format, for example:

```
EXPERIENCE Summary: <text>
INFORMATION Summary: <text>
CAUSE Summary: <text>
SUGGESTION Summary: <text>
QUESTION Summary: <text>
```

If a perspective is deemed absent by the model, no summary is produced for that label.

Evaluation Metrics To assess each perspective-specific summary, PerAnsSumm combines measures of *relevance* and *factuality*,

- **Relevance**: ROUGE (Lin, 2004), BLEU (Papineni et al., 2002), METEOR (Banerjee and Lavie, 2005), and BERTScore (Zhang et al., 2020b) quantify how well the generated summary aligns with the reference.
- **Factuality**: AlignScore (Zha et al., 2023) and SummaC (Laban et al., 2022) confirm that the summary is consistent with the original source text (i.e., it does not hallucinate or contradict).

These sub-metrics are aggregated into a final Task B score.

4 Methods

This section details the various modeling strategies we explore, including zero-/few-shot prompting, the MoA framework, and QLoRA supervised fine-tuning.

4.1 Zero-/Few-Shot Prompting

Zero-Shot Setup. We first experiment with prompting large language models using a instruction that specifies the task (either span identification/classification or perspective-based summarization). For instance, we provide definitions of the five perspectives (*cause, suggestion, experience, information, question*) and ask the model to extract or summarize accordingly (best prompt for each tasks are detailed in Appendix C). This approach requires no additional training or fine-tuning, leveraging the general knowledge embedded in instruction-tuned LLMs.

Few-Shot Setup. We provide 3–5 exemplars to the model via the prompt. We investigate two distinct methods for exemplar selection:

Manually Curated: We pick representative CQA threads that cover multiple perspectives and exhibit typical corner cases.

Embedding-Based Selection: We embed all potential demonstration samples from training set with a sentence-transformer (e.g., `all-MiniLM-L6-v2` in our case), cluster them using k-means, and then pick top-k samples based on proximity to the test query.

4.2 Mixture-of-Agents

Medical content requires both domain knowledge and nuanced understanding of different viewpoints. To overcome these limitations, we implement a Mixture-of-Agents (MoA) framework that leverages the complementary strengths of multiple language models working in concert. MoA is a framework for ensembling multiple sub-models (or agents) and integrating their outputs via an aggregator. We adapt and extend this method for our tasks. Specifically, we consider different numbers of layers (1, 2, or 3) in the MoA pipeline:

- **1-Layer MoA**: Each agent generates a partial response (e.g., predicted spans or short perspective-based summaries). An aggregator model then fuses these responses into a final output in a single step.
- **2-Layer MoA**: After collecting agent outputs, we employ an intermediate "verification" layer to refine or check consistency before passing the refined results to the final aggregator model.
- **3-Layer MoA**: We add an additional "hallucination detection" layer, which aims to filter out or correct unsupported statements before the final aggregation.

For our agent selection, we incorporate diverse models including open-source LLMs (LLaMA-3.3-70B-Instruct, Qwen-2.5-72B-Instruct, Deepseek-R1-Distill-LLaMA-70B) and closed-source models (GPT-4o, GPT-4o-mini). This diversity is intentional—each model brings different strengths in medical reasoning, language understanding, and factual recall. By combining them, we aim to create a system that outperforms any individual model, especially for complex medical content where perspectives might be subtle or require domain expertise.

We test various configurations to understand the optimal MoA architecture for each subtask. These configurations include combinations of open-source models only, GPT-4o only, and hybrid approaches where different model types handle different stages of the pipeline. For example, one effective arrangement uses GPT-4o for span identification/classification and a MoA ensemble for perspective-wise summarization based on those identified spans. We also explore the reverse configuration, as well as using MoA for both tasks. Through these experiments, we can measure the synergistic effects gained from mixing diverse LLMs and identify which models perform best at each stage of the process.

The multi-layer verification approach is particularly valuable for healthcare content, where accuracy is paramount. By adding verification and hallucination detection layers, we create checkpoints where potentially incorrect or unsupported information can be filtered or corrected before final aggregation, improving the reliability of the generated summaries.

4.3 QLoRA Supervised Fine-Tuning

While zero-/few-shot prompting relies on the generalization capabilities of LLMs, we also investigate QLoRA, a parameter-efficient fine-tuning approach. Through QLoRA, we can update a small set of low-rank adaptation parameters while keeping the majority of model weights frozen. This reduces both the computational overhead and memory usage compared to full fine-tuning.

Model	Setting	M-F1	W-F1	St-P	St-R	St-F1	Pr-P	Pr-R	Pr-F1	Overall
LLaMA-3.3-70B-Instruct	Zero-shot	0.5381	0.7299	0.0320	0.1218	0.0507	0.4530	0.6991	0.5498	0.3968
	3-shot w/ H	0.5390	0.7265	0.0339	0.1240	0.0513	0.4665	0.7163	0.5673	0.4031
	3-shot w/ C	0.5697	0.7676	0.0385	0.1311	0.0565	0.4954	0.7404	0.5974	0.4246
	QLoRA SFT	0.4788	0.6584	0.0256	0.1158	0.0447	0.4216	0.6681	0.5184	0.3664
GPT-4o	Zero-shot	**0.8949**	**0.9190**	**0.1756**	**0.2641**	**0.2110**	0.6578	0.7392	0.6961	**0.5697**
	3-shot w/ H	0.8176	0.8479	0.1552	0.2193	0.1818	0.6145	0.7124	0.6599	0.5261
	3-shot w/ C	0.8553	0.8723	0.1468	0.2546	0.1862	**0.6810**	**0.7525**	**0.7150**	0.5580
MoA	Best 1	0.8129	0.8478	0.1491	0.2072	0.1734	0.5512	0.6942	0.6145	0.5063
	Best 2	0.7682	0.7809	0.1443	0.1697	0.1560	0.5412	0.6512	0.5912	0.4753

Table 1: **Task A**(span identification/classification) results . "3-shot w/ H(uman)" means three manually curated examples were used for few-shot prompting; "3-shot w/ C(lustering)" means three exemplars were automatically selected via sentence-transformer embeddings. Metrics include Macro-F1 (M-F1), Weighted-F1 (W-F1), Strict Precision/Recall/F1 (St-P, St-R, St-F1), Proportional Precision/Recall/F1 (Pr-P, Pr-R, Pr-F1), and an Overall average.

5 Experiments

We employ a diverse set of open-source models (LLaMA-3.3-70B-Instruct (AI, 2024), Qwen-2.5-72B-Instruct (Qwen et al., 2025), and Deepseek-R1-Distill-LLaMA-70B (DeepSeek-AI et al., 2025)) and closed frontier model (GPT-4o and GPT-4o-mini (OpenAI et al., 2024)).

5.1 Experimental Data

We employ the PUMA[3] (Naik et al., 2024) corpus provided by PerAnsSumm shared task. It contains 3,245 Q&A threads, each with up to five perspective annotations (`cause`, `suggestion`, `experience`, `information`, `question`) and reference summaries per perspective. We follow official splits: 2,236 threads for training, 959 for validation, and 50 withheld for testing, while for the paper, we tested on the last 400 cases from valid set.

5.2 QLoRA Finetuning Implementation

We used `llama-factory` (Zheng et al., 2024) toolkit to simply fine-tune LLaMA-3.3-70B-Instruct under various hyperparameter settings. For additional fine-tuning details, see Appendix A.

6 Results

We evaluate our approaches on two tasks: **Task A** (span identification/classification) and **Task B** (perspective-based summarization), using the macro-averaged metrics described in Section 3.1 and 3.2.

[3]Perspective s**UM**marization d**A**taset

6.1 Task A: Span Identification and Classification

Table 1 presents the classification and span-matching results.

GPT-4o Zero-Shot remains the best overall single-model approach, scoring 0.5697 in Overall average, which notably outperforms all other models or methods. Detailed span identification results is described in Appendix B.

Few-Shot Prompting For both LLaMA-3.3-70B-Instruct and GPT-4o, embedding-based selection (0.4246 and 0.5580 overall) outperforms manually curated exemplars (0.4031 and 0.5261), showing better generalizability than human-chosen examples.

QLoRA Supervised Fine-tuning For Task A, our QLoRA-based fine-tuning of the LLaMA-3.3-70B-Instruct model (see Table 1) obtains an overall score of 0.3664, which is below the best zero- or few-shot baselines.

MoA Details. Best 1 is a 2-layer MoA with four open-source models in Layer 1 (two LLaMA-3.3-70B-Instruct + two Qwen-2.5-72B-Instrcut), one LLaMA-3.3-70B-Instruct in Layer 2, and an aggregator also based on LLaMA-3.3-70B-Instruct. As illustrated in Figure 2, a 2-layer configuration strikes the best balance between thoroughness and retaining valid outputs, outperforming both 1-layer and 3-layer variants. **Best 2** uses a similar 2-layer pipeline but swaps the sub-model composition to four temperature variants of LLaMA-3.3-70B-Instruct for Layer 1. Both surpass single LLaMA setups, underscoring MoA's ability to fuse multiple perspectives effectively.

Model	Setting	R-1	R-2	R-L	BLEU	MET	BS	AS	SC	Overall
LLaMA-3.3-70B-Instruct	Zero-shot	0.2476	0.0886	0.2156	0.0471	0.2777	0.8182	0.3096	0.2247	0.2786
	3-shot w/ H	0.2583	0.0968	0.2241	0.0487	0.2891	0.7612	0.2864	0.2345	0.2749
	3-shot w/ C	0.2733	0.0994	0.2398	0.0817	0.3055	0.8295	0.3151	0.2498	0.2993
	QLoRA SFT	0.2165	0.0778	0.1947	0.0315	0.2460	0.7960	0.2486	0.2033	0.2518
GPT-4o	Zero-shot	**0.4704**	0.2340	0.4038	**0.1307**	**0.4289**	**0.9116**	**0.4615**	**0.3031**	**0.4180**
	3-shot w/ H	0.4519	0.2291	0.3825	0.1193	0.3701	0.8821	0.4212	0.2543	0.3888
	3-shot w/ C	0.4515	**0.2524**	**0.4057**	0.1212	0.3987	0.8901	0.4552	0.2812	0.4070
MoA	Best 1	0.4372	0.2103	0.3611	0.1025	0.3305	0.8558	0.3913	0.2614	0.3688
	Best 2	0.4192	0.2055	0.3502	0.1096	0.3206	0.8512	0.3608	0.2853	0.3628

Table 2: **Task B**(perspective-based summarization) results. "3-shot w/ H(uman)" vs. "3-shot w/ C(lustering)" follows the same few-shot definitions as Table 1. Metrics include ROUGE (R-1, R-2, R-L), BLEU, METEOR (MET), BERTScore (BS), AlignScore (AS), SummaC (SC), and an Overall average.

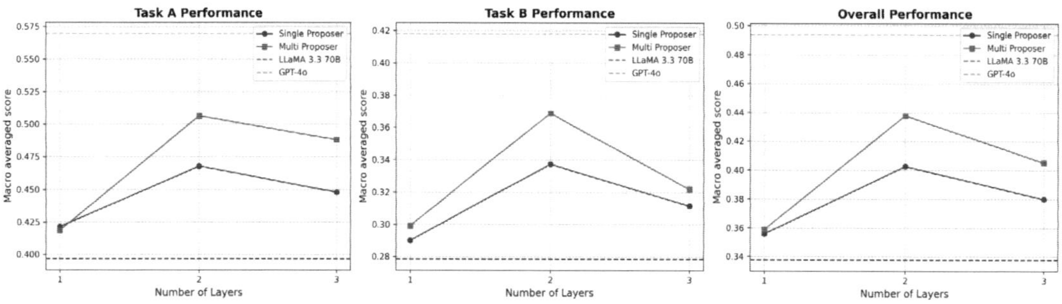

Figure 2: Performance comparison across different MoA layer counts.

MoA Best 1 at 0.5063, Best 2 at 0.4753 show strong improvements over single LLaMA-3.3-70B-Instruct baselines, though they still trail GPT-4o zero-shot. Nonetheless, MoA outperforms any single open-source LLM setting by a noticeable margin, 8% over LLaMA's best.

6.2 Task B: Perspective-Based Summaries

Table 2 shows the summarization performance, which is derived based on the best result spans from Task A, obtained using the optimal prompt detailed in Table 5 of Appendix C. Once again, the zero-shot GPT-4o approach leads with a general average of 0.4180, exceeding its 3-shot variants and aligning with the trends observed in Task A.

Few-shot Prompting For LLaMA-3.3-70B-Instruct, "3-shot w/ Clustering" yields 0.2993 overall vs 0.2749 with human-chosen examples and 0.2786 in zero-shot. Similarly for GPT-4o, sentence-transformer embedding based selection attains 0.4070, surpassing the human-chosen 3-shot (0.3888) while still slightly lower than the zero-shot GPT-4o (0.4180). Hence, while GPT-4o with zero-shot remains the single best, sentence-transformer embedding based few-shot tends to outperform manually curated exemplars.

MoA *Best 1* achieves 0.3688, while *Best 2* gets 0.3628, each notably exceeding LLaMA-3.3-70B-Instruct's best (0.2993). Although not rivaling GPT-4o, they confirm MoA's capacity to reduce hallucinations and unify multiple sub-model outputs.

QLoRA Supervised Fine-tuning For Task B, QLoRA fine-tuning yields an overall score of 0.2518 (Table 2), again lower than the corresponding zero- and few-shot results.

6.3 Ablation on Aggregators and Layering

Aggregator Comparison. Table 3 compares four aggregator models—LLaMA-3.3-70B-Instruct, Qwen-2.5-72B-Instruct, DeepSeek-R1-LLaMA-70B, GPT-4o-mini for the same MoA sub-model outputs (Best 1). LLaMA-3.3-70B-Instruct yields the highest Task A/B scores (0.5063 / 0.3688), while the GPT-4o mini aggregator drops to (0.4027 / 0.2981), showing that the aggregator choice is crucial.

Layering Comparison. Figure 2 illustrates how adding layers impacts MoA performance under two configurations:

- **Single Proposer:** Only LLaMA-3.3-70B-Instruct models are used to produce output

Aggregator	Task A	Task B
LLaMA-3.3-70B-Instruct	**0.5063**	**0.3688**
Qwen2.5-72B-Instruct	0.4719	0.3456
DeepSeek-R1-LLaMA-70B	0.4671	0.3411
GPT-4o-mini	0.4027	0.2981

Table 3: Performance comparison of different aggregators on Task A and Task B, holding the same MoA sub-model outputs as in "Best 1".

in each layer.

- **Multi Proposer:** LLaMA-3.3-70B-Instruct and Qwen-2.5-72B-Instrcut are combined to generate more diverse proposals.

In both cases, LLaMA-3.3-70B-Instruct is used as the aggregator, and the dashed lines indicate the zero-shot baselines (LLaMA: 0.3377 overall; GPT-4o: 0.4938 overall).

In the **Single Proposer** setting, the 1-layer model obtains an overall score of 0.3559, which increases to 0.4025 with 2 layers (a gain of 0.0466 points) but then drops to 0.3799 when using 3 layers. Similarly, in the **Multi Proposer** setting, the overall score rises from 0.3590 for 1 layer to 0.4376 for 2 layers (an improvement of 0.0786 points), before falling to 0.4050 with 3 layers.

These results indicate that adding a second layer consistently improves performance—yielding an improvement of roughly 14% over the LLaMA zero-shot baseline—while the third layer tends to over-correction, resulting in a performance drop. Thus, the 2-layer multi proposer configuration offers the best trade-off between enhancing overall accuracy and retaining valid outputs.

7 Conclusion

In this work, we addressed the challenge of perspective-aware summarization for healthcare Q&A. Our experiments show the recipe we tried and the final solution submitted for the challenge. With a bit disappointment, although MoA and embedding-based few-shot example selection improves the performance of open-source solution, the closed model, specifically GPT-4o in our case, still outperforms our best open-source solution by a large margin. Overall, our results highlight promising directions in leveraging large language models for multi-perspective healthcare Q&A, particularly when curated resources are scarce.

8 Limitations

Data size and quality could be one of major constraints. The generic training set might be too small to conduct effective finetuning. In our observation, Text span identification/classification annotations contain overlaps and ambiguities (e.g. extracted span starts with an incomplete word or punctuation), complicating the accuracy of perspective labels and gold summaries.

To apply an encoder-based model for span identification, we experimented with weighted NER finetuning (Appendix D). This approach assigns higher weights to underrepresented perspective categories to mitigate class imbalance. However, our results did not yield improvements, likely due to the inherent complexity and variability of user-generated content in the dataset. This suggests that alternative techniques, such as data augmentation or more robust fine-tuning strategies, may be necessary for handling imbalanced annotations effectively.

While MoA framework brings performance improvement, MoA configurations demand additional computational resources, especially in multi-layer or multi-agent setups.

Addressing these limitations, for example, through larger, more balanced datasets and more efficient aggregator layers, could further enhance perspective-aware summarization in real-world healthcare scenarios.

9 Future Work

To overcome current constraints, future endeavors could involve extracting more healthcare-related queries from broader corpora such as Natural Questions, followed by data augmentation via LLMs to create synthetic examples for underrepresented perspectives. A refined Mixture-of-Agents design could then integrate these enriched training sets for both classification and summarization tasks, thereby mitigating data scarcity, enhancing perspective coverage, and improving model generalizability across diverse healthcare topics.

Although our preliminary exploration shows that embedding-based selection boosts performance over manually curated exemplars, further studies on prompting construction techniques, like dynamic prompt construction (Gonen et al., 2022), retrieval-augmented prompting (Tang et al., 2025), or synthetic prompts (Kong et al., 2024), may lead to additional gains. We leave these investigations to future work, anticipating that such refinements will further enhance the robustness and scalability of perspective-aware summarization in the healthcare domain.

Acknowledgments

This research was supported by a grant of the Korea Health Technology R&D Project through the Korea Health Industry Development Institute (KHIDI), funded by the Ministry of Health & Welfare, Republic of Korea (grant number : HI19C1352).

References

Siddhant Agarwal, Md Shad Akhtar, and Shweta Yadav. 2025. Overview of the peranssumm 2025 shared task on perspective-aware healthcare answer summarization. In *Proceedings of the Second Workshop on Patient-Oriented Language Processing (CL4Health) @ NAACL 2025*, Albuquerque, USA. Association for Computational Linguistics.

Meta AI. 2024. Llama 3.3 model card and prompt formats. Accessed: 2024-12-06.

Satanjeev Banerjee and Alon Lavie. 2005. METEOR: An automatic metric for MT evaluation with improved correlation with human judgments. In *Proceedings of the ACL Workshop on Intrinsic and Extrinsic Evaluation Measures for Machine Translation and/or Summarization*, pages 65–72, Ann Arbor, Michigan. Association for Computational Linguistics.

Ernie Chang, Xiaoyu Shen, Hui-Syuan Yeh, and Vera Demberg. 2021. On training instance selection for few-shot neural text generation. *ArXiv*, abs/2107.03176.

Rochana Chaturvedi, Abari Bhattacharya, and Shweta Yadav. 2024. Aspect-oriented consumer health answer summarization. *Preprint*, arXiv:2405.06295.

Tanya Chowdhury and Tanmoy Chakraborty. 2018. Cqasumm: Building references for community question answering summarization corpora. *Preprint*, arXiv:1811.04884.

Tanya Chowdhury, Sachin Kumar, and Tanmoy Chakraborty. 2020. Neural abstractive summarization with structural attention. *Preprint*, arXiv:2004.09739.

DeepSeek-AI, Daya Guo, Dejian Yang, Haowei Zhang, Junxiao Song, Ruoyu Zhang, Runxin Xu, Qihao Zhu, Shirong Ma, Peiyi Wang, Xiao Bi, Xiaokang Zhang, Xingkai Yu, Yu Wu, Z. F. Wu, Zhibin Gou, Zhihong Shao, Zhuoshu Li, Ziyi Gao, Aixin Liu, Bing Xue, Bingxuan Wang, Bochao Wu, Bei Feng, Chengda Lu, Chenggang Zhao, Chengqi Deng, Chenyu Zhang, Chong Ruan, Damai Dai, Deli Chen, Dongjie Ji, Erhang Li, Fangyun Lin, Fucong Dai, Fuli Luo, Guangbo Hao, Guanting Chen, Guowei Li, H. Zhang, Han Bao, Hanwei Xu, Haocheng Wang, Honghui Ding, Huajian Xin, Huazuo Gao, Hui Qu, Hui Li, Jianzhong Guo, Jiashi Li, Jiawei Wang, Jingchang Chen, Jingyang Yuan, Junjie Qiu, Junlong Li, J. L. Cai, Jiaqi Ni, Jian Liang, Jin Chen, Kai Dong, Kai Hu, Kaige Gao, Kang Guan, Kexin Huang, Kuai Yu, Lean Wang, Lecong Zhang, Liang Zhao, Litong Wang, Liyue Zhang, Lei Xu, Leyi Xia, Mingchuan Zhang, Minghua Zhang, Minghui Tang, Meng Li, Miaojun Wang, Mingming Li, Ning Tian, Panpan Huang, Peng Zhang, Qiancheng Wang, Qinyu Chen, Qiushi Du, Ruiqi Ge, Ruisong Zhang, Ruizhe Pan, Runji Wang, R. J. Chen, R. L. Jin, Ruyi Chen, Shanghao Lu, Shangyan Zhou, Shanhuang Chen, Shengfeng Ye, Shiyu Wang, Shuiping Yu, Shunfeng Zhou, Shuting Pan, S. S. Li, Shuang Zhou, Shaoqing Wu, Shengfeng Ye, Tao Yun, Tian Pei, Tianyu Sun, T. Wang, Wangding Zeng, Wanjia Zhao, Wen Liu, Wenfeng Liang, Wenjun Gao, Wenqin Yu, Wentao Zhang, W. L. Xiao, Wei An, Xiaodong Liu, Xiaohan Wang, Xiaokang Chen, Xiaotao Nie, Xin Cheng, Xin Liu, Xin Xie, Xingchao Liu, Xinyu Yang, Xinyuan Li, Xuecheng Su, Xuheng Lin, X. Q. Li, Xiangyue Jin, Xiaojin Shen, Xiaosha Chen, Xiaowen Sun, Xiaoxiang Wang, Xinnan Song, Xinyi Zhou, Xianzu Wang, Xinxia Shan, Y. K. Li, Y. Q. Wang, Y. X. Wei, Yang Zhang, Yanhong Xu, Yao Li, Yao Zhao, Yaofeng Sun, Yaohui Wang, Yi Yu, Yichao Zhang, Yifan Shi, Yiliang Xiong, Ying He, Yishi Piao, Yisong Wang, Yixuan Tan, Yiyang Ma, Yiyuan Liu, Yongqiang Guo, Yuan Ou, Yuduan Wang, Yue Gong, Yuheng Zou, Yujia He, Yunfan Xiong, Yuxiang Luo, Yuxiang You, Yuxuan Liu, Yuyang Zhou, Y. X. Zhu, Yanhong Xu, Yanping Huang, Yaohui Li, Yi Zheng, Yuchen Zhu, Yunxian Ma, Ying Tang, Yukun Zha, Yuting Yan, Z. Z. Ren, Zehui Ren, Zhangli Sha, Zhe Fu, Zhean Xu, Zhenda Xie, Zhengyan Zhang, Zhewen Hao, Zhicheng Ma, Zhigang Yan, Zhiyu Wu, Zihui Gu, Zijia Zhu, Zijun Liu, Zilin Li, Ziwei Xie, Ziyang Song, Zizheng Pan, Zhen Huang, Zhipeng Xu, Zhongyu Zhang, and Zhen Zhang. 2025. Deepseek-r1: Incentivizing reasoning capability in llms via reinforcement learning. *Preprint*, arXiv:2501.12948.

Tim Dettmers, Artidoro Pagnoni, Ari Holtzman, and Luke Zettlemoyer. 2023. Qlora: Efficient finetuning of quantized llms. *Preprint*, arXiv:2305.14314.

Alexander Fabbri, Xiaojian Wu, Srini Iyer, Haoran Li, and Mona Diab. 2022. AnswerSumm: A manually-curated dataset and pipeline for answer summarization. In *Proceedings of the 2022 Conference of the North American Chapter of the Association for Computational Linguistics: Human Language Technologies*, pages 2508–2520, Seattle, United States. Association for Computational Linguistics.

Hila Gonen, Srini Iyer, Terra Blevins, Noah A. Smith, and Luke Zettlemoyer. 2022. Demystifying prompts in language models via perplexity estimation. In *Conference on Empirical Methods in Natural Language Processing*.

Karl Moritz Hermann, Tomáš Kočiský, Edward Grefenstette, Lasse Espeholt, Will Kay, Mustafa Suleyman, and Phil Blunsom. 2015. Teaching machines to read and comprehend. *Preprint*, arXiv:1506.03340.

Edward J. Hu, Yelong Shen, Phillip Wallis, Zeyuan Allen-Zhu, Yuanzhi Li, Shean Wang, Lu Wang, and Weizhu Chen. 2021. Lora: Low-rank adaptation of large language models. *Preprint*, arXiv:2106.09685.

Yilun Kong, Hangyu Mao, Qi Zhao, Bin Zhang, Jingqing Ruan, Li Shen, Yongzhe Chang, Xueqian Wang, Rui Zhao, and Dacheng Tao. 2024. Qpo: Query-dependent prompt optimization via multi-loop offline reinforcement learning. *ArXiv*, abs/2408.10504.

Philippe Laban, Tobias Schnabel, Paul N. Bennett, and Marti A. Hearst. 2022. SummaC: Re-visiting NLI-based models for inconsistency detection in summarization. *Transactions of the Association for Computational Linguistics*, 10:163–177.

Mike Lewis, Yinhan Liu, Naman Goyal, Marjan Ghazvininejad, Abdelrahman Mohamed, Omer Levy, Veselin Stoyanov, and Luke Zettlemoyer. 2020. BART: Denoising sequence-to-sequence pre-training for natural language generation, translation, and comprehension. In *Proceedings of the 58th Annual Meeting of the Association for Computational Linguistics*, pages 7871–7880, Online. Association for Computational Linguistics.

Chin-Yew Lin. 2004. ROUGE: A package for automatic evaluation of summaries. In *Text Summarization Branches Out*, pages 74–81, Barcelona, Spain. Association for Computational Linguistics.

Peter J. Liu, Mohammad Saleh, Etienne Pot, Ben Goodrich, Ryan Sepassi, Lukasz Kaiser, and Noam Shazeer. 2018. Generating wikipedia by summarizing long sequences. *Preprint*, arXiv:1801.10198.

Gauri Naik, Sharad Chandakacherla, Shweta Yadav, and Md Shad Akhtar. 2024. No perspective, no perception!! perspective-aware healthcare answer summarization. In *Findings of the Association for Computational Linguistics: ACL 2024*, pages 15919–15932, Bangkok, Thailand. Association for Computational Linguistics.

Shashi Narayan, Shay B. Cohen, and Mirella Lapata. 2018. Don't give me the details, just the summary! topic-aware convolutional neural networks for extreme summarization. In *Proceedings of the 2018 Conference on Empirical Methods in Natural Language Processing*, pages 1797–1807, Brussels, Belgium. Association for Computational Linguistics.

OpenAI, :, Aaron Hurst, Adam Lerer, Adam P. Goucher, Adam Perelman, Aditya Ramesh, Aidan Clark, AJ Ostrow, Akila Welihinda, Alan Hayes, Alec Radford, Aleksander Mądry, Alex Baker-Whitcomb, Alex Beutel, Alex Borzunov, Alex Carney, Alex Chow, Alex Kirillov, Alex Nichol, Alex Paino, Alex Renzin, Alex Tachard Passos, Alexander Kirillov, Alexi Christakis, Alexis Conneau, Ali Kamali, Allan Jabri, Allison Moyer, Allison Tam, Amadou Crookes, Amin Tootoochian, Amin Tootoonchian, Ananya Kumar, Andrea Vallone, Andrej Karpathy, Andrew Braunstein, Andrew Cann, Andrew Codispoti, Andrew Galu, Andrew Kondrich, Andrew Tulloch, Andrey Mishchenko, Angela Baek, Angela Jiang, Antoine Pelisse, Antonia Woodford, Anuj Gosalia, Arka Dhar, Ashley Pantuliano, Avi Nayak, Avital Oliver, Barret Zoph, Behrooz Ghorbani, Ben Leimberger, Ben Rossen, Ben Sokolowsky, Ben Wang, Benjamin Zweig, Beth Hoover, Blake Samic, Bob McGrew, Bobby Spero, Bogo Giertler, Bowen Cheng, Brad Lightcap, Brandon Walkin, Brendan Quinn, Brian Guarraci, Brian Hsu, Bright Kellogg, Brydon Eastman, Camillo Lugaresi, Carroll Wainwright, Cary Bassin, Cary Hudson, Casey Chu, Chad Nelson, Chak Li, Chan Jun Shern, Channing Conger, Charlotte Barette, Chelsea Voss, Chen Ding, Cheng Lu, Chong Zhang, Chris Beaumont, Chris Hallacy, Chris Koch, Christian Gibson, Christina Kim, Christine Choi, Christine McLeavey, Christopher Hesse, Claudia Fischer, Clemens Winter, Coley Czarnecki, Colin Jarvis, Colin Wei, Constantin Koumouzelis, Dane Sherburn, Daniel Kappler, Daniel Levin, Daniel Levy, David Carr, David Farhi, David Mely, David Robinson, David Sasaki, Denny Jin, Dev Valladares, Dimitris Tsipras, Doug Li, Duc Phong Nguyen, Duncan Findlay, Edede Oiwoh, Edmund Wong, Ehsan Asdar, Elizabeth Proehl, Elizabeth Yang, Eric Antonow, Eric Kramer, Eric Peterson, Eric Sigler, Eric Wallace, Eugene Brevdo, Evan Mays, Farzad Khorasani, Felipe Petroski Such, Filippo Raso, Francis Zhang, Fred von Lohmann, Freddie Sulit, Gabriel Goh, Gene Oden, Geoff Salmon, Giulio Starace, Greg Brockman, Hadi Salman, Haiming Bao, Haitang Hu, Hannah Wong, Haoyu Wang, Heather Schmidt, Heather Whitney, Heewoo Jun, Hendrik Kirchner, Henrique Ponde de Oliveira Pinto, Hongyu Ren, Huiwen Chang, Hyung Won Chung, Ian Kivlichan, Ian O'Connell, Ian O'Connell, Ian Osband, Ian Silber, Ian Sohl, Ibrahim Okuyucu, Ikai Lan, Ilya Kostrikov, Ilya Sutskever, Ingmar Kanitscheider, Ishaan Gulrajani, Jacob Coxon, Jacob Menick, Jakub Pachocki, James Aung, James Betker, James Crooks, James Lennon, Jamie Kiros, Jan Leike, Jane Park, Jason Kwon, Jason Phang, Jason Teplitz, Jason Wei, Jason Wolfe, Jay Chen, Jeff Harris, Jenia Varavva, Jessica Gan Lee, Jessica Shieh, Ji Lin, Jiahui Yu, Jiayi Weng, Jie Tang, Jieqi Yu, Joanne Jang, Joaquin Quinonero Candela, Joe Beutler, Joe Landers, Joel Parish, Johannes Heidecke, John Schulman, Jonathan Lachman, Jonathan McKay, Jonathan Uesato, Jonathan Ward, Jong Wook Kim, Joost Huizinga, Jordan Sitkin, Jos Kraaijeveld, Josh Gross, Josh Kaplan, Josh Snyder, Joshua Achiam, Joy Jiao, Joyce Lee, Juntang Zhuang, Justyn Harriman, Kai Fricke, Kai Hayashi, Karan Singhal, Katy Shi, Kavin Karthik, Kayla Wood, Kendra Rimbach, Kenny Hsu, Kenny Nguyen, Keren Gu-Lemberg, Kevin Button, Kevin Liu, Kiel Howe, Krithika Muthukumar, Kyle Luther, Lama Ahmad, Larry Kai, Lauren Itow, Lauren Workman, Leher Pathak, Leo Chen, Li Jing, Lia Guy, Liam Fedus, Liang Zhou, Lien Mamitsuka, Lilian Weng, Lindsay McCallum, Lindsey Held, Long Ouyang, Louis Feuvrier, Lu Zhang, Lukas Kondraciuk, Lukasz Kaiser, Luke Hewitt, Luke Metz, Lyric Doshi, Mada Aflak, Maddie Simens, Madelaine Boyd, Madeleine Thompson, Marat Dukhan, Mark Chen, Mark Gray, Mark Hudnall, Marvin Zhang, Marwan Aljubeh, Mateusz Litwin, Matthew Zeng, Max Johnson, Maya Shetty, Mayank Gupta, Meghan Shah, Mehmet Yatbaz, Meng Jia Yang, Mengchao Zhong, Mia Glaese, Mianna Chen, Michael Janner, Michael Lampe, Michael Petrov, Michael Wu, Michele Wang, Michelle Fradin, Michelle Pokrass, Miguel Castro, Miguel Oom Temudo de Castro, Mikhail Pavlov, Miles Brundage, Miles Wang, Minal Khan, Mira Murati, Mo Bavarian, Molly Lin, Murat Yesildal, Nacho Soto, Natalia Gimelshein, Natalie Cone, Natalie Staudacher, Natalie Summers, Natan LaFontaine, Neil Chowdhury, Nick Ryder, Nick Stathas, Nick Turley, Nik Tezak, Niko Felix, Nithanth Kudige, Nitish Keskar, Noah Deutsch, Noel Bundick, Nora Puckett, Ofir Nachum, Ola Okelola, Oleg Boiko, Oleg Murk, Oliver Jaffe, Olivia Watkins, Olivier Godement, Owen Campbell-Moore, Patrick Chao, Paul McMillan, Pavel Belov, Peng Su, Peter Bak, Peter Bakkum, Peter Deng, Peter Dolan, Peter Hoeschele, Peter Welinder, Phil Tillet, Philip Pronin, Philippe Tillet, Prafulla Dhariwal, Qiming Yuan, Rachel Dias, Rachel Lim, Rahul Arora, Rajan Troll, Randall Lin, Rapha Gontijo Lopes, Raul Puri, Reah Miyara, Reimar Leike, Renaud Gaubert, Reza Zamani, Ricky Wang, Rob Donnelly, Rob Honsby, Rocky Smith, Rohan Sahai, Rohit Ramchandani, Romain Huet, Rory Carmichael, Rowan Zellers, Roy Chen, Ruby Chen, Ruslan Nigmatullin, Ryan Cheu, Saachi Jain, Sam Altman, Sam Schoenholz, Sam Toizer, Samuel Miserendino, Sandhini Agarwal, Sara Culver, Scott Ethersmith, Scott Gray, Sean Grove, Sean Metzger, Shamez Hermani, Shantanu Jain, Shengjia Zhao, Sherwin Wu, Shino Jomoto, Shirong Wu, Shuaiqi, Xia, Sonia Phene, Spencer Papay, Srinivas Narayanan, Steve Coffey, Steve Lee, Stewart Hall, Suchir Balaji, Tal Broda, Tal Stramer, Tao Xu, Tarun Gogineni, Taya Christianson, Ted Sanders, Tejal Patwardhan, Thomas Cunninghman, Thomas Degry, Thomas Dimson, Thomas Raoux, Thomas Shadwell, Tianhao Zheng, Todd Underwood, Todor Markov, Toki Sherbakov, Tom Rubin, Tom Stasi, Tomer Kaftan, Tristan Heywood, Troy Peterson, Tyce Walters, Tyna Eloundou, Valerie Qi, Veit Moeller, Vinnie Monaco, Vishal Kuo, Vlad Fomenko, Wayne Chang, Weiyi Zheng, Wenda Zhou, Wesam Manassra, Will Sheu, Wojciech Zaremba, Yash Patil, Yilei Qian, Yongjik Kim, Youlong Cheng, Yu Zhang, Yuchen He, Yuchen Zhang, Yujia Jin, Yunxing Dai, and Yury Malkov. 2024. Gpt-4o system card. *Preprint*, arXiv:2410.21276.

Kishore Papineni, Salim Roukos, Todd Ward, and Wei-Jing Zhu. 2002. Bleu: a method for automatic evaluation of machine translation. In *Proceedings of the 40th Annual Meeting on Association for Computational Linguistics*, ACL '02, page 311–318, USA. Association for Computational Linguistics.

Qwen, :, An Yang, Baosong Yang, Beichen Zhang, Binyuan Hui, Bo Zheng, Bowen Yu, Chengyuan Li, Dayiheng Liu, Fei Huang, Haoran Wei, Huan Lin, Jian Yang, Jianhong Tu, Jianwei Zhang, Jianxin Yang, Jiaxi Yang, Jingren Zhou, Junyang Lin, Kai Dang, Keming Lu, Keqin Bao, Kexin Yang, Le Yu, Mei Li, Mingfeng Xue, Pei Zhang, Qin Zhu, Rui Men, Runji Lin, Tianhao Li, Tianyi Tang, Tingyu Xia, Xingzhang Ren, Xuancheng Ren, Yang Fan, Yang Su, Yichang Zhang, Yu Wan, Yuqiong Liu, Zeyu Cui, Zhenru Zhang, and Zihan Qiu. 2025. Qwen2.5 technical report. *Preprint*, arXiv:2412.15115.

Colin Raffel, Noam Shazeer, Adam Roberts, Katherine Lee, Sharan Narang, Michael Matena, Yanqi Zhou, Wei Li, and Peter J. Liu. 2023. Exploring the limits of transfer learning with a unified text-to-text transformer. *Preprint*, arXiv:1910.10683.

Lance A. Ramshaw and Mitchell P. Marcus. 1995. Text chunking using transformation-based learning. *Preprint*, arXiv:cmp-lg/9505040.

Lei Tang, Jinghui Qin, Wenxuan Ye, Hao Tan, and Zhijing Yang. 2025. Adaptive few-shot prompting for machine translation with pre-trained language models. *Preprint*, arXiv:2501.01679.

Yongjian Tang, Rakebul Hasan, and Thomas Runkler. 2024. Fsponer: Few-shot prompt optimization for named entity recognition in domain-specific scenarios. *Preprint*, arXiv:2407.08035.

Junlin Wang, Jue Wang, Ben Athiwaratkun, Ce Zhang, and James Zou. 2024. Mixture-of-agents enhances large language model capabilities. *Preprint*, arXiv:2406.04692.

Yuheng Zha, Yichi Yang, Ruichen Li, and Zhiting Hu. 2023. AlignScore: Evaluating factual consistency with a unified alignment function. In *Proceedings of the 61st Annual Meeting of the Association for Computational Linguistics (Volume 1: Long Papers)*, pages 11328–11348, Toronto, Canada. Association for Computational Linguistics.

Jingqing Zhang, Yao Zhao, Mohammad Saleh, and Peter J. Liu. 2020a. Pegasus: pre-training with extracted gap-sentences for abstractive summarization. In *Proceedings of the 37th International Conference on Machine Learning*, ICML'20. JMLR.org.

Tianyi Zhang, Varsha Kishore, Felix Wu, Kilian Q. Weinberger, and Yoav Artzi. 2020b. Bertscore: Evaluating text generation with bert. *Preprint*, arXiv:1904.09675.

Yaowei Zheng, Richong Zhang, Junhao Zhang, Yanhan Ye, and Zheyan Luo. 2024. LlamaFactory: Unified efficient fine-tuning of 100+ language models. In *Proceedings of the 62nd Annual Meeting of the Association for Computational Linguistics (Volume 3: System Demonstrations)*, pages 400–410, Bangkok, Thailand. Association for Computational Linguistics.

A Llama 3.3 70B QLoRA Supervised Fine-tuning Configs

As shown in Table 4, the following configuration was used for supervised fine-tuning using QLoRA for both Task A and Task B. The model was fine-tuned with 4 NVIDIA RTX A6000 GPUs. The only difference between the two tasks is the composition of the training dataset. This ensures that both tasks were fine-tuned under the same training environment, leveraging QLoRA to efficiently adapt the LLaMA-3.3-70B-Instruct model while maintaining computational efficiency.

B Confusion Matrix for GPT-4o Zero-Shot

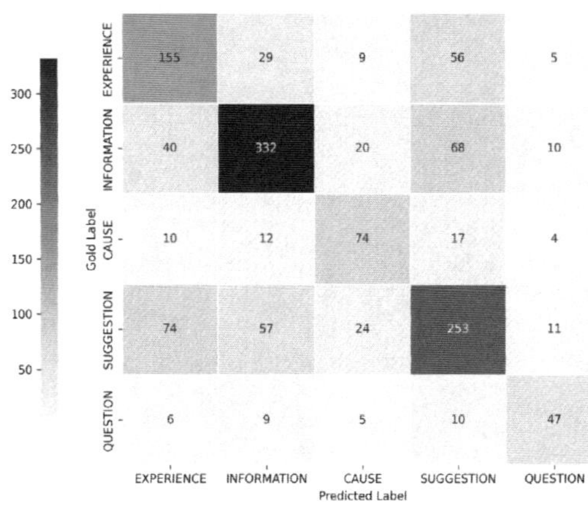

Figure 3: Confusion Matrix for GPT-4o Zero-Shot on Task A. Each cell indicates the number of samples in the corresponding gold-predicted label pair.

Figure 3 shows the confusion matrix (as a PNG image) for GPT-4o zero-shot on Task A (span classification). Rows correspond to the *gold* labels, and columns correspond to the *predicted* labels. Diagonal entries represent correctly classified samples for each perspective category, whereas off-diagonal entries indicate misclassifications (e.g., gold-labeled `EXPERIENCE` predicted as `INFORMATION`).

As illustrated in the confusion matrix, GPT-4o zero-shot achieves strong diagonal counts for each perspective label (`EXPERIENCE`, `INFORMATION`, `CAUSE`, `SUGGESTION`, `QUESTION`), indicating accurate predictions in most cases. The off-diagonal cells reflect scenarios where one perspective is mistaken for another, highlighting specific patterns of confusion (e.g., `EXPERIENCE` vs. `INFORMATION`). This strong performance aligns with our earlier quantitative results showing that GPT-4o zero-shot outperforms other baselines on span classification.

Parameter	Value
bf16	true
cutoff_len	3000
dataset	peranssumm_task
dataset_dir	data
ddp_timeout	180000000
do_train	true
double_quantization	true
eval_steps	5000
eval_strategy	steps
finetuning_type	lora
flash_attn	auto
gradient_accumulation_steps	2
learning_rate	5.0e-05
logging_steps	5
lora_alpha	16
lora_dropout	0.05
lora_rank	8
lora_target	all
lr_scheduler_type	cosine
max_grad_norm	1.0
max_samples	100000
model_name_or_path	{model_name}
num_train_epochs	3.0
optim	adamw_torch
output_dir	/path/to/output
packing	false
per_device_eval_batch_size	1
per_device_train_batch_size	1
plot_loss	true
preprocessing_num_workers	16
quantization_bit	4
quantization_method	bitsandbytes
report_to	none
save_steps	5000
stage	sft
template	llama3
train_on_prompt	true
trust_remote_code	true
val_size	0.3
warmup_steps	100

Table 4: QLoRA Supervised Fine-Tuning Configuration for LLaMA-3.3-70B-Instruct

C Prompt Example

In Table 5, we present an example of the best prompt format for GPT-4o in zero-shot for both span identification/classification and perspective-based summarization.

D NER Fine-tuning for Task A

In an exploratory experiment, we implemented a token-level BIO tagging(Ramshaw and Marcus, 1995) approach to perform span identification for Task A. In this method, each perspective is treated as a named entity with BIO labels (e.g., `B-INFORMATION`, `I-INFORMATION`, etc.), and the remaining tokens are tagged as `O`.

Data Preparation and Tagging. We first combined the question and answer texts and then tokenized the resulting sequence. Using the provided span annotations, we aligned token boundaries with the annotated spans to produce BIO tags. For instance, if an annotated span for the "CAUSE" perspective starts at character position s and ends at e, tokens falling entirely within this span are labeled as `B-CAUSE` for the first token and `I-CAUSE` for the subsequent tokens.

Class Weighting for Imbalance. To address class imbalance, we computed class weights as:

$$w_c = \frac{T}{n_c}, \quad \text{with } T = \sum_{c=1}^{C} n_c$$

where n_c denotes the total number of tokens belonging to class c, and T represents the total number of tokens across all classes. These weights were then incorporated into the cross-entropy loss function:

$$\mathcal{L} = -\frac{1}{N} \sum_{i=1}^{N} w_{y_i} \log \left(\frac{\exp(z_{i,y_i})}{\sum_{c=1}^{C} \exp(z_{i,c})} \right)$$

where $z_{i,c}$ is the logit for token i and class c, and y_i is the ground-truth label.

Observations. Despite applying class weighting, our NER fine-tuning did not yield significant improvements. We attribute this to the small dataset size and the inherent challenge of labeling extended, overlapping spans—conditions that differ substantially from typical NER tasks involving shorter entity mentions. Consequently, while promising in principle, further investigation with larger or more targeted datasets is required.

<table>
<tr><th>Task</th><th>Span Identification and Classification</th><th>Perspective-Based Summarization</th></tr>
<tr><td>System Prompt</td><td colspan="2">You are a helpful assistant.</td></tr>
<tr><td>User Prompt</td><td>You are an expert annotator specialized in perspective-aware Healthcare Answer Summarization.
First, validate that the document's content is aligned with the medical domain—ensure that it pertains to prevention, diagnosis, management, treatment of diseases, understanding of bodily functions, the effects of medications or medical interventions, or queries regarding wellness practices.
Next, for each text span in the 'Answers' section, carefully assess and assign the most relevant perspective(s) from the following definitions:<ul><li>INFORMATION: Knowledge about diseases, disorders, and health-related facts.</li><li>CAUSE: Reasons responsible for the occurrence of a medical condition.</li><li>SUGGESTION: Advice or recommendations to assist in making informed decisions.</li><li>EXPERIENCE: Individual experiences or anecdotes related to healthcare.</li><li>QUESTION: Inquiries for deeper understanding.</li></ul>Follow these instructions:<ul><li>Only annotate spans from the 'Answers' section.</li><li>Ensure the document is medically relevant.</li><li>Multi-perspective labeling is allowed.</li><li>If a span explicitly mentions quantitative details, include that in your annotation.</li><li>Avoid personal bias and exclude links or personal identifiers.</li><li>Review your annotations to cover all underlying perspectives.</li></ul>Format your response as: <code>span: "<extracted text>", label: "<perspective>"</code>.</td><td>While writing summaries, ensure that every essential idea and medical detail is captured from the extracted spans.
Each summary should:<ul><li>Be factually supported by the extracted spans.</li><li>Preserve all relevant insights and details.</li><li>Align clearly with the assigned perspective.</li><li>Avoid hallucinations, bias, or unverifiable content.</li></ul>Strictly adhere to the extracted spans to ensure factual consistency.
Use the following structure for each perspective:<ul><li>INFORMATION: "For information purposes, [summary]..."</li><li>CAUSE: "Some of the causes include [summary]..."</li><li>SUGGESTION: "It is suggested that [summary]..."</li><li>EXPERIENCE: "In user's experience, [summary]..."</li><li>QUESTION: "It is inquired whether [summary]..."</li></ul>Format your final summary as: <code>Summary: "<generated summary>"</code>.</td></tr>
<tr><td>Example Input</td><td><code>{Question} + {Context} + {Answers} + {User Prompt}</code></td><td><code>{Question} + {Context} + {Spans} + {User Prompt}</code></td></tr>
</table>

Table 5: Final prompt structure for Task A and Task B.

Abdelmalak at PerAnsSumm 2025: Leveraging a Domain-Specific BERT and LLaMA for Perspective-Aware Healthcare Answer Summarization

Abanoub Abdelmalak
University of Bonn, Bonn, Germany
ZB MED - Information Centre for Life Sciences, Cologne, Germany
abdelmalak@zbmed.de

Abstract

The PerAnsSumm Shared Task - CL4Health@NAACL 2025 aims to enhance healthcare community question-answering (CQA) by summarizing diverse user perspectives. It consists of two tasks: identifying and classifying perspective-specific spans (Task A) and generating structured, perspective-specific summaries from question-answer threads (Task B). The dataset used for this task is the PUMA dataset. For Task A, a COVID-Twitter-BERT model pre-trained on COVID-related text from Twitter was employed, improving the model's understanding of relevant vocabulary and context. For Task B, LLaMA was utilized in a prompt-based fashion. The proposed approach achieved 9th place in Task A and 16th place overall, with the best proportional classification F1-score of 0.74.

1 Introduction

Perspective-aware summarization of multiple text sources has recently been studied and used in different applications. One application is the reviews summarization on online shopping websites, where the summarization model can generate a summary that reflects the different perspectives of the reviewers or summarization of different news articles based on the news domain (Liu et al., 2021). Another application is the summarization of question-answering threads in healthcare communities, where the summarization model should be able to generate a summary that reflects the different perspectives of the users. The PerAnsSumm Shared Task - CL4Health@ NAACL 2025 (Agarwal et al., 2025) aims to improve healthcare community question-answering (CQA) by summarizing diverse user perspectives. The goal is to transform the enormous amount of knowledge that is available on these forums into structured information that could be beneficial to others.

The shared task is structured into multiple subtasks to systematically process community question-answering (CQA) threads. The first subtask involves identifying relevant answers and extracting specific spans that convey meaningful information. The second subtask focuses on categorizing these spans into the appropriate perspective classes. Finally, the third subtask entails generating concise summaries for each perspective class, ensuring that the diverse viewpoints present in the discussions are effectively captured. Task A emphasizes the identification and classification of perspective-specific spans, while Task B is dedicated to generating structured summaries. For further details and examples of the dataset, refer to the Appendix A.

The dataset used for this task is PUMA (Naik et al., 2024). It comprises 3,167 CQA threads with around 10,000 answers filtered from the Yahoo! L6 corpus. Each answer in PUMA is annotated with five perspective spans: 'cause', 'suggestion', 'experience', 'question', and 'information'. Based on these perspective and span annotations, summaries are crafted for each identified perspective. These summaries provide concise representations of the underlying perspectives contained within the spans across all answers. Each CQA thread includes up to five perspective-specific summaries.

2 Methodology

The proposed approach frames the first task as a sequence classification problem, where each sentence within an answer is assigned to one of the five predefined perspective classes. For the second task, a summary is generated for each perspective class, utilizing relevant information from the classified sentences. A pre-trained BERT model (Devlin et al., 2019) was fine-tuned on the training dataset to accurately classify sentences based on their perspective labels. For summarization, the LLaMA model (Dubey et al., 2024) was em-

Proceedings of the Second Workshop on Patient-Oriented Language Processing (CL4Health), pages 428–436
May 4, 2025 ©2025 Association for Computational Linguistics

ployed in a zero-shot manner, generating concise summaries for each perspective class without additional fine-tuning.

2.1 Dataset Preparation

The challenge organizers divided the dataset into training, validation, and testing sets. The training and development datasets included additional fields, such as ground truth perspective spans and perspective-specific summaries. However, these fields were not present in the testing dataset.

The training dataset was used to fine-tune the models for Task A. To accomplish this, answers needed to be broken into sub-sequences (sentences) before being fed into the BERT model. A comparison between the spans in the dataset and the actual text revealed inconsistencies. Some spans were incomplete, often missing letters at the beginning or end. This happened because the dataset was annotated based on the exact locations where the perspective appeared in the text. Therefore, Spacy (Honnibal et al., 2020) was not only used to split the text into sentences but the text was also tokenized using the Spacy tokenizer and the tokens were then compared with the tokens in the spans. Out of 22361 sentences, 15027 were found exactly in the labeled spans and 7334 were partially found (partially means that 45% of the larger span matches with the span in question) This criterion was used to filter the sentences that were used in the fine-tuning of the BERT model. Any sentences that didn't match were labeled as negative non-relevant sentences. The reason to restructure the training data is to make sure that the model is trained on the right data that will be used in the testing phase.

For more information on the data set, refer to the original paper by Naik et al. (2024).

2.2 Task A: Sentence Classification

This task is approached as two subtasks: eliminating non-relevant sentences and assigning relevant sentences to their corresponding perspectives. These tasks are modeled as a sequence classification problem, specifically, sentence pair classification, where the model takes the question and sentence as input, separated by the special token [SEP], and the first token [CLS] is used for classification. A set of experiments was conducted using only sentences without the question, resulting in lower training and validation F1-scores. Previous work by Chaturvedi et al. (2024) demonstrated through experimentation that encoder-based models (e.g., BERT, RoBERTa (Liu et al., 2019)) perform better in identifying the relationship between two sentences (in this case, the question and sentence). As a result, the basic BERT model with single sentences as input was used as a baseline.

Considering the nature of the dataset and the target of the models, the first choice model is COVID-Twitter-BERT (Müller et al., 2023) which is published on the Hugging Face model hub (Wolf et al., 2020). The model was originally pre-trained on COVID-related text from Twitter, which matches the same language used in the question-answering forums where people use informal language and also matches the use of health-related symptoms in that case which means it should have a richer dictionary of tokens.

2.2.1 Irrelevant sentences elimination

To achieve this, a COVID-Twitter-BERT model was fine-tuned on both question-sentence pairs and single sentences to classify sentences as relevant or not. The model was fine-tuned on the training dataset, with a sample of relevant sentences selected to balance the dataset (50%). The dataset only contained 2 labels (relevant and irrelevant). It was fine-tuned for 5 epochs with a batch size of 16 and a learning rate of 2e-5. The model was then tested on question-sentence pairs and single sentences, predicting the relevance of sentences in the validation dataset. Table 1 shows that the model achieved an F1-score of 0.74 in the development dataset.

2.2.2 Perspective Classification

A new instance of COVID-Twitter-BERT model was employed for classifying relevant sentences into their corresponding perspective classes. The model was fine-tuned on the training dataset for 5 epochs, using a batch size of 16 and a learning rate of 2e-5. Table 4 showed that it achieved an F1-score of 0.68 on the validation dataset. Additionally, Table 5 shows the performance of the best model on the different classes. Table 2 shows that the distribution of sentences across the perspective categories is imbalanced, which is a common issue in many datasets. To address this, a weighted cross-entropy loss function was utilized to assign more weight to the minority classes, helping to balance the model's sensitivity to different perspectives. The class weights were calculated based on the number of sentences in each class. The weights were calculated using inverse frequency as shown

Model	Precision	Recall	F1 (Macro)
COVID-Twitter-BERT (Single sentences)	0.74	0.73	0.74
BERT-base (Single sentences)	0.74	0.72	0.73
COVID-Twitter-BERT (Pairs)	0.75	0.73	0.74
BERT-base (Pairs)	0.75	0.72	0.73

Table 1: Performance comparison of models on precision, recall, and F1-score for identification of relevant sentences on the validation set to identify irrelevant sentences.

Perspective	No. Sentences
EXPERIENCE	2933
QUESTION	311
CAUSE	677
SUGGESTION	6695
INFORMATION	10723
O	4916

Table 2: Sentence count for each perspective category in the training set after using Spacy's en_core_web_sm model to tokenize each answer into sentences

Class	Weight
EXPERIENCE	7.28
QUESTION	68.61
CAUSE	31.52
SUGGESTION	3.19
INFORMATION	1.99

Table 3: Computed class weights for cross-entropy loss.

in Table 3.

2.3 Task B: Perspective-specific Summarization

The summarization process utilizes the **Meta-LLaMA-3.1-8B-Instruct** (Dubey et al., 2024) model to generate concise, perspective-specific summaries. The model runs with `bfloat16` precision and a maximum of 500 new tokens using the `transformers` pipeline.

A structured prompt ensures that the summary answers a given question while adhering to a predefined category and writing style. The model is instructed to avoid repeating the question or context and to generate a clear, one-line summary that explicitly references the subject. Each category follows a distinct tone: **EXPERIENCE** and **QUESTION** use a third-person perspective, **CAUSE** emphasizes causal reasoning, **SUGGESTION** adopts an advisory tone, and **INFORMATION** maintains a scientific style. The prompt structure ensures high-quality, structured outputs suitable for downstream analysis. A sample prompt can be found in the Appendix A.

The structure of the prompt is as follows:

- **Text Input**: The relevant text and the guiding question are provided to the model.
- **Category**: The prompt specifies the category under which the summary should fall (e.g., EXPERIENCE, QUESTION, CAUSE, SUGGESTION, or INFORMATION).
- **Writing Style**: The summary is generated according to the tone associated with the chosen category:
  - **EXPERIENCE** and **QUESTION**: Use third-person perspective and discuss the subject as users.
  - **CAUSE**: Focuses on causal reasoning and logical connections between events.
  - **SUGGESTION**: Uses an advisory tone, often starting with "It is suggested" when applicable.
  - **INFORMATION**: Presents information in a scientific and informative style.
- **Constraints**: The model is instructed to provide a clear, concise, one-line summary that explicitly references the subject of the question. The summary must not repeat the question or context and should follow the specified writing style.

2.4 Experimental Setup

For fine-tuning the BERT-based models, 2 A40 GPUs and AMD EPYC "Milan" 64-core/128-thread 2.00GHz CPUs were used. More details about it can be found in Appendix A. For the use of the LLaMA model in inference mode, 2 Nvidia A40 48GB GPUs were used.

For each of the BERT-based models, different settings and different datasets were experimented as follows:

Model	Precision	Recall	F1 (Macro)
COVID-Twitter-BERT (Single)	0.63	0.67	0.65
COVID-Twitter-BERT (Pairs)	0.67	0.69	0.68

Table 4: Performance of COVID-Twitter-BERT on precision, recall, and F1-score on the validation set to identify the different perspectives (EXPERIENCE and QUESTION, CAUSE, SUGGESTION and INFORMATION).

Class	F1-Score	Instances
CAUSE	0.42	274
EXPERIENCE	0.70	1248
SUGGESTION	0.76	3044
QUESTION	0.72	175
INFORMATION	0.79	4581
Macro Avg	**0.68**	9322

Table 5: F1-scores and instance count for each class, along with the macro average F1-score for the best-performing model on the validation set.

1. **BERT-base (Single sentences)**: BERT base-uncased fine-tuned on only the sentences from the answers.

2. **COVID-Twitter-BERT (Single sentences)**: COVID-Twitter-BERT fine-tuned on just the sentences from the answers.

3. **BERT-base (Pairs)**: BERT-base-uncased fine-tuned on the question-sentence pairs.

4. **COVID-Twitter-BERT (Pairs)**: COVID-Twitter-BERT fine-tuned on the question-sentence pairs.

This was applied to the irrelevant and relevant models and then was applied to the test data through the evaluation platform. For the model selection criteria and the model loss functions, the macro F1-score was used as the main evaluation metric. The models were fine-tuned using the Adam optimizer with a learning rate of 2e-5 and a batch size of 16. The models were trained for 5 epochs.

There were different data representations used for the fine-tuning as seen from the model names and also for the sentence processing after the classification. The consecutive sentences that were from the same class were merged to form a single sentence. This was done to see if it affects the exact matching results or not. Also, one experiment discarded the part where the sentences were classified as relevant or not to see if it affected the results or not. The results of the experiments are shown in Table 4. For the summarization part, the LLaMA model was used in inference mode. The model was run on the labeled sentences to generate the summaries for each perspective class.

3 Results and Discussion

This section presents the results of the experiments conducted on the PUMA dataset. The results are presented in two parts: the first part is the results of the sentence classification task and the second part is the results of the summarization task.

3.1 Evaluation

The BERT-based models were evaluated on the validation dataset after each epoch. The model with the highest F1-score was selected as the final model. For the sentence classification task, to get over the low classification scores for the minority classes, the weighted cross entropy loss function was used. The weights were calculated based on the number of sentences in each class. The weights were calculated using inverse frequency as shown in Table 3. The test phase For Task A (Span Identification and Classification), evaluation is conducted using the macro-averaged F1-score for classification. Additionally, span identification is assessed through Strict-matching and Proportional-matching methods to measure the accuracy of detected spans.

The evaluation of the summarization component focused on two key aspects: **relevance** and **factuality**. Relevance was assessed using **Recall-Oriented Understudy for Gisting Evaluation (ROUGE)** (R1, R2, RL) (Lin, 2004), **Bilingual Evaluation Understudy (BLEU)** (Papineni et al., 2002), **Metric for Evaluation of Translation with Explicit Ordering (METEOR)** (Banerjee and Lavie, 2005), and **BERTScore** (Zhang et al., 2020), measuring lexical and semantic overlap with reference summaries. Factuality was evaluated using **AlignScore** (Zha et al., 2023) and **Summary Consistency (SummaC)** (Laban et al., 2022), ensuring the generated summaries remained faithful to the original content.

Model	Macro F1	Strict F1	Prop. F1	Task A
Covid-Twitter-BERT	0.8859	0.1108	**0.7554**	**0.5931**
BERT	0.8584	0.1068	0.7518	0.5861
Covid-Twitter-BERT + Bingfire[1]	0.8859	0.1108	**0.7554**	**0.5931**
Covid-Twitter-BERT + Merge Sentences	0.8859	**0.1118**	0.7368	0.5872
Skip Irrelevance Step + Covid-Twitter-BERT + Merge Sentences	**0.8931**	0.1081	0.7437	0.5898

Table 6: F1-scores for classification, span matching, and Task A performance. The best values are in **bold**, and the second-best values are underlined.

Model	Task B Relevance	Task B Factuality
Covid-Twitter-BERT	0.2963	**0.2827**
BERT	0.2909	0.2691
Covid-Twitter-BERT + Bingfire	0.2774	0.2403
Covid-Twitter-BERT + Merge Consecutive Sentences	0.2963	**0.2827**
Skip Irrelevance Step + Covid-Twitter-BERT + Merge Consecutive Sentences	**0.3019**	0.2508

Table 7: Evaluation results for Task B: Relevance and Factuality. The best values are in **bold**, and the second-best values are underlined.

3.2 Results

This section reports the results from the challenge's evaluation platform. The results are presented in two parts: the first part is the results of the sentence classification task and the second part is the results of the summarization task.

Table 6 presents the F1-scores for classification, span matching, and Task A performance across several model configurations. The classification macro F1-score evaluates the overall classification performance across all classes, while the strict matching F1 and proportional matching F1 assess the model's ability to correctly identify and match spans at different levels of granularity. The Task A score provides an overall evaluation of the model's performance on the span identification and classification task. In the table, the best values are highlighted in bold, and the second-best values are underlined for easy reference.

The results indicate that the model pre-trained on data more similar to the task's dataset achieved the best overall performance. Additionally, switching the sentence tokenizer from Spacy did not impact the results, as it was only used during testing, not in the fine-tuning phase. Merging sentences did not affect the classification task but slightly improved the overall classification performance. Finally, skipping the relevance task did not enhance the results; in fact, it led to worse overall performance in the test phase.

While only one model and a single prompt were used in the summary generation task, the input text that comes from the first task was the factor that affected the results. The results show that a better classification contributed to a better result overall as shown in Table 7. While adding more sentences through skipping the irrelevance step did not affect the relevance of the summary, it affected the factuality of the summary.

4 Conclusions

The approach presented in this paper, as part of the PerAnsSumm Shared Task - CL4Health@NAACL 2025, aimed to enhance healthcare community question-answering (CQA) by summarizing diverse user perspectives.

A key aspect of the approach was the focus on accurately classifying sentences (parts of answers) into the correct perspectives while eliminating irrelevant text. To achieve this, a specialized BERT model (COVID-Twitter-BERT) was fine-tuned on the training data for each subtask separately. The results demonstrated that the model pre-trained on data more similar to the task's dataset achieved the best overall performance in Task A. The classification model achieved the best results in terms of proportional matching across the challenge, indicating that the data preprocessing for fine-tuning the model to classify the correct perspectives was highly effective. However, the identification of the correct spans was less accurate, even when merging sentences. This suggests that identifying the right sentence boundaries, in line with the dataset's standards, is notably different from the default boundaries applied in common libraries (e.g., SpaCy and Bingfire).

For the second task, which involves using sentences to generate summaries, only one model was tested in inference mode without any fine-tuning. The results demonstrated how the quality of the data from the first task can impact the results of the second. Specifically, better classification contributed to overall better performance in summary generation.

5 Limitations

In this work, the focus was on the classification of the sentences to the correct perspective classes. The results showed that the identification of the correct spans is low which can be highlighted as a limitation of this work. Additionally, due to time and human resources limitations, only one model (LLaMA) was used to generate the summary with few tweaks in the prompt and limited post-processing of the output text.

6 Future work

For future works, it is recommended to add more rules to identify the spans of the text. Or to only fine-tune a model to identify irrelevant parts of the text as a Named-Entity-Recognition task because in some cases it is only one or two words that are discarded which makes it costly in terms of the exact matching. Also, it is recommended to use more models to generate the summaries and to use more prompts to generate the summaries. Additionally, evaluating how fine-tuned summarization models can affect the results.

Acknowledgments

The author gratefully acknowledges the access to the Marvin cluster of the University of Bonn. The author would like to thank the organizers of the PerAnsSumm Shared Task - CL4Health@ NAACL 2025 for providing the dataset and the evaluation platform.

References

Siddhant Agarwal, Md Shad Akhtar, and Shweta Yadav. 2025. Overview of the peranssumm 2025 shared task on perspective-aware healthcare answer summarization. In *Proceedings of the Second Workshop on Patient-Oriented Language Processing (CL4Health) @ NAACL 2025*, Albuquerque, USA. Association for Computational Linguistics.

Satanjeev Banerjee and Alon Lavie. 2005. METEOR: An automatic metric for MT evaluation with improved correlation with human judgments. In *Proceedings of the ACL Workshop on Intrinsic and Extrinsic Evaluation Measures for Machine Translation and/or Summarization*, pages 65–72, Ann Arbor, Michigan. Association for Computational Linguistics.

Rochana Chaturvedi, Abari Bhattacharya, and Shweta Yadav. 2024. Aspect-oriented consumer health answer summarization. *arXiv preprint arXiv:2405.06295*.

Jacob Devlin, Ming-Wei Chang, Kenton Lee, and Kristina Toutanova. 2019. BERT: Pre-training of deep bidirectional transformers for language understanding. In *Proceedings of the 2019 Conference of the North American Chapter of the Association for Computational Linguistics: Human Language Technologies, Volume 1 (Long and Short Papers)*, pages 4171–4186, Minneapolis, Minnesota. Association for Computational Linguistics.

Abhimanyu Dubey, Abhinav Jauhri, Abhinav Pandey, Abhishek Kadian, Ahmad Al-Dahle, Aiesha Letman, Akhil Mathur, Alan Schelten, Amy Yang, Angela Fan, and 1 others. 2024. The llama 3 herd of models. *arXiv preprint arXiv:2407.21783*.

Suchin Gururangan, Ana Marasović, Swabha Swayamdipta, Kyle Lo, Iz Beltagy, Doug Downey, and Noah A. Smith. 2020. Don't stop pretraining: Adapt language models to domains and tasks. In *Proceedings of the 58th Annual Meeting of the Association for Computational Linguistics*, pages 8342–8360, Online. Association for Computational Linguistics.

Matthew Honnibal, Ines Montani, Sofie Van Landeghem, and Adriane Boyd. 2020. spacy: Industrial-strength natural language processing in python. *Zenodo*.

Philippe Laban, Tobias Schnabel, Paul N. Bennett, and Marti A. Hearst. 2022. SummaC: Re-visiting NLI-based models for inconsistency detection in summarization. *Transactions of the Association for Computational Linguistics*, 10:163–177.

Chin-Yew Lin. 2004. ROUGE: A package for automatic evaluation of summaries. In *Text Summarization Branches Out*, pages 74–81, Barcelona, Spain. Association for Computational Linguistics.

Siyi Liu, Sihao Chen, Xander Uyttendaele, and Dan Roth. 2021. MultiOpEd: A corpus of multi-perspective news editorials. In *Proceedings of the 2021 Conference of the North American Chapter of the Association for Computational Linguistics: Human Language Technologies*, pages 4345–4361, Online. Association for Computational Linguistics.

Yinhan Liu, Myle Ott, Naman Goyal, Jingfei Du, Mandar Joshi, Danqi Chen, Omer Levy, Mike Lewis, Luke Zettlemoyer, and Veselin Stoyanov. 2019. Roberta: A robustly optimized BERT pretraining approach. *CoRR*, abs/1907.11692.

Martin Müller, Marcel Salathé, and Per E Kummervold. 2023. Covid-twitter-bert: A natural language processing model to analyse covid-19 content on twitter. *Frontiers in artificial intelligence*, 6:1023281.

Gauri Naik, Sharad Chandakacherla, Shweta Yadav, and Md Shad Akhtar. 2024. No perspective, no perception!! perspective-aware healthcare answer summarization. In *Findings of the Association for Computational Linguistics: ACL 2024*, pages 15919–15932, Bangkok, Thailand. Association for Computational Linguistics.

Kishore Papineni, Salim Roukos, Todd Ward, and Wei-Jing Zhu. 2002. Bleu: a method for automatic evaluation of machine translation. In *Proceedings of the 40th Annual Meeting of the Association for Computational Linguistics*, pages 311–318, Philadelphia, Pennsylvania, USA. Association for Computational Linguistics.

Thomas Wolf, Lysandre Debut, Victor Sanh, Julien Chaumond, Clement Delangue, Anthony Moi, Pierric Cistac, Tim Rault, Remi Louf, Morgan Funtowicz, Joe Davison, Sam Shleifer, Patrick von Platen, Clara Ma, Yacine Jernite, Julien Plu, Canwen Xu, Teven Le Scao, Sylvain Gugger, and 3 others. 2020. Transformers: State-of-the-art natural language processing. In *Proceedings of the 2020 Conference on Empirical Methods in Natural Language Processing: System Demonstrations*, pages 38–45, Online. Association for Computational Linguistics.

Yuheng Zha, Yichi Yang, Ruichen Li, and Zhiting Hu. 2023. AlignScore: Evaluating factual consistency with a unified alignment function. In *Proceedings of the 61st Annual Meeting of the Association for Computational Linguistics (Volume 1: Long Papers)*, pages 11328–11348, Toronto, Canada. Association for Computational Linguistics.

Tianyi Zhang, Varsha Kishore, Felix Wu, Kilian Q. Weinberger, and Yoav Artzi. 2020. Bertscore: Evaluating text generation with bert. In *International Conference on Learning Representations*.

A Appendix

A.1 Dataset Insights

Here are some statistics of the dataset taken from the dataset publication (Naik et al., 2024). Figure 1 shows the examples from the dataset. While Table 8 shows the distribution of the dataset over the different perspectives.

	Information	Cause	Suggestion	Question	Experience
Train (2533)	4823/1961	646/342	4128/1547	325/249	1439/845
Validation (317)	643/246	108/49	549/208	42/32	170/108
Test (317)	631/242	81/45	499/188	44/31	181/100
Total (3167)	**6097/2449**	**835/436**	**5176/1943**	**411/312**	**1790/1053**

Table 8: Statistics of the original dataset (Naik et al., 2024)

A.2 Experiments of the different models combinations

There were different model combinations for Task A that were used but were not worth mentioning in the main body of the paper:

- Single step for Task A: The first experiments used one single model to identify all perspectives and also the irrelevant sentences as an extra class. However, this approach faced many issues due to the imbalance in data. The models are:
  - BERT model to identify all classes and irrelevant classes on pairs of questions and sentences
  - COVID-Twitter-BERT to identify all classes and irrelevant classes on pairs of questions and sentences
- 2-steps for Task A: The adopted approach in this paper was to approach the problem in 2 steps (identifying irrelevant sentences and then classifying the relevant ones from the correct perspectives) For that different formats of the dataset were used:
  - Pairs: The input data instances consist of pairs of questions and sentences.
  - Singles: The input data is only the sentences that should be classified.

  Different instances and models were tested:

  - BERT-base model.
  - COVID-Twitter-BERT
  - Biomed RoBERTa (Gururangan et al., 2020)

  Where the COVID Twitter BERT proved to be superior in terms of results.

A.2.1 Training Parameters

The models were fine-tuned on the training dataset for 5 epochs, using a batch size of 16 and a learning rate of 2e-5.

A.2.2 Hardware

The fine-tuning process was conducted using two Nvidia A40 GPUs and AMD EPYC "Milan" 64-core/128-thread 2.00GHz CPUs. Two Nvidia A40 48GB GPUs were utilized for inference with the LLaMA model.

[1]https://github.com/microsoft/BlingFire

Question: I was just diagnosed with gallstones in my gall bladder I really don't want to have surgery and have been told that there are other ways to get rid of the stones. Suggestions?	
Answer 1	Most gallstones are made of pure cholesterol. You might try a diet with low fat and very low saturated fats. Reducing the saturated fats will lower blood cholesterol and may (I'm not promising anything!) make the stones smaller. Lowering your total fat intake may also help reduce or prevent pain. Gallstones hurt because when you eat fat, the stomach senses it and tells the gallbladder to release some of the gall into the intestines to help digest the fat. If you have stones, that squeezing is about like squeezing a hand full of pointy rocks. However, I've had the surgery, and it really isn't a big deal. There is minimal scarring, ... If you leave the gallstones there, they can get large enough to damage the gallbladder, with the result of a bad infection and that can cause death, which is a very Bad Thing!"
Answer 2	Have you seen a gastroenterologist? They can do a minimally invasive procedure called an ERCP (Endoscopic Retrograde Cholangiopancreatography. An ERCP won't get rid of the stones that are in the gallbladder...just the stones that are stuck in the duct .... They can make a tiny cut in the duct and pull gallstones out with a small balloon. If the stone is too large, they have equipment that will crush the stone so it will pass freely. I had the surgery myself about 10 years ago. It's not as bad as you'd imagine, and you feel much better after it's over. You might still have phantom pain for a while, but it's nowhere near as bad as the pain you started with. A diet high in fat will make gallbladder disease worse, but you can't really get rid of the stones unless they pass naturally or you have them removed, either in surgery or with an ERCP.
Answer 3	The best remedy is surgery. I had surgery to have kidney stones removed. The surgery isn't as bad as you think it may be.
Perspective-based summaries	
Information	Reducing saturated fats may shrink gallstones as they're mostly made of cholesterol. Gallstone pain occurs when the gallbladder squeezes to aid digestion on fat consumption. An ERCP procedure by a gastroenterologist can remove stones stuck in the duct leading to the intestine. This minimally invasive technique involves extracting stones or crushing larger ones for easier passage, but it doesn't eliminate stones within the gallbladder itself.
Cause	Gallstones left untreated can harm the gallbladder, causing severe infection and potentially death.
Suggestion	To eliminate gallstones without surgery, a low-fat diet, particularly low in saturated fats, as it may help reduce pain associated with gallbladder disease. Ultimately, surgical or medical intervention like ERCP may be necessary for complete removal if stones don't pass naturally.
Experience	Multiple people shared their experience of undergoing surgery to remove kidney stones, assuring that the procedure wasn't as daunting as expected. Despite the possibility of post-operative discomfort, the relief from the original pain was significant.
Question	It was asked if the person had seen a gastroenterologist

Figure 1: Example from the dataset to show how the different perspectives are identified (Naik et al., 2024)

A.3 LLaMa Prompt

Figure 3 shows the prompt that was used to generate the perspective-oriented summaries. The prompt follows a structured format, where different placeholders represent key components of the input. Specifically:

- `text`: This refers to the list of sentences associated with a particular perspective. These sentences serve as the content from which the summary is generated.
- `question`: This represents the question that the summary is expected to address. It guides the summarization process by ensuring the generated output remains relevant to the intended query.
- `key`: This corresponds to the perspective class name, which helps differentiate between different viewpoints present in the dataset. By explicitly defining the perspective, the summarization model can tailor its output accordingly.
- `catch_phrase`: This is a perspective-specific command designed to shape the style or focus of the summary. It acts as a guiding phrase that reinforces the perspective's stance or emphasis. Figure 2 shows the different commands according to the corresponding key.

By structuring the prompt in this manner, the model is provided with clear instructions on how to generate summaries that are not only coherent but also aligned with the given perspective. This approach ensures that the summarization process remains consistent and interpretable across different perspectives, ultimately improving the quality of the generated outputs.

```
{"EXPERIENCE": "Use third-person
    perspective and talk about the
    people as users",
 "QUESTION" :"Use third-person
    perspective and talk about the
    people as users",
 "CAUSE" :"Use causality and chain of
    thoughts",
 "SUGGESTION" :"Use Advisory,
    Recommending tone and start by
    **It is suggested** when possible",
 "INFORMATION" :"Use scientific and
    informative tone"}
```

Figure 2: Custom commands to be entered in the summarization generation prompt to adapt the style to the required perspective

```
You are an expert in text analysis. Your task is to summarize the following text
    according to the given category.

### Text:
{text}

### Constraints:
The summary should answer a question regarding: {question}.

###Important: Do NOT repeat the question or the context. Only generate the summary.


### Category:
The summary should follow the {key} category.
### Writing Style:
{catch_phrase}.

### Instructions:
- Ensure that the summary is **one line**
- The summary **must explicitly reference the subject of the question**.
- The summary must not include the question.
- Follow the writing style specified for the given category.
- Ensure the summary is clear, concise, and relevant.
- Generate the summary as a **continuous paragraph** without bullet points.

### Summary:
```

Figure 3: The prompt used to generate perspective-oriented summaries where {text} refers to the list of sentences of one perspective, {question} is the question that the summary should answer, {key} is the perspective class name, and {catch_phrase} is a perspective-specific command.

UMB@PerAnsSumm 2025: Enhancing Perspective-Aware Summarization with Prompt Optimization and Supervised Fine-Tuning

Kristin Qi, Youxiang Zhu, Xiaohui Liang
Department of Computer Science, University of Massachusetts Boston
{yanankristin.qi001, youxiang.zhu001, xiaohui.liang}@umb.edu

Abstract

We present our approach to the PerAnsSumm Shared Task, which involves perspective span identification and perspective-aware summarization in community question-answering (CQA) threads. For span identification, we adopt ensemble learning that integrates three transformer models through averaging to exploit individual model strengths, achieving an 82.91% F1-score on test data. For summarization, we design a suite of Chain-of-Thought (CoT) prompting strategies that incorporate keyphrases and guide information to structure summary generation into manageable steps. To further enhance summary quality, we apply prompt optimization using the DSPy framework and supervised fine-tuning (SFT) on Llama-3 to adapt the model to domain-specific data. Experimental results on validation and test sets show that structured prompts with keyphrases and guidance improve summaries aligned with references, while the combination of prompt optimization and fine-tuning together yields significant improvement in both relevance and factuality evaluation metrics.

1 Introduction

Community question-answering (CQA) platforms have transformed how medical information is exchanged, allowing users to seek and provide answers that reflect different perspectives. These responses often include general medical knowledge, personal experiences, treatment suggestions, and insights from others with similar health concerns. However, given the large volume and different viewpoints of responses presented at different locations in the answers, it is difficult to extract accurate information efficiently. Perspective-aware summarization addresses this challenge by organizing responses based on their perspectives, helping users access relevant information more effectively (Naik et al., 2024).

Recent developments in large language models (LLMs) have shown strong performance in summarization tasks. LLM-generated summaries have demonstrated comparable or superior quality to reference summaries (Zhang et al., 2024; Liu et al., 2023). LLMs trained on medical information have enhanced their knowledge and reasoning capabilities for tackling complex problems in the healthcare domain. However, applying LLMs to perspective-aware summarization for medical CQA presents challenges: LLMs can struggle with accurately capturing distinct perspectives and effectively summarizing multiple viewpoints within long medical contexts. These challenges make it necessary to develop strategies for structuring summaries with improved accuracy.

In this work, we participate in the PerAnsSumm shared task (Agarwal et al., 2025), which focuses on developing methods for perspective span identification and perspective-aware summarization (Naik et al., 2024). Figure 1 presents an overview of our proposed approach. For perspective span identification, we employ the ensemble learning approach that integrates three transformer-based models (BERT (Devlin et al., 2019), RoBERTa (Liu et al., 2019), and DeBERTa (He et al., 2020)) with averaging to exploit individual model strengths and improve accuracy. For perspective-aware summarization, we leverage a pretrained LLM (Llama-3) (Dubey et al., 2024) and develop a suite of Chain-of-Thought (CoT) prompting strategies that incorporate keyphrases and additional guide information to enhance summary generation. To further improve the model performance in both relevance and factuality metrics, we apply prompt optimization using the DSPy framework (Khattab et al., 2023)

Proceedings of the Second Workshop on Patient-Oriented Language Processing (CL4Health), pages 437–444
May 4, 2025

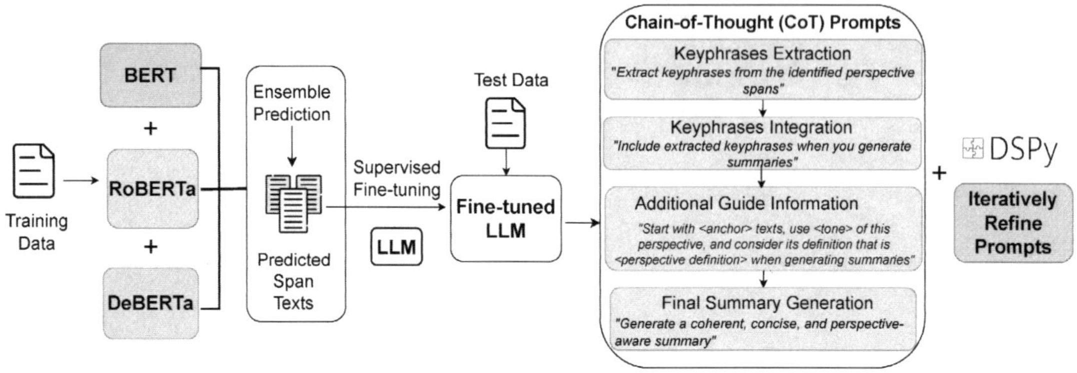

Figure 1: Detailed illustration of each component in our proposed approach for both tasks.

for automatic prompt refinement. We implement the 0-shot MIPRO optimizer within DSPy (Opsahl-Ong et al., 2024) for iterative prompt refinement. Additionally, we perform supervised fine-tuning (SFT) on Llama-3 (Prottasha et al., 2022) to adapt the model to the domain-specific data and context-aware requirements.

Our contributions are threefold:

- We integrate multiple transformer models through averaging prediction as our ensemble model. It exploits individual model strengths to achieve 82.9% F1-score on the test set and 83.9% on the validation set for perspective span identification.
- We design a suite of CoT prompting approaches incorporating keyphrases and guide information to break down summarization tasks into manageable steps. To enhance summary quality, we apply DSPy automatic prompt optimization. We also implement SFT to adapt the LLM to the domain-specific data.
- We conduct experiments that demonstrate the benefits of combining these approaches together. Particularly, the integration of DSPy-based prompt optimization with SFT significantly improves performance in both relevance and factuality evaluation metrics.

2 Related Work

Designing and optimizing prompts have become a crucial technique for guiding LLMs to generate more accurate and relevant responses for specific tasks. Recent techniques in prompt optimization have introduced various automated strategies that are better than manual prompt engineering. These approaches leverage different techniques, including gradient-based optimization (Pryzant et al., 2023), reinforcement learning (Zhang et al., 2022), and targeted word- or phrase-level edits (Fernando et al., 2023) to automatically search for optimal prompts. The DSPy framework (Opsahl-Ong et al., 2024) represents an development in this direction, yielding a modular approach that enables automatic prompt refinement.

DSPy is a programming framework that allows for chaining of LLM calls through composable modules. This technique facilitates the creation of dynamic and flexible systems that can automatically optimize both prompts and weights across multiple components. DSPy enables self-refine prompts to enhance performance during inference.

The DSPy framework includes several optimizer methods specifically designed to enhance performance on downstream tasks, such as OPRO and MIPRO optimizers (Opsahl-Ong et al., 2024). The OPRO optimizer leverages a stochastic mini-batch evaluation function to learn a surrogate model of the objective and refine instructions over multiple iterations. MIPRO optimizer employs a meta-optimization procedure to iteratively improve prompt construction.

Our approach applies the 0-shot MIPRO optimizer within DSPy framework to iteratively optimize instructions for generating perspective-aware summaries.

3 Dataset and Evaluation Metrics

3.1 Shared Task Description

The PerAnsSumm shared task comprises two main components that build upon each other, each addressing a different aspect of CQA.

Perspective Span Identification: Detecting and labeling text spans in answers that represent each of the perspectives, including Information, Cause, Suggestion, Experience, and Question. This task requires identification of specific perspective types that appear within response texts.

Perspective-aware Summarization: Generating summaries that preserve and reflect the identified perspectives and their span texts. This task creates summaries that are perspective-aware.

3.2 Dataset

The task dataset consists of CQA threads from medical forums (Naik et al., 2024). For each thread, responses contain multiple perspectives and summaries annotated for medical question-answer pairs. The dataset is divided into three parts: train, validation, and test. The training and validation sets are provided for model development, while the test set remains hidden. The training set contains labeled CQA threads with annotated perspective spans and reference summaries, while the validation set provides additional labeled data for hyperparameter tuning.

The training set contains 2236 samples, and the validation set contains 959 samples. Figure 2 illustrates the distribution of each perspective type percentage in training and validation sets. Train and validation sets have a consistent percentage distribution of each perspective.

3.3 Evaluation Metrics

Perspective-specific metrics include the macro-averaged F1-score to evaluate classification accuracy. Strict-matching and proportional matching scores assess the similarity between predicted and reference spans.

Summarization metrics include two aspects: relevance and factuality. Relevance evaluation metrics include ROUGE scores (ROUGE-1, ROUGE-2, ROUGE-L) to measure n-gram overlap, BERTScore to measure semantic similarity through embeddings, and BLEU and Meteor to evaluate precision and recall of generated summaries against references. The factuality evaluation metrics use AlignScore and SummaC. AlignScore checks whether all information in the summary is in the reference. SummaC measures factual consistency between the generated and reference summaries.

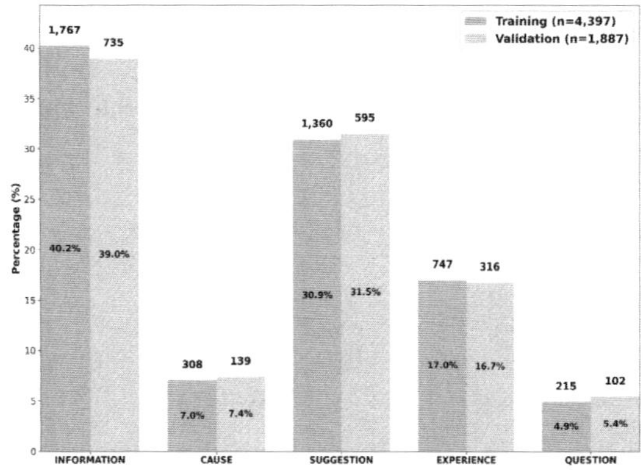

Figure 2: Percentage distribution of each perspective type in the training and validation sets. The values displayed on top of each bar represent the actual counts.

4 Method

This section describes details of our approach to addressing the shared task: ensemble learning for span identification and prompting strategies for summarization generation, including CoT, DSPy framework, and SFT.

4.1 Span Prediction with Ensemble Learning

We implement an ensemble learning framework that integrates multiple transformer models. Rather than relying on a single model's prediction, ensemble learning combines predictions from multiple models to achieve better results than any single model that could attain independently.

Our ensemble model implements three pre-trained transformer models, and we use their base models: BERT[1], RoBERTa[2], and DeBERTa[3]. These models have demonstrated strong performance in various language-related tasks. During

[1] https://huggingface.co/bert-base-uncased

[2] https://huggingface.co/FacebookAI/roberta-base

[3] https://huggingface.co/microsoft/deberta-base

inference, the ensemble model computes predictions through averaging that accounts for individual model predictions. Ensemble model is formally defined as:

$$P_{\text{ensemble}}(y \mid x) = \frac{1}{k} \sum_{i=1}^{k} P_i(y \mid x) \quad (1)$$

where $P_i(y \mid x)$ represents the prediction probability of the i-th model, and the final ensemble prediction is obtained by averaging the predictions of all k models.

5 CoT for Summarization

We leverage CoT prompting to enhance the reasoning and problem-solving capabilities of LLMs through breaking down the summarization task into smaller sequences of manageable steps. This approach guides the model to maintain high perspective alignment and summarization accuracy.

Our CoT prompting suite incorporates a structured four-step process:

1. **Keyphrase extraction:** We first prompt the LLM to identify and extract keyphrases from the identified perspective spans. This step elicits intermediate reasoning steps in the CoT.

2. **Keyphrase integration:** We prompt LLM to incorporate these extracted keyphrases when generating summaries. This step ensures that LLM preserves key information from the perspective span context.

3. **Guide information integration:** Our prompt incorporates a set of guide information referred to as the "guide" in our experiments. Following the prompt design templates established in PLASMA (Naik et al., 2024), our guide consists of three parts:

   - **Tone:** Perspective-specific tone instructions (e.g., informative tone for "Information", understanding-seeking tone for "Question").

   - **Anchor text:** Common start phrases found in reference summaries (e.g., *"For information purposes..."* for "Information" and *"It is inquired..." for "Question")*.

   - **Perspective definition:** Concise descriptions of each perspective's purpose and characteristic features.

   The model is prompted to integrate guide information using the format: *"Start with <anchor> texts. Use the <tone> tone of this perspective. Consider the following definition when generating the summary: <perspective definition>."*

4. **Summary generation:** Finally, we prompt the LLM to generate a coherent, concise, and perspective-aware summary: *"Focus on <perspective>-specific aspects in your summary. Now generate a concise and coherent summary."*

The prompt template details are shown in Appendix A. The above generation process is formalized as:

$$P_{\text{CoT}}(S \mid x, K, p) = \prod_{t=1}^{T} P(s_t \mid x, s_{<t}, K, p) \quad (2)$$

where x is the input text, K represents extracted keyphrases. p is the guide set for each perspective type. $S = \{s_1, s_2, \ldots, s_T\}$ represents the sequence of reasoning steps.

5.1 Prompt Optimization with DSPy

To further enhance summarization quality, we implement prompt optimization using the DSPy framework, which enables iterative refinement of prompts based on the context of each step. In each iteration, the DSPy compiler automatically generates multiple prompt variants (3-5) and selects optimal candidates through Bayesian optimization over the joint metric space. The challenge is defining a downstream metric that can enhance performance without having access to module-level labels or gradients.

Our downstream metric aims to balance each of the relevance evaluation metrics. Specifically, we define a composite metric that assigns equal weight (0.25) to each of four sub-metrics in the relevance category: ROUGE-L, BLEU, Meteor, and BERTScore. This process dynamically synthesizes prompts conditioned on the current step's context. The selection of the weights is based on the assumption that each sub-metric contribution is equal. The optimization objective is written as follows:

$$\mathcal{L}(T) = 0.25 \times \text{ROUGE-L} + 0.25 \times \text{BLEU} + 0.25 \times \text{Meteor} + 0.25 \times \text{BERTScore} \quad (3)$$

The objective function of optimization can be formulated as:

$$\mathcal{L}(T) = 0.25 \cdot \sum_{j=1}^{n} \log P(c_j \mid x, c_{<j}, \mathcal{M}(T)) \quad (4)$$

where $\mathcal{L}(T)$ is the optimization objective to be maximized. c_j is the generated summaries at step j, $\mathcal{M}(T)$ represents the LLM conditioned on optimized prompt T, and $P(c_j \mid x, c_{<j}, \mathcal{M}(T))$ is the probability of generating the next component c_j based on prior knowledge.

Optimizer: We select 0-Shot MIPRO, which provides a straightforward approach for optimizing instructions based on our balanced metric while remaining cost-effective within our computational budget constraints.

5.2 Supervised Fine-Tuning

SFT on LLMs has demonstrated its success in improving performance in various domains. We implement SFT on the Llama-3-8B-Instruct model[4] (Llama-3) using the Low-Rank Adaption (LoRA) technique (Hu et al., 2022). We fine-tune the model for two epochs on the training set. We report the results of summarization on both validation and test sets.

Implementation Details: All experiments were conducted on an NVIDIA A100 GPU with 40GB memory. We used a learning rate of $1e^{-4}$ with the AdamW optimizer and a batch size of 32. Token size was set to 256, temperature was at 0.1, and seed was at 42.

6 Results

We conduct all experiments using the Llama-3 model. Table 1 presents the results for span identification, while Table 2 presents the results for summarization.

[4]https://huggingface.co/meta-llama/Meta-Llama-3-8B-Instruct

7 Performance of Ensemble Models on Span Identification

We evaluate the performance of three individual transformer models (BERT, RoBERTa, DeBERTa) and their ensemble integration. Ensemble model exploits the strengths of individual models on different evaluation metrics. Table 1 presents comparisons on the validation set using three evaluation metrics: macro F1-score, strict match F1-score, and proportional match F1-score. The results on the test set are our final submission.

The ensemble model achieves an F1-score of 82.9% on the test set and 83.9% on the validation set. These results are between the best-performing (RoBERTa) and worst-performing (BERT) models. Additionally, we observe that different models outperform in different aspects of metrics: RoBERTa achieves the highest strict match F1-score, while DeBERTa performs better in proportional match. These results indicate how individual models can outperform in an evaluation while underperforming in others, which supports the ensemble methods that could combine strengths from multiple models. Our results could be further improved through advanced ensemble techniques, such as weighted combination strategies or hierarchical model structures.

Model	F1	Strict Match F1	Prop. Match F1
		Validation Set	
BERT	0.813	0.096	0.514
RoBERTa	**0.858**	**0.154**	0.546
DeBERTa	0.845	0.110	**0.559**
Ensemble	<u>0.839</u>	<u>0.120</u>	<u>0.540</u>
		Test Set Submission	
Ensemble	0.829	0.120	0.505

Table 1: Comparison of span identification performance on the validation and test sets. **Bold values** indicate the best scores, while <u>underscored</u> values show results from the ensemble model.

8 Summarization Performance

We experiment with multiple prompting strategies, including vanilla prompting, CoT, DSPy-based prompt optimization, and SFT. Table 2 presents the comparison across eight evaluation metrics. The test set performance is our final submission.

Category	R-1	R-2	R-L	BLEU	Meteor	BERTScore	AlignScore	SummaC
Baseline								
Vanilla Prompting	0.229	0.078	0.290	0.068	0.250	0.782	0.280	0.225
Chain-of-Thought (CoT) Prompting (Validation Set)								
CoT_keyphrase	0.310	0.110	0.315	0.074	0.268	0.797	0.300	0.238
CoT_guide	0.318	0.108	0.328	0.081	0.290	0.805	0.315	0.247
Prompt Optimization (DSPy)								
CoT_guide+DSPy	**0.390**	**0.212**	0.346	0.091	0.328	0.830	**0.370**	**0.291**
Supervised Fine-Tuning (SFT)								
SFT+CoT_guide+DSPy	**0.390**	0.165	**0.420**	**0.096**	**0.351**	**0.839**	0.366	0.251
Test Set Submission Results								
SFT+CoT_guide+DSPy	0.360	0.155	0.328	**0.096**	0.339	0.823	0.333	0.256

Table 2: Performance comparison of different strategies for summarization on the validation and test sets. *NOTE: CoT_guide indicates CoT+keyphrases+guide information.*

Our baseline uses vanilla prompting, where we directly prompt the LLM to generate concise and coherent summaries. Building on this, CoT approach with integration of keyphrases and guide information increases ROUGE-1 by +8.1% and BERTScore by +1.5%. These results indicate that structured reasoning and providing task-relevant external context can better guide LLM toward generating summaries with improved accuracy.

DSPy Optimization Impact: The application of DSPy optimization to the CoT+keyphrases+guide (*CoT_guide*) prompt strategy significantly improves performance. The DSPy framework iteratively refines prompts, leading to an additional increase across all relevance metrics (R-1, R-2, R-L, BLEU, Meteor, BERTScore), with average improvements of +25.6% on validation set and +9.1% on test set. Factuality metrics also show substantial improvements, with AlignScore and SummaC increasing by +17.0% and +4.7%, respectively. These results demonstrate that automated prompt optimization builds effectively on manual CoT design, and it scales summary quality through refinement of prompt precision and contextual awareness.

SFT impacts: Fine-tuning Llama-3 using domain-specific data further enhances the model's performance when combined with DSPy optimization. On the validation set, the SFT+DSPy combination improves performance over DSPy alone, with ROUGE-L improving by +21.4%, Meteor by +7.0%, and BLEU by +8.8%. Test set results reveal increases of +3.4% for Meteor and +5.5% for BLEU. While SFT substantially improves relevance metrics, its impact on factuality metrics is less effective, suggesting that fine-tuning primarily enhances the model's ability to generate content that aligns with reference summaries rather than improving factuality scores.

Findings: We observe that combining DSPy optimization with SFT demonstrates the benefits of integrating both approaches. Fine-tuning helps the Llama-3 model adapt to domain-specific features in medical CQAs, while DSPy optimization refines the prompt structure to better guide the model's summarization. This combination particularly achieves a better performance in relevance.

9 Conclusions

In this paper, we present our approach to the PerAnsSumm Shared Task. Our approach adopts ensemble learning with averaging individual model predictions for span identification, achieving an 82.9% F1-score on test data. For summary generation, we develop structured Chain-of-Thought (CoT) prompting with keyphrases and guide information and combine it with DSPy-based prompt optimization and supervised fine-tuning (SFT) of the Llama-3 model to improve summary quality.

Our experimental results demonstrate that the integration of keyphrases and guide information within CoT improves the alignment between generated summaries and references. Notably, automated prompt optimization through the DSPy framework substantially improves both relevance and factuality evaluation metrics, with average improvements of +25.6% on validation set. This reveals the effectiveness of iterative prompt refinement. Furthermore, combining DSPy optimization with SFT further enhances model performance, with particularly improvements in relevance metrics (ROUGE-L: +21.4%, Meteor: +7.0%, BLEU: +8.8%). Future work will compare our approach with other LLMs such as GPT-4 to identify factors that impact summarization quality. Moreover, we will explore designs for metric-based optimization strategies to improve alignments with references.

10 Limitations

Our approach reveals several limitations. First, we use Llama-3 as our LLM without benchmarking against API-based models such as GPT-4 or Claude-3. Compared with other teams' submissions, it indicates that Llama-3 underperforms relative to GPT-4 and Claude-3. Second, our implementation of MIPRO optimizer within the DSPy framework relies on the balanced metric formulation derived from empirical assumptions. This equal-weight approach may oversimplify the relationships between different evaluation metrics and potentially reduce accuracy. The generalizability of our prompt optimization strategy also remains an open question. Alternative optimizers, such as MIPRO with bootstrapped demonstrations or OPRO may yield further improvements. Lastly, our prompt design is tailored to the medical CQA. The prompt templates do not account for potential variability within summaries. These suggest room for future research.

References

Siddhant Agarwal, Md Shad Akhtar, and Shweta Yadav. 2025. Overview of the peranssumm 2025 shared task on perspective-aware healthcare answer summarization. In *Proceedings of the Second Workshop on Patient-Oriented Language Processing (CL4Health) @ NAACL 2025*, Albuquerque, USA. Association for Computational Linguistics.

Jacob Devlin, Ming-Wei Chang, Kenton Lee, and Kristina Toutanova. 2019. Bert: Pre-training of deep bidirectional transformers for language understanding. In *Proceedings of the 2019 conference of the North American chapter of the association for computational linguistics: human language technologies, volume 1 (long and short papers)*, pages 4171–4186.

Abhimanyu Dubey, Abhinav Jauhri, Abhinav Pandey, Abhishek Kadian, Ahmad Al-Dahle, Aiesha Letman, Akhil Mathur, Alan Schelten, Amy Yang, Angela Fan, et al. 2024. The llama 3 herd of models. *arXiv preprint arXiv:2407.21783*.

Chrisantha Fernando, Dylan Banarse, Henryk Michalewski, Simon Osindero, and Tim Rocktäschel. 2023. Promptbreeder: Self-referential self-improvement via prompt evolution. *arXiv preprint arXiv:2309.16797*.

Pengcheng He, Xiaodong Liu, Jianfeng Gao, and Weizhu Chen. 2020. Deberta: Decoding-enhanced bert with disentangled attention. *arXiv preprint arXiv:2006.03654*.

Edward J Hu, Yelong Shen, Phillip Wallis, Zeyuan Allen-Zhu, Yuanzhi Li, Shean Wang, Lu Wang, Weizhu Chen, et al. 2022. Lora: Low-rank adaptation of large language models. *ICLR*, 1(2):3.

Omar Khattab, Arnav Singhvi, Paridhi Maheshwari, Zhiyuan Zhang, Keshav Santhanam, Sri Vardhamanan, Saiful Haq, Ashutosh Sharma, Thomas T Joshi, Hanna Moazam, et al. 2023. Dspy: Compiling declarative language model calls into self-improving pipelines. *arXiv preprint arXiv:2310.03714*.

Yinhan Liu, Myle Ott, Naman Goyal, Jingfei Du, Mandar Joshi, Danqi Chen, Omer Levy, Mike Lewis, Luke Zettlemoyer, and Veselin Stoyanov. 2019. Roberta: A robustly optimized bert pretraining approach. *arXiv preprint arXiv:1907.11692*.

Yixin Liu, Kejian Shi, Katherine S He, Longtian Ye, Alexander R Fabbri, Pengfei Liu, Dragomir Radev, and Arman Cohan. 2023. On learning to summarize with large language models as references. *arXiv preprint arXiv:2305.14239*.

Gauri Naik, Sharad Chandakacherla, Shweta Yadav, and Md Shad Akhtar. 2024. No perspective, no perception!! perspective-aware healthcare answer summarization. In *Findings of the Association for Computational Linguistics: ACL 2024*, pages 15919–15932, Bangkok, Thailand. Association for Computational Linguistics.

Krista Opsahl-Ong, Michael J Ryan, Josh Purtell, David Broman, Christopher Potts, Matei Zaharia, and Omar Khattab. 2024. Optimizing instructions and demonstrations for multi-stage language model programs. *arXiv preprint arXiv:2406.11695*.

Nusrat Jahan Prottasha, Abdullah As Sami, Md Kowsher, Saydul Akbar Murad, Anupam Kumar Bairagi, Mehedi Masud, and Mohammed Baz. 2022. Transfer learning for sentiment analysis using bert based supervised fine-tuning. *Sensors*, 22(11):4157.

Reid Pryzant, Dan Iter, Jerry Li, Yin Tat Lee, Chenguang Zhu, and Michael Zeng. 2023. Automatic prompt optimization with" gradient descent" and beam search. *arXiv preprint arXiv:2305.03495.*

Tianjun Zhang, Xuezhi Wang, Denny Zhou, Dale Schuurmans, and Joseph E Gonzalez. 2022. Tempera: Test-time prompting via reinforcement learning. *arXiv preprint arXiv:2211.11890.*

Tianyi Zhang, Faisal Ladhak, Esin Durmus, Percy Liang, Kathleen McKeown, and Tatsunori B Hashimoto. 2024. Benchmarking large language models for news summarization. *Transactions of the Association for Computational Linguistics*, 12:39–57.

A Prompt Template

Prompt Template for the Chain of Thought (CoT)

You are a specialized medical summarizer trained to create perspective-aware summaries from community question-answering (CQA) content. Your task is to generate a concise, coherent summary that accurately reflects the {PERSPECTIVE} perspective from the provided context.

[Guidance Information]
Perspective: {PERSPECTIVE}
Definition: {DEFINITION}
Tone: {TONE}
Begin with: "{ANCHOR_TEXT}"

[Instructions]
1. Carefully read the perspective-based span texts below.
2. Extract keyphrases from the {PERSPECTIVE} perspective span.
3. Incorporate your extracted keyphrases when you generate the summary: {KEYPHRASES}
4. Generate a coherent, concise summary that:
  - Start with "{ANCHOR_TEXT}" texts
  - Use the {TONE} tone of this perspective
  - Consider the following definition when generating the summary: {DEFINITION}
  - Focus on {PERSPECTIVE}-specific aspects in your summary. Now generate a concise and coherent summary.

[Input Content]
Question: {QUESTION}
Context: {CONTEXT}
{PERSPECTIVE} Span texts:
{PERSPECTIVE_SPANS}

Follow the steps above to generate a perspective-aware summary that captures the essential {PERSPECTIVE} information from span texts. Let's think step by step.

Figure 3: Prompt template used in our approach.

Overview of the PerAnsSumm 2025 Shared Task on Perspective-aware Healthcare Answer Summarization

Siddhant Agarwal[1], **Md. Shad Akhtar**[2], **Shweta Yadav**[1],
[1]University of Illinois at Chicago, [2]IIIT Delhi
{sagarw38, shwetay}@uic.edu, shad.akhtar@iiitd.ac.in

Abstract

This paper presents an overview of the Perspective-aware Answer Summarization (PerAnsSumm) Shared Task on summarizing healthcare answers in Community Question Answering forums hosted at the CL4Health Workshop at NAACL 2025. In this shared task, we approach healthcare answer summarization with two subtasks: (a) perspective span identification and classification and (b) perspective-based answer summarization (summaries focused on one of the perspective classes). We defined a benchmarking setup for the comprehensive evaluation of predicted spans and generated summaries. We encouraged participants to explore novel solutions to the proposed problem and received high interest in the task with 23 participating teams and 155 submissions. This paper describes the task objectives, the dataset, the evaluation metrics and our findings. We share the results of the novel approaches adopted by task participants, especially emphasizing the applicability of Large Language Models in this perspective-based answer summarization task.

1 Introduction

Community Question Answering (CQA) forums such as Yahoo! Answers, Reddit, and Quora have transformed how people access information, especially with the rise of the internet. These sources facilitate the spread of information and knowledge across geographical boundaries and connect people with wide-ranging expertise and experiences. It is therefore no surprise that users of these forums discuss a broad range of topics, including healthcare concerns. However, within these forums, users often struggle to find relevant and reliable information given the plethora of answers. Further, these forums contain answers from users with a multitude of perspectives, such as their personal experiences or subject knowledge, which may or may not be relevant to what another user seeks. To this end, Naik et al. (2024) proposed the perspective-aware healthcare answer summarization task for CQA forums.

As seen in Figure 1, users' questions often receive answers from other users of CQA forums that contain a multitude of perspectives. For example, a user provides both a suggestion (*"try a diet with low fat and very low saturated fats"*) and their personal experience (*"I've had the surgery and it really isn't a big deal"*) in their answer. While such diverse insights can be valuable, they can also be overwhelming for users seeking specific information. Therefore, it is important to identify such perspective spans and provide a concise perspective-based summary of all answers (as shown in Figure 1). This allows users to obtain information relevant to their situation and assists them in making informed decisions.

The investigation of novel approaches for the task of CQA forum answer summarization has been limited with recent works being primarily reliant on Pre-trained Language Models (Naik et al., 2024) such as Flan-T5, leaving the utility of Large Language Models unexplored for the most part. Further, the majority of previous work has been limited by small dataset sizes (Bhattacharya et al., 2022; Chaturvedi et al., 2024) and the lack of a uniform benchmark. This work aims to fill this research gap by providing an accessible resource to researchers for developing and comparing novel techniques for perspective-aware healthcare answer summarization.

The PerAnsSumm 2025 Shared Task focuses on investigating novel solutions in the perspective-aware summarization of healthcare answers in CQA forums. This work aims to be a meaningful step forward in spearheading research in this direction and investigating the utility of recent advances in Natural Language Processing, such as the rise of Large Language Models (LLMs) in their application to the biomedical summarization domain.

Proceedings of the Second Workshop on Patient-Oriented Language Processing (CL4Health), pages 445–455
May 4, 2025

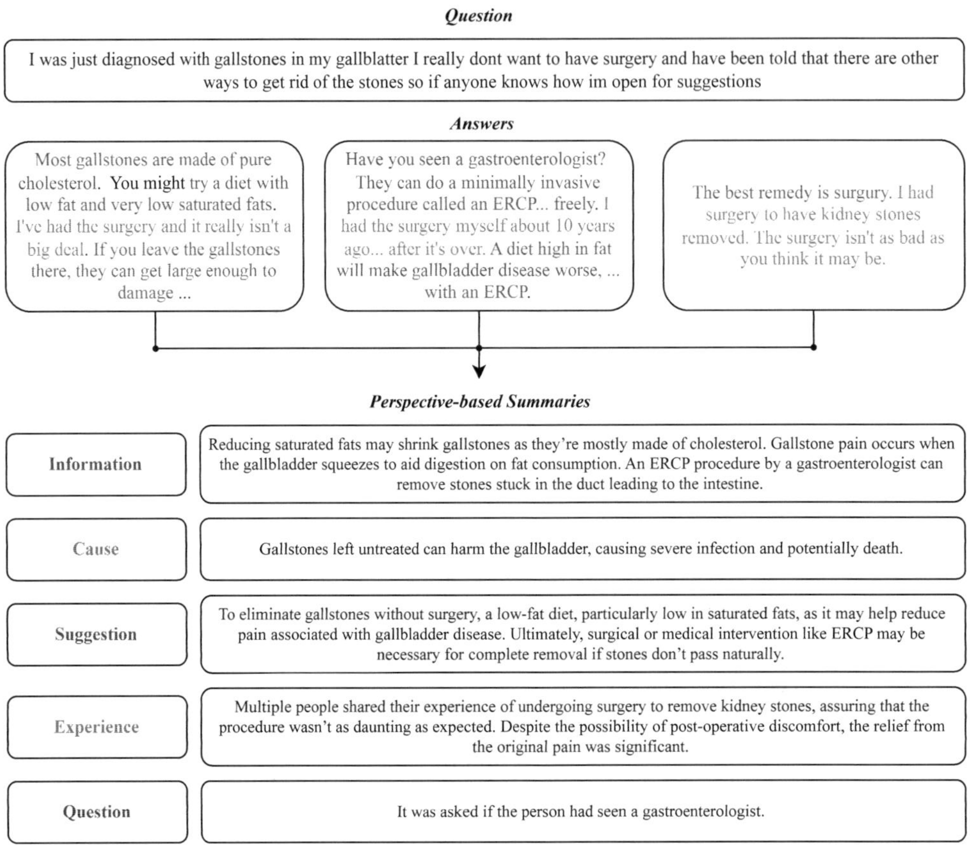

Figure 1: A description of the PerAnsSumm task with inputs and expected output. Colored spans in answers correspond to spans of different perspectives. The spans are utilized to generate a perspective-based summary for each class.

In this work, we present the findings of the PerAnsSumm 2025 Shared Task, hosted by the CL4Health Workshop at NAACL 2025. The shared task garnered significant interest, with 100 registered participants on the CodaBench[1] platform, with 23 teams participating and submitting a total of 155 valid submissions. The remainder of this paper describes key details of the shared task along with our findings and brief descriptions of the participating systems.

2 Task Description

The shared task involved two sub-tasks, (A) Span-Identification and Classification and (B) Summary Generation. These two sub-tasks aimed to capture the different ways in which a user may interact with a Community Question-Answering Forum when filtering based on the five defined perspectives – *'Information', 'Cause', 'Suggestion', 'Experience'* and *'Question'*.

TASK A – Perspective Span Identification and Classification. In this task, the participants were required to identify and accurately classify spans of text in the community answers of CQA threads according to the relevant perspective. For example, as shown in Figure 1: `Information` - *'gallstones are made of pure cholesterol'*, `Experience` - *'I had the surgery myself about 10 years ago'*, `Question` - *'Have you seen a gastroenterologist'*.

TASK B – Perspective-based Summarization. In this task, participants were required to provide a summary of all texts pertaining to the relevant perspective class. This may be looked at as a summary of the identified perspective-based spans or as a perspective-based summary of the answers in the CQA thread. For example, as shown in Figure 1: `Cause` - *'Gallstones left untreated can harm the gallbladder, causing severe infection and poten-*

[1]Available for continued access at: `https://www.codabench.org/competitions/4312/`

	Size	Information	Cause	Suggestion	Question	Experience
Train	2533	4823/1961	646/342	646/342	325/249	1439/845
Validation	317	643/246	108/49	549/208	42/32	170/108
Test (Seen)	317	631/242	81/45	499/188	44/31	181/100
Test (Unseen)	50	153/43	47/14	198/47	35/18	92/37

Table 1: Dataset Statistics describing the perspective-specific span count/summaries count in the split

tially death.'

Both tasks combined to address the underlying challenge of providing users with relevant content that is specific to their needs, and hence, allowing them to make informed decisions. We proposed these tasks as complementary, as identifying relevant perspective-specific spans allowed for improvements in the summarization task. However, the participating teams were given the option to participate in each task individually if they preferred.

3 Dataset

For this task, we utilized the PUMA dataset (Naik et al., 2024), containing 3167 total questions and 9987 answers. The dataset is divided into training, validation, and testing sets with detailed class-wise statistics given in Table 1. The PUMA dataset was developed using samples from the **L6 - Yahoo! Answers CQA** dataset [2] filtered on the Healthcare category. These samples were annotated by analyzing all answers for potential perspective labels and manually writing a perspective-based summary that is a concise representation of all perspective spans. As a result of this annotation, the dataset contained text spans in each answer, along with a perspective-based answer summary for each identified perspective class label for a question sample.

Naik et al. (2024) identified five perspective classes that correspond to the different ways in which users respond to questions on CQA forums. These perspectives were given as follows:

1. **Cause:** It underlines the potential cause of a medical phenomenon or a symptom. It answers the *Why* regarding a specific observation, offering insights to identify the root cause.

2. **Suggestion:** It encapsulates strategies, recommendations, or potential courses of action towards management or resolution of a health condition.

3. **Experience:** It covers first-hand experiences, observations, insights, or opinions derived from treatment or medication related to a particular problem.

4. **Question:** It consists of interrogative phrases, follow-up questions and rhetorical questions that are sought to better understand the context. They typically start with phrases like *Why, What, Do, How,* and *Did* etc, and end in a question mark.

5. **Information:** It encompasses segments that offer factual knowledge or information considering the given query. These segments provide comprehensive details on diagnoses, symptoms, or general information on a medical condition.

Through our utilization of this dataset, we hope to enable researchers to develop models which are capable of generating perspective-guided summaries for CQA answer forums. This would in turn enable users to make informed decisions when accessing CQA forums.

Since the original PUMA dataset was available to researchers upon request, we further annotated 50 samples as a new test set for the PerAnsSumm shared task. We followed the annotation guidelines as laid out by Naik et al. (2024) to identify relevant spans for each perspective class and manually created summaries for the identified perspectives. Submissions by the participants to the PerAnsSumm 2025 Shared Task were evaluated on this set of 50 newly annotated and unreleased samples.

4 Evaluation

In this section, we provide details about the evaluation metrics used for each of the two sub-tasks in the PerAnsSumm 2025 shared task.

Task A We evaluated submissions on 3 criteria - Classification (Macro F1 and Weighted F-1), Strict-matching (Precision, Recall and F-1), Proportional-matching (Precision, Recall and F-1). The overall score for task A combined these 3 criteria as it is the average of the classification-weighted F-1 score, the Strict-matching F-1 score and the Proportional-matching F-1 score. Classification metrics were based on framing the problem as a sample-level multi-label classification problem. Strict matching was defined as follows:

$$P = \frac{|\text{CorrectSpans}|}{|\text{PredictedSpans}|},$$

[2] `https://webscope.sandbox.yahoo.com/catalog.php?datatype=l&did=11`

$$R = \frac{|\text{CorrectSpans}|}{|\text{GoldSpans}|},$$

$$F_1 = \frac{2 \times P \times R}{P + R},$$

Proportional-matching was defined as follows:

$$P = \frac{\sum len(\text{MaximumOverlappingSpan})}{\sum len(\text{PredictedSpan})},$$

$$R = \frac{\sum len(\text{MaximumOverlappingSpan})}{\sum len(\text{GoldSpan})},$$

$$F_1 = \frac{2 \times P \times R}{P + R},$$

where MaximumOverlappingSpan refers to the sub-span of a predicted span that had the maximum overlap with each of the gold spans.

Task B Submissions were evaluated based on two criteria using multiple automatic metrics to assess both the relevance and the factuality of the generated summaries. These criteria were as follows:

1. *Relevance* - ROUGE-1,2 and L (Lin, 2004), BertScore (Zhang et al., 2020b), METEOR (Banerjee and Lavie, 2005) and BLEU (Papineni et al., 2002).

2. *Factuality* - AlignScore (Zha et al., 2023) and SummaC (Laban et al., 2022).

The overall score across both tasks was computed as an average of the Task A scores, the Task B Relevance scores, and the Task B Factuality scores. This was used in computing the final leaderboard positions. Implementation and hyperparameters used for all automatic evaluations were made available [3] to the participants before the evaluation stage.

5 Task Results

Table 2 presents the final leaderboard for the shared task based on the best performing submission of each team, according to the defined evaluation metrics. Task-wise results are given in Table 3 and 4.

In this section, we describe our findings and key results from the submissions.

⋆	Team	LLMs?	Score
1	WisPerMed	✓	45.71
2	YALENLP	✓	45.48
3	Team_ABC	✓	45.26
4	AICOE	✓	44.95
5	KHU_LDI	✓	44.92
6	LTRC-IIITH	✓	43.95
7	MNLP	✓	43.21
8	Team Airi	✓	42.38
9	DataHacks	✓	42.03
10	UTSA-NLP	✗	41.12
11	HSE NLP	✓	40.81
12	MediFact	✓	40.77
13	NU-WAVE	✓	40.46
14	Roux-lette	✓	39.96
15	Manchester Bees	✓	39.94
16	Abdelmalak	✓	39.07
17	Team_UMB	✗	38.24
18	massU	✗	38.15
19	RVK_Med	✗	37.50
20	TrofimovaMC	✗	36.98
21	TeamENSAK	✓	36.41
22	CaresAI	✓	34.05
23	LMU*	✓	17.26

Table 2: Final leaderboard for the PerAnsSumm 2025 Shared Task in order of average performance over the two sub-tasks. ⋆ denotes the rank column. Combined Average is the average of the average Task A and average Task B scores. * denotes the team participates in Task B only.

LLM usage As a part of the submission process, we asked participants to self-disclose the use of LLMs in their modeling approaches. Out of 23 participating teams, 18 teams disclose the use of LLMs in some capacity, with all of the top 10 teams utilizing LLMs. This highlights the growing prevalence and importance of LLMs in summarization and other NLP tasks. The growing trend of LLM utilization is highlighted further when compared to a similar task related to summarization in the biomedical domain, BioLaySumm 2024 (Goldsack et al., 2024), where only 18 of the 52 participating teams utilized LLMs. The rapidly evolving landscape of LLM research and its applications in the biomedical domain need careful evaluation, especially given the sensitivity of biomedical data and the related real-life implications. At the same time, we find this usage of LLMs as a positive signal of participants exploring novel techniques.

[3] Made available through a GitHub repository: `https://github.com/PerAnsSumm/Evaluation`

*	⋆	Team	Classification		Strict-matching			Proportional-matching			Avg
			macro	*weigh.*	*Prec.*	*Recall*	*F1*	*Prec.*	*Recall*	*F1*	
1	3	Team_ABC	86.97	91.73	22.05	27.81	**24.60**	62.15	80.29	70.06	**62.13**
2	7	MNLP	85.24	90.61	13.76	27.24	18.29	65.80	84.06	73.82	60.90
3	4	AICOE	86.56	91.40	17.65	27.43	21.48	65.97	71.59	68.66	60.52
4	2	YALENLP	84.39	89.02	15.71	28.57	20.27	63.72	82.18	71.78	60.36
5	6	LTRC-IIITH	**90.33**	**92.39**	19.15	22.29	20.60	67.74	68.33	68.03	60.34
6	12	MediFact	83.61	88.87	13.83	31.43	19.21	62.22	**84.93**	71.82	59.97
7	1	WisPerMed	87.75	92.11	17.26	23.05	19.74	62.36	73.80	67.60	59.82
8	16	Abdelmalak	88.59	91.30	8.53	15.81	11.08	**70.21**	81.74	**75.54**	59.31
9	5	KHU_LDI	79.09	86.18	18.68	**30.10**	23.05	57.16	81.84	67.31	58.85
10	13	NU-WAVE	81.24	87.19	20.48	22.86	21.60	57.02	72.26	63.74	57.51
11	14	Roux-lette	81.24	87.19	20.48	22.86	21.60	57.02	72.26	63.74	57.51
12	15	Manchester Bees	82.68	87.69	**22.67**	19.43	20.92	55.03	70.36	61.76	56.79
13	10	UTSA-NLP	73.59	84.26	16.87	18.67	17.72	59.66	67.64	63.40	55.13
14	11	HSE NLP	80.73	87.86	14.75	18.86	16.56	66.66	54.21	59.79	54.74
15	9	DataHacks	86.35	90.44	15.99	13.52	14.65	51.49	66.78	58.15	54.41
16	8	Team Airi	84.67	88.67	19.94	12.76	15.56	49.13	61.67	54.69	52.98
17	19	RVK_Med	89.84	92.07	0.19	0.19	0.19	58.01	72.05	64.27	52.18
18	18	massU	83.16	88.54	14.29	11.43	12.70	50.85	48.30	49.54	50.26
19	17	Team_UMB	82.91	88.26	12.66	11.43	12.01	52.32	48.77	50.48	50.25
20	20	TrofimovaMC	77.00	85.79	7.28	9.52	8.25	58.14	46.30	51.55	48.53
21	21	TeamENSAK	80.69	84.94	1.69	2.10	1.87	58.23	46.02	51.41	46.08
22	22	CaresAI	74.64	83.02	7.37	8.00	7.67	47.54	36.51	41.31	44.00

Table 3: Leaderboard for Task A of the PerAnsSumm 2025 Shared Task in order of average performance. ⋆ denotes the overall shared task rank column. * denotes Task A rank column. Classification scores are F1 scores. Average for Task A is calculated as the average of classification-weighted F1, Strict-matching F1, and Proportional-matching F1.

Comparing Task A and Task B performance We find that teams that perform well in Task A, which covers identification and classification, also tend to perform comparatively better in Task B, perspective-based summarization. It is observed that teams often utilize substantially different methods for both the tasks, with greater reliance on smaller pre-trained language models in the span identification task compared to the summarization task.

In-context learning as the new normal An interesting observation from the submissions is the reliance on novel in-context learning based approaches through innovative prompting strategies. Participants prefer inferencing on pre-trained large language models, utilizing their vast training knowledge as compared to fine-tuning models specifically for the task. This reliance is representative of the current shift in the NLP landscape from a pre-train and fine-tune to a pre-train and inference paradigm. This calls for the further development of models trained specifically on specialized domains, such as healthcare to advance research and boost model capabilities in these specialized areas.

6 Submissions

The PerAnsSumm 2025 shared task attracted submissions from 23 participating teams who made a combined total of 155 valid submissions that were evaluated by the task organizers. Out of these teams, 22 teams participated in both Task A and Task B, while 1 team participated in only Task B. Out of the 23 participating teams, 12 teams submitted system papers. Brief summaries of the approaches taken by these teams are described in this section. We also describe the baseline provided to participants as a starter code.

Starter Kit: We utilized the PLASMA model (Naik et al., 2024) as a strong starting point to the participants. This modeling approach showed promising results in the perspective-based answer summarization task (Task B). It utilized a perspective-conditioned prompt that is generated following a defined prompt template. Subsequently, the prompt was fed to the Flan-T5 model (Chung et al., 2022) with a prefix tuner to generate the summary. An energy-driven loss function was incorporated along with the standard cross-entropy (CE) loss to enforce the perspective attributes in the generated summary. This model represented the current state

*	★	Team	Relevance							Factuality			Avg
			R-1	R-2	R-L	BS	MT	BL	Avg	AS	SC	Avg	
1	1	WisPerMed	45.15	22.10	41.02	89.91	40.95	13.47	42.10	40.85	**29.58**	35.21	**38.66**
2	2	YALENLP	**46.90**	**23.14**	**42.87**	88.28	**44.54**	**15.71**	**43.57**	37.94	27.07	32.50	38.04
3	5	KHU_LDI	45.48	20.44	40.31	**90.12**	39.50	14.13	41.66	42.00	26.53	34.27	37.96
4	4	AICOE	43.45	18.69	38.78	86.58	38.44	11.24	39.53	42.60	27.01	34.80	37.17
5	8	Team Airi	38.42	18.68	35.19	76.80	33.93	13.96	36.16	47.28	28.72	38.00	37.08
6	3	Team_ABC	40.01	16.49	35.78	84.06	31.87	10.60	36.47	46.01	28.34	37.17	36.82
7	9	DataHacks	37.08	16.83	33.65	77.62	33.91	11.16	35.04	44.27	28.99	36.63	35.84
8	6	LTR-IIITH	39.46	17.41	35.12	83.11	34.07	13.38	37.09	41.84	27.01	34.42	35.76
9	7	MNLP	40.22	16.39	36.08	84.93	38.85	10.70	37.86	36.17	25.53	30.85	34.36
10	10	UTSA-NLP	34.38	12.61	30.53	76.87	31.16	10.24	32.63	45.03	26.20	35.62	34.12
11	11	HSE NLP	30.84	9.61	26.03	83.36	20.62	3.81	29.05	**51.50**	25.78	**38.64**	33.84
12	17	Team_UMB	36.02	15.46	32.78	82.32	33.93	9.58	35.02	33.26	25.62	29.44	32.23
13	18	massU	36.27	15.84	33.32	82.26	34.55	9.44	35.28	32.03	25.77	28.90	32.09
14	13	NU-WAVE	38.44	16.67	33.95	82.74	33.35	12.41	36.26	32.16	23.06	27.61	31.93
15	21	TeamENSAK	30.67	12.84	27.67	69.74	25.48	11.19	29.60	41.10	25.99	33.54	31.57
16	15	Manchester Bees	29.23	9.11	24.54	77.34	21.18	4.04	27.57	47.75	23.16	35.45	31.51
17	20	TrofimovaMC	28.76	9.12	23.85	81.77	19.31	2.13	27.49	46.79	23.04	34.91	31.20
18	14	Roux-lette	37.37	15.42	32.67	82.52	32.84	11.22	35.34	31.15	22.88	27.02	31.18
19	12	MediFact	34.85	14.75	32.12	83.36	31.20	10.78	34.51	31.21	24.48	27.84	31.18
20	19	RVK_Med	30.11	11.40	27.05	81.96	26.87	8.86	31.04	33.87	24.67	29.27	30.16
21	22	CaresAI	28.00	8.45	24.31	85.00	22.06	6.12	28.99	33.14	25.21	29.17	29.08
22	16	Abdelmalak	31.32	11.30	25.56	79.88	23.40	6.34	29.63	33.84	22.70	28.27	28.95
23	23	LMU	21.48	9.05	19.42	53.51	20.32	5.95	21.62	35.64	24.71	30.17	25.90

Table 4: Leaderboard for Task B of the PerAnsSumm 2025 Shared Task in order of average performance. ★ denotes the overall shared task rank column. * denotes Task B rank column. Task B metrics - R-1 (ROUGE-1), R-2 (ROUGE-2), R-L (ROUGE-L), BS (BertScore), MT (METEOR), BL (BLEU), AS (AlignScore), SC (SummaC). All metrics are F-1 scores wherever relevant. Average column is the average of the average Task B Relevance and Task B factuality average scores.

Team	Coherence	Consistency	Fluency	Relevance	Coverage
WisPerMed	4.40	4.40	4.47	4.00	4.07
YALENLP	**4.73**	4.53	4.60	4.20	4.40
Team_ABC	4.07	3.93	4.33	3.73	3.60
AICOE	4.27	4.00	4.40	3.73	3.80
KHU_LDI	4.53	**4.67**	**4.67**	**4.33**	**4.53**

Table 5: Human Analysis of 15 generated summaries for the top 5 ranking teams

of the art for the task of perspective-based answer summarization, and the source code for this model is provided to the participants in the starter kit as a part of the Shared Task.

WisPerMed Pakull et al. (2025) leveraged DeepSeek-R1 (DeepSeek-AI, 2025) in a zero-shot setting with structured prompting for Task A. They designed a detailed system prompt instructing the model to extract spans according to the given perspectives without modifying the original content. They instruct the model to return structured output for consistency and easy parsing. For Task B, they utilized two step pipeline with sequence classification and instruction tuning of the Mistral-7B model (Jiang et al., 2023). In the first step of this pipeline, they built a labeled answer dataset by associating the spans with their corresponding classes and using the Mistral model as a sequence classifier. In the next step, the perspective-specific subset of answers was used to generate perspective-aware summaries. The team achieved first rank on the leaderboard based on the average over Task A and Task B metrics, and also lead performance in Task B. Their approach exhibits close to peak performance across all aspects of the two tasks leading to a high overall rank compared to other teams' approaches which ace one set of metrics while falling behind on the overall task.

YALENLP Jang et al. (2025) utilized the zero-shot capabilities of GPT-4o (OpenAI et al., 2024b) for both Task A and Task B. They inference on GPT-4o without fine-tuning and rely upon the effectiveness of GPT4o to capture the diverse medical perspectives in CQA forums with promising results. They highlight that the generalizability of the GPT4o model allows for robust in-context learning and even surpasses few-shot configurations. They also utilized a Mixture-of-Agents (Wang et al., 2024) setup to enhance system performance through ensembling multiple open-source models, allowing them to compensate for the weaknesses of individual models. They exploited an intermediate verification layer to refine predictions and mitigate hallucinations. They achieved second rank on the task leaderboard with the best score Task B relevance metrics.

AICOE R et al. (2025) utilized a pipeline with a combination of two closed-source LLMs inferenced for both Task A and Task B. For Task A, they employed the OpenAI O1 (OpenAI et al., 2024a) and the Google Gemini-2.0 Flash models. The spans predicted by both these models are merged with a preference given to the Gemini-2.0 model based on an empirical review of performance. They then used these predicted spans as an additional input for Task B summarization using the Gemini 2.0 Flash model. They also highlight their experiments with fine-tuned open-source LLMs.

LTRC-IIITH Marimuthu and Krishnamurthy (2025) fine-tuned BERT-large (Devlin et al., 2019) and RoBERTa-large (Liu et al., 2019) models for span identification in the standard IO annotation format. They demonstrate the robustness of a fine-tuned RoBERTa model with the highest classification-weighted F-1 score for Task A. For Task B, they fine-tune BART-large (Lewis et al., 2020) and Pegasus-large (Zhang et al., 2019) models with an MLM (Masked-Language Modeling) objective for the BART model.

MNLP Lee et al. (2025) followed a two-stage Classifier-Refiner Architecture (CRA) to improve the classification of user-generated health responses in CQA forums. In the first stage, a classifier segments responses into self-contained snippets and assigns one of five perspective classes. If the classifier was uncertain, a refiner was triggered to reassess the classification using retrieval-augmented generation (RAG). The refiner retrieved the two most similar training examples based on all-MiniLM-L6-v2 sentence similarity and incorporated them as few-shot examples to enhance classification reliability. Additionally, they employed instruction-based prompting, tone definitions, and Chain-of-Thought (CoT) reasoning to guide the model's decisions and improve interpretability.

DataHacks Nawander and Reddy (2025) utilized the Mistral 7B (Jiang et al., 2023) model as their backbone for fine-tuning with LORA adapters. The same configuration of fine-tuning an LLM with Low-Rank Adaptation (Hu et al., 2022) was used for both tasks. They perform prompt engineering to restructure the input into the distinct sections of Question, Context, and Answer, allowing the model to better interpret details and leading to an observed improvement in model performance.

Team_UMB Qi et al. (2025) employed an ensemble learning approach combining multiple transformer models (BERT (Devlin et al., 2019), RoBERTa (Liu et al., 2019), and DeBERTa (He et al., 2021)) through weighted averaging for Task A. For Task B, they developed a suite of prompting techniques to leverage a pre-trained LLM (Llama-3 (Grattafiori et al., 2024)). Specifically, they used chain-of-thought (CoT) techniques with integrated keyphrases and additional guidance information. To optimize these prompts, they applied the DSPy framework with a designed downstream evaluation metric aimed at balancing relevance and factuality. Using the 0-shot MIPRO optimizer within DSPy, they iteratively optimized prompts to enhance summary generation capabilities. Furthermore, they demonstrated that incorporating supervised fine-tuning improved the quality of generated summaries.

MediFact Saeed (2025) presented a three-stage hybrid pipeline for Task A consisting of weak supervision with Snorkel, supervised learning with SVM and zero-shot classification using transformers. The transformer model was deployed in case of uncertainty in the predictions of the previous stages. For Task B, Saeed (2025) proposed an approach consisting of extractive summarization using the BART (Lewis et al., 2020) model and abstractive refinement using Pegasus (Zhang et al., 2020a).

Roux-lette Antony et al. (2025) used an LLM-based approach with semantic similarity-guided in-context learning (ICL). For Task A, they queried the Qwen-Turbo LLM (Qwen et al., 2025) by prompting it with 20 In-Context Learning samples selected from the training data using NVIDIA NV-Embed-v2 (Lee et al., 2024) text embedding model to obtain spans for each perspective. These spans were then processed through a matching pipeline that attempted exact matches first, followed by case-insensitive and fuzzy matching if needed. For Task B, they used a similar ICL-based approach, selecting relevant examples based on semantic similarity between the input text and training examples. The LLM leveraged these examples, along with the extracted spans from Task A, to generate perspective-aware summaries. The most effective prompt asked the model to replicate the annotation patterns observed in the ICL samples, ensuring that the summaries maintained alignment with human annotations.

Manchester Bees Romero et al. (2025) proposed an approach with Iterative Self-Prompting (ISP) with the closed source LLMs Claude and o1. They used the models to develop prompts for itself during inferencing in multiple iterations, allowing the model to refine the prompts. The effectiveness of this approach stands out with the team achieving the highest score in strict-matching precision.

Abdelmalak Abdelmalak (2025) primarily focused on Task A. They used SpaCy to tokenize the answers into sentences and then matched the labels based on proportional alignment with the reference data for training and development. Following this, they fine-tuned COVID-Twitter-BERT on two tasks: one to identify relevant sentences and the other to label each relevant sentence based on its perspective.

LMU Agustoslu (2025) participated only in Task B and evaluated a set of different prompting techniques for the summarization task. They achieved high performance in relevancy metrics through the use of fine-tuning and few-shot learning based approaches. Competitive performance was achieved in the factuality metrics by deploying a variant of Chain-of-thought reasoning known as SumCoT, which was designed for element extraction and text summarization tasks.

Human Analysis We conducted a thorough human analysis of the summaries by the top 5 teams based on five criteria defined by Fabbri et al. (2021). The human annotator annotates 15 summaries generated by the top 5 teams for this evaluation on a Likert scale from 1-5. These criteria are as follows:

1. **Coherence**- Is the generated summary coherently framed?

2. **Consistency**- Is the summary logically implied by the source answer?

3. **Fluency**- How well-formulated is the summary gramatically?

4. **Relevance**- Does the summary include only relevant and non-redundant information from the source answers?

5. **Coverage**- How well is the particular perspective covered in the summary?

The results of the human analysis based evaluation are given in Table 5. Based on this evaluation, we identified Team YALENLP (Jang et al., 2025) and Team KHU_LDI as consistently producing the highest quality of summaries. This observation is consistent with our evaluation using the automatic metrics where Team YALENLP (Jang et al., 2025) achieved the best scores in the relevance metrics. The high fluency and coherence scores for all teams are expected outcomes of using LLMs for generation, as these models are capable of producing high-quality, grammatically correct English text. However, relevance remains a weak point for all submissions, as the models often produce elaborate, unrelated, and irrelevant content. Consistency scores indicate how well the model follows the flow and logic of the user's answers, with Team KHU_LDI performing the best in this metric. Coverage is strong for some models, while others often miss key pieces of information, an issue that we believe can be mitigated by more effective utilization of the predicted spans as input.

7 Conclusion

This work presents an overview of the PerAnsSumm 2025 Shared Task, organized at the CL4Health Workshop 2025 which received 155 total submissions from 23 teams. The task aimed to identify and summarize perspective spans in answers in Community Question-Answering forums. Specifically, it contains two subtasks: (a) Perspective Span Identification and Classification and (b) Perspective-based Summarization. To this end, this task utilized the PUMA dataset (Naik et al., 2024) that was supplemented with a newly annotated test set for evaluation. We described relevant performance metrics for this task and provided an overview of our findings, as well as the approaches taken by the 12 teams that submitted system papers. We are optimistic that the provided resources will help foster further research toward the task of perspective-based answer summarization. To enable future work, we continue maintaining the CodaBench webpage for the Shared Task as a benchmark.

Limitations

The PerAnsSumm shared task involves generation of summaries which are evaluated automatically while presenting the leaderboard. This involves the selection of automatic metrics, which, while a strong indicator, may not be completely representative of actual summary quality. For this reason, we include a range of diverse evaluation metrics. Due to the number of participants, we conduct our human evaluation study only on the summaries generated by the top five participants which may be expanded to include all participants to determine the correlation between the human evaluation and automatic metrics in future work. Further, the wide use of LLMs in the shared task encourages us to define metrics more suited for evaluating LLM generated content in future runs of this shared task. These evaluations which were not included in the current shared task may include evaluating specifically for LLM hallucinations along with the current evaluation of factuality.

References

Abanoub Abdelmalak. 2025. Abdelmalak at peranssumm 2025: Leveraging a domain-specific bert and llama for perspective-aware healthcare answer summarization. In *Proceedings of the Second Workshop on Patient-Oriented Language Processing (CL4Health) @ NAACL 2025*, Albuquerque, USA. Association for Computational Linguistics.

Tanalp Agustoslu. 2025. Lmu at peranssumm 2025: Llama-in-the-loop at perspective-aware healthcare answer summarization task 2.2 factuality. In *Proceedings of the Second Workshop on Patient-Oriented Language Processing (CL4Health) @ NAACL 2025*, Albuquerque, USA. Association for Computational Linguistics.

Anson Antony, Peter Vickers, and Suzanne Wendelken. 2025. Roux-lette @ peranssumm shared task. In *Proceedings of the Second Workshop on Patient-Oriented Language Processing (CL4Health) @ NAACL 2025*, Albuquerque, USA. Association for Computational Linguistics.

Satanjeev Banerjee and Alon Lavie. 2005. METEOR: An automatic metric for MT evaluation with improved correlation with human judgments. In *Proceedings of the ACL Workshop on Intrinsic and Extrinsic Evaluation Measures for Machine Translation and/or Summarization*, pages 65–72, Ann Arbor, Michigan. Association for Computational Linguistics.

Abari Bhattacharya, Rochana Chaturvedi, and Shweta Yadav. 2022. LCHQA-summ: Multi-perspective summarization of publicly sourced consumer health answers. In *Proceedings of the First Workshop on Natural Language Generation in Healthcare*, pages 23–26, Waterville, Maine, USA and virtual meeting. Association for Computational Linguistics.

Rochana Chaturvedi, Abari Bhattacharya, and Shweta Yadav. 2024. Aspect-oriented consumer health answer summarization. *Preprint*, arXiv:2405.06295.

Hyung Won Chung, Le Hou, Shayne Longpre, Barret Zoph, Yi Tay, William Fedus, Eric Li, Xuezhi Wang, Mostafa Dehghani, Siddhartha Brahma, Albert Webson, Shixiang Shane Gu, Zhuyun Dai, Mirac Suzgun, Xinyun Chen, Aakanksha Chowdhery, Sharan Narang, Gaurav Mishra, Adams Yu, and 12 others. 2022. Scaling instruction-finetuned language models. *arXiv preprint*.

DeepSeek-AI. 2025. Deepseek-r1: Incentivizing reasoning capability in llms via reinforcement learning. *Preprint*, arXiv:2501.12948.

Jacob Devlin, Ming-Wei Chang, Kenton Lee, and Kristina Toutanova. 2019. BERT: Pre-training of deep bidirectional transformers for language understanding. In *Proceedings of the 2019 Conference of the North American Chapter of the Association for Computational Linguistics: Human Language Technologies, Volume 1 (Long and Short Papers)*, pages 4171–4186, Minneapolis, Minnesota. Association for Computational Linguistics.

Alexander R Fabbri, Wojciech Kryściński, Bryan McCann, Caiming Xiong, Richard Socher, and Dragomir Radev. 2021. Summeval: Re-evaluating summarization evaluation. *Transactions of the Association for Computational Linguistics*, 9:391–409.

Tomas Goldsack, Carolina Scarton, Matthew Shardlow, and Chenghua Lin. 2024. Overview of the BioLaySumm 2024 shared task on the lay summarization of biomedical research articles. In *Proceedings of the 23rd Workshop on Biomedical Natural Language Processing*, pages 122–131, Bangkok, Thailand. Association for Computational Linguistics.

Aaron Grattafiori, Abhimanyu Dubey, Abhinav Jauhri, Abhinav Pandey, Abhishek Kadian, Ahmad Al-Dahle, Aiesha Letman, Akhil Mathur, Alan Schelten, Alex Vaughan, Amy Yang, Angela Fan, Anirudh Goyal, Anthony Hartshorn, Aobo Yang, Archi Mitra, Archie Sravankumar, Artem Korenev, Arthur Hinsvark, and 542 others. 2024. The llama 3 herd of models. *Preprint*, arXiv:2407.21783.

Pengcheng He, Xiaodong Liu, Jianfeng Gao, and Weizhu Chen. 2021. Deberta: Decoding-enhanced bert with disentangled attention. In *International Conference on Learning Representations*.

Edward J Hu, Yelong Shen, Phillip Wallis, Zeyuan Allen-Zhu, Yuanzhi Li, Shean Wang, Lu Wang, and Weizhu Chen. 2022. LoRA: Low-rank adaptation of large language models. In *International Conference on Learning Representations*.

Dongsuk Jang, Alan Li, and Arman Cohan. 2025. Yalenlp @ peranssumm 2025: Multi-perspective integration via mixture-of-agents for enhanced healthcare qa summarization. In *Proceedings of the Second Workshop on Patient-Oriented Language Processing (CL4Health) @ NAACL 2025*, Albuquerque, USA. Association for Computational Linguistics.

Albert Q. Jiang, Alexandre Sablayrolles, Arthur Mensch, Chris Bamford, Devendra Singh Chaplot, Diego de las Casas, Florian Bressand, Gianna Lengyel, Guillaume Lample, Lucile Saulnier, Lélio Renard Lavaud, Marie-Anne Lachaux, Pierre Stock, Teven Le Scao, Thibaut Lavril, Thomas Wang, Timothée Lacroix, and William El Sayed. 2023. Mistral 7b. *Preprint*, arXiv:2310.06825.

Philippe Laban, Tobias Schnabel, Paul N. Bennett, and Marti A. Hearst. 2022. SummaC: Re-visiting NLI-based models for inconsistency detection in summarization. *Transactions of the Association for Computational Linguistics*, 10:163–177.

Chankyu Lee, Rajarshi Roy, Mengyao Xu, Jonathan Raiman, Mohammad Shoeybi, Bryan Catanzaro, and Wei Ping. 2024. Nv-embed: Improved techniques for training llms as generalist embedding models. *arXiv preprint arXiv:2405.17428*.

Jooyeon Lee, Luan Huy Pham, and Özlem Uzuner. 2025. Mnlp at peranssumm: A classifier-refiner architecture for improving the classification of consumer health user responses. In *Proceedings of the Second Workshop on Patient-Oriented Language Processing (CL4Health) @ NAACL 2025*, Albuquerque, USA. Association for Computational Linguistics.

Mike Lewis, Yinhan Liu, Naman Goyal, Marjan Ghazvininejad, Abdelrahman Mohamed, Omer Levy, Veselin Stoyanov, and Luke Zettlemoyer. 2020. BART: Denoising sequence-to-sequence pre-training for natural language generation, translation, and comprehension. In *Proceedings of the 58th Annual Meeting of the Association for Computational Linguistics*, pages 7871–7880, Online. Association for Computational Linguistics.

Chin-Yew Lin. 2004. ROUGE: A package for automatic evaluation of summaries. In *Text Summarization Branches Out*, pages 74–81, Barcelona, Spain. Association for Computational Linguistics.

Yinhan Liu, Myle Ott, Naman Goyal, Jingfei Du, Mandar Joshi, Danqi Chen, Omer Levy, Mike Lewis, Luke Zettlemoyer, and Veselin Stoyanov. 2019. Roberta: A robustly optimized bert pretraining approach. *ArXiv*, abs/1907.11692.

Sushvin Marimuthu and Parameswari Krishnamurthy. 2025. Ltrc-iiith at peranssumm 2025: Spansense - perspective-specific span identification and summarization. In *Proceedings of the Second Workshop on Patient-Oriented Language Processing (CL4Health) @ NAACL 2025*, Albuquerque, USA. Association for Computational Linguistics.

Gauri Naik, Sharad Chandakacherla, Shweta Yadav, and Md Shad Akhtar. 2024. No perspective, no perception!! perspective-aware healthcare answer summarization. In *Findings of the Association for Computational Linguistics: ACL 2024*, pages 15919–15932, Bangkok, Thailand. Association for Computational Linguistics.

Vansh Nawander and Nerella Chaithra Reddy. 2025. Datahacks at peranssumm 2025: Lora-driven prompt engineering for perspective aware span identification and summarization. In *Proceedings of the Second Workshop on Patient-Oriented Language Processing (CL4Health) @ NAACL 2025*, Albuquerque, USA. Association for Computational Linguistics.

OpenAI, :, Aaron Jaech, Adam Kalai, Adam Lerer, Adam Richardson, Ahmed El-Kishky, Aiden Low, Alec Helyar, Aleksander Madry, Alex Beutel, Alex Carney, Alex Iftimie, Alex Karpenko, Alex Tachard Passos, Alexander Neitz, Alexander Prokofiev, Alexander Wei, Allison Tam, and 244 others. 2024a. Openai o1 system card. *Preprint*, arXiv:2412.16720.

OpenAI, Aaron Hurst, Adam Lerer, Adam P. Goucher, Adam Perelman, Aditya Ramesh, Aidan Clark, AJ Ostrow, Akila Welihinda, Alan Hayes, Alec Radford, Aleksander Mądry, Alex Baker-Whitcomb, Alex Beutel, Alex Borzunov, Alex Carney, Alex Chow, Alex Kirillov, Alex Nichol, and 400 others. 2024b. Gpt-4o system card. *Preprint*, arXiv:2410.21276.

Tabea M. G. Pakull, Hendrik Damm, Henning Schäfer, Peter A. Horn, and Christoph M. Friedrich. 2025. Wispermed @ peranssumm 2025: Strong reasoning through structured prompting and careful answer selection enhances perspective extraction and summarization of healthcare forum threads. In *Proceedings of the Second Workshop on Patient-Oriented Language Processing (CL4Health) @ NAACL 2025*, Albuquerque, USA. Association for Computational Linguistics.

Kishore Papineni, Salim Roukos, Todd Ward, and Wei-Jing Zhu. 2002. Bleu: a method for automatic evaluation of machine translation. In *Proceedings of the 40th Annual Meeting of the Association for Computational Linguistics*, pages 311–318, Philadelphia, Pennsylvania, USA. Association for Computational Linguistics.

Kristin Qi, Youxiang Zhu, and Xiaohui Liang. 2025. Team_umb at peranssumm 2025: Enhancing perspective-aware summarization with prompt optimization and supervised fine-tuning. In *Proceedings of the Second Workshop on Patient-Oriented Language Processing (CL4Health) @ NAACL 2025*, Albuquerque, USA. Association for Computational Linguistics.

Qwen, :, An Yang, Baosong Yang, Beichen Zhang, Binyuan Hui, Bo Zheng, Bowen Yu, Chengyuan Li, Dayiheng Liu, Fei Huang, Haoran Wei, Huan Lin, Jian Yang, Jianhong Tu, Jianwei Zhang, Jianxin

Yang, Jiaxi Yang, Jingren Zhou, and 25 others. 2025. Qwen2.5 technical report. *Preprint*, arXiv:2412.15115.

Rakshith R, Mohammed Sameer Khan, and Ankush Chopra. 2025. Aicoe at peranssumm 2025: An ensemble of large language models for perspective-aware healthcare answer summarization. In *Proceedings of the Second Workshop on Patient-Oriented Language Processing (CL4Health) @ NAACL 2025*, Albuquerque, USA. Association for Computational Linguistics.

Pablo Romero, Libo Ren, Lifeng Han, and Goran Nenadic. 2025. The manchester bees at peranssumm 2025: Iterative self-prompting with claude and o1 for perspective-aware healthcare answer summa. In *Proceedings of the Second Workshop on Patient-Oriented Language Processing (CL4Health) @ NAACL 2025*, Albuquerque, USA. Association for Computational Linguistics.

Nadia Saeed. 2025. Medifact at peranssumm 2025: Leveraging lightweight models for perspective-specific summarization of clinical qa forums. In *Proceedings of the Second Workshop on Patient-Oriented Language Processing (CL4Health) @ NAACL 2025*, Albuquerque, USA. Association for Computational Linguistics.

Junlin Wang, Jue Wang, Ben Athiwaratkun, Ce Zhang, and James Zou. 2024. Mixture-of-agents enhances large language model capabilities. *Preprint*, arXiv:2406.04692.

Yuheng Zha, Yichi Yang, Ruichen Li, and Zhiting Hu. 2023. AlignScore: Evaluating factual consistency with a unified alignment function. In *Proceedings of the 61st Annual Meeting of the Association for Computational Linguistics (Volume 1: Long Papers)*, pages 11328–11348, Toronto, Canada. Association for Computational Linguistics.

Jingqing Zhang, Yao Zhao, Mohammad Saleh, and Peter Liu. 2020a. PEGASUS: Pre-training with extracted gap-sentences for abstractive summarization. In *Proceedings of the 37th International Conference on Machine Learning*, volume 119 of *Proceedings of Machine Learning Research*, pages 11328–11339. PMLR.

Jingqing Zhang, Yao Zhao, Mohammad Saleh, and Peter J. Liu. 2019. Pegasus: Pre-training with extracted gap-sentences for abstractive summarization. *Preprint*, arXiv:1912.08777.

Tianyi Zhang, Varsha Kishore, Felix Wu, Kilian Q. Weinberger, and Yoav Artzi. 2020b. Bertscore: Evaluating text generation with bert. In *International Conference on Learning Representations*.

Bridging the Gap: Inclusive Artificial Intelligence for Patient-Oriented Language Processing in Conversational Agents in Healthcare

Kerstin Denecke
Bern University of Applied Sciences
Quellgasse 21, 2502 Biel/Bienne
Switzerland
kerstin.denecke@bfh.ch

Abstract

Conversational agents (CAs), such as medical interview assistants, are increasingly used in healthcare settings due to their potential for intuitive user interaction. Ensuring the inclusivity of these systems is critical to provide equitable and effective digital health support. However, the underlying technology, models and data can foster inequalities and exclude certain individuals. This paper explores key principles of inclusivity in patient-oriented language processing (POLP) for healthcare CAs to improve accessibility, cultural sensitivity, and fairness in patient interactions. We will outline, how considering the six facets of inclusive Artificial Intelligence (AI) will shape POLP within healthcare CA. Key considerations include leveraging diverse datasets, incorporating gender-neutral and inclusive language, supporting varying levels of health literacy, and ensuring culturally relevant communication. To address these issues, future research in POLP should focus on optimizing conversation structure, enhancing the adaptability of CAs' language and content, integrating cultural awareness, improving explainability, managing cognitive load, and addressing bias and fairness concerns.

1 Introduction

Conversational agents (CAs) in healthcare - intelligent systems that enable natural language interaction - have the potential to improve access to healthcare services, enhance patient literacy (Wynia and Osborn, 2010), and empower individuals to make informed healthcare decisions. These systems are increasingly being used in a variety of applications, including medical history taking (Denecke et al., 2024), blended psychotherapy, and delivery of cognitive behavioural therapy (e.g., WoeBot (Sackett et al., 2024)). While early healthcare CAs were predominantly rule-based, the emergence of transformer-based models has opened up new possibilities for more dynamic, flexible and engaging conversations enabled through patient-oriented language processing (POLP) (Sarker et al., 2021).

A critical component of effective healthcare CAs is the ability of these systems to tailor communication to individual patient needs, taking into account factors such as health literacy, cultural context and linguistic diversity that is realized by artificial intelligence (AI), natural language processing (NLP), ideally incorporating POLP. While AI-driven CAs hold promise for improving access to healthcare, they also pose risks, particularly in terms of exacerbating existing inequalities. The design and implementation of these systems, including the AI models and datasets on which they rely, often fail to adequately represent diverse user populations, leading to biased outcomes and interaction barriers (Cross et al., 2024). Marginalised communities, already disproportionately affected by structural inequalities in healthcare, may be further excluded if AI fails to process and deliver health information in a way that meets their linguistic and cognitive needs. In addition, if patient-facing AI systems present excessive, irrelevant or poorly prioritised information, users may feel overwhelmed, hindering their ability to derive meaningful insights for their health concerns.

To develop inclusive POLP within healthcare CAs, the methods must be designed with fairness, adaptability, and user-centred communication strategies in mind. Inclusive AI involves integrating diverse human attributes and perspectives throughout the entire lifecycle of AI systems—from data collection and model training to implementation and governance (Zowghi and Bano, 2024). Nadarzynski et al. proposed a 10-phase roadmap for the design and implementation of inclusive CAs in healthcare (Nadarzynski et al., 2024), primarily focusing on system development and evaluation. In contrast, this paper takes a more specific approach, focusing on the linguistic and technical aspects required to achieve inclu-

Proceedings of the Second Workshop on Patient-Oriented Language Processing (CL4Health), pages 456–462
May 4, 2025 ©2025 Association for Computational Linguistics

sive POLP within healthcare CAs. While some general aspects of usability and accessibility will be discussed, our primary focus lies in ensuring that language processing within CAs effectively accommodates diverse patient populations.

In the era of digitisation and AI-driven healthcare, it is imperative to ensure that AI-driven conversational systems are not only functionally efficient, but also linguistically and culturally inclusive. Despite increasing discussions on AI ethics and responsible AI practices, there is still a lack of practical strategies to bridge the technology divide, especially for underserved populations.

This paper aims to address this gap by exploring concrete strategies for ensuring inclusivity in AI-driven healthcare CAs. Specifically, we explore aspects for improving POLP for ensuring that healthcare CAs account for linguistic diversity, varying levels of health literacy, and cultural sensitivities. The World Health Organization's 2021 Ethical Guidelines emphasise inclusivity, transparency and accountability as core principles for AI in healthcare (World Health Organization, 2024). Building on this framework, our study aims to contribute to the development of more equitable AI-driven healthcare solutions that prioritise inclusivity and accessibility for all patient demographics.

To achieve this, we address the following research questions (RQs):

- RQ1: How does inclusive AI impact POLP in healthcare CAs?
- RQ2: What NLP or other technologies are required to achieve inclusive POLP in healthcare CAs?
- RQ3: What are the most important future research directions for achieving inclusive POLP in healthcare CAs?

By answering these questions, this paper aims to contribute actionable insights for the design and implementation of fair, effective, and inclusive POLP in healthcare CAs. It is intended as starting point of research towards inclusive POLP for CA in healthcare.

2 Methods

To answer our research questions, we apply two steps. First, we use the facets of inclusive AI that have been collected in a recent review (Bokolo et al., 2025) and study how inclusive AI impacts on POLP within healthcare CA based on our experience in developing CAs.

In a previously conducted review (Bokolo et al., 2025), we retrieved papers that included the keyword "Inclusive AI" in their abstract from six databases (PubMed, PsycINFO, CINAHL, Academic Search Premier, IEEE Xplore, and Scopus). The included research studies should address inclusive AI in the context of healthcare. Out of 1377 papers, 18 were included with information extracted on strengths, weaknesses, opportunities and threats (SWOT). From this SWOT analysis, six facets of inclusive AI in healthcare were concluded: 1) Accessibility, 2) Equity, 3) Usability and Navigability, 4) Diversity and Cultural Sensitivity, 5) Mitigation of Disparities, and 6) Skill Development and Literacy. In more detail, accessibility asks AI technologies in healthcare to be designed in a useable manner by individuals with diverse needs (Accessibility). They should offer fair access and outcomes for everyone (Equity) and must be designed in a user-friendly manner (Usability and Navigability). AI technologies in healthcare should recognize and accommodate socio-demographic diversity (Diversity and Cultural Sensitivity), should mitigate existing disparities (Mitigation of Disparities). Users should be equipped with relevant skills to engage efficiently with AI technologies when used for healthcare purposes (Skill development and literacy).

We will consider these six facets and assess how inclusive AI impacts on POLP within CA in healthcare. In a second step, we suggest a research agenda for technologies and methodologies to address the identified impact factors.

3 Impact of Inclusive AI on POLP within Healthcare CA

This section is structured along the 6 facets of inclusive AI described in the section before. We will outline how inclusive AI shapes POLP within CA with regard to these specific facets.

3.1 Accessibility

Accessibility takes into account users with disabilities and different abilities such as visual, hearing, motor or cognitive impairments (Henni et al., 2022). An accessible CA must provide multimodal interaction to ensure that users with different abilities can effectively engage with it. This includes speech-to-text and text-to-speech capabilities for visually impaired or low-literacy users, keyboard-only navigation for those with motor impairments, and support for screen readers. In addition, the CA should provide high-contrast visual options, adjustable font sizes, and easy navigation to accommodate users with cognitive or visual impairments.

From a POLP perspective, the CA should:

- Use short, clear sentences to break down complex medical information.
- Offer step-by-step explanations for processes such as measuring blood pressure, ensuring better comprehension.
- Enable adaptive communication styles, allowing users to choose between brief responses and detailed explanations based on their needs.
- Provide direct answers with optional elaboration, offering additional details upon request.

To effectively implement these or similar features into healthcare CAs, adaptive language generation could be applied such as text simplification models to adjust the complexity of responses. User profiling and context-aware interactions consider the user's preferences for adapting answer length, style, etc.

A reverse Chain-of-Thought prompting, where the CA explicitly guides users through stepwise instructions (e.g., breaking a process into incremental, explainable steps for better user comprehension) could better guide through processes. Depending on the purpose of the CA, the conversation could be implemented as progressive disclosure where information is revealed gradually,

3.2 Equity

Studies show that limited health literacy is linked to poor health outcomes, increased healthcare costs, and health disparities (Gibney et al., 2020). Digital communication tools in healthcare, including CAs, have the potential to improve health literacy and empower individuals to take a more active role in managing their health (Fitzpatrick, 2023). In this context, CAs can play a critical role in providing equitable responses tailored to different socio-economic backgrounds, ensuring that all individuals - regardless of location, income or education - receive accurate and relevant health information formulated and presented in a way that addresses their reading skills, health literacy and data literacy (Nadarzynski et al., 2024).

Linguistic and culture inclusivity could be achieved by multilingual support, but needs also additional aspects such as cultural-appropriate health recommendations (see section 3.4). Trauma-informed conversational strategies (Berring et al., 2024) could be applied to address specific needs of users with trauma: NLP models should be designed to recognize distress and provide gentle, supportive responses. For example, if a user expresses suicidal thoughts, the CA should prioritize crisis intervention resources over generic health advice.

To address these and similar aspects related to equity, healthcare CAs should use simple, jargon-free language, integrating explanatory visuals, and providing localised health advice based on regional medical practices. Underlying AI models need to be trained on datasets that include diverse user groups to avoid biases that could lead to misinformation or exclusion of marginalised populations.

3.3 Usability and Navigability

Previous research also showed that user interfaces must be designed with consideration of the information requirements, cognitive capabilities, and limitations of end users in healthcare environments (Patel and Kushniruk, 1998). Therefore, healthcare CAs should be designed with an intuitive, patient-friendly interface that prioritizes clarity, guidance, and responsiveness (Denecke, 2023). For example, guidance would mean that the CA guides the user through the conversation, supports when the user has no idea what to write or say. Also structuring the dialogue could help or summarizing previously said aspects from time to time when the interaction gets long.

CAs should provide clear fallback options, such as the ability to speak with a human operator or access a help menu when the CA fails in recognizing user intent. They should maintain a consistent tone throughout the conversation which could be formal, friendly or empathetic. Proactive engagement would make the interaction more user-centric and intuitive. By anticipating what the user might need next, CAs can offer relevant information or actions before the user even asks. For example, if a user has been discussing symptoms of a cold, the CA might proactively suggest remedies or ask if they need a doctor's appointment. Based on previous interactions, the CA can suggest next steps or related information, making the user feel understood and supported.

Aspects mentioned for accessibility or equity could also support usability (e.g. clear, concise language).

3.4 Diversity and Cultural Sensitivity

Cultural factors have been identified to affect access to and uptake of digital health technologies among culturally and linguistically diverse populations (Davies et al., 2024; Whitehead et al., 2023). An inclusive patient-facing healthcare CA must be culturally competent and linguistically adaptable. This requires multilingual support with real-time translation capabilities to communicate in regional dialects and under-represented languages. In addition, the CA should be able to adapt health recommendations based on cultural beliefs, dietary restrictions and traditional medical practices. Avoiding gender bias in language, respecting gender identity pronouns, and acknowledging religious sensitivities in healthcare (e.g. fasting during Ramadan) are critical to making the CA more inclusive. By incorporating cultural nuances and linguistic diversity, healthcare CA can foster trust, improve engagement and increase the effectiveness of interactions, ultimately leading to better health outcomes for all communities (Davies et al., 2024).

3.5 Mitigation of Disparities

Individuals may struggle with limited health literacy, so it is essential for inclusive POLP in healthcare CA to simplify medical language and ensure that critical health information is easy to understand. Strategies to achieve this include dynamic simplification, where the CA adjusts its complexity based on the user's familiarity with medical terms, and interactive learning features such as visual aids, audio explanations and quizzes that reinforce understanding. The CA should proactively identify and clarify misunderstood terms and offer alternative explanations in simpler language to bridge gaps in understanding. Again, underlying data has to accurately represent different demographics, preventing the reinforcement of harmful stereotypes and the exclusion of marginalised groups.

3.6 Skill Development and Literacy

From a POLP perspective, skill development and CA literacy are essential to ensure that patients can effectively interact with healthcare CA, understand medical information, and make informed health decisions. To support skill development, healthcare CA should incorporate strategies to teach users how to engage with the CA, increase health literacy, and build confidence in using digital health tools. When users first interact with a CA, it should provide a guided onboarding experience that explains its capabilities, how to ask questions, and how to navigate responses and inform about the possibilities and shortcomings of the CA. Offering simple scenarios or guided exercises (e.g., "Try asking me about your symptoms!") can help users become comfortable with the interactions. Users may be unsure of how to phrase health-related questions effectively and what could the CA be asked. To address this, a CA can guide users by offering question templates (e.g. "You can ask me: 'What are the symptoms of diabetes?'").

4 Research Agenda for Inclusive Patient-oriented Language Processing in CA

The previous sections described the characteristics that inclusive POLP within a healthcare CA should provide. Considered from multiple facets, we can recognize that some aspects are of relevance to support multiple facets (e.g. concise language supports accessibility, equity and usability). Some technologies are already available to realize these aspects, while others still require research efforts. In this section, we are outlining possible research directions recommended for future research towards inclusive patient-oriented language processing within healthcare CAs. Table 1 lists some possible research questions for the future.

Conversation structure. Research is needed to determine how conversations in healthcare CA should be structured and how to implement these structures in POLP. A well-structured conversation flow ensures that information is delivered in a clear, understandable and digestible way. This minimises confusion and allows users to focus on key health information without unnecessary complexity. To achieve this, it is essential to analyse the linguistic and cultural barriers that affect communication with patients. These barriers can include low health literacy, non-native speakers and regional dialects. In addition, understanding how patients with disabilities - such as blindness, hearing loss or cognitive impairment - interact with health care CAs is crucial. Incorporating participatory methods during the design phase can help gather input from these user groups to ensure accessibility and usability.

Research area	Examples for possible research questions
Conversation structure	How should language simplification be implemented in healthcare CAs to ensure user comprehension of complex medical concepts?
Adaptability	How can CAs dynamically adapt to user's reading level, health literacy or cognitive load?
Cultural awareness	How can CA responses become culturally sensitive?
Explainability	How can explainability be included in the conversation flow without disturbing it?
Cognitive load analysis	How can a CA analyse a user's cognitive load in real time?
Bias and fairness-awareness	Which bias mitigation techniques could be implemented into healthcare CAs in general or into POLP specifically?

Table 1: Research areas and examples for research questions towards inclusive patient-oriented language processing in healthcare CA

Considering established rules of communication or best practices from patient-doctor interactions can help in designing effective conversation flows (Denecke, 2023).

Research could also explore how patients interpret and respond to medical terminology. Identifying areas where NLP-based language simplification or explanation of medical concepts is needed can improve comprehension. However, simplification must be carefully balanced, as excessive reduction of medical terminology may result in the loss of critical health information.

Cognitive load analysis. Interacting with a CA could be overwhelming when the conversation gets long and comprehensive. It could be studied whether NLP or other techniques can be used for real-time cognitive load detection (Zayim et al., 2023). This would mean signs of frustration, stress or cognitive fatigue could be recognized while the interaction takes place which in turn would allow to adjust CA responses accordingly. For example, inclusion of multimodal AI could offer an opportunity to address detected cognitive load by allowing for various modes of communication.

Cultural awareness. Another research direction regarding inclusive POLP within CA is how to consider cultural aspects in the health dialogue. Research could explore ways to incorporate cultural sensitivity into language models used in healthcare CAs. This may involve adapting conversation flows to align with cultural norms, addressing variations in health-related beliefs, or ensuring that medical terminology is explained in ways that resonate with different communities.

Adaptability. The previous three areas already indicate another important direction of research. While rule-based CAs capture the flow of conversations through predefined rules, LLMs and other AI methods offer greater flexibility and adaptability. Future healthcare CA can adapt their responses to the user's health literacy, reading level, cognitive abilities, or culture. Future research could explore adaptive models that dynamically adjust text complexity based on the user's level of comprehension or reading skills. Additionally, research could consider personalised AI for health literacy growth, enabling CAs to dynamically adapt their responses based on a patient's evolving comprehension of medical concepts. This will require the development of adaptive NLP models that assess a user's level of comprehension in real time and adjust explanations accordingly - offering simpler definitions for beginners, while gradually introducing medical terminology for more advanced users. Related to this, it could be studied how to realize a closed-loop-communication that ensures and verifies patient's comprehension by methods such as teach-back (Kreps, 2018).

Cultural adaptations can take multiple dimensions. The provided content can be tailored to align with the user's cultural context (e.g., dietary suggestions should respect cultural norms). Additionally, research could explore how the tone and structure of interactions adapt to different cultures. However, careful design is essential to avoid reinforcing stereotypes or generating biased responses.

Explainability. When transitioning from rule-based CAs in healthcare to LLM-based CAs, ensuring patient safety is crucial to maintaining control over the information provided. Research on explainability in conversational AI is essential for enhancing transparency and trust. AI-generated explanations of medical information should be interpretable, contextually relevant, and aligned with user expectations, while also ensuring they do not pose any risk to patients. Some approaches are already available for explainable CA such as the one presented by Nguyen et al. (Nguyen et al., 2023) or Garofalo et al. (Garofalo et al., 2023) .

Bias and fairness-awareness. Existing NLP models still have problems regarding fairness and come along with bias (Hovy and Prabhumoye, 2021). Therefore, research is necessary regarding bias detection and mitigation frameworks for gender, racial, disability, and socio-economic biases to be integrated in POLP within healthcare CA. Such advances in diverse and bias-aware dataset curation, along with fairness-driven fine-tuning of medical NLP models, are essential to mitigate model biases in POLP. Models capturing the peculiarities of specific user groups could help in handling local languages and developing specifically focussing solutions. This would require developing low-resource NLP models for underserved communities, integrating local dialects and indigenous languages.

5 Conclusions

This paper explored how patient-facing language processing in healthcare CAs should be designed to achieve inclusivity. Ensuring that healthcare CAs are accessible, equitable, usable, and useful to all individuals - regardless of their social or socio-economic background, cultural identity, health literacy, digital literacy, or cognitive abilities - is critical to their effectiveness as digital health interventions. These topics gain in relevance when moving from rule-based CAs to LLM-based systems as they allow for more flexibility.

We identified several key research directions for future work, including optimising conversation structure, improving the adaptability of CA language and content, integrating cultural awareness, improving explainability, managing cognitive load, and addressing bias and fairness concerns. These aspects are particularly important in healthcare settings, where CAs are used by a diverse patient population and must effectively support users with different needs.

Inclusive POLP is essential to prevent the unintentional exclusion of certain user groups, which could exacerbate existing health disparities and inequalities in healthcare. By prioritising inclusivity in the design of healthcare CAs, research can contribute to a more equitable and patient-centred digital health landscape.

6 Limitations

This work comes along with some limitations. While the facets of inclusive AI have been collected in a literature review, the impact of inclusive AI on POLP within healthcare CA was only reflected based on the experiences in CA development of the author. In future work, this should be verified by input from other experts in the field.

References

Lene Lauge Berring, Tine Holm, Jens Peter Hansen, Christian Lie Delcomyn, Rikke Søndergaard, and Jacob Hvidhjelm. 2024. Implementing trauma-informed care—settings, definitions, interventions, measures, and implementation across settings: a scoping review. In *Healthcare*, volume 12, page 908. MDPI.

Anthony Junior Bokolo, Kerstin Denecke, and Elia Gabarron. 2025. A literature review on inclusive ai in healthcare- a user-centered approach to potential benefits, challenges, and recommendations.

James L Cross, Michael A Choma, and John A Onofrey. 2024. Bias in medical ai: Implications for clinical decision-making. *PLOS Digital Health*, 3(11):e0000651.

Godson Kofi Davies, Martin Luther King Davies, Esther Adewusi, Kenechukwu Moneke, Olwaseun Adeleke, Lateefat Abiodun Mosaku, Abdulbasit Oboh, Damilola Sherifat Shaba, Isa Aisha Katsina, Joshua Egbedimame, et al. 2024. Ai-enhanced culturally sensitive public health messaging: A scoping review. *E-Health Telecommunication Systems and Networks*, 13(4):45–66.

Kerstin Denecke. 2023. How to design successful conversations in conversational agents in healthcare? In *International Conference on Human-Computer Interaction*, pages 39–45. Springer.

Kerstin Denecke, Daniel Reichenpfader, Dominic Willi, Karin Kennel, Harald Bonel, Knud Nairz, Nikola Cihoric, Damien Papaux, and Hendrik von Tengg-Kobligk. 2024. Person-based design and evaluation of mia, a digital medical interview assistant for radiology. *Frontiers in Artificial Intelligence*, 7:1431156.

Patrick J Fitzpatrick. 2023. Improving health literacy using the power of digital communications to achieve better health outcomes for patients and practitioners. *Frontiers in Digital Health*, 5:1264780.

Marco Garofalo, Alessia Fantini, Roberto Pellugrini, Giovanni Pilato, Massimo Villari, and Fosca Giannotti. 2023. Conversational xai: Formalizing its basic design principles. In *Joint European Conference on Machine Learning and Knowledge Discovery in Databases*, pages 295–309. Springer.

Sarah Gibney, Lucy Bruton, Catherine Ryan, Gerardine Doyle, and Gillian Rowlands. 2020. Increasing health literacy may reduce health inequalities: evidence from a national population survey in ireland. *International journal of environmental research and public health*, 17(16):5891.

Silje Havrevold Henni, Sigurd Maurud, Kristin Skeide Fuglerud, and Anne Moen. 2022. The experiences, needs and barriers of people with impairments related to usability and accessibility of digital health solutions, levels of involvement in the design process and strategies for participatory and universal design: a scoping review. *BMC public health*, 22(1):35.

Dirk Hovy and Shrimai Prabhumoye. 2021. Five sources of bias in natural language processing. *Language and linguistics compass*, 15(8):e12432.

Gary L Kreps. 2018. Promoting patient comprehension of relevant health information. *Israel Journal of Health Policy Research*, 7(1):56.

Tom Nadarzynski, Nicky Knights, Deborah Husbands, Cynthia A Graham, Carrie D Llewellyn, Tom Buchanan, Ian Montgomery, and Damien Ridge. 2024. Achieving health equity through conversational ai: A roadmap for design and implementation of inclusive chatbots in healthcare. *PLOS Digital Health*, 3(5):e0000492.

Van Bach Nguyen, Jörg Schlötterer, and Christin Seifert. 2023. From black boxes to conversations: Incorporating xai in a conversational agent. In *World Conference on Explainable Artificial Intelligence*, pages 71–96. Springer.

Vimla L Patel and Andre W Kushniruk. 1998. Interface design for health care environments: the role of cognitive science. In *Proceedings of the AMIA Symposium*, page 29.

Casey Sackett, Devin Harper, and Aaron Pavez. 2024. Do we dare use generative ai for mental health? *IEEE Spectrum*, 61(6):42–47.

Abeed Sarker, Mohammed Ali Al-Garadi, Yuan-Chi Yang, Jinho Choi, Arshed A Quyyumi, Greg S Martin, et al. 2021. Defining patient-oriented natural language processing: a new paradigm for research and development to facilitate adoption and use by medical experts. *JMIR Medical Informatics*, 9(9):e18471.

Lara Whitehead, Jason Talevski, Farhad Fatehi, and Alison Beauchamp. 2023. Barriers to and facilitators of digital health among culturally and linguistically diverse populations: qualitative systematic review. *Journal of medical Internet research*, 25:e42719.

WHO World Health Organization. 2024. Who releases ai ethics and governance guidance for large multi-modal models.

Matthew K Wynia and Chandra Y Osborn. 2010. Health literacy and communication quality in health care organizations. *Journal of health communication*, 15(S2):102–115.

Neşe Zayim, Hasibe Yıldız, and Yılmaz Kemal Yüce. 2023. Estimating cognitive load in a mobile personal health record application: A cognitive task analysis approach. *Healthcare Informatics Research*, 29(4):367–376.

Didar Zowghi and Muneera Bano. 2024. Ai for all: Diversity and inclusion in ai. *AI and Ethics*, 4(4):873–876.

Author Index